THE DIPLOMATS, 1939–1979

THE
DIPLOMATS
1939-1979

EDITED BY

GORDON A. CRAIG

AND

FRANCIS L. LOEWENHEIM

PRINCETON UNIVERSITY PRESS

PRINCETON, NEW JERSEY

LIBRARY OF CONGRESS CATALOGING-IN-PUBLICATION DATA

THE DIPLOMATS, 1939–1979 / EDITED BY GORDON A. CRAIG AND FRANCIS L. LOEWENHEIM.

P.   CM.

INCLUDES INDEX.

ISBN 0-691-03613-6 (CL)

1. WORLD POLITICS—1945–   2. STATESMEN—HISTORY—20TH CENTURY.

3. DIPLOMATS—HISTORY—20TH CENTURY.   I. CRAIG, GORDON ALEXANDER, 1913–

II. LOEWENHEIM, FRANCIS L.

D843.D544   1994

327'.09'04—DC20   94-1364

PHOTO CREDITS: THE EDITORS GRATEFULLY ACKNOWLEDGE THE FOLLOWING SOURCES
FOR PERMISSION TO REPRINT THE PHOTOGRAPHS. BILDARCHIV PREUSSISCHER
KULTURBESITZ: 1. UPI/BETTMANN: 5, 6, 7, 8, 9, 10, 11, 14, 16, 19, 22, 26, 28, 30, 31.
AP/WORLD WIDE PHOTOS: 12, 15, 18. TOPHAM/THE IMAGE WORKS: 17. GERMAN
INFORMATION CENTER: 23, 29. U.S. SIGNAL CORPS, FRANKLIN D. ROOSEVELT LIBRARY: 2, 4.
HOOVER INSTITUTION ARCHIVES, STANFORD UNIVERSITY: 3. POLISH INFORMATION
SERVICE: 13. WALTER LIPPMANN PAPERS, YALE UNIVERSITY LIBRARY: 20. JOHN F. KENNEDY
LIBRARY: 21. GERALD R. FORD LIBRARY: 25, 27. WHITE HOUSE PHOTO: 24.

IN MEMORY OF

Felix Gilbert

CONTENTS

ACKNOWLEDGMENTS

MICHAEL BRECHER expresses his thanks to Benjamin Geist for a rigorous reading of his chapter.

GORDON A. CRAIG expresses his gratitude to Professor Henning Köhler of the Friedrich Meinecke Institute of the Free University of Berlin, a longtime student of Konrad Adenauer and his politics; to Fred Luchsinger, formerly Bonn correspondent for the *Neue Zürcher Zeitung*, for advice and information during the writing of his chapter on the chancellor; and to William Z. Slany, historian, Bureau of Public Affairs, United States Department of State, for advice and information.

VICTOR H. FESKE expresses his thanks to the Avon Trustees for permission to quote from the papers of Anthony Eden, and to Dr. B. S. Benedikz and the staff of the Birmingham University Library for their generous assistance.

RENA FONSECA dedicates her chapter to Professor Franklin L. Ford, with affection and gratitude for his unwavering support and guidance.

JOHN LEWIS GADDIS thanks Professors Robert O'Neill and Adam Roberts and Dr. John Rowett, along with participants in the Oxford University seminar on United States Foreign Policy and the Cold War, for helpful comments on an oral summary of his essay.

RAPHAEL ISRAELI would like to acknowledge the assistance he received from Carol Bardenstein in the collection of materials and to express gratitude to the Harry Truman Institute for the Advancement of Peace, the Hebrew University of Jerusalem, whose facilities, library, and secretarial staffs have aided his research on Sadat.

PAUL GORDON LAUREN thanks Marilla Guptil, chief of the Archives Unit, United Nations Archives, and Brian Urquhart for advice and assistance.

FRANCIS L. LOEWENHEIM wishes to thank John B. Boles, Ira D. Gruber, Allen J. Matusow, Richard J. Smith, Gale Stokes, Matthew D. Taylor, and Martin J. Wiener of Rice University for their long continued interest and support and for reading all or portions of his chapters; Constance Menefee of the Cincinnati Public Library for timely assistance with government publications; Sally M. Moffitt of the Langsam Library of the University of Cincinnati for her unfailing helpfulness with books old and new; Josephine J. Wynne for patiently struggling with drafts and redrafts; and the indispensable staffs at the Truman, Kennedy, Johnson, Ford, and Carter presidential libraries, especially Jennifer A. Sterneman for carefully reading his chapters, and James A. Yancey, Jr., for locating an unpublished Carter interview, and Lida Fukumura and Leslie V. Vuylsteke of the UC Library for their expert assistance with copy and proofs.

ERNEST R. MAY thanks Philip Chen and Josh Tucker for research assistance—above and beyond the call of employment.

STEVEN MERRITT MINER acknowledges the assistance of Bruce Steiner and John L. Gaddis, his colleagues at Ohio University, in securing funding for his original research in Russia, and a grant from the Ohio University Research Council that enabled him to return to Russia in 1992. He wishes also to express gratitude to his former teacher Francis Loewenheim for more than a decade's counsel and to his parents, Donald and Margaret Miner, and his wife, Doreen, for unfailing support.

W. W. ROSTOW wishes to thank Robert Bowie, Douglas Brinkley, W. W. Cooper, Katherine Graham, Charles Kindleberger, Walter Korter, James Reston, and Edna, Eugene, and Elspeth Rostow for perspectives on Monnet, as well as Clifford Hackett, who was particularly generous with his time and his encyclopedic knowledge of Monnet's career.

PIOTR WANDYCZ gratefully acknowledges a travel grant from the Yale Center for International and Area Studies, enabling him to do research in Polish archives, as well as the assistance of the staffs of the New Archival Records (ANN) and the Foreign Ministry Archives in Warsaw, the Polish Institute and the Sikorski Museum in London, and the National Archives in Washington, D.C. He is indebted also to Professor Manfred Lachs and Henryk Birecki for valuable information and comments, and to Sir Michael Howard for advice concerning military matters.

GEOFFREY WARNER would like to thank Ernest Davies, Piers Dixon, Lord Mayhew, Lady Younger, and the staff of the Public Records Office in London for access to the documents on which his chapter is based. He is also grateful, for much mental stimulation on the subject of Bevin, to Anne Deighton, Mike and Saki Dockrill, Peter Hennessy, John Kent, Ann Lane, and John Young.

LIST OF CONTRIBUTORS

MICHAEL BRECHER is the Angus Professor of Economics and Political Science at McGill University. Among his books are *The Foreign Policy System of Israel* (winner of the Woodrow Wilson Book Award of the American Political Science Association, 1973); *Decisions in Israel's Foreign Policy;* and *Decisions in Crisis: Israel, 1967 and 1973*. His most recent book is *Crises in World Politics*.

RICHARD D. CHALLENER is professor of history at Princeton University. He was a contributor to *The Diplomats, 1919–1939*. His books include *The French Theory of the Nation in Arms, 1866–1939; National Security in the Nuclear Age; Admirals, Generals, and American Foreign Policy, 1898–1914;* and *Appeasement in Europe: A Reassessment of U.S. Policies*.

GORDON A. CRAIG is J. E. Wallace Sterling Professor of Humanities Emeritus at Stanford University and *Honorarprofessor* of the Free University of Berlin. He was coeditor of, and contributor to, *The Diplomats, 1919–1939*. His books include *The Politics of the Prussian Army, 1640–1945* (winner of the H. B. Adams Prize of the American Historical Association, 1956); *Germany, 1866–1945* (winner of the *Historikerpreis* of the City of Münster, 1979); *The Germans* (winner of the Political Book of the Year Prize of the Ebert Stiftung, 1988); *The End of Prussia: War, Politics and Diplomacy;* and (with Alexander H. George) *Force and Statecraft: Diplomatic Problems of Our Time*. He is a past president of the American Historical Association.

RICHARDSON DOUGALL retired in 1975 as deputy director of the Historical Office, Department of State, having served in that department under all of the secretaries of state with whom his chapter is concerned. He was principal editor for the coverage of the two Quebec conferences and the Potsdam Conference in the series *Foreign Relations of the United States*. He is also coauthor of *The Eagle and the Shield: A History of the Great Seal of the United States*.

VICTOR H. FESKE has been a lecturer in modern European history at Yale University. In 1993–1994 he is visiting assistant professor of history at Connecticut College.

RENA FONSECA is a postdoctoral fellow at the Center for Middle Eastern Studies at Harvard University. She received her Ph.D. from the Harvard University History Department, where she has served as lecturer on South Asian foreign relations. She is working on a study of the relationship between religion and nationalism in India, with comparative reference to the Middle East.

JOHN LEWIS GADDIS is Distinguished Professor of History at Ohio University and has also taught at the United States Naval War College, the University of Helsinki, Princeton University, and Oxford University. His books include *The United States and the Origins of the Cold War, 1941–1947; Russia, the Soviet Union, and the United States: An Interpretive History; Strategies of Containment: A Critical Appraisal of Postwar American National Security Policy; The Long Peace: Inquiries into the History of the Cold War;* and, most recently, *The United States and the End of the Cold War: Implications, Reconsiderations, Provocations.*

STANLEY HOFFMANN is the C. Douglas Dillon Professor of the Civilization of France and chairman of the Center for European Studies at Harvard University. Among his books are *Decline or Renewal? France Since the 1930s; Duties Beyond Borders;* and *Janus and Minerva.* He is working on a book on French nationalism.

AKIRA IRIYE is professor of history at Harvard University and a past president of the American Historical Association. His books include *After Imperialism; Across the Pacific; The Pacific Entanglement; The Cold War in Asia; Power and Culture,* and, most recently, *The Origins of the Second World War in Asia and the Pacific.*

RAPHAEL ISRAELI teaches Islamic and Chinese studies at the Hebrew University in Jerusalem, where he serves currently as the chair of the East Asian Studies Department. Among his books are *Man of Defiance: A Political Biography of Anwar Sadat; Palestinians Between Israel and Jordan; Muslims in China: A Study in Cultural Confrontation;* and, more recently, *Muslim Fundamentalism in Israel;* and *Muslims in China: A Critical Bibliography*

PAUL GORDON LAUREN is the Regents Professor at the University of Montana. Among his books are *Diplomats and Bureaucrats; Diplomacy: New Approaches in History, Theory and Policy; The China Hands' Legacy: Ethics and Diplomacy;* and *Destinies Shared.* His most recent book, *Power and Prejudice: The Politics and Diplomacy of Racial Discrimination* (winner of the Choice Award for 1989), has recently been translated into Japanese.

FRANCIS L. LOEWENHEIM is professor of history at Rice University. His books include *Political Community and the North Atlantic Area; Peace or Appeasement? Hitler, Chamberlain and the Munich Crisis; The Historian and the Diplomat: The Role of History and Historians in American Foreign Policy;* and *Roosevelt and Churchill: Their Secret Wartime Correspondence.* With Harold D. Langley, he is editing the personal diaries of Henry L. Stimson, 1929–1945.

ERNEST R. MAY is the Charles Warren Professor of History at Harvard University. In addition to various books on American history and diplomatic history, he is coauthor (with Richard E. Neustadt) of *Thinking in Time: The Uses of History for Decision-Makers* (winner of the 1988 Gravemeyer Award for Ideas Improving World Order). His most recent book is *American Cold War Strategy: Interpreting NSC68*.

A. JAMES MCADAMS is Associate Professor of Government and International Affairs at the University of Notre Dame. He is the author of *East Germany and Détente* and *Germany Divided: From the Wall to Reunification*. He is also coauthor of *Rebirth: A History of Europe Since World War II*.

STEVEN MERRITT MINER is associate professor of history at Ohio University. He is the author of *Between Churchill and Stalin: The Soviet Union, Great Britain, and the Origins of the Grand Alliance*, winner of the George Louis Beer Prize for 1990. He is working on a study of East-West cultural and political relations during the Second World War.

W. W. ROSTOW is professor emeritus of political economy at the University of Texas at Austin. He served in national security posts during the Kennedy and Johnson administrations. His books include *Essays on the British Economy of the Nineteenth Century; The Process of Economic Growth; The Stages of Economic Growth;* and *The World Economy: History and Prospects*. His most recent work is *Theorists of Economic Growth from David Hume to the Present, with a Perspective on the Next Century*.

NORMAN STONE is professor of modern history at Oxford University and fellow of Worcester College. Among his books are *The Eastern Front, 1914–1917* (winner of the Wolfson Prize for History, 1976); *Hitler; Europe Transformed, 1878–1919; The Other Russia;* and *The Russian Chronicles*.

PIOTR WANDYCZ is Bradford Durfee Professor of History at Yale University. Among his books are *France and Her Eastern Allies* and *The Twilight of French Eastern Alliances* (winners of the George Louis Beer Prize of the American Historical Association in 1962 and 1989, respectively); *Soviet-Polish Relations;* and *Czechoslovak-Polish Confederation and the Great Powers*. His most recent book is *The Price of Freedom: A History of East Central Europe*. He is a member of the Polish Academies of Sciences in Warsaw and Krakow.

GEOFFREY WARNER is a visiting senior fellow at the University of Birmingham, having taken early retirement from the Open University at the end of 1989. He has written *Pierre Laval and the Eclipse of France; Iraq and Syria 1941;* and many articles on the early history of the Cold War. He is currently writing a book on the origins of the Cold War and a study of British foreign policy since 1945.

SHU GUANG ZHANG is assistant professor of history at the University of Maryland at College Park. He is the author of *Deterrence and Strategic Culture: Chinese-American Confrontations, 1949–1958* and the forthcoming *Military Romanticism: China and the Korean War, 1950–1953.*

THE DIPLOMATS, 1939–1979

INTRODUCTION

IN 1919, IN A SADLY NEGLECTED BOOK called *Diplomacy and the Study of International Relations*, D. P. Heatley warned historians that, before they undertook to write about world affairs, they should try to acquire "the habit of mind that is required for appreciating questions of foreign policy." Above all, he continued, they should "never separate the study of policy . . . from the appreciation of the instruments on the understanding and use of which success depends, and [they] must test the character of the instruments by the work they have to do."

Among Heatley's contemporaries and the generation of historians who followed him, there was little understanding, let alone appreciation, of that advice. Many interesting books were written about the rivalries and contentions of the great powers, about what Philippe de Commynes in the fifteenth century had called "la bestialité de plusieurs princes et . . . la mauvaistié d'autres qui ont sens assez et expérience, mais ilz en veulent mal user," and about the wars that resulted from their impercipience or lack of restraint. But in most of these the emphasis was placed upon policy and upon the external political and economic forces that helped to shape it. Very little, on the other hand, was said about diplomacy, that body of principles and usages, of modalities and instruments that at any given time gives precise formulation to policy and effects its execution. The relationship between the nature of diplomatic practice and the conditions in which it operated, the appropriateness of the instrument to the task, generally went unremarked, as did the effect of change in one part of the equation that was not matched in the other.

This was a lamentable omission, and it was an awareness of how serious it was that, forty years ago, led the editors and contributors to *The Diplomats, 1919–1939*—of which the present volume is a sequel—to try to correct it. The period with which they were concerned was one in which the Great Powers, after the ravages of a war that affected every part of the globe, sought to create an international system to replace the one that had been destroyed in 1914, and in which, for a number of complicated political and economic reasons, they failed, at the cost of an even more terrible conflict. But it was also a period in which an important diplomatic revolution occurred, a complex of technological, socioeconomic and political changes that impinged upon the behavior of the members of the international community. The most dramatic of these, beginning with the war and continuing thereafter, were the steady growth of the number of active members in the international community and the simultaneous breakdown of its internal homogeneity as a result of that growth and, even more, of the intrusion into international politics of the ideologies of communism, fascism, and National Socialism, which had been unknown in the nineteenth century.

In telling the story of the interwar years, the contributors to *The Diplomats, 1919–1939* focused, to a degree unusual in the older works of diplomatic history, upon the diplomatic establishment itself. They set out to show how the usages and procedures of a diplomacy inherited from the past adjusted or failed to adjust to new circumstances and how this affected the coming of the war in 1939. In doing so, they saw the inadequacies of the League of Nations in the 1920s, the collapse of the system of collective security in the 1930s, and the agony of the final crisis in 1939 for the most part through the eyes of those whose professional duty it was to advise their governments about how the national interest could best be protected and promoted. These included the officials and staffs of the diplomatic establishment at home—the Foreign Office or Quai d'Orsay or Wilhelmstraße—as well as those who were sent to represent their governments in foreign capitals, to keep them informed about the attitudes and intentions of the governments to which they were accredited, and, whenever appropriate, to conduct negotiations.

Implicit in this approach there was inevitably an element of judgment. The contributors could not avoid asking themselves, for example, how sound the assessments were that diplomats like Sir Horace Rumbold and André François-Poncet or Robert Coulondre and Sir Nevile Henderson made of the personalities and motives of the dictators, or the degree to which Galeazzo Ciano and his diplomats encouraged Mussolini in his ill-considered ambitions, or how ready the Western foreign offices were to appreciate and act upon the reports that they received from abroad. No suggestion was made that the diplomats were responsible for the illusions and the follies of the interwar period, but that they had some part in bringing about the final *débacle* was admitted, and *The Diplomats, 1919–1939* attempted to delineate what that part was.

In general, the present volume has remained true to the method employed by its predecessor. It deals with the devastating global conflict that grew out of Hitler's assault on Poland in 1939, the subsequent genesis and development of the Cold War, the experiment with détente in the 1970s, and the threat, at the end of that decade, of the coming of new international tensions. As a whole, this period was one in which the hope of creating anything that could be called a world order was accepted by some as being impossible and by others as being undesirable. But it was a time, nevertheless, in which a bipolar international system evolved that, while never free of crisis and armed conflict, prevented war between the greatest of powers by a balance of terror and a mutual understanding of the consequences of its breaking down.

These were years in which the diplomatic community simultaneously contracted and expanded. Its most salient characteristic was the concentration of power and influence in the two great centers, Washington and Moscow, but these aggregates of power attracted allies and client states, and beyond these groupings (NATO and the Warsaw Pact) were states relatively new to the world of diplomacy that wished to remain free from the rivalry of the superpowers but nevertheless sought to influence it in various ways. The superpowers were never in a position to dominate world politics, either singly or together; the lesser powers sometimes created the crisis with which the greater ones had to deal and sometimes, by collective action in the United Nations, helped to solve them.

In contrast to the earlier volume, which was largely oriented toward Europe, and in which the Soviet Union played a relatively minor role and the United States a negligible one, *The Diplomats, 1939–1979* devotes much more space to the wider world. The diplomacy of statesmen like Zhou Enlai, Nehru, and Sadat claim as much attention as that of Ernest Bevin and Charles de Gaulle, although not as much as that of the Soviet Union and the United States in their new incarnation. These changes in balance and emphasis reflect the consequences to the international community of the Second World War, which humbled the aggressors and exalted the more self-sufficient of the victors, while destroying the colonial empires of others. Most of the problems that concerned the nations in this period grew directly out of the war.

The war also effected important changes in diplomacy itself. If, for example, less attention is paid in this volume than in its predecessor to the role in the diplomatic process of the resident ambassadors, this is because it was seriously diminished during the course of the conflict. Neville Chamberlain had never traveled by air until he set off to meet Hitler at Berchtesgaden in 1938, and Foreign Secretary Ernest Bevin was similarly a novice in this form of transport when he flew to attend the Potsdam Conference in 1945. But the British permanent under secretary for foreign affairs, Sir Alexander Cadogan, logged 87,500 miles of air travel in the course of the Second World War, and this was exceeded by the travels of his chief, Anthony Eden, to say nothing of the United States Secretary of State John Foster Dulles in the 1950s, who traveled so much that a journalist joked about his infinite capacity for taking planes. What this betokened was a growing tendency on the part of the foreign ministers, because of the supposed urgency of problems or an assumed need to impress the host government, to take over the duties of representation and negotiation traditionally assigned to the ambassadors and to reduce their role to that of reporters whose reports were often disregarded by the home office.

John Foster Dulles is reported to have said during his term as secretary of state, "Nowadays, when you can by overnight flight talk face to face with the foreign ministers of other countries, it's silly to go at it the old-fashioned way of exchanging notes, which take a month, perhaps, before you get as good an understanding, and then not as good as you can get by talking a few minutes face to face."[1] The results of this kind of diplomacy were often, it must be emphasized, unfortunate. In his chapter on the Suez crisis, Victor Feske tells us that Prime Minister Anthony Eden disregarded all of his Washington ambassador's warnings that the Americans were firmly opposed to any resort to force against Nasser and preferred to rely on an overoptimistic assessment by his chancellor of the exchequer, Harold Macmillan, whom he had sent to Washington as a special envoy to discuss the crisis with President Eisenhower. Macmillan had a rambling discussion with the president that lasted for about thirty-five minutes and concluded that Eisenhower would not object to a military strike, an erroneous impression that had many unfortunate consequences.[2] The incident supports the view of Philip M. Kaiser, himself a distinguished United States ambassador in Senegal, Budapest, and Vienna, who has written in his memoirs, "Ambassadors who know the politics, history, culture, and economics of the country to which they are assigned, who are in regular contact with its top officials and have earned their respect, and who know the mood of the country at any particular time are an essential antidote to the misunderstandings easily generated by instant communication and the quick visits of top officials."[3] But this sort of argument was not persuasive to Dulles or to Kissinger and Brzezinski after him, and the role of the ambassadors continued to wane throughout the period.

The war not only changed foreign ministers into ambassadors-at-large but converted heads of state to peripatetic activity as well. In the interests of alliance solidarity, the summit conference—not unknown in the diplomatic history of the years that followed the Paris Peace Conference of 1919—became the vogue during the Second World War and found its most characteristic manifestations in Teheran, the Second Quebec Conference, Yalta, and Potsdam. (That this development was not unconnected with the decline of the ambassador is illustrated by the fact that in 1943 the United States ambassador to Iran was not informed of the pending summit in Teheran until the participants had arrived on the scene.) There is a good case for the argument that summits generally create more problems than they solve, largely because they are bad places for the conduct of serious business and always arouse unreasonable expectations. The record of the wartime summits certainly tends to support Frederick the Great's dictum that heads of state should, whenever possible, avoid meeting each other. But despite their results, many of which seem in retrospect to have been unfortunate and avoidable if more traditional diplomatic methods had been used, diplomacy in this form proved to be contagious. Although Secretary of State Dean Rusk believed that the summit conference was the most unfortunate diplomatic invention of the modern era, he was a lonely exception to the general trend. Summitry was one of the principal characteristics of the Cold War, the phases of which can indeed be dated by the expectations aroused by them and the disappointments registered afterward.

In addition to these changes in traditional methods, the forty years that followed the outbreak of war in 1939 witnessed a decline in the former virtually uncontested position of the foreign office (and its equivalent in other countries) as the center of policy formulation and direction. This was a process that began during World War II for reasons that were originally justifiable—the desperate need to deal with overwhelming quantities of work by means of separation of function, establishment of auxiliary agencies, streamlining of chains of command, and other extraordinary measures—but it continued after the war, without the same justification, and its net result was often to deprive the foreign office of effective overview of policy and of the ultimate responsibility for advising the executive or head of state on policy choices. This was sometimes carried to an alarming extreme, as it was in the United States during the administration of Richard M. Nixon. The president and his national security adviser, Henry Kissinger, were so intent on preventing the Department of State from becoming involved in the sensitive discussions that they were conducting with the Soviet Union and Communist China that they repeatedly agreed to have the formal record of those conversations kept by representatives of their vis-à-vis, which prevented the department and its secretary, William P. Rogers, from learning what Nixon and Kissinger did not want them to know.[4]

Despite these developments, diplomacy in its more traditional forms was responsible for many successes in this period. One thinks of the ending of the Berlin blockade, for example, the protracted negotiation of the Schuman Plan, the London and Paris treaties of 1954 and 1955, and the various accords generated by Willy Brandt's *Ostpolitik*. It is well to remember, moreover, that resident ambassadors oversaw by far the greater part of the official relations between their countries and those to which they were accredited—all of the business, in fact, that was not likely to attract attention in the newspapers— and that, in time of crisis, they fulfilled the duties of representation and of protecting their own nationals, sometimes at great risk to their personal safety. William H. Sullivan, who was a member of the American Foreign Service during the whole of the period covered by this book and was United States ambassador in Teheran at the time of the Iranian revolution in 1979, wrote in his memoirs:

> For most of us, the period from 1939 to 1979 was a time of turmoil, but also a time of many satisfactions. The Chinese have an ancient curse: "May you live in interesting times." We lived in interesting times, and most of us did not feel accursed. I think we left a better world than we found. But that is for the historians to say.[5]

Following the example of the earlier volume, we have sought here to avoid separating the explication of policy from the appreciation of the instruments upon which policy depends for success. We have attempted also to provide the reader with the information that he needs to make his own judgment of the appropriateness of the diplomatic expedients brought to bear upon the problems of these four dangerous decades and the performance of the diplomats who employed them. But we have done so as individuals, with differing opinions and judgments about the events described, which the editors have not attempted to moderate or force into artificial agreement, any more than they have tried to regulate the mode of historical discourse that the individual contributor has selected for telling his part of the story of these years.

A final word on documentation. When *The Diplomats, 1919–1939* was published in 1953, the essential facts concerning the coming of the Second World War were fairly well established. This is distinctly not the case with respect to the four decades that followed. While the documentary record of Western diplomacy is largely complete to the mid-1950s, for the years since then it grows with exasperating slowness. For the history of nondemocratic states, communist or otherwise, the existing gaps are far larger, and despite the gratifying opening of archives in the former Soviet Union and the former German Democratic Republic in the last few years, it is clear that it will be a long time before scholars will be able to establish a complete and accurate record for such countries.

In completing this volume, therefore, the editors and the contributors have constantly been aware of what was not available to them, while making the most of what was, always keeping in mind Professor Herbert Butterfield's famous maxim that "history is all a process of unlearning." It is their hope that, as new documentary sources on this period are opened to historians, *The Diplomats, 1939–1979* will not be found significantly wanting.

October 1993   *G.A.C.*
                                                                                                F.L.L.

Notes

1. John Robinson Beal, *John Foster Dulles: A Biography* (New York, 1957), 154.

2. See below, Chapter 6.

3. Philip M. Kaiser, *Journeying Far and Wide: A Political and Diplomatic Memoir* (New York, 1992), 262.

4. One result of this practice—as William M. Franklin, the head of the department's Historical Office, confirmed following a careful review of the question at the Ford White House and the National Security Council in December 1974—was that Richard Nixon left office without the Department of State possessing a complete set of his summit discussions with Moscow and Beijing. See William M. Franklin to Francis L. Loewenheim, with related correspondence, White House Central Files, Subject File, F6 2-36, Gerald Ford Library.

5. William H. Sullivan, *Mission to Iran* (New York, 1981), 279.

PART ONE

THE WAR AND ITS AFTERMATH

1

DIPLOMATS AND DIPLOMACY DURING

THE SECOND WORLD WAR

Gordon A. Craig

FOR PROFESSIONAL DIPLOMATS, wartime is the most uncongenial of atmospheres. The institutional forms within which they are accustomed to work and the distribution of responsibility for the definition and executive of foreign policy are subject to pressures and demands to which they are not accustomed. Heads of state, normally absorbed in domestic affairs, now conceive it to be their duty to bring foreign policy under their personal control, often with the aid of special assistants and staffs with vaguely defined jurisdictions; other government departments, particularly those of Defense and the Treasury, demand their share in policy determination; the magnitude of the conflict and the multiplicity of unprecedented problems that require attention encourage the appearance of still other interlopers, in the shape of intelligence and security agencies and boards of economic warfare, and propaganda and public information organizations; and usurpations of function take place that challenge tradition and make control and coordination of policy difficult. Meanwhile, the soldiers, liberated from the unexciting routines of peacetime service, and convinced of their own indispensability and the priority of their own needs, are insistent that all aspects of policy be subordinated to the requirements of military strategy.

If the war is one of opposing coalitions, the interests and needs of allies now require heightened attention, and the traditional ambassadorial system begins to seem inadequate as a means of communication and consultation. The urgencies of decision-making in wartime appear to require the establishment of joint staffs and combined boards of one kind or another and the dispatching from capital to capital of special missions made up of experts and headed by celebrities not always known for any experience in foreign affairs. At the highest level, a progressive personalization of policy takes place that soon begins to affect the process of interallied negotiations. It is discovered that periodic meetings of allied heads of state are indispensable, and summit meetings are arranged that are designed as much to convince public opinion of allied will and solidarity as to facilitate allied operations, and that often result in agreements that are imprecise and establish precedents that mortgage the future. Meanwhile, the stakes in the conflict mount implacably, and victory seems ever more to be a prize worth any sacrifice, even if what is sacrificed includes a prudent regard for the vital interests of the nation, the vision of a desirable future, and the perspective and rationality that are required to make a sound connection between the two.

In the years that followed Hitler's attack upon Poland in 1939, the foreign services of all of the belligerent powers were subject to the pressures and problems created by the war and reacted in ways that reflected the nature of the political systems of which they were a part and their own particular traditions and political style. Of the three cases discussed here, the German one was for the professional diplomats the most humiliating and, in the end result, shameful. Proud of a tradition that began with Bismarck and was reasserted during the Stresemann years in the 1920s, the German foreign service saw its authority progressively thwarted and eroded after 1933 by the new Nazi rulers of the Reich, until in the end its power to check a foreign policy that many of its members regarded as potentially disastrous was nullified by a foreign minister who was uninterested in their opinions. Simultaneously, it was forced to condone and participate in the subversion of East European governments and the execution of the Final Solution of the Jewish question. The degree of its complicity in the latter was so palpable that the recovery of a German professional foreign service after the war was difficult and unpopular.

From any such fate, the British foreign service was protected by the constitutional powers of the foreign secretary and his direct relationship, through his parliamentary position, with the British people. Despite the novel and disturbing challenges raised by the war and the enhanced role of other government departments and agencies in policy functions as the conflict widened, the Foreign Office retained greater authority than any similar agency among the belligerent powers, and its efficiency in coordinating the instruments and modalities of policy left little to be desired from the first days of the conflict to the last. Its chief wartime problems were caused neither by interdepartmental rivalry nor civil-military disputes over prerogative but rather by the consequences to policy of the growing dominance in the last stage of the war of Britain's principal ally and, on a different level, by the difficulty of restraining an impetuous and willful prime minister. As one reads the diaries of the long-time permanent under secretary for foreign affairs, Sir Alexander Cadogan, it is difficult to decide whether his American or his Churchillian difficulties caused him the greater exasperation. Certainly his irritation over being lectured to by W. Averell Harriman at Teheran about how to conduct international conferences and how they usually developed ("I've forgotten a good deal more than he ever knew")[1] was almost as great as his *cri de coeur* at the Potsdam Conference about the behaviour of his prime minister ("He butts in on every occasion and talks the most irrelevant rubbish, and risks giving away our case at every point").[2]

As for the United States State Department, it too suffered from the high-handed and often painfully frivolous style of the chief executive, as well as from his tendency to reserve wide areas of policy for his private control and his preference for relying on special agents and emissaries who reported to him alone. While he was secretary of state, Cordell Hull was able to keep these tendencies under some measure of control. His successor, Edward Stettinius, was far less successful in this regard.

A greater problem and, in the long run, a more consequential one lay in the impossibility of persuading Franklin Roosevelt to interest himself in long-range planning. Aside from some vaguely conceived ideas about a new postwar order—in which peace would be secured by Four Policemen, one of which would be Nationalist China (surely not one of the president's most practical ideas),[3] and a fixed prejudice against colonialism that irritated his friend Churchill—Roosevelt had little interest in the future and almost none in what a postwar Europe might be like and what problems it might face. This was a source of grave concern to professional diplomats. Indeed, watching the course of American foreign policy in the last two years of the war, persons with any knowledge of the history of diplomacy may have had feelings akin to those of the Prussian diplomat Wilhelm von Humboldt, who in the last stages of the war against Napoleon Bonaparte had vainly urged his government to make a hard and fast agreement with its allies about boundaries, territorial claims, and other forms of compensation before peace negotiations got under way. Later, after the deliberations at Vienna had begun, Humboldt complained:

> The evil results caused by the postponement of many things from one epoch to another are now coming to light; one cannot postpone them any longer and yet does not know how to get out of the embarrassment they are causing. During the whole war we kept our eyes only upon the problem of overthrowing Napoleon . . . seizing upon everything that seemed to make that goal more certain and pushing aside everything that might even momentarily have delayed it. Therefore, we never reached a prior agreement with Russia about Poland. . . . That is all avenging itself now in the most shameful manner, and difficulties are springing up in places where, had we acted differently, we could have had a perfectly smooth path.[4]

I

The waning of the authority of the German Foreign Ministry was well advanced even before the coming of the war in 1939.[5] The note of self-confidence that prevailed in the Wilhelmstraße six years earlier—the feeling that the Nazis would be incapable of conducting foreign policy without the direction of the professional diplomats, who would be able to discourage dangerous ideas and keep policy within traditional channels—was not of long duration. To be sure, the new chancellor at first made no changes in the administration and personnel of the service, leaving both Konstantin von Neurath, an experienced diplomat who had served in Copenhagen, Rome, and London before being appointed foreign minister under Papen, and his secretary of state, Bernhard von Bülow, in their posts; and it is true also that the professionals were initially pleased by the direction taken by Hitler's policy and thoroughly approved of his withdrawal from the League of Nations and the Disarmament Conference in October 1933, which they regarded as a sign of a more assertive national emphasis in policy. But doubts began to arise in 1934, when the chancellor, against the strong objections of Rudolf Nadolny, his ambassador in Moscow, broke off the relationship with the Soviet Union that had been profitably pursued since 1922, and they grew rapidly as the Führer began to pay more attention to the policy advice of Joachim von Ribbentrop than to the foreign policy establishment.

Hitler provided the funds that enabled this self-confident amateur to have a foreign affairs institute of his own, appointed him special commissioner for disarmament questions in 1934 (a title that Ribbentrop believed gave him the authority to intervene in all aspects of policy), chose him to negotiate a naval agreement with Great Britain in 1935, although both the Foreign Ministry and the embassy in London declared this to be an impossibility, and, in recognition of his success in achieving it, made him ambassador to the Court of St. James in 1936, and finally, in the fateful reorganization of the government in February 1938, foreign minister of the Reich.[6] Even before this crowning indignity for the professionals, their control over policy was in disarray. In 1934, when Hitler appointed Franz von Papen ambassador to Vienna, Papen made his acceptance conditional upon his "being free from the jurisdiction of the Foreign Office and . . . responsible to Hitler alone."[7] In 1935, the Foreign Office learned of the projected repudiation of the arms clauses of the Versailles Treaty too late to be able to register its views, and the same was true of the sending of troops into the demilitarized Rhineland a year later, the legal justification of this action being prepared in the *Dienststelle Ribbentrop* rather than in the ministry's Legal Division.[8] An even more serious sign of loss of control was the fact that in 1937 German policy in the Far East underwent a radical change from the orientation toward Nationalist China favored by the Foreign Office to a close association with Japan. The new direction, which was inaugurated by the Anti-Comintern Pact of November 1936, was largely due to Ribbentrop's success, after the failure of his hopes for an Anglo-German alliance, in persuading Hitler of the potential uses of a global anti-British coalition.[9]

Meanwhile, the ambitions of other party agencies had begun to usurp the functions of the Foreign Office. In a bold policy grab in 1933, Joseph Goebbels had annexed most of the staff and the duties of its press section, and his Propaganda Ministry subsequently claimed control over the dissemination of cultural information that had formerly been the preserve of the Auswärtiges Amt.[10] Similarly, the party's Foreign Organization (Auslandsorganisation, or

AO), which was founded in 1931 to maintain contact with party members living abroad, began after Hitler's accession to power to develop a foreign service of its own, designed to assert party discipline over German nationals abroad. Despite Foreign Office complaints about the embarrassment caused by this and the disruption of the work of embassies in foreign capitals, Hitler not only supported the AO but in January 1937 issued an order giving its director a position in the Foreign Office with authority over all matters affecting Germans abroad.[11]

Party membership by Foreign Office personnel was not conspicuous in the early years of the National Socialist regime. Studies in the personnel files in the Berlin Document Center have indicated that fifty of the higher five hundred officials in the Foreign Office had become members of the National Socialist party by the end of 1933; the German Minister in Oslo, Ernst von Weizsäcker, referred to them as the "1933 *Spätlese*."[12] But further increase of that number remained modest until the years 1938–1943, when the size of the ministry greatly increased and when party membership gradually became obligatory. Thus, when Ernst von Weizsäcker was made secretary of state in 1938, his new chief made it clear to him that he would be expected to join the party and become an officer in the SS, and membership in the NSDAP was also a prerequisite of Adam von Trott zu Solz's admission to a position in the Foreign Office's Information Department in 1939. It need hardly be said that party membership was not necessarily equivalent to loyalty to Adolf Hitler and support of his aggressive policies. Ulrich von Hassell, ambassador in Rome until 1937, Werner von der Schulenburg, ambassador to Moscow until 1941, and Adam von Trott were all party members but were executed after July 1944 for their resistance activities; and Bernd von Haeften, on trial before the hyena-like Judge Roland Freisler for treason, declared that 60 percent of the Foreign Office personnel shared his oppositional opinions.[13]

Two features of Joachim von Ribbentrop's administration of the Foreign Office are worth emphasizing. The first was his belief that the ministry had no proper role in policy formulation, which was the prerogative of Hitler and himself. The establishment over which he presided was, in his view, little more than a technical apparatus. During the war, in a conversation with Weizsäcker's successor Steengracht von Moyland, he told the new secretary of state that his sphere of tasks included the handling of routine contacts with foreign diplomats in Berlin, the maintenance of discipline within the service, and the protection of the competencies of the ministry against other party agencies, but he specifically denied that it had a policy role.[14] The second notable characteristic of his tenure was the significant role played by the SS in the Foreign Office. Ribbentrop was a man who was probably disliked—for his arrogance, his intellectual pretensions, and his influence on Hitler—by as many of his party comrades as he was by the professionals in the ministry, but he was supported by Heinrich Himmler, the Reichsführer of the SS, who seems to have had a higher opinion of his talents than most people and was his intimate friend. Ribbentrop in his turn admired Himmler and was proud of his own commission in the SS, and in July 1940, after he had been promoted to the rank of SS-Obergruppenführer, he wrote to Himmler, using the intimate form of address:

> You know what my feelings are about your SS and how I admire its development, which is your very own work. I shall always regard it as a special honor to belong to this proud band of leaders, which is of decisive importance for the future of our Great German Reich.[15]

Both men apparently regarded the Foreign Office as an ideal place for the extension of SS influence, Himmler because of personal ambition, Ribbentrop because it might facilitate his influence on the operational aspects of Hitler's foreign policy. As a result, before the outbreak of the war, in addition to Weizsäcker, who was secretary of state of the Foreign Office and had the rank of SS-Oberführer, there were two secretaries *in* the Foreign Office, who held SS ranks: Wilhelm Keppler, *Staatssekretär zur besonderen Verwendung,* who had been in the SS since 1933, and Ernst Wilhelm Bohle, chief of the AO and SS-gruppenführer; and an under secretary, Ernst Woermann, head of the Political Division and SS-Oberführer. Other officials holding both diplomatic and SS rank directed the protocol, information and press, radio, and cultural-political divisions. In 1940, Martin Luther, a former member of the *Dienststelle Ribbentrop,* became under secretary of state and director of the Germany division, which had special competence for Jewish affairs. Luther was a SA-Oberführer.[16]

Ribbentrop's view of German foreign policy may be distinguished from Hitler's by its relative lack of any ideological component. He was much more the believer in a calculated use of power to secure the revision of the Versailles Treaty and the acquisition of an unassailable continental position for Germany, which could then be a base for the extension of overseas influence. The role of other powers in this conception was defined not by the factors of history, ideology, and race that determined Hitler's view, for instance, of France and the Soviet Union, but by pragmatic calculations about the extent to which they could contribute to the acquisition of Germany's goals.[17]

The weakness of Ribbentrop's grand design was that he was not a very good *Realpolitiker* (Neville Chamberlain, indeed, once described him to the British cabinet as stupid, vain, and incapable of understanding what was said to him)[18] and was bereft of any great sensitivity to either the material or the emotional components of policy. Always inclined to overestimate German strength and resources, he never perceived that pride and defiance can sometime compensate for physical inferiority. The easy German successes of the years 1935–1938 extinguished any residue of caution that he may once have had, and in any case his unwillingness to weaken his position with Hitler made it impossible for him to be less confident and unconditional than his Führer. Thus, both in 1938, during the Sudeten crisis, and in the final crisis of 1939, he favored resort to war on the grounds that the Western powers did not have the will to fight. In the former case, the soundness of his judgment was not put to the test, thanks to what may be considered the only victory that the Foreign Ministry ever won over its arrogant chief. Secretary of State Ernst von Weizsäcker was a man who was willing to cooperate with the Nazis in many ways that he doubtless regretted later on, but he was determined to do everything in his power to avoid their involving Germany in a war he was convinced it could not win. Because of this, he had encouraged German diplomats on post abroad to warn the governments to which they were accredited of the necessity of uniting against Hitler before it was too late;[19] and this was also the reason why—working with Neurath and Hermann Goering without Ribbentrop's knowledge—he drafted and communicated to Rome, by way of the Italian ambassador, Attolico, the text that Mussolini pulled from his pocket at Munich on 29 September 1938 and that served as the basis for a settlement short of war.[20]

Ribbentrop's confident judgment that the British would not go to war if Germany invaded Poland was belied in that famous scene in the Reich Chancellery on 3 September 1939, described by Hitler's interpreter Paul Schmidt, when the news of the British ultimatum arrived. "Hitler sat immobile, gazing before him. . . . After an interval that seemed an age, he turned to Ribbentrop, who had remained standing by the window. 'What now?' asked Hitler with a savage look."[21] The foreign minister's reputation with his master never completely recovered after that, despite his previous successes, including his important part in the negotiation of the Nazi-Soviet Pact only weeks before. Always one for grand conceptions, Ribbentrop continued to have dreams of coming up with a political initiative that would decisively change the course of the conflict and restore his fortunes. In 1940, when the destroyers-bases deal between the United States and British governments indicated that American intervention in the war might be just a question of time, he secured Hitler's authorization for negotiations with the Japanese and the Italians to transform the Anti-Comintern Pact into a tripartite pact that might intimidate the Americans. By the new agreement Japan recognized the right of its partners to establish a new order in Europe, in return for similar recognition of its Co-Prosperity Sphere in the Far East. In a clear threat to the United States, the third paragraph of the pact stipulated that the three signatories would "assist one another with all political, economic and military means if one of the three Contracting Parties is attacked by a Power at present not involved in the European war or the Chinese-Japanese conflict." In the United States the results of this were the opposite of what had been expected. News of the pact not only helped awaken the American people to the threat posed to its security by international fascism but helped elect Franklin D. Roosevelt to a third term as president, an event that must have seemed to Hitler to bring American intervention closer.[22]

Ribbentrop was undismayed by this and continued to design new projects. In

March 1943, for example, he was convinced that, after Germany's next significant military victory, the Führer should proclaim the establishment of a European Union of States (*Staatenbund*). This, he was convinced, would have any
number of remarkable effects: convincing the Russians that all Europe was
against them, weakening the will of the West and strengthening the opposition
to Roosevelt in the United States, helping recruit a couple of first-class SS
divisions in France, and relieving the beleaguered German forces in Tunisia.
This plan did not succeed in engaging the attention of the man it was meant to
impress.[23]

During the years of triumph and defeat, the Foreign Office, greatly bloated in
size compared with the modest establishment of Stresemann's day,[24] went
through the motions of foreign policy, maintaining contact with the missions
abroad and carrying on elaborate propaganda and information activities.[25] The
beginning of serious Allied bombing greatly handicapped its activities, and by
the end of 1943, although working staffs remained in Berlin, the greater part of
divisional personnel had to be evacuated to quarters in the Riesengebirge and
Thuringia, the Bodensee, and the neighborhood of Salzburg. In November
1943 a heavy raid inflicted serious damage on the ministry and destroyed the
greater part of its personnel files.[26] The Foreign Minister spent much of his time
away from the Wilhelmstraße, traveling from front to front in a special train,
keeping as close to Hitler as possible. His main concerns were to issue "speech
regulations" to the ministry for transmission to the missions abroad, telling
them how to react to the changing fortunes of war ("With respect to the ending
of the war," Weizsäcker wrote after receiving one of these in November 1943,
"we have to use the speech of unconditionality.")[27] and to protect his prerogatives from encroachments by the security services and other party agencies.
Thus, after complaints to Hitler about negotiations between party instances and
local authorities in the Netherlands, Norway, Switzerland, and "the Great
German Space," he managed to secure a directive that stated that "the province
of foreign policy is not appropriate for experimentation and personal endeavors" and ordered party and government agencies other than the Foreign
Office, which alone bore responsibility in this area, to cease their independent
activities in other countries and withdraw their agents.[28]

This victory, if that is what it was (for the offensive activities did not, and
probably could not have been expected to, stop completely), rather overlooked
the fact that Ribbentrop's real enemies were a lot closer to home, indeed, in the
Foreign Office itself. In February 1943, Under Secretary of State Martin Luther, a longtime associate of the foreign minister and the director of the ministry's powerful Germany division, was arrested for disobedience toward his
chief and was divested of his office and rank and sent to Sachsenhausen concentration camp, where he remained until the end of the war. Although the affair is
still murky, there is evidence that Luther had been conspiring with the chief of

Himmler's secret service, Walter Schellenberg, to overthrow Ribbentrop and was apprehended before the plans reached fruition.[29]

Meanwhile, an appreciable number of Foreign Office and embassy officials were involved in resistance activities. Before 1939 German diplomats in London, Bern, the Vatican, and Moscow fed information to their host governments and sought to encourage collective action against Hitler, and during the war years a group in the ministry's Information Division headed by Adam von Trott zu Solz maintained contact with the military conspirators. A former Rhodes scholar at Oxford, Trott had hated Hitler from the moment of his accession to power but combined this, in a way that confused his English friends, with a deep German patriotism and a belief in *Deutschtum*'s potential contribution to a new European civilization. He decided therefore to work against Hitler from within the system and used his position in the Foreign Office to travel as much as possible to neutral capitals whence he informed Allied contacts of the existence and plans of the resistance and tried to persuade them that evidence of interest and support on their part would increase military and popular support for a rising. He was also active in spreading abroad a knowledge of the activities of the Kreisau circle, led by Helmuth James von Moltke, and its views concerning the postwar organization of Europe.[30] Nothing in the end came of these activities, partly because of the studied indifference of the British and United States governments and more directly, of course, because of the failure of the bomb plot on 20 July 1944, which implicated Trott and other foreign service personnel and led to their death in frightful circumstances in the Plötzensee prison in Berlin.

Even so, the memory of their bravery may relieve in some part the shameful record of many of their colleagues. Despite his relative lack of ideological zeal, Ribbentrop thought it politically expedient not only to turn a blind eye to the activities of the SS officers in his own ministry (like the sinister *Staatssekretär* Wilhelm Keppler and his deputy envoy, Edmund Veesenmayer, who were deeply involved in the dissolution of the Yugoslav state in 1941 and the preparations for the occupation of Hungary in 1944)[31] but to promote cooperation between the foreign service and the security agencies, particularly in the field of Jewish policy.[32] The printed papers of the Foreign Ministry for the war years document its entire complicity in the Final Solution and include such damning documents as a communication from the ministry to the RSHA, stating that it had no objection to the dispatch of French Jews to Auschwitz,[33] a report from an SS agent in Slovakia saying that Ribbentrop had asked him to apply pressure on local authorities to speed up the liquidation of the Jews but to keep the Germany envoy out of the matter if possible,[34] and a memorandum of a conference on 1 July 1944 between a Foreign Office official and the SD chief Erich Kaltenbrunner concerning cooperation between the two agencies, with a review of their activities and problems in various areas.[35]

With its involvement in these squalid and criminal activities, the German foreign service dishonored its past and jeopardized its future.

II

During the Second World War, the British Foreign Office and the missions abroad had to suffer none of these humiliations. It is true that earlier there was some decline in their influence in technical and economic decisions and for a time on the overall direction of policy. In 1937 and 1938, Prime Minister Chamberlain clearly felt that the Foreign Office was unrealistic in its belief in the viability of collective security and too pro-French and anti-German in its orientation,[36] and he was inclined to depend on advisers from other departments and private confidantes, one of whom, in October 1938, told a member of *Dienststelle Ribbentrop* that "in all future moves [i.e., negotiations between Britain and Germany] it was important that all major questions be dealt with directly, thus by-passing the Foreign Office."[37] After the failure of the appeasement policy and the onset of war,[38] this situation gradually rectified itself, although lingering resentment in the Foreign Office and a feeling that Chamberlain had been more energetic in pursuit of peace than he had been in protecting Great Britain's interest and honor[39] found expression in an ardent desire for a change in political leadership.

Ironically enough, the change when it came did not promise to improve things. Sir Alexander Cadogan has written of Winston Churchill:

> The P. M. generally cared little for diplomats, who he thought inclined to give themselves airs for no particular cause and in some instances to owe their position to the operation of Buggins's turn, or for the F. O. as an institution, which he thought slow-moving, apt to search for smart paper solutions and to hedge its bets. Of their memoranda, he said that one should read only the odd-numbered or even-numbered paragraphs, since every alternate paragraph began "On the other hand."[40]

But Churchill, himself much given to combativeness, always appreciated that quality in others, and the refusal of his foreign secretaries and Permanent Under Secretary Cadogan to be intimidated or bullied by him or to fail to speak their own minds appeased his ardent spirit, particularly after Eden's return to the Foreign Office in December 1940. Thanks to the warm personal relations between the two, the Foreign Office probably had a much stronger role in the Second World War than it had during the prime ministership of Lloyd George in the First. In his meticulous and judicious account of British wartime foreign policy, Sir Llewellyn Woodward has written that, although the problems that the conflict engendered necessitated the foundation of new machinery and parallel agencies, like the Ministry for Economic Warfare and the Special Operations Executive, and although there were inevitable disputes, "the Foreign Office and the diplomatic Missions abroad remained the principal instruments for the formulation and execution of policy and the principal channels of communication between Government and Government."[41]

The fact that, from 1939 when Churchill was First Lord of the Admiralty until the end of the war, there was a highly active secret correspondence between him and the president of the United States[42] may seem to belie this, but after some early complaints by the British ambassador in Washington that he should be informed of these exchanges, Churchill saw to it that the Foreign Office and the embassy knew what he had said in his messages and consulted the Foreign Office and the war cabinet about proposals put to him by President Roosevelt.[43] In comparison with the American practice, it is striking to note the authority and trust that the prime minister and the war cabinet placed in the heads of mission—in 1944, when Eden was going to Moscow, he asked Cadogan if he would go as Foreign Office representative, and the permanent under secretary replied, "It would be as much a waste of time as was Teheran. If you have an Ambassador there, you must use him."[44] This trust was in general justified by the efficiency with which the ambassadors carried out the duties of representation, negotiated when necessary with local authorities, and kept the Foreign Office informed of political shifts that affected British interests.

All of this does not mean that perfect harmony prevailed. On the two most important issues, relations with the United States and with the Soviet Union, there were marked differences between the prime minister on the one hand and the Foreign Secretary and the professional Foreign Office staff on the other. Churchill always remembered with gratitude the aid that the United States had provided Britain in its darkest hour and, although occasionally irritated by Roosevelt's anticolonial pronouncements, was unhappy when not in full accord with his American ally. Except on the biggest of issues, he was disinclined to criticize it. Thus, after he had persuaded the Americans to substitute the North African operation for a cross-Channel landing in 1942, he could not be moved to take a strong line with them over their deal with Admiral Darlan, which Eden believed was a betrayal of the very principles that underlay Britain's war effort.[45] Similarly, he was inclined to associate himself much longer with Roosevelt's opposition to the formal recognition of Charles de Gaulle as putative leader of the government in France than Eden and the Foreign Office thought desirable.[46]

The professionals, after the first critical phase of the war was past, were inclined to believe that the prime minister should be less deferential to American opinion and prejudice, which they felt was excessively moralistic except in cases where United States interests were involved, and Eden, worried about the growing American economic dominance of the United States over Britain after 1942 and by evidence that the Americans were seeking to strengthen their position in Iran and Saudi Arabia at British expense, was inclined to agree.[47]

Differences between the Foreign Office and the prime minister existed also with respect to the Soviet Union. Churchill was less enthusiastic about the Anglo-Soviet Alliance of 1942 than Eden, who had negotiated it, feeling that the price paid—an implicit promise to support the Soviet claim to the Baltic states—was too high. He felt that the Soviets had no right to any special treatment, since "they entered the war only when attacked by Germany, having previously shown themselves utterly indifferent to our fate." But at a time when the Red Army was carrying the brunt of the fighting and public and parliamentary opinion was clamoring for closer union with the Soviet Union, the prime minister did not feel strong enough to dig his heels in. Eden was permitted to go his way, although it was predicted, among others by Under Secretary of State Sumner Welles, that his concessions would sooner or later lead to new Soviet demands.[48]

The foreign secretary hoped to forestall such difficulties by the establishment while the war continued of inter-Allied machinery for the planning of the postwar settlement in Europe and the international organization of security. He was encouraged by the fact that, at the Moscow meeting of Allied foreign ministers in November 1943, the Russians had agreed to the establishment of a European Advisory Commission in London that would examine problems that were bound to arise at the war's end and to make recommendations to the governments, and he was anxious to get it going.[49] At the same time, the Foreign Office had begun to work on plans for a postwar security organization that would avoid the procedural faults that had contributed to the destruction of the League of Nations.[50]

The prime minister, for his part, was always much too concerned with the military aspects of the war to pay much attention to these issues, and he believed in any case that they could not be addressed in any detail until the hostilities had come to an end. This is clear from his attitude toward the German question. During the meeting at Placentia Bay in 1941, Churchill told President Roosevelt:

> We must disarm the Germans and their accomplices but give no undertaking, which they can afterwards exploit, that we shall give them within any measurable time any sort of equality as regards arms. On the contrary, we must take care to see that we are sufficiently strongly armed to prevent any repetition, in Europe or the world of these catastrophes. On the other hand, we now take the view that impoverished neighbors are bound to be bad neighbors, and we wish to see everyone prosperous, including the Germans. In short, our intention is to make Germany fat but impotent.[51]

This indicated some thinking about mistakes made after 1918 but no reflection on difficult problems like punishment, partition, and reparations, on all of which Churchill was ambivalent. At Teheran, he reacted furiously to Stalin's suggestion that fifty thousand German officers should be killed,[52] but on other occasions he was less chivalrous and seemed intent on dispelling any suspicion on Stalin's part that the British would be soft on the Germans.[53] He never varied from the view, however, that Germany must be a member of the European family of nations in the postwar world.[54]

What Germany might look like after the war, Churchill left to the experts in the Foreign Office, without attending very carefully to their plans or considering himself bound by them.[55] There were in any case strong differences of perspective between the prime minister and the Foreign Office. Churchill, who thought in terms of tradition and continuity and believed that there was something imperishable about Great Powers, was interested in restoring the old European system, in ways that struck Eden's aides as antiquated and unrealistic. He was, for example, fascinated with Prussia, with which he had always had a love-hate relationship, and regarded it as a necessary bulwark against Russia, and between 1940 and 1942 played with various restoration and federation plans in which Prussia figured. The Foreign Office, after the conclusion of the Anglo-Soviet Pact, was anxious to build upon it by negotiating a Four Power Pact (Great Britain, the United States, the Soviet Union, and—in deference to President Roosevelt—China) that would regulate and control Germany, and their irritation over their failure to hold Churchill's attention is shown by an entry in the diary of Eden's private secretary in October 1942:

> P. M. has sent another foolish minute about our postwar plan. He wishes to put the clock back to the Congress of Vienna. With Roosevelt straining to put the British Empire in liquidation and Winston pulling in the opposite direction to put it back to pre–Boer War, we are in danger of losing both the Old and the New World.[56]

Because the prime minister instinctively opposed plans that might tie his hands and make concessions to the Soviets that would not be justified by the military situation at the end of the war—and perhaps because he overestimated Britain's military strength—he did not always feel bound by arrangements made by his diplomats and sometimes made impulsive and disruptive decisions. Thus, at the Quebec Conference in September 1944, he allowed himself to be talked into a plan sponsored by the United States secretary of the treasury, Henry Morgenthau, Jr., to turn Germany into a pastoral state, an aberration that infuriated his foreign secretary, who could hardly speak coherently about it.[57] Nothing came of the Morgenthau Plan, but it was symptomatic of Churchill's failure to comprehend how far his country was already committed by decisions made by the EAC, assumptions made at summit conferences, and the movements of armies. Even at Yalta, the prime minister seemed to assume that, as far as Germany was concerned, nothing had really been settled.[58]

Similarly, Churchill's failure to pay close attention to the Foreign Office plans for an international security organization—plans in which his permanent under secretary for foreign affairs, Sir Alexander Cadogan, played a leading role—caused confusion when the organization became the center of some contention at the Yalta Conference.[59] In a rare cabinet discussion of the subject on 4 August 1944, the security organization had been mentioned but, as Cadogan wrote in his diary, "P. M. [was] cynically jocular—which bodes ill. Neither he—nor anyone else—would take it seriously."[60] At Yalta, however, Cadogan wrote, "[The] silly old man, without a word of warning to Anthony or me, plunged into a long harangue about the World Organisation, knowing nothing whatever of what he was talking about and making complete nonsense of the whole thing."[61]

There was more irritation than rage in these Foreign Office outbursts. Churchill's frequent failures to master his brief before adopting firm and highly wordy stands was a burden that the professionals had to tolerate, and it was often troublesome to correct the damage done. But it usually could be corrected. At the conference at Dumbarton Oaks in the autumn of 1944, Cadogan made the most of the Foreign Office plans and worked out the key compromises that assured the foundation of the United Nations,[62] to which he would be the first chief of the British permanent delegation. In the meantime, the Foreign Office never forgot what they had in Winston Churchill. In the darkest of days after the fall of France, when Britain had stood alone, his leadership, as Sir Llewellyn Woodward has written, "had about it something adamantine and absolute; something which had not been known in English history since the years 1757–1759. Such power and insight brought a new direction in every branch of the State."[63] There could have been few people in the Foreign Office who failed to understand the tremendous burdens that the prime minister bore for five long years of war or to regard their relationship with him, even if intermittently contentious, as rewarding and inspiring.

III

Compared with the British diplomatic establishment, the United States Department of State and the American Foreign Service could not claim to be the principal instruments in the formulation and execution of wartime policy. The war years represented a period of remarkable growth for the State Department[64] but also one in which new agencies with an interest in foreign policy came into being—the Board of Economic Warfare, the Coordinator of Information (later Office of Strategic Services), the Office of War Information, and many others. Particularly after the involvement of the United States in the war, competition between these agencies and attempts to take over functions formally reserved for the State Department were persistent and protracted. The raids were, as often as not, successful, with the subsequent result that coordination of operations, and even exchange of information that would have facilitated coordination, became difficult.

Meanwhile, Secretary of State Cordell Hull was always more interested in questions of trade and Wilsonian concepts of world order than he was in grand strategy. The president valued him most for his influence on Congress but on other matters rarely saw him more than once a week and preferred, in any case, to do his State Department business through the under secretary, Sumner Welles. This tactic of controlling the department by dividing it against itself made Hull and Welles bitter enemies, and in August 1943 the secretary asked Roosevelt to choose between them, and the president was forced to let Welles go.[65] All things considered, the secretary was treated with little ceremony by the White House. At the Casablanca conference in January 1943, Roosevelt's chief of staff, Admiral William D. Leahy, was instructed not to divulge any information about the conference without the president's specific permission in each instance, and was placed in the embarrassing position of having to inform Secretary Hull, who had asked about how the conference would affect relations with Turkey, that this rule applied to him.[66] Similarly, at the Yalta Conference, Roosevelt did not see fit to inform Hull's successor, Edward R. Stettinius, Jr., of the agreement he had made with Stalin about Soviet intervention in the Japanese war, on the ground that it was a military affair.

As far as the chiefs of mission abroad were concerned, the president was no respecter of their authority or their feelings. He was much given to the use of private and personal representatives, like Harry Hopkins and W. Averell Harriman, who would descend upon an Allied capital and enter into relations with the head of government without consulting the United States ambassador or including him in the discussions. For the unfortunate envoy, this was humiliating. The journalist Harrison Salisbury once told an interviewer that, after Harriman's arrival in London as Lend Lease Administrator, he not only "took the glamour out of [Ambassador John] Winant's job; he substantively undercut his relationship with Churchill."[67] Admiral W. H. Standley in Moscow resigned his post after being repeatedly by-passed by special envoys and finally having to tolerate the arrival of Joseph E. Davies (a notoriously inefficient predecessor of his) with a special message from Roosevelt to Stalin, which, when Standley presented him to the Soviet leader, he refused to open in the ambassador's presence.[68] It is doubtless true that these extraordinary methods were sometimes necessary and had some short-term advantages, but they diminished the role of representation, and they were not a satisfactory substitute for continuous and fully informed political liaison on the highest level.[69] Moreover, their greatest disadvantage was that, in the last analysis, the only person who could speak authoritatively about the nature and direction of the United States policy was the president himself.

It is doubtful whether this was justified by Franklin Roosevelt's knowledge of or experience in foreign affairs. Enthusiasm for his high gifts of leadership has led his admirers to exaggerate his diplomatic skills, and Sumner Welles once wrote incautiously that he "brought to the conduct of American foreign relations more specialized qualifications than those possessed by any President since the days of John Quincy Adams."[70] In fact, when one thinks of Adams's long and varied career in foreign affairs, Roosevelt had no comparable experience; his only federal service before becoming president was as assistant secretary of the navy from 1913 to 1920; and his knowledge of Europe was based on annual trips to England, France, and Germany with his parents and governesses in the late 1880s and 1890s. His complete absorption in domestic politics from 1920 to 1933 had given him no opportunity to correct this weakness, and he tended to respond to the deterioration of the European situation in the thirties with the clichés of classical diplomacy[71] and the hope that, as he wrote to his ambassador in Vienna in December 1933, "German sanity of the old type that existed in the Bismarck days when I was a boy . . . will come to the front again."[72]

It was inevitable that he would find it hard to understand the character of the new dictators in Europe and the Far East.[73] He thought of great-power politics as a rational pursuit and assumed that it would continue to operate according to reasonable and generally accepted rules of procedure and accommodation, particularly in an age still suffering from the ravages of a terrible war and in the grasp of a worldwide economic depression. It was inconceivable to him that there were national leaders who repudiated such ideas and had no compunction about using war to secure their objectives. If this was naïveté, it was shared by many Americans, as well as by the press, distracted by the problems of the Depression, and the U.S. missions abroad. Although there were exceptions (the reporting of the Tokyo mission under Joseph Grew was of consistently high quality),[74] it has to be said that during his first term, the president was not particularly well served by his ambassadors, and the European heads of mission were for the most part all inclined to underestimate Hitler's intentions. Reports that held that the Führer was "a paranoiac, with a gift of eloquence of a kind halfway between Bryan and Billy Sunday,"[75] and that he would modify his objectives if the right approach was made[76] provided the president with neither the guidance nor the cautionary prescriptions that might have helped him, and their very diversity of view robbed them of any sense of urgency. Thus, Roosevelt tended to give Hitler the benefit of the doubt, and it was only after the Führer had repudiated the arms clauses of the Versailles Treaty in 1935 and sent his troops into the demilitarized Rhineland a year later, that he became vaguely alarmed and began to consider the possibility that "Hitler was an international gangster, a bandit who some day would have to be halted."[77] But he did not say so publicly, and even as late as October 1937, when he decided in the famous Quarantine speech in Chicago to test the public desire to collaborate in the restraint of the dictators, he was quick to retreat when he mistakenly believed the reaction was unfavorable.

When Hitler went on the offensive in 1938, therefore, Roosevelt had no strategy for opposing him. His proposal to Neville Chamberlain in January 1938 for a White House conference of world leaders to define and establish rules of international behavior was turned down by the British prime minister because it threatened to disrupt his own plan for driving a wedge between Hitler and Mussolini, but it was in any case unrealistic. William C. Bullitt wrote the president that, in view of Hitler's obvious designs on Austria, the plan was "as if in the palmiest days of Al Capone you had summoned a national conference of psychoanalysts to Washington to discuss the psychological causes of crime."[78] As Austria fell and the drama of Czechoslovakia began to unfold, he was unwilling to follow Bullitt's suggestion that he warn the German dictator that, if he continued on his present course, the United States would almost certainly be drawn into opposition to his designs,[79] and at the height of the Sudeten crisis he confined himself to sending a plea to Hitler urging him to continue negotiations, which ended with the awkward admission, "The United States has no political involvement in Europe and will assume no obligation in the conduct of present negotiations."[80] His subsequent expression of satisfaction with the Munich settlement was belied by Hitler's annexation of rump Czechoslovakia and the beginning of his propaganda campaign against Poland. In the face of this, the president had nothing to offer but a message to Hitler on 15 April 1939, asking him to pledge not to attack a list of thirty-one nations, which he appended, a request that was ridiculed by Hitler in a speech before the party faithful and may have given him the impression that he had nothing to fear from the United States.

The influence of the United States on the culminating events of 1939 was negligible, and there is no doubt that the strongly isolationist cast of American public opinion had much to do with this. Yet David Reynolds is surely correct in arguing that "the ambiguities of Franklin Roosevelt's policy grew as much out of his own character and attitudes as they did out of his celebrated deference to the dictates of public opinion,"[81] and surely the president's diplomatic démarches in 1938 and 1939 illustrated a lack of grasp of realities and perceptions outside the United States, a desire to play the great mediator, and a "concentration on easy rhetoric, rather than on politically hazardous and difficult action."[82]

On the other hand, if the president's diplomatic performance had been uninspired, his direction of American policy after the outbreak of the European war, while hesitant, tentative, and even contradictory in its tactics, was masterful in its overall strategy. To the military situation he responded with vigor and assurance. In July 1939, by a military order issued in his capacity as commander in chief, he moved the Joint Board of the Army and Navy, which coordinated the strategical plans of the two services, and the military and civilian agencies in charge of procurement and production programs into the new Executive Office of the President, thus concentrating the military power of the United States under his own control.[83] Despite his latent opposition to British imperialism (a feeling shared by the top layer of officials in the State Department, Sumner Welles, Assistant Secretary Adolf Berle, the head of the

European desk, Jay Pierrepont Moffatt, and Hull himself, all of whom in varying degrees shared a deep suspicion of perfidious Albion)[84] he had made a basic strategical decision long before hostilities began, namely, that if war came the United States would have in its own interest to support Great Britain. He hoped at the same time that if this support were vigorous enough, actual military intervention by the country might not be necessary.

This basic concept was implemented by four decisions. The first was Roosevelt's order in November 1938 for the creation of a plant capacity capable of producing ten thousand planes a year, a number later stepped up in May 1940 to fifty thousand. The second, strongly supported by Ambassador Bullitt and the secretaries of interior, the treasury, and war, Harold Ickes, Henry Morgenthau, Jr., and Henry L. Stimson, was a program of speeches and fireside talks to educate the American people to the reality of the threat and the necessity of opposing it by all steps short of war.[85] The third was the decision in May-June 1940 to commit the country to all-out military assistance to Great Britain, a step revealed to the American public for the first time in a speech in Charlottesville on 6 June and later given substance by the destroyers-bases deal and the Lend Lease legislation. Finally, the president decided in the spring and summer of 1941, against the strong reservations of General George C. Marshall, to establish garrisons and convoys in the Atlantic and to extend them in order to keep the supply line to Britain open as far as necessary.[86] There can be little doubt that this strategy made it easier for the British government to withstand German pressure for surrender after Dunkirk and helped sustain it during the dark days that followed.

But Franklin Roosevelt always had a surer touch with military questions than with those of international politics, and once the United States had become involved in the war his diplomatic deficiencies became obvious and troubling for his allies and his subordinates. Here his skills as a domestic politician worked against him. His compulsion to be liked, which often led him to feign agreement with an opinion rather than cause disappointment, was an important weapon in his domestic armory but didn't work in diplomacy, where geniality is not highly treasured and where basic issues and objectives are always at stake and promises are remembered. Roosevelt's cheerful fecklessness, as Anthony Eden once called it,[87] and his lighthearted changing of position were resented by those who had to pay the price for them. His genius at judging the strength of his public support in domestic affairs betrayed him in foreign politics, and his uncertainty about how far he could carry the country with him led him to be overcautious and unwilling to face up to problems that needed to be addressed, like the Russian position on Poland, or to give the public overoptimistic impressions of how close all problems in Europe and the Far East were to solution and how soon American troops would be home again. At the same time, his fascination with military problems led him to emphasize them to the neglect of long-term political planning. It is safe to say that he had no real plan for what was to happen in China after the Japanese were defeated, and that he was by no means certain in his mind how far the United States should be involved in the postwar European settlement.[88] All of these weaknesses were compounded by his secretiveness, his distrust of his allies and his total confidence in his own judgment, which, in the view of a British historian, encouraged him to entertain convictions about those with whom he was dealing that made him ill-informed and indeed myopic.[89]

It was perhaps the president's assumption that he was the leader of the wartime coalition from the moment he joined it and his utter confidence in his ability to talk people around that most irritated the British Foreign Office. Cadogan, for instance, had been infuriated by the mission of Sumner Welles to Europe in February 1940 and had exploded in his diary about the president's "awful, half-baked, idea of sending Sumner Welles (!) here with a flourish of trumpets to collect data on which Roosevelt is to proclaim bases of peace."[90] Foreign Office indignation was greater during one of the difficult stretches in the negotiations of the Anglo-Soviet Alliance of 1942. In his memoirs, Anthony Eden has written that in mid-February 1942 as the British and the Russians wrangled over the question of the Baltic states,

> Welles told [Ambassador] Halifax that the President had decided to make a direct approach to Stalin and was confident he could reach agreement with him. Halifax demurred at this, pointing out that it was with us that Stalin wished to sign a treaty and that this procedure might put me in a dangerous position. Here was the first of several occasions when the President, mistakenly I believed, moved out of step with us, influenced by his conviction that he could get better results with Stalin direct than could the three countries negotiating together. This was an illusion.[91]

It was a persistent one, however, which had its ultimate expression in Roosevelt's conduct at the Big Three summit meetings at Teheran and Yalta. In the former, where Allied second-front strategy was decisively revised in accordance with American and Soviet wishes, the president used questionable tactics to ingratiate himself with the Soviet leader, avoiding preconference consultation with Churchill and having three private sessions with Stalin, during which he emphasized his differences with the British prime minister with respect to the liquidation of British and French colonialism and told Stalin that he agreed in general with his host's ideas about the reconstruction of Poland but could not take a position on this until after the next presidential election, since he needed the votes of Americans of Polish extraction.[92] At Yalta, the president was so intent upon gaining assurances with respect to Soviet intervention in the war against Japan and Stalin's willingness to participate in the international security organization that had been designed at the conference at Dumbarton Oaks that he accepted assurances about the future government of Poland, which within months of the conference had proved to be worthless.[93] Nor was he willing to admit the truth when it became obvious. On 13 March 1945, as Secretary

Stettinius was assuring the cabinet that Yalta demonstrated "the Russian desire to cooperate along all lines" with the United States, Churchill cabled the president: "Poland has lost her frontier. Is she now to lose her freedom? . . . We are in the presence of a great failure and an utter breakdown of what was settled at Yalta." He argued that combined pressure upon Moscow was required.[94] Roosevelt denied that a breakdown had occurred and joked to his cabinet that he was having trouble, not with the Russians but with the British, who were perfectly willing for the United States to have a war with the Soviet Union.[95]

What is striking in all this is not merely the president's dogged belief that in the last analysis his personal influence with Stalin would overcome all differences, but his resolute refusal to think seriously about the European future. This was motivated in part by a disinclination to become involved in the kind of traditional agreements about balance of power and spheres of influence that were deeply alien to the American public conscience, in part by an often convenient but nevertheless deeply held belief that political decisions should wait upon military victory (which flew in the face of Clausewitz's warning of the perils that such delays were likely to cause),[96] and partly by a conviction that disputes over territory and sovereignty would be best regulated by the world organization that was in formation. The president might on occasion make future promises, as he did in June 1944, when he assured Stanislaw Mikolajczyk, prime minister of the Polish government in exile, that at the appropriate time he would help Poland retain Lwow, Tarnopol, and the oil areas in eastern Galicia, and would see that it received Königsberg, the rest of East Prussia, and Silesia, but his added remark that he was opposed to territorial settlements being made before the end of the war robbed the promise of any essential meaning and, given the movement of events, any real chance of fulfilment.[97]

One thing that can be said of the president's attitude is that it was consistent. Immediately after Pearl Harbor, when Foreign Secretary Eden and Sir Alexander Cadogan went to Moscow, Cadogan told the American chargé d'affaires that it would be a good idea for the United States and British governments to concert their attitude toward postwar problems and then present their joint view to the Soviets.[98] This suggestion elicited no response from Washington. Two years later, when the Allied foreign ministers agreed at Moscow to set up a European Advisory Commission to anticipate postwar problems and make recommendations for solving them, Secretary Hull discovered upon returning to Washington that neither the White House nor the Department of State had any enthusiasm for the idea. In consequence, as George F. Kennan has written in his memoirs, the American representative to the EAC was kept on such short leash that he could

come up with no thoughts and make no suggestion to his colleagues which had not come to him in instructions from Washington, and since Washington seemed to have a total absence of thoughts, and only the tardiest and most grudging of suggestions, this obviously limited drastically what the American representative could do.

When he went to London to serve as assistant to Ambassador Winant in his capacity as representative to the EAC, Kennan was warned by Assistant Secretary of State James C. Dunn to bear in mind "that in wartime the Department of State had only an advisory role with respect to matters of policy, and that it gave advice only when asked." In these circumstances, the American role in what planning was effected by the EAC could not be a distinguished one.[99]

Similarly, the high importance given by the American delegation at the Yalta Conference to the question of Soviet adherence to the new world organization unquestionably reflected the president's determination to assure that body's viability. But it was also a convenient method of avoiding other important issues. George Kennan, then counselor of the United States embassy in Moscow, wrote warningly at the time:

> An international organization for the preservation of peace and security cannot take the place of a well-conceived and realistic foreign policy . . . and we are being . . . negligent of the interests of our people if we allow plans for an international organization to be an excuse for failing to occupy ourselves seriously and minutely with the sheer power relationships of the European peoples.[100]

But such relationships could not be a major concern to a president who did not believe that there would be any American troops in Europe for more than two years after the conclusion of hostilities, and who had told Stalin that in postwar Europe British and Soviet troops would alone be responsible for any necessary ground operations.

Given this general aversion to planning ahead, it is little wonder that in March and April 1945 the commander of American troops in Europe, General Dwight D. Eisenhower, was deaf to British arguments that it would be politically advantageous to capture Berlin and Prague before the Red Army reached those capitals. Eisenhower made his own position clear by writing to General George Marshall, "May I point out that Berlin itself is no longer a particularly important objective,"[101] and was backed up by the Joint Chiefs of Staff and the White House, while the State Department was deaf to British protests.[102]

IV

It may be incautious, after these disparate observations, to attempt any general conclusion. Yet, whatever may be said in the way of explanation and palliation, it is difficult to avoid feeling that, on the whole, diplomacy during the Second

World War mortgaged the future, in the German case by complicity in the crimes of the Nazi regime, in the Western case by a failure to pursue a coordinated political strategy, and on the part of the Americans by focusing on the problem of overthrowing the dictators without sufficient thought about what would come thereafter. The configurations of the world of the Cold War are to be discerned in the crimes of commission and omission of those in charge of their countries' foreign policies. Even before the sound of the guns had died away, mankind had every reason to admit, in Wilhelm von Humboldt's rueful words, that "the evil results caused by the postponement of many things from one epoch to another [were] now coming to light."

Notes

1. David Dilks, ed., *The Diaries of Sir Alexander Cadogan O.M., 1938–1945* (London, 1971), 579.

2. Ibid., 765. See also Robert Rhodes James, *Anthony Eden* (London, 1986), 307.

3. On this, see Gordon A. Craig and Alexander H. George, *Force and Statecraft: Diplomatic Problems of Our Time*, 2d ed. (New York, 1990), 102–9. Robert Dallek has pointed out that the idea was not based on a sentimental concern for the Chinese but rather with the notion of supporting America's interest in the Far East. Robert Dallek, *Franklin Delano Roosevelt and American Foreign Policy* (New York, 1979), 428 f. The inadequacy of China's military strength for a major world role did not appear to worry the president.

4. Anna von Sydow, ed., *Wilhelm und Caroline von Humboldt in ihren Briefen,* (Berlin, 1910), 4:400.

5. See my account in Gordon A. Craig and Felix Gilbert, eds., *The Diplomats, 1919–1939* (Princeton, 1953), 406–36, and the more recent treatments by Hans-Jürgen Döscher, *Das Auswärtige Amt im Dritten Reich: Diplomatie im Schatten der Endlösung* (Berlin, 1986); and "Zur Geschichte des Auswärtigen Amts," in *100 Jahre Auswärtiges Amt. 1870–1970,* compiled by the Political Archive of the Foreign Ministry under the direction of Dr. Heinz Günther Sasse (Bonn, 1970), 42 ff.

6. Useful accounts of Ribbentrop's career are to be found in John Weitz, *Hitler's Diplomat: The Life and Times of Joachim von Ribbentrop* (New York, 1992), and Michael Bloch, *Ribbentrop* (New York, 1992), although neither is very useful in analyzing its subject's ideas. Better in this respect is Wolfgang Michalka, *Ribbentrop und die deutsche Weltpolitik 1933–1940* (Munich, 1980).

7. Franz von Papen, *Memoirs,* translated from the German by Brian Connell (London, 1952), 341.

8. Erich Kordt, *Nicht aus den Akten* (Stuttgart, 1950), 93, 129 f.

9. See Michalka, *Ribbentrop,* 210 ff., 247 ff.

10. Kordt, *Nicht aus den Akten,* 91 f.

11. Craig, in Craig and Gilbert, *The Diplomats,* 427 ff.

12. Daniel Koerfer, "Ernst von Weizsäcker im Dritten Reich: Ein deutscher Offizier und Diplomat zwischen Verstrickung und Selbsttäuschung," in *Die Schatten der Vergangenheit: Impulse zur Historisierung des Nationalsozialismus,* herausgegeben

von Uwe Backes, Eckhard Jesse, and Rainer Zitelmann (Frankfurt am Main, Berlin, 1990), 383. See also Paul Seabury in *The Wilhelmstrasse: A Study of Diplomats Under the Nazi Regime* (Berkeley, 1954).

13. *100 Jahre Auswärtiges Amt,* 46.

14. *Trials of War Criminals Before the Nurenberg Military Tribunals Under Control Council Law No. 10,* 14 vols. (Nuremberg, 1946–1949), 13:25.

15. Döscher, *Das Auswärtige Amt,* 152.

16. Ibid., pp. 157–81, 192 ff. On Luther, see Christopher R. Browning, "Unterstaatssekretär Martin Luther and the Ribbentrop Foreign Office," *Journal of Contemporary History* 12, no. 7 (1977): 313–44, and *The Final Solution and the German Foreign Office: A Study of Referat D III of Abteilung Deutschland 1940–1943* (New York, 1978).

17. See the interesting argument advanced by Michalka, *Ribbentrop,* 298 ff.

18. David Dilks, " 'We must hope for the best and prepare for the worst': The Prime Minister, the Cabinet and Hitler's Germany, 1937–1939," *Proceedings of the British Academy* 63, no. 9 (1987): 326.

19. Ernst von Weizsäcker, *Memoiren* (Munich, 1950), 162 ff.; Klemens von Klemperer, *The German Resistance Against Hitler: The Search for Allies Abroad, 1938–1945* (Oxford, 1992), 26–27.

20. R. A. Blasius, *Für Großdeutschland und gegen den großen Krieg: Ernst von Weizsäcker in den Krisen um die Tschechoslowakei und Polen* (Cologne, 1981), 58 ff.

21. Paul Schmidt, *Statist auf diplomatischer Bühne 1923–1945* (Bonn, 1949), 464.

22. William L. Langer and S. Everett Gleason, *The Undeclared War, 1940–41* (New York, 1953), 21–32; James V. Compton, *The Swastika and the Eagle: Hitler, the United States and the Origins of the World War II* (Boston, 1967), 195 ff; *Documents on German Foreign Policy, 1918–1945: From the Archives of the German Foreign Ministry* (Washington, D.C., 1949 and continuing), series D, XI, nos. 123, 141, 164.

23. *Akten zur deutschen auswärtigen Politik 1918–1945: Aus dem Archiv des Auswärtigen Amts,* series E (Göttingen, 1969 ff.), V, no. 229, p. 437 ff. (Aufzeichnung Ribbentrops, 21 Mar. 1943.)

24. Between 1938 and 1943, its personnel increased from 2,665 to 6,458 in number. *100 Jahre Auswärtiges Amt,* 44.

25. For its organization and personnel in 1944, see *Akten,* series E, VII, p. 695 ff.

26. *100 Jahre Auswärtiges Amt,* 46.

27. *Akten,* series E, V, no. 128, p. 219. See also I, no. 275, p. 511 (Ribbentrop to the Mission in Bern, 23 Feb. 1942).

28. Ibid., III, no. 286, pp. 488 ff. (Memorandum of Under Secretary of State Luther, 14 Sept. 1942); III, no. 302, pp. 519 ff. (Unsigned Memorandum, 20 Sept. 1942); IV, no. 124, pp. 222 ff. (Directive of Hitler, Führerhauptquartier, 4 Nov. 1942).

29. See Döscher, *Das Auswärtige Amt,* 256–61; and Browning, "Unterstaatssekretär," 332–40.

30. The literature on this is massive. See, among recent works, Klemperer, *German Resistance;* Peter Hoffmann, *German Resistance to Hitler* (Cambridge, Mass., 1988), and *Claus Graf von Stauffenberg und seine Brüder* (Stuttgart, 1992); Ulrich von Hassell, *Die Hassell-Tagebücher 1938–1944: Aufzeichnungen vom anderen Deutschland,* ed. Freiherr Hiller von Gärtringen (Berlin, 1988); Helmuth James von Moltke, *Briefe an*

Freya, 1939–1945, ed. Beate Ruhm von Oppen (Munich, 1988); Ulrich Sahm, *Rudolf von Scheliha 1897–1942: Ein deutscher Diplomat gegen Hitler* (Munich, 1990); Marie Vassiltchikov, *Berlin Diaries, 1940–45* (New York, 1987); and Giles MacDonogh, *A Good German: Adam von Trott zu Solz* (Woodstock, N.Y., 1992).

31. Döscher, *Das Auswärtige Amt*, 175 ff.

32. See especially John P. Fox, "German Bureaucrat or Nazified Ideologue? Ambassador Otto Abetz and Hitler's Anti-Jewish Policies 1940–1944," in *Power, Personalities and Policies: Essays in Honour of Donald Cameron Watt*, ed. Michael Graham Fry (London, 1992), 175–232, where the connections between the Foreign Office, particularly Martin Luther's Germany section, and the activities of Karl Theodor Zeitschel, head of the section for Jewish affairs in Abetz's Paris embassy and the fanatical Nazi and Jew hater Theodor Dannecker, Adolf Eichmann's *Judenreferat* in Paris, are spelled out.

33. *Akten*, series E, II, no. 56, p. 97 (Foreign Ministry to RSHA, 20 Mar. 1942). See also nos. 93, 177, 197, 230, 289.

34. Ibid., VI, no. 129, p. 223 (Note of SS-Oberführer Veesenmayer, 3 July 1943).

35. Ibid., VII, no. 148, pp. 148 f. (Memorandum of Vortagende Legationsrat Wagner for the Reich Foreign Minister, 1 July 1944). See also VII, nos. 7, 11, 18, 48, 49, 54, 66, 75, 101, 111, 127, 139, 148, 160, 162, 163, 189, 205, 220, 263, 309, 316, 317, 320, 352.

36. Chamberlain was not, of course, the first prime minister to accuse the Foreign Office of narrowness of view, dependence upon traditional concepts, and lack of realism. To some degree, Lloyd George and Ramsay MacDonald had shared this feeling. Gordon A. Craig, "The Professional Diplomat and his Problems, 1919–1939," in *War, Politics, and Diplomacy: Selected Essays* (New York, 1966), pp. 212 f.

37. *Documents on German Policy*, series D, IV, no. 306.

38. The best and most even-handed explanation of the failure of Chamberlain's policy is Donald Cameron Watt, *How War Came: The Immediate Origins of the Second World War, 1938–1939* (London, 1989). Among other things, he points out that Hitler's desire for war rendered any deterrent policy ineffective. For a defense of Chamberlain's policy against critics who fail to take into account the actual circumstances of the 1930s and the gap between British responsibilities and strength, see Dilks, "'We Must Hope.'"

39. This was Cadogan's conclusion by March 1939, although he had early supported Chamberlain's determination to secure an accommodation with Hitler. Dilks, *Diaries of Cadogan*, 54, 103, 161.

40. Ibid., 300.

41. Sir Llewellyn Woodward, *British Foreign Policy in the Second World War* (London, 1962), xxiv.

42. Francis L. Loewenheim, Harold D. Langley, and Manfred Jonas, eds., *Roosevelt and Churchill: Their Secret Wartime Correspondence* (New York, 1975); Warren F. Kimball, ed., *Churchill and Roosevelt: The Complete Correspondence*, 3 vols. (Princeton, 1984).

43. Woodward, *Foreign Policy*, xxiv.

44. Dilks, *Diaries of Cadogan*, 670.

45. Anthony Eden, *The Reckoning: The Memoirs of Anthony Eden, Earl of Avon* (Boston, 1965), 406. William L. Langer's attempt, in *Our Vichy Gamble* (Boston, 1947), to justify American policy on the grounds of *Realpolitik* is no longer as persuasive as it once seemed.

46. Eden, *The Reckoning,* 456 ff.; Woodward, *Foreign Policy,* xiv–xivi.

47. Rhodes James, *Eden,* 272. See also Gabriel Kolko, *The Politics of War, the World and United States Foreign Policy, 1943–1945* (New York, 1990).

48. On all this, see Steven Merritt Miner, *Between Churchill and Stalin: The Soviet Union, Great Britain, and the Origins of the Grand Alliance* (Chapel Hill, N.C., 1989). The pact was, of course, by no means one-sided and was accompanied, for instance, by a Soviet agreement to recognize the Sikorski government in exile and to free Polish prisoners of war and deportees so that they might fight the common enemy. See Eden, *The Reckoning,* 305 ff., 314 ff.

49. Ibid., p. 492. On the origins and work of the EAC, see especially Lord Strang, *Home and Abroad* (London, 1956), 199–225.

50. See especially Sir Llewellyn Woodward in collaboration with M. E. Lambert, *British Foreign Policy in the Second World War* (London, 1976), vol. 5, chaps. 61–63 and 65.

51. Ben Pimlott, ed., *The Second World War Diary of Hugh Dalton, 1940–1945* (London, 1986), 175.

52. Winston Churchill, *The Second World War,* 6 vols. (Boston, 1948 ff.), 5:330; Lord Moran, *Churchill: The Struggle for Survival, Taken from the Diaries of Lord Moran, 1940–1965* (Boston, 1966), 152.

53. Martin Gilbert, *1941–1945: Road to Victory,* vol. 7 of *Winston S. Churchill* (Boston, 1987), 1025.

54. Sir John Colville, *The Fringes of Power: 10 Downing Street Diaries, 1939–1955* (London, 1985), 363.

55. The general nature of Foreign Office thinking in 1943 is discussed in Woodward and Lambert, *British Foreign Policy,* vol. 5, chap. 61, and the continuation of planning in 1944 and 1945 in chaps. 64 and 66. See also the collection Reiner Blasius, ed., *Dokumente zur Deutschlandpolitik,* I. Reihe, Band 3: *1 Januar bis 31 Dezember 1942: Britische Deutschlandpolitik* (two half-volumes) (Frankfurt am Main, 1988). The best book on the subject is Lothar Kettenacker, *Krieg zur Friedenssicherung: Die Deutschlandplanung der britischen Regierung während des Zweiten Weltkriegs* (Göttingen and Zurich, 1989).

56. J. Harvey, ed., *The War Diaries of Oliver Hardy, 1941–1945* (London, 1978), 171.

57. Moran, *Diaries,* 190 f.

58. Kettenacker, *Krieg zur Friedenssicherung,* 542. In this account of Churchill's views on Germany, I have leaned heavily on my chapter on "Churchill and Germany," in *Churchill,* ed. Robert Blake and William Roger Louis (London, 1993).

59. See Woodward and Lambert, *British Foreign Policy,* vol. 5, chap. 65.

60. Dilks, *Diaries of Cadogan,* 653.

61. Ibid., 706.

62. See Woodward and Lambert, *British Foreign Policy,* vol. 5, chap. 63.

63. Woodward, *Foreign Policy,* xxix.

64. See below, Chapter 2.

65. See Dallek, *Roosevelt and Foreign Policy,* 421.

66. Admiral William D. Leahy, *I Was There* (New York, 1950), 173.

67. Rudy Abramson, *Spanning the Century: The Life of W. Averell Harriman, 1891–1986* (New York, 1992), 302–3.

68. Ibid., 347.

69. Woodward, *Foreign Policy,* xxxvi.

70. Sumner Welles, *The Time for Decision* (New York, 1944), 50.

71. See Klaus Schwabe, "Die Regierung Roosevelt und die Expansionspolitik Hitlers vor dem Zweiten Weltkrieg," in *Die Westmächte und das Dritte Reich, 1933–1939,* ed. Karl Rohe (Paderborn, 1982), 1:105.

72. Elliott Roosevelt, ed., *FDR: His Personal Letters, 1928–1945,* 4 vols. (New York, 1947–1950), 3:379.

73. This account of Roosevelt's policy before 1939 is based on my articles "Roosevelt and Hitler: The Problem of Perception," in *Deutsche Frage und europäische Gleichgewicht: Festschrift für Andreas Hillgruber zum 60. Geburtstag,* ed. Klaus Hildebrand und Reiner Pommerin (Cologne, Vienna, 1985), 169–94; and "Making Way for Hitler," *The New York Review of Books,* 12 Oct. 1989.

74. Joseph C. Grew, *Turbulent Era: A Diplomatic Record of Forty Years, 1904–1945.* Edited by Walter Johnson. 2 vols. (Boston, 1952). See also Waldo H. Heinrichs, *American Ambassador: Joseph C. Grew and the Development of the United States Diplomatic Tradition* (Boston, 1966).

75. *Franklin D. Roosevelt and Foreign Affairs,* vols. 1–3 edited by Edgar B. Nixon, vols. 4 ff. by Donald B. Schewe (New York, 1969 ff.), 1:505 (hereafter cited as *RFA*).

76. Ibid., 1:336.

77. *The Secret Diary of Harold L. Ickes,* 3 vols. (New York, 1953–1954), 2:213.

78. *RFA,* 8:122.

79. Orville H. Bullitt, ed., *For the President Only: The Correspondence Between Franklin D. Roosevelt and William C. Bullitt* (Boston, 1972), 279 f.

80. *Foreign Relations of the United States,* 1938, 1:684 f. (hereafter cited as *FRUS*). See also Dallek, *Roosevelt and Foreign Policy,* 165 f.; and Francis L. Loewenheim, *The Diffidence of Power: Some Notes and Reflections on the American Road to Munich,* Rice University Studies, no. 58 (1973), 48.

81. David Reynolds, *The Creation of the Anglo-American Alliance, 1937–1942* (Chapel Hill, N.C., 1982), 27.

82. Donald Cameron Watt, *How War Came: The Immediate Origins of the Second World War, 1938–1939* (London, 1989), 261.

83. Kent Roberts Greenfield, *American Strategy in World War II: A Reconsideration* (Baltimore, 1963), 52 ff.

84. Reynolds, *Anglo-American Alliance,* 28.

85. See William R. Rock, *Chamberlain and Roosevelt: British Foreign Policy and the United States, 1937–1940* (Columbus, Ohio, 1989).

86. See especially Waldo H. Heinrichs, *Threshold of War: Franklin D. Roosevelt and American Entry into World War II* (New York, 1988), 57–91.

87. Eden, *The Reckoning,* 433.

88. On all this, see the excellent assessment by Gaddis Smith, *American Diplomacy During the Second World War, 1941–1945* (New York, 1966), 8–12.

89. Watt, *How War Came,* 125.

90. Dilks, *Diaries of Cadogan,* 250.

91. Eden, *The Reckoning,* 375.

92. Gaddis Smith, *American Diplomacy,* 75–78; Robin Edmonds, *The Big Three:*

Churchill, Roosevelt and Stalin in Peace and War (New York, 1990), 248–359; Dallek, *Roosevelt and Foreign Policy,* 99, 429–39.

93. Gaddis Smith, *American Diplomacy,* 145–52; Edmonds, *Big Three,* 409–18; Dallek, *Roosevelt and Foreign Policy,* 514.

94. Churchill, *The Second World War,* 5:426.

95. Walter Millis, ed., *The Forrestal Diaries* (New York, 1951), 36–37.

96. See Clausewitz, *On War,* book 1, chap. 1, and especially book 8, chap. 6.

97. In a minute to the Foreign Office, the British foreign secretary wrote: "The poor Poles are sadly deluding themselves if they place any faith in these vague and generous promises. The President will not be embarrassed by them hereafter, any more than by the specific undertaking he has given to restore the French Empire." Eden, *The Reckoning,* 539 f.

98. *FRUS,* 1941, 1:204–5; Dilks, *Diaries of Cadogan,* 424.

99. George F. Kennan, *Memoirs, 1925–1950* (Boston, 1967), 164 ff.

100. Quoted by Gaddis Smith, *American Diplomacy,* 141.

101. Alfred D. Chandler, Jr., ed., *The Papers of General David Dwight Eisenhower: The War Years* (Baltimore and London, 1970), 4:2374.

102. Ibid., 4:2592–95; Forrest C. Pogue, *George C. Marshall: Organizer of Victory, 1943–1945* (New York, 1973), 548, 556, 568–74; David Eisenhower, *Eisenhower at War, 1943–1945* (New York, 1986), 662 ff.; Dilks, *Diaries of Cadogan,* 728, 735.

2

THE U.S. DEPARTMENT OF STATE

FROM HULL TO ACHESON

Richardson Dougall

IT IS SOMETIMES FORGOTTEN that Franklin D. Roosevelt's first secretary of state was Henry L. Stimson, who, in keeping with nineteenth-century practice, was held over from the Hoover Cabinet to avoid a break in the secretaryship between administrations. Stimson's service under Roosevelt lasted only a few hours, but it gave time for the new president to nominate Senator Cordell Hull of Tennessee as Stimson's successor, for the Senate to confirm the nomination, for Roosevelt to sign Hull's commission, and for Stimson, as his last official act, to countersign the commission.

His work as secretary of state completed, Stimson retired from office on the afternoon of 4 March 1933[1] and turned over to Hull a department that was very similar in size and organization to that which Stimson had inherited from Frank B. Kellogg four years earlier and indeed to that established in 1924 when Congress had reorganized the top levels of the department and had created the Foreign Service of the United States from the earlier diplomatic and consular services. It was one of the smallest departments in the United States government, with provision for its direction by the secretary, an under secretary, and four assistant secretaries—all political appointees of the president in power. Beneath this political layer,[2] the conglomeration of independent divisions and offices and their personnel remained largely untouched, although Hull found places in various crannies of the department for a few worthy Democrats who wanted jobs but did not aspire to high office. The geographic divisions—then, as now, considered the core of the department—were staffed at the officer level exclusively by white males. (One woman, Amy C. Holland, had been given the title of divisional assistant, at the junior professional level, in the Division of Near Eastern Affairs in 1931, but she continued to be listed as a clerk in the *Department of State Register* and was not moved above the salt until 1935.) Of the forty-three officers employed in those divisions on 1 July 1933, twenty-two were Foreign Service officers detailed for duty in Washington, and another thirteen had served in the past in the Foreign Service or in the diplomatic or consular services before their merger in 1924.[3] Foreign Service personnel carried over from the Stimson regime were in due course replaced on normal rotation. The other divisions and offices of the department were staffed largely by civil service officers and clerks, with a sprinkling of Foreign Service officers (about a dozen) in key positions, and with a substratum of messengers, chauffeurs, and laborers (mostly black) who were also a part of the civil service system.

Abroad, operating under the direction of the secretary of state, there were fifteen United States embassies and forty-seven legations, the heads of which served under presidential appointments—some political and some, at the president's option, recruited from the cadre of senior Foreign Service officers, who at that time had to resign from the Foreign Service to accept appointment as ambassadors or ministers. There were also sixty-five American consulates general and more than 180 consulates overseas, and about fifty miscellaneous offices, largely consular agencies.[4] Serving under the chiefs of the diplomatic missions and the heads of the consular offices were the officers and clerks of the Foreign Service. When Hull became secretary of state the Foreign Service officer corps contained a minuscule number of women, one of whom, Frances E. Willis, was destined much later to become the first female Foreign Service officer to be appointed to an ambassadorial post.[5] The service also included amidst its almost solidly white ranks Clifford R. Wharton, a black, who after a long series of assignments to posts in Africa eventually was to become minister to Romania and finally ambassador to Norway.

This mix of Foreign Service and civil service personnel systems, managed by two distinct personnel staffs in Washington, has been a subject of intermittent study whenever the administration of the Department of State has come under review, but it continued basically unchanged until enactment of new legislation in 1949, discussed below.

Roosevelt did not give Hull a free hand in the choice of his principal aides. Hull's first under secretary was William Phillips, replaced in 1937 by Sumner Welles, a Groton-Harvard product like the president, who had been a career Foreign Service officer for seven years beginning in 1922, and had then resigned from the service before he had reached the top career level and had received, during the Hoover administration, several special assignments with ministerial or ambassadorial rank. Considered very capable and somewhat arrogant, he served early in the Roosevelt administration as ambassador to Cuba and assistant secretary of state, but he never developed a relationship of trust with Hull, who felt undercut by Welles's direct access to Roosevelt, especially after Welles was appointed under secretary.[6] When this appointment was made, Hull's friend R. Walton Moore was promoted to the revived position of counselor, to rank immediately after Welles, but this position lapsed on Moore's death in February 1941. At the assistant secretary level, some appointees like Raymond Moley were definitely the president's men whom Hull could not control; others such as Jefferson Caffery, George S. Messersmith, Hugh R. Wilson, and G. Howland Shaw had formerly been career Foreign Service officers and worked well within the system; and others such as Francis B. Sayre (Woodrow Wilson's son-in-law), Breckinridge Long, Dean Acheson, and Henry F. Grady owed their appointments to political factors but formed relationships of mutual trust and respect with the secretary.

I

Cordell Hull had not been selected for wide experience in foreign affairs or for his administrative skills, and it surprised no one during his almost twelve-year tenure as secretary of state—the longest in the history of the nation—that he did not, indeed could not, give firm direction and control to the detailed workings of his department. He did, however, take personal charge of some aspects of foreign affairs, and in those areas he operated with considerable skill, remaining on cordial terms with President Roosevelt, whose off-hand style of running the White House and foreign policy in general and whose penchant for using special envoys[7] and for communicating directly with them, with ambassadors abroad, and even with the under secretary of state was maddening at times to the courtly southerner to whom the Department of State had been entrusted.

One of Hull's principal personal interests (carried over from his years in Congress) was a new system of bilateral trade agreements with many countries, and he moved aggressively at the beginning of Roosevelt's first term to obtain the legislative basis for such a system and then to negotiate a series of such agreements. Hull was involved personally in guiding the trade-agreements authorization act through the Congress, with somewhat wayward support from the president.[8] A new Division of Trade Agreements (later renamed several times) was established early in 1935, and its success in concluding a long list of bilateral agreements has usually been considered one of Hull's major accomplishments. A small Office of Philippine Affairs was set up to deal with new questions arising from the Philippine Independence Act of 1934, and the Division of Eastern European Affairs was revitalized by the preparations for and the aftermath of the negotiations that led to United States recognition of the Soviet Union in 1933.

On the broad stage of international negotiations Hull's personal participation was initially less successful. His first major international conference, the London monetary conference of 1933, was a dramatic failure and humiliation for the new secretary, whose position was undercut by Roosevelt. Hull's position was retrieved, however, by his participation in the inter-American conference held in Uruguay later the same year, where his efforts to implement Roosevelt's newly announced Good Neighbor Policy had solid results. He also headed the United States delegations to the inter-American conferences in Buenos Aires in 1936 and Lima in 1938, which were less successful. For the next few years the secretary stayed close to Washington, and when the president asked Hull to accompany him to the First Quebec Conference in 1943, he gave him very little to do. Hull's last conference abroad, the tripartite meeting of foreign ministers in Moscow in October 1943, should be counted a qualified success in that it led to the Teheran Conference, although Teheran, like the other summit confer-ences of World War II, had inadequate diplomatic preparation and left the most difficult and potentially insoluble problems for the heads of government to wrestle with in less than ideal situations, operating under intense time pressures far from the support systems that might have assisted them.

War clouds in Europe and continued tension in the Far East made for rough diplomatic waters during the first six years of Hull's secretaryship. Germany withdrew from the League of Nations, repudiated the military clauses of the Versailles Treaty, and announced plans for rearmament. The London naval conference of 1934–1935 was a failure. Italy began its campaign to conquer Ethiopia. The civil war in Spain involved countries far outside the Iberian Peninsula. Through an *Anschluß* Austria was united with Germany and ceased to be independent. Germany took over the Sudeten areas of Czechoslovakia and then the remainder of the country. Italy added Albania to its conquests. Japan continued its undeclared war in China. Finally, war erupted in Europe in Sep-tember 1939.

Meanwhile, the strong isolationist sentiment in Congress had led to the passage of the Neutrality Act of 1935. This act—parts of which Hull opposed—mandated an embargo on the shipment of arms to either belligerent in case of armed conflict, and required manufacturers, importers, and exporters of arms, ammunition, or implements of war to register with the secretary of state and to obtain a license for each import and export transaction. This led at once to the creation of the Office of Arms and Munitions Control (later the Division of Controls) in the Department of State to perform the duties mandated by the act. This office can thus be considered as the first of the special divisions set up in the department to deal with war problems. With the actual outbreak of hostilities in Europe, there was revised neutrality legislation and a change in the department's focus in implementing it.

While isolationist sentiment remained strong in the United States and the country remained neutral, there were more such creations in rapid order once Hitler began his blitzkrieg in the west. Night duty officers were assigned in the secretary's office to assess emergencies and call in policy officers as required. The Special Division was created in September 1939 to arrange for the repatria-tion of American citizens caught in the war zones, to handle what is generally referred to as "welfare and whereabouts" work, and to supervise the protection by twenty-four American diplomatic and consular offices of the interests of up to a dozen belligerent governments in the territories of or occupied by the Axis powers.[9] The next year a Division of Foreign Activity Correlation was set up; its functions had to do with resistance groups abroad and foreign-born groups in the United States who had relevant information. In mid-1941 the Division of

World Trade Intelligence was created to administer the Proclaimed List of Certain Blocked Nationals, which aimed to prevent trade with the United States by firms associated in any way with the Axis. Finally, in October 1941 a Board of Economic Operations was established in the Department of State, with Assistant Secretary Acheson as chairman. All of the economic wing of the department came under the aegis of this board, including later creations such as the Division of Exports and Defense Aid, the Division of Defense Materials, the Foreign Funds and Financial Division (soon split in two), and the American Hemisphere Export Office. Some of the units, whose basic functions were accurately reflected in their names, expanded very rapidly indeed, as the amount of detailed economic work to be done was astronomical. It should be noted that although Acheson chaired the Board of Economic Operations, some of the divisions mentioned came under the authority of Assistant Secretary of State Adolf A. Berle, Jr., so that there was not a clear line of authority on all economic matters.

Aside from problems that were specifically war-related, there was a slow expansion of the focus of foreign relations during Hull's middle years in office. Herbert Feis was named adviser on economic affairs in 1937 to give high-level attention to the complexities of international economic problems—this of course included some war-related problems, such as the preclusive buying of strategic materials. A new Division of Cultural Relations was set up in 1938 to cultivate international cooperation in intellectual and artistic fields, with emphasis at first on Latin America. A new Division of International Communications was established the same year to coordinate policy relating to international aviation, shipping, and telecommunications. In 1939 the president, under the Reorganization Act of that year, transferred to the jurisdiction of the Department of State the activities and personnel of the foreign services of the Departments of Commerce and Agriculture, thus consolidating a single Foreign Service of the United States. And in this period the chiefs of four geographic divisions were promoted seriatim to advisers on political relations—a glorified title that suspended them midway between the new chiefs of those divisions and the assistant secretary level, but which left them still very much in control of the divisions they supervised.

In the nonorganizational aspects of dealing with the war in Europe, mention should be made of Under Secretary Welles's mission to Italy and Germany in 1940 to see if any groundwork for peace could be found; the American agreement with the Danish minister in Washington for the defense of Greenland and Iceland against German occupation; the accreditation of an American ambassador to the government of occupied France established at Vichy; the "Atlantic Charter," drawn up at Roosevelt's first summit conference with British Prime Minister Winston Churchill (with Welles in attendance); a Lend Lease agreement negotiated with Great Britain involving the transfer of a number of destroyers to the British and the lease to the United States of naval and airbase facilities in the Caribbean and the Newfoundland area; and a slow transformation of the Good Neighbor Policy toward Latin America into a hemispheric system to protect the Americas from Axis infiltration. With respect to the European war in particular, President Roosevelt took an important personal role in deciding not only the general outlines of policy but also the details of its implementation.

In the Far East the deepening crisis in Japanese-American relations was, of course, a constant preoccupation of departmental officers, with Secretary Hull occupying a central position in policy-making and negotiating, relying in particular upon Stanley K. Hornbeck, adviser on political relations with respect to Far Eastern matters, and upon Ambassador to Japan Joseph C. Grew. Hull indeed was engaged in negotiations with a special Japanese envoy in Washington when, without prior notice, Japan launched the attack on American bases in Hawaii, which brought the United States into World War II on December 7, 1941 (Washington time). Four days later, Germany and Italy declared war against the United States, and the country was plunged into global warfare.

II

The country as a whole, its armed forces, and the civilian agencies of government, including the Department of State and the Foreign Service, were woefully unprepared for the enormous problems—military, economic, and diplomatic—of fighting a war on two fronts against powerful and well-prepared enemies. Although the Department of State had had a modest increase in size to staff the new divisions mentioned above, it was still a very small organization, which kept partially abreast of its responsibilities only by the investment of prodigious amounts of overtime by a dedicated staff. An immediate increase in staff was required, with no time for training except in the sink-or-swim circumstances of on-the-job performance. While the Foreign Service had been considerably enlarged by the reorganization plan of 1939, the commercial and agricultural attachés who had been absorbed into the service at that time did not have the skills most needed for wartime diplomacy and economic warfare.

In these circumstances it was probably inevitable that many necessary new tasks dealing with or impinging on foreign affairs were entrusted to agencies that were created out of chaos (and some would say into chaos) and that grew unrestrained in their attempt to handle the problems handed over to them. They went through periodic reshufflings and reorganizations and were far too numerous to list completely here. They included the Foreign Economic Administration, the War Production Administration, the Office of Lend Lease Administration, the Office of War Information, and the Office of the Coordinator of Inter-American Affairs—all these agencies sent personnel abroad. Lip service was usually paid to the coordinating and policy-making role of Secretary Hull and his department, but there were enormous interagency tensions, with many disputes and misunderstandings about the allocation of functions and the degree of control to be exercised by the chief of the diplomatic mission over other-agency personnel in his country. In some cases the Department of State was merely by-passed.

But the department itself had to have new staff to carry on its functions and to replace on a temporary basis men who were placed on military leave when they joined the armed forces. The procedures of Foreign Service and civil service examinations were too slow and cumbersome to meet immediate needs. Large numbers of employees were given temporary appointments, with no tenure, for service in Washington. Regular examinations for appointment to the Foreign Service were suspended for the duration of the war, and a Foreign Service Auxiliary was established for emergency overseas recruitment. The first Auxiliary officers, hired for posts in Latin America, were economic analysts, cultural relations assistants, information specialists, and vice consuls. As time went on, however, the Auxiliary was used to hire specialists in many fields for assignment all over the world as well as accounting and disbursing personnel and junior consular staff. By January 1946, auxiliary officers outnumbered career Foreign Service officers by 976 to 820.[10]

With so many young men called for military service, it was natural that many of the new employees were women. In some areas the department had for many years employed some professional women—in the Office of the Legal Adviser, for example—and now more women were hired for professional as well as clerical work, and during the war a growing number of them were assigned to the geographic divisions as well as to divisions dealing with such diverse subject matter as historical research, economic analysis, and postwar planning.[11] Blacks became more numerous in clerical and administrative positions and, in a quiet social revolution that occurred without incident and almost without being noticed, the Department of State cafeteria was desegregated and blacks and whites ate in the same room for the first time.

For more than two years the department tried to adjust its structure and its increased size within the confines of the 1924 organizational plan of a secretary, an under secretary, four assistant secretaries, and a growing collection of independent divisions. The work of many divisions was transformed almost beyond recognition. Passport and visa work, for example, was vastly expanded, as were the staffs assigned to that work—the personnel of the Visa Division increased from 47 in October 1940 to 278 by June 1942.[12] The Division of Communications and Records, responsible for telegraph traffic and the central files, was the largest division in the department, and during the course of the war its control of a central filing system practically broke down, as individual divisions began keeping their own files because of their inability to retrieve from Communications and Records the background papers urgently needed for

action purposes.[13] The Special (later Special War Problems) Division immediately was faced with the problems arising from the internment of Axis diplomatic staffs in the United States and of their American counterparts in Japan,
Germany, and Italy, and with the necessity for long and complex negotiations
that led eventually to the exchange of interned personnel. It also had to shift
gears from representing third-country interests in the Axis capitals to arranging
for neutral Switzerland to represent American interests in those capitals. It had
to deal with Switzerland, Sweden, and Spain, which between them represented
Axis interests in the United States, and it had special new functions for assuring
as best it could through the protecting governments that the Axis powers lived
up to their obligations under the Geneva Conventions concerning treatment of
prisoners of war.[14] The Division of American Republics was (with its superiors) much concerned with the Rio de Janeiro conference of 1942, which failed
to achieve unanimity on breaking off diplomatic relations with the Axis. The
Division of Near Eastern Affairs played an important role with respect to
American policy in the Allied invasion of North Africa later that year.[15]

Other new functions resulted in the creation of new divisions within the
department. Late in 1942, for example, an Office of Foreign Territories was
established (and abolished again soon after). An Office of Foreign Relief and
Rehabilitation Operations was also set up, headed by Governor Herbert H.
Lehman of New York, but jurisdictional disputes became so heated that the
president transferred the office and several economic divisions of the department to a new, independent Foreign Economic Administration.

The first major diplomatic document to emerge after the American entry into
the war was the Declaration by United Nations, signed by Roosevelt, Churchill,
and representatives of the Soviet Union and China on 1 January 1942 and signed
immediately thereafter by representatives of two dozen other countries and
eventually by many more. A draft of this declaration had been prepared in the
Department of State and was used by Roosevelt as a basis for discussion, and
into it British and Soviet suggestions were incorporated. This brief and broad
declaration of unity in the face of Axis aggression was the charter of the
individual countries known during the war collectively as the United Nations,
and it was representatives of those countries who much later, as the war in
Europe drew to a close, met to set up a world organization. The painstaking
preparations in this area were the province of the department's Division of
Special Research, headed by Leo Pasvolsky; it was later divided into Divisions
of Political and Economic Studies. The work of these divisions led first to the
Dumbarton Oaks Conferences in 1944 and then, the following year, to the full-
scale United Nations Conference on International Organization, which established the organization known also as the United Nations. Throughout the work
on these matters, the department made a special effort to obtain bipartisan
support for its proposals, and Hull's success in gaining the help of such promi-

nent Republicans as Senator Arthur H. Vandenberg, Governor Thomas E. Dewey, and John Foster Dulles was an essential element in bringing the proposals to fruition.

III

When Sumner Welles left his position as under secretary in September 1943, he was replaced by Edward R. Stettinius, Jr., who had been head of the independent agency in charge of Lend Lease operations. With his business background, Stettinius was expected to bring administrative skills to bear on the chaotic organizational arrangements in the Department of State. He moved quickly in that direction, and on 15 January 1944 a sweeping departmental order was issued to accomplish what he had in mind. Prepared by a small group of officers with a minimum of consultation with those affected, the order, which covered every area of the department, was literally sprung without notice, and some division chiefs read in the morning newspaper what was to happen to them and their divisions.

Basically, all the divisions were grouped into twelve offices, which were in turn assigned to the supervision of an assistant secretary or to that of the under secretary himself. The geographic divisions, now multiplied in number, were assigned to four geographic offices (headed by the four former advisers on political relations) reporting to the under secretary, and they were assigned coordinating responsibility for all matters affecting their respective areas. The under secretary also took on supervision of a new Office of Special Political Affairs, which was concerned with postwar planning. The economic divisions (except those dealing with transportation and communications) were for the first time brought under the control of a single assistant secretary (Dean Acheson). Administration and public information (including new divisions having to do with motion pictures and radio, with science, education, and art, and with labor and health) were assigned to another assistant secretary (G. Howland Shaw), congressional liaison to a third (Breckinridge Long), and transportation and controls (passports, visas, special war problems) to the only remaining assistant secretary (Adolf A. Berle).

This reorganization was obviously badly needed, but in their haste and secrecy the reorganizers overlooked some basic necessities, made a few errors, and failed to take into account the bruised egos of individuals who had enough clout to have their objections sustained. The initial order was therefore followed by a rash of modifying orders, several of which appointed special assistants to the secretary to oversee functions that had originally been assigned to the supervision of assistant secretaries or office directors.[16] And plans were begun for a complete overhaul of the implementing order in the light of experience.

At this juncture Secretary Hull, who had been in ill health for some time, resigned, effective 30 November 1944, and the president immediately replaced him by promoting Stettinius to the secretaryship. Meanwhile legislation had been making its way through Congress to create positions for two additional assistant secretaries in the Department of State. This legislation was approved early in December, so that the new secretary was able to take this into account when a further organization order (the "Christmas surprise") was issued on 20 December, to be followed, as usual, by further modifications.

Before the December order was issued the president had chosen Joseph C. Grew, a career officer who had been ambassador to Japan at the time of Pearl Harbor, to be the new under secretary of state (a return to the post that he had held in the 1920s); this was an obvious counterweight to offset Stettinius's comparative inexperience. All the assistant secretaries except one—Acheson—were let go, and Acheson was offered the assignment of liaison with Congress and international conferences. He later indicated that he thought it had been expected that he would turn down this assignment, after his years of struggle with wartime economic problems, but he accepted it at once.[17] Acheson's former assignments were given to William L. Clayton, as assistant secretary for economic affairs. The assistant secretaryship for administration was given to Julius C. Holmes, who had served in the Foreign Service and had executive experience in business and in the Army. The geographic areas were divided between Nelson A. Rockefeller, formerly head of an independent office dealing with Latin America (to continue in that field) and James Clement Dunn (to handle the rest of the world). The last assistant secretaryship went to the poet Archibald MacLeish, who had headed the government's Office of Facts and Figures, and who was assigned the field of public and cultural relations. Two high-level coordinating committees were established, with a joint secretariat to serve them both.[18] Once all these officers had taken their oaths, the white-haired Stettinius hired Constitution Hall for a departmental "assembly" to present Grew and his new "team" of six assistant secretaries to their subordinates. The team was thereafter referred to covertly as Snow White and the Seven Dwarfs.

Whether Roosevelt intended Stettinius as a long-term replacement for Hull or as a stop-gap until the end of the war will probably never be known. The new secretary, however, did his best to carry on the functions of his office, attending international conferences and carrying on diplomatic conversations, and he had some successes. As under secretary he had been chairman of the Dumbarton Oaks conversations on international organization, and the establishment of the United Nations was the apex of his secretaryship. He accompanied Roosevelt to the Yalta Conference and made a flying visit to Moscow before returning home. And he headed the United States delegation to the inter-American conference that drew up the Act of Chapultepec, which committed the signatories to consult as to appropriate measures to be taken in case of aggression or planned aggression.[19] Nevertheless, Stettinius is probably the least memorable secretary of state since William R. Day.[20]

IV

Although Stettinius remained as secretary of state under Harry Truman from April until the end of June, it is clear that the new president from the first considered this an interim arrangement—as one historian has put it, Stettinius was "a mannikin allowed to preside over the San Francisco Conference and then dismissed."[21] Truman obviously shared a general belief that Stettinius was not a strong secretary, and, being inexperienced himself in the field of foreign affairs, he felt the need for a secretary of state of much greater stature. He cannot have considered the matter long, because on the day following Roosevelt's death Truman broached with James F. Byrnes the possibility of his taking the position after Stettinius had seen to its conclusion the negotiation of the United Nations Charter. Byrnes, a former congressman, senator, and Supreme Court justice, had left the Court to take on such broad responsibilities in the White House that he had been dubbed an "assistant president" to Roosevelt; he had traveled with Roosevelt to the Yalta Conference; he was privy to the secret atomic-development project on which Truman had just been briefed—in short, he had the broad background that Truman wanted in his premier cabinet officer and potential successor to the presidency if Truman should die when there was no vice president.[22] The San Francisco Conference ended on 26 June, Stettinius's resignation was accepted the following day, and the new secretary took office on 3 July 1945. Three days later he left Washington with the president to attend the Potsdam Conference. The Department of State was left in Grew's charge, but immediately after Truman and Byrnes returned to Washington, Dean Acheson replaced Grew as under secretary.

At Potsdam, the final summit conference of World War II, Byrnes assisted Truman at all the plenary meetings with Generalissimo Stalin and Prime Minister Churchill (later Prime Minister Attlee) and negotiated in his own right at the frequent meetings at the foreign-minister level. One of the concrete agreements reached there established a Council of Foreign Ministers, in which France was also represented. The Potsdam Conference and two meetings of foreign ministers in 1945 and two in 1946, together with the initial meeting of the United Nations General Assembly and the sessions of the Paris Peace Conference in the latter year kept the secretary in Europe for more than six months all together and accounted for most of the seventy-seven thousand miles of travel that he chalked up between January 1945 and November 1946. It can be said that Byrnes instituted the tradition of the peripatetic secretary of state, which has been followed to some degree by all his successors.[23] While the heads of government reached what passed for agreement at Potsdam on other subjects, many of the issues they dealt with had to be considered in more detail and at greater leisure by the Council of Foreign Ministers.[24] That body, with its endless and repetitive arguments, eventually was successful in drawing up treaties of peace to be signed with Italy, Hungary, Rumania, Bulgaria, and Finland, and the conclusion of those treaties represented Byrnes's major achievement as secretary.

During Byrnes's secretaryship the Department of State was at the center of two important administrative developments, although the secretary himself was not closely concerned with them. The first was the absorption by the department of some of the continuing functions of various wartime agencies that were abolished after the end of hostilities. The research and analysis functions of the wartime Office of Strategic Services, for example, were transferred to a new intelligence apparatus established in the Department of State under the supervision of a special assistant to the secretary for intelligence—until Secretary Byrnes decided to split intelligence functions among the geographic areas.[25] The foreign functions, facilities, and personnel of the Office of War Information were placed under the supervision of the public affairs area of the department; and the economic divisions took over various fragmentary functions from abolished economic agencies, including such operational responsibilities as liquidation of foreign war surplus property.

The other major administrative development during Byrnes's tenure was the passage of two pieces of legislation in 1946 concerning the Foreign Service of the United States. Under temporary legislation approved in July, 166 Foreign Service officers were appointed from applicants who had served in the military forces, the merchant marine, or civilian agencies of the government.[26] (This made it possible for members of the Foreign Service Auxiliary and overseas employees of other agencies to be blanketed into the Foreign Service proper under comparatively simple examination procedures.) The Foreign Service Act of 1946, approved 13 August and effective 13 November, constituted a new organic law for the Foreign Service, replacing acts passed in 1924 and 1931.[27] For the first time Foreign Service officers could be appointed as ambassadors or ministers without resigning from the service. Positions in the Foreign Service were reclassified, salaries and allowances were raised substantially, and a new retirement system was instituted. A new building program for diplomatic and consular offices abroad was inaugurated, and the Foreign Service Auxiliary was abolished. Lateral entry was permitted at the middle and upper grades for candidates who had specified amounts of service in responsible positions in one or more government agencies. This act, drafted in large part by Foreign Service officers and passed with bipartisan support in Congress, formed the basis for the postwar Foreign Service. Although Byrnes was not personally involved in its drafting, he gave it his approval and strongly urged the president to sign it when the Bureau of the Budget raised objections to some of its provisions.

While Byrnes was secretary of state the overwhelming foreign policy problem—or cluster of problems—was what has come to be known as the advent of the Cold War, involving the relations of the United States and the West European powers with the Soviet Union. Not that problems with the Soviet Union began in July 1945; indeed one historian starts his study of the origins of the Cold War with the "formation of the Grand Alliance in 1941."[28] But wartime disagreements over such problems as German reparations, a postwar government for Poland, and communist domination of the Soviet Union's Balkan neighbors achieved a new virulence after the collapse of Germany, and the disagreements spread to almost every aspect of postwar Soviet-American relations.[29] Although for about two years the United States had a monopoly of atomic weapons, and although some historians have asserted that Truman and his advisers deliberately developed and pursued a policy of atomic diplomacy,[30] the Soviet government was probably aware that the United States had no further atomic weapons available immediately after the bombing of Nagasaki, and it correctly assessed American reluctance to start a third world war using atomic weapons.[31] In effect it ignored the small but growing American atomic arsenal and pushed to the limit of Western tolerance its own agenda for Europe and the Middle East based on its favorable geographic position and its formidable strength in ground troops and conventional arms.

Although Secretary Byrnes focused much of his personal attention on Europe, the Truman administration was greatly concerned about the immediate postwar situation in China, and in December 1945 the president sent General of the Army George C. Marshall as his personal representative to confer with both the Chinese government and with communist leaders. Marshall's mission was protracted, arduous, and ultimately unsuccessful. He did not finally return to the United States until January 1947.[32]

At first blush one might have expected that Byrnes, with his background in politics and with the experience on Capitol Hill that he shared with Truman, would have been entirely compatible with the president—far more compatible, one would think, than the soldier George Marshall or the patrician Dean Acheson who followed him. Yet, as it turned out, it was the latter two secretaries who established a relationship of complete confidence and trust with the president, while it was Byrnes who incurred Truman's wrath by failing to keep the White House sufficiently informed of the negotiations at Moscow during the meeting of foreign ministers there in December 1945 and by beginning to think of himself (as Truman put it in his memoirs) as "an Assistant President in full charge of foreign policy." Shortly after Byrnes's return from Moscow, the president (as he recalled later—although Byrnes disputed his recollection) read to the erring secretary of state a letter that made his dissatisfaction abundantly clear. Byrnes submitted his resignation in April 1946, when it was arranged that it would not take effect until later. When Byrnes's final negotiations on peace treaties with five European enemy states was approaching its conclusion, Truman asked his special envoy in China if he would be willing to serve as secretary of state. Having received an affirmative reply, the president announced acceptance of Byrnes's resignation the following January, and announced at the same time his selection of General of the Army George C. Marshall as Byrnes's successor.[33]

V

The president's choice for his third secretary of state was held in such high esteem as a man of great ability and integrity that his nomination was confirmed by the Senate without a committee hearing and under suspension of the rules to permit expedited action. Taking office on 21 January 1947, for what turned out to be a two-year tour of duty, General Marshall asked several members of Byrnes's top staff to remain, and both Under Secretary Dean Acheson and Under Secretary for Economic Affairs William L. Clayton agreed to stay on for a few months. Acheson was replaced in the middle of the year by Robert A. Lovett, with whom Marshall had worked during the war when Lovett had been assistant secretary of war for air. Clayton was not replaced, and economic affairs were split between two assistant secretaries, one a Byrnes holdover who stayed into the Eisenhower administration and the other a new appointee who stayed almost two years, about an average tenure among top departmental officials. The outstanding member of the new team was undoubtedly Lovett, who worked in close harmony with Marshall and the president.

On taking office Marshall was "horrified" at what he considered the complete lack of organization in the Department of State. His first moves, therefore, were to tell Under Secretary Acheson that he would act as chief of staff and to establish a central secretariat, which would function along the lines of the War Department General Staff. To carry out his desired changes he appointed one colonel in mufti to be his personal assistant and another to supervise the secretariat.[34] It could be said that this was Marshall's solution to the twenty-year-old problem of how to replace the particular skills of Assistant Secretary of State Alvey A. Adee. Adee, who had been an assistant secretary for almost forty-two years when he died in 1924, had been a one-man institutional memory and coordinating mechanism for the entire department, and, with a well-operated central file system, he had provided all that seemed necessary to keep operations running smoothly. His assistants later provided (at a lower level) a system of coordination and review, but that system was overstrained during the war years, and the collapse of effective central files has already been noted. The new secretariat, which in general operated well and has therefore been continued to the present day (with modifications, of course), provided a tight control for the flow of paper work at the top level of the department and for the filing and retrieval of documents once they had entered the system.

Marshall was also appalled that there was no planning staff separated from operational responsibilities and made one of his best personnel selections by naming career diplomat George F. Kennan to head a new Policy Planning Staff, with direct access to the secretary.[35] This staff was to develop long-term programs, anticipate problems, study broad politico-military problems, evaluate current policy, and coordinate all departmental planning activities—but Kennan's first assignment was to recommend in short order what Marshall should do about the mess in Europe.[36] Kennan organized a small staff and tried to assist the secretary by studying the conflicts between the views and recommendations of various offices of the department and suggesting ways in which those conflicts could be resolved, by helping to "infuse into the work of . . . subordinate offices an understanding of the larger concepts on the basis of which policy was being conducted at the top," and by relating day-to-day decisions to long-term American interests. He purposely excluded from planning papers the domestic political pressures that might influence—or indeed dictate—policy choices.[37] During Marshall's tenure as secretary, the Policy Planning Staff submitted studies on numerous facets of United States policy, and some of them, such as those on the "containment policy" toward the Soviet Union and those on the Marshall Plan, were influential in departmental decisions and operations.[38] A Policy Planning Staff has remained a part of the department's organization since that period, but after Kennan left (when Marshall had been replaced as secretary and the new team had determined that policy planning papers had to be cleared throughout the department before being presented to the top level) it never again served quite the same function that Marshall had had in mind.

When the National Security Council (NSC) was formed in 1947, the secretary of state was named a statutory member of the council, which had a very small staff and relied heavily upon the personnel of interested departments in the performance of its duties. Because of the stature of Marshall and his immediate successor and because of their very close relationship with President Truman, the Department of State contributed much to the smooth functioning of the council in its early years, and the secretary of state spoke with great authority and influence in its meetings. The seeds were there, however, for the later vast expansion of the NSC staff, for duplication of work, for rivalry between the NSC staff and personnel in the departments, and for the domination of the council's work by the president's national security adviser. During the Truman administration, however, the NSC was relatively harmonious, and Marshall was content to use it as a coordinating mechanism in bringing advice to the president.

Marshall's secretaryship will always be remembered because of the association of his name with the Marshall Plan. Anticipated by a speech in Mississippi by Under Secretary Acheson, and incorporating elements from papers prepared by Under Secretary for Economic Affairs William Clayton and by Kennan, a speech given by Marshall at Harvard University in June 1947 suggested American readiness to assist in the economic recovery of European countries that cooperated in formulating their needs. The Soviet Union promptly vetoed participation by its satellites, but other countries reacted positively. It took the rest of 1947 and all of the following year for the program of assistance known as the Marshall Plan to take shape and for the Truman administration to get through a Republican Congress (with much help from Senator Arthur H. Vandenberg) the necessary authorization and appropriation for the program and the legislation that created an independent Economic Recovery Administration to administer it. Marshall himself was much involved in negotiations with European and congressional leaders in laying the groundwork for the plan, which was to bear his name, and in supporting it in a series of public addresses. He was rewarded in 1953 with the Nobel Peace Prize.[39]

Marshall, like his predecessor and his successor, spent much time attending acrimonious meetings of the Council of Foreign Ministers, which still had before it the unfinished peace treaties with Germany and Austria and the problems arising from the quadripartite occupation of those two countries, particularly the fusion of the Western zones of Germany, currency reform, and elections for a West German government.[40] And crises elsewhere demanded his attention. The British government notified him early in his secretaryship that Britain could not sustain its program of economic and military aid to Greece and Turkey and suggested that the United States undertake the burdens that it could no longer bear. This led directly to the development of the Truman Doctrine, in which both Marshall and Acheson were much involved,[41] and to a large program of aid to Greece and Turkey and the establishment of aid missions in those countries that operated (much as wartime agencies had done) outside the normal bounds of the Department of State and the Foreign Service.

Another crisis in the foreign policy field arose when the Soviet Union began imposing, and then tightening, restrictions on travel between the western zones of occupation in Germany and the western sectors of Berlin, at least partly in reaction to a decision taken by the Western powers to form a West German government. The initial restrictions were announced on 30 March 1948, and, after the United States and British authorities had introduced a new deutschmark as the currency of their zones of occupation on 24 June, the Soviet Union closed rail and highway traffic into Berlin from the west completely. While much of the planning for the American reaction was carried on by the military and the White House, Lovett (who was acting secretary of state a good deal of the time) and Marshall (when he was in charge in Washington) were intimately involved in that planning, and Marshall even postponed a serious kidney operation because of the crisis. President Truman decided categorically that there would be no American withdrawal from Berlin, so the question to be decided was how to supply United States forces in that city and the German civilian population in the American sector of Berlin. Marshall informed the Soviet ambassador in Washington in early July that the United States occupied its sector of Berlin "with free access thereto as a matter of established right." The United States, he said, was willing to negotiate differences concerning the governance of Berlin, but not under duress. Meanwhile, an airlift to Berlin was begun, and it continued, supplying both civilians and military forces, until after Marshall's retirement as secretary. Within the Western coalition, the British and French governments were less inclined than Marshall to hold to a firm line in conversations with the Russians, and consultations on the subject with British and French representatives, military authorities, and the president took much of Marshall's attention during his final days in office, at which time both the blockade and airlift were still in place.[42]

During his two-year secretaryship Marshall continued to be concerned with the problems of China, which simmered on following his unsuccessful mission there; he headed the United States delegation to the United Nations General Assembly; and he gave active support to a British initiative that (after his retirement) led to the North Atlantic Treaty. He was instrumental in the continuation of bipartisan congressional support on many matters, and his cordial relationship with Senator Vandenberg was rewarded by the introduction and passage of the so-called Vandenberg Resolution of June 1948 in favor of American association (with safeguards) with European regional collective security arrangements. Marshall was also active in trying to shore up United States ties with Latin America. He attended inter-American conferences in Rio de Janeiro in 1947 and Bogotá in 1948. The Rio Treaty, signed at the end of the former conference, provided for action by all the signatories against an armed attack on any of the American republics, and Marshall was able to postpone action on Latin American requests for extensive United States economic aid. The Bogotá conference—interrupted by an unsuccessful revolution in the Colombian capital—revised the mechanics of the inter-American system and established the Organization of American States.

One major foreign policy decision during Marshall's term as secretary was taken by Truman against the secretary's advice, namely, United States de facto recognition of the provisional government of Israel effective immediately upon the relinquishment of the British mandate over Palestine. This move was clearly taken for domestic political reasons, and it was intensely embarrassing to American diplomatic representatives at the United Nations, whose position was undercut by it. One of Marshall's biographers reports that several of the secretary's friends are said to have urged him to resign over Truman's action, and that "Marshall supposedly replied that one did not resign because the President, who had a constitutional right to make a decision, had made one."[43]

Late in 1948, however, Secretary Marshall underwent surgery for the removal of a kidney, and he found it necessary to resign for reasons of health. His resignation took effect on 20 January 1949 as President Truman began his second term of office.

Early in Marshall's secretaryship Congress had passed legislation establishing a Commission on Organization of the Executive Branch of the Government, chaired by former President Herbert Hoover (known as the First Hoover Commission). The commission's studies on foreign affairs were entrusted to Harvey H. Bundy, formerly assistant to the secretary of war, and James Grafton Rogers, who much earlier had been an assistant secretary of state, with a former secretary of state and war, Henry L. Stimson, as adviser. This task force studied the Department of State and its relations with other parts of the government for almost a year and a half, and its report was not forwarded to Congress until January 1949, just a week before Marshall left office. Its conclusions represented a scathing criticism of the foreign affairs machinery of the United States, which Marshall had inherited and to some extent remodeled.

This report, which filled an entire booklet, recommended that cabinet-level committees be established to advise the president on domestic and foreign aspects of matters affecting foreign affairs; that the Department of State should not have operational responsibility for programs in the field of foreign affairs (such as foreign economic assistance and propaganda), but that it should establish policies (in conjunction with other interested agencies) and recommend choice and timing of the means for carrying out American policies abroad; that it should continue its traditional role with respect to representation abroad, collection and distribution of information and negotiation; that the internal organization of the department should center on four regional assistant secretaries, with additional high-level officers to supervise multinational affairs, planning, the executive secretariat, administration, and congressional relations, transferring to the geographic areas the officers carrying out functional duties, except for a very few functional specialists who would operate across geographic lines. The report also deplored the tension and mutual lack of respect between Foreign Service and civil service employees in the department in Washington, and recommended that over a period of years the senior levels of the two services be merged.[44]

The growing size of the department and the Foreign Service and the concomitant growth in size and power of the administrative arm of the department had led to their own problems. One diplomat of broad experience reflected later that the administrators hired to press the pants had been encouraged by the department's bureaucracy to wear them instead. *Rhynchophora publica* (the bureaucratic wood weevil), he said, had discovered "in Foggy Bottom the ideal environment in which to propagate."[45] Newsman Joseph Kraft, writing at a later period (but with wit that applied equally to the period under discussion), characterized the Department of State as a "fudge factory," deploring the fact that it had not been operated as an instrument for making decisions but had rather been run to conciliate interests and "avoid giving offense and rocking the boat."[46]

These problems and the implementation of the Hoover Commission report were left in the lap of the incoming secretary.

VI

On General Marshall's retirement Truman immediately replaced him by recalling to duty the veteran Dean Acheson, who, having served as assistant secretary under Hull and Stettinius and as under secretary with Byrnes and Marshall, had an unequaled background of departmental experience when he took his oath as secretary of state on 21 January 1949. Acheson was faced during his secretaryship with crises both foreign and domestic, and his performance has been judged so favorably that one writer has even called him "perhaps the greatest Secretary of State ever."[47]

Lovett had left the department with Marshall, and Truman soon selected James E. Webb, director of the Bureau of the Budget, to serve as under secretary. Webb's background was such that for three years he dealt with administrative matters and seldom participated in foreign policy matters,[48] although of course he served as acting secretary when Acheson was away. Webb was replaced early in 1952 by another noncareer under secretary, David K. E. Bruce, an able and elegant Virginian and a personal friend of Acheson's, who had been ambassador to France and who later was to serve as ambassador to West Germany and the United Kingdom—giving him a remarkable "triple crown" of three major West European ambassadorial posts. At the next level, Acheson's staff included Deputy Under Secretaries Dean Rusk (who accepted technical demotion in 1950 to take responsibility for Far Eastern affairs, and who was later to be a long-term secretary of state himself); John E. Peurifoy (a lateral entrant into the Foreign Service, who later served as ambassador to Greece, Guatemala, and Thailand); H. Freeman Matthews (a career officer who had been ambassador to Sweden and was later to serve in a similar capacity in the Netherlands and Austria); and Carlisle H. Humelsine (the head of Marshall's secretariat). Acheson's numerous assistant secretaries, in addition to Rusk, included Willard L. Thorp (for economic affairs, carried over from the Marshall staff), George W. Perkins (European affairs), and W. Walton Butterworth (Far Eastern affairs). The counselors of the department during Acheson's secretaryship were Charles E. Bohlen (carried over from Marshall), George F. Kennan (moved from the Policy Planning Staff), and then Bohlen again (when Kennan took a leave of absence). The post of ambassador-at-large was created for Philip C. Jessup, a noted international lawyer from Columbia University, and in that position Jessup carried out many top-level special assignments during the Acheson years.

The Hoover Commission recommendations for reorganizing the department had been carried over from the last days of Marshall's secretaryship, and many of them could not be carried out without new legislation. This took the form of an act "to strengthen and improve the organization and administration of the Department of State," which President Truman signed on 26 May 1949. This law increased the number of assistant secretaries from six to ten, two of whom could be named deputy under secretaries by administrative action (Rusk and Peurifoy, mentioned above, were the first to be so named). It also transferred to the secretary of state himself certain statutory powers that had previously been vested in subordinate officers, such as the director general of the Foreign Service. Peurifoy's area of responsibility—the administrative functions of the department—was reorganized immediately. Most of the divisions under his supervision were grouped into four new offices, one of which was headed by a new director of personnel, responsible for both Foreign Service and civil service employees. There remained, however, a Division of Departmental Personnel and a separate Division of Foreign Service Personnel, so that the two personnel systems continued to be operated separately, although both divisions reported to a single director.[49] Four assistant secretaries were given geographical responsibilities, while four other assistant secretaries were assigned to the fields of economic affairs, public affairs, congressional relations, and international organization affairs.

The next—and far more difficult—move was to carry out the Hoover Commission's recommendations concerning geographic centralization. Effective 3 October, four geographic bureaus were created, one under each regional assistant secretary. These bureaus also had various advisers—intelligence advisers, labor advisers, economic advisers, public affairs advisers, and so forth—who headed staffs taken from the former functional areas of the department. The economic area was reorganized into "staffs," and a Bureau of United Nations Affairs triumphed by surviving as a functional unit at the new, loftier, bureau level.[50] Meanwhile, a new layer of officers—deputy assistant secretaries—had appeared,[51] and the bureaus were made up of lower echelons of offices, branches, and sections. A month later it appeared that the department had not asked for enough additional assistant secretaries, and, to supply backing in Washington for the new civilian high commissioner for Germany, a separate Bureau of German Affairs was created, with a director who was given the rank of assistant secretary by administrative fiat.[52]

In his inaugural address in January 1949 President Truman defined several points for action, the fourth of which was establishment of a technical assistance program for underdeveloped and backward countries in all areas of the world. This "Point 4" program, as it was called, took some time to implement, and it was not until September 1950 that the necessary legislation had been passed. Responsibility was then assigned to the secretary of state. For this program—unlike the course taken in the establishment of an independent agency to operate the European Recovery Program—a new, autonomous agency was created *within* the Department of State, but for all intents and purposes (except that it reported to the secretary as its superior officer) it operated its new program independently, and had its own corps of employees both in Washington and abroad.

To turn from the administrative to the substantive problems that faced Acheson when he assumed charge of the State Department, the negotiations for the North Atlantic Treaty were far advanced. Marshall had had his staff, particularly Foreign Service officers John D. Hickerson (later assistant secretary for United Nations affairs and ambassador to Finland and the Philippines) and Theodore C. Achilles (later ambassador to Peru and counselor of the department) working on this subject for some time. Among the difficult issues still to be determined were the geographic scope of the treaty and the extent of a commitment to consider an attack against one signatory as an attack on all the signatories. Acheson had trouble on the latter point, even with Democratic members of the Senate Foreign Relations Committee, and had to engage Truman's help in getting the draft language approved. The treaty was signed on 4 April 1949 and became a cornerstone of United States policy in Europe for the next forty years. Because of its bipartisan support in the Senate, and perhaps even more because of the appointment (which Acheson supported) of General of the Army Dwight D. Eisenhower as the supreme commander of the forces under the treaty, the American commitment to the North Atlantic Treaty Organization survived a series of changes of administration in Washington.[53]

Acheson also inherited from Marshall the diplomatic problems attending the Soviet blockade of Berlin, and almost before he could be briefed on the subject, Stalin hinted to a Western journalist that rescinding the currency reform in the Western sectors of Berlin might not be a necessary prerequisite for the lifting of the blockade. Ambassador-at-Large Jessup was entrusted with long and difficult negotiations with Jakob Malik, the Soviet delegate to the United Nations Security Council, and eventually agreement was reached for the lifting of the blockade, effective 12 May 1949, in return for convening the Council of Foreign Ministers to consider the subject of Germany. While the British and French foreign ministers were in Washington for the signing of the North Atlantic Treaty, Acheson was able to establish with them a relationship of mutual trust and to reach agreement on a new occupation statute for Germany. A unified government for the three Western zones of Germany would have domestic self-government, subject to Allied control over German foreign and military affairs, and the Western military governors would be replaced by civilian high commissioners. Acheson won an interdepartmental dispute and his department, not the Army, was given responsibility for German affairs. When the Council of Foreign Ministers met in Paris, the Soviet representative showed no inclination to accept the Western initiatives, and almost no progress was made, but the Berlin blockade was not reimposed.[54]

In China, developments were far less favorable. Superior Communist forces took control of the mainland in 1949, and Generalissimo Chiang Kai-shek was obliged to remove his government to Taiwan, the American embassy in China moving with him. In the United States there was a great public and congressional outcry of "Who lost China?" Acheson was assigned much of the blame by some, but weathered the storm with the strong support of the president. Over the next several years, however, the careers of a number of "old China hands" in the Foreign Service were ruined, and those of others had to be redirected to other areas of the world.[55]

In September 1949 Washington learned that the Soviet Union had exploded an atomic bomb, and American officials realized at once that loss of the monopoly of atomic weapons would inevitably change the power base on which Soviet-American relations were conducted. The Truman-Acheson European policy was based on the Marshall Plan, the North Atlantic Treaty, and enough military power to deter possible Soviet aggression. Acheson therefore was constantly concerned to increase that power. He was a strong supporter of a larger budget for strength based on conventional weapons, and he supported the controversial decision to develop a "super" or hydrogen bomb.

In many respects the most compelling problem of Acheson's entire secretaryship was the invasion of the Republic of Korea by Communist armies from North Korea at the end of June 1950. The Department of State, with Truman's approval, called immediately for an emergency meeting of the United Nations Security Council. Thus the Korean War gave the first test—repeated forty-one years later when Iraq invaded Kuwait—of the ability of a multinational force to repel aggression under the aegis of the world organization. United Nations action in Korea was possible only because Soviet representative Malik was boycotting meetings of the Security Council on the ground that the Chinese seat on the council was occupied by a representative of the Chiang government. Malik therefore was not present to veto the two resolutions that the council passed in the first days of the crisis. The second of those resolutions recommended that members of the United Nations "furnish such assistance to the Republic of Korea as may be necessary to repel the armed attack and to restore international peace and security in the area." The United States was already giving air and naval support to South Korea, and ground forces followed immediately. The basic decisions on American action were made by Truman, but Acheson was the principal architect of the recommendations to the president, and it fell to him to engage other nations in forming the multinational force that fought under the command of General of the Army Douglas MacArthur. As with his major European initiatives, Truman was able to act in Korea with bipartisan domestic support.[56]

In the conflict in Korea both the State and Defense departments badly miscalculated the intentions of the Chinese Communist authorities. Acheson was in favor of fighting the North Korean forces above the thirty-eighth parallel, and he favored a United Nations General Assembly resolution calling for a unified Korea. MacArthur was permitted to carry the war almost to the borders of Manchuria. At this point the Chinese Communists attacked in great strength and threw his forces into full retreat. Eventually, the latter were able to fight back to positions approximately along the thirty-eighth parallel. The United

States then abandoned the immediate goal of a unified Korea and was willing to settle for a cease-fire based on the thirty-eighth parallel. Truman, after receiving advice from Marshall (now back in the cabinet as secretary of defense), from the Joint Chiefs of Staff, and from Acheson, relieved MacArthur of his Korean command, and the latter's successor, General Matthew B. Ridgway, was able (after a hint from the Soviet Union that such a course was possible) to enter into military negotiations for a Korean armistice. These negotiations soon became stalemated and remained so until after the end of the Truman administration.

One other aspect of Far Eastern diplomacy in the Truman-Acheson years remains to be discussed. Japan had surrendered in September 1945, and had been occupied since that date by forces under MacArthur's command; no peace treaty had been signed. Treaties with Germany and Austria were also unsigned, the situation in those countries being complicated by problems of quadripartite occupation in which the Soviet Union was a full partner. In Japan, MacArthur was the undisputed military commander, and it was possible for the United States and other allies to proceed with the negotiation of a treaty without Soviet participation. The negotiations were entrusted, with Acheson's approval, to John Foster Dulles, the Republican party's principal foreign policy expert, and thus escaped the partisan furor that accompanied any question concerning China. Acheson presided at a conference convened to sign—not to negotiate— the Japanese peace treaty, and it was signed at San Francisco in September 1951. The Soviet Union and a number of other countries did not sign the treaty, and indeed no peace treaty between the Soviet Union and Japan has yet been concluded as of 1993.

In February 1950 Senator Joseph R. McCarthy of Wisconsin gave a speech in Wheeling, West Virginia, in which (according to the press) he made the completely false statement that he had in his hand a list of 205 men who "were known to the Secretary of State as being members of the Communist Party and who nevertheless are still working [in] and shaping the policy of the State Department."[57] Acheson declined to protect himself from this and later attacks, leaving it to President Truman to support his good name. Despite the fact that the Department of State was exonerated by the Tydings Committee established by the Senate to investigate McCarthy's allegations, the internal security investigations called for by new legislation and McCarthy's continuing attacks on the department kept its personnel in a state of turmoil for several years and were devastating to morale.

As his days in office drew to a close, Acheson decided to time his resignation to coincide precisely with the end of Truman's term as president. The gentle civility of nineteenth-century transfers of authority, followed in 1933 by Secretaries Stimson and Hull, was inappropriate in an era where partisans of the incoming president had relentlessly heaped personal abuse upon the retiring secretary of state. Acheson's resignation was therefore made effective at noon on 20 January 1953. Under Secretary Bruce left at the same time, and the next ranking officer of the department, Deputy Under Secretary H. Freeman Matthews, a career Foreign Service officer, took the helm for a day as secretary of state ad interim until Secretary John Foster Dulles could be commissioned and sworn in. No secretary of state since then has handed his department over directly to a successor when a different party has won the presidency.

Notes

1. All dates for appointments and departures from office in this chapter are taken from Richardson Dougall and Mary Patricia Chapman, *United States Chiefs of Mission, 1778–1973* (Washington, D.C., 1973), principally from Appendix D, "Officers of the Department of State Commissioned by the President."

2. The political layer included a very limited number of personal assistants and secretaries to these senior officials.

3. *Department of State Register,* 1 July 1933 (Washington, 1933), particularly 7–9.

4. Ibid., 34–61.

5. Before Miss Willis became ambassador to Switzerland (1953), a few women had been given political appointments as chiefs of mission, notably Ruth Bryan Owen as minister to Denmark (1933), Florence Jaffray Harriman as minister to Norway (1937), and Perle Mesta as minister to Luxembourg (1949). Eleanor Roosevelt's service as a delegate to the United Nations should also be noted.

6. Concerning the friction between Hull and Welles, see Cordell Hull, *The Memoirs of Cordell Hull,* 2 vols. (New York, 1948), 2:1230–31, and Dean Acheson, *Present at the Creation: My Years in the State Department* (New York, 1969), 11–12. It may be expected that Welles's side of the story will appear in a biography now in preparation by his son Benjamin Welles. See also Frank Warren Graff, *Strategy of Involvement: A Diplomatic Biography of Sumner Welles* (New York, 1988).

7. The best known and most effective of these (although also perhaps the least objectionable from Hull's point of view) was the president's friend and close adviser Harry Hopkins. Hull and his department had greater problems with presidential envoys such as Patrick J. Hurley, Henry A. Wallace, and Lauchlin Currie.

8. Concerning Hull's accomplishments and problems, see Hull, *Memoirs,* and Julius W. Pratt, *Cordell Hull, 1933–44,* vols. 12–13 of *The American Secretaries of State and Their Diplomacy,* ed. Robert H. Ferrell (New York, 1964). Administrative changes within the Department of State during Hull's secretaryship are detailed in Graham H. Stuart, *The Department of State: A History of Its Organization, Procedure and Personnel* (New York, 1949), 318–411. A massive documentary record of American foreign policy during the period covered by this chapter has been published by the Department of State in its series *Foreign Relations of the United States (FRUS)* for the years 1933–1952.

9. See William McHenry Franklin, *Protection of Foreign Interests: A Study in Diplomatic and Consular Practice* (Washington, 1947), 109–15, 261–68.

10. William Barnes and John Heath Morgan, *The Foreign Service of the United States: Origins, Development, and Functions* (Washington, 1961), 245–47.

11. Homer L. Calkin, *Women in the Department of State: Their Role in Foreign*

Affairs (Washington, 1978). But by January 1953 there were still only sixteen women officers in the Foreign Service (p. 120).

12. Stuart, *Department of State, 355.*

13. The ultimate disposition of divisional and office files assembled during and after the war created a major problem. They obviously contained (with a great deal of duplicative and ephemeral material) many important documents of permanent value not duplicated in the central files. Eventually some such papers were incorporated into the central indexed files (many of the papers now filed under 740.00119 Potsdam, for example, fall in this category); others were packed in cardboard boxes and are still preserved as that historian's nightmare, the department's "lot files," which have poor finding aids but which are essential to the record of wartime and postwar diplomacy.

14. See Franklin, *Protection of Foreign Interests,* 115, 219–28, 266–72.

15. Stuart devotes almost an entire chapter to this subject. See *Department of State,* 365–71.

16. The reorganization (departmental order 1218) and its aftermath are dealt with in some detail ibid., 389–96.

17. Acheson, *Present at the Creation,* 89.

18. For details on departmental order 1301 of 20 Dec. 1944 and on its modifications, see Stuart, *Department of State,* 400–411.

19. Richard L. Walker, *E. R. Stettinius, Jr.,* in vol. 14 of *The American Secretaries of State and Their Diplomacy,* ed. Robert H. Ferrell (New York, 1965), 9–10, 39–53. See also Thomas M. Campbell and George C. Herring, eds., *The Diaries of Edward R. Stettinius, Jr., 1943–1946* (New York, 1975).

20. Day, McKinley's secretary of state for less than five months in 1898, is much better known for his later service as an associate justice of the Supreme Court.

21. Gaddis Smith, *Dean Acheson,* vol. 16 of *The American Secretaries of State and Their Diplomacy,* ed. Robert H. Ferrell (New York, 1972), 54. Stettinius, however, headed the delegation to the Preparatory Commission of the United Nations in London in 1945 and was the first United States representative to the United Nations.

22. Harry S. Truman, *Memoirs* (Garden City, 1955–1956), 1:22–23. James F. Byrnes, *All in One Lifetime* (New York, 1958), 280, indicates that he was offered the secretaryship in a second meeting with Truman on the second day following Roosevelt's death, and that he accepted the offer.

23. See the end papers in James F. Byrnes, *Speaking Frankly* (New York, 1947). See also *Foreign Travels of the Secretaries of State, 1866–1990* (Washington, 1990), 9–13.

24. For general coverage of Byrnes's secretaryship, see his two volumes cited above and George Curry, *James F. Byrnes,* in vol. 14 of *The American Secretaries of State and Their Diplomacy,* ed. Robert H. Ferrell (New York, 1965). See also Robert L. Messer, *The End of an Alliance: James F. Byrnes, Roosevelt, Truman, and the Origins of the Cold War* (Chapel Hill, N.C., 1982).

25. See Acheson, *Present at the Creation,* 127, 157–62. Acheson called this a "deplorable decision" and got it rescinded shortly after Marshall became secretary of state (p. 214).

26. Barnes and Morgan, *Foreign Service of the United States,* 255–56.

27. For a full analysis of the act see ibid., 256–66.

28. John Lewis Gaddis, *The United States and the Origins of the Cold War, 1941–1947* (New York, 1972), vii.

29. For a summary of the numerous and rancorous problems that developed between West and East, see Randall B. Woods and Howard Jones, *Dawning of the Cold War: The United States' Quest for Order* (Athens, Ga., 1991), which synthesizes much of the voluminous historical literature on the Cold War.

30. This school of historical revisionism was started with the publication of Gar Alperovits, *Atomic Diplomacy: Hiroshima and Potsdam; The Use of the Atomic Bomb and the American Confrontation with Soviet Power* (New York, 1965). But see the more recent work of John Lewis Gaddis, *The Long Peace: Inquiries into the History of the Cold War* (New York, 1987), 104 ff.

31. See a record (in translation) of Foreign Minister Molotov's conversation on the subject with Fedor Chuev in *Cold War International History Project Bulletin* (Spring, 1992), 20. Cf. Chapter 3, p. 86.

32. For a detailed account of Marshall's China mission, see Forrest C. Pogue, *George C. Marshall: Statesman, 1945–1959* (New York, 1987), 60–143.

33. Byrnes's account of his resignation is in Byrnes, *All in One Lifetime*, 387–88, 400–402. Truman's account is in his *Memoirs*, 1:546–53. The letter that Truman states he read to Byrnes in January 1946, and which he printed in full in his memoirs, had been published earlier in William Hillman, *Mr. President: The First Publication from the Personal Diaries, Private Letters, Papers and Revealing Interviews of Harry S. Truman, Thirty-Second President of the United States of America* (New York, 1951), 21–23. Byrnes denied flatly that Truman sent him or read him this letter, and stated that he would have resigned at once if he had received such a letter.

34. Pogue, *George C. Marshall: Statesman*, 149. Larry I. Bland, ed., *George C. Marshall: Interviews and Reminiscences for Forrest C. Pogue*, revised ed. (Lexington, Va., 1991), 561–62. For another assessment of Marshall's secretaryship, see Robert H. Ferrell, *George C. Marshall*, vol. 15 of *The American Secretaries of State and Their Diplomacy*, ed. Robert H. Ferrell (New York, 1966).

35. Pogue, *George C. Marshall: Statesman*, 150. Bland, *Marshall Interviews*, 561–63.

36. George F. Kennan, *Memoirs, 1925–1950* (Boston, 1967), 313, 325–27.

37. George F. Kennan, "The Original Planning Staff," *Foreign Service Journal* 69 (September 1992): 24–25.

38. Many of the Policy Planning Staff studies have been published officially in *FRUS*. Those for the first three years of the staff's existence have also been printed unofficially in *The State Department Policy Planning Staff Papers, 1947–49*, 3 vols. (New York, 1983). See Kennan, *Memoirs, 1925–1950*, 326 ff., for a summary of the work of the Policy Planning Staff with regard to the Marshall Plan, the containment policy, the Far East, the North Atlantic Treaty Organization, and Germany. See also Wilson D. Miscamble C.S.C., *George F. Kennan and the Making of American Foreign Policy, 1947–1950* (Princeton, 1992).

39. Pogue, *George C. Marshall: Statesman*, 197–257. See also Acheson, *Present at the Creation*, 226–35; James Jones, *The Fifteen Weeks* (New York, 1955); Charles E. Bohlen, *Witness to History, 1929–1969* (New York, 1973), 263–64. It may be noted that Marshall's Harvard speech was actually drafted by Bohlen, who, as a Foreign Service officer fluent in Russian, had been the presidential interpreter at the wartime summit conferences with Stalin and who in 1946 had been assigned as special assistant to the secretary. In August 1947 he reached the upper levels of the Department of State upon his appointment as counselor. In 1951 he was counselor again, and in later years he was

ambassador to the Soviet Union, the Philippines, and France, and deputy under secretary of state for political affairs. For recent economic interpretations of the Marshall Plan, see Michael J. Hogan, *The Marshall Plan: America, Britain, and the Reconstruction of Western Europe, 1947–1952* (New York, 1987), and Melvyn P. Leffler, *A Preponderance of Power: National Security, the Truman Administration, and the Cold War* (Stanford, 1992).

40. Pogue, *George C. Marshall: Statesman,* chaps. 12 and 17.

41. Ibid., 161–67; Acheson, *Present at the Creation,* 220–25; Jones, *Fifteen Weeks.*

42. Pogue, *George C. Marshall: Statesman,* chaps. 18 and 23. Concerning the willingness of Truman to use atomic weapons had the Berlin blockade led to war, see p. 315; and Avi Shlaim, *The United States and the Berlin Blockade, 1948–1949: A Study in Crisis Decision-Making* (Berkeley, 1983), 234–40.

43. Pogue, *George C. Marshall: Statesman,* 373. See also Clark Clifford, with Richard Holbrooke, *Counsel to the President: A Memoir* (New York, 1991), 3–23.

44. *The Organization of the Government for the Conduct of Foreign Affairs: A Report with Recommendations Prepared for the Commission on Organization of the Executive Branch of the Government* [Task Force H] (Washington, 1949), 1–5. The more detailed discussion of the general recommendations begins on p. 10.

45. Ellis O. Briggs, *Farewell to Foggy Bottom: The Recollections of a Career Diplomat* (New York, 1964), 159, 174.

46. Kraft's column released by Publisher's Newspaper Syndicate, 20 May 1966. This seemed so apt to Foreign Service officer John Franklin Campbell that he entitled his own later analysis of the department *The Foreign Affairs Fudge Factory* (New York, 1971) and quoted the pertinent portion of Kraft's column on the verso of his title page.

47. Evan Thomas (reviewing a biography of Acheson in his later years) in *The New York Times Book Review,* 8 Nov. 1992, 7.

48. Smith, *Acheson,* 396.

49. For text of the act, see *Department of State Bulletin* (hereafter *DSB*) 20 (26 June 1949): 835. The details of the administrative reorganization are printed in *DSB* 20 (29 May 1949): 702–3.

50. *DSB* 21 (31 Oct. 1949): 677–79.

51. *DSB* 21 (18 July 1949): 78.

52. *DSB* 21 (28 Nov. 1949): 835.

53. Smith, *Acheson,* 55–81. Acheson, *Present at the Creation,* 276–86. David S. McLellan, *Dean Acheson: The State Department Years* (New York, 1976), 145–55.

54. Smith, *Acheson,* 82–103. McLellan, *Acheson,* 155–63.

55. E. J. Kahn, Jr., *The China Hands: America's Foreign Service Officers and What Befell Them* (New York, 1975), 309–11.

56. Smith, *Acheson,* 177–200. See Glenn D. Paige, *The Korean Decision, June 24– 30, 1950* (New York, 1968), which may be compared with Rosemary Foot, *The Wrong War: American Policy and the Dimensions of the Korean Conflict, 1950–1953* (Ithaca, 1985), and its sequel, *A Substitute for Victory: The Politics of Peacemaking at the Korean Armistice Talks* (Ithaca, 1990).

57. This language is from a report by Frank Desmond of the Wheeling *Intelligencer* as quoted in Richard H. Rovere, *Senator Joe McCarthy* (New York, 1960), 125.

3

HIS MASTER'S VOICE:

VIACHESLAV MIKHAILOVICH MOLOTOV AS

STALIN'S FOREIGN COMMISSAR

Steven Merritt Miner

FEW THINGS illustrate the disparate verdict of the Second World War more neatly than the widely divergent fates of the Nazi and Soviet leaders. Those of Stalin's lieutenants who were able to survive him enjoyed remarkably long lives, a longevity all the more surprising given the mortal terrors they endured during their service to their *vozhd'*, or boss. These peaceful state pensioners would never have to answer to any Nuremberg-style tribunal for their actions; and, even after the collapse of the Soviet regime in 1991, plaques still adorn the apartment houses where they quietly lived out their retirement. Apparently some of these old Stalinists, such as Anastas Mikoyan and Georgii Malenkov—who, it is widely rumored, received baptism in the Orthodox faith before dying—were given to some regrets in later life.

Self-doubt seems to have been a stranger, however, to Stalin's best-known comrade, Viacheslav Mikhailovich Molotov, who was born Skriabin. As late as 1971 he would be photographed toasting "the great name of Stalin," and he would gratefully receive a portrait of his former boss for his birthday in 1981. Until his death at the age of ninety-six on 8 November 1986—fittingly enough one day after the sixty-ninth anniversary of the Bolshevik revolution—Molotov would remain loyal to the legacy of Stalin, even defending the prewar purges as necessary for the defense of socialism. Looking back over the decades, Molotov claimed that Stalin "did a great deal, and that is the most important thing. In those conditions nobody could have done better than Stalin—not only during the war, but also before and after the war."[1]

Molotov's attachment to his old boss is understandable, since without Stalin Molotov would most probably have passed through history unnoticed. After all, although Molotov would show himself to be a man of certain very great talents, he scarcely seemed the sort of figure destined to shine in politics. A laconic, sarcastic man with no flair for public speaking, Molotov seemed made by nature for the role of bureaucrat. With his pince-nez and his always-conservative suits, he looked like what he was: the offspring of a moderately prosperous provincial Russian family. Among his more freewheeling Bolshevik comrades, Molotov appeared like a bank clerk who had accidentally stumbled into a bohemian party. Even the malicious nicknames given him by his fellow Bolsheviks suggest contempt for Molotov's grayness and personal limitations. He was generally called "stoney-arse,"[2] and Lenin once dubbed him "comrade filing cabinet."

Perhaps as much as anything else, it was Molotov's very colorlessness that drew him to Stalin. At least until Stalin's last years, the two seemed ideally suited to one another. Molotov supplied the very talents Stalin needed during his rise through the Bolshevik hierarchy to supreme power—a legendary memory, huge capacity for work and organization, and a ruthlessness tempered by a dog-like loyalty toward his boss. Most importantly, Molotov clearly lacked the talent to be supreme leader. As his failure in the power struggles following Stalin's death would show, Molotov could only thrive as a number-two man.

Throughout Stalin's rise to prominence in the 1920s, Molotov could be found by his mentor's right hand, condemning "deviationists" of the left and right. He would later claim that his participation in battles against the "Trotskiites" and "rightists" had prepared him well for diplomacy, teaching him to think on his feet, debate, and speak without notes.[3]

During the collectivization of Soviet agriculture between 1929 and 1932 Molotov showed himself to be a hard-line Stalinist. Along with Stalin, he raised grain delivery quotas for peasants to such unrealistic levels that a famine resulted, causing millions of deaths by starvation. At the height of the famine, Molotov traveled through the Ukraine, where the devastation resulting directly from his policies was most intense, apparently without being moved by the mass suffering he witnessed.[4]

Molotov seems to have been unwavering in his belief that such vast human sacrifice was necessary in order to win the battle for communism. Feliks Chuev, a Soviet writer who came to know Molotov well during the last decades of his life, thought that Molotov's belief in the superiority of the socialist system, and its ultimate triumph over capitalism, was in fact a deeply held and unquestioned belief. Molotov, Chuev writes, was "unshakably convinced and did everything that was necessary to reach [the socialist] goal. Every event he fit into the struggle for socialism."[5]

The depth of his convictions gave Molotov a rigid moral self-confidence that served to enhance his already brutal character. He showed the same resolve and indifference to suffering that he had already demonstrated during the collectivization when Stalin launched his purges of the Soviet state and society. Molotov's signature has been found next to Stalin's on numerous lists of people condemned to death; on one day alone, 12 December 1938, Stalin and Molotov signed orders to have 3,167 people shot.[6] Far from doubting the necessity, wisdom, or morality of such massive repression, Molotov would later frequently defend the purges, claiming that "we acted correctly," since as a result "we had no fifth column during the war."[7]

On the eve of World War II, Stalin had no closer associate than Molotov. As president of the Soviet of People's Commissars, the latter took part in every major decision. His name, bust, and portrait appeared throughout the USSR, exceeded in frequency only by Stalin's own; towns, villages, collective farms, and the city of Perm were renamed after him, and one of the USSR's highest mountains was even redubbed Molotov Peak in the diminutive Bolshevik's honor. By 1939 Molotov was intimately familiar with all aspects of the Soviet state, lacking experience only in foreign affairs. Ironically, it was in this field that he would gain international renown.

I

Molotov's sudden and unexpected appointment as foreign commissar on 3 May 1939 triggered a shock wave throughout the world diplomatic community. Maksim Litvinov's dismissal was universally—and rightly—interpreted as a sign that the USSR would now be more open to approaches from the Nazis. Not only had Litvinov been a relatively consistent proponent of cooperation with the Western powers, even his personal style contrasted sharply with Molotov's abrupt manner. Sir William Seeds, then British ambassador to Moscow, wrote that the new foreign commissar was "a man totally ignorant of foreign affairs . . . to whom the idea of negotiations—as distinct from imposing the will of his party leader—is utterly alien." Seeds did allow, however, that Molotov possessed "a rather foolish cunning of the type of the peasant."[8]

German diplomats were understandably less disconcerted by Molotov's appointment. Perhaps because they understood the workings of totalitarian diplomacy, unlike Seeds, the Germans correctly believed that Stalin had appointed Molotov to his new post precisely because he would be Stalin's obedient tool. On 4 May 1939, for instance, Werner von Tippelskirch, counselor of the German embassy in Moscow, telegraphed the German Foreign Office that the appointment of Molotov, who, unlike Litvinov, was "no Jew," and who was "held to be [the] 'most intimate friend and closest collaborator' of Stalin," meant that the dictator would now bring the conduct of foreign policy more closely under his personal control.[9]

The German reading of Molotov's appointment was remarkably insightful. The new foreign commissar was indeed almost totally unfamiliar with the intricacies of foreign affairs. His only experience in this area had been several shadowy approaches to Berlin during the late 1930s, conducted apparently without the knowledge of Foreign Commissar Litvinov.[10] Molotov would later remark that he "never prepared specially" for diplomacy, having spent all of his early career in what he delicately called "party work." He assessed his chief failing as a diplomat to be his almost total ignorance of foreign languages; he could speak only Russian, though he could read some English, French, and German.[11] Despite these glaring shortcomings, however, Molotov enjoyed the one indispensible quality needed in totalitarian diplomacy: the dictator's current confidence.

Litvinov's sudden dismissal may have unpleasantly surprised both the foreign commissar himself and the rest of the Foreign Commissariat (NKID) personnel no less than the world at large. When he had met the British ambassador early on 2 May, for instance, he gave "no inkling" of the impending change.[12] Litvinov had even appeared near Stalin on the viewing platform of Lenin's Mausoleum during the May Day parade on Red Square, an honor usually thought to be reserved for those in good favor with Stalin.[13]

Despite these outward signs of calm, however, a storm was once more about to sweep through the NKID, as it had already done during 1937–1938. Molotov would later admit that his instructions on becoming foreign commissar were "to very strictly change almost the entire leadership" of the commissariat. Evgenii Gnedin, director of the NKID's Press Department from 1937–1939, who would survive the purge and the camps to publish his *samizdat* memoirs, writes that even as Litvinov stood on the Red Square viewing stand, "In the 'big house' on Dzerzhinskii Square [Lubianka prison and NKVD headquarters] the slanderous evidence against M. M. Litvinov and his coworkers was already being assembled. Feverish preparation for the 'case of the enemies of the people in the NKID' was underway."[14]

According to Gnedin's account, late in the evening of 2 May 1939, an investigative panel—composed of Molotov, Lavrenty Beria (recently appointed people's commissar for internal affairs), Georgii Malenkov (then a secretary of the Central Committee), and Vladimir Dekanozov (deputy people's commissar for foreign affairs and soon to be made ambassador to Germany)— assembled in the NKID building to interrogate, one-by-one, the high-ranking members of the Foreign Service. Litvinov was present, sitting quietly and dejectedly at the end of the table, as the panel probed for evidence of a treasonous conspiracy. The group interrogated Gnedin, who felt that the inquisitors were searching for information compromising to Litvinov personally.[15]

Litvinov may well have been the object of this witch hunt; to be sure there was no love lost between him and Molotov. At the time of this purge, the latter reportedly remarked to Fedor Gusev, party secretary at the NKID, "Enough of Litvinov liberalism. I am going to tear out that kike's wasps's nest by the roots."[16] Decades later, Molotov still regretted that Litvinov had somehow managed to slip out of his net, fulminating against his alleged "treachery" and remarking that "Litvinov only remained alive by chance."[17] Of course, this may have been no accident. Like most dictators, Stalin routinely retained people who might serve as a useful counterweight in the future to a current favorite, and even Molotov had to admit grudgingly that Litvinov "related well with Stalin."[18] As later events would show, after the Nazi-Soviet partnership collapsed unexpectedly in June 1941, Litvinov would once again render useful services for his boss.

The new foreign commissar was faithful to his master's instructions; he scythed ruthlessly through all levels of the NKID. The tempo of the purge reached a peak following the signature of the Nazi-Soviet Pact in late August 1939. And although there seems to have been no readily discernible pattern among those who disappeared into the Gulag, Litvinov appointees felt especially victimized.[19] For instance, Léon Helfand, the Soviet chargé d'affaires to Italy until his defection in 1940, told a British diplomat in September 1940 that "Maisky [Soviet ambassador to London] and Oumansky in Washington were the only Litvinovites left in [the Soviet] Foreign Service."[20] He might have added Aleksandra Kollontai, another long-time Litvinov ally who, in a later British ambassador's colorful phrase, was "one of the few 'Old Bolsheviks' still above ground."[21] All the others had been purged, had killed themselves, or, like Helphand himself, had defected.

Although the Stalin-Molotov blood purge of the NKID was odious, there could be no doubt in May 1939 that Soviet foreign policy was in the worst crisis since the revolution and civil war. If the situation did not demand such extraordinarily brutal measures, then at least it explains them. The reflexive Stalinist prescription for crises was invariably arrests, followed by ever-stricter control. "In general, we centralized our diplomacy," Molotov reflected later; "I say centralized, that is depending in everything on the center, on Moscow"; "ambassadors were only executors of detailed instructions. In our situation this diplomacy was unavoidable, and it achieved positive results." Nor did Molotov exempt himself from this stern discipline; he worked tirelessly to be—literally —his master's voice. "I saw, when I came to act in the capacity of minister of foreign affairs, especially after Stalin, many were surprised that I conducted myself so independently, but I was independent only within the boundaries of my directives. That is how a diplomat should perform."[22]

Slavish dependence on directives from Moscow certainly produced results, though at an incalculable price in lost flexibility. Soviet diplomats abroad needed constantly to look anxiously over their shoulders toward the center, fearful that a misstep could cause them to suffer their predecessors' fate. Furthermore, the new generation of Stalinist diplomats that stepped into the shoes of the purge victims lacked their elders' intimate knowledge of foreign countries and languages. The background and shortcomings of Andrei Gromyko, the most famous product of this process, were fairly typical. Trained as an economist, not a diplomat, Gromyko did not even know English when he was sent to Washington as first counselor to the embassy. Given his manifestly inadequate training, the State Department assessed him as "slow-witted and unimaginative." "It is not believed," the assessment continued, "that his qualifications or experience warrant his being left in charge of the Soviet Embassy."[23] Within two years the inexperienced and very young Gromyko would be ambassador to Washington; but, contrary to the State Department's assessment, he possessed all the qualities for success in Molotov's Foreign Commissariat—unswerving obedience and the ability to remain silent.

That Soviet foreign policy remained operative despite such rigidity is a testament in large part to Molotov's phenomenal capacity for work; this achievement is all the more impressive when one recalls that he continued to serve until 1941 in his capacity as president of the Council of People's Commissars (Sovnarkom). Even after Stalin assumed this title in the spring of 1941, Molotov remained his deputy and in fact continued to process the mass of the work. In addition, during the war Molotov would serve on the State Committee for Defense (GKO), Stalin's wartime inner cabinet. He would also be in charge of such crucial tasks as tank production and the Soviet atomic program.

The paperwork passing over his desk was breathtaking, ranging from reports on the potato harvest to the results of Supreme Soviet elections.[24] Some of the detail he was forced to handle was simply absurd. For instance, at the height of the war against Germany, he received a closely typed five-page document from a Central Committee member proposing a high-level state commission to establish the proper usage of the Russian letter *yo*.[25] Molotov was able to handle the flow of paper by being a stern, humorless taskmaster, demanding that his subordinates match his long hours at work and his grim attitude toward duty. He was so unforgiving that he apparently even regarded the catching of a cold as a sign of moral weakness. A proper overcoat, gloves, and scarf should be sufficient to ward off any illness. Failure to bundle up was a sign of self-indulgence.[26]

II

Molotov's name will forever be linked with the Nazi-Soviet Pact. In a return to the ancient Russian tradition where dubious deeds are invariably linked with the tsar's advisers rather than the tsar himself, the 1939 pact with Germany was long known popularly as the Molotov-Ribbentrop pact, much to the former's annoyance. In fact, however, Stalin directed the negotiations with the Nazis, and, even more than in later diplomatic events, the foreign commissar remained in the background during the events of spring-summer 1939.

By late winter 1939, the USSR's official policy during much of the decade— "collective security" against the German threat—had collapsed. Although a Soviet Union madly and murderously engaged in collectivizing agriculture and mercilessly purging the state and society could scarcely expect the outside world to regard it as a reliable partner, the fault for the disastrous state of affairs in 1939 did not lie entirely in Moscow. The sorry record of the Western powers in dealing with Hitler, the diplomatic failures from Spain to Munich, had given powerful support to the Soviets' already strong suspicions about Western reliability. At the outset of the new year, the USSR's position was perilous: excluded from the Munich Conference, without allies, the apparent object of the emerging Axis between Berlin, Rome, and Tokyo. Only Hitler's sudden shift in favor of Moscow rescued the Soviets from the diplomatic dead end in which they found themselves.

Although a change in German direction would make Nazi-Soviet rapprochement possible in 1939, there is every reason to believe that such a policy had long been the Soviets' preferred line. Such, at any rate, was the contention of Walter Krivitskii, a Soviet intelligence officer who defected to the West in 1937. Krivitskii argued that throughout the 1930s, despite the evident hostility between Hitler and Stalin, "the true picture of their relations was that of a persistent suitor who would not be discouraged by rebuffs. Stalin was the suitor. There was enmity on Hitler's side. On Stalin's there was fear." Stalin, Krivitskii continues, "had a profound contempt for the 'weakling' democratic nations, and an equally profound respect for the 'mighty' totalitarian states."[27]

Evidence indicating Stalin's preference for working with Germany can be found in his own rare public pronouncements on foreign policy. In a key speech to the Fourteenth Congress of the Soviet Communist Party in December 1925, Stalin argued that the results of the First World War drove the USSR to cooperate with Germany. In his view, the victors of the war, "Britain and America, as an Anglo-American alliance, are coming to stand at the head of the capitalist countries. Our country—the Soviet Union—is coming to stand at the head of those who are discontented with imperialism and engaged in a mortal struggle against it." Since the USSR was dissatisfied with the postwar order enforced by this "Anglo-American alliance," it stood to reason that Moscow should work with other revisionist powers. Soviet diplomacy, Stalin continued, should "work in the direction of rapprochement with those capitalist countries that were defeated in the imperialist war, with those capitalist countries which were most humiliated and came off worst, and which, owing to this, are in opposition to the ruling alliance of Great Powers."[28] Germany was clearly the country with which the USSR could cooperate most fruitfully.

Stalin made these remarks at a time when Germany and the USSR were already working together to undermine the Versailles order. Circumstances would change greatly following Hitler's rise to power eight years later and the consequent rupturing of ties between Berlin and Moscow. Nonetheless, there is every reason to believe that despite the prevailing heat between the two continental dictatorships, Stalin continued to seek some modus vivendi with Hitler between 1933 and 1939. Almost one year after his pact with Hitler, Stalin would echo his 1925 reasoning in remarks to the British ambassador to Moscow, Sir Stafford Cripps:

> During the pre-war negotiations with England and France, the USSR had wanted to change the old [European] equilibrium *for which these countries stood* [my emphasis], but . . . England and France had wanted to preserve it. Germany had also wanted to make a change in the equilibrium, and this common desire to get rid of the old equilibrium had created the basis for the rapprochement with Germany.[29]

Explaining the pact with Nazi Germany, Molotov would repeat his boss's reasoning:

> People ask, with an air of innocence, how could the Soviet Union consent to improve its relations with a state of the fascist type? Is that possible, they ask? But they forget that it is not a question of our attitude towards the internal regime of another country but of foreign relations between two States. . . . The countries that suffered the most in the war of 1914–18 were Russia and Germany. Therefore, the interests of the peoples of the Soviet Union and Germany do not lie in mutual enmity.[30]

At the time of Molotov's appointment as foreign commissar in May 1939, it was by no means clear in Moscow that a rapprochement with Germany would be possible. The Soviets had begun to send signals that some warming of relations might be in order. Soviet press attacks on Nazism became much more muted. And, on 10 March, in a speech to the Eighteenth Congress of the Soviet Communist Party, Stalin held out a famous olive branch to Berlin. He stated that "we are now witnessing an open redivision of the world into spheres of influence at the expense of non-aggressive states." The Soviet leadership, Stalin said, must "not allow our country to be drawn into conflicts by warmongers who are accustomed to have others pull the chestnuts out of the fire for them."[31] The diplomatic community in Moscow interpreted Stalin's remarks ominously; to one Estonian diplomat, the speech provided evidence that the former Soviet policy of collective security so "grandiloquently propagated by the Soviets for several years, was suddenly thrown overboard."[32] Any doubt about the thinking behind Stalin's speech was removed later in August, when Ribbentrop visited Moscow to sign the Nazi-Soviet Pact. Molotov "raised his glass to Stalin, remarking that it had been Stalin who—through his speech of March this year, which had been well understood in Germany—had brought about the reversal in political relations [between Moscow and Berlin]."[33] In truth, Stalin's speech differed little from previous Soviet speeches; he had even more than once used the chestnut metaphor to describe England's historical efforts to embroil the Continental powers in the past. What made Stalin's speech of 10 March stand out was the favorable German reaction.

Ironically, the Soviets received invaluable assistance in their approaches to

Germany not through their own efforts, but rather from their old imperialist rival, the British government. On 15 March 1939, Hitler broke the agreement he had made with Chamberlain in Munich when he ordered his army to occupy the Czech lands. The British prime minister, outraged at being betrayed by Hitler and concerned to deter further German territorial aggrandizement, extended a unilateral guarantee against German aggression, first to Poland and later to Romania. Subsequently, the French would extend their own guarantee to these two countries.

This proved to be a heaven-sent opportunity for the Soviets. At a stroke, the Western powers had given Moscow some much-needed diplomatic breathing room. Later, the British would learn from Léon Helfand, a Soviet diplomat who defected to London in 1940, that these guarantees had ended up harming British interests. Helfhand was

> asked whether this exclusion of Stalin from the Munich conversations had been a prime obstacle to an Anglo-Soviet agreement in 1939. He did not think so. He said that our great fault had been to give Poland the guarantee before we had got an agreement with Russia signed and delivered. He insisted that Stalin and Molotov believed that we should keep our word to Poland and therefore that the Western powers would embroil themselves without the Soviet needing to give any undertakings.[34]

Further evidence that the Soviet leaders believed the Western powers would indeed become embroiled with the Germans because of these guarantees is provided by Stalin's remarks to Ribbentrop in August. The latter minimized the British military threat and implied that London might be too weak to fight over Poland. Stalin disagreed, saying "that England, despite its weakness, would wage war craftily and stubbornly."[35]

Following the Anglo-French guarantees to Poland and Romania, the Soviets faced a choice. On the one hand, they could work toward an agreement with the Western powers to restrain Hitler. This would be risky, however; Britain and France might prove to be unreliable allies, sheltering behind their Maginot Line and watching as the Germans and Soviets bled each other white. Furthermore, ever-present in Soviet strategic thinking was the threat in the Far East. That other signatory to the Anti-Comintern Pact, Japan, was a constant worry in Moscow. In 1938 and periodically through 1939, the Japanese and Soviets clashed along the Mongolian border. Although the Soviets acquitted themselves very well in these clashes, should Moscow ally openly with the Western powers, and should this fail to deter Hitler, then the Soviets faced the daunting prospect of a war on two fronts, a continent apart, with dubious allies and an army that had during the previous two years lost forty thousand officers to political purges.[36]

On the other hand, rapprochement with Germany promised enhanced security and the possibility of territorial gain. Furthermore, should war break out between Nazi Germany and the Western Allies, this would only redound to Moscow's benefit.[37] In 1925, Stalin had given a hint as to how he might act when faced with such a choice. He told the Central Committee plenum that "if war breaks out we shall have to take action, but we shall be the last to do so. And we shall do so in order to throw the decisive weight in the scales, the *weight* that can turn the scales."[38]

The Soviets may have been inclined toward a deal with Berlin, but translating that wish into results was far from simple. The events of summer 1939 are familiar; the Soviets carried on two sets of negotiations: well-publicized talks with the British and French about a mutual security pact; and covert and tentative talks with Berlin. Historians have rightly stressed that the Western states were dilatory in their approaches to Moscow. During these protracted negotiations they did not press as energetically as they should have done for a military pact with the USSR.

At the same time, however, a careful reading of the Anglo-Franco-Soviet talks of June-August 1939 shows that the Soviets constantly raised thorny issues that delayed the talks, most notably questions relating to the states lying between Germany and the USSR. In particular, Moscow sought assurances from the Western powers that they would support Soviet moves against "indirect aggression" in the Baltic States. What Moscow was essentially demanding was the right to occupy the Baltic States in the event that any vaguely defined undesirable political developments occurred there. The British and French interpreted this Soviet demand, with some justification as later events would show, as evidence that the USSR intended to annex the Baltics at their convenience. Soviet prickliness over this and other questions served to prolong negotiations with Britain and France, giving the Germans time to produce suitably tempting counter offers.

It has long been unclear when precisely the Soviets decided to cast their lot with the Nazis rather than the Western Allies. Recent Soviet publications have shed some light on this question. The 2 August meeting between Ribbentrop and Georgii Astakhov, the Soviet chargé d'affaires in Berlin, was crucial. At this time the German foreign minister assured the Soviets that Berlin would not "export" National Socialism and sought the "normalization" of relations. Furthermore, Ribbentrop said, there were no "contradictions" between Soviet and German interests in the area stretching from the Baltic to the Black Sea.[39]

The following day, as a result of Ribbentrop's approach, Molotov called in the German ambassador, Count von der Schulenburg, to sound him out on the details. Molotov grilled the German on Berlin's position regarding Japan, about the "anti-Comintern pact," and alluded to the exclusion of the USSR from the Munich negotiations the previous year.[40] Evidently, Stalin and Molotov found Ribbentrop's comments and Schulenburg's explanations sufficiently tempting, for the following day, 4 August, Molotov informed Astakhov that Moscow wanted to continue exploring an improvement in relations.[41] When the Germans suggested the next day, however, that the two sides should conclude a trade agreement including a secret protocol concerning political-territorial questions, Molotov pulled back. He cabled Astakhov that such a secret protocol would be "inconvenient," and "would signify an inappropriate and incomprehensible rush forward."[42]

On 8 August, Astakhov sent a crucial letter. He said that the Germans were anxious for an agreement, showing this by halting all press attacks on the USSR and communism; furthermore, the Nazis were now explaining what they meant to include in a secret protocol. Ribbentrop's assurance that there were "no contradictions" between German and Soviet interests in the East meant that "the Germans wish to give us the impression that they would be prepared to declare their disinterest (at any rate politically) in the fate of the Baltic States (other than Lithuania), Bessarabia, Russian Poland (with changes to the benefit of Germany) and dissassociation from aspirations in the Ukraine." The German price was recognition of their claim to the rest of Poland and "a rejection of an Anglo-Franco-Soviet military-political agreement." The Germans' aim, Astakhov said, was "neutralizing us in the case of their [forthcoming] war with Poland."[43]

This was the pivotal note, and it evidently contained what Molotov and his boss wanted to hear. Three days later, Molotov answered Astakhov: "The enumeration of objects indicated in your letter of 8 August interests us."[44] Moscow was now being courted by both sides in the emerging crisis, and, as Helphand had said, Molotov was using this position to secure the better offer. Astakhov wrote from Berlin on 12 August: "Our negotiations with the Anglo-French military worry [the Germans] and they do not shy away from arguments and inducements of the widest order in order to forestall an eventual military agreement." Astakhov seemed genuinely shocked at the extent of the territory the Germans were willing to promise the Soviets in exchange for an understanding that would allow them to devour Poland free from the fear of two-front war. And, as Astakhov pointed out, these German promises preceded any serious negotiations.[45]

From these newly published messages between Moscow and Berlin, it is clear that the Kremlin knew that the Germans were yearning to invade Poland as soon as possible; Astakhov presciently estimated that an attack could come at the end of August or mid-September. He also gained the impression that the Germans believed they could avoid a world war by overrunning Poland so rapidly that the Allies would have to come to terms with the "real facts."[46]

By 15 August, Stalin had evidently been won over by German promises. Meeting Schulenburg on that day, Molotov spoke for the first time of a non-aggression pact between the two countries and of the forthcoming visit of Ribbentrop to Moscow.[47]

On the night of 23–24 August, Ribbentrop visited the Kremlin to negotiate the remaining details of the nonaggression pact and the secret protocol dealing with territorial changes. In the original protocol, the Baltic States—which in the Soviet reading included Finland—with the exception of Lithuania, fell into the Soviet sphere of influence. This was altered following the entry of the USSR into the war on 17 September; eight days later the Soviets proposed that Lithuania should fall within their sphere in exchange for which the Germans would receive more Polish land.[48] These changes were finalized during another round of negotiations on 27 September, and a supplementary territorial protocol was signed the following day.

The Soviets wasted little time translating German promises into concrete gain. A newly discovered record of the 27 September talks between Stalin and Ribbentrop sheds invaluable light on Soviet goals in the Baltic States. For decades, Moscow held that the USSR had annexed the Baltic States and established communist governments there only following the collapse of French resistance in June 1940. It is now clear that incorporation of the states into the USSR was Stalin's intent from August 1939 onward. The Soviet dictator told Ribbentrop that he and Molotov had already demanded that the Estonian and Latvian governments allow the establishment of Soviet bases on their territory:

> When asked by [Ribbentrop] whether this meant that the Soviet government intended to accomplish a slow penetration into Estonia and, possibly, Latvia, Mr. Stalin answered in the affirmative and added that nevertheless the present government system, ministries, etc., would be temporarily preserved in Estonia.
>
> Stalin said concerning Latvia that the Soviet government was going to make her a similar proposal. If the latter declines the proposal of a mutual assistance pact on the same conditions as proposed to Estonia, the Soviet Army will deal with it in the shortest possible time.[49]

During the negotiations with the Baltic States' leaders, Molotov played a role that would become familiar to world diplomats over the next decade: he supplied the threats of force behind Stalin's diplomacy, allowing his leader to masquerade as a relative moderate. On 24 September, for instance, he bullied Estonian Foreign Minister K. Selter. "If you do not wish to conclude a pact of mutual assistance with us, then we will have to resort to other means for the facilitation of our security, perhaps stronger, more complex [means]. I ask You, do not require us to use force in relation to Estonia."[50]

Molotov employed the same methods of intimidation with the representatives of the other two Baltic States, Lithuania and Latvia, reminding each of them that he possessed a blank check from Germany and that, as a result, they could expect no help from any quarter. He would later recall: "I should tell you secretly that I took a very hard line. The minister of foreign affairs of Latvia came to us in 1939, and I told him, 'You will not return until you sign the annexation agreement.'" "We were forced to such an extreme," he would claim, "But we did it, in my opinion, not badly."[51]

Such methods worked very well with the three small Baltic States, but

Molotov's threats failed to produce the desired results when applied to the representatives of Finland. That country chose to resist, much to Moscow's surprise; even more shocking, when the Red Army attacked Finland on 30 November 1939, it was not the expected walkover. Moscow learned both that the Finns were tough fighters and that the purge of Red Army leaders had sown dislocation and confusion among the ranks of the military.

There is every reason to believe that the Soviets sought to occupy the whole of Finland, as they would the Baltic States, and that the demand for Soviet bases on Finnish territory was simply a first step toward this end, again as it had been with the Baltics. Molotov would tell the Germans in November 1940 that he sought a settlement in Finland "on the same scale as in Bessarabia," which Moscow had incorporated into the USSR five months earlier.[52] Bogged down in Finland, taking large casualties, and afraid that the Western Allies might intervene on behalf of the Finns, the Soviets backed down and signed a moderate peace treaty with Finland on 12 March 1940.[53] Even after the war, the Soviets would not annex Finland, remembering the Western response to the Winter War of 1939–1940. Years later, Stalin would lament his "mistake" in not occupying Finland. "We were too concerned about the Americans," he said, "and they wouldn't have lifted a finger."[54]

Nazi-Soviet collaboration worked well for Moscow through June 1940. In that month, as world attention was distracted by the German offensive in France, Stalin made good on his promise to annex the Baltic States, which he did along with Bessarabia and Northern Bukovina.

Following France's surrender, however, points of conflict between the USSR and Nazi Germany began to take on a more serious tone. Stalin had hoped that France would offer more effective resistance and was concerned that German power was not unchecked on the continent. Nonetheless, especially after the British neutralized the French fleet at Oran, thereby depriving the Germans for the time being of sufficient seapower to challenge the Royal Navy, the Soviets once again began to believe—or at any rate act—as though the Germans needed them more than vice versa. When in the summer of 1940 the British ambassador to Moscow tried to persuade Stalin that the USSR should be concerned about German hegemony in Europe, the dictator remained unruffled: "M. Stalin said that he was not so simple-minded as to believe what individual German leaders said as to their not wanting to dominate Europe or the world. He was however aware of the physical impossibility of their dominating Europe or the world, which was the same thing." "Germany could not establish a hegemony over Europe without the domination of the seas," Stalin said.[55]

This calculus explains Soviet diplomacy during the period August 1939 through spring 1941. The Soviets believed that they were in a strong position relative to Germany; they did not have an unfinished war on their hands, as Berlin did, and so, the Soviets reasoned, Berlin needed Moscow more than vice versa. This conviction, apparently quite reasonable and yet ultimately mistaken, would explain the hard line Molotov would adopt in negotiating with Hitler in November 1940.

The Soviets became increasingly troubled by growing German assertiveness after the victory over France. Particular areas of concern to Moscow were Finland and Romania; the Germans stationed troops in the former, despite the fact that it fell within the Soviet sphere; and Germans remained active and highly visible in Romania, which again should have been in the Soviet zone. Furthermore, the Soviets were concerned that the Germans had fallen far behind in goods deliveries agreed to in the German-Soviet trade agreement of the previous February.

It was in part to iron out such matters that Molotov accepted Ribbentrop's invitation to visit Berlin. The German foreign minister issued the invitation accompanied by the customary barbs directed against Britain and containing a hint of further Soviet territorial gain. The Soviet foreign commissar should discuss with the Nazi leadership "the historical mission of the four powers—the Soviet Union, Italy, Japan, and Germany—to adopt a long-range policy and to direct the future development of their peoples into the right channels by delimitation of their interests on a world-wide scale."[56] As the results of Molotov's visit would demonstrate, the Soviets would prove vulnerable to such bait, especially to Hitler's promises that Moscow could share in the loot of the supposedly collapsing British empire, which Hitler would call "a gigantic world-wide estate in bankruptcy."[57]

Molotov met with the Nazi leaders from 12–13 November 1940. It was a high point of the foreign commissar's career, showing as it did that he possessed his boss's complete trust. As he told Hitler at one point during the negotiations, he had been given "exact instructions" from Stalin, and "everything that he was about to say was identical with the views of Stalin." There is every reason to believe that Molotov stayed completely in line with telegraphed directives from his boss in Moscow; that would explain why, in the first meeting with Ribbentrop, he refused to be drawn into speculative talk about a world-wide territorial division of the British empire between Germany, Italy, Japan, and the USSR. Later, having had an opportunity to communicate with Stalin, Molotov would prove more willing to talk about such things.

Throughout the meetings, the Germans tried to persuade their guest that British resistance was at an end—a claim made less convincing by the fact that one of the meetings was interrupted by a British air raid. Molotov remained unconvinced by Nazi blustering, tartly telling Ribbentrop: "The Germans were assuming that the war against England had already actually been won. If, therefore, as had been said in another connection, Germany was waging a life and death struggle against England, he could only construe this as meaning that Germany was fighting 'for life' and England 'for death.'"[58]

Molotov was, perhaps, too impervious to German boasting; he left the meetings persuaded that the Nazis were far more enmeshed in their war with Britain than they were admitting and that this would prevent them from attacking the USSR in the near term. Valentin Berezhkov, Molotov's translator and assistant during the Berlin meetings, writes: "This may seem surprising but [Molotov] believed that Hitler would not venture to start a war."[59] Berezhkov would later claim that Molotov returned to Moscow convinced that the Germans would not attack the USSR in 1941.[60]

Molotov's optimism was misplaced. The previous summer, Hitler had ordered his high command to prepare invasion plans against the USSR, and before the talks with Molotov he had ordered that, regardless of the meeting's results, "all preparations for the east already verbally ordered are to be continued."[61]

This disastrous misreading of German intentions and capabilities explains the next Soviet move. Having returned to Moscow and after briefing Stalin on the Berlin talks, Molotov summoned the German ambassador to the NKID. There he handed him one of the most important documents of the period of Nazi-Soviet collaboration. The note took the Germans up on their offer to share in the spoils of the British empire. The USSR would formally ally with the Axis powers, subject to four conditions: withdrawal of German forces from Finland; securing of Soviet interests in Bulgaria and the Turkish Straits; recognition that the area south of the Caucasus Mountains toward the Persian Gulf was within the Soviet sphere of "aspirations"; and renunciation by Japan of all rights in northern Sakhalin Island.[62]

The Soviets had overplayed their hand. Hitler would never reply to this offer, and throughout the winter and spring of 1941, it would become clearer every day that the Nazis believed they no longer needed to assuage Moscow. As Joseph Goebbels put it, "The Russian card is no longer trumps."[63] Throughout the first six months of 1941, the omens grew ever stronger that Germany was preparing to invade the USSR.

The Soviet failure to heed the warning signs and take timely action is one of the great mysteries of the Stalin era. It would seem that the dictator believed that if he could delay a German attack until late enough in the year, the Germans would have to wait until 1942 for a full season of warm-weather campaigning.[64] To this end, Stalin sought and achieved a nonaggression pact with Japan, signed in April; he also sought to avoid any action that might give the Germans a pretext to attack. Orders were even issued to the Soviet press so that no publication would "give any kind of pretext for conclusions that at this moment any kind of changes have occurred in the situation of Soviet-German relations and, much less, any pretext for any sort of diplomatic representation" by the Germans.[65]

Stalin received scores of warnings about the forthcoming German attack, but he apparently believed that these were the work of British intelligence, which was thereby attempting to enmesh him with Germany in order to save the British empire.[66] Stalin sent word down to the ranks of the intelligence services that warnings of German invasion plans were not welcome. Nonetheless, such warnings kept pouring in. One recently published document, dated 21 June 1941 from Beria to Stalin, dramatically illustrates the situation on the day before the German invasion:

> I again insist on recalling and punishing our Ambassador to Berlin, Dekanozov, who keeps on bombarding me [the People's Commissar of Internal Affairs] with 'reports' on Hitler's alleged preparations to attack the USSR. He has reported that this 'attack' will start tomorrow. . . .
>
> But I and my people, Iosif Vissarionovich, firmly remember your wise plan: Hitler is not going to attack us in 1941.[67]

III

On 22 June 1941, Stalin and Molotov had to face the unpleasant reality that their diplomacy had led directly to disaster. The Politburo met at 4:30 in the morning to discuss the attack.[68] To Mikoyan, who was present, Stalin appeared "depressed" and "shocked." He kept muttering, "So this is how that scoundrel Ribbentrop deceives."[69] The military situation was unclear in the first hours of the war; Klimenty Voroshilov and Georgii Malenkov believed that the German attacks constituted a "short adventure of the Germans," which would end after "several days," following much the same course as the clashes with Japan two years before.[70] In what in retrospect seems a spasm of wishful thinking, the Soviets appealed to the Japanese for "mediation" in this border skirmish.[71] When it became clear to the Kremlin that this was no simple crisis, but a battle to the death, Molotov was left to complain pathetically to German Ambassador Count von der Schulenburg, "Surely we did not deserve this"?[72]

Even after it became clear that this was a war, the mood in the Politburo remained optimistic. Endless propaganda about the invincible Red Army had apparently convinced the Soviet leaders themselves that the Germans would be repulsed by Soviet counterattacks.[73] Stalin was unsure enough about the situation, however, that he left to Molotov the unpleasant task of informing the nation by radio about the outbreak of war, saying: "I have nothing to say to the people. Let Molotov speak."[74] The Soviet dictator could not bring himself to speak publicly until 3 July, twelve days after the attack. In his address, Molotov adopted the line, "Our Cause is Just," which would become the guiding propaganda slogan of the war, appearing in posters, on the sides of tanks, and in graffiti throughout the USSR.

Whereas in the past it was believed that Stalin had some sort of nervous attack on being told of the German invasion, it has now become clear that this was not the case. Only after learning that his first orders to counterattack against the Germans had produced nothing but further losses did the full realization of the disaster finally sink in. Beginning on 28 June, Stalin failed to turn up in his

Kremlin office for two days. Since virtually every important military or political decision had to be approved by Stalin personally, Molotov was forced to act as his stand-in during this time. Finally, on 30 June, the Politburo members, led by Molotov, traveled to Stalin's "nearby" dacha to plead with their boss to return to the Kremlin.[75] Mikoyan recalled that Stalin appeared frightened that his underlings had come to arrest him, but Molotov assured his boss that he remained indispensable.[76]

Following the German attack, the chief Soviet diplomatic concern was how Britain and the United States would react. Would they extend assistance or leave the USSR to its fate? Moscow was reassured by Churchill's radio address on 22 June, in which the prime minister welcomed the USSR as an ally against Hitler. More worrisome, however, was the American reaction; the Soviet representative in Washington, Konstantin Umanskii, cabled Moscow warning that there was strong opposition in some circles to any assistance to the USSR.[77]

It was in part to appeal to American sensibilities that Maksim Litvinov made a reappearance. Litvinov had been under a cloud, and in some danger, since Molotov replaced him as foreign commissar in May 1939. Now that cooperation with the Western democracies was once again the order of the day, however, that well-known advocate of a Western orientation once again became useful. On 8 July, Litvinov made a radio appeal to the British and Americans to work with the USSR to defeat Hitler, and he came as close to any Soviet leader ever did, then or since, to admitting that the Nazi-Soviet Pact had been disastrous.[78] Perhaps for this reason, domestic Soviet radio stations were shut down without warning during Litvinov's broadcast, causing some ordinary Soviet citizens to believe that Moscow had been bombed or captured by German paratroops.[79]

Following his political resurrection, Litvinov would be sent to Washington as ambassador. He had apparently been chosen for the new assignment owing to his name recognition in the United States, the hope being that he could help to draw the United States into the war against Germany, or at least ensure that Lend Lease supplies would come flowing to Moscow. As he arrived in Washington on the morning of 7 December, however, part of his mission was achieved even before he officially assumed his post.

Throughout the autumn of 1941, the Soviets remained deeply concerned about American opinion, even holding a high-level meeting at the Foreign Commissariat to determine methods of influencing American public opinion favorably toward the USSR.[80] From this original conference sprang an elaborate network of organizations designed to mold Western—especially American—opinion in support of aid to the USSR. Even after the United States entered the war in December, the Soviets expended considerable effort designed to win over American opinion, thus ensuring a free flow of Lend Lease aid. Litvinov's role in all of this would be strictly limited, however; Molotov would keep his rival on a tight leash, ultimately even forbidding him to speak in public.[81] Even after being recalled to Moscow in 1943, Litvinov would remain critical of excessive centralization that gave no scope to ambassadors to respond to local circumstances.[82]

Molotov remained by his leader's side throughout the war, taking part in every significant diplomatic meeting or conference: he was present during Stalin's negotiations with the Polish government in exile in July; when Roosevelt's personal representative Harry Hopkins visited Moscow in August; when Lord Beaverbrook and Averell Harriman came to the USSR to discuss the delivery of Western military supplies to the Red Army; and when British Foreign Secretary Anthony Eden visited Moscow in December.

During such meetings Molotov generally sat silently beside Stalin, making few remarks other than to supply a missing detail. Occasionally he would play his accustomed role as hard-liner so that Stalin could masquerade as the moderate of the Kremlin. In May 1942, however, he got his first opportunity since the German invasion to travel abroad for negotiations. He flew first to London and then to Washington.

The reason for his journey was twofold: most importantly, he sought to gain a commitment from the Western Allies to open a second front in Western Europe. But he was also on a political mission for Stalin. As he told the British on 21 May, following his arrival in London, he sought recognition of the USSR's nonnegotiable politico-territorial demands, Moscow's "minimum conditions":

> When he spoke of "minimum conditions," he meant that his Government insisted on recovering the territory violated by Hitler, and they could make no concessions in this respect. Further, it was not sufficient simply to restore what existed before the war; the Soviet government must secure their north-western and south-western frontiers.[83]

In short, the Soviets demanded that their allies recognize Soviet territorial gains made during the period of Nazi-Soviet collaboration.

During meetings in Moscow the previous December, Stalin had seemed to promise British Foreign Secretary Anthony Eden that, should the British recognize the Soviet claim to the Baltic States, then the USSR would be more flexible over the reestablishment of the Soviet-Polish border. Restoration of the USSR's borders as they existed at the time of the German attack was, Stalin said, "what the whole war is about."[84]

Although as early as September 1940 the British had decided against recognizing wartime territorial alterations before a postwar peace conference, Eden returned to Britain as advocate of recognizing Stalin's demands. He reasoned that Britain would gain Soviet trust by such a move, thus creating a better climate for postwar Anglo-Soviet cooperation; furthermore, by thus enhancing Soviet power in the Baltic, the Soviet Union would act as a bulwark against any revival of German power after the war.[85] At first, Prime Minister Churchill disagreed with Eden, twice threatening to resign rather than recognize Soviet territorial gains made in collusion with the Nazis and against the will of the peoples involved.[86] Churchill would come around, however, when it became clear that the bulk of the war cabinet favored Eden's policy. The prime minister also believed that by thus accepting Soviet territorial claims, it would be easier to resist Moscow's demands for a second front in Europe during 1942.

One wrinkle in British plans was Roosevelt's opposition to a settlement of the Baltic question; the president even intervened personally, trying to convince Stalin to postpone the question until a postwar peace conference.[87] Owing to the considerations mentioned above, Churchill decided to proceed with recognition of Soviet Baltic demands despite American opposition; one consideration in his decision to do so may have been his realization that the Americans were more inclined than the British to agree to opening a second front that summer.

Thus, when Molotov flew to Britain on May 20, he arrived in the middle of an Anglo-American dispute over how to deal with Moscow. He also arrived at a time of crisis on the Soviet-German front. Earlier that month, Soviet forces had launched an offensive into the Ukraine designed to recapture Kharkov; by the time of Molotov's departure the offensive had begun to sour and would eventually result in the worst Soviet defeat since the first months after the German attack.

In this complex strategic-diplomatic situation, Molotov had to backtrack. After arriving in London, he demanded that the British recognize Soviet territorial claims, not only to the Baltic States but also to those areas of Poland seized by the Red Army in 1939. By the time of his departure from London on 26 May, however, he had agreed to sign an Anglo-Soviet agreement with no mention of frontiers, leaving territorial questions open for the time being. The reasons for this about-face remain uncertain, but the collapse of the Red Army's offensive may have added greater urgency to the need to secure a Western commitment to open a second front that summer. The Americans, who opposed signing a territorial settlement, were more inclined than the British to pledge an immediate second front. Molotov apparently sensed this, and so he shelved Soviet territorial demands for the time being—without renouncing them—and, after traveling to Washington, received a pledge from President Roosevelt that the Western Allies would open a European front that summer.

Molotov later claimed that neither he nor Stalin believed that the Allies would honor this promise, but he nonetheless regarded "as our greatest victory my trip in 1942 and its results." This was for two reasons: first, the Allied pledge would give a much-needed boost to Soviet civilian morale in the midst of the arduous second year of war; second, it would score propaganda points against London and Washington. "When in the name of the government [the Allies] pledged to open a second front, and then clearly did differently," Molotov later reflected, "people [would] see that it was impossible to trust such a leadership."[88] The resulting embarrassment might force the Allied governments to increase Lend Lease supplies in partial compensation.

This was typical of Molotov's dealings with his wartime Allies. They might be useful, but they remained suspect, potential enemies every bit as much as the Germans. In 1942, this was especially true of the British. Churchill thought Roosevelt's pledge of an immediate second front ill-advised, and in August he traveled to Moscow for his first meeting with Stalin, to explain why there would be no Allied landing in Europe that year.

As a result of Churchill's visit and his opposition to an early invasion of Europe, Moscow concentrated its propaganda fire on London. The Soviet press began to hint that London's heart was not in the war, that it was hoping to bleed Russia white while it stood aside. Soviet news reports began to question darkly why the British had not put Rudolf Hess on trial—were they still hoping to use him as a conduit for a separate peace with Germany? More ominously, as part of their campaign against the British, the Soviets began to scatter hints that a Nazi-Soviet separate peace treaty might be possible. In one extraordinary incident, an official at TASS suggested that, with the goal of increasing

> pressure on the British, [we should] create a transmitter, which would broadcast in the name of "a group of old German generals." The fundamental theme of the work of this transmitter—back to the policies of the "Iron Chancellor," peace with Russia and evidence of the record of the historic opponent of Germany—English imperialism.

This transmitter would broadcast materials lauding historical periods of Russian-German cooperation, citations from Nazi leaders during the period of the Nazi-Soviet Pact that would extol the benefits of partnership with Moscow, and stress how the English have historically benefited from Russo-German antagonism.[89]

Hints thus planted of a possible Soviet-German armistice may have spurred the Western Allies to make their declaration the next year committing themselves to "unconditional surrender." They may also have been moved by persistent rumors that Molotov had met with the Germans in early 1943—by some accounts in Sweden, by others behind German lines in the Ukraine. No solid evidence has ever emerged to substantiate these rumors, though they persist. Molotov later denied that he had angled for a separate peace in 1943—though the force of his disclaimer is undermined somewhat by the fact that he also denied the existence of a secret protocol to the Nazi-Soviet Pact.

Molotov's trip to Washington and London was his last major independent foray before his visit to San Francisco in 1945. He attended all the major wartime conferences—the foreign ministers' meeting in 1943, the Teheran Conference in November–December of the same year, Yalta in February 1945, and Potsdam that summer. His role in these conferences was invariably the same: when Stalin was present, he remained largely silent. When his leader was absent, he doggedly pursued Soviet goals, even if this meant angering his Western counterparts. He was never reluctant to exchange harsh words, a practice that would become almost routine following the defeat of Hitler.

Molotov's most famous verbal clash was with Harry Truman, following Roosevelt's death. Molotov had come to the United States for the establishment of the United Nations. After a particularly sharp exchange of words on 23 April with the new president about Soviet actions in Poland, Molotov exclaimed indignantly, though rather unconvincingly coming from one of Stalin's lieutenants, "I have never been talked to like that in my life." Truman, undaunted, snapped back, "Carry out your agreements and you won't get talked to like that."[90]

A great deal has been made about this exchange, showing as it supposedly does that the new president, unlike Roosevelt, was too impatient with the Soviets and brought unnecessary heat into relations with Moscow. Judging by his own account of the incident, however, Molotov was not especially disturbed. He thought Truman had "misfired," and he evaluated the new president as "a little dim-witted [tupovatyi]." Truman "was far from Roosevelt in intellect," Molotov would claim. "But they had one thing in common: Roosevelt was also a born imperialist."[91] Molotov was not specially disturbed by Truman's anger; he expected hostility—open or veiled—from imperialist leaders.

Truman had put his finger on a key issue: the Soviets were interpreting the Yalta accords flexibly, to say the least. This was Stalin's own policy. When Molotov had first read the drafts pledging free elections in Poland and other East European countries, he "went to Stalin with this document to say to him: 'this is a bit too much.' 'It's nothing,' Stalin replied, 'Go back to work. We can fulfill it in our own way later. It is a question of the correspondence of forces.'"[92] This is reminiscent of Stalin's remark to Milovan Djilas, Tito's envoy, that this was "not as in the past"; in this war the victorious armies would impose their social systems on the countries they occupied.[93]

As the war drew to a close, the Soviets quite clearly worked toward gaining unilateral security, not troubling themselves overly with Western reactions. They did this in Eastern Europe as well as with the atomic bomb. Molotov and Beria had been in charge of the Soviet bomb project since 1943, and recent revelations in Moscow make it clear that, so far as the fission bomb at least was concerned, Soviet espionage played the key role in enabling the USSR to construct a bomb as rapidly as it did. Soviet atomic scientist Iulii Khariton admitted that the first Soviet atomic weapon—though not the later fusion bomb—was a replica of the American weapon, made possible by espionage. In Khariton's estimation, successful espionage had shortened the Soviet atomic project by two years, and, one might add, saved countless rubles in the process.[94]

With the Soviet atomic bomb project already under way for two years, and with reports from agents flowing into Moscow about the progress on the Manhattan Project, it is small wonder that Stalin showed so little surprise when Truman mentioned during the Potsdam Conference that the Americans had exploded a powerful device. Molotov recalled:

> It seemed to me that he wanted to flabbergast us. But Stalin reacted very calmly. Truman decided that he had understood nothing. "The atom bomb" was not mentioned, but we soon guessed what was being spoken of. And we understood that [the Americans] were not in a position to unleash a war yet, since they had all of one or two bombs [to drop], which they dropped on Hiroshima and Nagasaki, and no more remained. But even if there had been more, they could not then play a special role.[95]

Even had the Americans been determined to practice "atomic diplomacy," the Soviets would not be bluffed. And within four years they would have atomic weapons of their own, though it would be some time after that before they could deliver them successfully.

Soviet foreign policy in the postwar years consisted of a peculiar mixture of arrogance and fear: arrogance springing from a conviction that they were on the crest of the future's wave; fear that their control over their empire was weak for all its apparent strength. The impressive Soviet victory over the Wehrmacht served to obscure the enormous price the Soviet people had paid in blood and treasure. Even within the USSR itself, not only was the extent of destruction beyond comprehension; in the western portions of the country, the reimposition of Soviet rule was more like another invasion than liberation. If the outside world stood in fear of Soviet expansion, this was largely because nobody outside of the USSR knew just how weakened by war the USSR was.

In this Molotov and other Soviet leaders were their own worst enemies. So anxious were they to mask any weakness that they successfully persuaded the world at large that their power was much greater than it was in fact. In reality, the Soviet grip on Eastern Europe was tenuous and had to rely almost entirely on force. This, apparently, was the reason the Soviets refused to receive Marshall Plan aid, or to allow their East European clients to do so. Molotov claims that, at first, the Soviet Ministry of Foreign Affairs wanted to "propose that all the socialist countries participate." But in the end, the Soviets decided that the fledgling rulers in Eastern Europe lacked sufficient "experience" to take American assistance without falling under imperialist hegemony.[96] This was in fact an admission of great weakness: the USSR could offer its allies very little in the way of positive incentives; it could only maintain control by force.

The weakness of the USSR's position in Eastern Europe was highlighted by Tito's break with Moscow, the success of which prompted Stalin to resort to his tried and true methods of control: he conducted purge trials of the East European communist leadership while eliminating any vestiges of precommunist civil society.

By 1949, when Stalin dismissed Molotov from his post as foreign minister,[97]

Soviet foreign policy stood bankrupt. Even where the Soviets looked strong, as in Eastern Europe, Moscow could only rely on fear to overawe the local population. The Soviets were capable of scaring the West, as they did during their blockade of Berlin; but they were unable to translate this fear into measurable gain. If, as has been suggested, the Soviet intention during the Berlin blockade was to forestall the establishment of an independent West Germany, then, for all the sound and fury, the blockade was a complete failure.

In the Far East, the situation was little better. The creation of a Communist China, although outwardly seeming to enhance Soviet power greatly, instead stored up problems for the future. When Stalin gave the green light for the North Koreans to invade the South,[98] the American reaction would come as an unwelcome surprise, and it would drive the first of many wedges between Moscow and Beijing. For all the fear that Soviet policy inspired in the West, the more that is revealed from Soviet archives, the clearer it becomes that Soviet power was more apparent than real and that Moscow's mischief-making was designed to—successfully did—mask this. It is a legitimate question whether by doing so the Soviets did themselves any great service.

IV

During his long career Molotov had been able to achieve what few other Bolsheviks had: he retained Stalin's confidence for more than three decades. But being the right-hand man of such a capricious tyrant remained a risky undertaking, even for one as slavishly loyal as Molotov. Toward the end of the 1940s, his long run of luck began to run out.

During Stalin's last five years of life the morbid suspicions that had occasionally gripped him began to increase, to become almost permanent. Whether Tito's successful challenge to Moscow's stewardship of the communist world, the recovery of Western Europe under the Marshall Plan contrasted with the sullenness of the East Bloc, the growing Cold War, suspicions of that traditional bugbear of Russian rulers, international Jewish influence, or merely the ravages of old age—whatever the source of his discontent, Stalin once again began to move against his high-ranking associates as he had done before 1937. And for once Molotov, who had for so long managed to be on the dispatching end of arrest warrants and death sentences, began to fear for his privileged position and indeed for his life.

His own personal and political crisis first emerged openly when he was replaced as foreign minister in March 1949 by Andrei Vyshinskii, the notorious prosecutor in the show trials of Nikolai Bukharin and other leading Bolsheviks during the late 1930s. Molotov remained in the Central Committee, but everyone in the upper reaches of the Soviet government was aware that he was under a cloud. In December of the same year, Stalin ordered Molotov's wife, Polina

Zhemchuzhina, arrested. When the Central Committee voted unanimously for this, Molotov could not bring himself to defend her; he abstained from voting.[99] When the general secretary of the Israeli Communist party, S. Mikunis, later asked Molotov why he had not defended his wife, he replied, "Because I am a member of the Politburo and I must obey Party discipline."[100] Only after Stalin's death would Molotov be reunited with his wife.

The reason for Zhemchuzhina's arrest remains a matter of speculation: perhaps Stalin harbored suspicions of her because she had been close to his own wife, who had committed suicide in 1932; perhaps her Jewishness ensured her arrest along with the other members of the wartime Jewish Antifascist Committee.[101] But then too many millions had disappeared into the maw of the Gulag to sustain the belief that there were always rational reasons for every arrest. Besides, the persecution of his minions' immediate family members was apparently one of Stalin's favorite tactics: Lazar Kaganovich warned his brother of his impending arrest, giving him time to commit suicide; the wife of Mikhail Kalinin, the figurehead president of the USSR, had been sent to the camps, only to be restored after her husband's death; the wife of Stalin's long-time secretary, Poskrebyshev, was also arrested, at which the dictator reportedly quipped, "We'll find you another wife."[102]

According to Khrushchev, Stalin began to suspect that Molotov had become an "agent of American imperialism." The germ of this extraordinary conviction was an incident during Molotov's visit to Washington in 1942. The foreign commissar had returned late to the USSR, making an unplanned side trip to New York. When passed through the mangle of the increasingly senile dictator's tortuous logic, this excursion suggested treason. "Stalin reasoned," Khrushchev recorded, "that if Molotov traveled by train then he must have had his own railway car. And if he had his own private railway car, then where did he get the money? Hence Molotov must have sold himself to the Americans."[103] Churchill may have helped to plant this particular seed of doubt in Stalin's mind, whether unintentionally or maliciously it is hard to say, during his visit to Moscow in August 1942. During an all-night conversation with Stalin and Molotov, the prime minister asked, "Was the Marshal aware that his Foreign Secretary on his recent visit to Washington had said he was determined to pay a visit to New York entirely by himself, and that the delay of his return was not due to any defect in the aeroplane, but because he was off on his own?" According to Churchill, Stalin laughed, but Molotov "looked rather serious at this."[104]

In his speech to the Nineteenth Party Congress on 16 October 1952, Stalin ruthlessly attacked both Molotov and Mikoyan. According to one eyewitness, the two disgraced men's faces "were white and lifeless" as the dictator outlined their supposed misdeeds. They later tepidly defended themselves against Stalin's attack, but they could scarcely have had any doubt that their fates were all but sealed.[105]

Following the Congress, Stalin no longer asked the two to his late-night dinners and films in the Kremlin or at his dacha, invitations that had long been the ultimate sign of membership in the "inner circle." Molotov and Mikoyan would find out from Khrushchev where the dictator was holding his sessions and turn up uninvited. This was no game; as Khrushchev later said, "they wanted to save themselves—and not just their positions in the Party and the leadership. They wanted to stay alive." Finally, Stalin tired of Molotov's and Mikoyan's persistence and ordered his guards to refuse them entry. Fortunately for the two Stalin died the following March, which almost certainly saved their own lives.

After Stalin's death, Molotov once again became minister of foreign affairs, a post he would occupy until 1956, when Khrushchev would dismiss him once and for all after the Twentieth Party Congress. Without the guiding hand of his old master, Molotov's second tenure as foreign minister was unremarkable; he was out of sympathy with Khrushchev and opposed any moves toward greater moderation in foreign or domestic policies. He fought against Khrushchev's attempts to normalize relations with Tito, and he urged a harder line in Poland. On important matters, such as the withdrawal of Soviet forces from Austria, Khrushchev simply circumvented the foreign minister.[106] Molotov's powerlessness soon became evident to foreign diplomats. The Yugoslav ambassador to Moscow, Veljko Micunovic, was "left with the impression that although Molotov is Minister of Foreign Affairs he does not hold in his hands the main threads of Soviet foreign policy, at least so far as Yugoslavia is concerned."[107]

Up until his death in 1986, Molotov would bemoan Khrushchev's supposed liberalism, blaming him for loosening the Soviet grip in Eastern Europe and denouncing his belief that war between the capitalist and socialist blocs was not inevitable. "That is a shortsighted Khrushchevite point of view," he would say in 1972. "It is very dangerous. We have to think about preparations for new wars."[108]

Molotov understandably opposed Khrushchev's decision to reveal in a very limited fashion at a secret meeting during the Twentieth Party Congress certain of Stalin's more egregious repressions of communists. He could scarcely do otherwise, since no revelation of even a fraction of Stalin's crimes could fail to mention his own role. It is a testimony to the willful self-deception of so many communists, both in the USSR and abroad, that Khrushchev's attack on Stalin, when it became public knowledge as it soon did, both shocked and surprised so many. Immediately some loyal communists began to speak about trials of Stalin's chief lieutenants.[109]

Molotov would never have to face trial, however; whether because he wanted to end Stalin's habit of killing his defeated rivals, or because he feared that trials might lead to uncomfortable questions about his own deep involvement in Stalin's repressions, Khrushchev did not have the so-called anti-Party group, the leading member of which was Molotov, arrested when he finally defeated them in 1957. Instead of a prison cell or a bullet, Molotov received a new posting, to be sure an exile of sorts: he became Soviet ambassador in Ulan Bator, Mongolia. Even in such a distant spot, he was shunned as a pariah by ambassadors from other communist countries and subject to petty humiliations and verbal attacks. The living conditions were also quite a comedown after his life with Stalin, and he complained to visitors of the harsh climate and the fact that wolves roamed the outskirts of the city. Nonetheless, Molotov retained his interest in foreign affairs, exulting to a visiting Yugoslav diplomat that the launch of Sputnik "might make the Americans and the West more realistic" about Soviet scientific might.[110]

The posting to Mongolia was not Molotov's final official appointment. For reasons that remain unclear, Khrushchev recalled Molotov from Ulan Bator in 1960 and appointed him Soviet representative at the International Agency on Atomic Energy in Vienna, where he remained until 1962, striking those who met him as a ghost of another historical age.

Following the Twenty-Second Party Conference in 1962, during which Khrushchev returned to his attacks on the Stalinist legacy in order to consolidate his own hold on power, Molotov was finally removed from all posts and sent into forced retirement. Perhaps most humiliating for a man with his beliefs, he was expelled from the party to which he had devoted his entire adult life. He would remain in this enforced, if materially comfortable, retirement, regularly appealing for reinstatement into the party and fulminating against any perceived liberalism or weakness on the part of Soviet rulers. Perhaps only Molotov could have faulted the Brezhnev leadership for insufficient reliance on force and excessive liberalism; but he would complain in 1976: "Now we stand before the West with our pants down. It has come to pass that the fundamental goal is not the struggle with imperialism, but the struggle for peace."[111] Molotov could genuinely claim that he had never been guilty of such heresy.

Even the most disgraced statesman, should he live long enough, might find himself restored to good graces. During the brief return to neo-Stalinism under the anachronistic and slightly ridiculous premiership of Konstantin Chernenko, Molotov had his party card returned and his period of expulsion removed from his record by decision of the Politburo on 12 July 1984. At the same session the Soviet leaders contemplated restoring Stalin's name to Volgograd, complaining that Khrushchev's denunciations of Stalin had done incalculable damage to the cause of communism. "Not a single one of our enemies has inflicted so much misfortune on us as Khrushchev did regarding his policies and his attitude toward Stalin," the head of Soviet armed forces, Marshal Dmitri Ustinov, complained. A recent addition to the Politburo, Mikhail Gorbachev, voted with the majority to restore Molotov, along with two other surviving lieutenants of Stalin, Malenkov and Kaganovich.[112]

Thus, Molotov died believing that his role in communist history had been vindicated, that the stain on his record engineered by Khrushchev had been removed. Dying in 1986, he did not live long enough to witness the headlong Soviet retreat from Eastern Europe, the secession from the USSR of the territories he and Stalin had added to the Soviet empire, and the ultimate collapse of the Soviet system itself. He died no doubt fully convinced that the network of socialist states that he had helped to create under Stalin, and which had given shape to the postwar world for more than four decades, would last indefinitely. That was merely the last of his political miscalculations; he would never understand the aspirations of common people, nor believe that they could shape history.

V

In his memoirs, Winston Churchill famously compared Molotov with the greatest foreign ministers of history. "In the conduct of foreign affairs," Churchill wrote, "Mazarin, Talleyrand, Metternich, would welcome him to their company, if there be another world to which Bolsheviks allow themselves to go."

Although one must give Molotov great credit as an indefatigable negotiator, the more we learn about the conduct and results of Stalin's diplomacy and Molotov's hand in its formulation and execution, the harder it becomes to agree with Churchill's generous observation. Churchill wrote the passage at a time when he still looked forward to being prime minister again, and he wanted to keep the lines open to Moscow for future negotiations. A little flattery in such circumstances was perhaps not out of line, but there is no need to give such evaluations too much weight.[113]

In the first place, it is hard to establish exactly to what extent Molotov had a hand in the formulation of policy, as opposed merely to executing the will of his boss. From the 1930s on Molotov was never known to diverge even slightly in public from Stalin's line. This did not necessarily mean that he never differed with his leader in private. On this question first-hand testimony is contradictory. Anastas Mikoyan, long a member of Stalin's inner circle, complained that Stalin-era propaganda portrayed Molotov as "very wise, just and good." In fact, Mikoyan claimed, Molotov was "a big half wit [*tugodum*], lacking the feelings of novel, courageous initiative, and a man for whom everything was vanity." "Those who were in Stalin's office frequently saw Molotov sitting next to him. But, as a rule, he sat and remained quiet. Possibly Stalin had Molotov there as a decoration in order to create the impression that he [Stalin] never decided important questions alone."[114]

Mikoyan's spiteful observations may have been motivated in part by personal rivalry. Nikita Khrushchev, whose political feuds with Molotov gave him no great cause to praise his older rival, would nonetheless admit: "While Stalin was still alive, I had a lot of respect for Molotov. In my eyes, Molotov was a man who sometimes might even question what Stalin said. More than once he raised his voice on my behalf, or on behalf of others who were suffering momentarily from Stalin's wrath."[115] In fact, Molotov only rarely defended anyone from Stalin's ire, the most notorious such incident being his failure to come to his wife's defense. Indeed, the only historian who has yet studied the archives for the period of Stalin's terror failed to find a single dissenting voice within the Central Committee on any death sentence.[116]

Even if one were to accept that Molotov was more than Stalin's yes-man, the Stalin-Molotov foreign policy fails to meet the criteria of great statesmanship on numerous counts. Most significantly, it lacked any overarching vision other than a grim determination to seize and control as much territory for the Soviet Union as possible—whether because of an obsessive need to secure Moscow's unilateral security, a desire to expand the bounds of communist control, or some combination of these drives, may never be known with final certainty. At times, Molotov's attachment to territorial gain could be quite inarticulate, an underlying feeling rather than any carefully considered policy. Khrushchev recounts how Molotov opposed withdrawal of Soviet forces from Austria in 1955. The latter could not think of any clear arguments in favor of retaining troops there; he simply opposed withdrawal with "an unbelieveable stubbornness, bordering on stupidity."[117] Fortunately, particularly so long as Stalin was alive, this acquisitive instinct was tempered with a caution very unlike Hitler's recklessness.

Molotov was proud of his achievements as foreign commissar; indeed, he seems to have taken far greater pride in his foreign policy successes than in any other area of his career. But his pride was in acquisition rather than in satisfaction at having created a better or more stable international situation. "I saw my task as minister of foreign affairs," he would comment in 1975, "as being how to expand [*rasshirit'*] as much as possible the boundaries of the Fatherland. And it seems to me that we and Stalin did not cope badly with this task."[118] To be sure, Molotov believed that the creation of a net of socialist states was a historically positive achievement. He "considered the main cause of his life to be the strengthening of the socialist order, the strengthening of the military, economic, and political role of our country and of all the socialist fraternity, [and] the weakening of imperialism."[119] But this assessment itself reveals the bankruptcy of his vision; by as early as 1948, it was clear that the Stalinist communist order in Eastern Europe, which Molotov regarded with such pride, could be maintained only through force, and with the backing of the Red Army. Only a man locked away in the Kremlin and profoundly out of touch with the people he ruled could believe that the nations of Eastern Europe were benefiting from the imposition of Stalin's communist order.

This crude standard of successful diplomacy as corresponding directly with territory acquired apparently confirms Litvinov's harsh condemnation of postwar Soviet foreign policy. In June 1946 he told American journalist Richard C.

Hottelet that the "root cause" of the nascent cold war was "the ideological conception prevailing here [in Moscow] that conflict between Communist and capitalist worlds is inevitable. . . . There has been a return to the outmoded concept of security in terms of territory—the more you've got the safer you are."[120]

The Soviets' obsessive concern with territory and total control mingled with a reflexive distrust of all statesmen not under Moscow's thumb. Molotov's routine assumption that all "capitalist" leaders were, sooner or later, bound to work against Soviet interests blinded him to the many opportunities the Grand Alliance presented to cooperate in the long term with Washington and London. In sharp contrast with Roosevelt's persistent, and Churchill's intermittent, efforts to assuage Soviet concerns, the diplomacy of Molotov and his leader could only on rare occasions be called genuinely cooperative. Molotov was, and would remain, consistently distrustful of any attempt by a Western leader to meet him halfway; he gave very little credit to Roosevelt's tireless approaches, for instance, dismissing the president as merely knowing better how to "dissimulate" than his successor, Truman.[121] Molotov would suggest that, far from wanting to work with Moscow after the war, Roosevelt hoped that the USSR would be so weakened by the struggle with Germany that Stalin would have to dance to Washington's tune. "They miscalculated on this," Molotov recalled, "but in this they were not Marxists, and we were. When they lost half of Europe they woke up."[122]

By no means did Molotov distrust only the Americans. In an especially revealing observation, he said: "[Ernest] Bevin—he was a Churchillite. An enemy. But Eden, Churchill's assistant, he was completely spineless, completely delicate and quite feeble. Eden, of course, I liked much better. It was possible to be on good terms with Eden. But with Bevin, that was impossible."[123]

Stalin and Molotov's deep suspicions of all non-Soviet governments inevitably permeated the lower ranks of the Soviet government as well; those who took talk of Allied friendship too literally were liable to be brought up short. In one instance, in March 1943 a Soviet press officer in the USSR's embassy in London, Rostovskii, relayed to Moscow an apparently harmless request from the BBC to station a permanent reporter in Moscow. Rostovskii reasoned that, since "millions of people listen" to the BBC, this would "give us the opportunity to spread information useful to our government among wide strata of populations abroad." Molotov rejected the request out of hand, minuting on the text: "Nobody from *Soviet* [underlined twice by hand] organs empowered com. Rostovskii to plead for the BBC."[124] It takes little imagination to guess the terror that must have struck Rostovskii's heart reading such a chilling remark, with memories of the recent purges of the NKID no doubt still all too fresh in all Soviet diplomats' minds.

If Soviet officials did not share their leaders' distrust of Western motives, then at any rate it clearly made sense to pretend otherwise. A letter from a

Soviet writer stationed in Murmansk, a copy of which was relayed to Molotov, shows how lower-ranking officials cast all actions by Allied personnel in the worst possible light. The writer, V. I. Beliaev, declared that four points concerning Allied officers stationed in Murmansk to administer Lend Lease were "beyond argument." First, they were "undoubtedly" preparing to use Murmansk as a jumping off point for a new anti-Soviet military intervention in the postwar period. Second, their spies were therefore studying "all facets of social life and in general all circumstances." Third, Allied officers were trying to act "irreproachable," all the better to mask their malign intent. Finally, the Allies were hostile to the NKVD, because they would not allow them to "create machinations against Soviet power" and treat the USSR as another Argentina— a haven for spies.[125]

Did Beliaev, and other mid-level officials like him, truly believe all of this, or did they merely tell their bosses what they thought they wanted to hear? No amount of new archival material is likely to answer such a question, since those who harbored doubts about the Kremlin's line were understandably unlikely to express these doubts in print.[126] It is no wonder, at any rate, that Molotov was so out of touch with the reality of the Soviet empire; it could scarcely be otherwise. The Stalinist terror had not only ensured rigid centralization and unquestioning obedience to the Kremlin on the part of Soviet officials; it also guaranteed that the Soviet leaders would receive reports that distorted reality to fit their own skewed worldview.

Viewed from the Kremlin, the postwar Stalinist diplomatic achievements— the creation of socialist states in Eastern Europe and Asia, the establishment of the USSR as a superpower on a par with the foremost capitalist nation, the United States, and the survival of the communist economic system in the face of a reviving and dynamic Western Europe—all these were great gains indeed by a country that in 1917 had nearly dissolved. Understandably, Molotov could choose to forget the dark side of his career and congratulate himself, a one-time tsarist political prisoner, on having played a formative role in the establishment of the communist international system.

It is tempting in the wake of communism's headlong retreat from Eastern Europe and the collapse of the USSR to dismiss these achievements as all hollow and unsustainable. Perhaps, however, Molotov for all his reactionary opinions, understood something fundamental that reforming communists like Khrushchev did not: the Soviet communist system could not liberalize; that path spelled doom. He may well have been out of touch with the aspirations of common people under "real existing socialism," but Molotov understood enough to realize that the Soviet system could only survive as an armed camp, shut off from the rest of the world. Gorbachev and his followers would disagree, and the Stalin-Molotov creation, which took four decades to build, would implode within five years.

Notes

1. Feliks Chuev, *Sto sorok besed s Molotovym: Iz dnevnika F. Chueva* (One hundred forty conversations with Molotov: From the diary of Feliks Chuev) (Moscow, 1991), 40. Since preparation of this chapter, Chuev's account has been edited and translated into English. See Albert Resis, ed., *Molotov Remembers: Inside Kremlin Politics; Conversations with Felix Chuev* (Chicago, 1993).

2. Roy Medvedev, *All Stalin's Men* (New York, 1984), 86.

3. Chuev, *Sto sorok besed s Molotovym*, 106.

4. Robert Conquest, *Harvest of Sorrow: Soviet Collectivization and the Terror-Famine* (Oxford, 1986), 114, 324.

5. Chuev, *Sto sorok besed s Molotovym*, 9.

6. Dmitrii Volkogonov, *Stalin: Triumph and Tragedy* (New York, 1991), 339.

7. Chuev, *Sto sorok besed s Molotovym*, 390.

8. Seeds to Halifax, 30 May 1939, in Sir Llewellyn Woodward and Rohan Butler, ed., *Documents on British Foreign Policy 1919–1939* (hereafter, *DBFP*), Third Series, vol. 5 (London, 1949–). 722.

9. Tippleskirch to Berlin, in Raymond J. Sontag and James Stuart Beddie, ed., *Nazi-Soviet Relations, 1939–1941* (Washington, D.C., 1948), 2. The Kremlin's dismissal of Litvinov and other Jews from the Soviet Foreign Commissariat was not missed in Berlin. Nazi diplomat Ernst von Weizsäcker, father of the current German president, observed in an internal memorandum dated 22 Aug. 1939 that the Nazi-Soviet rapprochement would not signify German abandonment of "the principles of the Anti-Comintern Pact." Under Stalin, however, Soviet policy had undergone "a decisive structural change," turning away from "world revolution" toward "an attachment to the idea of Russian nationalism." "Attention is drawn," Weizsäcker continued, "to the ejection of Jews from leading positions in the Soviet Union." "Circular of the State Secretary," *Documents on German Foreign Policy, 1918–1945* (hereafter cited as *DGFP*), Series D v. 7 (Washington, D.C., 1956), no. 180.

10. The best account of these as yet obscure approaches is in Evgenii Gnedin, *Iz istorii otnoshenii mezhdu SSSR i fashistkoi Germaniei: Dokumenty i sovremennye kommentarii* (From the history of relations between the USSR and Fascist Germany: Documents and contemporary commentary) (New York, 1977).

11. Chuev, *Sto sorok besed s Molotovym*, 106–7.

12. Seeds to Halifax, 4 May 1939, in *DBFP*, Third Series, vol. 5, 353.

13. *Pravda*, 2 May 1939.

14. Evgenii Gnedin, *Katastrofa i vtoroe rozhdenie* (Catastrophe and rebirth) (Amsterdam, 1977), 175.

15. Ibid., chap. 1, part 2.

16. Quoted in Arkady Shevchenko, *Breaking with Moscow* (New York, 1985), 147.

17. Chuev, *Sto sorok besed s Molotovym*, 97,

18. Ibid., 98.

19. For a discussion, now somewhat out of date, of the impact of the purges on the Foreign Commisssariat, see Teddy Uldricks, "The Impact of the Purges on the People's Commissariat of Foreign Affairs," *Slavic Review* 36, no. 2 (June 1977): 187–204.

20. Record of interview with Léon Helfand, 13 Sept. 1940, British Public Record Office, London, Foreign Office (hereafter, FO) 371 24845.

21. Stafford Cripps to Mallet, FO 371 29506.

22. Chuev, *Sto sorok besed s Molotovym,* 95, 98–99.

23. "Biographical Sketch of Mr. Andrei D. Gromyko, Counselor of the Soviet Embassy," 13 May 1941, United States National Archives, Washington, D.C., Record Group 59, 701.6111/1012.

24. Molotov's routine Sovnarkom correspondence occupies numerous volumes in the Tsentral'nyi Gosudarstvennyi Arkhiv Oktiabr'skoi Revoliutsii (Central archive of the October Revolution), fond 5446, op. 82.

25. Russkii tsentr dlia khraneniia i izucheniia nyneshnykh dokumentov (Russian center for the preservation and study of contemporary documents, hereafter RTsKhISD), Moscow, G. Aleksandrov to Molotov, fond 17, opis' 125, rolik 29.

26. This is from Vladimir Sokolov, who worked with Molotov, "Foreign Affairs Commissar Vyacheslav Molotov," *International Affairs* 6 (August 1991): 83–95.

27. W. G. Krivitskii, *In Stalin's Secret Service: An Expose of Russia's Secret Policies by the Former Chief of the Soviet Intelligence in Western Europe* (New York, 1939), 3.

28. J. V. Stalin, *Works* (Moscow, 1954), 7:288, 304.

29. Memorandum of conversation between Cripps and Stalin, 1 July 1940, British Public Record Office, London (hereafter, PRO), N6526/30/38.

30. Jane Degras, ed., *Soviet Documents on Foreign Policy 1933–1941* (Oxford, 1953), 3:367, 369.

31. Degras, *Soviet Documents,* 3:318, 322.

32. August Rei, *The Drama of the Baltic Peoples* (Stockholm, 1970), 249.

33. Sontag and Beddie, *Nazi-Soviet Relations,* 76.

34. Memorandum of interview of Léon Helfand by Sir Nevile Butler, PRO N6758/30/38.

35. Sontag and Beddie, *Nazi-Soviet Relations,* 74.

36. This was the figure given by the Soviets during the Khrushchev thaw, and it has been reaffirmed with the opening of the Soviet archives. Not all of the officers purged were shot, and many actually returned to active service following the German attack. The most famous such instance was the arrest and subsequent success of Marshal Rokossovskii. On the purges' impact on the Red Army, see Seweryn Bialer, *Stalin and His Generals: Soviet Military Memoirs of World War II* (New York, 1969), 57–88.

37. Valentin Berezhkov, Stalin's translator and Molotov's deputy during much of the war, confirmed that such reasoning underlay Soviet actions in spring–summer 1939. Author's interview with Berezhkov, 21 Sept. 1991.

38. Stalin, *Works,* 7:14.

39. Astakhov to NKID, 3 Aug. 1939, Ministerstvo inostrannykh del SSSR (hereafter, MID), *1938–1939,* vol. 2 of *God krizisa: Dokumenty i materialy* (Year of crisis: Documents and materials) (Moscow, 1990), 157–58.

40. Zapis' besedy narodnogo komissara inostrannykh del SSSR V. M. Molotova s poslom Germanii, F. Shulenburgom (Record of a conversation of the people's commissar of foreign affairs of the USSR V. M. Molotov with the ambassador of Germany, Schulenburg), 3 Aug. 1939, ibid., 159–63.

41. Molotov to Astakhov, 4 Aug. 1939, ibid., 175.

42. Molotov to Astakhov, 5 Aug. 1939, ibid., 177.

43. Astakhov to Molotov, 8 Aug. 1939, ibid., 178–80.

44. Molotov to Astakhov, 11 Aug. 1939, ibid., 184.

45. Astakhov to Molotov, 12 Aug. 1939, ibid., 185–86.

46. Astakhov to Molotov, 12 Aug. 1939, ibid., 186–88.

47. Zapis' narodnogo komissara inostrannykh del SSSR V. M. Molotova s poslom Germanii v SSSR.F. Shulenburgom (Record of a conversation of the people's commissar of foreign affairs of the USSR V. M. Molotov with the ambassador of Germany, F. Schulenburg), 15 Aug. 1939, 229–31.

48. Sontag and Beddie, *Nazi-Soviet Relations*, 102–3.

49. Lev Bezymensky, "What Did Stalin and Hitler Agree upon in 1939?" *New Times* 37 (1991).

50. Quoted in A. G. Dongarov and G. N. Peskova, "SSSR i strany pribaltiki (Avgust 1939–Avgust 1940)," *Voprosy istorii* (Problems of history) 1 (1991): 34.

51. Chuev, *Sto sorok besed s Molotovym*, 15.

52. Sontag and Beddie, *Nazi-Soviet Relations*, 240.

53. For a discussion of Soviet concerns regarding Allied intervention on behalf of Finland, see Steven M. Miner, *Between Churchill and Stalin: The USSR, Great Britain, and the Origins of the Grand Alliance* (Chapel Hill, N.C., 1988), 20–31.

54. Milovan Djilas, *Rise and Fall* (New York, 1985), 155. Molotov confirmed that the Soviets had been deterred by fear of American intervention. Chuev, *Sto sorok besed s Molotovym*, 93.

55. Cripps to Foreign Office, 1 July 1940, PRO N6526/30/38.

56. *DGFP*, series D vol. 11 (Washington, D.C., 1960), 291–97.

57. *DGFP*, series D vol. 11, 550–62.

58. Ibid., 562–70.

59. Valentin Berezhkov, *History in the Making: Memoirs of World War II Diplomacy* (Moscow, 1982), 39.

60. Author's interview with Berezhkov, 21 Sept. 1991.

61. Quoted in Barry Leach, *German Strategy Against Russia, 1939–1941* (Oxford, 1973), 77.

62. *DGFP*, series D vol. 11, 714–15.

63. Joseph Paul Goebbels, *The Goebbels Diaries, 1939–1941* (New York, 1983), 328.

64. Molotov's secretary in the Sovnarkom, Iakov Chadaev, quotes Stalin's secretary, Poskrebyshev, as saying that he "heard from Stalin's own mouth that it would be good to delay the start of the war by any means until the fall of 1941, when the roads would become impassible and the Germans might not decide to attack then until 1942." Chadaev, *Memoirs* (unpublished manuscript in Russian), vol. 2, part I, p. 909, personal archive of Georgii Kumanev.

65. N Pal'gunov to Upravlenie propagandy i agitatsii TsK(b), A. A. Puzin, 10 May 1941, RTsKhISD, Moscow, fond 17, opis' 125, rolik 1354.

66. For the enumeration of several such warnings, see Barton Whaley, *Codeword Barbarossa* (Cambridge, Mass., 1973).

67. Quoted in Arkady Vaksberg, *Stalin's Prosecutor: The Life of Andrei Vyshinsky* (New York, 1990), 220.

68. Iakov Ermolaevich Chadaev, *Memoirs*, 2:751 (unpublished manuscript in Russian), personal archive of Georgii Kumanev.

69. Quoted in Georgii Kumanev, "Vstrechi" (Meetings), *Sovershenno sekretno* (completely secret), no. 11 (1991).

70. Chadaev, *Memoirs,* 2:756.

71. John Erickson, *The Road to Stalingrad* (London, 1975), 125.

72. Gustav Hilger and Alfred G. Meyer, *Incompatible Allies: A Memoir History of German-Soviet Relations, 1918–1941* (New York, 1953).

73. Chadaev, *Memoirs,* 2:781.

74. Kumanev, "Vstrechi."

75. Volkogonov, *Triumph and Tragedy,* 410. Chadaev, *Memoirs,* 2:970–71.

76. Kumanev, "Vstrechi," Chadaev, *Memoirs,* 2:970–75.

77. "Iz telegramma posla SSSR v SShA v Narodnyi komissariat inostrannykh del SSSR," Ministerstvo inostrannykh del SSSR (From a telegram of the ambassador of the USSR in the USA to the people's commissariat of foreign affairs of the USSR), *Sovetsko-Amerikanskie otnosheniia, 1941–1945* (Soviet-American relations, 1941–1945) (Moscow, 1984), 1:42–44.

78. "Radio Address by Mr. M. M. Litvinov," 8 July 1941, United States National Archives, 740.0011 European War, 1939/13173.

79. 11 July 1941, B Dvinskii (Rostov) to Shcherbakov, RTsKhISD, Moscow, fond 17, opis' 125, rolik 1357.

80. 2 Oct. 1941, "Stenogramm soveshchaniia u tov Lozovskogo" (Stenographic record of a meeting at Com. Lozovskii's), RTsKhISD, fond 17, opis' 125, rolik 1352.

81. Sumner Welles memorandum, 7 May 1943, *Foreign Relations of the United States,* 1943, 3:522–24.

82. Litvinov to Lozovskii, 31 Jan. 1944, RTsKhISD, Moscow, fond 17, opis' 125, rolik 1393.

83. "First meeting with the Soviet Delegation at Number 10 Downing Street, 21 May, 1942," PRO N2902/5/38.

84. The complete British text of the Stalin-Eden talks is in PRO WP(42) 8. The much less complete Soviet text is in MID, *Sovetsko-Angliiskie otnosheniia vo vremia velikoi otechestvennoi voiny 1941–1945* (Soviet-English relations during the great patriotic war, 1941–1945) (Moscow, 1984), 1:184–98.

85. Eden memorandum to the War Cabinet, 28 Jan. 1942, W.P. (42) 48.

86. Churchill to Eden, 8 Jan. 1942, FO 371 32874.

87. See the text of Roosevelt's meeting with Litvinov on March 12. MID, *Sovetsko-Amerikanskie otnosheniia* (Soviet-American relations), Litvinov to Molotov, 12 Mar. 1942, 1:155–56. Also Halifax to Foreign Office, 13 Mar. 1942, PRO N1364/5/38.

88. Chuev, *Sto sorok besed s Molotovym,* 66–67.

89. Ia. Khavinson to Shcherbakov, 23 Sept. 1942, marked "Sovershenno sekretno" (Top secret), RTsKhISD, Moscow, fond 17, opis' 125, rolik 1366.

90. Harry S. Truman, *Year of Decisions,* vol. 1 of *Memoirs by Harry S. Truman* (Garden City, New York, 1955), 82.

91. Chuev, *Sto sorok besed s Molotovym,* 81.

92. Ibid., 76. It is interesting to contrast Stalin's apparent indifference to the meaning of the Yalta accords with various attempts by Western historians to explain Stalin's "reading" of the agreements. One recent history, for example, calls Stalin's "interpretation" of the Yalta accords, "a credible one." Melvyn P. Leffler, *A Preponderance of Power: National Security, the Truman Administration, and the Cold War* (Stanford, 1992), 33.

93. Milovan Djilas, *Conversations with Stalin* (New York, 1962), 114.

94. *New York Times,* 14 Jan. 1993. Molotov also attributes early Soviet success to "our chekists." Chuev, *Sto sorok besed s Molotovym,* 81.

95. Chuev, *Sto sorok besed s Molotovym,* 81.

96. Ibid., 88.

97. This term had replaced foreign commissar in 1946.

98. Professor Kathryn Weathersby, of Florida State University, has recently unearthed from the Soviet archives a text of Stalin's authorization of the attack. I learned this from personal conversations; it was later announced in the U.S. press.

99. Strobe Talbott, ed., *Khrushchev Remembers* (Boston, 1970), 260.

100. Quoted in Medvedev, *All Stalin's Men,* 99.

101. Louis Rapoport, *Stalin's War Against the Jews: The Doctor's Plot and the Soviet Solution* (New York, 1990), 110. Khrushchev also links Zhemchuzhina's arrest with the purging of the Jewish Antifascist Committee. Talbott, *Khrushchev Remembers,* 260.

102. Arkady Vaksberg, *Stalin's Prosecutor: The Life of Andrei Vyshinsky* (New York, 1990, 278.

103. Talbott, *Khrushchev Remembers,* 309.

104. Churchill, *The Hinge of Fate* (Boston, 1950), 497.

105. Konstantin Simonov quoted in Vaksberg, *Stalin's Prosecutor,* 305.

106. Strobe Talbot, ed., *Khrushchev Remembers: The Glasnost Tapes* (Boston, 1990), 75–78.

107. Veljko Micunovic, *Moscow Diary* (New York, 1980), 23.

108. Chuev, *Sto sorok besed s Molotovym,* 95.

109. See, for example, Vittorio Vidali, *Diary of the Twentieth Congress of the Communist Party of the Soviet Union* (Westport, Conn., 1974), 96.

110. Micunovic, *Moscow Diary,* 353.

111. Chuev, *Sto sorok besed s Molotovym,* 109.

112. David Remnick, "Report from Moscow: The Trial of the Old Regime," *New Yorker,* 30 Nov. 1992, 114.

113. As Churchill's subsequent correspondence with President Eisenhower would reveal, the prime minister hoped to draw on his wartime working relationship with Molotov to establish better relations with Moscow following Stalin's death. See Peter G. Boyle, ed., *The Churchill-Eisenhower Correspondence, 1953–55* (Chapel Hill, N.C., 1990), 31. At the same time, Churchill could be exasperated with Molotov's "insult, false charges, and outright vituperation" (p. 120).

114. Kumanev, "Vstrechi,"

115. Talbott, *Khrushchev Remembers: The Glasnost Tapes,* 77.

116. Dmitri Volkogonov, *Stalin: Triumph and Tragedy* (New York, 1991), 309.

117. Talbott, *Khrushchev Remembers: The Glasnost Tapes,* 77.

118. Chuev, *Sto sorok besed s Molotovym,* 14.

119. Ibid.

120. Richard C. Hottelet, five-part interview with Litvinov, published following the latter's death, *Washington Post,* 21–26 Jan. 1951.

121. Chuev, *Sto sorok besed s Molotovym,* p. 76.

122. Ibid., 67.

123. Ibid., 75.

124. RTsKhISD, Aleksandrov to Molotov, March 1943, fond 17, opis' 125, rolik 1358.

125. RTsKhISD, Moscow, A. Lozovskii to Molotov, 21 Mar. 1944, fond 17, opis'125, rolik 1391.

126. The bulk of Beliaev's letter recounts how the thuggish behavior of the NKVD in Murmansk was creating an unfavorable impression in the minds of Allied personnel. Allied sailors, upon learning that Soviet citizens who fraternized with them were often arrested, regarded this as "evidence of 'Bolshevik terror' and the influence of the dictatorship even in the private lives of the people." Perhaps Beliaev was trying to cloak his criticisms in politically acceptable form.

PART TWO

THE COLD WAR

4

ERNEST BEVIN AND BRITISH FOREIGN POLICY,

1945–1951

Geoffrey Warner

ERNEST BEVIN ALMOST FAILED to become foreign secretary in the British Labour government of 1945. When the Labour party won its landslide victory in the general election of July, he himself hoped to become chancellor of the exchequer, while the new prime minister, Clement Attlee, had virtually promised the foreign secretaryship to Hugh Dalton. At the last minute, however, Attlee changed his mind: Dalton went to the exchequer and Bevin to the Foreign Office. The reasons for the prime minister's change of heart are still much disputed, but it is clear that both King George VI and the outgoing foreign secretary, Anthony Eden, urged that Bevin should be appointed. In view of subsequent events, it is tempting to wonder whether their advice—which may or may not have swayed Attlee's final decision—was tendered because they believed that Bevin was likely to take a tougher line in policy, particularly with regard to the Soviet Union, but personal reservations about Dalton seem a more likely explanation.[1]

I

Born in 1881, the illegitimate son of a farm laborer's widow and an unknown father, Bevin was orphaned at the age of eight, left school at eleven, and worked in various blue-collar jobs before being appointed a full-time labor union official in 1911. He was almost excessively proud of these humble origins, which not surprisingly gave him a strong sense of empathy with the working class, or "my people" as he always liked to describe them. He gradually worked his way up through the union movement, helping to create what was to become by the end of the 1930s the largest labor union in the world, the Transport and General Workers Union, of which he was the general secretary until 1940, when his position as the most powerful leader of organized labor in the country led to his being invited to become minister of labor in Winston Churchill's wartime coalition government. He soon became a permanent member of the inner war cabinet and the prime minister's favorite among his Labour party colleagues, and his skill in mobilizing Britain's industry and human resources for the war effort played a vital part in the victory of 1945.[2]

On the face of it little of this would seem to have equipped Bevin for the task of running British foreign policy in the immediate postwar period, but he was in fact well informed on international affairs. He had traveled widely, visiting the United States, Europe, and Australasia between the two world wars, and he had taken part in a number of international negotiations within the International Labor Organisation. His union experience, moreover, had given him an awareness of the economic dimension of international relations, which was to bulk so large in the foreign policy of his impoverished country after 1945.

Bevin's personality was a strange mixture of Jekyll and Hyde. He was adored by his officials, not only because there was never any doubt that foreign policy was made in the Foreign Office while he was its head, but also because he was as solicitous of their welfare and conditions of employment as he had been of those of his union members. His word was universally regarded as his bond and his loyalty once given was unstinting. At the same time, as even his admirers have conceded, he was long-winded, vain, vindictive, profoundly suspicious, and prejudiced against—among others and in no particular order—Jews, Germans, Roman Catholics, and intellectuals of all kinds, groups that, when taken together, comprised a large proportion of those with whom he had to deal.[3] President Truman, who was definitely not an admirer, found him a "boor," a view shared on the other side of the Iron Curtain by the Russian diplomat, Andrei Gromyko.[4]

The new foreign secretary took office at a particularly unpropitious time. Before the Second World War Britain had been one of a number of more or less equal Great Powers in a multipolar world. After 1945, despite its victorious status as one of the "big three," it was a very poor third in a new bipolar world dominated by the United States and the Soviet Union. Although dwarfed by those of the Soviet Union, Britain's armed forces in 1938 were actually slightly larger than those of the United States: 381,000 to 323,000. By 1945 they were dwarfed by those of the United States as well. The figures were Britain 4.7 million, the United States 12.1 million, and the Soviet Union 11.6 million.[5] It was a similar story with respect to air power. In 1938 Britain was producing 236 aircraft a month compared to 625 in the Soviet Union and 150 in the United States. By the end of the war in 1945 the British figure had risen to 1,341 a month, but the Russian to 3,483 and the American to an astonishing 8,294.[6] While the Royal Navy continued to outrank that of the Soviet Union in 1945— reflecting Britain's position as a maritime as opposed to a continental power— it was only half as big as the United States Navy, instead of being roughly the same size as it had been in 1939.[7]

Things were equally depressing on the economic front. In 1938 Britain's per capita national income had still been 90 percent of that of the United States; ten years later it had fallen to 51 percent.[8] The country was also on the verge of bankruptcy. Over a quarter of its national wealth had been sold off to pay for the war, and as the economist Lord Keynes pointed out in a paper to the cabinet in August 1945, Britain was living beyond its means to the tune of £2 billion a year, a situation made possible only by American Lend Lease, Canadian Mutual Aid, and Sterling Area credits. Once the war was over, Keynes forecast a deficit of £1.7 billion on the balance of payments for the three years 1946–1948. Without remedial action, this would lead to "a financial Dunkirk," involving "a sudden and humiliating withdrawal from our onerous [foreign] responsibilities" and "an indefinite postponement of the realisation of the best hopes of the new Government [at home]."[9]

The foreign responsibilities to which Keynes referred were real enough. In 1945 Britain had significant numbers of troops in more than forty countries all over the world, to say nothing of the naval forces in the oceans in between. Even if the government wanted to reduce these wide-ranging commitments, it could not be done all at once. The result was that, proportionately, Britain had to bear a much heavier burden in the field of foreign and defense policy in the immediate aftermath of the Second World War than the much more powerful United States. In the fiscal year 1946, for example, 18.7 percent of men were in the armed forces in Britain compared to only 10 percent in the United States, and Britain spent 18.8 percent of its national income on defense, compared to the United States's 10.6 percent.[10]

It is a common criticism that Bevin and his advisers did not appreciate the decline that had taken place in Britain's international position. Nothing could be further from the truth. Foreign Office documents in the second half of 1945 are replete with references to Britain's reduced status,[11] and while it is true that Bevin told the House of Commons on 16 May 1947 that the government "do[es] not accept the view . . . that we have ceased to be a Great Power, or the contention that we have ceased to play that role," he had admitted in the privacy of the Foreign Office only ten days earlier that "for some time to come he had to bluff his way through in foreign policy, given the financial weakness of this country," and just over two months later was to appeal to the nation's miners to give him more coal to enable him to carry out an independent foreign policy.[12]

II

The situation that Bevin confronted might have been easier if the unity of the "big three" had survived the defeat of Germany and Japan, but it was already showing signs of breaking up as early as the fall of 1945. In a memorandum that he drafted on 8 November 1945, Bevin wrote that instead of the international cooperation under the aegis of the United Nations organization, which had originally been envisaged as the basis of the government's policy, "we are rapidly drifting into spheres of influence or what can be better described as three great Monroes." Long predominant in the Western Hemisphere, the United States was now attempting to extend its sphere of influence to include China and Japan, while the Soviet Union seemed to have settled upon one extending from Lübeck and the Adriatic in the west to Port Arthur in the east. Britain stood between the two, and Bevin warned that "if this sphere of influence business does develop it will leave us and France on the outer circle of Europe with our friends, such as Italy, Greece, Turkey, the Middle East, our Dominions and India, and our colonial empire in Africa: a tremendous area to defend and a responsibility that . . . would make our position extremely difficult."[13]

This revealing document displayed almost as much concern about the United States as the Soviet Union. Apart from Palestine—where Bevin felt that in order to cultivate the influential Jewish vote the Truman administration sought to play the traditional role of the harlot in exercising power without responsibility[14]—there were a number of issues upon which he was highly critical of American policy during his early years as foreign secretary. Although he supported the American loan of December 1945 on the grounds that it was the only feasible short-term solution to the financial problems which Lord Keynes had outlined in August, he did not like the way in which the United States administration attempted to link the ratification of the loan agreement with the acceptance of American plans for the acquisition of air-naval bases on British and Commonwealth territory.[15] He resented the United States's determination to run the occupation of Japan with minimal attention to the wishes of its allies,[16] and when he supported the decision to go ahead with the manufacture of British nuclear weapons, it was not the Soviet threat that he cited as justification, but the fact that Britain "could not afford to acquiesce in an American monopoly of this new development."[17]

Nevertheless Bevin was undoubtedly even more suspicious of the Soviet Union and believed that the principal threat to Britain's interests came from that direction. In common with many of his prejudices, Bevin's suspicion of the Soviet Union was deeply rooted in his experience as a labor organizer and intensely personal. Referring to his union's opposition to the loading of supplies destined for Poland in its war against the Soviet Union in 1920, he reminded left-wing critics of his policy in June 1946 that no one in his audience had done more to defend the Russian Revolution than he had. Yet all the thanks he got for it "was an attempt by the Communists to break up the Union that I built." "You have built the Soviet Union and you have a right to defend it," he recalled telling the Soviet ambassador on one occasion. "I have built the Transport Union and if you seek to break it I will fight you."[18]

After 1945, however, it was the Soviet Union's behavior in international affairs rather than memories of labor union battles in the 1920s and 1930s that fed Bevin's mistrust. In the first place, he was worried by the Russian sphere of influence in Eastern Europe. It was not so much its existence, which he understood and accepted, but its nature that he found so disturbing. As he told the House of Commons on 7 November 1945, "If security against attack and intrigue and the stirring up of difficulties is given, I cannot accept that the natural thing that follows from that is to close the door and prevent entry or any contact with those peoples for trade or anything else. I say that these are two separate and distinct things." Secondly, Bevin feared the extension of this sphere of influence, especially as it seemed to him that this was most likely to take place to the detriment of Britain's own position in the Mediterranean and the Middle East. He was particularly alarmed by the Soviet Union's demand for a United Nations trusteeship over Tripolitania in the former Italian colony of Libya. "One cannot help being a little suspicious," he told the House of Commons on the same occasion, "if a great Power wants to come right across . . . the throat of the British Commonwealth."[19] Privately, he expressed even greater concern, suggesting that the Russians' real objective was to gain entry to Africa, possibly with a view to obtaining access to the uranium of the Belgian Congo.[20]

Despite this suspicion of and hostility toward the Soviet Union, it would be unfair to characterize Bevin, as some recent scholarship has done, as one of the principal architects of the Cold War. He was certainly more reluctant to abandon hope of an agreement with Russians than either the United States or his own officials. Thus, when Bevin told the Paris meeting of the Council of Foreign Ministers on 10 July 1946 that unless Germany were treated as an economic unit, the British government would be forced to go its own way in its own zone of occupation, he was not, as some have alleged, engaging in a conscious ploy to bring about the division of the country. This is shown by his cautious reaction to the proposal that the U.S. secretary of state, James Byrnes, made on the following day. Although Byrnes announced his government's willingness to "join with any other occupying government or governments in Germany for the treatment of our respective zones as an economic unit," Bevin told his cabinet colleagues that the American was thinking in terms of a zonal merger that would exclude the Russians and that he (Bevin) had persuaded him "that it would be a mistake at this stage to commit ourselves irrevocably to a measure which implied a clear division between Western and Eastern Germany." Bevin only came round to accepting the American proposal, in fact, after he was assured by his officials that it was the only practical solution to the problem of the financial drain caused by the deficit in the British zone—which was the reason for his original ultimatum—and that it did not foreclose the possibility of the eventual unity of Germany.[21]

At the end of the same year Bevin gave an optimistic report on the outcome of the New York meeting of the Council of Foreign Ministers, which reached agreement on peace treaties with Italy, Romania, Bulgaria, Hungary, and Finland, to a skeptical Christopher Mayhew, one of his junior ministers. He cited the remark of the Soviet foreign minister, Viacheslav Molotov, on the boat back to Europe—"I think we are learning now to co-operate"—and attributed much of the toughness and bitterness of Russian diplomatic methods to the inexperience of their officials.[22]

In April 1947, while the new American secretary of state, General George C. Marshall, returned from the Moscow meeting of the Council of Foreign Ministers full of gloom and foreboding, Bevin agreed with Molotov that the conference had not failed, but had narrowed the differences between the participating governments and thereby improved the prospects for discussions at the next meeting. That this was not simply diplomatic politeness is shown by his private comment that "Mr. Molotov was beginning to come to a better understanding of the attitude of His Majesty's Government and . . . to show some sympathy for it."[23]

Marshall's response to the Moscow conference was his famous Harvard speech of 5 June 1947 in which he floated the idea of an economic recovery program for Europe, to be drawn up by the European countries themselves with the assistance of the United States. Bevin's reaction to this somewhat nebulous proposal is well known: the immediate summoning of a conference in Paris between Britain, France, and the Soviet Union at which the idea would be discussed. According to his private secretary, Pierson Dixon, "It was obvious to us from the beginning that the Russians could not come into any honest plan for European recovery," but this does not seem to have been Bevin's own reaction. When news of the Russian acceptance of the invitation reached him, he kept on repeating, "Perhaps they *will* play after all," and it is clear from Dixon's own account that even after Molotov attacked Marshall's proposal and announced his intention of returning to Moscow, Bevin was reluctant to accept that there was no possibility of agreement and that Britain and France would have to go ahead on their own.[24] It was not until the London meeting of the Council of Foreign Ministers in November–December 1947 that he finally gave up on the Russians.

What Bevin saw as the principal task of his foreign policy was to create a separate nexus of power that would preserve British interests and influence in a world increasingly dominated by the two superpowers. "He had a plan," he told the editor of *The Times* on 11 March 1946. ". . . Give him three years and he would build a new Commonwealth without regard for Russia or America." He would build it up, he said, as he had done his own Transport and General Workers Union.[25] "The British Empire," he assured newspaper correspondents on the following day, "isn't going to be either the 49th [American] State or the 17th [Soviet] Republic."[26]

Ideas concerning the elements that might constitute this separate nexus of power had been put forward by Bevin before he became a minister in the wartime coalition government. As early as September 1927, at the Trades Union Congress, he had advocated an economic union of Europe, a concept that he subsequently extended to include Europe's colonial empires. He was strongly in favor of closer cooperation between the member nations of the British Commonwealth.[27] During the war itself he demonstrated his concern to preserve Britain's "informal empire" in the Mediterranean and the Middle East, defending the wartime coalition government's policy in Greece before a Labour party conference on 13 December 1944 on the grounds that "the British Empire cannot abandon its position in the Mediterranean. On the settlement of these countries much of the peace of the future world depends."[28]

All these ideas reemerged after Bevin became foreign secretary in July 1945. His private secretary recorded in August 1945 that he "considers it important to carry the Dominions with us generally in our foreign policy," and he warned a few days later that "if the Dominions were to enjoy the advantages of belonging to the Commonwealth, they must fall in line with the general policy of the United Kingdom."[29] Unfortunately the Commonwealth proved unwilling to play the role envisaged for it by Bevin. Canada was adamantly opposed to any suggestion of greater centralization in matters of defense and foreign policy. Australia was an equally difficult partner, thanks to its unreliable foreign minister, Dr. Herbert Evatt, and its poor security. Moreover, like New Zealand and Canada, it was as keen to reinsure with the United States as with Britain. India, which became independent in 1947, was also a doubtful quantity from the point of view of security, and was in any case far from eager to follow London's lead after two hundred years of British rule. Paradoxically, the Commonwealth country that was to become Britain's closest partner during Bevin's term as foreign secretary was the Union of South Africa, which was hardly an exemplar of his brand of progressive social democracy, especially after the Nationalist victory in the elections of 1948.[30] Despite these difficulties, however, Bevin never gave up his hope of organizing the Commonwealth as an instrument of British power.

With regard to the Mediterranean and the Middle East, Bevin was determined that Britain must remain the predominant power in the area. Indeed, unknown to Parliament, press, and public, a fierce battle raged within the Labour government over the issue, a battle that was not settled until January 1947 and in which Bevin for once found himself pitted against Attlee. The prime minister believed that the advent of nuclear weapons and developments in air power rendered the old British imperial strategy in the Mediterranean and the Middle East obsolete. Moreover, the country could not afford it; the local regimes were unreliable and unstable; and British bases in the area could well be regarded by the Soviet Union as provocative. Bevin won the battle, although financial considerations were to compel a drastic reduction of British commitments in Greece and Turkey in the spring of 1947 and political turmoil a complete withdrawal from Palestine in May 1948, and it is doubtful whether he would have prevailed at all had the chiefs of staff not threatened to resign *en bloc* if Attlee had his way.[31]

Although Bevin shared the economic and strategic concerns of the chiefs of staff, his agenda was much broader. "We are the last bastion of social democracy," he wrote on 13 March 1946 in one of his memoranda justifying the British presence in the Mediterranean and the Middle East. "It may be said that this now represents our way of life as against the red tooth and claw of American capitalism and the Communist dictatorship of Soviet Russia." Any weakening of Britain's position in the Mediterranean, he argued, would "lead to the end of social democracy there and submit us to a pressure which would make our position untenable."[32] Bevin was also determined to steer British policy in the Middle East in a more progressive direction. "The benefits of the partnership between Great Britain and the countries of the Middle East," he told Lord Halifax, the British ambassador in Washington, on 12 October 1945, "have never reached the ordinary people and so our foreign policy has rested on too narrow a footing, mainly on the personality of kings, princes and pashas."[33] His intention, as he had informed the cabinet a few weeks earlier, was to "broaden the base upon which British influence rests and to this end . . . develop an economic and social policy that would make for the prosperity and contentment of the area as a whole." He was wary of both Russian and American ambitions in the Middle East. His policy of economic and social advancement, he maintained, would be "the most effective counter to Russian advances in the area . . ." and Britain "should not make any concession that would assist American commercial penetration into a region which for generations has been an established British market."[34]

Arab nationalism was to frustrate Bevin's efforts to strengthen the British position in the Middle East. His attempts to renegotiate the Anglo-Egyptian treaty of 1936 and the Anglo-Iraqi treaty of 1930, both regarded by nationalists as relics of imperialist domination, failed completely. Negotiations with the Egyptians broke down in December 1946 over the future of the Sudan, and the two countries were further than ever from a mutually acceptable agreement when Bevin left the Foreign Office in March 1951. A replacement treaty with Iraq was signed on 15 January 1948 aboard Lord Nelson's flagship, HMS *Victory,* in Portsmouth harbor, but it was almost immediately repudiated by the Iraqi regent after demonstrations and riots in Baghdad. The proclamation of the state of Israel in May 1948 did not help Britain's cause in the Arab world. Although the British government was powerless to prevent what happened, as the mandatory power it received much if not most of the blame from Arab nationalists. Even Bevin's schemes for economic and social improvement in the Middle East were crippled by lack of money and the reluctance of local governments to implement them. Unlike both his predecessors and successors, moreover, Bevin was unwilling to take action to overthrow these governments, however hostile they were toward British policy.[35]

The European dimension of Bevin's attempt to forge a British-led coalition between the superpowers was revealed as early as 13 August 1945, when he told his officials that "his long-term policy was to establish close relations between [Britain] and the countries on the Mediterranean and Atlantic fringes of Europe," adding a few days later that he hoped "to make the Ruhr industries a central pivot in the economy of an eventual 'Western Union.' "[36] The first concrete step came in the shape of the Anglo-French treaty of alliance, concluded at Dunkirk on 4 March 1947. Meanwhile, in January of the same year, Bevin had submitted a memorandum on European economic cooperation to the cabinet, which asked for a study to be made of the implications of "a full customs union." Both Dalton and the president of the board of trade, Sir Stafford Cripps, were unenthusiastic about the proposal, reflecting the deeply entrenched opposition of the economic departments to any notion of a European customs union. In the end the cabinet endorsed a suggestion for a broader study by a group of economists from outside the government.[37] This group, consisting mainly of Cambridge University faculty members, did not meet until the end of March, and by the time they were ready to report, their labors had been overtaken by General Marshall's initiative.

Although this was enthusiastically welcomed by Bevin, he was not prepared to fall in completely with American plans. In particular, he strongly objected to Britain's being treated as "just another European country."[38] He also pressed ahead with his own ideas. On 5 September 1947 he wrote to Attlee urging the study of a whole series of customs unions—empire, Commonwealth, combined empire and Commonwealth, and European—by "a high-level group." As he explained in a further minute to the prime minister on the sixteenth, he was convinced that "we must free ourselves of financial dependence on the United States of America as soon as possible. We shall never be able to pull our full weight in foreign affairs until we do," especially as he did not feel that Britain could rely upon American financial assistance. This objective, he feared, could not be attained merely by selling manufactured goods to a world that was becoming more and more industrialized. Raw materials were needed too. "Hence the importance not only of closer trade relations with the Commonwealth and Empire but also of an intensified effort for development within them." Later he warned one of his junior ministers to "go very slow on linking Colonial developments with the Marshall proposals. We must keep our hands free and not whet American appetites in the Colonial Empire."[39]

The question of colonial development and its relationship to the United States came up in conversations with the French prime minister, Paul Ramadier, in Paris at the end of September 1947. "With their populations of 47 million and 40 million respectively and with their vast colonial possessions," Bevin told the Frenchman, "they could, if they acted together, be as powerful as either the Soviet Union or the United States. It was only owing to their divisions that the Western democracies did not occupy the position that they might in the world today. In addition to their populations they possessed supplies of raw materials greater than those of any other country." He made the same point to the French foreign minister, Georges Bidault, in London on 29 November

1947. He "drew attention to the great resources of Western Europe, both in Europe and in their African Colonies. If properly developed these amounted to more than either the Soviet Union or the United States could muster, and should enable Western European Powers to be independent of either."[40]

In the meantime, however, the proposal for a European customs union had encountered the withering skepticism of the economic departments. Duff Cooper, the British ambassador in Paris and a political holdover from Eden's days at the Foreign Office, summed it up well when he wrote in October 1947 in the context of closer economic cooperation with France that both the treasury and the board of trade were opposed in principle. This was because they felt that while both countries were poor, Britain was still better off than France and would therefore make a bigger contribution if their resources were combined; and because they were "convinced that nothing in the world matters except dollars, and that therefore no country counts except the United States."[41] In the face of this opposition, Bevin was reluctantly forced to abandon his plans for a European customs union and to settle for the looser framework of the Organisation for European Economic Cooperation (OEEC).

By the end of 1947, Bevin was also finally abandoning any hope of agreement with the Soviet Union. When the London meeting of the Council of Foreign Ministers finally broke down, Bevin reacted with the speed of someone who had given a great deal of thought to the consequences. He told the Canadian high commissioner on 17 December 1947 that the United States had no plan to deal with the situation. "This meant that we in the United Kingdom must clear our minds and produce a plan for them." He did so on the same day for the benefit of General Marshall. Using an expression of the U.S. ambassador in London, Lewis W. Douglas, Bevin said, "The issue . . . was where power was going to rest." What was required was "some western democratic system comprising the Americans, ourselves, France, Italy etc. and of course the Dominions. This would not be a formal alliance, but an understanding backed by power, money and resolute action. It would be a sort of spiritual federation of the west." Although he was aware that the United States and France had written constitutions, he hoped that "the British conception of unwritten and informal understandings" would suffice for this purpose. He believed that if it were achieved "it would then be clear to the Soviet Union that having gone so far they could not advance any further."[42]

Early in 1948 Bevin presented no less than four separate memoranda for the consideration of his cabinet colleagues. A lengthy review of Soviet foreign policy concluded that while it was unlikely that the Russians were planning to start a war with either Britain or the United States, "the success of [their] expansionist plans would threaten, if not destroy, the three main elements of Commonwealth defence, the security of the United Kingdom, the control of sea communications, and the defence of the Middle East."[43] The remaining three papers set out his detailed proposals for meeting the Soviet threat. One, which dealt with Germany, argued in effect for the establishment of a west German state on democratic lines, which would not only prevent a Soviet takeover of the whole country but also act as a powerful magnet for the Germans in the Russian zone.[44] Another, which had been drafted by Christopher Mayhew, called for an all-out propaganda offensive against communism, the basis for which should be Britain's social democratic ideology. It was, the memorandum argued, for the British and not the Americans "to give the lead in the spiritual, moral and political sphere to all the democratic elements in Western Europe which are anti-Communist and, at the same time, genuinely progressive and reformist, believing in freedom, planning and social justice—what one might call 'The Third Force.' "[45]

This theme was taken up in the remaining memorandum, entitled "The First Aim of British Foreign Policy." Calling for the organization and consolidation of "the ethical and spiritual forces inherent in this Western civilisation of which we are the chief protagonists," it advocated the creation of "some form of union in Western Europe . . . backed by the Americas and the Dominions." But while "material aid will have to come principally from the United States, . . . the countries of Western Europe which despise the spiritual values of America will look to us for assistance in building up a counter attraction to the baleful tenets of communism within their borders." In publicizing his plans, Bevin emphasised, it was not his intention "to abandon the political principle for which we stand out of deference to American views."[46] On 8 January 1948 all four memorandums were endorsed by the cabinet.[47]

The new policy, taking up his 1945 idea of a "Western Union," was publicly launched by Bevin in his famous speech to the House of Commons on 22 January 1948, although there was naturally no mention of such covert measures as the proposed propaganda offensive or of the critical comments about the United States. The latter were also deleted from the copy of "The First Aim of British Foreign Policy" that was given to the Americans.[48]

Because the negotiations set in train by Bevin's speech led eventually to the conclusion of the North Atlantic Treaty in April 1949, it is tempting to conclude that "Western Union" was nothing more than bait to entice the United States into a commitment to defend Western Europe—"a sprat to catch the mackerel," as he himself was once supposed to have said.[49] It was certainly true that Bevin did want an American military guarantee. What worried him, and other British ministers, was a repeat performance of World Wars I and II, when the United States had not come into the conflicts until three and two years, respectively, after they had started. If a war broke out now, Bevin told the chiefs of staff on 4 February 1948, "America must be prepared to come in at once. He intended to make it clear to the Americans that we could not act as a mercenary army or defensive outpost for them." But "Western Union" was intended to involve much more than a transatlantic military alliance.[50]

As well as such fleeting notions as the harmonization of social welfare systems,[51] Bevin continued to attach considerable importance to plans for colonial cooperation between the European powers. He had referred at length to this in his speech to the House of Commons on 22 January 1948. "The organisation of Western Europe," he said, "must be economically supported. That involves the closest possible collaboration with the Commonwealth and with overseas territories, not only British but French, Dutch, Belgian and Portuguese . . . If Western Europe is to achieve its balance of payments and to get a world equilibrium, it is essential that these [colonial] resources should be developed and made available, and the exchange between them carried out in a correct and proper manner."[52]

When it came to the point, however, the Brussels Treaty of March 1948, which was the immediate outcome of Bevin's speech, did not cover colonial cooperation. The Benelux countries, which signed the treaty along with Britain and France, did not think it was a suitable framework for colonial cooperation because the Netherlands was not as deeply involved as Belgium and France, while Portugal, which was, was not a signatory. The British Colonial Office, too, was critical of Bevin's ideas. It did not believe that there was much scope for an increased colonial contribution to the economic problems of the metropole and regarded the notion of institutional cooperation between the colonial powers to that end as redolent of the old-fashioned imperialism from which it was trying to escape. If there had to be organization for colonial cooperation, the Colonial Office wanted it to be answerable to noncolonial powers as well, and when the OEEC was established it got its way. As John Kent has written, "This meant colonial economic co-operation was linked, not to the idea of Western Union and the Brussels Treaty Organisation, but to a body working with the American Economic Co-operation Administration in an Atlantic partnership. Bevin's ideas of the economic independence through the use of African resources were consequently dealt an administrative blow."[53]

III

Perhaps the most crucial development that helped to undermine Bevin's conception of "Western Union" was the wresting of the political initiative from his grasp by the federalist forces gathered at the Hague Congress in May 1948. A precondition of all his plans was that they should be implemented pragmatically, through a careful process of intergovernmental negotiation, and he had no patience with the protagonists of European federalism, whose grandiose schemes involving written constitutions and parliamentary assemblies he regarded at best as an irrelevance and at worst as a positive hindrance to the realization of European unity. "It is easy enough," he had remarked scathingly to the House of Commons in his speech of 22 January 1948, "to draw up a blueprint for a united Western Europe and to construct neat looking plans on paper. While I do not wish to discourage the work done by voluntary political organisations in advocating ambitious schemes of European unity, I must say that it is a much slower and harder job to carry out a practical programme which takes into account the realities which face us, and I am afraid that it will have to be done a step at a time."[54]

When M. Bidault took up the Hague Congress's call for a European parliament at a meeting of the consultative council of the Brussels Treaty powers in July 1948, Bevin was therefore not at all pleased. "Never 'eard such bloody rubbish!" he was overheard to mutter by the French ambassador in London.[55] Bidault's successor, Robert Schuman, did not even wait for the Brussels Treaty powers to complete their examination of the proposal before embracing another suggestion emanating from the organizers of the Hague Congress, which called for a preparatory five-power conference of members of parliaments to prepare for the convening of a European assembly. The British ambassador in Paris was informed on 28 August 1948 that Bevin felt "that on this issue the French Government are playing politics, that they have not really given any serious study to the matter and that he declines to be bustled into folly, simply to suit the temporary convenience of the French Government."[56]

In an effort to outflank the federalists, Bevin came up with a new suggestion: a "Council of Western Europe," consisting of annual meetings of the key ministers of the Brussels Treaty powers, who would be able to take the initiative and recommend policies for acceptance by the member countries. Such a council, he thought, "should be in the nature of a cabinet for Western Europe." He agreed that this additional machinery, together with that already set up, "would . . . constitute something in the nature of a Confederation," although he did not think that the term should be employed at this stage.[57]

A slightly modified version of this proposal was endorsed by the cabinet on 4 November 1948 and was referred, along with the original French suggestion of a European parliamentary assembly, to a meeting of governmental representatives of the Brussels Treaty powers. It is clear from what Bevin told Dalton, who headed the British delegation to this meeting, on 17 November 1948 that the foreign secretary envisaged the widest powers for his latest brainchild. It should deal, he said, with "economic affairs, rationalised defence, etc." Even the OEEC might be subordinated to it after the European Recovery Program ended in 1952. He reverted to his hope that "the Commonwealth and Western Europe might grow together . . . [and] make a really great Third Power in the world." But everything was contingent upon the new organization being a body of intergovernmental cooperation. "B[evin] was against a meeting of parliamentarians at this stage," Dalton recorded. "General debates, followed by no action, and fruitless controversies about federal constitutions, would make the peoples lose heart. . . . Decisions must be kept in the hands of governments and their representatives."[58]

The eventual outcome of the negotiations was a messy compromise between the British and French conceptions: a Council of Europe, which consisted of a committee of ministers and a parliamentary assembly, albeit one composed of delegates as opposed to directly elected members. Predictably, it satisfied no one and the early history of the council was bedeviled by a running conflict between the assembly, which sought to expand its competence, and the ministerial committee, with Britain in the van, which fought a rearguard action to preserve its prerogatives. Bevin thought he knew who was to blame, and he was very bitter about it. "We were hoping," he told the House of Commons on 13 November 1950, "that comradeship between the two [i.e., the committee and the assembly] would have grown up. . . . The European Movement killed it. . . . Two or three gentlemen in Europe, who were so anxious to pillory the Ministers because they did not belong to their parties at that moment, wrecked that great opportunity. I say that advisedly. A grave responsibility rests on those who did it."[59]

Whatever the reasons—Commonwealth indifference, bureaucratic resistance, or federalist rhetoric—it is clear that, by the beginning of 1949, Bevin was beginning to move away from his original conception of a "third force" in world affairs. An indication of his changing mood is contained in a memorandum of 25 January 1949, which he and Cripps jointly presented to the cabinet's economic policy committee. In contrast to his earlier view concerning the need for the closer economic integration of Western Europe, the memorandum drew attention to the dangers inherent in too much British involvement in it. As Cripps put it when the memorandum was discussed, "We must face the fact that if we tied our economy closely to these nations and they (or any of the more important of them) collapsed, it would be hard for us then to recover our position vis-à-vis the rest of the world."[60]

In February 1949 Bevin set up a British equivalent of the State Department's Policy Planning Staff inside the Foreign Office: the permanent under secretary's committee, the purpose of which was to advise him on long-term policy issues.[61] Whether by coincidence or design, the first paper that the committee produced addressed the question of a "third force" and came to the conclusion that it was neither practicable nor desirable. The Commonwealth, the committee pointed out, exhibited no political tendencies that suggested that it could be consolidated into a single unit, while from an economic and military point of view "the attraction exerted by the pound sterling and the Royal Navy is now less strong than that of the dollar and the atom bomb." Any attempt to force Commonwealth countries to choose between London and Washington, therefore, would certainly propel them in the direction of the latter, despite their emotional ties to Britain. As for Western Europe, "centrifugal tendencies are still strong" and the military and economic strength of its constituent states was so weak "that there can be no immediate prospect of welding them into a prosperous and secure entity without American help." Moreover, the committee argued, any attempt to establish a "third force" would only encourage

American isolationism and Soviet expansionism. In the circumstances, "the best hope of security for Western Europe lies in a consolidation of the West on the lines indicated by the Atlantic Pact." Bevin approved a summary of the committee's paper in March 1949 and circulated the complete document to the cabinet in October.[62]

In the meantime the North Atlantic Treaty had been signed on 4 April 1949. This has rightly been regarded as one of Bevin's triumphs. After all, it was he who had first put forward the idea of American military backing for his "Western Union" in January 1948, and he played a vital role during the long and sometimes difficult negotiations that led up to the conclusion of the treaty. He was certainly proud of what he had done. His permanent under secretary in the Foreign Office at the time, Sir William Strang, later wrote, "No single act during his term of office as Foreign Secretary gave him a more satisfying sense of achievement than the signature of the North Atlantic Treaty."[63] Nevertheless, Bevin did not obtain everything he wanted. The crucial Article 5 of the treaty, which contained the American military guarantee, was drafted in looser terms than he would have wished. Article 2, which spoke of the need for nonmilitary cooperation between the signatories, he would have preferred to do without altogether. Finally, he had not wanted Italy as one of the original members of the alliance, arguing that it would contribute little but ask for much.[64]

With the abandonment of his belief in a "third force," Bevin came to regard the Atlantic alliance, which he had originally conceived as a protective umbrella beneath which the "third force" could be built up, as an end in itself. Cold War developments, such as the Berlin blockade—on which Bevin took a very firm line—and communist successes in China and southeast Asia, no doubt reinforced the perceived need to draw ever closer to the only power capable of deterring aggression, but it was also true that developments continued to turn Britain away from Europe as well as propel it in the direction of the United States.

In a memorandum for the cabinet on 25 October 1949, which referred back to the one they had submitted to its economic policy committee exactly nine months earlier, Bevin and Cripps argued that economic union with Europe was now "less rather than more attractive than it was then." Instead of Britain's dollar position improving, it had deteriorated—indeed, the pound had been devalued by 30 percent in September—and although the European countries had been more successful than expected in controlling their inflation, they had not shown any sign of tackling the other fundamental weaknesses in their economies. Since Britain now had less resources to contribute to an economic union than it had in January, such a union was less likely to succeed. The experience of the summer, moreover, had shown just how difficult cooperation within the framework of the OEEC was. On the other hand, the devaluation discussions with the United States and Canada and the meeting of Commonwealth finance ministers had laid the foundations for "a new relationship with the United States and the Commonwealth," and since relations with these areas now took priority over relations with Europe, there were definite limits to the extent to which Britain could cooperate with the latter.

These limits had not been spelled out in January, but they were in October, and they revealed the distance that Bevin had traveled since his earlier espousal of a European customs union and a European central bank. The British government, the memorandum stated, should not accept "(i) loss of . . . responsibility for budgetary and credit policy, and for the management of the reserves; (ii) hindrance to our own efforts to reach and maintain equilibrium between the dollar area and the sterling area; . . . (iii) opening to European decision the size of the strategic dollar-earning and dollar-saving United Kingdom industries; [and] (iv) [proposals] materially affecting the system of Imperial preferences."[65]

Following the course marked out in the permanent under secretary's committee's report of March 1949, Bevin's objective was to create an Atlantic community. As he told the cabinet on 8 May 1950, "Our interests would best be served by the closest possible co-operation with the United States and Canada." This was because "it was clear that, even with the support of the Commonwealth, Western Europe was not strong enough to contend with the military danger confronting it from the East," which had been heightened following the communist victory in the Chinese civil war in October 1949, so that "the United Kingdom and Western Europe must be able to rely on the full support of the English-speaking democracies of the Western Hemisphere; and for the original conception of Western Union we must now begin to substitute the wider conception of the Atlantic community."[66]

At the same time, Bevin was still determined to preserve Britain's independence and influence, and he saw the United States's continuing support for European federation as an American ploy to exert indirect control. Everybody in Britain was anxious to remain independent of the United States, he told one of his junior ministers, Ernest Davies, on 24 April 1950. They wanted to cooperate with the Americans, but not to be dominated by them. "Now if you surrender your sovereignty to Europe," Bevin went on, "there will be an avenue of pressure at once on Great Britain through Europe by the financial power of the United States which will leave you in many cases in a minority." He had consistently believed, he said, "that the vital interests of the Commonwealth, the sterling area, or ourselves must be determined by ourselves." It might be another matter if the United States were prepared to join in on the same basis as everyone else, but he clearly felt that this was not the case.[67]

This was undoubtedly a factor in his hostile reaction to the Schuman plan for the integration of Western Europe's coal and steel industries, which was announced by the French foreign minister on 9 May 1950. The American secretary of state, Dean Acheson, has written eloquently of Bevin's angry suspicion that the plan had been "cooked up" between Acheson and Schuman, deliberately kept from him, and then made public before he had had a chance to examine it.[68] None of this was true, although the circumstances of Schuman's announcement gave it a degree of plausibility. What was indisputable was that the Americans welcomed the plan and were disappointed by Britain's refusal to take part in it.

IV

Political, personal, and international developments combined to complicate Bevin's task of organizing an "Atlantic community" in which Britain was the privileged partner of the United States. The Labour government fought a general election in February 1950, and although even more voters supported it than in 1945, the same was true of the Conservative opposition, and the vagaries of the British electoral system ensured that Labour ended up with an overall majority of only five seats in the House of Commons. It was inevitable that there would have to be another election before too long, and in the interim the government was clearly perceived to be living on borrowed time.

It was not only the government that was in this position, for Bevin was increasingly affected by ill health. A serious heart problem had been diagnosed as early as 1937, and when he was examined in 1943 his doctor "found not a sound organ in his body, apart from his feet." According to the same source, Bevin suffered "from angina pectoris, cardiac failure, arterio-sclerosis, enlarged liver, damaged kidneys and high blood pressure. He was overweight [as any photograph of him clearly shows], smoked and drank more than was good for him, took no exercise and was a poor sleeper." To the punishment that he inflicted on his own body, his workload at the Foreign Office added even more. He collapsed after a debate in the House of Commons in July 1946 and from then on was repeatedly assailed by severe attacks of angina and other bouts of illness, and was only kept going by the continuous administration of drugs. By 1950–1951 he was in a very bad way indeed. Alan Bullock notes that between the beginning of March and the end of July 1950 he was either in hospital or convalescing from surgery for a total of 85 out of 153 days, and he entered hospital again in January 1951, stricken with pneumonia.[69]

Attlee did in fact suggest to Bevin in the fall of 1950 that he should move from the Foreign Office to the Treasury, but he turned down the offer. Among other considerations, as his then private secretary subsequently remarked, was the fact "that he did not at all relish the idea of handing over the Foreign Office to one of his colleagues—for he did not think that any of them . . . was qualified to take on such a responsibility."[70] His vanity thus persisted to the end. It is impossible to be precise about the effect that illness had upon Bevin's foreign policy during his final year in office, but as we shall see, at least one of his junior ministers thought it was considerable.

Finally, the international situation took a marked turn for the worse during 1950 with the outbreak of the Korean War on 25 June. Although Britain and the United States were more or less in agreement over policy to be pursued in southeast Asia, there was an enormous rift between them over China when, despite American entreaties to stay its hand, Britain extended de jure recognition to the Communist regime on 5 January 1950. The reason for the decision, which Bevin communicated to Acheson on 16 December, 1949, was twofold. In the first place, there was the existence of "vast Chinese communities" in Malaya and Singapore. The British government had been advised, said Bevin, "that continued non-recognition is liable to cause trouble there which we cannot afford to risk." Secondly, the British government took the view "that to withhold recognition indefinitely is to play straight into the hands of the Soviet Union" and that "the only counter to Russian influence is that Communist China should have contacts with the West, and that the sooner these contacts are established the better."[71]

The Korean War exacerbated this division between Britain and the United States. Bevin was convalescing in hospital after surgery when North Korean troops crossed the thirty-eighth parallel, but he was shown the draft of the public statement that President Truman intended to make on 27 June and that had been communicated to the British government in advance. This statement announced four major decisions: (1) to extend U.S. air and naval support to South Korea; (2) to neutralize the island of Formosa, which was still held by Chiang Kai-shek's Nationalist forces, by placing units of the U.S. Seventh Fleet in the straits between it and the mainland of China; (3) to strengthen American forces in the Philippines and to accelerate military aid to the Philippine government; and (4) to accelerate military aid to French Indochina and to despatch a U.S. military mission to the area.[72] When Bevin was first shown the statement, he put his finger on the passage concerning Formosa and asked, "Why did they have to do that? Before we know where we are we'll all be in a world war for the sake of Chiang Kai-shek. . . . Why can't they keep it to Korea?"[73] Nevertheless, his considered advice to his cabinet colleagues was that the British government should not seek publicly to isolate Korea from the other issues raised in the proposed American statement, since "we did not wish to discourage . . . [the U.S.] Government from helping us and the French in resisting Communist encroachments in Malaya and Indo-China." Any resolution that the United States put to the United Nations, however, "should be confined strictly to events in Korea."[74]

Bevin took up the question of Formosa in a private message to Acheson on 7 July 1950, linking it with an approach he had recently made to the Russians with a view to restoring the *status quo ante* in Korea. If the Russians were willing to cooperate, Bevin thought, they would almost certainly raise both the issue of Formosa and that of Chinese representation in the United Nations, where, thanks to American support, the Nationalist regime still occupied the seat allocated to China in the Security Council and elsewhere. "Whereas the United States have the whole-hearted backing of world opinion in the courageous initiative they took to deal with the aggression in Korea," Bevin warned, "I do not believe that they could rely on the same support for their declared policy in connexion with Formosa." Many countries, especially in Asia, were concerned about the prospect of an extension of the conflict that might occur if the Chinese Communists tried to invade Formosa. Some undoubtedly believed that since the Communists controlled all mainland Chinese territory, it would be wrong to take any step that might prejudice the return of Formosa to China, as had been agreed by Roosevelt, Churchill, and Chiang Kai-shek in the Cairo Declaration of 1 December 1943.[75]

The administration in Washington was not at all happy with Bevin's attempts at peacemaking and still less with his views on China. Acheson made his irritation clear in a tough, uncompromising reply to Bevin's message and instructed the U.S. ambassador in London to "leave him in no doubt of [the] seriousness with which I view [the] implications of his message and the possible effect on our whole future relationship."[76]

Since that relationship was now the cornerstone of Bevin's foreign policy, it was not surprising that he was, in the ambassador's words, "a little taken aback at the vigor of [Acheson's] response."[77] He did send a spirited defense of his views to Acheson a few days later, but as the latter subsequently wrote in his memoirs, "The correspondence clearly had no future, so we dropped it."[78] Moreover, Bevin's words were not followed by actions. He told Dalton on 2 September 1950 that he wanted "to vote straight out at the start of the U.N. Assembly in favor of admitting the new Chinese government, even though this means voting publicly against [the] U.S.,"[79] but he did nothing of the sort. Similarly, when his new deputy, Kenneth Younger, tried to persuade the cabinet to discuss what Britain would do in the event of a clash between the United States and China over Formosa, Bevin vetoed the initiative. "He was afraid," wrote Younger, "of some decision which might tie his hands when the time comes."[80]

Despite his anxiety over the possibility of conflict between the United States and China, Bevin did not do as much as he might have to restrain the Americans from crossing the thirty-eighth parallel in October 1950, after the tide of war in Korea had turned in favor of the United Nations following the Inchon landings. The Chinese had warned that they would intervene in the war if this happened, and Bevin was in possession of an intelligence report that described "heavy mechanised transport traffic" moving "bumper to bumper" from Manchuria into North Korea.[81] Yet the most he was willing to do was to call upon the Americans to time future military operations so that there was the widest possible gap between the passage of the British-sponsored resolution that provided for the reunification of Korea and the crossing of the thirty-eighth parallel by United Nations troops.[82] This was because he himself believed in the need to reunite Korea by force in order to avoid the possibility of future aggression, and also because he feared that if the opportunity for a speedy victory was lost, Britain would be blamed. American troops crossed the parallel immediately after the passage of the U.N. resolution on 7 October 1950, a mere twenty-four hours after Bevin's appeal for a delay. Britain had hoped that the government of India would vote for the resolution, but it refused. On 9 October Bevin told the cabinet that "he believed that there was insufficient foundation for their apprehension that China or Russia might . . . be provoked into active intervention" by the passage of the resolution.[83] Along with many others, he was soon to be proved tragically wrong.

The outbreak of the Korean war had repercussions that went far beyond east Asia. One was the American demand for West German rearmament to strengthen the forces of the North Atlantic alliance in Europe. This was something to which the Labour government and the Labour party—although not the British military establishment—objected, and as Bevin arrived in New York in September 1950 for the North Atlantic Treaty meeting at which the Americans were expected to raise the issue, he made clear his opposition to journalists.[84] However, no sooner had the Americans threatened that if their allies would not accept the need for German rearmament, they would not send further troops to Europe or appoint a supreme commander for the alliance's forces—steps to which Bevin attached enormous importance as proof of a genuine American commitment to the defense of western Europe—than he swiftly changed tack. After bombarding his colleagues with a series of ever more importunate telegrams, he managed to secure their "general agreement to an acceptance in principle of German participation in Western defence," although it is obvious, even from the typically circumspect cabinet minutes, that there was a great deal of opposition to the idea, and as Dalton—a leading objector—subsequently noted in his diary, "There were some principles that were accepted but never applied."[85]

By December 1950 Bevin was changing tack again. He was impressed by the views of the French and of some of his own officials that the Russians might well regard German rearmament as a provocative act. The latter had warned the Western allies in October that they would not reconcile themselves to it and, as he put it in a message to Attlee, "It might be no less dangerous to ignore this warning in our present condition of weakness than it was to ignore the warning of the Chinese in regard to an approach to the Manchurian border by United Nations forces." This was said, of course, in the context of the massive Chinese intervention in the Korean War, which had turned the triumphal march of the United Nations forces toward the Yalu River into something approaching a rout, and he was writing to Attlee because the prime minister was in Washington for crisis talks with President Truman prompted by the latter's remarks at a press conference on 30 November in which he had seemed to be contemplating the use of nuclear weapons to redress the situation in Korea. It would be unwise,

Bevin thought, to push ahead with German rearmament when it looked as though "a large proportion of Allied military resources would be tied up [in east Asia] for a long time to come."

The chiefs of staff, together with some members of the cabinet, did not share Bevin's reservations, and he loyally summarized their views for the prime minister, leaving it to him to decide what to say to Truman.[86] In his reply Attlee pointed out that the Americans were now ready to proceed with the nomination of a supreme commander in Europe (General Eisenhower) and to despatch reinforcements to Europe, even though these would only be National Guard units. Since Britain had been pressing for these decisions for some time, he thought it would have been "unthinkable" to backtrack on German rearmament. "To have done so would, in the opinion of everyone here, have killed the present talks and dealt a body blow at the renewed Anglo-American partnership which seems to be developing."[87] Bevin was thus overruled, in part at any rate, by reference to his own policy of maintaining a "special relationship" between Britain and the United States.

Another result of the Korean War was a greatly accelerated rearmament program. After the outbreak of the war, the United States confronted its allies with a specific request to increase their expenditure upon defense. Despite the fact that Britain was already spending a higher proportion of its national income on defense than it was on the eve of the Second World War, it acceded to the American request, and the planned expenditure of £2.59 billion over the next three years was increased to £3.4 billion. But this was contingent upon aid being received from the United States to the tune of £550 million. It soon became clear, however, that the latter was not prepared to contribute anything like that amount.

In October 1950—by which time the cost of the defense program had risen to £3.6 billion as the result of a particularly generous increase in pay for the armed forces—Bevin and the new chancellor of the exchequer, Hugh Gaitskell, proposed that the negotiations for the greater portion of American aid should be carried out on a multilateral basis within the framework of the so-called Nitze Exercise. This was a scheme in which all the NATO countries would work out an equitable procedure for sharing defense expenditure within the context of the alliance. Their rationale was that, by the middle of 1950, the British economy was performing much better than had been anticipated at the beginning of the European Recovery Program, and the achievement of the government's target of financial independence was now in sight. "As the strength of sterling steadily increased," wrote the foreign secretary and the chancellor, "so did the power and influence of Britain. . . . [W]e were becoming able, for the first time, to sustain our world-wide commitments . . . [and t]he visible growth of economic independence gave us weight in the counsels of the nations." Direct assistance on the lines of the European Recovery Program, Bevin and Gaitskell argued, could lead Britain to forfeit that independence and lose the position it was just regaining as the principal partner of the United States in world affairs. They warned that Britain would then "be back again in the European queue" and would find itself "treated not as partners . . . but as just another necessitous European nation."[88]

When Attlee was in Washington in December 1950, he was put under strong pressure to increase Britain's defense effort still further. "We cannot stand any more for the time being," Bevin minuted on the record of the conversation during which the pressure was exerted, but the cabinet did. On 18 December it authorized him to say that the government had decided to increase and accelerate its defense preparations yet again and invited the chiefs of staff to work out the details. "In his talks in Washington," Attlee explained, "he had persuaded the Americans to accept Anglo-American partnership as the mainspring of Atlantic defence. Much of the advantage we had gained would be lost if we were now to be treated as merely one of the European countries which were being urged by America to make a larger contribution to the common defence effort. We should align ourselves with the Americans in urging the others to do more."[89] Once again Bevin found himself a prisoner of his own policy.

After the formal announcement by the United States at the NATO council meeting in Brussels in December 1950 that American troops already in Western Europe would be reinforced and that a supreme commander for the NATO forces would be appointed, Bevin is said to have remarked that he had nearly died three times in the course of the previous year, but had kept himself alive in order to see the Atlantic alliance properly launched, which had now been achieved.[90] It may be that these measures did help to deter Soviet aggression, but things did not look quite so clear-cut at the time. Indeed, the problem did not necessarily come from the Soviet side. Just a few days before the meeting, the chief of the imperial general staff, Field Marshal Sir William Slim, a distinguished soldier not prone to alarmism, told his colleagues on the chiefs of staff committee after a visit to Washington, "The United States were convinced that war was inevitable, and that it was almost certain to take place within the next eighteen months." The British did not hold this view and were still hopeful that war could be avoided, but the American attitude "was dangerous because there was the possibility that they might think that since war was inevitable, the sooner we got it over the better, and we might as a result be dragged unnecessarily into World War III."[91]

This concern persisted into the new year. On 10 January 1951 Attlee asked to see Bevin after talking to a number of military and other personalities "who were thoroughly alarmed about the American attitude to world affairs which they were afraid would end by dragging us into war."[92] We do not know the details of the anxieties concerning "the American attitude to world affairs," which those who talked to Attlee had expressed, but they were probably not dissimilar to those which Kenneth Younger set out in a contemporary diary entry.

So far, with the exception of her decision to resist N[orth] Korean aggression . . . [the United States] has hardly done or said a sensible thing over many months. By linking Formosa with Korea; by refusing to recognise Peking and by clinging to Chiang Kai-shek; by the rashness of MacArthur's military policy in Korea; and finally by the failure of any of her troops except the Marine Division to fight properly, she could not have played more completely into the hands of the Russians, or made it more certain that [the] USSR and China will be united in an expansionist policy in the Far East in the immediate future. Having been largely responsible for getting us into this dangerous situation, she is pressing for measures which may make it more dangerous still, without offering any prospect of putting effective pressure on [the] USSR or China. When you add to this, that simultaneously she has been pressing for immediate German rearmament, regardless of the risk of provoking the Russians at the moment of Europe's greatest weakness, you could scarcely get a more complete picture of dangerous stupidity on the part of a leading power.

What Younger thought might make the situation "more dangerous still" was the proposed United Nations resolution condemning the Chinese as aggressors and laying the foundation for sanctions against them. Although the British government was opposed to this policy, Younger thought there was "great reluctance to be tough with the Americans about it." In particular, he was very unsure of Bevin's position. "My impression of Ernie has been lamentable," he wrote. "Sometimes he seems very unwell, sometimes not so bad; but every time I have seen him so far he has seemed to me to be morally a broken man. I think the weakness is partly physical, and that he simply hasn't the stamina for taking difficult decisions. Just now the line of least resistance is to drift along behind the Americans, making ineffectual protests all the way."[93]

Bevin's response to Attlee's anxiety certainly gave little indication that he shared it. In a note to the prime minister, which sounded more like a reflection of the views of his officials than usual, he expressed the opinion that aggression was not in the American character and that the U.S. Constitution did not make it easy to carry out. He conceded that there was a risk that the Americans might drift into war as a result of ill-considered or impulsive acts, but this could be reduced by "wise diplomacy." In any case, there were no grounds for altering the view that the government had reached "after long deliberation" that neither the Commonwealth, nor Europe, nor the two combined were sufficiently powerful to stand up to the Soviet threat. Britain would simply have "to exert sufficient control over the policy of the well-intentioned but inexperienced colossus on whose co-operation our safety depends."[94]

This was easier said than done. When Bevin was laid low by pneumonia on 22 January 1951, Younger, who was temporarily in charge of the Foreign Office, succeeded on 25 January in persuading the cabinet to instruct the British representative at the United Nations to vote against the U.S. resolution that condemned the Chinese as aggressors. There then followed a concerted campaign by pro-American ministers and officials to overturn the decision. Gaitskell threatened to resign, the officials lobbied energetically, and the Americans made a small concession. Bevin was reported "too incoherent to be told" what was going on, but Gaitskell used an argument that he would almost certainly have endorsed: that to break with the United States "might have the most fatal consequences on Anglo-American relations. . . . It might lead to [their] virtually coming away from Europe which would . . . be the end for us." The decision was duly reversed on 26 January 1951, and the General Assembly passed the resolution on 1 February.[95]

Bevin returned from his convalescence on 1 March 1951, but his days in the Foreign Office were numbered. Younger saw him some days earlier and was profoundly depressed by their conversation. Newspapers of all political persuasions were critical of Bevin and were urging Attlee to replace him with someone else. "Ernie is convinced," wrote Younger, "that every word of this is inspired by one or other of his colleagues . . . [and] I felt positively contaminated by his petty bitterness. Whatever he may have been when he was a fit man he is a pathetic old wreck now, and in many ways contemptible. I think he could only be effective as a maker of trouble in the cabinet and the party."[96]

He did not get the chance. Attlee had finally come to the conclusion that he must go. Downing Street announced on the evening of 9 March that Bevin would be succeeded as foreign secretary by the lord president of the council, Herbert Morrison, and that he himself would become lord privy seal, a post without departmental responsibilities. The fact that the announcement came on the day that Bevin was celebrating his seventieth birthday, and that Morrison was his chief political enemy in the Labour party did nothing to soften the blow. As he left the Foreign Office for the last time, his private secretary recorded, "He looked old and frail and miserable."[97] Just over a month later, on 14 April 1951, he suffered another heart attack and died alone before help could reach him.[98]

V

Two and a half years later, on 4 November 1953, the foreign secretary in the Conservative government, Anthony Eden, unveiled a bronze bust of Ernest Bevin on the central stairway of the Foreign Office building in Whitehall. Also present for the occasion was the prime minister, Sir Winston Churchill, who made a short speech in which he described Bevin as "one of the greatest foreign secretaries that has ever been called upon to discharge his duties."[99] The ceremony symbolized the bipartisan consensus that had grown up around Bevin's foreign policy and that has persisted to this day.

This consensus may be summarized as follows: Bevin was swift to realize the threat posed by the Soviet Union after 1945; he was instrumental in arousing the sleeping American giant to a sense of its responsibilities in the matter; and he was a key figure in organizing the successful Western response to communist subversion and aggression. He was as much responsible for the implementation of the Marshall Plan as Marshall himself; and he was one of the principal architects of the North Atlantic Treaty, which not only kept the peace in Europe for more than forty years, but led to the collapse of the Soviet system.

There are some serious flaws in this analysis. If Bevin was suspicious of the Soviet Union, he was, as this essay has tried to show, suspicious of the United States as well, especially during his early years as foreign secretary. He also entertained hopes of a détente with the Soviet Union long after the Americans had given up. "He's always been horribly over-optimistic about bringing the Soviet Union to its senses," Christopher Mayhew wrote at the end of 1948, "and blames himself for not bringing a settlement about."[100] Nor did the United States need any coaching from Bevin to reach the conclusion that the Soviet Union was a threat to its vision of the world, as the work of scholars like Bruce Kuniholm, Marc Gallicchio, and Melvyn Leffler has demonstrated. As for the Marshall Plan and NATO, it is undeniable that Bevin did play an important part in their creation, but given the international context of 1947–1949, it is hard to imagine that the United States would not have moved to shore up Western Europe, both politically and militarily, even if he had never held office. Moreover, Bevin had some serious reservations about the implications of the Marshall Plan.

The consensus view of Bevin's foreign policy has always been challenged by a minority. At the time, there was a small but vociferous group of members of Parliament on the left of the Labour party, whose continual sniping exhausted Bevin's small reserves of patience and brought down the full weight of his displeasure and contempt upon their heads. Much of the platform of this group, which appeared as a pamphlet in May 1947, was not dissimilar to Bevin's own policy, notably their wish to preserve Britain's independence from the United States and to build up a socialist alternative to both communism and capitalism. But the rest of their critique—opposition to staff talks with the Americans, the renunciation of the atomic bomb, and the setting of a date for the withdrawal of British troops from Greece, Palestine, and Egypt—went far beyond what he was willing to tolerate.[101]

The Marxist left, of course, goes a lot further in its criticism of Bevin. A good example of their approach is John Saville's essay in *The Socialist Register* for 1984. According to Saville, the "central thrust" of Bevin's foreign policy "was pivoted upon a total opposition to the Soviet Union and to all those radical movements in Europe and elsewhere in which Communists played, or were thought to be playing, an important part. . . . [T]he overriding consideration was felt to be the communist threat to established orders. In this crucial regard, Labour was no different from the Conservatives," and Bevin was "Washington's man."[102]

At least two responses can be made to Saville and those who share his views. In the first place, even if Bevin was compelled to compromise with the "established orders," it is totally misleading to imply that he was little more than a capitalist stooge, deliberately setting out to preserve the status quo against "radical movements." In the case of Europe, he wanted, as this essay has argued, to establish some kind of social democratic alternative to both communism and capitalism. He also advocated profound social reforms in what would now be called the Third World, and it is hard to imagine a Conservative foreign secretary urging, as Bevin did, the distribution of British labor union rulebooks throughout the Middle East![103] Secondly, whatever reservations may be entertained concerning the postwar regime in Greece and French rule in Indochina—British support for which Saville criticizes particularly—they were an improvement upon the Stalinist thugs who would undoubtedly have succeeded them without that support, and who in the case of Indochina eventually did. Bevin's dislike of communism and its methods was amply justified.

A more effective critique of Bevin's foreign policy can be developed with reference to his own assumptions than to those of his opponents. His principal objective was not the implementation of "a socialist foreign policy"—whatever that may mean—but the preservation of Britain's independence and influence, and it was precisely in the realization of this objective that he conspicuously failed.

To some extent, of course, he was the victim of circumstance. As we saw at the beginning of this essay, Britain did emerge from the Second World War in a greatly weakened position. But Bevin's insistence upon the need to cling to every imperial position for as long as possible only made matters worse. The Labour government enjoyed some remarkable economic successes—unlike most of its West European neighbors, for example, Britain had achieved a surplus on its current balance of payments account as early as 1948—but it would undoubtedly have done even better if the country had not been saddled with such a heavy burden of defense expenditure. One of the first conclusions the new Conservative government came to after the general election of October 1951 was that the massive rearmament program that its Labour predecessor had launched in the new year was more than the country could afford. When the Meiji regime strove to preserve the independence of Japan in the second half of the nineteenth century, it based its policy upon the slogan of a strong economy and a powerful army. For all his economic expertise, Bevin overemphasised the latter at the expense of the former.

Bevin also allowed personal prejudice to come between him and the achievement of his principal aim. His violent antipathy to the very word *federalism,* together with his ignorance of and contempt for the realities of politics under the

Fourth Republic in France prevented him from seeing that successive French governments were no more eager to surrender their sovereignty to some federal entity than he was, and, moreover, shared his objective of an independent Europe, closely linked to but not controlled by the United States. If Bevin had shown a little more flexibility and understanding, a European community might have grown up around an Anglo-French instead of a Franco-German axis.

From the laudable desire that Britain should maintain its freedom of maneuver between the United States and the Soviet Union, Bevin's policy had moved in the direction of increasing dependence upon the former. By 1950–1951, everything was subordinated to the Atlantic alliance, which in turn led to an almost pathological fear of upsetting the Americans. Kenneth Younger was surely right when he wrote in January 1951 of the possible risks in breaking with the United States over the United Nations resolution condemning China as an aggressor. "I do not really believe that the action proposed would upset the Anglo-American alliance for more than a short time. After a spasm of rage . . . the Americans would revert to the policy which their national interest dictates." As it was, the Americans clearly felt that they could always count upon the British to support them, regardless of any misgivings. "We have got to stop this rot," Younger wrote, "if we ever want to have real influence upon them."[104]

With one dishonorable (Anthony Eden) and one honorable (Edward Heath) exception, there has never been a serious attempt by any British government to "stop the rot" of obsequious dependence upon the United States in matters of foreign affairs, a dependence that is no less real because it is dressed up in the rhetoric of the so-called special relationship. Even as these lines are being written (November 1992). Labour party politicians are attacking the Conservative government for jeopardizing this relationship by supporting George Bush in his unsuccessful presidential campaign against Bill Clinton, while the government hastens to reassure us that it remains intact. What other Western nation's leaders would feel the need to behave in such a pathetic fashion? The fact that Britain's still do is in large part the responsibility of Ernest Bevin.

Notes

This essay makes use of some earlier research I have published, and in particular, my essays, "The Labour Governments and the Unity of Western Europe, 1945–51," in *The Foreign Policy of the British Labour Governments, 1945–1951*, ed. Ritchie Ovendale (Leicester, 1984), 61–82; "The British Labour Government and the Atlantic Alliance, 1949–1951," in *Western Security: The Formative Years*, ed. Olav Riste (Oslo, 1985), 247–65; and "Britain and Europe in 1948: the View from the Cabinet," in *Power in Europe?* ed. Josef Becker and Franz Knipping (Berlin, 1986), 27–46. I have, however, changed my views on some issues since those essays were published.

1. Ben Pimlott, *Hugh Dalton* (London, 1985), 410–22.

2. Alan Bullock, *The Life and Times of Ernest Bevin,* vol. 1 (London, 1960); Vol. 2 (London, 1967).

3. Sir William Hayter, *A Double Life* (London, 1974), 77–78; Sir Frank Roberts, *Dealing with Dictators* (London, 1991), 124; Lord Strang, *Home and Abroad* (London, 1956), 292; Ben Pimlott, ed., *The Second World War Diary of Hugh Dalton 1940–45* (London, 1986), 677 (entry for 29 Nov. 1943); Christopher Mayhew, *Time to Explain* (London, 1987), 119–20; Alan Bullock, *Ernest Bevin: Foreign Secretary, 1945–1951* (New York, 1983), 90; *The Memoirs of Lord Gladwyn* (London, 1972), 176–77.

4. Eben Ayers diary, 7 Aug. 1945, Eben Ayers MSS, Harry S. Truman Library; Andrei Gromyko, *Pamyatnoye* (Moscow, 1988), 1:324–25.

5. U.S. Department of Commerce, Bureau of the Census, *Historical Statistics of the United States: Colonial Times to 1970,* part 2 (Washington, D.C., 1975), 1141; U.K. Central Statistical Office, *Annual Abstract of Statistics 1938–1948; 1938–1950* (London, 1949, 1952); Mark Harrison, *Soviet Planning in Peace and War 1938–1945* (Cambridge, Eng., 1985), 138.

6. Richard J. Overy, *The Air War 1939–1945* (London, 1980), 21, 150; *Velikaya Otechestvennaya Voina 1941–1945: Entsiklopediya* (Moscow, 1985), 35.

7. Bruce W. Watson, *The Changing Face of the World's Navies 1945 to the Present* (London, 1991), 34; Geoffrey Bennett, *Naval Battles of World War II* (London, 1975), 37, 52.

8. W. S. Woytinsky and E. S. Woytinsky, *World Population and Production* (New York, 1953), 389, 392.

9. Keynes memorandum, 13 Aug. 1945, *Documents on British Policy Overseas (DBPO)* I/III, no. 6.

10. David Sanders, *Losing an Empire, Finding a Role* (London, 1990), 50; Ritchie Ovendale, *The English-Speaking Alliance* (London, 1985), 21.

11. Peter J. Taylor, *Britain and the Cold War: 1945 as Geopolitical Transition* (London, 1990), 88.

12. House of Commons Debates (hereafter H. C. Deb.), vol. 437, col. 1965; Riches minute, 6 May 1947, Public Record Office (hereafter PRO), Foreign Office (hereafter FO) 371/62971/J2102/G (all quotations from Crown Copyright documents in the Public Record Office are reproduced by kind permission of the controller of Her Majesty's Stationery Office); *The Times,* 28 July 1947.

13. Bevin memorandum, 8 Nov. 1945, DBPO I/III, no. 99.

14. William Roger Louis, *The British Empire in the Middle East 1945–1951* (Oxford, 1984), sec. IV; Ritchie Ovendale, *Britain, the United States, and the End of the Palestine Mandate* (Woodbridge, 1989).

15. C.M. (45) 57, 29 November 1945, Confidential Annex, DBPO I/III, no. 132; Dixon minute, 26 Jan. 1946, DBPO I/IV, no. 18; Bevin telegram, 27 Apr. 1946, DBPO I/IV, no. 82.

16. Unsigned note, 3 Oct. 1945, DBPO I/II, no. 166.

17. GEN. 163/1, 8 Jan. 1947, PRO CAB 130/16.

18. Labour Party, *Report of the 45th Annual Conference . . . Bournemouth . . . 1946,* 167.

19. H. C. Deb., vol. 415, cols. 1338, 1342.

20. Hugh Dalton, *High Tide and After* (London, 1962), 50, summarizing his contemporary diary entry of 5 Oct. 1945.

21. Bevin statement, 10 July 1946, *Foreign Relations of the United States* (hereafter *FRUS*), 1946, 2:868–69; Byrnes statement, 11 July 1946, *FRUS*, 1946, 2:897; C.M. (46) 68, 15 July 1946, PRO CAB 128/6; Dean minute, 23 July 1946, PRO FO 371/55589/C8643.

22. Christopher Mayhew diary, 20 Dec. 1946. I am extremely grateful to Lord Mayhew (as he now is) for letting me see and quote from extracts from his unpublished diaries.

23. Unsigned minute, 25 Apr. 1947, PRO FO 800/447; Undated Bevin memorandum [but after 24 Apr. 1947], idem.

24. Francis Williams, *Ernest Bevin* (London, 1952), 265; Pierson Dixon diary, 2 July 1947. I am extremely grateful to Piers Dixon for letting me see and quote from those portions of his father's diaries that are not published in his biography, *Double Diploma* (London, 1968).

25. Donald McLachlan, *In the Chair: Barrington-Ward of "The Times" 1927–1948* (London, 1971), 280.

26. Pierson Dixon diary, 12 Mar. 1946.

27. Alan Bullock, *The Life and Times of Ernest Bevin* (London, 1960), 1:387–88, 440–44, 622–23, 648–49.

28. Labour Party, *Report of the 43rd Annual Conference . . . London . . . 1944*, 147.

29. Pierson Dixon diary, 7 Aug. 1945; Unsigned minute, 21 Aug. 1945, PRO FO 800/443.

30. John Darwin, *Britain and Decolonisation* (London, 1988), 147–50; Roberts minutes, 6 Apr., 10 July 1948, PRO FO 800/444; William Lyon Mackenzie King diary, 24 Nov. 1947, Cambridge University Microfiche Collection, ME 1222; Ritchie Ovendale, *The English-Speaking Alliance* (London, 1985), chap. 9.

31. Raymond Smith and John Zametica, "The Cold Warrior: Clement Attlee reconsidered, 1945–7," *International Affairs* 61, no. 2 (Spring 1985): 237–52; Richard J. Aldrich and John Zametica, "The Rise and Decline of a Strategic Concept: The Middle East," in *British Intelligence, Strategy and the Cold War 1945–51*, ed. Richard J. Aldrich (London, 1992), 236–74.

32. Bevin memorandum, D.O. (46) 27, 13 Mar. 1946, PRO CAB 131/2.

33. Bevin telegram, 12 Oct. 1945, PRO FO 800/484.

34. Bevin memorandum, C.P. (45) 174, 17 Sept. 1945, PRO CAB 129/2.

35. William Roger Louis, *The British Empire in the Middle East 1945–51* (Oxford, 1984), especially sec. I, chaps. 6 and 8, and sec. V, chap. 1; Wesley K. Wark, "Development Diplomacy: Sir John Troutbeck and the British Middle East Office, 1947–50," in *British Officials and Foreign Policy, 1945–51*, ed. John Zametica (Leicester, 1990), 228–49.

36. Unsigned, undated minute, DBPO I/V, no. 4; Dixon minute, 17 Aug. 1945, PRO FO 371/45731/UE3689/G.

37. Bevin memorandum, C.P. (47) 35, 18 Jan. 1947, PRO CAB 129/16; C.M. (47) 13, 28 Jan. 1947, PRO CAB 128/9.

38. Peterson memorandum, 24 June 1947, *FRUS*, 1947, 3:268–73.

39. Bevin letter, 5 Sept. 1947, PRO PREM 8/1146; Bevin minute, 16 Sept. 1947, PRO FO 800/444; Bevin telegram, 17 Nov. 1947, idem.

40. Unsigned minute, 22 Sept. 1947, PRO FO 371/67673/Z8461/G; Dixon minute, 29 Nov. 1947, PRO FO 800/465.

41. Duff Cooper letter, 16 October. 1947, quoted in Duff Cooper, *Old Men Forget* (London, 1953), 379.

42. Roberts minute, 17 Dec. 1947, PRO FO 800/444; Roberts minute, 17 Dec. 1947, PRO FO 800/447.

43. Bevin memorandum, C.P. (48) 7, 5 Jan. 1948, PRO CAB 129/23.

44. Bevin memorandum, C.P. (48) 5, 5 Jan. 1948, PRO CAB 129/23.

45. Bevin memorandum, C.P. (48) 8, 4 Jan. 1948, PRO CAB 129/23.

46. Bevin memorandum, C.P. (48) 6, 4 Jan. 1948, PRO CAB 129/23.

47. C.M. (48) 2, 8 Jan. 1948, PRO CAB 128/12, part II.

48. H. C. Deb., vol. 446, cols 383–409; enclosure to Inverchapel letter, 13 Jan. 1948, *FRUS*, 1948, 3:4–6.

49. Avi Shlaim, "Ernest Bevin," in Avi Shlaim, Peter Jones, and Keith Sainsbury, *British Foreign Secretaries Since 1945* (Newton Abbot, 1977), 48.

50. C.O.S. (48) 18, 4 Feb. 1948, PRO DEFE 4/10.

51. Roberts minute, 9 Feb. 1948, PRO FO 371/73048/Z1404/G.

52. H. C. Deb., vol. 446, cols. 398–99.

53. John Kent, "Bevin's Imperialism and the Idea of Euro-Africa," in *British Foreign Policy, 1945–56*, ed. Michael Dockrill and John W. Young (London, 1989), 47–76. The quotation is from p. 68.

54. H. C. Deb., vol. 446, col. 395.

55. René Massigli, *Une Comédie des Erreurs 1943–1956* (Paris, 1978), 156. This is a conjectural reconstruction of Bevin's original English.

56. Kirkpatrick letter, 28 Aug. 1948, PRO FO 371/73097/Z6885.

57. Bevin minute, 26 Sept. 1948, PRO FO 800/465.

58. Hugh Dalton diary, 19 Nov. 1948, Hugh Dalton MSS, British Library of Political and Economic Science, London.

59. H. C. Deb., vol. 480, cols. 1500–1501.

60. Cripps/Bevin memorandum, E.P.C. (49) 6, 25 Jan. 1949, PRO CAB 134/221; E.P.C. (49) 5th meeting, 26 Jan. 1945, PRO CAB 134/220.

61. Strang minute, 9 May 1949, PRO FO 371/76384/W3113/G; Ritchie Ovendale, "William Strang and the Permanent Under-Secretary's Committee," in *British Officials and British Foreign Policy, 1945–51*, ed. John Zametica, 212–27.

62. Strang minute, 23 Mar. 1949, PRO FO 371/76384/W3114/G; P.U.S.C. (22), 9 May 1949, DBPO II/II, no. 20.

63. Lord Strang, *Home and Abroad* (London, 1956), 289.

64. Nicholas Henderson, *The Birth of NATO* (London, 1982); John Baylis, "Britain and the Formation of NATO," in *The Origins of NATO*, ed. Joseph Smith (Exeter, 1990), 3–32.

65. Bevin/Cripps memorandum, C.P. (49) 203, 25 Oct. 1949, PRO CAB 129/37, part I.

66. C.M. (50) 29, 8 May 1950, DBPO II/II, no. 74.

67. Kinna minute, 24 Apr. 1950, Ernest Davies MSS. I am extremely grateful to Ernest Davies for letting me see and quote from his private papers. I understand that these have now been deposited in the British Library of Economic and Political Science in London.

68. Dean Acheson, *Present at the Creation: My Years at the State Department* (New York, 1969), 385.

69. Alan Bullock, *The Life and Times of Ernest Bevin* 1:614; Bullock, *Ernest Bevin: Foreign Secretary,* 287–89, 717, 827.

70. Sir Roderick Barclay, *Ernest Bevin and the Foreign Office 1932–69* (London, 1975), 49–50.

71. Bevin letter, 16 Dec. 1949, *FRUS,* 1949, 9:225–26.

72. For the text of Truman's statement, see *FRUS,* 1950, 7:202–3.

73. Transcript of Kenneth Younger interview with Richard Rose, 27 Dec. 1961, 37, Kenneth Younger MSS. I am extremely grateful to Lady Younger for granting me access to her late husband's diaries and papers.

74. C.M. (50) 39, 27 June 1950, PRO CAB 128/18.

75. Bevin letter, 7 July 1950, *FRUS,* 1950, 7:329–30.

76. Acheson letter, 10 July 1950, *FRUS,* 1950, 7:347–51; Acheson telegram, 10 July 1950, 7:351–52.

77. Douglas telegram, 11 July 1950, *FRUS,* 1950, 7:361–62.

78. Bevin letter, 15 July 1950, *FRUS,* 1950, 7:396–99; Dean Acheson, *Present at the Creation,* 418.

79. Ben Pimlott, ed., *The Political Diary of Hugh Dalton 1918–40, 1945–60* (London, 1986), 484.

80. Kenneth Younger diary, 5 Aug. 1950, Kenneth Younger MSS.

81. Scott minute, 4 Oct. 1950, PRO FO 371/84110/FK1023.

82. Bevin telegram, 6 Oct. 1950, DBPO II/IV, no. 64.

83. C.M. (50) 63, 9 Oct. 1950, PRO CAB 128/18; Anthony Farrar-Hockley, *A Distant Obligation* (London, 1990), chap. 10.

84. *The Times,* 13 Sept. 1950.

85. Bevin telegrams, 14 Sept. 1950, DBPO II/III, nos. 20, 21; C.M. (50) 59, 15 Sept. 1950, DBPO II/III, no. 27; Dalton diary, mid-February 1951, Hugh Dalton MSS, British Library of Political and Economic Science, London.

86. Bevin telegram, 6 Dec. 1950, DBPO II/III, no. 128. Bevin did not accompany Attlee to Washington because his health did not permit him to fly.

87. Attlee telegram, 6 Dec. 1950, DBPO II/III, no. 131.

88. Bevin/Gaitskell memorandum, C.P. (50) 247, 23 Oct. 1950, DBPO II/III, no. 79.

89. Unsigned minute, 7 Dec. 1950, DBPO II/III, no. 134; C.M. (50) 87, 18 Dec. 1950, PRO CAB 128/18.

90. Lord Ismay, *NATO: The First Five Years 1949–1954* (Paris, n.d.), 37.

91. C.O.S. (50) 206, Confidential Annex, 14 Dec. 1950, PRO DEFE 4/38.

92. Barclay minute, 10 Jan. 1951, PRO FO 800/517.

93. Kenneth Younger diary, 9 Jan. 1951, Kenneth Younger MSS.

94. Bevin minute, 12 Jan. 1951, PRO FO 800/517.

95. Kenneth Younger diary, 28 Jan., 4 Feb. 1951, Kenneth Younger MSS; Philip M. Williams, ed., *The Diary of Hugh Gaitskell 1945–1956* (London, 1983), 229–32 (entry dated 2 Feb. 1951); Pimlott, *The Political Diary of Hugh Dalton,* 503–4 (entry dated mid-February 1951).

96. Kenneth Younger diary, 25 Feb. 1951, Kenneth Younger MSS.

97. Barclay, *Ernest Bevin and the Foreign Office,* 51.

98. Alan Bullock, *Ernest Bevin: Foreign Secretary* (New York, 1983), 832–35.

99. *The Times,* 5 Nov. 1953. I am extremely grateful to Dr. Ann Lane of the historical branch of the Foreign and Commonwealth Office for this reference.

100. Christopher Mayhew diary, 15 Dec. 1948.

101. R. H. S. Crossman, Michael Foot, and Ian Mikardo, *Keep Left* (London, 1947), 46–47; Jonathan Scheer, *Labour's Conscience* (Boston, 1988), especially chaps. 2–3.

102. John Saville, "Ernest Bevin and the Cold War, 1945–1950," in *The Socialist Register 1984,* ed. Ralph Miliband, John Saville and Marcel Liebman, 68–100. The quotations are from 90, 92.

103. Unsigned minute, 10 Sept. 1945, PRO FO 371/45252/E6806.

104. Kenneth Younger diary, 9 Jan. 1951, Kenneth Younger MSS.

5

THE MORALIST AS PRAGMATIST:

JOHN FOSTER DULLES AS COLD WAR STRATEGIST

Richard D. Challener

FOR THE HISTORIAN writing in the last decade of the twentieth century, John Foster Dulles has become an anachronism. Though its wake is turbulent, the Cold War is over, and the name of Dwight Eisenhower's secretary of state conjures up unpleasant memories of the years of virulent Soviet-American confrontation, a time when world politics was a zero-sum game, with Soviet gains measured in terms of American losses. Dulles was the American spokesman for the conventional wisdom of the Cold War in its most frozen moments in the 1950s—the stern Presbyterian who thundered endlessly about the evils of atheistic communism, exhorted the West to defend its moral values against the Soviet onslaught, and preached the doctrine of massive retaliation as the remedy for alleged Soviet and Chinese expansionism. As one of the president's press secretaries remembered, "Dulles was a tough old boy. . . . He was a Roundhead, a Puritan, and I'm quite sure that in the Cromwell era his ancestors were chopping down the Cavaliers in the name of their religious beliefs."[1] Irreverent members of the Washington press corps labeled him a "card-carrying Christian."

John Foster Dulles, both because of Eisenhower's "hidden hand" style of leadership and the force of his own personality, dominated the foreign policy headlines throughout most of the 1950s. It was Dulles who seemed to be the engine of American foreign policy, the secretary to whom a largely disengaged president had delegated responsibility. But the passage of time and the opening of the Eisenhower papers in Abilene have radically altered that impression. Historians now recognize that Dwight Eisenhower governed as well as reigned and was fully involved in all major foreign policy decisions. Foreign policy was shared policy, the product of an evolving and close collaboration between two men with similar values and perceptions. Moreover, it is clear that Dulles, with the possible exception of the Japanese Peace Treaty, left no creative legacy like the imaginative plan of Secretary George Marshall, and that, although he wrote two books during his career, as well as countless articles, and delivered hundreds of speeches, historians will hardly regard him as a foreign policy theorist whose writings are to be compared with those of George F. Kennan or Henry Kissinger.

The record is, however, far from being entirely negative. As the stream of declassified official documents and policy papers of the Eisenhower years widens, Dulles is increasingly revealed as a much more complex and sophisticated secretary than his many detractors once imagined. The one-dimensional Roundhead is a caricature. A conference held in February 1988 to celebrate the hundredth anniversary of his birth produced papers, and eventually a book, that clearly demonstrated that, despite his fulminations against "neutralism," Dulles could embrace it when it seemed in the American interest, as he did in the case of the Austrian State Treaty in 1955, and that he was far more open to the idea of meaningful negotiations and agreements with the Soviet Union, provided they were closely monitored, than his public speeches ever suggested.[2] John Gaddis, who showed that the four decades after World War II are better described as the Long Peace than the Cold War, has argued that the secretary of state gradually developed a measured, judicious concept about the actual employment of atomic weapons, even at a time when, in his public posture, he advocated massive retaliation. Indeed—to use Gaddis's terminology —he practiced "self-deterrence" even when the Soviet Union, with no credible nuclear force, was extremely vulnerable. Moreover, Gaddis and others have argued that, instead of founding his policy upon an unshakable belief in a monolithic Sino-Soviet bloc, the secretary developed a complex strategy of pressure—the "wedge theory"—designed to exploit, if possible, the differences between mainland China and the Soviet Union and, over time, to separate Beijing from Moscow.[3]

I

John Foster Dulles, son of a Presbyterian minister, was born in Watertown, New York, a small and remote town near the Canadian border at the eastern edge of Lake Ontario. Valedictorian of the Class of 1908 at Princeton, he studied philosophy for a year in Paris (particularly the writings of Henri Bergson, although not very rigorously), and then entered the law school of George Washington University.[4] In 1911 he began his long career as a Wall Street lawyer with the prestigious and internationally minded law firm of Sullivan and Cromwell. The grandson of one secretary of state, John Foster, who had served the last eight months of President Benjamin Harrison's administration, and the nephew of Robert Lansing, who was Woodrow Wilson's secretary from 1915 to 1920, Dulles first came to Washington—at Lansing's request—during the First World War and, as a major in the Army, was posted to the War Trade Board. This position—which involved liaison and coordination functions with the War Industries Board and the General Staff—led in 1919 to his appointment to the

American delegation to the Paris Peace Conference as counsel on reparations matters, in which capacity he helped formulate the United States position, defended it in discussions with other governments, and, once the principles had been agreed upon, helped draft the reparations sections of the Versailles Treaty. When the treaty was signed, he remained in Paris at the president's request to work out the reparations and financial aspects of the treaties with Austria, Hungary and Bulgaria and subsequently participated in the first negotiations with the Germans concerning deliveries of shipping and coal and was the American member of the Inter-Allied Commission that established political authority in the areas of occupation. These were all experiences that influenced his European policy thirty-five years later.

The years that followed were devoted to the law, and in 1921, at the age of thirty-two, Dulles became partner in Sullivan and Cromwell, rising to senior partner five years later. He continued his interest in foreign affairs and gradually developed some reputation as a speaker and writer on the troubled issues of German reparations and allied war debts. The Great Depression, the rise of aggressive totalitarianism in its wake, and the disintegration of the system of collective security alarmed and engaged him, and, as the thirties advanced, he became gradually convinced that the Protestant churches might provide the dynamic to preserve world peace. After the onset of the European war in 1939, he began to devote increasing amounts of time and energy to their international activities and in early 1941 accepted the chairmanship of the Commission on a Just and Durable Peace, a blue-ribbon group established by the Federal Council of the Churches of Christ in America to establish the foundations of a new and liberal world order once the fighting in Europe had terminated.

Meanwhile, his political connections had flourished. A committed Republican, he had, as early as 1940, emerged as the principal foreign policy adviser to presidential aspirant Thomas E. Dewey, and in 1944 he helped write the foreign policy plank of the Republican's campaign platform and served as Dewey's liaison with the Department of State. An adviser to the United States delegation at the San Francisco Conference that founded the United Nations in 1945, Dulles, with Senator Arthur H. Vandenberg of Michigan, became one of the prime architects of the bipartisan postwar foreign policy,[5] his first direct participation in the foreign policy process occurring when he was named an American delegate to the first session of the UN General Assembly. Similar assignments followed: he served, for example, as a Republican adviser to Secretaries Byrnes and Marshall at the meetings of the Council of Foreign Ministers that took place between 1947 and 1949.

It was during these years that the problem of the Soviet Union became one of Dulles's major preoccupations, although he was slow to become a cold warrior. During the war, he had been as optimistic as Franklin D. Roosevelt about the possibility of continuing cooperation with the Soviets; afterward he was even inclined for a time to blame the disappointment of that hope on the American people. The trouble, he told an audience at the Princeton University bicentennial in 1946, was that Americans had lost their dynamic faith in the great American experiment that had once moved them and were, unfortunately, in no mood to make the UN into an agency of great purpose in the world. "We have lost our sense of purpose and our capacity to inspire and uplift"; in consequence American foreign policy had become ineffective, "impotent to breathe life into the UN."[6] Later in the same year he interpreted the challenge of communism "not as a measure of the capacity of the Soviet government but of the inadequacy of the West," which, as he endlessly insisted, had lost its faith and dynamism. Finding a fellow believer in the historian Arnold J. Toynbee, he became enamored of Toynbee's claim that the failure of Western civilization arose from the fact that it "has been living on its spiritual capital . . . clinging to Christian practice without possessing the Christian belief."[7]

His evolving views about the Soviet Union continued to be ambivalent. After his first attendance at the London foreign ministers meeting of September 1945, he strongly endorsed Secretary of State James F. Byrnes's refusal to yield on principle to the Soviets,[8] but he could also state that the Russians had every reason to challenge the American position and that "it was probably a good thing that it happened."[9] He initially excused the Soviet exercise of the veto in the UN as "natural," and frequently observed that wartime alliances inevitably fall apart and that great power tensions were, unfortunately, the norm of international relations. Perhaps, he speculated at a meeting of the Federal Council in March 1946, the negative behavior of the Soviets was a result of the misery caused by the war. Perhaps the Kremlin had erected barriers so that the Russian people would not know "that other peoples were so much better off than they were." There followed the Toynbeesque conclusion: the Soviet challenge should stimulate and not paralyze the search for peace.[10]

During the war, Dulles had become one of the favorite writers of Henry R. Luce, a fellow Republican and publisher of both *Time* and *Life* magazines, and it was for Luce that he wrote his first major article warning of the threat of Soviet expansionism. "Thoughts on Soviet Foreign Policy and What To Do About It" appeared as a two-part sequence in *Life* in June 1946 (with a later condensation in that most simplistic and widely read of journals, *The Reader's Digest*). Dulles's message was, at best, ambivalent. There were stern warnings: the Soviets fomented class hatred and sponsored global violence; the Soviet Union was a nation that relied on coercion; "the personal freedoms which they would take away constitute our most cherished political and religious heritage." There was a recommendation: "So long as Soviet policy seeks its own security by achieving a *Pax Sovietica*, the United States must resist all expansionist manifestations of Soviet policy." But the article was not yet a Cold War call to arms. Dulles's opening statement posited: "The most urgent task of American statesmanship is to find policies which will avert a serious clash with the Soviet Union." Stalin was a cautious realist—he "has pulled back and relieved the tension when unexpected resistance was encountered." Indeed, Dulles came close to the conclusion that the Soviets were opportunistic and would, in fact, respond rationally to external constraints. Ideological differences still did not figure prominently in his analysis, and he ended his article with a section that stressed what the UN could do to prevent "the violent clash we apprehend."[11]

To religious audiences, he preached a similar message. In confronting the Soviet challenge, Christians must never "surrender or compromise their faith," but they should understand that the existence of conflicting beliefs was natural, that change was not evil in itself, and that neither socialism nor free enterprise provided a perfect economic system.[12] Included in a carefully prepared statement on Russian-American relations for the Federal Council of Churches was the sentence: "The United States should set an example by renouncing the acquisition of new military bases so far distant from the continental United States and so close to the Soviet Union that the offensive threat is disproportionate to their defensive value to the United States and also incompatible with a policy designed to dissipate distrust and increase good will."[13]

Throughout these years he was slowly refining—and hardening—his position on the Soviet Union. What emerged was an ever-increasing emphasis upon the moral and religious differences between the Soviet Union and the West. In a lengthy statement prepared for presentation at the first meeting of the World Council of Churches in Amsterdam, he wrote with his characteristic bluntness: "In its foreign policy the Soviet Union shows its adherence to the theory that the ends which it seeks can only be achieved through violent means."[14] At Amsterdam he insisted upon a basic difference between the communist and Christian creeds: "Marxian communism is atheistic and materialistic. Its leaders reject the concept of moral law." According to Stalin, laws are merely the means whereby those in power carry out their will, and human beings have no rights which are God-given and therefore not subject to be taken away by man." At the same time, while arguing that the intellectual breach was complete, Dulles backed off from the ultimate implications of his critique. The Christian response must be by peaceful means; there should be no "holy war" against communism. "The danger is that those who face the Soviet challenge will feel that they must defend themselves on every count."[15]

In early 1951, President Truman—despite the harsh attacks that Dulles had levied on the Democrats in his unsuccessful attempt to win election as a Senator from New York the previous year—asked him to take over the long dormant negotiations for a peace treaty with Japan. It was by no means an easy assignment, involving far more than simply persuading Japan's former enemies of the international importance of "restoring Japan to a place in the society of nations." Dulles had to establish a relationship of confidence and cooperation with the Japanese government of Yoshida Shigeru, while at the same time persuading other governments, like that of the Philippines, that Japan was incapable of paying reparations; Australia and New Zealand were anxious about a possible recovery of Japanese military power; many East Asian countries wanted to place restrictions upon Japanese trade; and many also, with their suspicions of Western imperialism, balked at entering security relations with the United States.[16]

His approach reflected both Dulleses, the man who remembered the Versailles experience, and the evolving cold warrior. On the one hand, he was convinced that Japan must not be humiliated as Germany had been in 1919; it must not suffer the kind of economic disadvantages that had been imposed upon the Weimar Republic; and the peace must be—his favorite phrase from the war years—"creative and curative." Versailles was the model to avoid; Japan must be restored as a sovereign equal among nations.[17]

But at the same time, there was a clear Cold War purpose. Japan, like Germany, was a principal target of international communism. MacArthur's occupation, whatever its successes, had run its course. The United States, if it were to prolong it, would appear "as a jailer," and Japan would become ripe for communist exploitation. No less important, particularly since the Korean War had begun in the early stages of the negotiations, was the "security chain" that ran from Australia and New Zealand through Okinawa and Japan. This made it necessary to supplement the treaty with a series of security pacts, ranging from ANZUS to a separate U.S.-Japan security treaty (under which the Japanese "freely consented" to accept the stationing of American troops on Japanese soil). But Dulles insisted that, while remaining disarmed, Japan still had "a duty . . . to participate in the collective security planning of the free world." In the Cold War, everyone had to participate. "Today," Dulles sternly warned a Tokyo audience, "no nation has a right to refuse to make a contribution to collective security, and no nation has the right so to expose itself so that it can be seized, exploited and used as a weapon against its neighbor."[18]

During the early postwar years, as previously noted, Dulles remained primarily a Europeanist. But, with the collapse of Nationalist China, even while still working with the Democratic administration, he began to emerge as a severe critic of President Truman's ill-fated China policy. In January of 1950, for example, he cited for the first but by no means the last time Stalin's alleged dictum that "the road to victory in the West lies through revolutionary alliance with the liberation movement in the colonies and dependent countries."[19] The United States had "no policies or strategies to cope with the continuing encirclement from the East." And, a chronic Republican complaint of the day: "The Administration never did invite Republican participation" in attempts to devise them.[20]

These criticisms were muted, to be sure, by his involvement in the Japanese peace treaty negotiations and by Truman's response to the North Korean attack. But for Dulles the Korean War was fundamental in changing his views about the nature of the Soviet threat. (He was, of course, not alone, as witness the almost universal acceptance of NSC-68 with its call for massive rearmament to meet threats in any part of the globe.) Before June 1950, he had generally taken the view that the Soviet Union would not risk general war but rely primarily upon a strategy of civil war, coercion, sabotage, and terrorism to secure its malevolent ends. But the Korean War—instigated, he never doubted for a moment, by the Soviets—invalidated his previous assumptions. The Soviets, he now concluded, never forgot the importance of Asia and were quite willing to practice war there. Mao, in his blunt judgment, was "simply a creature of the Politburo."[21] Thus, with Korea and the Chinese intervention, the communist monolith became reality.

Immediately after the completion of the Japanese treaty, Dulles broke off all official ties with the Democratic administration and, positioning himself for the 1952 presidential campaign, began to write highly critical articles and strongly worded speeches that not only condemned Truman and Acheson for the "loss" of China but also castigated the policy of containment as "sterile" and "negative," dooming the United States to unsuccessful responses to Soviet aggressions. In the great political struggle in the Republican party between its Eastern liberal wing and the more conservative followers of Ohio Senator Robert Taft, Dulles unhesitatingly cast his lot with Dwight Eisenhower. During the ensuing campaign he soon emerged not only as the strident critic—whose overblown rhetoric promised, along with the "liberation" of subject peoples and the "unleashing" of Chiang Kai-shek, the restoration of initiative to American foreign policy—but also as Eisenhower's probable choice as secretary of state. Three weeks after his victory over Adlai E. Stevenson, the president-elect did name him to the position, thus beginning a tenure that lasted a little more than six years, until shortly before his death on 24 May 1959. He was, on the basis of his record, probably the best prepared of any individual in this century to hold the office he had, indeed, long sought.

II

During his first forty months in office Dulles delivered fifty-four speeches and held sixty-nine press conferences—media events that covered every phase of American foreign policy. There was, incidentally, only one significant article, his famous piece in *Foreign Affairs,* which attempted to spell out the meaning of massive retaliation, and even this was largely an attempt to correct the many misapprehensions that had arisen as a result of his earlier speech before the Council on Foreign Relations.

Dulles used his radio addresses and television appearances for many purposes over and above simply informing the public about major policy decisions and providing reports on developments on the international scene. One was to transmit signals to the leaders, especially the communist leaders, of other countries. One of his notable warnings to the Chinese Communists about pursuing further aggression was inserted in an otherwise routine speech to the American Federation of Labor in September 1953.[22] And, at least in the eyes of the secretary, it was an effective technique. In the aftermath of the Geneva Conference of 1954, John M. Allison, the ambassador in Tokyo, asked for guidance about American intentions. Dulles answered that the leaders of world communism read his speeches, followed his press conferences, and, as a consequence, had no doubts about the American response.[23]

More importantly, he firmly believed that his predecessor, Dean Acheson, had been gravely hampered by congressional opposition and lack of public support. Thus, Dulles's hard-line anticommunist speeches, for example, served the purpose of defusing the Republican right, especially those senators whose passion had long been the cause of Chiang Kai-shek. Indeed, building support with Senate conservatives was, from the beginning of his term in office, a major objective. Many Americans—not only Senator Joseph R. McCarthy— believed that Russian and Chinese communist successes were the result of subversives in the Department of State. Determined to demonstrate that there would be no Alger Hisses in the department during his watch, Dulles alienated many Foreign Service officers by demanding what he called "positive loyalty." Moreover, while he personally opposed McCarthy, he more than tolerated the introduction of McCarthyism into State Department personnel policy. Indeed, Dulles took home and read the dossier of every Foreign Service officer accused of disloyalty but, perhaps not surprisingly, never found any of them suitable for further employment.[24]

That there was a price to pay for this goes without saying—not only the loss of those members of the Foreign Service who were most experienced in Far Eastern affairs, the so-called China Hands, but the confidence of the service in general and of the professionals in the Department of State. Dulles accepted this, if not with indifference, at least with equanimity. He preferred in any case to work around the professional diplomats and to manage the conduct of foreign affairs with a small circle of trusted advisers, which included the distinguished San Francisco lawyer Herman Phleger, the tough-minded Harvard professor Robert R. Bowie, who headed the Policy Planning Staff and had the task of playing devil's advocate to Dulles, and Douglas Dillon, initially ambassador to France, who became an intimate confidant and was given unchallenged direction of foreign economic policy. In major diplomatic crises, Dulles also relied upon the skills of three men chosen personally by the president from his military staffs—Walter Bedell Smith, under secretary of state; Robert D. Murphy, deputy under secretary for political affairs; and Douglas MacArthur II, counselor—although they did not play key roles in policy-making.

Dulles firmly believed—again the Acheson example—that his foreign policy could not succeed without the support of the American people. The bitter debates over foreign policy (which, to be sure, he helped to foment) that had marked Truman's last years in office must be ended. America must speak with one voice. His many speeches to the American public also had this goal in mind. Dulles, at the same time, tended to believe that the American people could be all too easily tempted to let down their guard, to be seduced, for example, by the prospect of a summit conference. Hence it was always important, in addressing the public, to stress the ideological, moral, and spiritual differences that separated the free world from the communist one. His speeches were often classic examples of American exceptionalism, in which he emphasized core American values and the American mission as the city set upon the hill. To be successful in the great struggle against atheistic communism, the American people must, Dulles preached time after time, renew their dynamic faith in their democratic heritage and free institutions.

Even as secretary of state, he wrote his own speeches. "I don't recall," one of his close associates later remembered, "the Secretary ever having made a speech that he had not done, if not all, at least overwhelmingly most of the work on." Most speeches, invariably timed for thirty minutes, went through numerous drafts—ten, twelve, even more—and, on each the secretary spent at least twelve to fifteen hours. It was not a chore but a task he welcomed. "It is," he said once, "the only thing that forces me to think through each of these problems. Because in order to write a speech about it, you must think it through."[25] On occasion, to be sure, a staff member might be asked to compose "a sort of composite rough draft incorporating the views of the regional bureaus." But, while this was going on, the secretary was composing his own version, which, inevitably, he preferred. As one disillusioned assistant remembered it, "The truth, as I came to know it, was that the great Cold Warrior did not care for anyone who tried to put words in his mouth. . . . Once I knocked out his favorite word 'moral' nine times, and he put it back eight times."[26]

But if the final text, as delivered, was the work of the secretary, it had always been reviewed by many people both within and without the Department of State. As one in-house memo put it, "Comments from Mr. Dodge, Mr. Hollister, Mr. MacArthur, and Mr. Allen have been correlated with the text of your draft. Additional copies of your speech have been sent to Mr. Allen Dulles, Mr. Hoover, and Mr. McCardle, who have not yet had the opportunity to set forth their views in writing."[27] And the reviewers could sometimes be blunt. Gerard C. Smith, then special assistant to the Secretary of State for atomic affairs, once wrote, "The draft gives a net negative impression of the Summit and carries a heavy burden of 'moralizing' which has caused criticism from certain quarters in the past and which may obscure the important additional matters of substance."[28]

More importantly, Dulles and Eisenhower regularly exchanged copies of each other's major speeches and commented, in detail, upon matters of substance as well as style. The secretary always took great care to make certain that Eisenhower concurred with his major statements of policy. For example, before delivering a September 1953 speech warning the Chinese Communists against further aggression, he telegraphed the key sentences to Eisenhower, accompanying them with a note that he wanted to be sure that the president knew precisely what he intended to say and agreed with him.[29]

Finally, Dulles showed real skill in drawing at least certain members of the press corps into his corner. With some regularity, he held "backgrounders," informal meetings, often over drinks and dinner, with a small and select group of correspondents, men whom he trusted and with whom he was on close personal terms. On these occasions, participants have recollected, Dulles was frank and open, although he spoke "not for attribution." It was a successful device to reach such leaders of the Washington press corps as James B. Reston of the *New York Times,* Richard L. Harkness of NBC News, Peter Lisagor of the *Chicago Daily News,* John Robinson Beal of *Time-Life,* and James Russell Wiggins of the *Washington Post.*

Much of what Dulles had proclaimed in his strident campaign speeches can, naturally, be dismissed as rhetoric, part of the process of wooing the American voter with the prospect of change. But, even before he assumed office, he had a blueprint, a grand strategy for the United States to pursue in countering what he believed was Soviet aggression. It followed closely from his previous positions. On board the cruiser *Helena*, when Eisenhower was returning from his preinaugural and highly publicized trip to Korea, Dulles presented the president-elect with a number of propositions.[30] According to his analysis, the Soviet Union was pursuing its own strategy of trying to exhaust the United States by mounting a series of aggressive moves throughout the entire world at times and places of its own choosing. Moreover, it was targeting locations such as Korea and Indochina, where any American response came at high cost. The attempt to counter each and every aggression would be prohibitive, an absolutely unacceptable drain on American resources.

As Dulles saw it, under the Truman administration's policy of containment the United States had fought by the rules of the Marquess of Queensbury, even when the Soviets ignored them. The time had come for the United States to adopt bold, new policies, designed to match the Soviets at their own game. America should foment discord and unrest behind the Iron Curtain. It should seize the initiative in those particular areas of the world in which the United States itself held a commanding position. Thus, the "weak flanks" in Korea and Indochina could be secured by assembling "deterrent power" in the center directed at Communist China. It was important to act decisively and immediately. The communists expected conservative Republicans to be tougher than the more liberal Democrats they had just succeeded. If the Republicans merely continued the old policy of containment, then the Soviets would unquestionably expand the limits of what they felt they could get away with. Moreover, Dulles went on, with his penchant for painting worst possible scenarios, America's allies would lose their will to resist and "something akin to panic and complete disorder . . . may ensue." He conceded that there were dangers in his recommendations. But the possible costs were less than the risks of perpetuating the Truman-Acheson approach. To continue the failed policy of containment "means certain disaster."

In the spring of 1954, after the new administration had been in office for a little more than a year, the secretary of state produced a more reasoned memorandum that summarized his overall plan for countering "the aggressive strategy and techniques of Soviet communism."[31] There were four general objectives: first, the policy, in the contemporary shorthand, of "massive retaliation." The United States would deter "open and armed aggression by the capacity and willingness to retaliate at places and by means of our own choosing so that the aggressor would be hurt more than he could gain." Second, the United States must restore the strength of the West "by closing the Franco-German breach that has for a century caused the West to war with itself and expend its vigor in internecine strife." Third, the United States must find creative ways to exploit the internal contradictions within the Soviet sphere and promote the spirit of nationalism in Europe. The goal was to distract "the Soviet Communist rulers from indirect aggression by compounding their internal difficulties." Fourth, at the ideological level, the administration must take the lead in "vitalizing liberty and freedom within the free world so that it becomes a dynamic force countering the revolutionary spirit with which Communism imbues its followers."

These two papers summarize concisely the way in which the secretary conceptualized the Soviet problem and the broad outlines of his grand strategy to combat it.

Then and later, many people wondered if the secretary of state who made such recommendations was the same person who had in the 1930s been a strong advocate of "peaceful change," who had served later as passionate supporter of the UN, and who had been among the first to raise moral questions about the use of the atomic bomb at Hiroshima. On one occasion in the mid-fifties, Dulles was invited to speak at a meeting of the Federal Council of Churches. The delegates were about to endorse a resolution in favor of American diplomatic recognition of Communist China. Dulles flew in, delivered a strong speech against recognition, and flew immediately back to Washington. The delegates endorsed the resolution by a wide margin, many of them—especially those who had worked with him during World War II—doubtless wondering what had caused the change.[32]

That the change was real is clear enough. Dulles's involvement in international affairs as a delegate to UN meetings and as Republican adviser to the Truman administration, his increasing visibility as the Republican heir-apparent to the secretaryship of state, and his religious convictions—especially his firm belief that communism denied individual liberty and thus violated one of God's moral principles—all played their part in it. Even so, as his term as secretary would show, there were also many continuities. He had been and would remain strongly anticolonial. His belief that the historic rivalry between France and Germany was the root cause of recurrent warfare had been one of the reasons why, in the 1930s, he had opposed American involvement in another world conflict. His remedy—European unity—had long been an objective. Ever an American exceptionalist, he had always—as his brief flirtation with Clarence Streit's Union Now movement in the 1930s demonstrated—proclaimed the American federal system as an exemplar to the world. His public speeches had always proclaimed Christian and moral values; indeed, his moral objections to Soviet communism are not logically unrelated to his earlier criticisms of the churches for deifying the nation. Longstanding, too, was his conviction—nurtured by his earlier studies of Bergson and his understanding of Toynbee—that some nations are more dynamic and possess a stronger national purpose than others. Now, instead of Hitler's Germany, it was the Soviet Union, propelled "by the revolutionary spirit with which Communism imbues its followers" that possessed that dynamism. Whether writing about war and peace in the thirties, prodding the American people to accept internationalism in World War II, or developing a strategy to counter communism, Dulles always proclaimed that the dynamic was superior to the static and that America must rekindle a dynamic faith in its democratic principles.

III

The first of his policy prescriptions, and the one with which Dulles is most commonly associated, is "massive retaliation." This doctrine (Dulles preferred the clumsier but more accurate term massive retaliatory power) was intended to achieve multiple goals. Along with the New Look—the Eisenhower military posture that involved significant reductions in ground forces and increased emphasis on the Strategic Air Command (SAC) and the atomic bomb—it met a domestic objective of great importance to the fiscal conservatives who came into office in 1953. The recommendations of NSC-68—massive rearmament founded upon Keynesian assumptions that an ever-expanding economy could support both more guns and more social services—had made Republicans predict national bankruptcy. With massive retaliation and the New Look, the Holy Grail of fiscal Republicanism—the balanced budget—appeared to be achievable. Eisenhower (and Dulles, no less) always worried that excessive military expenditures—with their concomitant creation of what Eisenhower, in his valedictory address, would call the "military-industrial complex"—carried with them a threat to basic American institutions. They might, the president warned, lead to "the garrison state."[33]

Second, massive retaliation promised a magical technological solution to the problem of war by attrition, to the argument that the United States could not afford the attempt to match the Soviets or Chinese man for man in land warfare, where basic demography gave them overwhelming advantages. With its reliance upon SAC and the atomic bomb, massive retaliation would prevent America from being "nibbled to death" in future Koreas.

Above all, retaliation at places and by means of America's own choosing would restore American initiative as well as solve the problem of war by miscalculation. A potential enemy would be kept off balance and deterred by his realization that the United States could retaliate in ways that would maximize his own suffering. In theory, massive retaliation would minimize both costs and risks, since the United States would be relying upon those weapons of coercion in which it was supreme and because the enemy would understand the certainty of an American response.

Underlying the Dulles approach to international relations was the belief that war usually does not occur as a result of premeditation or clear intent but as a consequence of miscalculation by one side or the other. Despite the impact of Korea on his analysis of Soviet intentions, it is highly unlikely that the secretary of state really feared that the Soviet Union, whatever its capabilities, would embark upon war with the United States as a deliberate act. "War," he once advised the National Security Council, "is not inevitable. The greatest danger of war comes from miscalculation by our enemies as to our intentions if they aggress further."[34] He frequently used a few specific (and highly questionable) historical examples to "prove" his case: there would have been no European war in August 1914 if Sir Edward Grey had made clear Britain's determination to defend Belgium; no war in 1939 if FDR had made it clear to Hitler that the United States would provide material assistance to the Allies; and—a point much labored by Republican orators—no war in Korea if Dean Acheson had not told the National Press Club that South Korea lay beyond the American defense perimeter in East Asia.

Consequently, he developed what can best be termed the "certainty/ uncertainty" principle—the idea that both the Soviets and the Chinese communists must be made certain that the United States would respond to aggression, but they must also be kept in a state of uncertainty about the means to be employed, and the time, and even the place, of their employment. A transcript of a discussion during the first Quemoy-Matsu crisis states the essence of the principle: "Secretary Dulles outlined his theory of X and 2X—that any time the enemy wished to attain X we would exact a cost of 2X from him."[35] To Ambassador John M. Allison, seeking policy guidance after the 1954 Geneva Conference, Dulles began, at the theoretical level, with his familiar argument that the potential aggressor must know that he cannot prescribe the combat situations that suit him. Then, with specific reference to the post-Geneva situation, he stated that the United States had no intention of dispatching major military force to Southeast Asia, and, in fact, was planning to redeploy some of its troops from Korea. But at the same time—by permitting the Navy to patrol the offshore islands of Quemoy and Matsu and by sending patrol planes over the China coast—the United States was clearly demonstrating to the Chinese Communists that the United States had both the power to retaliate and the will to do so. His clear intent, he emphasized, was to impress upon the Chinese that "we are 'willing and able' to make the aggressor suffer at times and places of our own choosing, i.e., where our sea and air power are predominant." And, tying theory to practice, he argued that what was going on off the coast of China was an attempt to prevent war by miscalculation, and he prophesied that its success would deter further aggression in eastern Asia.[36]

An essential element of the secretary's certainty/uncertainty principle and of the idea of avoiding war by miscalculation was his attempt to articulate certain positions and establish certain lines that would make it clear to a potential enemy that any transgression of them would trigger an American response. During the 1954 Dienbienphu crisis, for example, Dulles declared that there was much value in drawing a line and saying no farther. Such a tactic, he went on, gave an opponent an opportunity to back off, to stay his hand, to reconsider. Further, it maximized the opportunity to rally allies to your own position.[37] The same logic informed his two successful attempts—with respect to Formosa and the Middle East—to secure congressional resolutions that would bind the legislature in advance to support whatever response the administration adopted to meet future communist threats in those areas. Both were intended to make it clear, without shadow of doubt, that the United States Congress backed the administration and that, unlike the situation in the Truman years, the executive and legislative branches spoke with one voice. The certainty of response would be established in the calculations of Moscow and Beijing.

Dulles, moreover, always emphasized, both in public and in private, the importance of will and determination. The nuclear deterrent simply would not work if the American people lacked the will to employ it. During a 1957 debate over military options for NATO, he burst out, "The real deterrent is not the divisions in Korea but the fact that we would, within minutes, wipe out the industrial complex of Manchuria if Korea were attacked. . . . The problem is not one of thinking through what . . . we would do under various hypothetical situations. We can have all the NSC position papers in the world, and they will persuade no one. What our allies want to know is the state of our will, of our determination."[38] Even when the Soviets had achieved their own nuclear deterrent, he emphasized the point in a speech to the National War College: "We must be able to deter . . . by retaliatory striking power, not merely the possession of that power but the will to use it. If there was a feeling on the part of the Communist rulers that even though we had the power we did not have the will to use it, or if our allies in other Free World countries felt that we had not the will to use it, then the mere possession of power would itself not operate as a deterrent. . . . It is essential to have the two elements to have an effective deterrent."[39] As McGeorge Bundy has noted, writing about Dulles and atomic weapons, "He had no irresponsible desire for their instant use, but he wanted nothing to inhibit the *threat* of such use."[40]

It followed that the public must be educated about the nuclear deterrent. After a discussion with the president in 1955, Dulles confided in a memorandum: "We reviewed the importance of education with respect to distinction between atomic missiles for tactical purposes and the big bomb with huge radio-active fallouts. . . . We went over the draft of my proposed talk and we discussed whether or not to make in it reference to atomic missiles. The president thought it might usefully be done in an incidental way."[41] Three days later, during the NSC discussion of the offshore islands crisis, the secretary made the same point: "Determination must be made whether in such defense atomic weapons will be used. . . . U.S. and world opinion must be prepared."[42]

On no less than three occasions, both Dulles and Eisenhower believed that the certainty/uncertainty principle had worked: the North Koreans and Communist Chinese had agreed to a Korean truce because of the veiled atomic threat that the war would be extended into Manchuria; and China had been deterred from intervening directly in Indochina in 1954 and from moving against Quemoy and Matsu.[43] Skeptical historians and deterrence theorists have expressed doubts that the atomic threat, whether veiled or explicit, was the catalyst in these cases, raising questions about the extent to which it really was Eisenhower's skillful manipulation of the conventional instruments of coercion in the second Quemoy-Matsu affair that defused the crisis;[44] and whether the Chinese were actually deterred at all. Chinese scholars have indeed suggested that the Communists may never have intended to seize the islands but, being themselves fearful of an American attack on the mainland, made their own threats to deter America.[45] Only one thing is clear about these cases: the documentation is still insufficient and the variables too plentiful to enable one to say with certainty much more than that the threats may have had some influence.

The Eisenhower administration, we now know from newly released documents, backed off from the logical implications of its stated policy of massive retaliation. Even when America's nuclear superiority was unquestioned, both the president and the secretary sensed the practical and moral dilemmas involved in its use. And it was more than just the lack of suitable targets. They came to understand that there were many potential confrontations in which nuclear weapons would be inappropriate. "We cannot," Dulles said in March 1955, "splurge our limited supply of nuclear weapons, without serious danger to the balance of power"—a statement that implied that they were instruments of general war and not for local aggressions.[46] But, in addition, there was sensitivity to the political repercussions that the use of the atomic bomb might produce. During the Dienbienphu crisis of 1954, which occurred in the midst of Dulles's prolonged efforts to secure French passage of his cherished European defense treaties, the secretary expressed the hope that nuclear weapons would not have to be employed in Southeast Asia. Given European sensitivities about the bomb, the political fallout of their real or suggested use might prevent ratification of the treaties.[47] More important, in the light of Hiroshima and Nagasaki, he and Eisenhower sensed the moral dilemma involved in dropping an atomic weapon upon another Asian nation. As Dulles noted during the first

Quemoy-Matsu crisis, the cause of Chiang Kai-shek would be damaged if an invasion of the mainland was preceded by American use of an atomic weapon.[48]

Both John Gaddis and McGeorge Bundy have written extensively about the Eisenhower administration and atomic weapons. The former has insisted that massive retaliation, as a policy, was "declaratory" rather than "actual," that the president and Dulles, in reality, practiced "self deterrence."[49] The latter emphasizes that the administration drew the line "between threat and action."[50] There were, to be sure, veiled atomic threats. Eisenhower and Dulles also believed that, in the event of all-out war, nuclear weapons would have to be employed, and the actual military plans of the Eisenhower years reflect that belief. And they were attracted to the potential of so-called tactical nuclear weapons, which would lessen the dangers of radiation and fallout. Still, on balance, the Gaddis/Bundy analysis holds. Massive retaliation was more declaratory than actual.

Moreover, any analysis of their views on the possible use of the atom indicates that it is inaccurate to think of a "tough" Dulles and a "soft" Eisenhower, with the former always the nuclear swordsman, the latter restraining his headstrong secretary. Rather, sometimes it was the secretary who was more cautious than the president. Neither was always consistent about considering the necessity to use the bomb or the dilemma it raised. Both can, in fact, be cited at many points on the spectrum.

IV

In the second Eisenhower administration—and especially after the Russians had launched *Sputnik* in 1957—there was mounting criticism that the New Look and massive retaliation had led to unbalanced forces. Critics charged the United States simply did not possess sufficient conventional military force to cope with challenges that were less than "massive." But Dulles himself, despite his emphasis upon massive retaliatory power, never totally neglected conventional forces. As early as December 1954, in a memorandum to the president, he expressed doubt that the Joint Chiefs and the Defense Department "were in reality planning to deal adequately with the possible 'little wars' which might call for punishment related to the degree and the locality of the offense but which would not justify massive retaliation against the Soviet Union."[51] After *Sputnik,* amidst the growing pressure to build more and better missiles, Dulles warned that such programs must not come at the expense of the conventional forces, which, he maintained, were essential to implement his policies.[52] Indeed, in Eisenhower's second term, the secretary became increasingly concerned about the so-called problem of "indirect aggression," which he defined as the fomenting of civil war in a country by a foreign power for its own ulterior motive.[53] The Lebanon crisis of July 1958 was to him a classic example of the problem and of the need to have conventional forces readily available to thwart indirect aggression.[54]

Throughout his term in office, Dulles seems to have been satisfied with the actual mix between American nuclear and conventional military power. Certainly, after *Sputnik,* he resented Democratic charges that the result of the New Look had been to create a situation in which, in any crisis, the only available option was "to go nuclear." But, at the same time, Dulles also appears to have relied upon the military wisdom of Eisenhower and to have trusted his judgment. His colleague Robert R. Bowie, for example, has long insisted that, when pressed to take a more active role in discussion of force levels, the secretary, deferring to Ike's views, declined to pick up the cudgels.[55] Dulles, moreover, had a strong sense of turf, as is shown by what happened both to Nelson Rockefeller and to Harold Stassen when they tried, unwisely, to insert themselves between him and Eisenhower in the policy-making process. Since he did not want the Joint Chiefs or the Defense Department infringing upon his diplomatic territory, he may well have believed it unwise for him to intervene too directly in theirs.

Nor did his understanding of the role of atomic weapons in national security policy remain static. As early as 1954—scarcely a year into the new administration —he realized that American supremacy in weapons and delivery systems would be relatively short-lived. Thus, sooner or later, the nuclear threat would lose much of its validity. By the time of Eisenhower's second term, he sensed that growing Soviet nuclear power was pointing in the direction of mutual deterrence. Both sides now understood that, in an all-out nuclear exchange, the level of destruction would be unacceptable.[56] General war, therefore, was much less likely. Still, with the development of Soviet missiles, he worried that the European allies might lose their will because they would come to believe that the United States, out of fear that its own cities would be incinerated, would not come to their defense. Indeed, in July 1958, when he met Charles de Gaulle, then developing his *force de frappe*, Dulles went to extraordinary lengths to try to convince the skeptical French leader that a separate French nuclear capacity was unnecessary since the United States could always be counted upon to defend France from attack.[57] Finally, after *Sputnik,* Dulles, if not in the forefront, was certainly one of the leaders in the administration in arguing that, while there was still time, there must be a thorough review of the totality of the American national security concept. It was, he informed Secretary of Defense Robert B. Anderson in 1958, "running into a dead end."[58]

But Dulles never completely abandoned the beliefs that he held so firmly in 1953. As late as April 1958, he was still busy exploring the possibility of tactical nuclear weapons—their role in creating an "effective defense . . . short of wholesale obliteration of the Soviet Union."[59] And while it might well have been only an example of his "declaratory" policy as well as his continued attempts to strengthen the will of an ally, he could still advise Prime Minister Harold Macmillan during the second Quemoy-Matsu crisis in 1958 that "there is also a question as to whether, if we did intervene, we could do so effectively without some use of atomic weapons; I hope no more than air bursts without fallout. That is of course an unpleasant prospect but one, I think, we must face up to because our entire military establishment assumes more and more that the use of nuclear weapons will become normal in the event of hostilities."[60] Then, when the president opted for caution, Dulles interjected, a bit plaintively, "But I thought we had acknowledged the risk of the political and psychological dangers of these weapons when we included them in our arsenals."[61]

Certainly, even after he had formally turned over the running of the Department of State to Christian Herter in the middle of April 1959, he clung to the conventional wisdom. The mounting crisis in Berlin produced one of his final theoretical statements: "There is a total failure to grasp or accept the whole concept of our deterring strategy. We can't rely on, whenever there is a threat, having to buy our way out by making concessions rather than standing firm and relying upon our nuclear power to keep the peace." Similarly, when Harold Macmillan and Selwyn Lloyd visited him in Walter Reed Hospital, he maintained his long-established views:

> I said that I quite disagreed with the Prime Minister's theory that, if we are threatened, we must negotiate, lest the public not support our being firm. I said that our present considerable strength is conceived as a deterrent to Communist imperialist aggression. It is a deterrent, and there is not going to be the war [over Berlin] of which the Prime Minister spoke. In being firm we have sometimes to take added risks, such as our sending troops to Lebanon and Jordan and holding Quemoy. But in that instance, I felt sure, our show of firmness and determination, coupled with our deterrent power, had avoided war.[62]

Dulles's grand strategy, this essay has stressed, placed great emphasis upon making potential aggressors certain about an American response but uncertain about its time, place, and means. But, in many ways, his approach created its own uncertainties, especially with the American public. In January 1954, Dulles made his most remembered speech on "massive retaliation" before that august body of the establishment, the Council on Foreign Relations.[63] The speech immediately raised fears that the administration, without consulting Congress or allies, was prepared to unleash the atom on slight provocation. The key sentence—written, ironically, not by Dulles but by Eisenhower—read: "The basic decision is to depend primarily upon a great capacity to retaliate instantly, by means and at places of our own choosing." The two words "instantly" and "primarily," as McGeorge Bundy has properly pointed out, raised questions and created uncertainty in the public mind about the administration's intentions.[64] Dulles attempted immediate damage control. The revised text of his January speech, which appeared in the April issue of the council's influential journal, *Foreign Affairs,* attempted to tidy up the language, emphasized that the crucial factor was to have the capacity for massive retaliation rather than the intent to employ it, and stressed that there were many circumstances in which thermonuclear power would not be appropriate.[65]

But it was the Quemoy-Matsu crisis of 1955 that best exemplified the inherent problems in the certainty/uncertainty principle. At issue in the resolution put before Congress were the circumstances under which the administration would use military force to defend both Taiwan and the off-shore islands. Moreover, Dulles and his advisers had—to use their own phrase—"fuzzed up" the text as a way to heighten communist uncertainty about how, where, and when the United States would respond to an attack. This in the interest of enhancing its deterrent force. But, an even more complicating problem was the fact that the administration doubted if the two islands were really defensible. There was resentment at Chiang for placing some of his best troops on Quemoy and Matsu, an attempt it was thought, to force the American hand. On the other hand, Dulles believed that the loss of the islands would have a devastating effect upon Nationalist morale. Consequently he and Eisenhower sought to walk a very fine line—to keep their options open so that they could intervene only if an attack upon Quemoy and Matsu appeared to be a clear prelude to an assault upon Taiwan itself.[66] But this, obviously, could not be communicated either to the Chinese or to the American public. The result was confusion. The "fuzzing up" transferred the problem of certainty/uncertainty to both the minds of the American and European peoples.[67] Indeed, any examination of the public records at this time demonstrates that, while the American people were prepared to accept the need to defend Taiwan, they were badly divided on the issue of defending the off-shore islands. Dulles, in this respect, was often his own worst enemy. Foreign policy, he knew, was complicated, and he doubted the ability of the general public to comprehend its subtleties. To get public attention, foreign policy must be made dramatic and simple, proclaimed in capsule phrases that would capture the headlines and the television audiences. In consequence, what are all too often remembered about the secretary are such simplistic phrases as "rollback," "liberation," "agonizing reappraisal," and, above all, "brink of war." To many discerning critics, Dulles appeared a simplifier, a reductionist who overdramatized.[68]

His problem was exemplified by a notorious article that appeared in *Life* in January 1956.[69] In a free-wheeling interview with three journalists, Dulles was attempting to define the essence of great-power confrontations and, especially, his conviction that, at a time of crisis, a leader cannot afford, in advance, to indicate that he will cave in or surrender. But the longer Dulles talked, the more he employed dramatic-sounding phrases to describe the three separate occasions when, in his view, the United States had been required to go to "the brink of war" to preserve peace. His graphic language—about how, for example,

President Eisenhower "came up taut"—plus the provocative editing that took place later in the offices of *Life* created the image that has, even four decades later, never totally disappeared, of John Foster Dulles as the brinksman who reveled in bringing the United States and the Soviet Union to the verge of nuclear Armageddon.

Dulles, in short, always had difficulty communicating to the public his ideas about how the certainty/uncertainty principle would actually work. Moreover, there was always a gap between his public speeches and what he wrote in private or official memoranda. While his public discourse was moralistic and his speeches all too often became sermons, his official memoranda were tightly written models of the legal brief, and often, indeed, relied on the value-free language of the social sciences. Anyone who compares a Dulles speech with a Dulles memorandum will be struck by the contrast in styles of language, depending upon the audience that is being addressed. And the gap sometimes extended to his dealings with foreign statesmen, most notably with Anthony Eden. Indeed, Eden once complained to Eisenhower that he simply could not comprehend what the secretary was driving at and was often left with the impression that Dulles thought he was "dumb." At the height of the Suez crisis, General Gruenther wrote the secretary a private letter in which he stated, directly and bluntly, that Dulles had failed to make the British and French understand what he really wanted to do about Nasser. "If I were one of your staff officers," Gruenther went on, "I would probably say something like this to you: 'Mr. Secretary, I don't know what it is that causes your approach to misfire on occasion, but certainly it does. I strongly recommend that at the earliest possible moment we have a private meeting of the three foreign ministers, or, better yet, the three heads of government to resolve what I think is a deteriorating situation.' "[70]

Dulles cannot, of course, be assessed simply on the basis of concepts of deterrence or the success or failure of what has been described here as the certainty/uncertainty principle. Certainly, he had been highly critical of containment, and he could find no position for its author, George F. Kennan, in a Dulles State Department. Yet, early in the new administration, the Solarium project, a thorough review of possible national security options—ranging from continuation of containment to the possibility of liberation—concluded that the only viable option was, in essence, an expanded version of the former.[71] Indeed, Kennan long remembered with satisfaction having presided over the White House session at which this conclusion was formally presented to the secretary.[72] Like most incoming administrations, the Eisenhower/Dulles team soon discovered that the windows of opportunity for radical change in American foreign policy were severely limited. Facing what Ronald Pruessen has labeled the "predicaments of power," the Eisenhower years are probably best remembered in terms of what they continued and extended from the Truman-Acheson legacy than for any radical departures.[73]

Certainly the dangers of "liberation" became apparent with the East German uprisings in June 1953, while doubts soon developed about the wisdom of "prodding the bear" through the presumed gaps in the Iron Curtain. The Hungarian experience in November 1956, when the United States was embarrassed by its failure to move when Soviet tanks crushed that revolution, effectively ended the idea of liberation of subject peoples. In public Dulles was a moralist; in practice, a pragmatist.[74]

V

Another policy objective that Dulles set forth in his 1954 memorandum had been to end the centuries of Franco-German rivalry. His experience at the Peace Conference of 1919 and on the reparations and Inter-Allied Commission on the occupied territories had given him rich experience in the relations between the two powers, and he was inclined to underestimate neither the political unreliability of the Germans nor the French fear of German strength. Like his predecessor as secretary of state, he hoped to win French confidence and to reduce the dangers of the "German question" by anchoring the new West German republic firmly within Europe. The key element in this plan was the European Defense Community (EDC), which would include West German troops, a matter of central importance for Pentagon planners. Dulles campaigned hard for the EDC, but the traumatic effect of the collapse of the French empire in Southeast Asia and of the great defeat of Dien Bien Phu in 1954, confronted the government of Pierre Mendès France with a French Assembly that was increasingly nervous about German rearmament; and, in the end—despite Dulles's threats of an "agonizing reappraisal" of American policy in Europe—Mendès was unable to win approval for EDC in the crucial Assembly vote in August 1954.

The crisis that followed, in which plans for the defense of Western Europe seemed to be in ruins, was not Dulles's finest hour. He had concentrated his efforts so exclusively—and so dogmatically—upon winning French approval for EDC that he had no alternative plan of action when they were unsuccessful. The French Assembly's negative vote therefore left American policy in disarray, the more so because, at this crucial juncture, the secretary's presence was urgently needed in Manila to energize the stalled negotiations for the South East Asian Treaty Organization (SEATO). The solution that was found for the European security problem—the establishment of a West European Union (WEU) "to promote the unity and to encourage the progressive integration of Europe," the admission of the German Federal Republic to it and to NATO, and a British pledge to maintain a standing force of infantry and tactical air in Europe—was largely due to the political adroitness an determination of Anthony Eden, although it would be unfair to assume that American influence on the result was wholly negative.[75]

However that may be, one positive result of the crisis and its aftermath was that Dulles developed a relationship of confidence and trust with Konrad Adenauer, the chancellor of the Federal Republic of Germany, that was a valuable element in the Western defense system, the two men becoming visible symbols of the so-called Policy of Strength, which was intended to cause dissension and defection among the Soviet satellites in Eastern Europe by its demonstration of Western power, unity, and indomitability. It is fair to say that their friendship drew strength from their mutual ambivalence about the German people and the future role of Germany in Europe. While both paid frequent lip serve to the idea of German reunification, Adenauer as a Roman Catholic was unenthusiastic about a united nation that would be dominated by Protestants from Prussia and Saxony, while Dulles never got over the fear that he expressed in 1947, when he said that a united Germany, independent of East or West, "would have an enormous bargaining power which, if skillfully used, can give Germany the mastery of Europe."

Adenauer, whose skepticism about his fellow Germans was profound, always feared that, under given circumstances, they would prove susceptible to Soviet seduction, and both Dulles and he rejected the Austrian formula of 1955—that is, neutralization—as a possible solution for the problem of German reunification, Dulles contending, in a conversation with Charles de Gaulle in July 1958, that "a disengaged Germany would constitute an element between the two blocs that would use bargaining and blackmail for its own ends, which could very well lead to another war."[76] The only solution that would prevent a resurgence of dangerous German nationalism was—both Dulles and Adenauer agreed, as Acheson and John McCloy had in their time agreed—unwavering German membership in the Western alliance, whose function of containing the Soviet Union thus came to involve an implicit containment of the Germans as well. Needless to say, neither Dulles nor Adenauer used the term double-containment publicly, although the closeness of their personal relationship, and what it seemed to promise in the way of American support, persuaded the German electorate to accept it enthusiastically, although not without strong elements of dissent.[77]

That strains would develop in the German-American relationship was inevitable. In the last analysis, it depended upon the confidence of the Germans in the will of the United States to defend them in the event of any Soviet attack. After *Sputnik* had heralded the coming of nuclear parity, that determination could no longer be taken for granted, and increasingly West Germans of all parties began to talk of the necessity of finding an alternative for the Dulles-Adenauer policy of unrelenting refusal to consider any concessions to the East. During the long Berlin crisis that began in November 1958, the old chancellor became highly critical of these tendencies and also of what he considered to be the willingness on the part of his Western allies, to make dangerous concessions to Khrushchev, although he generally spared Dulles the abuse that he heaped on Macmillan and Eisenhower. Ironically, however, as his faith in the United States declined, Adenauer turned increasingly to France, and the improvement of Franco-German relations that Dulles had desired was achieved in the Treaty of Friendship of January 1963. By that time, Dulles was long dead, and the Policy of Strength was beginning to be replaced by a more flexible one in both Germany and the United States.[78]

It is unlikely that he would have approved of this. There were moments in the mid–1950s when he thought he detected signs of substantial softening in the post-Stalin Soviet Union, which he attributed to internal domestic pressures, unrest within the satellites, and frustration produced by Western unity and the success of his own policy. The Russians were now much less likely to practice the "virulent aggression" that had marked the Stalin era. But this, he cautioned, was probably a mere change in tactics, and his speeches continued to cite Lenin's alleged remark that "promises are like pie crusts, made to be broken."[79] But he was at least willing to acknowledge that limited negotiations—provided that any agreements were rigorously monitored—might be of some utility, and this attitude even affected his initial approach to Khrushchev's Berlin ultimatum. And, over time, he came to believe that the Chinese Communists, riding the crest of recent revolutionary success, were more likely to commit direct aggression than the Soviets. The Russians were more cautious, more conservative, he believed, although his great worry about Khrushchev was not that he intended war, even over Berlin, but that he was mercurial and unpredictable.

Like Kennan, Dulles could envision the eventual breakup of the Soviet system. One reason, to be sure, was his repeatedly stated belief in the "force of freedom," which was confirmed by the uprisings in Hungary and Poland.[80] He regarded Suez as a "tragedy," in part because the Anglo-French-Israeli invasion had occurred at a time when the bankruptcy of the Soviet Union was, he felt, becoming apparent.[81] But he also argued that the forces of modernization and, especially, education would be a liberalizing force. Soviet education, to be sure, was largely in technical areas and not in the humanities, but Dulles was confident that an educated Soviet citizenry would eventually see through communist dogma and demand freedom. "The spread of education and industrial development create growing demands for greater intellectual and spiritual freedom, for greater personal security through the protection of law."[82] In one of the last formal speeches of his life, an address to the National War College in late November 1958, he reaffirmed his conviction: "If you deny the successes, then the change internally comes about."[83]

His record in the Far East is more problematical. To be sure, while he and Eisenhower always publicly supported Chiang Kai-shek, there is abundant evidence that they were frustrated, especially by the Nationalist leader's policies toward the offshore islands. Eisenhower complained, almost bitterly, about "that place where we are trapped" and, like Dulles, sought unsuccessfully to find solutions for the offshore islands other than complete dependence upon Chiang's many whims. As a result, instead of being "unleashed," Chiang was brought more effectively under the control of Washington and enjoyed less freedom of action under the Republicans than under the Democrats—in part because Dulles's militant speeches had completely defused the appeal of the Republican right, Chiang's most ardent defenders in the United States. Similarly, while publicly insisting upon the monolithic nature of the Sino-Soviet bloc, Dulles began to understand that Mao Zedung was not a creature of the Kremlin and that his regime had developed more than a little stability. While the secretary always loudly and publicly refused to consider diplomatic recognition of "Red China" or its admission to the UN, he maintained back channel communications with Mao's government—another example of the moralist as pragmatist.

He also developed what several recent historians have termed the "wedge theory," the idea of exerting pressure upon the Chinese Communists that would make Mao more and more dependent upon the Soviet Union and, over time, produce fissures within the "monolith."[84] But, whatever its merits, the "wedge theory," it could be argued, might well have hardened Chinese Communist fears of the United States, and Dulles's hard-line speeches undoubtedly did much to harden public opinion in the United States about the dangers of the Red Peril in Asia, thus making it politically impossible for any American leader, until the time of Richard Nixon, to begin making serious overtures to Beijing.

In Southeast Asia, Dulles had clearly wanted to intervene in the aftermath of Dienbienphu, for he believed that French weakness and timidity would cause dominoes to topple throughout all Southeast Asia. But his much-heralded plan for "united action" could never be implemented, a failure that underscores the fact that the United States, even at the height of its economic-political power, encountered both domestic and foreign constraints. Remembering the unpopularity of "Truman's war" in Korea, many members of Congress (with encouragement from the Army side of the defense establishment) worried about involvement in a land war in Asia; the Churchill-Eden government held back; and the French were unwilling (and probably unable) to continue the war on Dulles's terms. The secretary's support for Ngo Dinh Diem, the ruler of South Vietnam after 1955, eventually, but only temporarily, stabilized the situation in Vietnam; the dominoes did not fall; and Southeast Asia did not again become an area of crisis until after the secretary's death. Still, in the long, complex and lugubrious history of American involvement in Vietnam, it should be remembered that it was under Dulles that the basic American commitment was made, and the assumption accepted that the preservation of an independent South Vietnam was vital to the national security of the United States. In a very real sense, presidents from Kennedy through Gerald R. Ford were attempting to carry out and implement pledges and commitments first made by John Foster Dulles.

Dulles, as well as Eisenhower, recognized—and the record of their deliberations in the National Security Council during the Indochina debates sustains the point—the necessity of understanding the force of nationalism in the Third World, specifically the danger of tying the American cause to French colonialism in Southeast Asia. (Indeed, many of Dulles's bitter disagreements with the French, whether in Indochina or Algeria, arose from French colonial practices.) They also recognized that, given their recent emergence from imperialist control, the new countries in Asia and Africa would be suspicious of too close an association with the West. The secretary, especially in the aftermath of Suez, welcomed decolonization. On the other hand, skeptical that the new independent countries possessed the tradition or experience that would fit them for successful political and economic development, he also saw them as special targets for Soviet penetration and as vulnerable to Moscow's argument that the most rapid route to modernization was by adopting the Soviet model.[85] As Stalin's successor saw it, Third World nationalism might well provide the indispensable opening for communist forces to obtain power. Thus, for Dulles—and Vietnam is the classic case in point—resistance to communism took precedence over support of nationalism in the Third World.

How was one to deal with the changing nature of the Soviet threat? Running through the newly released documentation is Dulles's continuing resistance to summit conferences. "Better results," he confided to reporters during one of his not-for-attribution backgrounders, "come from regular negotiations. The history of U.S. presidents who have dealt directly has not been an outstanding success."[86] It was not simply that summits raised expectations that could not be achieved; more important was the possibility that they might produce a letdown in the will and determination of the American people. Thus, even when he took his first, tentative steps toward the suspension of nuclear tests in 1957, Dulles would describe them as "a good thing" because they warded off pressure for a summit. Near the end of his life, when an Eisenhower-Khrushchev summit to deal with the mounting Berlin crisis was still months away, he told Vice President Richard Nixon that he had spent the last year and a half of his life avoiding a summit. "Why go on at all?" Dulles asked?[87]

One aspect of Dulles's legacy remains particularly troubling. In both Iran (1953) and Guatemala (1954), covert actions became, for the first time in American history, a recognized instrument of official policy. A dangerous precedent was, in fact, institutionalized. Dulles, to be sure, had no qualms about the clandestine effort by the CIA that toppled the Nicaraguan left. It had, he felt, simply removed a communist "cancer" from the Western Hemisphere. Most of the decisions that led to these covert actions occurred at secret meetings between the two brothers, Foster of State and Allen of the Central Intelligence

Agency. As Richard Immerman has observed, their decision took place "behind permanently closed doors" that the historian, no matter how many official records are declassified, will never be able to unlock.[88]

VI

The Dulles record, then, is decidedly mixed. The secretary and the president succeeded in producing a Cold War consensus in American foreign policy. The bitterness and divisiveness over the fall of Nationalist China and the Korean War, which had marked the latter years of the Truman-Acheson era and carried over into the 1952 campaign, faded with time. The Republican right, once so noisy and prominent, was tamed, indeed, almost forgotten by 1956. In 1960 Kennedy and Nixon would debate the tactics rather than the fundamentals of American foreign policy.

Similarly, but probably inadvertently and unexpectedly, many of Dulles's policies and decisions turned out in time to create the preconditions for long-term stability in Soviet-American relations. He backed off from the theme of liberation and abandoned "prodding the bear" on the other side of the Iron Curtain; he "re-leashed" the Chinese Nationalists; and above all, and despite his stated and widely proclaimed deterrence policy of massive retaliation, he practiced "self deterrence."

After an hour and a half meeting with the secretary in the Oval Office on 10 January 1958, President Eisenhower wrote in his personal diary: "There is probably no one in the world who has the technical competence of Foster Dulles in the diplomatic field."[89] This is a meager assessment. Dulles's great achievement as secretary of state was to give the American people a foreign policy that they thought they understood and could support. He may not have been able to explain the complexities of his certainty/uncertainty principle to the American public, and there was always a gap between his public statements and his private discourse. But, with his long background in the churches, he had full command of the language of American Protestantism and could harness it to spread the word of American righteousness confronting communist evil, of the Free World standing against tyranny. And, like Ronald Reagan a generation later, he possessed a unique ability to preach the gospel of American exceptionalism, the mission of the United States to spread its institutions and its democratic ideology as a fitting model for a deeply divided world.

Notes

1. Interview with James C. Hagerty, Dulles Oral History Project, Mudd Library, Princeton University (hereafter cited as DOH).

2. Richard H. Immerman, ed., *John Foster Dulles and the Diplomacy of the Cold War* (Princeton, 1990). Also on the pragmatism of his diplomacy, Ronald W. Pruessen, "Beyond the Cold War—Again: 1955 and the 1990's," *Political Science Quarterly* (Spring 1993): 67 ff. For his views about the communist ideology and violence, see JFD to Avery Dulles, 3 Mar. 1947, Dulles Papers, Mudd Library, Princeton University (hereafter DP), Additional Papers.

3. John Lewis Gaddis, *The Long Peace: Inquiries into the History of the Cold War* (New York, 1987), esp. 123–46, 174–94.

4. For more detailed information about Dulles's career before he became secretary of state, see Ronald W. Pruessen, *John Foster Dulles: The Road to Power* (New York, 1982), and Mark Toulouse, *The Transformation of John Foster Dulles: From Prophet of Realism to Priest of Nationalism* (Macon, Ga., 1985). There are earlier biographies by Louis L. Gerson, Michael A. Guhin, Townsend Hoopes, and John Robinson Beal, the latter an authorized biography, which first appeared in 1957. Leonard Mosley, *Dulles: A Biography of Eleanor, Allen, and John Foster Dulles and Their Family Network* (New York, 1978), is notable only for its wealth of misinformation.

5. See Hua Qingzhao, *From Yalta to Panmunjom: Truman's Diplomacy and the Four Powers, 1945–1953* (Ithaca, 1953), 176 ff.

6. Richard D. Challener, "John Foster Dulles: The Princeton Connection," *Princeton University Library Chronicle* 50, no. 1 (Autumn 1988): 7–29.

7. "World Brotherhood Through the State," address to the Brotherhood of St. Andrew, Philadelphia, 8 Sept. 1946, and "Christian Responsibility for Peace," address to the General Conference of the Methodist Church, 4 May 1948, Dulles Papers, Speeches and Articles series (hereafter cited as DPSA).

8. Later, to be sure, he would claim that he and Arthur H. Vandenberg, the two Republican advisers to Byrnes, were the ones who had stiffened the resistance of the allegedly pliable secretary.

9. Report on the London Meeting of the Council of Foreign Ministers, Columbia Broadcasting System, radio broadcast, 6 Oct. 1945, DPSA.

10. Address before the Federal Council of Churches, Columbus, Ohio, 5 Mar. 1946, DPSA.

11. "Thoughts on Soviet Foreign Policy and What To Do About It," two-part article, *Life*, vol. 20, nos. 20, 22 (3 and 10 June 1946). Also a condensed version appeared in the August 1946 issue of *The Reader's Digest*.

12. "A Statement on Soviet-American Relations," Federal Council of Churches, November 1945, DPSA.

13. Ibid.

14. "The Christian Citizen in a Changing World," prepared for the World Council of Churches meeting at Amsterdam, 22 Aug.–4 Sept. 1948, DPSA.

15. Address at Assembly of World Council, Amsterdam, 24 Aug. 1948, DPSA.

16. Address to Governor's Conference, Gatlinburg, Tenn., 1 Oct. 1951; to Council on Foreign Relations, New York, 31 Oct. 1951, and his major article, "Security in the Pacific," *Foreign Affairs* 30, no. 2 (January 1952): 175–87, all in DPSA. On the treaty, see also below, chap. 11.

17. See his remarks at the Institute of Pacific Relations, Manila, 12 Feb. 1951; CBS broadcast, "Laying the Foundations for Peace in the Pacific," 1 Mar. 1951; Address

on Japanese Peace Treaty, English Speaking Union, London, 17 June 1951, all in DPSA.

18. Address before the American Chamber of Commerce in Japan and the Japanese Chamber of Commerce and Industry, Tokyo, 14 Dec. 1951, DPSA. The other Cold War concerns mentioned in this paragraph are to be found in the speeches previously cited, most notably the one to the Governors Conference on 1 Oct. 1951.

19. "The Importance of Spiritual Resources," Cold Spring Harbor, N.Y., 27 Jan. 1950, DPSA.

20. "The Balance of Power," Chicago, 10 Mar. 1950.

21. "Laying the Foundations for Peace in the Pacific," CBS broadcast, previously cited; "Chinese-American Friendship," China Institute of America, 18 May 1951; "The Free East and the Free West," National Conference of Christians and Jews, Cleveland, 29 Nov. 1951 (also a NBC broadcast), DPSA.

22. Address to the Seventy-second Annual Convention of the American Federation of Labor, St. Louis, 24 Sept. 1953, Department of State Press Release 514, DPSA.

23. Dulles to Ambassador John M. Allison, 20 Aug. 1954, DP, Chronological Series (hereafter cited as DPChron), box 9.

24. Richard D. Challener, "New Light on the Dulles-Hiss Relationship," *University*, no. 56 (Spring 1973), 1–3, 28–33. See also interview with Douglas MacArthur II, DOH. It should also be noted that Dulles, claiming that he had put his house in order, eventually resented Senator McCarthy's continuing search for subversives in the State Department.

25. Interview with John W. Hanes, Jr., DOH.

26. Interview with Burke Wilkinson, DOH.

27. John W. Hanes, Jr., to Dulles, 10 Apr. 1956, DPChron.

28. Gerard C. Smith to Dulles, 11 Sept. 1955, DPChron.

29. Dulles to Eisenhower, 23 Sept. 1953, DPChron.

30. "Helena" notes, 11 Dec. 1952, DP, Subject Series, Pre-Inauguration Materials. See also, in the same series, his talk with Selwyn Lloyd, 26 Dec. 1952.

31. Memorandum, "United States Foreign Policy," 16 May 1954, DP, White House Memoranda Series, General Foreign Policy Matters (hereafter cited as DPWHMS).

32. Interviews with Samuel M. Cavert, Frederick L. Flagley, Ernest A. Gross, DOH.

33. In addition to such biographies of as Stephen E. Ambrose, *Eisenhower: The President* (New York, 1984), see, in particular, John Lewis Gaddis, *Strategies of Containment* (New York, 1982), and Robert Griffith, "Dwight D. Eisenhower and the Corporate Commonwealth," *American Historical Review,* 88 (February 1982): 87–122.

34. Transcript of meeting of National Security Council, 31 Mar. 1953, DPWHMS.

35. Memorandum of Conversation Held in the Secretary's Office, 28 Mar. 1955, DPWHMS.

36. Dulles to Ambassador John M. Allison, 9 May 1954, DP, Subject Series (hereafter cited as DPSS).

37. Memorandum of Conversation on Indochina at the Secretary's Residence, 9 May 1954, DPSS, box 9. But not everyone was impressed. Indeed, the next line in the transcript reads: "Admiral Arthur W. Radford [Chairman of the Joint Chiefs of Staff] did not give the impression of being impressed by this line of thought."

38. Memorandum of Discussion at the State Department, 8 Nov. 1957, DP, General Correspondence and Memoranda Series, box 3.

39. "Current United States National Strategy," lecture at the National War College, 23 Nov. 1958, DPSA.

40. McGeorge Bundy, *Danger and Survival: Choices About the Bomb in the First Fifty Years* (New York, 1988), 256.

41. Memorandum of Conversation with the President, 7 Mar. 1955, DPWHMS.

42. Memorandum for the Record of National Security Council Meeting, 10 Mar. 1955, DPWHMS, Formosa Strait.

43. James R. Shepley, "Three Times at Brink of War: How Dulles Gambled and Won," *Life,* vol. 40, no. 3 (16 Jan. 1956), 70–80.

44. Bundy, *Danger and Survival*, 279–87.

45. Richard Ned Lebow and Janice Gross Stein, "Deterrence: The Elusive Dependent Variable," *World Politics* 42, no. 3 (April 1990): 336–69.

46. Memorandum of Meeting Held in the Secretary's Office, 28 Mar. 1955, DPWHMS, Formosa Straits.

47. Memorandum for the Record, 11 Mar. 1954, DPWHMS.

48. Memorandum of 28 Mar. 1955, DPWHMS.

49. Gaddis, *Long Peace*, 104–46.

50. Bundy, *Danger and Survival*, 245.

51. Memorandum of Conversation with the President, 22 Dec. 1954, DPWHMS, Meetings with the President.

52. Telephone Conversation with Robert B. Anderson, 2 Dec. 1958, DP, Telephone Transcript Series (hereafter cited as DP Tel Con).

53. Among his many speeches on this subject, see especially "Foundations of Peace," to the Convention of the Veterans of Foreign Wars, Department of State, Public Service Division, no. 70, 18 Aug. 1958, and "Background Remarks" at meeting of Executive Council of the AFL-CIO, Bushkill, Pa., 19 Aug. 1958, DPSA.

54. Telephone Conversation with Robert B. Anderson, 3 Dec. 1958, DP Tel Con.

55. Interview with Robert R. Bowie, DOH.

56. "Disarmament and Peace," radio and television address, Department of State Press Release 430, 22 July 1957, and "Dynamic Peace," speech to the Associated Press Annual Luncheon, Department of State Press Release 229, 22 Apr. 1957, DPSA.

57. Transcript of Meeting of 5 July 1958 with Charles De Gaulle, reprinted in *De Gaulle et les Américains: Conversations avec Dulles, Eisenhower, Kennedy, Rusk, 1958–1964,* ed. Bernard Ledwidge (Paris, 1984). See also interview with General Lauris Norstad, DOH.

58. Telephone Conversation with Robert B. Anderson, 30 Apr. 1958, DP Tel Con.

59. Memorandum of Conversation with the President, 1 Apr. 1958, DPWHMS.

60. Dulles to Harold Macmillan, 4 Sept. 1958, DPWHMS.

61. Memorandum of Conversation with the President, 4 Sept. 1958, DPWHMS, Meetings with the President.

62. Memorandum of Conversation with Christian Herter, 10 Apr. 1959, DP Tel Con, and Memorandum of Conversation in Walter Reed Hospital, 20 Mar. 1959, DPWHMS, Meetings with President.

63. "Evolution of Our Foreign Policy," speech to the Council on Foreign Relations, New York, Department of State Press Release no. 8, 12 Jan. 1954, DPSA.

64. Bundy, *Danger and Survival,* 155–57.

65. "Policy for Security and Peace," *Foreign Affairs* 32, no. 3 (April 1954): 353–64.

66. For the most recent discussion of China policy, see Nancy Bernkopf Tucker, "John Foster Dulles and the Taiwan Roots of the 'Two China' Policy," in Immerman, *Dulles and the Diplomacy of the Cold War,* 235–62. See also Memorandum for the Record, 11 Mar. 1955, DPWHMS; and, in the same series, Memorandum for the Record, 1 Apr. 1955; Memorandum of Conversation with the President, 4 Apr. 1955; Memoranda of Conversations with the President, Augusta, Ga., 18 and 27 Apr. 1955; and (especially for a thorough exposition of Eisenhower's ideas), Eisenhower to Dulles, Memorandum for the Secretary, 5 Apr. 1955.

67. In the midst of the crisis, Eisenhower attempted, in a five-page letter to General Alfred M. Gruenther, to describe the almost insoluble dilemma of explaining the Formosa policy to the American public. Papers of Dwight Eisenhower, 1 Feb. 1955, Whitman File (copy in DP).

68. This was one of Walter Lippmann's major criticisms of Dulles's diplomacy. See Ronald Steel, *Walter Lippmann and the American Century* (Boston, 1980).

69. Shepley, "Three Times at Brink of War."

70. General Alfred M. Gruenther to Dulles, 29 Oct. 1956, DP, General Correspondence.

71. For a general discussion of the Solarium project, see Robert J. Watson, *The Joint Chiefs of Staff and National Policy, 1953–54,* vol. 5 of *The History of the Joint Chiefs of Staff* (Washington, 1984), 11–14. Some of the problems in interpreting Solarium and Dulles's connection with it are briefly discussed in Immerman, *Dulles and the Diplomacy of the Cold War,* 274.

72. Kennan commentary at Dulles Centennial Conference, 25 Feb. 1988.

73. For Pruessen's appraisal of Dulles as secretary, see his chapter in Immerman, *Dulles and the Diplomacy of the Cold War,* 21–46.

74. For example, at the time of the Hungarian uprising, Dulles inserted a paragraph—all carefully worked out in advance with Eisenhower—into a speech given to the Texas Council of World Affairs in Dallas. It stressed that the United States did not look upon the East European countries as potential military allies but only as friends. The idea, he later confided to newspapermen in one of his backgrounders, was to convey a message to the Soviet Union, suggesting that "we had no desire to push forward hostile forces that would make these countries bitter enemies of the Soviet Union and reproduce the *cordon sanitaire* that France tried to create." See "The Task of Making Peace," speech of 27 Oct. 1956 in Dallas, Department of State Press Release 560, DPSA, and Background Press Conference on Suez and Hungary, 30 Oct. 1956, compiled by J. R. Wiggins, DP, Additional Papers, box 1.

75. Detlef Felken, *Dulles und Deutschland: Die amerikanische Deutschlandpolitik 1953–1959* (Bonn, 1993), 243, 245–55, 267, 270–71.

76. For a complete text of the July 5 meeting between de Gaulle and Dulles, see Ledwidge, *De Gaulle et les Américains*, 14–33. Dulles came prepared with a lengthy "talking paper," which he did not actually present to the new French leader but which he did discuss at length with both Ambassador Amory Houghton and General Lauris Norstad before-

hand. Various versions of the "talking paper," dated June 1958, and a memorandum of his 4 July conversations with American officials are in DP, Selected Correspondence.

77. For an interesting analysis, from the West German perspective, of "double containment," see Wolfram F. Hanrieder, *Germany, America, Europe: Forty Years of German Foreign Policy* (New Haven, 1989). On Dulles's ideas about Europe and his anxieties about the solidity of the Federal Republic's attachment to the West and his opposition to the idea of German neutrality, see Ronald W. Pruessen, "Beyond the Cold War—Again: 1955 and the 1990's," *Political Science Quarterly* v. 108 (Spring 1993): 72–76.

78. For a German discussion of the Dulles-Adenauer relationship, based on the latest documentation, see Felken, *Dulles und Deutschland.*

79. See such speeches as "Disarmament and Peace," Department of State Press Release 430, 22 July 1957, and an address to Chicago Council on Foreign Relations, 20 Nov. 1957, as well as his article, "Our Cause Will Prevail," *Life,* vol. 43, no. 26 (23 Dec. 1957), 12–13, DPSA.

80. Speech of 20 Nov. 1957 in Chicago, cited above.

81. Suez was, among many things, also a tragedy of miscommunication, as General Gruenther's letter, cited above, indicates. From the start, Dulles had believed that the use of force against Egypt would be counterproductive. At the same time, as he confessed in a candid backgrounder, "The real problem has been to find a solution that would give a blow to Nasser, that would eliminate his influence." And also to find a "just solution" that would recognize the rights of those nations that used the canal and whose economies depended upon it. But these signals, especially given Eden's mindset, were almost impossible to communicate. In his last public address, Dulles stated firmly that the United States had to make it clear, as a matter of principle, "even to its good friends, that we are opposed to the use of force in the settlement of international problems. . . . it seemed to us, in the fall of 1956, that the entire peace concept of the United Nations was at stake and that, if the article of the chapter involving the use of force were to become a dead letter, the world would revert to chaos." "The Role of Law in Peace," address to the New York Bar Association, Department of State, Public Service Division, series S, no. 79, 31 Jan. 1959, DPSA. A recent analysis of Dulles and Suez that stresses the mixed communications on both sides is William Roger Louis, "Dulles, Suez, and the British," in Immerman, *Dulles and the Diplomacy of the Cold War,* 133–58.

82. Address to the Chicago Council of Foreign Relations, 20 Nov. 1957, DPSA.

83. Speech to the National War College, 23 Nov. 1958, cited above.

84. See Gaddis, *Long Peace,* chap. 6, as well as Richard Melanson and David Mayers, *Reevaluating Eisenhower: American Foreign Policy in the 1950's* (Urbana, 1987).

85. Among many speeches on the subject, "Report to the Nation on his Recent Asian Tour," radio and TV address, Department of State Press Release 159, 23 Mar. 1956; "The Cost of Peace," address at Iowa State College commencement, Department of State Press Release 307, 8 June 1956; Remarks at Dinner of Council on Foreign Relations, 7 June 1957, DPSA.

86. Background Press Conference, 4 Apr. 1958, compiled by James Russell Wiggins, DP, Additional Papers.

87. Memorandum of telephone conversation with Mr. Greene, 24 Mar. 1959, DP Tel Con. But see also his lengthy discussion with Eisenhower when the president visited him

in Walter Reed Hospital shortly before his death. In it Dulles stressed that he opposed a summit conference because "the Soviets were trying to bring about a summit meeting not through good behavior but by coercing us with threats and with violations of our established rights." Memorandum of conversation with the President, 19 Mar. 1959, DPWHMS.

88. Immerman, *Dulles and the Diplomacy of the Cold War*, 275.

89. Robert H. Ferrell, ed. *The Eisenhower Diaries* (New York, 1981), 306.

6

THE ROAD TO SUEZ: THE BRITISH FOREIGN OFFICE

AND THE QUAI D'ORSAY, 1951–1957

Victor H. Feske

T HE TRIPARTITE DECLARATION of May 1950 represented a rudimentary attempt by Britain, France, and the United States to speak with a united voice on the issue of the Middle East. The four-paragraph document announced unilateral Western controls over weapons shipments into the region, while providing de facto recognition of Middle Eastern frontiers pending some further Arab-Israeli settlement. With its declared intent of promoting "the establishment and maintenance of peace and stability in the area," the agreement sanctioned, temporarily but indefinitely, the new Middle Eastern status quo. However, the three allies approached their mutual undertaking with divergent aims and assumptions that boded ill for the document's long-term efficacy.

With its gaze concentrated primarily upon Europe and the Far East, the Truman administration was generally content to allow Britain to take the lead in Middle Eastern affairs. But American sufferance of an auxiliary role always remained contingent upon the weaker partner's continuing demonstration of its willingness and capacity to defend the West's interests in the energy-rich region. Washington viewed the Middle East as a problem in Cold War geopolitics and expected her allies, both Britain and France, to embrace a similar perspective and accept the priorities thereby imposed.

However, for Britain, Middle Eastern policy was an altogether more complicated affair. The Attlee and Churchill governments took the ideological and strategic Soviet threat to the region very seriously indeed. But the translation of such concerns into a generic and, in some sense, altruistic defense of Western interests remained problematic, for they intertwined and often conflicted at every level with Britain's determination to retain some considerable measure of her traditional Middle Eastern preeminence. At stake were prestige and the influence that accompanied it, both deemed essential to a nation experiencing doubts about the postwar durability of its great-power status. So long as Britain's historic regional interests and Cold War imperatives converged, it was a comparatively simple matter to coordinate policy with Washington. Difficulties arose when the weakened junior partner attempted to pursue its own agenda, damaging, at least from the American perspective, the anti-Soviet common cause.

While Britain juggled dual roles, France followed a less fractured course. Faced with armed revolt in Indochina and rumblings in Tunisia, Morocco, and Algeria, the Quai d'Orsay directed its principal energies in the Middle East toward preserving as much as possible of the remnants of France's once imposing position of power and influence. The rationale for French policy revolved around a desire to remain dominant in neighboring North Africa and, more broadly, to conserve the trappings of a great power. The Fourth Republic's attempts to justify such narrow policies by internationalizing the context—that is, equating French colonial struggles with the global effort toward the containment of Soviet expansionism—were generally received with barely disguised skepticism by its Western allies.

In view of these incompatibilities, as well as the great discrepancy in economic and military strength between the United States on one hand and France and Britain on the other, it is hardly surprising that the Western Alliance should have come to grief in the Middle East. But institutional weaknesses within the diplomatic structure compounded problems already posed by divergent national interests. Fragmentation of authority and confusion of effort left both the Foreign Office in London and the Quai d'Orsay in Paris ill-equipped to deal with the complexities of the Middle East after 1951, rendering already daunting tasks of accommodation and coordination well nigh impossible.

I

Beginning with the shrill denunciations of old-style diplomacy in the 1920s, followed in quick succession by the diplomatic debacles of the 1930s and the taint of Munich, the British Foreign Office of the early 1950s looked back on four decades of eroding authority and prestige.[1] The "Eden-Bevin reforms"— unofficial name for the 1943 Foreign Service Act—did little enough to retrieve the situation, particularly in light of Churchill's wartime predilection for top-level summitry, which contributed to the appearance of the marginalization of the Foreign Office civil servant. The publication after 1946 of British interwar diplomatic documents and the 1951 defections of Burgess and Maclean provided fodder for postwar press and parliamentary critics alike.[2]

Moreover, the difficulties of the Foreign Service were more substantial than a negative public image. The increasingly artificial division into separate spheres of global economic affairs and international relations and the Foreign Office's relative neglect of the former encouraged encroachment upon its terrain by the Treasury and other cabinet departments. The post-1945 era, with its proliferation of new organizations and agencies, also provided other means for the formulation and execution of foreign policy outside of traditional diplomatic channels. Along with high profile summitry, the rise to prominence of the United Nations and the spectacular growth of intelligence services like MI6 impinged upon the Foreign Office's once exclusive domain.

Ernest Bevin's tenure as foreign secretary (1945–1951) helped to restore sagging morale among permanent officials. Strong-willed and well-liked, Bevin reclaimed the control of foreign policy previously lost to the prime minister. Officials under his direction applauded Bevin's recognition of the need for difficult choices and long-term thinking in light of Britain's diminished postwar strength. With a view toward the latter, he authorized the creation of the Permanent Under-Secretary's Committee in 1949 as a conduit for analyses of and recommendations on long-range questions by junior and senior officials.[3] This, to be sure, came late in the day, and the reassessment and reorientation of British foreign policy was far from complete when Bevin stepped down for reasons of health in March 1951. His successor, Herbert Morrison, appeared ill-suited to the ministerial post and therefore unlikely to continue the Bevinite restoration of the fortunes of the Foreign Service.[4]

Under the circumstances, the Foreign Office heaved a collective sigh of relief on Morrison's supersession by the veteran Anthony Eden following the October 1951 general election, a change viewed approvingly by senior officials as the return of "a professional diplomat as Secretary of State."[5] Eden, having twice before occupied the same cabinet post, was well versed regarding the inner workings of the office, and his blend of experience, charm, and sophistication combined with an extensive knowledge of international affairs to make his choice a popular one among his new subordinates. Prospects seemed auspicious for a harmonious concurrence of attitudes and policies between minister and officials.

But initial expectations of mutual compatibility were to be disappointed. Eden proved to be thin-skinned, reacting badly when faced with criticism or contradiction. His excitability caused problems, his frequent emotional response to questions of policy hindering flexibility.[6] Even his reported strong suit, the adroit handling of head-to-head discussions with foreign representatives, was often marred by personal vanity and a lack of proper discretion and reserve. After one such encounter with Molotov in 1954, Eden's private secretary, Evelyn Shuckburgh, complained of his master's public performance, "These politicians are two-thirds prima donnas."[7]

Eden's distaste for partisan politics created the false image of a man above the fray, when in reality he was extraordinarily sensitive to public opinion, in particular, to sentiment within Conservative ranks. He disappointed permanent officials, obsessed with the notion of continuity, in his resemblance to a "sea anemone, covered with sensitive tentacles all recording currents of opinion around him. He quivers with sensitivity to opinion in the House, the party, the newspapers."[8] By December 1953 Permanent Under-Secretary Sir Ivone Kirkpatrick was complaining of Eden's lack of "fixity at any point."[9]

Eden's reactive political antennae complemented a personal aversion to long-term thinking. He was more tactician than strategist, content to tackle finite, immediate concerns while postponing consideration of broader issues.[10] Even after years of close observation Shuckburgh could not quite make up his mind about his chief. At times he seemed unable to "bear long-term thoughts, and wants only to discuss how to answer this morning's telegrams." But even when it seemed that his eyes were not concentrating solely upon the next footfall, even on those occasions when it was clear that Eden could "*see* a little ahead," he remained "too keen on popularity to push far-seeing measures through."[11] This marked preference for thinking in the short term ensured the eclipse of the Permanent Under-Secretary's Committee established by Bevin. Eden's prejudices in that direction encountered only sporadic resistance from permanent officials suffering from chronic fatigue induced by overwork. Sir William Strang, permanent under-secretary from 1949 to 1953, recorded how inevitably "the mind revolted against the reading of discourses and articles that had no immediate bearing on day-to-day problems."[12] Without persistent encouragement and support from the foreign secretary, there was little incentive for his professional advisers to pursue long-term planning. Eden's failure in that regard was to cost him dearly in the Middle East.

Accustomed to Bevin's ascendancy over Attlee, the Foreign Office also experienced frustration at Eden's relative deference to the prime minister. While the foreign secretary did not shrink from clashes with Churchill during cabinet discussions on foreign policy, particularly over Egypt, he was frequently hesitant to press his advantage in argument. As a result, the normal cabinet decision-making process suffered from inefficiency born of procrastination. In part, Eden's anomalous position as Churchill's heir apparent explains this reluctance. The prime minister's stubborn refusal to step aside before 1955 represented a constant source of irritation to an already irascible Eden. Cautious and sensitive to a fault regarding his standing with the public and within the Conservative party, the foreign secretary fretted over the potential for self-inflicted damage from repeated conflicts with Churchill.

Churchill's intrusions into the formulation of foreign policy ventured beyond the forceful expression of his opinion in cabinet debate, going so far as to provide secret encouragement to the backbench Tory "Suez Group" in their opposition to Eden's 1953–1954 negotiations with Egypt.[13] Eden guarded his terrain jealously against encroachment by the prime minister[14] but still could not avoid creating the impression that there were "in effect two men acting as Foreign Secretary at the same time."[15] Like that of his chief, Eden's health was poor. He never completely recovered from a series of operations for cholangitis in the spring of 1953. With a convalescent Eden absent for nearly eight months of that year, Churchill assumed complete control of foreign policy. The Foreign Office found it nearly impossible to work with the headstrong and impulsive seventy-eight-year-old. Shuckburgh detailed the frustrations of "trying to conduct our foreign policy through the PM who is at Chartwell and always in the bath or asleep or too busy having dinner when we want urgent decisions."[16] The Foreign Office and an incapacitated Eden strenuously resisted Churchill's advocacy of a 1953 great-power summit with the Russians, a fixation linked by dismissive permanent officials to the "sentimental illusion that peace can be obtained if only the 'top men' can get together." It smacked of the "hubris which afflicts old men who have power, as it did Chamberlain when he visited Hitler."[17]

The prime minister repaid Foreign Office exasperation with interest. Contact between No. 10 and the office was kept to a minimum, Churchill preferring to deal with Strang alone or with Sir John Colville, his own joint principal private secretary responsible for foreign affairs,[18] purposely avoiding the crush of permanent officials with their "contrary and long-winded drafts."[19] Championing, as he believed it did, a policy of 'Scuttle' toward imperial responsibilities, Churchill thought the Foreign Office "an excellent institution for explaining us to other countries, but when its head is weak it seems to spend its time seeking agreements abroad at our expense."[20]

The "head" to which Churchill referred was, of course, Eden. Since the initial cabinet meeting of the new government, prime minister and foreign secretary had been locked in a prolonged struggle over the pace and direction of negotiations for a new Anglo-Egyptian treaty to settle the future of Britain's Suez Canal Zone military installations. Churchill, in favor of staying on in Suez despite all arguments to the contrary, accused the more conciliatory Eden of "throwing the game away."[21] Only two months before Eden's surgery, Churchill was raging against the foreign secretary's Egyptian policy of "appeasement," adding that "he never knew before that Munich was situated on the Nile."[22]

Churchill identified Eden with Foreign Office policy, a sentiment shared to a certain extent by the permanent officials themselves who viewed the Foreign Secretary as an ally in their efforts to combat prime ministerial extravagances.[23] Whether this favorable internal assessment was entirely accurate is something else again. Like the Foreign Office, Eden grasped the fundamentally reduced nature of Britain's postwar economic and military power. Sharing his officials' tempered pessimism about the future, he searched for a realistic formula to provide a better match between Britain's overseas commitments and its reduced circumstances. However, for Eden, Britain's first order of business was relations with the Empire and Commonwealth; the significance of the trans-Atlantic alliance with the United States and ties with Western Europe paled by comparison.[24]

The Permanent Under-Secretary's Committee had concluded in late 1949 that, for the foreseeable future, the cornerstone of British foreign policy should remain "close Anglo-American cooperation in world affairs."[25] Yet Eden's allegiance to the British-U.S. axis was never as firm and unequivocal as that of his predecessor Bevin or of his professional advisers. The foreign secretary entertained a low opinion of American diplomatic skills[26] and distrusted U.S. motives, blurting out in a fit of pique during the 1954 Geneva Conference that in addition to the Americans' desire to displace French influence and run Indo-China themselves, "they want to replace us in Egypt too. They want to run the world."[27] In a striking example of disregard for the realities of power, Eden informed the cabinet in October 1955 that in the Middle East, "We should not . . . allow ourselves to be restricted overmuch by reluctance to act without full American concurrence and support. We should form our own policy in the light of our interests in the area and get the Americans to support it to the extent we could induce them to do so."[28]

During their long association, Churchill always harbored doubts whether his protégé was quite sound on the fundamentals of foreign policy. The foreign secretary seemed bound up in detail, and his actions were "sometimes very foolish." Churchill fretted that Eden "would quarrel with the Americans over some petty Central American issue which did not affect Great Britain and could forget about the downtrodden millions in Poland."[29] Evelyn Shuckburgh believed that Eden "recognized the decline in the power and influence of Britain, but he could never quite reconcile himself to its inevitable consequences—growing American dominance and self-assurance in international affairs."[30] Ironically, the Foreign Office, while repeatedly quarreling with Churchill over details of policy, agreed with the prime minister's overriding dictum for Britain in the post-1945 world: "Never be separated from the Americans."[31]

In large measure, it was through concurrence with Foreign Office views on the necessity of a negotiated Canal Zone settlement with Egypt and the inadvisability of great-power summitry with the Russians—both stances clashing openly with Churchillian prejudices—that Eden's image as champion of the views of his permanent officials survived the internal tensions of his third term as foreign secretary. But upon advancing to the leadership in April 1955, Eden quickly assumed many of his predecessor's annoying traits. Shuckburgh was astonished "that A.E. should act so exactly in the manner of W.S.C., considering how he hated it when he was Foreign Secretary."[32] Harold Macmillan, the new foreign secretary, found that Eden had no intention of relinquishing control over foreign policy. From the outset it seemed quite clear to the independent Macmillan that "Eden wanted to get rid of me; he kept on sending me little notes, sometimes twenty a day, ringing up all the time. He really should have been both PM and Foreign Secretary."[33] Eden agreed, noting in his diary that he "thought Harold too woolly generally."[34]

Eden rectified this uncomfortable arrangement after only eight months by appointing as Macmillan's replacement Selwyn Lloyd, a man who openly admitted that he was out of his element and had been overpromoted.[35] Shuck-burgh recorded in his diary the Foreign Office suspicions concerning the cabinet reshuffle, which shunted Macmillan over to the Exchequer.

> The FO was astonished and depressed at losing H. M. . . . the change is *not* being made because A. E. is desperate for a good man to replace Rab [outgoing Chancellor R. A. Butler]; but rather because he is critical of H. M. as Foreign Secretary. I could see it all in a flash; he is *never* able to be loyal to anyone, and he does not like H. M. having a policy of his own.

Minister of State Anthony Nutting, the foreign secretary's political deputy, judged Lloyd "a pure mouthpiece of A. E."[36]

The Foreign Office was despondent at the prospect of a foreign secretary "who wants to be a cypher." It seemed to Permanent Under-Secretary Kirkpatrick that "Selwyn's only ambition is not to get into trouble." Because he offered no resistance, Lloyd found himself completely dominated by the prime minister. Eden bombarded him with phone calls, ringing up "poor Selwyn" thirty times over the Christmas 1955 weekend, while insisting that all written foreign office submissions receive approval from No. 10 before release. Shuckburgh, now under-secretary for Middle Eastern affairs, despaired at the mounting evidence that "we have no Secretary of State. We have a rather nervous official who has not the inclination or the courage to take decisions of any kind."[37]

When Eden reassumed the post of foreign secretary in the Churchill government of 1951, Shuckburgh, as private secretary, had found himself in the novel and not altogether comfortable position of "justifying the Office to the Secretary of State and defending startled officials" rather than, as with Herbert Morrison, "being concerned to explain and justify the Foreign Secretary to the Office."[38] As the Foreign Service's favorable disposition toward its new minister slowly crumbled, Eden reciprocated by losing faith in the loyalty and competence of his permanent officials. In Middle East affairs he developed a special mistrust because of a perceived pro-Arab bias within the diplomatic corps.[39] A suspicious Eden blamed the Foreign Office's "casual and inactive" attitude bred of prejudicial complacency for Britain's notable lack of success in the region.[40]

Relations appreciably worsened after Eden moved to No. 10. Previously the Foreign Office had coaxed him along tactfully in order to protect their policies as best they could from his impulsive intrusions.[41] After mid-1955 the degree of difficulty involved in these maneuvers soared. It seemed that desk officers and ambassadors were "alternately . . . rejected by the PM as no good, not on the job, unhelpful. . . . No one is trusted to the extent that his advice is regarded when unwelcome."[42] Shuckburgh sensed the growing chasm between Eden and his advisers, noting in his diary of 10 January 1956 a "feeling" that the coming Washington, D.C. visit by the prime minister and Selwyn Lloyd "is being prepared somewhere else, by someone else, and that although ostensibly I am going out to prepare it (on the Middle East side) I have not been told all."[43]

As difficulties with Egypt and the rest of the Middle East mounted in early 1956, Eden's dissatisfaction with his permanent officials kept pace. Complaints about pro-Arab sentiments gave way to denunciations of the "anti-Jewish spleen of you people in the Foreign Office!"[44] Even Nutting, a political appointee as minister of state and considered Eden's protégé, found himself unwelcome at No. 10.[45]

By the time Nasser seized the canal in July 1956, the estrangement of prime minister from Foreign Office was nearly complete. Shuckburgh's January suspicions of his own exclusion were well founded, for in formulating and pursuing Middle East policy, Eden was now ready to bypass his permanent officials, using the intelligence service MI6 as an alternative to normal channels in order to circumvent Foreign Office policy. By the summer of 1956, when the crisis broke, the Foreign Service had lost all of the ground made up during the Bevin administration, and more. Deliberately left out of the loop throughout the four-month Suez ordeal, the office exercised virtually no control over events, and morale sank to a new low.

II

While Britain enjoyed remarkable political stability between the close of the Second World War and the Suez Crisis of 1956—three prime ministers and only a single change of party—France was not similarly blessed, experiencing more than twenty alterations in government during the same period. The splintered nature of postwar French politics ensured the rule of a succession of barely distinguishable Left-Center coalitions, instability producing an impotent but functional form of stability.

Nowhere was this paradoxical outcome more apparent than in the control of foreign affairs. The Quai d'Orsay became a safe postwar preserve of the new Mouvement Républicain Populaire (MRP), with two of its leaders, Georges Bidault and Robert Schuman, monopolizing the key Foreign Ministry portfolio from the liberation until early 1954. Continuity of cabinet personnel from one coalition government to the next precluded the genuine parliamentary control of foreign policy by the National Assembly that might be the expected result of this sort of governmental volatility.[46] Conversely, chronic governmental impermanence strengthened bureaucratic control over policy-making within the Quai d'Orsay at the expense of cabinet politicians. Schuman complained that while he was serving as foreign minister, responsible for both Morocco and Tunisia, policy there was in fact made by the residents-general in defiance of his wishes.[47] The senior level diplomat Hervé Alphand recorded in his journal how Foreign Minister Bidault, paralyzed by "weakness and hesitation," tolerated without a word bureaucratic "indiscipline" and "les intrigues du Quai d'Orsay."[48]

Under the direction of its civil servants and the MRP, French foreign policy followed a fairly consistent course between 1946 and 1954, acknowledging with reluctance the necessity of the Atlantic Alliance as essential to French security and prosperity and edging resignedly into the anticommunist bloc led by the United States. Despite this coherent line, however, reservations within the Quai over alignment with the American camp remained considerable. The Western Alliance and NATO were expected to play their part in rebuilding and maintaining French global interests. Yet dependence on the United States led inevitably to the subordination of France's understanding of its own requirements for national defense to any American concept of global containment. As junior partner, the Fourth Republic had to rely upon convincing its doubtful ally of the perfect congruence of French desires and Western security interests. By 1956 this amounted to equating its suppression of nationalist revolt in Algeria with the performance of a crucial NATO defense task.[49]

The unspoken assumption was that there existed a viable alternative, that if the alliance finally proved itself incompatible with French national interests, a federated Europe led by France could form a nonaligned Third Force to balance the U.S.-USSR antagonism. There was a significant sentiment for nonalignment among the general populace throughout the life of the Fourth Republic.[50] It failed to find political expression while the Quai and the MRP dominated the formulation of policy. But in 1954 the question of German rearmament and a European Defense Community, the war in Indochina, and, finally, unrest in North Africa all enhanced the possibility for dramatic departures by removing foreign affairs from the narrow purview of the professional diplomats and returning it to the political center-stage. The further eclipse of the Quai bureaucracy before and during the Suez crisis merely accelerated this process.

The staff of the Quai d'Orsay in the early 1950s was a heterogeneous mixture, comprised of a large residue of veteran prewar officials mingled with novices acquired with some haste at the time of liberation in 1944–1945, supplemented by transfers of redundant personnel from other parts of the administration.[51] At least one contemporary observer equated the absence of postwar departmental 'purity' with internal weakness, noting the inability of the Ministry of Foreign Affairs "to defend its personnel, which now became heterogeneous, against the intrusion of foreign elements, Inspecteurs des Finances, *académiciens,* or mere Resistance fighters."[52] But this newly introduced *cadre complémentaire* never succeeded in forming a distinctive "party,"[53] and the young technocrats supplied to the Foreign Ministry after 1947 by the École Nationale d'Administration, diplomats "less burdened by history" than their predecessors according to one authority,[54] were still junior in station, relatively few in number, and lacking in influence by the mid-1950s. Career diplomats with service dating back to the Third Republic filled the vast majority of senior posts. Under the direction of men like René Massigli, Jean Chauvel, Roland de Margarie, Henri Roux, and Roger Seydoux, the Quai d'Orsay posted mixed results in the internal struggle to reestablish its pre-1939 power and prestige. In Franco-German relations, where technical economic questions predominated, other governmental agencies poached freely on the

Quai's formerly autonomous preserve. But in the Middle East, received wisdom went virtually unchallenged.

Although forced, at British insistence, to relinquish formal control over Syria and Lebanon at the end of the Second World War, the Quai still maintained in a mid-1954 confidential memorandum that "today as yesterday" cultural interests in Syria, Lebanon, the Holy Land, and Egypt continued as the prime motive for a French political presence in the Middle East.[55] The Quai balked repeatedly at British and American pressure to assist in the construction of a Middle East Defense Organization (MEDO). Although publicly the French stressed, as the prime motive for their recalcitrance, the provocative appearance of MEDO in the eyes of the Soviet Union,[56] the real calculation behind Quai opposition was the perceived threat of a Middle East alliance in which a dominant Iraq, led by Britain's old friend Nuri Said, would threaten French influence in Syria and Lebanon.[57] Resentment at their exclusion from a strictly Anglo-Saxon dialogue on Western policy toward the Middle East reinforced French intransigence.

Despite its signature on the Tripartite Declaration, France found that by the mid-1950s its views in the region were all but ignored in London and Washington. The Quai argued that France, to reaffirm its status as a regional power, should resist Anglo-Saxon initiatives in exact proportion to which the British and Americans excluded it from consultation and regarded its interest in the area as "bon marché."[58] It was this attitude that accounted for Anglo-American use of the terms "irrationally obstructive" and "nuisance value" when referring to French foreign policy.[59]

C. Douglas Dillon and Gladwyn Jebb, respectively U.S. and British ambassadors in Paris, both agreed in December 1955 that only the Quai d'Orsay and a few newspapers like *Le Monde* cared at all about France's "alleged" position in the Middle East; the average Frenchman remained unmoved by the possibility of Syria's absorption by Iraq.[60] Relative public indifference allowed Foreign Ministry officials to pursue their own agenda unimpeded. However, all of that was to change after the January 1956 election. A new coalition government headed by the Socialist Guy Mollet and with another Socialist, Christian Pineau, as foreign minister had very different ideas regarding the orientation of French policy in the Middle East.

Both Mollet and Pineau had been active in the resistance during the war. The new premier had witnessed at first hand German atrocities against Jews. Pineau spent more than a year at Buchenwald after his second capture by the Germans. His experiences there transformed him into a passionate advocate of Zionism. Sympathy for the Israelis extended to the realm of political ideology as well. At Mollet's first meeting with Director-General Shimon Peres of the Israeli Defense Ministry, the Frenchman outlined the dual nature of his attachment to the new Jewish state. "I know all about Nazi persecution. I was a victim myself. Why, the greatest Frenchman I ever knew was Léon Blum. He was my teacher, my guide. It is my warmest wish to visit Israel. I have many friends in the Labour movement there. Israel is developing the very model of a socialist society to which we in our French party aspire."[61] The Radical Maurice Bourgès-Maunoury, a cabinet veteran of Fourth Republic coalitions, assumed the defense portfolio in Mollet's government. Under the name Polycarpe he had served with great courage and distinction in the Parisian underground and as liaison to de Gaulle's Free French. His chief aide, Abel Thomas, was likewise a resistance veteran, and both men shared a sympathy and admiration for the Jewish struggle in Palestine.

Inevitably the leaders of the new government perceived the Quai as their adversaries and attempted to wrest Middle East policy from the grasp of the permanent officials, for in contrast to their political masters, any sympathy the Quai d'Orsay felt for Franco-Israeli cooperation stemmed from purely practical considerations. In its appraisal of General Moshe Dayan's August 1954 visit to Paris, the Quai insisted that such contacts did not signal any reversal of France's traditional regional policy. The relationship with Israel was merely expected to serve as a useful instrument with which to resist Anglo-Saxon encroachment in the Levant.[62] Abel Thomas branded all upper-level functionaries and ambassadors in the Foreign Ministry as pro-Arab.[63] Pineau also complained of a powerful Arab lobby within his department.[64] Shimon Peres did not believe the Quai d'Orsay was actively hostile toward Israel; rather he found their "attitude was one of aloofness."[65] Pineau dissented, openly accusing his permanent officials of anti-Semitism.[66] In any case, to the France of Mollet, Pineau, and Bourgès-Maunoury, "Israel appeared in quite another light, very different from that in which she was viewed by the sophisticated traditionalists at the Quai d'Orsay."[67]

Because of philosophical differences separating them from the career diplomats, the frustrating experience of previous French politicians with foreign policy leaks,[68] and also perhaps an inability to shake off the atmosphere of secrecy and suspicion so prudently nurtured during service in the wartime resistance, Mollet and his colleagues viewed the Quai with profound distrust while searching for means to bypass it. At his first meeting with Peres in early 1956, Abel Thomas cautioned that they must, in their dealings, "keep away as far as possible from the diplomatic crowd—they don't make foreign policy but policy that is foreign."[69] Pineau could not fault the intelligence of his civil servants, but he found their loyalty and discipline severely wanting. He observed that the high functionaries at the Quai d'Orsay seemed to feel that their opinion should prevail over government ministers. Warning of the serious consequences of "treachery" in diplomacy, Pineau judged that a new foreign minister who wished to break with the policies of his predecessors needed support from key bureaucrats who shared his ideas.[70] Failing that, circumvention was the only viable option.

Secret arms transfers between France and Israel began in 1954, but the scale

remained relatively small. Even after Nasser's large purchase of Czechoslova-
kian arms in the autumn of 1955, neither Edgar Faure (premier February 1955–
January 1956) nor Antoine Pinay (foreign minister February 1955–January
1956) evinced any great enthusiasm for increasing or even maintaining these
exchanges.[71] When Peres discussed with the head of the Quai's Levant Department the role France might assume to "correct the balance" of arms in the
Middle East, he received the disappointing reply: "As far as France is concerned, I fear that is the least reasonable and least likely course to be followed."[72] The deteriorating situation in Algeria added a new urgency to the
problem; Bourgès-Maunoury, Mollet, and Pineau all looked upon Egypt as
the key to French difficulties in North Africa. Arming Israel to counterbalance
the apparent increase in Nasser's military strength offered an attractive Algerian
by-product to its primary function of preserving Israeli security.[73]

Once again the Quai d'Orsay was unsympathetic. A November 1955 Paris
conference of all French representatives in the Middle East discussed the two
incompatible policy alternatives in the region: the traditional French policy of
friendship with all Arab countries in the area versus the adoption of a hard line
toward the Arabs in reaction to recent events in North Africa. The conference
decided unanimously in favor of the former option.[74] Pineau agreed that collaboration must continue with the Arab world, but he believed, as apparently his
permanent officials did not, that it was a moral impossibility for French Algerian policy to ever gain Arab approval or even acquiescence. In the end, Muslim
solidarity would overwhelm rational calculations of political or economic interest by the Levantine Arabs.[75]

All things considered, Mollet's government determined to arm Israel over
the Quai d'Orsay's objections or, if necessary, behind its back. Anglo-
American exclusion of France from Middle East affairs provided a convenient
pretext for ignoring the Tripartite Declaration and bypassing the Near East
Arms Coordinating Committee (NEACC). Repeated Israeli requests for shipments of tanks, artillery, and warplanes formed the backdrop for a power
struggle within the new administration, pitting the Quai against a Defense
Ministry backed by both Pineau and Mollet. The professional diplomats strenuously opposed bilateral arrangements between France and Israel, urging instead
that the responsibility, and odium, be shared equally with the British, Italians,
and Americans. At first Pineau seemed to side with his permanent officials,
agreeing that to shoulder "total responsibility" for arming Israel would "concentrate upon us the hostility of all the Arab states," creating generalized
Francophobia within the Muslim world with disastrous consequences for the
fragile situation in Algeria.[76]

However, the other Western nations were reluctant to cooperate, forcing
Pineau to reconsider. Meanwhile, at the meetings of the Interministerial Committee in charge of foreign arms sales the Defense Ministry and the Quai
d'Orsay were at loggerheads. In February and March 1956 Pierre Maillard,
director of the Quai's Africa-Levant Department, repeatedly requested either

the cancellation of arms contracts with Israel or immediate reference to the NEACC, while Bourgès-Maunoury fumed over imbecilic diplomatic obstruction.[77] Then at the 16 April meeting the minister of defense shocked the representatives of the Quai by informing them that he had obtained formal permission from Pineau for an additional Franco-Israeli weapons contract.[78]

Apparently betrayed by its own cabinet minister, an embarrassed Quai d'Orsay attempted to shore up its crumbling position. Henri Roux of the Africa-Levant Directorate challenged Bourgès-Maunoury's claim for the Defense Ministry's sole authority in the assessment and execution of arms sales, reasserting instead the Quai's prerogative to rule on the political advisability of such deliveries.[79] In May, Secretary-General René Massigli informed the Israeli ambassador in Paris that "he personally was vehemently opposed" to the sale of arms to Tel Aviv.[80] Such impassioned protests were, however, in vain, for in addition to fighting Pineau and Bourgès-Maunoury, the Quai found the premier himself ranged against them.[81] The outcome of this unequal contest was clear; by July François de Laboulaye of the Washington embassy was warning the Americans that, although the professional diplomats were "anxious to preserve the best possible position with the Arab countries" on the issue of arms sales to Israel, it was "difficult for the Quai d'Orsay to resist the pressure of other elements of the French Government."[82]

By the spring of 1956, the breach between politicians and bureaucrats, along with the mistrust that occasioned it, mirrored the unhealthy situation across the channel. In the coming Suez ordeal neither the British nor French diplomatic apparatus would function properly. In both Paris and London, cabinet ministers accepted as a given the monolithic opposition of their professional advisers and acted accordingly. This working assumption was, in fact, only partially correct, but its total embrace by Mollet, Pineau, Eden, and Selwyn Lloyd would subsequently weaken diplomatic initiatives against Nasser, hinder the free flow of advice requisite to informed judgments, and contribute to American estrangement.

III

After a May 1953 tour of the Middle East, President Dwight Eisenhower's secretary of state, John Foster Dulles, endorsed a shift in U.S. policy to deal with the Soviet threat. Previously, regional defense had been left to the United Kingdom, but now Dulles concluded from his discussions in Arab capitals that the "British position [is] rapidly deteriorating, probably to the point of nonrepair."[83] At the very moment the Americans were abandoning any notion of building Middle East defense policy around Egypt—Britain's preference—in favor of a Northern Tier perimeter anchored by the frontline states of Turkey, Iran, Pakistan, and Iraq, Eden was immersed in delicate negotiations over the future of a British military presence in Suez in which he hoped to link Egyptian participation in MEDO to British troop withdrawals from the Canal Zone.[84]

The treaty, signed in October 1954, did not live up to expectations, providing only for British evacuation of the base by June 1956, permission to re-occupy the Canal Zone in a military emergency, and maintenance of base facilities by British technicians. Eden had stressed to Eisenhower during discussions in January 1953 that "Egypt was the key to Middle East defence . . . that if we were to secure a satisfactory agreement [on the disposition of the Canal Zone and on MEDO], we must act together."[85] By the following January, however, in view of American reluctance to pressure Cairo, the foreign secretary admitted candidly that "the chances of Egyptians becoming our friends are slight." Determined not to cede British preeminence in the region to the Americans, Eden concluded that failure with Egypt necessitated that, in future, British "authority must be based on relations with Jordan and Iraq."[86]

Three years of opposition to Churchillian stubbornness over Egypt had established Eden's *bona fides* as sincere advocate of the Foreign Office position that negotiation of a treaty mandating British evacuation of the Canal Zone was both prudent and inevitable. However, the foreign secretary's commitment to this course was less than complete. During the early stages, an Egyptian formula setting out the "basis of negotiations," deemed adequate by Permanent Under-Secretary Strang and head of the African Department Roger Allen, aroused indignation in Eden, who claimed "he could not possibly get it through Cabinet and would not try." On several occasions the foreign secretary appeared close to siding with Churchill and breaking off negotiations altogether unless and until the Egyptians "behave better." His permanent officials related Eden's inconstancy to excessive concern over his personal standing within the Conservative party, the "sea anemone" recoiling from charges of appeasement leveled by a small but vocal "Suez Group" of backbenchers. Caught between advice from professional diplomats and criticism from party and press, Eden lurched from side to side, concluding optimistically in March 1954 that "Nasser is the man for us," reversing himself four months later while accusing his officials of wanting "to give everything away," then finally expressing enthusiasm for the final terms of the Anglo-Egyptian Treaty. Shuckburgh saw his minister's undulating resistance as an unflattering example of reason sacrificed to passion; Eden reacted badly to those who offered sound but "unpalatable" advice.

> It is like the ancient kings who slew the bearers of bad news. This has made me determined to be as difficult as I can possibly make myself over this Egypt issue. I am *certain* that we have to get agreement on the best terms available, and that A. E. has to be forced to get that accepted by Cabinet. He will be furious with all who press him into so disagreeable a task, and will call us all sorts of names.[87]

Watchful Foreign Office advisers labored unceasingly to combat disruptions of their carefully cultivated and slowly evolving plans by what one of their number described as Eden's "petulance to the point of unreason."[88]

Writing three decades later, Shuckburgh recognized that the tension between foreign secretary and civil servants issued from more than temperamental differences alone, for it was clear that Eden shared the Foreign Office view of the Middle East only "up to a point."[89] Discrepancies would eventually emerge, but in the aftermath of the signing of the Suez Base Agreement of 1954 the foreign secretary and his advisers were united over the course for the immediate future. The Baghdad Pact, lineal descendant of MEDO and outgrowth of an apparent reconciliation of Britain's new emphasis on the Iraqi-Jordanian axis with American interest in a Northern Tier defense, became the cornerstone of a revised British Middle East policy.

Yet, despite private assurances of its support for the Baghdad Pact, the United States refused to join the alliance. Britain was prepared to address what it believed to be the principal domestic reason for American coyness, that is, the opposition of a powerful pro-Israeli lobby to any U.S. military agreement with an Arab state. Eden's answer was to launch Project ALPHA, a joint Anglo-American attempt to broker a Palestinian settlement, secretly approaching first Nasser and then the Israelis with a comprehensive package of territorial adjustments, resolution of the disputes over Jerusalem and the Jordan River, and refugee compensation and resettlement.[90]

But the U.S. State Department also harbored doubts about too close a public association in the Middle East with an old colonial power like Britain. American adherence to the Baghdad Pact threatened to alienate "the support and friendship of rising nationalism" in the Arab world.[91] Washington based its reservations primarily on functional rather than ethical considerations; within the context of the Cold War a policy of intimacy with a weakened Britain in the Middle East appeared, from the American perspective, increasingly ill-conceived and short-sighted.

To Eden, Egypt, as the focus of pan-Arab nationalism, represented the key to overcoming this snag as well. Nasser, leader of Arab opposition to the Baghdad Pact, viewed Britain's friend Iraq as his country's main rival for primacy in the Middle East and the pact itself as simply another means of reintroducing Western influence into the region.[92] If, in conjunction with a Palestinian settlement based upon ALPHA, Egypt could be persuaded to join the alliance or, at the very least, cease its vocal opposition, Eden reasoned that American objections to their own accession to the Baghdad Pact would evaporate. Shuckburgh believed it was always Eden's intention "to base his Middle East policy on cooperation with Egypt."[93] The Suez Base Agreement of 1954 had cleared away one of the "unnecessary irritants" retarding Anglo-Egyptian relations, and the foreign secretary remained cautiously optimistic that Nasser might thereafter adopt a more reasonable and flexible attitude toward Western overtures.

However, following a February 1955 stopover in Cairo to bid personally for Egyptian backing of British plans for Middle East defense, a firmly rebuffed Eden reported to Churchill that, because of "jealousy" and "a frustrated desire to lead the Arab world," Nasser's mind was set firmly against the Baghdad

Pact.[94] Admitting the visit's failure, the foreign secretary predicted Cairo's continued denunciation of the pact and future Egyptian intrigue to depose Iraq's Nuri Said.[95] Yet Eden still refused to write Nasser off completely, continuing his endorsement of ALPHA despite the risks involved for Britain's relations with her traditional Arab friends[96] and telling Dulles that he "was even more convinced than ever that the Suez Canal base settlement was worth all it had cost."[97] Even the Egyptian purchase of Soviet arms from Czechoslovakia in September 1955 did not fully tip the balance. Certainly the Foreign Office was more aroused than the prime minister. Reacting to the news, Shuckburgh concluded Britain "must first try to frighten Nasser, then to bribe him, and if neither works, get rid of him."[98] Echoing this militancy, Deputy Under-Secretary Sir Harold Caccia minuted before the arms sale was formally announced, "We may have to get rid of Nasser, especially if he becomes publicly committed to the contract."[99] Foreign Secretary Macmillan was horrified and combative, recording in his diary, "We really cannot allow this man, who has neither the authority of a throne nor of a Parliament, to destroy our base and threaten our rear."[100]

By contrast, Eden's reaction remained subdued. Anthony Nutting recalled how the prime minister took the news with relative calm.[101] A month later in cabinet a conciliatory Eden excused the Egyptian arms purchase from the Soviet bloc as "understandable if regrettable" in view of Nasser's dependence on the support of the Egyptian army and the West's reluctance to supply the desired weaponry.[102] Rather than join in their rage at Nasser, the Foreign Office discovered to their horror that Eden proposed dealing with this latest unpleasant development by approaching the Soviets directly. His suggestion of a four-power consultation on the Middle East met with universal disapproval among the professionals and provoked this contemptuous aside from Shuckburgh, "Shades of W.S.C.!"[103]

Eden had hesitated, up to this point, to invite additional Arab states to join the Baghdad Pact for fear of inciting further Egyptian opposition. However, by late 1955, Nasser's unrelenting hostility forced a reevaluation of this policy of restraint. In an effort to cement the Baghdad-Amman axis as the new fulcrum of British influence in the Middle East, Jordan was now to be actively courted to become a full partner in the alliance. Still, Eden continued to look hopefully over his shoulder at Cairo, confiding to Macmillan on 6 November his uncertainty whether Jordan's inclusion in the Baghdad Pact would stoke the flames of Egyptian resentment or precipitate a more salutory, less aggressive posture from Nasser.[104] Unfortunately, Field-Marshal Sir Gerald Templer's December mission to Amman, to outline the British offer to King Hussein, was a complete failure, leaving Eden with the conviction, which proved correct, that Cairo was orchestrating Jordanian ministerial opposition to Western overtures. His patience now exhausted, Eden finally relinquished all hope of working with Nasser, vowing to have nothing further to do with the "cad."[105]

Eden never seemed to realize that it was a mistake to pursue Project ALPHA and Nasser's approval of the Baghdad Pact simultaneously. The two policies were incompatible, the price exacted for agreement on either certain to wreck the other half of the tandem. And further complicating the picture for the British was implacable French hostility. Augmenting Nasser's pan-Arab propaganda effort, French authorities used their still considerable influence in Lebanon and Syria to foment opposition to the Baghdad Pact, prompting Shuckburgh to characterize their attitude in the Middle East as "psychopathic."[106] Answering French complaints of exclusion from Anglo-American decisions, the British blamed the Czech-Egyptian arms deal on Paris's reckless policy of supplying military hardware to Israel.[107] Convinced that they were as bad or worse than Nasser, Eden pronounced the French "our enemies in [the] Mid East!"[108]

At first the Mollet government seemed to herald no change. Despite personal assurances to the contrary, the new French premier adhered to the Quai d'Orsay's policy of publicly attacking the Baghdad Pact.[109] Sir Gladwyn Jebb, British ambassador in Paris, judged Pineau favorably disposed toward appeasement of Nasser. When Jebb reported how the Socialist French foreign minister, "looking extremely tired," had urged the British to act as though Nasser was sincere in his denial of aggressive intentions toward Israel, an exasperated Eden minuted, "I hope he will pass out!"[110] But initial impressions proved overly pessimistic, for with the new administration in Paris cooperation slowly replaced antagonism over the Middle East. Jebb discovered Guy Mollet to be "pro-British."[111] As a Socialist and follower of Léon Blum, the premier's first priority was to use his position to further the creation of *l'Europe*.[112] In line with that determination, Anglo-French relations took precedence over relatively minor peripheral interests, since Mollet believed a unified Western Europe without Britain was unthinkable. His gaze remained focused on this goal throughout the entire Suez crisis, and he told Julian Amery a few days before the November landings at Port Said that if Britain and France prevailed alone against Soviet and American opposition, Eden, he believed, would be converted to the idea of a unified Europe constructed around an Anglo-French axis.[113]

Pineau shared his chief's grand ambitions and felt that he and Eden were on "the same wave-length" in their mutual desire for a measure of independence from the suffocating American embrace.[114] Difficulties in Algeria, for which the French blamed Nasser, argued for a quid pro quo: noninterference in Middle East defense arrangements in return for British diplomatic support for the French position in North Africa.[115] Bourgès-Maunoury called for a more significant break with traditional Quai policy: French adhesion to the Baghdad Pact without worrying about repercussions in Lebanon or Syria.[116] Further augmenting the movement toward congruence, French warnings about Nasser's links with the Soviet Union, issued repeatedly since mid-1955, now began to strike a responsive chord on the other side of the channel.

In September 1955 Shuckburgh and the Foreign Office had dismissed as "too clever a French supposition" Foreign Minister Pinay's claim to have intelligence of a comprehensive deal between Nasser and the Russians.[117] However, in November MI6 began forwarding intelligence from a Cairo-based operative code-named LUCKY BREAK with reported links to Nasser's inner circle. This material stressed the depth and breadth of Nasser's involvement with the Soviet Union.[118] Shuckburgh remained cautiously doubtful, recording in his diary on 29 November, "the evidence that Nasser is playing closely with the Russians is very disquieting—unless it has been planted on us, which I think is very possible."[119] The nonprofessionals were less skeptical, the prime minister's press secretary concluding from the MI6 reports: "It is clear that Nasser has gone further than I had ever supposed towards a tie-up with the Communists. . . . He must go."[120] Disillusioned with Nasser after the Czech arms deal and the Jordanian fiasco, Eden was receptive to the conclusions provided by LUCKY BREAK. In Mid-January he warned President Eisenhower about Soviet-Egyptian cooperation in the Middle East and its dire consequences for Western security. Privately Eden had taken to comparing Nasser to Mussolini, both men possessed of the identical ambition "to be Caesar from the Gulf to the Atlantic, and to kick us out of it all."[121]

Although the Foreign Office still retained some hope for Nasser's rehabilitation,[122] Eden had finally had enough. King Hussein's 1 March dismissal of Lieutenant General Sir John Glubb, British commander of Jordan's Arab Legion, often depicted as the catalyst that finally turned Eden against Nasser, merely provided dramatic confirmation that the prime minister's instincts were sound. As in the case of the December rebuff of Field-Marshal Templer in Amman, Eden blamed Egyptian intrigue for Glubb's ouster (although this time apparently with less justice). Tony Nutting claimed that the Glubb dismissal metamorphosed the prime minister: "From now on Eden completely lost his touch. Gone was his old uncanny sense of timing, his deft feel for negotiation. Driven by the impulses of pride and prestige and nagged by mounting sickness, he began to behave like an enraged elephant charging senselessly at invisible and imaginary enemies in the international jungle."[123]

Adding fuel to the flames were domestic pressures and the prime minister's disastrous Commons speech during the 7 March Middle East debate. Shouted down, Eden lost his temper and "made an ass of himself." To Shuckburgh he appeared "to be completely disintegrated—petulant, irrelevant, provocative at the same time as being weak."[124] These brutal observations by Nutting and Shuckburgh must be weighed against the knowledge that their own disenchantment with Eden was of long-standing. But, in her diary entry of 7 March, even Clarissa Eden admitted that recent events in Jordan had "shattered" her husband. "He is fighting very bad fatigue which is sapping his powers of thought. To-night's winding up of the debate was a shambles."[125] Certainly the prime

Minister's blood was up; he even entertained the idea of a military response, suggesting the reoccupation of Suez in force.[126]

The cabinet, the Foreign Office, and the Americans all appear to have concluded in unison that they could no longer do business with Nasser.[127] As always, the professional diplomats bent their efforts toward curbing Eden's impulsive nature. On 12 March, Nutting drew up a draft proposal for isolating Nasser by shoring up the Baghdad Pact, strengthening the Iraqi-Jordanian axis, detaching Saudi Arabia from Egypt, and withholding military and economic aid from Cairo, including financial support for the Aswan Dam. But Eden was in no mood to entertain thoughts of a moderate, long-term solution, exploding over the telephone to Nutting after reading the memorandum: "But what's all this nonsense about isolating Nasser or 'neutralising' him, as you call it? I want him destroyed can't you understand? I want him removed, and if you and the Foreign Office don't agree, then you'd better come to the Cabinet and explain why."[128] Despite this outburst, during Cabinet discussions of Nutting's proposals a week later, Eden declared himself "in full agreement" with the entire package. Lloyd was dispatched to Washington with the prime minister's blessing to enlist the Americans in this new strategy.[129]

The U.S. State Department was already independently considering measures similar to those outlined in Nutting's brief. Thus they were quick to endorse the Foreign Office proposal for concerted long-range Anglo-American action against Egypt. Designated Operation OMEGA, this strategy of diplomatic isolation now displaced Project ALPHA as the blueprint for Western cooperation in the Middle East.[130] Shuckburgh had cautioned in early March that, in order to check Nasser, American collaboration was indispensable.[131] And it now appeared to the Foreign Office that, having overcome Eden's irrationality, it had carried the day with its call for firm but moderate action.

But Anglo-American cooperation foundered on conflicting views of the issues at stake. For Eden, Nasser's Egypt was a dangerous and active foe, flirting with the Soviets, threatening the stability of the Jordanian and Iraqi regimes, strangling Britain's last hope to retain a credible Middle East presence. To Washington, Nasser resembled more of an irritant. It was the Northern Tier states that were truly vital to the policy of containment. Egypt occupied the second line of defense, more important in political than military terms. The United States advocated the reciprocal use of carrot and stick to prevent the alienation of Nasser and Arab nationalism from Western interests.

Dulles was quite explicit regarding American aims for the Anglo-American Middle East partnership.

> The primary purpose [of OMEGA] would be to let Colonel Nasser realize that he cannot cooperate as he is doing with the Soviet Union and at the same time enjoy most-favored-nation treatment from the United States. We would want for the time

being to avoid any open break which would throw Nasser irrevocably into a Soviet satellite status and we would want to leave Nasser a bridge back to good relations with the West if he so desires.[132]

There was little here to satisfy Eden's desire for the destruction of Nasser, and, despite his pledge of "full agreement" with OMEGA, he had already taken matters into his own hands. Employing the Permanent Under-Secretary's Department (PUSD)[133] to provide a direct liaison with the intelligence services, Eden bypassed the Foreign Office as well as the cabinet. With Permanent Under-Secretary Ivone Kirkpatrick's knowledge and approval, the prime minister mandated MI6 to proceed with covert operations aimed at Nasser's overthrow and replacement by friendlier rebel officers from the Egyptian military.[134]

Thus, the pattern whereby Eden perceived the Foreign Office as his adversary in Middle East affairs and acted accordingly was well established before Nasser's stunning nationalization of the Suez Canal on 26 July in response to the withdrawal of American financial backing for the Aswan Dam project. Immediately following the seizure, the prime minister appointed a Suez Committee of the cabinet consisting of himself, Macmillan, Lord Salisbury, and Lord Home.[135] The following morning this "War Cabinet" was reconstituted as the Egypt Committee with Selwyn Lloyd and Minister of Defense Sir Walter Monckton added to the original membership of four. All or some of the Chiefs of Staff as well as a few additional cabinet ministers, like Lord Privy Seal R. A. Butler, attended meetings frequently. Dominated by Eden, this small ad hoc committee defined and directed British policy throughout the crisis. Without a strong, independent, and determined foreign secretary to guard its prerogatives, the Foreign Office input was relegated to the Egypt Official Committee, a marginal group charged with little more than outlining the political aims of any hypothetical military action against Nasser.[136]

Eden's suspicions about the Foreign Office were almost certainly overwrought. At the outset, at least, some senior diplomats like Shuckburgh and Gladwyn Jebb looked with favor upon hints of a military response in the offing.[137] Eden received unwavering support from the permanent undersecretary throughout the prolonged ordeal. Kirkpatrick, posted to Berlin in 1933 and a veteran of pre-Munich diplomacy, was determined there would be no repetition of that dismal progression in the case of Nasser.[138] When, in late September, Shuckburgh ventured some mild criticism of the handling of Suez, Kirkpatrick, exhibiting the siege mentality of those in Eden's inner circle, rose in the prime minister's defense.

> He said the PM was the only man in England who wanted the nation to survive; that all the rest of us have lost the will to live; that in two years' time Nasser will have deprived us of our oil, the sterling area falling apart, no European defence possible, unemployment and unrest in the UK and our standard of living reduced to that of the Yugoslavs or Egyptians. He said that all the newpapers except *The Times* are

concerned only to criticize the Government for "making trouble" over Suez, while exonerating the brigand Nasser from any blame for his felony.[139]

Eden left it to this highly efficient and deferential subordinate to seal off all the usual Foreign Office telegraphic traffic, at all levels.[140] The office found attempts to express dissenting opinions rebuffed by their own head of department. To Assistant Under-Secretary Harold Beeley's warning of the grave consequences of the employment of force against Nasser, a sardonic Kirkpatrick responded, "It seems to me easy to enunciate these views . . . but it is more difficult to draw up a programme which will achieve the end, 'Defeating Nasser without resort to force' . . . I shall be grateful for ideas."[141] To at least one eyewitness, Kirkpatrick "appeared to participate in the enterprise with zest."[142]

Only three foreign service officials were privy to the extent of military planning and the decisions of the Egypt Committee: Kirkpatrick; Patrick Dean, superintending under-secretary of the PUSD and, as chairman of the Joint Intelligence Committee, responsible for coordinating relations between the FO and the fighting and intelligence services; and Geoffrey McDermott, Dean's deputy and Foreign Office adviser to MI6. McDermott recalled that instructions for the privileged trio, "passed down by word of mouth from Eden, were both clear and unusual. First, only we three were to be in on all the intelligence and planning. . . . Other under-secretaries, for instance the experts on economic matters, Middle Eastern problems, or Anglo-American relations, were to be kept in the dark as far as possible." Secrecy prevailed even within this tiny circle. McDermott found that on occasion Dean mysteriously disappeared for twenty-four hours or so. "On his return he vouchsafed no explanation; and, good subordinate official as I then was, I did not press for one."[143]

Only Kirkpatrick and Archibald Ross, Shuckburgh's successor as assistant under-secretary for Middle Eastern affairs, were informed of the visit by Albert Gazier[144] and General Maurice Challe to Chequers on 14 October and of their plan for Anglo-French military intervention concerted with an Israeli strike into Sinai. Inside the Foreign Office suspicions were rampant that "some funny business was going on."[145] Indeed, in Paris, Bourgès-Maunoury had quite frankly admitted as much to Jebb, indicating that heads of government were handling matters outside normal diplomatic channels.[146] Confirmation came on 16 October, when, over the ambassador's protest,[147] Eden and Selwyn Lloyd excluded Jebb from a meeting with Mollet and Pineau to discuss the Challe-Gazier proposal.

The French had taken similar precautions to ensure secrecy. As in London, a small cabal handled all details: Mollet; Pineau; Bourgès-Maunoury; Abel Thomas, adviser to Minister of Defense Colonel Louis Mangin; Gazier; Minister of War Max Lejeune; and Generals Challe and Paul Ely. A conspiratorial atmosphere, the legacy of common service in the resistance, dominated proceedings within this closed circle. The selection of a site for the famous Sèvres

Conference—a secluded villa once used by Bourgès-Maunoury as an underground safe house and owned by the Bonnier de la Chapelle family, whose son had been executed for the 1942 assassination of Vichyite Admiral Darlan in Algiers[148]—symbolized the psychological link with the recent past. These men believed they detected the hand of the Quai d'Orsay behind any manifestation of opposition or doubt.[149] Thus, as in London, the diplomatic professional found himself deliberately and systematically excluded from consultation by his political superiors. A bemused and somewhat discomfitted Jean Chauvel, ambassador to Britain, received explicit instructions not to accompany Challe and Gazier to their rendezvous with Eden at Chequers.[150] Henri Roux of the Africa-Levant Directorate was entirely truthful when on 27 September he assured the U.S. embassy that he knew nothing of additional transfers of Mystère IV aircraft to Israel.[151]

Perhaps to keep the Quai off balance, changes in key personnel preceded the Suez crisis: Ambassador Couve de Murville was moved from Washington to Bonn and replaced by Hervé Alphand; Louis Joxe assumed the post of secretary-general from Réné Massigli, who resigned in July, a victim, as he saw it, of ministerial determination to escape "la 'dictature' des fonctionnaires."[152] Certainly the latter substitution did nothing to lift the veil of secrecy. When Abel Thomas attempted to transmit a communication from Ben-Gurion on to Pineau and Bourgès-Maunoury—both then in London—using Joxe as an intermediary, he received a stiff reprimand for his trouble from Guy Mollet: "You are completely mad! Do you want all of our enemies at the Quai d'Orsay to know what is going on when we put them out of the running six months ago!" Mollet recommended the use of a public telephone in order to bypass the Quai's communications network.[153] During a 30 October conversation with Joxe, a suspicious Dillon received the distinct impression that the secretary-general was "under instructions to tell the US as little as possible at this time."[154] More likely Joxe's reticence was simply the result of ignorance.

Neither Eden nor Mollet was well served by this self-imposed isolation. The distrust felt by Pineau toward the Quai's senior officials, and the gulf established between politicians and civil servants as a result, ensured the foreign minister's complete surprise at Nasser's seizure of the Canal, with Couve de Murville's prediction of the inevitable Egyptian response to the bungled withdrawal of Western funds for the Aswan Dam going unheeded.[155] Assurances by poorly informed diplomats to American Ambassador Dillon that France was most anxious to avoid the use of force if at all possible, when contradicted by Pineau's belligerent expressions, must surely have deepened Washington's sense of duplicity of French policy over Suez.[156] Almost certainly the Quai d'Orsay would have resisted Mollet's schizophrenic use of the Soviet card.

Meeting with Dillon on 31 July, the French premier opened by equating Nasser's seizure of the canal with the invasion of South Korea, detailing the threat to the Free World of communist penetration into North Africa and the

Middle East. Dillon reported to the State Department how the line of reasoning changed abruptly as the interview drew to a close.

> As I got up to leave Mollet said he wished to tell me one more thing in greatest confidence which he had not mentioned previously. He said that it was made clear to him by the Soviet leaders when he was in Moscow [earlier that spring] that they were prepared, in concert with Nasser, to agree to bring about peace in Algeria on a basis acceptable to his government provided he would agree to come part way to meet their views on European matters. They did not ask that France make any dramatic moves, such as the abandonment of NATO, but only that she be less faithful to the West and become in effect semi-neutralist. Mollet said I must realize the temptation such an offer regarding Algeria offered to any French statesman.[157]

The professionals at the Quai would have been appalled at this clumsy and counterproductive effort to extort American support, employing what could only be interpreted as a barely disguised threat.

Mollet, at least, was not acting in a complete vacuum. He had the backing of the National Assembly, while public opinion was supportive.[158] Eden enjoyed no such luxuries. With the national press evenly split, the Labour party drifting from an initial position of forbearance to one of vocal opposition, and public opinion polls registering only lukewarm support for the hypothetical use of force, Eden found himself unable to rally broad-based, bipartisan support for intervention. Though never threatening their parliamentary majority, more disturbing still were the divisions within the Conservative party and, in the end, even the cabinet.[159] Out of choice, the prime minister neglected to cultivate an alternative base of support within Whitehall. On the single occasion Eden did solicit a Foreign Office opinion, he elected to disregard it. When consulted about the Gazier-Challe plan, Archibald Ross objected strenuously and the loyal Kirkpatrick labeled it "a crazy idea."[160]

Instead of listening to the arguments of the only two senior Foreign Office officials in the know, the prime minister relied on envoys like Harold Macmillan. An old friend of Eisenhower and hawkish on Suez from the beginning, the chancellor of the exchequer was dispatched to Washington in late September to ascertain the president's true attitude toward the crisis. After a rambling thirty-five minute conversation at the White House, during which Anglo-American differences over Suez were never systematically addressed, Macmillan reported to Eden his feeling that "Ike is really determined, somehow or another, to bring Nasser down. I explained to him our economic difficulties in playing the hand long, and he seemed to understand. I also made it clear that we *must* win, or the whole structure of our economy would collapse. He accepted this."[161] This satisfactory appraisal of American attitudes surely influenced Eden to disregard the clear and repeated warnings received from Eisenhower that the use of force by Britain against Nasser would result in "a serious misunderstanding between our two countries."[162]

Ambassador Sir Roger Makins, sitting in on the Macmillan-Eisenhower conversation and taking notes, came away with quite a different impression from that of the chancellor. Makins was "expecting Harold to make a statement, say something important on Suez—but in fact he said nothing. I was very much surprised. Nor did Ike say anything. I was amazed." The ambassador saw "no basis for Harold's optimism." He conceded the American desire for Nasser's removal, but stressed that in no way implied a sanction for military action.[163] Throughout the crisis, Makins reported accurately on the temper and intentions of the U.S. government: in July he predicted Dulles would brook no use of force as long as Nasser did not interfere with traffic through the canal; in October he echoed Eisenhower's warning to Eden that American public opinion was adamant against military intervention; in September he offered his own understanding of what was at stake.

> There are times perhaps (they are surely very rare) when we must take our own line because our national interest transcends even the need to uphold the Atlantic Alliance. But this, I think, is true only when there is an issue of profound substance dividing us. Here it is a case of our wanting to perform an operation (cutting Nasser down) one way and the Americans another. Ours may be better, but if we can keep their immense power working in our favour, is it not preferable to try theirs?[164]

This was the sort of detached analysis of the relation of Suez to Britain's long-term priorities in foreign policy consistently ignored by Eden during the crisis. When in late August Makins relayed Dulles's suggestion that public opinion in the United States, and likely in Britain as well, believed in the exclusion of military action until the affair was referred to the UN, Eden minuted "Mind his own business."[165] One suspects he meant Makins along with Dulles.

IV

Even without the restraining hand of the Foreign Office, Eden and Lloyd—if not Pineau and the French[166]—were close to agreement on a negotiated settlement by mid-October. This possibility, which would have brought OMEGA back into effect, ran afoul of an acute exacerbation of tensions between Israel and Jordan. Fearing an Israeli invasion of Jordan, triggering in turn an Iraqi response and a treaty-mandated British intervention against the Jewish state, Eden eagerly signed on to the Challe-Gazier proposal of 14 October.[167]

There were only Kirkpatrick and Ross to argue against the prime minister's impulses, and, because of the enforced isolation of these two from their colleagues, their warnings did not carry the full weight of official Foreign Office opinion. With Makins out of the loop, there was no one to emphasize repeatedly that it was Eisenhower, not Dulles, who had the final say on American policy.

Eden, tired and weak, using amphetamines to overcome exhaustion and barbiturates to counteract the effect of the prescribed stimulants, had no sober, independent voice to counsel him. The disadvantage of having appointed Selwyn Lloyd as foreign secretary was only too apparent. But even Lloyd's predecessor Macmillan, employed as emissary to Washington in an effort to short-circuit the Foreign Office, proved no more serviceable, offering the opinion that if an Anglo-French force seized the canal, "the Americans would issue a protest, even a violent protest in public; but that they would in their hearts be glad to see the matter brought to a conclusion. They would therefore content themselves with overt disapproval, while feeling covert sympathy."[168]

Eden's insistence on absolute secrecy argues for the conclusion that, despite reassurances from Macmillan and others, he still harbored doubts about the genuine benignity of the attitude of the U.S. government. In the end, he gambled that a successful use of force would unite the Conservative party and British public opinion behind his aggressive policy, while eliciting only a toothless and insincere objection from Washington. But in the awkward five-day delay between the initial bombings of Egyptian airfields on 31 October and the parachute drop at Port Said on 5 November, opposition at home and abroad mounted. Carried swiftly and ruthlessly to completion, the military operation might have wrought a diplomatic success in its wake.

After the combination of unbearable American economic pressure and hostility on the floor of the UN and the House of Commons forced a cease-fire, Lloyd held his famous meeting with the American secretary of state in his Walter Reed Hospital room on 17 November, where Dulles demanded of his startled visitor, "Selwyn, why did you stop? Why didn't you go through with it and get Nasser down?"[169] Some writers have dismissed this ambiguous exchange as essentially meaningless.[170] But five days earlier Dulles had expressed identical views to Eisenhower himself. "The British, having gone in, should not have stopped until they had toppled Nasser. As it was, they now had the worst of both possible worlds. They had received all the onus of making the move and, at the same time, had not accomplished their major purpose."[171] It is impossible to say exactly how the United States might have reacted to the fait accompli that never quite materialized. But even in the heat of the moment, while pondering how the U.S. could "possibly support Britain and France if in doing so we lose the whole Arab world," Eisenhower admitted that a permanent disruption in the Atlantic Alliance was "unthinkable," that "quite naturally, Britain not only has been, but must be, our best friend in the world."[172]

Quick and decisive military action might have salvaged opinion in the Foreign Office as well. Above all, the diplomats were embarrassed about their deliberately orchestrated ignorance. Without instructions and taken completely off-guard by the 30 October ultimatum to Egypt (and ostensibly to Israel), ambassadors were left to their own devices to explain London's policy to their host governments. One unlucky spokesman was actually busy explaining to journalists Britain's intention to invoke the Tripartite Agreement in response to the Israeli strike into Sinai at the very moment Eden rose in the Commons to announce the ultimatum.[173]

Personal and professional pique and practical disagreement over policy rather than moral outrage fueled most intradepartmental opposition. Shuckburgh objected to Eden's course of action because it seemed to suffer from "*every* fault," meaning that, because of vexations caused to the Americans, the UN, Parliament, and British public opinion, the cost-benefit ration was unfavorable.[174] One Treasury official, who wore a black tie to the office during the Suez operation in an apparent protest of conscience, later explained the real reason for his actions.

> I felt that [the landing in Suez] was not a bad move in policy terms, but that I personally had been duped, because I had been sent to discuss with the American State Department something quite different—the introduction of a Suez Canal User's Association which would deal with the Egyptians over the Canal and so on. I was very angry indeed at, as I thought, being used as part of a cover plan while the . . . preparations were being made. So I wore a black tie until the operation ended.[175]

Paul Henry Gore-Booth, deputy under-secretary for economic affairs, signed and circulated a "round-robin" protest memo—a radical enough innovation inside any disciplined bureaucracy—concerned mainly with the damage done to Britain's reputation. Kirkpatrick responded with an urgent top-level meeting on 5 November, the same morning as the parachute landings at Port Said, in order to contain any disaffection within the ranks. Although in retrospect some civil servants extravagantly recalled wondering at the time how, if at all, they differed from Hitler's Nazi accomplices,[176] when the dust finally settled only two permanent officials tendered their resignations. Despite the general feeling of astonishment, betrayal, and depression, many within the Foreign Office agreed with Dulles that, once "having gone in, surely we should have done the job."[177]

V

It is interesting to compare post-mortems on Suez by the Quai d'Orsay and the Foreign Office. French public opinion never turned against the war, Great Britain and the United States providing scapegoats to explain the failure of policy. Consequently Mollet's government did not fall. But although the Quai's chief adversary from January to November remained in office, it proved possible to effect a rapprochement between politician and civil servant. Mollet's greatest ambition—even at the darkest moments of the crisis—was to further the creation of *l'Europe*. As Konrad Adenauer had advised in conference with the premier on 6 November, just prior to French acceptance of a cease-fire, this humiliation in the Middle East could be turned to advantage in the pursuit of a loftier goal.

> France and England will never be powers comparable to the United States and the Soviet Union. Nor Germany either. There remains only one way for them to play a decisive role in the world, it is to unite to construct Europe. England is not yet ripe, but the Suez affair will contribute to the preparation of her spirits for it. We have no time to lose. Europe will be your revenge.[178]

The Quai, resigned to the irreversible compromise of its traditional Arab policy, was now transformed into a willing accomplice. The comportment of the United States and its cavalier treatment of French interests—first in Indochina, then in North Africa, and now in the Middle East (making France feel, as Joxe said, like a "defendant at the bar"[179])—called into question the value of the Atlantic Alliance. The professional diplomats concluded it necessary to make *l'Europe,* under French tutelege, a reality.[180] Psychologically Suez prepared the Quai d'Orsay, like the rest of the nation, for de Gaulle and the Fifth Republic.[181]

Britain drew a different lesson from her "climacteric."[182] As Adenauer had observed, England was not ready for a serious commitment to the construction of a unified Europe. With the brittle and shallow nature of her power exposed, ties with America assumed more importance than ever. The quick reestablishment of the "special relationship" required Eden's immediate exit. His departure (like the subsequent replacement of Kirkpatrick by Sir Frederick Hoyer-Millar in February 1957) was also necessary to heal the breach between Foreign Office and cabinet. With the more domestically oriented Macmillan at No. 10 and the tentative Selwyn Lloyd staying on as foreign secretary, the eclipse of the professional diplomat was at an end. It was under the guidance of, and in close cooperation with, the Foreign Office that the new prime minister embarked upon a campaign to overcome the estrangement between Washington and London.[183]

Notes

1. See Gordon A. Craig, "The British Foreign Office from Grey to Austen Chamberlain," in *The Diplomats 1919–1939,* ed. Gordon A. Craig and Felix Gilbert (Princeton, 1953), 15–48.

2. See Anthony Adamthwaite, "The Foreign Office and Policy-Making" in *The Foreign Policy of Churchill's Peacetime Administration 1951–1955,* ed. John W. Young (Leicester, 1988), 1–28.

3. Ritchie Ovendale, "William Strang and the Permanent Under-Secretary's Committee," in *British Officials and British Foreign Policy 1945–50,* ed. John Zametica (Leicester, 1990), 212–27.

4. Sir Roderick Barclay, *Ernest Bevin and the Foreign Office 1932–1969* (London, 1975), 94–106.

5. Evelyn Shuckburgh, *Descent to Suez: Diaries 1951–56* (New York, 1987), 11.

6. Ibid., 338–39.

7. Ibid., 193.

8. Ibid., 148. See also 120–21.

9. Ibid., 125.

10. See Anthony Eden, *Full Circle* (Boston, 1960), 10.

11. Shuckburgh, *Descent to Suez*, 346, 152.

12. Lord Strang, *Home and Abroad* (London, 1956), 280.

13. Julian Amery, "The Suez Group: A Retrospective on Suez," in *The Suez-Sinai Crisis 1956: Retrospective and Reappraisal*, ed. Selwyn Ilan Troen and Moshe Shemesh (New York, 1990), 110–26.

14. Robert Rhodes James, *Anthony Eden* (London, 1986), 345.

15. Shuckburgh, *Descent to Suez*, 126.

16. Ibid., 99.

17. Ibid., 91. See also Sir John Colville, *The Fringes of Power: 10 Downing Street Diaries 1939–1955* (London, 1985), 567.

18. Anthony Seldon, *Churchill's Indian Summer: The Conservative Government, 1951–55* (London, 1981), 381.

19. Colville, *Fringes of Power*, 674.

20. Lord Moran, *Churchill: The Struggle for Survival, 1940–1965* (London, 1966), 482–83.

21. Colville, *Fringes of Power*, 643.

22. Shuckburgh, *Descent to Suez*, 75.

23. See, e.g., ibid., 218.

24. Robert Rhodes James, "Eden," in Troen and Shemesh, eds. *The Suez-Sinai Crisis*, 103.

25. Foreign Office (FO) 371/76385/3/500G, PUSC (51), "Anglo-American Relations: Present and Future," 24 Aug. 1949.

26. Rhodes James, "Eden," 103–4.

27. Shuckburgh, *Descent to Suez*, 187.

28. CAB 128/29, C.M. 34(55).

29. Colville, *Fringes of Power*, 694. With the benefit of hindsight, Harold Macmillan argued that "Winston thought Anthony would wreck it—that's a reason why he held on for so long." Alistair Horne, *Harold Macmillan*, 2 vols. (New York, 1988–1989), 1:384.

30. Shuckburgh, *Descent to Suez*, 19.

31. Quoted in Martin Gilbert, *'Never Despair': Winston S. Churchill 1945–1965* (London, 1988), 1123.

32. Shuckburgh, *Descent to Suez*, 284.

33. Horne, *Harold Macmillan*, 1:379–80. See also Shuckburgh, *Descent to Suez*, 277.

34. Avon Papers (hereafter AP), Birmingham University Library, 20/1, Eden diary 17 Sept. and 3 Oct. 1955.

35. Shuckburgh, *Descent to Suez*, 127.

36. Ibid., 314.

37. Ibid., 325, 335, 315, 334, 337.

38. Ibid., 12.

39. See Selwyn Lloyd, *Suez 1956: A Personal Account* (London, 1978), 53, for Lloyd's agreement with Eden. On pro-Arab sentiments of British diplomats, see Ilan Pappé, "Sir Alec Kirkbride and the Anglo-Transjordanian Alliance, 1945–50," and Wesley K. Wark, "Development Diplomacy: Sir John Troutbeck and the British Middle East Office, 1947–50," in Zametica, *British Officials and British Foreign Policy,* 121–55 and 228–49; Wm. Roger Louis, "Britain at the Crossroads in Palestine, 1952–1954," *Jerusalem Journal of International Relations* 12, no. 3 (September 1990): 59–82.

40. Shuckburgh, *Descent to Suez,* 67. FO 371/113608 JE 1057, P.M.'s minutes, Macmillan to Eden, 29 June 1955.

41. Louis, "Britain at the Crossroads in Palestine," 76–77.

42. Shuckburgh, *Descent to Suez,* 346.

43. Ibid., 319.

44. Anthony Nutting, *No End of a Lesson: The Story of Suez* (New York, 1967), 89.

45. Ibid., 37–40. See also Rhodes James, *Anthony Eden,* 344, and Shuckburgh, *Descent to Suez,* 300.

46. J. B. Duroselle, "French Diplomacy in the Postwar World," in *Diplomacy in a Changing World,* ed. Stephen D. Kertesz and M. A. Fitzsimons (Notre Dame, 1959), 244–46.

47. Robert Schuman in *La Nef* (March 1958), quoted in Alfred Grosser, *La IVᵉ République et sa politique extérieure* (Paris, 1961), 52.

48. Hervé Alphand, *L'étonnement d'être: Journal, 1939–1973* (Paris, 1973), 237, 242.

49. See, e.g., Documents diplomatiques français (*D.D.F.*), 1955 (Paris, 1987), 1:690–91, doc. 300, Pinay to Couve de Murville (Washington, D.C.), 26 May 1955.

50. Jean-Pierre Rioux, *The Fourth Republic 1944–1958* (Cambridge, Eng., 1989), 138–39.

51. Herbert Tint, *French Foreign Policy Since the Second World War* (London, 1972), 234–36.

52. André Siegfried, *De la IIIᵉ à la IVᵉ République* (Paris, 1956), 243. This influx was certainly real. M. Couve de Murville and M. Hervé Alphand, successive ambassadors to Washington during the Suez crisis, were both former *inspecteurs des finances.* One Quai official judged two key diplomatic posts in the hands of these interlopers as "*pitoyable et décourageant.*" Jacques Dumaine, *Quai d'Orsay* (Paris, 1955), journal entry for 31 Jan. 1948, 350.

53. Duroselle, "French Diplomacy in the Postwar World," 214–18.

54. Grosser, *La IVᵉ République et sa politique extérieure,* 71.

55. *D.D.F.,* 1954 (Paris, 1987), pp. 119–21, doc. 54, "Réajustement de la politique francaise au Moyen-Orient après la visite du général Dayan," 11 Aug. 1954.

56. *D.D.F.,* 1955 (Paris, 1987), 2:657–58, doc. 296, Pinay to Couve de Murville, 13 Oct. 1955; 1956, I (Paris, 1988), doc. 22, pp. 39–42, Pinay to French ambassadors in Washington and London, 14 Jan. 1956.

57. *D.D.F.,* 1955, 1:474–75, doc. 204, "Problème du Moyen-Orient," 19 Apr. 1955.

58. *D.D.F.*, 1954, pp. 119–21, doc. 54, 11 Aug. 1954.

59. *Foreign Relations of the United States (FRUS)*, 1952–1954, 5 (part II): 1175–76, Fuller memo, 10 Sept. 1954; and FO 371/115468 V1022/1, Jebb to Kirkpatrick, 5 Feb. 1955 and V1022/15, Shuckburgh to Gardener (Damascus), 13 Apr. 1955.

60. Shuckburgh, *Descent to Suez*, 311–12.

61. Shimon Peres, *David's Sling* (London, 1970), 59.

62. *D.D.F.*, 1954, pp. 119–21, doc. 54, 11 Aug. 1954.

63. Abel Thomas, *Comment Israël fut sauvé: Les secrets de l'expédition de Suez* (Paris, 1978), 74.

64. Christian Pineau, *1956 Suez* (Paris, 1976), 65–66.

65. Peres, *David's Sling*, 44.

66. Pineau, *1956 Suez*, 66.

67. Peres, *David's Sling*, 44. See also Pierre Milza, "La relève des impérialismes au Proche-Orient," *L'histoire* 38 (October 1981): 20–22.

68. See René Massigli, *Sur quelques maladies de l'Etat* (Paris, 1958), 12, and Grosser, *La IVe République et sa politique extérieure*, pp. 60–63.

69. Grosser, *La IVe République et sa politique extérieure*, 57.

70. Pineau, *1956 Suez*, 64–66.

71. Michael Bar-Zohar, *Ben-Gurion: A Biography* (New York, 1977), 226–27, and Peres, *David's Sling*, 48–53.

72. Peres, *David's Sling*, 55.

73. PREM 11/1344, meeting between Eden and Mollet at Chequers, 11 Mar. 1956.

74. FO 371/115468, J. D. Scott (Beirut) to E. M. Rose (Levant Dept.), 3 Nov. 1955.

75. Pineau, *1956 Suez*, 66.

76. *D.D.F.*, 1956, 1:176–77, doc. 86, T. 1286-91, Pineau to Couve de Murville (Washington, D.C.), 10 Feb. 1956.

77. *D.D.F.*, 1956, 1:242–43, doc. 115, note by Pierre Maillard, 20 Feb. 1956.

78. *D.D.F.*, 1956, 1:623–24, doc. 258, note by Africa-Levant Directorate (Henri Roux), 19 Apr. 1956.

79. *D.D.F.*, 1956, 1:744–46, doc. 309, note by Africa-Levant Directorate, 11 May 1956; and doc. 416, pp. 1011–12, note by Africa-Levant Directorate (Henri Roux), 19 June 1956.

80. *FRUS*, 1955–1957, 15:614–15. doc. 335, 5 May 1956.

81. Thomas, *Comment Israël fut sauvé*, 63–64, 73–74.

82. *FRUS*, 1955–1957, 15:843–44, doc. 463, Geren memo, 16 July 1956.

83. Quoted in W. Scott Lucas, *Divided We Stand: Britain, the U.S. and the Suez Crisis* (London, 1991), 26.

84. David R. Devereux, "Britain and the Failure of Collective Defence in the Middle East, 1948–52," in *Britain and the First Cold War*, ed. Ann Deighton (London, 1990), 237–52. Wm. Roger Louis, "The Tragedy of the Anglo-Egyptian Settlement of 1954," in *Suez 1956: The Crisis and Its Consequences* ed. Wm. Roger Louis and Roger Owen (Oxford 1989), 43–71. Ritchie Ovendale, "Egypt and the Suez Base Agreement," in Young, ed. *The Foreign Policy of Churchill's Peacetime Administration*, 135–55.

85. Eden, *Full Circle*, 276.

86. FO 371/110819 V1193/8, Eden minute, 12 Jan. 1954.

87. Shuckburgh, *Descent to Suez*, 40, 125, 146, 118, 148, 150, 155, 226, 234.

88. Comment by Lord Sherfield (Sir Roger Makins) quoted in Richard Lamb, *The Failure of the Eden Government* (London 1987), 169.

89. Shuckburgh, *Descent to Suez*, 210.

90. Shimon Shamir, "The Collapse of Project Alpha," in Louis and Owen, eds. *Suez 1956*, 73–100. See also Shuckburgh, *Descent to Suez*, 205 ff.

91. *FRUS*, 1952–1954, 9 (part I): 207, doc. 67, Hoskins memo, 7 Apr. 1952.

92. Brian Holden Reid, "The 'Northern Tier' and the Baghdad Pact," in Young, ed. *The Foreign Policy of Churchill's Peacetime Administration*, 162–63, 172–74.

93. Shuckburgh, *Descent to Suez*, 214.

94. Rhodes James, *Anthony Eden*, 398.

95. *FRUS*, 1955–1957, 14:71, doc. 30, Dulles to State Dept., 24 Feb. 1955.

96. PREM 11/945, T. 2013, Eden minute, Dulles to Macmillan, 25 Aug. 1955.

97. *FRUS*, 1955–1957, 14:71, doc. 30, Dulles to State Dept., 24 Feb. 1955.

98. Shuckburgh, *Descent to Suez*, 281.

99. FO 371/113674 JE1194/152G, Caccia minute, 23 Sept. 1955.

100. Horne, *Harold Macmillan*, 1:376.

101. Nutting, *No End of a Lesson*, 21.

102. PREM 11/859, 20 Oct. 1955.

103. Shuckburgh, *Descent to Suez*, 282–84.

104. AP 20/20/111, Eden to Macmillan, 6 Nov. 1955.

105. Shuckburgh, *Descent to Suez*, 318.

106. FO 371/115468 V1022/15, Shuckburgh to Gardener (Damascus), 13 Apr. 1955. See also Shuckburgh, *Descent to Suez*, 308–9.

107. FO 371/115468 V1022/22, John Beith (Paris Embassy) to R. M. Hadow (Levant Dept.), 3 October 1955. See also Shuckburgh, *Descent to Suez*, 284, 290.

108. PREM 11/1344, Eden minute, Makins (Washington, D.C.) to FO, 19 Jan. 1956.

109. PREM 11/1344, Eden to Jebb (Paris), 25 Mar. 1956. FO 115/4548 1042/25/56G, FO to Washington embassy, 26 Mar. 1956.

110. PREM 11/1344, Eden minute, Jebb to FO, 19 Mar. 1956. Jebb was of the opinion that the Quai was much sounder in its attitude toward Nasser than Pineau. Jebb to FO, 20 March 1956.

111. Lord Gladwyn, *The Memoirs of Lord Gladwyn* (London, 1972), 223.

112. Gérard Bossuat, "Guy Mollet: La puissance française autrement," *Relations internationales* 57 (Spring 1989): 25–48. See also Jean-Paul Cointet, "Guy Mollet, the French Government and the SFIO," in Troen and Shemesh, eds. *The Suez-Sinai Crisis*, 127–39.

113. Amery, "The Suez Group," 124.

114. Pineau, *1956 Suez*, 45–46.

115. At least one Foreign Office official had suggested just such an arrangement in 1955. FO 371/115468 V1022/13, Sir Ralph Stevenson to Kirkpatrick, 15 Mar. 1955.

116. Hervé Alphand, *L'étonnement d'être*, 277. On succeeding Mollet as premier in June 1957, Bourgès-Maunoury assured Macmillan that France under his leadership was not opposed to the Baghdad Pact. PREM 11/1850 WF 1051/34, Bourgès-Maunoury to Macmillan, 15 June 1957.

117. Shuckburgh, *Descent to Suez*, 281–82. See also FO 371/115468 V1022/23, 11 Oct. 1955.

118. Wilbur C. Eveland, *Ropes of Sand: America's Failure in the Middle East* (New York, 1980), 169–71; Keith Kyle, *Suez* (New York, 1991), 84, 102; and Lucas, *Divided We Stand,* 109, 117.

119. Shuckburgh, *Descent to Suez,* 306.

120. William Clark, unpublished diary entry for 29 Nov. 1955, quoted in Kyle, *Suez,* 84.

121. Shuckburgh, *Descent to Suez,* 327.

122. FO 371/121271 V1075/39, G. G. Arthur memorandum, 7 Jan. 1956. In his diary entry for January 29 Shuckburgh mused, ". . . there is the $64 question of Nasser—do we write him off or try to work with him?" *Descent to Suez,* 327.

123. Nutting, *No End of a Lesson,* 27, 32.

124. Shuckburgh, *Descent to Suez,* 344–45.

125. Quoted in Rhodes James, *Anthony Eden,* 432.

126. Ibid., 344, 341.

127. CAB 128/30 C.M. 24(56), 21 Mar. 1956; Shuckburgh, *Descent to Suez,* 345–46. *FRUS, 1955–1957,* 15:352–57, doc. 192, Wilkins memo, 14 Mar. 1956.

128. Nutting, *No End of a Lesson,* 34–35. In 1986 Nutting claimed that Eden actually said, "I want him *murdered* can't you understand." Kyle, *Suez,* 99.

129. CAB 128/30, C.M. 24(56), 21 Mar. 1956.

130. For the fullest account of OMEGA see Lucas, *Divided We Stand,* 111–34.

131. FO 371/121235 V1054/70G, Shuckburgh to Kirkpatrick, 10 Mar. 1956.

132. *FRUS, 1955–1957,* 15:419–21, doc. 223, Dulles memo, 28 Mar. 1956.

133. Home of the PUSC, now sunk into obscurity.

134. Lucas, *Divided We Stand,* 100–103, 116–18. Eveland, *Ropes of Sand,* 168–71.

135. Horne, *Harold Macmillan,* 1:405.

136. Lucas, *Divided We Stand,* 141, 195.

137. Shuckburgh, *Descent to Suez,* 360. Gladwyn, *Memoirs,* 282.

138. *FRUS 1955–1957,* 15:366, doc. 198, Allen memo, 15 Mar. 1956; 16: 249–50, doc. 109, McCardle memo, 21 Aug. 1956.

139. Shuckburgh, *Descent to Suez,* 360–61.

140. Wm. Roger Louis, "American Anti-Colonialism and the Dissolution of the British Empire," *International Affairs* 61, no. 3 (Summer 1985): 414. Geoffrey McDermott remarked that it was "just about unique" that Eden never had a harsh or even "narking" word to say about Kirkpatrick. McDermott, *The Eden Legacy and the Decline of British Diplomacy* (London, 1969), 105.

141. FO 371/119128 JE14211/1390G, Beeley minute, 18 Aug. 1956, and subsequent minutes.

142. McDermott, *Eden Legacy,* 146.

143. Ibid., 133, 145.

144. Gazier, minister for social affairs in the Mollet government, was temporarily in charge of the Quai while Pineau was in New York.

145. McDermott, *The Eden Legacy,* 144.

146. Gladwyn, *Memoirs,* 282.

147. PREM 11/1126, Jebb to Lloyd, 17 Oct. 1956; Eden to Lloyd, 19 Oct. 1956.

148. Kyle, *Suez,* 316. See also Moshe Dayan, *The Story of My Life* (New York, 1976), 221–22.

149. See, e.g., Thomas, *Comment Israël fut sauvé,* 158.

150. Jean Chauvel, *1952–1962, Commentaire* (Paris 1973), 3:194–95.

151. *FRUS,* 1955–1957, 16:1253, doc. 637, Armstrong memo, 5 Dec. 1956.

152. Chauvel, *Commentaire,* 3:176.

153. Thomas, *Comment Israël fut sauvé,* 226–27.

154. *FRUS,* 1955–1957, 16:847–48, doc. 417, Dillon to State Dept., 30 Oct. 1956.

155. Kyle, *Suez,* 130, 144.

156. See *FRUS,* 1955–1957, 16:358–59, doc. 164, Dillon memo, 3 Sept. 1956; 16:461–62, doc. 201, Dillon memo, 10 Sept. 1956.

157. *FRUS,* 1955–1957, 16:74–77, doc. 38, Dillon to State Dept., 31 July 1956.

158. Jean-Pierre Rioux, "L'opinion publique ou 'le lion vieilli et le coq déplumé'," *L'histoire* 38 (October 1981): 35–37.

159. Leon D. Epstein, *British Politics in the Suez Crisis* (Urbana, 1964). See also Philip M. Williams, *Hugh Gaitskell: A Political Biography* (London, 1979), 418–43, and Anthony Adamthwaite, "Suez Revisited," in *British Foreign Policy 1945–56,* ed. Michael Dockrill and John W. Young (London, 1989), 239–41.

160. Nutting, *No End of a Lesson,* 95–96. Kirkpatrick's opinion was suppressed in the original edition of Nutting's book at cabinet insistence. However Alistair Horne cites the unexpurgated version in *Harold Macmillan,* 1:440, n. 106.

161. PREM 11/1102, Macmillan to Eden, 26 Sept. 1956.

162. FO 800/726 T. 1839, Eisenhower to Eden, 8 Sept. 1956.

163. Horne, *Harold Macmillan,* 1:429–30.

164. FO 371/119080, Makins to FO, 30 July 1956; 371/120329, Makins to Eden, 5 Oct. 1956; 800/740, Makins to Lloyd, 9 Sept. 1956.

165. Lamb, *The Failure of the Eden Government,* 203.

166. AP 20/25/85, Lloyd to Eden, 11 Oct. 1956.

167. This scenario is argued persuasively by Lucas, *Divided We Stand,* 227–36.

168. Harold Macmillan, *Riding the Storm, 1956–1959* (New York 1971), 157.

169. Lloyd, *Suez 1956,* 219.

170. See, e.g., Robert R. Bowie, "Eisenhower, Dulles, and the Suez Crisis," in Louis and Owen, eds. *Suez 1956,* 214.

171. Quoted in Lucas, *Divided We Stand,* 307.

172. *FRUS,* 1955–1957, 16:910–14, doc. 455, Gleason memo, 1 Nov. 1956; 16:943–45, doc. 475, Eisenhower to Hazlett, 2 Nov. 1956.

173. Anthony Sampson, *Anatomy of Britain* (London, 1962), 313.

174. Shuckburgh, *Descent to Suez,* 362.

175. BBC 2 interview in 1974 with William Armstrong, quoted in Peter Hennessy, *Whitehall* (London, 1989), 164.

176. Leo Pliatsky, *Getting and Spending: Public Expenditure, Employment and Inflation* (Oxford, 1982), 27.

177. Shuckburgh, *Descent to Suez,* 363–65. See also McDermott, *Eden Legacy,* 164, for the same sentiment.

178. Pineau, *1956 Suez,* 191.

179. *FRUS,* 1955–1957, 16:996–97, doc. 507, Dillon to State Dept., 5 Nov. 1956.

180. *D.D.F.* 1956 (Paris, 1990), 3:271–77, doc. 158, "Note de la Direction générale politique," 10 Nov. 1956. From London Chauvel reported favorably on the possi-

bility of Eden's replacement by Macmillan primarily based on the likelihood that the new government would support the construction of *l'Europe. D.D.F.*, 1957, 1:62–63, doc. 30, Chauvel to Pineau, 10 Jan. 1957.

181. For a discussion of the effects of the crisis on France see Maurice Vaisse, "Post-Suez France," in Louis and Owen, eds. *Suez 1956*, 335–40.

182. FO 800/728, "Memorandum on relations between the United Kingdom, the United States and France in the months following Egyptian nationalisation of the Suez Canal Company in 1956," 21 Oct. 1957.

183. See Horne, *Harold Macmillan*, 2:2–59.

7

KONRAD ADENAUER AND HIS DIPLOMATS

Gordon A. Craig

O NE OF KONRAD ADENAUER's most outspoken critics, Karl Georg Pfleiderer, used to say scornfully that the chancellor of the Federal Republic had come to foreign policy for the first time at an age when Bismarck was being sent into retirement.[1] The remark was charged with the condescension that professionals often show to amateurs, for Pfleiderer had served for twenty years in the Foreign Service, with posts at Milan, Peking, Moscow, Leningrad, Kattowitz, Paris, and Stockholm,[2] acquiring a knowledge of the world and its affairs that was unavailable to Adenauer. But it was also obtuse, assuming that nothing in Adenauer's long experience in municipal affairs would have any relevance to the tasks that he was called upon to deal with after 1949. The reverse, of course, was true. Adenauer's tenure as lord mayor of Cologne from 1917 to 1933 was the school in which he developed the talents that were so conspicuously successful in his postwar career: patience and a sense of timing in negotiation; tactical virtuosity in exploiting the critical moment when it came; great stubborness when under pressure; and a fertility of expedients that often enabled him, when he was the lonely exception to a consensual view, to postpone or defeat its acceptance. These were the gifts, sharpened rather than impaired by age, that were instrumental in bringing the great successes that Adenauer's policy enjoyed in the years between the Petersberg Protocol in 1949 and the regaining of West German sovereignty in 1955, and it was they that sustained him during the great Berlin crisis of the years from 1958 to 1962.

These political gifts were reinforced by a deep religious faith that was the principal source of his inveterate self-assurance and by the juristic rationalism in which he was trained as a youth, which imbued him with a sense of realism that, in his political thinking, prevented any conflict between moral principle and expediency. It is here perhaps that one finds the closest similarity between Konrad Adenauer and his greatest predecessor, with whom he has often been compared.[3] Also rooted in his Cologne years were Adenauer's supreme ability, indispensable to a democratic statesman, to explain complicated issues of policy so clearly that voters believed that they understood them and agreed with his position (a gift that was particularly effective during the Bundestag debate on the treaties of 1955), and his skillful interfactional diplomacy, full of feints, ruses, and subtle menaces, which held his often rebellious coalition behind him. In his best years, Adenauer was a formidable parliamentary politician, the first German chancellor, the *Deutsche Rundschau* wrote in an article celebrating his eightieth birthday, who had "fully mastered the technique of legitimate power."[4]

Finally, to a degree that proved incomprehensible to representatives of an older diplomatic school, like Karl Georg Pfleiderer, Adenauer possessed that indispensable gift of the great statesman, the kind of vision that senses the way in which the wheel is turning, that discerns the moment when modes of thought and action become outworn and must be discarded, that sees new possibilities and glimpses new futures. At a time when former Chancellor Heinrich Brüning, returning from his exile in Vermont to address the Rhein-Ruhr Club in Düsseldorf, was actually calling for a return to the Rapallo *Schaukelpolitik* of the 1920s,[5] Adenauer knew that that was all past and dead and that the Europe of national states was no longer relevant to the needs and hopes of Europeans. It was he who had the vision to discern that there could no longer be any European Great Powers in the old sense of the word, but that there could be a Europe, if statesmen knew how to create it. It was he who saw in the Coal and Steel Community not merely a useful form of economic collaboration but a symbol of Franco-German collaboration and something that could not help but change the way that Europeans thought about each other. It was this vision that made Adenauer more than a run-of-the-mill practitioner of foreign policy but, in the words of Christian Hacke, "a foreign policy revolutionary [who] led the . . . Federal Republic from its old geopolitical position in the middle into the political modernity of Atlantic civilization."[6]

That having been said, it is nevertheless precisely with Adenauer as practitioner of foreign policy that we must concern ourselves here, and before doing so it is necessary to remember that the political skills and the qualities of mind and character that made him one of the most original and successful political leaders of the postwar period were accompanied by temperamental traits that were offensive and self-defeating. He had a low opinion of the intelligence of other people and, in the case of his fellow-Germans, was given to fleeting comments on their herdlike instincts, lack of steadfastness, and mental and political instability. Admirable in his ability to distinguish between those things that were vital to his country's interest and those that were not, and to base his actions courageously upon that distinction, he was often indifferent to the fact that other nations had interests too, which did not, even when they were his allies, always coincide with Germany's. He was inclined to believe that he was a better judge of such things than they and, particularly after 1955, to read the worst into their refusals to agree with him. This strong strain of what can be called *Besserwissertum* was accompanied by a deep suspicion of the motives and loyalty even of his closest associates, which could take malicious and wounding forms when he came to believe that they might be encroaching upon his own prerogatives, and, not infrequently, by a lack of gratitude and even basic loyalty to people who had served him well.

These faults were reflected in Konrad Adenauer's diplomatic style, that is, in the way in which he conducted foreign policy and the nature of his relations with his diplomatic establishment, both in Bonn and in the missions in the field, and their results were generally regrettable. Because he was a suspicious man, Adenauer sought to control both the policy-making process and the knowledge needed to animate it. This tended to deprive other government agencies with foreign-policy functions, like the Foreign Affairs Committee of the Bundestag, of information that they needed for the adequate performance of their duties, while at the same time—in a way that is reminiscent of one of Bismarck's least admirable traits[7]—keeping German missions abroad inadequately briefed on the chancellor's true intentions and the direction of his policy. The inevitable result of this was incoherence and inefficiency and a not inconsiderable amount of dissatisfaction within the diplomatic establishment itself, and this was not the least important reason for the deterioration of Adenauer's control over the policy process during his last years of office.

I

The great tradition of German foreign policy began with Bismarck and ended with Hitler. Before Otto von Bismarck became minister president of Prussia in September 1862 and inaugurated the policy that eventuated in the proclamation of the German Empire in 1871, the diplomatic practice of the German states, with the exception of Austria, was provincial to the extreme, and even the Prussian service, filled with mediocre minds and lacking the kind of direction that would have developed systematic procedures and general rules of conduct, was in a sorry state, disorganized, undisciplined, and destitute of either uniform method or clear channels of communication.

To correct these conditions was Bismarck's first order of business when he moved into Wilhelmstraße 76, where the Prussian Foreign Ministry was housed in what had once been the home of one of Frederick William I's generals, and took over an office on the upper floor, which was filled with heavy mahogany furniture, a lion's skin, a rack for his meerschaum pipes, a thermometer disguised as a *Litfaßsaüle*, that characteristic feature of Berlin street life, and the portraits of the kings of Prussia, Bavaria, and Italy, of Helmuth von Moltke, and, after 1867, of the American president Ulysses S. Grant.[8] Amid this agreeable clutter, Bismarck, during the years in which he was founding the Reich, transformed the chaos of 1862 to order and efficiency and then, in the decade after the victory over France, expanded the foreign service to meet the needs of the empire. In the end, by his vigilant attention to the minutest aspects of the art of diplomacy and by the force of example, he transformed the

Foreign Ministry into a disciplined and superbly coordinated organization with a systematic command of the history and current condition of the international system, a specialized knowledge of all areas in which German interests were at stake, and the many auxiliary skills that are the necessary adjuncts of policy execution. Under his direction too, the diplomatic service was brought to a level of technical excellence that was probably unsurpassed in Europe. Conservative and nationalist in political coloration, his system survived the Great War and the collapse of the empire in 1918, was relatively untouched by movements of democratic reform in the first turbulent years of the Weimar Republic, and had a brilliant renascence during the long tenure of Gustav Stresemann as foreign minister from 1923 to 1929.[9]

Those, however, were the last good days for the German diplomatic establishment, although it was some time before this became clear. In the Brüning years there was no dearth of capable and independent-minded diplomats—one thinks of Rudolf Nadolny, who led the German team at the Disarmament Conference and was later ambassador in Moscow—but the period was overshadowed by the world economic crisis[10] and the most notable German diplomatic initiative was the unfortunate Customs Union Plan of 1931, which was a fiasco.[11] And after Brüning came Hitler, with respect to whom the professionals were, as we have seen,[12] too self-confident, so that they applied for membership in his movement in the expectation that this would allow them to continue to direct foreign policy as before, only to discover in the end that this merely made them accomplices in his criminal designs. Thus, despite the gallantry of a minority that carried on resistance against the Führer, both Foreign Ministry officials and envoys abroad did things during the war years that were difficult to forget when peace was restored, making the professional diplomatic caste suspect in the eyes of a public that was taking the first difficult steps toward democracy.

It was a long time before anything like the old diplomatic establishment was organized in the new Germany. Indeed, it was only in 1948–1949, after the Western zones had been combined and preparations were being made to establish a federal government in the western part of Germany, that members of the emerging political elite began to consider the possibility of a new Foreign Ministry. Study groups came into existence—in Stuttgart, a Bureau for Peace Questions, directed by the Bavarian Minister Anton Pfeiffer; in Frankfurt, a working group led by Hermann Pünder, the director of the *Wirtschaftsverwaltung* of the combined zones; in Darmstadt, a special commission set up by the minister president of North Rhine-Westphalia, Karl Arnold—which often included former diplomats in their membership, like Hans von Herwarth, who had served under Werner von der Schulenburg in Moscow and now worked with Pünder and Hans Kroll, who had been in the Foreign Ministry from 1929 to 1936 and in the embassy in Ankara from the latter year until the end of the war and was now associated with Arnold's commission.[13] There was much speculation about who would be appointed Foreign Minister when the federal government was organized; but all this came to an end when Konrad Adenauer was elected federal chancellor and in his first government declaration, on 20 September 1949, declared:

> Among the federal ministries a Foreign Ministry is lacking. Nor have I acceded to the proposals made to me for a Ministry of Interstate Relations. I have not done that because, in accordance with the Occupation Statute, foreign relations, including international agreements that may be concluded by, or in the name of Germany, are a matter for the Allied High Commission of the three zones.

Adenauer went on to say that this did not mean that the government was relinquishing the thought of any activity in this area. No action taken by government or the parliament in domestic affairs was without its foreign policy consequences.

> In consequence of the occupation, the Ruhr Statute, the Marshall Plan etcetera, Germany is involved with the outside world more closely than ever before. These matters will be dealt with in a State Secretariat that will be established in the Federal Chancery.[14]

This was a solution that doubtless accorded with Adenauer's personal preferences. He had no desire, as he began to plan his policy, to be burdened with a large organization of professional Foreign Service officers who might contest his judgments, and he was anxious to avoid the party and press attacks that such an organization would surely attract, given the Nazi connections of many of the professionals. So the *Dienststelle* for foreign affairs that took shape in the next eighteen months was remarkable for its modest size and its nonprofessional character. To be sure, two former diplomats were included in the team, but both were exceptions to the general rule. Herbert Blankenhorn had served in Washington, Helsinki, and Bern during the Nazi years, but there were signs that he had not been not trusted by the Nazis (he had been dismissed briefly in 1933) and in the last two years of the war he had had a relatively innocuous position in the Foreign Ministry's protocol office. Adam von Trott zu Solz, the *spiritus rector* of a resistance cell in the Information Section of the ministry, considered him, "next to [Hans Bernd von] Haeften, the most capable and sympathetic of the younger colleagues I have found in the office." Blankenhorn knew of Trott's resistance activities and was in touch with him after the failure of the bomb plot in July 1944, although he escaped arrest. From 1946 to 1948, he was deputy secretary general of the advisory board in the British zone, and then went to Cologne as secretary general of the CDU, becoming a close associate of Konrad Adenauer and serving as his closest adviser during the meetings of the Parliamentary Council. He had a wide acquaintance among Allied officials, soldiers, and security people and was the natural choice for liaison officer with the High Commissioners, which he became.[15]

The second professional diplomat whom Adenauer called to his side was Hans von Herwarth, who became chief of protocol in the new foreign section of the Chancery. He too had spent long years in the Foreign Service, but always as an outsider, both because of his Jewish blood and his resistance activities. Herwarth's personal contacts with American officials like Charles Thayer and Charles Bohlen were as close as Blankenhorn's with Englishmen like Noel Annan and Michael Thomas.[16]

For the rest, Adenauer's choices were determined by the nature of the tasks that were thrust upon him, for in the first months of his chancellorship he was more at the mercy of events beyond his control than some of the books about him suggest. As Hermann J. Rupieper has shown, it was the Americans, who by the end of 1949 had a considerable stake in Europe's future, who were the driving force in shaping West German policy.[17] At the end of November 1949, Secretary of State Dean Acheson sent a note to the American ambassador in Paris, David Bruce, for transmission to the French foreign minister, Robert Schuman, which read:

> Whether Germany will in the future be a benefit or a curse to the free world will be determined, not only by the Germans, but by the occupying powers. No country has a greater stake than France in the answer. Our own stake and responsibility is also great. Now is the time for French initiative and leadership of the type required to integrate the German Federal Republic promptly and decisively in Western Europe. Delay will seriously weaken the prospects of success.[18]

The French responded by coming forward with the plan for a Coal and Steel Community, which Jean Monnet proposed to Adenauer on 23 May 1950,[19] suggesting also, when the chancellor responded favorably, that he choose as delegation leader for the negotiations a professor with no Nazi associations. Adenauer appointed Walter Hallstein, professor of private and public law at the University of Frankfurt and sometime lecturer at George Washington University in the United States, a man with no political affiliations and a somewhat colorless personality, but with the broad knowledge and the legal skill that the times required.[20] Since the chancellor had neither the knowledge of, nor an interest in, the economic problems involved in the negotiation of the Schuman Plan, he gave Hallstein a free hand and, two months after he had begun his work, made him state secretary in the Federal Chancellory and, in effect, minister for foreign relations. A year later, Wilhelm Grewe, professor of public and international law at the University of Freiburg im Breisgau, joined the central organization with the special mission of conducting the negotiations for the revision of the Occupation Statute,[21] and in February 1952, after a number of short-range appointments, Felix von Eckardt, a journalist with long experience, became press and information director.[22]

Hallstein, Blankenhorn, Grewe, Eckardt, and Herwarth formed the heart of Adenauer's foreign policy team, aided by planning and support staffs and technical bureaus of various kinds that grew steadily until the total organization was more than a thousand strong in 1954. Adenauer was the strategist, the one who negotiated with the high commissioners and the one who explained and defended his policy before the Bundestag. Hallstein was the head of the planning staff and was responsible for preparing the instructions for negotiating teams. Blankenhorn was chief of the political section, roving ambassador, and, sometimes, collaborating with Eckart, drafter of the chancellor's speeches in parliament, a difficult task, given the old man's willfulness.[23] Eckart handled relations with the press, determined the nature and timing of releases of information about policy and, with Herwarth, planned the details of receptions for important visitors and the itineraries and schedules of the chancellor's trips abroad. This inner group was entirely loyal to the chancellor and worked together smoothly and effectively, although they learned to expect little in the way of gratitude from their lord and master, who took a malicious pleasure in playing one of them off against the other as a means of asserting his control.[24]

II

One weakness of the system was that it lacked a truly adequate foreign service. In a meeting of 15 November 1949, the high commissioners informed the chancellor that Germany would be authorized to participate in international organizations, after some constitutional questions had been cleared up, and that it had the right to establish consulates and other economic missions.[25] In the course of 1950, the chancellor took advantage of this to send three consuls general abroad: to London, Hans von Schlange-Schöningen, who had been a member of Brüning's cabinet and, after the war, had built the CDU organization in Schleswig-Holstein; to New York, Heinz Krekeler, an FDP deputy and former director of I. G. Farben; and to Paris, on the advice of a female friend of ardent Catholic persuasion, the art historian Walter Hausenstein. Other consulates were established in the years that followed, but at such a dilatory pace that the allies were annoyed. The American high commissioner, John J. McCloy, complained in May 1950 about "Adenauer's disinclination to take advice on foreign policy" and said his office had been "urging the Chancellor to get his consular service organized and into the field so that the Federal Republic can receive its own reports on the feeling towards Germany in other countries." Instead, he said, Adenauer preferred to rely upon "third-rate agents who pretend to have intimate contact with this or that leading political personality abroad and whose judgment and reliability are frequently open to question to say the least."[26] It was not until the first revision of the Occupation Statute in March 1952 authorized Adenauer to assume the title and functions of foreign minister and to establish a regular foreign service that any energy was shown in establishing missions abroad.[27]

The note of asperity in McCloy's report is to be explained less by the nature of Adenauer's policy than by the tactics that accompanied it. Both McCloy and Acheson had been impressed by Adenauer during their first meetings with him and had been convinced of the genuineness of his desire for reconciliation with France and for German integration in the Western community.[28] They were intermittently annoyed, however, by his persistent argument that, for the protection of their own interests, he was the most reliable German leader available and that, unless they were willing to make concessions to him (the end of dismantling, for example, or revisions of the Occupation Statute to give him greater freedom in foreign affairs), he was likely to be replaced by people who would be willing to negotiate with the Soviet Union for reunification at the price of neutralization or worse. They were aware of the strength of his argument, and they were conscious of the degree to which the defense of Western Europe was dependent upon the raising of German troops, but they became tired of Adenauer's complaints and demands at meetings of the high commissioners[29] and of Blankenhorn's uninvited appearances at three power meetings with lists of demands and suggestions in hand. Dean Acheson was heard to grumble that the Allies must disabuse the chancellor of the idea that Germany was the key to Europe and that concessions had to be made to it,[30] and on the question of wider freedoms in foreign policy for Adenauer both he and McCloy were unsympathetic. In July 1950, Acheson telegraphed to the American delegation to the Intergovernmental Study Group on Germany in London:

> We regard control of fonaffs as being of critical importance. There can be no doubt that the present Occ Stat in addition to our position through ECA gives us a position of great influence not only in Ger but in Eur. With Gers in conduct of their own for relations position of Allied HICOM and particularly our own position will be radically altered. . . . We wish to retain . . . greatest possible influence on internal development Ger in coming period.[31]

Both Acheson and McCloy suspected the British of wishing to loosen the controls in such a way as to enable them to deal with the Germans by bypassing HICOM.[32] McCloy, who feared that the death of Adenauer might herald the defeat of democracy and a return to nationalism and *Rapallopolitik*,[33] took the position that Allies should hold on to their reserve powers as long as possible and retain the right to veto treaties that endangered Allied policy and control the Federal Republic's relations with the eastern bloc even after it regained the right to its own foreign policy.[34]

In time, these American concerns were relieved by the chancellor's steadfastness in supporting the Schuman Plan and the EDC and his refusal to let his policy be influenced by the Soviet note of 10 March 1952. This had suggested a willingness on the part of Moscow to open negotiations for an ending of the division of Germany, but the Americans believed that it was intended to halt the momentum of German integration with the West, and they were relieved to find that Adenauer felt the same way.[35] At the same time, they were beginning to be apprehensive lest "distrust of [the Germans'] capacity to run their own affairs" might be counterproductive, actually impeding the progress of democracy in the Federal Republic.[36] Finally, mounting irritation over French foot-dragging on the military question made Acheson more tolerant of German complaints.[37] Thus, in pushing the negotiations of the EDC and the revision of the Occupation Statute on to their successful issue, the Americans and Adenauer's diplomats were the closest of allies (which was manifest in Washington in September 1951, for example, when Hallstein, Blankenhorn, and Grewe made their first appearance at a meeting of the Western foreign ministers),[38] and the signing of the EDC Treaty and the General (German) Treaty in December 1952 was one of the chancellor's greatest triumphs.

The bond between the Federal Republic and the United States became closer when the Eisenhower administration came to power at the beginning of 1953, a fact that was given symbolic expression when Adenauer visited Washington in April and was accorded all of the honors due to a close and trusted ally, including a visit to Arlington cemetery, where he stood by the tomb of the Unknown Soldier while the United States Marine Band played the two national anthems. The visit marked the beginning of the long and close relationship between the chancellor and the American secretary of state, John Foster Dulles,[39] and also the onset of a more aggressive note in German diplomacy, for it was preceded by a visit to Washington by Herbert Blankenhorn, to set the agenda for the political discussions and to make sure that, whatever their result, the wording of the final communiqué would help Adenauer in the elections that were coming in September.[40] This proved to be the beginning of a busy season for Blankenhorn. Adenauer had learned to his dismay that Winston Churchill was anxious to solve the German problem on the basis of reunification with neutralization. This idea was not popular with the prime minister's colleagues (Anthony Eden said sensibly that a reunited Germany would be too big to be controlled by either disarmament or neutrality),[41] and nothing came of it because of the East German rising of 17 June 1953 and Churchill's sudden illness. Even so, the chancellor was alarmed enough to send Blankenhorn back to Washington with a letter to Dulles suggesting the calling of a four power summit on Germany after the elections.[42] As Blankenhorn explained to his hosts, "The Chancellor's present feeling is that his whole position is in danger because of the prevalence of the idea that he is somewhat against German unification. Therefore, he must demonstrate his support of German unification and hopes to publish his letter to the Secretary of State."[43] Dulles proved amenable (he was so committed to Adenauer's reelection that three days before the poll he made a public comment about its importance to the Western cause), and he not only supported the conference idea but agreed that the Germans should have a consultative role in setting the agenda. This doubtless helped Adenauer win his great victory in the September elections. The Berlin Conference that followed in January was, however, without result,[44] except in committing the Western Allies more definitely to the idea of German unification than some of them desired to be. (Three years later Harold Macmillan was to call the whole idea "something of a fraud.")[45] The net result of all these maneuvers may have been to divert attention from the critical question of the erosion of French support for the 1952 treaties. Thus, the French Assembly's refusal to ratify the EDC Treaty in the fall of 1954 came as an unpleasant surprise—the French ambassador in Bonn described the mood there as "un émotion considérable dans laquelle il semble, toutefois, qu'il entre plus de regret et de consternation que d'irritation"[46]—and precipitated a major crisis in Western policy.[47]

III

Thanks to constructive thinking and nimble footwork on the part of British Foreign Secretary Anthony Eden, the situation was retrieved, the Germans were admitted to NATO, and the General Treaty was ratified.[48] But one result of the defeat of EDC was a major reorganization of the West German diplomatic establishment. For some time there had been mounting pressure upon the chancellor to give up the Foreign Ministry, partly because of a widespread perception that the combination of the duties of chancellor and foreign minister was too great a burden for a man of his age, but also because there was growing discontent in parliament and the CDU/CSU parliamentary delegation (*Fraktion*) about Adenauer's failure to keep them adequately informed about policy and ongoing negotiations. Adenauer responded to suggestions that he relinquish the ministry by evasions of one kind or another, generally arguing—as he did in the spring of 1952—that the critical nature of the international situation made a change inadvisable. At the end of 1954, however, the complaints became louder. There were rumors of sinking morale in the ministry itself, because of the uninspiring leadership of State Secretary Hallstein;[49] the foreign missions were said to be dissatisfied by the failure of the *Zentrale* to give them adequate instructions (Adenauer's lapidary comment on this was, "Then they'd have too much to say to me!"), and, worst of all, no one in Bonn seemed interested in what they had to report. It was said that Adenauer and Hallstein had been so confident that the French would sign the EDC Treaty that they had disregarded the warnings sent to them from Paris by Botschaftsrat von Walter, and that, indeed, this able Foreign Service officer was now being penalized for disagreeing with his chiefs by being denied his long overdue promotion to minister.[50] In the view of the press, the time had clearly come for a major shakeup, the more so because a more than adequate candidate for the post of foreign minister was at hand.

This was Heinrich von Brentano, descendant of a distinguished family that had originated in the area around Lake Como and included in its members the writer Clemens von Brentano (1778–1842) and the Berlin social reformer Bettina von Arnim. A bachelor and intensely private man, Brentano had been a co-founder of the CDU, had played an important part in the work of the Parliamentary Council in 1949, and had been elected unanimously as leader of the coalitions' parliamentary *Fraktion*. An effective and eloquent parliamentarian, who was known for his arts of conciliation, Brentano early developed a strong interest in foreign affairs. He was dedicated to the idea of European unity and, after the Federal Republic became a member of the Council of Europe in 1950, regularly took part in the meetings of the Straßburg Parliament. As leader of the *Fraktion,* he was critical of the chancellor's failure to collaborate with it, and often complained about this, but he was loyal to Adenauer and sought to assist him by such things as sending him lists of persons he felt especially qualified for posts abroad.[51]

Adenauer always reacted with suspicion when Brentano's name was proposed as his successor, in 1952 going so far as to accuse his backers of plotting against him and seeking to position Brentano for a takeover of the chancellorship.[52] Now he did his best to persuade everyone who talked to him about the appointment that Brentano was inexperienced, irresolute, and ill-prepared to deal with the problems facing the country.[53] When it was clear that he would have to give up the post, he fell back upon an idea that he had first tried out on Blankenhorn in September 1953 and which Blankenhorn had declared to be against the best interests of the ministry, an arrangement in which Brentano became minister but the chancellor reserved certain areas of state business for his own.[54] The reorganization was carried out in June 1955, making Brentano foreign minister, leaving Hallstein in place as state secretary but placing Grewe in direction of the Political Department, and appointing Blankenhorn and Herwarth as ambassadors to NATO and the Court of St. James respectively. But Adenauer wrote Brentano:

> I beg you not to misunderstand, if until further notice, in order that I can continue to use my relationship with Dulles effectively, I keep the direction of European affairs, the affairs of the USA and the SU, as well as conference matters *privately* in my own hands, in such a way that I am informed of everything, that you communicate the steps you are going to take promptly, just as I on the other hand will make appropriate communications promptly to you. Publicly that will not stand out unless there are compelling reasons. When such compelling reasons obtain, the chief of government in other countries too steps forward as the leader in foreign policy.

He added that he was writing at such length because it was important that they work in close agreement. He had full confidence in Brentano's capacities and sensitivity, but it took time to acquire the personal connections that were so extraordinarily important in the direction of "such delicate matters," and this was particularly so of the relationship with "such a unique and at first so reserved a man as Dulles."[55]

Brentano accepted this arrangement, although he must have suspected that it was bound to cause friction. But he could hardly have expected the flood of complaints, niggling in character but filled with suspicion and malice, that descended upon his head in the months and years that followed. The chancellor seemed bent upon discouraging any thought of private initiative on his part, objecting to Brentano's press statements, his relations with party leaders, and what he said to foreign ambassadors, and demanding written answers to his charges rather than clearing the air by open discussion. Early on, the foreign minister felt compelled to write a personal letter expressing outrage at the chancellor's willingness to believe the worst of him and to allow petty differences to obscure his long record of loyalty. This did not slow the avalanche of spiteful reproach (in January 1959, when Brentano sent Adenauer a letter congratulating him on his birthday, he received in return four pages of criticism of his recent conduct of office), nor did it deter Adenauer from traducing Brentano in discussions with other persons, including the federal president.[56] The chancellor had an unpleasant habit, moreover, of blaming his own faults upon the foreign minister and his staff, as he did, for example, after the Foreign Ministers Conference in Geneva in the summer of 1959, in which the Western case had been hopelessly muddled by his own objections to the allied negotiating position and his demand for last-minute changes,[57] but whose failure he later attributed to Foreign Ministry inefficiency.

In truth, Brentano was a better foreign minister than Adenauer deserved. He was dedicated to the objectives of the chancellor's policy and constantly on the watch to prevent things that might weaken it. He was a careful observer of tides of opinion in the Bundestag and sought constantly to improve communications between the chancellor and the parties, without great success. He was a student of mood swings in the Western capitals and was perhaps the first to detect the beginning of a weakening of the will to support Adenauer at all cost. Above all, he sought to discourage actions on Germany's part that would surprise and annoy its allies, and he was not, for example, enthusiastic about Adenauer's dramatic trip to Moscow in September 1955, which he regarded as ill-conceived and clumsy in execution. Ten years later, he was to say that when he went to Moscow Adenauer should have made the release of German prisoners of war a *condition préalable* to negotiation over diplomatic recognition and should have returned home immediately if this was refused. As it was, the Soviets got recognition on the cheap (for the prisoners, after all, meant nothing to them) and at a cost to the Federal Republic in the West of anger and a reawakening of talk about *Rapallopolitik* and unreliability.[58] In a report from Moscow on 14 September, the United States ambassador, Charles Bohlen, spoke of "a complete collapse of the West German position" and added that the "Soviets have achieved probably their greatest diplomatic victory in [the] postwar period." The agreement, he said, was "in flat contradiction insofar as I can judge from every assurance given [the] Western Powers both prior to and during the Moscow talks."[59]

It was at this point in his chancellorship that Adenauer's deep-seated pessimism about the human condition and his inveterate suspicion of others began to affect his judgment and weaken the coherence of his policy. Although his hopes of a continuing relationship with the Soviet Union came to nothing in the period after the Moscow meeting (which he characteristically attributed to the Foreign Ministry's failure to develop cordial relations with the Soviet ambassador in Bonn), he had an obsessive suspicion of new approaches to the Soviet Union by his allies, taking the line that any agreement was potentially disastrous. This sometimes flatly contradicted earlier positions. In December 1955, the German ambassador in London, Hans von Herwarth, had a talk with Sir Ivone Kirkpatrick of the British Foreign Office about the British position at the recent Foreign Ministers Conference in Geneva. The British had taken the line that the Western powers would be willing to conclude any reasonable security arrangement with the Soviet Union, provided it grant free elections in Germany and assure any future united German government complete freedom for its domestic and foreign policy. Herwarth said that Adenauer had told him that he wanted the British government to know that he did not think much of this. He had no confidence in the German people and regarded the integration of Germany with the West as more important than reunification.[60]

Adenauer was flattered to hear that, during a pause in the Geneva meetings, Dulles had said to the German observer, "If we love Germany, it is because we have unlimited confidence in the Federal Chancellor," but this did not prevent him from becoming increasingly critical of American policy.[61] Even his friend Dulles was not exempt from this. Dulles traveled too much, he said, implying that he was not intent enough upon the German question and, when Dulles pointed out to him in answer to a similar complaint that the United States was, after all, a world power, that worried him. Almost everything that happened in the world he saw in German terms and found troubling. The Austrian State Treaty, which freed Austria from Soviet occupation at the price of neutralization, was a "Schweinerei" that would encourage people to apply the same solution to Germany. The plan of the Polish Foreign Minister Rapacki for a nuclear-free zone in Germany and Poland he regarded as a "Russian trap,"[62] and the fact that George F. Kennan devoted his 1957 Reith Lectures to it and the disengagement idea in general struck him as an ominous circumstance.[63] The collaboration of the United States and the Soviet Union in the United Nations to force British and French troops out of Suez in 1956 he regarded either as politically naive or a sign that the United States was contemplating dividing the world with the Soviet Union. (Listening to his complaints about this in November 1956, American Ambassador James Bryant Conant was moved to observe that "it is clear [the] Chancellor is confused about our military policy and the whole atomic military picture.")[64] He began to lose his faith in Eisenhower, who was, he felt, now that Dulles was ill, falling under the influence of appeasers; in any case, like most of the people around him, the president was lazy and inattentive and had allowed the Soviet Union to win virtual nuclear parity with the United States because he wasn't watching. At the same time, the successful launching of the Soviet *Sputnik* in 1957 convinced him that the United States was falling behind in the race for world mastery, and that in these circumstances German dependence upon America might be dangerous.

His foreign minister shared some of these concerns, without allowing them to assume alarmist proportions. But he was worried by growing signs of deviation from the Adenauer policy within the government coalition, by criticism, for example, from the left wing of his own party and most of the FDP, of the so-called Hallstein Doctrine, which held that the Federal Republic would consider the establishment of diplomatic relations with the DDR by third states as an unfriendly act. Anything else, Brentano maintained, would weaken the Federal Republic's legitimacy as the only state that could represent all Germany.[65] The growth of talk, inside Germany as well as abroad, about disengagement also disturbed him, and in his gloomier moments he sensed a mood in the West that was leading it toward another Godesberg or Munich.[66] He agreed with Blankenhorn, who reported from his post at NATO in 1956 that "the picture offered by the Western alliance is a certain unanimity on the surface and growing fundamental differences, which no longer remain hidden from anyone."[67] His fears for the unity of the Western alliance became even darker when Charles de Gaulle assumed power in France in July 1958, and he wrote to Adenauer, "We must be quite clear about the fact that, from a certain standpoint, the new French government destroys European policy as a whole."[68]

On this last point, however, he was soon to discover that the chancellor had quite different views.

IV

Four months later, the diplomatic dovecotes were fluttered with a vengeance by Khrushchev's Berlin note, demanding that the Western allies withdraw their forces from the city and announcing that Soviet functions in the city would be turned over to the East German government. The next four years were never entirely free from the possibility that the Russians really meant what they said and would use force if they were resisted. In this period Adenauer's faith in the Anglo-Saxon powers steadily dwindled. His friend Dulles seemed bereft of expedients and vacillated between the devising of elaborate legal schemes that would give the Russians what they wanted without admitting it and blood-curdling brinkmanship scenarios that risked the use of nuclear weapons in Berlin.[69] At one point, President Eisenhower, without much reflection, suggested to Harold Macmillan that a willingness to recognize the Oder-Neisse line might be useful in solving the crisis. Macmillan himself—who was convinced that the chancellor's hard line showed that he was "aging rapidly" and had become "a bit potty"[70]—embarked on a personal visit to Moscow to see what he could come up with. All of this seemed to confirm Adenauer's deepest suspicions of imminent surrender to Khrushchev's desires. On the other hand, in September, at Colombey, he had had his first meeting with the new president of France and had succumbed to what Jean Lacouture has called a "coup de séduction réciproque et immédiate."[71] In an ally, Adenauer was convinced, power and vitality were the essential qualities, even if expressed in unconventional and even startling ways. Disregarding his foreign minister's apprehensions, he felt that he had found a kindred spirit in De Gaulle, a believer in Franco-German reconciliation, in Europe, and above all in resistance to Soviet blackmail.

We cannot attempt here to tell in any detail the story of the series of Berlin crises that filled the years 1958–1962.[72] Hans-Peter Schwarz, in a book based on a mastery of the literature and a thorough knowledge of public, party, and private archives, has written of Adenauer's diplomatic performance in these years that "with a combination of stubbornness and intermittent hints of willingness to compromise, the chancellor in fact succeeded in preserving the city unscathed through four years of intense Soviet pressure."[73] This is certainly overgenerous. That Berlin was not lost during this difficult period was due to a number of complicated factors: De Gaulle's unwavering refusal to negotiate under the pressure of ultimatums, which prevented the Western powers from uniting on a policy of concessions to the Soviet Union;[74] Khrushchev's disinclination to back his threats with military force; his mistake, after the U-2 incident, of breaking up the Paris summit in 1960, where he might indeed have gotten much of what he wanted (Adenauer remarked after the summit's collapse, "Wir haben nochmals fies glück gehabt!");[75] his decision in August 1961 to settle for half of what he wanted by authorizing the building of the Berlin Wall; and his subsequent folly in abandoning a concentrated for a diffuse strategy and becoming involved in the Cuban affair.[76] Yet if these were the determinative factors, Adenauer's role was far from unimportant. He contributed to the final result by stubborn opposition and detailed criticism of all Allied plans for meeting the Soviets halfway, by the production of elaborate but generally impractical solutions of his own, consideration of which slowed the process, and perhaps also by hints that he might meet with Khrushchev himself if worst came to worst, which would have greatly alarmed his allies.

When Herbert Blankenhorn left the Foreign Ministry in 1955, Adenauer played with the idea of making him a special ambassador whom he could use for his own purposes without the foreign minister always being aware of his activities. Blankenhorn resisted the idea, and it was dropped.[77] But in Hans Kroll, who went to Moscow as ambassador in 1958, the chancellor found an envoy that came close to what he had earlier sought. Kroll had been in the Foreign Service since 1920, serving in Lisbon, Madrid, Chicago, and San Francisco, and, after a hitch in the ministry, as counsellor of embassy in Ankara from 1936 to 1945. He returned to the service in 1950, was briefly on the staff of the consulate general in Paris before being seconded to the Ministry of Economics as east-west trade negotiator, then became ambassador in Belgrade from 1952 to 1955, and, from then until he went to Moscow, ambassador to Tokyo. He was, therefore, an experienced diplomat, but also a self-confident one and one who prided himself on his dynamic qualities.[78] His appointment to Moscow represented the achievement of a long-held dream, and it was his hope that he would be remembered as one of the great Moscow ambassadors, along with Otto von Bismarck, Lothar von Schweinitz (Bismarck's "mighty magus of the north"), Ulrich von Brockdoff-Rantzau, Rudolf Nadolny, and Werner von der Schulenburg.[79] It was said that he kept a copy of Bismarck's *Gedanken und Erinnerungen* on his bedside table and that, upon arrival in Moscow, he had announced, "I'm no cocktail ambassador! I didn't come here to eat caviar!"[80] He set out to make himself an *intimus* of Khrushchev and was soon unpopular with other Western ambassadors, Llewellyn Thompson in particular, for monopolizing the First Secretary's attention at diplomatic gatherings.[81] Khrushchev apparently recognized his uses and invited him to his dacha, and Kroll reported to Adenauer that the Soviet leader had repeatedly told him that the whole Berlin business could be solved quite easily if he and the chancellor could sit down together. The chancellor showed no sign of wishing to have such a tête à tête, but he may have suggested artfully that he had the option, and he always held a protecting hand over Kroll's head when the Foreign Ministry suggested that he be reined in or recalled.[82]

Whatever the reason for his tolerance in this case, Adenauer's suspicions of London and Washington grew darker, particularly after the Kennedy administration came to office at the beginning of 1961. His difficulties with the new president were in a sense prefigured, for, in much the same way as he had insisted upon believing in 1954 that the French Assembly could not fail to ratify the EDC Treaty, he had been confident before November 1960 that Richard M. Nixon would win the presidential election and had not taken the elementary precaution of instructing his embassy in Washington to maintain contact with the Democratic opposition.[83] Startled by the result, he convinced himself, after a meeting with the new president, that no great changes need be expected. A critical appraisal, however, by the embassy staff, of Kennedy's first hundred days—which mentioned the ignorance of, and lack of interest in, European affairs on the part of the people closest to the new president, compared to the Eisenhower-Dulles team—contradicted this view and, because it did so, reduced the chancellor to fury. He instructed the foreign minister to reprimand the Washington ambassador, Wilhelm Grewe, in terms more appropriate in a communication to a raw novice than in one to a man who had served for eight years in Bonn before going to Washington in 1958 and who had been called the *Spitzendiplomat* in the Federal Republic's Foreign Service.[84] Indignantly, the chancellor told Brentano that Grewe must be instructed

> to consider his judgements more carefully. I am shocked and angered by his dispatch and his—however guarded—judgement.
>
> We talked some weeks ago about a replacement of Ambassador Grewe. I beg you to consider whether that replacement should not take place very soon. Particularly in the present situation, we must place decisive value on having an ambassador in Washington with all of the qualities needed in that important post. Herr Grewe does not possess them.[85]

But the chancellor did not long abide by this unjust opinion or his favorable view of the new administration in Washington. The young president and his aides were alarmed by the state of the world and—particularly after the building of the Berlin Wall on 13 August 1961—were persuaded that a solution to the Berlin crisis was urgent but could not be reached by the unyielding tactics of the old man in Rhöndorf, who seemed to them to represent an age long past. They were too impulsive to study the treaty structure in which Berlin's freedom and Allied rights in the beleaguered city were imbedded, and they regarded Grewe, who had after all helped draft the treaties, as a bit of a bore for seeking to instruct them. Their eagerness for a settlement alarmed their own diplomats in Berlin. In the spring of 1962, Alan Lightner, the United States minister, said gloomily to a visitor that he had the gravest fears that the president would be lulled by the Soviets into giving up the city, adding, "We've just got to get Bobby [Kennedy] over here to see what's at stake!"[86]

His fears were probably confirmed by what happened in April. On the ninth, Foy Kohler and Charles Bohlen of the State Department came to Grewe with a sheaf of papers that they said represented proposals that Secretary Dean Rusk wished to use as a basis for talks with the Soviet ambassador, Dobrynin. They asked that German comments be returned to them within forty-eight hours. Noting that this hardly allowed time for serious consideration, the ambassador forwarded the papers to Bonn, where they caused a sensation in the Federal Chancellory, both because of their ultimative character and their substantive nature, which among other things envisaged the establishment of international agencies for the control of access routes to Berlin, the majority of whose members would come from small neutral countries, as well as plans for the exchange between East and West of pledges not to use force in their dealings with each other. Adenauer immediately convened a meeting of ministry officials and party leaders to consider what he regarded as a surrender to appeasement and what one of the participants said was a plan that would turn Berlin "into a dead city." The chancellor was probably not unaware of the fact that such a gathering would alert the press to the fact that something was afoot. In any event, on 13 April, shortly after Grewe had been instructed to communicate the federal government's concern over the proposed talks to the State Department, he received a telephone call from Kohler complaining about the fact that the American proposals had been leaked to the German press, a complaint repeated in stronger terms on the following day. This was followed by a telegram from Dean Rusk to the German foreign minister that was so sharp in tone—saying among other things that the United States government would in the future communicate its views only through its ambassador in Bonn—that Adenauer regarded it as an affront and, according to press accounts, hesitated to accept it.[87] One gained the impression, he said, that the whole affair was an American maneuver.[88]

What promised to become a major crisis in the Western alliance was quickly brought under control when the Kennedy administration decided that it was perhaps best not to drive Adenauer into the arms of De Gaulle and abandoned the Rusk proposals. In a sense this was a victory for Adenauer. It was secured in part, however, at the expense of his ambassador in Washington, who— according to the newspaper columnist Marquis Childs—was suspected by the White House of having long used the press to criticize and counter American policy (or, in Childs' words, of having been "the chief author of the leak system.") Despite the injustice of these charges, Grewe realized that his usefulness in Washington was at an end and submitted his resignation to Bonn. In accepting it, however, the chancellor did not defend his ambassador. Indeed, in a curiously ill-prepared and slipshod statement to the press, he gave the impression that he was disavowing Grewe's actions, damning him with faint praise in phrases like, "Sometimes, when there are complications, the innocent must suffer" and "I regard him as a very capable man. But you know how it is: Someone or other doesn't like your nose, and another doesn't like your ears."[89]

V

In April 1956, Jacob Beam of the State Department's Office of East European Affairs wrote to Assistant Secretary of State Livingston Merchant of a conversation he had had with Albrecht von Kessel of the German embassy staff. He wrote:

> Von Kessel told me yesterday afternoon in strict confidence that the government is having more and more difficulty with Adenauer because of his age and present state of health. He said Adenauer's non-lucid intervals outnumber those when he is his old self and that the same troubles are arising as occurred with Churchill.[90]

There may have been an element of wishful thinking at work here, for Kessel did not approve of the direction of Adenauer's policy and soon left the service. But with the passage of time the number of those who came to share his views about the chancellor's mental condition increased, and Adenauer's own actions—his announcement in April 1959, for example, that he would be a candidate for the presidency in succession to Theodor Heuss, only to reverse himself two months later—encouraged the belief that his judgment was impaired. His policy during the Berlin crisis struck many members of the Bundestag, including a significant section of his own party, as too intransigent toward the Soviet Union and too calculated to alienate the Anglo-Saxon powers. The weakness of his response to the building of the Berlin Wall in August 1961 was widely criticized, as was his declaration during the election campaign of September that the Soviet action had been a trick to help the Social Democratic party. In the wake of the election, in which the CDU/CSU lost its secure majority, the Free Democratic Party threatened to bolt the coalition unless Ludwig Erhard replaced Adenauer as chancellor. This was the most serious threat to the chancellor's position since 1949, and he responded to it with a brilliant demonstration of political skill that belied all of the rumors about his condition. By threatening to form a Great Coalition with the SPD, and actually entering into talks with the Socialist leaders, he forced the FDP into line and secured his leadership of the government. But this victory was bought at a price. In return for their continued support, the FDP insisted that Heinrich von Brentano be dropped as foreign minister, and, after some hesitation, the chancellor yielded.[91]

This was a more serious loss to Adenauer than he may have thought at the time. Brentano, who voluntarily withdrew from the cabinet when he saw that Adenauer did not intend to fight very hard to retain him, and who never forgave the chancellor for this repayment for years of loyalty, said in an eloquent letter of resignation, "Behind the demands for a change in the person, there stands in reality a demand for a change in the policy."[92] The truth of this had been shown when the chancellor, in the course of the interfactional negotiations, suggested that Walter Hallstein might be brought back from Brussels, where he had been president of the European Economic Community (EEC) since 1958, to take Brentano's place. This the FDP vetoed because of Hallstein's identification with the doctrine of nonrecognition of the east bloc states. The new foreign minister, Gerhard Schröder, had always been sympathetic to opening up contacts with the East, just as he was the strongest voice in the ministry for cooperation with Great Britain since Blankenhorn's departure in 1955. Thus, with the passing of Brentano, the balance within the Foreign Ministry was significantly altered. From now on it was to be a more self-assured, more independent agency, less under the chancellor's control (in the crisis over the proposals for the Rusk-Dobrynin talks in April 1962, Schröder sought to avoid the confrontation that Adenauer appeared to desire), and more likely to push for its own policies. Horst Osterheld, an Adenauer admirer of the purest water, noted in his diary his belief that Schröder would be "a stronger Foreign Minister than Brentano," but wondered whether he would be "loyal," adding "otherwise it could be difficult for him and [his relations] with the Chancellor, who is in any case already watchful."[93] Blankenhorn, always a believer in a strong and independent ministry, wrote with satisfaction after hearing Schröder speak in Paris, "What I like about the new minister are his great calm and the consequence with which he follows undeterred the road that he recognizes as the right one. There is no doubt that, in relation to the chancellor, he shows more self-assurance and independence than his predecessor."[94]

Almost defiantly, Adenauer held to his own policy. Although Schröder believed in an accommodation with the Western Powers, the chancellor became ever more convinced of their desire to appease the Soviets, and he was encouraged in this belief, as we have seen, by the heedless policy of the Kennedy administration. In his view, his only true ally was Charles de Gaulle, and, if he had until now had serious doubts about the plans that the general had spread before him in Rambouillet in July 1960 for a reform of NATO and of the procedures of EEC[95] and as late as February 1961 had said privately, "I am full up to the throat with distrust of De Gaulle!,"[96] he now became increasingly insistent that German policy should be reoriented around a Franco-German axis.

Adenauer had always been in favor of a reconciliation with France. That idea had been as much a part of his political faith as NATO, EURATOM, the Common Market, and European unification. But in turning toward De Gaulle in 1962 he was not merely celebrating—or reemphasizing—an old relationship; he was giving every indication of willingness to accept ideas that contradicted principles that had guided his policy since 1949. For De Gaulle did not believe in a genuine European community, but in a Europe of Fatherlands. He was not a supporter of NATO in its present form, but wanted fundamental changes in its command structure; and he was opposed to British membership in the Common Market. Herbert Blankenhorn, Adenauer's long-time adviser on foreign policy, was appalled. De Gaulle, he warned, was seeking to bind Germany to an alliance that would split Europe into two camps, an English and a French one, that would destroy NATO and lead the Americans to withdraw their troops from Europe, that would not be tolerated in the long run by the electorate, and that would destroy Adenauer's historical reputation. The suggested new course was simply not rational foreign policy.[97]

Blankenhorn's argument was so obviously logical that one must wonder about Adenauer's motives. They were probably mixed and, from the standpoint of policy, irresponsible. He was certainly moved by a desire to lash out demonstratively against Anglo-American policy, but his radical change of front was also a malicious attempt to undercut the Atlanticist policy of Ludwig Erhard, his putative successor, and to saddle him with a policy that he couldn't sustain. It savored also of a desire to defy his new foreign minister, who, he was convinced, was negotiating with the Americans behind his back. One could think of other motives, including a reversion to his old lack of faith in the German people, now that they were showing signs of waning faith in his judgment. When Blankenhorn said to him that Germany had twice committed the sin of binding itself to weak allies, in 1914 and in 1939, and that it must not make the same mistake again, he retorted that it was necessary to bind the Germans. Otherwise they would go over to the Russians or try to dance between the blocs. They were political dreamers, and they had gone soft.[98]

In any event, Blankenhorn was right. The suggested new course was unacceptable to the leaders of Adenauer's own party, who suspected that it would have disastrous political consequences, and they took advantage of the public outcry against the chancellor's behavior in the so-called *Spiegel* affair in October 1962 (when he sought to prosecute the editors of the Hamburg news weekly for high treason because of a story they had printed about NATO maneuvers) to exact a promise from him that he would retire from office in 1963.[99] Before that time came, he concluded a Treaty of Friendship with France, although one that was empty of significant political content.[100] In later years, this was to be celebrated as one of his greatest achievements; at the time it was much criticized in the West, particularly when it was followed almost immediately by General de Gaulle's veto of British membership in the Common Market.[101] On 1 February 1963, Dean Acheson sent Secretary Rusk a memorandum entitled "Reflections on the January Debacle," in which he wrote that the treaty was a political act that meant

> far more than the words written upon the paper. It means that Germany wants the best of all worlds. It wants to ride along with conflicting interests as far as possible without choosing and being in a position as long as possible to play one interest off against the other. To allow this is not in the American interest.

Acheson thought it would be necessary to send someone, preferably John J. McCloy, to point out to the chancellor that the United States would not look favorably upon an attempt on his part to explore "the road along which De Gaulle wishes [him] to embark."[102]

This was needlessly alarmist. The treaty marked a termination rather than a beginning. Herbert Blankenhorn, once one of Adenauer's greatest admirers, saw what Acheson failed to perceive, when he wrote sadly that history would probably regard this aspect of German policy as "the inadequate performance of a man who because of his age is simply no longer capable of defining a complex, correctly nuanced position for the Federal Republic in foreign affairs and drawing the right consequences."[103]

The long-time chancellor stepped down in October 1963, an event that foreshadowed a significant change in West German foreign policy, on the one hand a reaffirmation of the ties with the West, which had been so strained since 1958, but at the same time an end to the old inflexible Policy of Strength. Three months earlier, at the Political Society of the Evangelical Academy at Tutzing, there had been a meeting on German unification in the course of which Egon Bahr of the SPD argued for a new approach to the East, a "policy of small steps" that would bring about "change through rapprochement." The slogan *Wandel durch Annäherung* proved to have a wide public appeal, even to members of Adenauer's own party. It was to become the principle that animated the *Ostpolitik* of Willy Brandt after 1969, but long before that the first tentative steps were being taken in that direction by Gerhard Schröder under the chancellorship of Ludwig Erhard and by the Great Coalition that followed it.[104]

Konrad Adenauer remained unpersuaded that the new policy would be productive. In one of his last public speeches, at the CDU Party Congress in 1966, the former chancellor spoke once more for the policy that had been his and Hallstein's and Brentano's and Grewe's. Germany, he said, must remain armed and vigilant.

> We remain convinced that Germany must be reunited in peace. . . . I will not give up hope that one day the Soviet Union will realize that this division of Germany and, with it, the division of Europe, is not to its advantage. We must watch to see when the moment comes, and when a time nears, or seems to near, that presents a favorable opportunity, then we must not leave it unused.[105]

Notes

1. *Der Spiegel* (Hamburg), 1954/21, 22 June 1954.

2. Hans-Peter Schwarz, *Adenauer, Der Staatsmann, 1952–1967* (Stuttgart, 1991), 11.

3. Winston Churchill was not the only one to describe Adenauer as "the greatest German statesman since Bismarck."

4. *Deutsche Rundschau*, no. 82 (January 1956): 27.

5. Heinrich Bruening, "Die Vereinigten Staaten und Europa. Ein Vortrag im Rhein-Ruhr-Club, Düsseldorf" (Stuttgart, 1954); *New York Times*, 5 June 1954, 4.

6. Christian Hacke, "Revolutionäre deutscher Außenpolitik," *Die Zeit* (Hamburg), no. 46 (8 Nov. 1991): 17. See also Christian Hacke, *Weltmacht wider Willen: Die Außenpolitik der Bundesrepublik Deutschland* (Stuttgart, 1988), 40–47, 89–98.

7. See Gordon A. Craig, *From Bismarck to Adenauer: Aspects of German Statecraft* (Baltimore, 1958), chap. 4, "The Ambassador and His Problems from Bismarck to Hitler," especially 101 ff.

8. Bodo-Michael Baumunk, "Die Wilhelmstraße," *Die Zeit*, no. 43 (25 Oct. 1991): 12.

9. See Hajo Holborn, "Diplomats and Diplomacy in the Early Weimar Republic," in *The Diplomats, 1919–1939*, ed. Gordon A. Craig and Felix Gilbert (Princeton, 1953), especially 148–154. On Stresemann, see Peter Krüger, *Die Außenpolitik der Republik von Weimar* (Darmstadt, 1985), 207 ff.

10. See Josef Becker and Klaus Hildebrand, eds., *Internationale Beziehungen während der Weltwirtschaftskrise, 1929–1932* (Göttingen, 1982).

11. Edward W. Bennett, *Germany and the Diplomacy of the Financial Crisis, 1931* (Cambridge, Mass., 1962), chap. 3.

12. See above, Chapter 1.

13. Hans von Herwarth, *Von Adenauer zu Brandt: Erinnerungen* (Frankfurt am Main, 1990), 108 ff.; Hans Kroll, *Lebenserinnerungen eines Botschafters* (Cologne, Berlin, 1967), 173 ff.

14. Arnulf Baring, *Außenpolitik in Adenauers Kanzlerdemokratie* (Munich and Vienna, 1969), 12.

15. Ibid., 15; Herbert Blankenhorn, *Verständnis und Verständigung: Blätter eines politischen Tagebuchs* (Frankfurt am Main, Berlin, 1980), 30–62; Giles MacDonogh, *A Good German: Adam von Trott zu Solz* (Woodstock, N.Y., 1992), 272, 299; Klemens von Klemperer, *German Resistance Against Hitler: The Search for Allies Abroad, 1938–1945* (Oxford, 1992), 68 n., 299 n.; obituary, *The Independent* (London), 3 Sept. 1991, 23.

16. See his own account of his resistance activities in *Against Two Evils* and that of an American colleague in Moscow, Charles E. Bohlen, *Witness to History, 1929–1969* (New York, 1973), 69–83, 86–87. See also Baring, *Kanzlerdemokratie,* 16 f.

17. Hermann-Josef Rupieper, *Der besetzte Verbündete: Die amerikanische Deutschlandpolitik 1949–1955* (Opladen, 1991), 55.

18. *Foreign Relations of the United States (FRUS),* 1949, 3:622 ff.

19. Hans-Peter Schwarz, *Adenauer: Der Aufstieg, 1876–1952* (Stuttgart, 1986), 716–23; Konrad Adenauer, *Erinnerungen 1949–1953* (Stuttgart, 1976), 336 f.; Blankenhorn, *Verständnis,* 103–9; and below, Chapter 9.

20. Baring, *Kanzlerdemokratie,* 18.

21. Wilhelm Grewe, *Rückblenden 1976–1951* (Frankfurt am Main, 1979), 127 ff.

22. Baring, *Kanzlerdemokratie,* 45; Felix von Eckardt, *Ein unordentliches Leben: Lebenserinnerungen* (Düsseldorf, Vienna, 1967), 161 ff.

23. See, for an example of how difficult it might be, Eckardt, *Ein unordentliches Leben,* 268 f.

24. Baring, *Kanzlerdemokratie,* 20 f.

25. *Akten zur Auswärtigen Politik der Bundesrepublik Deutschland,* herausgegeben im Auftrag des Auswärtigen Amts von Hans-Peter Schwarz. Bd. 1. *Adenauer und die Hohen Kommissare, 1949–1951,* ed. Hans-Peter Schwarz and Reiner Pommerin (Munich, 1989), 10.

26. *FRUS,* 1950, 4:636, HICOM to Acting Secretary of State, 7 May 1950.

27. For dates of the establishment of consulates and other foreign missions, see *Die Auswärtige Politik der Bundesrepublik Deutschland,* published by the Foreign Ministry (Cologne, 1972), 929 ff.

28. *FRUS,* 1949, 3:308 ff.; Adenauer, *Erinnerungen,* 1:263 f.

29. *Adenauer und die Hohen Kommissare, 1949–51.*

30. Rupieper, *Der besetzte Verbündete,* 118.

31. *FRUS,* 1950, 4:753 f.

32. *FRUS,* 1950, 3:933 ff.

33. This was a fear shared by the French, and Jean Monnet used it as an argument to try to persuade the British to support the Schuman Plan, about which they were not enthusiastic. See Rohan Butler and M. E. Pelly, eds., *Documents on British Policy Overseas* (London, 1986), 2d series, vol. 1 (1950–1952), especially Nrs. 20, note 2, 22; Nrs. 460, 461.

34. Ibid., 755 ff. See Dean Acheson, *Present at the Creation: My Years in the State Department* (New York, 1969); and, on McCloy, Thomas Alan Schwartz, *America's*

Germany: John J. McCloy and the Federal Republic of Germany (Cambridge, Mass., 1991); and Kai Bird, *The Chairman: John J. McCloy, the Making of the American Establishment* (New York, 1992).

35. See Sir Frank Roberts, "Stalin, Khrushchev and the Berlin Crises," *International Affairs* (November 1991), 125; *FRUS*, 1952–1954, vol. 7 (1), 332 ff.; *Adenauer und die Hohen Kommissare 1952*, 24.

36. Rupieper, *Der besetzte Verbündete*, 126 f.; *FRUS*, 1951, vol. 3 (1), 1192–95.

37. *FRUS*, 1952–1954, vol. 7 (1), 2–11.

38. Ibid., 1951, vol. 3 (2), 1525 ff.

39. Rupieper, *Der besetzte Verbündete*, 310, f.; Schwarz, *Der Staatsmann*, 52–58. See also, Detlef Felken, *Dulles und Deutschland: Die amerikanische Deutschlandpolitik, 1953–1959* (Bonn, 1993).

40. *FRUS*, 1952–1954, vol. 7 (1), 405 ff., 416 ff.

41. Sir Frank Roberts, *Dealing with Dictators: The Destruction and Revival of Europe, 1932–1970* (London, 1991), 164.

42. Josef Foschepoth, "Wie Adenauer Churchill austrickste," *Die Zeit*, no. 19 (11 May 1984): 19; Schwarz, *Der Staatsmann*, 71 ff.

43. *FRUS*, 1952–1954, vol. 5 (2), 1606 f.; Blankenhorn, *Verständnis*, 160 ff.

44. *FRUS*, 1952–1954, vol. 7 (1), 601 ff., 754 ff., 865 f., 976 f.; Blankenhorn, *Verständnis*, 181–89; Schwarz, *Der Staatsmann*, 124 ff.

45. Alistair Horne, *Macmillan* (London, 1989), 1:120. On 23 June 1953, Selwyn Lloyd wrote to Winston Churchill that everyone, including the Soviet Union, the Western Powers and Adenauer, knew that a divided Germany was the best solution for a peaceful Europe, "but none of us dares to admit this openly because of its effects upon public opinion in Germany. So we all publicly support a united Germany, each of us with his private conditions." Foschepoth in *Die Zeit*, 11 May 1984. See also Wolfram F. Hanrieder, *Germany, America, Europe: Forty Years of German Foreign Policy* (New Haven, 1989).

46. *FRUS*, 1952–1954, vol. 5 (1), 1088. See also *Documents Diplomatiques Français*, 1954 (21 July–21 Dec.) (Paris, 1987), 283 (hereafter cited as *DDF*).

47. *FRUS*, 1952–1954, vol. 5 (1), 1088 ff.; *DDF*, 1954, 237, 244, 247 f.

48. See especially Roberts, *Dealing with Dictators*, 169–72.

49. In his memoirs, Wilhelm Grewe, who admired Hallstein for his legal and stylistic talents and his success in imposing systematic procedures and working methods on the ministry, admitted that he tended to be cold and pedantic and had been less than successful in giving it an esprit de corps. *Rückblenden*, 331 f.

50. See the interesting and well-informed article by Hans Ulrich Kempski, "Sand im Getriebe des Auswärtigen Amtes," *Süddeutsche Zeitung*, 21 Sept. 1954. In his memoirs, Walter Hausenstein, consul-general in Paris from 1950 to 1955, speaks of Hallstein's "primitive optimism" in the EDC question and Adenauer's irritation over reports that contradicted his mistaken view of the positive nature of Franco-German relations. *Pariser Erinnerungen: Aus fünf Jahren diplomatischen Dienst, 1950–1955* (Munich, 1961), 107, 147.

51. On Brentano, see above all Arnulf Baring, *Sehr verehrter Herr Bundeskanzler! Heinrich von Brentano im Briefwechsel mit Konrad Adenauer 1949–1964* (hereafter cited as Baring, *Brentano*) (Hamburg, 1974), 11 ff., 27, 35–42, 50, 52 ff., 56 ff., 74, 128 f., 130 ff.

52. Otto Lenz, *Im Zentrum der Macht: Das Tagebuch von Staatssekretär Lenz 1951–1953* (Düsseldorf, 1989), 413 f.

53. Schwarz, *Der Staatsmann*, 194.

54. Blankenhorn, *Verständnis*, 169 f.

55. Baring, *Brentano*, 151.

56. Ibid., 152 ff., 160, 162, 166 ff., 169, 171 f.; Schwarz, *Der Staatsmann*, 355 f.

57. Grewe, *Rückblenden*, 393 ff., 399.

58. Interview with Gordon A. Craig, 30 Aug. 1964, John Foster Dulles Oral History Project, Princeton University; Gordon A. Craig, *Tagebuch/Journal*, 16:50–52, Stanford University Libraries. See also Baring, *Brentano*, 174 f.; Adenauer, *Erinnerungen*, 2:487 ff.; Grewe, *Rückblenden*, 229 ff.; Eckardt, *Ein unordentliches Leben*, 383 ff.; Schwarz, *Der Staatsmann*, 207 ff.; Bohlen, *Witness to History*, 387.

59. *FRUS*, 1955–1957, 5:582 f. That Adenauer was conscious of the concern of his allies is shown by the fact that, a year later, meeting Dulles for the first time since his return from Moscow, he offered an explanation and justification. *FRUS*, 1955–1957, 26:110. See also p. 145. On French feelings about the trip, see *D.D.F.*, 1955 (Paris, 1988) 2:513–15.

60. Herwarth, *Von Adenauer zu Brandt*, 220 f. On the foreign ministers' conference, see Grewe, *Rückblenden*, 272.

61. Schwarz, *Der Staatsmann*, 291 f., 298, 302.

62. See below, Chapter 10. On Brentano's views of disengagement, see Baring, *Brentano*, 232.

63. He complained about this in a conversation with President Eisenhower in Paris in December 1957, and the president soothed him by saying that Kennan was "a headline seeker." *FRUS*, 1955–1957, 26:346 f.

64. *FRUS*, 1955–1957, 26:174.

65. For a clear discussion of this complicated matter, see Grewe, *Rückblenden*, 251 ff.

66. Baring, *Brentano*, 237.

67. Ibid., 194.

68. Ibid., 303.

69. See above, Chapter 5.

70. Horne, *Macmillan*, 2:119, 130.

71. Jean Lacouture, *Le Souverain, 1959–1970*, vol. 3 of *De Gaulle* (Paris, 1986), 293.

72. For a clear and reliable account, see Dennis L. Bark and David R. Gress, *From Shadow to Substance, 1945–1963*, vol. 1 of *A History of West Germany* (Oxford, 1989), 435–90. In his interesting analysis of the crisis, *History and Strategy* (Princeton, 1991), Marc Trachtenberg suggests that neither of the two major antagonists fully understood the motives of the other, that the Soviet goal was not Berlin but an accommodation upon Germany as a whole, and that President Eisenhower, and particularly President Kennedy, were made increasingly amenable to this idea by Soviet threats that were not always meant as such.

73. Schwarz, *Der Staatsmann*, 749.

74. Macmillan wrote in his diary on 18 June 1959, "De Gaulle will not play with me or anyone else. Adenauer is now half crazy. . . . Eisenhower is hesitant and unsure of himself." Horne, *Macmillan*, 2:133 f.

75. Ibid., 560.

76. Khrushchev's hesitations were certainly influenced by the fact that the Americans, thanks to the Penkovsky spy affair, knew the limitations of the Soviet nuclear armament. See Roberts, *Dealing with Dictators,* 220 f.

77. Schwarz, *Der Aufstieg,* 194.

78. His memoirs, *Lebenserinnerungen eines Botschafters,* are filled with stories about his correct judgments and about good advice of his that was sadly not taken. See 233, 244, 248, 451. He says that an acting head of the Foreign Ministry's personnel division told him, "Herr Kroll, you're too dynamic. We're afraid that, if you ever get in here, you'll shove us all up against the wall in no time" (p. 208).

79. On Brockdorff-Rantzau and Nadolny, see Holborn, "Diplomats and Diplomacy in the Early Weimar Republic," and Gordon A. Craig, "The German Foreign Office from Neurath to Ribbentrop," in *The Diplomats, 1919–1939;* on Schulenburg, the chapters on the German embassy in Moscow in Herwarth, *Against Two Evils.*

80. *Der Spiegel,* 1961/48, 22 Nov. 1961.

81. *Der Spiegel,* 1960/23, 15 June 1960.

82. Kroll describes his attempt, at the Geneva Foreign Ministers Conference of 1959, to persuade Brentano to act like Stresemann. *Lebenserinnerungen,* 404. On Brentano's suspicions of him, see Baring, *Brentano,* 378–80.

83. In August 1960, Horst Osterheld, a member of the embassy staff in Washington, was transferred to Bonn to become head of the Foreign Affairs Bureau of the Bundeskanzleramt. In his first meeting with Adenauer he predicted Kennedy's election but was apparently not taken seriously. Horst Osterheld, *"Ich gehe nicht leichten Herzens . . . "; Adenauers letzte Kanzlerjahre: ein dokumentarischer Bericht* (Mainz, 1986), 9.

84. *Der Spiegel,* 1959/24, 10 June 1959, 16.

85. Grewe, *Rückblenden,* 471.

86. Craig, *Tagebuch/Journal,* 12:106; 13:32.

87. According to Fred Luchsinger, Adenauer may have been outraged because Rusk, perhaps inadvertently, used the formulation "breach of confidence" instead of the less accusatory "breach of confidentiality." Craig, *Tagebuch/Journal,* 46:237. On the affair as a while, see Grewe, *Rückblenden,* 549–55; Schwarz, *Der Staatsmann,* 743 ff. and on its background, *Berlin Crisis 1961–1962,* vol. 14 of *Foreign Relations of the United States, 1961–1963* (Washington, 1994).

88. Osterheld, *"Ich gehe nicht leichten Herzens,"* p. 106.

89. Grewe, *Rückblenden,* 555.

90. *FRUS,* 1955–1957, 26:90.

91. See Daniel Koerfer, *Kampf ums Kanzleramt: Erhard und Adenauer* (Stuttgart, 1987), 574 ff., 590 ff.

92. Baring, *Brentano,* 373.

93. Osterheld, *"Ich gehe nicht leichten Herzens,"* 84.

94. Blankenhorn, *Verständnis,* 426.

95. See Lacouture, *Le Souverain,* 296 ff. It was probably after Rambouillete, that Adenauer said to Fred Luchsinger, the veteran correspondent for the *Neue Zürcher Zeitung,* "Sehen Sie, Herr Luchsinger. De Gaulle ist ein sehr gefährlicher Mann!" Craig, *Tagebuch/Journal,* 46:237.

96. Osterheld, *"Ich gehe nicht leichten Herzens,"* 20.

97. Schwarz, *Der Staatsmann*, 756.

98. Ibid.

99. On the politics of the affair, see Bark and Gress, *From Shadow to Substance*, 499–505; Koerfer, *Kampf ums Kanzleramt*, 675 ff.

100. Lacouture, *Le Souverain*, 307 f.

101. See Osterheld, *"Ich gehe nicht leichten Herzens,"* 194–203.

102. "Reflections on the January Debacle," 31 Jan. 1963. The Papers of Dean Acheson, Harry S. Truman Library, Independence, Mo.

103. Schwarz, *Der Staatsmann*, 822; Blankenhorn, *Verständnis*, 438 f.

104. See below, Chapter 18.

105. Schwarz, *Der Staatsmann*, 922.

8

THE FOREIGN POLICY OF CHARLES DE GAULLE

Stanley Hoffmann

I

CHARLES DE GAULLE became a statesman by accident. If France had not been defeated by Hitler's Germany in June 1940, he would have remained a military man—known primarily for his writings about mechanized warfare, if peace with Germany had been maintained, or else becoming one of France's top army commanders, had France waged a successful war. It was the fall of France that precipitated de Gaulle into statecraft. When, on 18 June 1940, he called on the French to resist and stated that France had lost a battle but not the war, when leaders better known and more prestigious than he failed to join him, he took all the responsibilities and burdens of his nation upon himself. He had to master a double task. From his exile in London, he had to raise, in metropolitan France and abroad, enough French forces to keep France among the Allies, whose victory he foresaw and passionately worked for. He also had to prevent France's calamitous fall and the armistice signed by Marshal Pétain from destroying France's standing in the world and from provoking irreversible losses of sovereignty and territories. What was at stake was status and honor—integrity, in all its meanings.

It was France's good fortune to have found a champion who had prepared himself throughout his forty-nine years for the leap that took him from France to London and from relative obscurity to world fame. When he wrote in his memoirs that, as a youth, he thought that the "interest of (his) life" would be to perform a noted service for a country he saw doomed to "gigantic trials,"[1] he may have referred to that unfinished essay he wrote in 1905 at age fourteen, in which "General de Gaulle," commander of the larger of two French armies, defeated the Germans who had invaded France in 1930.[2]

What stands out in these years is above all the challenge of Germany. De Gaulle's father had fought in the Franco-Prussian war of 1870–71; de Gaulle's Catholic and monarchist parents lived in the shadow of France's defeat and of the loss of Metz and Strasbourg. When the young Charles de Gaulle decided to become a soldier (and chose the infantry), a war with the German Empire appeared, if not imminent, at least probable. The young officer, serving under Colonel Pétain's orders, shared in the "nationalist revival" of pre-1914 France.[3]

When Captain de Gaulle, wounded in the battle for Verdun in 1916, became a prisoner of war in Germany, he spent his time reading, reflecting, and lecturing his fellow prisoners about history—and not only military history. He also observed what was happening to Germany. A study of the causes of the Reich's defeat was his first published book.[4] In the 1920s and 1930s, the two central concerns expressed in his writings were the nature of leadership,[5] on the one hand, and the need for an offensive, mechanized force capable of defeating a revanchist Germany and of protecting French allies and interests in Europe.[6] De Gaulle had only a brief experience in the French overseas empire—in Syria and Lebanon in 1929–1931. His conclusion was that France ultimately could only choose between a policy of force or withdrawal.[7] His main focus—like Clemenceau's earlier—was on the German threat. German was the one foreign language he knew, and his works have many references to Goethe and to Nietzsche. German discipline and collective power impressed him, as well as German culture; Germany's lack of "measure" made him anxious.

Another important element of de Gaulle's "preparation" is provided by the lessons he learned about the theme of some of his deepest reflections: civil-military relations. A soldier, convinced that force is the most important instrument of statecraft, and, in particular, that France was "created by the sword,"[8] de Gaulle held original views in two respects. One was his conviction that force must be at the service of a policy and that civilian control and direction are indispensable; it was Germany's violation of that precept that had led to its defeat in 1918. De Gaulle was, indeed, a Clausewitzian. Moreover, perhaps because he had been far away from the battlefield in the last phases of the First World War, he never shared the fatal tendency of France's commanders and statesmen to turn the "lessons" of France's victory into dogmas—so that when the Second World War began, the French army was hampered by the cult of the defensive and by instructions that were stuck in time around 1918. What de Gaulle had learned was something completely different: the need for initiative and innovation and the importance of circumstances.

A third major feature is a lesson he learned from his frustrations with French policy (diplomatic and military) in the 1930s: disenchantment with France's elites, and particularly with the institutions of the Third Republic (his letters from World War I show that his dislike of parliamentarians had started early).[9] Paralysis at home, and, increasingly, impotence and dependence on unreliable allies abroad, seemed to him to lead to disasters that could have been avoided. The military revolutions he deemed indispensable were rejected by France's civilian and military leaders, while the Germans put them into effect; the politicians failed again and again to resist and to stop Hitler, whose ambitions and frenzy de Gaulle analyzed correctly. It is impossible to understand his statecraft if one does not see where he came from and what he was determined to rule out in the future.

A last clue is provided by de Gaulle's character, which was partly shaped by his family's nature and beliefs. Studying de Gaulle, one senses a man who lived in the past and in the future, and for whom the present was just a moment linking the past and the future. As he explains in the first pages of his war memoirs, his parents looked at the political travails of pre-1914 France—the Dreyfus case, the separation of church and state—with sadness. It was the greatness of France's past that provided their consolation. The interwar period was one of intense and growing worry for de Gaulle, who was a voracious reader of France's history. Eager for action and leadership, *his* consolation was his determination to work for a future worthy of the past. In both directions, he lived in the long run. This, again, is not so usual, even among statesmen. Fidelity to France was both the spring of his rebellion and the core of his policy. France he saw as a melting pot of peoples, and he excluded none of its traditions and components.

His statecraft falls in two very different periods. One was the period from June 1940 to January 1946, when he resigned from his office as president of the government. The second period lasted from his return to power, as the Fourth Republic collapsed under the weight of the Algerian war, in May 1958, to his second resignation in April 1969. There are good reasons for distinguishing these phases. The circumstances were profoundly different. Between 1940 and 1946, de Gaulle was an embattled self-appointed and little-known leader fighting against enormous odds to lift France out of the abyss and to force France's allies to treat her as a member of their coalition, not as a defector—indeed, to treat her as a great power despite her fall and Vichy's betrayals. He had to do so with an extremely weak hand: his forces were small, he was dependent on Britain first, later on Britain and the United States, for resources and communications. France was slowly shifting from a shellshocked enthusiasm for Pétain to partly active but still largely passive support for de Gaulle and resistance, in conditions that, in 1944, came close to civil war. Even after the Liberation, the scene remained bleak, given the magnitude of France's losses, and the need to reconstitute a legitimate political system on the ruins left by the Third Republic and by Vichy.[10] Between 1958 and 1969, France faced two major crises— Algeria, where war had broken out in 1954, and May 1968—but de Gaulle began with the establishment of a suitable political regime (whereas he had resigned in January 1946 mainly because he saw himself helpless to prevent the Constituent Assembly from installing an unsuitable one). He had behind him a much wealthier and self-confident nation than the one he had found after the Liberation. Saving it from falling or jumping into chaos and civil war remained his fate, but it was, for all its difficulties, an easier task than the artificial respiration, the resurrection he had to perform in the 1940s.

A second reason for distinguishing the two periods is that the personality of the general was not quite the same. The de Gaulle of the war years was seen, and often resented, as an extraordinarily difficult person to deal with—prickly, haughty, cold, suspicious, often angry, angular, condescending, and sarcastic.

It was not only because of the obviously intense suffering that France's condition inflicted on him—his awareness both of France's plight, and of the failure of the French to behave in the way he wanted them to act, a failure that forced him, as he much later confided, to operate "as if" they were acting as he wished.[11] It was also because he was, so to speak, learning his job while performing it. He was a military commander with limited political experience, and a man of learning and reflection who suddenly faced ever widening burdens of statecraft. The de Gaulle of 1958 was not only older, but also more relaxed, avuncular, and serene—rounder both physically and in manner, far more sure of himself and of his place in history. The writing of his war memoirs had provided both catharsis and renewal. The de Gaulle of the war years never gave the impression of enjoying himself in the least; the "sovereign" of the Fifth Republic did often and obviously enjoy himself, and the turmoil he created. Whereas France's failure to heed his warnings in the 1930s had led to the greatest tragedy in her modern history, to a fall so deep that only he was left to save her, the failure of the French to listen to him after 1945 seemed to have mainly given him a chance for doing for her at last everything he had been incapable of accomplishing in the circumstances of 1945. What had been an epic tragedy the first time was now a splendid opportunity. One has only to look at the titles of his memoirs: the three volumes of the war memoirs are *The Call, Unity,* and *Salvation;* the planned three volumes of the memoirs of hope were to be called: *Renewal, Effort,* and *The End.*

II

This essay will concentrate on the second period, 1958 to 1969. However, the basic ideas de Gaulle brought to foreign policy, as well as his style, did not change. The circumstances shaped the specific designs he launched, but in both periods we find the same mix of pragmatism and principles. He knew exactly how he wanted France to behave and what kind of world and Europe he wanted for his country; he never wavered in this respect; it is this vision that will be discussed in this section. But precisely because his obstinate determination to do all that was possible to shape France's future required, in his view, that he never remain stuck in quagmires and dead ends, his daily practice could be so flexible and his diplomacy apparently so complex that some critics saw nothing but opportunism and empty showmanship, and forgot the conception at whose service all of his tricks and turns always were.

One of de Gaulle's successors, Valéry Giscard d'Estaing, liked to begin his statements with "observations" about France's or the world's situation, as if policy naturally followed from observation. In de Gaulle's case, it is not with his view of the momentary situation that one should begin, but with his permanent imperative; France's independence and greatness. Gaullism may or may not be a doctrine—Gaullists have kept arguing on both sides—but it is, above all, a call. To be more precise it is a call for a will—the will to keep France "mistress of herself," with free hands and no other commitments than those she has freely chosen to promote her interests. It is also the will to keep France, even if she is no longer a "mastodon," a nation of importance and weight, fighting for great causes. The will to independence and grandeur has, in de Gaulle's mind, the force and character of a categorical imperative. However, he was also willing to defend it in terms of its consequences: France's independence will be good for humanity in general and Europe in particular, and above all France's search for greatness will save the French from their permanent tendency to splinter and quarrel. Without a constant effort toward autonomy, and grand actions, France would become the victim of foreign machinations and internal demons.

From that fixed point, a whole series of effects follow. The first is, of course, the rejection of any commitment to a foreign state that could infringe upon France's independence and handicap her *grandeur*. The complicated story of de Gaulle's relations with Churchill and Roosevelt in 1940–1945 shows clearly that despite his physical dependence on Churchill's good will in 1940–1942, he insisted on being treated just like the regular governments from continental Europe in exile in London. The repeated crises between the Free French and the British in the Levant resulted from his conviction that the latter wanted to eliminate and to replace the French in Syria and Lebanon. FDR he saw, for all his greatness and charm, as a threat to French independence, because of the president's preference for leaders more tractable and docile than de Gaulle, and, because of an anticolonialism that masked the appeal of hegemony, as a threat to French overseas possessions. Above all, the "original sin" of Vichy was the Armistice of 1940, which amounted to accepting foreign domination— something, de Gaulle wrote, no French regime had ever done before.[12]

Another consequence was de Gaulle's suspicion of international organizations such as the United Nations and even more of supranational organizations, such as those that had been set up by the Fourth Republic with the guidance of Jean Monnet. Insofar as France risked having to submit to decisions made, either by other states in bodies functioning with a rule other than unanimity, or by irresponsible international civil servants likely to be manipulated by foreign powers, such organizations were potential traps that could not be tolerated.

A third consequence concerns France herself, and can be formulated as a paradox. On the one hand, de Gaulle is arguing for the primacy of foreign policy—an existential primacy: in a world of competing interests, forces, and designs, whoever neglects this primacy will have to pay a price that may well be enormous or even fatal. In his war memoirs, he notes with bitterness that, after the Liberation, French factions and media often failed to support him in his struggle for France's rights against the British or the Americans. The occasion for his resignation in 1946 was a quarrel between him and the Socialists (who were in his government) over the size of the military budget. In the 1960s, his fiscal and financial efforts at curbing inflation through strict wage controls in order to make France more competitive abroad, and his accumulation of monetary reserves placed at the service of his attack on the privileges of the dollar, led to equally severe criticisms at home and contributed to the workers' strikes of May 1968. But on the other hand, he realized that a nation's influence abroad depends on its internal strength.[13] Thus, it is the very primacy of foreign policy that requires a constant effort at creating and maintaining all the domestic prerequisites for strength on the world scene—national morale, political unity, economic efficiency, technological progress, social cohesion. Despite the legend that de Gaulle cared only for diplomatic and military matters, the leader of the Fifth Republic followed economic and social policy issues with great care.[14] In 1944–1945, his disdain for detail and his reliance on men with little experience, recruited among the Free French and from the Resistance, had led to a great deal of confusion and inertia.[15] After 1958, the creation of the position of prime minister, a person in charge of detail and daily management, and his reliance on a professional civil service of high quality, provided the president with the levers and relays he needed.

What was the best way for France to preserve her independence and to maximize her influence? Here, we turn to de Gaulle's view of the world. He saw it as a world of states, "i.e. what is least impartial and most interest-driven."[16] In a way that reflected the views of nineteenth-century liberals, he believed that stability would be greater if the actors were not just states, but nation-states, that is, "peoples" with a sense of distinctiveness, a will to live together, and a desire to have a common set of institutions.[17] He understood quickly the strength of popular aspirations for national self-determination and, especially in his second period, he supported them, from Biafra to Vietnam and from Quebec to Ireland. Ideologies either pass, or are the disguises of national interests; nations remain, with their claims or needs, and states persist, with their ambitions. However, stability is not automatic and self-perpetuating. The classicist de Gaulle believed that the guiding principle in foreign policy must be the principle of balance (this is how, in 1936, he had justified an alliance between France and the Soviet Union in a letter to his fervently anticommunist mother).[18] Any grave imbalance of power produces threats to the independence of states, and risks of war (just as in Europe "arbitrary centralization always provoked, in reaction, the virulence of nationalities").[19] A second requirement is hierarchy. All states are entitled to equal dignity and rights, but responsibilities are not equal—and he found nothing wrong in the idea of a great power's sphere of influence, as long as it did not threaten the overall balance of power.

De Gaulle remained convinced that a reasonably stable and peaceful world needed something like the concert of great powers that had existed—at times— in the nineteenth century. It is because of this belief that, in 1945, he had strongly supported the creation of the UN Security Council, and disapproved of the later shift—in a UN whose Security Council was paralyzed by the Cold War—from the Council to the General Assembly. Of course, France had to be a member of whatever new concert would take the place of the old one; and de Gaulle, in difficulty with the British and the Americans in 1943–1944, went to Russia in November 1944 in order to play his own game of balancing (but he found Stalin unwilling to play with him, and was convinced that he could obtain far greater benefits from practicing a concert policy with the United Kingdom and the United States only).

A last element of his view of the world was his conviction that Europe, the former "core" of world politics, needed to be restored and to regain an essential role. Being French, he once said, he was of course European; but the Europe he wanted had to be free from outside hegemonies and willing to resist them, and while her greatness was a worthy objective, France could not be absorbed and handicapped by Europe. France, as he had told Anthony Eden, was a great, that is, global, power.[20] If other Europeans did not follow his lead, France alone would have to speak for Europe's true interests, and move on.

From his categorical imperative and his view of the world, de Gaulle derived policy objectives and strategies for France, appropriate to the specific circumstances that he found. In 1944–1945, he had devised a double plan—for the short and for the long term. The short-term plan had two objectives. The first was aimed at destroying once and for all Germany's "aggressive capacity"[21]: French security vis-à-vis Germany was the prerequisite for France's renewal. The demands de Gaulle made were enormous: no more centralized Reich, a loose union of German states east of the Rhine, a long occupation of the Rhineland detached from the rest of Germany, an international regime for the Ruhr. None of France's major allies accepted this view, and at the time of his resignation, French diplomacy had achieved almost nothing; the policy continued for several years but was finally abandoned by de Gaulle's successors in 1949. The second objective was the return of France to what de Gaulle deemed her legitimate rank. Here, he was more successful. He wanted to regain control of all overseas possessions and protectorates before negotiating the terms of their emancipation (which he deemed inevitable in the long run), and, while tension in the Near East between France and England persisted, de Gaulle had sent an expeditionary corps to Saigon to wrest control of Indochina from Ho Chi Minh's forces. Even though France was kept out of Yalta (which led de Gaulle and the French to mythify Yalta as a cynical division of the world between the Soviets and the "Anglo-Saxons"), he did obtain for France a permanent seat in the Security Council and a zone of occupation—an important bargaining chip in his eyes—in Germany.

The short-term plan seems—not only in retrospect—remarkably *passéiste:* restoration overseas, and a resurrection of France's original anti-German schemes presented by Clemenceau in 1919. The long-term plan, however, showed that de Gaulle understood that the past would not suffice. He writes that he had a double design: a liberalization of the French Empire, and the establishment of a "grouping" of Western Europe comprising the states situated near the Rhine, the Alps, and the Pyrenees.[22] He wanted to make of this organization "one of the three planetary powers, and, if necessary someday, the arbiter between the Soviet and the Anglo-Saxon camps."[23] This grouping was supposed to offer the new Germany (or rather Germanies) a prospect of economic development and political rehabilitation (indeed, he insisted that France's occupation policy in Germany not be merely repressive and thought that France might give shelter to 2 million Germans).[24] It would serve as a magnet for the countries subjugated by Moscow in Eastern Europe. Grandeur, balance and hierarchy would all have been promoted by this design. But by January 1946, it had not gone beyond the stage of speculation.

When de Gaulle returned to power twelve years later, he found a very different world: a bipolar contest in which no "third grouping" had emerged, and in which France (with his partial blessing, during his period in the opposition) had chosen her camp. There was a unified (albeit federal) West Germany with its own army. Despite de Gaulle's attacks, France had become a part of the integrated military structure of NATO, under American command, and of three Communities that linked six of the states de Gaulle had had in mind in 1945, but that also entailed supranational features he loathed. The French had lost Indochina, granted independence to Tunisia and Morocco, were bogged down in Algeria, and had begun the decolonization of black Africa—on those issues, de Gaulle had gradually moved from intense colonialism in the late 1940s, to a far more liberal view in the mid-1950s.

On the other hand, as de Gaulle saw it, France had important assets: "for the first time in her history, she is not gripped by any threat from any nearby neighbor";[25] to be sure, the bipolar contest threatened peace, but he was convinced that nuclear weapons at the disposal of the West would powerfully reenforce "Russia's" interest in peace. Moreover, France herself was in the process of becoming a nuclear power and her economy was progressing at last. De Gaulle thus used the new circumstances to carry out a revamped version of his old program—"knowing very well that in such a matter nothing is ever accomplished exactly as one had wanted it,"[26] but endowed now with far more "credit outside and support within"[27] than in 1945.

Independence, once more, was essential—hence his determination to remove, sooner or later, France's forces from the integrated command of NATO, a plan he carried out by stages between 1959 and 1966. He was also determined to subordinate the Communities he had not created to the "grouping" he had in mind, which would differ from them in two ways—it would also deal with diplomacy and defense, and it would be strictly intergovernmental, without supranational authorities or majority rule. The failure in 1962 of the Fouchet plan, which incorporated these ideas, doomed the project, but the crisis over the financing of the Common Agricultural Policy in 1965 provided him with the opportunity both to curb the Common Market's Commission and to prevent the passage from unanimity to qualified majority in votes of the Common Market's Council, on issues deemed of essential importance by a member. The same concern for independence led him to reject the "Nassau formula" accepted at the end of 1962 by the United Kingdom—that is, the offer of American nuclear submarines in exchange for the subordination of France's nuclear force to NATO.

As for grandeur, it was going to take the form of a variety of designs aimed both at magnifying the role of France, and at moving toward the kind of world de Gaulle deemed to be in the general as well as in France's interest. The long-term objective was nothing less than the end of bipolarity, the return to a world of several major powers (hierarchy), in which the smaller states could avoid the servitudes of alignment and receive the help they needed for their development. Equilibrium required that, as long as the bipolar conflict persisted, Soviet efforts at breaking the delicate balance established between the military blocs in Europe be resisted; in the long run, it required a struggle against both of "the two hegemonies," the emancipation of those who were now subjected to either one, attempts at preventing either one or both from extending their control outside Europe, and a policy of European reunification "from the Atlantic to the Urals." Equilibrium, hierarchy, French grandeur, and security all required a careful policy toward Germany; it would combine the partnership already envisaged in 1945—and thus keep the Federal Republic oriented toward the West—with a strategy that would curtail the full independence of West Germany and preserve crucial elements of French superiority.

It is possible to distinguish three phases. The first lasted from 1958 to 1963. De Gaulle's main concern was the reconstruction of French power. The establishment of the Fifth Republic, with its strong presidency in charge of diplomacy and defense (1958), the financial plan against inflation and the devaluation recommended by the Rueff-Armand report of 1958, the successful explosion of the French atomic bomb (1960), the difficult liquidation of the Algerian war (and of France's colonial army) in 1962 were his main accomplishments. De Gaulle's acceptance of the Common Market, which surprised many who knew his reservations or had doubted France's economic capacity to meet its requirements, was largely caused by his conviction that opening France's borders to her partners would greatly accelerate her modernization.

Resisting American, Soviet, and other encroachments was the second task. Concerning the United States, de Gaulle not only rejected the strategy of flexible response and centralized American control of nuclear weapons advocated by the Kennedy administration, but also kept Britain out of the Common Market because of his conviction that the United Kingdom had never repudiated Churchill's preference for the United States over Europe. Concerning the Soviet Union, and against British and American temptations to reach a compromise with Moscow, de Gaulle took the firmest line in opposing Khrushchev's attempts to change the status of Berlin (a line that served both his strategy of equilibrium and his policy of attracting Adenauer). He also supported the United States during the Cuban missile crisis. His recognition of the Communist government of China, in early 1964, was another blow for a multipolar balance: like Nixon and Kissinger later, he thought that the fear of a China open to the West would help push the Soviet Union closer to the West. His hostility to Hammarskjöld's and the UN's intervention in the Congo in 1960 resulted from his conviction that the crisis there was a matter for the United States, the United Kingdom, and France, not for the "thing"—*le machin*—that is, an irresponsible international body, open to demagoguery and to Soviet machinations.

The third task was finding an appropriate framework for French activism. His first attempt was the famous memorandum of September 1958, in which he suggested that France, the United States, and England jointly devise a strategy for "political questions affecting world security"[28] and for the use of nuclear weapons in any part of the world. He does not appear to have ever believed that his allies would give him satisfaction, but the rejection (or rather the nonacceptance) of this proposal served as his justification for his offensive against NATO. Far more serious was his second attempt, which lasted two years (1960–1962) at creating a "European Europe," an "organized cooperation" among the six states that had already formed the Common Market, in order to coordinate their policies in the political, economic, cultural, and defense areas and to lead to a reform both of the Atlantic Alliance and of the existing Communities. A protracted negotiation led to the Fouchet plan of January 1962— which failed over Dutch and Belgian opposition, and, more fundamentally, because de Gaulle's view of the relationship Western Europe should have with the U.S. was shared by none of his partners, because his opposition to Britain's entry into the Communities was shared only by Adenauer, and because the other four were bothered by the Franco-German "axis."[29] A third and more modest attempt was made after that fiasco; it took the form of the Franco-German treaty of January 1963—a two-power version of the Fouchet plan. But the preamble adopted by the German Parliament showed that the Federal Republic did not share de Gaulle's approach to the United States and to European security, and that American influence prevailed in Bonn over France's.

The second phase of de Gaulle's diplomacy went from 1964 to the summer of 1968. On the one hand, de Gaulle, dissatisfied with his European partners' "subservience" to the United States, and with post-Adenauer Germany in particular, turned away from Western Europe. In the previous phase, not only had he decided to endorse the Common Market treaty despite its unwelcome features, but it was his own imperious insistence, and his somewhat paradoxical cooperation with the "supranational" Commission of the Common Market, which had led to the adoption, by the Community, of a common external tariff and above all of a common agricultural policy that served French interests and also gave genuine substance to the whole enterprise.[30] Now, his only efforts aimed at curbing supranationality and majority vote (1965) and at continuing to keep Britain out (1967).

On the other hand, after Khrushchev's retreat over Berlin and defeat in the Cuban missile crisis, de Gaulle thought that the time had come to launch a policy he had always thought necessary for the long run: "détente, entente and cooperation" with the Soviet Union. He believed that Moscow, threatened in Asia by Beijing, and checkmated by the United States over much of the world, had a long-term interest in becoming, as in the nineteenth century, a primarily European power. He knew how important the "German question" was for Russian security. He was looking forward to the day when the pressures of nationalism abroad and the difficulties of the regime at home would force Moscow to accept the emancipation of its European satellites, and he was offering to Moscow the prospect of a "European" settlement of the German question—one in which Germany would be gradually ultimately reunified, but with severe border and military restrictions, and under the control of its European neighbors. This vision of "Europe from the Atlantic to the Urals" clearly served all of his goals: a reduction of American as well as Soviet influence, a restoration of Europe's role in the world, a German solution that would meet Germany's national hope yet sharply curtail and contain its power.[31] But Moscow was not willing to let itself be convinced or seduced, and de Gaulle's visit to the Soviet Union in 1966 produced little beyond bilateral agreements. During the Middle East crisis of 1967, the Soviet leaders preferred dealing directly with the United States to the quadripartite "concert" suggested by de Gaulle. The Soviet invasion of Czechoslovakia in August 1968 put a brutal end to what can be called the first Western policy of détente. Events had been moving both too slowly—in the Soviet Union—and too fast—in Czechoslovakia.

During this phase, de Gaulle did not limit himself to his Soviet policy. He strove to give a global dimension to his battle against the "hegemonies," and in a period when the United States seemed to have become preponderant, the main thrust of de Gaulle's activism was aimed at the United States. He went to Phnom Penh to denounce American policy in Vietnam (1966). His visit to Canada in August 1967, which ended after his provocative call for a free Quebec, was—he tells us—caused not only by his sense of historic injustice (France's abandonment of her people in North America in the eighteenth century) but also by a desire to create a counterweight to the United States.[32] He went to Latin America to preach the gospel of independence and development, and generally appeared as a defender of the rights of Third World countries—as the one Western champion of decolonization who had no other goal than helping the newly independent states. (He tried to make Franco-Algerian cooperation exemplary despite the collapse of the 1962 Evian agreements and a multiplicity of Algerian pinpricks).[33] His decision, in May 1967, to condemn whatever state—Egypt or Israel—resorted to armed attack first, and his condemnation of

Israel when the Jewish state struck Egypt, resulted both from his desire to preserve the policy of rapprochement with the Arab world he had practiced since the end of the Algerian war, and from his conviction that a war in the Middle East could only reenforce the grip of the United States and of the USSR on their respective clients in the area. His support for Biafra resulted from his sympathy for national self-determination and pitted him against both the "Anglo-Saxons" and the Soviets.

His long offensive against the privileges of the dollar and his call for a different kind of international monetary system were another element of his global design—but, as in so many other domains, he failed to find enough support to shake up the status quo. The crisis of May 1968 made it financially impossible for him to persist in his policy of converting France's dollar reserves into gold.

The two crises of the summer of 1968 obliged de Gaulle to begin a third phase, which lasted only seven months. The first task was—again—to rebuild French strength, depleted by the riots and strikes of May and by the settlement the Pompidou government had negotiated with the unions. Global activism had to be curtailed. With Soviet domination reaffirmed in Eastern Europe, with a United States both weakened by Vietnam and willing to start negotiating its exit, de Gaulle returned to the West European framework he had neglected since 1963. During the financial crisis of November 1968, which had weakened the franc, de Gaulle, faced with Germany's refusal to revalue the deutschmark, in turn refused to devalue the franc—a refusal that required a strict anti-inflationary and therefore unpopular policy at home. He now made a tentative offer to Britain; he realized that France's partners saw Britain's entry into the Community as a sine qua non for its development, and that under certain conditions the United Kingdom's presence in a European entity could be a useful counterweight to Germany (or prod Germany into closer cooperation with France). He suggested to Ambassador Soames a revision of the treaty of Rome and the establishment of a four-power political concert or directory. The British government chose to exploit this offer against de Gaulle, and nothing came of it.[34] Then came the fatal referendum on decentralization, and de Gaulle's departure.

III

It was necessary to summarize de Gaulle's various designs and campaigns, both in order to show how he tried to define and promote French interests, and because of the importance, not of dogmas but of concepts or schemes in de Gaulle's mind. He had a global vision, and always subordinated his tactics and his means to that vision. He never separated France's "possession goals"—to use Arnold Wolfers' distinctions[35]—from the "milieu goals" he had formulated. He did not always reveal all aspects of his designs at once or fully. Yet those who found his policies confusing or hard to understand have really no excuse. He was a relentless pedagogue, and his speeches, press conferences, and memoranda left very little in the dark. In 1960, when he spoke before the U.S. Congress, Vice President Nixon asked him about his reputation for "machiavellianism"; he replied that since June 1940 "what I say and try to do is always as clear and straight as possible. Since many professional politicians and journalists don't imagine public action without deceit and betrayals, they see only cunning in my frankness and my sincerity."[36]

He was, indeed, frank, and undoubtedly he was sincere when he wrote that he had never struck at "the pride of any people or at the dignity of its leaders."[37] And yet, few statesmen have been more controversial, and provoked so much hostility. It wasn't only because his designs and schemes were incompatible with the objectives and policies pursued by many of the states with which he interacted. Clearly, "Atlanticists" in the United States, Germany, or Holland, European integrationists in France or Italy, British champions of the "special relationship," Soviet spokesmen for the Brezhnev doctrine, Israelis proud of the Six Day War, British Canadians, or idealistic admirers of Dag Hammarskjöld were unlikely to be very enthusiastic about the general's ideas and projects.

But this was only part of the story. The other part had to do with the general's style. It was unusual in a variety of ways. First of all, there was something grandiose—one needs the French word *démesuré*—about the man and his policies. For he did act upon the premise that France had a *vocation,* a mission, to be great, even if accidents of history temporarily reduced her power and influence—and that neither the French themselves nor foreigners had any right to challenge this assumption. De Gaulle's nationalism is remarkably similar to that of Michelet, who saw *la patrie* as a "great friendship,"[38] and France as indispensable to the progress of humanity—or to that of the Catholic and populist Péguy on the eve of the First World War. This could not but shock all those who resented as extravagant any national claim of exceptionalism, *and* those who could accept such a claim only from states whose power matched their ambitions. De Gaulle knew that France was only a middle power, in material terms, and that the days of Louis XIV and Napoleon were gone, but he also believed that only a sense of mission could keep the French from slipping even further—because of external and internal perils—and that France had enough material and spiritual cards left to stand straight and to aim high. Since he expressed this view incessantly and in ringing tones, it is not surprising that he was resented as much as he was admired. It was, most certainly, de Gaulle who could not be himself without *la grandeur*; the French, as he knew only too well, could accommodate themselves quite comfortably to mediocrity. But he identified with France, not with the French, and he saw his destiny as dragging the French upward. His foreign minister, Couve de Murville, a cool, competent, and skeptical patriot, described him as "sentimental";[39] I would rather say that he was a romantic, disciplined by his familiarity with classical authors and concepts.

One may ask why, with such views, de Gaulle nevertheless succeeded in fascinating quite a number of leaders, from Adenauer to Ben-Gurion. It was partly because of his epic wartime achievements, partly because of his mastery of language and sharpness of mind. But it was also because he seemed to embody what had so often made French nationalism attractive abroad—the universality of its appeal. De Gaulle preached both a particularly expansive notion of the *national* interest, and a sermon on international relations that stressed peace, balance, independence, generosity, *la querelle de l'homme*,[40] and the dignity of nations. De Gaulle's vision, in a sense, provided France with a surfeit of "soft power,"[41] to use Joseph Nye's concept; at the same time, he was putting French power, hard and soft, at the service of more than narrowly or selfishly French interests.

Another reason for the resentments and refusals he provoked was the panoply of tactics he used. His statecraft remained deeply marked by his past—that of a military champion of *Blitzkrieg*. He understood the need for cooperation as well as any of his critics—had he not cooperated with Churchill and, if not with FDR, at least with Eisenhower during the war, he would not have reached any of his goals. His plans for a "Europe of states," his calls for a variety of great power concerts, were invitations to cooperate. But there is no doubt that he felt more at home in maneuver and combat, in exhortation, imprecation, warning and confrontation, than in compromise and collaboration. Two of the three secretaries general of the presidency were career diplomats,[42] and so were several of his most trusted ministers; he wrote about many of his ambassadors with pride and praise.[43] Nevertheless, diplomacy was not his preferred mode of action. He told one of his ministers: "One doesn't negotiate in order to come to a conclusion ("*aboutir*") but in order to win."[44] He complained repeatedly about the tendency of diplomats to want always to deal, and about politicians who prefer "presenting France's case" to saying: "This is what we want."[45] In a clash with his foreign minister Bidault in December 1945 about how to react to a note in which France's allies tried to justify France's exclusion from the negotiation of peace treaties with Germany's allies in the Balkans, de Gaulle stated that "accepting with lamentations is the worst of all solutions,"[46] and that the Quai d'Orsay's style was to accept under reservations that are never realized. De Gaulle also disagreed with and overruled Couve, who wanted to let the negotiations with Britain about London's application to the Common Market drag on, in January 1963, and who, in 1966, would have preferred a more "diplomatic" and less "military" exit from NATO.[47]

Treaties—one of the supreme forms of diplomacy—were not highly valued by de Gaulle. He took the initiative for only very few (and they did not fare too well): the Franco-Soviet treaty of 1944, the Fouchet draft of 1961–1962, two technical agreements with the Soviets in 1966 were the only examples. A British offer, rather clumsily transmitted in 1944, was rejected, and the Franco-German treaty of 1963 was initiated by Adenauer.[48] As de Gaulle told his ambassador in Washington, commitments bring only troubles.[49] Treaties signed or commitments made by others were not considered sacred by him—we have already mentioned his attitude toward the Treaty of Rome and the North Atlantic Treaty, and he declared during the Middle East crisis of 1967 that the tripartite declaration of 1950 was no longer applicable. Indeed, he viewed such agreements and assurances with deep misgivings, because he suspected the French who signed them of having been too willing to consent to France's "submission" to foreign ideas and interests.[50]

Nor did he care for another form of diplomacy: mediation. He did not offer his good offices in the Vietnam War, although he let the Americans meet with their enemies in Paris. He was not interested, in 1967, in mediating between Tel Aviv and Cairo, even though many Israelis believed he was in a unique position to do so. Mediation meant being at the service of others, rather than carrying out one's own policy.

During the war, he had explained to Churchill, who wanted him to show greater flexibility toward FDR, that he—unlike the British leader—was "too poor" and too burdened to be able to bend.[51] But bending was not any more in his nature after the burdens had lightened and once he sat on the pinnacle of power. He always much preferred unilateral action—such as his moves against NATO and the construction of a purely French nuclear force, a costly undertaking, but one that did not leave France exposed to the kind of bad surprise that the American cancellation of the Skybolt missile inflicted on Britain in the fall of 1962. In de Gaulle's case, the line between unilateral action and shock tactics could be exceedingly thin, as was shown by his two "*non*" to Britain, his exit from NATO, and above all his apparently spontaneous but certainly deliberate call for the freedom of Quebec.

He also was determined never to appear as a supplicant, a "*demandeur.*" He could, on occasion, propose and suggest: the 1958 memorandum, the plan for an organized Western Europe, the call for détente, the conversation with Soames are examples of his initiatives. But he never wanted to be seen as *needing* something, out of fear that he might have to make dangerous concessions in exchange for what he might obtain. He carefully refrained from asking the United States to help France in nuclear matters and to give, in this respect, the same privileged treatment to France as U.S. law provided to the United Kingdom.[52] When Adenauer came to visit him at Colombey in September 1958, de Gaulle told him that France wanted nothing from Bonn, and, unlike the Federal Republic, did not "need" any organized Western Europe.

His one attempt at being "diplomatic" had not been very successful. His instructions to his prime minister about how to negotiate what was going to become the Fouchet plan, without attacking directly France's partners' attachment to NATO and to the Treaty of Rome, had led the Quai d'Orsay to go very far toward meeting those partners' demands for reassurances, without receiving any indication that *they* had really moved toward *his* conception of a "European Europe." De Gaulle, therefore, in January 1962 revised the draft himself, removed the key concessions, and thus provoked the final failure of the plan in April.[53] The fiasco was compounded when he then showed himself willing to restore the concessions he had canceled, for three of France's partners were no longer willing to compromise. But success at the cost of a wishy-washy compromise that would have papered over the fundamental clash of designs mattered less to him than the opportunity to stick to *his* design unencumbered. For instance, since the reform of NATO, which he had often called for, seemed unlikely to lead to any drastic loosening up of military integration and American predominance, he preferred to pull France out of the military structure rather than to go through a protracted diplomatic charade.

If he disdained making concessions that could have brought him some support in return, on what did he count for moving toward his goals? A first answer is that he wanted, as a prerequisite, success in resisting and obstructing the course others were, as he saw it, trying to force upon France. Believing, at the end of 1943, that the Allies never treated France as a genuine ally and never consulted him on their plans, he states that he felt justified "each time it would be necessary, to act for our own account and independently of the others. It would not go without clashes, but they would have to accept it."[54] In 1945, this same attitude led to France's rejection of the Potsdam agreement on a central administration for Germany; a few months earlier, his refusal to recognize the Lublin Committee as the government of Poland had almost led to a breakup of his talks with Stalin, and he had shown himself willing to return to Paris without any treaty unless Stalin yielded.[55] In the period covered here, his most spectacular refusal was the double rejection, in January 1963, of Britain's entry into the Common Market, and of America's nuclear proposals resulting from the Nassau meeting between Kennedy and Macmillan. Bidault had once said of him: "It tires him to say yes."[56]

If his adversaries refused, in turn, to let themselves be obstructed or stopped, he would see to it that the course they persisted in following would be costly.[57] The embargo on weapons to Israel—after many years in which France had been its main provider of arms—the policy of converting dollars into gold are two examples of his determination. Another one was the so-called policy of the empty chair—France's boycotting of the Common Market institutions in 1965, after the president of the Commission, Hallstein, had attempted to use the crisis over the financing of the Common Agricultural Policy as a means of increasing the resources and powers of the Commission and of the Parliament at the expense of the member states: the boycott ended with the Luxembourg "compromise," which, on the whole, gave de Gaulle what he wanted.

This does not mean that he was incapable of cooperating—on a basis established by him, and toward goals acceptable to him. The Common Market, from 1958 to 1965, is a good example of what could be achieved. The solemn reconciliation with Germany is another case in point. The practical agreements reached between NATO and France, and between Germany and France, after France's withdrawal from NATO (when he waited for the Germans to request that he keep French forces in the Federal Republic) are a third and important instance. The policy of cooperation with Algeria and other former French colonies is a fourth. But these arrangements were often less visible (and, as in the case of NATO, kept deliberately so) than the confrontations and the solo performances de Gaulle seemed to crave—or else the agreements were presented as French victories. It was, on the whole, only in his Third World policy that he celebrated cooperation unreservedly. There, he was the one who had something to offer, and (as in former colonies in black Africa) much to gain in exchange, and no entrapment to fear.

When neither unilateral action nor obstruction nor cooperation succeeded in bringing him closer to his objectives, he resorted to one last technique—prophecy and exhortations. If he could not change things, he could use his lucidity and his verbal gifts to explain how the present course of events would lead to disaster, or how things would ultimately move where he wanted them to go. By proclaiming this in as striking a way as he could, he hoped to push things in his direction. He often seemed far more concerned with stating positions for the distant future than with achieving immediate results—perhaps because he realized how little leeway for effective maneuver France actually had in a bipolar world, and he saw his options limited to either resignation to a status quo he disliked for himself and for France, or taking the "right" stand (right, that is, both for France and for the world) even if this was not followed by great effects in the short run. Thus, in his famous press conference of November 1967, he both warned about what would happen to Israel and to the Middle East if Israel did not put an end to its occupation of Arab lands, and he called for an independent Quebec. The long-term plan he outlined in the press conference he held on the twentieth anniversary of Yalta proposed a method for resolving the German problem and for reunifying Europe and Germany once the circumstances had become favorable. His simultaneous call for a new, more "objective" monetary system that would impose discipline on all and provide advantages to none, his plan for peace and neutralization in Vietnam, his exhortation to foreign countries to be or become "themselves" are all aspects of the kind of magisterial statecraft he liked to perform.

The power of the word was important to him, not just for its own sake—he had prefaced one of his early books with: "in the beginning was the word—no, in the beginning was action"[58]—but because, as an intellectual, he knew that nations and national feelings were largely the products of powerful rhetoric and galvanizing language. Indeed, he had proved it between June 1940 and the Liberation. Even if the walls of Jericho did not collapse at the sound of his trumpet, his words rang around the world as well as all over France and raised France's pride and prestige. This is why his diplomacy relied so heavily on the art of communication. As he himself put it,[59] his press conferences, twice a year, were events; he used them not only to explain his policies but to announce decisions. Even more important were the visits of foreign dignitaries to France, and, above all, his exhausting journeys abroad, aimed at spreading the gospel of France's greatness, at celebrating old or new friendships, at paying tribute to past joint achievements, at supporting new members of international society, or at calling for a new world order. If France could not, by herself, bring it about, she could at least, through him, carry her message everywhere. The politics of verbal magic aimed at changing people's minds and at striking their imagination. Was it effective, or illusory?

IV

Indeed, what did he actually achieve? It is easy to indict a diplomacy of sound and fury, which, at the time of his resignation seemed to have reached a dead end (as in January 1946). In terms of substance, as we have seen, every one of his designs for a new, multipolar balance had failed. The West European entity that would incorporate the existing communities and provide for coordinated foreign defense policies was never founded—only the Communities he had opposed or distrusted remained. Franco-German cooperation had not overcome the difference between de Gaulle's anti-Atlantic view of Europe's future and Germany's dependence on the United States for security. The Soviets flattered but did not listen to him. The nations of Eastern Europe remained under Soviet domination, those of Western Europe—except France—stayed under American command, in an unreformed NATO. The superpowers were on the verge of negotiating the kind of arms control he most disliked, for it seemed to him to consecrate the two hegemonies and to amount to collusion at the expense and behind the back of the Europeans. He had kept Britain out of the EEC, but at the cost of paralyzing it. Israel had become a client and dependent of the United States, and the Middle East one more battleground for the superpowers. The dollar's supremacy was not shaken (and when his prediction about some of the disadvantages of the monetary system came true, the United States changed the rules unilaterally, in 1971). The policy of independence may have drugged the French, but in reality they had not gotten any better deal than Britain and West Germany, countries that did not challenge the United States or the international system.

Another part of the indictment concerns the boomerang effects of the general's style. Was not the good will he accumulated in many Third World countries, or in Romania, more than offset by the resentments he raised in the United States, Britain, or Israel? Did not his shock tactics against Washington lead one administration—Kennedy's—to wage a successful counteroffensive so as to regain control of a wavering West Germany, in 1963, and the next administration—Johnson's—to ignore de Gaulle so as to provide him with fewer opportunities for making waves? Had his way of treating the United Kingdom as America's Trojan horse, eager to destroy the agricultural policy France had wanted in Western Europe and to tie the West European boat to the American battleship, not merely confirmed Britain's loyalty to the United States without deterring London from seeking entry into the EEC? Had his excommunication of Israel in 1967 not precipitated its leaders into the arms of the United States, the very outcome he most deplored?[60] Had his appeals to the Poles and the Romanians to act as independent nations not strengthened the Soviets' determination to preserve their domination in Eastern Europe? Above all, had his attempt at "seducing" Adenauer not been recurrently disrupted by the crises that resulted from his own haughty way of raising France to the status of a world power while the Federal Republic was to be kept within bounds—the 1958 memorandum that he had not shown to the chancellor, the French nuclear program that provoked Adenauer's anger in October 1960?[61] Had he not sabotaged the project that, along with détente, was closest to his heart—the organization of Western Europe—both by repeatedly attacking his partners' attachment to NATO and to supranational integration (as in his "toughening" of the Fouchet plan) and by presenting the smaller partners and a passive but prickly Italy with the fait accompli of the Franco-German axis? From the viewpoint of effectiveness, was he not his own worst enemy?

These charges were made, not only abroad, but in France, by commentators as sharp as Raymond Aron and Pierre Hassner,[62] and they are hard to refute. However, they miss two points. The first is that they neglect what he *did* achieve. If "France's future was in herself,"[63] then the task of domestic reconstruction and development that he pursued must be put in the credit column of his statecraft. A constitution that provided both stability and flexibility, a painful but ultimately successful process of decolonization that eliminated formidable burdens (far heavier than the benefits France still derived from her overseas possessions), the whole policy of economic transformation that aimed at and partially succeeded in modernizing French agriculture and in making an industrial country out of a traditionally rural one—these were major accomplishments, even if the decline of such relays between the president and the people as Parliament, parties, and interest groups led to the volcanic eruptions of May 1968, even if the policy of state-fostered and state-fed "national champions" in a *dirigiste* economy led to a number of industrial fiascoes.[64]

Another achievement was France's nuclear program. For de Gaulle, France had to be a nuclear power for a large number of reasons: because of the overall importance of nuclear technology, because nuclear weapons buttressed France's claim to *le rang*, because they gave France an asset that was kept away from Germany, because they made it more difficult for the United States to carry out a strategy of flexible response whose deterrent power he doubted. Fundamentally, France's nuclear arsenal was essential because it confirmed France's great power status (to this day, the five permanent members of the Security Council are the five openly declared nuclear powers), and because it provided France with a deterrent against war and blackmail.[65] De Gaulle believed—rightly—that for France and Europe any war, conventional or nuclear, would be fatal; that extended deterrence, that is, the American guarantee, was an uncertain and unreliable assurance now that each superpower could devastate the other; and that a national deterrent, even small, was a much better insurance policy. Like Khrushchev, he thought that no state was ready, by initiating an attack against a nuclear power, to court even a small risk of annihilation. France's nuclear force was, thus, a force for peace in a tense present, and an insurance policy for a cloudy future. The general did not bother about "theological" debates on the uses of nuclear weapons, because he doubted they would ever be used; and when he inspired General Charles Ailleret's famous "*tous azimuts*" doctrine in 1967, it was not so much another deliberate provocation of America, as another way of proclaiming that France was a global, not merely a European, power.[66] A third achievement was Franco-German reconciliation; it had begun under the Fourth Republic, but de Gaulle gave it a singular solemnity, and the treaty of 1963 created institutions that made it easier for the two countries to weather periods of mutual suspicion.

The second point that de Gaulle's critics miss is that the main thrust of his statecraft was most probably not short-term results. As his conversations with Adenauer make clear, he was well aware of the limits of France's power and of the formidable obstacles he faced. It has always seemed to this observer that de Gaulle had three main objectives. The first was to *protect* French autonomy and freedom of action, by loosening foreign grips, shedding obsolete burdens, increasing the forces, military and economic, at France's disposal, but also by avoiding responsibilities that exceeded France's means. This was, in a sense, de Gaulle's tribute to France's past, his way of being worthy of the leaders who, throughout history, had made France great and kept her free. The second goal was to *project* a vision of the future that could serve as a guide for action and a criterion for judging what others, and also his own successors, would do. It was important for him to *prendre date*, to stake a claim. "Against war, which is the history of men," let us "realize united Europe, which is the dream of the wise."[67] Of the failed Fouchet plan, he wrote that things would remain in suspense until one found out if it was, "for history, 'some armada sunk in an eternal lie' or else, for the future, a beautiful hope rising from the waves."[68] His policy of détente was another "dream of the wise," and he must have known that the circumstances were not ripe. But he felt he had a duty to take the initiative, because his plan was the only one that could ultimately reconcile Germany's desire for unity, Germany's neighbors' and Russia's need for security vis-à-vis Germany, the desire in the two halves of Europe for a reunification of the continent itself, and the ambition of France and Russia to be the key guarantors of a European settlement. The moment may not have been right, but if he waited, the fate of Europe would be sealed either by the superpowers directly, by a Soviet-German deal, or—as did happen—by a combination of the two. De Gaulle used to say that the future lasts a long time. He wanted to provide guidance for his successors.

A third objective, quite simply, was to fill the stage, to *perform* relentlessly in the present—a present that was indeed frustrating and constraining. What distinguishes de Gaulle's second "reign" from his first is the role of spectacle in his Fifth Republic statecraft. If one could not dislodge the two hegemons, one could at least share the stage with them, and get the spotlights focused on oneself because one's words and deeds grabbed the spectators' attention. He knew only too well that his successors would not be able or willing to steal the show as brilliantly as he had; had he not written, *à propos* of his first abdication, that "everyone . . . had, deep down, the feeling that the General took away with him something primordial, permanent, necessary, which he embodied because of History"?[69] He wanted to use his "personal equation" for France's glory. Glory could no longer be purely military (de Gaulle had never been a militarist and saw war as an often necessary but dirty business), but it could still be radiant, whatever the constraints of the international system and the limits on French power. To be both the *Tintin* of international politics—the smaller guy who thumbs his nose at the big bullies—and the tall prophet of "détente, entente and cooperation" and of national independence for all corresponded exactly to his character, and made France a global factor, if not a global power. De Gaulle's glow gave self-confidence to the French, and thus made them more capable of acting for independence and grandeur.

V

The general, after his fall, wondered if he had not written the last pages of France's grandeur. The question we must now ask concerns the legacy of his statecraft.

Something happened to French foreign policy, which de Gaulle would probably have observed without surprise but with some dismay. His heirs have had a tendency to turn into dogmas policies that he developed for specific circumstances, and that he felt free to drop or revise when the circumstances changed. Until the mid-1980s, it can be said that, with minor deviations, the French train kept moving on the rails set down by de Gaulle. (The deviations were Britain's entry into the EEC, on terms that had to be renegotiated for over ten years, the development of a French tactical nuclear arsenal of uncertain strategic significance, the popular election of the European Parliament, however without any increase of its powers, and France's acceptance of the post-1971 monetary system of floating exchange rates, which eased pressures on but did little to reduce the advantages of the dollar). Resistance to the American "hegemony" and distress at France's partners in Europe who continued to accept it persisted, and the crisis in Franco-American relations over Kissinger's "Year of Europe" and handling of the oil crisis of 1973 was handled by President Pompidou and Foreign Minister Jobert as if de Gaulle and Couve were still in power. The friendship of Giscard d'Estaing and Chancellor Schmidt revived the Franco-German motor of the European Community. The creation in 1977 of the European Council—a reunion of chiefs of state—and the timid beginnings of political (i.e., foreign policy) cooperation among the members of the EEC, were direct descendants of the Fouchet plan. During the Second Cold War, after 1979, President Mitterrand's support for the deployment of American missiles in Germany can be compared to de Gaulle's support for the United States in the Cuban missile crisis. Before that period of renewed tension, détente was pursued, tepidly by President Pompidou, naively by President Giscard d'Estaing, disappointingly by both—as before.

However, de Gaulle's absence made a vast difference in one important respect. Détente policy was snatched away from French hands, and the initiative passed to Willy Brandt and to Henry Kissinger: they had more to offer to the Kremlin than de Gaulle had ever had (*his* willingness to recognize existing borders was never accompanied either by a readiness to recognize "Pankow," or by a willingness to stop denouncing "Yalta" in order to be better able to transcend it later). Here, in an area de Gaulle deemed crucial, Gaullism without its founder faltered.

As long as bipolarity and a divided Europe still provided the main features of the international system, arguments for challenging the Gaullist legacy had been few: no other policy appeared to promise more. It is since 1985 that the legacy of Gaullism has been put in question. First, Mitterrand's *relance* of European integration led both to a de facto reenforcement of the Commission of the EC, under Jacques Delors, and—in the Single Act of 1987—to a shift to majority voting in the council that de Gaulle would probably have opposed. (He was aware of the paralyzing dangers of unanimity in a Community of many more states than the original six, but his remedy would probably have been the establishment of a hierarchy within the entity.) Secondly, and above all, the end of the Cold War, of Soviet domination in Eastern Europe, and of Germany's partition, the paradoxical advent of a "unipolar" world whose lone superpower is world-weary and battered by serious domestic problems, the ferocious return of nationalism on the ruins of communism, the disintegration of the Soviet Union, all this has created a new world in which the French position is anything but comfortable.

Herein lies another paradox: "the overcoming of Yalta" has occurred, the conditions for European and German unity described by de Gaulle in 1965 have been realized[70]—and yet France seems to discover today that it had more freedom of maneuver in the hated bipolar system than now. The main reason for this is that events actually did *not* follow de Gaulle's script so closely. He had not expected Soviet power and unity to collapse to the point of ceasing to offer any counterweight to American power and of having to accept Germany's reunification on Atlantic terms. Above all, he had not wanted Germany to be the principal partner of Moscow in setting the speed and the terms of its reunification, with Washington's blessing, and with France and the United Kingdom on the sidelines. The almost instant absorption of eastern Germany by the Federal Republic was definitely not part of his plan.

The new world is doubly unsatisfactory for France. On the one hand, the United States has, in some respects, reenforced its grip, not only in the Middle East, but in Europe, where NATO remains the only security organization. The United States continues to frown effectively against the development of any independent rival scheme, be it the Western European Union or the Franco-German corps, and the East Europeans turn to the United States rather than to Western Europe for security and reassurance. Here, the failure of de Gaulle's design for a West European entity with its own diplomacy and defense has weighed heavily on the orientations of the former Soviet satellites. The one organization that extends all the way to the Urals (and beyond), the Helsinki Conference, includes the United States and amounts to very little. On the other hand, despite the temporary disruptions caused by the absorption of the East German Länder, it is Germany, not France, that is the main beneficiary of the end of the Cold War in Europe. While Germany's unwillingness to send troops abroad condemns the Community to partial impotence, its economic power and renewed diplomatic self-confidence raise the fear of a "renationalized" German Reich—or of a Community dominated by the new Germany.

In such circumstances, "Gaullism" appears to have little left to offer, beyond rather fruitless resistance to Washington's claim of being the best interpreter of European interests. When Kissinger in 1969 asked de Gaulle how, in the general's intergovernmental scheme for Europe, he would be able to prevent German domination, the general answered *"par la guerre"*[71]—was it a cryptic joke or a serious thought? The crucial fact is that in the new international system where nuclear war between rival blocs is no longer a nightmarish possibility, atomic power, France's former trump card vis-à-vis Germany, is devalued. What matters now most in Franco-German relations is comparative economic power, and, in influence abroad, the capacity to send nonnuclear intervention forces, a capacity that is limited in France's case precisely because of the priority given to the development of a strong nuclear force. What matters even more abroad is economic power, but here two states that are not permanent members of the Security Council and which are nonnuclear, Germany and Japan, far outweigh France.[72]

In de Gaulle's days, the "Gaullist formula": enough West European cooperation to strengthen West Germany's ties to the West and to France—ties which

West Germany's status and security needs made imperative anyhow—but not so much of it that France's "free hands" would be tied, and the preservation of France's worldwide military autonomy, appeared to safeguard France's essential interests. Today, there is a need for a stark choice, with enormous risks whatever alternative is adopted. Should France, both in order to "contain" the new Germany and because of the sharp limits to her own effectiveness as an independent player, reverse gears and promote a policy of full West European integration? This would lead to a kind of West European federal state with its own diplomacy and defense, and with France's forces and nuclear arsenal at the disposal of such a state. It would, of course, constitute a repudiation of the whole Gaullist legacy. The West European enterprise would no longer be, as it has been so far,[73] a *means* for France, but a *goal*. The alternative policy is the Gaullist one of maximum autonomy—diplomatic, military, financial, and economic. But wouldn't it lead to an unfettered, dominant Germany—worse than "contained," dilute, and tempered German domination within a West European Federation—and demonstrate the present inability of France to reach any important national goal through purely national means?

Until now, French official policy has straddled the fence and tried to have the best of both worlds. But some critics argue that clinging to the phantasm of nuclear autonomy hampers the development of a collective West European defense entity, while other critics argue that the post-1985 attempts to "deepen" the Community not only handicap French freedom of maneuver in the economic and financial realms (where the franc is tied to the deutschmark and French growth is hostage of the Bundesbank) but also leave Eastern Europe in a no man's land de Gaulle would have found intolerable, because the insecurity of those states breeds chaos—as in Yugoslavia—leaves the field open to German economic influence, and provides renewed attraction for the United States.

The heirs of the general, in the neo-Gaullist party, are split. There are those who want a return to a strict policy of "free hands," pan-European and strictly intergovernmental cooperation, and French military autonomy—these are the Gaullists who voted against the Maastricht treaty.[74] There are those, like Jacques Chirac, who, essentially, want to continue to straddle the fence and who accept Maastricht because it both sets up a framework for the "containment" of Germany and remains sufficiently intergovernmental to preserve French autonomy in matters other than money and the economy. Whether de Gaulle would side with those who say "no" or with those who say "yes, if and as long as . . . ," is impossible to know. It is clear that he would reject the West European federal option, with passion and indignation, on behalf of French national identity. How he would overcome the paradox of France in 1993— having reached the goal of getting rid of Yalta, and finding the post-Yalta world even less suitable to French influence than the world of the two blocs—we shall never be able to find out (although we can guess that he would return to his idea of an "organized" Europe, extending as far east as possible, with its own diplomacy and defense, with a Franco-German core, and above all work to create a France sufficiently strong in all dimensions of power to remain the major partner in that association). Just as it took General de Gaulle to carry out fully de Gaulle's policy, it would take him to invent a new one. The problem with great statesmen such as a Bismarck or a de Gaulle, is that when they leave office or die, while their ideas may live and be endlessly analyzed, their skill dies with them.[75] But de Gaulle, of course, believed that their example would inspire others, some day.

Notes

MG   = *Mémoires de Guerre*
ME   = *Mémoires d'Espoir*
Inst. = Institut Charles de Gaulle, *De Gaulle en son siècle*
LNC = *Lettres, notes et carnets*

All the translations from de Gaulle's Memoirs are my own.

1. Charles de Gaulle, *Mémoires de Guerre,* single vol. ed. (Paris, 1989), 10.
2. Charles de Gaulle, *Lettres, notes et carnets, 1905–1918* (Paris, 1980), 13–29.
3. Cf. Eugen J.Weber, *The Nationalist Revival in France, 1905–1914* (Berkeley, 1968).
4. Charles de Gaulle, *La discorde chez l'ennemi* (Paris, 1924).
5. Charles de Gaulle, *Le fil de l'épée* (Paris, 1932).
6. Charles de Gaulle, *Vers l'armée de métier* (Paris, 1934).
7. *LNC, 1969–1970* (Paris, 1988), 250 (letter of 30 June 1930).
8. Charles de Gaulle, *La France et son armée* (Paris, 1938), 1.
9. Cf. Jean Lacouture, *Le rebelle,* vol. 1 of *De Gaulle 1890–1944* (Paris, 1984), 67. Lacouture's three-volume biography is the best account of the general's life and career.
10. The best description of France's situation is by Jean-Pierre Rioux, *La France de la 4e République. I: L'ardeur et la nécessité 1944–52* (Paris, 1980).
11. Cf. André Malraux, *Les chênes qu'on abat* (Paris, 1971).
12. *MG,* 593.
13. Cf. Hervé Alphand, *L'étonnement d'être. Journal* 1939–1973. (Paris, 1977), 321.
14. Cf. Institut Charles de Gaulle, *l'Europe,* vol. 5 of *De Gaulle en son siècle* (Paris, 1992), 174 ff.
15. Cf. Michel Debré, *Trois Républiques pour une France* (Paris, 1984), 1:411 ff; Jean Chauvel, *Commentaire* (Paris, 1972), 115.
16. *MG,* 796.
17. Cf. Inst., *Liberté et dignité des peuples,* vol. 6 of *De Gaulle en son siècle* (Paris, 1992), 60, on de Gaulle's political vocabulary.
18. *LNC, 1919–1940* (Paris, 1980), 441–43.
19. *ME,* (Paris, 1970), 181.
20. *MG,* 374.
21. *MG,* 642.

22. Cf. René Massigli, *Une comédie des erreurs* (Paris, 1978), 40–41.

23. *MG*, 775–76.

24. Inst. 5:313 ff; Pierre Maillard, *de Gaulle et l'Allemagne* (Paris, 1990), chap. 5.

25. *ME*, 174.

26. *MG*, 643.

27. *MG*, 644.

28. *LNC, 1958–1960*, 84.

29. G.-H. Soutou, "1961: Le plan Fouchet", *Espoir*, no. 87 (December 1992): 40–55; see also Robert Bloes, *Le plan Fouchet et le problème de l'Europe politique* (Bruges, 1970).

30. Cf. Inst., the essay by John Keeler, 5:155–67.

31. On de Gaulle's detente policy see Inst., *La sécurité et l'indépendance de la France,* vol. 4 of *De Gaulle en son siècle* (Paris, 1992), part 2, chap. 2.

32. *ME*, 253. On de Gaulle and Canada see Inst., vol. 6, chap. 9. When de Gaulle, after his resignation in 1969, went to Ireland, he gave a toast to "l'Irlande tout entière": Inst., 6:23.

33. Inst., vol. 6, chap. 2.

34. See Bernard Ledwidge, *De Gaulle* (New York, 1983), chap. 42.

35. In Arnold Wolfers, *Discord and Collaboration* (Baltimore, 1962), chap. 5.

36. *ME*, 258.

37. *ME*, 177.

38. Jules Michelet, *Le Peuple* (Paris, 1846).

39. Inst., 6:226.

40. Charles de Gaulle, *1958–1962,* vol. 3 of *Discours et Messages* (Paris, 1970), 86.

41. See Joseph Nye, *Bound to Lead* (New York, 1990).

42. Geoffroy de Courcel (1958–1962) and Etienne Burin des Roziers (1962–1967).

43. *ME*, 219.

44. Inst., 5:177.

45. *ME*, 180.

46. Jules Moch, *Rencontres avec de Gaulle* (Paris, 1971), 100–101.

47. Inst., 4:224.

48. Inst., 5:362, 418.

49. Alphand, *L'étonnement d'être,* 483; also 321.

50. *MG*, 217.

51. *ME*, 179–82.

52. Alphand, *L'étonnement d'être,* 311.

53. See Etienne Burin des Roziers, *Retour aux sources* (Paris, 1986), chap. 3; Inst., essay by G.-H. Soutou, 5:126–44; Maurice Couve de Murville, *Une politique étrangère* (Paris, 1971), 366 ff; Robert Marjolin, *Le travail d'une vie* (Paris, 1986), 322 ff.

54. *MG*, 532.

55. *MG*, 672.

56. Chauvel, *Commentaire*, 2:114.

57. *MG*, 644.

58. Epigraph of chap. 1 of *Le fil de l'épée.*

59. *ME*, 303.

60. Cf. Inst., essay by Elie Barnavi, 6:417–29.

61. See Michel Debré, *Trois Républiques pour une France,* 2:423–24.

62. See in particular Raymond Aron, *Le grand débat* (Paris, 1963).

63. *MG,* 461.

64. See Inst., *Moderniser la France,* vol. 3 of *De Gaulle en son siècle* (Paris, 1992), chaps. 4 and 6.

65. Alphand, *L'étonnement d'être,* 331–54.

66. See Jean Doise et Maurice Vaysse, *Diplomatie et outil militaire* (Paris, 1992), chap. 14.

67. *ME,* 202.

68. *ME,* 210.

69. *MG,* 883.

70. Charles de Gaulle, *1962–1965,* vol. 4 of *Discours et Messages* (Paris, 1970), 338–42.

71. Henry A. Kissinger, *White House Years* (New York, 1979), 110.

72. These points are developed further in my chapter in Robert Keohane, Joseph Nye, and Stanley Hoffmann, eds., *After the Cold War* (Cambridge, Mass., 1993).

73. Inst., 5:70–71.

74. A "nationalist" fraction of the Socialist party, led by J.-P. Chevènement, shares these views.

75. Among the books that deal with de Gaulle's foreign policy, in addition to Lacouture, *De Gaulle,* one should mention: A. W. de Porte, *De Gaulle's Foreign Policy, 1944–1946* (Cambridge, 1968), Edward Kolodziej, *French International Policy Under Georges Pompidou* (Ithaca, 1974), Lois Pattison de Menil, *Who Speaks for Europe?* (London, 1977), and Philip G. Cerny, *The Politics of Grandeur* (Cambridge, 1980). See also Stanley Hoffmann, *Decline or Renewal? France Since the 1930s* (New York, 1974).

PART THREE

A NEW EUROPE?

9

JEAN MONNET: THE INNOVATOR AS DIPLOMAT

W. W. Rostow

M Y MOST VIVID MEMORY of Jean Monnet is of his conversing with Charles de Gaulle. The French president towered physically over Monnet by almost a foot, but somehow the latter—square, comfortable, self-contained—seemed of at least equal specific gravity. With ties reaching back more than twenty years, they talked easily, as if it were natural that two Frenchmen should lead the contending forces that would, one way or the other, shape the future of Europe. And, besides, they had in their time made common cause.[1]

The conversation took place on the afternoon of 25 November 1963. The place was the large reception room on the eighth floor of the Department of State in Washington. The occasion was President Johnson's reception for the chiefs of state and other dignitaries from abroad who had come to President Kennedy's funeral. Aside from the tragic background, it was a bizarre setting; for the room was filled with mainly middle-aged to elderly men, emotionally drained, many experiencing jet lag. They were personages who were almost never seen without an entourage of appropriate officials; but here each was alone without even a prescribed protocol for opening a conversation: Prince Philip, Prince Bernhard, Anastas Mikoyan, King Haile Salassie, President Luebke, etc.—a kind of mobile Madame Tussaud's. Monnet was there as a friend of the Kennedy family.[2] He held no official position whatever, but one and all took it for granted that he belonged to that company.

For sixty-two years—from his fateful meeting with French Prime Minister René Viviani in the second week of September 1914, when he was 26, until his retirement as president of the Action Committee of the United States of Europe on 9 May 1975—Jean Monnet played a critical role as innovator in public policy, mainly as a highly unconventional diplomat. He was author of the Anglo-French system of joint supply during the First World War; deputy secretary general of the League of Nations in the interwar years; a catalytic figure in the rearming of the United States and the supply of American arms to its allies during the Second World War; an agent for the unification of France's wartime military and political effort under Charles de Gaulle, while keeping a certain distance from the leader; the modernizer of the French postwar economy; a trail-blazer for the unity of Western Europe by way of the Coal and Steel

Community, Euratom, and the Common Market; a tireless advocate on both sides of the water of a long-run Atlantic partnership; and the man who, from 1955 to 1975, gave support to these last extraordinary achievements by means of the Action Committee, a unique informal coalition of political, economic, and other leaders representing 70 percent of the Western European electorate, thus outflanking both Gaullists and Communists. As François Duchêne has correctly observed, Monnet built "a kind of shadow party" in support of his vision on both sides of the Atlantic.[3]

I

In a wry aside, Monnet once defined his "line of work":

> If there was stiff competition around the centres of power, there was practically none in the area where I wanted to work—preparing the future, which by definition is outside the glare of present publicity. Since I did not get in statesmen's way, I could count on their support. Moreover, although it takes a long time to reach the men at the top, it takes very little to explain to them how to escape from the difficulties of the present. This is something they are glad to hear when the critical moment comes. Then, when ideas are lacking, they accept yours with gratitude— provided they can present them as their own. These men, after all, take the risks; they need the kudos. In my line of work, kudos has to be forgotten.[4]

It was not quite like that, for Monnet was an innovator as well as an inventor of ideas. He shared or led in the process of translating ideas into action. He knew what it was to battle (or outflank or enlist) entrenched bureaucracies, opposing politicians, and even recalcitrant governments. And sometimes he lost. Still, his batting average was extraordinary, especially for a man prepared to commit himself to a cause he thought good if there was even "a chance of succeeding." Sure things do not require great innovators. In this essay I shall follow Monnet's lead in his *Memoirs,* written with the help of the distinguished writer François Fontaine, who was close to Monnet for more than thirty years. That book rings true for those who knew Monnet, his work, and his style. Even in English translation one can almost hear his voice. But it is overwhelmingly a book of what he did and how he did it rather than an autobiography. Neither didactic nor arrogant, it is, still, a handbook for the incipient innovator in public policy—a kind of *Poor Richard's Almanac* on how to get constructive things done in a world where governments still claim sovereignty, and bureaucrats ardently defend their turf and the status quo. And, in part, we know that is precisely what Monnet intended the book to be. In what follows, then, I shall try to lay out the main elements of what might be called Monnet's system.

At lunch with Katherine Graham during his wartime Washington years, Monnet remarked casually, "You know, you don't have to do much in life. I've only had one good idea, but that's enough." That idea appears in Monnet's *Memoirs* at the end of an extended passage on Antoine de Saint-Exupéry, who evidently formulated it quite independently, writing "Man's finest profession is that of uniting men." This, Monnet recognized, was what his professional life was all about. The dedication of *Memoirs* is, *"Nous ne coalisons pas des États, nous unissons des hommes."*

Embraced in this deceptively simple statement of mission is a complex intermingling of pragmatic, moral, and deeply personal judgments and impulses.

Pragmatically, Monnet perceived, starting in September 1914, that the pursuit of the war by France and Britain as two sovereign states, cooperating conventionally at arms length, might well lead to the defeat of both. And so he found his way to the French prime minister and persuaded him to let this twenty-six year-old cognac salesman go to London to persuade the British to set up integrated machinery for joint supply. Monnet was thus launched on a life-long struggle to overcome the mortal weaknesses of national sovereignty as the framework for solving the critical problems of the twentieth century—a conclusion that was cumulatively reinforced by Monnet's experiences in the League of Nations and as a banker in the Great Depression; by the desperate need in 1940–1942 to link a maximum U.S. war effort to those of its hard-pressed allies; by the initial post-1945 disarray of the West; and by the pattern of remarkable but still incomplete success that followed.

He perceived from the beginning that to move beyond the conventional coalition procedures of sovereign states to a regularized framework of common action required that officials be induced to focus on the solutions to a problem perceived to be common rather than on a zero-sum negotiation, in which gain by one participant meant loss for the other (or others). Moreover, "to talk about the same thing from the same set of facts," nations had to sit, in effect, on the same side of the table. To help produce this result, Monnet early hit on a device that runs like a *leitmotif* through his professional life: the balance sheet. This conventional business tool to which he was introduced by his father at the age of sixteen through the books of the family firm, demonstrated what had to be done by contrasting the current situation with what was necessary to achieve an agreed positive objective. In policy terms the bottom line defined the scale of what had to be done. In political terms the balance sheet was a way of strengthening those, like Franklin Roosevelt in 1941, who took the position with respect to U.S. military production that "it's not a matter of what we *can* do, but of what we *must* do," on which Monnet comments: "I recognized in his attitudes and decisions the same philosophy of action that I myself had acquired from different experience."

There was a moral dimension to all this bringing of men and sovereign governments together by focusing on a common problem. The effect was to reduce the sense of difference in power and resources among those at the table.

This recurrent strand in Monnet's operating style was clearly much affected by the limited successes and final failure of the League of Nations and his reflections upon them:

> We did not feel like people who were misunderstood or whose actions led nowhere. We got results. We overcame crises that were no less serious than those of Berlin or Northern Ireland today; we administered territories by new methods; we put a stop to epidemics. We developed methods of cooperation among nations which hitherto had known only relationships based on power. We placed great hopes in the development of the League, and the difficulties we encountered acted as a stimulus. It was only later that I realized how we had underestimated them, or rather how we had failed to dig deep enough. At the root of them all was national sovereignty. In the League Council, this prevented the general interest's being seen. At every meeting, people talked about the general interest, but it was always forgotten along the way: everyone was obsessed by the effect that any solution would have on him—on his country. The result was that no one really tried to solve the actual problems: their main concern was to find answers that would respect the interests of all those around the table. In this way, the whole organization fell into the routine of mere cooperation.

All this—indeed all Monnet had learned since 1914—came to a climax in his historic meeting in Bonn with Adenauer on 23 May 1950, an authentic turning point in modern European history:

> I already had some idea of how Adenauer looked, with his rigid figure and impassive face; but now I realized at once that I did not know him. The man before me was not self-assured, but anxious to know what I was going to say, and unable completely to conceal a degree of mistrust. Clearly, he could not believe that we were really proposing full equality; and his attitude was still marked by long years of hard negotiation and wounded pride. Our conversation lasted for an hour and a half. As it progressed, I saw the old man gradually relax and reveal the emotion that he had been holding back.
>
> "We want to put Franco-German relations on an entirely new footing," I said. "We want to turn what divided France from Germany—that is, the industries of war—into a common asset, which will also be European. In this way Europe will rediscover the leading role which she used to play in the world and which she lost because she was divided. . . . The aim of the French proposal, therefore, is essentially political. It even has an aspect which might be called moral". . . . Adenauer listened attentively and answered with warmth: "For me, like you, this project is of the highest importance; it is a matter of morality. We have a moral and not just a technical responsibility to our people, and that makes it incumbent upon us to fulfill this great hope. . . . I have waited twenty-five years for a move like this. In accepting it, my Government and my country have no secret hankerings after hegemony. History since 1933 has taught us the folly of such ideas. Germany knows that its fate is bound up with that of Western Europe as a whole."
>
> When we had finished, Adenauer rose to his feet.

"Monsieur Monnet," he said, "I regard the implementation of the French pro-posal as my most important task. If I succeed, I believe that my life will not have been wasted."

We took our leave. I can say of Adenauer what he said in his memoirs about me: "After that, we were friends for life."[5]

There was yet another converging element in Monnet's grand idea of bring-ing men and nations to act together, although like everything that is highly personal in his memoir, it emerges only in terse asides: "It was not in my nature to respect in established authority for its own sake"; "The will to dominate arouses my deepest feelings." One can, for example, feel Monnet's raw anger as he recounts Poincaré's rejection of a plan generated by the Secretariat in the early days of the League to set a limit on German reparations:

"If I understand you aright, gentlemen," said Poincaré, "this boils down to reduc-ing the amount of German debt?" "Not reducing, fixing. One cannot speak of a debt if it has no limit. I should say rather that we propose to free Germany from an unknown burden." At this, Poincaré stood up, flushed with rage. "Never, sir. The German debt is a political matter, and I intend to use it as a means of pressure." To dramatize his words, he drew from his pocket an extract from the Treaty of Ver-sailles and brandished it before our eyes.

And perhaps most germane, Monnet's response to Schuman's concern when French political pressure to annex the Saar strained Franco-German relations in January 1950: "Peace can be found only on equality. . . . we failed in 1919 because we introduced discrimination and a sense of superiority. Now we are beginning to make the same mistakes again."

As we shall see, Monnet often met opposition from men and institutions that wished "to dominate" as he conducted his sequence of innovations. His style in such struggles was, to the degree possible, nonconfrontational—quite often to mobilize alliances so overwhelming as to leave his opposition no realistic option except to acquiesce. At one point Monnet remarks: "Certainly mixed motives and murky conspiracies sometimes exist. But I have always ignored them, and they never did me any harm." In some cases, it took, in fact, considerable effort to frustrate those who opposed Monnet; and he did not always win.

In his youth, Monnet "longed to be a boxer."[6] If he had achieved his aspira-tion his style would not have been to slug it out in the center of the ring, but to slip his opponent's punches and patiently pursue his own strategy.

II

Most of Monnet's life was taken up with innovation; that is, putting ideas into action, often a process with many stages. And this is well reflected in the proportioning of his *Memoirs*. In person, Monnet impressed one as a man of action—an operator engaged in moving forward a course of action clearly defined. He was extraordinarily persuasive and tactically resourceful once launched on an enterprise; and as a matter of conviction and style his expositions were spare and simple as if he had given himself the redrafting instruction he often gave newcomers to his staff: "Too intelligent: rewrite." But Monnet was an inventor as well as an innovator: "I have never acted in any other way. First have an idea, then look for the man who can put it to work." This statement is made in the context of an explanation of why he sought an interview with the French prime minister in September 1914 to make the case for French advocacy to the British of "joint bodies to estimate the combined resources of the Allies, share them out, and share out the costs." This was at the time an utterly revolutionary idea. Where did it come from?

Monnet supplies a rather full account, which I shall paraphrase. Found to be medically unfit for military service, he surveyed the war effort to establish how he could be most useful. France was bearing the brunt of the battle on the ground, losing territory and important economic resources, suffering disproportionate casualties. Its balance of payments was deteriorating, and it was utterly dependent on foreign shipping for overseas supplies, having lost two-thirds of its iron and steel, half of its coal, as well as important agricultural land. But only a small part of the French merchant fleet had been requisitioned.

The British were better off: uninvaded, their fleet in command of the seas. Only a part of the merchant fleet had been requisitioned. Foreign trade was carried on in seminormal style with the French and British often bidding against each other for scarce overseas supplies and raising shipping rates as well as import prices in the bargain.

Germany, with a large industrial machine behind its powerful army on the offensive beyond German borders, was initially in a much better position to organize an efficient flow of supplies in the front and to the war economy.

Behind this dangerous asymmetry was Monnet's basic perception: unlike the wars of the nineteenth century, the basis for power lay in a capacity to mobilize "a nation's whole resources." Despite the rapidly deteriorating situation in the autumn of 1914, Monnet was confident, from his knowledge of the British, that they would in time organize a formidable army and retain control of the seas. The task was to mobilize efficiently the full resources the British could command with those available to France in ways that left neither side free to use its men, supplies, or shipping in ways that were not agreed by both.

Conscious that Britain and France had sovereign governments and parliaments, Monnet nevertheless felt sure the British would agree if France appealed to their loyalty and played fair—each contributing to the common cause what it could in manpower, production, and shipping.

This was the argument that led the French prime minister, after listening to his young crusading visitor, to commend Monnet to his minister of war; and by November 1914 Monnet was in London launched on a protracted step-by-step process of innovation in which he found in a British civil servant, Arthur Salter, a priceless comrade-in-arms.

The point here, however, is that behind Monnet's "idea" lay an extremely complex argument. It wove together a fresh assessment of a war that promised to be lengthy with the strengths and deficiencies of the antagonists in both the short and the long run. It captured the sharp asymmetry in the French and British situations and took into account inherited habits of mind that had to be overcome. It was based, moreover, on sufficient knowledge of the British to justify confidence that the concept of a truly integrated effort could in the end be brought to life.

Monnet prefaces his account with this observation:

I quickly realized what I had to do. It was clear that the Allies were going to face a formidable problem for which there had been no preparation: the coordination of their war efforts. If this was obvious to me, it was *because* I was so young, not *in spite of* the fact. It was a new problem, a twentieth-century problem, which someone without prejudices, without memories of the past, could see more easily than experts brought up on nineteenth century experience. For them, it was harder to realize that the basis of power had changed, that the war machine would now have to mobilize a nation's whole resources, and that quite new forms of organization would have to be invented. Germany, with a powerful army backed by immense industrial might, seemed to me better prepared for this new kind of warfare than the Allies, whose combined strength was weakened because they were preparing to fight separately instead of as one.

All this is quite true. But the weaving together of disparate elements into a coherent rationale for a new, precisely defined course of action was creativity—invention—of the highest order. And it requires no underlining to capture in this tale anticipations of the inventive talent exercised by Monnet not only during the Second World War but in the following three decades. In a sense the recurrent pattern of creativity explains what he may have meant when he told Katherine Graham that he only had one idea. But Monnet's bringing men together was not a process of simple repetition; for the problems Monnet addressed and for which he prescribed each had unique features requiring an assessment of its multiple facets and a bringing of his conclusions to bear in the form of a lucid proposal for action. He was, in short, an inventor whose simple style of exposition concealed the complexity and elegance of the creative process that lay behind it.

We know one rather charming fact about Monnet the inventor and problem solver: the role of lonely walks. The habit began in the Canadian Rockies when, at the age of eighteen, he was visiting the family firm's agents and customers: "It was a need I have felt ever since. I can hardly call it a form of recreation, on the contrary it seems to be the time, or the agent for the concentration of mind that precedes action." As André Herre, who with his wife served the Monnet family for more than thirty years, put it: "It's simple, Monsieur puts his idea in front of him, talks to it, and then decides."

Each in the sequence of Monnet's inventions required a period of intense concentration followed by a phase of equally intense innovation, a quite different kind of business. Then, when the innovation was successfully institutionalized Monnet became bored, disengaged, and moved on to the next problem. Some of his inventions failed, for example, the last-ditch effort to unite Britain and France in May 1940, a Monnet idea that Winston Churchill adopted, and the European Defence Community (EDC), which the French Assembly rejected in August 1954,[7] and the idea of creating a federal district within which all of the European institutions could be located. One innovation in which he participated failed, the League of Nations. In face of such setbacks, he simply moved on to the next challenge that had to be met if the values to which he was committed were to survive.

Analysts have noted that creative physical and social scientists have such an instinct to identify where the next great task lies;[8] and something similar could be said of great novelists, painters, and composers elaborating in successive creations their private grand designs. In the majestic succession of those that occupied his life—each of them with many phases—Monnet seemed to know with confidence what his next job should be, and the rhythm of his life provided for both phases of withdrawal (above all, to his country home in Houjarray), with time for long walks, sustained reflective thought, and extended exchanges with a few like-minded friends, and phases of extraordinary operational intensity, evidently supported by the great natural energy that he husbanded for such intervals of innovation.

III

There is always an element of mystery about the private process whereby an inventor hits upon a new idea. Often many factors are involved, swirling about until a clear and often simple solution emerges.[9] Innovation is quite different: a sustained operation conducted with others in the open.

In the case of Monnet, it is easy to summarize how he proceeded. Quite explicitly he made repetition a principle and a weapon.

> Once I have reached a conclusion that I want others to share, I am never afraid to repeat myself. . . . In fact, there are many advantages in getting the same formulae fixed in people's minds. My maternal grandmother used to be known as "Marie la Rabacheuse"—"Monotonous Mary." I think she had only a few very simple ideas, and to those she held fast.

Monnet applied this principle in his *Memoirs* as he described how he conducted his succession of adventures. In most cases his rules are stated several times; and they are seen in action even more often. It is, therefore, not difficult to derive from his account and the testimony of those who worked intimately with him, the maxims he applied as he "organized change."[10]

Timing Is Almost Everything

There are in the *Memoirs* at least seven explicit references to the critical importance of timing in the innovation of public policy.[11] The most illuminating, perhaps, is this: "People only accept change when they are faced with necessity, and only recognize necessity when a crisis is upon them."[12] Operationally, Monnet felt that "the flair to discern when the moment of possible action had come" was a fundamental requirement. It was equally important, therefore, to be patient until that moment: to observe without discouragement men in responsibility, in George Marshall's phrase, "fighting the problem," trying to get by with small modifications of familiar policies; denying, in the psychologist's sense, the magnitude of the problem that had to be confronted; from an *ex post* perspective, wasting invaluable time. Monnet did not regard such thrashing about as wasted, but as a necessary condition for later success. He knew that "wisdom and reform came only after great difficulties." And, as he looked back, he was willing to preface that aphorism with the word *always*. He summed up his proposition with the dictum: "There are no premature ideas: there are only opportunities for which one must learn to wait."

For the innovator, however, waiting was not a time for sterile meetings, bitter debates, and a growing sense of impending disaster. It was a time for honing the details of his solution; building a team of like-minded coconspirators, in most cases across national boundaries; creating a network of contacts that would guarantee access to the point of decision when the moment of decision in the midst of crisis arrived.

In the most literal sense, in these intervals of intensely busy, patient waiting for crisis, Monnet was "preparing the future." No man ever guided his professional life more completely by that dynamic, nonlinear conception of how history unfolds.

Embedded in Monnet's doctrine of timing was an implicit assumption. He assumed that statesmanship consists in carrying forward a long-run goal, in the face of many unpredictable circumstances, bringing gradually to life a great vision.[13] What he was asserting in his crisis doctrine was that: "Any reform carried out with a distant strategic aim in view must be in answer to current preoccupations."[14] That is how the long and the short-run come together. Indeed, it is another version of Monnet's doctrine of the potential efficacy of crisis.

The Balance Sheet Is a Link Between Invention and Innovation

For Monnet the balance sheet—where it was possible to draw one up—was a powerful link between invention and innovation. It was for Monnet a way of converting a broad, possibly vague statement of policy into a quantitative, concrete working task. Monnet first transferred this familiar tool of business into public policy in the course of the Anglo-French joint supply arrangements during the First World War. These came to crisis over the issue of creating a joint shipping executive as the war itself came to its climax.[15]

Multiple forces converged to put the Allies in mortal jeopardy in 1917–1918: a French offensive in April failed after losing 147,000 men and surrendering important French resources to the Germans; workers were striking in Paris; the German submarine offensive had widened and Allied losses mounted to an average of a half million tons a month, a rate higher than could then be matched by Allied ship-building. Britain as well as France was becoming increasingly dependent on overseas supply. Shipping to bring over American troops, desperately needed to turn the tide in the field, was a further massive requirement just over the horizon. After a tortured confrontation on 3 November 1917, an Anglo-French transport executive was agreed upon. Monnet, Arthur Salter, and their coconspirators at last had their way.

> A transport executive . . . would supervise all Allied and neutral ships, after specifications, their movements, and their cargoes. A continuing inventory of this sort was only imaginable by means of the extensive information network that was at Salter's command, . . . the new Executive should be able gradually to bring about the centralization of all supply programmes, and their adjustment in the light of what shipping was available. For the first time, machinery for large-scale economic information and action would be at the disposal of several countries; and it would oblige them to exchange data that had hitherto been kept secret.

The inventory Monnet describes here is a dynamic balance sheet employed as an executive policy-making tool from day to day. Despite further serious resource losses from the German offensive begun on 21 March 1918, Britain and France were supplied by the tough-minded Allied shipping executive at a marginal level; and 2 million Americans were in France on Armistice Day.

It was a close thing, even for Monnet. The urgent demands for information from the shipping executive and its often peremptory priority decisions offended many in the French bureaucracy including the minister of armaments, who tried to get Monnet transferred to the military. It required Clemenceau himself to keep Monnet at his post.

Monnet was to use the technique of the balance sheet on four other major occasions:

> Balance-sheets of this sort have been milestones in my work: the strength of our fleets in 1916, of our air forces in 1940, of Allied and Axis military power in 1942, of the French economy in 1945, and of the six-nation European Community in 1950. Each time, the need for appropriate action became obvious once the balance sheet was drawn up.

Networks Help Facilitate Innovation

Monnet had no elaborate theory of how to move from invention to innovation. Nevertheless there was a recurrent pattern in the way he went about his business, as he was well aware; and I know of no book on administration that describes how Monnet operated—or, indeed, any other freelance conspirator to do public good.[16]

At some risk of oversimplification I would identify four components in Monnet's recurrent pattern of operation:

—Links to the top;
—Dealing with the top;
—The small circle of co-conspirators;
—Intelligence from and support on the flanks: politicians, bankers, lawyers, activist professors, the press.

Innovation is a process of transferring a new policy from idea into action, seeing it through the vicissitudes of its teething stage until it is institutionalized and accepted as part of established policy. For that process to be set in motion a responsible executive decision is required. As time went on and Monnet's visibility and recognition grew, he developed access to the presidents and prime ministers that most interested him; but, even then, chiefs of government kept changing and intermediaries who supported his policies remained useful and even necessary.

Thus, reflecting on his first extraordinary intermediary in 1914, Monnet wrote: "Sometimes there have to be intermediaries, who may well be little-known, although they are very much aware of the responsibilities they are taking on. Fernand Benon was the first of many. Without him, I might never have come to deal with what my father called 'other people's business'—that is, public affairs."

William Bullitt performed Benon's role with respect to Franklin Roosevelt. Prime Minister Daladier (whom Monnet had met at a friend's home) introduced Monnet to Neville Chamberlain. Monnet does not supply an account of his first meeting with Churchill, but it probably arose as a simple matter of bureaucratic order because Chamberlain and Daladier had set up an Anglo-French Coordinating Committee, which Monnet chaired by joint appointment. But Sir Horace Wilson was a critically important intermediary who "staked all his credit" with Churchill, in support of Monnet's interventions. In a somewhat different way Walter Hallstein performed that function with Adenauer, but Monnet had already come to a deep understanding with Adenauer before Hallstein became Monnet's German colleague in bringing the Schuman Plan to life. Monnet met Truman in Roosevelt's entourage and Eisenhower in North Africa during the war. John Kennedy was surrounded by a battalion of Monnet's friends who might have served as intermediaries; but it did not take much persuasion to arrange his several talks with the president in April 1961, for Kennedy knew a great deal about Monnet—and favorably—by that time.

Once face-to-face with a chief executive, Monnet knew what to do from his 1914 interview with Viviani forward: to explain in spare, unvarnished, pellucid prose the case for the course of action he advocated, relating it to a major problem the executive immediately confronted. Monnet was an artist at this kind of exposition. He understood that executives, almost by definition, required an answer to the question posed by John Kennedy when an idea was put to him: "What do you want me to do about it today?" He also understood that executives were often more willing to innovate than their bureaucratic subordinates because they could not escape the sharp edge of the circumstances that pressed in on them. The costs of sticking with existing policy were thus more vivid, the costs of innovation less formidable than they appeared to most bureaucrats. A decision that appears inescapable to an executive may seem postponable to a bureaucrat; or, at least, somewhere the bureaucrat knows that the impending crisis, and the action it will bring about, will fall on the executive's shoulders, not his. And quite often—more often than one might suppose—executives are drawn to innovations by contemplating their place in history.

It is already clear in the story told thus far that Monnet as innovator operated habitually with a small inner group of men dedicated to the same objectives. As noted earlier, the process yielded a remarkable and cumulative series of friendships. Arthur Salter was the first. He and Monnet not only were brothers-in-arms in the First World War; they also worked in parallel on China's economic development in the 1930s and resumed their roles in joint Anglo-French supply in the Second World War. Salter remained a Monnet confidant, for example, among those he consulted in London on the possibility of Britain joining the Schuman Plan in 1950. Among others on the list of those who labored side-by-side in major enterprises was Ludwig Rajchman, ultimately founder of UNICEF; in Washington 1940–1942, Arthur Purvis, who headed the British supply mission in Washington, and, on the American side, Felix Frankfurter, Henry L. Stimson, John J. McCloy, Acheson, with two military men part of the rather open conspiracy to rearm America to the hilt: General James Burns and Lieutenant Colonel H. S. Aurand. Scarcely less involved were Philip and Katherine Graham, James Reston, and Walter Lippmann. Still closer were Stacy May and Robert Nathan, critically important to the working out of the final U.S. war production plan, which crystallized in 1941, officially adopted on 25 September and implemented with much grinding of gears after Pearl Harbor.

Then there were the remarkable goings on in Algiers, which proved an occasion for resolving, after a fashion, the Girard-de Gaulle conflict but also assembling much of what proved to be Monnet's core team for the postwar years. The French war effort, military and political, was united under de Gaulle with the face-saving device for Giraud of a jointly appointed Committee of

National Liberation. The process was conducted with maximum pain for a good many participants and observers. As Monnet observed: "Reasonableness was not on the agenda." But if Monnet found Giraud's and de Gaulle's egos too strong to unite, he contributed decisively to the emergence of the Committee of National Liberation. Some of Giraud's nominees to that committee, in effect a provisional cabinet, were both friends of Monnet and men who won de Gaulle's respect as Monnet foresaw, notably René Pleven, René Mayer, and a relatively new arrival on the scene, Maurice Couve de Murville.

As the war moved to a climax, Monnet was thrown into planning via UNRRA for immediate postwar emergency economic assistance. He attended an initial United Nations meeting in Washington in November 1943. But it was in Algiers that Monnet began to form the team whose key members would not only manage postwar emergency assistance but also design and implement the French modernization plan, and then move on to the tasks of unifying Europe. Among the initial members of this group of friends conspiring on behalf of a common vision, were René Mayer, Robert Marjolin, and Hervé Alphand, joined from the underground resistance by Etienne Hirsch as well as a major resistance leader, Henri Frenay, who moved over soon to a political career. Léon Kaplan joined the team a bit later as well as Félix Gaillard who served as Monnet's *chef de cabinet* for several years. Pierre Uri came to the Planning Commissariat in 1947, a brilliant and creative intellectual who became a critically important component of Monnet's core team. Later there would be Richard Mayne and François Duchêne (one English, the other English-Swiss) and Max Kohnstamm (from the Netherlands) at the Action Committee.

By and large, Monnet was consistently surrounded by much younger men. Perhaps with some exaggeration of age differentials, Monnet's administrative practice was among the phenomena that led Gunnar Myrdal to observe repeatedly that post-1945 Europe was built by a linking of men who knew Europe before 1914 (Monnet, de Gasperi, Adenauer, Schuman) and their grandchildren who fought on in the underground or from England. (Monnet referred to them as the Resistance generation). The figures from the interwar generation, Myrdal would say, were too conscious of their failures to be effective after 1945.[17] I believe historians will find a good deal in this insight.

It is remarkable that, in the midst of the most urgent problems of war, the reestablishment of legitimacy in French political life, and emergency assistance to its economy, Monnet led his close colleagues in protracted discussions on the long-run future of Europe. A note to the Committee of Liberation in Algiers as early as 5 August 1943, said in part:

There will be no peace in Europe if States re-establish themselves on the basis of national sovereignty, with all that this implies by way of prestige policies and economic protectionism. If the countries of Europe once more protect themselves against each other, it will once more be necessary to build up vast armies. Some countries, under the future peace treaty, will be able to do so; to others it will be forbidden. We experienced such discrimination in 1919; we know the results. Alliances will be concluded between European countries: we know how much they are worth. Social reforms will be prevented or delayed by the pressure of military expenditure. Europe will be reborn yet again under the shadow of fear.

The countries in Europe are too small to give their peoples the prosperity that is now attainable and therefore necessary. They need wider markets. . . . To enjoy the prosperity and social progress that are essential, the States of Europe must form a federation or a "European entity" which will make them a single economic unit. The British, the Americans, and the Russians have worlds of their own into which they can temporarily withdraw. France is bound up in Europe. She cannot escape. . . . The solution of the European problem is all important to the life of France.

Evidently, Monnet's postwar grand design for Europe had deep historical roots and was fast taking shape in 1943–1944.[18]

In addition to core collaborators who worked with Monnet for sustained periods on major innovations, he nurtured not merely contacts but friendships with a spectrum of characters who, in different ways, served his purposes.

In places like London, New York, and Washington, where the big decisions are made, my first talks have always been with men who cannot afford to make mistakes—bankers, industrialists, lawyers, and newspapermen. . . . One of them, André Meyer, I have known for forty years. I have been to see him every time I go to the United States. The same is true of Pierre-David Weill, George Murnname, Floyd Blair, and Dean Jay. . . . Nor did I fail to seek the opinion of Felix Frankfurter, until his death in 1965. After that I also went to see lawyers like Dean Acheson and George Ball, or university teachers like Robert Bowie, Walt and Gene Rostow, or McGeorge Bundy. None of them was ever far from public affairs and government. . . . Finally, I learned a very great deal from talks with friends in the press world—Phil and Kay Graham, Walter Lippmann, Joe Alsop, James Reston, David Schoenbrun, and Robert Kleiman.

Monnet maintained similar abiding ties in London and other centers of initiative. In a curious way these networks, taken together, constituted a kind of private, flexible, innovating bureaucracy for Monnet.

Haste Can be the Innovator's Friend, but Not Always

Monnet's view of the pace of innovation was paradoxical. There were times when he believed that haste was the innovator's friend, and he was not adverse to forcing the pace to secure a desirable result, as in Algiers in 1942, when he sought to unite the warring French factions by inserting into a speech of General Giraud such a degree of unqualified resistance rhetoric that Giraud's supporters objected.[19] On the other hand, he also understood that patience was more often the quality required. He lived by what might be called the Ibn Saud principle.

> Difficulties have this advantage: they can be used as a lever. I have never forgotten the words which Jacques Benoist-Méchin quotes in his fine biography of Ibn Saud. A Western visitor had asked him for the secret of his success. Ibn Saud replied: 'God appeared to me when I was a young man, and said something which has guided my actions throughout my life. He told me: "For me: everything is a means—even obstacles."'

This is how Monnet phrased the Ibn Saud principle in a particular context: the Anglo-French supply during the First World War.

> I never stopped insisting that only a joint overall organization could enable the German challenge to be met. But, as so often in my life, this simple idea had to go through a maze of complications—long and arduous discussions which seemed out of all proportion to what was at stake. . . . And yet to abandon a project because it meets too many obstacles is often a grave mistake: the obstacles themselves provide the friction to make movements possible.

In short, like anyone working at the margin to tip the course of history in benign directions, Monnet knew that "everything takes longer than one expects—which is why one must never set time-limits for succeeding." There were, thus, long frustrating intervals to be endured with patience as well as moments that called for bold action, well-prepared.

Details are Important

Like many other of Monnet's basic homilies in *Memoirs,* his major passage on the importance of details is stirred by recalling a particular moment: in this case the recruitment of René Pleven, then a young financial expert, to help Monnet in 1927 raise a dollar loan to stabilize the hard-pressed Polish zloty.

> At the beginning of 1927, Rajchman put me in touch with the Polish Government, and I went to Warsaw. A young financial expert who had been recommended to me by Pierre Comert has recalled how we made our headquarters at the Hotel Europeiski, where our feverish activity astonished the local population. It was René Pleven, later Prime Minister of France. . . .
>   I think that I was not always easy to live with. I asked a great deal of my colleagues, who found it hard to get used to my methods of work. But they soon saw that these were not really personal idiosyncrasies, because they reflected operational necessities to which I was subject myself. Certainly René Pleven took a little time to realize that we had to live simultaneously on American time and Polish time if we wanted to start a real dialogue. . . . Equally, like many others, it took him some time to agree to rewriting ten or twenty times a note "of secondary

importance" whose text was "more or less satisfactory." In fact, nothing that has to be done to attain one's aim is "secondary." Nothing should be an approximation, accepted out of tiredness or the lateness of the hour. Pleven also had to learn that to write a letter is not enough: one has to be sure that it has been sent, and to check that it has arrived.[20]

Monnet's attention to detail is attested by all who worked with him from day-to-day. But it was no compulsive quirk of character to be tolerated in an otherwise great man. It was to him an essential facet of the innovation process. An innovation is, by definition, a disturbance of the status quo. Those with a conscious or unconscious vested interest in things as they are normally greet an innovational proposal by raising points of possible difficulty. The successful innovator must anticipate such questions and be prepared to answer them credibly. This takes hard, imaginative work. Monnet's negotiation of the Schuman Plan is perhaps the best example of the exacting discipline required to bring to life a large revolutionary idea. An aside in Monnet's account of a critical conference on the Schuman Plan in June 1950 captures the genius of his basic tactic: he left room for accommodating points raised that he judged legitimate; but made sure work proceeded on the basis of his carefully prepared draft.

> For more than two hours I expounded the French draft, but without distributing the text, so as not to cramp the discussion. I intended to incorporate any important points made by the other delegations. . . .
>
> In fact, our working document, drawn up by Hirsch and Uri, was the only text of any substance. . . . but that, in my view, was not a mere matter of chance. I have never sat down to discuss anything without having a draft before me—and I care very little whether it be the first or the only text. . . . If the others accept it because it seems the best, or for any other reason, so much the better. To tell the truth, our suggestions have often been accepted in the absence of any competition. Generally, people come to the table empty-handed, out of either circumspection or sloth. In their hearts, they are pleased to find that a paper has been produced overnight. To produce it means staying up late.

Thus, Monnet not only brought to bear the passionate energy of the crusading innovator who knows exactly what he wants, but also exploited the "circumspection or sloth" of his potential opposition.

Concentrate on a Narrow Front

Chiang Kai-shek once remarked that he thought Monnet would make an excellent general. Others have made observations in the same vein. Indeed, Monnet did possess some of the key qualities of a great commander in the field: he drew to his side in each engagement a few first-rate lieutenants, for there are not many; he had both a large view of the field of engagement and took immense pains to generate a flow of accurate, detailed intelligence; he knew when to wait and when to strike swiftly. Perhaps above all, he understood the critical importance of concentrating effort and resources on a narrow front where a breakthrough would yield victory.

In the First World War quite explicitly he perceived that the mobilization of allied shipping around firmly held common priorities was essential for a victory barely won; and he brought to bear every ounce of sustained energy, every device of persuasion to bring that result about. In the Second World War, he early perceived that air power would prove decisive; and he put himself in a position to bring to bear his capacity for stubborn single-minded concentration to influence the setting of Franklin Roosevelt's 1941 production targets for victory—an effort in lobbying that John Maynard Keynes believed shortened the war by a year. So vivid was Monnet's sense of where the bottleneck lay that, with the war decided in his mind, he was by the end of 1942 prepared to turn to the next great task, although two and a half years of bloody fighting lay ahead. But the path to victory had been institutionalized. There were aspects of the future beyond victory to prepare.

Two nonmilitary exercises in the principle of concentration of effort are worth citing.

The first concerns the initial point of concentration of resources in the postwar French Modernization Plan. The economic ministries and their many departments were filled with statements of requirements. But they were uncoordinated, all competing for "limited resources of energy, man power and foreign currency."

> The question was: where to begin? Once again, I realized that this was the only question that mattered. Once you have made a start, all you need do is continue. But in order to begin, one needs to have clear ideas and decide on the simplest way forward. Common sense is not enough, even if in retrospect the decisions taken look obvious. . . . Admittedly, we could hardly go wrong by concentrating on energy and steel, where shortages were visibly paralyzing France's recovery. But even there we had to keep within bounds: we had to bear in mind the nation's available resources of raw materials, capital, foreign currency and above all, manpower.[21]

Thus, the initial bottlenecks to be broken were steel (which meant coking coal, as well) and hydro-electric power. To achieve the necessary concentration of investment resources required, in turn, that Monnet hold the line against strong pressures to disperse resources in the production of badly needed consumer goods and that he successfully enlist the financial support of the United States. After arduous efforts, he succeeded in satisfying both conditions. On the widened foundations of steel and power, and critical dollar assistance from the United States, the French economy flourished. By the end of the 1950s

French GNP per capita surpassed that of Britain for the first time in the modern era.

The second example concerns the line of Monnet's thought that brought him to the concept of the Coal and Steel Community. Late in March 1950 Monnet perceived Europe to be trapped in a deadlock. To clear his mind and find a path forward he escaped to the Alps for two weeks of walking with his guide from one overnight lodge to another. He emerged with several pages analyzing the state of affairs, "the reasons for acting, and so clear an idea of the direction in which to move, that from my point of view the time of uncertainly was over."[22]

The outcome again concerned coal and steel: the Schuman Plan. But this was no exercise in choosing the leading sectors required to break an economic bottleneck. Here are the elements in the deadlock Monnet perceived on his walk in the Alps:

—With Stalin's blockade of ground routes to Berlin and the Anglo-American airlift, the Cold War was at an extremely intense stage.

—Quite particularly, it threatened to engage overwhelmingly the recovering states of Western Europe.

—Meanwhile, as German recovery proceeded and the intensification of the Cold War posed inevitably the question of a German military role, Franco-German tensions rose. In the existing framework, France could only try negatively to maintain existing constraints on German power via indefinite Allied control. But this was inevitably a losing game as Germany moved toward partnership in an American-led anti-Soviet coalition: "France was beginning to feel inferior again as she realized that attempts to limit Germany's dynamism were bound to fail." A symbol of all this—and part of the substance—was the German desire to raise its steel production from 11 to 14 million tons as French production leveled off.

—Neutralism was rising in France and elsewhere in the West; but this had to be rejected. It would only increase western Europe's sense of impotence, tossed about by the contention of two non-European powers. Europe had to unite and find its own voice in the great affairs of the world.

—But for Europe to unite France and Germany first had to find firm common ground. And only France could initiate that process.

Here is how the pooling of coal and steel became the point of concentrated attack to break out of the corrosive deadlock.

All successive attempts to keep Germany in check, mainly at French instigation, had come to nothing, because they had been based on rights of conquest and temporary superiority—notions from the past which happily were no longer taken for granted. But if the problem of sovereignty were approached with no desire to dominate or take revenge—if on the contrary the victors and the vanquished agreed to exercise joint sovereignty over part of their joint resources—then, a solid link would be forged between them, the way would be wide open for further collective action, and a great example would be given to the other nations of Europe. The joint resources of France and Germany lay essentially in their coal and steel, distributed unevenly but in complementary fashion over a triangular area artificially divided by historical frontiers. With the industrial revolution, which had coincided with the rise of doctrinal nationalism, these frontiers had become barriers to trade and then lines of confrontation. Neither country now felt secure unless it commanded all the resources—i.e., all the area. Their rival claims were decided by war, which solved the problem only for a time—the time to prepare for revenge. Coal and steel were at once the key to economic power and the raw materials for forging weapons of war. This double role gave them immense symbolic significance, now largely forgotten, but comparable at the time to that of nuclear energy today. To pool them across frontiers would reduce their malign prestige and turn them instead into a guarantee of peace.

Monnet's exercise of generalship in this matter—formulated in a general's language—is illustrated in a sense in one of the nine drafts of the proposal for a Coal and Steel Community, a sentence that did not make it to the final draft: "The proposal has an essential political objective; to make a breach in the ramparts of national sovereignty which will be narrow enough to secure consent, but deep enough to open the way towards the unity that is essential to peace."

A final observation on this matter. Monnet was greatly assisted in pursuing the style and method of concentration of effort because he explicitly rejected a career in politics; and among the reasons for that rejection, in the immediate aftermath of the Second World War, was his awareness that it is of the nature of a politician's profession that he must operate over a wide front and spread himself thin.

> My work, unlike that of the quintessential politician, had not required an endless succession of fresh choices to be made in the infinitely complex situations that face the Government of a State. What I had undertaken, at every important turning-point in my life, had been the result of one choice and one choice only; and this concentration on a single aim had shielded me from the temptation to disperse my efforts, as from any taste for the many forms of power.

Monotony Has Its Virtues

I noted earlier Monnet's commitment to repetition as part of his working method. There were, I believe, four converging strands in his comfortable use of the style of his maternal grandmother "Marie la Rabacheuse":

First, all serious innovators have to be pedagogues; and all teachers (and advertising men) know that repetition is a powerful device. As Monnet wrote: "There are many advantages in getting the same formulae fixed in people's minds."

Second, Monnet operated in the worlds of bureaucracy, politics, and diplomacy. All are filled with men and women determined to maintain their status or that of the institutions or nations they represent. In the case of politicians with a possible future, the next election is never far from their thoughts. These people are, by profession, suspicious of those with whom they deal; and this attitude is generally not malign but simply a matter of self-protection. Contrary to a widely held view, political and diplomatic practitioners put an extremely high premium on integrity. One's word must be good, because there is no way to consummate every mutual understanding with a notary public let alone a treaty. In this highly competitive, zero sum, anxious world, no operator is more quickly identified and rejected than one who tells different stories to different people; for whatever the level of formal security classification, public life leaks like a sieve. The beginning of trust and credibility is often, therefore, knowledge that one tells the same story to everyone. Although Monnet's integrity was demonstrated in other ways, he understood quite well that literal repetition of his proposals and their rationale helped his cause.

Third, in good part Monnet repeated himself because, as he was well aware, a good deal of his professional life was repetitive. Here is how he evokes the issues at stake in the bureaucratic battle to create Anglo-American joint supply arrangements in Washington during the first half of 1942:

> The struggle to establish what came to be called the Combined Production and Resources Board went on until the beginning of June. I used the same arguments, and in some cases the same notes, that had convinced Daladier and Chamberlain in 1939—and when one remembers that they referred back to the experience of the Supreme War Council of 1916, one can see how little my preoccupation had changed. Why should it change, if men were still taking up the same attitudes and making the same mistakes? Only circumstances change, so that the forms of organization devised to deal with them must be different every time. What I proposed to Oliver Lyttelton, Beaverbrook's successor, and to Hopkins, and what they in turn, after many vicissitudes, persuaded Churchill and Roosevelt to accept, was a new structure, but one that for me at least embodied the same principle.

But I would guess another element entered the equation. Monnet never went to the university, and he was in no sense a conventional intellectual. He was not interested in playing with ideas. He did not relish elaboration and the elegance of complex structures. Words were literally operational instruments for him— almost like terms in an equation. He struggled to get them just right, but like a great engineer, he also sought elegance: the marriage of form and substance in the simplest way possible. Once having achieved such functional simplicity he saw no advantage and considerable cost in fussing about with alternative formulations.

Monnet himself captured this point—"necessity can always dispense with artifice"—in a page of praise for Jean Vergeot and his three assistants in the economic and statistical section of the Modernization Plan organization.

> In his orbit, three young economists—Jacques-René Rabier, Jacques Van Helmong, and Jean Ripert—practised the style which for years was to be that of the Planning Commissariat's publications: short sentences, numbered paragraphs marking the transition from one idea to the next without clumsy bridging passages, a limited number of concrete words, and few adjectives. It was an austere art, of which all three became pastmasters. Some people thought it the opposite of art, because it lacked virtuosities of form or wit. At that time there was a fashion for brilliant dialectical displays. Myself, I fancy that the reports of Monsieur Vergeot's team may well have worn better than some of the period's far more subtle writings. At all events, they can be re-read today. They expressed the necessity of the time—and necessity can always dispense with artifice.

Bureaucrats May Be Outflanked, Recruited, or Cleared Away by Crisis

In the *Memoirs* bureaucrats and bureaucracies generally appear—as they often do to all innovators—as elements of resistance. Explaining, for example, why he wanted the Modernization Plan organization attached to the prime minister's office, Monnet observes: "Traditionalists would have placed the whole Commissariat under one of the economic Ministries, and the whole weight of civil service tradition tried to drag it back in to this state of subordination every time there was a Cabinet change." When de Gaulle, his initial sponsor and protector, suddenly resigned in 1946, a bureaucratic effort to subordinate the Commissariat to the Ministry of Economic Affairs was launched. With his resignation in his knapsack like a field marshal's baton, Monnet promptly called on the new prime minister, Félix Gouin, and said:

> I have a high regard for the French civil service . . . but it is not equipped to produce a plan for changing the face of France. On the contrary, its job is to maintain the state of affairs entrusted to it. The senior civil servants who run it have every quality—except the spirit of enterprise. To transform France, we must first transform the French Establishment, and perhaps also the training that produces it.

Monnet's démarche succeeded in buying time; but he fought a recurrent battle with the Treasury—the natural enemy of innovation in most governments—more than holding his own. The most important victory was won with the help of two Americans, Ambassador David Bruce and the U.S. Treasury representative in Paris, William Tomlinson. They became Monnet's intimate friends, confidantes, and supporters. With their help the U.S. administration persuaded the French government to allocate to the plan hundreds of billions of counterpart funds (francs derived from sale in France of U.S. Marshall Plan supplies). In 1949, 90 percent of the Modernization Plan's funds derived from this source; in 1950, 50 percent. Those were the turning-point years in French recovery and growth.

But, in fact, Monnet's dealings with bureaucratic resistance was more var-iegated than outflanking bureaucracy with prime ministers or supportive Americans.

First, he sought allies in the bureaucracy itself. Monnet's characterization of the French civil service to Prime Minister Félix Gouin was no doubt just in institutional terms; but there were individuals of intellect and character ready to enter loyally into innovative ventures. In his earlier talks with de Gaulle, Monnet said: " 'I don't know exactly what has to be done,' I said; 'but I'm sure of one thing. The French economy can't be transformed unless the French people take part in its transformation. And when I say 'the French people,' I don't mean an abstract entity: I mean trade unionists, industrialists, and civil servants. Everyone must be associated in an investment and modernization plan." And this theme was formally written into the "Treatise on Method," the plan's procedural bible.

The upshot was that in the course of 1946 there were "350 members of the Modernization commissions and a further 500 in their sub-commissions all working toward the same goal." Many of the members were civil servants working side-by-side with producers and representatives of the working force. It was, perhaps, Monnet's grandest exercise in getting people—previously expert in negotiations with each other—on the same side of the table with a common definition of a problem that could only be jointly solved.

And, no doubt, without day-to-day participation of civil servants in the creation of the plan, it would never have been accepted by the ministries or carried out. Prime ministers and friendly outsiders are never enough to execute policy.

After the event, virtually all major historical occasions can be viewed as "inevitable"; but before the event the situation of France in 1945–1946 was not such as to make the Modernization Plan inevitable. The 1930s had been a cruel, essentially stagnant or regressive time for the French economy. Defeat and occupation had further reduced the French capital stock and widened the gap between the age of French industrial plant and those of Britain as well as the United States: productivity was perhaps one-third the American level, two-thirds the British. Monnet believed: "There was a very real danger, indeed, that France might content herself with frugal mediocrity behind a protectionist shield. This, after all, had been a national tradition." In assuming advocacy of a serious modernization effort, Monnet knew he had two critically important assets: "The new Resistance generation and . . . General de Gaulle." Thus, Monnet successfully exploited what proved to be a realistic possibility; but the immediate postwar situation did not constitute a crisis so palpable and acute that it forced radical action of the kind Monnet undertook. I make this point simply to underline that Monnet's third method for dealing with the bureaucracy was to wait patiently for the time that crisis itself—a moment of necessity—forced radical innovation, and the first rule above came into play, that is, swift, well-prepared action to translate the invention into reality.

Work Comfortably in an Environment of Disorder

Clearly, Monnet's trip of several months to North America at the age of eighteen as a brandy salesman was one of the formative experiences of his life. The venture was framed by his father's instructions: "Don't take any books. No one can do your thinking for you. Look out the window, talk to people. Pay attention to your neighbor." In addition to visiting agents and customers of the family firm, Monnet did, indeed, follow his father's instructions, and out of his observations came an almost Schumpeterian (or chaos theory) image of the process of change:

> In contrast to the static balance of the old Europe, this was the dynamism of a world on the move. Each had its merits; each could be explained. But the American expansion needed no explanation; it was spontaneous, like necessity itself. To my European eyes, this spontaneity looked like confusion; but I very soon ceased to think in those terms. I became convinced that there could be no progress without a certain disorder, or at least without disorder on the surface. . . . I also went to the United States, from New York to California. Everywhere I had the same impression: that where physical space was unlimited, confidence was unlimited too. Where change was accepted, expansion was assured. The United States had retained the dynamism of the Western pioneers, like those I had seen in action at Winnipeg. But to that they had added organization. To organize change—that, I saw, was necessary, and it could be done.

To Monnet, his self-defined mission of "preparing the future" was an exercise in "organizing change." The impact on him of North America, with its vivid contrast to the virtually static life of Cognac in which he had grown up, almost certainly encouraged him to think systematically in dynamic terms of change as a normal condition.

A part of his feeling for time and change related to human beings. Palpably, the Canadians and Americans of the West of 1906 were a different breed than the citizens of Cognac. They were comfortable in the midst of a still-unfolding frontier, their minds taken up with visions of the future as well as the dynamic reality all around them.

All this related in a way not easy to trace to one of Monnet's most fundamental recurrent propositions: human nature does not change, but attitudes and behavior can be altered by changing the setting in which people live and work; for example, industrialists and labor leaders jointly helping to set production targets in the French Modernization Plan or French and Germans working jointly to assure fulfillment of Europe's coal and steel requirements. Thus, also, his patient acceptance of the time required for painful experience and friction to prepare men's minds for the bold action required at "the moment of maximum danger."

The fundamental importance to Monnet's innovational style of this behaviorist view of human action in a dynamic setting suggests how fortunate he was never to have been subjected to a rigorous training in mainstream economic theory with its rigidly defined initial conditions, fixed parameters and relations, plus maximizing behavior. In the phrases of Monnet *père,* if one looked out the window and paid attention to one's neighbor it became clear that none of these conditions characterized the unfolding of life in the active world.

Innovations Must Be Institutionalized

Monnet's view of the critical importance of institutionalizing innovations is straightforward. It is set out, for example, in his talk to the first meeting of the Assembly of the Coal and Steel Community gathered in Strasbourg on 10 September 1952:

> The Union of Europe cannot be based on goodwill alone. Rules are needed. The tragic events we have lived through and are still witnessing may have made us wiser. But men pass away; others will take our place. We cannot bequeath them our personal experience. That will die with us. But we can leave them institutions. The life of institutions is longer than that of men; if they are well built, they can accumulate and hand on the wisdom of succeeding generations.

This perspective applied to institutions themselves. He felt it would take them time to evolve to their full stature; that it was important in that process to be "vigilant" and "resist the temptation to temporize" on the principles they were designed to preserve.

There is in this story, however, a bit of paradox. As an innovator, Monnet gave great attention to "laying solid foundations" to his enterprises. But once firmly institutionalized, Monnet quickly became bored and was off on his next adventure in shaping the future. Moreover he liked small organizations, was suspicious of large ones. François Fontaine reports:

> He fought as long as he could against proliferation. He had even hoped that Europe would function with small numbers of personnel, who would call on the services of independent experts for consultation whenever necessary. He was as anxious to surround himself with competent people as to get rid of them when they had served their purpose.[23]

On 6 August 1952, Theodore Achilles reported to Secretary of State Acheson from the Paris embassy: "In conversation with Monnet yesterday . . . was struck by his calm and pragmatic approach to development of High Authority, which he plans to keep small and develop only as its functional needs become clear in practice."[24] The same bias appears in an anecdote as told by Richard Mayne:

> One spring day in 1973, the Action Committee was meeting in the Berlaymont, the steel, glass, and concrete headquarters of the European Community's executive arm. As I guided Monnet through the labyrinth, I gestured at the rows of offices and the functionaries hurrying to and fro. "Isn't it odd to think that all this was once just a piece of paper on your desk?" Monnet's eyebrows rose, "Yes, it's extraordinary." Then, with a smile. "It's appalling."

But as the governments moved the institutionalization of Europe another step forward in December 1991 Monnet might well have said: "Even with Berlaymont, it's worth it."

These Ten Commandments for the innovator in public policy embrace, I believe, virtually all the major propositions to be derived from Monnet's own account—and others'—of his operating style. But one important element is missing, and it is not trivial: Monnet had, as they say, independent means. Having won out in 1926 in a painful confrontation with his father on his family firm's policy in the global brandy market,[25] the endangered business survived. Monnet probably sold out to his cousins his interest in the firm in 1960. Thus, he was never financially dependent on any one else's pleasure. This was a double blessing in the high-risk innovational business in which he was engaged: he could always take a stand on the merits as he saw them; and, of at least equal importance, those he dealt with knew this was the case. It added weight to the credibility—the palpable integrity—of Monnet's commitment to the causes he advocated.

And, one can add, this asset was fortified by his conscious and explicit rejection of a career in politics, a decision which, as noted above, permitted him to pursue the principle of concentration of effort to an extraordinary degree.

IV

My wife and I were married in the old registry office in St. Giles, Oxford, on 26 June 1947. We intended to spend a brief honeymoon in Paris before joining the faculty of the first session of the Salzburg seminar, to which we had been independently appointed. The only flight we could get left Croydon at about 6:00 A.M. on 27 June. Still early on a bright summer morning in Paris, having missed the usual trappings and company of weddings, we felt a need to present ourselves as a married couple to a friend. Having gotten to know Monnet quite well on his visit to Washington (March–June 1946) I called 18 rue de Martignac. Monnet promptly invited us around.

In the course of a conversation—centered on whether I should join Myrdal in the new but already beleaguered east-west United Nations Economic Commission for Europe in Geneva—Monnet said the following: "First, we must modernize France. Without a vital France there can be no Europe. Then we must unite Western Europe. When Western Europe unites and gathers strength, it will draw to it Eastern Europe. And this great East-West Europe will be of consequence and a force for peace in the world. Then the Economic Commission for Europe will be able to play an important role."

He then urged us to join the enterprise and recalled the abiding value in his life of his experience in the League of Nations.

I cite this story in part to underline how deeply rooted was his long-run vision of the future of Europe and how real that vision was to him even when focused on urgent short-run tasks in France. After all, we were talking only a few weeks after George Marshall's speech at Harvard, and French recovery, let alone its modernization, was at an early problematical stage. Monnet evidently lived by his own version of Winston Churchill's magisterial maxim: "Those who are possessed of a definite body of doctrines and of deeply rooted convictions upon it will be in a much better position to deal with the shifts and surprises of daily affairs than those who are merely taking short views, and indulging their natural impulses as they are evoked by what they read from day to day."[26]

The full range of Monnet's vision has not always been understood. It embraced France, all of Europe, Europe's relationship with the United States, and ultimately, a world at peace.

First, France itself. Monnet was aware that there was something paradoxical about Cognac. It was in many ways a classic French provincial town working to the slow, patient rhythm of wine production and aging, virtually unchanged over many generations. On the other hand, Cognac, north of Bordeaux, not far from the sea, sold its brandy throughout the world. At sixteen Monnet was sent not to distant Paris but across the bay to London, a major brandy market, to prepare himself to carry on the family firm. At eighteen he was dispatched to Canada and the United States. As Monnet points out, as distillers and salesmen Cognac's task was to provide worldwide outlets for the products of a very small district. He captures the paradox with this story of a visit to a family friend after his return from North America.

> I remember going to Segonzac, a village close to Cognac, to see M. Barrault. His vines covered gently undulating territory. I do not know whether it is these faint undulations, planted in perfect lines, or the sea air, or the slowness of the river, that has made travellers speak for so long of "the soft Charante." M. Barrault was in the vineyard, and I found him driving his own cart, dressed in an old tail-coat. Canada, its forests, its snows and its trappers, seemed to belong to another world. Even before I could ask him about the harvest, he said: "Well, what's the news from Winnipeg?"

Monnet was both a prototypical Frenchman of the countryside and, almost literally, a man of the world. Reticent, dignified, simple in language and manners, with intense but generally shielded family attachments, he was as free as such a good Frenchman could be of narrow nationalism.

> So, from the days of my childhood, while French society stagnated in its own parochialism, I was taught to realize that we lived in a world of vast distances, and it was natural of me to expect to meet people who spoke other languages and had different customs. To observe and take account of these customs was our daily necessity. But it did not make us feel different, or dependent. At Cognac, one was on equal terms with the British: in Paris, one was somewhat under their influence. So we avoided the proud or defensive nationalistic reactions that were beginning to permeate French politics. In later years, in my relations with other peoples, I have never had to fight against reflexes that I have never acquired.

His concern for France and its twentieth-century vicissitudes nevertheless played a larger role in the development of his vision than might appear. There is a strand of tight-lipped pain at the tragedies his country experienced; for example, the horrendous casualties suffered in the field in the First World War. Or, flying out of Bordeaux as his plan to unite Britain and France definitively failed. "As we followed the Charente coastline I thought of the big house in Cognac where my old mother was living, looked after by my sisters. It was four years before I saw them again." Or, in a letter to de Gaulle as France fell in 1940, "Like you, I have only one aim: to reawaken the energies of France and convince her that she cannot end like this." Or the Monnets' naming their second daughter, born in the United States in November 1941, Marianne: "The symbol of the French Republic that was to be reborn when our country again became free." Or, on his return to Paris in September 1944, after an absence of four years: "My heart ached to see how impoverished and exhausted people were, once the excitement of the Liberation had passed."

But it was not a simple, inescapable identification with his people that drove him to conclude: "The solution of the European problem is all-important to the life of France."[27] It was all Monnet had seen and experienced since 1914 of the limits of French power, in particular, and of narrow national sovereignty in general.

In the First World War, France had to rely on the British navy, British ships, American production and its Expeditionary Force to survive; again in the Second World War, France, defeated in 1940, could only assume a place of dignity in the world in association with Britain and the United States. And in 1950 he saw that there was no future for France in a narrow, negative nationalistic effort to limit German steel production or to prevent a German contribution to European defense. Thus he sought a solution to French relative weakness vis-à-vis Germany in the abandonment by both countries of narrow nationalism in favor of European solutions to both the steel and defense problems.

But there was more to it than that. Monnet believed the European solution was not merely essential for France but essential for Europe itself. In his decisive session with Adenauer on 23 May 1950 concerning the Schuman Plan, Monnet argued that the proposal was not merely the correct route to Franco-German reconciliation but that "in this way, Europe will rediscover the leading role which she used to play in the world and which she lost because she was divided." These were days, in the wake of the Berlin blockade and, within a month of the outbreak of the Korean War, when the Cold War was intense. Monnet felt a still fragmented Europe was in danger of getting caught up piecemeal in an American-led coalition before Franco-German tensions had been satisfactorily resolved by an authentic reconciliation as fellow Europeans, before Western Europe as a whole had established a collective identity.

In part, Monnet wanted a united Europe "to rediscover the leading role she used to play in the world," as he said to Adenauer. Monnet did not wish to see Europe—rescued from its nationalistic folly in the First World War by the marginal but critical intervention of the United States, in the Second World War by the Soviet Union and United States—trapped again in relative impotence by the dynamics of the Cold War. In this he was responding to postwar circumstances like a good many Europeans; although he utterly rejected either narrow nationalism or the neutralism that was a quite common stance. In fact, the vision he had in mind—Europe's ultimate mission—is quite different and stated well in the final paragraph of *Memoirs*:

> We cannot stop, when the whole world around us is on the move. Have I said clearly enough that the Community we have created is not an end in itself? It is a process of change, continuing that same process which in an earlier period of history produced our national forms of life. Like our provinces in the past, our nations today must learn to live together under common rules and institutions freely arrived at. The sovereign nations of the past can no longer solve the problems of the present: they cannot ensure their own progress or control their own future. And the community itself is only a stage on the way to the organized world of tomorrow.

In part of his being, Monnet remained the former deputy secretary of the League of Nations, who knew that ultimately its global objectives would have to be attained.

François Duchêne has noted: "Few contemporaries beyond a restricted circle of like-minded reformers ever fully grasped the paradox, in traditional, national terms, of Monnet's refusal to be a European nationalist, and his determination that a uniting Europe should achieve 'equality' with the United States. It is ironic that Gaullists saw Monnet as a pawn of the Americans (thus jettisoning Monnet's cherished goal of association in equality); while Kissinger, in the *Years of Upheaval,* viewed him as a subtler kind of European Gaullist proposing to obtain from America by stealth what de Gaulle hoped to snatch by defiance (thus jettisoning the stress on interdependence and cooperation). What they wrote off as camouflage, because neither would, nor could, see it through the same spectacles, was in fact the clue to his strategy and values.[28]

What about Britain and the United States, with which Monnet had, of course, older professional and human ties than with any other country except his own?

Sent to Edwardian London at the age of sixteen, Monnet never lost his admiration for the best in British life and character: stoutness in the face of adversity, integrity, fairness, a capacity for team play. His provincial reticence, understatement, quiet humor and capacity for reliable friendship not hastily established fitted well the style of British life. But he hardened his heart against British insularity, with its insistence on special status vis-à-vis continental Europe. He understood the deep geographical historical origins of this confident British sense of identity, which helped save the Western world in 1939–1942; but he insisted at critical moments that Europe proceed forward without dilution, without special arrangements for the British, counting correctly that, in the end, Britain would recognize reality and deal with it.

As for the United States, from his visit at the age of eighteen, he regarded American power and dynamism "as a fact of nature." Writing of his period in Washington (1940–1943), when American war production targets were set and implemented, Monnet concluded:

> When the total came to be counted at the end of the war, aircraft production had increased from a trickle in 1940 to the astonishing figure of 300,000. Once run-down automobile factories had produced 100,000 tanks. Shipyards hit by the Depression had built 184,000 ships. America's arsenals had manufactured 2.7m. machine-guns; her blast-furnaces had made 430m. tons of steel. That a country's economy could have expanded so rapidly in so few months seems obvious only to those who regard the power of the United States as a fact of Nature. No doubt, Americans have a natural bent for organization and expansion. But this does not exempt them from the need for effort and discipline. And their natural gifts become active only when they are led by energetic and responsible men. I had chosen to live among such men, and I was lucky enough to be able sometimes to suggest what they might do.

Indeed, earlier the 2 million Americans in Europe on 11 November 1918 were a critically important margin, as was later American support for the French Modernization Plan and then the unity of Europe.

Monnet advocated a Europe so unified as to be able to deal with the United States on the basis of dignity and equality; but he advocated positively a trans-Atlantic partnership. The problems he foresaw required the two great continents to work in harness for positive purposes. The policy required of the United States was, in a sense, paradoxical. Support for European unity risked, if it did not actually guarantee, creating a potential rival rather than a partner. But this view was never dominant in Washington, in part because the United States commanded sufficient power to protect its vital interests in the worst case but even more because the worst case was judged to be unlikely. A common heritage of democracy, a common stake in a world at peace, prosperous and reasonably stable, and the inevitably rising imperatives of interdependence would tip the balance favorably. Finally, a weak Europe, divided, using its resources inefficiently, incapable of bearing appropriate responsibilities on the world scene, would force upon the United States unmanageable burdens.

Since Monnet's death in 1979, the trans-Atlantic partnership has remained in place, as the European states—with more or less grace, unanimity, and efficacy—have learned the ways of cooperation. The final form of a united Europe—should there be a final form—is still hidden in the mists, but, by and large, the institutions of Europe continue to evolve in the living, nonlinear, essentially biological process that Monnet envisaged.

V

In a splendid youthful *bon mot* David Hume wrote, "These principles of human nature, you'll say, are contradictory, but what is man but a heap of contradictions?"[29] Certainly, like all of us, but perhaps a little more so, Jean Monnet was a man of contradictions: a provincial Frenchman who loved his country but acted in terms of a truly global vision; a shrewd observer and analyst of politics and power who was driven by idealism; a man who used—even exploited—his friends but whose friendships were authentic and enduring; in action, concentrated compulsively on the task in hand, but with a sure and explicit awareness of where his current objective fitted into his grand design; a superb listener, dependent upon lively give and take with colleagues, but prepared at the moment he thought right to step off on his own, at high risk. Monnet's "heap of contradictions" could evidently be extended. The simple point to be made is that, in the end, this complex man was all-of-a-piece and marvelously effective in a unique profession of his own fabrication.

Notes

1. For Monnet's relations with de Gaulle, including Monnet's later reflections, see Richard Mayne, "Gray Eminence," chap. 4 in *Jean Monnet: The Path to European Unity,* ed. Douglas Brinkley and Clifford Hackett (New York, 1991), 117–21. See also Douglas Brinkley, *Dean Acheson: The Cold War Years, 1953–1971* (New Haven, 1992), particularly p. 89, where Acheson is reported as writing in 1962, when he was concerned over De Gaulle's opposition to the grand design of European unity, that "while Monnet and his people . . . are good at organizing support for a new idea when the opponent is ignorance or inertia, . . . they cannot lead against De Gaulle. They have no power base."

2. I was then chairman of the Policy Planning Council at the Department of State and among those mobilized as hosts at the reception. Only the secretary and the under secretary attended the funeral as officials. I was invited as a family friend. Monnet and I,

who had known one another since early 1946, spent that painful day together. We were summoned to the reception from a Washington restaurant, where Monnet had his first martini in twenty-five years.

3. François Duchêne, "Jean Monnet's Methods," MSS., 57–58.

4. Jean Monnet, *Memoirs,* with an introduction by George W. Ball, translated from the French by Richard Mayne (New York, 1978), 230–31. Since this chapter is largely a set of reflections on this work, I have not felt it necessary to supply a footnote for every reference to it. When it has seemed necessary to call attention to particular passages, I have given page references. All unidentified quotations are from the *Memoirs.*

5. *Memoirs,* 309–11. François Fontaine, in his essay in Brinkley and Hackett, 43, refers to this meeting as "the true birth of Franco-German reconciliation and of the European Community." See also Konrad Adenauer, *Erinnerungen 1945–1953* (Stuttgart, 1976), 336 f., and Hans-Peter Schwarz, *Adenauer: Der Aufstieg, 1876–1952* (Stuttgart, 1986), 716–23. In his authoritative work, *Coal, Steel and the Rebirth of Europe, 1945–1955: The Germans and the French from Ruhr Conflict to Economic Community* (Cambridge, Eng., 1991), 367–69. John Gillingham pays tribute both to Adenauer and to Monnet, who he says "deserves exceptional credit for having preached tirelessly that national sovereignty was meaningless without industrial competitiveness. Monnet's success, he adds, was due not only to determination and vision but to American support. "No foreigner has ever occupied a position of trust comparable to Jean Monnet's in American affairs. . . . The Americans agreed to let Monnet run, and he set the course for Europe."

6. Monnet, *Memoirs,* 230. Quasi-confirmation of my view of Monnet as a boxer is his observation on how he came to deal with the German problem in proposing the Coal and Steel Community: "It was at this time, undoubtedly, and on that precise problem, that I realized the full possibilities of an approach which had long been familiar to me, and which I applied empirically in trying to overcome difficulties of all kinds. I had come to see that it was often useless to make a frontal attack upon problems, since they have not arisen by themselves but are the product of circumstances. Only by modifying the circumstances—'lateral thinking'—can one disperse the difficulties they create. So, instead of wearing myself out on the hard core of resistance, I have become accustomed to seeking out and trying to change whatever element in its environment that was causing the block. Sometimes it was a minor point, and very often a matter of psychology" (p. 291).

7. See above, Chapters 5 and 7.

8. See, for example, Paul A. Samuelson, "A Theory of Induced Innovation Along Kennedy-Weiszäcker Lines," *Review of Economics and Statistics* 47 (November 1965): 353–55.

9. One of the best descriptions of the creative process is James D. Watson, *The Double Helix* (New York, 1968), where the author writes that, amid the confusion of the search, he knew that the truth would be "simple as well as pretty."

10. François Duchêne has described Monnet's working style on the basis of both personal experience and extensive interviews with others in Brinkley and Hackett, eds. *Monnet,* 184–209, and in his longer unpublished manuscript, "Monnet's Methods."

11. I have in mind, for example, Monnet, *Memoirs,* 62, 64, 113, 171, 291, 418, and 428.

12. Ibid., 64. The phrase is actually quoted from Sir Arthur Salter's memoirs,

describing the crisis circumstances in which at last the Allies agreed, on 3 Nov. 1917, to pool their shipping and allocate by need. Salter noted that "the way for the advance was prepared mainly by Jean Monnet.

13. Writing of Franklin Roosevelt, Monnet observed, "A great statesman is one who can work for long-time goals which eventually suit situations as yet unforeseen." *Memoirs*, 114.

14. This formula is quoted in Duchêne, "Monnet's Methods," 34.

15. The story is told in Monnet, *Memoirs*, 61–71.

16. In the mainly (but not wholly) academic literature on innovation in public policy, Nelson W. Polsby, *Political Innovation in America* (New Haven, 1984), is unique. From secondary sources Polsby examines in some depth eight innovations in science and foreign and domestic policy.

17. Myrdal quite consciously built the secretariat of the Economic Commission on this principle, combining senior officers in their sixties, several retired from government service, with men in their thirties or younger.

18. For a 1944 formulation of Monnet's postwar vision in an interview with John Davenport in *Fortune*, see *Memoirs*, 222–23.

19. Ibid., 188.

20. Ibid., 103. A later example of Monnet's obsession with detail concerns the drafting of the treaty for the Coal and Steel Community (pp. 296–97): "Between . . . Sunday, April 16, and Saturday, May 6, there were nine different versions. Whether this is few or many I cannot judge. In these matters I have only one rule, which is to work as long as is necessary, starting again a hundred times, if a hundred attempts are needed for a satisfactory result, or only nine times, as in the present case."

21. Ibid., 235.

22. Ibid., 298.

23. Fontaine in Brinkley and Hackett, eds. *Monnet*, 56.

24. *Foreign Relations of the United States, 1952–1954*, 6 (1): 149.

25. Monnet, *Memoirs*, 99–102. Monnet's father had built the firm on a reputation for cognac of the highest quality, which required aging for long periods. Monnet cognac found itself losing market share to blended brands, and its financial viability was endangered. Monnet's father sought to hold on to the traditional method, which tied up capital in inventory. Jean finally won out "against someone I loved . . . [and] against ideas that deserved great respect."

26. Winston S. Churchill, *The Gathering Storm* (Boston, 1948), 210.

27. Monnet, *Memoirs*, 222. This sentence is from a note written on 5 August 1943 from Monnet to the Committee of National Liberation in Algiers.

28. Duchêne in Brinkley and Hackett, eds. *Monnet*, 204 f. See also Kissinger's view, in *Years of Upheaval* (Boston, 1982), 138–39, that Monnet was "that most unusual of revolutionaries, who overturned the prevailing order without alienating the upholder of existing institutions." Kissinger is less persuasive when he argues that Monnet's "premises did not differ much from those of Charles de Gaulle." He appears to have forgotten that Monnet was for several years deputy secretary general of the League of Nations and never turned away from the vision that it incorporated. To the intense narrow nationalism that De Gaulle invoked he was always inflexibly opposed.

29. David Hume, *Philosophical Works*, ed. T. H. Green and T. H. Grose (London, 1912), 3:238.

10

ADAM RAPACKI AND THE SEARCH

FOR EUROPEAN SECURITY

Piotr Wandycz

O N 2 OCTOBER 1957, in a speech before the General Assembly of the
United Nations, the foreign minister of the Polish People's Republic,
Adam Rapacki, proposed the creation of a nuclear-free zone in Central
Europe. The Rapacki Plan, as it came to be called, may have been the only case
in which the United States and other Western powers discussed "political and
military questions of larger than bilateral interest separately with a junior member of the Soviet bloc."[1] Was it really a Polish initiative, or was it a Soviet
gambit with Warsaw serving as the messenger? Rapacki insisted that his plan
"had its origins in Polish national interest, in the Polish historical experience, in
the contemporary Polish socialist way of thinking, and in the most vital international interests of our country."[2] It would be a mistake to take this as mere
propaganda, but it needs nevertheless to be examined in its international context
as well as in the light of Poland's unique place in the Soviet system.

I

During the three years that preceded Rapacki's speech, a series of momentous
developments shaped the nature of the Cold War and the confrontation between
East and West. In December 1954, the strategy of NATO, hitherto based upon
the defense of Western Europe by conventional forces backed by the threat of
nuclear deterrence, shifted to the immediate and direct use of tactical nuclear
weapons against the aggressor. This affected West Germany, which by the Paris
accords of October 1954 had regained virtual sovereignty and become a member of NATO. Engaging itself to raise a Bundeswehr that was fully integrated in
and subordinated to that command, and promising not to produce atomic or
bacteriological arms on its territory, Bonn was forced to come to grips with the
reality of a possible nuclear conflict on German soil. The NATO air exercise
"Carte Blanche" in August 1954 indicated that in a conflict in which tactical
nuclear weapons were used German casualties would reach millions. This
seemed a horrible price to pay for membership in the Western alliance, and the
rearmament question seriously divided German public opinion.

In 1953 Moscow exploded the hydrogen bomb and thus entered the path that led to nuclear parity between the superpowers. Seeking to woo the West Germans away from NATO before their formal admission had been consummated in May 1955, the Soviet Union appeared to hold out the example of the Austrian State Treaty of 1955 as an alternate course: neutralization would bring with it both German unity and independence. This was not lost upon those in the West who believed in a détente with the USSR, but the opportunity, if that is what it was, was let pass. After 1955, Moscow seemed reconciled to the existence of two German states, and the German Democratic Republic became a member of the Warsaw Pact. The division of Europe became deeper, although—despite John Foster Dulles's rhetoric about the "liberation" of Eastern Europe and "massive retaliation"—there was still some apparent willingness in Washington to engage in limited détente. At the Geneva Summit in July 1955, President Dwight Eisenhower proposed a worldwide arms control system—the "Open Skies"—an idea that turned out to be not very realistic. The same was true of Premier Bulganin's elaborate scheme for the withdrawal of all foreign troops from Europe, the prohibition of nuclear weapons, and the reduction of conventional forces leading to a gradual dismantling of both NATO and the Warsaw Pact, culminating in a collective security pact.

More meaningful, and from the German viewpoint more dangerous, was Prime Minister Eden's plan, the earlier versions of which had been presented in 1954. It called for the reunification of Germany through elections—a unified German state assuming the international obligations of the GDR (which included a recognition of the Polish border on Odra-Nysa [the Oder-Neisse])—and a demilitarized zone east and west of the above border. This would be accompanied by reduction of forces and armaments in countries neighboring Germany, and a European collective security pact. What Eden had mainly in mind was local disarmament, but Bonn not unnaturally feared an East-West deal over the heads of the Germans—with lip service paid to reunification—relegating them to an inferior position. Adenauer's subsequent trip to Moscow in September 1955, during which he established diplomatic relations with the Soviet Union, stemmed from desire to have direct contact with the superpower even if it represented another step toward the acceptance of the status quo.

Bonn made it clear, however, that it would have no diplomatic relations with any other state that recognized the GDR. This, coupled with an adamant opposition to the recognition of the Oder-Neisse border, limited the Federal Republic's freedom to maneuver vis-à-vis East Central Europe, and helped to sustain fears of German revisionist designs upon that region.

The Geneva Summit enjoined the foreign ministers to discuss a security pact for Europe, as well as limitation, control and inspection of armaments and the establishment of a zone between East and West where some accord could be reached on armed forces. While disarmament questions were referred to the United Nations commission, which grappled with them for years to come, the question of a denuclearized or demilitarized zone in Europe began to be approached from various angles in the West and East. In the former, it led to a debate over "disengagement" or phasing troops out of defined areas as a means of reducing the danger of conflict along the Iron Curtain divide and stabilizing the European situation. In Moscow, Gromyko showed increased interest in the Eden Plan and treated it as a point of departure for concepts of zones of limited armaments covering Germany's neighboring countries.[3]

In December 1955, the NATO Council called on the United States to place tactical atomic weapons at the disposal of its West European allies, a move related to the reduction of the size of conventional armies. The Germans, who regarded the projected half-million strong Bundeswehr as part of a sizable conventional defense system, began to worry lest their army be treated as "cannon fodder" while the Anglo-Saxon troops enjoyed the advantage of nuclear equipment. Thus Bonn began to show interest in atomic arms, wishing also to enhance German partnership in NATO. A slow and painful reappraisal of German security policies was on the way.

If 1955 could be viewed as a watershed in the postwar evolution of Europe, 1956 became a crisis year, showing the weaknesses of both blocs. The conflict in the Middle East, which saw Britain, France, and Israel pitted against Egypt, revealed serious differences between Western Europe and the United States. True, when Moscow threatened Paris and London with nuclear missiles, Washington responded by warnings of retaliation, but it also applied pressure on its allies. The political unity of NATO was somewhat impaired.

Khrushchev's denunciation of Stalinism at the Twentieth Party Congress included a formulation of basic principles of Soviet foreign policy: peaceful coexistence, rejection of inevitability of war, and the approval of various forms of transition to socialism. The suppression of the November rising in Hungary by Soviet tanks showed, however, that Moscow set clear limits to the autonomy of its satellites. The uprising also discredited Dulles's "liberation" doctrine by demonstrating the unwillingness and inability of the United States to give military assistance to a nation struggling to free itself. The Hungarian revolution, and even more the "Polish October," which brought Władysław Gomułka to power in the teeth of Soviet opposition, forced Moscow to abandon "the old principles governing the relations" with countries of the Eastern Bloc. New methods would include "loud conversations and quiet settlement of issues."[4] How would this affect Warsaw's foreign policy, if indeed one could speak of one, rather than a reflection of the Kremlin's line? We need now to turn to the Polish scene.

II

The roots of Polish communist thought on international affairs go back to Rosa Luxemburg's internationalism. Scornful of the "social-patriotic" stance of the Polish Socialist party (PPS), the communists subordinated Poland's fate to the

Russian Revolution. Their behavior in the 1919–1920 war and thereafter branded them in the eyes of many Poles as Soviet agents. True, a certain critical (national) trend in the Polish Communist party (KPP) did exist, but without affecting its main line. Disgraced by the party's dissolution by the Comintern on the grounds of infiltration by enemy elements, the surviving Polish communists in the USSR passively witnessed the Ribbentrop-Molotov Pact and the fall of their country. The German invasion of the USSR and the Great Patriotic War changed all this. Patriotism became respectable.

The conceptualization of foreign policy principles was the work of a group of former KPP members, led by Alfred Lampe, whose writings on Poland's place in Europe have been described as "the definitive statement" of Polish communist foreign policy.[5] Lampe's goal was a reliable alliance with a fully committed Soviet Union, completed by alliances with other states east of Germany. He regarded German enmity toward Poland as perennial and saw the only protection against it in Russia.

Polish history, according to Lampe, demonstrated the criminality of anti-Russian policies, which were motivated mainly by class considerations and had led to Poland's partitions. In the interwar period, this line had been continued by "bourgeois-landlord" circles, which sought to protect the country by an impossible balancing act between Germany and the Soviet Union. The Polish government in London could not depart from this tradition, and for that reason it could not be trusted by Moscow. Since Soviet Russia could never allow the existence of a Poland that conducted an unfriendly policy toward it, only a united Polish left led by the communists could overcome this liability.[6]

A "democratic Poland" (the word communism was avoided in public utterances) would thus not only resolve domestic socioeconomic and political problems but bring external security. Poland's eastern borders—the bone of contention between the USSR and the Polish government in London—would no longer be those of 1939 but be traced in accordance with the rights of Ukrainians, Belorussians, and Lithuanians. Poland would expand westward to the Oder River and include East Prussia, not only as a compensation for Nazi war ravages, but as a contribution to stability in Central Europe. The Polish communists discounted the possibility of Soviet-German collaboration at Poland's expense. As one of them put it, the Ribbentrop-Molotov Pact was contrary to the very nature of the Soviet state. As Moscow's ally, Poland could exert "real influence on the development of relations in Europe."[7]

Lampe's contribution lay essentially in adroitly combining the internationalist element of the KPP tradition with concern for national security of the Polish state. This linkage was later described as "the most original feature of the foreign policy of People's Poland."[8] The claim to originality may be disputed—the anti-German and pro-Russian trend based on historical and contemporary analyses was dominant in the nationalist credo of Roman Dmowski—but it still provided a rationalization for the Communist rule in Poland and for the recognition of the dominant role of the USSR in East Central Europe. Did it assume blind subservience to the Kremlin? In the case of Lampe and of Władysław Gomułka, the Communist underground leader within Poland, it did not. For Gomułka, the Polish-Soviet alliance was a "historical necessity"; future relations between Warsaw and Moscow would be based on national self-determination. Writing at roughly the same time as Lampe, he visualized Poland as a bridge of "peace and friendship between the USSR and Europe."[9] The emphasis on peace was deliberate, for the Communists propagated the formula of USSR winning the war while Poland would have to win the peace. Assuming continued cooperation between the Big Three, the Communists insisted on alliance with Britain and the United States and spoke of a revival of Franco-Polish friendship. In the Lublin Manifesto of 22 July 1944 one can find a combination of all these concepts: friendship with USSR; recognition of Ukrainian, Belorussian, and Lithuanian rights; a return of Poland's old medieval lands in the west; the notion of a Slav dam against German aggression based on a Soviet-Czechoslovak-Polish pact; and the above-mentioned alliances with the West. These principles were synthesized in an important article of July 1945.[10]

The collapse of the Grand Alliance, the beginnings of the Cold War, and the use of the German card by the United States, as in Secretary Byrnes's Stuttgart speech in 1946, alarmed the Poles. Fears of a third world war were genuine enough, and peace was more than a mere slogan. The Stalinist system, however, left no room for autonomous Polish thinking on international matters. The program of the United Polish Workers party (PZPR) of 1948 took the enmity of the West for granted and identified completely with the USSR. Poland became a pawn. It was told to reject the Marshall Plan, and its cities became launching pads for various Soviet-sponsored activities: Szklarska Poręba for the Cominform, Wrocław for the Peace Congress, Warsaw for the Pact of 1955.[11] Gomułka's views on national independence became suspect; accused of Titoist nationalist deviation, he was removed from his leading position in the party in 1948 and later imprisoned.

Gomułka's return to power in 1956 was made possible by the de-Stalinization process, which culminated in the "Polish October." Gomułka spoke of a "Polish way to socialism" and, while attaching the greatest value to the alliance with the USSR, insisted on placing it on a footing of equality of both partners. All this aroused some suspicion in Moscow, even though Khrushchev, seemingly impressed by Gomułka's toughness, his distrust of intellectuals, and his genuine devotion to communism, seems to have found common ground with the Polish leader.[12]

The conduct of Polish diplomacy was placed in the hands of Adam Rapacki—foreign minister since April 1956, but now a member of the Politburo—and his associates. The son of a well-known theorist of the cooperative movement, partly educated abroad and with a good knowledge of foreign languages, Rapacki was characterized as pragmatic, liberal, and ambitious.[13] After his return from imprisonment in a German POW camp, he joined the Polish Socialist party, recreated mainly by leftist radicals and crypto-communists. Supporting those who favored close collaboration, and eventually a merger, with the Communist party, Rapacki held several cabinet positions in the postwar years. Yet, like other socialists, he remained attached to PPS's old tradition of patriotism, and shared the socialists' concern for cooperation with social democracy in the West and Czechoslovakia. The coming of the Cold War and the influence in the West of German socialists (regarded as nationalistic and anti-Polish) contributed to Rapacki's closer identification with the communists without destroying the essentials of his socialist outlook.

Rapacki was a reserved man with few friends, but with a reputation for loyalty and personal integrity even among his political opponents.[14] He had played no major role in the "Polish October" and his relations with Gomułka do not appear to have been intimate.[15] Was his position in the Politburo strong? If so, it resulted from his personal prestige and international standing rather than from any political power base.[16] The American ambassador called him "courteous and agreeable" although not very friendly toward the United States.[17] He was effective in contacts with journalists and moved easily in international circles,[18] and it was characteristic of him to combine a belief in historical determinism with a pragmatic approach. Adherence to basic foreign policy concepts was for him a matter of principle, and he defined these concepts as: "Unity in relations with socialist countries; solidarity in relations with nations fighting for liberation from all forms of colonial dependence; and peaceful coexistence in relations with states having socioeconomic systems different from ours."[19]

Rapacki's two deputies were Marian Naszkowski and Józef Winiewicz. The former was reputed a Moscow man, the latter was a prewar journalist of rightist leanings, later an official of the Polish government in London specializing in German affairs, and in 1946–1955 Warsaw's ambassador to Washington, a career that smacked of opportunism. Winiewicz was undoubtedly an intelligent man, and foreign observers commented on his elegant manners, command of languages, and wide political horizons, as well as on his wit and occasionally mischievous behavior. They did not doubt his Polish patriotism.[20]

Closer to Rapacki was the director general of the ministry, the former socialist Przemysław Ogrodziński, and the heads of the political and legal departments, Henryk Birecki and Manfred Lachs.[21] To a well-informed German journalist, the English-educated Lachs appeared to be the leading figure in this group. Endowed with a broad European perspective, he believed that Poland could play a larger role in international relations while remaining within the Soviet bloc only if it contributed to a relaxation of international tensions. Without a détente, Warsaw's position would be precarious. Lachs's expertise in international law was to play a major part in foreign policy initiatives under

Rapacki's leadership.[22] It is with this group in mind that Birecki wrote about politicians who "notwithstanding the circumstances of their ascendancy to power had conceptions of international relations that differed from those of Stalin and Molotov." These people sought "to extend the margin of maneuver" in foreign policy, although it was admittedly a narrow margin as produced by the Soviet Union, internal constraints, and the presence of the Red Army.[23]

Accompanied by Premier Józef Cyrankiewicz, Gomułka made his first trip to Moscow in November 1956, where they subscribed to a joint declaration that reaffirmed the Soviet statement of 30 October on the equality of status and sovereignty between the states of the Eastern Bloc. This was followed by formal agreements dealing with Soviet troops in Poland, repatriation of Poles from the USSR, and economic matters. On 17 November Khrushchev had addressed a letter to the Western powers in which he proposed an inspection zone one thousand miles wide in Europe, the reduction of armed forces, the banning of the atomic bomb, a gradual liquidation of foreign bases, and eventually a nonaggression accord between NATO and the Warsaw Pact. The next day at the reception for Gomułka he declared that, if the British and American troops were withdrawn from Germany, he would withdraw his own from Hungary and Poland.[24] Coming in the midst of the Hungarian crisis, this did not sound very convincing, but Gomułka was seemingly impressed. On his return to Warsaw, he suggested to Rapacki that the Foreign Ministry look into the problem of freeing Central Europe from the threat of a nuclear armament race.[25]

Was this the origin of the Rapacki Plan? Not really. It is clear that studies of central European security were already under way in Warsaw in the spring and summer of 1956,[26] and in the Foreign Ministry files there is a memorandum from that time speaking of the growing interest of the great powers, now that the Cold War was beginning to wane, in creating "a definite region in Europe of greatly reduced forces and armaments." "Poland," this memorandum stated, "was vitally interested in strengthening peace in this very area," which was defined as consisting of Denmark, Belgium, France, the Netherlands, Luxembourg, Germany, Poland, and Czechoslovakia.

The paper proposed that these countries conclude an accord banning the use of force and reducing troop levels and military budgets. Within a smaller zone (Germany, Denmark, the Benelux countries, and the parts of France, Poland, and Czechoslovakia adjacent to Germany) a complete ban on nuclear weapons would prevail, including production, stockpiling, tests, and the use of arms that could be fitted with nuclear missiles and rockets. A system of inspection and controls by member states and neutrals (Austria, Switzerland, Yugoslavia) would be introduced. Membership in NATO and the Warsaw Pact would be unaffected. The memorandum suggested that after consultation with friendly states a proposal along the lines described would be submitted to the countries concerned, as well as to the four great powers. Having received their reactions in September–October, the final proposal would be presented at the eleventh session of the United Nations in November 1956. The memorandum concluded with the suggestion of normalizing relations with West Germany through individual visits, articles, and meetings. Catholic circles were to be involved.[27]

The crisis in the fall of 1956 undoubtedly affected the proposed agenda. The foreign ministry, however, continued its work. How original was the final outcome and Rapacki's own input? Naturally, as Lachs expressed it, "ideas are not born in a vacuum, they are in the air."[28] It is also clear that Polish diplomacy "took the Soviet concepts for a starting point to develop a peace offensive directed at NATO countries."[29] The emphasis on Polish national interest that one finds constantly repeated in private and public utterances must be taken seriously.[30] As mentioned, national interest required a lessening of international tensions—political and military—to provide greater room for domestic and international maneuver. The center of this tension was Germany, whose return to "Weltmacht" was the principal cause of Poland's concern. Gomułka in particular was obsessed with Germany becoming a nuclear power, and this dominated Polish planning.[31]

In December 1956 it was proposed at the NATO Council that European forces be given tactical nuclear weapons, and in April 1957 the United States declared itself ready to place them, as well as the "flying bomb" type Matadors (ca. five-hundred mile range), at the disposal of NATO troops, West German included. Warheads would, however, remain under American control. In view of the deep-seated divisions in Germany regarding the equipment of the Bundeswehr with nuclear arms, and the September parliamentary elections, the NATO Council decision was postponed until its December meeting.

The timing of the Polish initiative was clearly connected with these developments.[32] To test possible reactions, a trial balloon was launched in the form of an article concerning a nuclear free zone in Central Europe in the periodical Świat a Polska in the spring of 1957. The Foreign Ministry felt that given the apparent failure of vast schemes advocated by the Soviet Union,[33] only a concrete and limited plan would be treated seriously and receive support from West European leftist and other groups that favored "disengagement" and feared the specter of an atomic war.

The extent of consultation with the USSR, East Germany, and Czechoslovakia seems to have been rather limited. The Soviet chargé in Warsaw voiced approval of the Polish initiative and suggested that it be accompanied by a Czechoslovak statement.[34] Previously, Warsaw had evaded a request from Prague for documentation of a Polish project, apparently fearing lest Czechoslovakia try to seize the initiative itself.[35]

What became known as the Rapacki Plan was announced in general terms on 2 October 1957. It boiled down to the following offer: should both German states agree to a ban on production and stockpiling of nuclear arms on their territory, Poland would make a similar engagement.[36] With Czechoslovakia and subsequently East Germany adhering to the Polish plan, a nuclear free zone would comprise four states.

The initial response to the Rapacki speech was one of indifference; his initiative sounded like another Soviet overture.[37] By December, however, this changed, the idea itself and the whole issue of nuclear strategy becoming subject to serious debate. The launching of the Soviet *Sputnik* on 4 October, preceded by the firing of the first ICBM, raised fears concerning Moscow's nuclear capabilities. Would the United States be willing to defend Western Europe with the use of nuclear arms if such action carried the danger of a Soviet retaliation against America itself? This may have been a premature question, but one likely to become real in the near future.

In the prestigious Reith lectures delivered on the BBC in October and December, George Kennan urged a basic revision of Western policies based on the nuclear deterrent. Basically, Kennan argued that an armed West Germany would make any future negotiations with the East much more difficult, political and military issues being inseparable. A voluntary Soviet withdrawal from East Germany and East Central Europe could only be achieved at a price: disengagement and a neutralized zone in the region. East European satellite leaders might well be "our allies" in endeavors to reach an accord with Moscow, claimed Kennan. Thus it would be "far more desirable to get the Soviet forces out of Central and Eastern Europe than to cultivate a new German army for the purpose of opposing them while they remain there." Kennan mentioned the Rapacki proposal among others, but deemed none of them fully acceptable.[38] Still, the Poles were encouraged.[39]

In Britain, the Labour party espoused the concept of disengagement as voiced by its leader Gaitskell. It was based on the assumption that, while a nuclear deterrent was necessary, it had to be accompanied by a positive and imaginative policy. War was most likely to arise out of a local dispute escalating to a major crisis. Hence, one had to eliminate potential danger spots, notably along the Iron Curtain. The best hope would be a "disengaged zone" comprising all of Germany, Czechoslovakia, Poland, Hungary, perhaps even Romania and Bulgaria, in which troops would be subject to controls and the territorial status quo guaranteed, Oder-Neisse border included. Gaitskell distinguished between "full" disengagement, which was unlikely to be accepted, and a more modest scheme that the West could propose in response to the Rapacki Plan. Limited to *nuclear* disarmament alone, it was insufficient, but could be a "basis for discussion." Notable was the fact that for the first time Poland, Czechoslovakia, and East Germany were seen in a barter-like arrangement as an equivalent for West Germany. Outright opposition to the plan meant playing into Soviet hands.[40]

German socialists shared some of these views, as evidenced, for instance, in the electoral debates in May where the SPD argued that after a nuclear conflict nothing would be left of the German people. Their electoral defeat notwithstanding, the socialists continued to voice interest in the Rapacki Plan. The former French socialist defense minister, Jules Moch, also supported a "thinned out" zone. In both Germany and France, however, the governments were strongly opposed to Rapacki's ideas and to the notion of disengagement, as was true also in the United States and to a larger degree in Great Britain. Kennan's views were subjected to ridicule on military grounds, and Dean Acheson was to engage him in a heated polemic, arguing that disengagement would lead to isolation of Germany and carry with it the danger of another Ribbentrop-Molotov Pact and the abandonment of Eastern Europe to the Soviets. Moscow would be satisfied only by a liquidation of NATO.[41]

Acheson's conviction that the West should deal only from a position of strength was to prevail at the NATO Council meeting in December. Conscious of that, Rapacki sought to influence Western public opinion, and especially Britain, which the Quai d'Orsay regarded as "softer" than the others on the question of denuclearized zones.[42] True, Macmillan's Foreign Secretary Selwyn Lloyd told Rapacki that the British regarded the "buffer zone concept" as "outdated" and that the Polish plan would result in American withdrawal from Europe.[43] Even so, a special study group to examine the various plans was set up in London, and the British felt that Dulles and Adenauer took an unnecessarily intransigent attitude.[44] In January 1958, Warsaw was gratified by the British gesture of giving it a copy of Macmillan's reply to Bulganin's note, because the latter had contained a reference to the Rapacki Plan.[45]

During the winter, Rapacki held talks with Western envoys, gave speeches and interviews, and launched a veritable propaganda campaign centering on Britain and the United States. In his instructions to missions, he recommended different approaches to different countries. The dangers of German hegemony and the similarity between the Rapacki and Eden plans were to be pointed out to the British. Rapacki himself expressed hope to the British ambassador that at the NATO meeting the British would take into account "our position and our interests." Anticipating possible questions about what Poland could do to liberalize the policy of the USSR, the foreign minister advanced the formula that Warsaw's possibilities "depended to a large degree on détente, hence on the policy of the West."[46]

Rapacki's speech in the foreign affairs commission of the *sejm* on 13 December stressed two tendencies in the West—the peaceful and the hegemonic-militaristic-revisionist—and he expressed worry about the successes of the latter. Poland, he said, promoted "constructive coexistence." The use of this term and the unmistakable overtures to Germany were of special importance in the speech. Similar points were made in interviews for *Die Welt* and *Le Monde,* respectively, on 12 and 15 December, except that Rapacki told the French that his proposal was intent on preventing a local incident that could cause an all-European war and place France against Poland.[47]

In December 1957, the NATO Council approved the installation of American IRBMs in Europe—Thors in Britain and Jupiters in Italy and Turkey—and the equipment of the Bundeswehr with tactical weapons that could use either conventional or nuclear explosives. The question of Europe's own defenses was raised by Paul-Henri Spaak, but treated unfavorably by the United States and Germany. While Spaak was to refer to Rapacki's Plan as a "dangerous trap," and the French and Benelux leaders were to denounce it after the meeting, the NATO Council reached a consensus that while the plan was unacceptable, it deserved, together with other similar schemes, serious study and possibly counterproposals.[48]

In January 1958, the interest of the Western press was aroused by the exchanges between Bulganin, Eisenhower, and Macmillan concerning a summit to discuss nuclear issues, nonaggression pacts, and a nuclear free zone. It was obvious that the attitude of Washington was of crucial importance.[49] John Foster Dulles, who in Lukacs's pat phrase elevated the "political ideology of anti-Communism into superior moral principle,"[50] objected to any disengagement schemes on power-political and ideological grounds, claiming at a press conference on 11 January 1958 that a nuclear free zone would be the first step toward neutralization of Germany and would deepen the dependence of Eastern Europe on the USSR. The Polish ambassador listed as reasons for Washington's negative attitude toward the plan its unwillingness to negotiate at this point with the East and its conviction that the plan would lead to Germany's neutralization, which was unacceptable on military grounds. He added that the Polish origin of the plan was therefore questioned.[51]

This last aspect was important. Gomułka's Poland was represented in Washington as an example of peaceful self-liberation. Economic aid sent to Warsaw was sometimes perceived as a means of weaning it away from Moscow. Could the Rapacki Plan present the United States with "possibilities for making a diversionary move and causing trouble between the Poles and the U.S.S.R.," mused Jacob Beam, the American ambassador in Warsaw? He believed that the Poles were genuinely interested in a neutral zone as "means of alleviating Soviet controls." Their "motives in proposing and advocating the plan" were linked with fears that the stationing of nuclear weapons in West Germany would increase Soviet demands on Warsaw. Recognizing "the Secretary's aversion to neutral zones of any kind," Beam limited himself to "suggesting that some advantages might be drawn from the present situation."[52]

Secretary Dulles made his position crystal clear in a circular to missions. While the Rapacki Plan "might have some surface attraction," it posed "totally unacceptable risks." Like other Soviet proposals, it presumed that Germany would remain divided. To deny Bonn nuclear weapons was contrary to NATO strategy, leaving aside the fact that such limitations were discriminatory because they were not applicable to other members of NATO. The proposal was aimed at those in the West who favored disengagement and believed that reduction of tensions would facilitate the settlement of the German problems. These were "erroneous" and "dangerous" views. If the Rapacki Plan was indeed a Polish initiative, this was "interesting." It might indicate Warsaw's desire to resolve the East-West deadlock, as well as reflect worries lest the nuclearization of West Germany lead to Soviet demands for nuclear facilities in Poland and Czechoslovakia and to a restoration of controls weakened in 1956. (Indeed, the communiqué issued after the Moscow meeting of communist parties in November 1957 commemorating the anniversary of the Bolshevik Revolution represented an attempt to reassert controls, although it did not destroy the seeds of pluralism.) Dulles recognized the usefulness of exploiting potential differences between Warsaw and Moscow, but the advantages one could derive from it would not "warrant us in incurring risks to our own security." He concluded that the Rapacki project did not contribute anything new and was, in fact, "highly dangerous."[53]

The State Department, after reiterating that the plan "would have [the] effect of undermining the Western position," informed the missions that no counterproposals were contemplated. It enjoined American diplomats, however, to give "clear recognition" to the Polish character of the plan, even if there were doubts about it. One had to do it subtly so as "to avoid placing Poland in [a] position of feeling constrained to issue denials of Soviet interference."[54]

III

What exactly was the nature of the connection between the Rapacki Plan and Moscow's policy? Rapacki asserted in the *Die Welt* interview that it was a Polish initiative "advanced after consultation with other signatories of the Warsaw pact." Gomułka later cited the plan as an example of a Polish move in accord with the policy of the bloc, but not "simply some sort of an echo of Soviet policy." He stressed "[our] own deliberations and studies."[55] Ranking Polish officials said that, while the general idea of withdrawing foreign troops from Europe had "Soviet parentage," even Moscow's proposal of November 1956 had "originated from Polish suggestions." Winiewicz went "so far as to say," that what the Poles wanted was a military neutralization of the four states, for they were "only looking out for themselves and wished to avoid nuclear war, which could result in [the] destruction" of their country.[56] There is no doubt that there was "a partial interdependence of our initiative with the Soviet initiatives aiming at . . . general solutions," as a Polish note put it.[57] But differences also existed.

As we know, Rapacki's statement at the United Nations had been approved by the Soviets, but Khrushchev had apparently wished to exploit it propagandistically, treating it as merely a piece of the larger scheme. Khrushchev and Gromyko expressed open approbation only at the 21 December meeting of the

Supreme Soviet and in Bulganin's letter of early January. The Poles suspected that the reason was the general interest the plan had aroused in the West.[58] There was hardly unqualified endorsement, since the Soviets were objecting to the introduction of eventual controls in the denuclearized zone, and were still thinking of enlarging the area to Scandinavia and the Middle East. This would destroy the concrete and limited character of the Rapacki proposal.[59] All this made the Polish foreign minister so discouraged that he would remark pointedly and gloomily in the presence of the Soviet ambassador that Poland was making no official announcement of its plans to the West. To his collaborators, Rapacki commented on the funeral of his project.[60]

On 29 January the minister, accompanied by Lachs, went to Moscow for talks with Gromyko and top officials of the Foreign Ministry. The exchanges, which may have been assisted by a secret Gomułka-Khrushchev encounter a few weeks earlier, were difficult. Eventually, the Soviets agreed to leave the door open for controls in the nuclear free zone, as well as for an agreement on limitation of conventional weapons. The Polish formula that exempted Bonn from negotiating or signing an accord together with East Germany was accepted. Finally, the Polish side induced Gromyko to support their opposition to a Bulgarian project applying the denuclearized concept to Italy and the Balkans, and other regional schemes that could damage the chances of the Rapacki Plan.[61] The Moscow talks showed that the Polish point of view was taken seriously, even though some criticism of Polish ideological "revisionism" persevered.[62]

The final communiqué, the usual verbiage aside, spoke of the willingness to consider effective controls and referred to conventional weapons. It is hard, therefore, to accept Ambassador Beam's opinion that the Soviets had "regained control" over the developing stages of the Rapacki Plan.[63] If anything, Warsaw now had the green light from Moscow as well as support from East Berlin and Prague.[64] A circular informed the missions on 8 February of moving to the "next stage of our diplomatic action." Four days later an internal "strictly secret" memorandum reviewed the issues. "Package deals" and "general settlements" were criticized as ineffective, but the chances for limitations of conventional arms and effective controls appeared good, although the matter had to be handled carefully for "understandable reasons." The proposal was seen as a "pilot scheme" for future disarmament arrangements.[65]

On 12 February 1958, Rapacki sent to Gomułka and the top leadership a note and the text of the memorandum, which was drawn up after consultation with Moscow and which took into consideration some of the Czechoslovak and East German observations. The document would still be submitted unofficially to the Soviet ambassador and made known to the other two allies for last-minute comments. Two days later it would be formally presented to the ambassadors of the Four Powers, Czechoslovakia, GDR, Belgium, and Canada. Sweden would be asked to transmit the document to Bonn. The question of a future summit would also be raised.[66] The First Rapacki Plan, as it came to be known, was launched.

As compared with the original statement of October 1957, the Polish memorandum contained new or elaborated features. The most important ones were: an extension of the nuclear arms prohibition to equipment and installations; a prohibition of the use of nuclear weapons by the great powers *against* the zone; a ground and aerial inspection mechanism with neutral representatives besides those of the Warsaw Pact and NATO; and a complex-sounding provision (IV, 3) meant to allow West Germany to undertake obligations through a unilateral statement avoiding joint participation with the GDR.[67] This ingenious idea ascribed to Lachs made it possible for Bonn to avoid jeopardizing its position vis-à-vis East Germany by appearing to renounce the Hallstein Doctrine.

It was obvious that the German issue was central for the Poles. Rapacki had broached the subject of a denuclearized zone with the German ambassador to Belgrade in the fall of 1957, but the subsequent breach of German-Yugoslav relations closed this channel of communication.[68] The Rapacki Plan at no point raised the issue of a solution to the German problem—to avoid encroaching on the Soviet domain—but it was a question very much on the Polish minds. Gomułka denied any connection between the plan and German unification but hinted that it would create conditions conducive to unification. A nuclearized Germany would be a threat to all, and while the Germans had the right to unite, he added rather undiplomatically that it would be no misfortune if Germany stayed divided.[69]

Rapacki phrased this question in a slightly different fashion. According to him, the German issue was "the central international problem of the thousand-year history of the Polish state." NATO policies encouraged revanchist and expansionist German tendencies, and in the long run it would not be a question of the West restraining Germany, but of Germany dragging along the West. The German question could only be resolved through international détente, and his plan was a step in this direction. Indeed he pretended that "a desire for a peaceful solution of the German problem" was its main inspiration.[70]

The Polish memorandum and a note accompanying it, which suggested informal talks, was sent to Bonn via the Swedish ambassador. Foreign Minister Heinrich von Brentano, who had earlier publicly questioned the Polish character of the Rapacki initiative, was barely persuaded by his secretary of state to acknowledge its receipt in a curt, almost rude note. The German press, however, gave it extensive coverage, urging the government to study the plan carefully. The formula that allowed Bonn to avoid contact with Pankow was appreciated, and the notion of controls was welcomed. But obviously the discussion had to turn around two basic issues: German unification and the military implications for Germany and the West.

Bent on German reunification, SPD leaders argued during the great Bundestag debate of March 1958 on the arming of the Bundeswehr that the Rapacki Plan was evidence that the Poles were taking their destiny in their own hands, and that their plan for détente favored reunification. Having talked to Lachs, Helmut Schmidt asserted that "he sees things as I do."[71] Since the socialists continued to oppose arming the Bundeswehr with nuclear weapons, Adenauer adroitly brought the final discussion to a vote for or against NATO. He won when the parliament decided on 25 March (against the nays of the SPD and many FDR abstentions) that the Bundeswehr should be equipped with "the most modern weapons." As has been aptly put, "the integration of the Federal Republic into the nuclear defense concept of NATO was also a decision against the Rapacki Plan."[72]

The motives of Adenauer were political rather than military. To the chancellor, the true cause of East-West tension was not the threat of an armed confrontation but a divided Germany. Although at certain times Adenauer sought a direct contact with Moscow as a reassurance,[73] he aimed at Germany's freedom through integration with Western Europe. This put off any chance for unification for the foreseeable future, but Adenauer believed in the eventual weakening of the USSR under the West's pressure. The main dangers to be avoided were falling prey to Soviet expansionism or to a four-power deal at Germany's expense. The Bundeswehr was for Bonn, above all, a way to partnership with the West. The Rapacki Plan, in Adenauer's thinking, would sever the Federal Republic from the West and solidify the division of Europe. Germany would find itself in an inferior position, and the territorial status quo, which included the Oder-Neisse border, still contested by most Germans, would be reaffirmed. A denuclearized zone could only make the Warsaw Pact's superiority in conventional arms more dangerous; the prohibition of a nuclear strike against the four-state zone was deemed an insufficient safeguard.[74] If an East-West détente was ever to be realized, it would have to be *with* and not at the expense of the Federal Republic. The incompatibility of German and Polish policy objectives was obvious.

Rapacki refused to treat the German aide-mémoire delivered on 25 February as a substantive reply to the Polish memorandum.[75] He had sought to influence the German debate by, among other things, an interview which appeared in *Der Spiegel* on 24 March in which he took the line that as long as Germany was a crucial factor in military strategies its chances of unification were nil. One could not think in purely military terms, he remarked, adding that the Warsaw Pact military was also unhappy with some aspects of his plan. As a position paper sent to all Polish missions put it, "If one thought exclusively in military categories, any disarmament would be nonsensical, and an armament race would be the only sensible way of coexistence among nations." The paper admitted that Warsaw had not proposed any solution to the problem of Germany, and it believed that a divided Germany was abnormal. But what was wanted was a united but "peaceful" Germany.[76]

The Western powers could hardly respond with a "flat, uncompromising rejection," as Schmidt described Bonn's note. Their objections to the full version of the Rapacki Plan centered on its omission of the question of German reunification and on nuclear disarmament provisions that favored the Soviet Bloc given its superiority in conventional armaments. The main difference between Washington and London was that while the former was unwilling to treat the memorandum as a basis for discussion, the latter was inclined to do so.

Presenting the text to Ambassador Beam, Rapacki repeated twice that Warsaw would hope for American observations that could facilitate fruitful exchanges. He expressed his support for the great powers summit, hoping that an agreement on the Polish proposal would make a contribution to its discussions. Indeed, Polish expectations of a summit were high at this point, and a team was organized to provide material on the Rapacki Plan for the participants.[77]

As in the past, Beam appealed to Washington to give at least full credit to the Poles for wishing to reduce tensions, and try to "make capital of [the] fact [that] Soviet interference had at certain stages confused and complicated true understanding of Polish intent." The ambassador urged Washington to "encourage [the] concept or at least exploit [the] illusion that Poland is trying to exert some independence in foreign affairs." He added that neither the Soviets nor the East Germans "seem to be enthusiastic about the Rapacki Plan in its unadulterated Polish form." At the same time, Beam suggested the use of an argument that the Rapacki Plan really jeopardized "European and Polish long range interests."[78] He probably meant that the plan was unlikely to promote the cause of Poland's independence of the USSR, a point made by Polish political emigrants in a memorandum for John Foster Dulles. Their document stressed that the only result of the plan would be "the strengthening of the Soviet Bloc at the cost of the Free world." The steps that ought to be taken in East Central Europe should involve a withdrawal of the Soviet forces from Poland and the rest of the area. Only the end of the Soviet occupation, followed by a final recognition of the existing Polish-German frontier, could become the basis of a security settlement.[79]

The Polish ambassador to the United States, Spasowski, was told at the State Department that an exclusion of nuclear arms in one area did not resolve the basic security problem. Nor did the Rapacki Plan offer a solution to the German issue. He asked if the inclusion of conventional weapons would make the plan more attractive, and understood from a cautious reply that it might. In Warsaw, Beam was warning the Poles against exaggerated hopes.[80]

It seemed clear that the NATO High Command preferred direct contact with its adversary and a frontline rather than a buffer zone. The United States was unwilling to experiment with any form of disengagement, whatever the merits of the Rapacki Plan might have been. Raymond Aron commented that the existing situation in Europe may have been abnormal but it was clear-cut, and an abnormal situation appeared less dangerous than an equivocal one.[81] Thus,

American diplomacy concentrated on making sure that its viewpoint would be accepted by its NATO allies. This prolonged the process of replying to Warsaw until May.

In the case of Britain, Prime Minister Macmillan suggested in early 1958 to Eisenhower the need to work out a joint policy of disengagement as proposed by Eden and now "elaborated by the Poles in the Rapacki Plan."[82] While British objections to the plan as spelled out in *The Times* on 19 March were basically the same as Washington's, the government subjected the Polish proposal to a close study, and Labour members in the House of Commons questioned the wisdom of rejecting it before the summit. Foreign Secretary Selwyn Lloyd stressed his government's sympathy for Warsaw's desire to reduce international tensions, but insisted on a common and negative perception by NATO of the military and political aspects of the plan.

The draft British reply evoked criticism in Washington as being not nearly negative enough. Although the State Department wished London's reply to be parallel to the American one and delivered simultaneously in Warsaw, it had to be satisfied with a somewhat hardened final version, which, however, still expressed hope for the settlement of the main issues through conferences.[83] The Americans hoped that Paul-Henri Spaak, who was also disturbed by the "weak British position" on the Rapacki Plan and the summit, would help to dispel "some of the fuzzy thinking about the Rapacki Plan." Spaak proved unable, however, to affect the Belgian reply, which was uncoordinated with NATO and said that the plan made a real contribution to efforts to resolve armament questions.[84]

The position of Paris, as summed up on 20 February in *Le Monde,* was strongly negative. Security could not be separated from the German issue, and the Rapacki Plan for all its legal niceties would result in a de facto recognition of East Germany, a weakening of the bonds between West Germany and NATO (giving Bonn greater independence), would encourage neutralism and lead to American withdrawal from Europe. The Quai d'Orsay believed that, whatever Warsaw's reasons, Polish tactics were coordinated with Moscow and that there was no chance of driving a wedge between the two. Still, for the sake of French public opinion—Jules Moch and Guy Mollet among others publicly expressed interest in the plan—it was inadvisable to sound too negative. Hence, lip service was paid to "new elements" and a "deep interest" expressed. The domestic upheaval that brought de Gaulle to power in May further delayed the response to Warsaw, the general wishing for no Franco-Polish *malentendus* regarding Germany.[85]

In these circumstances, the Quai d'Orsay favored a short reply avoiding detailed comments and concentrating on military matters. It noted the lack of distinction in the plan between offensive and defensive nuclear weapons, which was important for NATO strategy since it relied on nuclear artillery and anti-aircraft defenses. Control of conventional armaments needed to be introduced.

The American note of 3 May, the presentation of which preceded those above, was of crucial importance for the Poles. Somewhat to Ambassador Beam's surprise, Winiewicz did not take Washington's rejection of the plan as final, and even expressed satisfaction over the careful consideration given the plan as well as the expressed appreciation of Polish motives. Noting the American point that only universal measures of nuclear disarmament could bring a solution, Winiewicz declared that, given the difficulty of reaching a general agreement, surely a first step, however limited, had to be made. He added that the Polish memorandum foresaw the possibility of discussing conventional armaments, although the ongoing remilitarization of Germany made it difficult. As on earlier occasions, Beam questioned the validity of Polish fears of Germany, but otherwise did not comment on Winiewicz's point that Warsaw would study American objections and continue discussions.[86]

Rapacki, as he declared at the United Nations on 1 October, did not consider the plan dead. Warsaw publicized the expression used in the Canadian reply, the most favorable of all, namely that it was a "first step." It also noted a certain softening of Bonn's tone toward Poland.[87] While beginning to work on a new version of the plan, the Foreign Ministry decided against its formal presentation at the United Nations and sought to dissuade Czechoslovakia from any such move.[88] Instead, Rapacki went in late October to Norway, which he used as a sounding board for a revised project. The trip had been preceded by a tour by Winiewicz of the Scandinavian countries, during which he held preliminary talks with Norway's Foreign Minister Lange, who had shown a definite interest in the Rapacki Plan.[89] In early October, Rapacki himself talked to Lange and Canadian Foreign Minister Smith in New York. The Polish statesman felt that further discussions ought to be based on the acceptance of the principle of disengagement, the inclusion of Germany, as well as the linking of denuclearization of Germany with future reductions in nuclear armaments in general, a preliminary accord on conditions, timely and mutually advantageous arrangements, before any demand for withdrawal of all foreign troops. Once again Rapacki emphasized that his was a "pilot project."[90]

Surveying the actual stage of the debate on the Rapacki Plan, a ministerial position paper sought to deal with salient objections to the plan, particularly the charges that it brought military advantages to the Soviet bloc, which it questioned, quoting some figures.[91] From his UN post, Ambassador Michałowski listed reasons for resuming a diplomatic offensive: the growing opposition in the West to the armaments race, a ferment within NATO, and Soviet diplomatic initiatives that could place Warsaw in an embarrassing situation. Indeed, it seemed that Moscow had grown lukewarm in its interest for regional arrangements and was reverting to general proposals, as for instance its 15 July offer of a treaty of European friendship and cooperation, with troop reductions and aerial control eight hundred kilometers east and west of the Iron Curtain. While the Polish goal remained delaying German armaments, the tactics, according to

Michałowski, ought to be such as to "break up" the opposition to the Rapacki Plan and "above all isolate Dulles' policy." He recommended a two-stage approach, which Warsaw eventually adopted.[92]

Rapacki's speeches in Norway, in which he aired the idea of tying reduction of conventional arms to nuclear limitations, were designed to test international reactions. These proved to be limited. He then came out with the statement at a press conference in Warsaw on 4 November 1958,[93] where he unveiled what has often been referred to as the Second Plan based on a two-stage approach to the creation of a denuclearized zone in Central Europe. During the first phase, a ban would be imposed on the production of nuclear weapons; neither launching devices nor armaments for troops that did not possess them would be permitted. The implementation of these measures during the second phase would coincide with a reduction of conventional forces. Appropriate controls would operate in both stages. Rapacki explained to the missions abroad that the modified plan was not to be presented as a formal document through diplomatic channels so as to avoid, as long as possible, its rejection and also to achieve a certain propaganda effect.[94]

American, British, and French ambassadors in Warsaw agreed that the new features of the plan amounted, among others, to the acceptance of the American nuclear presence in West Germany during the first stage, as well as introduction of controls. The Poles apparently sought to maintain their international prestige, to gain credit as independent negotiators and to exploit a link to the Western socialists. Unlike Gomułka, who spoke of West German rearmament, Rapacki distinguished between "possessors of atomic weapons" and others.[95]

The State Department admitted that Rapacki's new move was "clever" and "professed an attitude of reasonableness." The modifications were "clearly tailored to appeal to certain segments of opinion" in the West, but they did nothing to alter fundamental U.S. and Western objections and thus did not merit serious substantive consideration." Soviet capability to launch a nuclear attack would leave the denuclearized zone at its mercy; Germany would remain divided. A reduction of conventional forces, in the absence of a Western nuclear shield, would not stop the USSR—given its geographic proximity and superiority in manpower—from rushing in troops. Since production of nuclear armaments in the four states of the zone neither existed nor was being seriously contemplated, Rapacki's proposal aimed at the maintenance of the status quo. The State Department assumed that the Soviets were hoping for the new proposal to create friction among the Western states, which did not mean that the "Poles did not have their own reasons." These included the avoidance of heavy military expenditures to counter West German armaments, and some hope for bringing about partial withdrawal of Soviet troops from Poland and East Germany.[96]

American diplomacy did not wish to appear to be "taking the lead publicly" in rejecting Rapacki's proposal, and Washington wanted Spaak to schedule a discussion at the NATO council.[97] It was clear that Bonn was bound to reject the Second Rapacki Plan. Although on 8 November, a governmental bulletin recommended its study, once the Khrushchev note had inaugurated the long Berlin Crisis, Franz-Josef Strauss called all those who supported the plan "potential criminals."[98] Paris viewed it dangerous because it seemed more plausible and took some Western criticism into consideration. Moreover, the French objected to a discrimination between their army and the nuclear-equipped Soviet and American troops.[99] The British were somewhat confused by the term *freeze* used by Rapacki, and the Polish embassy in London had to explain that it did not apply to reinforcement of units that already had nuclear weapons. As before, Labour expressed a qualified approval, although the "shadow cabinet" had no intention of getting involved in any discussion with the Poles, while the Conservatives opposed the plan but wished to be circumspect. Faced with questions in the House of Commons on 19 and 26 November and 4 December, the government was able to avoid taking a stand by stressing that no official Polish proposal had been submitted. When the Polish ambassador handed in an aide-mémoire on 18 December, he was told that the Berlin Crisis had altered the international situation and the Rapacki Plan could only complicate matters.[100]

IV

Indeed, Khrushchev's move on 27 November, which opened the Berlin Crisis, seems to have given "a first class funeral" to the Rapacki Plan. The Polish "attempt to develop a foreign policy line of their own had been frustrated."[101] How accurate is that assessment? Was there any link between the Second Rapacki Plan and the Berlin Crisis?

In early November 1958, Gomułka went to Moscow for talks with Khrushchev. As the Polish embassy in Moscow opined, the journey marked the end of the phase during which Poland had seemed revisionist and somewhat untrustworthy. While not everything that Warsaw did was approved by the USSR, the post-October period was over.[102] While continuing to voice support for the Rapacki Plan (a month later, on 22 December in the interview for *The Observer,* for instance), Khrushchev resorted to a "shock initiative" regarding Berlin. Rapacki allegedly had an inkling of what was coming and may have discussed it on the telephone with Gomułka, but the speech that Khrushchev delivered to the Polish-Soviet friendship society was known to Gomułka only the day before.[103] In that speech, the substance of which he subsequently repeated in an official note to the three Western powers on 27 November, the Soviet leader said that the status of West Berlin had become abnormal and its occupation must end. The USSR was willing not to interfere with Western access to the city for the next six months but thereafter the West would have to negotiate with East Germany, which would assume full control. This amounted to an ultimatum. The ultimate object was seemingly to prevent the nuclearization of the Federal Republic by detaching it from NATO at the price of an East German withdrawal from the Warsaw Pact.[104] Yet Khrushchev seemed also willing to work for an accord with Germany, even an armed one, as he told Walter Lippmann in an interview that was unpublished in the USSR.[105]

Allegedly Gomułka returned from Moscow depressed, foreseeing a worsening of relations with the West as well as increased influence for Walter Ulbricht in Moscow.[106] Was he also aware that Khrushchev's move could be interpreted as an attempt to invalidate the Potsdam agreement, which defined the German-Polish border? Or did Gomułka's fear of a nuclearized Germany dominate other considerations, and was Khrushchev's reassurance that the USSR guaranteed the Oder-Neisse border enough for him?[107] Be it as it may, Gomułka's verbal attacks on West Germany and the support he voiced for Moscow's policies contrasted with the tone of Rapacki's pronouncements.[108] The foreign minister suggested, however, that were it not for the nuclear armaments and territorial revindications of West Germany, the Berlin Crisis would not have become so acute.[109] A few months later, addressing a party congress, he asserted that the Soviet initiative "came at the right time; the Poles were consulted and there was "full unanimity" of views.[110] Did he believe that the Soviet brutal move might force the West to engage in a more meaningful dialogue and eventually permit a reconsideration of his own plan? In his speech, if we dismiss all of the communist verbiage, we find the word "coexistence," which Rapacki defined as a "common search for solutions in controversial matters."

It was clear that both Gomułka and Rapacki continued to treat the plan as the chief element of Polish foreign policy. No occasion was missed to refer to it. When a State Department official told Spasowski that the real enemy of the Rapacki Plan was Khrushchev, who had boasted that he could destroy the West with nuclear arms, the ambassador remarked that the plan "would bring about the withdrawal of Soviet forces from Poland."[111] The premise that an East-West détente would increase Poland's security remained valid. The Poles kept noting various disengagement plans, which continued to be advocated in the West, hoped to bring the Rapacki Plan to the summit, and proposed that its military-technical aspects, which the West had questioned, be examined by a conference of experts. Harold Macmillan's journey to Moscow in early 1959 aroused Warsaw's interest as a welcome change in the atmosphere.[112] By contrast, Nixon's visit to Poland and Russia in early August raised the East-West temperature. Gomułka, annoyed by the warm reception of the vice president by Warsaw crowds, was tough and vented anti-German feelings "with a vehemence that became embarrassing."[113]

The 1960 summit in Paris to which Polish diplomacy attached some hopes proved a dismal failure. Eisenhower came under brutal attacks by Khrushchev. The Poles, Ambassador Beam commented, "had the good manners to stand aloof."[114] This posture may have earned Gomułka a friendly reception at the State Department when he came to New York to address the United Nations. He judged the moment opportune to advocate the Second Rapacki Plan on 17 September 1959, in spite of the Soviet delegate's opposition.[115]

Gomułka came to insist that technological advances allowed the United States to defend Germany with intercontinental rockets, while there was no likelihood of a communist expansion into a proposed military vacuum in Central Europe.[116] Such views may have been shared to some extent by President Kennedy, who seemed to attach less importance to nuclear armaments in Central Europe. Unlike his predecessor, he felt that the East-West division had to be overcome before Germany could be united, not vice versa. The Kennedy-Khrushchev Vienna summit was, however, another failure, and the erection of the Berlin Wall in 1961 brought the confrontation to a dangerous level. Rapacki was critical of a situation in which Berlin appeared the paramount issue, and the German question a by-product. Berlin could be used as a means of pressure, but what mattered was stopping German rearmament and achieving recognition of the GDR and Polish-German borders.[117] Again the Rapacki Plan appeared relevant. Winiewicz had recalled it on 27 November 1961 at the Political Commission of the General Assembly. Kennedy declared in March 1962 that the concept of a nuclear free zone deserved investigation.

On 28 March 1962 Rapacki submitted a third version of his plan to the Disarmament Convention in Geneva. It contained two new features: membership of the zone could be expanded to include other participants who wished to join; it prohibited the creation of new bases and installations for stockpiling or servicing nuclear weapons in the zone during the first phase. The Soviet Union did not like the second provision but eventually went along with the Polish proposal. The United States rejected it on 3 April on the grounds that it did not affect the nuclear arsenal in the USSR, jeopardized the military balance, and would create an illusion of progress while, in fact, increasing the dangers.[118]

The Cuban crisis demonstrated the fragility of peace, but it also was shock therapy, as proved by the installation of the White House–Kremlin "hot line" and the Test Ban Treaty. Polish diplomacy greeted the latter accord and returned doggedly to the advocacy of the Rapacki Plan. In what was the longest and most elaborate argument for it, an article in the January 1963 issue of *International Affairs,* "The Polish Plan for a Nuclear-Free Zone Today," the foreign minister maintained that the project was more valid than ever, since it had never been clearer than now that the balance of power needed to be replaced by a balance of security. On 28 December, Gomułka delivered a speech that contained a five-point plan for slowing down the arms race and facilitating disarmament talks and a nuclear freeze in Central Europe. Khrushchev seemed to second him in his New Year's Eve address in so far as he proposed banning the use of force in the search for solutions to territorial issues.[119]

In January 1964, the two leaders met secretly. Moscow was at this point in conflict with China and experiencing troubles with Romania. The United States was involved in Vietnam, and the Western alliance appeared shaky, with France maneuvering on its own and Bonn, after Adenauer's retirement from office, seeking a direct contact with the USSR. In this somewhat fluid situation, Khrushchev thought it a good moment to make overtures to Bonn. Gomułka was dismayed and sought to persuade the Soviet leader that Germany would be a direct threat to Poland should Soviet-Polish relations be weakened. Khrushchev spoke of the heavy burden of common defense borne by Moscow and allegedly proposed to withdraw troops from Poland. Gomułka did not accept this offer.[120] It may well be that this encounter made him decide to revive the old plan as based on his own speech. Rapacki was apparently hesitant, but the Gomułka Plan, as it became known, was embodied in the 29 February 1964 memorandum, and this time submitted directly also to Bonn. It was basically a proposal for a nuclear freeze in Central Europe, and it made it clear that it did not mean a renunciation of the full-blown Rapacki Plan.[121] The Polish minister repeated this point at a press conference on 5 March and in his speech at the Untied Nations in December. This was really the swan song, and the 1968 Crisis in Poland saw the resignation of Rapacki. True, his spirit was to be reflected in the partial nonproliferation treaty of July 1968, and the Polish-German treaty of 1970, while not a direct outcome of the Rapacki Plan, corresponded to its goals. His initiative would be mentioned by Willy Brandt, and recalled as late as May 1987 by General Wojciech Jaruzelski.

V

How should we assess a plan that had at least in 1957–1958 seemed to offer a glimmer of a chance for East-West détente? From the 1950s perspective of the Polish People's Republic the Rapacki Plan made good sense. It "felicitously combined Soviet and Polish interests" and could be regarded "as an independent initiative, even though it fitted in logically with the Soviet disarmament proposals."[122] There is a certain paradox here. Had not the Rapacki Plan been approved by Moscow, it would not have been treated seriously in the West. On the other hand, its Polish character gave it a certain appeal and credibility. Another paradox is that while its emphasis was on nuclear disarmament—and there was obviously fear of Central Europe becoming a battleground—it pursued mainly political aims.[123] While a third world war was not completely absent from calculations of either John Foster Dulles or Viacheslav Molotov, its likelihood was not great. The remaining options were either an evolutionary process in which the West would peacefully triumph over the USSR or an ongoing détente that would combine international stability with domestic socioeconomic progress and possible reforms. The former option, which did not appear to promise to materialize in the near future—and if it meant liberalization of East Central Europe, appeared almost like wishful thinking—was subscribed to by the Western governments and the Polish political emigrés. The Rapacki Plan was based on the second option, and its "minimalist" program sought to improve Poland's position *within* the Soviet Bloc. Warsaw and the Poles abroad were united only with respect to the German threat and the desire for normalization.

The plan never stood much of a chance. The West was unwilling to abandon its basic concept of dealing from a position of strength, and if one looks at the international developments from the perspective of the 1990s, this policy did in the end triumph. But it was impossible at the time to predict that this would be so. One can only speculate about what might have happened if the plan had been accepted. It might have strengthened détente tendencies in Europe and led to a process that culminated in the Helsinki accord of 1975 much earlier. Or, inversely, the plan might have contributed to a Soviet-German rapproachement and their joint domination of Europe. Was the rejection of the plan as a basis for discussion a "diplomatic failure on the part of the West," as Helmut Schmidt believed?[124] Perhaps, but it is really futile to pursue speculations that can never be proved or disproved. The Rapacki Plan must be evaluated in the context of its time as an interesting and ingenious attempt to promote European stability and Polish interests as the government in Warsaw perceived them. As such, it and its authors surely deserve a place in diplomatic annals.

Notes

1. Jacob O. Beam, *Multiple Exposures: An American Ambassador's Unique Perspective on East-West Relations* (New York, 1978), 94. Fullest survey and documentation are in Andrzej Albrecht, *Plan Rapackiego: dokumenty i opinie* (Warsaw, 1984), and his *The Rapacki Plan: New Aspects* (Warsaw, 1963). See also Ryszard Liczmanowski, *Adam Rapacki* (Warsaw, 1989). The most recent treatment is Teresa Łoś-Nowak, ed., *Plan Rapackiego a bezpieczeństwo europejskie* (Wyd. Uniw. Wrocławskiego, "Nauki polityczne," 48, Wroclaw, 1991.)

2. Adam Rapacki, "The Polish Plan for a Nuclear Free Zone Today," *International Affairs* 39 (January, 1963): 3.

3. See Eugene Hinterhoff, *Disengagement* (London, 1959), and Michael E. Howard, *Disengagement in Europe* (London, 1958). During the period 1946–1954, some twenty projects appeared.

4. Report for the first half of 1957 in Ambasada PRL, Moskwa, Archiwum Ministerstwa Spraw Zagranicznych, Warszawa, z. 7 t. 34 w. 4 (hereafter AMSZ).

5. See Anatole C. J. Bogacki, *A Polish Paradox: International and the National Interest in Polish Communist Foreign Policy, 1918–1948* (Boulder, Colo., 1991), 92–99. Cf. Vojtech Mastny, *Russia's Road to a Cold War: Diplomacy, warfare, and the politics of Communism, 1941–1945* (New York, 1979), 100, and Stefania Stanisławska, "Rodowód polityki zagranicznej Polski Ludowej," *Sprawy Miedzynarodowe* 17, no. 7 (July 1954).

6. See an appraisal of anti-Russian and anti-Soviet sentiments in Poland in Alfred Lampe, "Zagadnienia," *Zeszyty Historyczne* 26 (1973). The proper date of the document is 1943.

7. Respectively, Ryszard Frelek, "Koncepcje polskiej polityki zagranicznej w mysli i praktyce politycznej PPR," *Sprawy Miedzynarodowe* 3 (1967): 109, and Mieczysław Rakowski, *Polityka zagraniczna PRL* (Warsaw, 1974).

8. Adam Kruczkowski in Frelek, "Koncepcje," 109.

9. Bogacki, *Polish Paradox,* 75.

10. Ibid., 168–70; cf. Rakowski, *Polityka,* 37, 39.

11. See comments in Romuald Spasowski, *The Liberation of One* (San Diego, 1986), 348.

12. See report for the second half of 1957, Ambasada PRL, Moskwa, AMSZ, z. 7 t. 34 w. 4; see also note on conversations 16–17 July 1957, Archiwum Akt Nowych, KC PZPR, Warszawa, P. 1225, T. 87 (hereafter AAN KC PZPR).

13. Hansjacob Stehle, *The Independent Satellite* (New York, 1965), 231–32; cf. Józef Winiewicz, *Co pamietam z długiej drogi życia* (Poznán, 1985), 573.

14. It is worth recalling that Rapacki resigned in 1968 rather than condone the anti-Semitic purge of his ministry.

15. Andrzej Werblan's introduction to Adam Rapacki, *Przemówienia, artykuły, wywiady 1957–1968* (Warsaw, 1982), 16.

16. See Mieczyslaw Manelli, *War of the Vanquished* (New York, 1972), 6.

17. Beam, *Multiple Exposures,* 83.

18. Naszkowski's comments on the documentary film "Plan Rapackiego," Embassy of the Polish Republic, Washington, D.C.

19. Rapacki, *Przemówienia,* 366; also 21.

20. Beam, *Multiple Exposures,* 83.

21. Rapacki's warm feelings toward Birecki are visible in a private letter shown to the author.

22. See Hansjacob Stehle, "Erschreckend unrealistisch: Der Rapacki-Plan und einer seiner 'Väter' Manfred Lachs," *Die Zeit,* 4 Dec. 1987. See also Manfred Lachs, "Kollektive Sicherheit, Abrüstung—Teillösungen," *Neue Juristische Wochenschrift,* 11 July 1958. On Lachs, Ogrodziński, Birecki, and Winiewicz as "fathers of the Rapacki Plan," see R. G. Johnson to the State Department, 11 Mar. 1958, State Department, National Archives (hereafter SDNA), Record Group 59, 640.0012/3-1158. Cf. Łoś-Nowak, *Plan Rapackiego,* 22. A close relationship apparently existed between Rapacki and the ambassador to the United Nations, Jerzy Michalowski.

23. Henryk Birecki, "Le mécanisme de la formation de la politique étrangère dans les démocraties populaires: Le cas de la proposition polonaise de création d'une zone dénucléarisée en Europe Centrale," *Politique Étrangère,* no. 2 (1970): 198. The article was read and approved by Rapacki.

24. See Hinterhoff, *Disengagement,* 192.

25. Winiewicz, *Co pamietam,* 252.

26. Interview, *The Sunday Times,* 3 Jan. 1958; Polish text, Rapacki, *Przemówienia,* 48.

27. Memorandum, penciled in 1956, AMSZ, z. 23 t.163 w. 14.

28. *The Sunday Times,* 3 Jan. 1958; Stehle, "Erschreckend." I did not find other drafts mentioned to me by Manfred Lachs.

29. See respectively Stehle, "Erschreckend," and Rakowski, *Polityka,* 111.

30. "We do not conceal (the fact) that the basic motive for advancing the proposal to create a de-atomized zone was Polish national interest," Ministry circular, 5 Mar. 1958, AMSZ, z. 23, t. 163, w. 14. Cf. Winiewicz, *Co pamietam,* 557; Werblan, in Rapacki, *Przemówienia,* 12; Marian Dobrosielski, "Der Rapacki-Plan noch immer aktuell," in *Zwanzig Jahre Ostpolitik: Bilanz und Perspektiven,* ed. Ernst Ehmke, Karlheinz Koppe, Herbert Wehner (Bonn, 1986), 103.

31. Rapacki allegedly said that improved West-East relations were "indispensable in securing Polish independence and sovereignty" and that "disputed Polish western frontiers determined Polish foreign policy and tied our hands," Manelli, *War,* 4–5; cf. Stehle, *Independent Satellite,* 227; cf. David Stefancic, "The Rapacki Plan: A Case Study of East European Diplomacy," *East European Quarterly* 21, no. 4 (Winter, 1987): 404. Gomułka's preoccupation was stressed by Lachs in conversation with the author. On weakening some of Gomułka's anti-German remarks in the interview for *The Times,* see note of Winiewicz, 20 Feb. 1958, AMSZ, z. 23 t. 164 w. 14.

32. The most recent included Bulganin's letters of 20 Apr. and 20 July, and Khrushchev's remarks for American TV on 2 June 1957.

33. Stehle, *Independent Satellite,* 222–23.

34. Naszkowski-Bernov conversation, 18 Sept. 1957, AMSZ, z. 23 t. 57 w. 7.

35. See Stehle, *Independent Satellite,* 22–25; Eugeniusz Gajda, *Polska polityka zagraniczna, 1944–1974* (Warsaw, 1974), 170; note, 15 May 1957, AMSZ, z. 23 t. 163 w. 14.

36. Summary in James Ozinga, *The Rapacki Plan* (Jefferson, 1989), 33–35.

37. Beam to Sec. of State, 14 Dec. 1957, SDNA 640.0012/1-2457; cf. note of Winiewicz, AAN KC PZPR, P. 125, T. 87.

38. George Kennan, *Memoirs 1950–1963* (Boston, 1972), 239–47.

39. Lachs invited Kennan to come to Warsaw, where he gave a talk.

40. See Hugh Gaitskell, "Disengagement: Why? How?" *Foreign Affairs* 36, no. 4 (July, 1958). Also Milnikiel, tel. 13 Jan. 1958, AMSZ, z. 9 t. 699 w. 53. Also U.S. Embassy, London to State Dept., 27 Jan. 1958, SDNA, 640.0012/1-2758.

41. Dean Acheson, "The Illusion of Disengagement," and Kennan's reply "Disengagement Revisited," *Foreign Affairs,* respectively, 36, no. 3 (1958), and 37, no. 2 (1959).

42. Helga Haftendorn, *Security and Detente: Conflicting Priorities in German Foreign Policy* (New York: 1985), 56, 96.

43. See Ozinga, *Rapacki Plan,* 86–87; Winiewicz, *Co pamietam,* 567.

44. Barbour and Whitney to Sec. of State, 14 and 28 Jan. 1958, SDNA, 640.0012/1-1458 and 1858; also Milnikiel tel., 10 Jan. 1958, AMSZ, z. 9 t. 697 w. 58.

45. Sir Eric Berthoud visit, 16 Jan. 1958, AMSZ, z. 9 t. 695 w. 53; also Winiewicz, *Co pamietam,* 566–67.

46. Rapacki notes, 2 Dec., AMSZ, z. 9 t. 622 w. 47, and Dec. 4, 1957, AAN KC PZPR, P. 125. T. 87. Also tel. to Spasowski, Milnikiel and note on conversation with Berthoud, 6, 9, and 10 Dec. 1957, respectively, AMSZ, z. 9 t. 622 w. 47, t. 697 w. 53, and t. 698 w. 53.

47. Text in Rapacki, *Przemówienia,* 33–43.

48. Burgess to Sec. of State, 25 Jan 1958; also Tuthill, Beam, and Young to Sec. of State, 4 Jan., 14 Jan., 7 Feb., SDNA, 640.0012/1-2458; 640.0012/1-458, 640.0012/ 1-1458, 640.0012/2-758.

49. See Harold Macmillan, *Riding the Storm 1956–1959* (New York, 1971); also Spasowski tel. and Ministry reply, 14 and 16 Dec. 1957, AMSZ, z. 9 t. 622 w. 47; Spasowski and Michałowski tel., 13 and 19 Jan. 1958, z. 9 t. 624 w. 47; Małcużyński note, 11 Jan. 1958, z. 9 t. 698 w. 53.

50. John Lukacs, *A New History of the Cold War* (Garden City, N.Y., 1966), 106.

51. Michałowski letter, 19 Jan. 1958, cited by Winiewicz, AMSZ, z. 23 t. 163 w. 14.

52. Beam to Leverich, "official-informal," 24 Dec. 1957, SDNA 640.0012/12-2457.

53. Dulles to missions, 21 Jan. 1958, SDNA 640.0012/1-2158.

54. Herter to missions, 28 and 29 Jan. 1958, SDNA 640.0012/1-2458. Compare Spasowski tel., 23 Jan 1958, AMSZ, z. 9 t. 697 w. 53.

55. *The Times,* 18 Feb. 1958.

56. Respectively note on Ogrodziński-Berthoud conversation, 9 Dec. 1957, AMSZ, z. 9 t. 697 W. 53, and Beam to Sec. of State, 7 Feb. 1958, SDNA, 640.0012/2-658.

57. Note on meeting of principal ambassadors, 10–11 March 1958, AMSZ, z. 23 t. 163 w. 14.

58. Embassy, Moscow report, 2d half of 1957, AMSZ, z. 7 t. 34 w. 4.

59. Naszkowski note, 3 Jan 1958, AMSZ z. 23 t. 163 w. 14; Beam to Sec. of State, 14 Jan and 6 Feb. 1958, SDNA, 640.0012/1-1458, and 640.0012/2-558; Beam, *Multiple Exposures,* 95–96.

60. Beam to Leverich, Dec. 24, 1957, SDNA, 640.0012/2-2457. Winiewicz assumed that "consultations with our allies must have gone badly," *Co pamietam,* 552.

61. On Moscow talks, Stehle, *Independent Satellite,* 225–26; for Polish-Bulgarian talks, 30–31 Jan. 1958, AMSZ, z. 23 t. 57 w. 7; also Winiewicz, *Co pamietam,* 570–71.

62. Embassy, Moscow, 1st half 1958, AMSZ, z. 7 t. 35 w. 5.

63. Beam to Sec. of State, 6 Feb. 1958, SDNA, 640.0012/2-658.

64. For meetings with Germans and Czechoslovaks, 8 Jan. 7, 8–9 Feb. 1958, AMSZ, z. 23 t. 39 w. 5, and z. 23 t. 164 w. 14.

65. Circular, AMSZ, z. 23 t. 164 w. 14, and memo, 12 Feb. z. 9 t. 696 w. 53.

66. AAN KC PZPR P. 125 T. 87.

67. Text in Ozinga, *Rapacki Plan,* 143–46.

68. Stehle, *Independent Satellite,* 224.

69. Gomułka's interview, *The Times,* 18 Feb. 1958.

70. Rapacki, "Polish Plan." On the connection between the Rapacki Plan and West German–Polish relations, see Łoś-Nowak, *Plan Rapackiego,* 63–74.

71. Cited in Stehle, "Erschreckend."

72. Haftendorn, *Security,* 97.

73. As exemplified by conversations with Ambassador Smirnov and Anastas Mikoyan in March 1958 and the suggestions for an "Austrian status" for East Germany. See Haftendorn, *Security,* 98, and Konrad Adenauer, *Erinnerungen 1955–1959* (Stuttgart, 1967), 369–95.

74. Haftendorn, *Security,* 62–63.

75. Ozinga, *Rapacki Plan,* 86; Beam to Sec. of State, 1 March 1958, SDNA, 640.0012/3-158.

76. Draft, 3 March 1958, AMSZ, z. 23 t. 163 w. 14.

77. Beam to Sec. of State, 15 Feb. 1958, SDNA, 640.0012/2-1458. Also note, 27 Mar. 1958, AMSZ, z. 23 t. 163 w. 14. On the team, see z. 9 t. 695 w. 53.

78. Beam to Sec. of State, 21 Feb. and 21 Mar. 1958, SDNA, 640.0012/2-2058 and 3-2158.

79. Memorandum of the Executive Committee of the Polish Council of National Unity, 3 Mar. 1958, signed by J. Starzewski, Polski Instytut i Muzeum Sikorskiego, London, archives, kol. 408/145. Among émigré political parties NiD (Independence and Democracy) passed a resolution on 30 Mar. 1957 that advocated a withdrawal of all foreign troops from Eastern Europe and West Germany, banning atomic and restricting conventional weapons and the signature of a security pact assuring against interference in domestic affairs. See Hinterhoff, *Disengagement,* 421. On negative reaction to Rapacki Plan of Polish-American press, see a caustic note, 19 Feb. 1958, AMSZ, z. 9 t. 624 w. 47.

80. Respectively note on Jandrey-Spasowski conversation, 4 Mar. 1958, SDNA, 640.0012/3-458, and on Beam-Ogrodziński talk, 15 Mar. 1958, AMSZ, z. 9 t. 624 w.47. On the émigré political writings concerning a neutral zone and the Rapacki Plan, see Łoś-Nowak, *Plan Rapackiego,* 77–90.

81. Mentioned in Kennan, *Memoirs,* 253–55.

82. See Macmillan, *Riding the Storm,* 464.

83. See documentation in SDNA, 640.0012/4-1858, 4-1958 and 4-2258, also 3-2858, and AMSZ, z. 9 t. 695 w. 53, t. 700 w. 53, t. 703 w. 53.

84. See dispatches and press cuttings in SDNA, 7405/1-2858, 2-3158, 1-3158, also 640.0012/4-1958 and 4-2258.

85. See conversations of Birecki with Roziers and de Carbonelle, 11 Apr., 1 Oct., 15 and 16 Dec., AMSZ, z. 23 t. 163 w. 14 and w. 5. Also Houghton to Sec. of State, 20 Feb. 1958, SDNA 640.0012/2-2058, and Murphy-Alphand conversation 1-258.

86. Text of reply in Ozinga, *Rapacki Plan,* 151–53; note on conversation, 3 May 1958, AMSZ z. 9 t. 623 w. 47, and Winiewicz to Spasowski, 4 May 1958, z. 9 t. 624 w. 47. Cf. Winiewicz, *Co pamietam,* 566. Beam's later comment that "the Poles felt they had acquitted themselves of their duty to the Soviet bloc and had enhanced their international standing in carrying out their mission" (*Multiple Exposures,* 96) does not quite tally with his views of the time.

87. Rapacki, *Przemówienia,* 62–73; cf. Beam to Sec. of State, SDNA, 640.0012/3-158. On American advice to Bonn, Bruce to Sec. of State, 19 May 1958, 640.0012/5-1958.

88. Winiewicz's conversations, 23 July, 1 Aug. 1958, AMSZ, z. 23 t. 57 w. 7. Vojaček had been referring to the Rapacki Plan as a Polish-Czechoslovak Plan, see 9 Jan. 1958, AMSZ, z. 23 t. 163 w. 14.

89. See Embassy Oslo to State Dept., 19 Mar. 1958, SDNA, 640.0012/3-1958, also Winiewicz, *Co pamietam,* 554.

90. Note on conversation, AMSZ, z. 9 t. 626 w. 47.

91. Typewritten draft received from Prof. Lachs. Cf. military statistics in Ozinga, *Rapacki Plan,* 104–5.

92. Michałowski tel., 8 Oct. 1958, AMSZ, z. 9 t. 626 w. 47.

93. Rapacki, *Przemówienia,* 74–86.

94. Rapacki tel., 8 Nov. 1958, AMSZ, z. 9 t. 701 w. 53.

95. Beam to Sec. of State, 6 Nov. 1958, SDNA, 640.0012/11-658.

96. State Department circular, 8 Nov. 1958, SDNA, 640.0012/11-858.

97. Ibid.

98. Stehle, "Erschreckend."

99. Lyon to Sec. of State, 12 Nov. 1958, SDNA, 640.0012/3-158. Also Milnikiel-Ogrodziński tel., 24 and 25 Oct. 1958, AMSZ, z. 9 t. 701 w. 53.

100. Milnikiel tel., 11 Nov., 18 Dec. 1958, 21 Jan. 1959, AMSZ, z. 9 t. 704 w. 53, and t. 701 w. 53.

101. Stehle, *Independent Satellite*, 230.

102. Embassy report, 2d half of 1958, AMSZ, z. 7 t. 35 w. 5.

103. Bennett Kovrig, *The Myth of Liberation: East-Central Europe in U.S. Diplomacy and Politics Since 1941* (Baltimore, 1973), 229; Stehle, *Independent Satellite*, 39.

104. See Adam B. Ulam, *Expansion and Coexistence: The History of Soviet Foreign Policy 1917–67* (New York: 1968), 619–20.

105. Embassy report, 2d half of 1958, AMSZ, z. 7 t. 35 w. 5.

106. H. Birecki's letter of 16 June 1992 to the author.

107. Stehle, *Independent Satellite*, 39.

108. Report, Embassy London, 14 Nov. 1958, AMSZ, z. 9 t. 782 w. 61.

109. Interview in *The Observer*, 22 Nov. 1958; Polish text in Rapacki, *Przemówienia*, 89.

110. Speech at Third Party Congress, 18 Mar. 1959, Rapacki, *Przemówienia*, 95.

111. Kohler-Spasowski conversation, 29 Jan. 1959, SDNA, 640.0012/1-1959.

112. See Gede-Khrushchev conversation, 3 Mar. 1959, AMSZ, z. 23 t. 39 w. 5. List of proposals in Hinterhoff, *Disengagement*, 429–32.

113. Beam, *Multiple Exposures*, 106.

114. Ibid., 108.

115. Rapacki's note, July 26, 1962, AAN, KC PZPR, P. 125, T. 87.

116. Cited by Stehle, *Independent Satellite*, 235.

117. Rapacki's undated letter to "Dear Comrade," AAN, KC PZPR, P. 125, T. 87.

118. See Rapacki's notes, 26 and 27 July 1962, AAN, KC PZPR, P. 125, T. 87. Also, Ozinga, *Rapacki Plan*, 122; Albrecht, *Plan Rapackiego*, 31.

119. Albrecht, *Plan Rapackiego*, 20–21. Gomułka, however, had no ready answer when asked by Lippmann how one could enforce the Rapacki Plan if a future German government decided to defy its provisions. Confidential note (not for publication) on interview with Gomułka on 19 Nov. 1962. Yale University Library, MS, group 326, Walter Lippmann Papers, ser. 111, box 74.

120. Nicholas W. Bethell, *Gomulka: His Poland and His Communism* (New York, 1969), 242; Sergei Khrushchev, *Khrushchev on Khrushchev* (Boston, 1990), 49; *Khrushchev Remembers* (Boston, 1970), 118–20. Did Rapacki have Khrushchev in mind when he wrote about "short-sighted calculations of bribing GRF" (*Przemówienia*, 368)? For Mikoyan's observations to Bruno Kreisky about armaments being the only area in which the USSR could economize, see Matthews to Sec. of State, 22 Mar. 1958, SDNA, 640.0012/3-2158.

121. Winiewicz, *Co pamietam*, 572; Birecki, "Le mécanisme," 205; Karol Małcużynski, *Plan Gomułki* (Poznań, 1964).

122. Respectively Zbigniew Brzezinski, *The Soviet Bloc: Unity and Conflict* (Cambridge, Mass., 1971), 365, and Haftendorn, *Security*, 61.

123. Albrecht, *Plan Rapackiego*, 52.

124. Helmut Schmidt, *Defense or Retaliation: A German Contribution to the Consideration of NATO's Strategic Problem* (London, 1962), 150.

1. Hitler and his Diplomats: At Führer's headquarters rehearsing for weekly newsreel following French armistice, 22 June 1940. From left Walther Hewel, Steengracht von Moyland, Franz von Sonnleithner, Joachim von Ribbentrop, Hitler

2. Roosevelt and his Diplomats: At Alexandria after Yalta, February 1945. Seated from left John G. Winant, Roosevelt, Edward R. Stettinius, Jr., Harry L. Hopkins

3. Molotov and Friend (i): With translator and Hitler, in Berlin, Nov. 1940

4. Molotov and Friend (ii): With Franklin D. Roosevelt at White House, June 1942

5. Between Stalin and the Court of St. James: Ivan Maiskii, Soviet ambassador to Britain, 1932–1943

6. Ambassador Arriving: Maxsim Litvinow at Washington airport, 7 December 1941. On left George T. Summerlin, State Department chief of protocol

7. Looking Diplomatic:
Cordell Hull and Sumner
Welles at White House,
May 1940

8. Secretaries of State
Coming and Going:
George C. Marshall
and Dean Acheson,
April 1947

9. Socialists as Diplomats: Ernest Bevin and Clement R. Attlee, July 1945

10. Reshapers of American Foreign Policy: Harry S. Truman, Robert A. Lovett, George F. Kennan, Charles E. Bohlen, Nov. 1947

11. Fathers of a New Europe: Jean Monnet and Robert Schuman, Nov. 1951

12. Restorer of Japanese Respectability: Shigeru Yoshida at Washington reception, 8 November 1954

13. Searcher for European Security: Adam Rapacki

14. United Against Communism: Konrad Adenauer and John Foster Dulles

15. Toward a New Global Alignment: Jawaharlal Nehru and Zhou Enlai, Delhi, 1 Jan. 1957

16. Builders of a Better World: Trygve Lie and Dag Hammarskjöld, April 1953

17. The Eve of Suez in Paris, 26 September 1956. From left: Christian Pineau, Sir Anthony Eden, Guy Mollet, Selwyn Lloyd

18. Charles de Gaulle Meets the Press, Paris, May 1958

19. Representing Israel:
Golda Meir and Abba Eban
in Washington, March 1957

20. The Columnist and the
Dictator: Jozef Tito and Walter Lippmann (Mrs. Lippmann
on left), Nov. 1953

21. Inside the Cuban Missile Crisis: Anatoly F. Dobrynin, Andrei Gromyko, and John F. Kennedy at the White House, 18 October 1962

22. Between Peace and War: Dean Rusk at News Conference, July 1964

23. Makers of Ostpolitik: Egon Bahr and Willy Brandt

24. The Peacemakers: Le Duc Tho and Henry A. Kissinger, Paris, January 1973

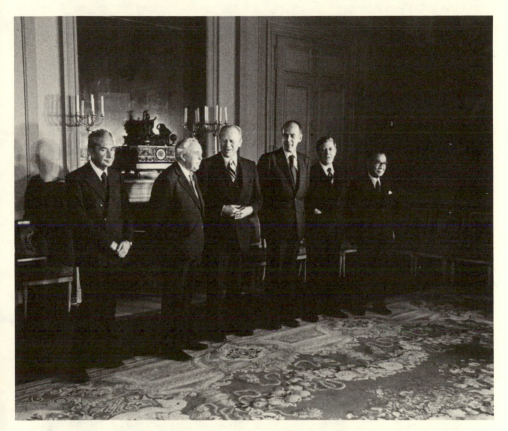

25. Inaugurating Economic Summitry at Rambouillet, Nov. 1975. From left: Aldo Moro, Harold Wilson, Gerald R. Ford, Giscard d'Estaing, Helmut Schmidt, and Takeo Miki.

26. The Icebreakers: Menachim Begin and Anwar Sadat, April 1979

27. New Faces of the 1970s (i): Deng Xiaoping, George Bush, and Gerald R. Ford at Peking, Dec. 1975

28. New Faces of the 1970s (ii): Helmut Schmidt, Dietrich Genscher, and Cyrus R. Vance, March 1977

29. Polite Adversaries: Helmut Schmidt and Erich Honecker at Helsinki, July 1975

30. Embrace at the Summit: Jimmy Carter and Leonid Brezhnev at Vienna, June 1978

31. The Diplomat Unarmed: William H. Sullivan at Tehran, Feb. 1979

PART FOUR

THE WIDER WORLD

11

JAPAN RETURNS TO THE WORLD: YOSHIDA SHIGERU

AND HIS LEGACY

Akira Iriye

O N 8 SEPTEMBER 1951, at the San Francisco opera house, Japanese Prime Minister Yoshida Shigeru put his signature on a document that brought to a formal end the state of war that had existed between Japan and forty-eight countries. These included the United States, Britain, France, the Netherlands, and many Asian countries. The peace treaty, however, was not signed by several other nations against which Japan had also fought a war, most notably China and the Soviet Union. Thus the occasion that marked Japan's readmission to the community of nations also demonstrated the divided nature of that community.

Should Japan have agreed to such a "partial peace," as it was called? For the San Francisco peace treaty had the effect of identifying the nation's fate with the United States and its definition of the world. That definition had two aspects. One was the global order institutionalized by the United Nations. A clause in the peace treaty obligated Japan to accept article two of the United Nations charter, which called on the member states to "settle their international disputes by peaceful means" and to "refrain . . . from the threat or use of force against the territorial integrity or political independence of any member or state." In accordance with such principles, the United Nations was even then engaged in a war on the Korean Peninsula. For Japan to sign a peace treaty amidst the Korean War was, therefore, to see itself as a member of the world organization with all the obligations such membership entailed. But the very fact that United Nations forces were engaged in a war against North Korea, to which the Soviet Union and the People's Republic of China had been giving their support (albeit short of direct military involvement in the former's case) showed that the world was fast becoming divided into two camps. Underneath the seeming unity symbolized by the United Nations, international affairs had become characterized by bi-polarity, a division of most of the world into the U.S.-led and the USSR-led blocs. In this second definition, Japan was clearly signaling its adherence to the former against the latter. That was why so many in Japan denounced the peace treaty as confirming and rigidifying the division. It would be far better, they argued, to wait until there emerged a truly unified international community and then rejoin the world.

For Yoshida such thinking was, as he said, unrealistic and, worse, irresponsible.[1] Not only would it be futile to wait for the United States and the Soviet Union to come together, it would be in Japan's interest to side explicitly with the former. As for China, he recognized the need to work out a peace treaty with the country with which Japan had been at war longer than with any other, but here, too, he believed that the crucial thing was to follow the U.S. lead, for only the latter was intent on ending the state of war and allowing Japan to rejoin the world. Washington had not recognized the People's Republic of China, and the two powers were in fact colliding in Korea, so to follow the United States amounted to putting off any chance of restoring normal relations with mainland China. Yoshida was willing to accept this risk, and indeed he even acceded to the U.S. Senate's insistence that Japan sign a peace treaty with the Republic of China, the Nationalist regime on the island of Taiwan. He was not happy about taking such a step, for he did not share the view that the Taipei regime spoke for the Chinese people, but he bowed to the necessity of deferring to American wishes.[2]

In taking such action, Yoshida helped shape postwar Japan's destiny. It was he who, more than anyone else in Japan, paved the way for the country's emergence from defeat onto the world arena and who defined the nature of that emergence as being in a state of dependence on the United States.

I

For Yoshida (1878–1967) the road to San Francisco had been a long one. It must not, however, have been unpredictable. For he came from a background that virtually ordained that he would play a role in reconciling Japan and the United States. A career Foreign Service officer during the halcyon days of prewar Japanese diplomacy, he exemplified its essentially Western orientation.[3] The country's foreign policy after its entry into the family of nations in the 1850s had aimed at achieving equal status with the Western powers—equal in international law, in military arms, in economic resources, in prestige, in race relations. By the time Yoshida reached one of the top positions available to a career bureaucrat—vice minister of foreign affairs—in 1927, some at least of these goals had been achieved. During the 1920s Japan was one of the principal international actors, sharing power and responsibility in Asia and the Pacific with the United States and Great Britain. "International cooperation" entailed acting closely with these nations in ensuring regional stability. Although the Anglo-Japanese alliance, the best symbol of Japan's great-power status, was abrogated at the Washington conference of 1921–1922, it was replaced by a broader framework (the nine-power treaty, the five-power treaty, the four-power treaty, and many other agreements) built upon cooperation among Tokyo, London, and Washington. To be sure neither Shidehara Kijûrô, the key figure in Japanese diplomacy at that time, nor Yoshida denied that Japan had special interests in China which limited the scope of cooperation with the other countries on the continent, but they understood that Japan's international standing and especially its economic needs dictated the maintenance of friendly relations with Washington and London.

Shidehara's leadership in Japanese foreign policy came to an end when the Manchurian crisis erupted, eroding civilian authority in the nation's external affairs. Yoshida, however, was not immediately eclipsed. He served as ambassador to the Court of St. James during 1936–1939 and tried to interest British officials in reviving the Anglo-Japanese alliance, in spirit if not in name. He believed that only such a step could prevent Japan from becoming totally isolated in the world. Time was against him, however, for by then the various treaties and agreements worked out at the Washington and other conferences had been violated and abrogated, mostly by the Japanese military, and international affairs were drifting further and further away from any sort of cooperativeness. Still, Yoshida did what he could to prevent what many now believed awaited Japan, the path of unilateralism in Asia that would end up pitting it against the Anglo-American nations. He retained some confidence that he could influence the course of events in part because of his family ties; he was the son-in-law of Count Makino Nobuaki, the high court official in the 1930s who had been Japan's chief delegate at the Paris peace conference and who had been a strong advocate of cooperative diplomacy. Through Makino, Yoshida came into contact with others who shared the view that it was nothing short of idiocy to antagonize the Anglo-American powers and to take sides with revisionist forces exemplified by Nazi Germany and Stalinist Russia. During 1939–1941 he was one of the few civilians (he no longer held any official position) who argued for maintaining a peaceful relationship with these countries even at the expense of making concessions in China. To the very end, and indeed even after Pearl Harbor, Yoshida remained in touch with the American ambassador, Joseph C. Grew.

When war with the United States and Britain came, Yoshida immediately went to work to prepare for what he privately predicted would be a certain defeat of his country.[4] He had to be extremely circumspect lest he and like-minded people be frustrated in their endeavor to pave the ground for such an eventuality, but the longer the war lasted, and the worse it grew for Japan, the bolder these conspirators became. One climax came in February 1945 when Yoshida worked closely with Konoe Fumimaro, the former prime minister and a court noble, to draft a memorandum for the attention of the emperor. The "Konoe memorandum" reflected Yoshida's view that a long, disastrous war must be brought to an end as quickly as possible, for otherwise the country would be thrown into confusion and chaos, from which only radicals would benefit. He saw a connection between the extremism of right and left, and worried that a prolonged war would turn the fanatical militarists and chauvinists into revolutionaries to the detriment of political stability, especially the preservation of the imperial institution.

For having had a hand in drafting the memorandum, Yoshida was arrested by military police and imprisoned for seventy days. Clearly, he was advocating, albeit through the emperor, a policy that opposed the war. But his reasons were conservative, to preserve Japan's political stability and societal cohesiveness. To him both were intimately linked to maintaining a cooperative attitude toward the Anglo-American powers. It had been a horrendous mistake to alienate them and identify Japan's fate with the antidemocratic, antiliberal regimes of Germany and the Soviet Union. The emperor seems to have shared such a view, even though for a while he had been captivated by visions of a grand revisionist (i.e., anti–Anglo-American) alliance.[5] Neither the emperor nor Yoshida, however, was able to change the nation's set course overnight, and it would take many more weeks to reorient its foreign affairs so as to end the conflict. In this final drama of war termination, Yoshida played only a minor part because he was chastened by the imprisonment, and also because many others now joined the movement to bring the war to an end. As is well known, the cabinet of Admiral Suzuki Kantarô, appointed in April 1945 (shortly before the death of President Franklin D. Roosevelt), saw its mission as the termination of the Asian-Pacific war. Yoshida does not seem to have wanted, or even to have been asked, to participate in these efforts of the new cabinet. Suzuki turned to another diplomat, Tôgô Shigenori (foreign minister at the time of Pearl Harbor), to head the Foreign Office to initiate and conclude the war-terminating process.

The disastrous war convinced Yoshida once again that Japan should never have strayed from the course set during most of its prewar history, to base its foreign affairs on a structure of political and economic cooperation with the Anglo-American powers. Now that the "new order" strategy had brought ruins and humiliation to the nation, it was clear that Japan must revert to the earlier orientation and reconfirm its commitment to working closely with the United States and Great Britain. The country really had no alternative, now that American forces, helped to some extent by those from the Commonwealth countries, occupied the defeated nation. But to Yoshida, the defeat and the occupation were a good opportunity to tie Japan's destiny once again with the Americans and the British. Many who thought like him and, for this reason, had been driven underground or silenced for several years, now emerged as the leaders of postwar Japan. Yoshida was joined by others like Shidehara Kijûrô and Ashida Hitoshi, both former professional diplomats, and they took turns becoming prime minister. It may be said that the continuity of postwar Japan with the pre-1931 phase of modern Japanese politics and diplomacy was ensured when these men emerged as the new leaders.

It was not something that came naturally to Yoshida. Temperamentally, he was not given to enjoying making political deals and offering compromises. Rather, he liked to stand above the fray of daily politics. But he had no choice. Once he was recruited to head the reestablished Jiyûtô (Liberal party), he threw himself headlong into the game of parliamentary politics. It should be recalled that at that time Japan had no foreign policy; the Ministry of Foreign Affairs was drastically restructured by order of the occupation authorities, its primary function now being to serve as a liaison between the government and those authorities, centered at the General Headquarters under General Douglas MacArthur. There were, of course, no embassies abroad; all Japanese diplomats were repatriated, and some senior Foreign Service officers were "purged"—they were not to hold governmental office. With little to do, many former diplomats had to support themselves and their families by taking up farming, retailing, teaching, and other occupations.

Yoshida was one of the luckier former diplomats in that he was not purged and had sufficient resources for providing minimum comfort. He, as well as others like Shidehara and Ashida, believed the time would come sooner or later when the occupation would end and the former enemies would offer Japan a chance to reenter the international arena. It would be extremely important to be prepared for such an eventuality and to make a careful study of Japanese foreign affairs strategies after the nation regained sovereignty.

Much of this preparation was carried out by younger officials, but there is no reason to doubt Yoshida's thinking was fully congruent with theirs.[6] Their shared assumption was that Japan would never again attempt to conquer neighboring countries through force, but that it would seek to protect and promote national interests primarily through economic means. It would be essential to resume trade in order to obtain, and pay for, food, energy resources, and other raw materials; and this in turn would necessitate reindustrialization. In the meantime, it would be important to maintain domestic order so as to prevent social tensions and political upheavals that could only undermine such economic endeavors. All these objectives indicated the need to turn to the Anglo-American powers, in particular the United States, for assistance and cooperation.

This did not mean, at least initially, that Japan would not seek good relations with other countries, in particular China and the Soviet Union. The former would be especially important for trade; now that the dream of Asian empire had been shattered, it would be all the more important to reopen trade opportunities in mainland China. The Soviet Union, too, would have to be befriended if only to ensure Japanese security. The idea of Japan's maintaining good relations with the United States, Britain, China, and the Soviet Union had been implicit in the "Yalta system," the product of the February 1945 conference by the leaders of the three Western allies.[7] There Roosevelt, Winston Churchill, and Joseph Stalin had agreed in essence to continue their wartime cooperation into the postwar period and, in Asia, to include China as a regional partner. Japan would be kept under their control but would eventually be permitted to be reintegrated into the community of nations. Within a few years after 1945, however, the Yalta formula was steadily undermined. By 1950, with China now under a Communist regime and the Soviet Union confronting the United States in Europe, it appeared that the Yalta framework was not going to work and that some alternative scheme would have to be defined. Then came the Korean War.

II

The North Korean attack on the south shocked the Japanese like nothing else since the war. They had accepted the new constitution and its underlying idealism, as expressed in the preamble that "we have determined to rely for our security and survival upon the justice and good faith of the peace-loving peoples of the world." Now, all of a sudden, the idea hit home that not all peoples had eschewed aggression and that Japan's own security might fall victim to another war. For Yoshida and other leaders in Tokyo, however, the outbreak of the Korean War provided an opportunity to formalize the basic orientation of the country's foreign affairs. General MacArthur, also responding to the crisis on the Korean Peninsula, encouraged such a step, with the result that within weeks of the North Korean invasion of the south, some outlines for Japan's immediate future became drawn.

As Yoshida saw the new situation, the North Korean aggression belied the principles that had sustained the new constitution and compelled the nation to take a more realistic look at its own security problem. He would certainly have agreed with Ashida, the former prime minister, when the latter wrote for the July 1950 issue of the popular monthly, *Bungei shunjû,* that "Japan must declare itself to belong to one side in the divided world."[8] The Korean War clearly demonstrated, he argued, that military force was still the determinant factor in international affairs. It followed that Japan, regardless of the constitution, must undertake at least modest rearmament. Yoshida shared such views, which were in perfect accord with his Anglo-American oriented thinking. He, too, believed the time had come to tie Japan's sovereignty and security more explicitly to the military power of the United States. The nation must regain independence and put an end to the foreign occupation, but it could not expect to protect itself without the assistance of the United States. The idea of coupling the regaining of sovereignty with yielding part of that very sovereignty so as to provide bases for U.S. forces had been mentioned by some, notably Ashida, even before this time, but Yoshida persuaded himself that the war in the neighboring country made this the only viable solution for the country's future.

General MacArthur as well as officials in Washington thought along similar lines. For the United States to respond decisively to the Korean conflict was tantamount to redefining national security objectives in Asia and, most fundamentally, to scrapping the Yalta formula. For it was taken for granted that the Soviet Union was behind the North Korean attack and that the People's Republic of China, which had just signed a thirty-year treaty of alliance with Moscow, was also an accomplice in violating the peace. This view of China, of course, was confirmed in the fall of 1950, when waves of Chinese "volunteers" entered Korea and engaged United Nations troops as the latter approached the Manchurian border. With the two communist states thus identified as aggressors, the Yalta definition of postwar regional order was no longer tenable.

What was to take its place? Leaders in Tokyo and Washington had a ready answer: a new security arrangement that would combine the forces of Japan, the United States, and other anticommunist countries in Asia and the Pacific in order to check Soviet and Chinese expansionism. This new strategy would eventually develop into a collective security system tying together the defences of Japan, South Korea, Taiwan, the Philippines, Australia, and New Zealand within the overarching umbrella of American military power. The emerging Japanese-U.S. security connection was to be the first piece of this grand construction.

Not that Yoshida and other Japanese saw the development so clearly in 1950. They had the constitution to worry about before embarking on a radical new security policy. Besides, as will be noted, they did not always identify with Washington's adamantly anti-Beijing stance. Still, both Japanese and Americans were architects of the new regional order in which the two nations would play a central role.

The first step, which came immediately after the outbreak of the Korean conflict, was the establishment of a seventy-five thousand–man police reserve force. MacArthur suggested, and Yoshida implemented, the creation of the quasi-army primarily in order to maintain Japan's domestic order, now that the bulk of U.S. forces was being shifted to the Korean Peninsula. Despite its dubious constitutionality, there was little debate on the new army, primarily reflecting the growing pessimism that the constitution's pacifism could be realized. It should also be noted, however, that by opting not to revise the constitution in order to accommodate the new development, the Japanese, above all Yoshida, were accepting the argument that an armed force purely for self-defense was not prohibited by the constitution. The latter, they asserted, forbade the creation and use of military force for aggressive purposes, not for defense. History might have suggested that the line separating aggression and self-defense was often in the eye of the beholder, but by choosing to accept such reasoning Yoshida could maintain that there was no departure from the main course of postwar Japanese foreign policy, which, after all, had reversed the more revisionist, unilateralist, and aggressive orientation of the 1930s and the war years. In other words, the rearmament was a confirmation, not a rejection, of the new approach to international affairs. This was ingenious reasoning, for by arguing that way Yoshida could retain some flexibility in determining how much further the nation would push its military strengthening, and to what extent it would spend national resources on defense.

In any event, Japanese rearmament was an important initial step for the establishment of a new regional security arrangement. The rest of the arrangement would be worked out in due course, but in the meantime the most important next step as far as Japan was concerned was the convening of a peace conference to put a formal end to the Second World War. Washington was now ready and eager for a peace conference, sensing the need for incorporating an independent Japan into an Asian collective security system. Between January and July of 1951, a series of conversations were held in Tokyo between Prime Minister Yoshida and John Foster Dulles, America's chief negotiator for a peace treaty.

It will not be necessary to chronicle in detail those negotiations.[9] Suffice it to note that Yoshida's hand was as clearly visible there as Dulles's. The two were in basic agreement on a number of points. All restrictions placed on Japan as a defeated nation would be removed; it would resume trade and other economic activities in the international arena; and its occupation by foreign troops would formally come to an end. At the same time, its security for the time being would be entrusted to the United States, with which Japan would conclude a security treaty. That the peace treaty and a security pact were inseparable was something both Yoshida and Dulles accepted as the point of departure.[10] That such a coupling would make it practically impossible to obtain the agreement of the Soviet Union, the People's Republic of China, and other communist countries was also assumed as an inevitable, if regrettable, corollary. The basic premise, of course, was that the world had become rigidly divided into two camps, and that Japan must make a choice—unless it chose nonalliance and neutrality.

Could, and should, Japan have done so? Yoshida and his supporters adamantly denied such a possibility, arguing that neutrality without armament was totally unrealistic, whereas neutrality through military strengthening would be detrimental both to the national economy and regional stability. To join the American alliance system was a way of choosing a third alternative, to ensure national security without massive rearmament and to prevent international isolation through a visionary scheme of unarmed neutrality.

Critics, on the other hand, did not easily succumb to the Yoshida-Dulles realism. If anything, now that serious negotiations for a peace treaty had begun, Japanese pacifists, opposition party members, intellectuals, labor leaders, and many others stepped up their campaign for a "total peace," a comprehensive and not "partial" peace treaty that would be accepted by all fifty-odd former belligerents, above all by the Soviet Union and China. The opponents' argument took on an air of added urgency because of the Korean conflict. Deeply worried that Japan, which was already serving as a base for American military operations in the peninsula, might become steadily drawn into the war and into an even larger conflict between the nuclear powers, they mobilized the press, labor unions, and universities and worked through the opposition parties, especially the Socialist party, to derail the Yoshida-Dulles negotiations. The debate between the two sides was often acrimonious. (Japan was still an occupied country where freedom of expression and assembly were restricted, and indeed the Communist party's organ, *Red Flag,* was banned in the wake of the out-break of the Korean War. Still, the American occupation authorities did not overtly seek to suppress expression of opinion on the peace negotiations.) Yoshida was so irritated by what he took to be his opponents' naïveté that he called them visionaries and pedants without an understanding of the realities of international politics.

To the extent that opinion polls in those days reflected public sentiment, it would appear that the Japanese people by and large supported the government's position on the necessity of concluding a "partial" peace.[11] Even if the public favored a speedy end to the occupation by an early conclusion of such a peace treaty, however, there was much stronger opposition to coupling it with a security arrangement with the United States, which would mean continued presence of American forces on Japanese soil. Here not just pacifism and neutralism but nativist, xenophobic, and radical sentiments joined forces to create a significant political movement. It may well be, on the other hand, that Yoshida's strategy of presenting the peace treaty and a security pact as one package succeeded in splitting the opposition, for part of it accepted the peace treaty. This was best revealed when the Socialist party was unable to take a unified stand on the new arrangements; those who supported the peace treaty but not the security treaty with the United States were pitted against those who were opposed to both. No agreement was possible between the two positions, and in October 1951, just before the Diet ratified the peace treaty, the party was split into Right and Left Socialists.[12]

On one issue, however, Yoshida and his opponents were in essential agree-ment. That was the question of China. To be sure, the prime minister had to realize that the People's Republic and the Soviet Union had signed an alliance directed at Japan, that they were both implicated in the North Korean attack on the south, that American forces were fighting against Chinese, and, therefore, that there was virtually no chance that the United States would invite the Beijing regime to a Japanese peace conference. Nevertheless, Yoshida recognized that Japan had certain interests and concerns that compelled it to approach China from a somewhat different perspective. It was not that he shared the Asianist sentiment of many of his countrymen, the view that Japan should maintain a close relationship with China because both were Asian countries and held much in common. As he was fond of saying, Japan was a "maritime" nation and its survival hinged on extensive trade with the great industrial and commercial nations of the West. Moreover, in politics, economy, and social conditions, it was more a "Western" than an "Asian" country.[13] It followed, then, that to focus on its ties to China and other countries and to slight Western nations was wrong, as the disasters of the 1930s and the war had clearly demonstrated. This did not mean, however, that Japan could ignore China, a huge potential market against which the country had waged an aggressive war. Yoshida shared his countrymen's sentiment that the recent past and future economic prospects dictated a policy of an eventual, if not immediate, rapprochement with the People's Republic of China. (The relationship with the Republic of China on Taiwan, too, would have to be kept in mind, of course, but neither Yoshida nor his opponents accepted that the island regime represented the Chinese people as a whole.) In the meantime, Japanese trade with mainland China had been carried on, albeit on a modest scale, and the business community as well as officials in Tokyo expected that sooner or later the Chinese would turn to Japan for consumer products and goods they needed for reconstruction.[14]

The China question, therefore, emerged as a potentially troublesome issue in Yoshida's negotiations with American officials. Dulles understood Japan's predicament, but Washington had already decided, when the Korean War broke out, to interpose U.S. ships in the Taiwan Strait in order prevent the Communists from forcefully unifying the country by conquering Taiwan, thus in effect dividing China. It was the Republic of China that the United States continued to recognize as the legitimate regime, whereas it pressed the United Nations, in late 1950, to condemn the People's Republic as a violator of the peace. In such a situation, for Japan to sign a "partial" peace treaty might make it difficult to improve relations with Beijing.

Indeed it did, and in fact Japan's problems were compounded when the United States Senate insisted that Tokyo sign a treaty of peace with the Nationalist government in Taiwan. When the San Francisco peace conference was convened, neither Beijing nor Taipei had been invited. Washington had decided on this course to save itself embarrassment since Britain and several other participants, not to mention the Soviet Union, had already extended recognition to Beijing, and they insisted that if China were to send a delegation to San Francisco, it would have to include representatives of the People's Republic. So it transpired that the peace conference was held without representatives of the one country with which Japan had been at war for the longest time and in which it had caused the largest amount of casualties and damage. The state of war with China, in other words, would persist.

The Senate's insistence that a peace treaty be signed with the Taipei government was probably the toughest challenge Yoshida had to face as prime minister. He had no qualms about signing a "partial" treaty in San Francisco, or a security pact with the United States. But to conclude a Chinese peace treaty with the Nationalists would not only antagonize the Chinese on the mainland and make a future rapprochement with Beijing that much more difficult; it would run into solid domestic opposition. His solution was ingenious: he would sign an instrument of peace with Taipei, as otherwise the Senate might not approve the San Francisco treaty, but at the same time declare that the provisions of the instrument would apply only to areas under effective control of the Nationalist government. In other words, the Taipei treaty would not prevent Tokyo or Beijing from negotiating another peace settlement in the future.

Much to Yoshida's relief, neither Dulles nor the Senate rejected this solution, and at home there was general agreement that a worse disaster had been prevented. So, on 28 September 1952, Tokyo and Taipei duly signed their peace treaty. Chiang Kai-shek, the Nationalist leader, had already declared that China would not seek reparations from Japan, and a document accompanying the treaty stated that "as a symbol of generosity and goodwill" toward the Japanese people, the Republic of China would refrain from seeking repayment for war damages. This extreme generosity was in line with America's and other Western nations' similar decision not to press for reparations. There is little doubt that Japan was a beneficiary of the Cold War tensions, which urged upon those countries the need for its speedy reincorporation into the international community. (The peace treaty did, however, provide for reparations payments to the Asian countries Japanese forces had occupied during the war.)

<h2 style="text-align:center">III</h2>

On 28 April 1952, the San Francisco peace treaty went into effect. Yoshida, who would remain as prime minister until the end of 1954, could take pride in the achievement. But for him the task of national reconstruction had just begun. At that time, despite the windfall revenue from the U.S. forces' "offshore procurement" orders, the Japanese economy still had not recovered the level attained during 1934–1937. Much more would be needed to revitalize the economy, to restabilize politics, and to reestablish a sense of national purpose. These were tasks Yoshida took upon himself to accomplish. His assignment was not an easy one, especially since the end of the occupation meant the reentry into positions of prominence of political, economic, and intellectual leaders who had been tried as war criminals, "purged" from public positions, or otherwise forced to remain inactive. Many of them now came out of seclusion and openly challenged Yoshida for leadership in the government and in the Liberal party. Japanese politics became quite fluid, even as the economy sputtered. Intellectuals, many of whom refused to accept the security pact if not the peace treaty itself, remained alienated, even as waves of McCarthyism in America and thought-reform campaigns in China affected Japanese opinion and tended to polarize it.

Yoshida's contribution in such a situation was to utilize what was left of his political life for reconfirming the basic orientation of Japanese foreign policy that had been formulated before the peace conference. Japan would tie itself unequivocally to the United States in the global Cold War, but at the same time it would focus on economic recovery, eschewing a large-scale military build-up. Japanese defense spending, which used to comprise between 20 and 40 percent of government outlays even in peacetime, was now only slightly over 10 percent. And the ratio continued to decline; while defense expenditures increased by 50 percent between 1952 and 1960, total public spending nearly doubled, so that by the end of the decade the ratio was down to 9 percent, a lower percentage than those for education or social welfare.[15] In the meantime, as national income began to grow, increasing from $14.1 billion in 1952 to $33.3 in 1960, the ratio of defense spending to the GNP fell to 1.4 percent by the end of the decade, the lowest figure among the major nations of the world. Japan was clearly steering a different course from the prewar years.

It is not difficult to detect Yoshida's influence in such a development. If some confirming evidence was needed for his national security strategy, it was amply provided by the Washington talks of October 1953 between Walter S. Robertson, assistant secretary of state for Far Eastern affairs, and Ikeda Hayato, chairman of the Liberal party's policy committee, who represented the prime minister. The talks were preliminary to the conclusion of a new mutual security agreement that would replace and continue the 1951 security pact. The United States government insisted that Japan create a 350,000-man military force as part of its contribution to the defensive alliance, but the Japanese resisted, convinced that such a large force would not only not be needed for the preservation of national security—there was no thought that a Japanese military force would be dispatched overseas—but would also be too costly for an economy just beginning to recover from the war. In the end, the negotiators agreed that Japan would establish a self-defense force of 110,000. What it lacked in firepower and mobility would be provided by U.S. forces stationed in Japan, especially Okinawa, which was not to be returned to full Japanese sovereignty until 1972. Yoshida was pushed out of his office in December 1954 by some party insurgents headed by Hatoyama Ichirô, one of the "de-purgees" (i.e., those whose had been purged during the occupation), but neither Hatoyama nor his successors significantly departed from Yoshida's basic posture.

The other important aspect of his strategy—to increase national wealth through reindustrialization and revitalization of foreign trade—was also pushed with vigor after 1952. It should be noted that Japan was still a net importer of goods at that time, and it remained so throughout the 1950s and well into the 1960s. In 1952, the nation imported $2.3 billion worth of goods, whereas its exports amounted to only $1.3 billion. Huge amounts of imports were, of course, necessary to obtain raw materials that were essential for Japanese industry. Since such imports could not really be controlled and, if anything, were expected to grow further, it was imperative to look for overseas markets to reduce trade deficits as much as possible. Because the United States, though Japan's biggest customer, always recorded trade surpluses toward the latter, it was natural that Japanese officials and businessmen should look in the direction of Asia for markets. That would primarily mean China and Southeast Asia, areas to which Japan had sought to extend its sway in the name of the Greater East Asian Coprosperity Sphere. There was little self-conscious embarrassment about returning to these markets, since the instrument of expansion would now be purely economic, not military. Indeed, for Yoshida and others, the establishment of trade connections with other Asian countries, unaccompanied by military force, should demonstrate postwar Japan's peaceful intentions and promote the region's economic interdependence, whatever the reality of Cold War confrontations.

Such implied dualism—Japan becoming incorporated into the U.S.-led alliance system but carrying on trade activities that were not confined to that framework—became the basis of Tokyo's China policy after 1952. To be sure, Yoshida had decided to sign a peace treaty with Taiwan and, moreover, Japan became bound by the guidelines established by the COCOM (Coordinating Committee for Export to Communist Areas) that restricted trade with communist nations. This, however, did not deter Japanese businessmen from entering into a trade agreement with Chinese authorities as early as June 1952, barely a month after the peace treaty went into effect. The Japanese government was not officially involved in the negotiation, as it had not recognized the Beijing regime, but, of course, it took full cognizance of what the businessmen were doing and justified the policy of "separating politics from economics."[16] This, too, was in line with Yoshida's overall strategy, and Japanese trade with the People's Republic of China continued to grow to such an extent that by 1956 it exceeded that with Taiwan. In the meantime, as soon as Japan regained its sovereignty, it became a member of the International Monetary Fund, and steps were taken to seek admission into the General Agreement on Tariffs and Trade. (The efforts bore fruit in 1955, thanks in no small degree to U.S. support, which overcame the European countries' reluctance to let Japan into the agreement lest it enable the country to compete aggressively in the world markets.)

When Yoshida stepped down in 1954, Japan had not yet joined the United Nations. Neither had it concluded a peace treaty with the Soviet Union. It would appear that for him these two objectives, inherently important as they were, were of lower priority than the need to ensure security and to resume trade. Although the San Francisco peace treaty had specified that Japan would accept the obligations under the United Nations charter, Yoshida did not vigorously push for Japanese membership in the world organization. He must have realized that any such application would meet with a Soviet veto. And Moscow would oppose Japanese membership so long as Tokyo refused to negotiate a peace treaty. The two issues were thus closely linked, and it was to be the task of the succeeding Hatoyama cabinet to solve both together. In 1956 Foreign Minister Shigemitsu Mamoru—another prewar diplomat (and wartime foreign minister) who had been tried as a war criminal and received the light sentence of seven years' imprisonment—traveled to Moscow to conclude an agreement restoring diplomatic relations between the two countries. Although this step did not amount to a peace treaty, it led to the Soviet Union's willingness to let Japan join the world organization. These were important landmarks in postwar Japanese diplomacy. They did not, however, alter the basic orientation that had been defined under Yoshida's leadership. Japan remained a very passive member of the United Nations for years to come, and to this day it has not succeeded in concluding a peace treaty with Russia.

What about the basic ideology, the intellectual underpinnings and world-views that had sustained Yoshida's postwar diplomacy? Did Japanese leaders and people share his perspectives on the nation's modern history and its relationship with others? It would seem that by and large they accepted the basic proposition that Japan must identify itself with the Anglo-American nations, above all the United States, not simply because their protection was needed for national security but also because, fundamentally, they stood for values and philosophies that the Japanese had once found congenial and that should guide their destiny after the end of the occupation. Many, to be sure, argued that Yoshida's strategy belied the very values the Western democracies espoused; remilitarization, however small-scale, and the continued presence of U.S. forces were contrary to the spirit of the postwar constitution, which, after all, had been an American product. The radical critique would not abate until prosperity brought greater domestic cohesion in the 1960s. In the meantime, right-wing nationalists came out of seclusion after 1952 and began urging national reconstruction along a different path that would be less modeled after Anglo-American democracy. Many of them urged revision of the postwar constitution, and indeed this would become a goal of the Liberal Democratic party when it was established in 1955 through the coalescence of conservative and centrist politicians, including those who had earlier belonged to Yoshida's Liberal party. On the other hand, the fact that no constitutional revision was ever attempted may attest to the widespread acceptance of the framework of postwar democratization.

If anything, after 1952 American influence in Japan not only did not abate but even increased. Not just American military personnel but businessmen, tourists, and scholars visited Japan, constituting by far the largest contingent of foreigners residing in the country. On their part, Japanese merchants, manufacturers, and journalists, as well as young scholars and students eagerly crossed the Pacific to live, observe, and study in the fabulously rich, friendly country that awaited them. The coming to the United States of twenty-five hundred Japanese intellectuals, on Fulbright and other grants, during 1952–1960 may have been one of the most significant developments in postwar U.S.-Japanese relations, for most of them were destined to return to their country and emerge as the leaders in government, business, journalism, and academia. Their role in spreading favorable images of America, in accustoming the Japanese to view the United States as a model and as an inspiration, is incalculable. To the extent that Japanese perspectives on their country's national and international affairs were subtly molded by these experiences, as well as by the presence of American people, goods, and ideas in Japan, it would be difficult to escape the conclusion that by and large those perspectives reinforced the visions and ideas held by Yoshida Shigeru as he steered the nation from defeat to independence.

IV

Yoshida's legacy, then, was a powerful one. Postwar Japan's security policy, economic strategy (including its China initiatives), and political/ideological orientation closely followed his own thinking. He was by no means the only postwar leader who developed a comprehensive vision for the defeated country's future. But fate placed the nation's leadership in his hands longer than in anyone else's, and those who came after him basically accepted his vision. Despite attacks from right and left, the legacy provided an essential continuity to postwar Japanese domestic and foreign affairs. It was only in the late 1980s and the early 1990s that voices began to be heard and forces marshaled to reorient Japanese politics and foreign policy. But the fact that these efforts have thus far not succeeded, except partially (such as the sending of military force to Cambodia, a step Yoshida might not have disapproved), indicates the strength of the legacy. In the coming decades, Japan's domestic and external affairs will undoubtedly change, but that their essential definition has lasted for nearly a half century speaks eloquently for the unique conjunction of accident and design that produced the Yoshida strategy. To the extent that the world today accepts Japan, and Japan the world, more readily than fifty years ago, we shall need to give due credit to one man who spanned the history of modern Japan.

Notes

1. Yoshida Shigeru, *Kaisô jûnen* (Tokyo, 1957), 2:52–53.

2. Hosoya Chihiro, "Japan, China, the United States, and the United Kingdom, 1941–1952," *International Affairs* 60 (Spring 1984): 247–59.

3. The best study of Yoshida's diplomatic career is John W. Dower, *Empire and Aftermath: Yoshida Shigeru and the Japanese Experience, 1878–1954* (Cambridge, Mass., 1979).

4. Ibid., chap. 7. For the unusually close relationship between Grew and Yoshida, see Iokibe Makoto's essay in *Ningen Yoshida Shigeru,* ed. Kurihara Ken (Tokyo, 1991).

5. See my essay in *FDR and His Contemporaries: Foreign Perceptions of an American President,* ed. Cornelis A. van Minnen (New York, 1992).

6. Akira Iriye and Warren I. Cohen, eds., *The United States and Japan in the Postwar World* (Lexington, Ky., 1989), 83–85.

7. On the Yalta system, see Akira Iriye, *The Cold War in Asia* (Englewood Cliffs, N.J., 1974).

8. Akira Iriye, *Shin Nihon no gaikô* (Tokyo, 1991), 65.

9. The best scholarly treatment of the making of the Japanese peace treaty is Hosoya Chihiro, *San Francisco kôwa e no michi* (Tokyo, 1984).

10. Yoshida, *Kaisô jûnen;* 3:108–109.

11. Iriye, *Shin,* 75–77.

12. Masamune Kimihiro, *Sengo-shi* (Tokyo, 1985), 1:344.

13. Akira Iriye, *Nihon no gaikô* (Tokyo, 1966), 158–59.

14. Akira Iriye, *China and Japan in the Global Setting* (Cambridge, Mass., 1992), chap. 3.

15. Iriye, *Shin,* 91–92.

16. Iriye, *China,* 106.

12

IN THE SHADOW OF MAO: ZHOU ENLAI

AND NEW CHINA'S DIPLOMACY

Shu Guang Zhang

C OMRADE ZHOU ENLAI," said Foreign Minister Qian Qichen at the March 1989 Conference on Zhou's Diplomatic Thought and Practice, "made the most outstanding contribution to New China's diplomacy in an all-around way during his 26-year tenure as a [foreign] policy maker, commander, and practitioner."[1] At this conference, organized by the Ministry of Foreign Affairs, more than fifty senior and junior diplomats—most of them were long-time aides of the former premier—"studied" (*yan jiu*) Zhou's diplomacy in the light of their own experience. Almost all the participants praised their former leader's "always correct" judgments and his "unusual" vigor, remarkable wisdom, and realistic leadership style; but no one seriously touched on a critical question: to what extent was Zhou free to pursue his objectives in his own way?

Khrushchev remembered Zhou as "Mao Tse-tung's [Mao Zedong's] most influential and most brilliant adviser," and he even admitted that "Stalin regarded him with respect. We all consider him a bright, flexible, and up-to-date man with whom we could talk sensibly."[2] Zhou's role was precisely what Khrushchev portrayed. Indeed, he had always been subject, willingly or unwillingly, to Mao's direction. This was an important dimension of the former premier's leadership style. Therefore, the nature of the Mao-Zhou working relationship and the restrictions that Mao exerted on him are worthy of examination.

I

There can be little doubt that Zhou played a significant role in shaping China's foreign policy. He served as the People's Republic's first foreign minister from October 1949 to February 1958 and as premier of the State Council from 1949 until his death on 8 January 1976. During his tenure Zhou won both domestic and international recognition as being responsible for the formulation and execution of China's foreign policy during the Cold War. Nevertheless, he had always insisted, "We owe all our achievements to Chairman Mao's brilliant leadership."[3] Zhou was a modest person, but more important, he had long submitted to Mao's personality cult in the course of the Chinese Communist revolution.

Zhou Enlai was a Western-educated Marxist-Leninist as a young man. Although he was initially exposed to communism in Japan, he, like many Chinese student nationalists of the 1920s, looked to the West for an explanation of China's desperate condition of internal collapse and humiliating foreign exploitation. Zhou expanded his revolutionary vision in London, Paris, and Berlin from 1920 to 1924. At the age of twenty-six he returned to China. Enjoying the respect and trust of the Comintern, he was to assume a senior Communist leadership position. Driven by a vigorous spirit and radical zeal, he immediately plunged into the first wave of Chinese Communist revolution. Because of his outstanding leadership in organizing the armed struggles of the Guangzhou and Shanghai workers, he was elected to the Chinese Communist party (CCP) Politburo at the Fifth Party Congress (27 April–9 May 1927), assuming the positions of general secretary and minister of military affairs. In the latter capacity, he directed the famous Nanchang Revolt on 1 August 1927 and the fourth and fifth campaigns to resist the Kuomintang's (KMT) "surrounding and suppressing" attacks on the CCP central base in southern Jiangxi from December 1931 to August 1934.[4]

Nevertheless, Zhou soon found out that China's political situation was much more complicated than was suggested in his European readings of Marx on labor and capital. Following a radical or "leftist" line, he had encountered one setback after another in the armed struggles he directed. At this critical juncture, Mao's influence emerged. Unlike Zhou and many other senior CCP leaders, Mao never studied abroad. As a self-educated Communist, he understood Chinese history better than Marxist-Leninist theories and advocated adapting Marxist-Leninist theory to the realities of the Chinese situation. To him, a victorious Chinese Communist revolution could only be achieved through mobilization of Chinese peasants to undertake a guerrilla war. In Jiangxi, Zhou twice criticized Mao, who had long been perceived as a "pacifist," "rightist," and "narrow-minded nationalist." At the central Politburo meeting in early October 1932, Zhou pointed out that Mao's "passive waiting and retreating" strategy was "incorrect." However, he admired Mao's ability and experience in military affairs and insisted that Mao not be deprived of his military command; but he could not stop the passing of a resolution to remove Mao from the position of the general political commissar of the First Front Army, the back-bone of the CCP Red Army.[5] Given his reluctant denunciation of Mao, the radical-dominated central leadership forced Mao to give up the command of the Red Army in January 1934.

Mao's principles of "fighting no battle we are not sure of winning" and "fighting no battle unprepared" (*buda wu bawu zhi zhan* and *buda wu zhunbei zhi zhan*) were soon proven correct. In early October 1934, having failed to resist the

KMT's fifth "surrounding and suppressing" campaign, the seriously decimated Red Army began a general retreat or Long March to northwest China. On 1 January 1935, the CCP Politburo held an enlarged meeting at Zunyi in Guizhou province. Convinced that Mao would be the only person to salvage the Red Army, Zhou along with Wang Jiaxiang and Zhu De proposed to restore Mao's military leadership. Faced with the desperate situation, the participants discredited the "radicals" and restored Mao's command.[6] This paved the way toward a fundamental change of Zhou's role in the CCP central leadership.

Zhou further demonstrated his endorsement of Mao's leadership, when, during the Long March, he strongly resisted a motion by the First Group Army Commander Lin Biao at the May 1935 Politburo meeting that Mao should be removed. While rebuking Lin's "mistaken" ideas, Zhou highly praised Mao's mobile warfare strategy.[7] As the threat of Japanese expansion in China grew in the early 1930s, Zhou firmly supported Mao's decision to change the CCP revolutionary aim into "a long-term national revolutionary war." He not only completely accepted Mao's "united front" strategy, but was fully devoted to the efforts of seeking alliances with the Nationalist authorities and other noncommunist elements during the anti-Japanese war.[8] When the CCP, under Mao's leadership, greatly expanded its power and influence, Zhou subordinated himself to Mao without the slightest reservation. Addressing the office staff of the CCP central leadership on 2 August 1943, he was "completely convinced that Mao Zedong's leadership of the Chinese revolution is correct." Zhou explained:

> With Comrade Mao Zedong's leadership and instructions, our Party has been so guaranteed that [we] never lost direction or took a wrong road especially at many critical and important junctures in the past years.
>
> It has been never clearer that all those who have discredited Comrade Mao Zedong's leadership and ideas are now proven to be deadly wrong.
>
> The 22-year history of our Party testifies that Comrade Mao Zedong's ideas have developed into a Chinese-style Marxist-Leninist or Chinese Communist revolutionary line throughout the Party's entire history.

Concluding that "Comrade Mao Zedong's direction is the only direction of the Chinese Communist Party and Comrade Mao Zedong's line is the only line of the Chinese Bolshevization,"[9] Zhou called upon the entire party to follow Mao's leadership unconditionally.

Zhou's full-hearted support of Mao defined their working relationship for the most of Zhou's career. Regarding himself as Mao's assistant, Zhou adhered to the practice that Mao would always make strategies (*fangzhen*) and policies (*zhengce*) while he himself would be responsible for execution and operations; he would at most exercise "guiding leadership" (*zhidao*), make operational principles or set standards for taking actions (*xingdong zhunze*). His diligent, careful, and intelligent way of handling details won him recognition as Mao's most capable aide in dealing with external and internal relations.

Within this operational context, Zhou assumed many of the burdens of the CCP's external affairs in the 1930s and 1940s. It is important to note that during this period Zhou completely adopted Mao's pragmatism. He echoed Mao's attack on "dogmatism" in the party and urged other CCP leaders to maintain a flexible attitude to achieve a new understanding of domestic and international politics. He regarded Mao's teaching of "seeking the truth from the facts" as the most helpful guide in decision-making and policy execution. More important, he defended the utility of "diplomatic method" (*waijiao shouduan*) as the means of discriminating between, and extracting concessions from, competing powers in order to secure Chinese Communist influence and power.[10]

Zhou Enlai worked very closely with Mao in the construction of a united front. In order to turn the KMT Northeast China Army against the Japanese in Manchuria instead of attacking the CCP base in northern Shanxi, Mao instructed Zhou to travel secretly to the Northeast Army headquarters in early April 1936. He did his best to persuade General Zhang Xueliang to cease assaulting the CCP forces and exacerbated Zhang's strong dislike of Chiang Kai-shek's "non-resistance" policy toward the Japanese expansion. This was the very first success of Zhou's personal diplomacy.[11] Zhou also successfully carried Mao's orders to resolve the Xian incident of 12 December. After kidnapping Chiang Kai-shek and forcing him to resist Japan, Northeast Army Commander in Chief Zhang cabled Mao for advice. Believing that supporting a peaceful solution of the crisis would win the CCP both domestic and international endorsement, Mao sent Zhou to Zhang's headquarters in Xian. Once again Zhou did not disappoint Mao. Although caught in a very complicated situation, he was finally able to work out a peaceful solution of the incident.[12]

During the CCP-KMT coalition to resist Japan from 1936 to 1945, Zhou carried the united front strategy further by winning domestic and international support for the CCP. As the CCP's chief representative in the nationalist government, he spent more than seven years at Chongqing. The major objective of his mission, Mao directed, was to protect the CCP interests in the new coalition government. Relatively free of Mao's direct control, he brought his experience of struggle and cooperation to the exigencies of the negotiating table with the KMT. Meanwhile, he established a wide contact with the West. A major target of his diplomacy was Americans in China. Many U.S. officials were impressed by Zhou's personality and analytical approach. Through contact with Zhou, Washington's "China hands" felt that the CCP, in contrast to the KMT, had evidently achieved a remarkably realistic understanding of Chinese political, economic, military, and social conditions. Some believed that "the CCP leaders were realists because they were Chinese."[13]

Mao supported Zhou's diplomatic overtures, which he conceived as "the beginning of our participation in the unified international anti-fascist front and the start of our diplomatic work." The CCP chairman welcomed the dispatch of the U.S. Army Observation or the Dixie Mission to Yanan, then CCP's headquarters, in June 1944.[14] More important, the arrival of Franklin D. Roosevelt's special envoy to China, General Patrick J. Hurley, in early September drew the immediate attention of Mao and Zhou. They sent CCP senior leaders Dong Biwu and Lin Boqu to ask Hurley for Washington's support. The general flew to Yanan on 7 November and met with Mao and Zhou to discuss the American role in bringing about a postwar coalition government in China and supporting the CCP's active participation and made several promises including a guarantee of the CCP's legitimate political status and equal treatment of the CCP forces. Encouraged by this prospect, Mao decided to send Zhou to Chongqing again for detailed negotiations with the Nationalist government.[15]

Before Zhou could reach any substantial agreement with the Nationalists, however, the Japanese surrendered in early August 1945. Chiang cabled the CCP headquarters on 11 August inviting Mao to "talk with him face to face on all the important issues." Encouraged by the situation, Mao stated at the enlarged CCP Politburo meeting on 23 August that peace was possible and an early outbreak of nationwide civil war was avoidable. Proposing a new line of "peace, democracy and unity," the CCP chairman decided to accept Chiang's invitation and even told other CCP leaders that "we should be prepared to make concessions." At first, Zhou was worried about Mao's personal security and proposed to undertake some preliminary talks to probe Chiang's real intentions. When Mao persisted, Zhou gave in and assumed full responsibility for preparation and operation of the negotiations.

Mao flew to Chongqing on 27 August and did not return until 11 October. Hoping that Washington would be able to curtail the Nationalists, the CCP leadership took the negotiations very seriously. To show their sincerity, Mao and Zhou were prepared to concede eight of the CCP-controlled "liberated areas" in central China, and to accept a national military reorganization that would have left the CCP with ten divisions and the KMT with fifty. During these tedious negotiations, Mao and Zhou cooperated perfectly; while Mao made all the principal decisions, Zhou took care of every detail.[16]

The two parties, however, could not agree on how to form a coalition government in China; neither could George C. Marshall's mediation in late 1945 and early 1946 prevent the country from another civil war. Chiang exercised his military option by attacking the CCP "liberated areas" in central China in late June 1946, eastern China in mid-July, and northern China in October. Under Mao's instructions, Zhou Enlai stayed in Nanjing, the capital of the Nationalist government, until November 1947, when the CCP-KMT talks on a peaceful settlement in postwar China were officially ended. Zhou was practising Mao's strategy of "fight, fight, talk, talk" [da da tan tan]. He believed in Mao's judgment that the CCP would gain political advantages through the continued negotiations. He later explained that his continuous presence at the negotiation table, although there was little to negotiate, would prove to the world that the KMT, not the CCP, was fully responsible for starting the war.[17] Mao confirmed in his talks with Zhou and Liu Shaoqi in Yanan on 21 November that the negotiations in Nanjing achieved the goal of "educating the [Chinese] people. . . . Only by making it clear who is responsible for spoiling [the peace] and going to war shall we not lose the popular support and sympathy."[18]

Zhou, like Mao, was good at "uniting a high degree of flexibility with a high degree of principle." It is true that he talked a lot about principle in terms of Marxist-Leninist theories, but his major concern was his party's political interest, which, through the 1930s and 1940s, consisted of the survival, expansion, and ultimately acquisition of power in China. Zhou's early diplomatic experience showed his prodigious talent in exercising flexibility under seemingly tortuous and intractable political circumstances. This talent was soon to become legendary.

Leaving all the decision-making to Mao, Zhou became completely devoted to policy execution. He was often cited as the author of *wuqin,* meaning "get busy with the five parts of one's body." During his negotiations with the KMT, he urged his aides to "get busy with their eyes in reading Mao's writing and the Party's directives; to exercise their ears in collecting opinions and information; to use their tongues in disseminating Party policies; to use their hands to take notes and write personal observations and proposals; and to use their legs to go out and make contacts rather than waiting at home."[19]

More important, many of the Chinese philosophic teachings that Mao praised highly became important guides to Zhou's diplomatic actions: "Do as one sees fit, or *jianji xinqshi,*" "Gain mastery by striking only after the enemy has struck, or *hou fa zhi ren,*" "Return as good as one receives, or *lai er buwang fei li ye,*" "Give tit for tat, or *zhenfeng xiang dui,*" "Retreat ninety li so as to give way to another to avoid a conflict, or *tuibi san she,*" "Shoot the arrow right at the target, or *you di fang shi,*" "Where there is precaution, there is no danger, or *youbei wu huan,*" and "seek common ground while reserving differences, or *qiutong cun yi.*"[20]

II

When the Chinese Communists founded the People's Republic in October 1949, the focus of their political concerns was on China's national security. It is evident that the CCP leadership defined the country's security interests in terms of national autonomy, independence, and power status. These certainly became the primary aims of New China's foreign policies.

How diplomacy would best serve the purpose of national security was closely related to the CCP leadership's understanding of the Cold War international relations. Its perception of immediate and potential threat, in particular, played a crucial role. Even before the nationwide victory over the KMT, Mao and Zhou began to treat the United States as China's most dangerous enemy.

Ever since the CCP-KMT fighting had resumed shortly after the Second World War, Mao Zedong had consistently worried that the United States might directly involve its armed forces in assisting Chiang Kai-shek against the CCP forces. They were especially concerned that U.S. Marines in China might occupy some coastal cities such as Yantai, Qingdao, and Shanghai and use them as military bases for further action.[21]

The CCP leadership's concern over American military intervention became intensified as the Chinese Communists approached nationwide victory. "The Current Situation and the Party's Tasks in 1949," a CCP Central Committee document drafted by Mao, dated 8 January 1949, asserted that Chiang's rule was doomed unless the United States rescued him. Mao warned that it was likely that (a) "the US would send armed forces to occupy some of China's coastal cities and directly fight against us;" (b) the U.S. might "throw in their own forces to blockade China's ports;" and (c) even if America did not intervene directly, it would surely try to undermine the CCP's rule through "sabotage, espionage and political infiltration." Since "the imperialists will not change their [aggressive] nature in the near future," Mao urged, "the entire Party must take [these] possibilities into full consideration" throughout the year. Zhou Enlai echoed Mao's concern by pointing out at the same time that "there exists a possibility of U.S. military intervention, but we are fully prepared."[22]

Why was Mao so concerned about U.S. military intervention? How did his perception of this threat evolve? First, Mao's theoretical concept of the "intermediate zone," which grew out of his understanding of the Cold War, played a crucial role. The crux of his theory was that, although the United States and the Soviet Union were confronting each other, they were separated by "a vast zone which includes many capitalist, colonial and semi-colonial countries in Europe, Asia, and Africa." Mao calculated that "before the U.S. reactionaries have subjugated these countries, an attack on the Soviet Union is out of the question."[23] The Cold War period was thus one in which the United States would fight for this vast intermediate zone, and general war with the USSR would come only after the United States had consolidated its hold on countries within the zone. Since any anti-American or pro-Soviet forces within the zone would weaken, in one way or another, American capabilities for fighting the Russians, the United States would have to wipe out those forces first.[24] To Zhou, Mao's "intermediate zone" argument made sense; indeed like other CCP leaders, he regarded the Truman Doctrine, the Marshall Plan, the rehabilitation of Germany and Japan, the U.S. occupation of South Korea, and especially, American military assistance to the KMT and the stationing of U.S. Marines along China's coast as strong evidence of a U.S. struggle for this "intermediate zone."[25]

Both Mao and Zhou distrusted America's China policy. They had not had much experience in dealing with the Americans, but from those few occasions where contacts had taken place, they had felt cheated and humiliated. The

Marshall Mission of 1946, they first believed, had been intended to mediate China's civil war impartially, but the outcome was a rude awakening to the CCP. "The policy of the U.S. Government," Mao asserted, "is to use the so-called mediation as a smoke screen for strengthening Chiang in every way and suppressing the democratic forces in China through Chiang Kai-shek's policy of slaughter so as to reduce China virtually into a US colony." Moreover, in light of continuing American military and economic aid to the KMT, the CCP leadership concluded that to expect America to maintain neutrality was only wishful thinking. U.S. aid, Mao pointed out, would certainly "enable him [Chiang] to wage a civil war on an unprecedented scale."[26] Based on these considerations, Mao quickly jumped to a regretful conclusion: "[Since] it was the first time for us dealing with the U.S. imperialists, we did not have much experience. As a result, we were taken in. Now with the experience we won't be cheated again." Zhou Enlai also asserted in late 1946 that after dealing with Marshall, "we have found out that the real intention of the U.S. is to dominate China alone." In his view, Washington could "no longer play the game of fraud [*pian ju*]."[27]

Indeed, the activities of U.S. military forces in China worried the CCP leaders. "U.S. naval, ground and air forces," Mao claimed in August 1949, "did participate in the war in China." Mao believed that "all these were acts of direct participation in the war, even though they fell short of an open declaration of war and were not large in scale, and although the principal method of U.S. aggression was the large supply of money, munitions and advisers to help Chiang Kai-shek fight the civil war."[28] Especially when the CCP intelligence noticed "the sudden increase of [U.S.] marine activities in Qingdao" in the late spring of 1949, the CCP leader felt the imminent threat of American military action.[29]

Even in late 1949, when immediate U.S. armed intervention seemed to be less likely, the Chinese Communist leaders were stressing U.S. long-term—if not short-term—hostility. Mao explained in August that the absence of direct intervention by the United States "was determined by the objective situation in China and the rest of the world, and not by any lack of desire on the part of the Truman-Marshall group, the ruling clique of American imperialism, to launch direct aggression against China." In his view, the United States had placed China as a top priority in its efforts to control the "intermediate zone," because, "China, the center of gravity in Asia, is a large country with a population of 475 million; [thus] by seizing China, the United States would possess all of Asia. With its Asian front consolidated, American imperialism could concentrate its forces on attacking Europe."[30]

It was within this context that Zhou directed the practice of New China's diplomacy. He designed the very first diplomatic principle of "sweeping the house clean before inviting guests." This encompassed several specific policies. He insisted on refusing to recognize the official status of Western countries' embassies and consulates. In response to CCP local authorities' request on how to deal with Western diplomats in big cities, Zhou directed on 10 November 1948 that "since Britain, America, and France and other [Western] countries have not recognized our government, we will not recognize their diplomats and merely treat them as ordinary foreign residents."[31] He explained on 23 November that "non-recognition of American, British, and French diplomatic relations with the KMT government will put us in a positive diplomatic position." However, nonrecognition "does not mean no diplomatic relations with these countries for ever, nor does it mean non-differentiated treatment of these countries." Zhou did present one condition: any foreign government that wanted to form diplomatic relations with the CCP government must sever its relations with the Nationalists on Taiwan.[32]

Zhou's stand was what Mao wanted. On 19 January 1949, Mao approved Zhou's draft of "Directives on Diplomatic Work [*guan yu waijiao gongzuo zhishi*]," which made it clear that the CCP government "will not be bound by any humiliating rules and traditions in diplomacy." In general terms, the document stressed that Western countries' "privileges in China must be abolished and the independence and liberation of the Chinese nation must be realized." The document, however, directed that "we must deal with each individual case realistically and carefully; after all, we must appropriately handle the relationship between principle and flexibility in diplomacy so as to stand firm and adaptable."[33] Zhou confirmed in April that there would be no compromise of China's "independence," but he stated: "We are willing to cooperate with all countries that treat us as equals." China would welcome foreign aid, but only on the basis of an acceptance of China's national equality.[34]

"Sweeping the house clean," however, did not mean to drive away all the foreigners by force; and Zhou was especially concerned about not provoking the West, especially the United States. The 19 January directives on diplomatic work made it clear that local CCP authorities should not confiscate any foreign properties, including investment, trade, customs, press, or radio stations.[35] Between March and May, the central leadership issued a number of instructions to the local authorities that appropriate measures must be taken to avoid provoking the foreigners in China. On 25 April Zhou Enlai instructed Deng Xiaoping in particular that the lives and property of the Americans and the British in Nanjing "shall be by all means protected; we should see to it that these foreigners will not be humiliated, and we need not register them." As a Chinese historian has noted, "The idea was to avoid a direct confrontation with western powers and not to give them any pretext to interfere in China's internal affairs."[36]

Nevertheless, the widely felt anti-American sentiment in China and CCP's strong sense of insecurity made Zhou's cautious diplomacy wishful thinking. The Angus Ward incident of late 1949 became the first diplomatic conflict between the United States and Communist China. Ward was the American consul general at Shenyang, known in the West as Mukden. The CCP forces seized control of that city in October 1948, but Ward and his staff remained and continued to exercise their diplomatic function. A conflict emerged in November when Ward refused to hand over a radio transmitter as requested by the CCP Shenyang Military Control Commission. The local authorities took it as intentional disregard of their authority and open violation of Chinese sovereignty. They then decided to place Ward and his staff under house arrest on 20 November. The United States responded vigorously, strongly condemning the Chinese Communists as being "illiterate in the language of international diplomacy and decency." Angered by the American criticism, on 24 October 1949, the Shenyang authorities had Ward and four other consulate employees arrested for "violating Chinese security." Soon afterward Secretary of State Dean Acheson announced at a news conference that the United States would not consider diplomatic recognition of Communist China until Ward and his staff were released.[37]

The Chinese Communists responded more vigorously. In January 1950, the Military Control Commission of Beijing requisitioned the former military barracks of the American diplomatic compound in Beijing. Mao explicitly supported these actions. "I endorse . . . the requisition of foreign military barracks," he cabled another CCP senior leader Liu Shaoqi on 13 January; "we have to prepare for the United States to withdraw all consulates in China." He further explained: "It is extremely favorable to us that the United States withdraw its diplomats"[38] Rather than trying to avoid the escalation of this conflict, Zhou went along with Mao's hard line. Like Mao, he had no faith in immediate diplomatic relations between the United States and the PRC, and he was busy with negotiations with other countries including the USSR, Bulgaria, Romania, Hungary, Korea, Czechoslovakia, Poland, Outer Mongolia, East Germany, Albania, Burma, India, Vietnam, Denmark, Sweden, Switzerland, and Indonesia. Moreover, Zhou was frustrated when his requests for representation in the United Nations Security Council and membership in the UN General Assembly were blocked by the Americans. Washington not only barred the PRC from taking China's UN seats but, with its Cold War propaganda, focused international attention on the CCP's lack of genuine responsibility in the international community.[39]

Beijing could no longer play an "equal distance" game between the Soviet Union and the United States, even if Zhou had wanted to. Mao had already considered seeking military alliances to encounter the perceived American threat. From late 1949 to early 1950, however, the CCP chairman remained concerned about China's coastal security. He, in particular, feared that the United States might initiate a military conflict either from the Taiwan Strait, French Indochina, or the Korean Peninsula. Unfortunately, available materials are insufficient to recount how the leadership had come to such a conclusion. Yet, as Zhou Enlai revealed later, he shared Mao's belief that "it is almost inevitable [for China] to confront American imperialists from any one of these three areas," and actually considered which one "would be the best battlefield for us to fight [should military conflict break out]."[40] Shortly after the People's Republic was founded in October 1949, the Beijing authorities began disposing troops for coastal defense. In a telegram of 31 October to the Fourth Field Army Commander Lin Biao, Mao pointed out that "the focuses of our national defense are on three areas, centering around Tianjin [north China], Shanghai [east China] and Guangzhou [south China]."[41]

Mao calculated that his new regime would have to identify itself with the Soviet Union. His reasoning was simple: it could never be a mistake to ally with an enemy's enemy. Yet such an alliance, to the CCP leaders, would not be easy to achieve, given the history of Moscow's suspicious attitudes toward Mao's CCP. The CCP leadership knew that Stalin was particularly worried that Mao could become a Chinese Tito.[42] In an attempt to eliminate Stalin's distrust, Mao decided in May 1949 to dispatch a secret mission of top leaders to Moscow. Liu Shaoqi and Zhou Enlai, assisted by Wang Jiaxiang, were in charge of the preparations. Two months later, Liu led a five-person delegation to the Soviet Union. In Moscow, Liu had four meetings with Stalin and his top aides. At these meetings, Liu reported back, Stalin apologized for not offering as much help to the Chinese Communists as they should have but instead "hampering your revolution to some extent . . . because we did not know China's situation very well." The Kremlin leader expressed his willingness to help.[43]

It seemed that Stalin had changed his attitude toward the CCP. However, the Chinese leaders felt that he remained ambivalent about how to "help" the Chinese Communist government. Under this circumstance, Mao chose to move decisively. On the eve of the party's twenty-eighth anniversary (30 June 1949) the CCP chairman made his "lean-to-one-side" speech, and released it to the public the next day. For the first time, the CCP proclaimed that it would only lean to the side of the Soviet Union and not to any other.[44]

In early September 1949, Mao decided to visit Moscow and deal with Stalin face to face. However, he was not sure how much the Kremlin would do to meet CCP demands, and how his visit should proceed. In order to probe Stalin's intentions, Mao in a 9 November telegram to Wang Jiaxiang, the CCP representative in Moscow, instructed Wang to ask Stalin if he would want Zhou Enlai to accompany Mao to Moscow. Mao was hopeful that if Stalin let Zhou, CCP's best negotiator, come with him, that would indicate the Kremlin's sincere intention to provide substantial assistance to the CCP.[45] But because of Mao's subtlety or Moscow's reluctance, Mao left for Russia in early December without Zhou Enlai.

Even though Mao departed with a sense of uncertainty, he met a splendidly cordial welcome in Moscow. Upon his arrival, Stalin and almost all of the Soviet top leaders held a state banquet in Mao's honor. The Soviet leader once again apologized, this time in front of the East European communist leaders, for the mistakes that he had made and told Mao, "Now you are a winner, and as a winner, no criticism should be imposed on you." Then Stalin asked what the Soviet Union could do to help the Chinese comrades, inquiring what Mao really wanted from him. Interestingly, Mao could have given a truly blunt answer, but did not. "For this trip," Mao replied, "we expect to create something that should not only look nice but taste delicious." Mao actually meant to achieve a substantial Sino-Soviet relationship rather than a postured friendship, but his Chinese-style metaphor was so ambiguous that when it was translated into Russian, no one understood what it really meant. Shi Zhe, the main translator present, recalled that Lavrenti Beria even could not help laughing at it. When Stalin asked again, Mao replied: "I want to send for Premier Zhou Enlai." Stalin felt even more puzzled: "If we can't decide on what to achieve, why do we need to have Zhou here? What for?"[46]

For the next two weeks Mao remained patient but still ambivalent with regard to his real intentions in Moscow. Stalin, however, repeatedly urged Mao to express exactly what he wanted. But Mao still beat around the bush, insisting that Zhou Enlai should come to Moscow and that Zhou should present the whole package.[47] The Kremlin appeared to have run out of patience. On the day after Mao's comments to Tass, Anastas I. Mikoyan and Viacheslav Molotov informed him that Stalin had authorized them to talk with Mao about the possible results of the visit. Beginning to see the Soviets' sincerity, Mao listed three alternative outcomes:

(1) We may sign a friendship and military alliance treaty as well as new economic cooperation agreements, [so as] to settle the Sino-Soviet relationship on the basis of these new treaties. In this case, Zhou must come to Moscow. (2) We may sign an informal agreement to set some general guide-lines for the future Sino-Soviet relationship. (3). We may just sign a communique to confirm the friendly relationship between the two countries. Therefore in cases (2) and (3) Zhou need not come.

When Molotov and Mikoyan responded, "we will go along with the first [option]," Mao immediately cabled Beijing, instructing Zhou to leave China for Moscow in five days. But Mao still did not seem to be in a hurry because he specifically wanted Zhou to "take the train not airplane."[48]

Once the Soviets agreed to work on a military alliance treaty, Mao wanted Zhou to have serious and comprehensive negotiations over future Sino-Soviet relationships. He instructed on 5 January: "We must have a full preparation for the coming negotiations [with the Soviets], which should include all the issues that our Central Committee is concerned with. Now that it is going to be a formal negotiation, we should proceed with it in all possible ways, and make all our positions clear [to the Soviets]."[49]

Zhou was now faced with a difficult task. When the negotiations started, the Soviets did not seem to be willing to accommodate all the Chinese demands. The biggest difficulty for Zhou was to obtain an explicit commitment from the

Soviet Union to assist China if it was invaded, an objective he regarded as the key to the military alliance treaty. The first Soviet-drafted version of the treaty stated that if one side was invaded by a third party, the other side "is supposed to [*de yi*] to offer assistance." For Zhou, this was not enough because it did not make clear the binding liability of a military alliance. He bent all his efforts to get a clarified version out of the Russians: "is supposed to" was to become "must devote all its efforts [*jiejin quanli*]." It took quite a time for Zhou and his aides to bargain over this with the Russians. Zhou was quite happy with the final text, though, which provided: "If one side is attacked by a third party, the other side must devote all its efforts to provide military and other assistance."[50]

Zhou did an excellent job, as he had to, because Mao had explicitly set the task for him: "The basic spirit of the alliance treaty should be to prevent the possibility of Japan and its ally [the United States] invading China," and "once the treaty is concluded we will be able to use it as a big political asset to deal with imperialist countries in the world."[51] Zhou also expressed relief in his departure address that the alliance treaty had "made the Chinese people feel that they are no longer isolated; to the contrary, they are much stronger now than ever before."[52]

III

Beijing also attempted to secure smaller allies. Concerned about the increase of American influence in Indochina, the CCP leaders offered political and material support to Ho Chi Minh's Vietnamese Communist movement. Zhou Enlai played a major role in establishing this relationship. As early as the spring of 1947, long-wave radio communications had been set up between CCP headquarters in Shanxi and Ho's Indochinese Communist party. Through this connection, Zhou Enlai maintained frequent contact with Ho, particularly "sharing information and discussing important issues concerning both nations' liberation movement."[53] Ho sent a personal representative to Beijing in November 1949 with a letter addressed to Zhou Enlai. Ho hoped to convince the Chinese leaders that a Communist victory in China would provide a great opportunity for the Vietnamese to overthrow the French. "In order to seize the opportunity of defeating the opponent," he stressed, "we are desperate for your help."[54]

Mao wanted Zhou to establish a close tie with the Vietnamese Communists. In early January 1950, Ho sent his foreign minister, Huang Minh Chian, to Beijing, seeking the PRC's diplomatic recognition and the establishment of formal relations. When Mao was informed of the Vietnamese request in Moscow, he instructed Zhou Enlai on 17 January that "recognition and diplomatic relationship should be granted to the Viet Minh Government at once."[55] At the same time, he drafted an official reply to Ho Chi Minh, in which he stressed that "the establishment of our diplomatic relationship . . . will serve the purpose of strengthening the friendship and cooperation of our two nations in our common course." On 19 January Beijing publicly proclaimed its willingness to establish diplomatic relations with the Viet Minh, thus becoming the first country to do so. Moreover, in order to find more supporters for the Viet Minh, Mao appealed to Moscow and East European communist countries to grant diplomatic recognition.[56]

Zhou Enlai received Ho Chi Minh in Beijing in mid-January of 1950. During his secret visit, Ho talked a great deal about what the Chinese could do to advance his cause. Zhou clearly understood what Ho was seeking, but hesitated to make any commitment without Mao's endorsement. He then suggested that Ho should go to Moscow and talk directly with Mao and Stalin. Ho Chi Minh immediately contacted the Soviet ambassador to Beijing, requesting that arrangements be made for his visit. With Moscow's approval late that month, Ho went to Moscow with Zhou, who was sent there by Mao to negotiate the details of a Sino-Soviet alliance treaty.[57]

In Moscow, Ho Chi Minh met with Mao and Stalin several times to discuss how the Soviet Union and the People's Republic of China could assist the Vietnamese revolution.[58] In one meeting, Stalin explicitly explained to Ho that he was "sincerely concerned about the Vietnamese struggle," but he preferred that "the Chinese comrades take over the principal responsibility of supporting and supplying the Vietnamese people." Mao agreed to give some thought to how that could be appropriately accomplished when he returned to Beijing.[59] In order to secure Mao's promise, Ho Chi Minh addressed a memorandum to Zhou Enlai, outlining the main points of the Stalin-Mao-Ho talks and asking Zhou to verify them. He also reminded Zhou that he would wait for him in Beijing to discuss detailed arrangements for China's military assistance.[60]

Both Mao and Zhou wanted to enhance the security of the Sino-Vietnamese border, too. Viet Minh domination of that area would diminish the potential threat to the border security before it became real. Zhou had made it clear to Ho Chi Minh in early 1950 that the Vietnamese struggle against the French was a part of the Chinese struggle against imperialism in Asia, for if Vietnam remained controlled by the imperialists, China's southern border would be exposed to a direct threat.[61] Mao also telegraphed Ho in May, stressing the importance of "the eternal unity of the peoples of the two countries, China and Vietnam, and their common effort in the cause of peace in Asia."[62] Clearly from then on, if not earlier, a central objective in Beijing's diplomacy toward Indochina was to secure a buffer zone on the Sino-Vietnamese border and prevent Indochina from falling under permanent French or American control. The PRC, indeed, became the main supplier of military materials to the Viet Minh during this period.

To diminish American influence in the Korean Peninsula, Beijing could have offered the same type of assistance to the North Korean Communists as to the Viet Minh. The PRC leaders obviously understood the importance of Communist control in that peninsula, and they had no problem working with Kim Il-sung and his followers, who, along with more than ninety thousand soldiers of Korean origin, had fought the Japanese side by side with the Chinese Communists in Northeast China throughout World War II. However, since Moscow had been giving North Korea military assistance since late 1948, the Chinese stayed uninvolved in Kim's preparations to attack South Korea.

There is no doubt that Zhou placed good diplomatic relations with Pyongyang as one his priorities. Shortly after the inauguration of the PRC, the two governments officially recognized each other and established formal diplomatic relations. Zhou selected his longtime aide Ni Zhiliang as Beijing's first ambassador to North Korea. As head of the government, Zhou also signed three agreements with North Korea on 7 January 1950, which established Sino-North Korean postal services, telephone, and telegraphic lines. The premier also had the People's Central Government Commission ratify these agreements on 1 February 1950.[63] Zhou accepted Kim's request in January 1950 that all the officers and soldiers of Korean origin be turned back to North Korea. After a few rounds of negotiation, he endorsed a Sino-North Korean agreement, which stated that "altogether 14,000 soldiers of Korean origin would be returned to North Korea along with their weapons and equipment."[64]

At the outbreak of the Korean War in the summer of 1950, Washington's announcement of its intention to intervene in Korea and the sending of the Seventh Fleet into the Taiwan Strait highly alarmed the Beijing authorities. It seemed that United States policy toward East Asia was just as they had predicted. On 27 June Mao authorized Zhou to proclaim that the objective of the Truman administration's decision to intervene in the Taiwan Strait was to prevent the People's Republic from liberating Taiwan and was an act of aggression that the CCP leadership had fully anticipated. Zhou asserted that the United States had instigated Syngman Rhee to initiate the Korean conflict as a prelude to an American grand strategy of invading Korea, Taiwan, Vietnam, and the Philippines.[65] To cope with the sudden crisis, Zhou employed diplomacy first. Condemning the disposition of the Seventh Fleet in the Taiwan Strait as a "violation of the United Nations Charter," he urged the UN secretary general that the PRC should now be involved in UN deliberations on the Korean crisis. On August 26, Zhou revealed to the public that a "legally appointed" Chinese delegation to the UN General Assembly was ready to leave for New York. He also cabled the UN Security Council on 30 August complaining of American violations of Manchurian airspace and insisting that the council should invite his government to the discussions of a Korean settlement.[66]

Under Mao's instructions, Zhou directed the preparations for possible military involvement in the Korean War. On 7 July he chaired a national security meeting involving the PRC's high-rank military commanders, at which they for the most part discussed how to strengthen the Sino-Korean border defense, and how to prepare for possible United States military expansion. They all agreed that "it is necessary to 'prepare an umbrella before it rains [*wei yu choumu*],' " and suggested the immediate establishment of an individual Northeast Border Defense Command and deployment of the Fourth Field Army's Thirteenth Army Group, which had been stationed in Henan, Guangdong, and Hunan provinces as strategic reserves of national defense, into Northeast China. Zhou specified that all the troops designated as the Northeast Border Defense Army (NBDA) should be positioned along the Sino-Korean border by the end of July, the People's Liberation Army (PLA) General Logistics Department should begin movement of arms and supplies right away, and the PLA's General Political Department should lay out detailed plans for political mobilization.[67] Three days later, Zhou Enlai called another national security meeting to discuss the details of force deployment in Northeast China. Zhou in particular stressed the urgency of military preparations and directed that the Fourth Field Army and Northeast Military Commands should fully support the formation and dispositions of the Northeast Border Defense Army. He then talked in detail with the commanders about specific issues such as places of force deployment, establishment of supply depots, and air defense measures.[68]

Zhou also arranged to acquire first-hand battlefield information through diplomatic channels. As early as 28 June 1950, Acting Chief of Staff Nie Rongzhen proposed to Zhou that China should dispatch a military observation mission to Korea. Nie suggested that Chai Chengwen, a senior CCP intelligence staff member and then the director of military intelligence of the Southwest Military Command, be named to head this group. Zhou approved Nie's proposal and personally arranged for Chai's new assignment. On the night of 30 June, together with Deputy Foreign Minister Zhang Hanfu and First Deputy Minister of Military Intelligence Liu Zhijian, Zhou gave Chai instructions in person. "Now that war has broken out in Korea," he explained, "the United States Truman Government not only has sent troops to Korea and the Taiwan Strait, but also plans an overall [force] deployment for further aggression in Asia. They [American leaders] want to link the Korean issue with that of Taiwan and other parts of the Far East. Therefore, we need to send some people [to Korea] to maintain a direct contact with Comrade Kim Il-sung." However, Zhou did not like the idea of sending Chai as an independent Chinese military observer. It would be better, he instructed, "to place Chai's mission under the cover of China's embassy [to Pyongyang]." Zhou then wanted Zhang and Liu to assist Chai in organizing such a mission, which, he requested, should be in North Korea in a week.[69]

On the morning of 8 July, Zhou met with Chai's mission before they left for Pyongyang. He stressed that "we anticipate that, since the United States will muster more countries to send troops to Korea and, therefore, it is very difficult to prevent a prolonged war in Korea, a series of issues will emerge to complicate the overall situation [in the Far East]." Under this circumstance, Zhou directed that "your main task is to maintain close contact with the North Korean

Labor Party [leadership] and the North Korean People's Army [command], and send back information on any change of the war situation as quickly as possible."[70] China's military intelligence mission arrived in Pyongyang on 10 July. Shortly after, Kim Il-sung personally welcomed Chai and his aides. "At the outbreak of the war," Kim explained, "I requested Premier Zhou that China send army and division rank commanders to Korea. Finally, you are here." At Chai's request, Kim directed the establishment of a direct telephone line between his headquarters and Chai so that, Kim stressed, "you can contact me whenever you want."[71]

By late summer the Beijing authorities became increasingly worried about a possible United States/United Nations amphibious action in North Korea. Zhou called Chai Chengwen and the Chinese ambassador to Pyongyang, Ni Zhiliang, back to Beijing on 1 September. In his briefing, Chai pointed out that General Douglas MacArthur might prepare to launch an amphibious landing in North Korea. Zhou interrupted Chai by asking: "If a sudden change in the [Korean] situation requires us to participate in the war, what would be the difficulties that we will encounter?" Chai replied: "In my view, an immediate problem concerns transportation and [Korean language] interpreters. We could not guarantee railway [transportation], and highways [in Korea] are narrow and in poor condition. We could not acquire supplies [in North Korea] because there are no stocks of food and munitions there; and it is impossible for a large army to live on captured enemy supplies." Zhou took Chai's report very seriously and passed it to Mao and all the other CCP Politburo Standing Committee members.[72] When meeting Lee Sang-chok, Kim Il-sung's personal representative in Beijing, Mao stated that "the United States is a real tiger capable of eating human beings." Pointing at three sea ports, including Inchon, along Korea's western coast on a map, he stressed that "we ought to prepare for [the possibility] that American troops might take a circuitous route around the front lines and land at any one of these ports to strike at the rear of the Korean People's Army." Mao and Zhou urged Lee to report to Kim Il-sung and "begin military preparations for possible U.S. landing action immediately."[73]

Despite Beijing's warning, North Korea was not prepared for MacArthur's landing at Inchon on 15 September 1950. Shortly after the U.S./UN amphibious operations began, the North Korean Peoples Army (NKPA) fell into immediate disarray, and its offensive in South Korea soon collapsed. Beijing was now becoming increasingly worried about the drastic setback of the North Koreans. Minutes after receiving the news of the Inchon landing, Zhou Enlai directed the immediate dispatch of five more high-ranking PLA officers to North Korea. Their main task, Zhou specified in his meeting with these officers on 17 September, included "observing the general situation [in North Korea], inspecting Korea's topography, and preparing battlefield information."[74]

North Korea's resistance to the U.S./UN advance deteriorated in late September. More importantly, it appeared imminent that the U.S./UN forces would cross the thirty-eighth parallel. Without immediate Chinese military action, the North Koreans would soon be overrun. At midnight on 1 October, Kim Il-sung called an emergency meeting with Chinese Ambassador Ni Zhiliang in Pyongyang, asking Ni to pass his request to Zhou that the Chinese government should move the Thirteenth Army Group across the Yalu River within the next few days. In order to win more time for a Chinese military deployment, Kim told Ni that his troops would "fight with life and blood" to delay the enemy movement north.[75]

China's entry in the Korean War seemed almost certain by late September 1950. From a diplomatic standpoint, however, Zhou asserted that China would be in a better position to intervene if the U.S./UN forces crossed the thirty-eighth parallel and marched north toward the Sino-Korean border. On 22 September, a Ministry of Foreign Affairs spokesman issued an official statement that "we clearly reaffirm that we will always stand on the side of the Korean people—just as the Korean people have stood on our side during the past decades—resolutely to oppose the criminal acts of American imperialist aggression against Korea and their intrigues for expanding the war." On 24 and 27 September, Zhou twice cabled United Nations headquarters to protest the United States air intrusion over Andong. Appearing as *Renmin Ribao*'s headline news, Zhou's statement read: "The flames of war being extended by the United States are burning more fiercely. If the representatives of the majority of states attending the UN General Assembly should still be pliant to the manipulation of the United States and continue to play deaf and dumb to these crimes of aggression by the United States, they will not escape a share in the responsibility for lighting up the war-flames in the East."[76]

On 1 October, U.S./UN forces began crossing the thirty-eighth parallel. Twenty-four hours later, American ground troops were moving into North Korea en masse. It was on that day that Mao finally made up his mind on China's military intervention. "We have decided," he informed Stalin on 2 October, "to send troops into Korea in the name of the People's Volunteer Army, to fight the United States and its running dog, Syngman Rhee's forces, and to aid the Korean comrades." Mao explained to the Kremlin leader that "we believe that this is a necessary step because, should the Americans occupy the whole of Korea, the Korean revolutionary force would be completely destroyed and the American invaders would become more rampant; all of this would be detrimental to the entire East [Camp]."[77]

Zhou Enlai, however, insisted that China should issue a last-minute warning. He was cautious in wording the warning message, which, he thought, should not be too belligerent to lose the sympathy of the neutral countries. Describing how China would react to the continued American advance in North Korea, Zhou chose the Chinese verb *guan*. He then spent considerable time with his English translator, Pu Shouchang, discussing how to translate the word *appropriately*.[78] At 1:00 A.M., 3 October, Zhou called the Indian ambassador to

Beijing, K. M. Panikkar, to his office for an emergency meeting. "The American forces are endeavoring to cross the 38th parallel with the intention to expand the Korean conflict," he told Panikkar, "if they really want to do so, we will not sit still and do nothing. We surely will respond in an appropriate fashion [*women yao guan*]. Please inform your Prime Minister of our stance."[79]

In the meantime, Zhou wanted to secure a Soviet guarantee of military assistance to China before the Chinese forces undertook combat actions in Korea. On 8 October, accompanied by interpreter Shi Zhe and confidential secretary Kang Yimin, he flew to Moscow. Joined there by Lin Biao, Zhou went to see Stalin at the Kremlin leader's summer resort on the Black Sea. At the 9 October evening meeting with Zhou, Stalin stated that the USSR would provide supplies and dispatch Soviet air forces to protect Manchuria and the northern and eastern China coasts if China would send ground troops into North Korea. Zhou intended to drive a hard bargain. Rather than accepting Stalin's offer, he replied that China needed Soviet assistance to modernize its military and "is not yet ready to send forces [to Korea]." Disappointed at Zhou's response, Stalin requested that China allow the North Korean government and military to reorganize in Manchuria, and that, in return, the USSR would provide the Chinese with military aid. Without further bargaining Zhou went back to Moscow the next morning. A few hours after, he was surprised to receive a telegram from Mao that "now that majority of the Politburo members support the idea of dispatching troops into Korea right away, we have made a final decision [on military intervention in Korea]." This telegram placed Zhou in a very awkward position for asking for Soviet military support. This time the Kremlin leaders did not hesitate to reduce the amount of munitions and supplies they had previously promised. Zhou felt even more frustrated when Molotov informed him that the Soviet Air Force was "not yet ready to assist the Chinese military action in Korea."[80] Zhou Enlai tried his best to change Stalin's mind, and after three more days of negotiations, he secured Moscow's agreement to equip one hundred Chinese infantry divisions with leftover World War II military materials and augment China's coastal air defense with its air forces in the Far East.[81]

Zhou came back to Beijing with mixed feelings: disappointed, frustrated, and most of all worried. Only a year after the foundation of the New China, the CCP leadership was plunged into an international conflict that it had never prepared to fight and was fighting almost alone.

IV

China's involvement in the Korean War placed the new government in a very difficult situation. The already war-torn national economy had to be rebuilt, the party had to consolidate its political control over the mainland, and more important, the Chinese people had to be persuaded to fight a war on foreign soil. As premier, Zhou Enlai had clearly realized the need for a peaceful international environment, so as to further the process of economic restoration and political reorganization. However, this had never been easy. It took him another twenty years to accomplish this goal.

Zhou's first task was to achieve a cease-fire in Korea. It was fortunate that Mao had no intention to "liberate" the whole of Korea. Mao wanted first to restore Korea's physical status quo, meaning that there should be no American or South Korean troops north of the thirty-eighth parallel. "We will never agree to start an armistice negotiation," Mao explained in his 4 December instructions to Peng Dehuai, "unless the US imperialists withdraw back south of the 38th parallel." In the second place, he wanted to restore Korea's political status quo. Mao insisted that China would accept a final settlement of the war only when "the Korean people are allowed to elect their own government under UN supervision with as much Chinese and Soviet participation as possible." To achieve these objectives, Mao envisioned, the Chinese forces would "be prepared to fight for at least one or a few more years."[82]

After the Chinese forces secured a foothold around the thirty-eighth parallel, the PRC leaders began seriously to consider a peace settlement. On 3 June 1951, when Kim Il-sung arrived in Beijing, Mao and Zhou Enlai succeeded in persuading him to accept "the restoration of the 38th parallel [as a short-term political objective], and phased withdrawal of all foreign troops [from Korea] through negotiations and political settlement of Korea's future by peaceful means [as long-term goals]."[83] Under Mao and Zhou's instructions, CCP's senior leader Gao Gang and Kim Il-sung went to Moscow to report to Stalin in mid-June. Concerned with Korea's military situation, Stalin agreed that truce talks should begin as soon as possible. Stalin also went to considerable lengths to clarify with Kim and Gao the nature and format of the armistice negotiations, timetable for cease-fire, and the final peace settlements.[84]

When Soviet ambassador to the UN Malik announced on 23 June new proposals for cease-fire and armistice, Beijing was not surprised. Zhou Enlai responded by announcing on 1 July that China would send a delegation to Kaesong to talk with U.S./UN representatives on 10 July.[85] Zhou selected First Deputy Foreign Minister and CMC intelligence Director Li Kenong and Director of the Press Bureau of the Ministry of Foreign Affairs Qiao Guanhua, Zhou's best foreign affairs aides, to direct the talks behind the scenes. Beijing requested Peng to "arrange a special working resort for Li and Qiao which should be one or two kilometers away from where actual meetings take place" so that they could discreetly monitor the negotiations.[86] Before Li and Qiao left Beijing, Mao and Zhou instructed them to "work hard to produce positive outcomes."[87]

Mao, however, expected the cease-fire talks ultimately to reach a peace treaty. After the negotiations started on 10 July, he closely supervised the work of the Chinese team. Every night China's official negotiators Deng Hua and Xie

Fang would meet with Li and Qiao to brief them on the day's negotiations; Li and Qiao would report to Zhou Enlai, who would immediately relay the information to Mao. Mao's instructions would then go back through Zhou to Li and Qiao and then Deng and Xie.[88] Throughout the negotiations, Mao consistently maintained that the withdrawal of all foreign troops from Korea should be given top priority by the Chinese delegation. In his 11 July telegram to Li Kenong, Mao pointed out that "[we] must hold on to [our] position of having all [foreign] forces withdrawn." When the U.S./UN representatives refused to put this issue on the agenda for the armistice talks, Mao instructed the Chinese delegates to protest. "We have sufficient reason to put forward this position," he cabled Li on 17 July, "since all the foreign troops came to Korea to fight, not to visit, why is it that a cease-fire negotiation is only authorized to discuss cessation of hostilities and has no authority to talk about withdrawal of all the troops?" In his view, there was no reason to exclude this issue from the truce talks. He explicitly directed Li that "we must insist that these negotiations are authorized not only to discuss a cease-fire but to negotiate the withdrawal of [foreign] troops." Undoubtedly, what Mao expected was a peace negotiation that would settle the Korean conflict and not merely arrange a temporary armistice agreement. He made it very clear in editing a proposed response by Kim and Peng to the UN Commander, General Matthew Ridgway, that "all misunderstandings over minor issues should be avoided . . . [so as] to guarantee carrying out negotiations for a peace treaty [*heping tanpan*] smoothly."[89]

The truce talks, though, did not proceed as well as Mao expected. He came to believe that Washington was not yet ready to settle the Korean conflict peacefully. He instructed Peng on 26 July that the Chinese units should be "actively" preparing for military action because it was unclear "whether the enemy truly intends to talk about peace."[90] He also maintained that China should never accept a peace settlement under U.S./UN military pressure. On 14 November, Mao directed the Chinese negotiators that "we must apply flexible tactics [in negotiation], and never show any [sign] of anxiety to achieve peace." He explained that "although achieving peace now is in our favor, we should not be afraid of letting the war drag on."[91] In response to Li Kenong's report on a U.S./UN initiative to adjourn the negotiations, Mao agreed to quit the talks. "We are not afraid of letting the war continue," he explained, "[we] must be prepared for the possibility that [the conflict] will drag on for a considerable length of time before it is resolved. As long as we are not anxious to end the war, the enemy will be at wit's end."[92]

The Panmonjum negotiations dragged on interminably. The armistice talks were stalled primarily over the exchange of prisoners of war. Zhou Enlai found it difficult to convince Mao to take a conciliatory stand; moreover, Stalin stubbornly told the Chinese and North Koreans not to give in on the prisoner of war (POW) issue. In mid-August 1952, Zhou Enlai once again travelled to Moscow to confer with Stalin. Regarding the Korean truce talks, Stalin made it clear at his meeting with Zhou on August 21 that "it is right to press the United States to change its stand . . . [because] it is illegal for the United States not to repatriate POWs." The Kremlin leaders also stated: "If the enemy detains 30% of [Korean and Chinese] POWs, then we ought to hold 13% of the [U.S./UN] POWs [captured by us], so as to demonstrate that we do not believe that our POWs would refuse to return." By doing this, Stalin stressed, "the enemy will be compelled to change its position." During his talks with Kim Il-sung, Zhou, and Peng Dehuai on 1 September, Stalin again pointed out that "there is no need to accept the American proposal on the POW issue, which concerns our principles. We may detain either less than or the same number of POWs held by the enemy."[93]

The Chinese stood firm. Mao explained: "We will agree upon a cease-fire only when political and military situations are favorable to us. To accept the enemy's proposal under pressure means to sign a peace treaty under coercion [*Jie chengxia zhi meng*] which is detrimental to us." Because both sides were unwilling to compromise, the talks broke off indefinitely in October 1952. When the Chinese negotiators consulted Beijing in February 1953 on whether or not to resume the talks, Mao answered that "if we initiate resumption of the negotiation . . . it would make [our] opponents think that we are anxious to achieve a peace settlement that would render an impression of weakness." He argued that "my sense is that action is worse than inaction; [we] shall let the war continue until the United States is willing to make compromises."[94]

Zhou Enlai was finally able to break the log jam in March 1953. Stalin's death apparently removed a major roadblock of the Korean truce talks, while at the same time Mao shifted his attention from the Korean War to domestic politics, especially campaigns against dissidents. After another trip to Moscow to attend Stalin's funeral, Zhou issued a statement on 30 March designed to renew the deadlocked armistice negotiations. He showed a new spirit of compromise by agreeing to turn over prisoners of war who failed to declare themselves in favor of repatriation to a neutral nation supervisory commission for determination of their status.[95]

As the military conflict in Korea approached its end in the summer of 1953, Zhou prepared to change Beijing's belligerent foreign policy toward a more conciliatory diplomacy. Addressing a group of Chinese diplomats on 5 June, he asserted: "The major contradiction in today's world is that of peace or war. We advocate the resolution of all international disputes through peaceful negotiations. . . . We should practice peaceful co-existence and peaceful competition in [an international community of] different systems; this is now the focus of our [foreign] policy." This type of diplomacy was possible, he explained, "[because] the American war threats will widen the gap between the United States and the Western European countries and cause most of the nations in Asia, Middle East and North Africa to keep a distance from America. . . . [The people's] voice for peace will sound stronger and stronger."[96] Zhou first tried his conciliatory diplomacy to improve Sino-Indian relations. Meeting with an Indian delegation in Beijing on New Year's Eve of 1953, he pointed out that "we have already established several basic principles in Sino-Indian relations: they include mutual respect for territorial integrity and sovereignty, non-aggression, non-interference in each other's internal affairs, equality and mutual benefit, and peaceful co-existence."[97] These soon became Zhou's famous "five principles" of international relations.

Zhou's nonbelligerent diplomacy paid off at the Geneva Conference of 1954. In mid-February 1954, Soviet Foreign Minister Molotov cabled Zhou that the Berlin meeting of the Big Four foreign ministers—the USSR, the United States, Great Britain, and France—had agreed to include the Indochina issue on the agenda of the forthcoming Geneva Conference for a Korean settlement, which would include the PRC as an "invited" power.[98] With Mao's approval, Zhou immediately accepted the invitation and began a thorough preparation for the conference. In early March, Zhou supervised the drafting of the key document "Our Estimation of the Geneva Conference and Preliminary Instructions on Our Preparation." It pointed out that "the United States, France and Britain disagree with each other, especially on the Indochina issue, and they have great difficulty in reconciling their views"; the internal conflicts of the Western bloc could be further "exploited to our advantage." The instructions then directed that "our delegation at Geneva should take all possible initiatives and seize every chance to contact the British, the French, and the neutral [countries] . . . [so as] to make our views of a settlement and preference for peace known and understood by them." The document directed that the Chinese delegation should try hard to generate positive outcomes. To this end, "we should concentrate on the issues which contain no big differences of opinion and try to accomplish at least a tentative agreement on them. We shall not allow the conference to end without any result."[99]

Zhou was truly anxious to achieve a substantive result at Geneva. In early April he made a special trip to Moscow to consult the Soviet leaders on the upcoming talks. Both Khrushchev and Molotov expressed low expectations on the Geneva conference. Zhou, however, argued differently: "That China, [North] Korea, and Vietnam can jointly participate in this international conference is itself an unexpected event and is one of our [diplomatic] victories. It will be a bigger success if we can take this opportunity to express our positions and principles on all the issues and make explanations on certain questions so as to resolve some disputes." Since it was the first time that Beijing had taken part in such a conference, Zhou insisted that "the Chinese and Soviet [delegations] must keep close contact, so as to exchange opinions and information, rectify different stands, and support each other's actions." To show his sincerity, he asked Soviet Foreign Minister Molotov to teach the Chinese delegates "how to act appropriately on diplomatic occasions" before they went to Geneva.[100]

Zhou came to Geneva with a delegation of more than two hundred on 24

April. Two days after the conference started, he made his first speech, in which he claimed:

> The Chinese government and people have all along favored peace and opposed war. We have not invaded others, and we will not invade other countries. We respect the rights of the peoples of other countries to choose and to safeguard their own way of life and state system and to be free of foreign intervention; at the same time we would require that other countries adopt the same attitude toward us. [101]

Zhou could not have done better in reiterating his "five principles of peaceful co-existence"; but he had little control over the North Korea delegate, Nam Il, who kept blasting American "imperialism." Neither did the United States delegate, John Foster Dulles, give Zhou's conciliatory diplomacy much support. Even when there seemed to be hardly any chance for an agreement on Korea, however, Zhou insisted on "taking those views that are shared in common as a positive basis for moving forward in the talks, and at the same time in those areas where there was some disagreement, seeking a method for their solution."[102]

Zhou was determined to achieve a substantive agreement on the Indochina question. While he genuinely followed Molotov's lead in the Korean sessions, he was now ready to take a policy initiative of his own. When the news of the Viet Minh's success at Dienbienphu reached Geneva on 7 May, Zhou was greatly encouraged. He calculated that, after such a defeat, the French would no longer hesitate to accept a peaceful solution to the Indochina problem, and that the British would certainly lend their support. Without British and French cooperation, the United States would eventually have to accept peace terms in Indochina. [103]

Zhou's expectation was practically realized at Geneva by mid-June 1954. The new Mendès France government of France proclaimed that it would agree to restore peace in Indochina on two conditions: a temporary partition of Vietnam, and self-determination and neutralization of Laos and Cambodia under the supervision of an international control commission. British Foreign Minister Eden had actually initiated these proposals. Zhou undoubtedly liked the proposed settlement, but worried that the Viet Minh might not accept the conditions. To persuade the Vietnamese, Zhou flew back to China and met with Ho Chi Minh at Liuzhou, Guangxi province, on 3 July. He explained to Ho that the Viet Minh was now at the crossroads of either continuing to fight or accepting peace now, with the option of resuming the fight later. It would be wise, Zhou stressed, for Ho to cease hostilities with the French and consolidate control now, and look for other opportunities at a later date. "We should do our best to support the Mendès [France] Government," he said to Ho, "so that we can prevent the war-like elements in France from overthrowing [it]. This would be certainly beneficial to both of us." Ho took Zhou's advice and accepted the conditions. [104]

On his way back to Geneva, Zhou stopped at Moscow. Here he reached agreement with the Kremlin leaders that "if we rejected Mendès' proposal, the United States would seize the chance to replace the Mendès government with a more belligerent one. That would make the settlement of the Indochinese conflict even more difficult."[105] Zhou pushed his personal diplomacy further by flying to neutral Berne, Switzerland, on 23 June to meet the new prime minister of France. Zhou and Mendès France "had a frank exchange of views on the Indochina settlement and achieved a better understanding of each other's positions." Zhou personally, at Mendès France's request, undertook to persuade the Vietnamese to speed up the negotiations.[106] As a result of Zhou's efforts, the Chinese, Vietnamese and Soviet delegations jointly proclaimed their acceptance of the Mendès proposal. That paved the way for final signing of the Geneva Accords on Indochina on 21 July, providing for an immediate cease-fire in Indochina, a partition of Vietnam, and neutralization of Laos and Cambodia. This settlement satisfied the Chinese, since most of Vietnam was under the control of a friendly government and "no foreign forces or military bases or military alliance" would be placed in Laos and Cambodia.[107]

Zhou himself was very pleased with the result. On the way back to Beijing, his aides asked the premier to reflect on his Geneva experience. He commented:

(1). The solution of all international disputes can always be based on negotiation and consultation. As long as both sides have a good will and understand each other, no matter how complicated the issue is, there will be a path toward its solution.

(2). At a conference all the formal speeches and debates are read line by line from a prepared text [zhaoben xuanke], and speakers often indulge in exaggeration without substance for the purpose of either saving face or propagandizing. This is not aimed at resolving practical problems and can not do so.

(3). Activities after a formal meeting including private contacts provide an opportunity for participants to have a frank exchange of views, probe into each other's intentions, put one's cards on the table, negotiate and bargain and reach detailed agreements. These are the practical and fine methods used to resolve problems.

(4). To find effective solutions always requires mutual understanding, accommodating each other's needs, yielding to the other's reasonable demands, and showing consideration for each other's interests, so as to seek a common ground for an agreement. If neither side can agree on certain issues, they ought to be shelved for the time being. This is what compromise is all about. . . .

(5). When we deal with small and weak nations we must pay special attention to their face [mian zi]; in other words, we must never hurt their national pride. As a major power we should and could understand this.[108]

When his aides wholeheartedly congratulated him on his success, Zhou immediately warned them that "you must not brag about what we have achieved [at Geneva] and more important, you must never praise me when you are back home." At a Foreign Ministry ceremony party in Beijing, one of Zhou's aides proposed a toast to the premier's great leadership and remarkable achievement at Geneva. Zhou immediately cut him short and toasted: "Let us drink to Chairman Mao's leadership and health!"[109]

Zhou Enlai was keenly self-conscious about his subordination to Mao. Not long after, indeed, he found that he could hardly bring himself to submit to the chairman's increasingly radical foreign policies. It is important to note that Mao was getting over-optimistic about confronting the United States after Geneva. Reconfirming his thesis that "imperialism and all reactionaries are paper tigers," Mao believed that "tension diplomacy" or "limited belligerency" would be the best choice for China to win international prestige. Mao personally implemented his "tension diplomacy" by initiating the crises in the Taiwan Strait in 1954–1955 and 1958. The PLA's massive bombardments of the Kuomintang-held offshore islands, Jinmen (Quemoy) and Mazu (Matzu), Mao thought, would draw the focus of international attention on China and pressure Washington to bow to Beijing's demands. Sufficient evidence demonstrated that Zhou went along with hot-headed Mao even though the chairman was heading a very different and dangerous route that the cautious premier would not have taken by himself.[110]

Zhou clearly sensed Mao's dislike of his conciliatory foreign policy, especially toward the United States. In 1956 Mao had already considered having Marshall Chen Yi, one of the chairman's few close friends, replace Zhou as the foreign minister, and he made the change officially in February 1958. During his two private meetings with Chen in June, Mao revealed his discontent with what he regarded "a conservative foreign ministry," which had been so far run by Zhou. Mao specifically criticized the Foreign Ministry's "catering to Americans," and explicitly instructed Chen to rectify this "bureaucracy" by organizing a self-criticism campaign among the senior diplomats. Zhou did not protest but accepted Mao's criticism, and soon changed his tone about Beijing's foreign policy. He claimed at a Foreign Ministry meeting in 1958 that New China's diplomacy should aim "to consolidate socialism, fight against the United States, and bring down imperialism."[111]

A much graver and more devastating challenge to Zhou's conciliatory diplomacy came in the late 1960s. The premier and his foreign policy apparatus were swamped in the "red sea" of the Cultural Revolution. The Red Guards, who allegedly were responsible for propagandizing "Mao Zedong Thought" around the world and making China the "center of world revolution," found Zhou's "five principles of peaceful co-existence" at odds with Mao's revolutionary diplomatic lines. Zhou felt powerless to prevent the Red Guards in the Foreign Ministry from extending the Cultural Revolution to foreign countries, which, in his opinion, was "an active interference in the domestic politics of other states, particularly in those states which had large Overseas Chinese communities."[112] As the Cultural Revolution radicals stressed that foreign policy was a "secondary consideration in the minds of the social revolutionaries," China's diplomatic machine practically ceased to function. From 1967 to 1969 all its ambassadors abroad—except the ambassador to Egypt—were called back to take part in "the studies of the Cultural Revolution." Zhou was thus rendered powerless to take any major diplomatic initiatives.[113]

China's foreign policy, however, saw a turning point in 1969. Mao not only tried to improve the deteriorating relationship with the Soviet Union but, more important, began to consider normalizing the two-decade-long confrontational relationship with the United States. The CCP chairman was compelled to compromise by the worsening conditions that his rule encountered. The biggest challenge now came from the Soviets. The invasion of Czechoslovakia in August 1968 and the Brezhnev Doctrine with which Moscow justified its invasion forced Mao to take a realistic stand in the face of the Soviet threat. The two serious border clashes between the Red Army and the People's Liberation Army over Zhenbao (Chenpao) Island in the Ussuri in March 1969 proved that the military threat from the north was real. China had long concentrated on the American danger in the southeast—the Taiwan Strait and Indochina. As a military strategist Mao understood that China could not afford to fight a two-front war. Domestic difficulties also caused Mao to worry. While the Soviet Union had increased its military capability in East and Central Asia, China's armed forces were involved in a myriad of civil chores. Without regular training, and with most of the field armies underequipped and undermanned, the PLA's combat capability was declining and becoming unreliable. Moreover, the Cultural Revolution, which called for workers and peasants to leave their productive posts and join the political struggle, and the material assistance the Chinese gave to the Vietnamese to fight the Americans, pushed the nation's economy to the edge of total collapse.[114] Although Mao continued to call for preparations to fight against foreign aggressors, he was compelled to listen to Zhou's voice in these moments of danger from outside.

Zhou was now able to resort to diplomacy on the basis of peaceful coexistence. He wanted first to restore China's institutions of foreign policy. In the spring of 1969, he requested that the Foreign Ministry send all ambassadors back to their diplomatic posts. Talking to the would-be-ambassador to Hanoi, Wang Youping, on 4 June, the premier made it clear that it was time the senior diplomats undertook appropriate measures to diminish the Cultural Revolution's "abnormal influence" on diplomatic work.[115]

Zhou took his first major diplomatic initiative by meeting with Soviet leader Alexei Kosygin at the Beijing airport on 11 September 1969. Kosygin was passing through on his way home from the funeral of Ho Chi Minh. Zhou spent three and a half hours talking to the Soviet leader on how to resolve the Sino-Soviet conflict. While stressing that Beijing and Moscow could continue "the debate on ideological issues," he believed that state-to-state relations should be maintained on the basis of the five principles of peaceful coexistence. "We have no intention to fight a war [with your country]," Zhou explained; "we can't even take care of our own domestic problems, and why should we want to fight a war? Neither China nor the Soviet Union has any reason to fight a war over border disputes, because these disputes can be resolved fairly through peaceful negotiations." He therefore suggested signing a cease-fire agreement and then resuming the talks on the border conflict. He also proposed restoring the exchange of resident ambassadors, expanding trade activities, and improving transportation and communication between the two countries. Kosygin verbally agreed with Zhou, but took no immediate action after he returned to Moscow. Twice, on 18 September and 6 October, the Chinese premier wrote to Kosygin urging him to act upon their conversation.[116] The Sino-Soviet tension was finally relaxed when the shooting stopped, border talks were reopened, ambassadors were exchanged, and normal trade was resumed.

Zhou Enlai was anxious to take on a bigger diplomatic initiative. In early 1969, he perceived some changes in the Sino-American relationship after Richard Nixon was inaugurated as president. Zhou immediately directed the Foreign Ministry to "strengthen the observation and analysis of American policy trends so as to find out about America's strategic intentions and exploit possibilities of coming into contact with [*jiechu de keneng*] the United States."[117] Therefore, whenever he received reports on the shifts in Washington's rhetoric regarding China, no matter how subtle or minor, Zhou immediately sent them to Mao. Sometimes he would visit Mao in order to analyze these changes together with the chairman. By constantly feeding Mao with information on the positive attitude of the Nixon administration toward China, Zhou intended to make sure that Mao would consistently be on his side. Slowly but surely, Zhou's initiative became Mao's decision.[118]

Zhou was largely responsible for the overture to normalize the relations between the PRC and the United States. After more than three years of diplomatic activity, he finally got to shake hands with President Nixon in Beijing on 21 February 1972. This special moment started a new chapter in Sino-American relations. Many have written both convincingly and vividly about how Beijing and Washington dealt with each other and endeavored to melt the diplomatic iceberg.[119] One can hardly add anything new to the literature until more official documents become available on both sides.

It is true that Zhou made a remarkable contribution to the eventual Sino-American rapprochement. His intelligence, diligence, subtlety, flexibility, and personality became a legacy in PRC diplomacy. However, his role should not be overestimated. New materials have explicitly disclosed that Zhou worked very closely with Mao on policy-making and execution. He never took a step without either consulting Mao or securing Mao's endorsement. It is interesting to note that Zhou would merely regard himself as "Chairman Mao's good student and long trusted aide," and nothing more.

V

In China, Zhou Enlai is still well respected as a "fine" leader for his political performance and leadership style. On 27 June 1981, the Chinese Communist party publicized a resolution on party history that explicitly criticized Mao's poor political judgment during the Cultural Revolution, and pointed out that Zhou "found himself in an extremely difficult situation throughout the 'Cultural Revolution' . . . but still managed to minimize the damage caused by the lunatic ultra-left."[120] However, there has yet to be a posthumous reappraisal of how Zhou managed to cope with the difficult situation in which PRC's diplomacy operated.

Zhou had never had the freedom to pursue his foreign policy goals. There can be little doubt that, as an imperious and despotic leader, Mao exerted strong control over party and government policy-making. Zhou showed so much deference to Mao that he was practically responsible for the creation of Mao's personality cult. In retrospect, the CCP chairman frequently misperceived external threats such as the United States in the 1950s and 1960s and the USSR in the late 1960s and early 1970s and misjudged the international aspect of such conflicts as those in Korea, the Taiwan Strait, and Indochina. Zhou followed every policy line of Mao. There has been no indication that he had ever challenged Mao's "tension diplomacy" or "short-term belligerency," which were clearly at odds with his conciliatory diplomacy. Indeed, Zhou was as much to blame as his "beloved master" for the implementation of these policies.

Zhou was an astute, well-traveled observer, but did not escape the fate of many other prime ministers or *chengxiang* in traditional China. Centuries of a rigid hierarchy of power have nurtured a strong sense of subordination among the Chinese officials. The Confucian traditions of "gentleman behavior or *junzi,*" no matter how much the Chinese Communists tried to discredit them, have reasserted themselves again and again in Chinese politics. Within this political context, Zhou could hardly find much freedom in executing his domestic and foreign policies. There is, however, no evidence that he had ever wanted to act on his own.

Notes

1. Qian Qichen, "Seriously Study Zhou Enlai's Diplomatic Thoughts and Practices," in *Yan Jiu Zhou Enlai: Waijiao Sixiang yu Shijian* (Study Zhou Enlai: Diplomatic Thought and Practices), ed. Division of Diplomatic History, Ministry of Foreign Affairs (Beijing, 1989), 1.

2. Nikita S. Khrushchev, *Khrushchev Remembers* (Boston, 1970), 372.

3. Shi Zhe, *Zai Lishi Juren Shenbian: Shi Zhe Huiyilu* (Working with historical giants: Shi Zhe memoirs) (Beijing, 1991), 565.

4. *Zhou Enlai Zhuan: 1898–1949* (Biography of Zhou Enlai: 1898–1949) (Beijing, 1989), 221–41. Also see Ronald C. Keith, *The Diplomacy of Zhou Enlai* (London, 1989), 1.

5. Ren Bishi, Xiang Ying, and Deng Fa, "Explanations on the Disputes at the Ningdu Meeting," 12 Nov. 1932, cited in *Zhou Enlai Zhuan*, 255–57; telegram, Zhou Enlai to the CCP Central Politburo, 12 Nov. 1932, *Zhou Enlai Zhuan*, 255; Zhu De, Wang Jiaxiang, and Peng Dehuai, "Order of the First Front Army," 12 Oct. 1932, *Zhou Enlai Zhuan*, 256.

6. Manuscript, Chen Yun, "Outlines on the Zunyi Meeting Resolutions," February 1935, cited in *Zhou Enlai Zhuan*, 283.

7. *Zhou Enlai Zhuan*, 286.

8. Ibid., 304–11.

9. Ibid., 553–54.

10. Keith, "The Diplomacy of Zhou Enlai," 14.

11. *Zhou Enlai Zhuan*, 306–10.

12. *Zhou Enlai Nianpu: 1898–1949* (Chronicle of Zhou Enlai: 1898–1949) (Beijing, 1989), 332–42.

13. Keith, "The Diplomacy of Zhou Enlai," 15. Also see *Zhou Enlai Zhuan*, 417, 490–92.

14. Telegram, Mao to Zhou, December 1941, *Zhou Enlai Zhuan*, 541.

15. *Zhou Enlai Zhuan*, 564–65, 570–73.

16. *Zhou Enlai Nianpu*, 615–18; *Zhou Enlai Zhuan*, 591–605.

17. *Zhou Enlai Zhuan*, 609–37.

18. Ibid., 662–63.

19. Keith, "The Diplomacy of Zhou Enlai," 5.

20. Yao Zhongming, Yang Qinghua, "Basic Characteristics and Influence of Zhou Enlai's General Diplomacy," in *Yan Jiu Zhou Enlai*, 46–47.

21. *Zhongguo Renmin Jiefangjun Liushinian Dashi Ji* (The chronicle of important events in PLA's sixty-year history], ed. Historical Research Division, Chinese Academy of Military Science (Beijing, 1988), 344.

22. CCP Central Committee document, drafted by Mao Zedong, "Current Situation and Our Tasks in 1949," 8 Jan. 1949. The complete text is printed in *Wenxian Yu Yanjiu* (Manuscripts and research) 10 (October 1984): 1–3. Zhou Enlai, "Report on Current Situation," 16 Jan. 1949, *Zhou Enlai Nianpu*, 808.

23. Mao Zedong, "Talks with the American Correspondent Anna Louise Strong," August 1946, in *Selected Works of Mao Tse-tung* (Peking, 1977), 4:99. Also see Lu Dingyi, "The Explanation of Several Basic Questions Concerning Post–World War II International Relations," *Jiefang Ribao* (Liberation daily), 4 Jan. 1947, 1. (Lu was a senior CCP official in charge of political propaganda, and the article was drafted by Mao himself.)

24. Mao, "Talks with the American Correspondent Anna Louise Strong," August 1946, *Selected Works of Mao*, 4:99.

25. Lu Dingyi, "Explanations of Several Basic Questions," 1. Also see telegram, the CCP Central Committee to Liu Ningyi, March 21, 1948, cited in *Zhou Enlai Nianpu*, 767.

26. Mao Zedong, "The Truths about US 'Mediation' and the Future Civil War in China," 29 Sept. 1946, *Selected Works of Mao,* 4:109.

27. Mao's comment is cited in He Di, "The Development of the CCP Policy Toward the US, 1945–1949," *Lishi Yanjiu* (Historical studies) 3 (June 1987): 17–18.

28. Mao Zedong, "Farewell, Leighton Stuart," 18 Aug. 1949, *Selected Works of Mao,* 4:434. As early as 1946, Zhou Enlai had pointed out that "to support Chiang Kai-shek, the U.S. has in fact stationed its troops [in China] and provided ammunition and financial assistance [to Chiang]," Minutes of Zhou-Stuart Talks, 6 Aug. 1946, *Zhou Enlai Nianpu,* 685.

29. He Di, "Development of the CCP Policy," 21.

30. Mao Zedong, "Farewell, Leighton Stuart," 18 Aug. 1949, *Selected Works of Mao,* 4:433; "Cast Away Illusions, Prepare for Struggle," 14 Aug. 1949, *Selected Works of Mao,* 4:428.

31. Telegram, Zhou to each CCP branch, 10 Nov. 1948, *Zhou Enlai Nianpu,* 796.

32. Telegram, Zhou to Lin Biao and Luo Ronghuan, *Zhou Enlai Zhuan,* 739–40.

33. CCP document, "Directives on Diplomatic Work," 19 Jan. 1949, *Zhou Enlai Nianpu,* 809.

34. Cited in Keith, "Diplomacy of Zhou Enlai," 39.

35. CCP Document, "Directives on Diplomatic Work," 19 Jan. 1949, *Zhou Enlai Nianpu,* 809.

36. Telegram, Zhou to the General Front Command Commission, 25 Apr. 1949, *Zhou Enlai Nianpu,* 824. Chen Xiaolu, "China's US Policy, 1949–1955," in *Sino-American Relations, 1945–1955: A Joint Reassessment of a Critical Decade,* ed. Harry Harding and Yuan Ming (Wilmington, Del., 1989), 186.

37. Chen Jian, "China's Road to the Korean War: A Critical Study of the Origins of Sino-American Confrontation, 1949–1950" (Ph.D. diss., Southern Illinois University, 1990), 64–82.

38. Ibid., 77.

39. Keith, "Diplomacy of Zhou Enlai," 35–36.

40. Zhou Enlai's address to the Korean veterans, 17 Feb. 1958, cited in Yao Xu, "A Wise Decision to Resist America and Aid Korea," *Dangshi Yanjiu Ziliao* (Research and materials of the CCP history), 24 Oct. 1980, 7.

41. Telegrams, Mao to Liu Shaoqi, 13 and 17 Jan. 1950, *Jianguo Yilai Mao Zedong Wengao* (Mao's manuscripts since the founding of the People's Republic of China) (Beijing, 1987), 1:235, 241.

42. Steven Goldstein, "Communist Chinese Perceptions, 1945–1950," in *Uncertain Years: Chinese-American Relations, 1947–1950,* ed. Dorothy Borg and Waldo Heinrichs (New York, 1980), 253.

43. *Shi Zhe Huiyilu,* 406–15.

44. Mao Zedong, "On the People's Democratic Dictatorship," *Renmin Ribao,* July 1, 1949, 1.

45. Telegram, Mao to Wang Jiaxiang, 9 Nov. 1949, *Mao Zedong Wengao,* 1:131.

46. *Shi Zhe Huiyilu,* 436–37.

47. Ibid., 14.

48. Telegram, Mao to the CCP Central Committee, "On Zhou's Participation in Moscow Negotiations," 2 and 3 January 1950, *Mao Zedong Wengao,* 1:211.

49. Telegram, Mao to the CCP Central Committee, January 5, 1950, *Mao Zedong Wengao,* 1:215.

50. Wu Xiuquan, *Zai Waijiaobu Banian* (My eight years in the Ministry of Foreign Affairs, January 1950–October 1958) (Beijing, 1983), 8–9.

51. Telegram, Mao to the CCP Central Committee, 2 Jan. 1950, *Mao Zedong Wengao,* 1:213.

52. *Zhonghua Renmin Gongheguo Duiwai Guanxi Wenjian Ji, 1949–1950* (Collected documents of foreign relations of the PRC) (Beijing, 1957), 1:81.

53. Zhang Yisheng, "The Revolutionary Friendship Between Premier Zhou and Chairman Ho," *Yindu Zhina Yanjiu* (Indochinese Studies) 3 (March 1981): 14.

54. Ho's letter is cited in Huang Zhen, *Hu Zhiming Yu Zhongguo* (Ho Chi Minh and China) (Beijing, 1987), 123–24.

55. Telegram, Mao to Liu Shaoqi, "On Our Reply to The Viet Minh Government," 17 Jan. 1950, *Mao Zedong Wengao,* 1:238–39.

56. Mao Zedong's reply to the Viet Minh, 19 Jan. 1950, *Renmin Ribao,* 19 Jan. 1950, 1; telegram, Mao and Zhou Enlai to Liu Shaoqi, 1 Feb. 1950, *Mao Zedong Wengao,* 1:254. They told Liu that the Soviet Union had agreed to recognize the Viet Minh, and that Mao had already sent his request to the embassies of East European countries to Moscow. Mao stated that "I am so glad to see that the Viet Minh will join the anti-imperialist and democratic big family."

57. *Mao Zedong Wengao,* 1:124–25.

58. Wu, *Zai Waijiaobu Banian,* 13.

59. Hoang Van Hoan, *Changhai Yishu: Huang Wenhuan Geming Huiyilu* (A drop in the ocean: Hoang Van Hoan's revolutionary reminiscences) (Beijing, 1987), 259.

60. Huang, *Hu Zhiming Yu Zhongguo,* 125.

61. Ibid., 126.

62. Telegram, Mao to Ho Chi Minh, 20 May 1950, *Renmin Ribao,* 20 May 1950, 1. Also see *Xinhua Yuebao* 3, no. 2 (June 16, 1950): 290.

63. Huang Daoxia, ed. *Zhonghua Renmin Gonghoguo Sishi Nian Dashi Ji: 1949–1989* (The chronicle of important events in PRC's forty-year history) (Beijing, 1989), 6.

64. Nie Rongzhen, *Nie Rongzhen Huiyilu* (Nie Rongzhen Memoirs) (Beijing, 1986), 748.

65. Premier Zhou Enlai's Proclamation, 28 June 1950, *Renmin Ribao,* 28 June 1950, 1.

66. *Dangdai Zhongguo Waijiao* (China Today: Diplomacy) (Beijing, 1987), 124.

67. Nie Rongzhen to Mao, 7 July 1950, *Mao Zedong Wengao,* 1:428, n. 2; also see Qi Dexue, *Chaoxian Zhanzheng Juece Neimu* (Inside stories of decision makings in the Korean War) (Shenyang: Liaoning University Press, 1991), 30.

68. Du Ping, *Zai zhiyuanjun Zhongbu* (My Years at the CPV Headquarters) (Beijing, 1989), p. 14. Minutes of this meeting have as yet to be released.

69. Chai Chengwen, *Banmendian Tanpan* (Panmumjom negotiations) (Beijing, 1989), 35–37.

70. Ibid., 39–40.

71. Ibid., 41–45.

72. Ibid., 77–78.

73. Sun Baosheng, "Mao Zedong Had Predicted the US/UN Landing Attack in Inchon," *Junshi Shilin* (Studies of Military History) 5 (1990): 13.

74. Chai, *Banmendian Tanpan,* 79.

75. Ibid., 80.

76. A Statement by Ministry of Foreign Affairs, 22 Sept. 1950, *Renmin Ribao,* 23 Sept. 1950, 1. Also see Allen S. Whiting, *China Crosses the Yalu* (New York, 1960), 104–9.

77. Telegram, Mao to Stalin, "On Our Decision to Dispatch Troops to Fight in Korea," 2 Oct. 1950, *Mao Zedong Wengao,* 1:539–41.

78. Division of Diplomatic History, Ministry of Foreign Affairs, ed., *Xinzhongguo Waijiao Fengyun* (State of Affairs of New China's Diplomacy) (Beijing, 1990), 97.

79. Minutes of Zhou-Panikkar meeting, 1:00 A.M., 3 Oct. 1950, Chai, *Banmendian Tanpan,* 81.

80. Kang Yimin's recollections, cited in Qi Dexue, *Chaoxian Zhanzheng Juece Neimu,* 62–63; *Shi Zhe Huiyilu,* 495–97.

81. *Shi Zhe Huiyilu,* 499–502.

82. Telegram, Mao to Peng, 4 Dec. 1950, cited in *Zhongguo Renmin Zhiyuanjun Kangmei Yuanchao Zhan Shi* (Combat history of the CPVs in the war to resist America and aid Korea) (Beijing, 1989), 76–77.

83. Chai, *Banmendian Tanpan,* p. 125. Also see Qi Dexue, *Chaoxian Zhanzheng Juece Neimu,* 177.

84. *Shi Zhe Huiyilu,* 508.

85. Editorial, 25 June 1951, *Renmin Ribao,* 1; CCP Central Committee, "Instructions on Issues Related to Korean Cease-Fire Negotiation," 3 July 1951, cited in Qi Dexue, *Chaoxian Zhanzheng Juece Neimu,* 188.

86. Telegram, Mao to Peng and Kim Il-sung, 25 June 1951, Qi Dexue, *Chaoxian Zhanzheng Juece Neimu,* 187; Telegram Mao to Peng and Kim Il-sung, 2 July 1951, *Mao Zedong Wengao,* 2:379–80.

87. Chai, *Banmendian Tanpan,* 129–30.

88. Telegram, Mao to Li Kenong, 9 July 1951, *Mao Zedong Wengao,* 2:390–91; telegram, Mao to Li Kenong, 12 July 1951, *Mao Zedong Wengao,* 2:405; telegram, Mao to Li Kenong, 1:45 A.M., 14 July 1951, *Mao Zedong Wengao,* 2:409; Mao to Li Kenong, 10:00 A.M., 14 July 1951, *Mao Zedong Wengao,* 2:412–13; Mao to Li Kenong, 11:00 A.M., 14 July 1951, *Mao Zedong Wengao,* 2:414; and Mao to Li Kenong, 6:00 P.M., 14 July 1951, *Mao Zedong Wengao,* 2:415.

89. Telegram, Mao to Li Kenong, 7:00 P.M., 11 July 1951, *Mao Zedong Wengao,* 2:392; Mao to Li Kenong, 17 July 1951, *Mao Zedong Wengao,* 2:422; Mao to Li Kenong, 1:00 P.M., 14 July 1951, *Mao Zedong Wengao,* 2:415.

90. Telegram, Mao to Peng Dehuai, 26 July 1951, *Mao Zedong Wengao,* 2:426.

91. The Central Military Commission instruction, 14 Nov. 1951, cited in Xu Yan, *Diyici Jiaoliang* (The first encounter) (Beijing, 1990), 277.

92. Telegram, Mao to Li Kenong, 28 Dec. 1951, *Mao Zedong Wengao,* 2:642–43.

93. *Shi Zhe Huiyilu,* 510–12.

94. Telegram, Mao to Li Kenong, 14 July 1952, Xu Yan, *Diyici Jiaoliang* 285; telegram, Li Kenong, Deng Hua, Xie Fang to Mao, August [undated] 1952, cited in Qi Dexue, *Chaoxian Zhanzheng Juece Neimu,* 217; Li, Deng, and Xie to Mao, 22 Aug. 1952, *Chaoxian Zhanzheng Juece Neimu,* 217–18; Mao to the Chinese delegation at Panmumjom, 6 Feb. 1953, *Chaoxian Zhanzheng Juece Neimu,* 288.

95. Keith, "Diplomacy of Zhou Enlai," 57.

96. *Zhou Enlai Waijiao Wenxuan* (Selected works of Zhou on diplomacy) (Beijing, 1990), 62.

97. Ibid., 63.

98. *Dangdai Zhongguo Waijiao,* 64–65.

99. Huang, *Ho Chin Minh yu Zhongguo,* 139.

100. *Shi Zhe Huiyilu,* 539–41.

101. Cited in Keith, "The Diplomacy of Zhou Enlai," 62.

102. Ibid., 66.

103. Wang Bingnan, *Zhongmei Huitan Jiunian Huigu* (Nine years of the Sino-American ambassadorial talks) (Beijing, 1985), 4.

104. Ibid., 5; also see Huang, *Hu Zhiming Yu Zhongguo,* 139–41.

105. *Dangdai Zhongguo Waijiao,* 66–67.

106. *Shi Zhe Huiyilu,* 556; also see Keith, "Diplomacy of Zhou Enlai," 75.

107. Wang, *Zhongmei Huitan Jiunian Huigu,* 6.

108. *Shi Zhe Huiyilu,* 563–64.

109. Ibid., 565.

110. Zhang Shu Guang, *Deterrence and Strategic Culture: Chinese-American Confrontation of 1949–1958,* (Ithaca, N.Y., 1992), chap. 7 and 8.

111. Chen Xiaolu, "Chen Yi and China's Diplomacy," unpublished paper, 4.

112. Keith, "Diplomacy of Zhou Enlai," 150–41.

113. Liao Xinwen, "The Feeling Hidden in the Mind of a Senior Diplomat," *Renmin Ribao—Haiwaiban* [People's daily—overseas edition], 8 Jan. 1992, 2.

114. Li Ke and Hao Shenzhang, *Wenhua Dageming zhong de Renmin Jiefangjun* (The People's Liberation Army in the Cultural Revolution) (Beijing, 1989), 225–41.

115. Liao, "The Feeling Hidden in the Mind of A Senior Diplomat," 2.

116. Gong Huiping, "The Meeting of Zhou Enlai and Kosygin at the Beijing Airport and Its Indications," in *Yanjiu Zhou Enlai,* 170–75; Letter, Zhou to Kosygin, 18 Sept. 1969, *Zhou Enlai Waijiao Wenxuan,* 462–64.

117. Wang Li and Qiu Shengyun, "Zhou Enlai and the Process of Opening the Door to Sino-American Relations," in *Yanjiu Zhou Enlai,* 203.

118. Ibid., 203–4.

119. Excellent English language books include Henry A. Kissinger, *White House Years* (Boston, 1979), 684–787; John W. Garver, *China's Decision for Rapprochement with the United States, 1968–1971* (Boulder, 1982); Dick Wilson, *Zhou Enlai: A Biography* (New York, 1984); and Keith, "Diplomacy of Zhou Enlai," 181–209. A good Chinese language book is Qian Jiang, *Pingpang Waijiao* (Table tennis diplomacy) (Beijing, 1988).

120. Cited from Keith, "Diplomacy of Zhou Enlai," 209.

13

NEHRU AND THE DIPLOMACY OF NONALIGNMENT

Rena Fonseca

Long years ago, we made a tryst with destiny, and now the time
comes when we shall redeem our pledge. . . . At the stroke of
the midnight hour, when the world sleeps, India will awake to
life and freedom. A moment comes, which comes but rarely in
history, when we step out from the old to the new, when an
age ends, and when the soul of a nation, long suppressed,
finds utterance. . . .

The achievement we celebrate today is but a step, an opening of
opportunity, to the greater triumphs and achievements that await
us. Are we brave enough and wise enough to grasp this
opportunity and accept the challenge of the future?

. . . We have . . . to work, and work hard, to give reality to our
dreams. Those dreams are for India, but they are also for the
world, for all the nations and peoples are too closely knit together
today for any one of them to imagine that it can live apart. Peace
has been said to be indivisible; so is freedom, so is prosperity
now, and so also is disaster in this one world that can no longer
be split into isolated fragments.

This is no time for petty and destructive criticism, no time for ill
will and blaming others. We have to build the noble mansion of
free India where all her children may dwell.[1]

WITH THESE WORDS, on 15 August 1947, a slight man in a white
tunic addressed the Indian Constituent Assembly. Jawaharlal Nehru
stood at a dramatic crossroads: after centuries of colonial rule, India
was independent. But despite the stirring words, Nehru's voice was tired.[2]
Later, he confessed that he was haunted by a sense of inner failure at this
moment of greatest triumph. Even as he delivered his historic midnight address
to the Constituent Assembly, his mind was filled with images of his beloved city
of Lahore in flames, another victim of the unfolding horror of partition. While
the seemingly endless butchery continued to engulf the country's northwest

frontier, staggering problems of poverty and communal strife loomed in the rest of India.

India was the first major developing country to gain independence from a colonial power in this century. The means had been as revolutionary as the end; Gandhi's nonviolent independence struggle, unique in the annals of modern history, had caught the imagination of the world. Both the character and the success of the Indian national movement served as an example for other colonized Asian and African countries, which were poised to join the great shifts in power that would follow the Second World War.

The independence of India marked a death as well as a birth. It was the beginning of the end for an empire on which the sun had not set for two hundred years. The ravages of the Second World War, the rise to power of a Labour government in London, and the weakened state of Europe's economies, made it merely a matter of time before other colonies followed India in declaring their independence. A structural upheaval was imminent that was every bit as significant as the collapse of the Hapsburg and Romanov empires after the First World War, or the dissolution of the Soviet Union and the Eastern Bloc in our own time. After the long humiliations of occupation and colonization, hundreds of millions of former colonial subjects would soon embark on the delicate business of giving reality to their dreams, and of establishing new relationships with their erstwhile rulers—this time as equals.

I

To millions of ordinary Indians, Nehru is affectionately remembered as *Chacha* Nehru (Uncle Nehru). He was endowed with the name during his intimate partnership with Gandhi—correspondingly known as *Bapu* (Father)—during the struggle for independence, and the name stuck during his long tenure as India's first prime minister.[3]

The memory of Nehru in the West is more complicated than in India. During the mid-fifties, the eminent journalist Harold Isaacs, interviewing prominent Americans for their views on India and China, found that virtually all of his interviewees had formed a strong personal impression of Nehru, ranging from the deeply admiring to the harshly critical. Indeed, Nehru had come to be so closely identified with India that he seemed the very personification of modern India's strengths and weaknesses.

"Like Gandhi, though for different reasons," Isaacs observed, "Nehru commands enormous and sometimes adoring admiration, as a leader, an intellectual, a sensitive, complex, gifted and even tragic man. Nehru may symbolize the conscience of the West for its past role in Asia; it is not easy to justify a history in which such a man could be so long imprisoned or held to be inferior. But he has no saintly aura about him. Many also see him as vain, arrogant, unwise, naive or even plain foolish. . . . It is one measure of [his] impact that reactions to Nehru among Americans are so numerous, so strong, so varied, and often so downright personal."[4]

In the crucial independence year, 1947, Herbert Rosinski, a German military historian, visited New Delhi as a senior adviser to the Indian Defense Ministry. Rosinski had the benefit of two extended conversations with Nehru, covering a great sweep of subjects—the state of the world, the future of Asia, the problems of underdevelopment, the differing temperaments of Indians and Germans, the importance of seapower in history, and above all the specter of another world war. On his return each evening, Rosinski recorded his impressions in a series of letters to his wife, subsequently collected in an unpublished document entitled "Conversations with Nehru."

"Conversations" provides a rare and fascinating glimpse into Nehru's personality, through the eyes of an unusually meticulous, sensitive observer. Conversing with the prime minister, Rosinski reported, was "a very strenuous exercise".[5]

> Nehru is shorter than one expects from the pictures, and seems somewhat older. His face . . . is tired. His features tell of the tension that weighs upon him. The complexion is unexpectedly dark, almost a light bronze.
>
> But all these externals are completely eclipsed by the overwhelming animation (*Lebendigkeit*) that is his basic characteristic. It's a quite unusual kind of animation, full of contradictions. . . .
>
> His interest, when aroused . . . is of an intensity difficult to describe. He goes right to the innermost heart of every question, sets it in the broadest context, and pursues questions that interest him over a considerable period of time. On the other hand, he breaks off just as abruptly when he is dissatisfied with an answer or doesn't like the trend of the conversation. . . .
>
> But all these sharply arresting traits—the penetrating intensity of his mind and interest, his dictatorial manner of conducting a conversation, his nervous leaping from one topic to another—are outweighed and transfigured by the infinite humanity (*Menschlichkeit*) that is his other basic characteristic. . . . Behind all the trenchancy of judgement and expression, and all the onesidedness, one has the sense of a quite unique humanity, one that has completely transcended the bitterness of his past experiences and really does contemplate the great political questions from an elevated human vantage point. . . .
>
> The impression was overwhelming, and the strain no less so."[6]

Jawaharlal Nehru was born in 1889, into a family of Kashmiri Brahmins in the city of Allahabad. His father Motilal had a flourishing legal practice, and a generous household "sheltering a large family of cousins and near relations, after the manner of Hindu families."[7] Despite this setting, Jawaharlal by his own admission had a rather lonely childhood, for he was much younger than the rest and so "was left a great deal to my own fancies and solitary games." He also listened to the conversations of the grown-ups around him, which often revolved around "the overbearing character and insulting manners of the English people, as well as Eurasians, towards Indians, and how it was the duty of every Indian to stand up to this and not tolerate it."[8]

Nonetheless his father, whom the boy adored and feared, was often visited by English friends. Motilal also hired English and European governesses and tutors for his children, including the part-Irish F. T. Brooks, who helped develop in Jawaharlal a taste for the novels of Scott, Dickens, and Thackeray, as well as for Mark Twain and Sherlock Holmes stories. The result was that, from a very early age, "much as I began to resent the presence and behaviour of the alien rulers, I had no feeling whatever, so far as I can remember, against individual Englishmen. . . . [Indeed] in my heart I rather admired the English."[9]

This childhood exposure to—and affection for—the race whose presence in India he would spend much of his adult life fighting distinctively shaped young Jawaharlal's view of the world. It gave him even as a ten-year-old an unusually international frame of reference, in sharp contrast to the much more parochial upbringing of the man he would later love and follow, Gandhi.

At fifteen, Jawaharlal found himself suddenly transplanted into the very different world of the English public school. After an initial period of homesickness he soon settled in at Harrow, where he was bored by his classmates' endless conversations about games, but greatly interested in the general election of 1905, which brought the Liberals to power. From Harrow, Nehru moved on to Trinity College, Cambridge, where he grew interested in the ideas of Bertrand Russell and the Fabian Socialists, but otherwise spent "three quiet years with little of disturbance in them, moving slowly on like the sluggish Cam." Cambridge was followed by two years in London, ostensibly training at the Inner Temple while in fact he enjoyed the life of a dandy, and still managed to pass his bar examinations "with neither glory nor ignominy."[10] By the time he was ready to return to India, he was, in his own words, "a bit of a prig, with little to commend me."[11]

Nehru's education in the West sowed many of the ideas that would later form the basis of his policies. As his biographer Michael Brecher has pointed out, it also "set him apart in the Indian National Congress, a solitary figure in a middle-class, traditional-minded General Staff, guiding a petty-bourgeois and peasant army. Although he accepted the stern discipline imposed by Gandhi and functioned as a member of a team, Nehru's approach to strategy and tactics revealed the Western rationalist. . . . In a wider sense it made Nehru alien in his own society . . . 'a queer mixture of the East and the West, out of place everywhere, at home nowhere.'"[12]

Nehru was many things to many people—some of them contradictory and paradoxical. A product of Harrow and Cambridge, he spent most of his adult life fighting the British and spent nine years in British prisons. But once free, he strove to keep India in the Commonwealth. A fervent secularist, he was himself adored by most of his countrymen with something almost approaching religious veneration. Almost thirty years after his death, and many biographies and thousands of words down the road, it is still impossible to riddle out all the contradictions in his character. Was he a moralistic hypocrite, as his detractors believed, or a well-meaning but self-deluding ideologue, an Indian Don Quixote tilting at windmills, full of utopian ideas? Was he, in the words of an American admirer, "one of the three great statesman of the century, alongside Churchill and Roosevelt," or was he instead (to quote a critic) "an arrogant, anti-American, pro-Communist, high class aristocratic, stiff-necked Hindu"?[13]

The best source on Nehru is Nehru himself. This is rare for statesmen, who tend to write as much to conceal as to reveal. Nehru was an exception. His prolific prison writings are sensitive, passionate, and extraordinarily candid: we see the man in his greatness as well as his smallness, warts and all. These are by far the best source on his thought and development, the sense of a commanding moral destiny for himself and for India, and the sudden, intensely personal moments of illumination. His speeches—usually extemporaneous—though frequently moving, do not always have quite the same transparent honesty as his written reminiscences and reflections, perhaps because they were addressed to a public audience.

A democrat by conviction, a Brahmin by breeding and instinct, Nehru was perceived by some as warm and charming, and by others as cold and aloof. In many ways a solitary, even lonely figure, he nonetheless had a great love of the crowd, and all his life drew extraordinary energy from the cheering thousands everywhere amassed to greet him.

No one was more aware of these contradictions than Nehru himself. In November 1937, when he was forty-eight years old and had completed two terms as president of the Congress party, a prominent Calcutta journal published an article that acutely probed his character:

> What lies behind that mask of his, what desires, what will to power, what insatiate longings? These questions would be interesting in any event, for Jawaharlal is a person who compels interest and attention. But they have a vital significance for us, for he is bound up with the present in India, and probably the future, and he has the power in him to do great good to India or great injury. . . .
>
> Men like Jawaharlal, with all their capacity for great and good work, are unsafe in a democracy. He calls himself a democrat and a socialist, and no doubt he does so in all earnestness, but. . . . a little twist and Jawaharlal might turn a dictator sweeping aside the paraphernalia of a slow-moving democracy. . . .
>
> In normal times, he would just be an efficient and successful executive, but in this revolutionary epoch, Caesarism is always at the door, and is it not possible that Jawaharlal might fancy himself a Caesar? Therein lies the danger for Jawaharlal and for India. . . . We want no Caesars."[14]

The essay was submitted anonymously, by someone hiding behind the nom-de-plume Chanakya, and the editor had published it in good faith. In time, the reason for its sophistication and intimate understanding of its subject became evident: the author was Jawaharlal himself.

II

Indians still refer to the period from 1947 to 1964 as the "Nehruvian era," so profound was Nehru's impact on their country's life. Every important area of government was critically shaped by the prime minister's ideas: home affairs, economic planning, agriculture, industry, foreign policy, defense, atomic power, space research. He sometimes even held several portfolios simultaneously, a situation that furnished much grist for the mill of political cartoonists.[15] Most Indians consider Nehru's foundation-laying and institution-building contributions rather like the combined legacies of Washington, Jefferson, and Lincoln in this country. (However, some critics, like his biographer Michael Edwardes, condemn him as "an inefficient executive and an incompetent administrator, who could not delegate even if he wanted to.")[16] Nehru's philosophical beliefs established the foundations of the Indian state: democratic government, secularism and socialism at home, and nonalignment abroad.

Nehru emerged as first prime minister by consensus: he was not even formally nominated by the Congress party. He was simply the acknowledged leader of the Congress and the designated political heir of Gandhi.[17] Once in office, he swiftly and effectively asserted his authority against challenges both from within the party and from the opposition. In 1950, his only real political rival, Sardar Vallabhai Patel, died, after which he rapidly consolidated his hold on the party organization, working with dissident factions and carefully building relationships with formidable state party bosses.[18] Nehru's government managed to combine the strength of the central government—dominated by the Congress "High Command"—with effective state governments run by powerful Congress regional leaders. Eventually, however, as every Congress member knew, ultimate authority rested in New Delhi.

In addition, Nehru established generally tolerant working relations with an array of opposition parties, sometimes himself seeming to lead the opposition, so outspoken was his criticism of his own party. In the 1952 general elections, the Congress party won a landslide victory, which firmly established it as the uncontested center of power and which effectively demolished Nehru's serious political opposition. Indeed, so much did the prime minister become the mainstay of the Congress and the country that, until the end of his days, even after his influence and his health were fading, he had only to threaten to resign to melt opposition to him and help persuade people to his point of view.

Under Nehru, India launched a new economic experiment. The Nehruvian brand of "mixed socialism" combined limited free enterprise with economic planning, a marriage in which, it was hoped, the private and public sectors would cooperate in providing for the nation's needs. The goal was "self-reliance": to achieve self-sufficiency in food, power, and essential commodities in the shortest possible time. New Delhi's economic policy, like its foreign policy, was primarily concerned with the preservation of Indian independence, and with the enhancement of India's prestige. Rather like a Victorian gentleman exhorting the wonders of progress, when he opened a great power dam in the Damodar Valley Nehru proclaimed: "These are our temples."[19]

For the first seventeen years of its existence, therefore, India's government was a striking paradox: a constitutional democracy governed continuously by one party, and that one party dominated by one man. Notwithstanding this concentration of power, the fact that India is still a functioning democracy—in contrast to most developing countries—owes much to Nehru's guiding influence. India contains what is probably the most diverse national society on earth. Its people speak twenty-four major languages (and hundreds of minor ones), follow five major religions, and organize their lives around an intricate social system comprised of thousands of castes. Western observers, viewing the divisions and centrifugal forces that rocked the Indian Union during the forties and fifties—including communal riots, state and language riots, and secessionist strife—were sometimes given to predicting the Balkanization of India. But despite the odds, the country and its democratic system survived, in no small measure due to Nehru's liberal, democratic, and secular beliefs: beliefs that acquire special significance in light of the rising xenophobia afflicting India today. As his biographer Vincent Sheean has pointed out, Nehru was the first Indian leader to acquire secular power in a purely secular way and to wield it without once claiming any form of religious sanction.[20]

Nehru's other great gift to India was his internationalism, a quality that, above all the others, marked him out as a statesman. In contrast to so many of his counterparts, Nehru believed deeply that the destinies of all nations were critically intertwined, especially in the new nuclear world. Nehru's breadth of vision distinguished him from many of his Congress colleagues, and went a long way toward neutralizing the more parochial and xenophobic elements in the government. He ceaselessly argued the need for the country to look *forward* and *outward*. "We do not wish to be isolated," he stressed. "We wish to have the closest contacts, *because we do from the beginning firmly believe in the world coming closer together and ultimately realizing the idea of what is now being called One World.*"[21]

Nehru brought to the office of prime minister a full-blown and controversial set of ideas about the practice of diplomacy, which won many critics and adherents. His policy of nonalignment, later much misunderstood and fuzzed-over (a problem partly his own doing), was neither the unworldly and utopian set of high ideals it is often portrayed as, nor, as some of its critics hold, merely a cynical fig leaf for opportunistic motives. In keeping India nonaligned, Nehru was hoping both to enhance India's prestige and to protect the country from having to commit its strained resources in binding commitments to either bloc.[22]

India was one of the first nations to face a dilemma that would soon confront every developing country: how simultaneously to preserve freedom and security and advance economic growth. Even the richer nations of Europe, rebuilding their economies after the war with the help of the Marshall Plan, were struggling with the conflicting need for guns and butter. For developing countries like India, the choice was between guns and bread. Nonalignment, as Nehru envisaged it, would keep India out of military entanglements, out of war, and give it the necessary breathing space to concentrate on internal development.

Nehru's doctrine was built around several interlocking ideas: peaceful coexistence with other nations (including those with different governing philosophies, such as communism and capitalism); the maintenance of independence by refusing to join foreign alliances or to have foreign military bases on Indian soil; active efforts to find peaceful solutions in the event of third-party conflicts, which Nehru called "dynamic neutrality"; and vigorous support of freedom movements against imperialism. Nonalignment, Nehru insisted, was not passive or negative (on which grounds he objected to the word "neutralism") but was highly dynamic, demanding great alertness to important issues in which India might have a stake.

To Nehru, the world of the forties and fifties seemed ominously armed and divided. The postwar polarization of the world into American and Soviet blocs seemed to him a dangerous and frightening development, one which must inevitably lead to another catastrophic world war. This anxiety was a persistent theme in his speeches and conversations. It fed the fear that the Cold War would drag India into another conflagration. In 1954, during a visit to Sri Lanka, Nehru said: "It would be a tragedy of infinite magnitude if we should be checked and baulked and our policy set at naught because of the troubles and quarrels of others. . . . We do not want that at this critical moment in the history of our respective countries, war should upset the plans we have laid and the dreams we have dreamed."[23] Nevertheless, his reaction to the threat of war was not a defensive battening-down of the hatches in isolation (in sharp contrast to Mao and Khomeini in later years). Instead he sought to make common cause with other new states, which, like India, were struggling to preserve their independence and to stay out of the Cold War.

To many new Afro-Asian nations, the Cold War was insidious, a Trojan horse of imperialism. Instead of military conquest and outright annexation, they suspected that the new strategies for expanding Western influence would be primarily political, economic, and intellectual. The struggle for the minds and hearts of Africans and Asians would take the form of seduction by means of economic aid, military alliances, and ideology (democracy versus communism, capitalism versus socialism). To these nations, the old exploitative ends hadn't changed, though the means were increasingly sophisticated. In this landscape, nonalignment had considerable appeal to new nations as an alternative to military alliances. In the glow of new independence, it caught on as a posture in much of the Third World because it seemed to meet the concerns of developing countries in ways lacking in both the American and the Soviet approaches, and because it was not tied to a specific ideology or religion.

The Afro-Asian nations were at a dramatic new crossroad, but, at least in some ways, history was repeating itself. There was a striking resemblance between Nehru's rhetoric in 1947 and George Washington's farewell address to the American people in 1795: "A passionate attachment of one nation for another produces a variety of evils. . . . 'Tis our true policy to steer clear of permanent alliances with any portion of the foreign world."[24]

In 1947, the memory of the humiliations of British colonialism among Indian leaders was as fresh as it had been for the Americans two and a half centuries earlier. Indeed, as early as the 1920s, Congress party resolutions had declared that India would oppose all imperialistic wars. As he traveled the world during the 1920s and 1930s, Nehru vocally condemned all forms of political oppression, and projected India's national movement as a model for anticolonial struggles everywhere.

The fight for independence also taught the Indian nationalists the lesson that moral force could triumph over physical force, even that of the mighty British Empire. With independence, that lesson would be applied to the larger world stage.

> [Gandhi] taught us the doctrine of non-violence . . . as an active and positive instrument for the peaceful solution of international differences. He showed us that the human spirit is more powerful than the mightiest of armaments. He . . . pointed out that means and ends can never be separated, for the means ultimately govern the end.
>
> . . . All this may seem fantastic and impractical in the modern world. . . . And yet we have seen repeatedly the failure of other methods. . . . I have become . . . convinced that so long as we do not recognize the supremacy of the moral law in our national and international relations, we shall have no enduring peace.[25]

Today all this might sound rather naive. But for Nehru, at least at the beginning, there was no necessary conflict between moral means and practical ends: he agreed not with Clausewitz ("war is an extension of diplomacy by other means") but with Aristotle, regarding politics as an extension of ethics. Political power, he felt, must serve "the pursuit of peace not through alignment, but through an independent approach to each controversial or disputed issue, the liberation of subject peoples, the maintenance of freedom, both national and individual, the elimination of racial discrimination, the elimination of want, disease, and ignorance which afflict the greater part of the world's population."[26]

At the heart of these lofty goals was a passionate belief in India's rightful destiny as a great power. India, Nehru often reminded his audiences, encompassed a complete and ancient civilization of a richness and longevity few other nations could boast. Now, freed from the shackles of imperialism, India was destined to play a shining role in the important affairs of the day. "India comes now, I think, into the forefront in world affairs. . . . India, not because of any ambition of hers, but because of the force of circumstances, because of geography, because of history and because of so many other things, inevitably has to play a very important part in Asia. And not only that; India becomes a meeting ground between what might roughly be called East and West. Look at the map."[27]

With hindsight, given the gulf between the vision and the reality of India today, these hopes may seem like the delusions of an overblown ambition. But at the time, India seemed to exemplify the aspirations and problems of the developing world. Given its relatively orderly transition to democratic government and its population of 350 million, it also seemed a likely future leader of what would eventually come to be called the Third World. Which way India decided to go would be important: its decision would inevitably serve as a touchstone for other developing nations. With China "lost" to communism, there were initially high hopes in many Western capitals that India, with its democratic leadership and strong civic institutions, might lead a resurgent Asia. Nehru's own conviction was contagious: "I saw the star of India rising far above the horizon. . . . We dare not be little. . . . Destiny has cast a certain role upon this country."[28]

III

What does independence consist of? It consists fundamentally
and basically of foreign relations. That is the test of
independence. All else is local autonomy. . . . Our policy will
continue to be not only to keep aloof from power alignments, but
[to] try to make our independence . . . with no hostile
background in regard to any country . . . we approach the whole
world on a friendly basis.[29]

Nonalignment acquired special significance from the configuration of the international landscape in which it was conceived. The Second World War left the world with a unique balance of forces, a landscape transformed simultaneously by the process of decolonization, with all its attendant conflict and upheaval, and by the polarization of the world in an accelerating Cold War. In this landscape, the Indian subcontinent presented a special challenge to the superpowers.

To the United States, India was a cornerstone of the developing world, and also a rather uncomfortable country, distant and a bit strange. On the one hand, its democratic system and British-educated leadership made it seem a natural ally of the United States, a fine place to demonstrate the success of free enterprise and democratic development. On the other hand, India's geographical proximity to the Soviet Union, its poverty, its socialist economy, and its leaders' postcolonial suspicion of Western motives made it seem a dangerously fertile field for communism.

To Secretary of State John Foster Dulles and other Washington hardliners, Nehru was annoyingly obtuse, blind to the important moral differences between the American and the Soviet systems. In a world threatened by communism and totalitarianism, Indian "neutralism" was "an obsolete conception," and "except under very exceptional circumstances . . . an immoral and shortsighted conception."[30] In Washington, the frustration with Nehru ran high. "That is one area of the world," President Eisenhower told Dulles in 1953, "where even more than in most cases, emotion rather than reason seems to dictate policy."[31]

To Nehru and his followers, America was the myopic and self-serving party. In its insistence that Asian countries "stand up and be counted" as American friends, Washington was being simplistic and foolish. After all, wasn't the United States itself once "the greatest and the noisiest of all neutrals"?[32] Further, they felt, by ignoring New Delhi's natural claim to the status of dominant power in the region (a claim accruing from India's sheer size and strength), and by equating India with Pakistan, the Americans were doing precisely what they complained India was doing: they were equating inherently different and unequal powers.

In all the hyperbole characteristic of the fifties, the Indian rhetoric of socialism, anticolonialism (edged with anti-Westernism), and nonalignment ran smack into the rhetoric of capitalism and anticommunism then pouring out of the United States. The moralizing tone sometimes adopted by Nehru, and far more abrasively by Krishna Menon, his ambassador to the United Nations (later defense minister) grated on American and Western nerves. The result was that although some of Nehru's most vocal and prominent admirers were Americans, the most strident (and to the Indians, painful) public criticism of Nehru and nonalignment also issued from the United States. Throughout the fifties and sixties, India and the United States remained at loggerheads because each failed to support the other on a central preoccupation: India refused to join the American campaign against communism, and the United States refused to make the eradication of colonialism a top priority.

The Soviet Union, for its part, was also initially mistrustful of nonalignment. In the early days of the Cold War, Moscow regarded Nehru as a capitalist-bourgeois, almost a running dog of U.S. imperialism. But after the United States signed a military alliance with Pakistan in 1954, the Soviet attitude began to undergo a distinct change. In 1955, Khrushchev made a highly successful visit to New Delhi. As the Soviet Union set out to woo India, it offered public reinforcement in some areas crucial to Nehru: it agreed that India was a great power, supported its nonaligned foreign policy, and backed the Indian position on Kashmir in the United Nations.

Indeed, perhaps the truest test of Nehru's lofty ideals, by the nature of things, was the one closest to home: Kashmir and Pakistan. Few nations are paired in a deadlock the way India has been with Pakistan (the Arab-Israeli conflict is the only comparable analogy in this century). The deadlock has been all the more fierce for the bitterness and bloodshed that accompanied partition, and because of the very different ideologies governing the two nations. In 1947, many Indians still questioned the right of Pakistan to exist; Pakistan, for its part, lived in the shadow of India with a real (if sometimes deliberately exaggerated) fear of Indian hostility.

In October 1947, barely two months after independence, war erupted between India and Pakistan over Kashmir. The Kashmir issue, like the Palestinian problem, is proving to be one of the most intractable conflicts of the century. Ruled under the aegis of the British raj as a princely state, Kashmir had to make a choice in 1947 and join either India or Pakistan. The departing British left it to the rulers of the Indian princely states—565 in all—to decide to which of the two countries they wished to accede. While there was a Hindu majority in Jammu, in the south of the state, Kashmir as a whole was overwhelmingly Muslim, and so a fierce controversy developed as to which side Kashmir should join.

The Pakistanis felt that Kashmir rightfully belonged to them by virtue of its large Muslim population. The Indians, on the other hand, argued that it was impossible to cede or divide the Valley of Kashmir, as it contained the strategic routes to Ladakh, on the Tibetan border. Nehru and his advisers also felt that Kashmir, a Muslim state, had to stay in India as a proof of Indian secularism. In addition, Nehru, himself a Kashmiri, was deeply attached to his homeland, a bond evident from many lyrical passages in his writings about the beauty and grandeur of Kashmir.

Hari Singh, the maharajah of Kashmir, wavered on the issue of accession until well after independence. In September 1947, Muslim tribesmen, mostly Pathans, with the active support of Pakistani officials, decided to force the moment to a crisis, and advanced on the state's capital, Srinagar, looting and raping as they went. The maharajah, in a panic, fled to Jammu and appealed to India to intervene. The Indian government replied that Hari Singh must first accede to India, which he did on 26 October. Shortly after, Indian troops surrounded Srinagar and drove the tribesmen back, gradually pushing them out of the valley as well. Fearing that India would take over the whole of

Kashmir, the Pakistani government now provided the Azad Kashmir (Free Kashmir) forces with material and weapons to help them consolidate their hold over the northwest area of the state, and sent in Pakistani soldiers to serve as "volunteers."

Nehru, meanwhile, had announced that the issue would eventually be settled with a plebiscite, perhaps held under the auspices of the United Nations, but that first the aggressors must leave Kashmiri soil. Pakistani Prime Minister Liaquat agreed, provided the Indian forces withdrew. Nehru rejected this offer, and, convinced of the legality of India's case, took the problem to the United Nations on 31 December 1947.

In the UN Security Council's debate, Pakistani Foreign Minister Zafrullah Khan presented the Pakistani case forcefully and effectively. He accused Nehru of the genocide of Indian Muslims, among other things, and of obtaining Hari Singh's signature by questionable means. Compared with Khan's powerful advocacy, the Indian representative's presentation was brief and weak. The Security Council responded by altering the scope and title of the debate, which was changed from the Jammu-Kashmir Dispute to the India-Pakistan Dispute. To Nehru's indignation, instead of focusing on India's charges of aggression, the United Nations' discussion now widened to include the broader general question of India's relations with Pakistan. "The fundamental issue has been slurred over and by-passed," he fumed.[33]

In December 1948, the Security Council issued a resolution calling for a cease-fire line, which was accepted by both belligerents and which left the Indians in control of most of the Kashmir Valley, while the Pakistanis consolidated their hold in "Azad Kashmir." For the next few years, the dispute was constantly before the UN, which turned out several resolutions and potential mediators, to little effect. Both India and Pakistan agreed to a plebiscite "in principle," but they could never agree on the conditions for the referendum, and still have not done so, two wars and more than forty years later.

The 1947 Kashmir crisis marked India's debut on the international stage, and left Nehru deeply disillusioned both with the United Nations and with Pakistan. Disillusionment turned to dismay when it became clear that Pakistan was going to make common cause with the Truman administration and join an American military alliance, ostensibly to contain communism. In May 1954, Washington and Karachi signed a Mutual Defense Assistance Treaty, and later Pakistan joined both SEATO and the Baghdad Pact, thereby becoming America's "most allied ally." Nehru bitterly criticised the American program to develop and equip the Pakistani defense forces. American assurances that the arms supplied to Pakistan would only be used against communist countries did little to assuage his fears (with good reason, as the war of 1965 was to prove). The conviction mounted in India that Pakistan's main, if not sole, purpose in joining the pacts was to continue its aggression against India. Nor did it soften the blow that President Eisenhower offered a similar arrangement to India. The Pakistani arms deal helped motivate Nehru to some of his feverish diplomatic activity during the mid-fifties, when he worked ceaselessly to spread India's influence in the nonaligned movement.

In contrast to his suspicion of the motives of India's western neighbor, and of the idea of an Islamic theocracy, Nehru had an almost romantic attachment to India's huge eastern neighbor, China. China's civilization and Mao's revolution had long had a deep fascination for him. His powerful sense of affinity with China was shared by other leading intellectuals in the Indian independence movement, who saw in China a fellow Asian Gulliver, struggling to free itself from the shackles of European imperialism. While the Indian nationalists were not communists themselves, there was both sympathy for the Chinese revolution and a practical recognition that India was going to have to do business with whatever regime came to power in its massive northeastern neighbor. Thus, shortly after Mao's men won their war in 1949, India recognized Communist China, and thereafter sought tirelessly to gain it a seat in the United Nations.

Every one of Nehru's most cherished principles in foreign affairs—nonalignment, self-reliance in defense, an "area of peace" around India—depended on peaceful co-existence with China and a peaceful northeastern border. Indeed, Nehru's vision of Asia resurgent was of a continent led by its two giants, India and China. This was still over a decade before the Great Leap Forward, almost two decades before the horrors of the Cultural Revolution, and the prospect of an Indian-Chinese *entente cordiale* did not then seem all that farfetched. (On the other hand, Nehru and Mao would have made an odd couple indeed, an Oxbridge-educated Brahmin schooled in Gandhian nonviolence with a peasant revolutionary who wielded the power that grows out of the barrel of a gun.)

In 1950, two crises arose to test Nehru's vision of an Indian-Chinese entente: the Korean War and the invasion of Tibet. North Korea's invasion of South Korea in June 1950 sent shock waves through the developing world. Suddenly, naked aggression was being perpetrated by one Asian nation on another, rather than by a Western aggressor on an Asian victim.

In the United Nations, India voted for the resolution identifying North Korea as the aggressor and calling upon its forces to withdraw. In New Delhi, isolationist legislators in Parliament, responding to Nehru's obvious interest in mediating the conflict, protested that India would be entangled in a war that was not her business. The prime minister replied that he had never intended India to be "permanently neutral," for that would mean "a permanent retirement from public affairs, a kind of national *Sanyasa*."[34] Soon Nehru was moving away from his early pro-Western position and toward a middle ground from which he could offer India's services as a mediator.

In July, Nehru sent a peace proposal to Stalin and Secretary of State Acheson, suggesting, among other steps toward conciliation, the seating of the People's Republic of China in the UN, and direct negotiations between China, the United States and the USSR to resolve the crisis. The proposal managed to offend both the United States and the USSR, which promptly rejected it. Meanwhile, the UN operation in Korea was gaining ground, and by October the UN was debating whether its forces should cross the thirty-eighth parallel and push the North Korean troops back into their homeland. India opposed this move, especially after its ambassador in Beijing, K. M. Panikkar, was told by no less than Zhou Enlai himself that if American forces crossed the divide, China would be forced to intervene.

President Truman, considering this a bluff, decided to continue the advance. Nehru, for his part, pursued efforts to sponsor Chinese entry into the United Nations, while his UN representative tried, together with other Asian and Arab representatives, to find a joint solution for peace talks, an alternative to a resolution condemning the Chinese entry into the war. The latter passed, however, the Asian-Arab efforts failed, and India, despite its efforts to act as a neutral "honest broker," found itself alienated from both Washington and Moscow.

By the autumn of 1952, India was once again involved, this time on a sensitive issue over which the principals were deadlocked: the exchange of prisoners of war. In November, the Asian and Arab states, led by India's new representative to the UN, Vijayalakshmi Pandit (Nehru's sister), set out to find a solution. An Indian draft resolution (painstakingly drawn up after much behind-the-scenes effort) was rejected first by the United States and then by the Soviet Union. Then the Americans decided that if Moscow had rejected the proposal it must have some merit, and reversed their earlier stance. Eventually the resolution passed with considerable noncommunist support, and after Stalin's death in March 1953, the Chinese and the North Koreans finally accepted its terms. India, as head of the Neutral Nations Repatriation Commission, was charged with the difficult task of repatriating the prisoners of war.

By the end of the Korean War, despite—or perhaps because of—its vigorous efforts to mediate and not to be tied to any one side in the dispute, India had so roused suspicions among the belligerents, especially the United States, that, at the latter's insistence (supported by South Korea), it was excluded from the peace conference that was convened in Geneva in 1954. Nehru's efforts left both Washington and Moscow feeling that India could not be relied upon for consistent support. Like a small boy in a schoolyard who, with the best of intentions, tries to break up a fight, India not only failed to stop the conflict, but isolated itself in the process.

Although the Korean War occupied considerable attention, other developments, in Indo-China, also presented New Delhi with a policy dilemma. On the one hand, India was staunchly opposed to imperialism, and to a continued French colonial presence in Indo-China. On the other hand, Ho Chi Minh's communist ties, the Cold War confrontation that seemed to be gathering, and Nehru's concern to avoid entangling India militarily all pointed to the wisdom of keeping a low profile. Prudence prevailed. Nehru carefully avoided taking sides in the conflict, and when he stopped over in Hanoi en route to China in 1954, made sure he visited Saigon on the way back.

Early in 1954, expressing his concern at the growing deliveries of Chinese and American materials into the area, and the potential escalation of the conflict, Nehru appealed for a cease-fire, to be followed by "direct negotiations between the parties immediately and principally concerned."[35] At a conference in Colombo, even as the great powers were meeting in Geneva to discuss a settlement, five Asian governments endorsed a peace proposal based on Nehru's ideas. The eventual Geneva accords on Indo-China closely resembled those ideas, including provisions for a cease-fire, for the transfer of sovereignty from France to Vietnam, Cambodia, and Laos, and for the end of military ties between outside powers and these states. The Geneva accords also established three International Commissions of Supervision and Control for Vietnam, Cambodia, and Laos, comprised of Indian, Polish, and Canadian members and chaired by India.

Nehru's diplomatic skills and statesmanship, deployed with varying degrees of success in Korea and Southeast Asia, were less effective in dealing with an ominous development unfolding much closer to home: China's invasion of Tibet. Tibet had long been a region of great strategic importance for China, which first attempted to take over the country in 1910. This was one thing that hadn't changed under communism: Mao's revolutionaries evidently shared the traditional Chinese belief that the Middle Kingdom had a duty to spread its superior culture among the barbarians on China's borders.

In 1950, Mao sent an army to "liberate the oppressed and exploited Tibetans and reunite them with the great motherland," and to protect them from the "forces of imperialism" (although, in fact, there were only ten white men in the country at the time).[36] Nehru, faced with the prospect of war with China if India attempted to expel its forces from Tibet (a war India's neglected defense forces were not equipped to fight), chose instead merely to express India's concern, a response which did not significantly impede the occupation of Tibet. Not surprisingly, the diplomatic exchanges over the invasion marked a turning point in India's relationship with China, which was to grow steadily warmer over the next few years.

In 1954, Nehru and Zhou Enlai signed an agreement based on the *Panchsheela,* or five principles: (i) mutual respect for each other's territorial integrity and sovereignty, (ii) mutual nonaggression, (iii) noninterference in each other's internal affairs, (iv) equality, and (v) peaceful coexistence.[37] The *Panchsheela,* which closely resembled the central principles of the United Nations Charter, were visibly absent in practice in the Chinese government's dealings with the Tibetans. But the mood in India was nonetheless rosy. While official speeches proclaimed a new era of Indian-Chinese friendship and cooperation, ordinary Indians echoed the official optimism with the Hindi slogan: *"Hindi-Chinee-bhai-bhai!* [Indians and Chinese are brothers!]

The high point of the policy of friendship with China, from Nehru's point of view, came at the Bandung Conference in 1955. For almost thirty years, Nehru had dreamed of an Afro-Asian community of nations working in close cooperation. The Bandung Conference seemed to him the beginning of the realization of that dream. China made its debut at the conference, ushered in by India, and Nehru's *Panchsheela* were signed by twenty-nine African and Asian nations, including China, Laos, Cambodia, and the Democratic Republic of Vietnam. Many Indians—possibly including Nehru himself—regarded Bandung as India's finest hour on the world stage. However, ironically, it was at this very stage that Nehru's influence in Asian councils, vis-à-vis that of China, started to decline.

For while the "spirit of Bandung" was much bandied about, and the conference members were vocal in their opposition to Western colonialism and nuclear weapons, when it came down to the meat-and-potatoes of Asian diplomacy —to matters of Western economic aid and the military alliances that were keeping some illegitimate regimes in power—a great many differences surfaced. In a forum in which nearly one-half of the states present were in fact aligned with the West, Nehru's high-flown injunctions against the evils of alliances struck a strident and patronizing note.

The politeness and moderation of Zhou Enlai made a striking contrast.[38] Meanwhile, unbeknownst to Nehru, the Chinese delegation, relatively unknown, deeply resented his attempt to take China under the Indian wing. As Neville Maxwell observed in his controversial book, *India's China War,* to the Chinese (already irritated by bourgeois capitalist India's assumption of "older brother" status in Asian councils), Nehru's apparent kindliness must have appeared patronizing in the extreme. The friction arose partly from a mirror-image problem. The Indian ambassador to Beijing, K. M. Panikkar, later recalled, "[The] independence of India was welcome, but of course it was understood that China, as the recognized Great Power in Asia after the war, expected India to know her place."[39] Apparently, the memory rankled for years. Almost a decade later, in 1964, Zhou Enlai told a group of visiting members of Parliament from Sri Lanka, "I have met many leaders of the world throughout my career. I met Khrushchev. I met Chiang Kai-Shek. I've met American generals. But I have never met a more arrogant man than Nehru."[40]

Though relations with China formed the centerpiece of Nehru's bilateral diplomatic initiatives, he worked busily to extend the nonaligned net westward as well as eastward. One natural ally was Marshal Joseph Tito, who had proclaimed Yugoslavia's neutrality in the face of Stalin's expulsion of his country from the Cominform, and whose independence therefore depended on some kind of nonalignment. In December 1954 Tito visited New Delhi, and was met by crowds chanting "*Viva* Marshal Tito!" and "Marshal Tito *ki jai!* [Victory to Marshal Tito!][41] He later recalled that meeting Nehru was like meeting someone he had known a long time.

The joint Indo-Yugoslav declaration of 22 December 1954, was a vigorous affirmation of the principle of "dynamic neutrality": "The President and the Prime Minister desire to proclaim that the policy of non-alignment adopted and pursued by their respective countries is not 'neutrality' or 'neutralism' and therefore passivity, as sometimes alleged, but is a positive, active and constructive policy seeking to lead to collective peace, on which alone collective security can really rest."[42] Nehru returned Tito's visit in July 1955, and the two leaders announced their agreement not only in concept and principle but on such specifics as the need to control atomic weapons, potential solutions to the problems of Germany and Formosa, and the need to represent Communist China in the United Nations.

Meanwhile Nehru was also cultivating Egyptian President Gamal Abdel Nasser, whom he had first met during a visit to Cairo in February 1955. Concerned that Nasser might succumb, in the wake of Pakistan, to American pressure to join the Baghdad Pact, Nehru was pleased to reach an agreement with Nasser in July that "involvement in military pacts or alignment with great powers does not serve the cause of peace."[43]

In July 1956, Nehru, Tito, and Nasser met at Brioni, in a conference which, while it did not solve any specific problems, signaled to the rest of the world that the nonaligned movement was alive, well, and getting stronger. Coming so soon after Bandung, it seemed to be a triumph of diplomacy for Nehru, whose net now embraced a great many nations.

But soon two events occurred that severely tested the high ideals articulated at Bandung and Brioni. Nehru passed one of these tests and failed the other. On the 29 October, after Nasser nationalized the Suez Canal, Israel attacked Egypt, and this attack was followed on 5 November by a joint Anglo-French invasion. Nehru's response was swift and unequivocal: "In my experience of foreign affairs, I've come across no grosser case of naked aggression than what England and France are trying to do."[44] On 31 October he cabled Nasser: "This is a reversal of history which none of us can tolerate."[45]

Yet, when Soviet tanks rolled into Hungary to crush the uprising in Budapest, Nehru's response, like that of many of his counterparts in the Afro-Asian world, was much more equivocal. He expressed India's "concern and distress," but there was nothing like the ringing condemnation of aggression with which he reacted to the invasion of Egypt. To the acute embarrassment of many Indians, in the United Nations India abstained from the vote condemning the Soviet aggression in Hungary, and opposed another resolution demanding the withdrawal of Soviet troops. This double standard raised a storm of criticism both within and outside India. In Parliament Nehru faced some angry questions, while abroad even his staunchest admirers were shaken, and his critics provided with much grist for their mill. After several weeks, Nehru did come out with several offsetting statements more critical of the Soviet Union, but by this time it was too late, and the damage had been done.

In spite of the debacle of Hungary, one relationship important to New Delhi improved during the late fifties and early sixties: the relationship with the United States. When John F. Kennedy was inaugurated president, celebratory parties warmed the dining rooms of New Delhi's diplomatic elite. Kennedy's inaugural address, with its emphasis on independence for the new states of the Third World ("we shall not always expect to find them supporting our view"), seemed to be ushering in a less ideological, more flexible America. The Indian-American "honeymoon" of Kennedy's first year in office is vividly captured in the frequent letters that flew back and forth between him and Nehru, covering Laos, the Congo, economic aid, Berlin, nuclear testing, and a host of other subjects. Relatively free of hedging, innocent of bureaucratese, they are notable for a warmth and clarity quite remarkable in official correspondence.[46]

The two men worked well together on several thorny issues. In Laos, a confused civil war was under way, compounded by the intervention of the Soviet Union, Communist China, and the United States, with no clear solution in sight. Nehru served as a line to Khrushchev for Washington, and, at Kennedy's urging, reconvened the International Control Commission for Laos, which managed to obtain a ceasefire. Eventually, in July 1962, after many alarms and diversions, a new Geneva accord was concluded, with fourteen governments agreeing to guarantee the coalition Laotian government. Similarly, in the bloody civil war that was unfolding in the Congo, Indian troops, flown to the area in American military aircraft, formed the backbone of the United Nations operation, placing considerable strain on New Delhi's already meager defense budget. Despite continuing controversy and fierce domestic opposition, Nehru (with periodic encouragement from Kennedy) stuck to his commitment, and the Indian troops stayed to the end, eventually returning to India in 1963.

Nehru's good personal relationship with Kennedy proved crucial for India, in a way he had never anticipated. On 20 October 1962, just as the discovery of Soviet missiles in Cuba was breaking in Washington, twenty thousand Chinese troops invaded India, pouring in over the Thagla Ridge in the Himalayas. Using heavy artillery and tanks, they drove back the Indian forces stationed on the border with ease, and took heavy casualties.

The invasion was the culmination of a border dispute that had been simmering between New Delhi and Beijing for over three years and had come to a head in the autumn of 1962. Repeated border incursions since 1959 had been accompanied by a fruitless dialogue between Indian and Chinese officials, and an unsuccessful summit meeting between Nehru and Zhou Enlai had been held in New Delhi in 1960. The two areas in dispute were at opposite ends of the Himalayas—the North East Frontier Agency, or NEFA, a heavily forested area in the east, and Ladakh in Kashmir in the west, where the Chinese now occupied the bleak, eighteen-thousand-foot-high Aksai Chin plateau.

In late 1961, after repeated border clashes, the Indian Joint Chiefs had warned Defense Minister Krishna Menon that a war might be brewing. Notwithstanding this intelligence, Nehru had embarked on a risky "forward policy": one of establishing Indian military posts behind the posts already staked out by the Chinese. As the Chinese mounted their massive invasion, the Joint Chiefs' worst fears were realized. The Indian Army was ill-equipped to fight in rugged mountainous terrain, and hundreds of troops were sent to fight in the Himalayan snows in cotton summer uniforms and canvas shoes. Morale among the men was low after fifteen years in which the army had been considered a low priority, and five under the disastrous stewardship of Krishna Menon, during his tenure as defense minister. Despite a brave fight, poorly equipped and unprepared as they were for battle, the army collapsed with humiliating speed. As *Time* magazine put it, the Indian army was caught critically short of "almost everything but courage."[47]

To the Indian people, who had been reassured by the prime minister's brave words (in Parliament and elsewhere) that India was ready for anyone, the army's collapse was a great shock. Psychologically, economically, and militarily, the nation had not been prepared for war. Panic swept the country, and cities as far south as Bombay began to prepare for Chinese bombing attacks.

Despite the scale of the crisis, Nehru stayed in power. The extent of the Indians' adulation of their leader was borne out by the fact that in the first shock, there was more sympathy than blame for Nehru: some thirty Congress members of Parliament meeting the prime minister in New Delhi on 23 October complained not that the country had been misled by the government, but that Nehru, Parliament, and the country had been misled by Krishna Menon. When a stunned and tired Nehru faced a conference of state ministers on 25 October, he confessed, "We were getting out of touch with reality in the modern world and living in an atmosphere of our own creation. We have been shocked out of it, all of us."[48]

In the West, there was a certain amount of *Schadenfreude* that India, "which had tended to be non-aligned eastward and to lecture westward," had been brought down to earth.[49] But there was also widespread sympathy expressed in the American and British press. The Chinese attack was seen by many as a major assault on the bastion of Asian democracy. *The Daily Telegraph* warned that it was "the first round of the struggle for the Asian mind between the Communist and non-Communist giants of the subcontinent."[50]

The reaction of the nonaligned nations, which India had aspired to lead, was disappointingly equivocal by contrast. Only Ethiopia and Cyprus came out openly in support of India, and as for the Middle East, expressions of support from the Arab world were conspicuous by their absence. The reasons for this are not hard to find. Arab leaders must have found themselves in an awkward place, since Pakistan, a fellow Islamic nation (and a member of Central Treaty Organization, in keeping with the ancient Indian tenet of statecraft that "the enemy of your enemy is your friend," had commenced boundary negotiations with China.

However, the real blow for the Indians was the Russian reaction. The Soviet Union was the nation most likely to be affected and embarrassed by a dispute between India and China. American analysts later concluded that the Chinese invasion had been at least partly motivated by Beijing's desire to force the Soviets to declare their hand in the Sino-Soviet dispute, in which China's conflict with India was enmeshed. The Soviet Union was suddenly faced with having to choose between its communist ally or an important potential partner, or, as Khrushchev put it, of having to take sides between "a brother and a friend."[51] Caught between a rock and a hard place, the Soviet Union initially leaned toward China. Under pressure from Khrushchev to accept the Chinese cease-fire proposals, a desperate Nehru now decided that the only place left to turn was the United States.

Indeed, the United States was the only one of the big powers whose reaction reflected any sense of urgency. President Kennedy's letters to Nehru in the immediate aftermath of the invasion were warm and personal: "Our thoughts are with you in your hour of trial. . . . As you move down the road, you know you carry with you my understanding, sympathy and friendship."[52]

On 26 October, barely a week after the initial Chinese onslaught, the Indian ambassador in Washington, B. K. Nehru, delivered to the White House Nehru's plea for support. The ambassador explained that after the humiliating defeats India had so recently suffered, his prime minister found it difficult to ask explicitly for military aid. He was hoping instead that the president in his reply would offer "support" rather than "military assistance," on the basis of "sympathy" rather than an "alliance."[53] Kennedy, who had already decided to help the Indians on a military assistance basis rather than the usual cash sale basis, assured the ambassador that the United States was not interested in drawing India into a military pact. He also asked whether the prime minister had asked Khrushchev for arms, and suggested that Nehru tell the Soviet premier "to put up or shut up."[54]

In public, Kennedy's official response to Nehru's appeal was couched in language sufficiently warm and vague to save face for the prime minister, but also specific enough to imply the comfort of forthcoming United States military aid. On 29 October, reassured that India would not be entangled in an alliance, Nehru made a formal request for military aid, and barely five days later, the first big American C-130 transport planes began to arrive in Calcutta, loaded with light artillery and infantry weapons.

November 20 was a day of great panic in the northeastern sector, as a wave of Chinese troops swept forward over the border, threatening oil-rich Assam. The next day, just hours before Kennedy announced the departure to India of a high-level American mission, the Chinese, presumably anxious to stave off further

American involvement, declared a "unilateral" cease-fire, and informed Nehru that Chinese troops would unconditionally withdraw to their earlier positions.

Meanwhile, alarmed at the prospect of an American military pact with its principal enemy, Pakistan was vociferously protesting Kennedy's support, and let it be known that this would adversely affect its attitude to the Western alliance. The generals in Karachi bitterly resented what they saw as an American decision to make no distinctions between its loyal allies and erstwhile neutrals. In October Pakistani President Ayub Khan had come under fire for being "soft" on India, when he resisted the generals who urged an attack on Kashmir while Indian forces were concentrated in the Himalayas.

In December 1962, Karachi announced the opening of border talks with Beijing. A flurry of diplomatic activity ensued, and a much-publicized Pakistani-Chinese entente gathered momentum in the following months. By June 1963, the popular Karachi paper *Dawn* was quoting Zhou Enlai as promising that China would defend Pakistan "around the world."[55] A few weeks later, Pakistan's foreign minister, Zulfikar Ali Bhutto, warned in Parliament that any attack on Pakistan by India would involve the intervention of "the largest state in Asia."[56] For the Indians, the Sino-Pakistani entente was a frightening development, raising the prospect of a joint Pakistani-Chinese pincer attack. Thereafter India intensified its efforts to assure the country's security by negotiating for military transfers from both the United States and the Soviet Union.

China's invasion of India left Nehru's foreign policy in ruins. India had been deceived and then attacked by its supposed friend and neighbor, had been abandoned by the Soviet Union and by its nonaligned brethren, and had been forced to beg for help from the nation whose policies it had most loudly criticised, the United States. The humiliation was complete. For Indians in general, it was the end of innocence, and of any shred of belief in friendship with other nations as the guarantee of security. Defense Minister Krishna Menon was forced to resign in ignominy, India's defense budget more than doubled, and the nation started a searching and agonized reappraisal of its policies.

For Nehru, already in poor health, the invasion was devastating. He never recovered, and faded rapidly in the next year, though he was still enough himself to defy his doctors' orders to rest: "Let them go to hell. If I lie down in bed for even a week, I know I will not get up."[57] He died on 27 May 1964 at the age of seventy-four.

IV

Jawaharlal Nehru had "the vitality that moves history."[58] "The mind is ultimately a slave to the heart", he wrote in 1937, with prescient insight.[59] Nehru's strengths were tied to his greatest weaknesses. His emotional attachment to an internationalist view of the world made it hard for him to see that world as it actually was, with all its partisan and narrow nationalist interests. The same broad horizons that made Nehru India's greatest modern statesman also prevented him from seeing the real conflicts of interest that exist between nations. Further, Nehru's equation of Western capitalism with disguised imperialism, and his admiration for the Soviet Union, despite its record, were deeply ingrained. These ideological biases made him slow to recognize some of the complicated realities with which India had to deal.

If Nehru's policies failed to live up to his ideals, it would be wrong to let his failures obscure his achievements. The nonaligned movement has shaped the world we live in, and has been an important part of the developing world's struggle for equality and self-definition. That it was formed at all in the hostile postwar environment is a testament to his dynamism and leadership.

In examining Nehru's career with hindsight it is useful to distinguish between nonalignment *as a movement* and *as a foreign policy for India,* though Nehru himself frequently blurred the boundary between these distinctions. He vigorously denied any desire for the nonaligned states to form a third bloc or grouping; his whole policy, he reminded the Indian Parliament, was opposed to the alliance of nations in "camps" and "blocs." Nonetheless, his dream was clearly to lead a community of Afro-Asian nations cooperating in nonaligned solidarity, committed to his principles and to resisting the Cold War.

In the first flush of independence, nonalignment was a fairly simple idea. But the developing world soon grew into a very complicated place. The great variations in the conditions, ideologies, and leadership of the nonaligned nations led most of them to place self-interest, in the form of real or de facto military alliances, above Nehru's global moral imperatives. Some of the regimes embraced by the nonaligned movement consistently violated the values embodied in the *Panchsheela:* tolerance, pluralism, and peaceful co-existence. From the initial partnership of Nehru, Tito, and Nasser, the nonaligned movement steadily deteriorated during the sixties and seventies, eventually embracing such men as Gaddafi and Saddam Hussain, dictators from whom Nehru would have recoiled. No one can be held accountable for the degeneration of a movement after his time, but even while Nehru was alive the movement's weakness was beginning to show.

Nehru frequently stressed that the internationalist and moral principles undergirding nonalignment would serve and advance, not undermine, India's national interests. In retrospect, this does not seem to have been the case. Nationalism and internationalism need not necessarily compete, but any nation's domestic and foreign policies must be philosophically consistent in order to be effective. Within India, Nehru was vigorous in fighting communism, religious obscurantism, and xenophobia, and steadfast in upholding democracy and secularism as the founding values of the Indian state. However, abroad he was not sufficiently alert to the absence of these values among India's partners.

His singular focus on Asia and his suspicion of Western designs were both understandable, growing as they did out of India's experience with colonialism, and out of the fear of a Cold War–inspired nuclear war. But they also prevented him from seeing things he did not want to see, such as the territorial designs of India's neighbors.

As a foreign policy for India, nonalignment failed in the critical area of security. Foreign policies have traditionally served one purpose above all others: the protection and enhancement of an individual country's security. India's security suffered from Nehru's wishfulness and from his inattention to developments on the ground.

In the case of China, even if he started out with warm hopes of Asian solidarity, after 1950 there was plenty of evidence of Beijing's potentially aggressive intentions. Nehru should have adjusted his policies, and India's military budget, accordingly. China's invasion of Tibet and then of India itself demolished Nehru's policy—and his illusions—in the most brutal manner.

Nor did the policy of "friendship with all nations" win that many friends. India's tendency to "tilt," at different times in Nehru's career, toward China (throughout the early fifties), toward the Soviet Union (in 1956), and toward the United States (in 1962) created considerable confusion and mistrust among bloc powers. During and after the Korean War, they took turns in shutting India out of their deliberations either because they did not believe in or did not trust its principle of "dynamic neutrality." After the debacle of 1962, the nonaligned world was conspicuously silent, and only the United States (and, in its wake, Great Britain) rallied to India's defense.

However, nonalignment was by no means a complete failure; it has also brought considerable benefits to India. It has enabled the country to receive critical economic and military assistance from both superpowers, and simultaneously to retain a certain independence and flexibility. Today India has an impressive military force, with weapons from sources as diverse as Great Britain, France, and Czechoslovakia, but it suffers no foreign military bases on its soil. Nehru's fundamental principles, such as the importance of supporting anticolonial movements (e.g., in Vietnam and South Africa), and the need to stay out of military alliances, continue to direct Indian foreign policy today.

Nonalignment presaged the multipolar world in which we now find ourselves. If he were alive today, Nehru would have been exhilarated by the end of the Cold War, saddened by the catastrophe of Yugoslavia, and profoundly depressed by the communal violence in his own country. Believing as he did that the fabric of our "one world" is closely knit, he probably would have seen the intolerance erupting around the world as a harbinger of widespread and dangerous unraveling. The ethnic and racial violence in Yugoslavia and the revived Hindu-Muslim fratricide in India would have conjured up for Nehru hideous memories of the carnage that accompanied India's birth.

On the other hand, he probably would not have succumbed to gloom long. As he wrote to his daughter Indira in 1943, "Life is a queer business. . . . We are apt to slide along it without much thinking so long as everything is normal. . . . We may not understand much in this changing world, but we can endeavour to make ourselves effective instruments for thought and action, whatever might happen. . . . Do you remember what Beethoven said, Beethoven of all men in the wide world to be stricken with the misery of deafness? 'I shall seize fate by the throat. It shall never wholly overcome me.' "[60]

Notes

1. Jawaharlal Nehru, Speech in the Constituent Assembly, 14 Aug. 1947; in *Jawaharlal Nehru: An Anthology,* ed. Sarvepalli Gopal (Delhi, 1983), 76.

2. From the recording of Nehru's voice played at the Nehru Memorial Museum, New Delhi.

3. The fact that Indians have dubbed their nation's founders "Father" and "Uncle" says something about the Indian attitude toward political authority—and also about Indians' deep affection for Gandhi and Nehru.

4. Harold R. Isaacs, *Scratches on Our Minds: American Views of India and China* (New York, 1958), 303.

5. Herbert Rosinski, "Conversations with Nehru" (Boston, 1985), 12. Unpublished document loaned to the author by Franklin L. Ford, Harvard University.

6. Ibid., 11–14.

7. Jawaharlal Nehru, *An Autobiography* (London, 1989), 1.

8. Ibid., 1–6.

9. Ibid., 6.

10. Ibid., 17–25.

11. Ibid., 26.

12. Nehru's words quoted in Michael Brecher, *Nehru: A Political Biography* (London, 1959), 2–3.

13. Isaacs, *Scratches on Our Minds,* 307–12.

14. "The Rashtrapati," *Modern Review,* November 1937, in Gopal, *Nehru: An Anthology,* 565.

15. One of these cartoonists depicted Nehru as a one-man Indian orchestra simultaneously playing several different instruments, including a pair of cymbals—with his toes.

16. Michael Edwards, *Nehru: A Political Biography* (London, 1971), 245.

17. For an excellent discussion of postindependence government and politics, see Paul R. Brass, *The Politics of India Since Independence* (Cambridge, 1990).

18. After Sardar Patel's death, his candidate for Congress president, P. Tandon, was forced to resign, and Nehru's supremacy was never again seriously threatened.

19. Nehru quoted in Vincent Sheean, *Nehru: The Years of Power* (New York, 1960), 11.

20. Sheean, *Nehru: The Years of Power,* 25.

21. Jawaharlal Nehru, *Independence and After* (New York, 1959), 257 (my emphasis).

22. I am indebted to Charles H. Heimsath and Surjit Mansingh for their competent work on nonalignment and Indian diplomacy, in *A Diplomatic History of Modern India* (Bombay, 1971). I am also grateful to Carolyn Barnett for her fine unpublished paper on nonalignment, which pointed me to some useful sources.

23. Nehru, reported in *The Hindu,* 2 May 1954, quoted in Raju G. C. Thomas, "Nonalignment and Indian Security: Nehru's Rationale and Legacy," *Journal of Strategic Studies* 2, no. 2 (September 1979): 153–71.

24. George Washington quoted in Chester Bowles, "A Fresh Look at Free Asia," *Foreign Affairs* 33, no. 1 (October 1954): 54–71.

25. Nehru, *Independence and After*, 302–3.

26. Nehru quoted in Gandhijee Roy, *The Non-Aligned Diplomacy of Mrs. Indira Gandhi* (New Delhi, 1979), 32–33.

27. Nehru, Speech in the Constituent Assembly, 8 Mar. 1949. In Jawaharlal Nehru, *India's Foreign Policy: Selected Speeches, September 1946–April 1961* (New Delhi, 1961), 21–22.

28. Speech to the Constituent Assembly, 8 Nov. 1948, Nehru, *Selected Speeches,* 17–20.

29. Speech in the Constituent Assembly, 8 Mar. 1949, Gopal, *Nehru: An Anthology,* 367.

30. John Foster Dulles's speech at Ames, Iowa, made on 9 June 1956. From "Debating Neutralism," Editorial, *New York Herald Tribune,* 15 July 1956, quoted in Gordon A. Craig, *War, Politics and Diplomacy: Selected Essays* (New York, 1966), 250.

31. Eisenhower to Dulles, 16 Nov. 1953, quoted in Dennis Merrill, "Eisenhower, Dulles and India: Accommodating Immoral Neutralism, 1953–1958" (paper presented at the American Historical Association Annual Convention, December 1987).

32. Craig, *War, Politics and Diplomacy,* 256.

33. Nehru's speech of 7 Sept. 1948, in Jawaharlal Nehru, *Independence and After* (New York, 1950), 97; quoted in Charles H. Heimsath and Surjit Mansingh, *A Diplomatic History of Modern India* (Bombay, 1971), 153.

34. *Sanyasa* refers to a way of life involving the renunciation of worldly ambitions. Nehru quoted in Heimsath and Mansingh, *Diplomatic History of India*, 66.

35. Nehru's speech in the Lok Sabha, 24 Apr. 1954. Nehru, *Selected Speeches,* 399.

36. Mao quoted in Alex Shoumatoff, "Letter from Lhasa," *Vanity Fair,* May 1991, 88.

37. *Panchsheela* is the transliteration often used by modern Indian scholars, and is perhaps closest to the Hindi; *panca-sila* and *panchshila* are other commonly used transliterations.

38. K. M. Panikkar quoted in Neville Maxwell, *India's China War* (New York, 1972), 274.

39. K. M. Panikkar quoted in Maxwell, *India's China War,* 274.

40. Report of Zhou's meeting with some members of the Parliament of Sri Lanka, *Ceylon Observer,* 11 Oct. 1964. Quoted in Sarvepalli Gopal, *Jawaharlal Nehru: A Biography* (Delhi, 1984), 3:271.

41. M. J. Akbar, *Nehru: The Making of India* (London, 1989), 481.

42. Ibid.

43. Heimsath and Mansingh, *Diplomatic History of India,* 75.

44. Nehru quoted in A. Appadorai and M. S. Rajan, *Indian Foreign Relations and Policy* (New Delhi, 1985), 268–69.

45. Nehru's words quoted in Akbar, *Nehru,* 501.

46. The Kennedy-Nehru correspondence is available in the John F. Kennedy Library, Boston. See the President's Office Files; Countries: India, box 118a.

47. *Time* quoted in Brig. J. Dalvi, *Himalayan Blunder* (Bombay, 1969), 406.

48. Speech to the conference of information ministers of the states, reported in the *National Herald,* 26 Oct. 1962. Quoted in Gopal, *Nehru: A Biography,* 3:223.

49. Paul Gore-Booth, *With Great Truth and Respect* (London, 1974), 294.

50. *The Daily Telegraph* quoted in Maxwell, *India's China War,* 388.

51. Khrushchev quoted by T. N. Kaul, then Indian ambassador to Moscow. Author's interview with T. N. Kaul in New Delhi, August 1985.

52. Letters from Kennedy to Nehru on Oct. 22, and Dec. 6, 1962, John F. Kennedy National Security Files, Country File: India, Nehru Correspondence.

53. Theodore C. Sorensen, *Kennedy* (New York, 1966), 663.

54. Author's interview with B. K. Nehru, New York, 1987.

55. *Dawn,* quoted in S. M. Burke, *Pakistan's Foreign Policy* (London, 1973), 293.

56. Bhutto quoted in Burke, *Pakistan's Foreign Policy,* 293.

57. Nehru quoted in T. N. Kaul, *Diplomacy in Peace and War* (Delhi 1979); quoted also in Gopal, *Nehru: A Biography,* 3:266.

58. A phrase used by Theodore H. White to describe John F. Kennedy, in *America in Search of Itself* (New York, 1982), 3.

59. "The Rashtrapati", *Modern Review,* November 1937, in Gopal, *Nehru: An Anthology,* 564.

60. A letter to Indira Gandhi, 14 Aug. 1943. In Gopal, *Nehru: An Anthology,* 191–92.

14

EBAN AND ISRAELI FOREIGN POLICY

DIPLOMACY, WAR, AND DISENGAGEMENT

Michael Brecher

ABBA EBAN'S TENURE as Israel's foreign minister ended almost twenty years ago. Yet he remains the best-known Israeli in the chancelleries of the world and at the United Nations, where he was the consummate advocate of a state under siege. To many who heard his masterly flow of words he was the Churchill of post–World War II diplomacy.

Among the members of Israel's foreign policy–national security inner circle,[1] Eban was the most distant in background and experience from the new Israeli *sabra* society, its aspirations, its behavior, its approach to war and peace, and its attitude toward the rest of the world. Yet his Zionist roots were deep. Born in South Africa in January 1915 to Lithuanian immigrants, he went to England as an infant. His grandfather was a "fanatical Hebraist," and the young Aubrey was bilingual (English-Hebrew) at the age of five. His mother was secretary to Zionist leader Nahum Sokolow. And Eban himself came to the attention of the preeminent figure in world Zionism, Chaim Weizmann, as a talented public speaker in the Zionist cause in the hostile environment of England during the late 1930s. By then he was a fellow of Pembroke College, Cambridge, after a brilliant academic record: he graduated from Cambridge University in 1938 with a First in both classics and oriental languages and literature—Arabic, Hebrew, and Persian.

Eban worked briefly with Weizmann and Shertok (later Sharett, Israel's first foreign minister) at the London office of the Jewish Agency in 1939. He was a near-participant in the Dunkirk disaster of 1940. Thereafter his war service brought him increasingly into contact with the *yishuv,* the Jewish community in Palestine: in 1942, as liaison officer at Allied headquarters in Jerusalem; and two years later, as chief instructor at the Middle East Arabic Centre in Jerusalem. After demobilization in September 1946, he gave up his academic career and joined the Political Department of the Jewish Agency, the forerunner of Israel's Foreign Office. In the spring of 1948 he made his first appearance on the UN stage, pleading with passion the cause of an independent Jewish state.[2]

For most of the next quarter century he was the unrivaled voice of Israel: from 1948 to 1959 as permanent representative to the UN; from 1950 to 1959 as ambassador to the United States; and from 1966 to 1974 as foreign minister. And as Israel's preeminent diplomat, his status, while in Washington and New York, was higher than in his early cabinet years, as minister without portfolio, minister of education, and deputy prime minister, from 1959 to 1966. All three prime ministers until then, David Ben-Gurion, Moshe Sharett, and Levi Eshkol, had great faith in his ability to explain Israel's actions even when they aroused misgivings abroad, notably retaliation for raids into Israel from Egypt, Jordan, and Syria.

Eban was not only "present at the creation" of Israel's foreign policy in 1947–1948. From his Washington embassy and his UN mission in New York, he was directly involved in several major decisions during Israel's first decade. One was the (unsuccessful) quest for a mutual defense agreement with the United States, vigorously pursued from 1951 to 1955. Another was Sharett's decision to decline China's offer of diplomatic relations in 1955.[3] But the most consequential was his role in the decision to offer *conditional* withdrawal from Sinai in 1956–1957. In fact, at no time during his distinguished career of public service—as diplomat, minister, and parliamentarian from 1948 to 1988—were Eban's talents more effectively displayed than in 1956.

I

It began with an eloquent defense of the Sinai Campaign on 1 November at the special session of the UN General Assembly:

> Surrounded by hostile armies on all its land frontiers, subjected to savage and relentless hostility, exposed to penetration, raids and assaults by day and by night, suffering constant toll of life amongst its citizenry, bombarded by threats of neighboring governments to accomplish its extinction by armed force, overshadowed by a new menace of irresponsible rearmament, embattled, blockaded, besieged, Israel alone amongst the nations faces a battle for its security with every approaching nightfall and every rising dawn.[4]

Six days later Ben-Gurion created an international uproar with his "victory" speech to the Knesset, declaring the 1949 armistice agreement with Egypt "dead and buried" and the armistice lines no longer valid. The USSR was talking of military intervention. The United States threatened to cut off all material aid if Israel did not agree to withdraw from Sinai. The UN General Assembly passed several resolutions condemning Israel. And similar pressure mounted from Israel's loyal ally, world Jewry.

At a long and tense cabinet meeting on 8 November, "the Government decision was to leave the decision to Ben-Gurion." The prime minister decided to withdraw—in principle. At that point, the head of the United States Department in Israel's Foreign Ministry, Yaacov Herzog, urged an attempt to make withdrawal conditional, to be based on a formula that Eban had recommended that morning from Washington. It read: "The Government of Israel declares her willingness to withdraw her forces from Sinai *when satisfactory arrangements are made with the international force that is about to enter the Canal Zone.*" In an extraordinary act, Ben-Gurion left the choice—between unconditional and conditional withdrawal—up to Eban. The ambassador chose to pursue the second option and secured the approval of Secretary of State Dulles. Ben-Gurion's parting remark to Eban was phrased by witnesses as follows: "If you really take the responsibility that it is feasible, then I agree."

Most diplomats since World War II, perhaps earlier, would undoubtedly share the elation that Eban expressed over this diplomatic triumph: "In an age in which heads of government have usurped the negotiating functions of ambassadors in response to the vogue of summitry . . . , the idea that an ambassador can decide between sensitive and potentially explosive courses seems unreal even in retrospect."[5]

The Sinai case reveals an important role for a diplomat in decision-making under high stress. It is true that the strategic decision to withdraw was taken by Ben-Gurion before consulting Israel's envoy to the United States. At the same time, Eban's role was innovative. And the burden of responsibility placed upon him on 8 November was very heavy. Finally, the formula permitted phased withdrawal and therefore ample time to secure concessions, the raison d'être of the political struggle to follow.

For the most part, in 1956–1957 and later, Eban was the advocate, negotiator, and implementor of Israel's foreign policy par excellence. This was evident throughout his years as foreign minister (1966 to 1974), when Israel experienced several major foreign policy and national security upheavals: crisis and war in May–June 1967; the struggle over UN Security Council Resolution 242 in the autumn of 1967; the War of Attrition and the Rogers Proposals in 1969–1970; crisis and war in 1973–1974; and the disengagement agreements between Israel and Egypt and between Israel and Syria in 1974. It is on Eban's role during his tenure as foreign minister that the following pages will focus. But first it is necessary to note his conception of diplomacy and to explore his images of Israel and the world, as a key to his behavior.

II

Eban has always been an admirer of the "old" diplomacy, while recognizing the enormous changes in diplomatic practice wrought by Wilsonian ideology and modern technology. This is evident in his voluminous writings, nowhere more clearly than in a lengthy disquisition on "Diplomacy: Old and New," where his point of departure, approvingly, was François de Callières's classic eighteenth-century guide to the art of negotiation and the personal qualities required of the diplomat. He countered the oft-stated claim that diplomacy leads inevitably to appeasement thus: "If compromise and resistance are both excluded from the repertoire of diplomacy, there is precious little left." On the perennial debate over chance and predictability in international events, his view was unequivocal and self-assured: "Surely all evidence indicates that most international situations really *are* unique. Since they deal with contingency and purpose, they cannot be traced by rigorous formulas." Yet his erudition did not extend to the large body of international theory, especially decision-making analysis: "A scientific system . . . that makes no allowance for contingency, emotion and personality is unlikely to lead to better solutions than the admittedly imperfect classical method has been able to achieve."

Like virtually all members of the diplomatic guild, Eban deplored the depreciation of the role of ambassadors in the conduct of interstate relations. He often criticized the increasing "vogue of summitry," as noted above. But he concluded his discourse with, for Eban, a muted judgment: "It would be internationally harmful if professional diplomats were to lose their sense of vocation through being constantly outflanked by their political masters."[6]

Eban's view of the world during the first decade of Israel's independence and beyond focused on the Arab/Israel conflict, Israel and the Middle East, and Israel's right to security. At the global level, the principal perceptual components were the United States, the UN, and Jewry.

Typical of his image of the centrality of the United States was his remark in March 1955 that Israel's alleged isolation was false, that it had friendly relations with the majority of states and that, "in this process of establishing relations . . . with other peoples, our strongest reliance has been upon friendship with the United States."[7]

Until 1955 Eban and other Israeli decision-makers thought that they could ignore the Soviet Union's role in the Arab/Israel conflict. The violent anti-Zionist and anti-Semitic character of Stalin's last years, the break in diplomatic relations in 1953, the massive Soviet-inspired Czech arms transfer to Egypt and Syria in 1955, and the Soviet threat of grave damage to Israel at the height of the Suez War–Sinai Campaign in 1956 restored the historic Jewish image of a hostile Russia. Soviet patronage of Israel's Arab enemies during the next decade and Moscow's incitement of Syria and Egypt during the May-June 1967 crisis deepened Eban's mistrust of Soviet intentions. This reality, along with the role of the United States in the aftermath of the Six Day War, strengthened his predisposition to perceive the superpowers through a pronounced pro-American lens.

Like Sharett, Eban recognized the UN's limitations and its shortcomings in the Arab/Israel conflict, notably Secretary-General U Thant's abrupt withdrawal of the UN Emergency Force (UNEF) from Egypt in May 1967. At the same time, he persistently acknowledged its contributions to Israel's independence. And more generally he perceived the UN as a stabilizing element of great value in the global system as a whole. For Israel, he observed, the paradox was that, while the UN was congenial to the universalist element in Israel's heritage, the Arabs' numerical advantage, then 13-1, was most marked in that sphere.

A notable *lacuna* in Eban's image of global politics was Asia: as with most Israeli leaders, his view was concentrated on America and Europe, along with a recognition that Israel's diplomatic, economic, and military presence in Africa, at its peak in the 1960s, had political value for the resolution of the Arab/Israel conflict. Finally, Eban attached great significance to Israel's links with Diaspora Jewry; but, like most Israelis, he defined the latter's primary function as organizing "Jewish solidarity and free world opinion in favor of Israel . . . , a political role of crucial importance."[8]

Among his peers in the inner circle, Eban articulated the clearest image of the Middle East as a region of world politics. In a sweeping survey of the area and its peoples, caught up in "the tide of nationalism," he declared in 1959:

> While full respect is due to the rights of Arab nations, it remains true that the Middle East has not been in the past, is not now, and can never be in the future an exclusively Arab domain.
>
> The inner, progressive truth about the Middle East is to be found not in the word, "unity" but in the greater words "diversity" and "tolerance". . . . There is not one Arab nationalism alone. . . . There is not only Islam."[9]

This concept of a pluralist, multinational, and multicultural Middle East was to acquire the status of quasi-official Israeli doctrine. No one gave it such persuasive exposition as Eban.

On the critical question of Israel's proper place in the Middle East, Eban advocated a policy of cooperative coexistence. He also urged an outward "Mediterranean orientation . . . in concert with a renascent Europe and an emerging Africa."[10] And when he became foreign minister, he emphasized the "natural right" theme: "Israel is not an invader, an interloper into the Middle East. Israel sprang from this region, and Israel is returning to it."[11]

Along with, in fact as part of, his pluralist image, Eban was capable of effusive tribute to Arab civilization: "There is an Arabic literature of such versatility and range as to constitute a full humanistic education in itself. . . . [Moreover], the Arab mind has achieved radiant insight into the natural sciences."[12] At the same time he criticized what he termed imperfections in the Arab national movement: its lack of altruism; its obsession with the negative; its exclusive concentration on the political aspects of national freedom; the contrast between its political success and social irresponsibility; and its indifference to the wider interests of international order.[13]

In his perception of the conflict and of the Arabs, Eban was the most lucid exponent of the Weizmann-Sharett conciliatory, dovish approach to relations with Israel's neighbors.[14] Thus, soon after assuming the portfolio of foreign minister, he cautioned: "Such kind of talk and thought [ideas like 'The Arabs only understand the language of force'] is fundamentally wrong. As Jews we must be sensitive to any national 'typology'. . . . It is our duty to screen public speeches for insulting innuendoes and any derision of Arab culture."[15] Throughout his public life he advocated keeping all options open to facilitate a negotiated settlement, against the contrary mood of "fortress Israel" associated with Ben-Gurionism and expressed in policy terms as no concessions for peace.

III

The first major external challenge to Israel during Eban's tenure as foreign minister was the May-June crisis of 1967. That upheaval not only led to Israel's most decisive military victory (the Six Day War or June War). It also transformed the Arab/Israel balance of power and the geopolitical map of the region. Indeed, the territorial legacy of 1967—Israel's acquisition of the Golan Heights from Syria, the West Bank and East Jerusalem from Jordan, and Sinai from Egypt—was to shape the military and political agenda of the conflict for the next quarter of a century.

Two wars—the War of Attrition, 1969–1970, and the Yom Kippur War (the October War), 1973–were initiated by Arab states in attempts to regain the "lost territories." Resolution 242, the only UN document to win the acceptance of all parties to the conflict, enshrined the principle of "land for peace" in the aftermath of the 1967 crisis. An array of peace plans was generated by that upheaval, reinforced by the 1973 earthquake, notably: Allon (1967, Israel); Resolution 242 (1967, UN); Rogers (1969, the United States); Hussein (1972, Jordan); Begin (1977, Israel); Camp David Accords (1978, the United States); Fahd (1981), Fez (1982, Arab); Reagan (1982, the United States); Brezhnev (1982, USSR); Shultz (1987, the United States); and Shamir-Rabin (1989, Israel). And even the Madrid process, beginning in October 1991, can be traced to the problem of revising the territorial results of the 1967 war. In short, the 1967 crisis-war was a watershed in the forty-five-year-old Arab/Israel conflict. And since Eban was Israel's premier diplomat during the momentous events of 1967, his role during that upheaval and the struggle over Resolution 242 provides a valuable basis for evaluating his—and Israel's—diplomacy in conditions of high stress and high stakes.

The 1967 crisis, as Eban correctly noted later, was "born in Syria," where a militant, Alawi minority Ba'athist regime had come to power in February 1966. To overcome its internal insecurity and external isolation the Damascus regime immediately called for a guerilla-type "total war of liberation" against Israel, the recurrent theme of Syria's public posture into 1967. It was reiterated on 17 April 1967, ten days after the trigger to an international crisis then seemingly remote, an air battle in which six Syrian Migs were shot down.

The 1967 crisis unfolded rapidly. In each phase Eban's role was important; and in the agonizing "waiting period" at the height of the crisis it was central. During Israel's precrisis period (7 April–16 May), the onset phase, the cabinet made a contingent decision on 7 May to launch a limited retaliation raid against Syria if it did not desist from supporting a campaign of transborder terror.[16] This was followed by several Israeli public threats by Prime Minister–Defense Minister Eshkol, Chief-of-Staff Rabin, and others, and a formal message to the Security Council on 11 May that Israel "regards itself as *fully entitled to act in self-defence as circumstances permit.*"[17] The danger of these threats being misperceived was acknowledged in a typical display of Ebanesque sarcasm: "There were some who thought that these warnings may have been too frequent and too-little co-ordinated. . . . If there had been a little more silence the sum of human wisdom would have remained substantially undiminished."[18]

On 14 May, disquieting but not yet ominous news arrived in Jerusalem—of a state of alert in the Egyptian army and the movement of Egyptian forces into Sinai. Rabin responded in terms of standard operating procedure, moving some regular army units to Israel's Southern Front. Eban tried to "hold the fever down" by reassuring Egypt and other Arab states on the fifteenth, via the UN, as he did the Soviet ambassador to Israel two days earlier, to no avail, that there were no Israeli troop concentrations threatening Syria and that Israel had no intention of initiating hostilities.[19]

On the seventeenth three graver signals reached Israeli leaders: first, Egypt's demand—and UN Secretary-General U Thant's abrupt consent—that UNEF forces be withdrawn immediately from the border, where they had served as an effective cushion against direct collision between the armies of Egypt and Israel for a decade after the end of the Sinai Campaign; second, the crossing of two additional Egyptian army divisions into Sinai; and third, an Egyptian overflight of Israel's nuclear research center at Dimona in the Negev. These three hostile events and acts sharply increased the Israeli perception of threat and added an awareness of time pressure for response, as well as of a higher likelihood of war; that is, they triggered the change from precrisis to full-scale crisis.

Israel's crisis period, coinciding with the escalation phase of the crisis as a whole, falls into three distinct subperiods: apprehension and mobilization, 17–22 May; delay and diplomacy, 23–28 May; and resolution, 29 May–4 June.

The first was dominated by four decisions on mobilization, designed to convey Israeli resolve. The most important, by the defense minister and the General Staff on 19 May, calling for large-scale—but not yet full—mobilization of Israeli Defense Forces (IDF) reserves, was approved by the cabinet two days later. Eban was an active participant in the intense decision-making process, as a member of the eight-man Ministerial Committee on Defense, as well as the full cabinet; and he supported these decisions unreservedly, in accord with his atypically Ben Gurionist view about bargaining from strength: "With Israel weak," he declared on the seventeenth, "the Arabs will not make peace. With a strong Israel they will be compelled to make peace."[20]

Although diplomacy was subsidiary at this stage, it was not inactive. On the seventeenth Eban instructed Israel's UN representative to call the attention of the secretary-general to his predecessor's (Dag Hammarskjold) commitments in 1956 when UNEF was formed, namely, to prevent belligerency in the Straits and to consult within the UN if its removal was requested. The next day, the foreign minister expressed Israel's objections to the withdrawal of UNEF to the ambassadors of the three Western powers. Most important, he drafted Eshkol's reply to Lyndon Johnson's first communication during the 1967 crisis, in which the president warned Israel against retaliatory action, pressure he was to exert frequently during the next twelve days: in essence, Eban urged the United States to reaffirm publicly the guarantees given Israel in the past, notably by Johnson to Eshkol in 1964.

On the nineteenth, Eban made a last attempt to enlist Soviet support for a policy of restraint: he proposed to Ambassador Chuvakhin "a reciprocal de-escalation of troops in the South" and requested Soviet cooperation to this end. The ambassador's demeanour "expressed a sadistic delight with Israel's predicament." And his response led Eban to conclude: "it was almost indecently clear that what the Soviet Union 'had in mind' was not how to reduce tension, but how to bring it swiftly to the boil."[21]

That day, too, an Eban-drafted letter from Eshkol to Charles de Gaulle emphasized that Israel would not take military action against Egyptian forces at Sharm-e-Sheikh, the southern tip of the Sinai Peninsula, "until or unless they close the Straits of Tiran to free navigation by Israel." Similar messages were sent to France's foreign minister, Couve de Murville, and Britain's foreign secretary, George Brown. In Eban's words: "Between May 18 and 20, we informed the leading maritime powers that if the Straits of Tiran were closed, Israel would stop short of nothing to cancel the blockade." The purpose, he added, was to prevent any misunderstanding of Israel's intention: "One thing was now clear. If Nasser imposed a blockade, the explosion would ensue not from 'miscalculation', but from an open-eyed desire for war."[22]

With Nasser's announcement of the closure of the Tiran Straits, at midnight on 22 May, the 1967 crisis escalated sharply. And for the next six days diplomacy became the prime instrument of coping with the new threat confronting Israel. This was the period of Eban's most influential role during the crisis as a whole. This is evident from the six decisions made between 23 and 28 May, all but one by the cabinet, sometimes acting as the Ministerial Committee on Defense:

23 May —to postpone for forty-eight hours a decision on whether to go to war;—to approve Eban's journey to Washington to explore American intentions;

25 May —to warn the United States administration, through Eban, that there was a danger of an imminent Egyptian attack (Eshkol's decision);

26 May —to await Eban's return before making a decision on the opening of the Straits by force;

28 May —to opt for further waiting, in order to give the maritime states more time to open the Straits; and—to keep the armed forces on full alert.

In short, the second subperiod began and ended with cabinet decisions to opt for diplomatic rather than military means to resolve the 1967 crisis.

At the 23 May meeting Eban shaped the discussion on options, by virtue of his knowledge of the "commitments" made by the Western powers and other maritime states in 1957 as an inducement to Israel to withdraw from the Sinai Peninsula.[23] His case for delay and diplomacy was strengthened by a cable from Israel's minister in the Washington embassy, Ephraim Evron, on 23 May, containing a formal request from President Johnson to delay any action for forty-eight hours. Moreover, Ambassador Avraham Harman and Evron had been informed by Under Secretary of State Eugene Rostow that the United States had decided to appeal to the UN Security Council in the matter of the Straits. Even Israel's military commanders attending the cabinet meeting concurred in the delay, in reply to Eban's question whether anything would be lost by a few days of intensive diplomatic activity. On his tactics for coping with the crisis, he recalled:

> Instead of joining either of the two camps, the one arguing for immediate action and the other for indefinite waiting, I made a compromise proposal for a 48-hour period of disengagement, after which we should resume our consultations and take our decision. This suggestion was the only restraining proposal which I submitted at any stage of the 1967 crisis, before, during or after the Six Day War.

In the end, Eban's lucid exposition and draft resolution carried the day, along with Eshkol's addition on the need to consult Washington.[24]

The path of diplomacy and Eban's role in the 1967 crisis reached their peak during the next four days. First in Paris, then in London and, most important, in Washington, the foreign minister advocated Israel's cause and sought assurances of support from the Western powers. De Gaulle's position during their conversation on the twenty-fourth—and throughout the crisis—was inauspicious: "Israel must not make war unless she is attacked by others. It would be catastrophic if Israel were to shoot first. The Four Powers must be left to resolve the dispute. France will influence the Soviet Union towards an attitude favorable to peace." Eban's claim that Egypt's blockade and Nasser's threats constituted the opening of hostilities led to a reaffirmation that opening hostilities meant firing the first shot: "I advise you now not to be precipitate. Do not make war." This amounted to a disavowal of all previous French commitments and pressure to acquiesce in Nasser's fait accompli.

Harold Wilson was more accommodating. According to Eban, the British prime minister assured him that "the Cabinet had met that morning and had reached a consensus that the policy expressed in the blockade must not be allowed to triumph; Britain would join with others in an effort to open the Straits."

Upon his arrival in Washington, Eban found an alarming cable, signed by Eshkol, about a drastically deteriorating military situation, with an instruction to inquire whether the United States "would regard an attack on Israel as an attack on itself." Despite his skepticism and "better judgement," he conveyed the report to his American interlocutors. Secretary of State Rusk and his advisers "did not share the appraisal that any Arab states were planning an immediate attack on Israel."[25]

At his meeting with the president, Eban summed up his presentation in the form of two questions: "In relation to the Gulf of Eilat [Aqaba]—do we fight alone or are you with us? And what is the practical and public expression of the United States commitment to Israel's security?"

Johnson's reply was unmistakable:

> "What you can tell your Cabinet is that the President, the Congress and the country will support a plan to use any and all measures to open the Straits. But we have to go through the [UN] Secretary-General and the Security Council and build up support among the nations."
>
> And he cautioned: "Israel will not be alone unless it decides to go alone." (He repeated this three times.)[26]

Armed with conditional support from Johnson and Wilson—but constrained by pressure for more time to forge an international flotilla to open the Straits—Eban returned to Israel late in the evening of 27 May for another crucial cabinet session. His sober report focused and shaped the discussion. He acknowledged his failure to win de Gaulle's backing for an interceptive Israeli military strike. Wilson would cooperate, within and outside the UN, but only in concert with the United States. And while Johnson did not promise anything concrete, he would act in the matter of the Straits. Thus, in Eban's atypically defensive words, expressed two years later:

> At the risk of further disruption of the prevalent mythology about the May 27 discussions, I must write that its atmosphere remained composed and mutually respectful at every stage. The conjecture [about his] threatening resignation is the more far-fetched of many fictions which imagination and intrigue have woven around the May 27 meeting. At no point was I swimming against any tide.

A sharply divided cabinet meeting lasted until the next morning and then adjourned; the tenor of the speeches clearly indicated a 9-9 split on the issue whether to go to war immediately.

The cabinet reconvened in mid-afternoon on 28 May. In the interim, pressure from the Western powers had increased sharply, the most important being a letter from the American president and a message from his secretary of state: "As your friend," wrote Johnson to Eshkol, "I repeat even more strongly what I said yesterday to Mr. Eban. Israel just must not take pre-emptive military action and thereby make itself responsible for the initiation of hostilities." The call for further restraint proved decisive, as Eshkol admitted soon after the war: "Had we not received Johnson's letter and Rusk's message, I would have urged the Government to make the decision to fight. . . . I did not want him [the president] to come afterwards and say, 'I warned you in advance and now you cannot make any claims whatever on the United States and its allies'." The result was a near-unanimous cabinet decision (17-1) to delay military action, by implication, for at least another two weeks.[27]

The Cabinet's decision on 28 May in favor of further delay was the peak of influence for diplomacy in coping with Israel's 1967 crisis. The last week of the crisis period, 29 May–4 June, fell into two subperiods: 29 May–1 June, dominated by growing pressure to form a National Unity Government, with Dayan as minister of defense; and 2–4 June, during which the decision process to go to war was consummated.

The last of a cluster of provocative Arab acts leading to Israel's decision for war was King Hussain's journey to Cairo on 30 May to sign a defense agreement with Egypt: Jordan's troops were placed under Egyptian command. For Eban and other Israeli leaders it was reminiscent of the tripartite Arab alliance—Egypt, Syria, and Jordan—in October 1956 that helped to trigger the Sinai Campaign. Chief-of-Staff Rabin later identified this as making war irrevocable: "In my opinion Israel should have fought on the 30th of May."[28] Eban too recalled: "By his journey to Cairo on May 30 Hussain had made it certain that war would break out."[29]

On the same day, Eban told the world press that Israel intended to act against the blockade of the Straits, "if possible with others, if necessary alone"; and he used a memorable phrase, describing Israel as "a coiled spring" that would act "in days or at most in weeks, certainly not in months." The same day, the head of Israel's foreign intelligence agency (Mossad), Meir Amit, was dispatched to Washington in an effort to discern the likely American attitude to Israeli military preemption. "It became totally clear that they were not planning to do a thing."[30]

By the thirty-first the extent of the American commitment to Israel had become blurred. American documents and Johnson's memoirs referred to a disposition "to make every possible effort" to open the Straits, not to "the assurance that the United States would take any and all measures to open the Straits of Tiran," the formula used in Eshkol's letter to Johnson on 30 May, which Eban drafted. Eban dismissed the "semantic point" as "insignificant"; but was it?[31]

On 1 June, Eban shifted his position in favor of preemptive military action.

The catalyst was a "document . . . which had a decisive effect on my attitude," a report received that afternoon from Evron about a conversation with "a highly placed American," Justice Abe Fortas, a confidant of Johnson: "The American friend understood that 'time was running out and that it was a matter of days or even hours.' But he believed that 'if the measures being taken by the United States prove ineffective, the United States would now back Israel,'" Eban added: "The significance of this formulation, in my view, was the absence of any exhortation to us to hold our hand any further." He was fortified in this view by Rusk's reported press comment, in reply to a question about restraining Israel: "I don't think it is our business to restrain anyone." However, Eban exaggerated the significance of his act: "In constitutional theory the Foreign Minister is one of many whose votes have equal weight. In practice, however, his vote, if given for military action, has the strength of ten"[!][32]

By 1 June it became clear that the international naval flotilla under the aegis of the United States and the United Kingdom was breaking up before it ever assembled. And within Israel a political crisis had reached its peak, with the replacement of Eshkol by Dayan as defense minister. The denouement of the crisis—for Israel—was at hand, despite a French Cabinet statement on the second that "the state which will be the first to open hostilities will have neither her approval nor her acclaim."[33] The French also imposed an arms embargo on Israel, to take effect on 5 June.

On the third the new defense minister, Dayan, succeeded in creating an impression that Israel would wait another week or two: thousands of soldiers were given a weekend leave and were visible at Israel's beaches. Yet as Eban recalled: "Everyone in responsible positions knew that the die had been cast." And so it was: late that evening an ad hoc meeting of Israel's political, military and bureaucratic leaders, twelve persons, decided unanimously to recommend to the cabinet the next day the decision to go to war against Egypt, but not to attack Jordan unless Jordan attacked first. The decisive input was the assessment by General Amit, just returned from Washington after meetings at the highest level of the United States administration, that if Israel acted alone the United States would not object.[34] There was also a consensus that the Soviet Union would not intervene militarily and that the United States would provide diplomatic support after the war.

On the fourth, Iraq acceded to the Egypt-Syria-Jordan defense pacts, and an Iraqi armored division entered Jordan on its way to the Israel border.

At a seven-hour Israel cabinet meeting that day, sixteen ministers and, soon after, the two left-wing Mapam members approved a Dayan-initiated resolution "to take military action in order to liberate Israel from the stranglehold of aggression which is progressively being tightened around Israel." The timing was left to the prime minister and defense minister. Eban, to the consternation of the doves in the cabinet, supported military action, since, "by every juridical definition, Egypt had made war against us"; and he assured his colleagues that "we shall not repeat the situation of 1956 when the United States refused to speak to us."[35]

Diplomacy had now given way to force as the primary instrument in coping with Israel's 1967 crisis. The result was the Six Day War, 5–11 June, Israel's most decisive military triumph over its Arab adversaries.[36]

Twenty-five years later, many questions about that watershed event in world politics remain unresolved. Did Nasser seek war with Israel aimed at politicide or was his objective merely the restoration of the pre-1956 [Sinai Campaign] status quo? Did the Soviet Union try to prevent escalation to war in the last week of the crisis? Was U Thant's abrupt withdrawal of UNEF a legitimate exercise of the Secretary-General's authority; and did it contribute decisively to the outbreak of war? Did American policy in May and early June aim at preventing war, that is, restraining Israel (red light), or was it permissive of a preemptive military strike (green light), or was it something else?

An attempt to answer these intriguing and important questions is beyond the scope of this chapter.[37] Highly salient, however, is the effect of diplomacy on Israel's decisions and therefore on the outbreak of the Six Day War. This issue, too, remains a focus of controversy because of its implications for men and politics in Israel since 1967.

Eban made the case for diplomacy at the cabinet and Ministerial Committee on Defense meetings on 23, 27, and 28 May. "The question is not whether we must resist, but whether we must resist alone or with the support and under-standing of others." Before Israel responded militarily, there were several powerful reasons for diplomatic activity: to explore Soviet intentions; to test the willingness of the Western powers to fulfil their 1957 post–Sinai Campaign commitments to break Israel's isolation; and to consult with friendly states, first and foremost with the United States, to ensure their diplomatic support if victory were achieved on the battlefield. Moreover, diplomacy involved no military danger. And finally, diplomacy was designed to ensure American support, especially the delivery of arms, in case of war. "Otherwise we may win a war and lose a victory."[38]

In Eban's words a year after the Six Day War:

> The problem of possible Soviet intervention had to be explored. In face of the constant warnings that Israel would pay a heavy price if it acted, a countervailing influence had to be secured; even if Israel won, there was a danger that she would be forced back to the situation existing before the crisis; this, too, had to be explored. The United States had committed herself in 1957; this was the time to test these commitments; a short wait was not dangerous militarily; and it took only several days to establish that, if Israel moved, there would be benign support from the United States, with all that entailed.[39]

In his unpublished (1969) memoir on the 1967 crisis and war, Eban wrote, in defense of the *Hamtana,* the "waiting period," from 23 May to 4 June:

From the tension of a week's delay Israel would reap a good harvest. Her resistance would be borne along on the wave of a universal public opinion mounting day by day to a climax of ardent support. Her military position would become predictably better, and that of Egypt worse, than on May 28. . . . Most important [Israel's restraint] would give [it] a strong claim to their [U.S. and U.K.] political support on the morrow of victory. But [he acknowledged] all these benefits lay in the future; they would emerge slowly and painfully from the clouds.

And when the Israeli preemptive strike began, on 5 June, Eban recalled:

Even before the first results of our air action were known I was overcome by a vast relief. Everything that could be done to defend honour and interest without war had been exhausted. The righteousness of our action would impress the world, and the United States could not argue this time about our basic rectitude or claim that we had not involved it frankly in our predicament."[40]

Not all agreed. Advocates of an activist approach to all foreign policy–national security challenges to Israel criticized the role of diplomacy and, in particular, Eban's role during the 1967 crisis. There were two highly vocal antidiplomacy groups: senior officers of the IDF, led by Ezer Weizman, the chief of military operations, but excluding Chief-of-Staff Rabin; and the hawkish ministers from the left-nationalist Ahdut Ha'avoda (Unity of Labor) party, Yigal Allon, Israel Galili, and Moshe Carmel. Their arguments, dramatically expressed at the "revolt of the generals" in a meeting with Eshkol on 28 May and by the politicians at the cabinet meetings on 23, 27, and 28 May, were essentially the "other side of the coin": the Soviet threat was a bluff; a victorious Israel would be able to dictate the terms of a cease-fire; the 1957 "commitments" by the powers were worthless; and time was working in favor of the Arabs, that is, the military gap seemed to be narrowing. In short, only self-reliance and military preemption could overcome the crisis, and the sooner the better.[41]

After the war some of the generals and politicians acknowledged the tactical utility of diplomacy during the 1967 crisis; others did not. One of the most scathing critics was Teddy Kollek, long-time aide of Ben-Gurion and, since 1965, a consistent advocate of Arab/Jewish coexistence as mayor of Jerusalem. In his memoirs he poured scorn on Eban's interpretation of the merits of the "waiting period" in 1967:

It seemed to us that Eshkol's hesitation about attacking derived from weakness, not wisdom. Later, his supporters gave statesmanlike reasons for the endless delay. . . . Much of this was nonsense (even after the American or British ships would have gone through, the Straits could have been closed again). It was good for some favorable editorials in newspapers and a few kind words on American television, yet it made no more difference in the United Nations than if we had attacked on May 15. . . . The fact that all turned out well was his [Eshkol's and, by clear implication, Eban's] good fortune and a result of Moshe Dayan's leadership and the army's state of preparedness."[42]

What does the evidence indicate? First, the IDF was not ready for war at the beginning of the "waiting period." So Chief-of-Staff Rabin informed the cabinet on 23 May; and he agreed to a delay! As Eban correctly noted in his memoirs: "Not a single voice was raised at the May 23 meeting in favor of immediate military response."[43] In fact, on the twenty-first, when asked what diplomacy could do, Rabin reportedly told Eban: "Time. We need time to reinforce the south."[44] Moreover, "at the May 27 meeting there was no pressure from the army for immediate action." And on the twenty-eighth, after the near-equal split the previous day, only one of eighteen ministers voted in favor of immediate military action.[45]

Eban has long felt wounded by the "virulent attacks" on the *Hamtana*, which was identified primarily with his diplomacy. "The paradox is that seventeen ministers, not one, voted for that decision [28 May], and the campaign against the decision came after the war, when it had proved to be utterly triumphant. It was as though something in the national character made Israel intolerant of her own success." He quoted Rabin as having stated in March 1969 that, but for the decisions of the "waiting period" and diplomacy, "it is doubtful if Israel would have been able to hold firm at the cease-fire lines and in the political arena two years after the war." He also cited a public opinion poll in August 1969 that 63 percent viewed the "waiting period" as an act of wise statesmanship, and the views of foreign commentators who viewed diplomacy as crucial to the success of Israel's preemptive military attack on 5 June.[46] And he referred to the view of U.S. Supreme Court Justice Abe Fortas, a confidant of Johnson, as expressed to Evron on 31 May 1967:

> If Israel had acted alone without exhausting political efforts it would have made a catastrophic error. It would then have been almost impossible for the United States to help Israel and the ensuing relationship would have been tense. . . . If Israel had fired the first shot before the United Nations discussion she would have negated any possibility of the United States helping her. Israelis should not criticize Eshkol and Eban. They should realize that their restraint and well considered procedures would have a decisive influence when the United States came to consider the measure of its involvement.[47]

The debate over the effectiveness of diplomacy in Israel's 1967 crisis has become enmeshed in personalities and politics. Nonetheless, several themes emerge from the evidence. First, the thirteen-day "waiting period" did not lead to Israel's military defeat: if diplomatic activity did not contribute to a decisive victory from 5 to 10 June, it certainly did not hinder that outcome. Secondly, there is evidence that diplomacy did aid Israel's war effort: when the Soviets threatened to intervene to defend the Damascus regime, on 6, 9, and 10 June,

Johnson made it unmistakably clear to Brezhnev, using the hot line, that the United States would not tolerate Soviet military intervention or Israel's defeat on the battlefield. Moreover, contrary to its critics, diplomacy as practiced by Eban during the "waiting period" was not directed to "crisis management" in the sense of *avoiding* war. Rather, it was designed to enhance Israel's capacity *to wage war* when war came. As such, it was highly successful. The assessment of Eban, Fortas, and others was vindicated; diplomacy strengthened Israel's military capability by making President Johnson much better disposed to support Israel in a war against what some perceived as a formidable Arab coalition, the outcome of which was uncertain.[48]

IV

Within hours of the outbreak of the Six Day War a new phase of Israel's perennial political struggle began at the UN and in Washington. As early as 5 June Eban was aware of three dangers: of Soviet military intervention in support of Egypt and Syria; of a UN cease-fire resolution calling for a return to the positions on 4 June, that is, the 1949 armistice lines; and of the condemnation of Israel by governments and public opinion, forgetful of Egypt's threats from 22 May to 4 June.

Eban's first diplomatic success was to separate the cease-fire, on 10 June, from a call for Israel's withdrawal: a Soviet draft resolution on the thirteenth received only four Security Council votes in support of condemning Israel's "aggressive activities," and only six votes in support of the demand for Israel's "withdrawal behind the [1949] armistice lines." Ironically, the same day a leading Israeli newspaper, *Haaretz,* called for Eban's dismissal. But Eshkol stood loyally behind his embattled foreign minister, and the incident passed. Then, at an emergency session of the General Assembly, a Yugoslav draft resolution calling for Israel's withdrawal to the 4 June lines received only fifty-three votes on 4 July, far short of a two-thirds majority.[49]

The severance of diplomatic relations by the USSR and all of its East European clients except Romania immediately after the Six Day War was a serious setback to Israel's diplomacy. That void lasted more than twenty years. (The East European states and, later, Russia and the successors to the USSR established relations with Israel only in 1989–1990.) But the most important challenge for Israeli diplomacy in the aftermath of the war was the struggle in November 1967 over the phrasing of a UN Security Council resolution that was designed to lay down the principles of a fundamental settlement of the Arab/Israeli conflict.

The landmark UN contribution to *peacemaking* in the Arab/Israel conflict, Security Council Resolution 242, was primarily the achievement of the British representative to the UN, Lord Caradon. Eban's role was secondary, but not unimportant. Two rival proposals competed for Security Council support at its deliberations beginning on 9 November 1967: an India-Mali-Nigeria draft that called for total Israeli withdrawal without any reference to peace; and an American draft that called for formal Arab/Israel peace but left open the scope of Israeli withdrawal, with boundaries to be negotiated by the parties.

Eban held what he regarded as successful talks with Prime Minister Harold Wilson and Foreign Secretary George Brown on 6 November over the American draft; in fact, they were sympathetic but did not instruct Lord Caradon to vote in its favor. The United States representative, Arthur Goldberg, adopted a strong pro-Israel stance in his address to the Council on the fifteenth: "Historically, there have never been secure or recognized boundaries in the area. . . . An agreement on that point is an absolute essential to a just and lasting peace just as withdrawal is." Despite the fact that the American draft proposed permanent peace and negotiated boundaries—different from the 1949 armistice lines, as well as the 1967 cease-fire lines—as well as a mediation not an arbitration role for the envisaged UN representative, it aroused suspicion and opposition in Israel's cabinet, making Eban's diplomatic task even more difficult. In the end both the India-Mali-Nigeria and American drafts failed to get a Council majority. The initiative then passed to the United Kingdom.

Lord Caradon's first draft, discussed with Eban on the eighteenth, contained elements much less favorable to Israel than the American one, though it retained the core principle of "land for peace." And the proposed UN representative's mandate was to be confined to ensuring Israel's withdrawal. Moreover, in order to win the support of Argentina and Brazil, the British delegate added, though only in the preamble, the principle of "the non-admissability of the acquisition of territory by force." Eban was not impressed: "In point of fact," he declared, "no such principle exists in international law. The boundaries of most states which are not islands reflect the results of past wars, some of them recent. . . . [And] the European security system established after the Second World War was based on the concept that territorial changes by war were not only 'admissable' but internationally vital."

Eban made it clear to Lord Caradon that Israel would not acquiesce in the British draft. More important, the United States indicated that its approval depended upon Israeli and Arab acceptance. The result was important changes. The goal was stated as "the establishment of a just and lasting peace." The UN representative would have to "promote agreement" between the parties. And on the most controversial aspect, Israel's withdrawal was specified as from "occupied territories," not from "all the occupied territories" or "the occupied territories."

Several Soviet, Arab, and Third World attempts to broaden the scope of withdrawal, including a plea by Prime Minister Kosygin to President Johnson on 21 November to "interpret" the resolution as referring to "all the territories," came to naught. A final threat to the revised British draft came from the known intention of Argentina and Brazil to put forward a competing draft based on the Latin American resolution at the emergency session that failed to secure a majority, namely, total withdrawal in exchange for the end of belligerency, that is, "land for partial peace." According to Eban, Israeli diplomacy played a crucial blocking role: "Our ambassadors in Buenos Aires and Brasilia . . . almost wore out their welcome through the assiduity of their representations, and I was soon to find new pastures for them to graze." Finally, on 22 November, Resolution 242 was approved unanimously by the Security Council. The Soviet (and Indian) delegate added that his vote was on the "understanding" (assumption) that withdrawal meant from "all the territories." But Lord Caradon, the architect of 242, stated before the vote: "The draft resolution is a balanced whole. To add to it or detract from it would destroy the balance and also destroy the wide measure of agreement we have achieved together. It must be considered as a whole as it stands."[50]

V

The next major challenge for Israeli diplomacy occurred during the War of Attrition, which Nasser launched in March 1969 to compel Israel's withdrawal from the Sinai Peninsula.[51] The catalyst was several American initiatives to break the impasse in the protracted Arab/Israel conflict. Rogers's Plan A flowed from the American posture of "more even-handedness" acquired during the first year of the Nixon administration. In the words of the secretary of state:

> Our policy is and will continue to be a balanced one.
> We have friendly ties with both Arabs and Israelis. To call for Israeli withdrawal . . . without achieving agreement on peace would be partisan toward the Arabs. To call on the Arabs to accept peace without Israeli withdrawal would be partisan toward Israel. Therefore, our policy is to encourage the Arabs to accept a permanent peace based on a binding agreement and to urge the Israelis to withdraw from occupied territory when their territorial integrity is assured.

Rogers then set out "three principal elements" to implement the formula of "land for peace": "a binding commitment by Israel and the U.A.R. to make peace with each other"; resort to indirect negotiations—the 1949 Rhodes procedure leading to the Armistice Agreements—to work out "the detailed provisions of peace relating to security safeguards on the ground"; and the "withdrawal of Israeli armed forces from U.A.R. territory to the international border between Israel and Egypt." There was also a reaffirmation that "we cannot accept unilateral actions by any party to decide the final status of the City [Jerusalem]."[52]

The contents of Rogers Plan A were widely at variance with the five principles of Israel's policy toward the Arabs laid down in Prime Minister Eshkol's speech of 1 December 1967: "permanent peace"; "direct negotiations" and "peace treaties between Israel and her neighbors"; free navigation for Israeli shipping through the Suez Canal and the Straits of Tirana; the determination of "agreed and secure borders," to be incorporated into a peace treaty; and "a settlement of the refugee problem within a regional and international context" —after the establishment of peace.[53]

The announcement of Rogers Plan A on 9 December 1969, following eight months of Soviet-American discussions—the Two Power Talks—created a sense of crisis in the Israel government. The cabinet was summoned to an emergency session that culminated in an unqualified rejection of the American plan on the eleventh.[54] Rejection was extended to the Yost Document (Charles W. Yost was then the U.S. permanent representative to the UN), which applied the principles of Rogers Plan A to the Israel-Jordan dimension of the conflict, including withdrawal from the West Bank and Gaza, apart from marginal territorial changes. The Knesset concurred: on 29 December it rejected Rogers Plan A and the Yost Document by 57-3, with two abstentions.[55]

Eban's role in the struggle over Rogers Plan A was noted in Kissinger's memoirs. As early as mid-March 1969, during their discussion in Washington:

> Eban took vigorous exception to the very concept of Four-Power and Two-Power talks, on the ground that the deck would be stacked against Israel in either group. Eban stressed the one Israeli demand that he calculated was least likely to be met by the Arabs: the insistence on direct negotiations and Arab signatures on a joint peace treaty. . . .
>
> Eban objected strongly to our formulations regarding borders. . . . Eban rejected the notion of big-power guarantees as well. . . . In the final analysis, Eban saw nothing intolerable in the status quo. . . . The next visitors were Arab. They were no more tractable.[56]

Eban's memoir on the Rogers Plan was dismissive—and fundamentally wrong:

> The Rogers plan was undoubtedly one of the major errors of international diplomacy in the postwar era. It had arisen out of another attempt to secure American-Soviet agreement. . . . The United States made no attempt to give operative effect to the Rogers proposals, and the bilateral relations between us were not affected.[57]

In reality, the Rogers Plan of 1969 has been the unshakable foundation of United States policy toward the Arab/Israeli conflict during the past twenty-four years.[58] Eban misjudged its importance and persistence.

While Rogers's sweeping peace-making Plan A failed to secure the approval of the major protagonists, the cease-fire segment of his Plan B was, in the end, more successful. Nixon told Eban at their meeting on 24 May 1970 that the flow of arms to Israel would continue and that the United States was planning an initiative for a cease-fire in the War of Attrition, then in its fourteenth month. The secretary of state stated this intention publicly on 7 June. Yet Rogers Plan B came as a surprise to Prime Minister Meir when it was presented to her on the nineteenth.

In essence, the proposal was for a cease-fire of at least three months, effective 1 July 1970, and a commitment by Egypt and Israel, and Israel and Jordan to "designate representatives to discussions" under Ambassador Gunnar Jarring's auspices aimed at a "just and lasting peace." The document specified the two key provisions of Resolution 242—mutual recognition of each other's sovereignty, territorial integrity, and political independence; and Israel's withdrawal from occupied territory.[59]

On 21 June Israel's cabinet decided, unanimously but without a vote, to reject the proposal and to communicate its reaction in the form of a special dispatch to Nixon. Ambassador Rabin, surprisingly, with Eban's later approval, objected to the tone of this message and did not send it. In fact, summoned to Jerusalem, he persuaded the cabinet to soften its tone but not its substance. Then the unanticipated occurred: on 22 July Egypt's foreign minister notified Rogers that Egypt accepted his formula, albeit with qualifications.

For the next week Israel experienced mounting American pressure to acquiesce. The main instrument of American diplomacy was a dispatch from Nixon to Meir containing many assurances, notably American acknowledgment that: Israel's borders would not be the same as those on 4 June 1967; the United States would not be a party to an imposed settlement; Israel's withdrawal would occur only after a contractual peace agreement was reached; the United States would continue the supply of arms; and it would assure Israel of large-scale economic aid.

This was followed by intense debate among the leaders of all the coalition parties, further bargaining in which Israel sought "clarifications" and "assurances." Finally, the cabinet voted 17-6 on 31 July "to endorse the latest peace initiative of the US Government," largely in response to "appeals of the President of the U.S., and without abandoning its commitment to its basic policy guidelines and authorized statements." The Knesset added its approval on 4 August, 66–28, with nine abstentions. And what turned out to be a three-year cease-fire went into effect on the seventh, ending the War of Attrition.

The most far-reaching consequence of Israel's acquiescence in Rogers Plan B was a domestic political upheaval. The National Unity Government, formed at the height of the 1967 crisis with the inclusion of Dayan and the right-wing Gahal bloc led by Begin, dissolved because of the latter's refusal to legitimize Israel's commitment to withdraw forces from Sinai and the West Bank. In short, the anomaly of a democratic polity without a parliamentary opposition came to an end. But the Labor Alignment–dominated coalition retained a comfortable majority, 76 out of 120.

Eban's role in the decision process on Rogers Plan B, which he recognized as "another major decision," was secondary. This is evident in the brevity and tone of his description of these events in his memoirs. He noted his own "call for a 'cease-fire and peace offensive' in February 1970," which Meir "had contemptuously rejected." And he summarized his 24 May meeting with Nixon, which he termed "play[ing] my part in preserving our balance of air strength." Most important, he acknowledged that the power of decision lay elsewhere: "The operative fact . . . is that Moshe Dayan [then defense minister] and Golda Meir [prime minister] bear the major responsibility for Israeli policy during the war of attrition. Rabin [then ambassador to the United States] [and, by implication, Eban himself] could only advise; Golda and Dayan alone could decide."[60]

VI

The 1973 crisis-war unfolded very differently from that of 1967. There was no "waiting period" in which diplomacy was the primary instrument of Israeli crisis management. Moreover, Israel did not preempt; rather, Egypt and Syria launched a surprise attack against Israel in an attempt to recover the "lost territories." Yet diplomacy played a modest role in the onset phase (13 September–4 October).

The background to these diplomatic overtures was recalled by Eban:

> There were to be talks between newly-appointed American Secretary of State Kissinger and all the concerned Foreign Ministers, and a meeting with King Hussain in mid-October. Kissinger told Eban in August: "This can't go on, let's talk in October." He held two rounds of talks, one a dinner party for all who were willing to attend, and a separate talk with Egypt's foreign minister. "Zayyad said there was not going to be war. Kissinger told him that, after the Israeli elections [scheduled for 31 October], Eban could come back for talks, and the Egyptians agreed. And at our October 4th meeting Kissinger said: 'You come back in November, let's hope Zayyad will come back, and then we shall see how we can get the negotiations going'."[61]

But the path of diplomacy was rudely interrupted by war.

Israel's precrisis period had begun on 13 September with an air battle in which thirteen Syrian Migs were shot down against the loss of one Israeli Mirage. A series of incremental actions were taken between 26 September and the outbreak of war on 6 October to strengthen Israeli defenses on the northern front. A meeting of Israel's kitchen cabinet on 3 October accepted the estimate of the IDF's Intelligence Branch that the probability of war was very low; a call-up of reserves was considered unnecessary. The situation could await the next scheduled cabinet session on 7 October!

Of his last low-key conversation with Kissinger before the war, on 4 October, Eban recalled:

> There were no American warnings [of an Arab military attack] specifically. . . .
> There was, on both sides, a leniency about the interpretation of the facts . . . in
> favor of contingencies other than war . . . right up to October 5th. In my talks with

Kissinger on October 4, five minutes were spent on the situation on the borders. . . . Then he said, "since nothing dramatic is going to happen in all likelihood, let's get on to the negotiations [scheduled for the beginning of November]."[62]

That near-disastrous estimate continued until the early hours of the sixth, when new irrefutable intelligence information indicated that war was imminent.

Eban's role during the 1973 war was much less prominent than in 1967. As in the Six Day War, the generals were in full command, notably Defense Minister Dayan, Chief-of-Staff David Elazar, and Haim Bar-Lev, a former chief-of-staff. Even in the realm of diplomacy he was not preeminent: diplomatic activity in America was shared with Ambassador to the United States Simcha Dinitz, a trusted aide of Meir who had served as director-general of the prime minister's office. The foreign minister concentrated on the UN dimension of the political struggle, with the ambassador taking the lead in bilateral matters, though they worked in tandem for much of the time.

Eban was in frequent contact with Kissinger in New York: on 6 October, when the secretary of state made last-minute efforts to prevent the outbreak of war; and on the seventh and succeeding days over Israel's initial concern about a possible Security Council call for a cease-fire in place. To the surprise of Eban, Kissinger, and many others, Meir was disposed to accept such a cease-fire on 12 October, even though it meant acknowledging early Arab military gains. Fortunately for Israel, President Sadat of Egypt rejected the proposal. And the IDF's decisive victory in the major tank battle of the October–Yom Kippur War on the fourteenth, set the issue of a cease-fire aside for several days—until Soviet Premier Kosygin, during a hasty visit to Cairo on 16–18 October, provided Egypt's president overwhelming evidence showing that the tide of battle had turned in favor of Israel, with the IDF's crossing of the canal early on the sixteenth.

In the meantime, from the twelfth to the fourteenth, Eban and Dinitz concentrated on the increasingly urgent task of overcoming the delay in the launching of an American airlift to replenish Israel's seriously diminished stockpile of advanced weapons. It took President Nixon's direct intervention to resolve an apparent impasse between Kissinger and the Pentagon and to set the airlift in motion on the fourteenth.

Eban returned to Israel on the nineteenth to assist in coping with a new challenge, a determined Soviet attempt to impose a cease-fire so as to forestall the imminent military collapse of its Egyptian client, with the cooperation of the United States if possible, alone if necessary. Despite known Israeli objections to a superpower *Diktat,* Kissinger rushed to Moscow on 19 October at Brezhnev's request and acceded to the Soviet demand for an immediate cease-fire, legitimized as a UN Security Council resolution. The USSR, for its part, dropped the demand that all forces on the battlefield return to the positions held on 6 October. There was to be no room for diplomacy and bargaining: it was take it or leave it.

Israel's response emerged from a late-night cabinet meeting on 21–22 October. Superpower collusion was viewed as ominous. The substance of their *Diktat* indicated a mixed balance sheet. On the positive side, Israel's military gains since IDF forces crossed the Suez Canal would be preserved. Moreover, an enduring political goal, the principle of negotiation, too, was incorporated in UN Resolution 338, passed by the Council on the twenty-second. On the other side of the ledger, with a few more days the IDF would have destroyed Egypt's Third Army, almost replicating the victory of 1967, but at the cost of heavy casualties.

In Eban's words:

> While I joined my colleagues in expressing criticism of the Moscow procedure, I ventured to remind them that on substance Resolution 338 was a staggering victory for Israel. . . . We had secured the stabilization of the cease-fire in an international document . . . , as well as the first international confirmation of the duty to negotiate peace. I suggested that we accept the cease-fire on those terms before anyone changed his mind.

Most important, in Eban's view, was the human dimension:

> Many arguments flowed into our decision, but the most decisive was probably the prospect of losing a thousand dead who would never return, in order to capture a mass of Egyptian prisoners whom we would have to restore to their homes in a short time.

Eban also acknowledged the influence of "pressure by the powers" in the unanimous cabinet decision. In fact, a message from Nixon arrived while the cabinet was in session, urging Israel's acceptance of the cease-fire resolution. And Prime Minister Meir acknowledged to the Knesset: "We responded to the U.S. call and that of its President in appreciation and esteem of the positive policy of the United States in the Middle East at this time."[63]

The cease-fire was to take effect in the evening of 22 October, but it remained elusive. Fighting continued on the Sinai front, as Egyptian commando and infantry units tried to break the encirclement of the Third Army, and the IDF acted to tighten its vise on the beleaguered force. This was in accord with another cabinet decision, on the evening of the twenty-second, following Kissinger's face-to-face report on his deliberations in Moscow, first to an angry Meir alone and then to the kitchen cabinet, with Eban present: it was decided that "if the Egyptians failed to live up to the cease-fire, the Israel Defense Forces will "repel the enemy at the gate."

Israel came under mounting American pressure to stop the fighting, including a phone call from Kissinger to Meir on the evening of the twenty-third, emphasizing his commitment to the Soviets on the cease-fire. That day, too, the Security Council passed another cease-fire resolution (339), calling for the immediate dispatch of UN observers to the battlefield.

The last days of the war—24–26 October—were as dramatic as its outbreak, the surprise attack on the sixth. More ominous was the eruption of a direct superpower crisis on the twenty-fourth, due to multiple miscalculations by the United States and the USSR. It was triggered by Sadat's formal request to both Nixon and Brezhnev to send troops (or monitors) to ensure (or supervise) the cease-fire. That, in turn, led the Soviet leader to send an urgent letter to the president calling for the dispatch of a joint force, with a threat to consider unilateral intervention if the United States refused. Washington responded by placing its strategic forces around the world on medium-high alert, "DefCon 3." The result was the brief "nuclear alert" crisis, the gravest superpower confrontation since the missile crisis of 1962.[64]

Its effect on war termination in the Middle East was immediate. American pressure on Israel to cease military operations—without the surrender of Egypt's Third Army—mounted swiftly on the twenty-fifth: from Kissinger to Dinitz in Washington and by phone to Dayan and Eban; and by phone conversation from Nixon to Meir. There were too many unknown factors to permit further delay, it was argued: possible Soviet military intervention; possibly disastrous effects on détente and future peace talks. Once more, Israel's cabinet held a late-night session on 25 October.

Eban, as always, had a vivid recollection of the high-stress deliberations and the reasons for acceptance of Resolution 340. The Security Council renewed its demand for an "immediate and complete cease-fire" (the third in four days) and decided "to set up immediately under its authority a United Nations Emergency Force" to supervise the cease-fire; troops from the five permanent members were excluded.

> Yes, consideration was given to the possibility that American supplies would be stopped, though this was not said in the [Nixon] letter. It was a matter of casualties if the war goes on, the Soviet threat, and a break with the United States. The continuation of good relations with the United States was more important than a greater military victory. . . .
>
> The threat of Soviet intervention was real and visible. . . . In the Cabinet there was a consensus that the Soviets might intervene unless the Cabinet responded, it was that persuasive. . . .
>
> The Cabinet meeting of the 25th lasted until 04.00 in the morning. The entire meeting was devoted to the question, do we accept the cease-fire or do we not? The decision was unanimous. The decisive factor was the Soviet threat, and the preparedness of the United States for a confrontation.[65]

A closely related contentious issue was the encircled Third Army: the United States delivered an ultimatum—that Israel agree to a one-time permit allowing a convoy of food, water, and medical supplies to pass through IDF lines to the besieged Egyptian force. A negative response would create a crisis with the United States. As Eban recalled in his most recent memoirs:

Each of us (at the 25–26 October meeting) had to vote for a clear choice: Should we attempt the destruction of Egypt's Third Army at the risk of Soviet intervention, or should we ensure American support and the saving of Israeli lives by accepting the cease-fire and allowing the Third Army to be saved? . . .

Kissinger's warnings and the danger of Brezhnev's action were not the only impulses that led the Israeli government to accept the cease-fire. . . . Our own commanders were not unanimously in favor of another round. . . . One of the estimates was that it would cost a thousand casualties.[66]

The Egypt-Israel segment of the October–Yom Kippur War came to an end on 26 October. The 1973 war followed the pattern of its predecessors. Israel's war aims were victory on the battlefield and maximal destruction of the enemies' military capability. Arab war aims were victory if possible, but if not, the employment of war as an extension of diplomacy to break a political stalemate. As long as the Arab side had the upper hand, there was little or no pressure from the superpowers. As soon as Israel regained the military initiative, there was intense pressure for a cease-fire, directly and through the UN. The Soviets used military threats to achieve its goals; the United States used pressure. In the end, the military outcome was much more blurred than in 1967.[67] As such, it prepared the ground for a meaningful but prolonged quest for Arab/Israel peace, still in process two decades later.

VII

Diplomacy returned to center stage in the aftermath of the 1973 war: first, in direct talks at Kilometer 101 leading to the Six Point Agreement on 11 November 1973; then, at the one-day Geneva Peace Conference, on 21 December; and third, in the negotiations leading to Disengagement Agreements between Israel and Egypt and between Israel and Syria in 1974. What role did Eban play in these early stages of a prolonged Arab/Israel peace process that led, five years later, to the peace treaty between Egypt and Israel?

The Kilometer 101 talks were held between the military of Egypt and Israel; and an agreement was negotiated by Generals Gamassi and Yariv, with valuable intervention by Kissinger. Eban was not involved in that first direct Arab/Israeli agreement, which, he noted correctly, "appears in retrospect to be technical and even subsidiary, but it had great importance at the time. It reversed the cycle of conflict and set up a process of negotiation."[68]

By contrast, Eban was the central Israeli figure at the Geneva Peace Conference on 21 December. To some, that episode was a one-day wonder. Indeed it has not reconvened to this day. It is also true that the absence of Syria and the Palestinians ensured its demise. Yet at the time it offered hope of serious negotiations among the major parties to the Arab/Israel protracted conflict. And it provided an important precedent for face-to-face talks among most of the principal adversaries.

Eban played a notable role: in setting the ground rules for the conference, at a meeting with Kissinger on 14 November; in persuading Israel's prime minister of the wisdom of convening the conference before the Israeli general elections, rescheduled for 31 December; and in proposing the formula for a symbolic UN presence, namely, convening the conference, but without a substantive voice in its deliberations.

A side benefit was a much-publicized meeting between Eban and the Soviet foreign minister on 21 December. While there was no breakthrough toward the resumption of diplomatic relations, severed during the Six Day War, Gromyko reportedly declared: "The Soviet Union recognizes that Israel has an undoubted right to exist like any other independent state in the world. If anybody violates this principle, we will oppose that with great force." Moreover, he reportedly specified the 4 June [1949 Armistice Agreements'] lines "as the only secure and recognized boundaries of Israel." He also implied a willingness "in principle" to consider the resumption of diplomatic relations. Although this did not come to fruition until the collapse of the Soviet Union in 1991, and although the Geneva Conference never reconvened after its single day of deliberations, it provided an important precedent for Israel's negotiations with Egypt in the late 1970s, and with Syria, Lebanon, Jordan, and the Palestinians in the early 1990s. As such, the Geneva Conference of December 1973 served as a building block in the Arab/Israel peace process.[69]

Far more important in the quest for peace were the disengagement agreements of 1974 between Israel and its main Arab adversaries, Egypt and Syria. The architect of disengagement was the United States secretary of state who, through a dramatic innovation, shuttle diplomacy, was able to bring the reluctant adversaries together. The major obstacles were, as expected: Israel's insistence on a quick exchange of all prisoners of war; Egypt's and Syria's preoccupation with regaining control of "every inch" of their soil held by Israel; Israel's wish to cede minimal territory, in accord with the dictum, "a piece of land for a piece of peace"; and Egypt's and Syria's unwillingness or inability to go beyond de facto nonbelligerency.

Eban's role was two-fold—decision-making and communication. He was a member of Israel's negotiating team or kitchen cabinet, along with Meir, Allon, and Dayan, usually Galili, with Chief-of-Staff Elazar and other senior IDF officers and several senior officials of the Foreign Ministry also in attendance; Peres and Rabin were added to the negotiating team vis-à-vis Syria. As such, Eban participated in the making of Israel's key decisions on disengagement: regarding Egypt, the framing of Israel's proposals on 1 January 1974, which the cabinet, the next day, authorized Dayan to present to Kissinger; abandonment of the demand for a clear-cut Egyptian declaration of nonbelligerency as part of the Disengagement Agreement (15 January); and acceptance of the agreement (17 January); regarding Syria, return of part of Kuneitra, the principal town on the Golan Heights, by dividing it into Israeli, Syrian, and UN zones; yielding one of the three strategic hills near Kuneitra; making minor concessions on the size of the UN buffer zone and the thinning out of forces on both sides; accepting an indirect American assurance in a memorandum of understanding on the cessation of Syria-supported terrorist activities; and, finally, accepting the disengagement agreement with Syria, which was signed on 31 May 1974. The guns on the Golan Heights ceased firing the same day.

Eban's other function was to receive reports from Kissinger about Egypt's and Syria's negotiating stance, at their daily, sometimes more frequent, trips from Ben-Gurion Airport to Jerusalem and to communicate these reports to the prime minister and his other senior colleagues. As Eban recalled: "The shuttle had exhausting effects on my own physical and political strength."

Notwithstanding these two functions, Eban's role and influence in 1974 was considerably less important and visible than in the "waiting period" of 1967 or even in the framing of UN Resolution 242. The main reason was that the basic issues in the negotiation of disengagement were military or strategic, falling more under the jurisdiction of Defense Minister Dayan, Allon, hero of the 1948–1949 War of Independence, and the IDF commanders. With respect to both Egypt and Syria these issues were: the extent of Israel's withdrawal, in Sinai and the Golan Heights; the size of forces to remain in the areas of the thinned-out forward lines on both fronts; and the presence, size, and composition of the UN force in the proposed buffer zones. There were several Israeli political demands: a call for a formal Egyptian announcement on "the end of belligerency" and guaranteed free passage through the Suez Canal for ships and goods bound to and from Israel; and a demand for a Syrian commitment to cease terrorist activities. Egypt and Syria did not accept any of these, and the disputes were resolved through the technique of Israeli-American memoranda of understanding.

There is also "literary" and quantitative evidence that Eban's role in the disengagement process was less than preeminent, in fact, less important than that of others, notably Defense Minister Dayan. His own account of the five weeks of disengagement talks with Egypt and the months with Syria is very brief and vague about Israel's decision-making, compared with his detailed memoir on 1967 (9 pages compared to 108 in his autobiography, 6 pages compared to 72 in *Personal Witness*).[70] He acknowledged Kissinger's pivotal role in the negotiations, "although disengagement had been decided in principle by the Geneva Conference." Like Kissinger, he was not averse to chiding a colleague's diplomatic style. He described "shuttle diplomacy" as a "procedure [that] was dictated very largely by his [Kissinger's] taste for centralized responsibility. He showed a candid lack of reverence for the professional skills at the disposal of the State Department"—another indication of Eban's strong preference for the "old" diplomacy, noted earlier.[71]

Kissinger's memoir on the disengagement negotiations is also instructive. Almost all of the eight citations to Eban on the talks with Egypt and Israel are matter-of-fact references to meetings with him and others on the "negotiating committee" or are lighthearted in tone; for example, when the deal with Egypt was struck, Kissinger termed it "a good agreement"; Allon replied that it was "not a bad agreement"; "'Not bad' is Hebrew for 'good', explained Eban the diplomat." The five references to Eban in Kissinger's very long discussion of the disengagement talks relating to Israel and Syria were even less substantive.

By contrast, Kissinger devoted considerable space to his meetings with Dayan, notably, the latter's presentation of Israel's plan for disengagement with Egypt, in early January 1974, which Kissinger referred to throughout as "the Dayan Plan," and "Dayan's new plan" for disengagement with Syria, presented in Washington on 29 March 1974. Of interest, too, was Kissinger's portrait of Dayan, so very different from his assessment of Eban (see below):

> He was acutely sensitive. Self-centered, poetic, aloof, a brilliant manipulator of people and yet emotionally dependent on them, Dayan at his best had the most fertile and creative mind of Israel's leaders. When he felt rejected [as he did in the aftermath of the October–Yom Kippur War] he would withdraw and turn bitter.
>
> Badly bruised by the assaults on him, he had played a role in the discussions that ranged from the sullen to the sardonic. . . . [However], once a decision had been made—and others had assumed the responsibility—Dayan was constructive, imaginative and helpful as ever.[72]

The successful outcome to the disengagement negotiations—a major diplomatic feat—coincided with the end of Eban's tenure at the Foreign Ministry. Meir resigned as prime minister and was succeeded by Rabin, with whom Eban had a correct but mutually disdainful relationship. Rabin offered him what he regarded as a humiliating portfolio, the Ministry of Information. And so, as he recalled sadly in his autobiography, he left the cabinet on 4 June 1974 for what he perceived as exile to the political wilderness.

It was not quite so: he remained a member of parliament for another fourteen years, part of the time as chairman of its prestigious Foreign Affairs and Security Committee. But he became increasingly disenchanted with Israeli public life, after twenty-six years in highly visible and influential positions as diplomat and minister. And at the end, in 1988, he suffered further ignominy: denial of a "safe seat" on the Labor party list for the Knesset elections, first by exclusion from the select group of party leaders who were granted the top seven places on the list and then by defeat in several highly publicized ballots within the party's Central Committee.

VIII

Eban's role in the crises and wars of 1956 and 1967 were the high points of his diplomatic career. He remained Israel's preeminent diplomat until 1974. But his influence on the shaping of Israel's foreign policy diminished over time.

A widely held image of Eban, especially among Israeli hawks and activists, but also extending to the attentive and mass publics, is that of a diplomat who pursued the path of conciliation, compromise, and concession. This, combined with his sophisticated, biblical Hebrew, his intellectualism, his lack of service in the IDF and apprenticeship in a political party, made Eban the odd man out among the rising young leaders in the Mapai (Labor party) establishment during the 1950s and 1960s, notably Allon, Dayan, and Peres, and senior long-serving officers in the IDF, such as Rabin and Weizman.[73]

The reality was very different. Although a professional diplomat—of very high quality—Eban was a practitioner in the classic *realpolitik* tradition. He viewed diplomacy as one of several instruments of statecraft, a complement to war, especially in a protracted conflict such as that confronting Israel since the pre-independence years. There were times when war was necessary, as in 1967—*once the crucial preparatory stage of diplomacy, the "waiting period," had achieved its goals*. Often war was thrust upon Israel, as in 1948, the War of Independence, and in 1973, the October–Yom Kippur War. Eban recognized that, at such moments, diplomacy had to play a secondary role; but even then it was important, as in ensuring active support from one or more major powers, especially from Israel's principal patron, the United States. And in the aftermath of war—whether in the 1967 struggle over an international consensus regarding the path to peace (Resolution 242) or in the 1973–1974 struggle over a new relationship with Israel's major adversaries, Egypt and Syria (Disengagement Agreements)—diplomacy was necessarily at the forefront of Israel's strategy.

Most important, Eban the diplomat was a tough and able negotiator, yielding only the minimum necessary to achieve the Israeli goal and only when the cost of compromise and concession was judged to be less than the benefits of the outcome. No one praised Eban's diplomatic skills more gracefully than a fellow member of the club of distinguished foreign ministers in the post–World War II era, and an adversarial partner in multifaceted negotiations from 1969 to 1974.

Henry Kissinger first paid tribute to Eban's eloquence:

> I have never encountered anyone who matched his command of the English language. Sentences poured forth in mellifluous constructions complicated enough to test the listener's intelligence and simultaneously leave him transfixed by the speaker's virtuosity. . . . No American or British personality ever reminded me so acutely that English was, for me, after all, an acquired language.

Yet Kissinger was not averse to poking fun at Eban's oratory: on 8 October 1973, at the Security Council deliberations, "I told Eban to sacrifice eloquence to length if possible—a painful sacrifice for the Israeli Foreign Minister."

As to Eban's skills as a diplomat, he continued:

> Eban's eloquence—unfortunately for those who had to negotiate with him—was allied to a first-class intelligence and fully professional grasp of diplomacy. He was

always well-prepared; he knew what he wanted. He practiced to the full his maxim that anything less than one hundred percent agreement with Israel's point of view demonstrated lack of objectivity. Even a most sympathetic position—say ninety percent—was deplored as "erosion," "weakening," or "loss of nerve."

[And, like so many], I was not always sure whether Eban's more matter-of-fact colleagues in Jerusalem appreciated his eloquence as much as I did.[74]

As so often, his formidable talents have been recognized more generously abroad than at home. A pity; for the record reveals that Eban, the diplomat, made important contributions to Israel's unfinished quest for security. He was, too, a persistent fighter for peace. This is not exceptional in the diplomatic profession. What makes Eban's role significant is that, at crucial moments, he was able to persuade his (often reluctant) colleagues to pursue the path of compromise and accommodation in the larger interests of national security and peace. This achievement, in the turbulent recent history of the Middle East, assures him a place of distinction in twentieth-century diplomacy.

Notes

1. Michael Brecher, *The Foreign Policy System of Israel: Setting, Images, Process* (Oxford, 1972), chap. 10.

2. For informative accounts of Eban's pre-state years, see Robert St. John, *Eban* (New York, 1972), chaps. 1–14; *Abba Eban: An Autobiography* (New York, 1977), chaps. 1–5; and Abba Eban, *Personal Witness: Israel Through My Eyes* (New York, 1992), chaps. 1–6.

3. See, respectively, Nadav Safran, *The United States and Israel* (Cambridge, Mass., 1963), chap. 13, and Michael Brecher, *Israel, the Korean War and China* (Jerusalem, 1974).

4. The text of Eban's 1 Nov. 1956 address to the UN is reproduced in the enlarged 1969 edition of his selected speeches, *Voice of Israel* (New York, 1969), 276–92; the extract is from 279–80.

5. Eban, *Personal Witness*, 277–78. This analysis of Israel's decision to withdraw is based mainly upon Eban's (1957) unpublished "The Political Struggle in the United Nations and the United States Resulting from the Sinai Campaign, October 1956–March 1957," and the author's interviews with Prime Minister Ben-Gurion, Foreign Minister Meir, Ambassador to the UN Eban, and many Foreign Ministry officials at the time. These are cited in Brecher, *Decisions in Israel's Foreign Policy* (Oxford, 1974), chap. 6 and 602–9. For the crucial U.S. (Eisenhower-Dulles) role, see Steven L. Spiegel, *The Other Arab-Israeli Conflict: Making America's Middle East Policy, from Truman to Reagan* (Chicago, 1985), 71–82, and Isaac Alteras, *Eisenhower and Israel: U.S.-Israeli Relations, 1953–1960* (Gainesville, Fla., 1993).

6. Abba Eban, *The New Diplomacy: International Affairs in the Modern Age* (New York, 1983), chap. 9; the quotations are from 381, 383, 384, and 364.

7. "The Lofty Peak," speech before the Assembly of Jewish Organizations, Washington, 6 Mar. 1955, *Voice of Israel,* 190.

8. "Israel in the Community of Nations," Address to the Twenty-sixth World Zionist Congress, Jerusalem, 5 Jan. 1965, *Voice of Israel*, 187.

9. Eban, *The Tide of Nationalism* (New York, 1959), 47–48.

10. Eban, "Reality and Vision in the Middle East," *Foreign Affairs* 43, no. 4 (1965): 632, 635–36.

11. "Extracts from the Budget Speech of the Minister for Foreign Affairs of Israel, Mr. Abba Eban, delivered in the Knesset on March 23, 1966." Issued by the Government Press Office, Jerusalem.

12. Eban, *Tide of Nationalism*, 23.

13. Eban, "Nationalism and Internationalism in the Middle East," 29 Feb. 1952, in *Voice of Israel*, 71–73.

14. This was in sharp contrast to two prominent followers of Ben-Gurion's hawkish path in foreign and security policy: Moshe Dayan, chief-of-staff of the Israel Defense Forces (IDF) in the Sinai Campaign of 1956 and defense minister during the Six Day War of 1967 and the October–Yom Kippur War of 1973, and Shimon Peres, who later held every major portfolio and served as prime minister in the 1980s. See Moshe Dayan, *Story of My Life* (Jerusalem, 1976), part III; and Shimon Peres, *David's Sling* (New York, 1970). See also Brecher, *Foreign Policy System*, chap. 12; Uri Bialer, *Between East and West: Israel's Foreign Policy Orientation 1948–1956* (Cambridge, 1990), part I; and Gabriel Sheffer, *Moshe Sharett: A Political Biography* (New York, forthcoming), chap. 34.

15. "An Interview with Mr. Eban," *New Outlook* (Tel Aviv) 9, no. 7 (82) (September 1966): 17–18.

16. A formal text of this decision has never been published. Eban referred to it in his illuminating account of the 1967 crisis, as a decision "early in May 1967 to pursue a strategy of 'limited response' . . . the exact opposite of the generalized warfare which the Soviet Union then and thereafter attributed to us" ("To Live or Perish," [unpublished, 1969], 33). Later, in his *My Country: The Story of Modern Israel* (London and Jerusalem, 1973), 164, he specified the 7 May date and elaborated: "Only if all this [defensive remedies and verbal warnings] failed and violence had to be met by force would its response come into effect. Even then, it would be swift and of local scope, falling short of a general confrontation and *leaving the existing borders intact*" (emphasis added). A more cryptic version is to be found in his revised autobiography, *Personal Witness*, 353.

17. Letter from Permanent Representative of Israel to President of the Security Council on 11 May 1967—UN Document S/7880. On Israeli warnings between 9 and 14 May, see *Middle East Record 1967* (Jerusalem, 1971), 179–80, 186–88.

18. Eban interview with the author, 22 July 1968, and Eban "To Live or Perish," 35.

19. In that context, Eban has consistently accused the Soviets of primary responsibility for the 1967 crisis and war: "Grave events seldom have a single cause," he wrote two years later. "But there can be no doubt that the decisive link in the chain of events which unfolded in May 1967 was forged, in both senses of the word, by the Soviet Union." As conclusive evidence he cited a remark in Nasser's speech on 22 May announcing the blockade of the Straits of Tiran, which made it "plain that Soviet informants had spurred him to the dangerous course on which he had embarked." "On 13 May," Egypt's president declared, "we received accurate information (—passed on to a visiting Egyptian parliamentary delegation headed by Anwar el-Sadat—) that Israel was

concentrating on the Syrian border . . . eleven to thirteen brigades . . . (and had made a) decision . . . to carry out an attack on Syria starting on 17 May. On 14 May we took action." Eban, "To Live or Perish," 37–38. Almost twenty-five years later, Eban wrote, pithily: "There is no room for doubt that the 'information' supplied by the Soviet Union on 13 May was the proximate cause of the 1967 war" (*Personal Witness,* 354).

20. Eban, Speech in Rehovot, Israel, reported in *Maariv* (Tel Aviv), 18 May 1967 (Hebrew).

21. Eban, "To Live or Perish," 57, 60. A detailed *aide-mémoire* of the Eban-Chuvakhin talk is reproduced on pp. 57–60. Cryptic versions are given in *Abba Eban: An Autobiography,* 325, and Eban, *Personal Witness,* 361.

22. The text of these messages is in Eban, "To Live or Perish," 63–65. They are briefly noted in *Abba Eban: An Autobiography,* 327, and Eban, *Personal Witness,* 361.

23. Eban, "To Live or Perish," 78–81, and Eban, *Personal Witness,* 279–84. For a less positive interpretation of the evidence on "commitments" see M. Brecher, *Decisions in Israel's Foreign Policy* (Oxford, 1974), 296–303.

24. A perception of Eban's pro-U.S. bias and the fear of being drawn into formal commitments led some ministers to urge that someone else, notably Eban's predecessor as foreign minister, and prime minister during the War of Attrition (1969–1970) and the October–Yom Kippur crisis and war (1973–1974), Golda Meir, then a Mapai party leader, be sent to Washington for this delicate diplomatic mission. But she, Eshkol, and others rejected the idea.

On the 23 May meeting see: Eban, "To Live or Perish," chap. 4, 72–89; the quotation is from 155–56; *Abba Eban: An Autobiography,* 332–38; *Personal Witness,* 367–69; St. John, *Eban,* 417–20; Menachem Begin, "A Chapter from a Book to be Written," *Maariv* (Tel Aviv), 18 June, 2 July, 1971 (Hebrew); Shlomo Nakdimon, *Towards the Zero Hour: The Drama that Preceded the Six Day War* (Tel Aviv, 1968) (Hebrew), 43–60; Zeev Schiff, "The Three Weeks that Preceded the War," *Haaretz* (Tel Aviv), 4 Oct. 1967 (Hebrew); M. Brecher with Benjamin Geist, *Decisions in Crisis: Israel, 1967 and 1973* (Berkeley, Calif., 1980), 117–23.

25. This cable, reinforced by an even more alarming one within hours, was instigated by Chief-of-Staff Rabin and the director-general of the prime minister's office, Yaacov Herzog. It was an unsuccessful high-risk attempt to compel the U.S. president to make a far-reaching commitment to Israel or to leave it free to act. Rabin attributed the idea to Herzog. Yitzhak Rabin, "Six Days and Five More Years," *Maariv* (Tel Aviv), 2 June 1972 (Hebrew), and *The Rabin Memoirs* (Boston, 1979), 86–89.

Eban expressed surprise and "deep perplexity," in "To Live or Perish," 111–15, 119–20. Twenty-five years after the crisis, in uncharacteristic, undiplomatic language, he expressed outrage and delivered a scathing personal attack on this unwarranted intrusion into a delicate and crucial diplomatic mission: "This cable sticks in my mind as an act of momentous irresponsibility." He referred to "this eccentric cable" and to the "hypochondriac cables. . . . One of the causes was the nervous indisposition of the chief of staff, Yitzhak Rabin [during the 1967 crisis], through what was charitably defined as nicotine poisoning. . . . The entire basis of my mission had suddenly been changed. . . . I was being called to present a demand that had no justification and that would only invite rejection. . . . The cable lacked wisdom, veracity and tactical understanding. Nothing was right about it" (Eban, *Personal Witness,* 382–83).

26. The main source for Eban's discussions with de Gaulle, Wilson, and Johnson is "To Live or Perish," chap. 5, 90–149; the quotations are: de Gaulle, 95, 99; regarding Wilson, 105; and Eban-Johnson, 139, 140. On the controversy surrounding Johnson's "commitment" to Eban, see n. 31 below. See also *Abba Eban: An Autobiography,* 341–59; Eban, *Personal Witness,* chap. 19, 371–91; St. John, *Eban,* 420–34; Lyndon B. Johnson, *The Vantage Point* (New York, 1971), 293–94; and Harold Wilson, *The Labour Government: A Personal Record, 1964–1970* (London, 1971), 401–4. (De Gaulle, in his *Memoirs of Hope* [London, 1971] has three fleeting passages on the Suez crisis, none on the exchange with Eban.) For analyses, see Brecher with Geist, *Decisions in Crisis,* 127–29, 131–33, 135–38; and William B. Quandt, "Lyndon Johnson and the June 1967 War: What Color Was the Light?" *Middle East Journal* 46, no. 2 (1992): 206–14.

27. The primary source for Eban's role at the 27–28 cabinet meetings is his "To Live or Perish," chap. 6, 150–78; the quotations are from 159–60. Abbreviated versions are to be found in *Abba Eban: An Autobiography,* 367–71; Eban, *Personal Witness,* 396–99; St. John, *Eban,* 437–39. Eshkol's statement is from an interview with the editors, *Maariv* (Tel Aviv), 4 Oct. 1967 (Hebrew). Other sources for these meetings are: Levi Eshkol, statement in the Knesset, 29 May 1967, *Divrei Ha-Knesset,* vol. 49, cols. 2283–85, in H. M. Christman, ed., *The State Papers of Levi Eshkol* (New York, 1969), 95–104; Moshe Gilboa, *Six Years–Six Days: Origins and History of the Six Day War* (Tel Aviv, 1969), 155–57 (Hebrew); Winston Burdett, *Encounter with the Middle East* (London, 1970), 266–67; Nakdimon, *Towards the Zero Hour,* 117–23, 128–29; Brecher with Geist, *Decisions in Crisis,* 142–48.

28. Rabin, "Six Days and Five More Years," *Maariv* (Tel Aviv), 2 June 1972 (Hebrew).

29. Eban, "To Live or Perish," 184–87, *Abba Eban: An Autobiography,* 380, and interview with M. Brecher, 8 Aug. 1968. President Johnson's national security adviser, Walt Rostow, shared this somber view in *The Diffusion of Power: An Essay in Recent History* (New York, 1972), 417–19.

30. Amit interview with Benjamin Geist, 13 July 1973.

31. Eban, "To Live or Perish," 196, 198. The president's national security adviser, Walt Rostow, conveyed his concern about Eshkol's more far-reaching formulation, to Israel's No. 2 in Washington, Evron, on 31 May; and Evron warned of the implications of the apparent weakening of the U.S. commitment (pp. 197–98). Johnson reportedly "became angry, claiming that he had not given Israel a blank check in the form of a promise to use 'any and all measures', but rather had stressed that he would make every effort within his constitutional authority" (Quandt, "Lyndon Johnson and June 1967 War," 217). Johnson, in his memoirs (*Vantage Point,* 293), quotes himself as having told Eban: "You can assure the Israeli Cabinet, we will pursue vigorously any and all *possible measures* to keep the strait open" (emphasis added). Eban, in his revised autobiography (*Personal Witness,* 398), quotes this sentence to prove that "the semantic point was insignificant."

32. As quoted in Eban, "To Live or Perish," 200, 201, 203. There is a slightly different wording of the key operational phrase by Fortas in *Abba Eban: An Autobiography,* 385: "to stay our hand *much longer*" (emphasis added). Eban identified the "highly placed American" in 1992 as Fortas and omitted reference to the phrase, "to stay our hand," *Personal Witness,* 405. And Peres referred to the Evron report elliptically:

"Even in certain circles in Washington the view was heard [at the end of May] that the only one able to find a way out of the impasse was Israel herself. This view reached the ears of Jerusalem" (*David's Sling*, 236).

33. *Documents on Palestine*, 49–50.

34. The Amit assessment was reinforced by two other events in the diplomacy of the last days of the 1967 prewar crisis period. One was Evron's report from Washington on his separate meetings with Walt Rostow, Secretary of Defense McNamara, and Rusk on 2 and 3 June: although they knew from him and Amit that "time was running out," none warned Israel not to take military action. The other was Fortas's reported remark to Harman on the third as he was leaving Washington for the inner cabinet meeting: "Rusk will fiddle while Israel burns. If you're going to save yourself, do it yourself." As reported in Quandt, "Lyndon Johnson and the June 1967 War," 219–21.

35. The Eban quotations, on 3 and 4 June, are from "To Live or Perish," 228, 243–44.

The full text of the cabinet war decision was published by the government of Israel on the fifth anniversary of the Six Day War. The English translation is in *Jerusalem Post*, 5 June 1972.

On the last days before the war, see also: Dayan, *Story of My Life*, chap. 19; *Abba Eban: An Autobiography*, 395–400; Eban, *Personal Witness*, 400–407; Nakdimon, *Towards the Zero Hour*, 169–278; Burdett, *Encounter with the Middle East*, 309–16; Brecher with Geist, *Decisions in Crisis*, 151–70.

36. On the military aspects of 1967, especially the balance of forces and the Six Day War, see: Dayan, *Story of My Life*, chaps. 20, 21; Trevor N. Dupuy, *Elusive Victory: The Arab-Israeli Wars, 1947–1974* (New York, 1978); A. Hashavia, *A History of the Six Day War* (Tel Aviv, 1968); Chaim Herzog, *The Arab-Israeli Wars* (New York, 1982); International Institute of Strategic Studies, *The Military Balance 1966–67* and *1967–68*, and *Strategic Survey, 1966* and *1967* (London, 1967, 1968); Donald Neff, *Warriors for Jerusalem: The Six Days that Changed the Middle East* (New York, 1984); E. O'Ballance, *The Third Arab-Israeli War* (London, 1972); Nadav Safran, *From War to War: The Arab-Israeli Confrontation 1948–1967* (New York, 1969), appendices B, C.

For Eban's memoirs on the war period, much of which he spent in America defending Israel's interests at the UN and in Washington, see "To Live or Perish," chap. 8, 251–76, *Abba Eban: An Autobiography*, 414–24, and Eban, *Personal Witness*, 415–26.

For a crisis perspective on the war, that is, 5–10 June as the "end-crisis" period of Israel's 1967 foreign policy crisis, see Brecher with Geist, *Decisions in Crisis*, chap. 8.

On the U.S. role in the 1967 crisis and war see William B. Quandt, *Decade of Decisions: American Policy toward the Arab-Israeli Conflict, 1967–1976* (Berkeley, 1977), chap. 2, and Spiegel, *The Other Arab-Israeli Conflict*, 136–53.

37. Suffice it to note the central finding from a careful reexamination of U.S. policy in the 1967 crisis. Based upon newly available primary sources, William B. Quandt opted for a "yellow-light" interpretation. "During the first two weeks of the crisis, in the latter part of May, Johnson seems to have genuinely hoped to avoid a war in the Middle East . . . (mainly by) trying to restrain the Israelis. . . . Toward the end of May, however . . . Johnson abandoned the policy of making an all-out effort to prevent war. . . . The red light turned yellow—but not quite green. For the Israeli cabinet, that was enough." "Lyndon Johnson and the June 1967 War," 198–228. The quotations are from 199, 228.

38. *Abba Eban: An Autobiography*, p. 334; Eban, *Personal Witness*, 368–69.

39. Interview with Eban in Herzliya, Israel, 8 July 1968.

40. Eban, "To Live or Perish," 168–69, 252.

41. Interview with Allon, 26 July 1968.

42. Teddy Kollek, *For Jerusalem* (Jerusalem and Tel Aviv, 1978), 190.

43. Eban, *Personal Witness*, 369.

44. *Abba Eban: An Autobiography*, 333.

45. Eban, *Personal Witness*, 396, 399.

46. These quotations and citations are from *Abba Eban: An Autobiography*, 373.

47. Eban, "To Live or Perish," 200–201; and Eban, *Personal Witness*, 405.

48. This discussion of Israel's behavior during the 1967 crisis and war draws upon the author's interviews with many of the participants, between 1968 and 1973, notably Allon, Ben-Gurion, Eban, Eshkol, Meir, Peres, Harold Wilson, and senior officials of Israel's Foreign Ministry.

These and other primary sources, and the rich secondary materials on 1967, are cited in Brecher, *Decisions in Israel's Foreign Policy,* chap. 7 and 609–15; and in Brecher with Geist, *Decisions in Crisis,* chaps. 2, 5, 8, and 439–45.

49. Eban's lengthy unpublished memoir on the June-July political struggle is in "To Live or Perish," chap. 9, 309–446. Abbreviated versions are in *Abba Eban: An Autobiography,* chap. 15; and in Eban, *Personal Witness,* chap. 21.

50. The text of Resolution 242 is in UN Document S/8247; the India-Mali-Nigeria draft is in S/8227; and the US draft is in S/8229.

For Eban's unpublished memoir on the struggle over Resolution 242, see "To Live or Perish," 450–75; the quotations are from 469, 474. Abbreviated versions are in *Abba Eban: An Autobiography,* 449–53; and Eban, *Personal Witness,* 455–459.

Goldberg's remark is from UN Document S/PV 1377, 15 Nov. 1967, 37. He reiterated the U.S. view in "Withdrawal Needn't be Total: An Interpretation of Resolution 242," *Washington Star,* 9 Dec. 1973, B-3.

Lord Caradon's remark is from UN Document S/PV 1382, 22 Nov. 1967, 31. He discussed the background of Resolution 242 in the *Sunday Times* (London), 5 July 1970, reprinted in his *A Plan for Peace* (London, n.d.).

British ministers, too, emphasized that Israeli withdrawal was envisaged as less than total. According to George Brown, foreign secretary at the time: "This resolution . . . does not call for Israeli withdrawal from 'the' territories recently occupied, nor does it use the word 'all'. It would have been impossible to get the resolution through if either of these words had been included." *In My Way* (London, 1971), 233.

And Foreign Secretary Michael Stewart declared in the House of Commons on 9 Dec. 1969: "As I have told the House previously, we believe that these two things ['withdrawal from territories' and 'secure and recognized boundaries'] should be read concurrently and that the omission of the word 'all' before the word 'territories' is deliberate" (*Weekly Hansard* [House of Commons], no. 812, 5–11 Dec. 1969, Debate on Foreign Affairs, col. 261).

51. On the fourth round of warfare in the protracted conflict see Yaacov Bar-Siman-Tov, *The Israeli-Egyptian War of Attrition, 1969–1970* (New York, 1980).

52. The text of Rogers Plan A is in Department of State Press Release, no. 371, 9 Dec. 1969.

53. A partial text is in *The Israel Digest* 60, no. 25 (15 Dec. 1967).

54. An English translation of the text is in "Israel Rejects Territorial Settlement by Outsiders," *Jerusalem Post*, 12 Dec. 1969.

55. The official Israeli response was blunt and accusatory: "The Cabinet rejects these American proposals [both Rogers Plan A and the Yost Document], in that they prejudice the chances of establishing peace. . . . The proposals . . . cannot but be construed by the aggressive Arab rulers as an attempt to appease them, at Israel's expense." The statement was reportedly drafted by an ad hoc committee of seven ministers, including Eban. *Haaretz* (Tel Aviv), 23 Dec. 1969 (Hebrew). The English version of the text is in *Jerusalem Post*, 23 Dec. 1969.

The parliamentary vote is in *Divrei Ha-Knesset*, 61:344–45.

56. Kissinger, *White House Years* (Boston, 1979), 359–60. Kissinger's somewhat disparaging views on the Rogers Plan are set out in pp. 373–77.

57. *Abba Eban: An Autobiography*, 464.

58. The Rogers principles were expressed in the Reagan Plan of 1 Sept. 1982 and in the Schultz Plan of 1987, though the phrasing differs.

59. The text of Rogers Plan B is in *New York Times*, 23 July 1970; *Jerusalem Post*, 31 July 1970; and "Note to the Secretary-General on the Jarring Mission for the Information of the Security Council" (S/9902, 7 Aug. 1970).

60. Eban's account of the "crisis" over Rogers Plan B is in *Abba Eban: An Autobiography*, 466–68, and *Personal Witness*, 487–91. The quotations are from Brecher, *Decisions in Israel's Foreign Policy*, 496; *Abba Eban: An Autobiography*, 467; and Eban, *Personal Witness*, 490, 487, 487.

For analyses of the Rogers plans from the U.S. perspective see Quandt, *Decade of Decisions*, chap. 3, and Spiegel, *The Other Arab-Israel Conflict*, 181–96. For an in-depth study of Israeli perceptions and Israel's decision process on Rogers Plans A and B see Brecher, *Decisions in Israel's Foreign Policy*, chap. 8.

For a detailed chronicle of the background to these plans, reactions by the parties, and the relevant document, see Bernard Reich, *Quest For Peace: United States–Israel Relations and the Arab-Israeli Conflict* (New Brunswick, N.J., 1977), 90–114, 119–20, 134–51, 153, 159–65, and 207–12.

61. Interview with Eban in *Herzliya* (Israel) 15 July 1974. This account was reaffirmed in *Abba Eban: An Autobiography*, 498.

62. Interview with Eban in *Herzliya* (Israel) 15 July 1974.

Kissinger's account concurred: "Our own reporting was a mirror image of Israel's. . . . Clearly, there was an intelligence failure, but misjudgment was not confined to the agencies. . . . Still, despite this event [the sudden airlift of Soviet dependents from Egypt and Syria] and the Egyptian military exercises, our morning briefings assured us that Egypt and Syria were not planning for war." *Years of Upheaval* (Boston, 1982), 464–65.

According to Quandt, too, the U.S. intelligence community held the view that "the option of a political alternative made an Arab-initiated war implausible" (*Decade of Decisions*, 168).

63. The Eban quotations are from *Personal Witness*, 537, and *Abba Eban: An Autobiography*, 530; the Meir quote is from *Divrei Ha-Knesset*, vol. 68, col. 4508, 23 Oct. 1973. See also Dayan, *Story of My Life*, 443–44.

64. For an illuminating case study of the superpowers' flawed crisis management in 1973, drawing on hitherto unavailable sources on Soviet behavior, see R. Ned Lebow and Janice G. Stein, *We All Lost the Cold War* (Princeton, N.J., 1994), part II.

65. Interview with Eban in *Herzliya* (Israel) 15 July 1974. These views were also noted in *Abba Eban: An Autobiography,* 528–30.

66. Eban, *Personal Witness,* 538–39. In his earlier memoir Eban wrote: "It was believed that the Soviet Union would not hesitate to land supplies by helicopter to relieve the Third Army. The Soviet Union would then be physically involved in the war against Israel." *Abba Eban: An Autobiography,* 535. See also Dayan, *Story of My Life,* 447–48; and Golda Meir, *My Life* (London, 1975), 371–72.

Pressure for a "one-time permit" was followed by an appeal for another—from Nixon himself—and then his insistence that the Third Army be supplied as long as Kissinger was negotiating in Egypt. Israel reluctantly agreed.

67. Eban's accounts of the 1973 crisis and war are in *Abba Eban: An Autobiography,* 500–537, and *Personal Witness,* 522–39.

Kissinger's much more detailed memoir—on the war, the cease-fire, and the nuclear alert crisis—is in his *Years of Upheaval,* chaps. 11 and 12. His references to interactions with Eban during the war are sparse: on 6 Oct., the first day of the war (pp. 454, 455, 458, 474, 475); on 8 and 12 Oct., regarding the Security Council meetings (pp. 487, 489, 509); and on 13 Oct., regarding the airlift (p. 513). Kissinger's memoir devotes much more attention to meetings and discussions with Dinitz.

Nixon's account is in his *RN: The Memoirs of Richard Nixon* (New York, 1978), 920–22, 924, 926–28, 930–32, 935, 936–40, and 941–42.

For valuable analyses of the U.S. role see Alan Dowty, *Middle East Crisis: U.S. Decision-Making in 1958, 1970, and 1973* (Berkeley, Calif., 1984), chaps. 10, 11, 13; Quandt, *Decade of Decisions,* chap. 6; and Spiegel, *The Other Arab-Israeli Conflict,* 236–67.

On Israel's perceptions and its decisions during the 1973 crisis and war, see, in addition to the Eban memoirs, Arye Bar-On, *Moshe Dayan and the Yom Kippur War* (Tel Aviv, 1993) (Hebrew); Dayan, *Story of My Life,* part VII; Meir, *My Life,* chap. 14; Brecher with Geist, *Decisions in Crisis,* chaps 3 and 6 and the bibliography, pp. 445–51. As with the 1956 and 1967 upheavals I benefited from interviews with many of the Israeli decision-makers in 1973–1974.

On superpower relations with their clients in 1973–1974, see Yaacov Bar-Siman-Tov, *Israel, the Superpowers, and the War in the Middle East* (New York, 1987), chap. 5.

A valuable collection of articles on the Arab view of the October War is Naseer H. Aruri, ed., *Middle East Crucible: Studies on the Arab-Israeli War of October 1973* (Wilmette, Ill., 1975). For the view of a prominent Egyptian, see Mohamed Heikal, *The Road to Ramadan* (London, 1975).

68. *Abba Eban: An Autobiography,* p. 540. On the talks leading to the Six Point Agreement, see Brecher with Geist, *Decisions in Crisis,* 304–7, based largely on the author's interviews with Eban, Mordekhai Gazit, then director-general of the Foreign Ministry, and Yariv, in July–August 1974; Kissinger, *Years of Upheaval,* 750–53; and Quandt, *Decade of Decisions,* 216-20.

69. Eban's account of the Geneva Conferences are in *Abba Eban: An Autobiography,* 543–55, and *Personal Witness,* 545–53; the quotation regarding Gromyko's words is from *Personal Witness,* 551. Kissinger's memoir is in *Years of Upheaval,* 792–98.

70. Dayan devoted 27 pages to the 1973–1974 disengagement process, in *Story of My Life,* compared to 64 pages to the 1967 crisis-war and 69 pages to the October–Yom Kippur War.

71. The quotations are from *Abba Eban: An Autobiography,* 558, 557, and 558.

72. Kissinger's memoir on the disengagement negotiations is in *Years of Upheaval,* chaps. 18, 21, and 23. The quotation on the Allon-Eban banter is from p. 837; Kissinger's comments on Dayan are from pp. 1042 and 1085. See also Quandt, *Decade of Decisions,* 224–45; Reich, *Quest for Peace,* 255–68 and 286–94; and Spiegel, *The Other Arab-Israeli Conflict,* 269–80.

73. For a comparative analysis of the first four then-young leaders—their background, personality, and perceptions of the global setting, the Middle East, and the Arabs—see Brecher, *Foreign Policy System,* chap. 14.

74. Henry Kissinger, *White House Years,* 358–59, and *Years of Upheaval,* 487. He also referred to Eban's tough negotiating stance in the context of the disengagement negotiations in January 1974 (*Years of Upheaval,* 833).

15

SADAT: THE CALCULUS OF WAR AND PEACE

Raphael Israeli

I F ANWAR SADAT's eleven-year term as president of Egypt was one of the most turbulent, and most pregnant with problems, in his country's history, he himself proved to be its most energetic and creative leader in modern times. During his presidency he not only overcame the daunting domestic problems left by the sudden death of his predecessor, Gamal abd-al-Nasser, but led his country from the depths of defeat in the Six Day War of 1967 to the daring military venture against Israel in October 1973. Then, in a startling and audacious volte-face, he turned from war to diplomacy and created an environment and a state of mind, among Arabs and Israelis, that facilitated the conclusion of the Egyptian-Israeli peace accords of 1979.

I

There was hardly anything of significance in Sadat's background to prepare him for his presidency. His humble village origin, his military career, his underground activity against the British during the Second World War, even his clandestine participation in the Free Officers movement after the war,[1] did not distinguish him much from other officers of the Egyptian military who had grown up in monarchical Egypt under the British colonial regime. The July 1952 Revolution, which put an end to the monarchy and catapulted the young and inexperienced Free Officers to power, for the first time also brought Sadat closer to the corridors of political rule. However, because of Nasser's towering figure,[2] Sadat almost slipped into oblivion, always filling either protocolary roles assigned to him by Nasser, or obediently sitting on the sidelines and admiring the master strokes of his great mentor. He duly earned the title of "Bikbashi Sahh" (literally "Colonel Right") because he reputedly always responded with "Sahh" ("Right") to anything that Nasser said.

During the two decisive wars of 1956[3] and 1967,[4] Sadat was far removed from the focus of power, which was more and more monopolized by Nasser. He had founded and edited, for a few years, the mouth-piece of the regime *Al-Gumhuriyya* (The Republic) and in that capacity mingled with intellectuals, writers, journalists, while serving the regime by presenting to the public the points of view of the ruling elite, distilled, screened, and censored to suit Nasser's purposes. Then, he was appointed as the speaker of the "Parliament," a body that was neither more representative of the people, nor more vigorous in the use of legislative authority than its model of emulation, the Supreme Soviet. Sadat was well content to fulfill his ceremonial duties at the head of that rubber-stamp body, and it never occurred to him in those years that the functions of the Parliament ought to derive their validity from the sovereign authority vested in the people.[5]

Sadat's political career prior to his ascendance to the presidency also took him to a one-year ministership (1954–1955) in one of Nasser's cabinets, and then to a position as secretary of the Islamic Congress (from 1955). After the 1967 war, which resulted in Egypt's defeat, Nasser, who was suffering from lingering diabetes, removed one of his pro-Soviet associates, Ali Sabri, from the prime ministership and strengthened his own grip of the apparatus of government. In December 1969, while Nasser was away at the Arab Summit of Rabat, he surprisingly named Sadat his deputy, giving him a decided advantage over other candidates to inherit his position.

II

Nasser died of a heart attack on 28 September 1970, and Sadat, whom many thought an unlikely successor, stepped in as acting president. To Sadat it seemed perfectly logical that he should succeed: after all, he had been Nasser's representative at the Islamic conference; he had been vice-president and had carried out whatever troubleshooting missions Nasser had delegated to him. Furthermore, Sadat had always maintained a good working relationship with the Soviet ambassador in Cairo, which gave him crucial contact with Egypt's major source of political, military, and economic aid. So, despite his later declarations that he had never believed he would succeed Nasser, despite the latter's reticence on the subject, and despite the claims of Sadat's detractors that others were more worthy of the presidency, Sadat had probably been grooming himself for this moment for years. At long last his time had come. At first, however, he was cautious, as though uncertain of his ability to fill the gap left by Nasser, and in speech after speech, he promised to carry out Nasser's aims and to be guided by his ideas on socialism, Arab unity, national honor, anti-imperialism, Egypt's leadership in the Arab World, nonalignment in the international scene, the alliance with the Soviet Union, and the perennial anti-Israel and anti-Zionist commitment.

Concretely, Sadat faced problems of major proportions, which, as the head of a autocratic government, he bore the supreme and personal responsibility to resolve. He had to set his priorities and act accordingly. First, he consolidated his personal power by neutralizing all the other contenders for the presidency and by allying himself with the wishes of his people: more apparent freedom and democracy, more care for the people's needs, more leeway to marginal groups in society. But foremost on his mind was the question of war and peace, which involved not only his direct struggle with his arch-enemy, Israel, but also his relations with the Arab world and his narrow field of maneuvering between the great powers.

Jews, Zionism, and Israel were, throughout most of Sadat's presidency, the main preoccupation not only of Egypt's foreign policy, but also of the Egyptian media, public discourse, religious sermons, official statements, and inter-Arab and inter-Islamic relations. The three words, often used interchangably, were assumed to refer to an implacable and redoubtable enemy, who had to be overwhelmed if Egypt were to retrieve its national pride. Jews, Zionists, and Israel were treated, under Sadat, on three separate though incremental levels: the Arab-Islamic tradition; the anti-Semitic literature imported from Europe; and the concrete grievances hurled at Israel as a result of the escalation of the Arab-Israeli conflict.

From the Arab-Islamic tradition, the Egyptians, like most other Arabs, borrowed the concept of *dhimmi*,[6] which depicted the Jew as a despicable, unreliable, and cunning creature, as compared with the noble, proud, and honorable Egyptian-Arab. It does not stand to reason, according to this worldview, that Jews could establish a state of their own in a land that used to be Islamic, and its very establishment was an affront to Islam and Arabism. The Jews, then, had to be reduced to mere adherents of a faith and as such sent back to their countries of origin. Jews had no characteristics of nationhood, and therefore their alleged movement of national liberation, Zionism, could only be a false one, and Israel, the state they created, could only be evil. Taking from Arab/Islamic history the antecedents of the Mongol and Crusader invasions, Sadat concluded that the new Zionist invasion could not take roots in Palestine and was bound to be removed ultimately when the Arabs pooled their resources or united.

Sadat, who was particularly fond of American westerns and had a private projection hall in his home, repeatedly warned his countrymen that, unless the Arabs stood up for a war of existence against Israel, they might become like the American Indians. He liked to compare Israeli generals to General Custer, and concluded that the American Indians had succumbed to their invaders because of their tribal differences and disunity. Hence the necessity for the Arabs to unify under Egypt's leadership in order to stop the invasion. Very often Sadat also compared his country to Russia during the Second World War, implying that he was, like Stalin, the hero of the Great Patriotic War, while the Israelis were likened to the Nazis, who fell upon their innocent prey, adopting the same blitzkrieg tactics, terror and mass murder, seizing territories and hostages, and threatening further aggression. The only note of hope that Sadat introduced to his people in this context was that under his leadership Israel, like Nazi Germany, was bound to be vanquished, for that was the historical lot awaiting all dictatorships.

Sadat regarded the war against Israel as a long-term mission of the Arabs. He urged his people to arm the young generation so as to sustain this protracted struggle, which would, by necessity, end in the eradication of Zionism from the area. For Israel was an alien body, implanted by world imperialism in the heart of the Arab world in order to undermine and subvert it. Since Israel's actions had no legitimacy, any counteraction adopted by the Arabs was to be considered as a legitimate act of self-defense, while Israel's attempts to defend herself were illegitimate acts of aggression. Thus, for example, when Israel destroyed the Suez Canal cities during the War of Attrition in 1969–1970 or shot down a Libyan airliner in 1973, or killed Palestinian leaders on several occasions, it ipso facto put itself beyond the pale of nations.

The problem of Qawmiyya (Pan-Arab nationalism) versus Wataniyya (local patriotism)—of Arab unity, on the one hand, and each individual country's separate interests on the other—was one of the most difficult issues confronting his brand of nationalism. For he was conscious not only of the threat of Israel, which was magnified by Arab disunity, and the ambitions of the great powers, which by their very nature cultivated Arab internal dissent, but also of the opposition of domestic regimes in the area that did not see eye-to-eye with his conduct of international affairs. In attempting to promote Arab unity and to reconcile his foreign policy with it despite the fact that it was rejected most of the time by radical Arabs, Sadat was, of course, seeking the impossible. It was his belief, however, that in time his Arab opponents would by necessity come to see the light if he persisted in pursuing Egypt's interests, which were consistent, he believed, with Arab interests. Meanwhile, he was willing to face reality. If unity was not feasible, then cooperation between Arab countries ought to be pursued as an attainable goal. Prior to the 1973 war, when the entire Arab world was skeptical and incredulous about Egypt's military capacity and resolve, Sadat made sure to prepare the grounds by informing Libya and Sudan, Saudi Arabia and the Gulf States about the impending war, without giving them any details, but also without attempting to harness them, let alone mobilize them, to the war effort. Only Syria, which was an essential military partner and a confrontation state in its own right, was made an intimate partner to the war plans. Before that, in 1972, Sadat had imparted to the Saudi king his intention of removing the Soviet experts from Egypt. And so, without dictates, intrigues, plots, and subversion, he achieved a modicum of cooperation, for the most part passive and quiescent, on the part of the Arabs.

There is little doubt that Egypt's rising modern nationalism has been inter-twined with the great powers' presence in, relations with, and attitudes toward that country. Not only had the long British occupation conditioned the reactions, often violently so, of the Egyptian nationalists since World War I, but during World War II, young officers of the Egyptian army, including Sadat himself, were prepared to collaborate with Nazi Germany in their anti-British drive. The Egyptian Revolution of 1952, which was engineered by the Free Officers and led by Nasser, was essentially directed against the British and their puppet Farouq regime in Cairo. Thereafter Nasser's pressure on the British to evacuate the Suez Canal area, his nationalization of the canal and his alliance with the Soviet bloc, all illustrated how important anti-Western rhetoric and defiance—including the nationalization of foreign properties in Egypt—were in the campaign to forge and inspire national spirit.

Sadat inherited that line of policy and agreed with it. But he also knew that Egypt needed at least one strong ally to supply it with the material means to defend its independence. Repudiation of the West necessitated turning to the East, and, having acted as liaison officer with the Soviet Union during the Nasser years, Sadat was not unaware of the danger of too great dependence upon Moscow. That danger became actual almost immediately after he had taken power. In May 1971, after his Corrective Revolution,[7] he was pressured by President Podgorny of the Soviet Union to sign a treaty of friendship that he both loathed and resented. But he had little choice, for he had begun the countdown for his much-advertised Year of Decision in 1971, and without Soviet supplies could not expect to accomplish it. It was a frustrating relationship, thanks to the obfuscations and delays and postponements of Soviet bureaucrats, and it made Sadat and Egypt the laughingstock of the Arab world because of their inability to deliver on their aggressive promises. In fury Sadat struck out at his great friend in Moscow. In July 1972, he ordered all Soviet advisers out of Egypt in what was not only an act of retaliation for promises unfulfilled but a nationalistic reaction to the many reports Sadat was receiving from his army officers about the haughty behavior of the Soviet experts and the humiliations suffered by Egyptians who had to work with them.

Indeed, Sadat presented the expulsion to his people as an act of liberation. For the Soviets had been unable to resolve any of Egypt's burning national problems, to shore up the sinking economy, to force Israel out of occupied Sinai, or to supply the Egyptians with adequate means to do that job themselves. Instead, they had committed themselves to a series of Brezhnev-Nixon summitry shows, which in effect preserved the status quo in the Middle East at the expense of Egypt. Sadat feared that the no war–no peace situation favored by the superpowers merely perpetuated Israeli occupation of Egyptian territory, thereby demonstrating Egypt's inability to regain it either diplomatically if possible or militarily if necessary. That was too much to bear in terms of national honor. Hence his resolve to achieve his objectives without the Soviets and, in a sense, despite them. A new definition of Egyptian nationalism emerged: a self-reliant Egypt, fighting alone, or with Arab allies, ostensibly without the connivance of any great power, to achieve Egyptian national goals.

But there was another great-power element in the conflict, the United States, which despite its mediation efforts in August 1970 and its achievement of a cease-fire, was perceived by Sadat as siding unreservedly with Israel. He feared that the endless three-to-six month extensions of the cease-fire agreements mediated by the United States would inevitably mean that the borders defined in those agreements would come to represent a fait accompli, which would be intolerable. He saw as a precedent the temporary 1948–1949 armistice line, which the world soon accepted as Israel's border. So Sadat needed progress or movement of some kind, and he could not initially expect much from Israel or the United States. If he could just make Israel withdraw a trifle, so that he could reassert the semblance of Egyptian control over the East Bank of the Suez Canal, that would be a start, because it would show that Israel could be made to retreat. Once the principle of withdrawal had been established, then world opinion might pressure Israel to withdraw further. Recognizing that it was essential to have the United States on his side, because of Israel's total dependence on it, Sadat decided to accept Security Council Resolution 242,[8] despite his earlier objections to it. He also accepted the Jarring Mission[9] and showed eagerness to conclude some arrangement under UN auspices, knowing that the automatic support he would get there from the Soviet bloc and the Third World virtually guaranteed sympathy for his cause.

But progress on this front did not promise to come quickly or to be dramatic, and all major powers seemed determined to achieve relaxation in the Middle East. Sadat came to the conclusion, therefore, that, unless he imposed movement by military means, the status quo of no peace–no war would take root and become a permanent reality. He decided to go to war.

III

The drama of October 1973 was so orchestrated by Sadat that it came as a total surprise to the Israelis, the Arabs, and the world. Paradoxically, he had warned of the coming war and its inevitability so often that world attention had become bored with such declarations, dismissing them as "empty rhetoric." Indeed, most people in the Middle East and elsewhere remained skeptical of Sadat's intentions and, even more, of his ability to act upon them. In a masterly ploy that should have made many an intelligence agency suspicious, he had desisted from declarations about the war or anything else from July 1973 onwards, only breaking his reticence once, in September 1973, when he addressed the Conference of the Non-Aligned in Algiers. The paradox is that he should have maintained his pattern of bragging and boasting up until the outbreak of the war if he wanted to achieve total surprise; reversing what was expected of him, he opted to keep silent. His successful gamble was coupled with a very careful campaign of disinformation and an elaborate circumstantial analysis of what he considered to be "Israel's security theory."

First, Sadat believed that Israel's strategy was founded on its power of deterrence, which it thought no Arab country would dare to challenge. To launch a powerful, concentrated surprise attack, when and where the enemy least expected it, was likely to shake that self-confidence. Second, Israel counted upon fighting on only one front at a time, which optimized its chances of success. Sadat therefore thought in terms of a simultaneous attack on the Egyptian and Syrian fronts, forcing Israel to divide its forces. He also stacked additional weapons, ammunition, and strategic supplies on his flank in Libya and at his rear in the Sudan, ensuring a firm stance in the event of an Israeli counterthrust. Third, Israeli doctrine called for the rapid transfer of hostilities to enemy territory in order to spare the destruction of its own lands; if Egypt and Syria launched a massive, simultaneous surprise offensive, such transfer would be impossible.

Fourth, Israel always assumed that any war must be brief and devastating, yielding victory before the great powers could intervene to stop Israel's advance. This blitzkrieg-style of war was essential to Israel because of its shortage of manpower and its reliance on total mobilization of its able-bodied men and women, which in turn brought about the temporary immobilization of its industrial production. Sadat would counter that by preparing for a long, protracted war, which he could endure because of his practically limitless manpower and the support he was to get from his Arab brothers. Fifth, because of its small population, Israel greatly feared high numbers of casualties; Sadat devised a massive attack with deadly weapons that would inflict heavy losses and was prepared to absorb a high ratio of Egyptian dead and wounded and still pursue the offensive. Sixth, Israel's fate hinged largely on a hurried, though admittedly well-organized, mobilization of its reserves; a surprise attack that developed rapidly would forestall this. Seventh, Israel's strategy had always depended on taking the initiative, for only if it could dictate the moves and force the Arabs onto the defensive, as it had done in the past, would it be able to end the war quickly. Sadat this time was determined to play the Israeli game and dominate the pace and form of the conflict. Finally, Israel had always relied on the superiority of its air power to check any surprise Arab attack, allowing time for its reserves to mobilize and deploy against Arab land forces; Sadat decided to position a screen of air defense missiles along the canal to foil Israel's plans.

To secure most of these advantages, Sadat desperately needed to effect a total surprise in his offensive. He was able to keep secret within Egypt, and from all Arab leaders save the Syrians, the date of the outbreak of the war, on which he had agreed with President Assad in August. Indeed, no more than a handful of top officers knew the details. He and his General Staff chose 6 October because it fell on a Saturday during the Yom Kippur festival in Israel, a time when everybody would be fasting and praying in synagogues and Israeli defenses were sure to be lax. By 2 P.M. on that day, the fasting Israelis would be exhausted, and the sun would be setting west of the Suez Canal, blinding Israeli defenders on its eastern side and so facilitating the task of the attacking Egyptians. The fact that October was also the month of Ramadan, when all Muslims fasted, was conversely thought to be beneficial, because the Israelis would be unlikely to believe that Egyptians would attack at that time. Sadat secured special permission for his soldiers to eat before they launched the attack.

In the months preceding the October war, Sadat traveled to many Arab capitals to deliver his appeals on the theme of Arab unity. He urged the Arabs to desist from "lifting their daggers against each other" and from "rejoicing at their brothers' distress," even if it was impossible for them to be united, for solidarity was the sole countermeasure that the Arabs could put forward to foil imperialism and Zionism, both perceived by Sadat as outside forces of invasion. Sadat had been depressed by the failure of his country's abortive union with Syria[10] and with the Federation of Arab Republics,[11] but he had learned three lessons from these disappointments: that the essence of cooperation was far more important than any constitutional form it might take; that there were major differences within the Arab world as a result of geographic, economic, social, cultural, and personal variations that were caused by "the history of imperialist conquest" and had to be tolerated (despite Sadat's belief in the cultural predominance of "7,000-year-old Egypt" and his not infrequent disdain for the rest of the Arab world); and that any semblance of unity could be achieved only by deeds rather than by enthusiastic speeches and zealous declarations of sentiment and intention. Sadat realized full well that while Arab unity potentially held much promise, it could also result in Arab disarray if hurriedly and recklessly executed.

In August 1973, Sadat made his supreme attempt to bridge the gap between "Right and Left," "progressives and reactionaries" in the Arab world. Significantly, his tour began with Saudi Arabia. Sadat had long talks with King Faisal and told him he was going to war soon, though he did not give an exact date. Faisal urged him not to stop the war too early, before he could reap its fruits. Sadat turned then for support to the nonaligned countries and the members of the Islamic conference. At the meeting of the latter body in Benghazi, Libya, in early 1973, Hasan al-Tuhami, the Egyptian deputy prime minister, who had been sent by Sadat to gain an Islamic consensus for Egypt, was elected as the organization's secretary general, and the resolutions adopted at the end of the conference lent, as expected, unconditional support to Egypt and other Arabs in their effort to liberate their lands from Israeli occupation. In May 1973, Sadat went to the Conference of the Organization of African Unity in Addis Ababa, Ethiopia, where he made an impassioned speech in which he tried to explain to the Africans that Israel and South Africa were two racist entities, which harbored aggressive designs against the black continent—Israel from the north and South Africa from the south—and that, therefore, there was no escape from the necessity to fight them both. He expressly said that Egypt was gearing up for a war that would help all Africans.

In September, Sadat went to the Non-Aligned Conference in Algeria, where he repeated the same arguments and extracted a resolution supporting Egypt's right to liberate its lands. There, he enhanced his position even further by violently attacking American policy toward developing countries, contending that what the Americans called a "war to conquer deserts" was nothing more than a new scheme to control the resources of the developing nations, which amounted to a revival of colonialism. Faced with the double threat of world imperialism and world Zionism, the nonaligned should, asserted Sadat, "effect the transition from words to deeds," and he implied that Egypt was going to lead the way by defying both threats.

The United States and Western Europe were a quite different story. Sadat entrusted his national security adviser, Hafez Isma'il, with the task of explaining Egyptian attitudes to them, even though he entertained little hope of swaying them toward unequivocal sympathy for the Arab camp. The United States had become a "lost cause" for Sadat, as he felt that it had lent its blessing to Israel, "slamming all doors" in his face. He therefore concentrated on the major European countries: Britain, France, Italy, and Germany. All of them assured Sadat's envoy that their position toward Resolution 242 remained unchanged. (After the March 1973 Beirut raid launched by Israeli commandos, France and Great Britain had voted in favor of the Security Council resolution censuring Israel.) Sadat regarded this response as the direct outcome of his diplomatic campaign and was encouraged by it.

In July 1972, when Sadat expelled the Soviets, Henry Kissinger, Nixon's national security adviser, had agreed to meet an Egyptian representative to discuss this development. Previously, whenever the Americans had questions about the Soviet presence in Egypt, Sadat had reassured them that, if an Israeli partial withdrawal were effected, he would no longer need it. Furthermore, he had always explained that he had granted the Soviets port facilities in Egypt, not bases, which was an indication of the provisional status of their mission in Egypt. Now that the Soviets were ousted, the Americans again evinced interest in Sadat, but the meeting of the parties did not take place until February 1973 in Paris. On that occasion, Kissinger was understood to have reiterated to Sadat's envoy that Egypt was compelled to search for a peaceful settlement with Israel because it was incapable of defeating it militarily, and until the existing military situation altered, there was simply no way that Egypt could advance any demands. Sadat was dismayed by these talks, which he immediately reported to the Soviets.

Following Nixon's meetings in Moscow and Peking in 1972, Sadat was advised by some European countries, and by moderate Arab states that maintained good relations with the United States, not to leave the doors of Washington open to Israelis alone. So, after initial contacts had proved that America's desire to renew the dialogue with Egypt was genuine, Sadat dispatched Hafez Isma'il to Washington, where he met President Nixon, Secretary of State William Rogers, and Kissinger. In those meetings, Isma'il reported Sadat's resolve to go to war because he could no longer endure the status quo. Nixon promised to try a new peace initiative that would strike a compromise between Egypt's sovereignty and Israel's security concerns. Sadat was unpersuaded by this, because he perceived the Americans as asking him to make one-sided concessions, such as total demilitarization of the Sinai, which would drive a wedge between Egypt and the rest of the Arab world. What was more, there was, in his view, total agreement between Israel and the United States on Middle East policy, and he saw the continuation of American military aid to Israel as proof of an alliance. In an interview in *Newsweek* in which Sadat said that the United States government was making a grave mistake in continuing to believe that the Egyptians were crippled and unable to act, he warned: "Mark my words, the situation here will be much worse than Vietnam, because U.S. interests are at stake. . . . Americans always use computers to solve geo-political equations, and they have always been misled. McNamara warned Johnson that by feeding the wrong data into the computers, he was getting all the wrong answers. McNamara was right and Johnson was wrong and compelled to abdicate. They simply forgot to feed Vietnamese psychology into the computer. . . . The U.S. has overlooked one factor—Arab psychology."[12]

IV

The war broke out on 6 October 1973. Initially, the Egyptian thrust into the Sinai made important gains, as did the coordinated Syrian attack in the north. But on 14 October, the United States government, which up until then had resisted domestic pressure for aid to embattled Israel, began a massive airlift to that country, and the fortunes of war shifted almost immediately. On the Golan Heights, the Syrians began to give way, an Egyptian drive to support them was repulsed, and on 16 October Israeli forces under General Sharon pushed between the Egyptian Second and Third armies on the Suez Canal and began to encircle the latter.

When the Israeli breakthrough began, Prime Minister Kosygin of the Soviet Union had been in Cairo for three days, attempting to impress upon Sadat the fact that the military situation, as the Soviet Union knew from its satellites and other intelligence sources, was turning against Egypt and that he ought to seek a cease-fire. Suspicious of the Russians since the beginning of the war, Sadat bluntly refused to accept this advice and vowed to continue the battle. This position, however, he could not afford to maintain in view of reports from the front on 16 October, and two days later he asked Kosygin to use his good offices to seek a cease-fire in place on the Sinai front.

This was as close to an admission of defeat as Sadat ever came, and throughout his later career he continued to describe the "Great Crossing" as a victory. In reality, had a cease-fire not been imposed upon Israel by the superpowers, its troops would have trapped the Egyptian armies east of the canal, destroying the entire force that Sadat had committed to the battle. This would, in all likelihood, have ended his career in disgrace. That he avoided this is to be explained by the urgent desire of the superpowers to end the war and, subsequently, by Sadat's decision to place his fortunes in the hands of the Americans and the diplomatic skill he showed in his dealings with them. Despite mutual suspicion and intermittent crises, Moscow and Washington were of one mind about the war. The Soviet Union, to whom the Arab states had appealed for assistance at the outset of hostilities, had no desire to become involved in the fighting but, on the other hand, could not tolerate an overwhelming Israeli victory without jeopardizing its whole position in the Middle East. The United States was aware that prolongation of the hostilities would increase the economic hardship being suffered by its European allies as a result of the oil embargo imposed in mid-October by the OPEC states out of sympathy for Egypt and Syria and hence favored a quick termination of the fighting.

In an impressive example of superpower collaboration, Henry Kissinger flew to Moscow at General Secretary Brezhnev's request and, on 22 October, negotiated a cease-fire in place. Unfortunately for Sadat, Israeli troops paid little attention to this, and their breaches of its terms and those of a modified cease-fire line on the twenty-fourth led to a dangerous crisis in late October, when the Soviet government alerted their airborne forces and threatened President Nixon with unilateral intervention if the Israelis were not forced to comply. The president responded by placing American forces on DefCon III, a precautionary alert status that greatly increased the danger of a superpower confrontation. At the same time, however, he brought the Israelis under pressure, and they stopped their advance, agreeing to a new cease-fire line that was somewhat more favorable to them than that of 22 October.[13]

Once hostilities ended, Sadat was quick to understand that the Americans were in the best position to produce a conciliatory mood in Israel, so that both sides would gain something from the closer definition of the cease-fire and a chance for disengagement of forces, as a prelude to a general settlement, might emerge. He began to hope for the rapid removal of the Israeli presence on the west bank of the canal, which bore witness to Israel's success in the war and cast doubt on his own claims of victory. On 29 October, he sent his new acting foreign minister, Isma'il Fahmi, to Washington to prepare the ground for Kissinger's next visit to the Middle East, during which he was to launch the first disengagement talks and inaugurate what came to be known as shuttle diplomacy. Kissinger arrived in Cairo on 6 November and immediately established a working rapport with Sadat, which very quickly grew into a warm close personal relationship. Indeed, Sadat's amiability and Kissinger's bent for analysis and wit somehow combined into instant chemistry that was to outlast Kissinger's ability to fulfill Sadat's expectations of him.

During these meetings, Sadat voiced concerns about Israel's advance beyond the 22 October cease-fire line, initially adopted by the Security Council, but Kissinger presented him with two choices: either he continue to press for the reestablishment of the now-defunct 22 October lines, or work for a large-scale disengagement of forces that would ultimately bring about a much larger Israeli withdrawal from their position west of the canal and the securing for Sadat of territorial gains in the Sinai. Kissinger hinted that he preferred the second option. Sadat, according to Kissinger, "sat brooding, saying nothing for many minutes and then he astonished me. He did not dispute my analysis. He did not offer an alternative, violating the normal method of diplomacy—which is to see what one can extract in return for concessions—he said simply that he agreed with both my analysis and my proposed procedure."[14]

He had not yet completely abandoned the military option and massed his troops for attack against the Israeli enclave west of the canal; but this was mostly intended now to help break the deadlock. Meanwhile, shuttling back and forth between Aswan and Jerusalem in January 1974, Kissinger elicited a series of Israeli proposals and an equal number of Sadat counterproposals. For Sadat it was humiliating to seem to yield to any Israeli offer of settlement, but it looked judicious and magnanimous of him to be collaborating with a super-power and accepting its suggestions. On January 13–14, the final obstacles were removed, and Sadat overruled his disgruntled chief-of-staff, Gamasi, and foreign minister, Fahmi, and had the disengagement agreement formally signed at Kilometer 101 on the road to Cairo. He was later harshly criticized by hard-line Egyptians and rejectionist Arabs for his deal with Israel, and especially for renouncing the right to station Egyptian tanks in Suez, and for agreeing that Israel could retain the Sinai strategic passes, which Sadat had desperately but unsuccessfully sought to take over during the war. On the last day of the disengagement talks, 18 January, Kissinger carried a letter to Sadat from Prime Minister Golda Meir stating her hopes for a permanent settlement. Someone whispered in Sadat's ear that the disengagement agreement had just been signed at Kilometer 101, and in an outburst of relief and gratitude, Sadat rushed to Kissinger, kissed him on both cheeks, and dramatically announced that he was taking off the military uniform that he had worn since the eve of the war, "never to wear it again except for ceremonial occasions." That, he said, was in re-sponse to Golda Meir's letter.

At that point, Sadat was very sensitive to insinuations that he had abandoned the Soviets and embraced the Americans instead. His image of himself as a loyal friend to whomever had helped him in time of distress simply did not allow him to switch sides without first finding a plausible justification for doing so. At first, he was apologetic; he denied Soviet contentions that he had relin-quished socialism, and stressed that, just as Egypt had elected the path of socialism for its own sake, and not in order to please anyone, so today he needed no comment from the outside on his regime and on the brand of socialism he chose to implement. Sadat stressed that since both superpowers were guarantors of the cease-fire, he had no interest in antagonizing either of them; on the contrary, he was interested in maintaining good relations with both.

V

Upon the completion in May 1974 of the disengagement agreement between Israel and Syria, under Kissinger's auspices, Sadat was eager to continue the momentum and pressed for the convening of the Geneva Conference, where Israel and all Arab parties, including the PLO, were to participate, but he soon realized that such a meeting, because of its complexity and multilateral composition, was not likely to bear any fruit. He turned again to the United States, and through Kissinger's mediation a new disengagement agreement was signed between Egypt and Israel, the latter further withdrawing from the Mitla and Giddi strategic passes and relinquishing the oil fields it exploited in the Sinai. This second disengagement, which brought Sadat solidly into the American orbit, also made him aware that the step-by-step policy under American sponsorship had run its course, and it was now time to make preparations for an overall settlement in Geneva, or elsewhere. At the same time, however, he was not yet ready for a full-fledged peace arrangement with Israel that entailed diplomatic relations and normalization. He repeatedly declared in various press interviews, that after so many years of enmity, bloodshed, and bitterness, complete normalization of relations with Israel was too much to expect. In his generation, he said, the most that could be hoped for was a state of non-belligerency, which would be achieved once Israel retreated from occupied Arab territories and restored Palestinian rights; the rest would be decided by coming generations. He said in one of those interviews that he distinguished between a "peace treaty" and a "peace agreement," expressing his readiness to sign the latter, but not the former.

Despite his reservations about a peace accord with Israel, and his assurance to the Arabs that the fact that the second disengagement agreement had been signed by the Egyptian chief of staff meant that this was a military and temporary agreement, he could not mitigate the attacks of the Arab rejectionists, notably the Syrians and the PLO. They accused him of having signed "separate" and "partial" agreements with Israel, despite the resolutions of the Arab summits that prohibited him from doing so. Sadat reproved the Arabs for their failure to realize that "90% of the cards were in American hands, and that without the United States they stood simply no chance of achieving any of their national goals. If the United States could be useful to the Arabs why not take advantage of its services?" He proclaimed that unless the Arabs understood the reality of the new era, and undertook a bold and realistic analysis of world affairs, they would remain bogged down in their trivial bickering and internecine hatreds, which would certainly not help them regain lost territories nor resolve the painful and long-standing Palestinian problem. Egypt, for its part, Sadat assured the Arabs, would continue to shoulder its national responsibility, without compromise, on both scores.

Sadat informed the Arab leaders who wished to listen to him that he would remain within the agreed parameters of Arab strategy, but he reserved the right to act freely and expect the Arabs to trust his judgment. His was a "triangular strategy," he announced. The base of the triangle, which consisted of his commitment to the agreed double strategy of the Arabs, remained fixed, while the apex was movable and corresponded to the shifting tactics he adopted in his day-to-day conduct of politics. As long as the base was firm, as long as he did not lose sight of the ultimate goals, the tactics he adopted mattered very little. Confident of his newly formulated strategy, Sadat was ready to counterattack. He denounced radical Arab critics as narrow-minded and myopic. His arsenal of imagery was never exhausted: his Arab critics were "sharp-shooters who witnessed the quick depletion of their faulty ammunition," and whose "ammunition was mere talk, while ours, of which we have plenty, is step-by-step action."

At the outset of 1977, Sadat faced very serious disturbances at home, and he was visibly shaken and disappointed by his people and gave a great deal of thought, in isolated retirement, to some spirited initiative that might produce a dramatic new development in an otherwise hopeless situation. He knew full well that without such lifeline he would be doomed to sink deeper into his domestic quagmire, away from the limelight that international affairs had thrust upon him. He had irreversibly abrogated the Treaty of Friendship with the Soviets a year earlier, and he had committed himself to the American-sponsored peace negotiations with Israel. Therefore, his best hope lay in continuing in that direction.

The second disengagement would run its course by September 1978, and the Americans still seemed unable to extract further territorial concessions from Israel. True, Sadat had threatened that if the Geneva Conference did not materialize and Israel failed to retreat from all Arab territories, he would have to resort to war again, but could he venture once again into a military operation that held no promise? Now that he had lost Soviet support and the Syrians had become his harshest critics, now that Israel was on constant guard against a repetition of the 1973 calamity, what chance did he stand? His economy was so feeble that the further pressure of a new war might deal it a devastating blow from which it would never recover. And what would happen to all his guarantees of Egyptian stability without which foreign investors would not have risked their investments in his programs? A war would only lose investors and halt or destroy the new development projects, thereby exacerbating even further the already difficult economic situation.

On the international level, Sadat had only the Americans to lean on. They had given him generous economic aid since the end of the war, but he could hope for a major, steady, and long-term commitment only if he proved that he was definitely heading for a peaceful settlement. Moreover, in any major war, he would be dependent on sophisticated equipment that he could only obtain in the West, and he was fully aware that the American Congress would not vote massive military aid to Egypt if there were any indications that such military hardware was to be used against Israel. Again, only the Americans could help avert Soviet subversion of Egypt's independence, which Sadat feared was a real possibility, for Libya, on his western border, was gradually becoming a store-house of Soviet weaponry, and the Soviets were at the same time cultivating a Marxist government in Ethiopia to the south, where the major branch of the Nile originated. To stand up to those challenges, it was essential to pacify the Israeli front and elicit a deeper military and economic commitment from the United States, which would balance the Soviet threat and support a sus-tained domestic recovery. All this boiled down to some sort of American-sponsored settlement with Israel. Sadat would have preferred to retrieve Arab territories, solve the Palestinian problem, and accept American military and economic aid without having to pay the price of recognizing and making peace with Israel. But he also knew that Israel was adamant about formal recognition, direct negotiations, and a contractual peace treaty that would provide for diplo-matic relations with its Arab neighbors. Would such a price be acceptable to Egyptians and other Arabs? Would the Israeli government be receptive to an initiative along these lines?

As Sadat was pondering his options, two major developments hastened his decision: the installation of a new administration in Washington and the rise to power of the Likud party in Israel. President Jimmy Carter's initial declara-tions, which favored a "homeland for the Palestinians" and condemned Israeli settlements in the occupied territories, were encouraging, but it was too early to conclude in which direction American foreign policy was moving. In Israel, the ascendence of Menachem Begin was also something of a puzzle to Sadat. He had viewed the Rabin government, which preceded Begin's, with disdain, seeing Israel's ruling "troika" (Rabin-Allon-Peres) as weak, divided, and inde-cisive. For Sadat, collective rule was an unmistakable expression of lack of energy and resolve. He could not strike a deal with such diffuse leadership. He needed to respect a man in order to measure up to him, challenge him, haggle with him, and finally come to a deal with him on the basis of parity. Moreover, it took a strong leader, as Sadat believed himself to be, to take the necessary hard decisions that he intended to extract from Israel during the forthcoming negotia-tions. Finally, only a stable and decisive leader, respected by his people, could be expected to deliver whatever he pledged. As Sadat saw it, Begin, the former chief of an underground organization, who had acquired prominence in Israel's political system by sheer resilience and tenacity of character, was exactly the kind of leader Sadat needed to deal with. When he went to Rumania in

October 1977, he had his feelings about Begin confirmed by President Nicholas Ceauşescu, who had welcomed the Israeli prime minister to Bucharest that summer and had time to assess his capabilities. Sadat was assured that Begin was indeed the right kind of man for him.

Much of 1977 was spent by the Americans in seeking a formula agreeable to the contentious parties in the Middle East, with the latter submitting draft treaties, agreements, memoranda, and messages, which the United States government sorted out, synthesizing some of the more constructive elements and eventually drafting proposals of its own. But soon Sadat realized that President Carter was unable to force the Israelis' hand and decided to explore the avenue of direct contact with Israel. He proceeded so secretly that even his foreign minister, who was in charge of negotiations with the Americans, was kept in the dark. Begin responded by requesting either a meeting with Sadat or a lower-level meeting between the two governments. Sadat was not averse to the idea and, when he learned in August 1977 that Begin was to visit Rumania, he sent his trusted representative, Sayyid Mar'i, the speaker of the Egyptian Parliament and a personal friend and relative, to Bucharest to gauge Begin's views. That contact made President Ceauşescu a mediator of sorts between Begin and Sadat, and paved the way for further contacts in Morocco between Israelis and Egyptians. In October, Sadat visited Rumania and received a personal confirmation from Ceauşescu regarding Begin's attitude. After much reflection, Sadat made up his mind and let it be known that he was prepared to meet Begin and was willing to circumvent all the procedures of Geneva, the mediation of the great powers, and the impotent United Nations. Rather than let others determine the rules of the game, why should he not take "his fate into his own hands," as he often liked to say? Why should he drift down a course charted by others, rather than launch his own "initiative," which would attract international attention, stun statesmen and countries around the world, and give the Israelis such a jolt that they would be rid of their fears and suspicions forever?

Sadat was taken by the idea of going to Jerusalem, but he did not want to appear to be "going to Canossa" to submit to his arch enemies. What he wanted was not to see Begin, not to beg for anything, but to address the Knesset, to tell the Israeli people that they had nothing to fear and that, in return for their evacuation of Arab territory, he would be prepared to make peace with them. In a way, he saw his demands as an act of defiance against the Israeli government, a *beau geste* toward the Israeli public, and a bold manifestation of statesmanship and vision on his part, which he was sure the world would appreciate. Since Egypt was unable to defeat Israel militarily, as he admitted to his inner circle, why not retrieve lost Arab territories by a stroke of peace, rather than pursuing the fruitless and costly path of war? Internally, Sadat presented his "journey of peace" to Jerusalem as a courageous, risk-taking attempt to break the impasse in the Arab-Israeli dispute. Immediately his shattered domestic image and all the ridicule surrounding him since the 1977 riots were forgotten, as the Egyptian media launched a campaign of praise and adulation for the "hero of peace," who was willing to defy the enemy and to lecture the people of Israel over the heads of their own government, on the subject of peace. To Egyptian Muslims, who were as shaken as the rest of the Arabs, he simply explained that he was going to pray at Al Aqsa Mosque in Jerusalem during the Feast of the Sacrifice. An Arab head of state, who was prepared to go into the lion's den to pray in Islam's third holiest place, something that many a Muslim would have liked to do, could only elicit adulation and popular support.

When he convened his National Security Council on 5 November, Sadat astonished all present by stating that he was prepared to speak to the Israeli Knesset if it "could save the blood of my sons." General Gamasi, the general who had collaborated with Sadat since the 1973 war and had been rewarded with the position of war minister, alone raised his voice in dissent, an act that cost him his post. Others were too stunned or too frightened to speak up. On 16 November, Sadat flew to Damascus, where he had a violent exchange with Assad, who totally condemned the peace initiative. Sadat told the press corps trailing him that despite Assad's opposition, he was going to Jerusalem. That was the first time he himself had made an official statement on the subject. Then he retired to his home in Ismai'iliyya to prepare for his trip by prayer, solitude, and meditation. It was there that he got Fahmi's letter of resignation as Egypt's foreign minister.

The peace initiative was making headlines around the world, and now that the Jerusalem trip had become official Sadat was at the center of attention. He explained that by going to Jerusalem he would resolve "70% of the conflict" and smash "the psychological barrier" that had separated Jews and Arabs over the past century. In his view, that barrier consisted of two elements: the conventional Arab-Muslim conception of Israel as a "foreign body" transplanted into the Arab world, which was therefore to be rejected; and the simultaneous feeling in Israel of being under constant threat, hence the "siege mentality" and "garrison-state" mode of life that had developed there. Sadat also believed that Israel's obsessions with survival, self-defense, and security, which were the result of a long history of persecution, culminating in the Holocaust, could be overcome if he stated openly that he recognized Israel and its need for security. In return, Israel should withdraw from all occupied Arab lands and accord the same measure of recognition to the Palestinians. That was to be the thrust of his address to the Knesset. He also thought that by pledging that there would be "no more war after October," he would alleviate Israel's fear and at the same time reassure the international economic community that he was determined to create a situation of peace and stability on his borders, which he hoped would encourage foreign investors to embark on development plans for Egypt.

Sadat's visit to Jerusalem created a new atmosphere of euphoria both in Israel and in Egypt, and broke the "psychological barrier," as Sadat would have it, but in terms of substance it was only the opening of a long and arduous process of negotiation. His symbolic visits to various sites, such as Al Aqsa Mosque and the Holocaust Memorial, culminated in his speech to the Knesset, where he laid down his demands: in return for a total withdrawal of Israel from all territories occupied in 1967, he recognized Israel's legitimacy and right for security and peace. He admitted all the past wrongs that the Arabs had meted out to the Jews, but he also castigated the Israelis for establishing a country in a land that "was not their own," while denying the Palestinians the right to nationhood. Sadat regarded his own sacrifice, his trip to Jerusalem, as so significant and far-reaching, that he likened it to the Sacrifice that Abraham, "the father of Arabs and Jews," was prepared to make for the sake of the Lord. Then, obliquely referring to the storm his trip had caused in the Arab world, he reiterated that Egypt would not sign a separate peace with Israel, because that could be a recipe for continued confrontation between Israel and the Arab world. Nor would he consent to an agreement between Israel and all Arabs that would leave the Palestinian problem unresolved. He stated that he was not expecting to sign another disengagement agreement in the Sinai, but wished to establish a permanent and true peace that would rule out further wars and bloodshed. Finally, he emphasized once more the need to produce a reasonable national solution for the Palestinian people, since Palestine remained the "core of the Arab-Israeli conflict."

When Sadat departed from Israel on 21 November, he left behind him a trail of excitement and expectation. Although nothing practical emerged from that highly publicized visit, it paved the way for more meetings and visits. Indeed, in a series of sessions in Egypt and Israel, attended by either the heads of states or their foreign ministers, the two parties began to iron out the modalities of the agreement to be concluded between them. To overcome the stalemate that developed, Prime Minister Begin floated the idea of an "autonomy for the Palestinians" in the context of a peace settlement between Israel and its neighbors. But the euphoria of November 1977 began to wane: the Jerusalem-Cairo axis, which was to become the focus of the peace initiative, was short-lived and soon gave way to a renewed American involvement in the peace process, so much so, that Sadat himself came to regard America as "a partner," not merely as an observer or catalyst. Sadat's instant rapport with Begin in Jerusalem, on the other hand, was soon transformed into suspicion and discord, because the terms of the peace could not be agreed upon. Begin clearly wanted to conclude a separate peace with Sadat and viewed the process as a bilateral one, while Sadat, bound by the Arab summits in which he had participated, wished to see himself a representative of all Arabs, or at least of the helpless Palestinians.

The main point of dispute between the parties resided in the fact that neither was satisfied with the flexibility of the other. Israel claimed that in return for its vast concessions and its readiness to give up most of Sinai, including the oil wells and the strategic passes, it expected Egyptian flexibility on the question of continued Israeli presence in the northern Sinai settlements[15] and the military air bases.[16] Sadat retorted that Sinai was "his" territory and Israel was doing him no favor in evacuating it in its totality. Therefore, it was he who awaited Israeli generosity toward the Palestinians, in return for the tremendous risks he had taken in launching his peace initiative and in defying the Arab consensus against negotiations with, and recognition of, Israel. Recriminations between Sadat and Begin in the media, where strong anti-Jewish sentiments were sometimes barely hidden, did not help ease the tension.

Fortunately for Sadat, President Carter too became exasperated by the slow pace of the peace process. He was himself beleaguered at home, with inflation and unemployment rising and his own popularity plummeting. The peace initiative became his best bet and his central preoccupation. In addition, he had himself invested so much energy and time in the peace efforts, and had made so much of his mediating role between Sadat and Begin, that he might well have to pay the full price of failure if the peace process were not brought to fruition and presented as his own personal achievement. In August 1978, he invited the two leaders to his presidential retreat at Camp David.

For thirteen consecutive days (5–17 September 1978), the three leaders were closeted in the camp, and in an atmosphere of haggling, bargaining, cajoling, and threats, in which Carter played a major role, an agreement was finally produced. The breakthrough occurred in the final two days of the talks, when a double instrument of peace, instead of the one the conference had set out to achieve, was signed at Carter's insistence. Begin could then claim that the two documents, the first an Egyptian-Israeli treaty, and the second a memorandum on the question of Palestinian autonomy, stood independent of each other and permitted Israel to fulfill the one while negotiating the other until it satisfied its requirements. Sadat too had a face-saving formula, whereby he could argue that what he had achieved was the beginnings of a comprehensive peace with Israel, and that he had refused to be bought off with a quick and comfortable separate peace for Egypt. What was more important for Sadat was that Israel had agreed to a total evacuation of the entire Sinai Peninsula, and undertaken to enter into negotiations concerning Palestinian autonomy and the ultimate status of the occupied territories in the West Bank and Gaza, in conjunction with Jordan and representatives of the Palestinians. The two parties had also given their word that they would do their utmost to sign the peace treaty within three months, that is, by 16 December 1978.[17]

Under heavy pressure from Carter, Begin gave up all Israeli settlements in Sinai and agreed to evacuate the air bases with the understanding that the U.S. would help build new ones within Israel's frontiers. In return, Sadat agreed to an autonomy formula that deviated only slightly from Begin's plan. Sadat soon discovered that the Camp David accords were not satisfactory, because Israel saw itself free to continue to settle the West Bank and Gaza, and he therefore invoked the "linkage" between the two diplomatic instruments that had been signed simultaneously at Camp David as one package, signifying, to his mind, that Israel should refrain from any unilateral step that might prejudice the future of the Palestinian autonomy provided for in the accords. Sadat was under pressure from his critics and his colleagues to resist the Israeli fait accompli by refusing to sign the peace treaty by 16 December 1978, unless the Israelis mended their ways. Despondent and wearied by this controversy, he elected not to go to Oslo to accept the Nobel Peace Prize, which had been awarded to him jointly with Begin, sending his confidant and in-law, Sayyid Mar'i, in his place. He was said to have felt personally insulted by the Nobel Prize Committee's decision to share the prize, believing that he deserved it for his audacity and vision, while Begin had merely taken the ride without paying for the ticket. If it were not for President Carter's tireless personal efforts, it is doubtful that the accords would have been signed in March 1979 on the White House lawn.

VI

Sadat was murdered on 6 October 1981, before he could see the full fruits of his peace efforts. He had confided in his wife, Jihan, back in 1979, that after the conclusion of the peace treaty, he had a sense of having fulfilled his role as Egypt's president. He also told his wife, on various occasions, that a leader should know when to step down and hand things over to the next generation. He sensed that the string of accomplishments that he had attained during his presidency, and which he referred to with relish as his "great annual breakthroughs"[18] had culminated in his visit to Jerusalem in 1977, the Camp David accords in 1978, and the peace treaty in 1979. Nevertheless, he had not resigned his post, despite the fact that at some point he had given this serious consideration, presumably because—at least, this is what he told his wife and what was stated in his posthumous memoirs—he wanted to remain in office until the return of Sinai was completed in April 1982 and to ensure that all went as he had planned. It seems that Sadat's imminent and urgent sense of the end of his presidency did not surface until early 1981, during his last difficult months in office.

In terms of statesmanship, there is no doubt that Sadat's personality came to be distilled to its very essence in his daring moves in war and in peace. No modern Arab leader before or after him has so skillfully, so resolutely, and against such great odds mobilized his people, and the rest of the Arabs, in such a great venture as the 1973 war, from which he emerged politically victorious, in spite of his near-disastrous military setback. Sadat will always also stand out as the first modern Arab leader to envision peace with an enemy bitterly hated and resented as the necessary price to pay for the recuperation of Arab lands lost during the protracted Arab-Israeli conflict. His capacity to turn trends around, to swim courageously against all streams, to defy foes and allies alike, and to emerge on top of seemingly lost situations, was perhaps his most unique and productive quality.

Sadat also effected a major breakthrough on yet another level. He showed the Arabs that by war and aggression they were not only incapable of overwhelming Israel, but that in trying to do so, they lost the support of most democracies in the world. Sadat realized that only dictatorships like those in the Soviet bloc and the Third World mobilized automatically behind the Arabs. Therefore, as soon as he began democratizing his own society and throwing in his lot with the West, he comprehended that a corollary of westernizing and democratizing was to embrace the peaceful way of negotiation. Despite the boycott to which the Arab states subjected him, as a result of his breaking their anti-Israel consensus, he was able to wave before their angry and envious eyes his novel strategy that bore undeniable fruit: without firing a shot, without losing a soldier, he talked Israel into withdrawing from Arab territory, something no war and no threats had ever achieved.

Sadat's harshest critics, among whom were Isma'il Fahmi and Ibrahim Kamal, the two successive foreign ministers who had resigned during the peace process, were particularly incensed because the peace agreements he had signed had, in their view, tied Egypt's hands and isolated it from the Arab world. To them, Israel's incursion into Lebanon in 1982 proved that the Begin government was pursuing a policy of destroying Arab states one by one, having neutralized its major Arab antagonist, Egypt. The blame for all this was put squarely on Sadat's shoulders, and even his hitherto universally acclaimed "October victory" was put into question. Others claimed that the war had been handled recklessly, and that Sadat's military expertise had been faulty. What was worse, they contended, was that when time came for negotiations, Sadat proved to be weak, playing into the hands of Kissinger and Begin. These arguments turned into a full-fledged litany of accusations against Sadat by Muslim fundamentalists, who simply and directly dubbed him as "traitor." His murder at the hands of these groups was a clear message in this respect.

Sadat's controversial legacy has nonetheless had remarkable consequences: boycotted and isolated Egypt has regained its place at the head of the Arab world, exactly as Sadat had predicted; and none other than his vice-president, Hosni Mubarak, has been the man who ensures the durability of the peace accords achieved by Sadat. Certainly, Mubarak has neither the stature nor the glitter of Sadat, but by maneuvering essentially within the perimeters drawn by his predecessor, and by facing the same threats as those directed against his departed mentor, Mubarak cannot distance himself very much from the legacy he inherited. One major difference between the two presidents emerges nevertheless: while Sadat was willing to pay the price of retrieving his territories by granting peace to Israel, Mubarak, having recovered all those assets, can now take that peace as a hostage to his inter-Arab policies whenever he feels so inclined. His adherence to Egypt's commitment to peace with Israel is not unconditional: Israel has to earn it every day anew by a standard of behavior to Egypt's liking. When Israel launched its incursion into Lebanon in 1982, Mubarak withdrew his ambassador from Tel-Aviv, replacing him with a second-rank diplomat; and the peace between the two parties became definitely cold. Israelis go en masse to Egypt, but no Egyptians are encouraged or allowed to embark on the reverse trip. Israel is still attacked almost daily, in the most vitriolic anti-Semitic terms, in the government-owned and controlled media. Almost no economic or cultural exchanges are cultivated by the Egyptians, and even the Israeli-planned farms established in the Delta area are regarded with suspicion and sometimes hostility by the Egyptian media. When the Taba dispute marred the relationship between the parties in the late 1980s, Israel was assured that following its withdrawal from that last piece of territory, relations with Egypt would warm up.[19] Israel retreated, but nothing happened.

The Palestinian issue cropped up again before and after the Intifada broke out in 1987, and this development was taken as yet another roadblock standing in the way of improved relations between Israel and Egypt. At that point, some considered future improvements in the chilly relationship to depend on the outcome of the 1992 Israeli elections. Since that time, some observers believe that renewed progress hinges on Israel's readiness to withdraw from additional territory and to accommodate the Palestinians, possibly at great risk to her own security and survival. Viewed from that vantage point, Anwar Sadat's legacy may end up being judged, not as a breakthrough toward a durable peace, but as the first slice of the Israeli salami that Hosni Mubarak, with the eager assistance of other Arab states, has been sharpening his knife to slice ever faster.

Notes

1. The Free Officers was a narrow circle of Egyptian officers who were animated by the hope of rescuing their country from the corruption of the monarchy, which had contributed to the humiliating rout of the army during the First Arab-Israeli War (1948–1949). Sadat and Nasser were among the founders of the group, and, like others among their colleagues, reached positions of power and responsibility after the coup that toppled the monarchy in July 1952.

2. Gamal-abd-al-Nasser, the leader of the Free Officers, engineered the July 1952 coup and henceforth had the predominant position in Egyptians politics until his death in September 1970.

3. The Sinai War (October–November 1956), when Israel colluded with Great Britain and France to attack Egypt after Nasser's nationalisation of the Suez Canal in July, ended with the total withdrawal of the three invading powers. Nasser was credited with this achievement. See above, Chapter 6.

4. The Six-Day War of June 1967, launched by Israel following Nasser's closure of the Tiran Straits in the Gulf of Aqaba, ended in the total rout of the Egyptian, Syrian, and

Jordanian forces, and the occupation by Israel of the Sinai, the Golan, and the West Bank.

5. Ironically, Sadat later accused Nasser of "too much democracy" when the Leader of the Revolution refused his colleagues', including Sadat's, demands that dictatorship be installed in Egypt after the successful coup of the Free Officers, and insisted that he had opted for democracy. Only his threats to resign forced them to yield to his determination. See Raphael Israeli with Carol Bordenstein, *Man of Defiance: A Political Biography of Anwar Sadat* (London, 1985), 371 f.

6. *Dhimmi* are protected and tolerated subjects of the Judaeo-Christian tradition, living under the rule of the Muslim state. See, for details, Bat Yeor, *The Dhimmi* (London, 1986).

7. This was a set of principles announced by Sadat in May 1971 to set the 1952 Revolution on a new course after he had purged his rivals for the presidency.

8. See above, Chapter 14.

9. Gunnar Jarring, Swedish scholar and diplomat, was entrusted by the United Nations in early 1971 to mediate a permanent settlement between Israel and its Arab neighbors.

10. At the apex of Nasser's popularity, he was talked into a union with Syria in 1958. It ended in discord three years later.

11. One of Nasser's last feats of diplomacy was the creation of the Federation of Arab Republics in 1970. Intended to embrace Egypt, Syria, the Sudan, and Libya, it was never an effective league.

12. *Newsweek,* 10 Apr. 1973.

13. On the war and the oil embargo, see especially *The Adelphi Papers* (published by the International Institute for Strategic Studies), especially nos. 111 (*The Arab-Israeli War, October 1973: Background and Events*), 117 (*Oil and Influence: The Oil Weapon Examined*), and 136 (*Oil and Security: Problems and Prospects of Importing Countries*). See also Muhammad Heikal, *The Road to Ramadan* (New York, 1975), and Nadav Safran, *Israel, the Embattled Ally* (Cambridge, Mass., 1978).

14. Henry A. Kissinger, *Years of Upheaval* (Boston, 1982), 638–41.

15. During its ten-year occupation of the Sinai, Israel had built two townships and a score of flourishing agricultural settlements inhabited by some six thousand people.

16. Two major air bases were built in the Sinai by Israel, which provided it for the first time with air depth, and it was therefore reluctant to renounce them.

17. Much has been written about the peace process, including autobiographical notes by Carter and Sadat. Perhaps the most telling accounts are Moshe Dayan, *Breakthrough* (London, 1981); Isma'il Fahmi, *Negotiating Peace in the Middle East* (Baltimore, 1983); Eitan Haber, *The Year of the Dove* (New York, 1979); and Ezer Weizman, *The Battle for Peace* (New York, 1981).

18. In his speeches Sadat liked to claim one major achievement for each of the years of his presidency: 1971, the Corrective Revolution; 1972, the expulsion of the Soviets; 1973, the October War; 1974, the disengagement agreement; 1975, the second disengagement; 1976, the Open Door policy; 1977, the peace initiative; 1978, Camp David; 1979, the peace agreement; and 1980, the beginning of Israel's evacuation of the Sinai.

19. Taba is a tiny beach west of the Israeli port of Eilat. It remained in Israel's possession after the evacuation of the rest of the Sinai and was restored to Egypt in 1990.

16

THE DIPLOMATS AND DIPLOMACY OF

THE UNITED NATIONS

Paul Gordon Lauren

THE FIRST OCCUPANT of this position in diplomacy ominously described it as "the most impossible job in the world."[1] "It was a challenge beyond my wildest dreams," he later wrote, "a nightmare" and "the target of criticism from right, left and center" from the great and the small powers of the world alike.[2] His successor stated publicly, "Nobody, I think, can accept this position . . . knowing what it means, except from a sense of duty."[3] Others who followed used similar language, describing their job as a "cockpit of world tensions" and the center of heavy burdens of international politics.[4] Still others maintained from their own personal experience that the position imposed "tasks of extraordinary difficulty," represented the focal point "where the big and little crises of the world converge," the place where one receives blame "time and again by one group of nations or another," and where one is "expected to embody the conscience of mankind and be all things to all men."[5]

Outside observers looking in at the nature of this job described it with admiration and respect as "a very formidable institution in world politics," representing "the world's chief civil servant," serving as "a spokesman for mankind," and being "a supranational, quasi-political, diplomatic post without equal." They also agreed that it presented "impossible," "thankless," and "almost superhuman" tasks with "a kind of built-in prescription for a heart attack or a stroke."[6] *Le Monde* described the position as simply "one of the most difficult jobs in the world,"[7] and the Associated Press observed that it was "the loneliest diplomatic job on earth."[8] The subject that attracted all these comments like a lightning rod, was, of course, the secretary-general of the United Nations.

I

The concept of the United Nations and its secretary-general emerged from the Second World War. The political leaders and diplomats who agreed on the Atlantic Charter in August 1941 and the Declaration by United Nations in January 1942 first raised the idea of some system of general postwar security and introduced the name United Nations. Then, significantly, in October 1943, U.S. Secretary of State Cordell Hull, Soviet Foreign Minister V. M. Molotov, and British Foreign Secretary Anthony Eden signed the Moscow Declaration pledging a continuance of wartime cooperation and explicitly recognizing "the necessity of establishing at the earliest practicable date a general international organization."[9]

Committed to this objective in peace as well as victory in war, the Americans, Soviet, British, and Chinese began to hammer out the details of what would be called "the most ambitious order-building experiment in history."[10] In 1944 they gathered together at the Dumbarton Oaks Conference to determine the precise nature of this postwar organization for maintaining peace and security in the world. Their assumption—and it proved to be a major assumption— was that the cooperation and unity of purpose among the Great Powers in war would continue in peace. "This time, as we fight together to get the war over quickly," said President Franklin Roosevelt before Congress, "we work together to keep it from happening again." He said that the time had arrived in diplomacy "to spell the end of the system of unilateral action, the exclusive alliances, the spheres of influence, the balances of power, and all the other expedients that have been tried for centuries—and have always failed." Instead, he concluded, "We propose to substitute for all these a universal organization in which all peace-loving nations will finally have a chance to join."[11]

The Big Four submitted the proposals drafted at Dumbarton Oaks to other nations for consideration and invited them to attend the United Nations Conference on International Organization during the spring of 1945 in San Francisco. In a spirit of euphoria, speakers from fifty countries described the conference as a "landmark" and "a milestone in the long march of man to a better future," and declared from the podium: "For there can be no doubt any more that for us, for the human race, the hour has struck. Mankind has arrived at the crisis of its fate, the fate of its future as a civilized world."[12] Time and time again the delegates were urged to avoid the mistakes of the past, to rise above their own parochial national interests, and to promote the common international good for the future of all. During the course of negotiations, the delegates agreed to establish a world organization pledged "to save succeeding generations from the scourge of war,"[13] but, importantly, made it one without power of sovereignty over decision-making or enforcement, and one composed entirely of independent nation-states that could give or withhold their cooperation as they wished. The Great Powers insisted on the lion's share of authority over collective security and provided that the Charter would authorize the creation of a Security Council on which they would have permanent membership and the power of veto over any decision they did not like. All other nations aspiring to increase their influence as much as they could wanted a "Parliament of Man," where they might confer on the basis of equality, and thus voted for articles in the Charter to establish the General Assembly. In addition, the majority of delegates supported a critical article declaring: "Nothing contained in the present Charter shall authorize the United Nations to intervene in matters which are essentially within the domestic jurisdiction of any state."[14] All of these provisions could have been easily anticipated, for they accurately reflected the global balance of power as well as the traditional and expected prerogatives of sovereignty.

What emerged as new departures in the Charter, however, were articles addressing much larger, and closely interrelated, principles that clearly expanded the claims of the organization in international affairs and eventually proved to be powerful forces for change. One of these, intensively supported by these small nations who once had been exploited by colonialism, took the form of the Declaration Concerning Non Self-Governing Territories, announcing that "the interests of the inhabitants of these territories are paramount," supporting the aspirations of political self-determination, and putting the world on notice that the age of imperial possessions was drawing to a close. Added to this was the principle of promoting economic and social justice around the world by enhancing higher standards of living, social progress, and development. In addition, and with the passionate support of those nations and groups in particular who themselves had been victims of racial discrimination or had suffered from the recent horrors of the Nazi Holocaust, the Charter pledged to promote and encourage "universal respect for, and observance of, human rights and fundamental freedoms for all without distinction as to race, sex, language, or religion."[15] Moreover, and in words that would greatly influence those diplomats charged with upholding these provisions, the Charter spoke about the organization's special responsibility, not to individual nations alone, but to the world as a whole, and not simply to governments, but to "all peoples."[16]

Reactions to these provisions varied enormously, and thereby initiated a debate over the Charter that continues to the present day. To many enthusiastic delegates, the Charter marked an unprecedented achievement—"one of the great moments in history"[17]—in which diplomats finally realized the importance of principle and agreed to create an international organization responsible for maintaining global peace and security. Indeed, the extravagance of the optimism among true believers was so great in the wake of the exhaustion of six years of catastrophic war that the Charter "seemed too good to be true" and raised exaggerated hopes that later would make them especially susceptible to bitter disappointment and disillusionment.[18] Others worried either that the Charter went much too far in creating "world government" that would threaten national sovereignty or, conversely, that by giving such prominence to nation-states and failing to include enforcement procedures it did not accomplish enough.[19] Those diplomats and observers with more experience and perspective, however, viewed the Charter neither as a magnificent achievement nor as a horrendous tragedy; but rather, in the words of President Harry Truman, as an essential "first step" toward the grand experiment of order-building for the world.[20] They believed that they had accomplished about as much as could be expected, given the circumstances, traditions, and prejudices of the time. As scholar John Stoessinger writes:

> In not attempting the impossible, the founders of the United Nations were realists. But in seeking to go to the very limits of the possible, they were also visionaries. And necessarily so, for the idea of the United Nations had to take into account the full import of the cruel paradox that, in the nuclear age, the national sovereignty of nations would have to be controlled by an international order, but that this international order would have to be created and even controlled by sovereign nations. The plan therefore had to combine the dictates of national power with those of international order.[21]

Perhaps this is what Lord Halifax of the British delegation had in mind when he told his colleagues that they had forged an instrument of many compromises that would work for peace only if the member nations were prepared to make sacrifices for it, and that the Charter marked "the beginnings of a long and challenging endeavor."[22]

No one would confront the demanding challenges of this endeavor more directly and intimately than those who served in the position of secretary-general of the United Nations. Beginning with the earliest planning stages, the founders of the new organization envisioned a strong executive leader and international diplomat. Roosevelt, for example, wanted the position to be filled by someone called the "World's Moderator."[23] The Charter recognized this intent and established that the chief administrative authority of the organization would be vested in the secretary-general, with full responsibility over an international civil service in the Secretariat and with the duty of preparing an annual report on the state of global peace and security. Then, in a radical departure from previous practice in diplomacy, the Charter provided the potential for far-reaching political powers for the secretary-general. In the first place, it enabled the various organs of the United Nations to entrust this individual with unspecified "other functions" and charge him with carrying out important and at times highly controversial decisions in the political arena. Moreover, and marking a complete innovation, the Charter gave the secretary-general the broad right to "bring to the attention of the Security Council *any* matter that in his opinion may threaten the maintenance of international peace and security."[24] Thus, in matters of the highest importance and urgency to order-building in the world, secretaries-general received from the Charter not only a status equivalent to that of a member state, but also a considerable reservoir of political authority on which they could draw or not as their own temperament, judgment, courage, and patience might suggest. In all of this the critical presumption was that the secretary-general would be able to serve both the principles of Charter and the interests of the membership.[25]

Other sources confirm this initial desire for strong and highly qualified leadership on the part of the secretary-general. One internal U.S. State Department document, for example, argued that the person holding this position "must be a first-rate diplomat with an exceptional capacity to resolve issues and construct patterns of cooperation," "gifted with an abundance of tact," and in possession of an "established reputation" capable of commanding confidence.[26] The department maintained that the secretary-general "should be a man of recognized competence and prestige in the field of foreign affairs."[27] The array of diplomats, including British Foreign Secretary Ernest Bevin, participating on the Preparatory Commission designed to fill in the details of the Charter prior to the first session of the United Nations, reached the same conclusion. They recognized that the fulfillment of the administrative duties of the office alone would require considerable abilities, and that performance of the political responsibilities would require even more, perceptively observing:

> Under Article 99 of the Charter, moreover, he has been given a quite special right which goes beyond any power previously accorded to the head of an international organization, viz: to bring to the attention of the Security Council any matter (not merely any dispute or situation) which, in his opinion, may threaten the maintenance of international peace and security. It is impossible to foresee how this Article will be applied; but the responsibility it confers upon the Secretary-General will require the exercise of the highest qualities of political judgment, tact, and integrity.

"The Secretary-General, more than anyone else," they concluded, "will stand for the United Nations as a whole. In the eyes of the world . . . he must embody the principles and ideals of the Charter to which the Organization seeks to give effect."[28]

To deal with the many problems of postwar diplomacy for the world, most member states creating the United Nations and the position of its secretary-general thus wanted a strong statesman and an international diplomat of the first order. What they obtained instead was Trygve Lie, and the explanation lies in the emergence of the era of confrontation and the beginnings of the Cold War.

II

The actual selection of the first secretary-general took place several critical months after the smiles of the San Francisco Conference and the harmonious cooperation of drafting the Charter. During that time the world watched as the Big Three failed to reach agreement at the Potsdam Conference on several fundamental features of the postwar world, as the Soviet Union secured its troop positions further in Eastern Europe and entered the war in Asia, and as the United States detonated the first atomic bombs over Hiroshima and Nagasaki. With the end of the war and the elimination of the common threat that had held them together, the coalition partners of the "Grand Alliance" began rapidly to fall victim to their own national passions, histories, interests, and perspectives. Two days after the beginning of the first session of the United Nations meeting in London in January 1946, for example, the presence of Soviet troops in Iran was brought before the Security Council, quickly followed by a countermove by the Soviet Union complaining of British forces in Greece and Indonesia. Within weeks, Winston Churchill delivered his "Iron Curtain" speech condemning Soviet behavior. In the words of one participant, "the clouds were gathering fast,"[29] and heretofore enthusiastic supporters of the United Nations painfully watched a pattern emerge that came to plague the entire experiment from its birth: "the moral infection of Great Power disagreement."[30]

In this setting, the diplomats vainly attempted to find a leader with the skills and reputation that the envisioned position of secretary-general required. They considered the names of several distinguished, well-known, and very capable individuals: Paul-Henri Spaak of Belgium, Lester Pearson of Canada, Jan Masaryk of Czechoslovakia, Anthony Eden of Great Britain, and Dwight Eisenhower of the United States, among others.[31] According to the terms of the Charter, however, the secretary-general could be elected only after a two-thirds vote of the General Assembly based upon the unanimous recommendation of the permanent members of the Security Council. Here, the Great Powers argued, as they would many times again, about the relative importance of personal competence, political orientation, and geographical distribution. The Soviets, for example, adamantly refused to support anyone tied to the West and, even more important, given subsequent events and evidence, appear to have concluded that they did not want a politically strong and highly qualified individual with independent views in the position of secretary-general.[32] Lengthy and often serpentine negotiations resulted in a compromise that pleased almost no one except perhaps Soviet Foreign Minister Andrei Gromyko, who personally and skillfully engineered the outcome: the first secretary-general of the United Nations would be the relatively unknown Norwegian foreign minister, Trygve Lie.

Although he had served as a member of the Norwegian delegation to the San Francisco Conference, Lie possessed precious little experience in international politics. He came from a poor family, participated actively in the Norwegian Labor Party, gained success as a trade union negotiator, and through time rose to become a member of the cabinet, serving as minister of commerce and as minister of justice. International opinion questioned his fitness to be secretary-general, describing him as a second-rate "mediocrity" completely "out of his depth."[33] An internal memorandum of the British Foreign Office judged Lie as being "somewhat unstable" and possessing an "unreliable character,"[34] and historical adviser Charles Webster wrote privately that he was "a poor choice" who stood "on the verge of being a stooge."[35] Even reports from Norway itself indicated a response that was "doubtful and unenthusiastic" about his election, and the American mission in Oslo wrote candidly that "he is clearly not an ideal

choice for Secretary-General." "He is ebullient, somewhat mercurial," it continued, stating that although Lie would likely work loyally in attempting to
make the United Nations a success, the "gravest reservation would be on the
ground of his lack of experience . . . plus his lack of broad educational and
cultural background and training."[36] Lie, to his credit, did not claim talents or a
background that he did not possess, and in his memoirs declared that he had
been "catapulted" into the position. "It seemed to me," he wrote, "that presid-
ing over . . . the United Nations would demand a profound experience in
international relations and an expertness in the languages of diplomacy—
qualifications I could not claim." Consequently, he asked, "Why had this
awesome task fallen to a labor lawyer from Norway?"[37]

Why, indeed? Those who founded the United Nations and drafted the Charter
understood that the whole vast and grand experiment could work only if the
Great Powers reached agreement in finding qualified personnel and cooperated
in an international spirit that transcended mere national interests. The very first
process of selection proved to be a disillusioning experience for them. It indicated from the beginning the emergence of conflicting and highly politicized
perceptions of the role of the United Nations and its secretary-general, depending upon the differing foreign-policy objectives of the member states. The
selection also emphasized that Lie and his successors would likely be placed
squarely and unenviably in the midst of a worldwide confrontation and power
struggle known as the Cold War, which would severely and painfully limit them
and the institution of the United Nations. The election of Lie, in the words of
one diplomat, marked a "compromise between Soviet and Anglo-American
views" that was likely to affect the future of the organization.[38]

To build and staff the new United Nations and guide it through the shoals of
this international struggle, to walk the narrow line between the two camps of
East and West, to confront whatever unanticipated problems might develop in
the world, and simultaneously to bring the principles of the Charter to fruition,
as one commentator observes, "would have taxed an Olympian god let alone a
mere mortal."[39] Lie's lack of experience, short temper, insecurity, linguistic
shortcomings, which fostered the impression that he lacked intellectual credentials as well, and the perception that he was somehow "Moscow's man" simply
made the problem worse and the tasks more formidable. Nevertheless, with a
determination that perhaps only one who actually has been the first occupant of
a newly created position with great public expectations can fully appreciate, he
set out to do his job by trial and error. In administrative affairs, he began hiring
staff for the Secretariat, building the headquarters in New York, developing a
myriad of operating procedures, providing services for translating and the
reproduction of documents, and creating a precedent that the secretary-general
could propose any matter for the agenda within the scope of the Charter and
make personal statements about his views as a spokesman "for the Organization
as a whole."[40] In the critical and sensitive area of political affairs, Lie often

moved with more exuberance than discretion, intending to be an activist and making the secretary-general, as he described it, "a force for peace." He knew that the powers of the office conferred by the Charter were unique, providing him with "a very special place in the structure of the United Nations" and "world political responsibilities which no individual, no representative of a single nation, ever had before." Yet, Lie also understood, as he stated with insight: "This role, with all its potentialities and its pitfalls for the future, had to be weighed against the hard political realities of a world by no means ready to accept either the outlook or the responsibilities of world citizenship."[41]

It did not take long for those "hard realities" to manifest themselves. Soviet troops in Iran, the fate of General Francisco Franco's Spain, and internal chaos in Greece during 1946 all presented problems for Lie; for in taking a stand that supported one of the Great Powers, he thereby alienated another, if not all of the rest. Even at this early date, American leaders confessed that they "had made a mistake in picking a dud as Secretary-General."[42] His opposition to the Truman Doctrine was regarded as being provocative, and his resentment that the United States largely excluded the United Nations from active involvement with the Marshall Plan in 1947 drew the wrath, if not the contempt, of British Foreign Secretary Ernest Bevin and American Secretary of State Dean Acheson. In agitation they rebuffed his efforts to mediate the Berlin Crisis of 1948, telling Lie that the United Nations might play some role in the future should the situation deteriorate, while the annoyed Soviets conveyed their opinion that the situation in Germany was none of his business. When he dared to suggest in a public speech that both East and West were equally guilty for escalating their differences, that from the perspective of history the Cold War would be a passing phenomenon, and that the United Nations could function much better if the Great Powers would employ it properly and live up to their promises under the Charter, a storm of criticism descended upon him. Some diplomats close to Lie even described him as "a disaster."[43] It was even worse when he worried publicly that the creation of the North Atlantic Treaty Organization might threaten genuine collective security, weaken the United Nations, and thereby increase tensions in the Cold War.

Only when international problems appeared too intractable or insoluble by other means did the Great Powers turn to the United Nations, as evidenced when the British desperately wanted out of the tangled web of politics and emotion in the Middle East and requested that Lie bring the difficult question of Palestine before the organization. Learning as he went with little to guide him other than a desire to prevent a war, Lie did so, and the majority in the General Assembly adopted a plan in 1947 calling for a termination of the British mandate in the area and the partition of Palestine into separate Arab and Jewish states. Widespread disturbances followed among angry Palestinian Arabs who protested the partition, and the British withdrawal in May 1948 and the abrupt reversal of American support for previous negotiations and immediate recognition of the state of Israel by the United States led immediately to the outbreak of war. For his role in supporting the United Nations partition plan and seeking an international force to protect the peace in this crisis, Lie was warmly praised by Abba Eban, who would become Israel's foreign minister, and other Jewish leaders as "a pillar of strength," yet he was widely and vehemently condemned by those sympathetic to the Arab cause.[44] Lie concluded from the experience that there would be "long-standing and considerable" involvement by the United Nations in Palestine in the years ahead,[45] and the subsequent history of several wars and countless acts of violence in the area certainly and tragically proved his prediction to be correct.

War in the Middle East proved to be only a prelude to other conflicts, for in June 1950 the North Koreans launched a surprise invasion of South Korea, thus launching the Korean War and marking, in the words of one observer, "one of the great watersheds in the history of international organization."[46] Lie viewed this armed aggression as a clear-cut attack not only upon the freely elected government of the Republic of Korea but also upon the United Nations and the principles of the Charter that he had sworn to uphold. His response in condemning the attack and mobilizing international support to stop it was "immediate, unequivocal, and influential," as described by the editors of his public papers, and the secretary-general's initiative in the Security Council "put the full weight and prestige of his Office squarely on the side of the first collective armed resistance to aggression ever taken by or under the auspices of an international organization."[47] This time the United States agreed with Lie, wanted to consult with him, and spoke glowingly of his courage, "unusual skill," "good judgment," and "understanding mind."[48] Although all forces were placed under American command and its controversial commander, General Douglas MacArthur, the war remained a United Nations effort, sanctioned and supported by the vast majority of the international community.

Lie and the United Nations found a notable exception to this support, however, among the Soviets. In supporting communist allies in North Korea and then the People's Republic of China, they vehemently opposed United Nations action in the Korean War. They viewed such activity as fundamentally incompatible with the Charter, and argued that by taking control out of the Security Council (where they possessed the veto to block any action) by means of the Acheson-inspired "Uniting for Peace Resolution" and placing it instead in the General Assembly (where they and their satellites could muster only a minority of votes), the United Nations was acting illegally. Whereas Lie regarded his stand on Korea as his "best justified act" of seven years as secretary-general, the Soviets, who had strongly supported him up to this point, now completely reversed themselves, tearing into him with accusations of becoming "an accessory to the American aggressors" and using *Pravda* to declare: "Dropping his mask, Mr. Trygve Lie . . . became one of the direct and active accomplices of US armed intervention in Korea."[49]

These highly visible crises and wars tend to attract the greatest attention, but they should not obscure other efforts made by Lie and the United Nations during his tenure that had profound long-term consequences both for the organization and for global politics. Even when prospects of reaching agreement appeared dim or nonexistent during conflict, for example, Lie supported the maintenance of negotiations and the value of the United Nations as the one permanent and universal diplomatic community where the machinery for communication could be mobilized at a moment's notice. In 1947 Lie opened the first meeting of the Trusteeship Council by declaring that it signaled "the beginning of a new and weighty responsibility for the United Nations" for addressing the needs of hundreds of millions of subjected peoples around the world by working toward the goal of their "self-government or independence."[50] During the following year, the United Nations initiated its assistance program for developing countries, extended its help to refugees, and adopted the revolutionary Universal Declaration of Human Rights to help end racial discrimination and set international standards of basic human rights for all people.[51] In 1949 Lie renewed his call for universal membership and urged the extension of member status to newly emerging nations irrespective of race or ideology, especially those in Africa and Asia, and encouraged them to play a role in world affairs. He continued this argument in 1950 when, despite the overwhelming opposition of the United States and criticism for being "a stooge of the Reds," he publicly supported membership in the United Nations for the People's Republic of China, thereby earning the begrudging admiration of James Reston in the *New York Times* for his "bold try" to "act in what he believes to be the best interests of the United Nations, even if they [the Great Powers] do not like it, and that is something of an innovation in the history of the security organization."[52] Moreover, his further initiatives and mission in 1950 for a twenty-year program for peace brought praise from Albert Einstein, who wrote, "You are one of the very few who in the midst of the bewilderment and confusion of our time has succeeded in keeping his vision clear, and whose urge to help remains undeterred by obstacles and narrow allegiances."[53]

Yet, despite these efforts and an occasional word of public or private praise, the implacable hostility of the Soviets toward Lie in the wake of his stand on the Korean War doomed his continuation in office. First, they vetoed his appointment for a second five-year term in the Security Council; then, when the majority in the General Assembly decided to support him anyway by simply extending his current term, the Soviet delegate declared for all to hear: "If Trygve Lie is appointed Secretary-General of the United Nations for any supplementary period whatsoever, the Government of the Soviet Union . . . will have no dealings with him and will refuse to regard him as the Secretary-General."[54] Their subsequent conduct in insulting him personally and boycotting him politically, however much it might be deplored, in the end ruined him. It not only made his life exceedingly difficult, but proved to be brutally effective in forcing even his supporters to realize that he could no longer hope to serve the interests of the organization and retain the confidence of the member states as envisioned by the Charter.[55] This unrelenting coercion from the Soviets, exacerbated by what he called "the purgatory" of pressure from McCarthyism in the United States, hysterically claiming that he was harboring communist sympathizers within the Secretariat, finally forced Lie, at the end of 1952, to announce his resignation.[56]

The experience of Trygve Lie underscored the great dilemma, if not the inherent contradiction, of international statesmanship. To be an effective spokesman for the principles of the Charter and the interests of the world community as a whole, the secretary-general must at times be able and willing to take a stand on major, controversial, political issues. But in this process, he must simultaneously retain the confidence of all the national actors who consider their own interests to be paramount.[57] This is critical, for a secretary-general must rely upon precisely this confidence of others in the prestige and moral force of the office rather than armed forces for influence and leverage in world politics. As the Soviet representative sarcastically reminded Lie on one occasion, he was not a commander in chief of troops, but only "of his workers in the Secretariat [and] . . . mimeograph machines."[58] Lie's successors, particularly those who also attempted to provide leadership during the period of confrontation in the Cold War, were forced to confront this agonizing problem as surely as he.

Perhaps it was with these larger thoughts in mind that during his last rather unpleasant and difficult months in office,[59] and at a time when Soviet diplomats said that his retirement was "long overdue"[60] and press reports announced that "The UN Is Dying,"[61] Lie spoke about the future of this grand experiment of the United Nations. With insight born from experience, he observed:

> Our Organization reflects the imperfections of our time, but it is also an expression of the most constructive forces for our world and a symbol of hope for the future. . . . The limitations of our Organization have been well tested. I would like to stress, however, that in my opinion its potentialities for peace have been less well explored.

For this purpose, Lie frankly concluded, "more than faith in principles and purposes of the United Nations is needed. Stamina and a wise recognition of realities are required."[62]

III

These necessary qualities of faith, stamina, and wisdom appeared to be possessed in much greater supply by Lie's successor, Dag Hammarskjöld. But few of the Great Powers on the Security Council knew this at the time, nor were they necessarily interested in the long-term future of an influential United Nations. Instead, their attention focused upon the immediate chore of finding someone to fill the position of secretary-general who would protect their own national interests. Once again, the politics and diplomacy of the selection process revealed that they could not agree and that a serious stalement would result unless a compromise candidate could be found. At precisely this juncture in the negotiations, Stalin died. The internal struggle within the Kremlin added to an already complicated situation, and the Soviets appeared to have decided that a more moderate image in world affairs might be to their advantage. In this setting, compromise seemed possible, and negotiators considered that their safest bet might be a Scandinavian. The French proposed the idea of a civil servant in the Swedish Foreign Ministry named Dag Hammarskjöld. Although the State Department possessed only "sketchy information" about him and considered that "he may be as good as we can get," the former ambassador to Sweden offered praise for his abilities and said "that the United Nations would be lucky to get Hammarskjöld and that they could do a lot worse."[63] The British ambassador described him as "absolutely straight and reliable, extremely frank, and painstakingly honorable,"[64] and Eden believed him to be an "excellent candidate" who should be supported.[65] Moreover, and not unimportantly, at the time there appeared to be little in his past that would indicate that he might ever present a threat as too strong or too active a leader. In fact, Lie actually opposed Hammarskjöld's candidacy, believing that he would be no more than an unobtrusive "clerk" never capable of leading or inspiring the order-building experiment.[66] But it was precisely his presumed restrained, behind-the-scenes, self-effacing, technocratic, administrative style as a civil servant rather than as a politician that seemed to fit exactly what was wanted. Thus, once the Soviets concurred and the Nationalist Chinese agreed to abstain in the voting, the rest followed quickly, and in the spring of 1953 Hammarskjöld became the second secretary-general of the United Nations.

It would be difficult to imagine two individuals more different than Trygve Lie and Dag Hammarskjöld. In sharp contrast to his predecessor, Hammarskjöld possessed a patrician pedigree, a brilliant mind, a stellar academic record, and a mastery of several languages. Those who knew him described him in extraordinary terms, speaking of him as "an exceptional human being of rich talents" with "moral courage" and a "conciliatory spirit" who provided "an exhilarating spectacle of principle and intellect in action."[67] Brian Urquhart, a man who worked closely with him for years, wrote:

All of Hammarskjöld's great gifts would have had far less effect without the personal impression he made on most of the people who dealt with him. His integrity, disinterestedness, and purity of intention were clear even to those—and there were many—with whom he strongly disagreed. . . . Dag Hammarskjöld was that most unusual of creatures, a truly good man.[68]

These personality traits were enhanced by his administrative experience as the chairman of the National Bank of Sweden, permanent under-secretary of the Ministry of Finance, and cabinet adviser on financial and economic problems. He also possessed considerable diplomatic experience in positions within the Foreign Ministry and as a delegate to the Organization for European Economic Cooperation, Council of Europe, and the United Nations General Assembly. Thus, when Hammarskjöld arrived at the United Nations, he brought many assets and promised to assist "those who make the decisions which frame history." Anticipating the tasks ahead, he observed that a mountain climber and the secretary-general needed much the same qualities: "perseverance and patience, a firm grip on realities, careful but imaginative planning, [and] a clear awareness of the dangers but also of the fact that fate is what we make it."[69]

Hammarskjöld would establish far more precedents than he would follow, and in this regard began his tenure with the enormous good fortune of a couple of initial years relatively free from major East-West clashes. Changes in leadership in both the Soviet Union and the United States brought about a temporary relaxation of tensions and an armistice in Korea. This allowed him to build up a vital store of confidence from both sides in the Cold War before circumstances forced him to take a more active role.[70] In addition, he attempted to learn from the mistakes of the past and to develop an approach to political disputes differing in two important respects from that of his predecessor. First, he wanted to gain authority for his actions in advance from the Security Council or the General Assembly. Second, as far as possible, he wanted to carry out his diplomatic activity quietly behind the scenes with patience and without publicity, as he did in 1954, when he flew to Beijing to negotiate privately and successfully with Chinese Premier Zhou Enlai for the release of eleven American airmen. The former would gain him the confidence of the major powers, he hoped, and the latter would make possible agreements without serious loss of face for any nations.[71]

Hammarskjöld soon found himself needing every one of these skills and more in dealing with the two major political struggles of our time: the Cold War and the fight for independence among former colonial territories. Indeed, the vast majority of votes taken in the United Nations before, during, and after his tenure involved one or both of these battles. One of the earliest problems in this regard was the fact that for nine years the East-West confrontation had prevented many newly emerged states from gaining admission into the United Nations. This logjam was finally broken under Hammarskjöld's leadership in 1955, by an arrangement for admitting sixteen new member states. This, in turn, began a process that many observers see as one of the most important, if not the most important, contribution of the United Nations to international order: namely, actively assisting in the greatest extension of freedom in history with the transfer of power from largely white, European colonial masters to independent states and their nearly one billion people around the world.[72]

Hammarskjöld subsequently oversaw the admission of many new states, most of them coming from Africa and Asia and clearly indicating the direction of the future. As Hammarskjöld's assistant, Andrew W. Cordier, anticipated early in the process, this admission "will certainly change some of the existing balances in the United Nations."[73] Through time these changes included an important shift in focus from the Security Council to the General Assembly, a new priority given to problems of racial discrimination like apartheid and to economic development, and a strengthening of the position of the secretary-general. In fact, the influence of these new states, the General Assembly, and the secretary-general grew hand in hand as they increasingly spoke together of the need for an "independent position" of the United Nations representing all states, not just the Great Powers, in world affairs.[74]

The Middle East has confronted all secretaries-general with turmoil, and Hammarskjöld was certainly no exception, as he discovered with the outbreak of the Suez Crisis. Egyptian President Gamel Nasser's sudden nationalization of the Suez Canal provided an excuse for an invasion of Egypt by Israeli, British, and French forces in 1956. With two permanent members of the Security Council accused of military aggression, the Arabs and Israelis locked in mortal combat, and the Soviet Union threatening to intervene, the United Nations faced a crisis of the first magnitude. In this situation, Hammarskjöld responded with great skill, energy, and ingenuity, pushing the limited resources of the Secretariat and the mechanisms of the organization to their practical extremes. As he confided privately at an early stage, "We have to play the ball with both guts and prudence. In such a situation I would be very sorry indeed if we were stopped by unnecessary diplomatic red tape."[75] Thus, for the first time he publicly rebuked two Great Powers, stating that he had no choice but to be "a servant of the principles of the Charter" and take a principled stand against aggression.[76] Then, since the states involved blocked action by Security Council, he turned to the General Assembly for authorization to negotiate a ceasefire, arrange for the withdrawal of Anglo-French-Israeli forces, and create an unprecedented experiment in the form of an international peacekeeping force, known as the United Nations Emergency Force (UNEF), to keep the warring parties apart. The enormous authority and confidence thus given to Hammarskjöld by the Assembly proved to be justified, for each one of these measures was successful and ultimately provided the means of depriving the Soviets of any grounds for military intervention, keeping the Egyptians and Israelis away from each other's throats, and at the same time allowing the British and French to extricate themselves from their mistake with some semblance of dignity.[77]

His skillful diplomacy and resourcefulness at overcoming seemingly insurmountable obstacles in the Suez Crisis not only brought a new respect to the United Nations, especially in its innovative creation and use of peacekeeping forces as a potentially significant instrument for international crisis management, but also to Hammarskjöld himself. President Dwight Eisenhower praised him publicly and indicated the growing position of the secretary-general in world affairs, and even those who disagreed with him acknowledged his remarkable resolution of purpose and abilities under pressure. Such heightened respect helps to explain why within a period of only a few months of having to act against the policies of three permanent members of the Security Council, he was unanimously elected in 1957 to a second five-year term as secretary-general, and one marked with a growing tendency in both the General Assembly and the Security Council to describe Hammarskjöld as "surely our supreme international civil servant" and to grant him broad powers.[78]

This experience strengthened his position and emboldened him to act in a more active and public political role than his previous pattern of "quiet diplomacy" might have suggested. When he first entered the office he had described the secretary-general's role as that of "an instrument, a catalyst, and perhaps an inspirer."[79] Now, however, he enunciated a concept of powers and responsibilities that came much closer to the concept of a leader rather than an instrument. Hammarskjöld said, for example, that in this order-building experiment he believed it "to be his duty to use his office, and, indeed, the machinery of the Organization, to its utmost capacity and to the full extent permitted at each stage by practical circumstances." In fulfilling this task, he explained, he ought to be instructed when possible, but then added: "I believe that it is in keeping with the philosophy of the Charter that the Secretary-General should be expected to act also without such guidance, should this appear to him necessary in order to help in filling any vacuum that may appear in the systems which the Charter and traditional diplomacy provide for the safeguarding of peace and security."[80] Yet with prescient foreboding, on his own copy of this speech, Hammarskjöld penciled in the last few words of the Lord's Prayer, and on the same day wrote in his revealing and posthumously published diary, *Markings*, that he considered the course now set "into the storm."[81]

When the storm hit Hammarskjöld, it struck with violence, and it began in the Congo. What made it so momentous and dangerous was that the two powerful struggles of the Cold War and decolonization combined, and that Hammarskjöld's sense of the responsibilities and integrity of his office and the institution of the United Nations directly challenged the interests and sensibilities of the most powerful member states. The crisis started when the Belgians precipitously withdrew from their colonial possessions in the Congo in 1960, suddenly leaving this strategically important and mineral-rich area vulnerable to external pressure, and when the Congolese leaders issued a request for the urgent dispatch of military assistance to their territory, Hammarskjöld decided to respond affirmatively to the new nation's appeal. After consulting the African delegations and members of the Security Council, he explicitly invoked his powers under Article 99 of the Charter for the first time and recommended the creation of another peacekeeping force. The Council approved his request and authorized him to take action that would eventually lead to the creation of an independent nation against seemingly insurmountable odds and be seen by many as "the UN's greatest success."[82] Once again he set out with courage and skill, as he had earlier in successfully negotiating in China for the release of American airmen, in the Middle East at the time of Suez, in Lebanon and Jordan during 1958 for the withdrawal of foreign troops, and in using his good offices in South Africa and establishing a United Nations presence in Laos during 1960.[83] Now he simultaneously performed administrative, military, political, and diplomatic assignments as circumstances required. This quickly earned him the praise of the world press, including Walter Lippmann, who wrote of the invaluable role of the United Nations "as it is now administered with the genius of Mr. Dag Hammarskjöld."[84] James Reston of the *New York Times* went further, observing that he was "tireless," "infinitely patient," "sensitive," and "knows exactly what his job will let him do and forbid him from doing," and concluding: "This remarkable man is proving to be one of the great natural resources in the world today, and it is difficult to think of another in the field of world diplomacy who could do the job as well."[85]

This adulation did not last long. Within a few months Security Council unanimity broke down, the Congolese government itself shattered into three competing and warring factions with the subsequent collapse of any semblance of law and order, the African states split in their decision about what action to take, the Belgians attempted to retain some of their former influence by sending troops into territories under dispute, and the major contestants of the Cold War chose to support their own favorites in the Congo deliberately outside of the context of peacekeeping efforts by the United Nations. Once this occurred, writes Joseph Lash, "the Secretary-General was pulled down from his pinnacle of influence and the United Nations was shaken to its foundations."[86] The Congo became for Hammarskjöld what Korea had been for Lie; and, in both cases, the Soviets led the attack. "The Congo is slipping through our fingers," said an enraged Soviet Premier Nikita Khrushchev to his confidants, warning ominously: "We have to get rid of him by any means."[87] Knowing in advance that the fervently nationalistic French President Charles de Gaulle had already also complained that the United Nations and Hammarskjöld were guilty of undue interference in world politics, Khrushchev decided to escalate the assault in the General Assembly itself and in the full light of publicity. Here, as he literally pounded the desk to draw attention, and with Gromyko at his side, Khrushchev accused Hammarskjöld of siding with colonialists and capitalists, violating the conditions of his office, and exceeding his authority. For these reasons, he suddenly exclaimed to a shocked assembly, "the post of Secretary-General . . . should be abolished."[88]

Hammarskjöld correctly viewed this vehement attack as a challenge not just to him, but to the United Nations and its future, and thus became forcefully determined to defend at all costs two positions: the independence of the secretary-general and of the Secretariat, and the concept of the United Nations as a politically active organization that could take practical measures in conflict situations to preserve peace and security. In defending these two positions his style changed dramatically, and he responded to his critics with a spirit, frankness, and single-mindedness that bore little resemblance to his cautious and quiet approach of years past.[89] The central issue, he said from the podium when he rose to speak, "is a question not of a man but of an institution." The principles of the Charter, he said, might well become an obstacle for those seeking certain political gains, but the secretary-general must never betray the trust given to him by caving in to unwarranted criticism or expediency. "I would rather see that office," he declared, "break on strict adherence to the principle of independence, impartiality, and objectivity than drift on the basis of compromise."[90] When Khrushchev renewed the attack and called for him to resign, Hammarskjöld responded by saying that he would leave whenever the majority wanted him to leave, but he would not be intimidated by Great Power pressure designed to emasculate the organization. "It is not the Soviet Union or, indeed, any other big powers who need the United Nations for their protection," he said, "it is all the others." In the end, he declared: "I shall remain in my post."[91] When he finished, the Assembly, now composed mostly of small and medium-sized states themselves wanting to resist Cold War pressures, rose to a standing ovation with an emotional roar of approval and applause. Yet, within less than a year, this joy turned to sorrow; for while on a fateful mission to bring peace to the Congo, his plane crashed in Africa, and Hammarskjöld was dead.

IV

The crisis produced by Hammarskjöld's tragic death temporarily immobilized the United Nations and seriously jeopardized the secretary-generalship. Profound grief and a sense of irreparable loss mixed with deep anxiety in the wake of this void of leadership. There were predictions that there would never be another secretary-general of Hammarskjöld's stature, and that perhaps there would never even be another secretary-general. The reason for this was that the Soviets held out against appointing any successor at all. They preferred instead to eliminate the position of secretary-general entirely and replace it with their idea of a troika, or three-headed directorate composed of representatives from the major power blocs, and thereby to drastically weaken central authority within the United Nations. Bitter arguments raged between delegates from the Soviet bloc and the rest of the membership. Most agreed with the assessment of one experienced diplomat that restructuring of the organization would present a major "setback to the concept of an independent international Secretariat [that] will turn the United Nations . . . into a mere talking shop."[92] Consequently, in the end, and especially with the strong support of the nonaligned Third World countries, the majority decided that any effort to install a triumvirate would only produce anarchy and paralysis within the United Nations and perhaps destroy the entire order-building experiment in the process.[93] Thus, the membership steadfastly refused to alter the position of secretary-general as created by the Charter and in November 1961 named as the acting secretary-general for the remainder of Hammarskjöld's term the permanent representative of Burma to the United Nations, U Thant.

The election of Thant satisfied two groups of nations. The first of these were those Great Powers, like the Soviet Union, who once again wanted a quiet, nonactivist man. Neither the undistinguished Lie nor the civil servant Hammarskjöld had turned out in accordance with their hopes and, in the blunt words of one internal British Foreign Office minute, "we should not wish a new Secretary-General to be given anywhere near the latitude of action which Mr. Hammarskjöld took upon himself."[94] It thus appeared that this slight, unassuming, deeply religious Buddhist described as "Mr. Clean" and a "Burmese Boy Scout" might finally be different.[95] Secondly, his election directly reflected the growing prominence of the new Afro-Asian membership within the United Nations, who wanted someone from their own region with their own experience and not another white European to be secretary-general. They viewed Thant's background as his greatest asset. Born in a town near Rangoon, he became a high-school teacher of English and modern history, frequently writing articles as a freelance journalist focusing upon national issues and supporting Burmese independence. He entered government service as a press director and then became a member of the delegation of Burma to the United Nations, subsequently spending the next nine years quietly gaining diplomatic experience within the organization. "An imperturbable citizen of the world," wrote the *New York Times* at the time of his appointment, "Mr. Thant in his daily life spans the Occident and the Orient."[96]

Thant would need this ability to span continents and issues in order to lead effectively as secretary-general. In terms of the Cold War, he would have to make every effort to hold a delicate course among the Great Powers and to avoid the problem of his two predecessors when they adopted strong positions that alienated the Soviet Union. In terms of the Africans and Asians, who regarded him as one of their own, he would have to guide the process of decolonization and address their international agenda concerns while avoiding the anti-Western demagoguery and emotionalism of many of his supporters, or what one official in the British Foreign Office described as "wild anti-colonial crusades."[97] Moreover, he would have to work at a time of catastrophe in the history of the United Nations and as secretary-general in the shadow and the memory of an Olympian figure like Hammarskjöld. "Few men," wrote *Le Monde*, ever had received "a legacy so burdensome."[98]

From the start, Thant discharged his responsibilities with thoughtfulness, patience, a strong sense of duty, and a marked lack of dogmatism. He was far more prepared to decentralize work and responsibility and to listen to advice than his predecessor, and demonstrated a remarkable inner calmness and staying power that resulted from Buddhist meditation.[99] This quickly impressed his colleagues, including the representative of Canada, who observed that "of all his attributes, integrity may be the most important, for it is from integrity that he seems to derive strength."[100] These several traits could be seen immediately as he approached the inherited conflict in the Congo, following the instructions of the Security Council that authorized the Secretary-General, for the first time, actually to use force in order to restore law and order on behalf of the central government. In conducting these operations, Thant knew that the United Nations was on trial in Africa, being carefully watched to see if it could protect newly independent states from the Cold War, assist them disinterestedly in their development, and do so with a minimum of interference in their own sovereignty. He accomplished these tasks with patience and discretion, and his own proposal known as a Plan of National Reconstruction brought peace and independence to the troubled Congo within three years.

One of Thant's greatest accomplishments occurred during the most threatening incident of the entire Cold War: namely, the Cuban missile crisis of October 1962.[101] When the United States discovered that the Soviets had been secretly placing nuclear missiles on the island of Cuba despite explicit promises to the contrary, it reacted with a naval blockade, military mobilization, and an ultimatum, and the world stood still on the brink of possible nuclear annihilation. Governments, organizations, and private citizens around the globe immediately sensed the gravity of danger and sent Thant hundreds of telegrams, letters, and other forms of communication emotionally begging him to "do something" for "the sake of the world" and for "unprotected people everywhere."[102] In this situation, he made it clear that his concept of the secretary-generalship as an agency of mediation was similar to that of his predecessors by initiating direct communications with the major antagonists, offering his good offices, serving as a go-between, and suggesting a way out to avert war. According to Urquhart, who worked very closely with Thant, "He was *the* person who created the ladder down which both the United States and the Soviet Union climbed to resolve the Cuban Missile Crisis."[103]

As the secretary-general of the United Nations, Thant provided an impartial central point of reference during the crisis to which both sides could respond positively without the appearance of weakness or surrender.[104] Thus, he could propose that Khrushchev suspend all arms shipments to Cuba and order his ships to stay out of the intercept area, that President Kennedy do everything possible to avoid direct confrontation with Soviet ships bound for Cuba, that Cuban Premier Castro suspend construction on the missile sites, and remind them all that "the path of negotiation and compromise is the only course by which the peace of the world can be secured at this critical moment."[105] Courage and wisdom on the part of many individuals made it possible for this proposal to serve as the basis of defusing the crisis, and the existence of the

United Nations made it possible to have an international observation and super-vision mechanism to ensure the terms of settlement acceptable to all sides. When the crisis was over, Thant in his characteristically modest way directed praise away from himself and gave it instead to the organization, declaring: "The man in the street, lined up behind one side or the other, did not realize how much his survival depended on what the United Nations *did* to help the rival factions gain the time they both needed to effect the compromise that eventually came about."[106] Others who knew the inside details gave him the credit. A highly unusual letter sent to Thant in both English and Russian, for example, stated: "On behalf of the Governments of the United States of America and the Soviet Union we desire to express to you our appreciation for your efforts in assisting our Governments to avert the serious threat to the peace which recently arose."[107] The fact that this letter to Thant was jointly signed by the two nations who just had brought the world to the brink of nuclear disaster provided a hopeful glimmer that perhaps the intense Cold War era of confrontation might possibly give way to a new era of negotiation.

U Thant's successes in Cuba and the Congo were followed by others, particu-lar in the interrelated areas of decolonization, development, and racial equality. Here he spoke and acted with a deep, and sometimes painful, passion and personal experience unknown by his predecessors. "The outstanding difference that distinguished me from all other Secretaries-General of the League of Nations or of the United Nations," he poignantly wrote in his memoirs, "lay in the fact that I was the first non-European to occupy that post. . . . I had first-hand experience of colonialism at work. I know what hunger, poverty, disease, illiteracy, and human suffering really mean."[108] For this reason, he forcefully worked in the face of great political and economic difficulties to facilitate independence for colonial countries and increase their membership in the United Nations, to extend technical assistance to developing nations, to bridge the gap between the rich and poor or the North and the South, to promote basic human rights and fundamental freedoms around the world, and to address issues of racial discrimination, which he described as a "wicked virus" and "a consummate and intolerable evil,"[109] by such means as creating the Special Committee on the Policies of Apartheid and negotiating the important Interna-tional Convention on the Elimination of All Forms of Racial Discrimination.[110]

One of Thant's greatest frustrations during his tenure was his inability to bring the parties to the Vietnam war to the conference table. He viewed the war and its tragic loss of American and Vietnamese lives as a moral issue, and feared that it might easily escalate to include the People's Republic of China and the Soviet Union. His initial behind-the-scenes efforts to use his good offices drew a public protest from President Lyndon Johnson for meddling and from the Chinese, who accused him of being a "tool of the imperialists."[111] Archival material reveals that these public criticisms were repeated in private, as indicated when Secretary of State Dean Rusk showed "strong irritation" whenever Thant suggested that perhaps more could be gained in Vietnam by negotiating than by fighting.[112] Yet, at exactly the same time, other American political figures, notably J. William Fulbright, chairman of the Senate Foreign Relations Committee, actively encouraged him to "press forward in an effort to bring hostilities in Vietnam to an end."[113] In this situation, Thant acutely understood the dilemma faced by his predecessors when faced with serious international crises. He observed:

> Now, there are but two alternative courses of action for me. I might stand by, make no further effort and observe the Vietnam conflict lead the world to possible disaster. Or, I might try once again to make a constructive move, regardless of the likely attitudes of the parties concerned toward such an initiative by me. Mindful of my responsibilities under the Charter and of my broad duty as Secretary-General of the United Nations to do whatever I reasonably and legitimately can in the pursuit of peace, I have decided that I must exert a new effort.[114]

He thus doggedly pursued his efforts to find a way to end the war with little thought to his own personal reputation or the political disadvantages of inserting himself into the conflict, suggesting secret meetings, cease-fires, bombing halts, and unconditional negotiations. Interestingly enough, it was his line of approach to ending the Vietnam War that Henry Kissinger eventually took up with success, but only hundreds of thousands of casualties later.[115]

If Vietnam presented Thant with one of his greatest frustrations, the decision to withdraw the United Nations Emergency Force from the Middle East in 1967 aroused more public criticism than any of his other actions. After years of peace between Egypt and Israel, Nasser suddenly demanded that the UNEF instituted by Hammarskjöld be removed immediately from Egyptian soil. Thant strongly opposed this action, and was the only person willing to go personally and try to persuade Nasser to reconsider a decision that was likely to have disastrous consequences.[116] Nasser, on a course of self-destruction, brusquely refused to change his mind; and, since the peacekeeping force required the permission of the host state to operate on its sovereign territory, Thant believed that he had no legal or practical choice but to instruct the United Nations forces to withdraw.[117] Egypt then closed the Strait of Tiran to Israeli shipping, and with this threat to their security and the unparalleled military opportunity to having no buffer force to deter them, the Israelis launched the first strikes of the 1967 Six Day War, taking territory in Jerusalem, much of the Sinai, the West Bank, the Gaza Strip, and the Golan Heights. Seeking to divert criticism of Israeli behavior and conquests, Foreign Minister Abba Eban ignored the fact that his country would never allow United Nations forces on its own territory and disingenuously accused Thant of making "one of the major diplomatic blunders of all time."[118] Others followed suit and similarly found it convenient to use the secretary-general as a scapegoat rather than admitting their own failures and deliberate unwillingness to use the United Nations as a means of finding a diplomatic solution.[119]

In other instances besides the seemingly intractable Middle East, of course, both Thant and the United Nations were able to find successful solutions in peacemaking and peacekeeping. Personal representatives sent to Cambodia and Thailand, Rwanda and Burundi, Equatorial Guinea, and Bahrain all helped to diffuse potentially dangerous situations. The dispatch of observers to Yemen in 1963, of forces to Cyprus in 1964, of a military mission to the border of India and West Pakistan in 1966, and of observers along the new cease-fire line between Egypt and Israel following the 1967 war all helped to keep contentious parties from each other's throats. Nevertheless, there were great disappointments as well, including financial difficulties for the United Nations, and during his later years in office Thant became discouraged when it appeared that some of the member states simply refused to honor their explicit promises under the Charter to "refrain in their international relations from the threat or use of force against the territorial integrity or political independence of any state,"[120] as in the case of the Soviet invasion of Czechoslovakia in 1968 or the American military intervention in the Dominican Republic in 1965 and invasion of Cambodia in 1970. On other occasions he found himself, like both his predecessors and his successors, frustrated when member states turned to him only after their own solutions had failed and then expected miraculous and immediate results, prompting him to write: "Great problems usually come to the United Nations because governments have been unable to think of anything else to do about them. The United Nations is a last-ditch, last-resort affair, and it is not surprising that the Organization should often be blamed for failing to solve problems that have already been found to be insoluble by governments."[121]

When Thant stepped down at the end of his second term as secretary-general at the end of 1971, he had served in the office for ten long and sometimes lonely years. Critics who expected more in terms of accomplishments or style complained that he lacked dynamic energy and vigor, possessed little imagination or magnetism, and failed to provide sufficient administrative leadership. Some accused him of being a moralist, placid, overly cautious, "quiet to the point of torpor," and as one "who spent most of his time twiddling his thumbs."[122] Others, like the *Washington Post* acknowledged that his tenure coincided with growing disillusionment with the organization, but argued that he "was also the man who may have prevented the disintegration of the United Nations at a critical time."[123] *The Times* in London commented not only on his political achievements, but also his personal qualities by concluding:

He was above all a humane man, unswayed by prejudice or vanity, and in spite of his great eminence and public successes he maintained throughout his Secretary-Generalship a genuine modesty and open-mindedness which was irresistible to those he dealt with. With him it was possible to say and do things which would have been impossible with someone of a more complex or devious character.[124]

V

Issues of character would eventually be raised about U Thant's successor, but in 1971 the member states of the United Nations were not thinking that far ahead and wanted only to find an acceptable secretary-general. Once more the selection process reopened all the old questions above the relative importance of personality, competence, diplomatic experience, political orientation, and place of national origin. Many outside observers again urged members to be bold for once and appoint a strong individual who would be able to realize the principles of the Charter. *Newsweek,* for example, argued that a new selection presented the United Nations with "a golden opportunity to revitalize itself."[125] It an editorial entitled "Good Opening for Man of Initiative," *The Times* proposed that "the time has come for the delegates in New York to look for a man of energy and originality."[126] Boldness, initiative, originality, and strong leadership in a secretary-general always had scared the Great Powers in the past, however, and they apparently saw no reason to change course and take any serious risk that might threaten their own sovereignty and prerogatives now. Consequently, by a vote of eleven for, one against, and three abstentions, the members of the Security Council recommended that the new secretary-general be the permanent representative of neutral Austria, Kurt Waldheim.

Waldheim possessed an unusual history, and his life and personality reflected a strange interplay between national and international affairs. He had been born in 1918, scarcely one month after the armistice that marked the end of the First World War and the collapse of the Austro-Hungarian Empire into a shadow of its former imperial self. His academic career included graduation from the Consular Academy in Vienna, a doctorate in international law, and the study of languages, all designed to facilitate a career in diplomacy. Like other young men of his age, world events seriously interrupted his plans, and after Hitler's occupation of Austria he was drafted into the German army. Waldheim's years as an intelligence officer in the Wehrmacht during the Second World War, and his lack of candor about the precise nature of his military service in German units that committed atrocities in the Balkans, would later come to haunt him and cast a dark shadow over his other considerable accomplishments.[127] Immediately after the war, he entered the Austrian diplomatic service, and his star rose dramatically as he held various positions within the Foreign Ministry, eventually becoming minister of foreign affairs. Overseas assignments included Paris, Ottawa, and service as representative to the United Nations, where he carefully cultivated other delegates. Although some worried about his excessive ambition, attraction to pomp, desire for public acclaim, seeming lack of conviction (hence a nickname of Rubber Kurt),[128] absence of modesty, and failure to answer questions about his military activities during the war—all of which stood in marked contrast to Thant—other traits attracted their attention. "He was regarded as fair, tenacious, discreet, and pleasant to all," writes one of Waldheim's biographers. "He threatened nobody and charmed nearly everyone . . . [and] was keenly aware that the Great Powers were looking for a discreet administrator, a workaholic . . . not another moralist who would use the United Nations as a forum to lecture them, offering alternative policies, and generally meddling in their business."[129] He could be counted on, stated *Newsweek* more bluntly, "not to make waves."[130]

Waldheim's first year in office actually surprised a number of observers, for he directly challenged several member states by speaking out publicly and taking initiative. He offered his good offices to help end the Vietnam War and took public note, for example, of reports condemning American planes bombing the dikes of North Vietnam, thereby incurring the ridicule of President Richard Nixon.[131] In addition, he deliberately took on several states over the difficult subject of terrorism. After the murder of eleven Israeli athletes by Palestinian guerrillas during the 1972 Olympic Games in Munich, Waldheim appealed for all "to turn away from senseless violence and to redouble their efforts to find peaceful solutions."[132] Toward this end, he insisted on placing the subject of international terrorism on the agenda of the General Assembly, but only after overcoming the objections of the Arab states and their supporters in the Soviet Union and the People's Republic of China. These actions suggested to at least one delegate that Waldheim might have "a lot of steel beneath the velvet."[133]

Waldheim, like his predecessors, needed both steel and velvet in dealing with the Middle East. Indeed, when Egyptian President Anwar Sadat launched a surprise attack on Israel in October 1973 during the Jewish holiday of Yom Kippur, the fourth Arab-Israeli war confronted the fourth secretary-general. Appeals from around the world came to Waldheim, including those from U.S. Secretary of State Henry Kissinger, to use his influence to bring the fighting to a halt and keeping it from spreading. Only after several weeks of fighting and the appearance of dangerous signs of escalation, however, did the members of the Security Council authorize Waldheim to dispatch United Nations peacekeeping troops to the area. He moved quickly and decisively, and within forty-eight hours the new United Nations Emergency Force II began to provide the mechanism that arranged for the successful supervision of a cease-fire, exchange of prisoners, transfer of displaced civilians, withdrawal of troops, creation of a buffer zone between the rival armies, and establishment of the UN Disengagement and Observer Force on the Golan Heights. These successes, greatly facilitated by cooperation between the United States and the Soviet Union and by Kissinger's shuttle diplomacy, provided a source of great satisfaction to Waldheim and the United Nations, demonstrating what the secretary-general and the organization could accomplish if only permitted by the Great Powers. Some observers described Waldheim's actions here as his "finest hour";[134] while others, including Nixon and Kissinger, acknowledged the vital role played by the United Nations during this period, realizing that there were certain tasks such as peacekeeping that could not be exercised unilaterally, even by a Great Power.[135] Through time, and with the active involvement of President Jimmy Carter, these successes also built a framework for negotiation that eventually led to the Camp David Accords of 1979, the first peace treaty between Israel and any Arab state.

Successfully employing peacekeeping forces in the Middle East encouraged Waldheim and the United Nations to use them in other troubled and volatile areas as well. One example was Cyprus, where in 1974 an ill-considered military coup d'état organized by Greece precipitated an invasion by Turkey. When the Great Powers began to equivocate in their response and indicated that they were unprepared to help save a small country from attack, Waldheim uncharacteristically became indignant over a matter of principle and insisted that they take action through the Security Council and authorize some kind of protection. His prodding, personal visits to respective leaders of the dispute, and the enlargement of the peacekeeping force on Cyprus eventually helped to create a cease-fire, protect the civilian populations, evacuate foreign nationals, establish a buffer zone across the island, restore law and order, and initiate direct contact among the disputants and thereby avoid a recurrence of fighting. He dispatched the similar peacekeeping UN Interim Force in Lebanon during 1978 in all but impossible circumstances. "Who else" other than the United Nations, asked Waldheim, "could have intervened in those situations" without precipitating an even greater crisis?[136]

In addition to these crises, the middle of Waldheim's tenure in office coincided with the assumption by the Third World of the majority within the United Nations, and thereby the loss of control by its traditional Western leaders. No longer could the West, particularly the United States, regard the General Assembly as a convenient refuge from Soviet vetoes in the Security Council and a place to get its way. In fact, the Assembly became inclined to assume positions clearly objectionable to the West. During 1974, for example, the majority passed the Declaration for the Establishment of a New International Economic Order, demanding far-reaching concessions from the industrialized countries, and then invited Yasir Arafat, the leader of the Palestine Liberation Organization, to deliver an address before the assembled delegates. The following year, the General Assembly passed an emotion-laden and explosive resolution declaring Zionism a form of racism and racial discrimination.[137] Although later rescinded, this resolution, among others, precipitated much public outcry about irresponsible behavior, especially in the United States, where there was much talk of punishing the United Nations. Not everyone, of course, blamed the entire organization like this. As the British ambassador observed: "I see little to be gained by attacking the institution of the United Nations because of the idiocies of some of its members. It is rather like complaining about Parliament when you lose a vote in the House of Commons."[138]

In keeping with its mission under the Charter, the United Nations continued to be vitally concerned in self-determination and decolonization, as it had since its beginning. Here, Waldheim appeared to take a particularly surprising interest, stating: "Since I myself come from a country that for years was under foreign domination, I feel great sympathy for oppressed peoples."[139] Consequently, he worked diligently and traveled extensively on behalf of those peoples in the so-called hard core of Africa under the control of Portugal, Southern Rhodesia, and South Africa. These included Angola, Mozambique, Guinea-Bissau, Zimbabwe, and Namibia, all of which eventually and successfully gained their independence and thereby joined so many others in the phenomenal postwar movement of decolonization.[140]

In the other major postwar phenomenon of international politics, the East-West struggle of the Cold War, Waldheim experienced a remarkable good fortune unknown to all of his predecessors. Because of the efforts of diplomats like Kissinger, Gromyko, and Zhou Enlai, among others, a thaw known as détente began to characterize some, but not all, of the relationships between the United States, the Soviet Union, and the People's Republic of China. Consequently, the United Nations and its secretary-general, which in the past had been severely handicapped by the international rivalry among these Great Powers, began to experience a new freedom to address issues that in the past always had been submerged by Cold War pressure. Under Waldheim's direction, for example, the United Nations held a number of meetings designed to deal with problems of a global nature that transcended national and ideological boundaries. These included the United Nations Human Environment Conference, Conference on the Law of the Sea, Conference on Science and Technology for Development, World Food Conference, World Population Conference, World Conference to Combat Racism and Racial Discrimination, and World Conference on the International Women's Year.[141]

When Waldheim's ten years of service as secretary-general ended in 1981, the assessments of his performance, not surprisingly, were mixed. Waldheim could justifiably look back with pride on a number of important personal and institutional accomplishments. These ranged from the use of good offices and successful peacekeeping missions to initiatives in dealing with terrorism, decolonization, and planetary concerns. The United Nations had managed to survive much of the Cold War and some of the worse excesses of its members, and Waldheim had managed to fulfill his duties under the Charter without seriously offending any of the member states and thereby earning, at least in some quarters, the title of a "diplomat's diplomat."[142] Others viewed the record very differently, describing Waldheim as "an ambitious mediocrity"[143] and his performance as secretary-general as "lackluster" and "uneven and unspectacular."[144] They focused instead on his unseemly campaign for an unprecedented third term in office and his inability to help secure the release of American hostages held in Teheran, to inspire confidence among the Great Powers, to stem the tide of financial difficulties within the United Nations, or to be forthcoming about his own wartime past. As such, the legacy of Waldheim's tenure presented both difficulties and prospects for the United Nations and its secretary-general as they approached the future.

VI

Few could have foreseen that under a new secretary-general the United Nations would play an ever-larger and more active role in global diplomacy. In selecting a successor to Waldheim, for example, the Security Council recommended Javier Pérez de Cuéllar, a former professor of international law and relations and a career diplomat from Peru with many years of experience at the United Nations.[145] "He was a quiet, serious person," according to Urquhart, "who knew who he was, had no pretensions or election debts, and wanted to get on with the job, which he already knew a great deal about."[146]

In this regard, he knew the importance of patience for any diplomat, but especially for a secretary-general. When the Reagan administration decided to withdraw a large part of its assessed contribution to the United Nations, Pérez de Cuéllar patiently waited for the storm to eventually wear itself out or change direction, and worked behind the scenes to minimize the financial crisis and low morale that it caused. He used the same long-term approach in working toward independence for Namibia and ending apartheid in South Africa.[147] In addition, he presided over the fortieth anniversary of the United Nations and its ambitious order-building experiment, attended by some seventy heads of state or government and virtually all foreign ministers, and carefully attempted to rebuild their confidence in the organization and its potential.

Under the leadership of Pérez de Cuéllar, the United Nations performed a string of successes. This is not the place or the time to consider all of these in detail, but they were so impressive that the often critical *New York Times* declared 1988 "The Year of the UN."[148] These ranged from successfully negotiating the Soviet withdrawal from occupied Afghanistan, a cease-fire for the deadly Iran-Iraq War, and new talks between Greek and Turkish Cypriots, to the removal of Cuban troops from Angola and the declaration by the Palestine Liberation Front that it would recognize the binding nature of United Nations resolutions on the right of the state of Israel to exist. The ten-thousand-member United Nations peacekeeping forces were awarded the Nobel Peace Prize during the same year. Moreover, and in sharp contrast to several decades of his country's efforts to limit the power of the organization and its secretary-general, Soviet President Mikhail Gorbachev made a breathtaking announcement before the General Assembly that he intended to reduce his armed forces unilaterally and submitted a far-reaching plan calling for a greatly enhanced role for the United Nations in global affairs.

With the subsequent, world-shaping collapse of the Soviet Union and the apparent end of the Cold War, the United Nations and its secretary-general had reasons to believe that they could build upon the hard and constructive work of their predecessors and play ever more active and important roles in international politics. Their belief was confirmed when the Security Council held a meeting described as "one of the most important in the history of the United Nations,"[149] and authorized the use of force, if necessary, to expel Iraqi President Saddam Hussein and his troops from occupied Kuwait to "restore international peace and security in the area."[150] When Hussein refused to leave Kuwait voluntarily, the United Nations embarked on a massive undertaking of political and military complexity and successfully mobilized a coalition to eject Iraqi forces forcibly and restore sovereignty to Kuwait. "For once the concept of collective security as envisioned in the UN Charter worked," wrote a contributor in *Foreign Affairs,* and "the United Nations reclaimed a major role in international relations."[151]

Such a role appeared as though it might well continue. As a result of all this considerable diplomatic activity and the dramatic political changes that made much of it possible, the United Nations and its secretary-general attracted considerably more attention than they had at other times. Indeed, a number of states appeared to have discovered new virtues in the United Nations that they had often neglected and abused in the past. This, in turn, led many thoughtful observers and participants alike to devote significant attention to how the institution might best respond to the needs of the future. "After forty-five uncertain, and sometimes bleak, years, the prospects for international cooperation are brighter than at any time since the Second World War," concluded an international study entitled *A World in Need of Leadership: Tomorrow's United Nations.*[152] Others expressed similar enthusiasm for an increasingly dynamic and invigorated role for the United Nations in global diplomacy,[153] and in a special issue called "Beyond the Year 2,000: What to Expect in the New Millennium," *Time* predicted that in the future "cooperation with the U.N. will be the norm" and that "the world will have to utilize the powers of the U.N." to solve its problems.[154] The world appeared "on the threshold of a positive new era in international relations," said Pérez de Cuéllar. But he noted the new challenges of the next century and cautioned that the future of the United Nations was by no means clear when stating:

> The retreat of the ice mass [of the Cold War] . . . has also exposed some basic realities: conflict, the actualities of ethnic strife, gross political and economic inequalities, disregard for human rights, and increasing threats to our planet, brought about both by mankind's cavalier conduct towards earth's resources and

the needs of the growing human family. If our Organization is to maintain its relevance in the eyes of the world, then it must measure up to these issues with renewed vigor.[155]

Whether the United Nations would be able to rise to this challenge in the future would be largely determined—as it always had been in the past—by the will and the action of its member states. "We must remember, the United Nations is a mirror of its members," observed Thant. "It shall be as strong or as weak as its members want it to be."[156] Since the organization was created as an association of sovereign and independent nation-states, it possessed no sovereignty of its own, and depended completely for its effectiveness upon the capacity of its members, especially the Great Powers, to reach accommodation. This applied not only to critical differences of opinion over international policy, but also to the selection of the secretaries-general and the degree to which they are enabled to honor their pledge to uphold the principles of the Charter for the entire world as a whole, all without physical power and without seriously offending the sensitivities of any of the nearly one hundred and eighty politically diverse and culturally heterogeneous member states.[157] "It is a path strewn with booby-traps,"[158] according to one secretary-general in words echoed by them all, that goes through an organization whose membership since its founding has more than tripled in size. By comparison, the tasks of other diplomats in the postwar era representing only the interests of their own nation-states often seem infinitely simpler and easier.

In addition to these structural and legal limitations, the diplomats of the United Nations were forced to confront all the problems between East and West in the Cold War, the dismemberment of colonial empires, struggles between new international authority and traditional national sovereignty, intense controversy between the developed North and the developing South, wars and revolutions, the threat of nuclear weapons with a destructive capacity unprecedented in history, and the failure of member states to honor their promises under the Charter. Moreover, they often faced exaggerated expectations, sharply divergent opinions about the appropriate role of the United Nations, deliberate assaults against some of the secretaries-general, and criticism from many sources. "On the seas we sail," said Hammarskjöld with nautical imagery,

> we have to face all the storms and stresses created by the ideological, economic, and social conditions of our world. Aboard this new *Santa Maria* we have to meet the impatience of those sailors who expect land on the horizon tomorrow, also the cynicism or sense of futility of those who would give up and leave us drifting impotently. On the shores we have all those who are against the whole expedition, who seem to take a special delight in blaming the storms on the ship instead of the weather.[159]

When one considers all of these factors, what is surprising is not that the United Nations and its secretaries-general did so little, but that they accomplished so much. In the face of these seemingly insurmountable problems, the institution evolved and the experiment survived. At times, it even prospered. Contributions to peacemaking and peacekeeping, preventive diplomacy, mediation and conflict resolution, relief operations, advancement of human rights and racial equality, promotion of self-determination and social and economic development, extension of global health and education, and efforts to address complex interdependence and the well-being of the planet established undeniable achievements. And, throughout it all, the organization remained the one and only permanent place in the world where the diplomats of all blocs, interests, races, and ideologies could meet in both formal and informal settings and be represented in deliberations in critical diplomatic problems.

In the process, this ambitious experiment in order-building for the world also managed to keep alive a vision. It was a vision of a larger international community of men and women united by a common desire for peace and justice rather than divided by human frailties and the anarchy of parochial interests. It was one hopeful of a future better than the past. In this regard, observed Hammarskjöld, "The United Nations reflects both aspiration and a falling short of aspiration. But the constant struggle to close the gap between aspiration and performance now, as always, makes the difference between civilization and chaos."[160] Perhaps it is in precisely this struggle that the greatest legacy of the diplomats and the diplomacy of the United Nations is to be found.

Notes

1. Trygve Lie, as cited by Dag Hammarskjöld, United Nations (hereafter UN), Secretary General (hereafter SG)/299, 1 May 1953.

2. Trygve Lie, *In the Cause of Peace: Seven Years with the United Nations* (New York, 1954), 17, 417.

3. Dag Hammarskjöld, UN, SG/616, 26 Sept. 1957.

4. U Thant, *View from the United Nations* (Garden City, 1978), xviii; and Javier Pérez de Cuéllar, UN, SG/SM/4674, 16 Dec. 1991.

5. Kurt Waldheim, *Der Schwierigste Job der Welt* (Vienna, 1978), 11–14.

6. See the comments by Richard Walker in Robert Jordan, ed., *Hammarskjöld Revisited: The UN Secretary-General as a Force in World Politics* (Durham, 1983), xv; "A Spokesman for Mankind," *Saturday Review,* 18 Nov. 1967; Alec Collet, "Kurt Waldheim," *The City: East and West* (November 1972), p. 4; and the typed manuscript entitled "U Thant and the Vietnam Papers" by James Boyd of the *Washington Evening Star,* 22 June 1971, in United Nations Archives/Departmental Archival Group (hereafter UNA/DAG)-1/5.2.1.9, Papers of the Secretary-General [Thant Papers], box 17.

7. "Portrait: Un bouddhiste réaliste," *Le Monde,* 17 July 1962.

8. George Bria, "A Personality in the News," Associated Press release, 19 Sept. 1972.

9. "Declaration of Four Nations on General Security," in U.S. Department of State, *Foreign Relations of the United States* (hereafter *FRUS*) 1943 (Washington, D.C., 1963), 1:756. The Chinese signed the declaration as well.

10. John G. Stoessinger, *The Might of Nations: World Politics in Our Time* (New York, 1979), 296.

11. Franklin D. Roosevelt, 1 Mar. 1945, in U.S. Congress, *Congressional Record, 79th Cong.*, 1st sess., vol. 91, part 2 (Washington, D.C., 1945), 1622. For a discussion of Roosevelt's plans for postwar security, see Gordon A. Craig and Alexander L. George, *Force and Statecraft* (New York, 1990), 101–9; and for the British perspective, Britain, Public Record Office/Foreign Office (hereafter PRO/FO), 371/40708 and 371/40716, among others.

12. Jan Smuts, Verbatim Minutes of the Sixth Plenary Session, 1 May 1945, in United Nations Information Organization (hereafter UNIO), *Documents of the United Nations Conference on International Organization, San Francisco, 1945,* 22 vols. (London and New York, 1946–1955), 1:420–421. Also see Ruth Russell, *A History of the United Nations* (Washington, D.C., 1958).

13. United Nations Charter, Preamble.

14. Ibid., Article 2, Paragraph 7.

15. Ibid., Article 1, among others. For more discussion on this point, see Paul Gordon Lauren, *Power and Prejudice: The Politics and Diplomacy of Racial Discrimination* (Boulder and London, 1988), 150–55.

16. United Nations Charter, Preamble.

17. See Verbatim Minutes of the Closing Plenary Session, 26 June 1945, in UNIO, *Documents,* 1:688 ff.

18. Brian Urquhart, *A Life in Peace and War* (New York, 1987), 93.

19. For a more recent complaint about the United Nations as constituting "world government," see Robert W. Lee, *The United Nations Conspiracy* (Boston, 1981), especially ix.

20. Harry Truman, 26 June 1945, in UNIO, *Documents,* 1:715–16.

21. Stoessinger, *The Might of Nations,* 300. Also see Inis L. Claude, Jr., *Swords into Plowshares: The problems and progress of international organization* (New York, 1964), especially 65–67.

22. Lord Halifax, 26 June 1945, in UNIO, *Documents,* 698.

23. See H. G. Nicholas, *The United Nations as a Political Institution* (New York, 1967), 165.

24. United Nations Charter, Article 99 (my emphasis).

25. See Nicholas, *United Nations,* 166–67; and Brian Urquhart, *Hammarskjöld* (New York, 1972), 50.

26. United States, National Archives (hereafter US/NA), Record Group 59, Lot File 55 D 323, Bureau of United Nations Affairs, box 2, undated paper written by Andrew Cordier entitled "United Nations Secretary-General."

27. US/NA, Record Group 59, Alger Hiss Files, box 25, Briefing Book, Secret, USGA/1a/3, 26 Dec. 1945.

28. UNA/DAG-1/2.3, Office of the Under-Secretary-General for Special Political Affairs [Urquhart Papers], box 2, "Report of the Preparatory Commission," 87.

29. Urquhart, *A Life in Peace and War,* 99.

30. Nicholas, *United Nations,* 47.

31. US/NA, Record Group 59, Alger Hiss Files, box 25, Briefing Book, Secret, USGA/1a/3, 26 Dec. 1945.

32. See the early anticipation of this development in US/NA, Record Group 59, lot file 55 D 323, Bureau of United Nations Affairs, box 2, undated paper entitled "United Nations Secretary-General."

33. See the many comments in James Barros's extensive biography, *Trygve Lie and the Cold War: The UN Secretary-General Pursues Peace, 1946–1953* (DeKalb, 1989), 19–51; Urquhart, *A Life in Peace and War,* 100; the revelations of personality in the Andrew Wellington Cordier Papers at Columbia University, Catalogued Correspondence, Lie [hereafter cited as Cordier Papers]; and Brian Urquhart, interview by the author, 14 Aug. 1992.

34. Britain, PRO/FO, 371/57053, memorandum entitled "Monsieur Lie," dated March 1946.

35. Sir Charles Webster Papers, London School of Economics, Webster Diary, vol. 15, entry of 3 Feb. 1946.

36. US/NA, Record Group 84, US Mission to the United Nations, box 34 B, telegram no. 1876, Secret, from Osborne (Oslo) to Stettinius (London), 30 Jan. 1946.

37. Lie, *In the Cause of Peace,* 4, 17.

38. Britain, PRO/FO, 371/57237, minute by Clifford Heathcote-Smith, 20 Feb. 1946.

39. Barros, *Trygve Lie and the Cold War,* ix.

40. Trygve Lie, 26 June 1946, in UN, General Assembly (hereafter GA), *Official Records, 1946,* Document A/65, "Report of the Secretary-General on the Work of the Organization," vi.

41. Lie, *In the Cause of Peace,* 39–40.

42. Thomas M. Campbell and George C. Herring, eds., *The Diaries of Edward R. Stettinius, Jr., 1943–1946* (New York, 1975), 474.

43. Britain, PRO/FO, 371/78794, Letter from Alexander Cadogan (United Nations) to Gladwyn Jebb, 11 Aug. 1949.

44. Abba Eban, as cited in Barros, *Trygve Lie and the Cold War,* 206.

45. Trygve Lie, as cited ibid., 209.

46. Arthur W. Rovine, *The First Fifty Years: The Secretary-General in World Politics, 1920–1970* (Leyden, 1970), 236.

47. Andrew W. Cordier et al., *Trygve Lie, 1946–1953,* vol. 1 of *Public Papers of the Secretaries-General of the United Nations,* 8 vols. (New York, 1969–1977), "Introduction," 20–21.

48. Extract from Daily Secret Summary No. 75, in *FRUS,* 1950, 2:136.

49. Lie, *In the Cause of Peace,* 323, 368–69, citing *Pravda.*

50. Trygve Lie, 26 Mar. 1947, in UN, Trusteeship Council, *Official Records,* 1–5.

51. See Lauren, *Power and Prejudice,* 174–182; and Albert Verdoodt, *La naissance et signification de la Déclaration universelle des droits de l'homme* (Louvain, 1964).

52. Lie, *In the Cause of Peace,* 262; and James Reston, "Lie Makes a Bold Move," *New York Times,* 22 Mar. 1950.

53. UN, M/640, 21 Apr. 1950, translated letter from Albert Einstein to Trygve Lie, 18 Apr. 1950; and Cordier Papers, United Nations Files, box 116.

54. Andrei Vyshinsky, 31 Oct. 1950, in UN, GA, *Official Records, Plenary Sessions, 1950,* 262.

55. Nicholas, *United Nations*, 56.

56. Lie, *In the Cause of Peace*, 385; Cordier Papers, Catalogued Correspondence, Lie, 1952; and UNA/DAG-1/5.1.1, Papers of the Secretary-General [Lie Papers], box 2.

57. See Stoessinger, *Might of Nations*, 327.

58. Andrei Vyshinsky, as cited in Lie, *In the Cause of Peace*, 347.

59. Barros, *Trygve Lie and the Cold War*, 341; and Brian Urquhart, interview by the author, 14 Aug. 1992.

60. Soviet delegates, as cited in Britain, PRO/FO, 371/107049, Telegram no. 278 from Gladwyn Jebb (United Nations) to Foreign Office, 7 Apr. 1953.

61. See Joseph P. Lash, *Dag Hammarskjöld: Custodian of the Brushfire Peace* (New York, 1961), 56.

62. Trygve Lie, "Address to the General Assembly," UN, SG/286, 7 Apr. 1953; and "Farewell Address Over UN Radio," UN, SG/294, 24 Apr. 1953.

63. US/NA, Record Group 59, box 1251, Telegram 10370 from Lodge to Dulles, "Eyes Only," and Memorandum for the Files, "Secret," both dated 30 Mar. 1953.

64. See Britain, PRO/FO, 371/107050, letter from R. B. Stevens (Stockholm) to Gladwyn Jebb, 10 Apr. 1953.

65. Anthony Eden, as cited in Memorandum of Conversation, 31 Mar. 1953, ibid. Also see the excellent discussion in Barros, *Trygve Lie and the Cold War*, 333–41.

66. Urquhart, *Hammarskjöld*, 15.

67. Among many, see U Thant, *Toward World Peace: Addresses and Public Statements, 1957–1963* (New York, 1964), 108; Lash, *Dag Hammarskjöld*, 208, 212; Urquhart, *Hammarskjöld*, 30, 32; Henry P. Van Dusen, *Dag Hammarskjöld: The Statesman and His Faith* (New York, 1967); and Mark Zacher, *Dag Hammarskjöld's United Nations* (New York, 1970).

68. Urquhart, *Hammarskjöld*, 33, 596. Urquhart confirmed this opinion written in 1972 during interviews by the author of 14 and 18 Aug. 1992.

69. Dag Hammarskjöld, "Statement on Arrival at Idlewild Airport," UN, SG/287, 9 Apr. 1953.

70. See Nicholas, *United Nations*, 168.

71. See Stoessinger, *Might of Nations*, 328.

72. Among many, see Clark M. Eichelberger, *UN: The First Twenty-Five Years* (New York, 1970), 92; and Lauren, *Power and Prejudice*, 197–232.

73. Letter from Cordier to Lie, 7 Feb. 1956, in Cordier Papers, Catalogued Correspondence, Lie.

74. Lash, *Dag Hammarskjöld*, 174–75; and Urquhart, *Hammarskjöld*, 595.

75. Private letter from Hammarskjöld to Cordier, Confidential, 21 Apr. 1956, in Cordier Papers, Catalogued Correspondence, Hammarskjöld.

76. Dag Hammarskjöld, 31 Oct. 1956, in UN, SG, *Official Records, 1956*, 751 Meeting, 1–2.

77. Nicholas, *United Nations*, 169–73; Urquhart, *Hammarskjöld*, 133–230; and E. L. M. Burns, *Between Arab and Israeli* (New York, 1963).

78. Sir Leslie Munro, 26 Sept. 1957, UN, GA, *Official Records, Plenary Meetings, 1957*, 175.

79. Dag Hammarskjöld, "Statement on Arrival at Idlewild Airport," UN, SG/287, 9 Apr. 1953.

80. Dag Hammarskjöld, "Statement Before the General Assembly on Reappoint-

ment to a Second Term," UN, SG/616, 26 Sept. 1957. Also see Nicholas, *United Nations,* 173; and Lash, *Dag Hammarskjöld,* 139.

81. Urquhart, *Hammarskjöld,* 253; and Dag Hammarskjöld, *Markings,* translated by Lief Sjoberg and W. H. Auden (New York, 1964), entry of 9.26.57, p. 156.

82. Among others, see Craig and George, *Force and Statecraft,* 113; and for some of the internal details, see UNA/DAG-1/5.1.2, Papers of the Secretary-General [Hammarskjöld Papers], box 6, and Cordier Papers, Catalogued Correspondence, Hammarskjöld.

83. See UNA/DAG-1/5.1.2, Papers of the Secretary-General [Hammarskjöld Papers]; and DAG-1/2.3.16, Office of the Under-Secretary-General for Political Affairs [Urquhart Papers].

84. Walter Lippmann, "Today and Tomorrow—The Congo and the UN," *New York Herald Tribune,* as cited in Urquhart, *Hammarskjöld,* 413.

85. James Reston, "United Nations: A Refuge of Sanity," *New York Times,* 10 Aug. 1960.

86. Lash, *Dag Hammarskjöld,* 233.

87. Nikita Khrushchev, as cited in Arkady Shevchenko, *Breaking with Moscow* (New York, 1985), 102.

88. Nikita Khrushchev, 23 Sept. 1960, in UN, GA, *Official Records, Plenary Meetings, 1960,* 82. Also see B. Ponomaryov et al., *History of Soviet Foreign Policy, 1945–1970* (Moscow, 1974), 347–50.

89. See Urquhart, *Hammarskjöld,* 260.

90. Dag Hammarskjöld, "Statement Before the General Assembly," UN, SG/964, 26 Sept. 1960.

91. Dag Hammarskjöld, "Statement Before the General Assembly," UN, SG/966, 3 Oct. 1960.

92. Britain, PRO/FO, 371/160984, Despatch no. 23 from Patrick Dean (United Nations) to Earl of Home, Confidential, 3 Oct. 1961.

93. See Cordier Papers, United Nations Files, box 100, file entitled "Troika: Public Statements"; and the retrospective Max Harrelson, "U Thant on a Tightrope," *The Sun* (Baltimore), 31 Oct. 1965.

94. Britain, PRO/FO, Office, 371/160984, minute from H. E. J. Hale, 10 Oct. 1961.

95. "Integrity Is Key to U Thant's Character," *Times Union,* 8 Oct. 1961; and Brian Urquhart, interview by the author, 14 Aug. 1992.

96. "Imperturbable Burmese," *New York Times,* 2 Nov. 1961.

97. Britain, PRO/FO, 371/160984, minute by P. H. Scott, 13 Oct. 1961.

98. "Portrait: Un bouddhiste réaliste," *Le Monde,* 17 July 1962.

99. See UNA/DAG-1/2.3.16.2, Office of the Under-Secretary-General for Special Political Affairs [Urquhart Papers], box 270, file 2064.

100. Despatch no. 82, from C. S. A. Ritchie (United Nations) to Undersecretary of State for External Affairs, Confidential, 1961, a copy of which is on file in Britain, PRO/FO, 371/166893.

101. Ramses Nassif, *U Thant in New York, 1961–1971: A Portrait of the Third UN Secretary-General* (New York, 1988), 25, describes this as Thant's "greatest achievement in his ten-year tenure."

102. These fascinating communications can be found in UNA/DAG-1/5.2.2.6.1, Papers of the Secretary-General [Thant Papers], box 1.

103. Brian Urquhart, interview by the author, 18 Aug. 1992. Also see the judgment in James G. Blight and David Welch, *On the Brink: Americans and Soviets Reexamine*

the Cuban Missile Crisis (New York, 1989), 83–84, 268, 367; and James G. Blight and David Welch, "The Eleventh Hour of the Cuban Missile Crisis: An Introduction to the ExComm Transcripts," *International Security* 12, no. 3 (Winter 1987/88): 9.

104. Urquhart, *A Life in Peace and War,* 193.

105. U Thant, 24 Oct. 1962, in UN, SC, *Official Records, 1962,* 1024th Meeting, p. 23.

106. U Thant, *View from the United Nations,* xvii.

107. Letter from the United States and Soviet Union to Thant, 7 January 1963, in UNA/DAG-1/5.2.2.6.1, Papers of the Secretary-General [Thant Papers], Box 2.

108. U Thant, *View from the United Nations,* 36.

109. U Thant, "Africa and the World Community," UN, Press Release SG/SM/3/Rev.1, 4 February 1964.

110. Many examples of his work in these areas can be found in UNA/DAG-1/5.2.7, Papers of the Secretary-General [Thant Papers], boxes 2 and 3.

111. U Thant, *View from the United Nations,* 58–71.

112. The words are those of Ralph Bunche describing a meeting between Thant and Dean Rusk on 20 June 1967, in UNA/DAG-1/5.2.2.1.2, Papers of the Secretary-General [Thant Papers], box 3, "Selected Confidential Papers," "Secret."

113. Letter from J. William Fulbright to Thant, 20 Dec. 1966, in UNA/DAG-1/5.2.3, Papers of the Secretary General [Thant Papers], box 3.

114. UNA/DAG-1/5.2.2.3.2, Papers of the Secretary-General [Thant Papers], box 1, Envelope 4, "Vietnam: For Perusal of the Secretary-General Only."

115. See Urquhart, *A Life in Peace and War,* 190; and paper by James Boyd entitled "U Thant and the Vietnam Papers," 22 June 1971, in UNA/DAG-1/5.2.1.9, Papers of the Secretary-General [Thant Papers], box 17.

116. See the account in Nassif, *U Thant,* 72 ff.

117. UNA/DAG-1/5.2.2.1.1, Papers of the Secretary-General [Thant Papers], box 4, file entitled "Notes on Withdrawal of UNEF."

118. See the comments of Max Harrelson in Cordier, et al., *U Thant, 1965–1967,* vol. 7 of *Public Papers of the Secretaries-General of the United Nations,* "Introduction," 15.

119. UNA/DAG-1/5.2.2.1.1.2, Papers of the Secretary-General [Thant Papers], box 3, "Selected Confidential Papers on the Middle East," "Secret."

120. United Nations Charter, Article 2, Paragraph 4.

121. U Thant, *View from the United Nations,* 32.

122. See Shevchenko, *Breaking with Moscow,* 132, 293; Alan James, "U Thant and His Critics," *The Yearbook of World Affairs, 1972* (London, 1972), 43–64; and James Barros, "The Importance of Secretaries-General of the United Nations," in Jordan, *Hammarskjöld Revisited,* 32–33, 37.

123. "U Thant: Long Service for Peace," *Washington Post,* 26 Nov. 1974.

124. "U Thant," *The Times* (London), 26 Nov. 1974. Also Brian Urquhart, interview by the author, 18 Aug. 1992.

125. "The UN: Will It Run or Punt?" *Newsweek,* 27 Sept. 1971.

126. "Good Opening for Man of Initiative," *The Times* (London), 1 Oct. 1971.

127. See Robert E. Herzstein, *Waldheim: The Missing Years* (New York, 1988); Simon Wiesenthal, "Waldheims Wahl und die Folgen," *Ausweg* (June, 1986): 1–2, 4; Gordon A. Craig, "The Waldheim File," *New York Review of Books,* 9 Oct. 1986; and his own account in Kurt Waldheim, *In the Eye of the Storm* (Bethesda, 1986).

128. See "UNO: Steuerfrei zur Macht," *Sonntagsjournal* (Zurich), Nr. 36/72 (1972); and Brian Urquhart, interview by the author, 18 Aug. 1992.

129. Herzstein, *Waldheim*, 221, 225. Also see Daniel Patrick Moynihan, *A Dangerous Place* (Boston, 1978), 83–84.

130. "United Nations: Velvet and Steel," *Newsweek*, 25 Dec. 1972. Also see Shirley Hazzard, *Countenance of Truth: The United Nations and the Waldheim Case* (New York, 1990), 73.

131. UNA/DAG-1/5.3.2.3.0, Papers of the Secretary-General [Waldheim Papers], box 1, file entitled "SG's Consultations and Offer of Good Offices—1972"; and Charles Yost, "Bailing Out the Superpowers," *Christian Science Monitor*, 19 May 1972.

132. UNA/DAG-1/5.3.2.1.5, Papers of the Secretary-General [Waldheim Papers], box 1, file entitled "Middle East—Incident at Munich Olympics," statement of 6 Sept. 1972.

133. As cited in "United Nations," *Newsweek*, 25 Dec. 1972. Also see William F. Buckley, Jr., *UN Journal: A Delegate's Odyssey* (New York, 1974), 248; "76 Votes for Terror," *Washington Post*, 13 Dec. 1972; and "UN wollen Wurzeln des Terrors bekämpfen," *Die Presse*, 25 Sept. 1972.

134. Des Wilson, "A Man for All Nations," *London News* (April 1980).

135. See UNA/DAG-1/5.3.2.1.1, Papers of the Secretary-General [Waldheim Papers], "Peacekeeping Operations"; Kurt Waldheim, *Challenge to Peace* (New York, 1980), 4, 79–92; Urquhart, *A Life in Peace and War*, 234–53; and Shevchenko, *Breaking with Moscow*, 254–59.

136. Waldheim, *Der Schwierigste Job der Welt*, 17.

137. See Lauren, *Power and Prejudice*, 237–39.

138. Ivor Richard, as cited in the excellent discussion by Urquhart, *A Life in Peace and War*, 264.

139. Waldheim, *Der Schwierigste Job der Welt*, 179.

140. See UNA/DAG-1/5.3.2.4.0, Papers of the Secretary-General [Waldheim Papers], box 1; and Lauren, *Power and Prejudice*, 240–66.

141. See UNA/DAG-1/5.3.3.4.0 and DAG-1/5.3.3.4.3, Papers of the Secretary-General [Waldheim Papers].

142. Alan James, "Kurt Waldheim: Diplomat's Diplomat," *The Yearbook of World Affairs, 1983* (London, 1983), 81–96.

143. Urquhart, *A Life in Peace and War*, 228.

144. Seymour Finger and Arnold Saltman, *Bending with the Winds: Kurt Waldheim and the United Nations* (New York, 1990), 79, 85.

145. He had served as the ambassador of Peru, the secretary-general's special Representative in Cyprus, and as the Under-Secretary-General for Special Political Affairs. See the introductory statement entitled "Secretary-General Pérez de Cuéllar" in the finding aid to UNA/DAG-1/2.3.16.5, Office of the Under-Secretary-General for Special Political Affairs [Urquhart Papers].

146. Brian Urquhart, personal interview, 18 Aug. 1992; and Urquhart, *A Life in Peace and War*, 334.

147. See Pérez de Cuéllar, "Statement to the Council for Namibia," UN, SG/SM/3232, 7 Jan. 1982; and "Statement to the Anti-Apartheid Committee," UN, SG/SM/3234, 11 Jan. 1982.

148. Paul Lewis, "1988 Was, at Long Last, the Year of the UN," *New York Times,* 1 Jan. 1989. Also see Craig and George, *Force and Statecraft,* 153–54.

149. James A. Baker III, as cited in "Security Council Votes Use of 'All Necessary Means,'" UN, SC/5237, 29 Nov. 1990.

150. Security Council Resolution 678, as cited in ibid. Also see Pérez de Cuéllar, "Secretary-General Urges Iraqi President Hussein to Withdraw Forces at Once," UN, SG/SM/4536, 15 Jan. 1991.

151. Alvin Z. Rubinstein, "New World Order or Hollow Victory?" *Foreign Affairs* 70, no. 4 (Fall 1991): 54, 58.

152. Brian Urquhart and Erskine Childers, *A World in Need of Leadership: Tomorrow's United Nations,* Development Dialogue series (Uppsala, 1990), 7.

153. See Richard A. Falk et al., ed., *The United Nations and a Just World Order* (Boulder and London, 1991); Bruce M. Russett and James Sutterlin, "The U.N. in a New World Order," *Foreign Affairs* 70, no. 2 (Spring 1991); and Peter Baehr and Leon Gordenker, *The United Nations in the 1990s* (New York, 1992).

154. Bruce Nelan, "How the World Will Look in 50 Years," *Time,* Special Issue (Fall 1992), 37.

155. Pérez de Cuéllar, "Farewell Statement of the Secretary-General," UN, SG/SM/4677, 20 Dec. 1991.

156. Thant, as cited in Nasssif, *U Thant,* 134.

157. On the nature of this difficulty for anyone serving as Secretary-General, see James Barros, "The Importance of Secretaries-General of the United Nations," 25–37; Urquhart, *Hammarskjöld,* 5–51; Leon Gordenker, *The UN Secretary-General and the Maintenance of Peace* (New York, 1967); Stephen M. Schwebel, *The Secretary-General of the United Nations* (Cambridge, Mass., 1952); and Rovine, *The First Fifty Years,* 415–63.

158. Kurt Waldheim, *Challenge of Peace,* 6; and notes 1–5 above.

159. Dag Hammarskjöld, "Address Before the American Association for the United Nations," United Nations, SG/336, 14 Sept. 1953.

160. Dag Hammarskjöld, "Statement Before Members of the New York State Legislature," United Nations, SG/420, 28 Mar. 1955.

PART FIVE

DÉTENTE AND ITS LIMITATIONS

17

DEAN RUSK AND THE DIPLOMACY OF PRINCIPLE

Francis L. Loewenheim

ON 12 DECEMBER 1960, President-elect John F. Kennedy announced his selection of Dean Rusk, a senior official in the Department of State in the Truman administration and currently president of the Rockefeller Foundation, to be the new secretary of state. Rusk was well-known in Washington, and his nomination was greeted with warm and widespread approval on both sides of the Atlantic.[1]

On 12 January 1961, Rusk appeared for his confirmation hearing before the Senate Foreign Relations Committee, and there, too, he received a cordial reception, with Democratic Senator Wayne Morse of Oregon remarking that "the President-elect and the Congress and the American people are very fortunate to have a man with such an outstanding background and as great ability as yours to advise the President-elect on foreign policy in the troubled years ahead."[2] Although Rusk had met with the committee on numerous occasions since the mid-1940s, in accordance with long-standing custom, he was invited to describe his background and experience, personal and professional, that had led John F. Kennedy to nominate him to head the oldest department of the United States government. Had Rusk, at fifty-one, not been so reserved and self-effacing about his own life and achievements, this is some of what he would have told the senators on that occasion.

I

David Dean Rusk—he dropped the first given name early in life—was born on a small farm in Cherokee County, Georgia, on 9 February 1909.[3] His father had studied to be a Presbyterian minister, but a throat ailment had kept him from the pulpit. The Rusks, a large family, were "poor . . . [but] proud poor," as the secretary later put it, and in 1913 they moved to Atlanta, where his father became a postal clerk, and young Dean a student at Boys' High School, a top all-city academic institution, proceeding after graduation in 1927 to Davidson College, which his father had attended, as had Woodrow Wilson for a year.

Economic straits proved no bar to personal achievement. Young Rusk was an outstanding student, athlete, and ROTC officer. He took a lively interest in events of the day and became a lifelong Wilsonian. In 1931 he applied for and received a coveted Rhodes scholarship to attend Oxford University. Rusk's interviewers were headed by Josephus Daniels, Woodrow Wilson's secretary of the navy, later Franklin D. Roosevelt's ambassador to Mexico, then editor of the *Raleigh News and Observer*. Asked how he explained his simultaneous interest in international peace and continued active service in the Reserve Officers Training Corps, Rusk replied: "The great seal [of the United States] has arrows in one claw and an olive branch in the other. The two must go together. Armed force and world peace are two sides of the same coin."[4]

The wider world Rusk found awaiting him at St. Johns College in September 1931 was a deeply troubled and discouraging place. The economic and international troubles Woodrow Wilson had gloomily foreseen a dozen years earlier were rapidly coming true. Imperial Japan had recently invaded Manchuria, and no one had stopped it. Great Britain, like the rest of the Atlantic world, was in the depth of depression. Rusk long remembered the "foreboding mood" of the time.

Many at Oxford, Rusk wrote later, "felt that Britain was overextended. . . . Capitalism came under sharp and skeptical questioning. . . . Antiwar sentiment was strong at Oxford; slightly more than a decade earlier an entire generation of Oxford men had gone to war and many failed to return. . . . debates at the Oxford Union, university lectures, and casual conversation all reflected this legacy of tragedy and confusion. I am personally convinced that this combination of pacifism, isolationism, and public indifference . . . contributed immeasurably to the events that led to World War II."[5] Some of his time Rusk spent in Germany, at the universities of Hanover and Hamburg and the Hochschule für Politik in Berlin, just as Hitler was coming to power. The destruction of political and academic freedom he witnessed made a lasting impression on him. Even worse, he recognized that few in the Western democracies appeared to care much about what was happening in Germany, and what the Third Reich portended for the peace of Europe and the world.

The United States Rusk returned to in the autumn of 1934 was little more encouraging. Understandably preoccupied with their own terrible slump, Americans were consumed by disillusionment and isolationism. American intervention in the World War had been a terrible mistake, never to be repeated.[6] Rusk was one of the more fortunate young people. He joined the faculty of Mills College, a prestigious women's college in Oakland, California, as associate professor of government, and soon became dean of the faculty as well. But the attitude and outlook of his students, the academic and political world around him deeply concerned him.

Even in the pacifist mid-thirties, Rusk deplored illusions about "peace at any price" as well as the increasingly fashionable talk about avoiding war by "peaceful change," a dangerously vague notion that appealed, for example, to John Foster Dulles at the time. As Rusk wrote in the *Mills Quarterly* in February

1935: "There are blessings of peace and costs of war . . . but there are also costs of peace and blessings of war. . . . Perhaps ambition and selfishness may be modified by pacific negotiations, but if irreconcilable claims are not withdrawn [presumably a reference to the growing political and territorial ambitions and demands of Germany, Italy, and Japan], war will result." Rusk would not have been too proud to fight for what he believed was right.

In Washington, meanwhile, there was little to hope for, internationally speaking. At the outset of his administration, President Roosevelt talked of supporting former Secretary of State Henry L. Stimson's nonrecognition policy, designed to deny Tokyo the diplomatic and political fruits of aggression in China.[7] But before long, the president appeared to accept the dominant isolationist tide. In a campaign speech in August 1936, he summed up his foreign policy: "I have seen war. . . . I hate war."[8] Two years later, when he heard that Neville Chamberlain was headed for Munich, he sent the prime minister a terse congratulatory message: "Good Man."[9]

Such developments did nothing to reduce Rusk's concern. "Once, in my international relations class with perhaps a dozen students present, I gave expression to my feelings about the passivity of the democracies in refusing to face up to Japanese and German aggression. I nearly shed tears before my astonished students, I felt so strongly about what was happening."[10] In the 1960s, Rusk remembered those days and was determined not to help repeat them.

At the time, the United States did nothing to stop the march of force. The gathering storm thoughtful observers had seen drawing near arrived in 1939. Following the fall of France, the United States at last enacted a draft law, and in December 1940 Rusk, who had retained his commission as a reserve officer in the U.S. Army, dating back to his college days, was ordered to report for active duty as an infantry officer at the Presidio army base, on the shores of San Francisco bay.[11]

Thus began Rusk's meteoric professional rise. After ten months at Oakland, word of his talents had reached Washington, and in October 1941 he was summoned to the War Department, there to be put in charge of a new G-2 (intelligence) branch covering British-held areas in South Asia and the Pacific, from Afghanistan to New Zealand. But he had no desire to spend his war years at a Pentagon desk, and in May 1943 he moved to New Delhi, where General Joseph W. Stilwell, the U.S. commander in the region and top military adviser to Generalissimo Chiang Kai-shek, had learned of Rusk's attainments in Washington. Before long, Stilwell appointed him deputy chief of war plans for the entire China-Burma-India theater.

Rusk's South Asian years were a learning experience on a par with his time in Oxford and Hitler's Germany. The rickety old imperial system in the area had been destroyed by Japan's army. China, though nominally one of the Big Four, was on the verge of disintegration, with no new political or military center in sight, including Mao's guerrillas, then lightly regarded by Moscow and Washington alike. In 1941–1942 Rusk had been troubled by the disastrous consequences of U.S. military unpreparedness. But FDR's eloquent utterances and principles, from the Four Freedoms to the Atlantic Charter, provided no concrete foundation for the postwar world. Rusk knew—it was an open secret around the world—that Roosevelt and Churchill disagreed fundamentally about postwar India and China.[12] But what about French Indo-China, whose strategic importance the president had recognized long before Pearl Harbor? When Stilwell's headquarters questioned Washington on the subject in early 1945, the reply came back: "The President [had declared] 'I don't want to hear any more about Indo-China.'"[13] A few months later, FDR was dead, and Indo-China would become a problem for President Truman and his successors.

His labors at General Stilwell's headquarters, especially his impressive reporting on military-political affairs, had attracted considerable attention in high places at the War Department, and in June 1945 Rusk—by then colonel—was back at the Pentagon as a member of the prestigious Operations Division of the War Department General Staff, in charge of long-range planning. For the next two years, he alternated between positions at the War and State departments, and in March 1947 Secretary of State George C. Marshall asked him to head the department's Office of Special Political Affairs (SPA), better known as the United Nations desk. In February 1949 he became the first assistant secretary of state for United Nations affairs.[14] Finally, in May 1949 Dean Acheson, Marshall's successor, appointed Rusk to be deputy under secretary of state, the third highest position in the department.[15]

One of his first important Washington assignments—hurriedly completed at the Pentagon, on the night of 10 August 1945, with another young colonel, Charles H. Bonesteel III, a fellow Rhodes scholar at Oxford—was to draw a demarcation line for Korea, dividing the former Japanese-occupied country into what came to be Communist North and noncommunist South Korea.[16] As it turned out, the supposedly temporary boundary, the thirty-eighth parallel, survived the 1950–1953 war into the 1990s.

As for George Marshall, Rusk had first met the renowned Army chief of staff in 1941–1942, but he worked much more closely with him after his return from New Delhi in the summer of 1945. Like countless others, military and civilian, Rusk soon fell under Marshall's spell. "He was," Rusk reflected in the 1980s, "the most extraordinary man I ever knew . . . a strong influence on everyone who served with him. He taught us how we should conduct ourselves in public life [and] he knew how to delegate responsibility. He thought that a secretary of state should do those things which only the secretary can do. If others could do something, he expected them to do it."[17] Marshall's determination to judge issues in a nonpersonal, nonideological manner became a model for Rusk. In Rusk's case, as will be seen, Marshall's style also became the source of more than occasional criticism.[18]

It seems fair to add at this point that none of Rusk's Washington assignments after the war meant more to him than his United Nations labors. As a strong supporter of the League of Nations, he was determined to make the new world organization work. "The U.N. is my client," he would respond, when some of his State colleagues taxed him for being overly attentive to its role. "I personally have never lost my enthusiasm for the U.N.," Rusk wrote in his memoirs. "My service heading the United Nations desk . . . was among the most fulfilling and exciting times of my life."[19] And his interest and support for the UN did not cease when he became secretary of state, when he repeatedly sought to have the world organization deal with such dangerous and otherwise intractable disputes as those over Berlin, the Cuban missile crisis, and the Vietnam war.

About Harry Truman, Rusk was enthusiastic, but not without some qualifications.[20] He thought American postwar demobilization far too rapid, and the president's Greek-Turkish aid program, soon to become known as the Truman Doctrine, rather too sweeping in its global implications. About the communist takeover of mainland China, Rusk was deeply concerned, but he also recognized American inability to prevent Mao's eventual triumph.[21] The consequences of a Communist China, of course, no one in Washington—Rusk included—could foresee.

Meanwhile, there were more immediately pressing issues for him to attend to. First there was the future of Palestine, which Great Britain had thrust into the United Nations' lap in early 1947.[22] Rusk, then in charge of United Nations Affairs, could accept either partition, which the Arabs rejected, or a new UN mandate, which the Jewish leaders found totally unacceptable. For an independent new Jewish state he showed little enthusiasm. Above all, he bitterly complained about what he regarded as excessive "Zionist" influence at the White House.[23] Rusk had not forgotten the suffering of Jews in Nazi Germany and Hitler's Europe, but in the Middle East, he saw a new international tragedy in the making.

Looking back nearly forty years later, Rusk felt no reason to regret or apologize for his position. "In retrospect," he wrote,

> a workable solution for Palestine may not have been possible. . . . We in the American delegation and others scoured the underbrush for every possible solution. But I think the actual creation of a Jewish state in Palestine, at the expense of Arab peoples who had lived there for centuries, was something the Arab world simply couldn't take . . . it is not easy for Americans, living halfway around the world with an entirely different culture and historical tradition, to understand what the creation of a Jewish state in Palestine meant to Arabs who had shared that same land for centuries.[24]

Even more explosive was the situation around West Berlin, after Joseph Stalin, in June 1948, imposed a ground blockade of the former German capital, designed to drive the Western occupiers out. Rusk persuaded Truman and

Secretary of State Dean Acheson, with whom he was on increasingly close and cordial terms, to take the issue to the United Nations, and it was there that, in early 1949, a face-saving compromise—the so-called Jessup-Malik agreement, essentially restoring the *status quo ante*—was eventually agreed to.[25] But the freedom and security of West Berlin remained far from assured. A decade later, Nikita Khrushchev would raise it forcefully anew.[26]

If Stalin learned anything from his inability to prevent the establishment of a new West German state and to drive the Western powers out of West Berlin, it was that far more fertile fields awaited him overseas, in the former colonial parts of the world. If a frontal attack on the United States, Britain, and France was clearly unpromising, prospects appeared considerably brighter in the Far East and Southeast Asia, and it was in that direction that the Cold War increasingly shifted after 1949–1950.

In March 1950, Acheson had, at Rusk's request, appointed him assistant secretary of state for Far Eastern affairs. It was in effect a step down from his current post as deputy under secretary of state.[27] But FE, as it was known, was where the action promised to be, and Rusk never shied away from action. In late June 1950, Communist North Korea suddenly struck south, and once more there loomed the specter of conflict, direct or indirect, with Communist China or perhaps even the Soviet Union.

In the first flush of General MacArthur's striking victories, Rusk supported the territorial reunification of North and South Korea, as previously voted by the United Nations. After the intervention of the Chinese Communists—and the massive retreat of MacArthur's forces—Rusk agreed that a return to the *status quo ante* was the most desirable outcome.[28] Even so, armistice negotiations dragged on for two years, and were not finally concluded until July 1953, when Dwight D. Eisenhower was in the White House and John Foster Dulles secretary of state.

In the meanwhile, the problem of Southeast Asia had begun to emerge from its dormant stage. At the Wake Island conference with General MacArthur on 15 October 1950, President Truman, for instance, had declared: "We have been working on the French in connection with Indo-China for years without success. . . . this is the most discouraging thing we face. . . . [We] have worked on the French tooth and nail to try and persuade them to do what the Dutch had done in Indonesia but the French have not been willing to listen."[29]

Fifteen months later, in March 1952, a State Department draft policy paper stated: "The strategic importance of Indo-China derives from its geographical position as a key to mainland Southeast Asia . . . [however] the U.S. should not employ U.S. armed forces in Indo-China."[30] In fact, Communist-sponsored or supported insurgency soon became a mounting problem for Paris and Washington. In July 1954, French authority in Indo-China ceased, but the United States refused to sign the Geneva peace agreement that followed, and so did the newly formed South Vietnamese government. Inspired by NATO's apparent deterrent success, Eisenhower and Dulles now came up with a Far Eastern counterpart, the South East Asia Treaty Organization (SEATO). As in Europe, so in the Pacific, the United States declared that "aggression by means of armed attack . . . would endanger its own peace and safety," and each of the eight signatories promised to meet the common danger in accordance with its constitutional processes.[31]

By that time, Rusk had left the State Department for the presidency of the Rockefeller Foundation. But he had not lost his interest in international—especially Pacific—affairs, though he believed the idea of SEATO was anything but sound or wise. In any event, Eisenhower's prestige produced its rapid ratification. But no one, least of all Rusk, knew the enormous cost the new treaty would ultimately exact.

The 1954 Indo-China crisis was followed by the crisis over Suez in 1956[32] and the making of a new confrontation over Berlin in November 1958, when Khrushchev suddenly proposed signing a peace treaty with the so-called German Democratic Republic, which might set the stage for another Berlin blockade.[33] Finally, in Laos, one of the Associated States of Indo-China, the 1954 neutralization agreement was coming apart. So great was the possibility of a Communist takeover that, in December 1960, Eisenhower declared himself ready for unilateral American intervention to keep a Communist Laos from dragging all Indo-China into the communist camp.[34] At a meeting with President-elect Kennedy, just before his inauguration, Eisenhower remarked that Laos was the key to all Southeast Asia.[35] In a matter of weeks, all these problems would land on Dean Rusk's desk.

II

Even before he was elected president, John F. Kennedy was determined to be his own secretary of state. "It is the President alone," he had told the National Press Club in January 1960, "who must make the major decisions on our foreign policy." He was looking, Arthur M. Schlesinger, Jr., recalled later, "for someone who would be wise in counsel, persuasive on the Hill, and effective in modernizing what he regarded as an unduly passive and conservative Foreign Service."[36]

Having no preferred candidate of his own, the president-elect lost little time consulting senior members of the foreign policy establishment—including Dean Acheson, Chester Bowles, Clark Clifford, Robert A. Lovett, and John J. McCloy—all of whom had worked with, and spoke highly of, Rusk. Kennedy had given some thought to appointing J. William Fulbright of Arkansas, the chairman of the Senate Foreign Relations Committee, but decided against him because of his avowed segregationist views. W. Averell Harriman, whom some of Kennedy's inner circle favored, was never considered for reasons of age.[37]

Kennedy had read with interest Rusk's illuminating article "The President"—one of his Elihu Root Lectures at the Council of Foreign Relations in early 1960—published in the April 1960 issue of *Foreign Affairs*.[38] Unlike Acheson, who guided President Truman's principal moves in foreign affairs, Rusk viewed his personal role as secretary of state rather like that of George C. Marshall. He intended to be the president's top adviser on foreign policy, but would make no effort to transcend that role, although Rusk left no doubt that on some issues—for instance, summitry—he had strong views, which might well conflict with those of the president he served.

Kennedy had not previously met Rusk, and they had only two meetings, both fairly short, before the president-elect announced his decision to appoint him. But Kennedy was familiar with his background, his performance and views on important issues, and, some later hostile claims to the contrary,[39] there is no reason to believe that Kennedy ever regretted his choice or planned to replace him in a second Kennedy administration.

The department Rusk returned to in January 1961, after a decade's absence, was a very different institution from the one he had left in the last year of the Truman administration. The senior officials of the Marshall-Acheson era had, with few exceptions, departed, and Rusk made no effort to import a new team of his own, as John Foster Dulles, for instance, had done at the beginning of the Eisenhower administration. About some senior appointments, for example, that of Chester Bowles as under secretary of state, Rusk had not been consulted. Adlai E. Stevenson, the 1952 and 1956 Democratic standard-bearer, named American representative to the United Nations, would doubtless have preferred Rusk's position, but the two men got on amicably until differences over Vietnam reportedly developed between them before Stevenson's sudden death in July 1965.[40] With G. Mennen Williams, the former Michigan governor, likewise appointed earlier as assistant secretary for African affairs, Rusk shared a firm belief that the United States should adopt a far more positive and supportive role toward the emerging black states of that continent.[41]

No secretary—and no president—inherits a warm bed, and Rusk returned to some very familiar problems and others that soon promised to become no less serious. As Kennedy and Rusk saw it, American policy during the 1954 Indo-China crisis and the 1956 crisis over Suez had done serious damage to relations between Washington, London, and Paris. The Eisenhower-Dulles penchant for contracting new alliances, modeled after NATO, the president and secretary found disconcerting, and no one could be certain what Nikita Khrushchev had in mind when, in early 1961, he announced strong Soviet support for what he called "wars of national liberation." If anything seemed fairly clear in January 1961, it was that the Cold War was about to get much colder.

In general, Kennedy and Rusk would probably have agreed that Eisenhower and Dulles had a distracting tendency to talk rather loosely on occasion,[42] and too often found themselves reacting to Soviet or Chinese Communist moves. In addition, American military policy seemed to have become increasingly inflexible, with dangerously facile slogans like "massive retaliation" replacing carefully thought-out policy alternatives. To these accumulated problems the question of what to do about Fidel Castro had been added in 1959–1960. Replacing the long-time Cuban dictator Fulgencio Batista, who owed much of his twenty-eight-year tenure to the benign indifference of the Roosevelt and Truman administrations, Castro soon embarked on a sharp turn to the Marxist left. Massive nationalization programs and a brutally repressive totalitarianism began to characterize his openly pro-Moscow regime. By early January 1961, Eisenhower decided to break diplomatic relations with Castro.[43] He also approved a plan, drawn up some months earlier by the Central Intelligence Agency, to train several thousand Cuban exiles in Guatemala to land on their home island to attempt to overthrow the Castro regime.[44]

Kennedy had first learned of the scheme at a briefing shortly after the election.[45] Rusk presumably knew nothing about it until he became secretary of state, but lost no time expressing his opposition to it. To the secretary, it constituted a clear violation of Article 15 of the 1948 Charter of the Organization of American States, which declared that "no state or group of states has the right to intervene, directly or indirectly, for any reason whatever, in the internal affairs of any other state, [not only with] armed force, but also any other form of interference or attempted threat."

Although a few other senior members of the administration, including Attorney General Robert F. Kennedy, also strongly opposed the project, the president determined to proceed on schedule. When the outnumbered and outgunned exiles were humiliatingly defeated by Castro's forces, Rusk—unlike some other State Department officials, notably Under Secretary Bowles—kept his disagreement to himself. It was an expression of loyalty the president appreciatively remembered.[46]

The Bay of Pigs operation proved a disaster in several ways. It suggested the new Kennedy administration was unable to handle a major new foreign policy challenge close to America's shores. More important yet, it created the impression of confusion and uncertainty in high places, an impression that was not entirely unwarranted. As if to counter that appearance, the president decided to press ahead with a two-day summit with Nikita Khrushchev in Vienna, in early June, prefacing that encounter with a brief meeting with President de Gaulle in Paris. Rusk had often cautioned against such meetings, and Kennedy's sessions with the French and Soviet leaders only confirmed the secretary's long-standing doubts.[47] The de Gaulle meeting produced little more than polite generalities, the summit with Khrushchev "a very harsh confrontation at the very top of the two governments," as Rusk put it later.[48]

Some recent accounts contend that Vienna was a political disaster, if not a humiliation, for the president.[49] The official American record, now available save for a few deletions, does not support that contention. Kennedy gave as good as he got.[50] As Rusk viewed it, "for the first time" the president "saw the full weight of Soviet pressure and the full weight of the ideological commitment of the Soviet Union." On the central issue of Berlin—in particular Khrushchev's repeatedly stated intention to sign a separate peace treaty with East Germany—Kennedy may have failed to persuade the Soviet leadership that the Western powers would not be bullied or otherwise forced out of the former German capital, but perhaps no one could have persuaded Khrushchev otherwise at the moment. As a matter of principle, Kennedy and Rusk were not prepared to yield an inch. They were ready to talk the issue to death. The question was whether Moscow was prepared to keeping on talking.

Within a matter of weeks, the Berlin situation was assuming crisis proportions from the Communist point of view. Month after month, thousands of East Germans had been fleeing to the West, many of them professional or otherwise skilled people the so-called German Democratic Republic could ill afford to lose. In 1960 alone almost two hundred thousand people had fled west. In 1961 the number continued steadily to rise, with no end in sight. In July 1961 alone, over thirty-thousand people fled to West Berlin. On Saturday night, 13 August 1961, the East German authorities, in agreement with Moscow, finally produced a striking response to the exodus.[51] It was the building of a massive concrete wall, through the heart of Berlin.[52]

What was the most appropriate Western response to the dramatic Communist challenge? Some high American officials or advisers recommended a military probe to see if the Russians planned to follow up construction of the wall with another blockade on the model of 1948. Former Secretary of State Dean Acheson suggested another air lift, and, if that failed, dispatching two American armored divisions on the Autobahn from West Germany.[53] As for Rusk, he believed the Western powers should simply stand their ground, while refusing to attack the wall, which, in any case, was located inside Communist territory. Rusk "saw nothing that we could negotiate. We already had a policy, and it had stood firm for fifteen years. It was the Russians who wanted a new policy, who wanted to change the status quo." The secretary favored passing the Berlin problem back to the United Nations, but that was as far as he was for the moment publicly prepared to go.[54] His unheroic caution produced widespread criticism in West Germany, where right and left momentarily united in fearing a possible American betrayal of the Federal Republic.[55]

As Rusk put it later, the United States was faced

> with a situation where we did not like what was happening, but we did not see any alternatives that would improve the situation. The idea that you would knock down the Wall would mean that at best you would simply move the Wall back fifteen or twenty feet. There was no way to prevent the East Germans from erecting barricades to prevent their own people from leaving East Germany. We were not prepared to fight a war over the issue of the Wall since it did not intrude into the

responsibilities of the Western powers for West Berlin and in itself did not interfere with access to the city so that it was not an issue of war as far as the West was concerned.[56]

From Khrushchev's vantage point, on the other hand, the wall appeared to be a striking success. For one thing, it put an end to the massive outflow of population from the East, and—perhaps he foresaw—it brought nearer the time when the Western governments would feel compelled to recognize the division of Germany and the sovereignty of the self-styled German Democratic Republic, although, as it happened, both Rusk and Khrushchev were out of office by the time that important concession was finally agreed to by the Western democracies as part of Willy Brandt's *Ostpolitik* in 1970–1971.[57]

In March 1962, the opening of the seventeen-power disarmament conference at Geneva further complicated relations with Chancellor Adenauer, still deeply displeased with "the Anglo-Saxons" for their allegedly insufficiently hardline response at the climax of the Berlin crisis in July-August 1961.[58] As noted earlier in this volume, the Western German leader was especially angered by a proposal Rusk presented to Soviet Foreign Minister Gromyko that provided, among other things, for the establishment of committees, composed of equal numbers of East and West Germans, to deal with technical contacts between the two states, and to establish an international access authority, including an East German member. The proposal was apparently leaked to the press in Bonn, which allowed Adenauer to assert that it, in effect, granted international recognition to East Germany.[59]

A renewed chill settled in between Bonn and Washington, but the secretary was hardly surprised by this turn of events. Right or wrong, many senior State Department officials had long regarded Adenauer as hopelessly "inflexible." As Rusk recalled nearly thirty years later in his memoirs:

> Although I occasionally became irritated with the old chancellor, I could never remain angry with him. He was a great figure in German life who had brought Germany out of a terrible war onto a sound democratic footing. But he lived in a world of shadows and needed constant reassurance about the loyalty of the Americans to NATO and to Germany. John Foster Dulles had to give him assurances every few months about American support, and I was expected to as well. Adenauer had a great affection for Dulles and used to remind me of it often. Every time I called on him, he would spend the first ten minutes reminiscing about the "good old days of John Foster Dulles." I found this rather amusing because I had known Dulles well, and Dulles had told me about the problems he had with Konrad Adenauer.[60]

The apparent end of the Berlin crisis produced something of a relaxation of tensions in Europe, but not in the Caribbean or in Southeast Asia. Apparently persuaded that Kennedy's response in Berlin represented a fundamental lack of presidential will, by late spring 1962 Khrushchev embarked on his most audacious scheme of all—the placement of nuclear missiles in Cuba. The origins and objectives of the impetuous Soviet leader's action have long been debated.[61] But about the possible consequences of his success there could be little doubt. At one stroke, it might alter the global military-political balance decisively in Moscow's favor. It would provide the Soviet Union with an invaluable springboard for further political-military activity in the Western hemisphere, in violation, among other things, of the Monroe Doctrine, for over a century and a quarter one of the pillars of American foreign policy. As Rusk told a closed door session of the Senate Foreign Relations Committee in May 1961, Soviet missiles in Cuba "could reach parts of this country which may be more difficult to reach otherwise [and this would] impose a degree of blackmail upon the United States in dealing with our problems in all parts of the world."[62]

Rumors of Soviet missiles being stationed in Cuba had been circulating in Washington since mid-1962, but the administration was inclined to dismiss such reports as politically inspired. Rusk himself demonstrated his usual circumspection. Asked on 30 September 1962 about "the Soviet arms build-up in Cuba in terms of the total Soviet cold-war strategy," he contented himself with telling John Scali, the ABC State Department correspondent, that "the Cuban situation . . . is . . . a very serious problem for us and has to be treated as such."[63] By 14 October, however, U-2 overflights provided incontrovertible evidence of Soviet perfidy, and tension was hardly reduced when Soviet Foreign Minister Gromyko in a meeting with President Kennedy declared that Soviet assistance to Cuba "was solely for the purpose of contributing to the defense capabilities of Cuba."[64]

At first, on 18 October the secretary opposed a surgical air strike to destroy the Soviet weapons "because we didn't first try diplomatic avenues and because an air strike would inevitably kill Russian advisers." But diplomacy, or attempts at diplomacy, were no longer working, leading Rusk subsequently to declare that "if the Soviets had not stopped working on the missile sites by 23 October, we should announce our intent to attack and destroy the sites the following day, telling Khrushchev that any response on his part would mean war."[65]

As with the Berlin crisis in August 1961, the secretary thought it essential to take the Cuban issue at once to the United Nations. Adlai Stevenson, he wrote later, "presented our case brilliantly," as indeed he did to millions watching the Security Council proceedings on national television. Although in the event, the missile crisis was ultimately resolved directly between Washington and Moscow, Rusk believed that prolonged discussion in the Security Council "lessened the chance that one side would lash out with a spasm and do something foolish. The UN earned its pay for a long time to come just by being there for the missile crisis."[66]

Rusk recognized that not "since World War II have we had a crisis anywhere that compares" with the Cuban missile crisis. Yet he disagreed with those who maintained that the crisis marked a fundamental turning point in the Cold War, because, as he put it later, "I think the Soviets drew from the Cuban missile crisis the conclusion that they must enter a program of substantial expansion of their nuclear forces, which they, in fact, did."[67] Washington—meaning the president and the secretary of state—drew another conclusion. The reduction of nuclear tensions had long been one of their principal objectives, and in May 1963 the State Department initiated a new series of discussions with Soviet Ambassador Anatoly Dobrynin, looking toward a treaty barring most nuclear tests, which would not require inspection. It was a position Rusk strongly supported, even in the face of vigorous military opposition expressed by General Maxwell D. Taylor on behalf of the Joint Chiefs of Staff.[68]

President Kennedy himself set forth his position in his notable address at the American University in Washington on 10 June 1963. "I speak of peace," he declared on that occasion, "because of the new face of war. . . . I believe we can help the leaders of the Soviet Union adopt a more enlightened attitude," and he announced that discussions "will shortly begin in Moscow looking toward early agreement on a comprehensive test ban treaty."[69] This promise was fulfilled on 5 August 1963, when the United States, Great Britain, and the Soviet Union signed a treaty pledging themselves not to conduct nuclear weapons tests in the atmosphere, in outer space, or under water, but were permitted to continue with underground testing.[70] Rusk was anxious not to exaggerate the significance of the test ban agreement. As he told a news conference on 16 August 1963:

"I got the impression . . . during these past few weeks that we are not involved in a comprehensive discussion . . . looking toward some negotiated détente across the board. I do have the impression that it is worth exploring particular points—for example . . . in the surprise attack field. . . . But this is speculative. One can be wrong by tomorrow morning. We just have to keep working at it and see what can happen."[71]

If the peaceful end of the Cuban missile crisis and the signing of the nuclear test ban treaty signaled an improvement in bilateral U.S.-Soviet relations, in Southeast Asia the long-distance conflict between Washington, Moscow, and Peking continued steadily to mount. The Kennedy-Khrushchev summit appeared to point toward some kind of neutralization agreement for Laos, and such an agreement was indeed signed at Geneva on 23 July 1962.[72]

The secretary recognized the strategic importance of the Laos agreement.[73] As he told the annual convention of the Veterans of Foreign Wars in Minneapolis on 13 August 1962, "If the agreement is faithfully executed . . . Laos will cease to be an avenue of supply and reinforcement for the Communist aggression against South Viet-Nam."[74] But the agreement became a dead letter as soon as it was signed, and the Vietnamese situation, which had been troubling at the outset of the Kennedy administration, soon turned increasingly serious, if not critical. From the first days of the administration, as Rusk recalled later, "President Kennedy felt very strongly that we had commitments in Southeast Asia and that those commitments had to be supported and that it was necessary not to permit a gradual assumption of or overrunning of Southeast Asia by Hanoi or by Hanoi and Peking."[75] In effect, the American position was quite simple and also enormously complicated. Like Germany and Korea, Washington regarded Vietnam as a country divided as result of the Cold War. Since the mid-1950s, South Vietnam had been increasingly recognized internationally as a sovereign state. American policy was to maintain that sovereignty against subversion and thinly disguised attack from Communist North Vietnam. For a short time after the 1954 Geneva conference, those attacks appeared to have ceased. But they resumed in 1957–1958, even before Nikita Khrushchev had given a Soviet blessing to "national wars of liberation."[76]

What seriously complicated Washington's problem was that the South Vietnam government was an increasingly unrepresentative and repressive regime headed by President Ngo Dinh Diem and members of his family. Rusk himself was at first reluctant to send American forces to shore up the Saigon government. As he put it at a meeting of the National Security Council on 5 May 1961, "If United States troops were put in South Viet-Nam, it could complicate the forthcoming Geneva conference on Laos."[77] Six months later, the direction of American policy had begun to change, and in a draft memorandum to President Kennedy, dated 7 November 1961, Rusk wrote that he, Secretary of Defense Robert S. McNamara, and the Joint Chiefs agreed that the "fall of South Viet-Nam to Communism would lead to the fairly rapid extension of Communist control, or complete accommodation to Communism, in the rest of mainland Southeast Asia and in Indonesia. The strategic implications worldwide, particularly in the Orient, would be extremely serious."[78]

The memorandum suggested communicating to "the Communist bloc our firm and clear determination to intervene with United States combat forces . . . unless they took prompt steps to halt their support of the Viet Cong." But this, the memorandum argued, required that "we now take the decision to commit ourselves to the objective of preventing the fall of South Viet-Nam to Communism and the willingness to commit whatever United States combat forces may be necessary to achieve this objective" and the document went on to propose that "we communicate this decision by suitable diplomatic means to the Communist bloc and selected friendly countries."

This is not the appropriate place to review the gradual intensification of the Vietnam War, or of Rusk's role in the buildup of American forces in South Vietnam. But several points need to be emphasized in this connection. To begin with, until the pertinent records of all the principal participants—Communist and noncommunist—are finally opened, no fully balanced account of the war can be written. Furthermore, although Rusk generally agreed with Defense Secretary McNamara on matters of strategy and tactics, he never shared the latter's trusting faith that Pentagon computer whiz kids, trendy new military theories, and steadily intensified bombing would suffice to break the enemy's will and power of resistance. If anything, Rusk's World War II experience in the China-Burma-India theater of war induced a healthy skepticism about the possible effectiveness of air power.

So month after month, high-level U.S. civilian and military missions departed for South Vietnam, often returning frustrated by the massive problems facing its government and the slowly expanding United States military establishment there. Still, confidence and optimism were the watchword in high places in Washington. In mid-February 1962, for instance, Attorney General Robert F. Kennedy visited Saigon and promised that American troops would remain until Communist aggression had been defeated. "We are going to win in Vietnam," he declared. "We will remain here until we do win. . . . I think the American people understand and fully support this struggle. . . . I think the United States will do what is necessary to help a country that is trying to repel aggression with its own blood, tears and sweat."[79]

With the exception of George Ball, the independent-minded under secretary of state,[80] the Kennedy administration seemed united on the proposition that Vietnam must somehow be saved. As the president noted in his State of the Union address in January 1962, in Vietnam the United States was facing not a "war of liberation" but "systematic aggression."[81] The Congress, the foreign policy establishment, the media, and public opinion generally supported this view.[82] As Rusk saw it, "Southeast Asia was vital to the security of the free world and that if the communists continued to press, they would press just as far as they could until they were stopped. I also took seriously the commitments of the SEATO collective security pact as the principal means for preventing World War III. . . . We made the NATO [North Atlantic Treaty Organization] commitment. We made commitments on the other side of the Pacific."[83]

This view was shared, as Rusk noted, by the free nations of Southeast Asia, especially Thailand, the Philippines, Australia, New Zealand, and Malaysia. As they saw it, "it was necessary to halt [the] southward pressure of the Communist world . . . if they were to have any security for the future." You see, he said later, "we did not seriously consider in 1961, '62 and '63 the alternative of doing nothing and allowing South Vietnam to be overrun by North Vietnam. . . . We more or less took courage in hand and acted on the basis that the American people at the end of the day would support what was necessary to make good our commitments in Southeast Asia."[84]

By mid-1963, Washington's concern was not merely with South Vietnam's external security but with its internal order, or lack thereof. As time passed, the United States ambassador in Saigon appeared to take on the role of an American proconsul, deeply, yet not decisively, involved in the endless round of Byzantine machinations and plots,[85] culminating in the abduction and brutal murder of President Diem and his brother Ngo Dinh Nhu on 2 November 1963. As the recently published records of the Department of State make clear, for those actions Washington bore no direct responsibility. Whether there were any suggestions along those lines that were not formally recorded remains uncertain at this writing.

By the autumn of 1963, day-to-day official American policy could be described as drifting or uncertain, but its overriding objective was firmly restated by President Kennedy in a message to Diem, dated 23 October 1963, the eighth anniversary of the establishment of the Republic of Vietnam. "On this occasion," Kennedy declared,

I wish once again to express the admiration of the American people for the unfailing courage of the Vietnamese people in their valiant struggle against the continuing efforts of communism to undermine and destroy Vietnamese independence. The United States of America has confidence in the future of the Republic of Viet-Nam, in its ability both to overcome the present communist threat to their independence, and to determine their own destiny. We look forward to the day when peace is restored and when the Vietnamese people can live in freedom and prosperity.[86]

With those sentiments, Secretary Rusk heartily concurred. Three weeks later, the president headed south for his final tragic journey.

III

Like Harry Truman, Lyndon Johnson cordially disliked and distrusted his charismatic predecessor, and from his first days in office he was determined to show that he could do better at home and abroad. Continuity became a central theme of the new administration. Johnson would retain Kennedy's team and carry out his programs and policies, foreign and domestic. As he told a cheering joint session of Congress: "This nation will keep its commitments from South Vietnam to West Berlin,"[87] and he meant it. All this Dean Rusk found most admirable, and between the secretary and the new president a special bond soon emerged. They were both, after all, poor boys from the rural New South, and were to spend not a few hours reminiscing about the long, hard road that had brought them together at the top. Moreover, like Rusk, Johnson had come of age politically in the 1930s. There was no need for the secretary to remind him about the dangers of appeasing dictators and countenancing international aggression.[88]

In foreign affairs, then, Johnson was determined to follow a two-track policy. He hoped to continue to improve relations with the Soviet Union, and he would seek both diplomatic accommodation and military security for South Vietnam. He wanted no wider war, but he was determined that South Vietnam be left alone to live as it pleased. In early June 1964, Johnson sent Under Secretary George Ball to see General de Gaulle, to tell the French president that "our ultimate objective was a political solution that would insure the independence of South Vietnam. . . . it was therefore essential that the South Vietnamese have the right to call for help from whatever outside source it wishes."[89]

As it happened, Ball's mission to de Gaulle was only the first of numerous peace efforts Johnson and Rusk soon began to undertake. In June and August 1964, the secretary encouraged J. Blair Seaborn, the chief Canadian delegate on the International Control Commission, established by the 1954 Geneva conference, to go to Hanoi to see if a serious diplomatic dialogue could begin. But Rusk's efforts were promptly dismissed by the North Vietnamese leadership, who demanded instead, for the first of countless times, that the United States unilaterally withdraw from South Vietnam and that Communist Viet Cong guerrillas be made part of a coalition government in Saigon.[90]

For a time in mid-summer 1964, the Vietnam situation appeared to hang uneasily in the balance. As Rusk told a news conference on 1 July:

> I know that everyone would like to see the future clearly. So would we in government. I am sure other governments would like to do the same. But perhaps mercifully that is withheld from ordinary human beings, and we don't have the crystal balls that will tell us what all those involved in this situation will be doing and deciding in the next weeks and months. But our own purposes and determinations there are very simple.[91]

On 2 and 4 August 1964, there were sensational reports of U.S. warships— the destroyers *Maddox* and *C. Turner Joy*—being attacked by North Vietnamese torpedo boats while on intelligence patrol in the Gulf of Tonkin, some sixty-five miles off the North Vietnamese coast. To the president and his senior advisers, this was a challenge that could not be ignored. At 6:45 P.M. on 4 August, Johnson held an extended urgent meeting with congressional leaders of both parties at the White House. The secretary reported: "This was a serious decision to attack our vessels on the high seas. . . . We . . . propose to call for the Security Council and also to report to our Allies. . . . We would make it as clear as we can that we are not going to be run out of Southeast Asia, but that we have no national ambitions either in a war to the north."[92]

Two days later, following additional discussion with congressional leaders, Johnson asked for, and the Congress promptly approved, a joint resolution authorizing the president "to take all necessary measures to repel any armed attack against the forces of the United States and to prevent further aggression." The resolution further reaffirmed American obligations under the 1954 SEATO treaty, and declared that the maintenance of peace and security in Southeast Asia was "vital" to American national interests and world peace. In subsequent years, a bitter debate developed over charges that the Johnson administration had deliberately waited for an incident, or the appearance of an incident, to obtain such sweeping authority. For this serious charge, no persuasive evidence has been produced. Indeed, appearing before the Senate Foreign Relations

Committee on 20 February 1968, Defense Secretary McNamara, himself by then disenchanted with the war and about to leave the administration, declared: "The suggestion that in some way the United Stated induced the incident on August 4, with the intent of providing an excuse to take the retaliatory action which we in fact took, I can only characterize such insinuations as monstrous."[93]

Soon after the Gulf of Tonkin incident, the United States found itself in the midst of the 1964 presidential campaign. Against the hawkish Republican nominee, Sen. Barry M. Goldwater of Arizona, Johnson was determined to be the "peace candidate." As he summed up his position in an address to the American Bar Association in New York City in mid-August 1964:

> Some others are eager to enlarge the conflict. They call upon us to supply American boys to do the job that Asian boys should do. They ask us to take reckless action which might risk the lives of millions and engulf much of Asia and certainly threaten the peace of the entire world. Moreover, such action would offer no solution at all to the real problem of Viet-Nam. America can and America will meet any wider challenge from others, but our aim in Viet-Nam, as in the rest of the world, is to help restore the peace and to reestablish a decent order.[94]

Abandoning the secretary of state's traditional neutrality in presidential contests, Rusk did not hesitate to campaign for Johnson. I think, he told a news conference on 14 September 1964, "there may be some Americans who expect miracles from the United States in these far-off and distant places. Let me remind you once again that there are a billion and a half people in Asia, half of them in the Communist world, half of them in the free world. We are not going to find answers for a billion and a half people by simply saying to them, 'Now just move over and we Americans will settle these things for you.' That is not the way it's going to happen."[95]

Did Johnson's campaign in 1964—like Woodrow Wilson's in 1916 and Franklin D. Roosevelt's in 1940—send the wrong signal to Hanoi, Peking, and Moscow? Rusk was one of those who thought that might have been the case. As he later told Columbia University historian Henry F. Graff, "dictatorships underestimate democracy's willingness to do what it had to do." Perhaps, the secretary continued, "the Communist world misunderstood our presidential campaign. The President kept saying he did not want a wider war. Perhaps the Communist side believed it could widen the war without appropriate American response."[96]

Be that as it may, by early 1965 the South Vietnamese situation had turned critical. A year earlier, Rusk had returned from several visits determined that Vietnam would not turn into another Korea. Now Johnson's military chiefs, with strong support from McGeorge Bundy, his national security adviser, declared that the United States must choose between increasing American forces there significantly at once or risking the collapse of South Vietnam. It was a decision in which the secretary fully concurred.[97] So American military involvement, on the ground and in the air, began to grow. At the time of President Kennedy's assassination, there were over 16,000 U.S. soldiers in Vietnam; by 15 June 1965 about 75,000, and by the end of the year 150,000, while one thousand had been killed in action.

As American military involvement rose, so did Johnson's determination to seek what might be called an economic and social solution to the conflict. In a major address at Johns Hopkins University on 7 April 1965, he offered "a billion dollar American investment" for a massive plan of cooperative development for the entire country."[98] In effect, the president proposed a New Deal for South East Asia, open to North Vietnamese participation, much as General Marshall had been prepared for communist participation in the European recovery program that bore his name. The immediate reaction to the president's address, at home and abroad, appeared highly favorable. But within a short time, it became clear that Hanoi would not be moved, and soon the dramatic effect of his proposal began to dissipate.

Meanwhile, as Rusk was well aware, the national consensus on Vietnam was beginning to show serious strains. Dissident Senate Majority Leader Mike Mansfield of Montana was increasingly joined by men like Senator Robert F. Kennedy of New York and Republican Senators George D. Aiken of Vermont and Jacob M. Javits of New York. By early 1966 their ranks had been augmented by Democratic Senators Frank Church of Idaho, Albert Gore of Tennessee, Eugene J. McCarthy of Minnesota, and Claiborne Pell of Rhode Island. The leading "dissenter," undoubtedly, was J. William Fulbright of Arkansas, the chairman of the Senate Foreign Relations Committee. In late January 1966, Fulbright used a pending foreign aid authorization bill as an opportunity to hold extensive public hearings on Vietnam. The secretary doubtless quickly sensed that American Vietnam policy was being challenged by a band of reservationists, much as Woodrow Wilson's League of Nations had been nearly fifty years earlier.[99] The new reservationists declared themselves opposed to unilateral American withdrawal from Vietnam. In fact, their vague and convoluted proposals for what they called "a political settlement" left little room for doubt about their ultimate objective.

Once more, Rusk sought to follow a middle course. "There seems to be very little interest and support" for "abandoning South Vietnam," he told the committee. The same held true for the "alternative of rushing into a general war or a larger war, get it over with as quickly as possible, regardless of cost." That, he declared, "leaves the position of firmness coupled with prudence. . . . But unless we make it clear to the other side that they will not succeed, there is no avenue to a peaceful settlement that has any chance of producing the peace that we are after."[100]

Unsurprisingly, the Fulbright hearings did nothing to reduce the growing national debate. On the contrary, the hearings might well have led Moscow,

Peking, and Hanoi's Washington-watchers to believe that they might yet achieve politically in the United States what they had, thus far, failed militarily to achieve in Vietnam. Yet while the political debate heated up, American military escalation continued likewise. By mid-1966, there were about 393,000 American servicemen in Vietnam, with more probably soon to come. Rusk fully supported the escalation. "We arm to parlay," Winston Churchill had argued after World War II. "We escalate to parley" was the new U.S. strategy, but the strategy did not work. The Communist side stubbornly rejected all diplomatic approaches until "the unconditional cessation of the U.S. bombing raids and other acts of war."

Meanwhile, in public and private U.S. peace efforts continued. Some of these diplomatic initiatives remained strictly confidential for many years, as the secretary wanted them to be. Some quickly became public knowledge. A detailed accounting of them was given by the compilers of the so-called Pentagon Papers in 1967–1968. But when those purloined records were turned over to the *New York Times* in 1971, the four separate volumes dealing with U.S. peace efforts were deliberately withheld.[101] It was not until 1983 that these volumes were finally published by the University of Texas Press under the title *The Secret Diplomacy of the Vietnam War: The Negotiating Volumes of the Pentagon Papers,* including some extensive deletions the State and Defense Departments continued to insist upon for security reasons.[102]

It should be noted that, while the Vietnam conflict continued to escalate, so also did administration efforts to improve relations with Moscow. That dual approach, which remained unchanged to the end of the Johnson administration, was not greatly appreciated in Western Europe, where London, Bonn, and Paris began to view Vietnam as a major stumbling block in the way of improved East-West relations.[103] Rusk did not take kindly to that position. Asked in a public television interview in May 1967 whether "the Vietnam war places strains upon our alliances," he impatiently responded, "I think that is non-sense—because if you want to put some strain on our other alliances, just let it become apparent that our commitment under an alliance is not worth very much. Then you will see some strains on our alliances."[104] The secretary was deeply angered by what he regarded as a lack of West European support, political and otherwise. "All we needed," he told a British journalist, "was one regiment. The Black Watch would have done. . . . Well, don't expect us to save you again."[105]

In mid-1967, the secretary's attention was distracted by a sudden new crisis in the Middle East, a region generally quiescent, if not stable, since the Suez crisis eleven years earlier. The episode began when Col. Gamal Abdel Nasser, the Egyptian dictator, on 18 May 1967 summarily demanded the withdrawal of UN peacekeeping forces from the Sinai, and, having achieved that objective, promptly closed the strategic Gulf of Aqaba to Israeli shipping, in flagrant violation of President Eisenhower's specific assurances in 1956–1957 that the waterway would remain open. Understandably fearing a massive coordinated Arab attack, on 5 June 1967 the Israeli government ordered a preemptive strike of its own.

It was a conflict the United States had understandably sought to avoid, and Rusk was anything but pleased with the Israeli government's performance. Nearly twenty years earlier, he had shown little sympathy with Israeli political needs and aspirations, and his outlook had hardly changed in the meantime. Not surprisingly, the president and the secretary rejected out of hand Israel's sudden plea for an immediate American-Israeli military alliance.[106] But they were not displeased by Israel's victory in the short war that followed, although the administration had serious reservations about Israel's extensive territorial gains, including the Sinai Peninsula, the West Bank, the Gaza Strip, and the Old City of Jerusalem.

The secretary himself was deeply concerned about the long-run impact and consequences of the Six-Day War. As he concluded gloomily in his memoirs in 1990: "I hope events will prove me wrong, but the intractable nature of the divisions between Jews and Arabs and even between moderate and extremist Arabs almost defy solution. . . . I don't believe the Arabs are willing to accept Israel's right to exist as a nation, nor is Israel prepared to make the necessary territorial concessions. I don't believe peace is possible until Israel agrees to withdraw from all territories seized in the June 1967 war."[107]

With the Middle East situation quieted down for the time being, in September 1967 the administration determined to make another peace effort in Vietnam. For months, numerous critics of the war had been calling for some kind of de-escalation of the fighting, or reduction of American bombing, which the Communists had long been demanding. Addressing the National Legislative Conference in San Antonio, President Johnson declared: "The United States is willing to stop all aerial and naval bombardment of North Vietnam when this will lead promptly to productive discussions. We, of course, assume that while discussions proceed, North Vietnam would not take advantage of the bombing cessation or limitation."[108]

As if to demonstrate that he was now reconsidering all possibilities, the president decided to summon what came to be known as "the wise men," an illustrious group of present or former senior government officials, including former Secretary of State Dean Acheson, former Under Secretary of State George Ball, General Omar Bradley, former National Security Adviser McGeorge Bundy, former top Korean war negotiator Arthur H. Dean, former Treasury Secretary C. Douglas Dillon, General Matthew B. Ridgway, former Deputy Defense Secretary Cyrus R. Vance, Supreme Court Justice Abe Fortas, former Under Secretary of State for Political Affairs Robert D. Murphy, W. Averell Harriman, Ambassador Henry Cabot Lodge, General Maxwell D. Taylor, and former top White House aide Clark Clifford. They met with the president for the first time on 2 November 1967.[109]

For the moment, "the wise men" strongly concurred with current U.S. strategy. Their far-reaching discussions—to which Rusk was only an occasional contributor—left little doubt that they saw no alternative course at present. All who commented "agreed that there is great improvement and progress." Acheson "predicted there will not be negotiations because that's not how the Communists operate. Instead there will be a subsiding of hostilities when the Communists finally give up." McGeorge Bundy and Clark Clifford were among those agreeing with Acheson. As for getting out of Vietnam altogether, "there was unanimous agreement that we should not." Said Bundy: "As impossible as it is undesirable." George Ball added that the U.S. should "clearly show the other side that we are creating the conditions to let them stop fighting." Clifford said wars will always "be unpopular" in America, but "we must go on because what we are doing is right. . . . recognizing this fact, I hope we don't get frustrated."[110] Belatedly, there was also some discussion of how to mobilize public opinion more effectively in support of the war, an area in which the administration had been curiously lagging, but no concrete agreement was reached in that regard.

In sum, the meeting of "the wise men" may have reassured the president, but it did nothing to improve the situation in Vietnam or on the diplomatic front, and, before long, fresh demands began to be voiced for a further softening of the American position. To Rusk, however, the "San Antonio formula," as it soon became known, was not open for further discussion. As he instructed the American embassy in New Delhi in January 1968, the Indian government should be informed that "it will do no good . . . to try to negotiate us down from the San Antonio formula without having something solid from Hanoi that moves tangibly in the direction of peace." Instead, Rusk went on, Hanoi was "pouring its forces in and through the demilitarized zone," so "we must decide whether to get out of [their] way or stop [them]. We have decided to stop [them]."[111]

Within a matter of days, the war reached another violent turning point. During the Tet holiday, on 31 January 1968, about eighty-thousand North Vietnamese regulars and Viet-Cong guerrillas struck with unexpected ferocity at major urban areas throughout South Vietnam. For a few hours, even the security of the American embassy compound in Saigon appeared in doubt. It is true that, within three days, the Communist Tet offensive was beaten back, and it was clear that the Communist side had suffered enormous casualties. But the psychological effect was devastating. Whatever they might say in public, Johnson and Rusk soon realized that the political mood in the United States had been changed, perhaps irreversibly, as a result.[112]

Senator Fulbright quickly saw his opportunity and on 11–12 March 1968 held a second series of televised committee hearings on Vietnam. The secretary appeared as a witness for nearly twelve hours, unfailingly patient and polite as always, but unready to yield further ground. "Most of the proposals that we get," he declared, "are variations of one sort or another of efforts that have already been made at one time or another." Clearly he held out no hope for early negotiations with Hanoi, for which pressure appeared to be mounting steadily.[113]

Against that background, on 25–26 March 1968 the president summoned "the wise men" a second time. He was planning soon to deliver another major address to the nation on Vietnam, and he wanted their counsel and, he hoped also, their continued support. Instead, Johnson quickly found their mood transformed by the events of Tet and its political aftermath at home. Leading off, McGeorge Bundy declared: "There is a very significant shift in our position. When we last met we saw reason for hope." Acheson concurred: "Neither the effort of the Government of Vietnam nor the effort of the U.S. government can succeed in the time we have left. . . . We cannot build an independent Vietnam." Said George Ball: "I share Acheson's view. I have felt . . . since 1961 that our objectives are not attainable." Acheson added that Supreme Court Justice Abe Fortas—a trusted Johnson adviser and strong supporter on Vietnam—"had said we are not trying to win a military victory. The issue is can we by military means keep the North Vietnamese off the South Vietnamese. I do not think we can." Virtually all participants agreed there should be a reduction in U.S. bombing, as a way of trying to open serious negotiations. Rusk, long anxious to do all he could for peace, had no difficulty agreeing.[114]

On Sunday night, 31 March 1968, the president went on national television to tell the country what he had in mind in Vietnam. He announced a significant reduction in American bombing, but his declaration was overshadowed by the dramatic announcement with which he closed his address: "I shall not seek, and I will not accept, the nomination of my party for another term as your President."[115] In later years, it became conventional wisdom to assert that Johnson had been driven from office—or at least discouraged from seeking another term—by rising public opposition to the war. In fact, as the secretary well knew, the president had made up his mind months earlier, probably by the autumn of 1967. He had been in increasingly poor health for some time, and remembering the fate of Woodrow Wilson and Franklin Roosevelt, had decided it was time to leave. It was a judgment Rusk fully understood, his own strength long taxed to the limit.[116]

In a matter of days, Johnson appointed a negotiating team headed by Ambassadors-at-Large Averell Harriman and Cyrus R. Vance, formerly deputy secretary of defense, to go to Paris to meet with North Vietnamese representatives, to see if serious negotiations were at last possible. There followed six increasingly trying months. Harriman, with an eye on the upcoming U.S. presidential election, thought only a dramatic diplomatic breakthrough could save the embattled candidacy of Vice President Hubert H. Humphrey.[117] The South Vietnamese government was fearful of inadequate representation or further damaging concessions before substantive negotiations with Hanoi commenced. As Rusk recalled later:

There were times when Harriman's suggestions went further than the president and I wanted to go. During the summer he advocated a phased withdrawal of American troops that might have left North Vietnamese soldiers in place in South Vietnam. That, to me, was outright surrender. But I cannot fault Harriman or our team in Paris. They tried their best to move difficult negotiations forward under circumstances heavily complicated by the attitudes of both the South and the North Vietnamese.[118]

It remains one of the unexplained paradoxes of the Vietnam era that the protracted war did not lead to a parallel freeze in American-Soviet relations. In fact, as noted above, from his first days in office, Johnson was determined to continue to improve relations with Moscow, and his efforts were far from unsuccessful. As he recalled proudly in his memoirs: "The sum of our efforts was the conclusion of more significant agreements . . . in the years 1963–1969 than in the thirty years after we established diplomatic relations with the Soviet regime."[119] Doubtless the most important of these agreements was the nuclear nonproliferation treaty, nearly two years in the making, and finally signed by fifty-six nations at the White House on 1 July 1968. As Rusk told the Senate Foreign Relations Committee ten days later, "Nuclear proliferation could add a new and dangerous dimension to historic ethnic and territorial disputes between nations. . . . In short, nuclear weapons proliferation could stimulate a preventive war."[120]

This is not to say that the Brezhnev-Kosygin regime in Moscow had fundamentally altered its outlook on international affairs. For several years, the United States had been encouraging improved relations between West Germany and the Soviet Union and a general relaxation of tensions in Central Europe. Washington watched with hopeful admiration as a Marxist reform movement in Czechoslovakia, headed by Alexander Dubček, sought to achieve a measure of political and ideological autonomy. Here, in sum, were the roots of what was later to become known as "détente," but Moscow was clearly having none of it. On the evening of 20 August 1968, Ambassador Anatoly Dobrynin urgently requested an immediate meeting with the president, to inform him that, "at Prague's request," forces of the Warsaw Pact—numbering more than five hundred thousand—were moving into Czechoslovakia to snuff out what in that country and the West had become known as "socialism with a human face."[121]

The brutal Moscow-directed invasion of Czechoslovakia put a sudden end to what Johnson and Rusk had hoped would be another significant step in the improvement of East-West relations, the beginning of negotiations on the limitation of strategic nuclear arms (better known as SALT I). Indeed, the president had looked forward to traveling to the Soviet Union to initiate the talks before the November elections. With hundreds of Soviet tanks rumbling in the streets of Prague, such a trip was obviously out of the question. To the president's and the secretary's deep disappointment, it remained for the next administration to see what it could accomplish in the vital field of arms control.

That left the formal opening of Vietnam peace talks as the principal remaining item on the Johnson-Rusk diplomatic agenda. Behind the scenes, there was bitter disagreement about what specific assurances to demand of Hanoi before all American bombing of North Vietnam ceased and "productive negotiations" finally began.[122] The South Vietnamese government, understandably anxious about what the forthcoming negotiations might ultimately lead to, made its own last minute demands, hoping perhaps to obtain a more favorable settlement from a Republican negotiating team, in the event Richard Nixon won the election.

Following increasingly impassioned exchanges between Washington, Paris, and Saigon, Rusk—although this was unlike him—at last became rather impatient with the South Vietnamese leadership, before peace talks got under way on 8 November. They were to last more than four years, and to end with a document ironically called "Agreement on Ending the War and Restoring Peace in Vietnam," finally signed in Paris on 27 January 1973.[123] In a characteristic mixture of personal pride and ill-concealed rage, Nixon told a press conference: "We finally have achieved a peace with honor. . . . I know it gags some of you to write that phrase, but it is true."[124]

In fact, it was not true. Rusk was tragically correct when, in the late 1980s, he described the agreement as "in effect a surrender,"[125] and went on to say: "Any agreement that left North Vietnamese troops in South Vietnam meant the eventual takeover of South Vietnam. We knew this from North Vietnam's failure to comply with past agreements. If in 1961 President Kennedy and his advisers had had the 1973 agreements to look forward to, we wouldn't have made the effort. We could have had peace at any time on the basis by which we finally pulled our troops out in 1973. Our basic position throughout the Johnson years was that any settlement must require the withdrawal of North Vietnamese forces."[126] Twenty-seven months later, on 30 April 1975, Hanoi's forces marched into Saigon. For the Republic of Vietnam it was all over. Rusk's pursuit of the diplomacy of principle, seemingly, had failed.

IV

Rusk's departure from the State Department, on 20 January 1969, came to him as an enormous relief, for his eight-year tenure—second in length only to that of Cordell Hull under Franklin D. Roosevelt—had been exhaustively demanding.[127] Johnson conferred upon him the Presidential Medal of Freedom—the highest decoration awarded a civilian[128]—and to Mrs. Rusk he sent a deeply felt personal message: "The man who had served me most intelligently, faithfully and nobly is Dean Rusk."[129]

If the secretary's last years at the department had been almost unrelievedly difficult, in some ways even more painful times were to follow. Unlike some of his predecessors (and successors), who unhesitatingly condescended to the presidents they had once served,[130] he remained deliberately silent about his years in Washington. As he probably realized all too well, he could readily have made headlines and received the plaudits and rewards of the left-leaning academic and media establishments had he been willing to abjure the policies he had helped to shape or supported during the Kennedy and Johnson years. But the former secretary saw no reason to repudiate his carefully considered ideas and actions.

As a result, unlike Dean Acheson, who was never long out of the limelight after he left office in 1953,[131] Rusk found himself for years the subject of professional ostracism, journalistic condescension, and a deplorable lack of academic courtesy. For example, when the senior class at Mills College, where he had been a professor and dean of the faculty before World War II, invited him to return to deliver the commencement address in 1982, he was greeted with a carefully orchestrated antiwar protest. Like W. W. Rostow, another unrepentant Kennedy-Johnson loyalist, who found himself barred from a permanent post at leading institutions on both coasts and found a congenial new academic home at the University of Texas at Austin, in 1970 Rusk accepted the Sibley professorship of international law at the University of Georgia Law School, a position he held with great distinction until his retirement in 1984 at the age of seventy-five.

A generation later, how can we assess Dean Rusk's years as secretary of state? Of criticism—strong, petty, acidulous—there has long been no shortage. Robert Kennedy's proverbial hostility, for instance, is too well known to require more than passing mention.[132] In 1992, Averell Harriman's authorized biographer summed up many criticisms of Rusk's performance. The secretary, Harriman believed, "still had the personality and habits of a professional staff man. He could brilliantly distill convoluted policy debates into their purest expression and strip arguments clean of rhetoric. He made discretion and integrity a fetish, striving always to emulate his hero, George Marshall. . . . Personal differences made him uncomfortable; and if there were differences, he had a habit of keeping his opinion to himself as long as a matter remained unresolved. He held back when sharp exchanges arose in the presence of the president, preferring to remain after all the others had been heard and give his own recommendations in confidence. It was a style that made Harriman boil."[133]

Such criticisms, and others like them, probably came as no surprise to Rusk, and it seems unlikely that he took such attacks—and the reasoning behind them—seriously.[134] From all indications, he brought to the office a carefully defined view of what constituted the proper role of the secretary of state. As a student of comparative politics, he was well aware of the fact that, unlike his counterparts in London or Bonn, the American secretary of state possessed no constitutional or political autonomy. An Ernest Bevin or Willy Brandt would have been unthinkable in Washington. Instead, from his first days in charge of Foggy Bottom to his last, the secretary considered himself to be the president's top personal adviser on foreign policy, as well as head of the department principally charged with carrying out that policy. In the absence of persuasive evidence to the contrary, there is good reason to believe that his understanding of his position was essentially the same as John F. Kennedy's, and that Rusk experienced no difficulty adapting to Lyndon Johnson's rather more expansive view of the secretary's proper role.

To be sure, on some issues—for example, the Bay of Pigs operation and the larger question of summitry—Rusk disagreed with John F. Kennedy, and undoubtedly communicated his disagreement to the president. On the other hand, having done so, it never occurred to the secretary to consider resigning as a matter of conscience, when the president decided not to follow or to overrule his advice. For as some of his critics caustically noted, Rusk's role model was indeed George C. Marshall, and although the general, for instance, strongly disagreed with President Truman's position on the recognition of the new state of Israel in May 1948, the renowned Virginian never considered resigning as a matter of principle,[135] as Anthony Eden, for example is often (if quite mistakenly) supposed to have done in early 1938,[136] and as Cyrus R. Vance was in fact to do as Jimmy Carter's secretary of state in April 1980.[137]

As the arguments over Vietnam became increasingly envenomed in the 1960s, the secretary was often accused of being a Cold Warrior of the John Foster Dulles school, and it was not infrequently asserted that Rusk suffered from what might be called a "surfeit of history," that is to say that he viewed contemporary events largely as a replay of the pre–World War II era. This assessment of Rusk constitutes a serious misreading of his political outlook and diplomatic positions.

It is correct to say that, like Kennedy and Johnson, Rusk sought to avoid repeating the errors of Western politics and diplomacy before World War II. But he was no less concerned about similar mistakes after 1945, to which he frequently referred. And it is likewise true that his wartime military service in south Asia led him to appreciate the importance of the Pacific world in a way that most Atlantic-oriented officials and politicians in Washington probably did not. In any case, Berlin, Cuba, and Vietnam not withstanding, the secretary's search for improved relations with the communist world—including mainland China—never ceased.[138] Now and then, he would employ the term *détente*, usually associated with the Nixon-Kissinger 1970s. More often, Rusk would talk about "building bridges." But whatever his terminology, his overriding objectives remained always the same: the reduction of international tensions in an age of ominously spreading nuclear weapons and technology, the advance of human freedom throughout the world,[139] and, last but far from least, the reliability of America's pledged word.[140]

Those were and remained Rusk's principal themes, although he later acknowledged having underestimated Hanoi's readiness to absorb severe military punishment for its aggression against South Vietnam, and correspondingly overestimated American willingness to stay the course until the political independence of South Vietnam was assured, or at least, until Hanoi, Peking, and Moscow accepted South Vietnam's right to determine its future destiny as it saw fit.[141] As regards one other central issue Rusk remained utterly and proudly inflexible. Human freedom, the principle of self-government and self-determination, he strongly believed, was for all people, white and nonwhite, throughout the world. As the antiwar movement left little doubt, it was an idea whose time had apparently not yet arrived in the civil rights 1960s.[142]

In sum, it would not seem to stretch historical parallels unduly to suggest that, in our knowledge and assessment of Johnson, Rusk, and the international world of the 1960s, we stand in the early 1990s about where we stood in the 1930s as regards Woodrow Wilson, whose national and international stature and reputation had been strikingly diminished by the shattering defeat of the League of Nations in 1919, a stature and reputation which—as the late William L. Langer once demonstrated—was revived only during World War II.[143] Rusk, who remained in touch with intellectual trends and developments, was probably not unaware of the fact that, as the World War I president's illuminating personal papers, for decades tightly closed by his misguidedly devoted widow, began at last to be published in the 1960s and 1970s,[144] Wilson's historic place in American and international history was reaffirmed beyond further serious challenge.[145]

So, like Lyndon Johnson, Rusk understandably trusted in the early opening and publication of the full historical record of all principal powers of the 1960s. It is hardly accidental that, both in his memoirs and his regrettably still unpublished oral histories of Kennedy and Johnson, Rusk repeatedly urged historians to look up the *contemporary* record and to base their conclusions on *that* record. As noted above, it was the publication of the so-called negotiating volumes of the purloined Pentagon Papers in 1983 that confirmed the secretary's continued determination to seek a lasting diplomatic settlement of the Vietnam war. Unfortunately, a decade later, the newly available documents remain virtually unknown, and most histories and other accounts of the war make no mention of them, as if they had never appeared or did not exist in the first place.[146]

Since 1988, the Department of State has published a special series of illuminating volumes on Vietnam in its noted documentary series, *Foreign Relations of the United States*.[147] As this is written, in late 1993, the remaining volumes covering the years from 1965 to 1968 are yet to appear. But the available record, published and unpublished, leaves no doubt about Rusk's performance as secretary of state. Throughout those years, he had pursued high principles—principles as old as the American diplomatic tradition itself—and he had good reason to believe that, when all the pertinent evidence finally became available, his imperturbable search for a meaningful reduction of international tension in the age of nuclear danger would be vindicated at last.

In the end, some readers may wonder if Dean Rusk was, to use the parlance of the Vietnam era, a hawkish dove or a dovish hawk. Understandably intriguing as it is, the question is impossible to answer categorically. We can, however, assuredly say this: All his adult life, he was a firm believer in certain fundamental values and principles, especially those enshrined in the Charter of the United Nations.

Rusk eschewed headline-making talk and reserved his most important counsel for the president of the United States. Above all, he was deeply concerned about the continuing possibility of atomic war in an era of ever more powerful and proliferating nuclear weapons. That concern led him to pursue peace and human freedom as deliberately and passionately as any modern American statesman.

Notes

1. The *Washington Post,* 13 Dec. 1960, for example, described Rusk as "a hard-minded yet imaginative man who knows the complexities of a changing world without being awed by them . . . a brilliant public servant." *The Times* of London reported from Washington, 13 Dec. 1960, that "above all, somewhat like Mr. Kennedy," Rusk "is a man who starts from realities rather than dogmas. . . . Presented with the Gordian knot, he would settle down to untie it. He has shown a valuable ability, often lacking here, for seeing the United States as others see her and understanding the doubts her policy sometimes arouses."

2. *Senate Committee on Foreign Relations,* 87th Cong., 1st sess., *Hearings on the Nomination of Dean Rusk, Secretary of State-designate* (Washington, D.C., 1961), 18.

3. For Rusk's account of his family background and early years, see his *As I Saw It,* as told to Richard Rusk, edited by Daniel S. Papp (New York, 1990), a work of unfailing interest and importance that repays careful reading and study, chaps. 1–2; and the invaluable biographical account of Thomas J. Schoenbaum, *Waging Peace and War: Dean Rusk in the Truman, Kennedy and Johnson Years* (New York, 1988), based on a wealth of unpublished materials (henceforth cited as Schoenbaum, *Rusk*), chap. 1.

4. Rusk, *As I Saw It,* 62.

5. Ibid., 66.

6. See, for instance, Warren I. Cohen, *The American Revisionists: The Lessons of Intervention in World War I* (Chicago, 1967), chaps. 5–7; William E. Leuchtenburg, *Franklin D. Roosevelt and the New Deal, 1932–1940* (New York, 1963), 215 ff; and Francis L. Loewenheim, ed., *The Historian and the Diplomat: The Role of History and Historians in American Foreign Policy* (New York, 1967), 44 ff.; Rusk, *As I Saw It,* chap. 5.

7. Frank Freidel, *Franklin D. Roosevelt—Launching the New Deal* (Boston, 1973), 118 ff.

8. *The People Decide—1936,* vol. 5 of *The Public Papers and Addresses of Franklin*

D. Roosevelt (New York, 1938), 289. For the background and significance of Roosevelt's Chautauqua address on 14 Aug. 1936, see Francis L. Loewenheim, "FDR Speech Dramatic—and Wrong," *Houston Post,* 16 Aug. 1986.

9. In fact, Ambassador Joseph P. Kennedy failed to deliver the president's message as specifically instructed by Under Secretary of State Sumner Welles, and it never reached Chamberlain. See Francis L. Loewenheim, "The Untold Story of FDR and Munich— and its Cover-Up," *Houston Chronicle,* 1 Oct. 1978.

10. Rusk, *As I Saw It,* 90.

11. For Rusk's account of his wartime military service, see ibid., 99 ff., and Schoenbaum, *Rusk,* 73 ff.

12. See, for instance, Francis L. Loewenheim, Harold D. Langley, and Manfred Jonas, eds., *Roosevelt and Churchill: Their Secret Wartime Correspondence* (New York, 1975), 183–84, 190–92; and James MacGregor Burns, *Roosevelt: The Soldier of Freedom* (New York, 1970), 238 ff.

13. Rusk, *As I Saw It,* 422. See also Walter LaFeber, "Roosevelt, Churchill and Indo-China 1942–1945," *American Historical Review* 80 (Dec. 1975): 1287 ff.

14. For Rusk's early postwar career, see Rusk, *As I Saw It,* chap. 8; and Schoenbaum, *Rusk,* chap. 4.

15. Dean Acheson, *Present at the Creation: My Years at the State Department* (New York, 1969), 255.

16. Bruce Cumings, *Liberation and the Emergence of Separate Regimes 1945– 1947,* vol. 1 of *The Origins of the Korean War* (Princeton, 1981), 120–21. See also 12 July 1950 memorandum from Rusk to G. Bernard Noble, Chief of the Division of Historical Policy Research, *Foreign Relations of the United States: 1945* (Washington, 1969) 6:1039.

17. Rusk, *As I Saw It,* 130–35. Paul Y. Hammond, *LBJ and the Presidential Management of Foreign Relations* (Austin, 1992), 44. For Marshall's view of those years, see the authorized biography of Forrest C. Pogue, *George C. Marshall: Statesman* (New York, 1987), chaps. 20–23.

18. See below, 524–25.

19. Rusk, *As I Saw It,* 155–56.

20. For Rusk's view of the Truman years, see ibid., 156.

21. Ibid., 157.

22. See, for instance, Alan Bullock, *Ernest Bevin: Foreign Secretary 1945–1951* (New York, 1983), 332 ff., 559 ff, and above.

23. Rusk, *As I Saw It,* 145, 153.

24. Ibid., 152.

25. Acheson, *Present at the Creation,* 272 ff.

26. See below, 505, 507–8.

27. See Acheson, *Present at the Creation,* 431–32. As Acheson recalled the episode in his memoirs: "Dean Rusk came to me with an offer that won my high respect and gratitude. He said that he was applying for demotion from his then post of Deputy Under Secretary for substantive matters. He would, if I wished, take on . . . responsibilities for Far Eastern Affairs. The area and its problems were not unfamiliar to him, as he had served on General Stilwell's staff in the China-Burma-India theater during the war and had, as part of his present duties, been in close touch with them. The President would, I told him, be as happy and grateful as I was for this offer 'above and beyond the call of duty'—as, indeed, it was—and I accepted it at once. He served faithfully and suc-

cessfully in this most difficult of posts. Years later, when President-elect Kennedy in December 1960 asked me to make recommendations for the Secretaryship of State in his Cabinet, I told him this story and placed Dean Rusk's name very high on the list."

28. Rusk, *As I Saw It*, 175.

29. *Foreign Relations of the United States* (henceforth cited as *FRUS*), 1950, vol. 7, *Korea* (Washington, D.C., 1976), 958.

30. *FRUS*, 1952–1954, vol. 13 (part 1), *Indochina* (Washington, D.C., 1982), 83.

31. For the text of the treaty, see *Department of State Bulletin* 31, no. 795 (20 Sept. 1954): 393–96.

32. See above, chapter 6.

33. See above, chapter 7.

34. *FRUS*, 1958–1960, vol. 16, *East Asia-Pacific Region; Cambodia; Laos* (Washington, D.C., 1992), 1029.

35. Stephen E. Ambrose, *The President*, vol. 2 of *Eisenhower* (New York, 1984), 614. According to Fred Greenstein and Richard H. Immerman, the president-elect may have "misperceived" what Eisenhower was trying to convey. "What Did Eisenhower Tell Kennedy About Indo-China? The Politics of Misperception," *Journal of American History* 72, no. 2 (September 1992).

36. Arthur M. Schlesinger, Jr., *Robert F. Kennedy and His Times* (Boston, 1978), 222.

37. For the background of Rusk's appointment, see especially Harris Wofford, *Of Kennedys and Kings: Making Sense of the Sixties* (New York, 1980), 78 ff.

38. Dean Rusk, "The President," *Foreign Affairs* 38, no. 3 (April 1960): 353–69.

39. See, for instance, Edwin O. Guthman and Jeffrey Shulman, eds., *Robert Kennedy: In His Own Words* (New York, 1988), 287.

40. As John Bartlow Martin, *Adlai Stevenson and the World* (New York, 1977), 242 ff., makes clear, these differences have been considerably exaggerated.

41. For Rusk's strong views on civil rights see Rusk, *As I Saw It*, 586 ff. See also Arthur M. Schlesinger, Jr., *A Thousand Days: John F. Kennedy in the White House* (Boston, 1965), chap. 21, for the administration's policy toward Africa, white and black.

42. Rusk, *As I Saw It*, 398, 426–28. Schoenbaum, *Rusk*, 328, 332.

43. Richard E. Welch, Jr., *Response to Revolution: The United States and the Cuban Revolution, 1959–1961* (Chapel Hill, 1985), 59–60.

44. Ambrose, *The President*, 608–10.

45. Schlesinger, Jr., *A Thousand Days*, 233.

46. Chester Bowles, *Promises to Keep: My Years in Public Life 1941–1969* (New York, 1971), 332, and Rusk, *As I Saw It*, 212. As Rusk elaborated in an interview at Athens, Georgia, on 18 May 1987: "I had been a colonel of infantry, chief of war plans, for General Stilwell, in World War II. As a colonel of infantry, I knew that this Cuban brigade didn't have a chance in hell in the Bay of Pigs. But in the spring of '61 I was not a colonel of infantry, I was the Secretary of State. And I did not throw myself into the military aspects of that problem in the way that the President should have." Quoted in James G. Blight and David A. Welch, *On the Brink: Americans and Soviets Reexamine the Cuban Missile Crisis* (New York, 1989), 177–78.

47. For a reliable summary of these meetings, see Schlesinger, Jr., *A Thousand Days*, 349–65.

48. Rusk, *As I Saw It*, 220–21.

49. See, for example, Michael Beschloss, *The Crisis Years: Kennedy and Khrushchev 1960–1963* (New York, 1991), 194 ff.

50. See Francis L. Loewenheim, "Records Refute Kennedy 'Weakness' During Cold War Summit," *Cincinnati Post,* 21 June 1991, now confirmed by the official American record published in *Berlin Crisis 1961–1962,* vol. 14 of *Foreign Relations of the United States 1961–1963* (Washington, 1994), 87–88. Nor does the available record substantiate the widely held theory—repeated, for example, in Richard Reeves, *President Kennedy* (New York, 1993)—that after the Bay of Pigs and the Vienna summit, the president "had to take a stand against Communism somewhere," and that he chose Vietnam. In early 1963, Kennedy repeated his innermost feelings in a personal letter to the sister of an American helicopter gunner killed in Vietnam (quoted in Reeves, *Kennedy,* 449–50):

> Americans are in Vietnam because we have determined that this country must not fall under Communist domination.
>
> It is also apparent that the Communist attempt to take over Vietnam is only part of a larger plan for bringing the entire area of Southeast Asia under their domination. Though it is only a small part of the area geographically, Viet Nam is now the most crucial. . . . Your brother was in Viet Nam because the threat to the Viet Namese people is, in the long run, a threat to the Free World community, and ultimately a threat to us also.

51. Rusk, *As I Saw It,* 223–24. "We were appallingly badly prepared," Willy Brandt wrote later in his memoirs, *My Life in Politics* (New York, 1992), 48.

52. See Peter Wyden, *Wall: The Inside Story of Divided Berlin* (New York, 1989), 26–29.

53. Douglas Brinkley, *Dean Acheson: The Cold War Years 1953–71* (New Haven, 1992), 148 ff.

54. Rusk, *As I Saw It,* 222. See also *Berlin Crisis 1961–1962,* passim.

55. Hans-Peter Schwarz, *Die Ära Adenauer: Epochenwechsel 1957–1963* (Stuttgart, 1983), 144 ff. Jean Edward Smith, *Lucius D. Clay: An American Life* (New York, 1990), 650 ff.

56. Dean Rusk, Oral History Interview, John F. Kennedy Library, 13 Mar. 1970, 175.

57. See below, chapter 18.

58. See Hans-Peter Schwarz, *Adenauer: Der Staatsmann, 1952–1967* (Stuttgart, 1991), 650–71, and Hans Jürgen Küsters, "Konrad Adenauer und Willy Brandt in der Berlin-Krise 1958–1963," *Vierteljahrshefte für Zeitgeschichte* 40, no. 4 (October 1992): 527 ff.

59. See above, chapter 7. See also Hans W. Gatzke, *Germany and the United States: A 'Special Relationship?'* (Cambridge, Mass., 1980), 190 ff. The shadowy scheme called International Access Authority is briefly illuminated in *Berlin Crisis 1961–1962.*

60. Rusk, *As I Saw It,* 225.

61. For the latest documentary accounts and assessments, see, for instance, Blight and Welch, *On the Brink,* and Lawrence Change and Peter Kornbluh, eds., *The Cuban Missile Crisis, 1962: A National Security Archive Documents Reader* (New York, 1992).

62. Quoted in Robert Smith Thompson, *The Missiles of October: The Declassified Story of John F. Kennedy and the Cuban Missile Crisis* (New York, 1992), 129.

63. *Department of State Bulletin* 47, no. 1216 (15 Oct. 1962): 595.

64. Schlesinger, Jr., *A Thousand Days,* 805. See below, chapter 21.

65. Rusk repeatedly defended his own role as well. As John Hightower of the Associated Press reported on 22 Aug. 1965, Rusk "said that the responsibility of the

Secretary of State was to advise the President and he did not think he should commit himself before all the facts were in." Quoted in Graham T. Allison, *Essence of Decision: Explaining the Cuban Missile Crisis* (Boston, 1971), 319, note 72. As Rusk put it in an interview in Athens, Georgia, 18 May 1987, "I felt that as Secretary of State I should withhold my judgment and take a look at the work of each of the working groups and then make a recommendation to the President as Secretary of State." Quoted in Blight and Welch, *On the Brink,* 176.

66. Rusk, *As I Saw It,* 412. See above, chapter 16.

67. Rusk never doubted the madness of nuclear war. As he put it in an 1987 interview, "those who really understand nuclear weapons understand that nuclear war is simply that war which must not be fought. . . . Unfortunately, people with brains have injected a lot of complications into what is utterly simple. The idea of limited nuclear war is nonsense. The idea of a prolonged nuclear war from which one side can emerge with some sort of advantage is nonsense." Quoted in Blight and Welch, *On the Brink,* 180. "I believe," Rusk said, "that the Cuban missile crisis was the most dangerous crisis that the world has ever seen. . . . With fumbling on either side, this could have resulted in nuclear war" (p. 179).

68. Glenn T. Seaborg with the assistance of Benjamin S. Loeb, *Kennedy, Khrushchev, and the Test Ban* (Berkeley, 1981), 220 f.

69. For the text, see *Public Papers: John F. Kennedy, 1963* (Washington, D.C., 1964), no. 232.

70. For the text of the test ban treaty, see *Department of State Bulletin* 49, no. 1259 (12 Aug. 1963): 239.

71. *Department of State Bulletin* 49, no. 1262 (2 Sept. 1963): 358.

72. For the text of the Laos agreement, see *Department of State Bulletin* 47, no. 1207 (13 Aug. 1962): 259–63.

73. Rusk, *As I Saw It,* 428 ff.

74. *Department of State Bulletin* 17, no. 1210 (3 Sept. 1962): 344. "The global struggle for freedom and against Communist imperialism," Rusk said, "is our main business in the State Department" (p. 343).

75. Dean Rusk, John F. Kennedy Library, Oral History Interview, 2 Dec. 1969, 7.

76. See, for instance, N. S. Khrushchev, *The National Liberation Movement: Selected Passages 1956–1963* (Moscow, 1963), 23–24.

77. *FRUS, 1961–1963,* vol. 1, *Vietnam 1961* (Washington, D.C., 1988), 125.

78. Ibid., 550–51.

79. *New York Times,* 19 Feb. 1962, 1. For Rusk's important role in this episode and the bombing halt announcement that followed, see the carefully documented account of David M. Barrett, *Uncertain Warriors: Lyndon Johnson and His Advisers* (Lawrence, Kan., 1993), 142 ff., 148 ff., and 153 ff.

80. For Ball's retrospective account, see his memoirs, *The Past Has Another Pattern* (New York, 1982), chap. 24. See also David L. DiLeo, *George Ball, Vietnam and the Rethinking of Containment* (Chapel Hill, 1991).

81. *Public Papers: John F. Kennedy, 1962* (Washington, D.C., 1963), 12–13.

82. Public opinion tended to be divided on specific issues but generally supportive of the war until the end of the Johnson administration. See Peter Braestrup, *Big Story: How the American Press and Television Reported and Interpreted the Crisis of Tet 1968 in*

Vietnam and Washington (Boulder, 1977), 679 ff., and William Conrad Gibbons, *The U.S. Government and the Vietnam War: Executive and Legislative Roles and Relationships,* vol. 14, January–July 1965 (Princeton, N.J., 1989), 141 ff.

83. Rusk, *As I Saw It,* 427. But in his memoirs Rusk also wrote: "Although I was out of government and watching only from the sidelines I thought the SEATO Treaty was a mistake . . . but I think the die for American commitment to Southeast Asia was cast in 1955. When the United States signed that treaty, SEATO became the law of the land and linked Vietnam to the general structure of collective security."

84. Ibid. According to Lawrence J. Bassett and Stephen E. Pelz: "In spite of Rusk's claim, the Eisenhower administration had not formally committed Kennedy to defend South Vietnam." See "The Failed Search for Victory: Vietnam and The Politics of War," in *Kennedy's Quest for Victory: American Foreign Policy 1961–1963* ed. Thomas G. Paterson (New York, 1989), 230.

85. See, for instance, Roger Hilsman, *To Move a Nation: The Politics of Foreign Policy in the Administration of John F. Kennedy* (New York, 1967), chaps. 31–33.

86. *Public Papers: John F. Kennedy, 1963* (Washington, D.C., 1964), 815.

87. Lyndon B. Johnson, *The Vantage Point: Perspectives of the Presidency, 1963–1969* (New York, 1971), 18 f; *Public Papers: Lyndon B. Johnson, 1963–1964* (Washington, D.C., 1965). All the same, from his first days in office, Johnson was deeply concerned about the Vietnam War. On 30 November 1963, in a telephone conversation with an old personal friend, Donald C. Cook, head of the American Electric Power Service Corporation, there was the following exchange ("The Johnson Tapes," *The Economist,* 2 Oct. 1993):

> LBJ: I want to start looking for some good people because our great problem . . . we need top-flight people. . . . for instance, we've got nobody to run the war in Vietnam for us . . . and we need the ablest man that we've got . . . the toughest chief of mission you can have. . . . [Henry Cabot] Lodge [ambassador to South Vietnam, appointed by President Kennedy in June 1963] is just as much an administrator as he is a utility maintenance [man] . . . and he just . . .
> DC: He never had to do it. . . .
> LBJ: He never had to do it and doesn't know one damn thing about . . . just leaks to the press and keeps everybody fighting each other. . . . We need an able tough guy to go there . . . and now that's not anything to be desired by anybody. . . . I don't imagine those eight or ten thousand boys out there desire it either—but we've got to either get in or get out . . . or get off . . . and we need a damn, tough cookie . . . somebody that can say, now, this is it . . . and has enough judgment to realise that he can't make . . . Vietnam into an America overnight.

88. For the Johnson-Rusk relationship on Vietnam, Barrett, *Uncertain Warriors,* supersedes all previous accounts; see especially 17, 31, 68, 87–88, 130, 133–34, 142–43, 154, 156, 158, 167, 169, 191, 228, 241, and 249.

89. *FRUS, 1964–1968,* vol. 1, *Vietnam 1964* (Washington, D.C., 1992), 466.

90. Rusk, *As I Saw It,* 461–62; Johnson, *Vantage Point,* 67–68; Victor Levant, *Quiet Complicity: Canadian Involvement in the Vietnam War* (Toronto, 1986), 178 ff.

91. *American Foreign Policy: Current Documents, 1964* (Washington, D.C., 1967), 975.

92. *FRUS, 1964–1968,* vol. 1, *Vietnam 1964,* 615.

93. Quoted in Ernest Gruening, *Many Battles* (New York, 1973), 472, to which McNamara added on that occasion: "Even with the advantage of hindsight, I find that the essential facts of the two attacks appear today as they did then, when they were fully explored with this committee and other members of Congress" (quoted in Deborah Shapley, *Promise and Power: The Life and Times of Robert McNamara* (Boston, 1993), 454). The Defense Secretary's unequivocal statements did not keep Gruening from asserting that "it is not incorrect to say that the United States was lied into the war." See also below, note 101.

94. *Public Papers: Johnson, 1963–1964*, 2:953. A quarter of a century later, when he had become bitterly anti-Vietnam, McNamara told a biographer: "I don't believe that the President, or I, or Dean Rusk, or [National Security adviser McGeorge] Mac Bundy were planning, in the sense of anticipating or embarking upon 'overt war' with North Vietnam in 1964. I know that the President didn't intend 'overt war' and I didn't intend 'overt war' in 1964. Johnson didn't have plans for military action other than to continue as we were" (quoted in Shapley, *McNamara*, 305).

95. *American Foreign Policy: Current Documents, 1964*, 998.

96. Quoted in Marvin Kalb and Elie Abel, *Roots of Involvement: The U.S. in Asia 1784–1971* (New York, 1971), 187 n.

97. See Brian Van DeMark, *Into the Quagmire: Lyndon Johnson and the Escalation of the Vietnam War* (New York, 1991), 83–84. For a long time, the overwhelmingly antiwar writing on Vietnam maintained, or suggested, that Johnson took the major escalation decisions largely on his own, following limited consultation with a few of his more hawkish advisers. That improbable view, contradicted by a wealth of available evidence, is disposed of by Barrett's impressively detailed *Uncertain Warriors*.

98. For the text of the address, see *Public Papers: Johnson, 1965* (Washington, D.C. 1966): no. 172.

99. The latest account of this fateful struggle is in August Heckscher, *Woodrow Wilson* (New York, 1991), 587 ff.

100. Quoted in *The Vietnam Hearings* (New York, 1966), 293–94. For the complete text, see *Supplemental Foreign Assistance: Fiscal Year 1966—Vietnam, Hearings Before the Committee on Foreign Relations*, United States Senate, 89th Cong., 2d sess., S. 2793 (Washington, D.C., 1966).

101. Preparing his memoirs for publication in 1971, Johnson was determined not to be "scooped" by publication of the Pentagon Papers. For a summary of the administration's peace efforts, and what happened to them, see *Vantage Point*, 579–91. If the *New York Times* made any efforts to obtain the withheld material, or was seriously concerned by the imbalance created by its unavailability, the story has not come to light. For James Reston's subsequent defense of the *Times*, of which he was at that time vice president, see his *Deadline: A Memoir* (New York, 1991), 328 ff. For Rusk's understandable criticism of the Pentagon Papers, see *As I Saw It*, 575–577. Some years after the *New York Times*'s publication of portions of the Pentagon Papers, William P. Bundy, during most of 1964 assistant secretary of state for Far Eastern affairs, and in a position to know about such matters, told an interviewer: "I must say I consider [those *New York Times* stories based on this material] to put it mildly, uneven and in some respects quite misleading, particularly misleading on the 1964 period and whether there was a Johnsonian decision that he was going to get into this war, that he was concealing this during the election year, that the Gulf of Tonkin was a put-up job. All of that I think is

historically wrong and put together by innuendo and by the misleading use of snippets of evidence, that it's bad history." Quoted in Michael Charlton and Anthony Moncrieff, *Many Reasons Why: The American Involvement in Vietnam* (New York, 1978), 186.

102. Edited by Professor George C. Herring of the University of Kentucky, the 906-page volume remains indispensable even with its occasional deletions. As of late 1993, the State Department was unable to say when those passages would at last be made available.

103. See, for instance, Harold Wilson, *The Labour Government 1964–1970: A Personal Record* (London, 1971), 355 ff. and Ben Pimlott, *Harold Wilson* (London, 1992), 458 ff.

104. *Department of State Bulletin* 61, no. 1456 (22 May 1967): 787.

105. Quoted in Robert M. Hathaway, *Great Britain and the United States: Special Relations Since World War II* (New York, 1990), 91.

106. For an account of this episode, see Abba Eban, *Personal Witness: Israel Through My Eyes* (New York, 1992), 382 ff.

107. Rusk, *As I Saw It*, 389–90.

108. *Public Papers: Lyndon B. Johnson, 1967* (Washington, D.C., 1968), 2: no. 409.

109. The best minutes are probably those in meeting notes file at the Lyndon B. Johnson Library, on which the following is based, but see also Clark M. Clifford with Richard Holbrooke, *Counsel to the President: A Memoir* (New York, 1991), 454 ff., and Brinkley, *Dean Acheson*, 247–48.

110. By the time he published his memoirs in mid-1991, Clifford was not inclined to dwell on his more hawkish positions before 1967–1968.

111. Rusk, *As I Saw It*, 467.

112. On the gap between what happened in Vietnam and what many Americans were persuaded to believe, see Peter Braestrup, *Big Story: How the American Press and Television Reported and Interpreted the Crisis of Tet 1968 in Vietnam and Washington* (New Haven, 1983).

113. Rusk quoted in *New York Times*, 12 March 1968, 16. For the complete text, see *Foreign Assistance Act of 1968: Part 1—Vietnam. Hearings Before the Committee on Foreign Relations,* United States Senate, 90th Cong., 2d sess., S. 3091 (Washington, D.C., 1968).

114. See Tom Johnson's notes at the LBJ Library and the accounts by and about Clifford and Acheson.

115. *Public Papers: Lyndon B. Johnson, 1968–1969* (Washington, D.C., 1970), 1:476. For the background of Johnson's address, see also his *Vantage Point*, 365 ff., and Francis L. Loewenheim, "LBJ Had Concluded His Day Was Over," *Houston Post*, 27 Mar. 1988.

116. Rusk, *As I Saw It*, 483, 534. "In retrospect," Rusk wrote in his memoirs, "I worked too hard at my job. One reason George Marshall was so effective at State was that he did only those things which only the Secretary of State can do."

117. This aspect of Harriman's Paris labors is (understandably) downplayed by his authorized biographer Rudy Abramson, *Spanning a Century: The Life of W. Averell Harriman 1891–1986* (New York, 1992), chap. 25, but confirmed by his unpublished papers at the Library of Congress, as well as Abramson, p. 667. To Harriman, "ending the war was an urgent matter . . . but even that paled in comparison to the necessity of keeping Nixon out of the White House."

118. Rusk, *As I Saw It,* 490.

119. Johnson, *The Vantage Point,* 476. In his memoirs, *Multiple Exposure: An American Ambassador's Unique Perspective on East-West Issues* (New York, 1978), 149, 152, Jacob D. Beam recalls:

> When I was assigned to Prague in August 1966, de-Stalinization had not yet caught up with Czechoslovakia, and Secretary Rusk realized there was little that could be accomplished there. He asked me, however, even at the risk of our appearing naive, to start off by trying to interest the Czechoslovak government in a reasonable and independent approach to the Vietnamese conflict. . . .
>
> I soon came to the conclusion that President Johnson's program of "building bridges" with Eastern Europe was neither for [President Antonin] Novotny nor for me."

120. *Department of State Bulletin* 59, no. 1514 (29 July 1968): 132.

121. According to Willy Brandt, then West German foreign minister, President de Gaulle complained to Chancellor Kurt Georg Kiesinger "that the Federal Republic had encouraged the Prague reformers and must thus take some of the blame for the tragedy, and—as a kind of confidential aside—that Brezhnev had previously ascertained from President Johnson that the United States would do nothing." *My Life in Politics* (New York, 1992), 205. See also Francis L. Loewenheim, "The LBJ Papers and the Assault on Prague," *Plain Dealer* (Cleveland), 27 Aug. 1988.

122. For Clifford's one-sided version, see his *Counsel to the President,* 536 ff.

123. For the full text, see *Department of State Bulletin* 68, no. 1755 (12 Feb. 1973): 169–88.

124. *Public Papers: Richard Nixon, 1973* (Washington, D.C., 1975), no. 12. See also Stephen E. Ambrose, *Ruin and Recovery 1973–1990,* vol. 3 of *Nixon* (New York, Simon and Schuster, 1991) p. 56.

125. Rusk, *As I Saw It,* 491. For a contemporary view, see Francis L. Loewenheim, "The Terms Amount to Surrender," *New York Times,* 1 Dec. 1972.

126. Rusk, *As I Saw It,* 491.

127. "I almost floated like a balloon," he said after watching Nixon take the oath of office. Lyndon Johnson felt a similar sense of relief. Schoenbaum, *Rusk,* 491.

128. *Public Papers: Lyndon B. Johnson, 1968–1969* (Washington, D.C., 1970), 2: no. 691.

129. Warren I. Cohen, *Dean Rusk* (Totowa, N.J., 1980), 316.

130. This unrewarding genre appears to have begun with Robert Lansing's writings on Woodrow Wilson. Its most recent examples are the autobiographical accounts of Alexander M. Haig, Jr., concerning his short-lived term as secretary of state under Ronald Reagan.

131. This is a notable feature of Brinkley's interestingly detailed *Dean Acheson— The Cold War Years.*

132. See, for instance, Schlesinger, Jr., *Robert Kennedy,* 433.

133. Abramson, *Harriman,* p. 614.

134. See, for instance, the conclusion of Cohen, *Dean Rusk* (330): "In the mid-1960s, some liberals shed their universalism and recognized the irrelevance of liberal democracy and a Eurocentric peace system for much of Asia and Africa. They concluded, as more radical thinkers had long before, that anti-Communism was senseless when Communism might be the best alternative offered a people. Rusk, however,

remained loyal to his President and to an earlier vision. He thus betrayed his own better instincts, the interests of his country, the principles of the UN. Much may be said in mitigation, but never enough."

135. See Pogue, *Marshall: Statesman*, 371 ff., to which may be added Francis L. Loewenheim, "Israel's Recognition Nearly Didn't Happen," *Houston Post*, 14 May 1988, and "Israel Recognition Didn't Come Easily," *Sunday Oregonian*, (Portland), 14 May 1989, based on the unpublished Clifford papers at the Harry S. Truman Library.

136. See Francis L. Loewenheim, "An Illusion that Changed History: New Light on the History and Historiography of American Peace Moves Before Munich," in Daniel R. Beaver, ed., *Some Pathways in Twentieth Century History: Essays in Honor of Reginald Charles McGrane* (Detroit, 1969), 177–178, 184–85. Written in 1966–1967, its conclusions are confirmed by the *Documents on British Foreign Policy 1919–1939*, 2d series, vol. 19, *European Affairs, 1 July 1937–4 August 1938*, edited by W. N. Medlicott and Douglas Dakin, assisted by Gillian Bennett (London, 1982), chaps. 5–7.

137. See Cyrus Vance, *Hard Choices: Critical Years in America's Foreign Policy* (New York, 1983), chap. 18, and David McLellan, *Cyrus Vance* (Totowa, N.J., 1983), 160–61.

138. The opening of Mao's Cultural Revolution, with its hyperxenophobic anti-Westernism, did nothing to dissuade Johnson from continuing to seek improved relations with Peking. See, for instance, his elaborately drafted nationally televised address to the American Alumni Council on 12 July 1966. *Public Papers: Lyndon B. Johnson, 1966* (Washington, D.C., 1967), no. 325.

139. This emerges unmistakably from his carefully crafted speeches and statements, published in *The Winds of Freedom* (Boston, 1963), which unfortunately cover only the period from January 1961 to August 1962.

140. "For Rusk," as Johnson's top domestic aide, Joseph A. Califano, put it in his memoirs, *The Triumph and Tragedy of Lyndon Johnson* (New York, 1991), 36, "the fundamental point was to stand by our word."

141. Rusk, *As I Saw It*, 472–73.

142. Ibid., 581 ff., 586 ff.

143. William L. Langer, *Explorations in Crisis: Papers on International History*, ed. Carl E. Schorske and Elizabeth Schorske (Cambridge, Mass., 1969), 300 ff., 348–49.

144. See the indispensable volumes of Arthur S. Link and associates, eds., *The Papers of Woodrow Wilson*, especially vol. 41 (24 January–6 April 1917) (Princeton, N.J., 1983), and its sequels.

145. See, for instance, the new generation of (West) German scholarship represented by Klaus Schwabe, *Woodrow Wilson, Revolutionary Germany and Peacemaking, 1918–1919: Missionary Diplomacy and the Realities of Power* (Chapel Hill, 1985).

146. Clifford, *Counsel to the President;* Kai Bird, *The Chairman: John J. McCloy: The Making of the American Establishment* (New York, 1992), chap. 26; and Abramson, *Harriman*, are among major recent accounts ignoring the "negotiating volumes" of the Pentagon Papers. Shapley, *McNamara*, lists them in her bibliography, without having made evident use of them. For their continuing significance, see Francis L. Loewenheim, "Times Used [Only] Part of Pentagon Papers," *Oregonian* (Portland), 10 June 1991.

147. See, for instance, the discussion of these volumes, in *The Economist*, 18 Jan. 1992 and 16 May 1992.

18

THE NEW DIPLOMACY OF THE

WEST GERMAN *OSTPOLITIK*

A. *James McAdams*

THE WISDOM behind the West German *Ostpolitik* of the late 1960s and early 1970s now appears self-evident. At the time, the Soviet Union and the United States had attained military parity in the contest over Europe's future, and hence all of the leaders of the Federal Republic of Germany (FRG), Willy Brandt, Walter Scheel, and Helmut Schmidt, seem to have reached the only rational conclusion open to them about their country's options. Since the superpowers were no longer willing to treat the still unresolved matter of Germany's national division as a pressing concern—by this point, most Western policymakers barely gave the issue a second thought—it made sense for them to put the challenge of living with the continental status quo ahead of their faint hopes of ever changing it. Nor was this an entirely unwelcome decision. Over the years, the majority of West German public officials had grown fatigued, even exasperated, in seeing their state drift away from the more conciliatory policies of its allies in Washington, London, and Paris. They were also pained at having the Federal Republic regarded as a permanent focus of suspicion throughout the Soviet bloc. At last, it seemed, the FRG could become a force for stability in Europe.

Thus, the détente initiatives were born that we associate with the West German *Ostpolitik:* Bonn's renunciation-of-force agreements with Moscow and Warsaw in 1970, and with Prague in 1973; the behind-the-scenes maneuvering that helped to facilitate the four-power Berlin accord of 1971; the delicate negotiations with the German Democratic Republic (GDR), resulting in the inter-German transit agreements and *Grundlagenvertrag* (Basic Treaty) of 1972; and finally, the FRG's out-front role in the European discussions that culminated in the Helsinki Final Acts of 1975. As reasonable as all of these diplomatic breakthroughs may appear today, however, the historian must avoid the temptation of assuming that the FRG's reconciliation with the East was merely a matter of will. While Bonn may have profited by portraying itself in the 1970s as a continental peacemaker, the challenge behind the *Ostpolitik* was in getting to the point in the first place where the hopeful reformers of West German foreign policy could begin to act upon their ideas.

One impediment was always clear. No one doubted that the Soviet Union's acquiescence was essential to improve East-West relations. Yet, even as the leaders of the USSR warmed to the idea that they would benefit from a friendlier relationship with the Federal Republic, they were never entirely free of the contrary influences of their allies in the GDR. And here, for a time, Moscow's options were limited. Throughout the 1960s, Walter Ulbricht, the first secretary of the East German Socialist Unity Party (SED), stubbornly opposed any easing of tensions at all with the FRG, as long as Bonn refused to recognize his country's sovereignty and maintained its claim, the so-called *Alleinvertretungsanspruch,* to speak for the whole German people.

Somewhat less evident, however, West Germany itself was the source of an equally serious impediment to a new Eastern initiative, since the early advocates of the *Ostpolitik* had the misfortune of operating within a climate of intense domestic turmoil. In particular, their political opponents argued against undue haste in opening ties with the Soviet bloc, on the grounds that every step taken in this direction might have the unintended consequence of solidifying the inter-German divide even more than it already was. As a result, Bonn frequently failed to act in ways one might have anticipated. Caught as the West German government was between the obstructionist potential of the GDR and equally forceful attacks on the *Ostpolitik* coming from within the FRG, one could justifiably wonder how it would ever satisfy both groups of its critics simultaneously.

I

On the face of it, the construction of the Berlin Wall on 13 August 1961 would seem to have been sufficient cause for the enunciation of a radically new Eastern policy.[1] As Willy Brandt would write in one of his many memoirs in 1976: "[In] August 1961 a curtain was drawn aside to reveal an empty stage. To put it more bluntly, we lost certain illusions that had outlived the hopes underlying them— illusions that clung to something which no longer existed in fact."[2] Of course, this was how Brandt saw things in the second half of the 1970s, after the signing of the treaties with Moscow and its allies, after the "regularization" of relations with East Berlin—one could still not use the word "normalization"—and a couple of years after he had put aside the pleasures and the burdens of being chancellor. Yet, Brandt's world had been different in the early 1960s. He was mayor of West Berlin at the time of the wall's erection, and while he and some of his more astute advisers may have vaguely recognized the need to set a new stage in their country's relationship with the communist East, it would be a mistake to imagine that the overcoming of old illusions was as easy or as straightforward as he later implied. Political conditions alone in the FRG would not have allowed for it.

True, there was a great deal about the wall's construction that seemed to demand an immediate break with past West German policy. One possible lesson was that, contrary to the logic of Konrad Adenauer's "policy of strength," national salvation was not to be found by relying solely on the agencies of the Western alliance. Since the late 1950s, doubts had been growing about the West's commitment to Adenauer's uncompromising stand on relations with the East, especially his insistence that any reconciliation presupposed a settlement of the problem of German division.[3] With the sealing of the sectoral boundary between East and West Berlin, therefore, one might have expected such doubts to be confirmed. Technically, the city's three Western occupying powers, the United States, Great Britain, and France, could have responded to the violation of their rights in Berlin by demanding, at the threat of the use of force, that the Soviets immediately reopen the border. But instead, with John F. Kennedy setting the tone for subsequent policy, they emphasized only their determination to defend *West* Berlin, thereby signaling their intention in the months and years to come to search for ways of reducing the likelihood of future conflicts with the East.[4]

Another possible lesson was that any dreams one may have still cultivated about national reunification were not likely to be realized in the foreseeable future, and certainly not as long as one hundred–plus miles of barbed wire, steel fencing, and concrete fortifications encircled the island city of West Berlin. This was the unmistakable message that Brandt's confidante and press spokesman, Egon Bahr, sought to convey at the Evangelical Academy at Tutzing on 15 July 1963. As long as the USSR was committed to keeping the dictatorial East German regime in power, Bahr reasoned, Bonn's best hope of transforming the GDR ("the Zone") lay in convincing its leaders, through a deliberate reduction of tensions, that it was in East Berlin's interest to open up to the West: change through rapprochement.[5] At the time, one could hardly have accused Bahr of writing off the goal of German unity, though in later years the charge may have been justified. Rather, his conception of how best to handle the GDR, like that of many other German intellectuals—Karl Jaspers, Rudolf Augstein, Peter Bender[6]—was of a long-term process, of "many steps and many stations." The central goal was to keep the fading memory of a united nation and of German commonalities alive.[7]

If only policy-making were so sensible. That Bonn took as long as it did to open up to the East in the 1960s, indeed that even the idea of a new *Ostpolitik* would become the subject of a fierce and acrimonious debate in the FRG, can practically be accounted for by mentioning one word—Adenauer. First, there was the man himself. Even in his twilight years as chancellor, Adenauer was still obdurate to the point of opposing publicly many potentially fruitful initiatives—overtures to the Soviet Union, new approaches on the German question—that he himself privately supported.[8] He scarcely made a secret of his bitterness at what he perceived to be a betrayal of American responsibilities to hang tough with his country in the fight against Soviet expansionism; in his eyes, Kennedy and Rusk were feeble substitutes for Eisenhower and Dulles.[9] Furthermore, we now know that the octogenarian was himself in far worse health than his aides ever admitted; he suffered his first heart attack in February 1962.[10] "The chancellor is growing old," long-time intimate Heinrich Krone solemnly recorded in his diary at year's end.[11]

But there was also another, equally imposing Adenauer. This was Adenauer the mystique, the embodiment of West Germany's postwar recovery of sovereignty. Beyond the chancellor's distinctive personality, if there is a key to his extraordinary ability to monopolize political power in the Federal Republic's formative years, it is to be found in the diverse domestic constituency that was able to find comfort in and then rally around his—and his party's—leadership.[12] Importantly, even as his personal authority had begun to wane within the Christian Democratic Union (CDU), these divergent tendencies remained to confound would-be innovators of West German foreign policy.

For example, there were still quite vocal lobbies, such as the various expellee organizations representing the Silesians, Pomeranians, and Sudeten Germans, which actively campaigned against even the slightest move to seek an understanding with the East. Such steps, they claimed, would end all hope of restoring Germany to its prewar boundaries. Yet, even as the West German public began to doubt that the lost territories of the Reich would ever be recovered, a more immediate fear was that well-meaning reformers might inadvertently jeopardize the remaining leverage that Bonn had over the GDR. With conviction, many mainstream conservatives worried that every effort to establish formal relations with the member states of the Soviet bloc would carry with it the simultaneous risk of cementing the division of Europe and, with it, the division of the German nation as well. Finally, these critics were joined by another group of individuals—including the leader of the Bavarian Christian Social Union (CSU), Franz Josef Strauß—for whom a strict adherence to the "policy of strength" was a crucial proof of West German sovereignty. For them, national reunification itself may not have been a pressing goal, but a tough stand on communism was still the best way of showing that the FRG's international options would not be dictated by anyone, even its Western allies.[13]

It is no wonder, then, that so many of the early efforts to work out the kinks and contradictions in the FRG's foreign policy goals, both at the end of Adenauer's reign and during the short-lived chancellorship of Ludwig Erhard, were marked by frustration and uncertainty. Consider the federal government's attempts to free itself of the self-imposed limitations of the Hallstein doctrine in the immediate aftermath of the wall's construction. It was widely recognized within the higher circles of the CDU, and even more so by the ruling party's coalition partners in the Free Democratic Party (FDP), that the official policy of breaking relations with countries that dared to recognize the GDR had done nothing to serve Bonn's interests. Originally, the policy had not even been meant to have the hard and fast proportions of a doctrine;[14] but with time, and with the legalistic interventions of the Foreign Office's bureaucracy, Bonn had found itself in the uncomfortable position of having to sever relations with Yugoslavia in 1957 and then having to rebuff an offer by the Polish government to normalize relations, which it had only recently solicited. Making matters worse, by the early 1960s, it was clear that this uncompromising stand had not at all weakened the East German regime. Far from merely having shut itself out of Eastern Europe, the West German government faced the very real possibility, as the GDR's representatives campaigned for their country's recognition in the Third World, that it might have to break diplomatic ties with a host of developing states as well.[15]

The attempt to counter these problems was at the heart of Gerhard Schröder's "policy of movement" (*Politik der Bewegung*), following his appointment as foreign minister in 1962: how to square the circle between refusing to accept the finality of the continental status quo while nevertheless coming to terms with the reality of the communist states of Eastern Europe.[16] Schröder reaffirmed his government's continuing displeasure with any regime that chose to recognize East Berlin. Yet, by offering to exchange subambassadorial trade missions with all of the governments in the region, he at least managed to introduce that needed element of flexibility to West Germany's foreign policy that had been lacking under Adenauer's leadership. By 1964, in fact, all of the Soviet bloc regimes, save Czechoslovakia and the GDR, which was not invited, had agreed with Bonn to open trade offices in their capitals.

Despite all this, it must be emphasized that there were equally consequential limitations upon Schröder's East European breakthroughs which, by the mid-1960s, had led much of the energy behind his initiatives to evaporate. From the first, the foreign minister's freedom of movement was sharply circumscribed by his domestic critics. For good reason, some observers wondered aloud whether Schröder would not have been happier as a member of the FDP—which had sponsored his appointment to the Foreign Office, against Adenauer's opposition—or perhaps even of the Social Democratic Party (SPD). Whether the attacks came from his predecessor, Heinrich von Brentano, Franz Josef Strauß, or even Adenauer himself, it seemed that few of the CDU or CSU prominence had to look far to find grounds for displeasure with his policies—he was too attentive to the Americans, not attentive enough to Germany's national ideals, and supposedly far too eager to appease the FRG's enemies.[17]

Yet Schröder was himself symptomatic of the continuing limitations resulting from his government's inability to deal with the existence of a rival German state, the GDR. While he routinely insisted that one of his chief goals was to improve the living conditions of those Germans trapped behind the wall, he parted company with Egon Bahr and other reformers on the desirability of any official contacts with the Ulbricht regime: "The Federal Republic is and must remain the *single,* truly legitimate international spokesman for all Germans."[18] Then, too, Schröder scarcely concealed the fact that an underlying aim of the "policy of movement" was to undermine the GDR by isolating it within its own camp. Once this objective became clear, and this did not take long, both East Berlin and Moscow were quick to restrain their socialist allies in East Europe from making any more conciliatory moves in Bonn's direction.

The same stubbornness was also in evidence in the way the new West German chancellor, Erhard, handled just about every opportunity to restore contacts between the two German populations. When, in winter 1963, the city government of West Berlin received a surprise invitation from one of Ulbricht's emissaries to enter into negotiations over special passes that would allow citizens of Berlin's western sectors to visit the East during the Christmas holidays, ruling-mayor Brandt and his advisers came under the immediate fire of the Bonn government. Erhard personally denounced the East German overture as a "trojan horse," shrewdly crafted by Ulbricht to undermine the FRG's claims to any special relationship with West Berlin, which indeed it may have been.[19] But this was also the first opportunity for the city's divided residents to see each other in over two years. The Christmas pass agreement was eventually reached, with the result that a staggering 1.2 million West Berliners were able to visit the East between 18 December 1963 and 5 January 1964. Still, the chancellor gave in reluctantly, and only in the face of both overwhelming public support for the undertaking and behind-the-scenes pressures from his FDP coalition partners.

That Erhard had no intention, however, of revising his views on the GDR became very clear when East Germany was not even included in his administration's famous "peace note" to the East of 25 March 1966. Formally, the declaration had all of the earmarks of a serious effort by Bonn to get back into step with its Western allies by ending all doubt about the FRG's determination to live in peace with its neighbors.[20] Erhard offered to sign treaties with all of the Eastern states renouncing the use of force in settling international disputes. Nevertheless, the declaration was also the product of a difficult compromise among internal forces within the Federal Republic, and therefore full of the kinds of qualifications that were bound to alienate even those to whom it was addressed. For example, although the "peace note" spoke hopefully about an improvement of relations with Poland, its authors flatly ruled out any discussion of Bonn's recognition of that country's westernmost, Oder-Neisse boundary. Similarly, the document acknowledged the Soviet Union's professions of interest in avoiding future wars, but then accused the Soviet government of continuing to make "unmistakable and massive threats" against the FRG.[21]

II

One should not make the mistake of assuming, however, that the impediments to an improvement in West Germany's relations with the states of the Soviet bloc lay solely with the Federal Republic. Walter Ulbricht's East German government was capable of raising serious obstacles of its own to the process. The GDR was not just any Soviet satellite but, given its location and strategic importance, central to the stability of Moscow's imperium in Eastern Europe. More than is commonly assumed, the Soviet leadership could rarely afford to ignore its ally's pleas for caution and restraint in its efforts to improve relations with the capitalist West. In addition, the GDR's leaders were not averse to upsetting progress in East-West relations when this suited their purposes. In the city of West Berlin in particular, thanks to its location in East Germany's midst and the vulnerability of the transit routes linking it with the FRG, they enjoyed a priceless lever, which they could, and did, use on occasion, by disrupting traffic to demonstrate their displeasure with Western policies.

But what exactly did they want of the West? Had the SED regime simply hoped to compel the FRG to alter one or another of its policies—the convening of political assemblies in West Berlin, for example, or the refusal to exchange official representatives—it is conceivable that some sort of early accommodation might have been reached. Yet, the GDR's objectives were much more fundamental. We now know, based upon the materials coming out of East German archives, from personal memoirs, and as a result of interviews with many of the individuals involved, just how much the country's leaders conceived of themselves as being locked into a win-or-lose battle with the FRG over whether they or their adversaries would retain the legitimate right to speak for the whole German nation.[22] Moreover, we are also beginning to get a picture of Walter Ulbricht himself which is considerably more complex than the "apparatchik par excellence," with the famous memory for faces and details and the iron sense of discipline.[23]

Many of those who worked closely with the SED first secretary in the 1960s insist that Ulbricht really believed, even after the wall's construction, that there was a possibility that Germany might one day be reunified under socialism. Therefore, in their view, the GDR could not have afforded to convey even the slightest suggestion of a willingness to compromise on the national question.[24] Of course, it does strain credulity to think that East Germany's leaders were preparing for an imminent proletarian uprising in the industrial sweatshops of the Ruhr and Saarland. It is much easier to imagine, however, that a leader like Ulbricht—and a communist at that, who had seen his party, the Communist Party of Germany (KPD), sorely underestimate the national question in the Weimar Republic—would have been extremely reluctant to allow the FRG to acquire full title to German national identity. The SED was already suspect enough in the eyes of the East German population as a result of the events of 13 August 1961. Hence, one could hardly have expected him to take any step toward Bonn that could have further undermined the GDR's slim claim to authority.

These circumstances may best help to account for Ulbricht's manifest eagerness throughout the 1960s to stay on the offensive on the national theme. Until almost the end of the decade, he was the routine source of proposals for inter-German dialogue (e.g., for an all-German confederal council) whose primary intent seemed to be to demonstrate that his government alone, and not that of the "Bonn ultras," was intent upon bringing the two German peoples back together again.[25] To listen to Ulbricht, one might have thought that his was the sole voice of reasoned compromise: "Whoever insists on a policy of 'everything now or nothing,'" he lectured in late July 1963, in an all-knowing reference to the logic of the FRG's position, "will certainly end up with 'nothing.'"[26] Yet, in every instance, Ulbricht was also noticeably careful to frame his proposals in a way that brought no risk to his country. He repeatedly raised demands of Bonn—for the GDR's full diplomatic recognition, for West Berlin's complete separation from the FRG—which, had they been accepted or even discussed, would have undoubtedly strengthened the East German cause. And when they were rebuffed, as was almost always the case, it was no problem at all to shift the onus of responsibility for the absence of dialogue to the FRG.

Ulbricht must have known all along that his maximal demands would get nowhere with a West German government that explicitly eschewed official relations with the GDR. In one provocative instance in 1966, however, one could get a hint of the intrinsic flaw to this strategy of exploiting the FRG's silence, which would later become fully exposed with the Brandt-Scheel *Ostpolitik*. In early February, as had been its custom for years, the SED leadership drafted an open letter to the delegates of the upcoming annual congress of the SPD, proposing that the two parties discuss forming an alliance against CDU/CSU policy on the national question. With equal regularity in the past, the Social Democrats had dismissed such overtures as empty propaganda. On this occasion, however, the party's executive committee chose to call the SED's bluff. On 18 March, it responded with a counterproposal, announcing its readiness to participate in a broad exchange of parliamentarians from both parts of Germany provided that they be able to discuss the practical problems of national division openly.

At once, the leaders of the SED were caught in a bind that was to haunt all of their later contacts with the FRG. On the one hand, for Ulbricht in particular,[27] this was an unexpected opportunity to promote the GDR's image as actively interested in the destiny of the German nation. Who, after all, was better suited to demonstrate the GDR's international acceptance than representatives of the very country that denied the existence of a socialist Germany? On the other hand, an equally strong case could be made—and was made by other members of the East German leadership[28]—that even this slight opening to the FRG carried the risk of undermining the GDR. For the first time in years, public talks with the SPD (a counterrevolutionary organization, if ever there was one in SED lore[29]) would present average East German citizens with a visible, alternative conception of German nationhood. No one could be sure how this would affect their loyalties to the GDR.

For several months, those who favored taking up the Social Democratic proposal appeared to have the upper hand. On 26 March East Berlin responded with its own offer, a one-time exchange of speakers in which representatives of both parties would travel to an East and a West German city to defend their respective national policies. Had the meetings come to pass, this would have been the first serious contact between major political parties from the two states. Nonetheless, as the date of the speakers' exchange neared, those arguing for caution within the SED evidently convinced the majority of the party leadership that the risks of the undertaking outweighed its potential gains. At the end of June, the party withdrew its offer to take part in the exchange, using the specious argument that Bonn was not prepared to guarantee its members' safety while traveling in the FRG.

Most likely, little of substance would have come from the talks between the SED and the SPD, a West German party that had still not risen to power. The significance, however, of the GDR's abrupt retreat cannot have been lost on those in the West who were searching for a way to articulate a new *Ostpolitik*. Apparently, it was just as important to convince the GDR to relax its inhibitions about contacts with the FRG as to form a working consensus within West Germany about the desirability of greater dialogue with the East.

III

One of these two conditions seemed to be fulfilled, at least partially, in December 1966 with the fall of Ludwig Erhard's coalition with the FDP and its replacement by the Grand Coalition government between the CDU/CSU and the SPD. The importance of the Social Democrats' inclusion in the governing coalition in Bonn can hardly be overstated. Suddenly, a party that was in no way beholden to the Adenauer legacy was in a position to reshape official policy toward the East. As well, the fact that Willy Brandt joined the new CDU chancellor, Kurt Georg Kiesinger, as foreign minister had the added advantage of placing an avowed proponent of a more flexible foreign policy into an office where he could take the initiative toward the Soviet bloc.

There is little to dispute about the personal dynamism that Brandt brought to the job of, as he saw it, helping the FRG to be "more independent—more adult, so to speak."[30] With Egon Bahr assuming the post of planning chief in the ministry, the Foreign Office took immediate steps to break with many of the self-imposed constraints of its past and to embrace more outward-looking policies that were, in Brandt's appealing testimony, "directed toward everyone and against no one."[31] In January 1967, Bonn took the first concrete steps toward abandoning the Hallstein doctrine by establishing full diplomatic ties with Romania.[32] Only a year later, in January 1968, the Federal Republic reestablished relations with Yugoslavia, more than a decade after its predecessors had severed ties with Belgrade. During the same period, the Foreign Office also increased efforts behind the scenes to improve the quality of contacts with its counterparts in Poland and Czechoslovakia. And, completing the diplomatic offensive that Gerhard Schröder had begun half a decade earlier, the FRG finally opened a trade mission in Prague in August 1967.

One should, however, be wary of attributing all of the responsibility for these initiatives to the new foreign minister. To be sure, for the most conservative members of the Union parties, Brandt's every step may have seemed to fulfill the kind of dire warnings of irresponsible Social Democratic radicalism that Adenauer had made in the CDU's glory years.[33] Nevertheless, Brandt's positions on the national question and the kinds of relations he was willing to entertain with the East were still considerably more cautious than those to be found in other political circles at the time; this was particularly true of the FDP, whose leaders were desperately searching for a new identity as a result of their exclusion from national office in 1966.[34] Brandt was no newcomer to the demands of modern electoral politics, and he generally did not need to be reminded by his risk-averse colleagues in the SPD leadership, such as party boss Herbert Wehner, that the Social Democrats' long road to power could be easily impaired with the collapse of its coalition with the CDU/CSU. Moreover, having just arrived in Bonn, he and Bahr were also in the unenviable position of having to fight daily battles with an entrenched Foreign Office bureaucracy to see to it that their visions of a new diplomatic posture were realized in fact.[35]

Another reason for moderating our praise for Brandt is that at least some credit is due to his superior, Kiesinger. As an individual who had more than once been denied the national spotlight thanks to his former membership in the National Socialist Democratic Workers party (NSDAP) (since 1933, no less), Kiesinger may well have found his single chance for personal redemption in his appointment as chancellor. Very much the Atlanticist and devotee of the notion that the Federal Republic could meet its own ends only when it was marching in step with its allies, he was the first West German leader to give voice to the unspoken premise behind the break with Adenauer's "policy of strength." National reunification would remain a central goal of the FRG, but it was only conceivable after the conditions had first been created on the European continent to make it desired by all. "A reunified Germany," he declared on 17 June 1967, the anniversary of the 1953 workers' uprising in East Berlin,

> has a critical size. It is too big to play no role in the balance of power and too small to maintain the balance of powers around it. It is therefore very difficult to see how a [reunified] Germany could associate itself with one side or the other, given the continuation of the present European political structure. For this reason, one can only conceive of the growing together of the separated parts of Germany as part of a process in which the East-West conflict itself in Europe is overcome.[36]

This tribute to the FRG's European setting was more than just a gratuitous political exercise. Like Brandt, Kiesinger explicitly endorsed the opening of diplomatic relations with all of the estranged states of Eastern Europe. His approval was central to confidential talks with the Soviet Union, which led in late 1967 to the first discussions of a treaty renouncing the use of force in disputes over European borders. The chancellor's most striking step of all, however, was toward the GDR, for in the first months after assuming office, he came closer than any West German leader before him to accepting East Germany's existence on a de facto basis. Although he refused to entertain the prospect of diplomatic relations with East Berlin, Kiesinger nevertheless engaged in a brief exchange of letters with the East German prime minister, Willi Stoph, between May and September 1967, in which he openly raised the possibility of improved contacts between the German populations. As Bonn had been in the custom of returning the GDR's official correspondence unopened since the mid-1950s, this brief contact practically broke the deadlock between the two states.

Admittedly, Kiesinger's critics in the SPD were not far off the mark when they accused the chancellor in later years of simultaneously impeding progress in the very initiatives he helped to introduce. Thanks to countervailing pressures from within his own party's ranks and from the CSU—and his own frankly conservative instincts on the handling of the German question—Kiesinger was just as often a brake upon the *Ostpolitik* as a facilitator. He railed against those—the *Anerkennungspartei,* as he called them, the "party of recognition"—who wanted to go beyond his own modest gestures to the GDR to support East Berlin's full recognition. He also directly criticized Brandt on occasions when he felt his foreign minister had gone too far to accommodate East European demands (e.g., after Brandt called for a settlement of the Oder-Neisse issue with Poland at the SPD's Nuremberg conference of March 1968). Finally, in the wake of the August 1968 Soviet invasion of Czechoslovakia, Kiesinger seemed to become all the more dubious about the value of any further efforts to normalize relations with the USSR.

Nonetheless, it is undeniable that the most formidable barrier to an easing of tensions between the FRG and the Soviet bloc was presented, not by the CDU/CSU or by its chancellor, but rather by the GDR, of which its response to the Grand Coalition was no exception. During a brief period in late fall 1966, when the composition of the West German governing coalition was still in question, Ulbricht's government had not been above dispatching upbeat signals about the possibility that an arrangement might be worked out between the FDP and the SPD.[37] However, when the Social Democrats chose instead to throw in their fortunes with the Union parties, East Germany's leaders could not contain their displeasure over what they perceived to be an unholy alliance between a workers' party—even one that had been guilty of all kinds of bourgeois deviations—and the forces of reaction.[38] At the SED's seventh congress in mid-April 1967, Ulbricht denounced the new coalition as being nothing more than a cleverly disguised version of the old Adenauer and Erhard regimes, in which Franz Josef Strauß evidently, and not Brandt, held the real strings of foreign policy-making power.[39] Similarly, in the subsequent exchange of letters between Prime Minister Stoph and Kiesinger, the East German government showed that if there was to be even the slightest hope of progress with the FRG, all of the giving would have to come from the West. The GDR would only consider expanding contacts when Bonn first recognized its sovereignty unconditionally.

Had such inter-German exchanges been merely isolated events, they alone would have been sufficient to dampen any hopeful prospects of cooperation between the blocs. But, the fact that Ulbricht also immediately began to campaign for a show of unity among his allies in response to the Grand Coalition's Eastern initiatives proved to be an even greater obstacle. As a direct counter to Bonn's establishment of relations with Romania, officials from the GDR Ministry of Foreign Affairs rushed to negotiate bilateral treaties of friendship and cooperation with Czechoslovakia and Poland in March 1967. These agreements not only emphasized both states' solidarity with the GDR but also halted moves already in evidence in Prague and Warsaw to emulate Bucharest's opening to the FRG; similar agreements followed with Hungary and Bulgaria. With Moscow's backing, East German authorities then used a 24–26 April Warsaw Pact meeting in Karlovy Vary to lobby for a common stand among their allies (excluding Romania, which chose not to attend) against the West German *Ostpolitik*. In what later became known as the "Ulbricht doctrine," because of the policy's resemblance to the Hallstein doctrine, the signatories to the conference's concluding document agreed to make any further contacts with the FRG contingent upon Bonn's acquiescence to long-standing East German demands. These included the Federal Republic's readiness to abandon all of its claims to represent the German nation and its willingness finally to recognize, among other supposedly unchallengeable aspects of the European status quo, "the border between the two German states."[40]

IV

In view of the barriers that East Berlin was still able to lay in the path of an easing of European tensions, historians have for good reason treated the formation of the Social-Liberal coalition government of October 1969, and especially Willy Brandt's appointment as its chancellor, as the first serious indication that the East-West impasse might be ended. At last, it seemed, the remaining ambiguities in West German foreign policy would be resolved and Bonn would cease to be a major obstacle to better ties with the East. What may be somewhat more open to debate, however, is why the subsequent SPD-FDP *Ostpolitik* was the unquestionable success that it turned out to be. Was it mainly the chancellor's confident vision of his country's role in a new "European peace order" that convinced his neighbors to view the FRG in a more favorable light? Or, was it instead his and his advisers' equally appreciable tactical skill in going beyond customary diplomatic and political channels to achieve this end?

Brandt's inaugural address of 28 October 1969 was indisputably a diplomatic tour de force. In one brilliantly crafted statement, the chancellor managed to give the Eastern bloc just enough of what it wanted—or at least, what *most* of its members wanted—to overcome many of the traditional arguments that had been used against the FRG in the past. At the same time, he preserved just enough of the essentials of his country's national policy to justify his new venture. In an unmistakable departure from the strictures of the Hallstein doctrine, Brandt announced his administration's readiness to assume diplomatic relations with every state in the world that was friendly to the Federal Republic, expressly singling out Poland and Czechoslovakia as countries with which his government hoped soon to resolve outstanding differences. Also, he welcomed Soviet proposals, first broached in 1966, for the convening of a European-wide conference on continental security. Most significant, Brandt seemed to remove the greatest obstacle of all to improved relations with the East by going at least halfway toward meeting the GDR's major demands. Although he emphasized that the FRG would never accept East Germany as a foreign state ("*nicht Ausland*") and maintained, in the same breath, that his administration would persist in its efforts to preserve the "cohesion [*Zusammenhalt*] of the German nation," he stressed that the FRG was at last prepared to deal with the East German leadership as a sovereign entity. Not only did he conspicuously eschew all of his predecessors' paeans to the FRG's right to represent the entire German population—he conceded for the first time officially that there were now "two states [existing] in Germany"—but he even failed to mention the most sacred of shibboleths, national reunification.[41]

These shifts in emphasis must have been appealing to many of Brandt's listeners. Yet, his tactical choices in the months to come may actually have guaranteed that the message behind the new policy was received in the East. Officially, the FRG was interested in talking to all powers "sharing our desire for peaceful cooperation,"[42] but one did not have to scratch very far beneath the surface of the chancellor's diplomatic niceties to see that the primary focus of the *Ostpolitik* was the USSR. Well before the formation of the Social-Liberal coalition, he, Bahr, and State Secretary Ferdinand Duckwitz had quietly conducted exploratory discussions on this subject with Soviet Ambassador Semyon Tsarapkin in Bonn; in June 1968, Brandt even managed to confer secretly with Tsarapkin's equivalent number in East Berlin, Pyotr Abrassimov. Few would admit it openly, but the Soviet-backed invasion of Czechoslovakia two months later, in August, seemed to confirm the wisdom of an approach that made the USSR the centerpiece of West German policy. One could only make inroads into the socialist bloc with Moscow's explicit consent, and definitely not against its wishes.[43]

What stands out about the new coalition's Eastern policy in late 1969 and early 1970 was the speed with which Brandt went about living up to this reasoning. For one thing, he was better positioned politically than anyone since Adenauer. Having just occupied the foreign minister's office, he could not only preserve the continuity of an increasingly more thoughtful direction toward the East; he also quite literally raided the Foreign Office of some of its most able staff to fill his own team of advisers in the chancellery. Indeed, with Walter Scheel's appointment as the coalition's foreign minister, it is no exaggeration to suggest that Brandt did not even suffer the inconvenience of having to give up his cabinet *Ressort* for international affairs. True, Scheel, a decent and well-meaning individual, was sensitive to the intricacies of consensus building among the FRG's quarreling parties, but he lacked even the most remote experience with his new post. It would take months, if not years, before he could begin to fathom the byzantine procedures of his ministry.[44]

Brandt, in any case, very quickly made it clear that he was not about to wait for routine political and bureaucratic processes in Bonn to weigh the merits of the *Ostpolitik*. On 30 January 1970, he sent Bahr to Moscow as his special envoy with the specific task of effecting the Soviet breakthrough and gaining the Kremlin's support for what were to become the Eastern treaties. To expedite the talks, Bahr was subordinate to no one but the chancellor, and hence free to decide all questions of consequence himself. Thus, when he returned to Bonn on 22 May with the rough outlines of an agreement in hand, the product of three grueling rounds of negotiations with Soviet Foreign Minister Andrei Gromyko, there were very few individuals in the Foreign Office or even the chancellor's own cabinet who had even an inkling of what had been under way.[45] The so-called Bahr paper, in essence the basis of the Moscow Treaty of August 1970, was the most delicate of compromises. By emphasizing the "inviolability" of all existing borders in Europe, it gave the Soviets just enough of what they wanted to convince them that the agreements to come with Warsaw, Prague, and even East Berlin would help to solidify their imperial claims in East Europe. At the same time, though, by acknowledging four-power rights in Berlin and Germany as a whole, the Bahr-Gromyko understanding also managed to hold open the slimmest of prospects that the German nation might one day be reunited following the peaceful revision of those same borders.[46]

To put it mildly, many onlookers, both inside and outside of the FRG, were frustrated as a result of their deliberate exclusion from Brandt's dealings with the Soviets, although there was very little that they could do to restrain the West German government. For example, Polish leader Wladyslaw Gomułka had sought to make a conciliatory gesture of his own toward the FRG as early as May 1969, by calling for an amicable settlement of the Oder-Neisse dispute; over the following summer, he had even received Brandt's private assurances that his wish would be fulfilled with the formation of a new government in Bonn. The galling aspect of the West German-Soviet deliberations in 1970, however, was that they had all of the force of a fait accompli. Although Gomułka ultimately received the accommodation he sought, it was a sorry testimony to his country's limited sovereignty that the rudiments for the Polish agreement with the Federal Republic had already been established in Moscow.[47]

Policymakers in the United States, too, experienced some anxiety about the course of the *Ostpolitik*. Here as well, however, their discomfort had less to do with any disagreement over fundamentals than with the fact that they were not free to manage all of the ramifications of Brandt's opening to the East. As Richard Nixon's national security adviser, Henry Kissinger, put it in a note to the president, the danger was that West Germany's leaders were getting into something far bigger than the interests of the FRG alone:

> It should be stressed that men like Brandt, Wehner, and Defense Minister [Helmut] Schmidt undoubtedly see themselves as conducting a responsible policy of reconciliation and normalization with the East and intend not to have this policy come into conflict with Germany's Western association. . . . But their problem is to control a process which, if it results in failure, could jeopardize their political lives and if it succeeds could create a momentum that may shake Germany's domestic stability and unhinge its international position.[48]

Kissinger probably meant to say that the greatest offense of the West German *Ostpolitik* was that he personally was not in charge of it.[49] Nevertheless, it was impossible to object to the new policy on grounds of principle, for the goals of the Brandt government closely paralleled those of U.S. policy toward the East. In fact, in the delicate four-power negotiations with Moscow over the future of Berlin—regarded by the Americans as the precondition for serious talks between the superpowers about limits upon strategic arms—Kissinger showed no hesitation in turning to Bonn. He used Egon Bahr in the way that he was utilized best, as a secret backchannel conferee with U.S. ambassador to the FRG Kenneth Rush, to guarantee that when the Quadripartite Accord on Berlin was finally ready for signing in 1971, West Germany's interests in maintaining ties with the city were fully incorporated into the agreement.[50]

In contrast, the Social-Liberal coalition encountered much more serious opposition to its policies from the CDU/CSU, which found itself for the first time in the FRG's history excluded from the government. This is not to say that there were no leading members of the Union parties with the ability to appreciate the merits of the *Ostpolitik*. Some, like the *Fraktion*'s parliamentary leader and later CDU chairman, Rainer Barzel, simply believed that Brandt and Bahr could have gotten much more than they did from the Soviet Union. In their view, the Moscow Treaty and its attendant accords had been negotiated in far too much haste and therefore failed to pay sufficient attention to the FRG's national obligations, above all in the question of reunification.[51]

The dilemma for the opposition forces, however, and a very consequential blessing for the ruling coalition, was that the CDU/CSU could never devise a convincing alternative of their own to Brandt's policy. Because many members believed that it would only be a short time before the Union found itself once again in control of the government, they were wary of compromise with the SPD on tactical grounds. Others were adamantly opposed to any long-term agreement with Moscow that failed to include a comprehensive peace settlement with the East. Yet, with public support for Brandt's initiatives growing and the chancellor's popularity rising with every achievement—in October 1971, he was awarded the Nobel Peace Prize[52]—it became evident that the conservatives could also not afford to vote against the Eastern treaties when they were presented for ratification in the Bundestag.

In this context, the CDU/CSU leadership made a crucial, and eventually fatal, decision. On 21 April 1972, Barzel called for a constructive vote-of-no-confidence against Brandt, reasoning that the best strategy was to bring the Union parties back to power and only then, with the aura of legitimacy to support them, to devise an effective basis for modifying Brandt's and Bahr's diplomacy. Had the gamble paid off, there can be little doubt that the character of the *Ostpolitik* would have been significantly altered. That Barzel was unable to unseat the chancellor, however, proved to be an electoral bonanza for the Social-Liberal coalition. Not willing to be relegated to the position of naysayers in the public mind—the unhappy platform that the SPD had monopolized in the 1950s—the majority of the CDU/CSU had no other option than to abstain in the final vote over the treaties, thereby strengthening its reputation for indecisiveness. In November 1972, Brandt then seized upon his advantage by allowing his government to fall. As a result, the subsequent elections to the Bundestag were transformed into a victorious national referendum over the fruits of the Eastern policy.

There was, however, one piece to the elaborate puzzle of the *Ostpolitik* that proved all along to be the elusive part of the Social-Liberal coalition's diplomatic offensive. This was the GDR. In fact, it says something for the difficulty of effecting significant historical change that, had the serendipitous play of fortune not intervened, Brandt's and Bahr's skillful manipulation of their neighbor's interests might never have been enough to overcome Walter Ulbricht's opposition to the FRG's new politics in the East. Of course, it cannot have hurt that the West German government had successfully enlisted the Soviet Union in the cause of creating a more stable framework for relations among the states of East-Central Europe. Ulbricht did not have to be a fortune teller to see that when Gromyko and Bahr began meeting in early 1970, they were bound to discuss themes centrally related to GDR priorities. Thus, not wanting to be left out, the SED first secretary was quick to put his country at the forefront of conspicuous efforts to promote dialogue between the blocs. The best-known of these were two highly publicized meetings between the East German premier, Stoph, and Willy Brandt, in Erfurt on 19 March and in Kassel on 21 May 1970.[53]

However, Ulbricht was still firmly wedded to the proposition that the GDR was a fitting model for the German future and hence that its interests should be fully incorporated into any comprehensive European agreements.[54] On one issue in particular, the fate of Berlin, his sense of priorities and those of the USSR seemed destined to collide.[55] By 1970, Soviet leaders had already made up their minds that some sort of compromise had to be reached with the city's three Western occupiers, even if this meant, to quote the Communist Party chief, Leonid Brezhnev, respecting "the wishes of West Berlin's population."[56] Yet, for all of his fabled devotion to Moscow, Ulbricht showed that he was prepared to engage in verbal combat with his ally to guarantee that the GDR's stake in the city's future was preserved, including its right to supervise the transit routes linking Berlin with the FRG.[57]

In these differences, the seeds of a major conflict were growing between Moscow and East Berlin, which might easily have held up the Quadripartite Accord. Nonetheless, fortune intervened in a form entirely unrelated to the vagaries of foreign policy-making. Since the mid-1960s, Ulbricht had enjoyed nearly unanimous support for his policies in the SED politburo, in part due to his efforts to spur on the East German economy to compete with the model of affluence so successfully implemented in the FRG. Yet, by the turn of the decade, his measures had become dangerously unrealistic, finally threatening to bring the country's economy to a standstill.[58] One after another, Ulbricht's old allies drifted away from him. As a consequence, just as the Soviets decided that their own *Westpolitik* was no longer compatible with the first secretary's obstructionism, the East German leadership was ready as well to fill his post with a more compliant candidate, Erich Honecker.[59]

In this sense, Ulbricht's removal from the SED's top position on 3 May 1971 may properly be regarded as lifting the last major impediment to Bonn's opening to the East. It was not that Honecker was any less apprehensive than his predecessor about the implications of the West German offensive. Who could know for sure, after all, whether the GDR had really been able to develop a stable identity in the years since the erection of the Berlin Wall, one that would suffice to survive a new order of relations with the West? Honecker at least had the good sense not to challenge the priorities of his allies in Moscow. Within a year, negotiations were ready to begin, with Egon Bahr again representing the FRG, on the inter-German agreement that would serve as the capstone to the *Ostpolitik*.

When the *Grundlagenvertrag* was finally initialed on 7 November 1972, it could not be all things to all people. For example, it failed to satisfy those in the West who had hoped to arrive at a definitive statement of the national ties binding both of the Germanies to a common destiny. The treaty did, however, provide for an unprecedented level of contacts between the two states, in communications, cultural and sports exchanges, and especially in the all-important matter of travel opportunities for average citizens to and (to a lesser extent) even from the GDR.[60] In these limited respects, the wall was transcended. Similarly, while the GDR's leaders were unable to secure from Bonn everything that they had consistently sought in the past (i.e., de jure recognition of their authority), they too had reason to be pleased with the treaty. In particular, the FRG promised to base its future actions on principles East Berlin held dear, the "inviolability of borders and respect for the territorial integrity and sovereignty of all states in Europe."[61] Apparently, the last of the foundations had been laid for a new era between the FRG and its former adversaries in the Soviet bloc.

V

Ostpolitik was a major breakthrough, although not in the sense that it guaranteed that Bonn's relations with its Eastern neighbors in the 1970s were harmonious or free of turbulence. Rather, the novel development was that it suddenly became possible to liken the FRG's interactions with these states to the foreign policies of other members of the Atlantic alliance, at least to the extent—and this was an important qualification—that Bonn's activities were no longer burdened by the vagaries of the German national question.

Well before the last *i* was dotted on the Eastern treaties, Leonid Brezhnev demonstrated his country's eagerness to entertain a new relationship with the Federal Republic by inviting Brandt in September 1971 to make an unprecedented visit, without protocol or state delegations, to his residence in Oreanda. This tête-à-tête between the two leaders, which covered subjects as wide-ranging as Moscow's strained ties with China, the requisites for a renunciation-of-force agreement with Czechoslovakia, and the possibility of negotiations on continental troop reductions, was then followed by a splashy official visit by Brezhnev himself to Bonn in May 1973. Heeding the general secretary's call for the Soviet and German peoples to perform a "heroic deed" for the sake of European peace, the Brandt government produced a sweeping, ten-year treaty on economic cooperation with Moscow.[62]

Much has been made about the fact that the ebullient tone that characterized West Germany's ties with Moscow at this point was lost a year later when Helmut Schmidt succeeded Brandt as federal chancellor in May 1974. Certainly, Schmidt did not share his predecessor's idealistic flare and ability to capture the popular imagination with images of future European order; his was much more the efficient style of a bank president or corporate chief executive.[63] But, as a former defense minister and devout believer in the virtues of the strategic balance between the superpowers, the new chancellor was, at least as much as Brandt, committed to the idea that the FRG had to search for common points of interest with the Soviets, if only out of necessity.[64] On his first official trip to Moscow after assuming office, in October 1974, Schmidt assured his hosts that his administration had every intention of maintaining continuity in its relations with the USSR. In fact, in several respects, West German–Soviet ties actually burgeoned during his tenure; by 1977, for example, total trade turnover between the two countries had more than quadrupled.[65]

Admittedly, there were also notable respects in which the good spirits that had accompanied the signing of the Moscow Treaty in 1970 were no longer present at the end of the decade. In many ways, Bonn's relationship with the Kremlin could even be said to have soured, despite the fact that both states endeavored to paint a happier picture of their ties on the occasion of Brezhnev's second visit to the West German capital in May 1978. Four years earlier, multilateral talks had begun in Vienna on the reduction of conventional forces on the continent—a major concern for the Federal Republic, given its geographic location—but these sessions had become increasingly bogged down in technicalities. More disconcerting for the West German government, and for Schmidt in particular, the Soviets had taken advantage of a loophole in the Strategic Arms Limitation talks and engaged in a massive build-up of their intermediate-range nuclear missile force, so-called SS-20s, stationed in the westernmost parts of the USSR. Despite Brezhnev's protests on the eve of his Bonn visit that only a "pathologically perverted imagination" could think the Soviet Union was pursuing any but its most basic defense needs, Schmidt feared, rightly it would seem in retrospect, that Western security would be imperiled if NATO did not respond in kind.[66]

These tensions ultimately led to the deployment of a new generation of intermediate-range nuclear missiles (INF) in the West in 1983 and a marked deterioration in West Germany's relations with Moscow. Yet, in view of the disputes that had once separated the two states, was this really a return to past animosities? At the time, all of Bonn's allies shared the very same anxieties about how best to respond to the Soviet arms build-up. In this sense, to the extent that the INF conflict, and other disagreements to come with the USSR, were removed from the esoteric German quarrels of old, it was easy to conclude that the Federal Republic was still on the road to a more normal foreign policy.

The same point can be made for Bonn's relations with the People's Republic of Poland in the 1970s, the health of which was equally dependent upon the Schmidt government's ability and inclination to separate old national obsessions from the more straightforward task of building better bilateral ties. For, even more clearly than in the case of the USSR, West German–Polish relations were burdened by these antagonisms in the period between 1970 and 1974. Some members of the administration saw the Warsaw Treaty as a ready vehicle for promoting the cause of ethnic German emigration from western Poland; hence they reacted with anger when their new interlocutors failed to comply exactly as desired. Naturally, the Polish government denounced these pressures as unwarranted interference in its internal affairs, and likewise became embittered when the FRG failed to come through with previous assurances of substantial economic aid.[67]

Yet, here too, Bonn eventually showed a willingness to rise above such differences. Perhaps it was the historical burden of Polish-German relations—a "primary interest for Germany," as Schmidt expressed it—that compelled the federal government to reach for an accommodation.[68] Following intensive discussions with Polish party chief Edward Gierek, on the eve of the signing of the Final Acts of the Helsinki Conference of European Security and Cooperation in late July 1975, the chancellor was finally able to announce a meeting of minds. In return for millions of marks in credits and direct financial payments to Poland, it was agreed that upwards of 120,000 ethnic Germans would be allowed to emigrate to the FRG over the next four years.

This was by no means an isolated case of West German conciliation in Eastern Europe. In subsequent years, the meeting at Helsinki proved to be a turning point in Bonn's relations with the socialist bloc. Given the inroads already made in the East, Schmidt even seems to have discovered a role for the FRG in acting as a "bridge" (to use his distinctive terminology) between East and West.[69] Between November 1975 and January 1978, virtually every East European leader of prominence could be found in Bonn negotiating broad-ranging agreements of political and economic cooperation, from Poland's Gierek to Todor Zhivkov of Bulgaria, Janos Kádár of Hungary, and Gustav Husák of Czechoslovakia. By the end of the decade, furthermore, Schmidt had managed to make reciprocal visits to almost all of his new discussion partners' capitals. Looking on, one might have thought the *Ostpolitik* complete.

VI

In view of these accomplishments, the record of FRG-GDR ties in the 1970s will appear much less heartening. For all of the speeches held in both German capitals after 1972 about the need "to create the bases of good-neighborly relations and of peaceful cooperation in living next to each other" (Egon Bahr), the Basic Treaty can hardly be said to have resolved many of the most serious antagonisms separating the Germanies.[70] In many ways, the inter-German relationship may even have been worse as the 1970s came to a close.

On the surface, these shortcomings were not always apparent. Viewed from a merely quantitative standpoint, for example, there were some impressive signs of progress on both sides of the national divide. For the first time in a decade, thanks both to the inter-German agreement and to the Quadripartite Accord, visitors literally flowed into the East from West Germany and West Berlin; nearly 7 million Westerners were able to travel to the GDR in 1972, and more than 8 million in 1973. Relatedly, the GDR became the obliging recipient of hundreds of millions of Deutsch-Marks annually, for new roads and rail-ways, for postal and telephone communications, and for visa fees and currency exchange requirements, as the FRG sought to solidify its gains by enmeshing the East German regime into its détente-minded policies.

Nevertheless, just beneath this image of cooperation, Bonn and East Berlin did not seem to want to get along. It was undoubtedly the closeness of the German situation, the fact that millions of their fellow countrymen were still confined behind barbed wire and concrete, that kept Schmidt and his colleagues from investing more of their time and energy in cultivating stronger ties with their counterparts in the East German politburo. "Until just yesterday," the chancellor was to write in his memoirs in 1990, "the GDR was a big prison."[71] Thus, despite repeated offers from the SED to host a visit by Schmidt, it was only by chance that he and Honecker happened to meet in the 1970s. This was during the Helsinki Conference, and only then for two brief and largely un-productive exchanges.

Then, too, ties between the FRG and the GDR were also strained by a nagging tendency on the West German side: the temptation to take advantage of every loophole and ambiguity in the *Grundlagenvertrag* and the Berlin accord to reaffirm the FRG's narrow understanding of the inter-German relationship. So it was, for example, that in 1974 Schmidt's outspoken foreign minister, Hans-Dietrich Genscher, then regarded by nearly everyone as a hard-liner on West Germany's international priorities, went out of his way to provoke the GDR and the Soviets, by conspicuously erecting a Federal Environmental Protection Office in West Berlin. For the East, Genscher's move was a blatant violation of a stipulation in the Berlin agreement that the city not be treated as a "constituent part" of the FRG, and for a time it proved to be a serious impedi-ment to any further business with East Berlin.

Yet, the East German government was hardly free of culpability in these questions. Assuredly, Erich Honecker was no Ulbricht. Whatever idealistic convictions the latter may have had about one day ruling a reunified and *social-ist* Germany, his successor replaced these dreams with, in his eyes, a more pragmatic emphasis on simply winning over the GDR's population to what had already been achieved. This meant ending all discussion about the openness of the German question. "There is no unity between the socialist German Demo-cratic Republic and the imperialist FRG," Honecker proclaimed in a defining policy statement in 1972, "and there will never by any unity."[72]

Still, the retreat from the GDR's national goals was by no means sufficient to assure concord with the other Germany, if only because the concrete implica-tions of East Berlin's agreements with Bonn forced it to engage in defensive measures of a new type. Faced for the first time since 1961 with the assault upon its social order of millions of resuscitated contacts between long-separated families and friends, the Honecker government was at pains to insure that its citizenry would be insulated from the adverse effects of the opening to the West: punishing dissident intellectuals when they went too far with their critiques of socialism, muzzling Western reporters, and even creating an entire class of individuals, so-called secret-carriers (*Geheimnisträger*), who were forbidden any contact with the FRG. Who could be surprised, then, that as the Schmidt government watched the communist regime depart from many of the high expectations of the early Eastern policy, the inter-German relationship was bound to suffer all the more.

VII

While both the FRG and the GDR were able to find grounds for disappointment in each other's behavior, it was somewhat less apparent, because more subtle, that one fundamental change had nevertheless begun to work its way into the *Ostpolitik*. Bonn's traditional emphasis on national reunification had slowly but surely lost the primacy of place that it once enjoyed among official West German priorities. Of course, few politicians in the FRG would have been willing to go so far as to write off the long-term aim of bringing the two German populations back together again; this would remain a formal goal of Schmidt's administration and of his successors. By the same token, however, many West German officials were increasingly disposed to view their government's national policy in much less confining terms than had formerly been the case under Adenauer.[73]

On 11 July 1973, Egon Bahr was invited back to Tutzing to reflect upon the progress that had been made in East-West relations since his initial address to the Evangelical Academy a decade earlier. If anything stood out about his remarks, it was the almost clinical manner in which he described the FRG's options and above all, his disinclination even to treat German reunification as a concrete objective. In particular, looking back at how he had viewed the concept of "change through rapprochement" in 1963, Bahr stressed:

> Then, it seemed to me to be the only possibility of realizing unity [*staatlichen Einheit*], following a temporally limited interim phase. Today, it is clear that the mistake in my thinking lay not in the theoretical feasibility [of the concept] but instead in the fact that events took a different course. . . . Today, one could say that the old concept is no longer applicable to a limited transitional period but rather to an unbounded [period of time], so long as there are still two German states and the Basic Treaty retains its validity.[74]

Nor was Bahr's aversion to speaking about the prospect of national reunion atypical. When Helmut Schmidt outlined the priorities of his administration in his inaugural address on 17 May 1974, the word *reunification* did not even cross his lips. To the extent that he even mentioned the inter-German relationship, it was only to suggest that "despite all the difficulties and reverses," the federal government would do its best to improve its ties with the GDR.[75]

No doubt, much of this shift in West German rhetoric can be attributed to the practical imperatives associated with the new politics of compromise with the East, what Bahr aptly characterized as *"Koexistenz auf deutsch."*[76] But, just behind the scenes of official policy-making in Bonn, there was another wish, that the FRG finally be able to transcend the circumstances that had recurrently made it an object of suspicion by its neighbors. As Schmidt would later caution his colleagues at a closed session of the SPD Bundestag *Fraktion* in February 1979, even his country's successes in dealing with its old adversaries in the Soviet Union and Eastern Europe had had the effect, paradoxically, of re-awakening anxieties in Europe about West German intentions:

> The Germans must be careful because they have grown relatively stronger in the course of the last ten or fifteen years. One reason for this strength is the greater room for maneuver that we have acquired as a result of the Ostpolitik, the treaties with Moscow, Warsaw, and Prague, and the four-power treaty on Berlin. We have to be careful to avoid the danger that one day others will regard our country as having become too big and too important.[77]

Thus, the logical recourse for many decision-makers in Bonn was to deemphasize that single aspect of FRG policy that still set their country definitively apart from its neighbors—the active pursuit of national reunification.

Perhaps historians will one day conclude that this shift, the greatest conceivable retreat from the "policy of strength" of Adenauer's time, helped West Germany's leaders to portray their state in an agreeable light in the 1980s. But in view of what was to come a decade later in 1989, when the possibility of German unity was thrust upon the FRG by events outside its control, they will undoubtedly also be struck by the ironic impact of the *Ostpolitik,* which seemed to prepare them for a different age of quiet accommodation with the status quo.

Notes

1. This approach is taken by almost all scholarly studies of the *Ostpolitik*. See, for example, William E. Griffith, *The Ostpolitik of the Federal Republic of Germany* (Cambridge, Mass., 1978), 102.

2. Willy Brandt, *People and Politics: The Years 1960–1975*, trans. J. Maxwell Brownjohn (Boston, 1978), 20.

3. Even Adenauer had private doubts about how rigorously the policy should be applied. Behind the scenes, he was involved in a few efforts to strike a deal with the Soviets on the national question. See Griffith, *Ostpolitik,* 84–87.

4. See Walter Stützle, *Kennedy und Adenauer in der Berlin Krise, 1961–1962* (Bonn-Bad Godesberg, 1973).

5. *Dokumente zur Deutschlandpolitik* (hereafter, *DzD*), series IV, 9:572–75. Bahr was not the first to broach such ideas. A full year earlier, an adviser to the Free Demo-

cratic Party, Wolfgang Schollwer, touched off a controversy within the party by explicitly—although not publicly—recommending that Bonn enter into relations with the GDR to keep alive the chance of national reunification. See ibid., series IV, 8:376–89.

6. See Peter Bender, *Neue Ostpolitik* (Munich, 1986), 118. Some were later to go even further than Bahr, for example, Karl Jaspers, *Wohin treibt die Bundesrepublik?* (Munich, 1966), and later, Bender himself, *Zehn Gründe für die Anerkennung der DDR* (Frankfurt, 1968).

7. See Bahr's speech at Tutzing, in *DzD*, series IV, 9:572–75.

8. On these, see Griffith, *Ostpolitik*, 84–86.

9. "Don't trust the Americans," he told Heinrich Krone in early February 1961, "They are doing everything they can, at our expense, to come to an understanding with the Russians." Cited in "Aufzeichnungen zur Deutschland- und Ostpolitik, 1954–1969," in *Adenauer Studien III*, ed. Rudolf Morsey and Konrad Repgen (Mainz, 1971), 168.

10. See Hans-Peter Schwarz's poignant account in *Adenauer, Der Staatsmann: 1952–1967* (Stuttgart, 1991), 709–12.

11. Cited ibid., 712.

12. On Adenauer's relations with the party, see Arnold J. Heidenheimer, *Adenauer and the CDU* (The Hague, 1960).

13. A revealing account of this complex individual is Klaus Bloemer, "Außenpolitische Vorstellungen und Verhaltensweisen des F. J. Strauß," *Liberal*, July–August 1980, 609–24.

14. Not only was the Hallstein doctrine not a doctrine, but its author was not even its namesake, State Secretary Walter Hallstein. The policy's real architect was Wilhelm Grewe, later Adenauer's quarrelsome ambassador to the United States.

15. These fears became particularly acute following an official visit by Ulbricht to Egypt in 1965. As FDP chairman Erich Mende warned: "Wherever the Federal Republic displays its flag, so too will Ulbricht's separatist flag be raised. This allows the Soviet zone to assert itself in politically important areas of our earth and to proclaim its own right to rule Germany." Cited in Boris Meissner, ed., *Die deutsche Ostpolitik: 1961–1970* (Cologne, 1970), 101.

16. For Schröder's rationalization of his policy, see his 4 November 1963 interview, in ibid., 71–72.

17. See Clay Clemens, *Reluctant Realists: The CDU/CSU and the West German Ostpolitik* (Durham, N.C., 1989), 41–47.

18. See his 4 November 1963 interview, in Meissner, *Die deutsche Ostpolitik*, 73, italics added.

19. See Klaus Hildebrand, *Geschichte der Bundesrepublik Deutschland: Von Erhard zur Großen Koalition, 1963–1969* (Stuttgart, 1984), 94. Ulbricht later claimed that the Christmas visit agreement confirmed the "sovereign as well as factual existence" of the GDR. *Neues Deutschland*, 4 Jan. 1964.

20. The desire to avoid international isolation was, for many CDU insiders, the primary motive behind the "Note on Disarmament and the Securing of Peace." See the less than enthusiastic rationalization by party stalwart Eugen Gerstenmaier, *Streit und Friede hat seine Zeit* (Frankfurt, 1981), 455.

21. "Note der Bundesregierung zur Abrüstung und Sicherung des Friedens" in Meissner, *Die deutsche Ostpolitik*, 120–24.

22. Author's interviews in East Berlin with Jürgen Hofmann, 29 May 1989; Heinz Hümmler, 31 May 1989; Herbert Häber, 1 June 1989; and Gerhard Keiderling, 21 Mar. 1990. Also, see GDR Oral History Project (Hoover Institution) interview with Otto Reinhold, 23 Mar. 1990. For provocative documents see Rudolf Herrnstadt, *Das Herrnstadt Dokument: das Politburo der SED und die Geschichte des 17. Juni 1953*, ed. Nadja-Stulz Herrnstadt (Reinbek bei Hamburg, 1990).

23. Wolfgang Leonhard, *Spurensuche* (Cologne, 1992), 92.

24. Author's interviews with Herbert Häber, 28 Apr. 1988 and 1 June 1989.

25. For Ulbricht, only the GDR was truly entitled to represent the German people. "Here where the GDR is," he affirmed in April 1965, "is the foundation of peace, here the people decide. [This] is Germany." *Neues Deutschland*, 28 Apr. 1965.

26. *Neues Deutschland*, 1 Aug. 1963.

27. See his defense of exploratory talks with the SPD on "basic questions," at the twelfth plenum of the Central Committee of the SED on 4 Apr. 1966. Central Party Archives, Institute for the Workers' Movement, Berlin (hereafter, CPA), IV 2/1/192.

28. For a hint of opposition to the talks, see Heinz Hoffmann's remarks before the same plenum, CPA, IV 2/1/193.

29. Suspicions about the danger of being too close to the "Social Fascists" were always just below the surface of SED rhetoric, due to the messy circumstances behind the formation of the Socialist Unity Party in 1946 and the forcible merger of the Eastern German SPD with the KPD.

30. See Brandt, *People and Politics,* 169.

31. See the foreign minister's address in Bucharest on 4 Aug. 1967, in Meissner, *Die deutsche Ostpolitik*, 217.

32. This marked about-face in policy was justified by appealing to a "birth defect" theory: the Soviet bloc states were not to be held responsible for a condition (i.e., relations with the GDR) with which they had practically been born.

33. Yet, Brandt can hardly have been considered a radical, if one only recalls his overtly pro-Atlanticist postures in the late 1950s and early 1960s, not to mention the fact that his reaction to the wall's erection was, if anything, stronger than Adenauer's. See Hans-Peter Schwarz, *Geschichte der Bundesrepublik Deutschland: Die Ära Adenauer, 1957–1963* (Stuttgart, 1983), 150–52.

34. See Arnulf Baring, *Machtwechsel: Die Ära Brandt-Scheel* (Stuttgart, 1982), 95–99.

35. One does not have to read too much between Brandt's lines to see that even the minister was expected to demonstrate appropriate respect for the established routines of the Foreign Office: "I was fortunate enough to work with efficient subordinates, some of them first-class. I seldom had cause to complain of disloyalty and demonstrated my confidence by eschewing the introduction of too many outsiders." *People and Politics*, 153. Later, as chancellor, Brandt went around the Foreign Service bureaucracy as often as he could.

36. Cited in Bender, *Neue Ostpolitik*, 136. Also see Kiesinger's press conference of 20 Jan. 1967, in Meissner, *Die deutsche Ostpolitik*, 174.

37. See Ulbricht's speech in *Neues Deutschland*, 14 Nov. 1966.

38. For a sample of the SED's indignation, see Ulbricht's interview with *Neues Deutschland*, 30 Nov. 1966.

39. See Ulbricht's speech of 17 Apr. 1967, in *DzD*, series V, 1:949–68.

40. See the statement of 26 Apr. 1967, in *DzD*, series V, 1:1047–54. For background, see Michael J. Sodaro, *Moscow, Germany, and the West: From Khrushchev to Gorbachev* (Ithaca, 1990), chap. 3.

41. For Brandt's speech, see Meissner, *Die deutsche Ostpolitik*, 380–83.

42. Ibid., 381.

43. See Günther Schmid. *Entscheidung in Bonn* (Cologne, 1979), 20.

44. See Baring, *Machtwechsel*, 269–71.

45. See Schmid, *Entscheidung*, 36–37; and Baring, *Machtwechsel*, 272–83, 311–12.

46. See Schmid, *Entscheidung*, 79.

47. Bonn sought to assuage the Polish government's consternation, however, by writing the Warsaw Treaty to emphasize the FRG's respect for, if not total recognition of, the Oder-Neisse border. On this, see Bender, *Neue Ostpolitik* pp. 176–77.

48. Henry A. Kissinger, *White House Years* (Boston, 1979), 408–9.

49. In private conversation with Foreign Office veteran Paul Frank, Kissinger admitted as much: "I will tell you one thing. If there is eventually to be a détente policy with the Soviet Union, then *we* will make it!" See Frank's pseudonymous adventures of diplomat Caspar Hilzinger, *Entschlüsselte Botschaft: Ein Diplomat macht Inventur* (Stuttgart, 1981), 287.

50. Kissinger, *White House Years*, 807–10, 823–33. So secret were these talks that William P. Rogers, the American secretary of state at the time, was unaware of their existence until the Berlin accord was practically completed.

51. Rainer Barzel, *Im Streit und umstritten* (Frankfurt, 1986), 138–40.

52. For Barzel's anguished observations about the chancellor's competitive advantage ("Now nothing was rational anymore"), see his *Auf dem Drahtseil* (Munich, 1978), 137–38.

53. Notably, both meetings came at Ulbricht's initiative, and not that of the Soviets, who were somewhat anxious to find (not unlike the Americans) that an ally was making German policy on its own. Author's interview, Herbert Häber, 21 Mar. 1990.

54. See, for example, his oral report at a meeting with the Soviet leadership, 3 Dec. 1969. CPA, IV 2/1/230, Berlin.

55. However, misgivings about the first secretary's arrogance and "sense of superiority" were by no means rare in Moscow. See, for example, Leonid Brezhnev's discussion with Erich Honecker, Ulbricht's eventual successor, on 28 July 1970, in Peter Przybylski, *Tatort Politbüro: Die Akte Honecker* (Berlin, 1991), 280–85.

56. *Pravda*, 30 Nov. 1970.

57. See his speeches in *Neues Deutschland*, 1 Jan. 1971 and 14 Jan. 1971.

58. An illuminating account is Gerhard Naumann and Eckhard Trümpler, *Von Ulbricht zu Honecker* (Berlin, 1990).

59. Ulbricht's loss of power, after twenty-two years of predominance, was filled with pathos. As it became clear that he would soon be replaced, he dispatched a pleading note to Brezhnev on 12 Mar. 1971, following a *Kur* in the Soviet Union, inquiring whether it would not be "useful to notify the press that you [*Sie*] have received me for a friendly exchange of views." In the Ulbricht *Nachlass*, CPA, Berlin.

60. See "Vertrag über die Grundlagen der Beziehungen zwischen der Bundesrepublik Deutschland und der Deutschen Demokratischen Republik," in Bundesministerium für innerdeutsche Beziehungen, *Zehn Jahre Deutschlandpolitik* (Bonn, 1980), 205–7.

61. Ibid., 205.

62. Brandt, *People and Politics*, 360.

63. An able characterization of the new chancellor is Wolfgang Jäger and Werner Link, *Geschichte der Bundesrepublik Deutschland: Republik im Wandel, 1974–1982* (Stuttgart, 1987), especially 9–10, 275–77.

64. Helmut Schmidt, *Menschen und Mächte* (Berlin, 1987), 22.

65. Sodaro, *Moscow, Germany, and the West*, 248.

66. Cited ibid., 271. For Schmidt's worries, see *Menschen und Mächte*, 64.

67. Bender, *Neue Ostpolitik*, 208–9.

68. "For when things go badly for [Poland]," Schmidt later wrote, "the painful memories will almost inevitably return of the injuries suffered by the Polish people over the last two hundred years." *Die Deutschen und ihre Nachbarn* (Berlin, 1990), 482.

69. For Schmidt's historical perspective, see *Menschen und Mächte*, 47.

70. On 21 Dec. 1972, *Zehn Jahre Deutschlandpolitik*, 212.

71. Schmidt, *Die Deutschen und ihre Nachbarn*, 27.

72. *Reden und Aufsätze* (Berlin, 1977), 1:438.

73. On this general theme, see A. James McAdams, *Germany Divided: From the Wall to Reunification* (Princeton, 1993).

74. "Egon Bahr am 11. July 1973 in der Evangelischen Akademie Tutzing," *Deutschland Archiv* (August 1973), 866.

75. "Regierungserklärung vor dem Deutschen Bundestag," *Bulletin* (Bonn: Presse und Informationsamt, May 18, 1974), 597.

76. See "Egon Bahr," 867.

77. Proceedings of the SPD Bundestag *Fraktion*, 6 Feb. 1979, Archives of the Friedrich Ebert Stiftung, Bonn.

19

RESCUING CHOICE FROM CIRCUMSTANCE:

THE STATECRAFT OF HENRY KISSINGER

John Lewis Gaddis

THE PUBLIC LIFE of every political figure is a continual struggle to rescue an element of choice from the pressure of circumstance."[1] So the most prominent American diplomat of the middle and late Cold War, Henry Kissinger, summed up what he had learned from his eight years of official responsibility, first as President Richard Nixon's national security adviser, then as secretary of state to both Nixon and his post-Watergate successor, Gerald R. Ford.[2] It was an uncharacteristically ungrandiose observation. After all, no statesman of the postwar era worked harder to build a reputation for indispensability; few in any era have had so keen an appetite for power, or such skill in hanging onto it. No twentieth-century American who was not himself a president sparked greater controversy about his own involvement in the events of his time, and it would be difficult to think of any public figure who has himself chronicled that involvement at greater length, or with such care.

It comes as something of a surprise, therefore, to find Kissinger retrospectively picturing the role of the statesman, not in terms of a "great man" theory of history—and certainly not in such a way as to recall the "lone cowboy" image he once improbably invoked to describe himself[3]—but rather in a manner suggesting the life of a harassed clerk, desperately seeking room for maneuver in an oppressive environment within which he has no choice but to function. "The statesman's responsibility is to struggle against transitoriness and not to insist that he be paid in the coin of eternity," Kissinger insisted in one of those heavy aphorisms that punctuate his memoirs. "He owes it to his people to strive, to create, and to resist the decay that besets all human institutions."[4]

So pessimistic a view of what statecraft could accomplish was extraordinary coming from an American. For whatever may have been the case in other countries, resignation, world-weariness, and the cultivation of despair have never worn particularly well in the United States. Kissinger's role in reshaping American foreign policy is all the more remarkable, therefore, given the attitude he brought to it. His image as a jet-setting "superstar"[5] was unprecedented for any diplomat, and nothing short of bizarre given who he was.

Kissinger was, to begin with, a refugee. The first naturalized citizen ever to become secretary of state, he had been born a German Jew and had experienced at first hand, not just the persecution of the Nazi regime, but also the subsequent dislocation of emigration. He was, as well, an intellectual—a university professor, think-tank consultant, and sometime government adviser—with little of the experience in diplomacy, business, or law that most makers of American foreign policy have had. Portly, bespectacled, speaking with an accent that thickened as he aged, Kissinger seemed utterly implausible as an object of public acclaim. Even more unfashionably, he was also a historian. The author of an early and respected book on the restoration of peace in Europe after Napoleon's defeat in 1815 and a keen student of Bismarck's diplomacy half a century later,[6] Kissinger had resisted the preoccupation with theory that had come to dominate the study of international relations in American universities.[7] His "realism," if that is what it was, came from steeping himself in the history of diplomacy, not from any systematic attempt to construct, or to endorse, a "science" of politics.[8]

"Luck," Kissinger the historian had once written, "is but the residue of design."[9] Perhaps so, but Kissinger—who had chosen, unpresciently, to link his fortunes with the political career of Nelson Rockefeller—can hardly have crafted his own entry into the world of statecraft. That design was Richard Nixon's, and the calculations that caused the president-elect to offer the position of national security adviser to Kissinger late in November 1968 are still not completely clear. Kissinger thought that Nixon wanted to "demonstrate his ability to co-opt a Harvard intellectual; that I came from Rockefeller's entourage made the prospect all the more interesting."[10] Nixon recalled having concluded, from Kissinger's academic writings, "that we shared a belief in the importance of isolating and influencing the factors affecting worldwide balances of power."[11] Both explanations ring true, as does a third one, advanced a bit cynically by one of Nixon's biographers: "They sensed in each other, in their first meeting, a shared love of secrecy and surprise, a strong sense of contempt for the bureaucracy, for established methods, for regular procedure. They were both born conspirators."[12]

It is too easy to assume, in looking at the Nixon-Kissinger relationship, that it was Kissinger who had the ideas and Nixon who authorized their implementation. Throughout his long career, observers of Nixon consistently underestimated his own conceptual abilities, which could be formidable.[13] Nor should one conclude, because Kissinger had been a professor, that he was inexperienced in the manipulation of power. That was precisely the theme he had studied as a historian; and as he once remarked, the rivalries that exist within academic establishments can be just as protracted, bitter, and self-absorbing as those within and among governments—it is only that the stakes are so much smaller.[14] Not until the archives of the Nixon-Kissinger era are fully open for research will we be able to sort out who influenced whom in this strange partnership; and even then, since so much that occurred between them was not written down—or taped—the issue may well remain unresolved.

What is clear now, though, is that it was Kissinger, not Nixon, who had the more durable impact on policy. With an amazement that still showed when he composed his memoirs a decade later, Kissinger has described how his own image of indispensability had come to exceed that of the president as the Watergate scandal worsened in 1973 and 1974.[15] Given his own involvement in the events leading up to that affair, it is significant that Kissinger was one of the few top Nixon administration officials to emerge unscathed from it, and that he went on to assume primary responsibility for foreign and national security policy during the two and a half year incumbency of Gerald Ford. Whoever may have had the ideas, it turned out to be Kissinger who retained the power.

How wisely he wielded it is a question journalists and historians began debating long before Kissinger left office.[16] As is usually the case with recent and controversial subjects, these accounts have tended toward hagiographic or hypocritical extremes: few balanced appraisals exist, even now.[17] Nor is there any consensus on what constitutes "success" in statecraft in the first place.[18] Do we mean by it attaining one's stated objectives, or resisting those of others? How much time is to be allowed to reach these goals? What balance should one expect between the guidance that principle provides and the expediency that effective action usually demands? All of these issues arise in seeking to evaluate Henry Kissinger's public career. The place to begin, though, is where Kissinger himself began, with the study of history.

I

"History is not, of course, a cookbook offering pretested recipes," Kissinger cautioned in his memoirs. "It teaches by analogy, not by maxims. It can illuminate the consequences of actions in comparable situations, yet each generation must discover for itself what situations are in fact comparable."[19] And yet, those same memoirs, like most of Kissinger's other writings, stagger under the weight of maxims drawn from historical experience. The following occur within a page of his assertion that maxims teach nothing at all: "If history teaches anything it is that there can be no peace without equilibrium and no justice without restraint." "History knows no resting places or plateaus. All societies of which history informs us went through periods of decline; most of them eventually collapsed." "There is a margin between necessity and accident, in which the statesman by perseverance and intuition must choose and thereby shape the destiny of his people." "To hide behind historical inevitability is tantamount to moral abdication; it is to neglect the elements of strength and hope and inspiration which through the centuries have sustained mankind."[20]

It is hardly surprising that the author of a long and ponderous undergraduate thesis on "The Meaning of History" should have concluded that history does have meaning.[21] What is interesting about this precocious literary effort is that Kissinger was already attempting, as a student at Harvard in the early 1950s, to apply historical lessons to the realm of policy. The study of history, he insisted, was not just an academic exercise; it was the "key to action."[22] But the capacity to act resided, paradoxically enough, in a recognition of constraints: opportunities for human freedom existed only within an acknowledgement of human limitations. The theme is an ancient one in religion, to be sure, but the young Kissinger substituted historical forces for Original Sin.[23] It was only by accepting inherited circumstances and transcending them *inwardly*—even if one never overcame them outwardly—that the opportunities for creative statecraft lay.

Kissinger's doctoral dissertation, subsequently published as *A World Restored,* applied these abstractions to the problem of how peace had been made after the Napoleonic Wars. Prior to Kissinger, few historians had found much to admire in the principal architects of that settlement, the Austrian foreign minister, Klemens von Metternich, and the British foreign secretary, Lord Castlereagh. If anything, these statesmen had been frowned upon for trying to restore an antiquated status quo, and in the case of Metternich for his suppression of challenges to it. Kissinger was impressed, though, not by how reactionary the Concert of Europe had been, "but how balanced." It might not have met the test of idealism, but it had given its generation "perhaps something more precious: a period of stability which permitted their hopes to be realized without a major war or a permanent revolution."[24]

The problem with wars and the revolutions that often caused them, Kissinger insisted, was that they overthrew the constraints that made freedom possible. The principal characteristic of a revolutionary power was "*that nothing can reassure it*. Only absolute security—the neutralization of the opponent—is considered a sufficient guarantee, and thus the desire of one power for absolute security means absolute insecurity for all the others." Diplomacy, which Kissinger defined as "the art of restraining the exercise of power," could hardly function in such a situation; as a consequence, sooner or later, war was likely to break out.[25] And in the modern era, far more than in that of Metternich and Castlereagh, war would be the ultimate denial of freedom.

Given these views, it might seem odd that Kissinger also admired the man most responsible for overthrowing the post-1815 settlement: Otto von Bismarck. But Bismarck, Kissinger emphasized, had been a "white revolutionary," not a "red" one. By transforming the Prussian state into a unified German empire, Bismarck had indeed upset an existing equilibrium; he had done this, though, "in the guise of conservatism." Having established that empire, he conducted its foreign policy with "an agility of conception and a sense of proportion which, while he lived, turned power into an instrument of self-restraint."[26] As a result, he was able for almost a generation "to preserve the peace of Europe by manipulating the commitments and interests of other powers in a masterly fashion."[27]

The systems of Metternich and Bismarck failed, however, to survive their founders. Both men, in Kissinger's view, had turned the balancing of power into the juggling of power: they confused statecraft with performance. So dextrous were Metternich's combinations, Kissinger wrote, in words that he could as easily have applied to Bismarck, that they made "the *tour de force* of a solitary figure" seem like "the application of universal principles."[28] Lesser men lacked the skill to sustain such systems, and bureaucracies—which Kissinger always regarded as repositories of mediocrity[29]—could not even come close to doing so. But to seek stability and sustain it in a chaotic world, even if temporarily, was for Kissinger as close as historical figures ever come to heroic accomplishment. To fail grandly, in his minimalist view of what history allows, was to succeed.

II

How much history would allow the Nixon administration was an open question when it took power early in 1969. The painful wound that was the Vietnam War—all the more painful for being largely self-inflicted—still transfixed the nation; and although President Lyndon B. Johnson had made the decision to undertake no further escalation in Southeast Asia, he had left office with over half a million American troops still in place there. Peace negotiations with the North Vietnamese and their Viet Cong surrogates had settled little more than the shape of the conference table. The adversaries, allies, and neutrals Johnson and his advisers had sought to impress by involving the United States in that conflict had witnessed a display of costly incompetence, not resolve. Meanwhile, public confidence in government had been severely shaken: not since the Civil War a century earlier had so many Americans objected so vociferously to the path their leaders had chosen to follow.

All of this, in turn, distracted attention from a geopolitical event of fundamental importance: the emergence of the Soviet Union, for the first time ever, as an approximate military equal of the United States. The NATO alliance had never matched the conventional forces available to the Warsaw Pact, to be sure, but American superiority in nuclear weapons and the means of delivering them had, heretofore, compensated for that disadvantage. As a result, the Soviet Union had backed down from a series of challenges it had initiated, beginning with the 1948 Berlin blockade and culminating in the Cuban missile crisis of 1962. In the wake of that last episode, however, as Americans were becoming more deeply enmeshed in Southeast Asia, the Russians had begun the mass production of real rockets, not just the rhetorical ones with which Nikita Khrushchev had sought to supplement his unimpressive arsenal. By the time the Nixon administration took office, the USSR had achieved numerical parity with, and was indeed about to surpass, American strength in intercontinental and submarine-launched ballistic missiles.[30]

How these new capabilities would influence the conduct of Soviet foreign policy was not yet clear, but the Kremlin leadership did appear to have taken on a new steadiness and determination since Khrushchev's deposition in 1964. Evidence of this would come four years later, when Leonid Brezhnev and his Politburo colleagues dealt decisively, if brutally, with the movement for reform that had emerged in Czechoslovakia. Moscow's influence elsewhere in the world seemed unaffected by the suppression of the "Prague spring," a fact that gave ominous significance to the "Brezhnev Doctrine," a proclamation by the new Soviet leader that implied the use of force to ensure the survival of *any* Marxist system that might henceforth be threatened, whether from within or without.

The stalemate in Vietnam and the Soviet achievement of strategic parity showed how much the position of the United States had eroded since President Kennedy's 1962 triumph in Cuba. One could account for this reversal in two ways. It could have been, as the Marxists insisted it was, the reflection of historical inevitability: having embarked on a futile crusade to hold back revolutionary nationalism, the United States had exhausted itself, and now had no choice but to yield global leadership to the nation that had more accurately aligned its policies with the forces of history, the Soviet Union. It could also have been the case, though, that long-term trends still favored the United States and its allies; but that American leaders had, through their own mismanagement, failed to calculate correctly long-term interests. Kissinger embraced elements of both explanations, with a resulting ambivalence that reveals much about his policies.

The hegemony the United States had enjoyed after 1945 had indeed been a temporary condition, Kissinger believed, made possible only by the way World War II ended. Europe and Japan were bound to regain their strength sooner or later; and the Soviet Union, also severely weakened at the time the Cold War began, had long since harnessed the power of nuclear weapons and the influence of communist ideology to challenge American authority. "Nothing we could have done would have prevented the Soviet Union from recovering from the war and asserting its new power," Kissinger insisted. "We never fully understood that while our absolute power was growing, our *relative* position was bound to decline."[31] It simply was not possible for *any* great power—no matter how wise its policies—to maintain a position of preeminence indefinitely.

But American policies, in Kissinger's view, had not been wise: the United States had had little experience functioning in a world of equals. For two centuries, the nation had oscillated "between overinvolvement and withdrawal, between expecting too much of our power and being ashamed of it." The Cold War had removed any possibility of isolation; Americans had yet to adjust, however, to the requirements of involvement. "The deepest cause of our national unease was the realization—as yet dimly perceived—that we were becoming like other nations in the need to recognize that our power, while vast, had limits." Vietnam had brought these contradictions into the open, and as a consequence the Nixon administration had been the first of the postwar generation "that had to conduct foreign policy without the national consensus that had sustained its predecessors largely since 1947."[32]

Kissinger saw the new administration's task, therefore, very much as a rescue mission: as one of preserving as much freedom as possible within an international environment from which the United States could no longer retreat, but in which its hegemony could no longer be taken for granted. The situation was neither promising nor hopeless: the nation would at last, however, have to grow up. Like all postadolescents, it would need all the patience, the wisdom— and, not least, the resignation—that are supposed to come with maturity.

III

Neither Kissinger's personal history nor his training in history encouraged him to assume any connection between democratic procedures and successful statecraft. States maintained their influence only because they preserved their power, and that fact gave authoritarian regimes, where power could be seized, focused, and directed, an inherent advantage. "The Soviet leadership is burdened by no self-doubt or liberal guilt," Kissinger pointed out with a hint of envy in 1979. "It has no effective domestic opposition questioning the morality of its actions. The result is a foreign policy free to fill every vacuum, to exploit every opportunity, to act out the implications of its doctrine. Policy is constrained principally by calculations of objective conditions."[33]

The triumph of authoritarianism was by no means foreordained, though. The very nature of such governments made orderly successions difficult. There was little to admire in Soviet economic performance over the years. The Communist party had evolved into a defender rather than a challenger of privilege: "Sooner or later," Kissinger predicted, "this essentially parasitic function is bound to lead to internal pressures, especially in a state comprised of many nationalities." The advent of nuclear weapons had reinforced an instinct for survival —and the compromises necessary to ensure it—that dated back to Lenin: "Soviet leaders have no intention of committing suicide." It would be foolish "to expect the Soviet leaders to restrain themselves from exploiting circumstances they conceive to be favorable." But the West could, through its own actions, see to it that such circumstances did not arise. "It is up to us to define the limits of Soviet aims."[34]

The difficulty was that this task required clarity and consistency in the foreign policy of the United States, qualities the American political system seemed to preclude. Public opinion, together with the congressional and media attitudes through which it filtered, tended toward extremes of euphoria or despair when it came to relations with the Soviet Union: both distorted the realities the West actually confronted. The requirement that every foreign policy maneuver be weighed against its domestic costs discouraged serious thinking about long-term objectives. Meanwhile official bureaucracies sought to perpetuate existing policies, whether they were working or not. "It seemed to me no accident that most great statesmen had been locked in a permanent struggle with the experts in their foreign offices, for the scope of the statesman's conception challenges the inclination of the expert toward minimal risk."[35]

What was necessary, therefore, was to find ways in which democratic states could behave with authoritarian purposefulness when their global interests required it, without at the same time sacrificing those democratic principles that provided the reason such states existed in the first place. Only in this way could the United States compete in an international environment it could no longer dominate. One simply could not apply, in one's policies toward the outside world, the same principles by which one ran one's society at home: the cold and cruel conditions of world politics did not allow such luxuries.

The office Kissinger occupied in the new Nixon administration reflected this tension between constitutional constraints and the need for operational flexibility. The National Security Council had been formed in 1947 to coordinate diplomacy with military, economic, and intelligence capabilities in a manner never before attempted in the United States: fighting the Cold War, it was thought, demanded nothing less. Until the Kennedy and Johnson administrations, the presidential assistant for national security affairs had had little more than clerical responsibilities; but under McGeorge Bundy and Walt Rostow the job had become a top White House advisory position, despite the fact that it did not require congressional confirmation.

Because Nixon distrusted bureaucracies as much as did Kissinger, even if for different reasons—he thought them dominated by liberal, Nixon-hating Democrats—he sought to centralize control over all aspects of foreign policy within the National Security Council. As a result, Kissinger's authority went well beyond what Bundy's and Rostow's had been. The more traditional agencies of government, especially the Department of State—to whom Nixon appointed William P. Rogers, the least memorable secretary of state of the Cold War era—were left with little to do.

Kissinger's influence depended totally, however, upon satisfying his mercurial yet morbidly suspicious chief. This meant accommodating himself to Nixon's distinctly odd working habits; it also required unquestioning support for questionable policies. When a series of news leaks provoked frantic efforts within the White House to track down their sources, Kissinger readily cooperated, even to the point of authorizing telephone wiretaps on journalists and several of his own subordinates: he thereby helped set in motion practices that eventually led to Watergate.[36] When others in the administration resigned in protest over the president's decision to invade Cambodia in the spring of 1970, Kissinger stayed on, thereby earning Nixon's gratitude but ensuring the enmity of former academic colleagues.[37] When Nixon insisted on heavily bombing Hanoi over Christmas 1972, primarily to soothe the anxieties of a nervous

South Vietnamese government, Kissinger did not protest.[38] Indeed, it is difficult to conceive of anything that could have happened during Nixon's presidency that might have caused Kissinger to resign, apart from a significant
restriction of his own authority, something that never took place.[39]

Kissinger's justification for these compromises was that, without them, he
would never have been in a position to accomplish anything.[40] One must retain
power, after all, if one is to rescue choices from circumstances. And just as the
growing military strength of the Soviet Union and intensifying domestic opposition to the Vietnam War presented circumstances in which choices were badly
needed, so Kissinger also regarded his own brooding president as a kind of
circumstance: one that could at times be arbitrary and unpredictable; but one
also capable of being managed discreetly through careful statecraft.[41]

Principles were by no means absent from Kissinger's calculations. He understood, perhaps better than most of his contemporaries, what the tyranny of authoritarianism was really like; he sensed, more clearly than many of his academic
counterparts, how easily the aspirations of revolutions can be perverted. The
issue, for him, was one of sequence, not priorities. Power and its prudent use
were neither more nor less important than principles, but they were antecedent:
one had to have a certain amount of stability, together with the authority to take
advantage of it, before one could begin to address issues of right and wrong.[42]

In his article on Bismarck, published just before he entered the new Nixon
administration, Kissinger had devoted several pages to an exchange of correspondence between the Prussian statesman and the man who had "discovered"
him, Leopold von Gerlach. In it Gerlach had taken Bismarck to task for trying
to improve Prussia's relations with Napoleon III's France, "for only he is
reliable who acts according to principle and not according to changing concepts
of national interest." Bismarck had responded by denying that "a properly
conceived Prussian policy requires chastity in foreign affairs even from the
point of view of utility." The differences here, Kissinger noted, were fundamental: "Gerlach tested policy by absolute moral scruples; Bismarck considered success the only acceptable criterion."[43] Kissinger the historian considered Bismarck to have failed, because although the Iron Chancellor himself had
substituted self-restraint for the constraints Gerlach would have found in moral
principle, Bismarck's successors had shown no such wisdom, and a great war
had been the result. But Kissinger the courtier knew that Gerlach's methods
would get him nowhere at the particular court to which he was attached: if one
was to achieve praiseworthy ends in the Nixon administration, it would have to
be by Bismarckian means.

IV

Bismarck had been a "genius," Kissinger wrote in 1968, because he had sought
"to restrain . . . contending forces, both domestic and foreign, by manipulat-

ing their antagonisms."[44] The key to understanding what Kissinger tried to do with the power he accumulated lies in this Bismarckian tactic of balancing rivalries. It might have been possible in the past to achieve stability through hegemony, much as Rome, for several centuries, had managed to do. But in the modern world, bids for hegemony, whatever their source and however admirable their intentions, were bound sooner or later to generate resistance, repression, and the instability that inevitably accompanied them. The preeminence of the United States at the end of World War II might have given rise to illusions that the Americans and their allies could carry off something like a Pax Romana, but the realities—as the events of the 1960s clearly demonstrated—had turned out to be very different.

The original strategy of containment, as articulated by George F. Kennan and put into effect by the Truman administration during the late 1940s, had had equilibrium as its objective: the idea had been to restrain Moscow's ambitions by peaceful means, in the expectation that the Soviet Union would eventually abandon its expansionist goals and become a "normal" great power. Rivalries with other such powers would not cease, but a balance among them—Kennan had in mind the United States, the Soviet Union, Great Britain, a West European community centered around Germany, and Japan—would keep the peace.[45]

In the hands of its subsequent architects, though, containment had evolved—much to Kennan's chagrin[46]—into a search for military superiority over the Soviet Union. Efforts to facilitate that nation's integration into the established international order had received little attention; the maintenance of alliances and the credibility that sustained them overshadowed the objectives these priorities were supposed to accomplish.[47] One undertook commitments, after all, for some purpose: to deter an adversary, to reassure an ally, to advance one's own interests. When commitments *became* interests—as had happened in Vietnam, where a single commitment was being honored extravagantly despite its failure to fulfill any of these larger purposes—then a rethinking of strategy was obviously in order. "Our dilemmas were very much a product of liberal doctrines of reformist intervention and academic theories of gradual escalation," Kissinger recalled. "The collapse of these high aspirations shattered the self-confidence without which Establishments flounder."[48]

Compounding these problems had been an unnecessary proliferation of adversaries. Because Americans assumed that a revolutionary ideology directed Moscow's policies, they fell too easily into the habit of believing that wherever similar ideologies existed, so too did Moscow's influence. But Kissinger was certain that ideology counted for less in world politics than did state interests. Hence, even though a nation might portray itself as revolutionary—as the USSR and the People's Republic of China had long done—over time, ideological enthusiasms wore thin and national priorities moved to center stage.[49]

It was difficult, however, for democracies to deal with ideologies. They tended either to disregard the role of such doctrines altogether, or to make ideology the all-determining explanation for the actions of states that adhered to them. The United States had followed the first procedure during World War II, when Franklin D. Roosevelt had sought to deal with Josef Stalin as if he had been Winston Churchill. But by 1950 the nation had shifted to the opposite extreme, so that even casual professions of Marxism were sufficient to mark states as adversaries, without regard to whether they possessed the intentions— or the means—of harming American interests.[50] The illogic of this procedure had also become evident in Vietnam, where the Johnson administration had made immense investments in manpower, materiel, and reputation to contain Ho Chi Minh, a leader some American officials had long acknowledged to be as much a nationalist as a communist. Meanwhile, they had done nothing to prevent the Soviet Union from undercutting the strategic superiority upon which the most fundamental elements of Western security had rested since the earliest days of the Cold War.

The first requirement for restoring the balance of power, therefore, was to regain a clearer sense of what constituted a threat to that balance in the first place. For Kissinger, this was not North Vietnam, or even China, but the Soviet Union, the nation that alone combined hostility toward the United States with the capacity to act upon it. It followed, then, that the strategy of containment needed to be refocused on its original target, and purged of the ideological distractions that had caused the United States unwisely to expand the number of adversaries it confronted.

It made sense, from this perspective, to return to Kennan's multipolar concept, amended to take into account the relative decline of Great Britain over the past several decades and the simultaneous emergence of China.[51] Nixon made this thinking explicit when he announced casually in 1971—with greater candor than Kissinger was prepared for[52]—that the United States, the Soviet Union, Western Europe, Japan, and China would dominate world affairs during the last third of the twentieth century. "I think it will be a safer world and a better world," the president argued, "if we have a stronger, healthy United States, Europe, Soviet Union, China, Japan, each balancing the other, not playing one against the other, an even balance."[53]

At the same time, though, maintaining a balance of power—or restoring one—was as much a matter of the psychological impressions one made as of the actual power one wielded. One could not withdraw too quickly from exposed positions, however unwise it might have been to take them up, without undermining one's credibility as an actor of consequence in the international system. "We could not simply walk away from an enterprise involving two administrations, five allied countries, and thirty-one thousand dead," Kissinger insisted, "as if we were switching a television channel." It was true that Charles de Gaulle had abandoned a long-standing French commitment in Algeria with minimal loss of credibility, but he had taken four years and he had done it "as an act of policy, not as a collapse, in a manner reflecting a national decision and not a rout."[54]

Kremlin leaders were poised to exploit any sign of weakness, Kissinger claimed: "The choice of Soviet tactics is . . . determined by their assessment of the 'objective correlation of forces,' which as Marxists they pride themselves on discerning."[55] Even if they were right, therefore, and historical circumstances were in fact working to reduce American power and influence in the world, the United States could never afford to acknowledge this because whatever was left of its authority would evaporate if it did so. "It seemed to me important for America not to be humiliated, not to be shattered. . . . it was precisely the issue of our self-confidence and faith in our future that I considered at stake in the outcome in Vietnam."[56]

The essence of the problem, then, was to find a way to withdraw from Vietnam without appearing to have been forced to do so; to regain the initiative in world affairs without giving evidence of ever having lost it; and to accomplish all of this within the awkward institutional framework that the American constitution demanded. The task would have been worthy of a Metternich or a Bismarck; those statesmen, in turn, would have found much that was familiar in the methods Kissinger used in attempting to accomplish it.

V

The first of these methods was to offer revolutionaries respectability. If American interests required recreating and sustaining a global balance of power, then it followed that that balance should include all major states. It would make no sense to exclude certain great powers because one disapproved of them, as the architects of the Versailles Treaty had sought to do with a defeated Germany and a revolutionary Russia after World War I; rather, the model should be that of 1815, when Metternich and Castlereagh had moved immediately after the defeat of Napoleon to bring France back into the Concert of Europe. They had done this because they understood that, if an international order is to survive, all of its major participants have to have at least some interest in its perpetuation. This could hardly happen if any of them bore lasting grudges against it.

The diminishing importance of ideology in the Soviet Union and China served, in Kissinger's mind, something of the function that Napoleon's downfall had for Metternich and Castlereagh: it raised the possibility—albeit by far less dramatic means than the Battle of Waterloo—that normal states might emerge from the two greatest revolutions of the twentieth century. Such a development would lessen the danger of nuclear war, a prospect Kissinger had worried about increasingly ever since years earlier he had wrestled with—but failed to solve—the problem of how nuclear weapons might be made a rational instrument of warfare.[57] The decline of ideology would allow the multipolar international environment that Nixon had foreseen and that Kissinger believed would be more stable than the bipolar one that had emerged from World War II.

By making it possible to balance potentially hostile powers against one another, this new configuration would also compensate for the relative decline in American strength that the erosion of bipolarity had brought about.

Therefore, an important element in Kissinger's strategy was to defer—elaborately at times—to the Soviet leaders' long-standing desire to have their country treated as a legitimate equal of the United States, and not just in military terms. The recognition had long been present in Washington that it would be dangerous to try to humiliate the Russians; hence, John F. Kennedy's careful efforts to help Khrushchev find as graceful an exit as possible from the humiliation he had inflicted on himself by placing missiles in Cuba. But not since Roosevelt had an American administration been willing to recognize the Soviet Union as a collaborator in the search for international order rather than as a challenger to it.[58] It was Kissinger's particular contribution to perceive how much Brezhnev and his associates craved that kind of recognition: "Despite all the ideological invective, we were the model of a great power that the Soviet Union sought to emulate, lagging some fifteen years behind us in evolution."[59]

At the same time, Kissinger used the principle of legitimacy in another way to put the Russians on the defensive. Having come to this position independently of one another prior to the 1968 election,[60] he and Nixon were prepared to reverse long-established American policy, acknowledge the victory of communism in China, and bring that indisputably great but isolated power back into the international system. The Russians could hardly object, since they had been urging American recognition of the People's Republic since its founding in 1949. Kissinger's dramatic trip to Beijing in July 1971 and the official Nixon visit that followed early in 1972 caused great nervousness in Moscow, however, because ideology had long since ceased to be a source of solidarity in Sino-Soviet relations. To the extent that ideology remained important at all in the modern world, in Kissinger's view, it was more as a cause of *disagreement* among communists than as a source of danger to the West. The real threat to Western security—and to that of China also, as the Chinese communists were coming to realize—was the growing military might that Moscow could command. Disputes over ideology could actually *restore* a balance that would benefit the United States and its allies; hence the advantage of offering respectability to Mao Zedong and the revolution he had made.

Despite their differences, both the Soviet Union and China responded warmly to the Nixon administration's acknowledgment of their legitimacy: the Russians because they sought parity with the United States in prestige as well as missiles; the Chinese because they shared Washington's interest in containing the Russians. In a twist of strategy Bismarck would surely have appreciated, by agreeing to accord both of its Cold War rivals the status of normal states, the United States gained the leverage to play each off against the other. The Russians and the Chinese achieved the respect they desired, but only by becoming objects of American manipulation.

Legitimization worked less well, though, in dealing with smaller revolutionary powers, as Kissinger was to discover in his long and unfruitful negotiations with North Vietnam. For unlike its counterparts in Moscow and Beijing, the Hanoi leadership still thought it could achieve total victory. "The North Vietnamese considered themselves in a life-and-death struggle," Kissinger recalled. "They did not treat negotiations as an enterprise separate from that struggle; they were a form of it."[61] Domestic pressures to withdraw American forces from Vietnam left the Nixon administration little choice but to negotiate; paradoxically, though, the very fact of *not* being a great power gave the Vietnamese Communists a kind of immunity from concerns about respectability. Ideology still dominated their behavior, and as Kissinger the historian—if not Kissinger the diplomat—had seen, "it is the essence of a revolutionary power that it possesses the courage of its convictions, that it is willing, indeed eager, to push its principles to their ultimate conclusions."[62]

But Kissinger also recognized—as neither the Johnson administration nor the North Vietnamese had been able to do—that the future of the world would not be determined in the jungles and swamps of Southeast Asia. Hanoi's militancy was frustrating for those who had to deal with it and ultimately humiliating for the United States, against whom it did, in the end, prevail; but that militancy was also an artifact in an era that was moving beyond ideology. Kissinger sensed this fact, even if his preoccupation with credibility kept him from fully acknowledging it. North Vietnam's victory, in the end, proved not be a portent of things to come, much less the first in a line of toppling dominoes. Instead, the evolution of larger revolutionary powers into normal states reduced Indochina "to its proper scale," as Kissinger put it: "a small peninsula on a major continent."[63]

VI

Making revolutionaries respectable was not enough in itself to secure American interests, though, for other nations could hardly be expected to act against interests of their own. One had to induce such states to define their interests in ways that corresponded to those of the United States, and it was here that the second instrument of Kissinger's statecraft—"linkage"—came into play. Offering rewards and threatening punishments was hardly a new idea in the history of diplomacy, but it was not one that had figured prominently in the history of American foreign policy, for reasons Kissinger located squarely within the American national character.

"Linkage," he pointed out in his memoirs, "is not a natural concept for Americans, who have traditionally perceived foreign policy as an episodic enterprise." American universities trained their students in specialization, not generalization. The legal profession emphasized facts and distrusted abstractions. Bureaucracies organized themselves according to regions or functions, not expansive visions or long-term perspectives. As a result, Americans preferred to deal with issues separately: "to solve problems on their merits, without a sense of time or context or of the seamless web of reality." And yet success in diplomacy required "a sense of history, an understanding of manifold forces not within our control, and a broad view of the fabric of events." Without such an awareness of interconnections, there could only be incoherence: "The absence of linkage produces exactly the opposite of freedom of action; policymakers are forced to respond to parochial interests, buffeted by pressures without a fixed compass."[64] At one level, then, linkage merely meant imposing a badly needed conceptual discipline upon the making of American foreign policy.

Kissinger saw linkage as operating at two other levels, however. One of these involved bilateral relations with other states, especially the Soviet Union. "We proceeded from the premise that to separate issues into separate compartments would encourage the Soviet leaders to believe that they could use cooperation in one area as a safety valve while striving for unilateral advantages elsewhere. This was unacceptable."[65] The United States would therefore offer the USSR certain things it wanted: increased agricultural exports and technology transfers, credits to finance them, an end to discriminatory tariffs against Soviet imports, recognition of post–World War II boundaries in Central and Eastern Europe, the acceptance of Moscow's position as a superpower with global, not just European, interests. But Washington would expect concessions, in return, on things the United States wanted: limiting the Soviet strategic weapons buildup, assistance in arranging an acceptable end to the Vietnam War, an acknowledgment of American, British, and French rights in West Berlin, joint action to keep Third World crises from escalating. All of these issues would interrelate in Kissinger's strategy, with progress on each requiring cooperation in most of the others.

But linkage was also necessary with respect to the international system as a whole, and to maintaining American influence within it. "Displays of American impotence in one part of the world, such as Asia or Africa, would inevitably erode our credibility in other parts of the world, such as the Middle East," Kissinger argued. "Our posture in arms control negotiations could not be separated from the resulting military balance, nor from our responsibilities as the major military power of a global system of alliances." The idea here was to impress, not just the Soviet Union, but anyone anywhere who might seek to challenge American interests. "We saw linkage, in short, as synonymous with an overall strategic and geopolitical view. To ignore the interconnection of events was to undermine the coherence of *all* policy."[66]

Kissinger was surely right to criticize the absence of linkage in the policies of his predecessors: if Vietnam demonstrated anything at all, it was how easily an excessively compartmentalized approach to world affairs can cause a nation's leaders to lose their sense of proportion. His insistence that distinctions be made between vital and peripheral interests, that the connections *between* policies be reestablished in the minds of policymakers, that the effects they produced should bear some relationship to the efforts that went into producing them— all of this served to revive, within a remarkably short period of time, a clarity of purpose and direction in American foreign policy that had been sorely lacking.

How well linkage worked in dealing with the Russians is more difficult to say. It certainly did not succeed in producing a more favorable settlement in Vietnam, for the simple reason—not fully grasped by Nixon and Kissinger until after they left office—that Moscow never had the influence they assumed it did with the leadership in Hanoi.[67] Nor did the economic inducements Kissinger had promised the Russians materialize: the difficulty here was the need for congressional approval, and the determination of Senator Henry M. Jackson, Democrat of Washington, and other critics of the Soviet Union to require additional concessions in the form of relaxed emigration procedures for Soviet Jews and dissidents.[68] The opening to China, however, did clearly unsettle the Russians, placing them in a position from which they felt they had to compete with the Chinese for Washington's favor.[69] And Kissinger managed brilliantly to convince Brezhnev and his advisers that they needed a strategic arms control agreement more than the United States did, despite the fact that it was the Russians, not the Americans, who were increasing their strategic arsenal. Kissinger did this, with strong support from Nixon, by threatening to sacrifice arms control if the Russians did not cooperate in helping to resolve a series of otherwise unconnected crises in Cuba, the Middle East, and on the Indian subcontinent. Together with the China initiative, these developments so rattled the Kremlin leaders that when Nixon authorized the bombing of Hanoi and Haiphong in May 1972, fully expecting the Soviets to respond by canceling the summit that had been scheduled for later that month, they did not do so.[70]

When applied at the level of the international system, though, linkage was much less successful. The reason, almost certainly, is that Kissinger had always been vague about just whom his efforts at linkage were supposed to impress. Their overall objective was clear enough: to maintain American credibility in the world. But credibility with respect to what, and with whom? Kissinger's failure to be more precise on this point left him subject to some of the same confusion that had afflicted Johnson and his advisers: like them—and like policymakers in several preceding administrations—he retained a tendency to see credibility as an end in itself, without regard to the purposes it was intended to achieve.[71] It is not at all clear, for example, that the slow and painful American withdrawal from Vietnam—a withdrawal designed primarily to retain the image of American potency in world affairs, and only secondarily to preserve the South Vietnamese government—impressed anyone at all, least of all the North Vietnamese. Certainly the domestic turmoil this policy produced, together with Nixon's own disastrous response to those disruptions, turned out to be as costly as can be imagined for his administration, since it led to the president's near impeachment and unprecedented resignation.

Linkage came naturally, Kissinger's most perceptive biographer has noted, "to someone who was both a brilliant conceptualizer and slightly conspiratorial in outlook, who could feel the connections the way a spider senses twitches in its web."[72] The image illustrates both the advantages and disadvantages of this practice. Linkage required that Kissinger occupy the policy-making center, which ensured coherence; but it also imposed extraordinary demands on him. To be alert to every twitch in the web; to have to rush off and repair damage here, while other damage might be occurring over there, meant a life full of crises, with little time for reflection or reconsideration.[73] It resembled, as nothing else, the condition of being buffeted by pressures that Kissinger had described as resulting from the absence of linkage. The fact that it was up to him—and increasingly to him alone, as Nixon became more and more distracted by Watergate—to be the fixed compass lent an impermanence to his entire strategy that was the opposite of what Kissinger had intended.

"The characteristic of a stable order is its spontaneity," Kissinger had written in *A World Restored*; "the essence of a revolutionary situation is its self-consciousness."[74] But Kissinger was unable to make the transition from linkage—which involved the suppression of spontaneity—to the long-term stability spontaneity was supposed to produce. Kissinger the historian had often written of the Greek goddess Nemesis, who frustrated the wishes of her worshippers by fulfilling them literally.[75] The idea of linkage placed Kissinger literally at the center of the web, precisely the position that Metternich and Bismarck had occupied. It did not, however, ensure the perpetuation of his policies, anymore than it had for the heroes upon whose careers he had modeled his own.

VII

A third method central to Kissinger's statecraft was—there is no getting around it—deception. Like other Kissingerian practices, there was nothing particularly novel about this: diplomats have been defined for centuries as men sent to lie abroad for their countries. With the onset of the Cold War, a culture of secrecy had developed within the United States government that was well in place while Kissinger was still a Harvard undergraduate. But as more is revealed about what went on behind the scenes during the Nixon and Ford administrations, it is becoming clear that Kissinger relied unusually heavily upon bending the truth, not just in his dealings with foreign statesmen but also with his own friends, associates, and at times even the presidents for whom he worked. He did this with such frequency that when biographers began interviewing those who had known him for many years a sad fact began to emerge: although most of them still admired him, few still trusted him.[76]

The roots of Kissinger's reputation for deviousness were both personal and professional. Despite his own denials,[77] there can be little doubt that the experience of growing up in Nazi Germany instilled a deep sense of insecurity, intensified by the necessity of having to make a new life in a foreign country and in an alien tongue. Mixed with this, and perhaps a product of it, was an intense ambition that caused Kissinger to attach himself repeatedly to powerful patrons. His manner toward them could easily slide from respect to deference to obsequiousness; but he also loved to gossip about them behind their backs. Not surprisingly, he came to be seen as chameleon-like: he was far more likely to take on the coloration of those around him than to resist it.[78] The experience of working for Richard Nixon, himself the least psychologically secure president in modern history, can only have magnified tendencies already present in Kissinger's personality. Their relationship was uneasy because each recognized something of himself in the other.[79] But perhaps that is also what made it work as well as it did.

One of the ways Kissinger used deception had to do with his own position in the Nixon White House. The president could hardly have announced his determination to put Kissinger in charge of foreign policy: the State Department bureaucracy would have protested, and Congress would almost certainly have investigated. Nixon and Kissinger chose instead to keep the traditional bureaucracy intact but to make their own alternative arrangements—keeping them as invisible as possible—for handling the issues that most concerned them. These generally took the form of secret meetings set up through "back-channel" communication links, a form of diplomacy that Kissinger made his specialty. He became particularly adept at appearing conspicuously at Washington social events, often with a striking movie starlet in tow, and then slipping away in the dead of night to a waiting Air Force plane that would whisk him—still in black tie—to some secret meeting halfway around the world, where bemused Russian or Chinese or North Vietnamese negotiators would be waiting. Neither the State Department nor the Congress nor the press would have any idea of what was going on, even though the Russians, the Chinese, and the North Vietnamese obviously did. The effects at times could be very odd, as when Kissinger once complained furiously to the Soviet ambassador because a Soviet diplomat had casually leaked the American position on arms control to the designated American negotiator on arms control, Gerard Smith, who of course had known nothing about it.[80]

But the Nixon administration's reliance on deception involved much more than Kissinger's "back-channel" negotiations. Nixon himself had long believed in the virtues of unpredictability: in disconcerting adversaries by springing surprises on them, thereby gaining leverage even when one's capabilities were declining.[81] Because democracies were not well-equipped to practice this art, though, it was necessary to be able to act, not just to negotiate, beyond the realm of public scrutiny. The secret bombing of Cambodia in 1969 established the precedent for such practices: Nixon and Kissinger not only lied when they denied that it was taking place; they even went so far as to devise a clumsy false command structure so that most of the Air Force itself, including the crews actually dropping the bombs, would—supposedly—not know where they were falling.[82] Similar lies disguised unsuccessful efforts by the Central Intelligence Agency, at the insistence of the White House, to prevent the democratically elected Marxist president of Chile, Salvadore Allende, from taking office in 1970.[83] Kissinger went to Beijing in 1971 without giving the slightest warning to the Chinese Nationalists, the Japanese, the State and Defense departments, or the Congress—to say nothing of the Russians—that he was planning to do so: in this case, the success of the maneuver overcame grave reservations about how it had been done.[84] And shortly after becoming secretary of state, Kissinger used deception with at least equal skill to recoup from the surprise October 1973 Egyptian-Syrian attack on Israel by maneuvering the Russians out of any role at all in a Middle East settlement, while promising repeatedly to respect their interests there.[85]

Recalling his China triumph while writing his memoirs, Kissinger made a point of quoting the late United Nations Secretary-General Dag Hammarskjöld to the effect that "the most dangerous of all moral dilemmas" occurred "when we are obliged to conceal truth in order to help the truth to be victorious."[86] With an inscrutability his Chinese hosts would have admired—but had had no need to teach him—Kissinger let this quotation hang without comment at the end of his account. The reader is left to wonder: is concealing truth in order to ensure that truth prevails the right thing to do or not?

It would be naive to expect that any government, however principled and however democratic, can function without a certain amount of deception. The situation Kissinger confronted in 1969 was one that required craftiness if he was to rescue whatever opportunities were left for the United States to regain the initiative in the unpromising situation it had gotten itself into. Kissinger's own position in government required adapting his own behavior to the devious and convoluted habits of his chief: the alternative was to follow the path of those who resigned on principle but thereby condemned themselves to impotence in shaping policy. Secrecy may have been necessary in some instances to overcome bureaucratic inertia or to ensure confidentiality: it is difficult to see how the opening to China could have come about, with such immediate success, in any other way. And there were points during negotiations with the Soviet Union over limiting strategic arms, or with the North Vietnamese over ending the fighting in Indochina, or in efforts to arrange a cease-fire after the 1973 Middle East war, when the existence of "back channels" proved useful in determining the other side's intentions.

The difficulty with deception, though, is that one cannot for long sustain it. One cannot continue to deceive even dense people without their eventually catching on; and most of the people Kissinger thought it necessary to deceive were by no means dense. One cannot master the intricacies of complex negotiations without expert advice, and there were embarrassing instances in which Kissinger's "back channel" approach suffered from its absence. One cannot conduct negotiations in secret without arousing the suspicions of those whose lives will be affected by the outcome, whether they are allies like the South Vietnamese or the Israelis, or the constituencies whose support one needs at home. One cannot conclude agreements and expect them to stick if they have been crafted in such a way as to allow opposing sides—as happened with both the SALT agreements and the Vietnamese peace accords—to interpret deliberately imprecise language in their own respective ways.[87] And, most important, one cannot build the base of legitimacy upon which the long-term future of any policy must rest by relying indefinitely upon less than legitimate means. The establishment of order may well necessarily precede the achievement of justice; but one does, sooner or later, have to get on toward that ultimate destination.

VIII

The transition from Richard Nixon to Gerald Ford liberated Kissinger from the byzantine atmosphere within which he had had to work for the past five years: the new president's open and uncomplicated personality could hardly have been more different from that of his predecessor.[88] Ford's almost total lack of experience in foreign policy made Kissinger's position more secure than it had ever been. His reputation for indispensability had become so strong, in fact, that the press found itself agonizing—most uncharacteristically—over how much to make of the information that was beginning to come out about Kissinger's involvement in wiretapping and covert operations during the Nixon years.[89] No comparable restraint had been evident in the media's handling of the former president himself.

But even as Kissinger's authority was expanding, his freedom to operate with few domestic constraints was contracting. Becoming secretary of state made Kissinger accountable to the Congress for the first time; and although he proved to be almost as adept at charming legislators as he had been in winning over foreign statesmen, the effort took time, energy, and careful preparation. Kissinger's new position also made it more difficult for him to operate behind the scenes; meanwhile the Watergate scandal and subsequent congressional investigations of the Central Intelligence Agency had made it clear that the public's willingness to tolerate secret diplomacy—and the press's willingness to cooperate in keeping it secret—was rapidly waning.

With Nixon out of office and with Ford obviously following Kissinger's lead in foreign policy, the new secretary of state—despite his generally good relationship with the press—was also becoming an inviting political target. The issue upon which he appeared most vulnerable was that of human rights, and by the end of 1973 attacks were coming from both the left and the right. Liberals had long criticized Kissinger's tendency to see Southeast Asia, Latin America, and Africa solely in Cold War terms: his preoccupation with global stability, they argued, had caused him to neglect the requirements of regional and local justice. But now conservatives were finding Kissinger's policy of détente with the Soviet Union—especially its implied acceptance of Moscow's sphere of influence in Eastern Europe and its allegedly naive agreements on arms control —to be reminiscent of Roosevelt's supposed "sell-out" at Yalta three decades before. And by making congressional approval of the 1972 Soviet-American trade agreement contingent upon an increase in the emigration of Soviet Jews to Israel, one of Kissinger's strongest critics, Senator Henry M. Jackson had found a way to rally both liberals and conservatives against his policies.[90]

Kissinger was well aware of how unusual—and unsustainable—had been the conditions under which he had operated while Nixon was in the White House. Much had been accomplished during those years, he later acknowledged, but the president's administrative approach "was weird and its human cost unattractive. . . . I do not consider the methods employed desirable in the abstract; certainly, they should not be regularly pursued."[91] It would have been easy for Kissinger to have adopted a "do as I say, not as I did" attitude on this matter, letting others worry about incorporating his achievements within a political and institutional framework capable of perpetuating them. To his credit, he did not adopt this course: unlike Metternich and Bismarck he sought to respond to the criticisms he was encountering, to adapt his policies to new circumstances, and even to build a moral consensus behind what had hitherto appeared to be amoral policies.

The "new" Kissinger went on display first in the Middle East, where after arranging a cease-fire in the October 1973 war, he embarked on a dogged and ultimately successful effort to negotiate a disengagement of Egyptian, Syrian, and Israeli forces and to begin a search for long-term peace. Characteristically, Kissinger took on the role of chief diplomat himself, shuttling repeatedly between Cairo, Jerusalem, and Damascus to deal with issues whose intricacy would have frustrated almost anyone else; quite uncharacteristically, though, he conducted these negotiations for the most part in the open, with a traveling press corps that was often taken into his confidence. He did not seek to paper over fundamental conflicts with sweeping but vague agreements, as he had done in Vietnam; rather, he patiently sought specific step-by-step accords. And for whatever reason—it has been suggested that Kissinger's negotiating style lent itself particularly well to the convoluted politics of the Middle East—these negotiations do not appear to have left the residue of distrust toward him personally that several of his other diplomatic efforts did.[92]

Old habits, to be sure, did not entirely disappear. The collapse of Portugal's African empire in 1974—and the possibility that communists might be allowed into the Portuguese government itself—provoked thinly veiled threats directed at Lisbon and an abortive covert attempt, which did not remain covert, to overthrow the Marxist regime that had taken power in Angola.[93] Kissinger regarded the final collapse of the Vietnamese peace settlement in the spring of 1975 as a humiliating blow to American credibility and desperately sought last-minute military assistance for the Saigon government; it took the cool common sense of President Ford to acknowledge reality and declare the Vietnam War over once and for all, something Kissinger could not quite bring himself to do.[94] And it was Ford, not Kissinger, who first saw the value of stressing the human rights provisions of the August 1975 Helsinki agreement, a multinational acknowledgment of existing boundaries in Central and Eastern Europe long sought by the Soviet Union, but one that ultimately undermined Soviet authority there.[95]

Kissinger did, however, show himself willing to learn from his mistakes. After the Angolan intervention became public, he surprised his critics and reversed a long-standing policy of supporting white minority rule in southern Africa. By the summer of 1976 Kissinger was calling openly for the overthrow of Ian Smith's regime in Rhodesia, and working skillfully to persuade the South African government—itself still run by a white minority—to facilitate that process. Africa henceforth, he implied, would be viewed as Africa, not as a diplomatic chessboard on which gains for the Soviet Union automatically meant losses for the United States.[96]

Worried about the extent to which concerns over human rights issues were disrupting his carefully crafted linkages, Kissinger had already begun another new and unexpected initiative: he set out to educate the American people on the proper relationship between morality and foreign policy. In a series of speeches delivered in 1975 and 1976, he sought to place his own geopolitical realism into a framework compatible with American ideals. The most important of these "heartland" speeches,[97] as Kissinger called them, was entitled "The Moral Foundations of Foreign Policy" and delivered at Minneapolis in July 1975. It stands both as an expression of what Kissinger wanted the nation to think about the relationship between ideas, interests, and the practice of diplomacy, and also as an indication of what he himself had learned.

Kissinger began with what was, for him, a familiar theme: the uniqueness of the American experience. The luxuries, first of isolationism and then of an almost immediate transition to global hegemony, meant that Americans had not had to wrestle with the difficult question of how principles and policies relate to one another: the United States had at first set itself apart from the world, but then had thought it possible to remake the world to resemble itself. American power and influence had declined since the early days of the Cold War, however: "Today we find that—like most other nations in history—we can neither escape from the world nor dominate it." It followed that "we must conduct diplomacy with subtlety, flexibility, maneuver, and imagination in the pursuit of our interests." Those interests, ultimately, had to be moral in character: "This nation must be true to its own beliefs, or it will lose its bearings in the world. But at the same time it must survive in a world of sovereign nations and competing wills."

It was unrealistic to expect some 150 other nations, "barely a score of them . . . democracies in any real sense," to share American values; but almost all of them shared with Americans the desire for peace and security. The United States had cooperated with undemocratic states in the past to pursue such common interests, most notably by aligning itself with Stalin's Russia to defeat Hitler's Germany in World War II. Cooperation was all the more important now, when the possibility of nuclear war threatened democracies and autocracies alike.

The United States would never be indifferent when democracy was at issue; it could never establish congenial relations with repressive states. "But truth compels a recognition of our limits. The question is whether we promote human rights more effectively by counsel and friendly relations where this serves our interest or by confrontational propaganda and discriminatory legislation." The issue was "whether we have the courage to face complexity and the inner conviction to deal with ambiguity, whether we will look behind easy slogans and recognize that our great goals can only be reached by patience, and in imperfect stages."[98]

Several points are worth noting about this speech, and several others like it that Kissinger gave during his final years in office. First, the time and trouble Kissinger lavished on these pronouncements—together with his earlier impressive "state of the world" reports as national security adviser—do not suggest indifference to the role of public opinion in a democracy; just the opposite. Kissinger was fully prepared to turn his talents as an educator to the task of winning support for his policies. Whether he understood how best to convey his ideas is open to question, since neither the press nor the public paid much attention to these educational efforts. But to argue that Kissinger neglected the task itself[99] seems less than fair.

Nor are these the pronouncements of a cold-blooded cynic, with no concern at all for issues of morality and principle. Despite Kissinger's admiration for Metternich and Bismarck, it is difficult to conceive of either of them speaking in these terms: Kissinger's background, his experiences, and ultimately the nature of his responsibilities and of the world in which he had to execute them could hardly have been more different. The criticisms Kissinger the historian had made of his nineteenth-century heroes has received no greater attention than the public speeches of Kissinger the statesman: so powerful is the temptation to impose simple categories on both those who make history and those who write about it.

Most striking about Kissinger's speeches, though, is what they reveal of his most fundamental assumptions concerning the history of his own times. There is in these pronouncements, as in many of Kissinger's private comments and in his memoirs, a sense that democratic institutions are and will remain islands in a sea of undemocratic regimes. There is no anticipation that democracy instead of authoritarianism might be the wave of the future; one would get not the slightest inkling, from any of Kissinger's writings or statements during his years of public responsibility, that Soviet power would decline even more rapidly than American power; that the force of moral principles would, to a large extent, eventually bring about the collapse of Moscow's influence, the end of the Cold War, and the disintegration of the Soviet Union itself.

This failure of foresight was hardly unique to Kissinger.[100] But it does raise questions about what caused him to take so pessimistic a view of American prospects in the world. First, Kissinger, like most others of his generation, was a product of World War II and the Cold War. There would have been little, in the experiences of these years, to lead one to believe that the role of ideas could possibly outweigh the role of power. Second, Kissinger as a historian had studied men who had gained their prominence by manipulating power, not by articulating ideas: had he chosen instead to write about Marx, or Gandhi, or even Thomas Jefferson, he might have found it easier to acknowledge the limitations traditional forms of power sometimes reveal when confronted by ideas. Third, Kissinger knew little, and by all accounts cared even less, about economics: he thereby missed the significance of a new industrial revolution that was going on around him—one based on computers and the flow of information—that would ultimately make the very basis of Soviet power obsolete. Finally, Kissinger tended to assume that the only thing nations and cultures had in common was the desire for security. That the desire for liberty might also be transnational and crosscultural in nature, in the end, eluded him.

IX

By the time Henry Kissinger left government in January 1977, he had become a political liability. Faced with Ronald Reagan's challenge for the 1976 Republican presidential nomination, Ford had felt it necessary to disassociate himself symbolically, if not in substance, from the entire concept of "détente"; and although the president was renominated, his Democratic opponent, Jimmy Carter, made Kissinger's "Lone Ranger" style and alleged indifference to human rights a major theme of his campaign. When President-elect Carter named as his national security adviser a former academic rival of Kissinger's, Zbigniew Brzezinski, it became apparent that Kissinger himself would have no influence at all within the new administration, despite the fact that it continued many of his policies.

Nor would he have significant roles to play, as it turned out, in the Republican administrations that followed. Reagan had been as suspicious of Kissinger as Carter, but for different reasons: where Carter distrusted Kissinger's realism,

Reagan objected to his pessimism. Convinced that the Soviet Union, not the United States, was declining, Reagan was ultimately able to achieve a long-awaited reconciliation with Moscow, but by means far removed from anything Kissinger had contemplated. It would be the ultimate imbalance of Soviet collapse that would end the Cold War, not Kissinger's conception of a balance arrived at through making the Soviet Union a normal state. By the time the Bush administration took office, Kissinger's political influence had been reduced to that of a grumbling television talking head—despite the fact that he remained a media celebrity, and had also carved out a lucrative third career for himself as an extraordinarily successful international business consultant.[101]

History's verdict on Henry Kissinger will not be in for some time yet, and it is not easy to anticipate what it might be. The success with which Kissinger the historian reevaluated the reputations of Castlereagh, Metternich, and Bismarck long after their deaths ought to give one pause: who knows what some future historian might do about Kissinger the statesman? It was characteristic of Kissinger to provide his own suggestions in the form of a twenty-seven-hundred-page memoir—which despite its length covered only two-thirds of his time in office. And by limiting his definition of success in statecraft to the rescuing of choices from circumstances, he did what all good politicians do when their reputations are on the line: he lowered expectations.

Kissinger, it turns out, was wrong about many things, not least of which was the direction in which historical circumstances were proceeding. He saw himself as desperately sticking fingers in dikes when in fact the ocean on the other side was receding. That does not mean, though, that there had never been an ocean there at all, or that the dikes were never in danger of collapsing. One never knows when some small action may set in motion some great historical trend: when a choice rescued from circumstance can actually alter circumstances. It is just possible that some future Kissinger will see the current Kissinger, for all his faults, as having been, like Metternich and Bismarck, in just the right place at just the right time—thereby fulfilling in history, as well as in life, the man's truly incorrigible determination to be at the center of it all.

Notes

1. Henry A. Kissinger, *White House Years* (Boston, 1979), 54.
2. Kissinger retained his position as national security adviser after Nixon appointed him secretary of state in August 1973, holding both positions until October 1975. At that point, Ford named Maj. Gen. Brent Scowcroft as his national security adviser, but he kept Kissinger as secretary of state through the end of his administration in January 1977.
3. Kissinger, *White House Years*, 1409–10.
4. Ibid., 55.

5. For a good account, see Walter Isaacson, *Kissinger: A Biography* (New York, 1992), 355–70.

6. See Henry A. Kissinger *A World Restored: Metternich, Castlereagh, and the Problems of Peace, 1812–22* (New York, 1957); and "The White Revolutionary: Reflections on Bismarck," *Daedelus* 97 (Summer 1968): 888–924. For Kissinger's characterization of himself as a historian, see *White House Years,* 54–55.

7. For an interesting assessment of the policy consequences such perspectives produced, see D. Michael Shafer, *Deadly Paradigms: The Failure of U.S. Counterinsurgency Policy* (Princeton, 1988).

8. A useful discussion of Kissinger's realism is Michael Joseph Smith, *Realist Thought from Weber to Kissinger* (Baton Rouge, 1986), 192–217.

9. Kissinger, *A World Restored,* 173.

10. *White House Years,* 12. Kissinger's description of how Nixon worked himself around to offering the position, and how Kissinger worked himself around to accepting it, pp. 7–16, is revealing of both men.

11. Richard Nixon, *RN: The Memoirs of Richard Nixon* (New York, 1978), 340.

12. Stephen E. Ambrose, *Nixon: The Triumph of a Politician, 1962–1972* (New York, 1989), 233.

13. Ibid., 113–17. Ambrose goes so far as to claim that, although Kissinger played a crucial role in executing Nixon administration foreign policy, he did so "as agent, tool, and sometimes adviser, not as a generator of ideas. The basic thrust of Nixon's innovations came from the President, not the National Security Adviser" (p. 655).

14. Isaacson, *Kissinger,* 72.

15. Henry A. Kissinger, *Years of Upheaval* (Boston, 1982), 414–23.

16. See, for example, David Landau, *Kissinger: The Uses of Power* (Boston, 1972); Marvin L. and Bernard Kalb, *Kissinger* (Boston, 1973); Stephen R. Graubard, *Kissinger: Portrait of a Mind* (New York, 1973); Henry O. Brandon, *The Retreat of American Power* (New York, 1973); John G. Stoessinger, *Henry Kissinger: The Anguish of Power* (New York, 1976); Edward Sheehan, *The Arabs, Israelis and Kissinger: A Secret History of American Diplomacy in the Middle East* (New York, 1976).

17. The best of the Kissinger biographers, Walter Isaacson, discusses the controversial nature of his subject in *Kissinger,* 14.

18. See, on this point, Robert D. Schulzinger, *Henry Kissinger: Doctor of Diplomacy* (New York, 1989), 238–39.

19. Kissinger, *White House Years,* 54.

20. Ibid., 55.

21. Henry A. Kissinger, "The Meaning of History: Reflections on Spengler, Toynbee and Kant" (A. B. thesis, Harvard University, 1951). The most thorough attempt to explain this still-unpublished thesis is Peter Dickson, *Kissinger and the Meaning of History* (New York, 1978); but see also the succinct evaluation in Smith, *Realist Thought from Weber to Kissinger,* 194–99. Isaacson, *Kissinger,* 64–67, recounts the circumstances in which Kissinger composed this thesis, still the longest ever done at Harvard.

22. Quoted in Smith, *Realist Thought from Weber to Kissinger,* 194.

23. Ibid., 198.

24. *A World Restored,* 5.

25. Ibid., 2. Emphasis in original.

26. Kissinger, "White Revolutionary," 889–90.

27. Ibid., 920.

28. Kissinger, *A World Restored*, 322. For an almost identical comment about Bismarck, see Kissinger, "White Revolutionary," 921.

29. See his essay "Domestic Structure and Foreign Policy" in Henry A. Kissinger, *American Foreign Policy*, 3d ed. (New York, 1977), especially 17–26.

30. Kissinger, *White House Years*, 124, 196.

31. Ibid., 61–62. See also Kissinger's speech, "The Permanent Challenge of Peace: U.S. Policy Toward the Soviet Union" (delivered to the Commonwealth Club, San Francisco, 3 Feb. 1976), in Kissinger, *American Foreign Policy*, especially 303–4.

32. Kissinger, *White House Years*, 57, 65.

33. Ibid., 116–17.

34. Ibid., 117, 119–20.

35. Ibid., 39.

36. This episode is well-covered in Isaacson, *Kissinger*, 212–33, 600–601. Kissinger's own explanation appears in *White House Years*, 252–53, and *Years of Upheaval*, 118–22.

37. Kissinger, *White House Years*, 514–15.

38. Ibid., 1448–49.

39. Kissinger had been contemplating resignation, in part because he feared losing his authority, prior to his appointment as secretary of state in 1973. *Years of Upheaval*, 6–7.

40. Schulzinger, *Henry Kissinger*, 41.

41. "What extraordinary vehicles destiny selects to accomplish its design," Kissinger wrote of Nixon in 1979. *White House Years*, 1475.

42. See Isaacson, *Kissinger*, 31, 76.

43. Kissinger, "White Revolutionary," 914–18.

44. Ibid., 888.

45. I have discussed Kennan's views at greater length in *Strategies of Containment: A Critical Appraisal of Postwar American National Security Policy* (New York, 1982), especially chaps. 2 and 3.

46. Kennan's growing opposition to official policy is eloquently documented in his *Memoirs*, 2 vols. (Boston, 1967, 1972).

47. "Central Issues of American Foreign Policy," in Kissinger, *American Foreign Policy*, 86.

48. Kissinger, *White House Years*, 297.

49. Schulzinger, *Henry Kissinger*, 77–79. For an early Kissinger discussion of the differences between statesmen and prophets, see *A World Restored*, 187.

50. This does not mean, though, that American officials necessarily believed in the existence of an international communist monolith, controlled from Moscow. For more on this, see John Lewis Gaddis, *The Long Peace: Inquiries into the History of the Cold War* (New York, 1987), 147–94.

51. See Kissinger's essay "Central Issues of American Foreign Policy," in Kissinger, *American Foreign Policy*, especially 74; also Kissinger's address to the October 1973 Pacem in Terris III Conference, in *American Foreign Policy*, 128–29.

52. Kissinger, *White House Years*, 748–49.

53. *Public Papers of the Presidents: Richard M. Nixon, 1971* (Washington, D.C., 1972), 806; *Time* 94 (3 Jan. 1972): 15. See also Schulzinger, *Henry Kissinger*, 59–60.

54. *White House Years*, 227–28.

55. Ibid., 119. See also 203, 413.

56. Ibid., 229.

57. Henry A. Kissinger, *Nuclear Weapons and Foreign Policy* (New York, 1957), had been an early and controversial effort to show how a limited war might be fought, if necessary, with nuclear weapons. Kissinger subsequently repudiated his own findings, concluding that there was no way that nuclear weapons could be used without the risk of escalation to all-out war.

58. For more on this point, see John Lewis Gaddis, *The United States and the End of the Cold War: Reconsiderations, Implications, Provocations* (New York, 1992), 35–39.

59. Kissinger, *White House Years*, 640. Kissinger was here summarizing the views of former ambassador to the Soviet Union Llewellyn Thompson.

60. Isaacson, *Kissinger*, 334–36. See also Kissinger, "Domestic Structure and Foreign Policy," in Kissinger, *American Foreign Policy*, 38–39.

61. Kissinger, *White House Years*, 260.

62. Kissinger, *A World Restored*, 3.

63. Kissinger, *White House Years*, 1049.

64. Ibid., 129–30. See also "Domestic Structure and Foreign Policy," in Kissinger, *American Foreign Policy*, 29–34.

65. Kissinger, *White House Years*, 129.

66. Ibid.

67. Isaacson, *Kissinger*, 168.

68. Ibid., 611–21.

69. See, for example, Kissinger's comparisons of the Soviet leadership's lack of self-assurance with the Chinese leaders' abundance of it, in *White House Years*, 1056, 1138–39.

70. I have tried to describe this sequence of events more fully in *Strategies of Containment*, 320–29; and in *Russia, the Soviet Union, and the United States: An Interpretive History*, 2d ed. (New York, 1990), 268–83.

71. See, on this point, Isaacson, *Kissinger*, 648, 656, 675, 684.

72. Ibid., 166. Kissinger himself, as noted above, stressed the need to be aware of the "seamless web of reality" in shaping policy.

73. For a revealing look at two not untypical weeks in Kissinger's life, see Isaacson, *Kissinger*, 285–315.

74. Kissinger, *A World Restored*, 3.

75. See, for example, ibid., 1.

76. See, on this point, Margaret Garrard Warner, "Kissinger: Betrayal of the Apostles?" *Newsweek*, international ed., 120 (5 Oct. 1992): 24.

77. Isaacson, *Kissinger*, 29–30.

78. Ibid., 140. Although, interestingly, Kissinger did not demand comparable deference from his subordinates, chiefly, Isaacson thinks, because he welcomed a good argument (p. 279).

79. Isaacson, *Kissinger*, 139–46, is particularly good on the similarities, but also the differences, in Nixon's and Kissinger's personalities. See also Ambrose, *Nixon: The Triumph of a Politician*, 490–91.

80. Isaacson, *Kissinger*, 324–25. Smith has described the frustrating effects of these procedures in his memoir *Doubletalk: The Untold Story of SALT* (Garden City, N.Y., 1981).

81. See, on this point, Gaddis, *Strategies of Containment,* 299–300.

82. Kissinger, *White House Years,* 242–54.

83. Ibid., 653–83.

84. Ibid., 733–63. In this as in several other instances, though, Secretary of Defense Melvin Laird, himself no novice when it came to deviousness, had been monitoring Kissinger's progress by means of National Security Agency intercepts of his own and foreign government communications. Isaacson, *Kissinger,* 200–202.

85. Kissinger, *White House Years,* 512–72.

86. Ibid., 763.

87. These criticisms are all effectively made in Isaacson, *Kissinger,* 320, 325, 431–36, 450–57, 481–82, 527, 541.

88. Ibid., 602–4.

89. Ibid., 584–86; Schulzinger, *Henry Kissinger,* 169–70.

90. Kissinger, *Years of Upheaval,* 979–98; Isaacson, *Kissinger,* 611–21.

91. Kissinger, *White House Years,* 840–41.

92. Isaacson, *Kissinger,* 551–53; Schulzinger, *Henry Kissinger,* 157–62. Kissinger's own lengthy account appears in *Years of Upheaval,* 747–853, 935–78, 1032–1110.

93. Isaacson, *Kissinger,* 673–92.

94. Ibid., 635–48; Schulzinger, *Henry Kissinger,* 184–209.

95. Isaacson, *Kissinger,* 660–63.

96. Ibid., 673–92. See also Kissinger's address, "Southern Africa and the United States: An Agenda for Cooperation" (delivered in Lusaka, Zambia, 27 Apr. 1976), in Kissinger, *American Foreign Policy,* 365–81.

97. Isaacson, *Kissinger,* 658–59.

98. "The Moral Foundations of Foreign Policy," 15 July 1975, in Kissinger, *American Foreign Policy,* 195–213. See also an earlier address by Kissinger, "The Nature of the National Dialogue" (delivered to the Pacem in Terris III Conference in Washington, 8 Oct. 1973, in *American Foreign Policy,* 115–39.

99. As Isaacson does in *Kissinger,* 242.

100. See, on this point, John Lewis Gaddis, "International Relations Theory and the End of the Cold War," *International Security* 17 (Winter, 1992/93): 5–58.

101. Isaacson, *Kissinger,* 730–59, provides one of the few accounts of this aspect of Kissinger's life.

20

ANDREI GROMYKO AS FOREIGN MINISTER

THE PROBLEMS OF A DECAYING EMPIRE

Norman Stone

THE PREDECESSORS of Andrei Gromyko as Soviet foreign minister were such as any man might wish for. Against that background, Gromyko could appear to be an angel of light, and Gromyko served almost for a generation as a socialist with an apparently human face. There had been Molotov (1890–1986), then Vyshinsky, then Molotov again, and then the colorless nonentity Dmitri Shepilov[1] before Gromyko's appointment in 1957. In comparison to these, almost anyone would have counted, in Western eyes, as an improvement. Molotov had given the world one of the few Russian words that it knows—*nyet,* summing up the obduracy and the haggling over small matters with which Western diplomats had been confronted when they encountered their Soviet opposite numbers. Molotov had also been involved with the most lurid episodes of Soviet foreign policy—the pact with Hitler, the division of Poland, the takeover, after 1945, of Eastern Europe. Vyshinsky, who had masterminded the great show trials of the 1930s, was not liked, either, as he lectured the United Nations on the sins of the Americans in a manner that combined the professor and the murderer.

Molotov gave up the Foreign Ministry in 1949, under the usual late-Stalinist cloud (his wife was imprisoned, ostensibly as an Israeli agent), but he got back in 1953 after Stalin's death. Khrushchev dismissed him in 1956, because he was a liability as far as relations with the Yugoslav Communists were concerned. It was Gromyko who effectively took over. Whatever his defects, he was, in terms of public relations, considerably less of a disaster than Molotov had been, for he was quite young (born on 18 July 1909) and personable. Gromyko therefore outlasted Molotov by quite a long head. He rose steadily; he became a member of the Politburo in 1973, and was named first deputy chairman of the Council of Ministers in 1983. He was to serve until the early years of Mikhail Gorbachev, giving way to Shevardnadze in 1985, and continued as president until 1988. Gromyko died in 1990, living, therefore, almost long enough to see the end of the state that he had served. In fact, his life was longer than its own, for he died within months of its ending.

I

Andrei Gromyko was involved in the American section of the Foreign Ministry, went to Washington, ultimately as ambassador, and so was a participant in the main decisions from the start of the Second World War in 1939, through the Teheran, Yalta, and Potsdam conferences that settled important interallied matters, and the great Soviet-American clashes of the Cold War. His influence on all of these matters is far from clear—to this day, there have not been many revelations in the Russian press about it: he was a technician, carrying out the will of the Politburo in much the same style as an earlier Russian foreign minister, Prince Alexander Gorchakov, who had said of his service under Tsar Alexander II, "I am a sponge to be squeezed in the hand of my master."

For instance, when the Soviet Union invaded Afghanistan in December 1979, Gromyko seems not to have taken a major part in the decision: he was present, and no doubt might have objected, but he seems not to have done so—the affair being mainly decided by a few politicians, including the minister of defence, D. M. Ustinov (apparently against the advice of the active military, Akhromeyev, and Ogarkov). Their idea was to stabilize matters, but they blundered into a long war through their initial support for Babrak Karmal and his clumsy ways. The minutes of the decision itself have now become available. They are laconic—to the point of referring to the "country A"—and reveal little as to who argued what.[2] Gromyko's influence is not clear.

Nor does his personality shine very much in the memoirs or journalistic reports. His start, replacing much more experienced people who had fallen victim to the purges in the later 1930s, was not particularly auspicious. According to Charles E. Bohlen, he was "ill at ease and obviously fearful of making some social blunder."[3] Later, he improved, of course. He danced well.[4] According to David Owen,[5] he could give a very lively party, even in the middle of tense negotiations, and join in the Russian folk songs ("but that he was ready to acquiesce in brutal suppression I never doubted"). He did not drink. This came in usefully when he talked, with American opposite numbers, who did indeed drink and sought to develop the useful gambit of *in vino veritas*. His wife was quite handy with medicines when required. But a perceptive American journalist, Don Oberdorfer, needing "color" for his pieces on disarmament negotiations, found none in Gromyko. His fellow countryman, George Shultz, though attempting to be a dry-as-dust Protestant businessman-cum-professor, failed to do so, and provided much more endearing anecdotes.[6]

Although Gromyko was present at various meetings of the Central Committee or the Politburo that took this or that essential decision, or that overthrew this or that prominent Soviet politico, he does not make much appearance in the record, or in anyone's memories of the event. He was good at wording UN resolutions, according to Khrushchev. Otherwise, there is little that is said about him, and in various Russian memorials of the period, his role is by no means prominent.[7] There was, certainly, one moment when it appeared to be decisive—the election of Gorbachev as party leader in March 1985, but, then too, in all probability, Gromyko just waited to see which majority would "emerge" before joining it. On that occasion, he made the only remark, in his long life, that history will remember: Gorbachev had, he said, a nice smile, but he had iron teeth. Those iron teeth in due course chewed up old Gromyko.

Gromyko wrote some memoirs, published not long before his death, in 1989.[8] They are a curiosity. Soviet memoirs were notoriously empty and "windy," very long on abstraction, very short on fact, character sketch, and anecdote. This was always odd, because, in the old days, Russian statesmen had been capable of rather interesting memoirs: one thinks of Sergei Witte, for instance, or even the exiled grand dukes. Nikita Khrushchev had written memoirs that did indeed have a human face, writing them in secret, being "bugged" by the KGB and therefore found out, then being ticked off in the Kremlin, and finally smuggling the memoirs out to the West. There have, of course, been some powerfully written books by once-Communist exiles—Kravchenko, for instance. And there was a very, very odd book by Ivy Litvinov, wife of Gromyko's chief in Washington (and earlier foreign commissar), revealing all manner of shenanigans in high places in the 1930s. Perhaps we should be charitable toward official memoirs, written so often by people trained in self-censorship (and, after all, Vice President George Bush's autobiography sold far fewer copies than did his wife's book about their favorite dog). But the officially published Soviet memoirs tended almost always toward the "Wooden Language" that communism deployed; and if ever they were published in the West, it was normally as part of some deal in countertrading of the questionable kind that made the fortune of Robert Maxwell and his like. Not long after the August coup of 1991, details were published of the subsidies paid, directly or indirectly, to western communist parties, or agents of influence. Official Soviet memoirs, or the works of, say, Ceaușescu, were a job-lot that went along to satisfy the vanity of some aging despot.

Gromyko's memoirs are not in the same category: they are certainly about something, and you can read them without being bored after a page or two. On the other hand, they lie—and lie almost with insulting obviousness. According to his account, there was, for instance, no secret protocol to the Nazi-Soviet Pact of August 1939: there was no provision for the division of Poland, Romania, the Baltic States. Yet, within weeks of the publication of his memoirs, the original document, outlining the Nazi and Soviet spheres of influence, was revealed from Soviet archives; and in any case, since the Nazis had had their own copy, the document was hardly a real secret. In the same way, Gromyko in the *Memoirs* sticks to the official line that South Korea caused the Korean War,[9] without Stalin's having any initiative as regards North Korea, whereas we now know that Stalin told Kim-Il-Sung to invade the South, sending a telegram to that effect. Cuba, according to Gromyko, got rockets in 1962 as a "purely defensive measure," and Mao was "on the whole a nice man."[10] We are told that Trotsky should be studied for his role in the revolution, but deserved his expulsion from the USSR.[11] His murder by Stalin is not mentioned. Gromyko even contrives to tell lies about the shooting down of the Korean airliner on 31 August 1983, maintaining that it was obviously carrying out espionage for the Americans. Yet, within a year or two, *Isvestiya* and others were admitting that a terrible mistake had been made. Altogether then, the Gromyko memoirs are impressive mainly for their desperate effort to disguise the fact that they are merely repeating the party line.

Nevertheless, Gromyko's memoirs are not inhuman. Especially in the early chapters, he is quite revealing. It is rather a worthy story of a Russian life that, in other circumstances, would probably have been very creditable, even inspiring.

Gromyko was born in 1909 in a village not far from Gomel, in White Russia. The family was poor—the father a worker on the land, the little Andrei helping make ends meet by drifting timber down the river—but there were many good points. Gromyko senior had four years of primary education and was a patriotic soldier in the First World War. There was a community nearby of Old Believers. They had suffered persecution and responded with puritanism—never drinking, but taking keenly to education, attitudes that the Gromyko family also adopted. In 1918, Andrei was already reading atheistic pamphlets and ambitiously devising his move upward out of the peasantry. Under communism, that kind of ambition meant sacrificing friends, and of this there is an early example. The Gomel region contained large numbers of Jews, and Gromyko mentions a Jewish boyhood friend, but did not apparently keep up with him. Nor does he go into Jewish questions in general, although they were obviously very important. Much later on, when the Americans made a great fuss about the lack of human rights for Soviet Jews, Gromyko in the memoirs could hardly bring himself to discuss it: it was interference in an internal matter, he said, and the reader can draw his own conclusions from this refusal to enter upon the matter. For the lies in Gromyko's book are not just the explicit ones; the implicit ones are worse. They bear out what the great anticommunist writers always said: that the USSR was the Kingdom of the Lie.

Still, there is more to Gromyko's memoirs than straightforward mendacity. He describes his move upward into the Communist party, via the headship of a school in Smolensk and studies in political economy. Then he got to Moscow, and by 1936 "after three years of post-graduate study," including English, became part of the Institute of Economics, with a side-suit in botany. This last he owed to his peasant background, but he had studied it because, as a good Communist, he had been involved in the collectivization of agriculture. This, as we now know, caused millions of deaths through starvation. Peasants would not join collectives willingly, giving up their own land, or their chance of owning land, and they had to be coerced. Gromyko was a small cog in the machinery of coercion, though again this is not a subject that he treats at any great length.

At any rate, in the later 1930s he transferred his attention away from the horrors of Soviet agriculture and took an interest in the economy of the West, by this time in the Academy of Sciences. In 1939, he joined the party's Central Committee's diplomatic commission, met Georgii Malenkov and Viacheslav Molotov, and was invited into the diplomatic service. Various things can be read into this record. There is the outstanding peasant ancestry. There is the impeccable work record, unblemished by drink or much else (he was married very early, to another correctly Soviet specimen). There were, then and later, no indiscretions; there was almost nothing resembling a joke, though in later life there could be a barbed comment or two, and there was not as much sheer grimness as was found elsewhere in the Soviet machine. Henry Kissinger tells of meeting him for the first time at a session of the United Nations General Assembly in 1969. "He walked up to me at a reception and said 'You look just like Henry Kissinger.' I replied, 'And you look just like Richard Nixon.' He gave me a wary look and then his face creased with a smile as he nudged me with his elbow."[12]

As regards political beliefs, Gromyko, even in the later 1980s, could record: "I had felt drawn to reading Lenin when I was still a youth, and the profundity of his views consistently impressed me. But there were words and ideas I still did not always understand, so I made a vow: if I didn't understand something, I would read and re-read it, and think it over, and . . . keep on at it until I did understand. I have kept this vow in relation to Lenin all my life." The thoughts of Chairman Mao will have inspired similar devotion from acolytes with their careers to think of.

In fact, party schools that taught Marxist-Leninism were formidable training grounds. As Wolfgang Leonhard has shown,[13] they gave their inmates a kind of political calculus. Bare boards, Spartan ways, pseudonyms, and lengthy lessons were the rule. A thorough knowledge of Marxism in history and theory gave students a rather good understanding of Western societies. It also gave them an extremely high tolerance of tedium. Diplomatic representatives of the Soviet Union, Gromyko in the lead, were extraordinarily tough when it came to the fine print of negotiation, and could drive their opposite numbers mad in the pursuit of detail. They bored for victory. When they had to take over a country in crisis, they were very good at dealing with committees. Lesser mortals at trade union meetings, especially, got bored with amendments and regulations; they went off for a drink, leaving the field open for a Communist-dominated caucus to vote as it pleased. With a base in the trade unions and a paramilitary wing, Communists could then look for allies. Even before, in 1914, Lenin had been quite catholic in his approach to these. By the mid-30s, Communists had become very good at appealing to whichever group they needed. They had made something of a common platform with proto-Nazis in Germany in the early

1920s—"National Bolshevism"—and combined with proper Nazis against the socialists a decade later. They could talk the language of social and land reform with social-minded Catholics, the ancestors of the "Liberation Theology" priests of today. They could, with liberals, talk women's rights, ecology, planning. And when they entered upon an alliance, they were good at dominating it. These methods, in Spain during the civil war, were given a dress rehearsal.

In Gromyko's era, the mid-forties, the play was staged properly in Eastern Europe. A Monsignor Plojhar would emerge as "stooge," standing in for the Catholic Party in Prague when the Communists needed an ostensible Catholic representative. In much the same way, the liberally minded surgeon, Juan Negrín, had been manipulated by the Communists when he headed the republican government in civil-war Madrid. In later years, attempts could be made to woo the feminists or the ecologists or the peace movement, each of which had its "stooge" elements.

This was Gromyko's background, though he gives us little information about it. And he shone, reaching a very senior diplomatic post while still a young man. He was only thirty when he became head of the American section of the Commissariat of Foreign Affairs. The reason for his appointment so young— he does not say this—was that the purges had greatly thinned the ranks of the foreign services. The Communists had, early on, used "cosmopolitan" people for these—men of Jewish origin, such as Constantine Oumansky, who controlled the foreign journalists when Malcolm Muggeridge had his winter in Moscow for *The Manchester Guardian* in 1931, and who was made ambassador to Washington before being recalled and killed in 1941. Gromyko became deputy to the ambassador, and in 1943, ambassador; then in 1946, representative at the United Nations; then deputy foreign minister shortly after; the first deputy foreign minister in 1949; then candidate member of the Central Committee and ambassador to London; then, in 1953, back to the Foreign Ministry as deputy, becoming a full member of the Central Committee in 1956. In 1957, he became foreign minister, holding the office for nearly three decades. Having been one of the bright young men of the Soviet state, he became a member of its gerontocracy.

The observations that he has to make are not unreadable, but they omit so much as to make them routine. Gromyko praises those Americans whom the Soviet Union could either buy or gull, and dismisses those whom it could not. In the later thirties, to Gromyko's great disapproval, the American press "were . . . spreading a mass of myths, for example, that the Soviet people were starving." Ambassador Laurence A. Steinhardt, for instance, did "nothing" for Soviet-American "relations," meaning that he saw through the USSR, and, after the war, as ambassador in Czechoslovakia, behaved with conspicuous humanity in helping people to escape. By contrast, says Gromyko, Joseph E. Davies was "better," and "business-like." In 1937–1938, when Davies was ambassador, he was solemnly telling Washington that the purge trials were actually "about" a real conspiracy, and were not just the put-up job we now know them to have been. Later on, Davies was influential in Hollywood, as far as the wilder flights of Soviet propaganda were concerned. And of course he had his reward, acquiring, during his embassy, an enormous quantity of icons, paintings, furniture, and porcelain, which the regime had forced their owners to sell. There is, in Gromyko's comments, one notable piece of ingratitude. In Russian eyes, Roosevelt's vice president, Henry Wallace, counts as a gull. He was taken to see labor camps that had been prettified for his visit. The prettification was only superficial, and a less naive observer would have seen the misery that it purported to conceal. Wallace saw nothing, and went on and on in praise of the progressive Soviet regime. Gromyko by way of gratitude dismisses him as "petty bourgeois," fearing "monopoly capitalism" and wanting to find some "middle way" between it and socialism.

The Gromyko memoirs, after 1945, become little more than a travelogue, interspersed with name-dropping—Baruch, Einstein, Stevenson, et al. Soviet foreign policy is judged in an atmosphere of utter self-satisfaction. The other side are the war mongers. They raise human rights, but, really, these have to be weighed in balance against other human rights, such as not to be unemployed or starving. The Soviet Union was cheated over the atomic bomb: there was no international agreement over it, and so Moscow had to go ahead on its own. There were various bits of progressive agreement, pioneered by Gromyko— nonproliferation in 1968, prohibition of the testing of weapons of mass destruction on the sea bed (1971), and of toxic weapons (1972). There was an antiballistic-missile treaty in 1972, and a SALT I (Strategic Arms Limitation Treaty) in 1972. There would have been another one, but the Americans did not ratify it. President Jimmy Carter and Secretary of State Cyrus Vance had engaged upon the process, but then they weaseled out of it and egged Congress secretly into nonratification while pretending, themselves, to promote it. This, Gromyko says, had apparently to do with the Soviet invasion of Afghanistan in 1979, but in fact had to do with something more sinister. In May 1978, NATO had decided to increase its budget for fifteen years, taking U.S. strength over the next five-year period to its highest level ever. In December 1979 came the "extremely dangerous" decision to put new medium-range nuclear missiles into Western Europe. In Germany, Helmut Schmidt, as chancellor, allowed this, whereas, once safely in opposition, he could safely denounce it without fear of responsibility. These people, says Gromyko, were all very difficult and untrustworthy. He alone never confesses a mistake, and he has very few words of condemnation for anything that his own side did or does. In other words, his is a most peculiar book. In theory, it is a product of *glasnost* and all that. In practice, it is—the first chapters apart—just more cardboard.

It is necessary to concentrate on Gromyko's memoirs, given that there are not many other sources that reveal anything much as to his personal role. Even the quite recent spate of discoveries in the Russian press has spared Gromyko. He was a technician, affably noncommittal in private, obstinate and niggling, where necessary, in public. No one had much affection for him, and no one had much dislike, either. It is evident from his career that ambition greatly mattered. Thus, he became extremely proficient at English quite early on (to the point of correcting interpreters), though he may have concealed this when, in the later 1930s, he moved into the diplomatic service (after all, at the time, superb knowledge of any language could have counted as compromising). He also acquired a thorough knowledge of classical diplomatic forms and techniques, partly perhaps by studying Western diplomatic manuals like Sir Ernest Satow's *Guide to Diplomatic Practice* and Jules Cambon's *Le Diplomate,* which had been approved reading in the Soviet diplomatic service in the Chicherin period and later. We can find some reflection of this, not only in his obliquely expressed discomfort at Khrushchev's ruder methods, but in two well-known incidents in the course of his tenure as foreign minister.

The first was the famous meeting between Gromyko and Ambassador Dobrynin, on the one hand, and President John Kennedy, Secretary of State Dean Rusk, and Ambassador Llewellyn Thompson, on the other, on 18 October 1962, as the Cuba crisis was coming to a head. Gromyko was later to describe this meeting as "the most complex discussion" of his diplomatic career,[14] and he did so probably because, although he was not aware that the president had learned of the presence of Soviet missiles in Cuba, he knew that he would be under pressure to explain recent Soviet military aid to the Castro government. Using a classical diplomatic ploy, he took the initiative, raising the Cuban issue himself and expressing the fear, which he said was widely shared, that the United States was bent on launching a second invasion of Cuba and going on to emphasize the inappropriateness of military action when negotiations were available.[15] Recent Soviet actions he described as efforts to increase the defense capabilities of the Cuban people and in no way offensive or contrary to international law. Since the exasperated president, unwilling to foreclose options, did not ask him directly about the missiles,[16] Gromyko did not feel called upon to volunteer any information and retired in great good humor, doubtless feeling that he had put the Americans on the defensive by making charges that they would have sooner or later to deal with. Whether the president was justified in muttering, "That lying bastard!" as Gromyko left the room doubtless depends upon one's tolerance for the niceties of diplomatic discourse.[17]

Gromyko's respect for the principles of classic diplomacy could on occasion assume comic proportions. In 1977, after forty pages of text had been agreed to by the Soviet and American negotiators of the SALT II Treaty, President Jimmy Carter sent Secretary of State Cyrus Vance to Moscow to propose a new basis for the treaty. Gromyko rejected this with indignation, whereupon President Carter made some unhappy comments to the press, with an implied threat concerning what would happen if Soviet obduracy continued. Gromyko then gave an extraordinary press conference in the form of a lecture to the benighted

Americans on diplomatic protocol, with special emphasis on the impropriety of the president's leaping into print before his own emissary had returned home to report on the success of his demarche.[18]

Whatever Presidents Kennedy and Carter may have thought about Gromyko, Henry Kissinger, who worked closely with him during the years of détente, admired him, writing in his introduction to the English edition of Gromyko's memoirs that he was "one of the ablest diplomats whom I have met." He gives, to be sure, little evidence to support this judgment, aside from saying that Gromyko was a master of that heavy silence that often makes Western negotiators nervous and inclined to offer small concessions for the sake of livening up the proceedings. But Kissinger adds significantly that, amid tumult and confusion, Gromyko protected his country and guarded its weakness.[19] This is a shrewd point and should be examined from a wider perspective.

II

The workings of the Soviet machine were never such as to make the role of any one man—Stalin apart—at all plain. Much of our information came from defectors, and there was an occasional revealing episode: for instance, in the SALT I negotiations, General Staff representatives ordered Foreign Ministry officials from the room so that they would not overhear technical details released to the American delegation.[20] The party clearly led—a kind of muscle, running through the administration fat. But there was also a machinery of state, which undertook the formalities of government. For long, Western commentators argued as to whether "the state" might matter as much as "the party." In the USSR itself, efforts were sometimes made to reform the system, by removing power from old party bosses and awarding it to local executives. Sovietologists learnedly pondered the significance of this. But, somehow, right up to the end of the Gorbachev era, the party would reassert itself. The result was a strange system, in which some parts worked, and others quite manifestly did not. How did this country combine rockets on the way to Venus with the rising death rates and the awful pollution that everyone knew so well?

Some day we shall have a good account of this. For the moment, it is the anticommunist classics that seem to have stood the test of veracity, classics that, in their day were dismissed as "Cold Warriors," contributing only negativity to the cause of "peace." Robert Conquest on the Great Terror of the 1930s has survived rather better than Professor Jerry Hough's updating of *How Russia is Ruled* by the late Merle Fainsod, which makes the extraordinary claim that the number of victims of Stalin's purges runs into at most the thousands, and more probably the hundreds.[21] Leszek Kolakowski's *Main Currents of Marxism*, which ends in frank mockery of its subject, has stood a similar test.[22] And on the real, as distinct from the fictitious way in which the Soviet Union managed its affairs, Alain Besançon in France offers the sharpest analysis.[23] It would be wrong to expect Gromyko to descant upon, or perhaps even fully to understand, what he was doing—just as it would be unfair to expect an expert golfer to explain the theory of ballistics or an opera diva to talk learnedly about harmonics. Nevertheless, Besançon's essay, *Court traité de la soviétologie,* offers a remarkable guide to Soviet foreign policy and accounts for a great part of Gromyko's own career.[24]

Observers have been greatly bewildered by Soviet foreign policy. The people lived at a level of poverty unknown outside the Third World. In fact, if you saw Soviet "cooperators" coming back from Somalia or Bangladesh, loaded down with boxes of ball-point pens and the like, you might even think that at home they lived on a Third World level generally. Yet here was a country with enormous weaponry, and the scale of its armaments reached, in Sakharov's account, 40 percent of the domestic product. We now know, even, that the CIA itself greatly underestimated the scale of armaments expenditure, perhaps because it is anyway difficult to distinguish between it and sophisticated industrial expenditure, perhaps because of a residual unwillingness to believe that Soviet official figures (under 10 percent) were just made up. Professors Bogomolov and Shatalin, in 1989, told Congress that the proper figure was about 25 percent. Given that, the United States was not really challenging the Soviet Union. How was this to be explained? It was not as if Soviet spokesmen talked the language of war. Quite the contrary, for "peace-loving" and "coexistence" formed their stock-in-trade. In the same way, they talked the language of rights and brotherly love, and went on oppressing their own people in ways that defied comprehension. Indeed, as Souvarine had said, the very title of the state— Union of Soviet Socialist Republics—amounted to four lies, just for a start. How, asked the Cyrus Vances and Jimmy Carters, could this country become a country like others?

There was a well-known theory on this, which went back even to the days when Lenin was in exile. If only you were nice to the Bolsheviks, they would lose their ferocious temper. Russian noblemen and businessmen had contributed to their funds before the revolution. The West traded with the new state, not long after. At the time of Stalin's five-year plans, it was first the Germans and then the Americans who came to the fore with credits and technical assistance, guiding the construction, for instance, of the great Dneprostroy dam, designed to supply hydroelectricity for Ukranian industry. Beginning with the later 1950s, credits and technical assistance were again devoted to the USSR— whole automobile factories, and, in the 1970s, millions of tons of food, for which the American taxpayer paid. The Besançons and Conquests, who said that the West was saving the Soviet Union, did not make themselves popular and were only vindicated when the system itself collapsed in 1991. Nevertheless, they had been right. As Besançon has written,[25] "The Soviet State . . . understood how to make government and private credit-granting institutions compete with each other, to combine severity in negotiation and punctilious-ness in interest payments, and finally to bind the creditor more and more tightly, forcing him to lend more in order to guarantee the security for what had already been lent." He quotes in this context Flaubert's banker, Dambreuse of *l'Educa-tion sentimentale,* trying to come to terms with the revolutionaries of 1848: "He would have paid money in order to be bought." In similar terms, Lenin had said that the capitalists "will sell us the rope with which we shall hang them." There always were Robert Maxwells who would do perhaps corrupt countertrade. But there were also well-meaning diplomats, who would do anything to encourage the USSR to become "a state like any other." There was, for instance, German *Ostpolitik.*

This was part of a system of alternations. The USSR was ruled by the party, which had its methods of control. For many decades, many people in the West were deeply mystified by this: institutions that acted for an ideology and actu-ally stood for what their denizens purported to believe in. The system—controlling, after all, an enormous mass—appeared from the outside to be desperately clumsy and slow-moving. Nevertheless, in its own terms it worked. For years and years, it survived economic backwardness of an increasingly serious order. The armed forces, which were clearly the privileged part of the system, were rather carefully controlled by the party, which had its own *zam-polits* right down to company level, and its—in effect—spies from the KGB's Third Chief Directorate, inside, but not under, the military command. As James Sherr has said, "Democratic centralism concentrates power in a few hands and at the end of the day produces decision rather than fudging." It was, he wrote in 1987, "alive and well," despite the economic troubles.[26]

This machinery was well made for a kind of alternating policy, which Besan-çon has so well outlined. The party was a species of parasite on a host body, civil society. When the host threatened to collapse (into drunkenness, thievery, near-sabotage of work, etc.) the parasite would let up: so, in Besançon's model, the revolutionary "War Communism" of 1918–1921 gave way to the New Economic Policy, and even an element of what became known as *glasnost.* This alternation went on through the history of the USSR. In foreign affairs, it had its equivalent. The party could go ahead with revolution, exporting it as necessary (and latterly to Nicaragua, Angola, the Horn of Africa, etc.). Meanwhile, there was also an orthodox machinery of state—embassies, classic foreign relations, and the rest. The Leninist aim was to use the enemy's strength against it: in this case, to push "disarmament" in return for credits, which could then be used ingeniously for better, though lesser, armaments. Thus, *Ostpolitik*—and it was Brezhnev, in Bonn, who first used the expression "common European home"—could be turned against the West Germans, whose hard currency could be used to subsidize movements against the emplacement of cruise missiles in Western Europe. Alternations in policy—now *détente,* now "hard line"—succeeded each other at decade-long intervals, but they were essentially the same policies.

Besançon and Sherr were of course much-criticized, even reviled, in the West for their revelations of this process. However, disarmingly, Boris Ponomaryov, head of the International Department of the Communist Party's Central Committee, supported them: "The policy of peaceful co-existence . . . does not hold back the revolutionary struggle, but promotes its upsurge."[27]

For the West, doing business with the Soviet Union was always problematical. It could involve transfers of technology that might find hostile military purposes. It might in the eyes of some observers stave off the crisis of the entire Soviet system, as it had done before. On the other hand, there was some possibility that, if the West were "nice," then the Soviet Union would join the existing world settlement. These arguments were particularly powerful for Germany. West Germany, after 1947, had recovered from the war at extraordinary speed and had built up enormous capital. Could this not somehow be used to make life easier for the 15 million people who were quite literally imprisoned, since 1961, within the German Democratic Republic and behind the wall? These thoughts were common enough, by the end of the 1960s, on the German left, and they acquired respectability through the FPD, the balance-of-power party, the stalwarts of which tended to make the running in foreign policy, Hans-Dietrich Genscher in particular.

"Reconstructing Petty-Bourgeois Europe" would make a good title for European history after 1945. The old elites had often been discredited by what had happened during the Thirties and the War. Democracy reigned, and two mass-parties took over in alternation—Christian Democrats and Social Democrats—with quarrels of their own, which sometimes loomed larger than much more important disputes with communism. With due care, could not their natural divisions be exploited? Was there not now, in the later 1960s, a good chance for Moscow to play the card of German *Ostpolitik?*[28]

For Moscow, this meant getting solid returns in return for what seemed to be superficial concessions. The Berlin Wall, put up in August 1961, had stopped the endless hemorrhage of skilled workers from East Germany, the economy of which then appeared to work. There were of course incidents, as people tried to escape the prison, and were shot—over 175 of them, sometimes in lurid and obscenely cruel circumstances. There were many, many old-age pensioners who just wished to rejoin their families in the West, and there were Western families who wanted to visit relatives in the East. Every year, there were incidents, as this or that well-meaning West German, or East German dissident, fell foul of the regime, was imprisoned for the usual vast sentence, and gave much for the most aggressively hostile Western propaganda to chew on. Concessions might be made over all of this: people released from East Germany, in return for Deutschmark payments.

In return for painfully drawn-out negotiations over "human rights" and other, in Soviet eyes, small change, there were tangible benefits to be won. Arms control was one. Commercial credit was another. A general avoidance of diplomatic static on the wavelengths was necessary for both of these, and here is where Gromyko came in. He was good at making things correct and businesslike. He did not give personal offense in the style of Molotov, and did not push his opposite numbers into a corner. Helmut Schmidt and Jimmy Carter detested each other a great deal more cordially than either disliked Gromyko. And the Soviet Union did rather well out of the various *Ostpolitik* deals that were sorted out in the later 1960s and the 1970s. There is even a case to be argued that *Ostpolitik* put off the crisis of communism for nearly two decades.

No Leninist would have been altogether surprised at what happened in West Germany after the sacrifices of the postwar recovery. The Social Democrats, internally divided over "capitalism," needed an external cause. There were many businessmen who looked with wonderment at the great potential market in the East, and thought that, with government help, they could penetrate it. Cheap energy might be had, a very important question, given the first and second oil shocks, of 1973 and 1979, which caused great trouble for the Western economies. Nationally minded Germans could also argue, as they had done in the past, that the only hope for German reunification lay in agreement with Moscow, and not in NATO. There were also many Germans, some of whom are now embarrassed by reminders of what they said, suggesting that in East Germany there was, after all, socialism and that it had created a certain prosperity. The Trier *Politologe* Jens Jesse, compiled a *sottisier* of these sayings and though the Social Democrats were well to the fore—insisting, for instance, even as late as 1988, on the scrapping of the federal institution for the study of East Germans' crimes against humanity—the other parties were also in evidence.

The elections of September 1969 led to the formation of a left-liberal government, under Willy Brandt, with Walter Scheel as foreign minister (and his party colleague Hans-Dietrich Genscher as minister of the interior). Implicitly, Brandt offered recognition of East Germany, although this meant abrogating much of the official West German stance since the constitutional laws of the later 1940s and the early 1950s. Egon Bahr did preliminary work, in Washington and elsewhere, in pursuit of his own beliefs. In August 1970 there was a broad Moscow treaty, essentially of nonbelligerence; and before then Bahr had already begun to discuss in Moscow a West German recognition of all the eastern borders. There followed negotiations with Rumania, Hungary, Poland, Czechoslovakia, and others, which laid the basis for a human traffic: German marks bought Germans who wanted to emigrate, and had the right to reside in Germany according to the constitution.

The advantages for the USSR were manifest. In the first place, economic arrangements were made. Oil and gas were to be sent by pipeline into Germany, and on 1 February 1970 at Essen agreements were signed. Over twenty years, Germany was to be sent 2.5 billion DM worth of natural gas (in the prices of 1970). The pipeline, already running from Siberia to Bratislava, was to be extended for this purpose. Mannesmann then promised to supply 1.2 million tons of large-diameter steel pipes and other equipment, while a consortium of seventeen banks, the Deutsche Bank in the lead, offered credit to pay for this (guaranteed by the German taxpayer). In July 1972 at Düsseldorf, there was a similar deal. Again, 1.2 million tons of high quality equipment would be supplied by Mannesmann, and again the banks lent money—1.2 billion DM,[29] repayable in 1983. These arrangements went together with a new agreement on trade, and there followed (to 1973) various new arrangements with the USSR, East Germany, and Eastern European states (e.g., to set up diplomatic relations with Hungary and Bulgaria). In return—and only after some humiliating obstacles had been placed, ostensibly by the East German regime—assorted concessions were made as regards access to money for *Autobahnen,* and the wait on the border was reduced from the usual day or even two days to a few hours.

Ostpolitik continued in the later 1970s as well. The deals were renewed with the USSR, on terms that greatly benefited Moscow: another 20 billion DM in 1981, stretching through at a fixed price to 1986, even though, in the meantime, the world price of gas fell by half. When martial law was proclaimed in Poland, President Reagan wished sanctions to be imposed by NATO as a whole, but not even Margaret Thatcher would agree to this, let alone the Germans and the French, even though what was proposed amounted to a ban on sensitive drilling equipment. In return for agreeable-sounding noises on human rights—the Helsinki follow-up conferences of 1977–1978 in Belgrade, and those of 1980–1983 in Madrid—*Ostpolitik* took its course. Even in petty ways, the Communists took their profit. Old-age pensioners and children visiting relatives in East Germany had to change a compulsory 20 or 25 DM at the border, and continue this for every day spent in the East, giving East Germany some 150,000 DM every year. Intra-German trade leapt up, some of it guaranteed a safe passage into the European Community as tariff-free imports. In time, the great bulk of the West German left-wing parties had been won round to greater accommodation, on lines of socialist unity, with the East German Communists. Right up to the end of their regime, liberal-minded West Germans (and a great number of media commentators further west) were still asserting that East Germany had its own patriotism, its high standard of living, its enviable welfare arrangements. Lenin had a good phrase for dealings with the West. You could always find, he said, "useful idiots," people who thought only of the wrongs of their home countries, knew nothing of Russia, and supposed that the Soviet Union had righted its equivalent wrongs. Paul Hollander has written of such "useful idiots," whether for Moscow, or for Hanoi and Managua.[30]

Andrei Gromyko had an essential part in all of this. We can only say that, as a technician, he was very efficient. No doubt he had dirty hands, somewhere along the line, but nothing in print makes this plain. And he was, in his own terms, quite successful. The Soviet Union *did* continue to be a Great Power, and *did* obtain money from, in effect, discreetly made blackmail. It *did* continue its arms effort, and if its leaders ever gave thought to the proper Leninist line, of spreading revolution around the globe, then they were, in their own terms, quite successful. They kept their country together, at a standard of living that at least met the desideratum of the former Austrian prime minister, Count Taaffe, who once said, "In politics I have no higher ambition than the achievement on all sides of a supportable level of dissatisfaction." Under Gorbachev, an effort was made—with Gromyko's ostensible blessing, though we can imagine the clenching of his teeth—to "sell" the Soviet Union even more vigorously. That effort went far out of control. In its great days, it had represented something of a Ptolemaic System. Marxist-Leninism was the political astronomy of the previous century. Its adepts, faced with more and more evidence that planets went round suns, tried to square this with the existing system, adding ever more complicated epicycles. The Gorbachev epicycle was the last in that sequence, of which Gromyko had been a distinguished element. And now, we shall see.

Notes

1. Shepilov was the main loser in the interparty battle of 1957. He lived into the 1980s in a waterless flat in the outskirts of Moscow. Molotov was humiliated for decades, but was readmitted to the party in 1984. Before he died, he recorded some memoirs, though they are not revealing. See above, chapter 3.

2. Vitaly Korotich, ed., *The Best of Ogonoyok* (London, 1990), 95 ff., and private information from Vladimir Bukovsky.

3. Charles E. Bohlen, *Witness to History, 1929–1969* (New York, 1973), 65.

4. According to Khrushchev, during a Soviet visit to Indonesia in the 1950s, Gromyko was "our top dancer" at the parties given by Sukarno. *Khrushchev Remembers: The Last Testament*, translated and edited by Strobe Talbott (Boston, 1974), 320. Comments on Gromyko's diplomatic role here and in *Khrushchev Remembers: The Glasnost Tapes*, edited by Strobe Talbott (Boston, 1990), are infrequent.

5. David Owen, *Time to Declare* (London, 1988), 336–37.

6. Don Oberdorfer, *The Turn: The United States and the Soviet Union from the Cold War to a New Era, 1983–1990* (London, 1992). George P. Shultz, *Turmoil and Triumph: My Years as Secretary of State* (New York, 1993). For other American descriptions of Gromyko in action, see for example *Berlin Crisis 1961–1962*, vol. 14 of *Foreign Relations of the United States 1961–1963* (Washington, 1994).

7. Yu. V. Aksyutin, ed., *N. S. Khrushchev Material K. bibliografii* (Moscow, 1989), especially the essay by N. Alekseyev, 67–81, on the Cuban crisis of 1962.

8. Andrei Gromyko, *Memoirs*, foreword by Henry A. Kissinger, translated by Henry Shukman (New York, 1989).

9. Ibid., 164 f.

10. Ibid., 175, 252.

11. Ibid., 266.

12. Foreword to ibid., x.

13. Wolfgang Leonhard, *Child of the Revolution* (London, 1958).

14. James G. Blight and David A. Welch, *On the Brink: Americans and Soviets Reexamine the Cuban Missile Crisis,* 2d ed. (New York, 1990), 392, n. 80.

15. Ibid., 391, n. 76; and, on the pervasiveness of this concern in Moscow, p. 327.

16. Ibid., 44–45, 336; Arthur M. Schlesinger, Jr., *A Thousand Days: John F. Kennedy in the White House* (Boston, 1965), 805.

17. Dino A. Brugioni, *Eyeball to Eyeball: The Inside Story of the Cuban Missile Crisis,* edited by Robert F. McCort (New York, 1989), 285–87; Raymond L. Garthoff, *Reflections on the Cuban Missile Crisis,* revised ed. (Washington, D.C., 1990), 47.

18. See below, Chapter 22.

19. Gromyko, *Memoirs,* x f.

20. James Sherr, *Soviet Power: The Continued Challenge* (London, 1987), 9.

21. Jerry F. Hough and Merle Fainsod, *How the Soviet Union Is Governed* (Cambridge, Mass., 1979).

22. Leszek Kolakowski, *Main Currents of Marxism* (Oxford, 1978).

23. Alain Besançon, *Passé russe, présent soviétique,* new ed. (Paris, 1986).

24. Alain Besançon, *Court traité de la soviétologie* (Paris, 1976).

25. Alain Besançon, *Anatomie d'un spectre* (Paris, 1981), 425.

26. Sherr, *Soviet Power,* 94.

27. Ibid., 97.

28. The best book on this is Dennis L. Bark and David R. Gress, *Democracy and its Discontents, 1963–1991,* vol. 2 of *A History of West Germany*, 2d ed. (Oxford, 1993), 151–223, 303–39.

29. Ibid., 170.

30. See Sidney Hook, Vladimir Bukovsky, and Paul Hollander, *Soviet Hypocrisy and Western Gullibility* (Washington, D.C., 1987).

21

SOVIET AMBASSADORS FROM

MAISKII TO DOBRYNIN

Steven Merritt Miner

ALL EMBASSIES are foreign outposts of the mother country. Soviet embassies, even more than those of other countries, were islands of the
motherland adrift in a hostile sea. Little is known of life on these
islands; even with recent revelations from the Soviet archives, very little light
has been shed on the functioning of Moscow's diplomatic outposts. One thing
has become ever clearer, however: Soviet ambassadors were kept on a much
tighter leash than their Western counterparts, at least from Stalin's time through
the collapse of the USSR. Nothing has emerged from the Soviet archives to
indicate that ambassadors were involved deeply in the policy-making process;
instead, Soviet diplomats abroad were charged with executing foreign policies
crafted in Moscow.

The virtual exclusion of Soviet diplomats from policy-making did not mean
that their activities were unimportant; the chief task of Soviet ambassadors in
noncommunist countries was instead presentation. This could take the form of
simple delivery of notes between Moscow and the leaders of the host country,
or, more frequently, it would involve appealing to the Western public.

Very few Soviet diplomats wrote about the nature of diplomacy. One exception was Valerian Zorin, a former diplomat who attempted to compose general
guidelines for Soviet diplomats serving in noncommunist countries. He wrote
that Soviet officials in such postings should do their utmost to help shape public
opinion in order to prevent the formation of hostile blocs by "the use of fissures
in [the capitalist] camp, by the maximal use of imperialist contradictions, by the
winning over to one's side of allies, even though [they may be] temporary and
unstable."[1] Zorin writes that the task of one section within a Soviet embassy,
generally under the leadership of a counselor or the first secretary, should be to
study and monitor "the internal politics of the country, maintain contact with
political parties, with ruling parties and oppositionists, with those individuals,
views and activities which have important significance for an understanding of
the basic tendencies of political development in the country."[2]

In one of several versions of his memoirs, Ivan Maiskii, the Soviet representative in London from 1932 to 1943, claimed that a Soviet ambassador in a

Western country had to be not only a discreet diplomat but also a master of public relations if he hoped to advance the Soviet Union's interests. "In countries of bourgeois democracy, like Britain, the USA, Scandinavia [*sic*] and some others," he wrote, "an Ambassador must know how to speak." It is not enough merely to meet privately with the leading figures of society; a Soviet ambassador must also be able to deliver his message to the public under widely varying circumstances: "at a crowded dinner arranged by some large organization, at the meeting of a learned corporation interested in the ambassador's views . . . at a lecture in a university . . . at a meeting of workers," and so forth. Maiskii warned that "an Ambassador who avoided such speeches would lose at once his prestige, and begin to be regarded only as a postman for transmitting notes from one government to the other." This would undercut "the possibility of influencing, in the sense he desires, public opinion in the country where he is accredited, and in the long run [would] injure the State that sent him there." Maiskii writes that each of his public speeches "was an excellent opportunity for telling the truth about the USSR or dealing a blow at defeatist moods," and that his chief problem was selecting which meetings to attend, in view of the veritable flood of invitations to speak that he received.[3]

In Washington, Maksim Litvinov, equal to Maiskii in his ability to present a forceful Soviet case, was also swamped by invitations, ranging from a mass meeting at Madison Square Garden calling for an immediate second front to more humble requests to address the chamber of commerce of a midwestern city.[4] During the war, other, less prominent, Soviet officials also spoke whenever possible to interested groups and even to school children, invariably closing with a call to open a second front.[5]

Both Maiskii and Zorin stress the importance for Soviet diplomats of establishing contacts in the host country with individuals and elements favorably inclined toward the USSR, whether communist or merely "progressive," that is, sympathetic to the current needs and policies of the Soviet Union. As Zorin pointed out, these people and groups need not be entirely of one mind with the USSR, so long as they held certain views congruent with Soviet policy at a given time. Zorin was simply reflecting Soviet practice. In a high-level meeting held in October 1941 to discuss how to influence American public opinion, Konstantin Umanskii, who had been Soviet ambassador to the United States, echoed Zorin's guidelines. He stated that the "most effective routes" for the Soviet propaganda message were "foreign correspondents, foreigners in general." For this reason, he told the meeting, Soviet officials should "cultivate them, reeducate them, even if they are hostile to us. We have espionage agents, and they are at work. Despite the fact that [these foreign contacts] might be drunks, still we need to use them, we need them."[6]

Litvinov, after his arrival as ambassador to Washington on 7 December 1941, frequently met or dined with such sympathetic figures as Joseph E. Davies and Henry A. Wallace. Indeed, Davies was so keen to assist the USSR in its war

against Germany that he apparently rejoiced on learning that his own country
had been attacked. According to Litvinov, when Davies was informed of the
Japanese bombardment of Pearl Harbor, he exclaimed "thank God." Maiskii,
too, was able to draw on his long experience moving among Britain's elite (in
addition to having lived in Britain before the revolution, he had been in London
since 1932, first as plenipotentiary [*polpred*] and then, from 1941–1943, as
ambassador [*posol*]).[7] Both before and during the war, he met regularly with
such left-wing intellectuals and political figures as Sidney and Beatrice Webb
and Sir Stafford Cripps; he also developed a good working relationship with
Lord Beaverbrook, the press baron and wartime cabinet minister, whom he met
frequently.[8] The contacts Maiskii cultivated before the war bore invaluable fruit
during the Grand Alliance.

In addition to meeting with sympathetic individuals in order to advance their
country's message, Soviet ambassadors in the United States and Great Britain
also made use of numerous political and "cultural" associations either controlled or funded directly by Moscow or the American or British Communist
parties. Some of these remained in close contact with the Soviet embassies in
Washington and London. A partial list of such groups operating in the United
Kingdom during World War II, prepared by Britain's Ministry of Information,
was divided into two categories: those associations "under strong Communist
influence," and those "materially directed by or being run to serve the interests
of the [British] Communist Party." In the first category were the International
Council of Students, the British-Soviet Women's Committee, the Women's
Parliaments, and the Society for Cultural Relations Between the Peoples of the
British Commonwealth and the USSR (the SCR). In the second group were the
Joint Committee for Soviet Aid, the National Council (or Conference) for
British-Soviet Unity, the Russia Today Society, and the Anglo-Soviet Friend-
ship Committee.[9]

The proliferation of such groups served Soviet interests well for several
reasons: their sheer number suggested that support for Soviet policy was widespread among the publics of the United States and Great Britain, although a
close look at the membership rosters reveals that these groups invariably drew
from the same well. A great many people belonged to more than one such pro-
Soviet friendship society. Furthermore, most of these societies were inspired or
funded by communist parties, or financed and guided directly from Moscow;
yet, had that fact become known, they would have been dismissed as mere
mouthpieces of Soviet propaganda, thereby losing their ability to influence
Western opinion, through such means as placing articles in the "bourgeois"
press. For this reason, the Soviets took great pains to mask the controlling hand
of Moscow behind the scenes of such groups.

These tactics could pay big dividends. The British Ministry of Information,
for instance, approved cooperation with the British SCR, believing that, although it was sympathetic to Moscow, it was not communist controlled. As an

internal Soviet Central Committee memorandum reveals, however, this was not the case: "Societies of Cultural Relations with the USSR in England, America, Sweden [and] China publish regular journals from materials sent by VOKS [the Soviet All-Union Organization of Cultural Contacts with the Soviet Union] and with money VOKS sends in secret [*sekretnom podarke*] for these ends to our foreign friends." The memorandum suggests that such ostensibly independent societies were in fact kept on a short leash: "Frequently some articles included in these journals are of a tone or character that are unwelcome to us. In such instances VOKS gives a special order, [and] these mistakes are corrected in the following issue and the entire line of the journal is examined and controlled by us."[10]

As a result of such covert tactics, during the period 1941–1945, the Soviets were able to funnel thousands of articles into the Western press with readers being given no indication of the actual Soviet source. Soviet Central Committee records show that both Maiskii and Litvinov, even after they had returned to the USSR after 1943, continued to pay great attention to the task of swaying Western opinion; and they both waged a running battle with more reactionary figures, such as Foreign Commissar Viacheslav Molotov, who showed little sensitivity to, or patience with, the delicate problems of attempting to influence Western opinion.

In one of his last communications to Moscow before his recall to the USSR, Litvinov argued forcefully that sophisticated and persistent propaganda directed at the American and British voting publics was an essential tool being underused by Soviet diplomacy. On 2 June 1943, in a telegram sent to Stalin, Molotov, and other members of the Politburo, Litvinov, who had been forbidden to make public addresses since early 1943, wrote: "[We must] place our ambassador in a position where he can speak frequently in front of the American public, explaining our general policy, or certain aspects of it, at present and in the future." In Litvinov's view, "serious pressure" on public opinion was virtually the only means by which the USSR could compel the Western Allies to hasten their landing on the European Continent. Furthermore, careful preparation of public opinion could prove vital for the postwar settlement as well. He wrote: "If we virtually settle the problem of our Western borders ourselves, there will be no major counteraction on the part of the U.S. However, since we'll need U.S. assistance for that, American public opinion will be vital." To present the Soviet case more forcefully to the American public, Litvinov suggested that "a number of people who can speak English fluently" should be dispatched at once from Moscow and "some reliable Americans" should be hired to translate and edit Soviet political materials for American consumption.[11]

Unfortunately for Litvinov, the leadership back in Moscow would prove unwilling to take such radical steps; Stalin and Molotov were in the process of making Soviet diplomacy more, rather than less, centralized. A year later, after his return to the USSR, Litvinov would still be lamenting Molotov's unwillingness to allow a more adaptive approach to propaganda in the West.

I

During the years of Nazi-Soviet collaboration, from August 1939 to June 1941, the prestige of Soviet diplomats in the Western capitals had reached a new ebb. The American ambassador to Washington, Konstantin Umanskii, had made himself especially unpopular during these years; he was widely disliked in Washington political circles for his abrasive personality and his frequent diatribes against American and Western policies. Furthermore, the American government had good reason to suspect that the ambassador and his staff had engaged in espionage during the period of the Nazi-Soviet Pact.

Evidence continued to mount during 1940 and 1941 that the Nazis and Soviets were pooling intelligence information about American defense preparations. The FBI, for instance, learned through a confidential source that Konstantin I. Ovchinnikov, the air attaché during Umanskii's tenure, had worked very closely with the German air attaché in Washington, Captain Peter Riedel, "to obtain information of value to the German and Russian Governments. [Ovchinnikov and Riedel] habitually exchanged information concerning the United States and apparently felt they were working together against this country." In one particularly egregious incident in May 1941, Ovchinnikov and his associate, Colonel Pavel F. Berezin, arrived "unannounced" at the Army's Edgewood Arsenal of the Chemical Warfare Service, demanding to be given classified technical documents and pretending that they could not understand English when asked on whose authority they had been sent. Secretary of War Henry L. Stimson wrote after this that the "repeated attempts of these Soviet officers working under the protection and with the aid of their diplomatic status, to obtain confidential military information in an illegal and surreptitious manner is adequate grounds for requesting their recall."[12] The orders were soon given, and Ovchinnikov and his associates were sent home.

Thus, relations between Moscow and Washington were under a cloud when news of the German invasion broke in 22 June 1941. The invasion presented Soviet ambassadors in the United States and Great Britain with a seemingly insurmountable set of problems. Overnight, the Soviets needed to mend fences with the United States and Great Britain; Moscow was especially concerned to prevent being left to fight the Wehrmacht alone; furthermore, if the USSR hoped to win, it would need material assistance from the Western democracies.

In the weeks following the Nazi attack, Ambassador Umanskii bombarded the Roosevelt administration with demands for assistance, while studiously disregarding the extreme displeasure caused in Washington by the Soviet

Union's recent collaboration with Hitler's Germany, about which the president and the State Department had been kept well-informed by the Moscow embassy. The ambassador's scornful dismissal before June 1941 of American warnings of an impending German attack did not strengthen his position, nor did the fact that, with the exception of the president, most senior officials in Washington, including Secretary of War Henry L. Stimson and Army Chief of Staff George C. Marshall, thought that the prospects of Soviet survival were dim. Under the circumstances, it was not Umanskii's diplomacy but Roosevelt's personal intervention that led to the dispatch of Lend Lease assistance to the Soviet Union in the last months of 1941, and it was only with the arrival of Umanskii's successor, Maksim Litvinov, whose earlier calls for collective action to halt the spread of Axis aggression were well remembered in Washington, that American-Soviet relations began to improve and the flow of American assistance to pick up momentum.

In London, after the Soviet Union became a belligerent in June 1941, Maiskii characteristically grasped at once the critical need for measures designed to persuade Western public opinion of two things: first, that, despite the initial German successes, the USSR would survive and prevail;[13] and second, that, like Britain, the Soviet Union was a nation fighting for its survival against the Nazis and not, as some continued to believe, a communist giant bent on conquest and expansion.

Maiskii displayed a remarkably subtle understanding of Western, and in particular British, opinion. This was, no doubt, the result of his long residence in Britain, both before the Bolshevik Revolution, when he had been an émigré from tsarist Russia, and again during his long appointment in London during the 1930s.[14] Later, this very understanding of Britain would land Maiskii in mortal danger when, in 1953, during Stalin's last days, he was arrested and accused of betraying the USSR. At that time, Maiskii would attempt to expiate his sins, telling his interrogators that "having spent long years abroad, he had allegedly lost his feeling for his native land and no longer knew which was his real home, the USSR or England. To all intents and purposes, England had become closer to him than the Soviet Union."[15]

Whatever one makes of such a comment, Maiskii's feel for British opinion served Soviet foreign policy well during the war. He displayed this touch when he met with British Foreign Secretary Anthony Eden on 22 June 1941, shortly after news of the German attack reached London. The ambassador suggested that an active program of positive cultural propaganda about the USSR, focusing in particular on prerevolutionary Russian history and literature, might slowly reshape British attitudes toward the USSR. As Eden later recounted to Duff Cooper, at that time Britain's minister of information, Maiskii said he understood "how deeply the dislike of Communism was rooted in this country," and that "nothing could be more unfortunate" than if rumors were to spread that the Foreign Office, in its desire to foster better relations with the USSR, was "lending itself to the popularising of Communist creeds." Maiskii said, "It was rather of the literary and artistic plane that he spoke." He suggested publication of an inexpensive edition of Lev Tolstoi's *War and Peace,* the object being to inform the Western reading public about how Russia had repulsed an earlier Western invader.[16]

Navigating the labyrinthian corridors of Britain's wartime bureaucracy, Maiskii diligently pursued the idea of cultural propaganda. On 12 July for example, he met Duff Cooper, with whom "he dealt at length with the importance of cultural propaganda and suggested that a committee should be set up to plan a programme of BBC talks, music, films, etc." When Cooper proved receptive, Maiskii further proposed a committee, to be headed by Mme. Maiskii and Lady Cripps, the wife of Sir Stafford Cripps, who was then Britain's ambassador in Moscow. The committee should deal with cultural propaganda in all its many facets. This seemed a good idea to the minister, who said he would "be glad to consider" it. A short while after this conversation, Cooper wrote a note to Eden expressing his opinion that "such a committee [as suggested by Maiskii] could do no harm."[17] Nevertheless, as he had earlier warned Eden, "It is difficult to see how we could boost modern Russian culture without implying some approval of the [Communist] experiment that has been going on there for the last 24 years."[18] Cooper had put his finger on one of the central dilemmas of the Grand Alliance: the conflict between the ideals and aspirations of the Western democracies and the Communist state, and the need to suppress these differences so long as Germany remained undefeated.

Through astute diplomacy, Maiskii did all he could to heighten this dilemma. The occupants of the Soviet Union's London embassy systematically monitored every aspect of British life that touched on the USSR in even the most peripheral way. Maiskii and G. Zinchenko, first secretary at the embassy, regularly complained to British authorities about even the apparently most trivial slights to the Soviet Union in print or in broadcasts (in 1943, Maiskii appointed Zinchenko to be the "competent official" for the Soviet embassy's liaison with the BBC).[19] To cite just a few examples from many, on 8 October 1942, Zinchenko suddenly appeared at the Ministry of Information complaining about a BBC historical play that, in his view, "contained falsifications of history, passages hostile to the Soviet regime, and remarks insulting to the memory of Lenin." He asked indignantly for "an explanation as to how it was possible for such a play to be produced by the BBC, considering the general happy relations between our two countries." Evidently, the offending play, entitled "Supreme Command," had dealt with German history in the closing stages of the previous world war and had referred to the German High Command's "ingenious plan" of returning Lenin to Russia in order to contribute to the disintegration of that country's fighting morale.[20]

Seven days later, Maiskii himself appeared in the Ministry of Information and, like Zinchenko, complained that British authorities were allowing "misinformation and slander" about the Soviet Union to be spread. He complained about a series of lectures on politics given by the Army Bureau of Current Affairs, and in particular by a "Miss Rosita Forbes," who, in the ambassador's view, was willfully denigrating the USSR. He "asked why the Ministry of Information did not provide the Army Bureau of Current Affairs with official speakers' notes on Russia's geography, economic potential and military organisation, and help the Army Bureau of Current Affairs to sort out its lecturers." Maiskii did not seem in the least mollified when Peter Smollett, the head of the Soviet section of the British Ministry of Information,[21] pointed out that, on balance, the great bulk of Army current affairs lecturers were decidedly favorable to the USSR—indeed, at one time the head of the Bureau had complained to Smollett that he was frequently accused of being "pro-Bolshevik."[22]

The tireless work of Maiskii and his assistants was comprehensive: they monitored such widely varying activities as radio broadcasts, provincial speeches, army lectures, school curricula and textbooks, and teacher training programs. As a result of this careful scrutiny, Britain's propaganda chiefs found themselves trying to hew to a very narrow line: attempting to say nothing in praise of Soviet Communism while simultaneously trying to say no evil of the USSR and thus bring down the wrath of their volatile ally. In practice, these conflicting goals proved impossible to reconcile. By as early as November 1941, Sir Orme Sargent, an under-secretary at the Foreign Office, noted despairingly that "we think it is time that the whole question [of BBC broadcasts about the Soviet Union] was reconsidered at a meeting. Much practical experience has been gained and among other things we find that, since the British Broadcasting Corporation naturally must give talks on present day Russia and cannot of course expose the less pleasant side, their talks cumulatively tend to build up a picture of a Soviet paradise."[23]

Careful Soviet monitoring of critical statements in the Western media had a much deeper effect than is generally realized and must rank as a truly important diplomatic triumph for Soviet ambassadors in the United States and Great Britain. Not only did the incessant badgering by Maiskii, Litvinov, Andrei Gromyko, and Fedor Gusev cause the Americans and British to watch their words carefully; the Western Allies also engaged in self-censorship for fear of offending Moscow. Of course, critical comment continued to appear in the American and British press, but, when publishers or prospective authors consulted government officials, the latter invariably toned down or eliminated entirely remarks critical of the USSR. Even recent history, especially anything relating to the origins or operation of the Nazi-Soviet Pact, was distorted or suppressed. British Foreign Office officials, for instance, persuaded Admiral Drax to postpone publishing his memoirs—as it turned out, permanently. In the summer of 1939, Drax had led the Franco-British military delegation to Moscow during the failed negotiations for a mutual defense pact between the Western democracies and the Soviets. It was felt that his memoirs might reflect

badly on Soviet diplomacy and trigger an ugly and avoidable diplomatic incident.[24] In another case, the Foreign Office was instrumental in preventing
publication by the Royal Institute of International Affairs of a booklet on Soviet
politics on the grounds that, though accurate, the work in question might offend
Soviet sensibilities.

The Americans, too, tried to avoid excess friction in the alliance by restraining publication of critical accounts about life in the USSR. When, for example,
Viktor Kravchenko defected to the United States in April 1944, American
diplomat Charles Bohlen agreed that the United States would accept him only
with the proviso that he not publish his memoirs. In the opinion of one student
of Soviet defectors, even this might not have prevented Kravchenko's forced
repatriation to the USSR, had he not taken the precaution of making his defection known to the press.[25] By 1946, with the Cold War beginning, however, the
State Department was apparently no longer concerned about offending Moscow, and Kravchenko proceeded to publish his bitterly critical—and best-
selling—account of his experiences in the Soviet Union.

II

Assessing the significance and impact of the Soviet ambassadors' persistent
cultural monitoring is no simple matter, since numerous factors other than
Soviet activity clearly contributed to the formation of Western public opinion
about the USSR. Overall, however, the results were distinctly limited, though
not insignificant. And, even more important, the Soviets in the end proved to be
their own worst enemies in the war for Western hearts and minds.

In the first place, the centerpiece of Soviet propaganda in the West was the
campaign for a second front in Europe; in London Maiskii and in Washington
Litvinov worked tirelessly to obtain an Allied commitment to land in France as
soon as possible. And yet, one could be forgiven for doubting that all the ink
spilled and breath wasted for the cause advanced the landing date by one hour.
To be sure, the second front campaign embarrassed Western leaders, but in the
end the decision to land in France was made for reasons only loosely connected
with any moral imperative to assist the USSR. If Soviet influence in Washington and London was all-pervasive, then it becomes difficult to explain why,
when judged by any reasonable standard, this most important of campaigns was
a signal failure.

Furthermore, it is not clear that the sharp rise in Western interest in and
admiration for the Soviet Union was caused so much by the efforts of Soviet
diplomats and propagandists as by the more tangible and impressive successes
of the Soviet armed forces against the Wehrmacht. Certainly the Soviets themselves believed that their new-found popularity in the West owed more to the
deeds of the Red Army than to effective propaganda. In Britain, judging from

the Home Office's weekly intelligence summaries, public interest in the Soviet Union waxed during those periods, such as early 1942, when British martial fortunes were sharply on the wane.[26] By the same token, by 1943, the British public was showing distinctly less interest in such things as "Anglo-Soviet weeks" and Soviet news in general. The novelty of being allied to the mysterious communist giant had worn off—it had become less mysterious; and the entry of Allied troops first into Italy and then into France tended to eclipse Soviet military feats in the Western press and popular imagination, even though Soviet gains remained impressive.

In the United States, the romance for things Soviet was never as widespread as it was in Britain. One study of American opinion during the war relates that a poll in 1942 ranked Russians twelfth among foreign nations most admired, behind the English, Canadians, South Americans (as one category), and, most surprisingly, Germans (who ranked seventh).[27] In part, of course, this can be explained by forces no more sinister than the presence in the United States of so many people of German descent, as opposed to much fewer from Russian immigrant stock. Nevertheless, despite such enthusiastic outbursts as the film version of *Mission to Moscow,* and *Life* magazine's 1943 issue devoted to Stalin, distrust of the USSR remained stronger in the United States than in Great Britain; the residue of suspicion from the Finnish War, religious antipathy to communism, and the presence of numerous East European immigrants with little love for Russia—tsarist or Soviet—conspired to inhibit the growth of a true American sympathy for the Soviet Union.

When assessing the contribution of the Soviet embassies' propaganda to the development of the Soviet wartime image in the West, one should remember the importance of the alliance and the war against Hitler as factors bonding the USSR with the Western democracies. In light of the common struggle against Hitler, it is not so surprising that a wave of pro-Soviet sympathy should have swept the United States and Britain, but rather that it was not more pervasive and lasting. To explain this paradox, one must look at the shortcomings of Soviet propaganda and the limited appeal of the Soviet system in general.

The Soviet diplomatic and propaganda machine was at times capable of great sensitivity and subtlety in dealing with the Western public. But there were distinct limits to Soviet finesse, and these became more apparent in mid-1943. In Britain, one of the greatest Soviet diplomatic assets was Ivan Maiskii; his experience and personal contacts patiently cultivated over more than a decade were invaluable resources for Soviet diplomacy. Although certainly no matinee idol, Maiskii was as popular as any Soviet diplomat would ever be in Britain; indeed, to this day his portrait hangs in London's Tate Gallery. Similarly, in Washington, Maksim Litvinov, the former people's commissar of foreign affairs, had the highest profile of any serving diplomat, and as a result he enjoyed greater influence than many among the grayer ranks of the Soviet diplomatic corps. Like Maiskii, Litvinov enjoyed a measure of public esteem. The two were, so far as one can tell, political allies; according to Maiskii, they maintained personal direct contacts during their concurrent tenures in Washington and London.[28]

In late spring 1943, both were suddenly recalled to Moscow for reasons that remain obscure. Over the years, the Soviets gave contradictory explanations at different times, as indeed did Litvinov himself; and, in his memoirs, Maiskii recounts a chronology that is incorrect, casting doubt on his version of events. The reasons for their recall may remain unclear, but the negative impact on the flexibility of Soviet diplomacy became apparent almost at once.

Their replacements were two as yet unknown figures: Fedor Gusev in London and Andrei Gromyko in Washington. In 1943, neither enjoyed any stature in the West. Gusev had only embarked on diplomatic work in 1937—that year of rapid promotions in the Soviet bureaucracy; and Gromyko, though bound for great things, had trained as an economist and only entered diplomatic service in 1939.[29] Indeed, Gromyko scarcely knew any English; when he told Stalin about this, the latter replied that Gromyko should visit American churches, since this was the best way to learn a language rapidly.[30] The State Department thought little of the new ambassador to Washington; an anonymous American analyst had earlier judged Gromyko to be "slow-witted and unimaginative." "It is not believed," the assessment continued, "that his qualifications warrant his being left in charge of the Soviet Embassy."[31]

The near-simultaneous withdrawal of Litvinov and Maiskii was one of the first visible signs of a process under way in the Soviet foreign commissariat during 1943. The new men, creations of the Stalinist system with no prerevolutionary past and beholden to the regime for their rapid promotion—often literally over the dead bodies of their predecessors—began to assume positions of authority. When Molotov had been appointed Foreign Commissar in 1939, Stalin had ordered him to purge the diplomatic service and bring it more closely into lock step with Moscow's dictates.[32] Molotov had executed his master's will faithfully; but the unexpected turn of events in June 1941 had interrupted the process. That the old Bolshevik Litvinov, and his political ally and old Menshevik Maiskii, could now be removed from their posts was due to the fact that by 1943 the military outlook was favorable and it was no longer imperative to retain the more independently minded duo in Washington and London as a sop to Western sensibilities.

Gromyko's very inexperience may have been one of his chief assets, along with his lack of flamboyance and his almost martial loyalty. Indeed, Stalin had told him during their first meeting in the Kremlin that "diplomats are like soldiers"; they must be prepared to follow orders and make unexpected moves if that is required by their superiors.[33] According to Viktor Kravchenko, who defected from the Soviets' Washington embassy shortly after Gromyko became ambassador, a system of dual authority was rigidly enforced in the Soviet embassy at this time; that is, while continuing to act as figurehead, the ambassador was in reality no longer in charge of the embassy. This job fell to an outwardly subordinate figure who may well have been from the NKVD.[34] It should be no surprise that such men were less attuned to the peculiarities of Western politics and public opinion, and Soviet propaganda in the later war years suffered a commensurate decline. Nor did the growing inter-Allied disputes, over such questions as Katyn, the Warsaw uprising, and the fate of the liberated countries, contribute to greater Western public trust of the Soviet Union. It was at this time that Litvinov began to air doubts about the direction of Soviet policy to various Western diplomats and journalists. Litvinov claimed, among other things, that Molotov "had removed from the Foreign Commissariat every important official who had any experience with the outside world and any personal knowledge of the . . . Western democracies."[35]

Recognizing the limited influence of Soviet diplomacy in the Western democracies should not, however, obscure the real Soviet gains made by Litvinov, Maiskii, and the staffs of their embassies. The Soviets failed to gain the desired second front; nor did they win over enough of the Western public to forestall the rapid growth of bitter anti-Soviet feeling during the Cold War. Indeed, the postwar collapse of Western illusions about the Soviet Union, misconceptions fostered by years of uncritical wartime propaganda, no doubt contributed to this bitterness. Despite such failures, however, Soviet diplomats and propagandists had contributed to the framing of political discourse in the West during the war. The existence of the Grand Alliance and the overwhelming need to rid the world of Hitler were not the only factors inhibiting critical debate about the nature of the Soviet Union and its war aims; the eternal vigilance of Soviet officials, their untiring efforts to seek out political allies and to isolate open enemies, were to a large degree successful. And, in the process, American and British diplomats were constrained in voicing their growing doubts about Soviet policy, until concrete actions—especially Soviet policy in Eastern Europe—had built a popular consensus to counter Moscow's power. By that time, however, many opportunities had been lost.

This is another way of saying, as Soviet historians and diplomats so often did, that the popular will exercised a restraining hand on Western diplomats' freedom of maneuver. But, as the Lenin of *What Is to Be Done* would surely have agreed, the existence of a popular opinion on any given question is unlikely to be politically decisive unless there is some agent to give it shape and focus. This was the role filled by Soviet ambassadors in the West.

III

It would take more than two decades to undo the damage Stalin had done to the Soviet diplomatic service. The greater stability of the *nomenklatura* that settled in over the Soviet Union after the death of the great dictator had a beneficial effect on Soviet foreign relations. Diplomats were able once again, for the first time since the ill-fated first generation of Soviet Foreign Service officers, to develop their linguistic skills and familiarity with foreign political systems. The foremost product of this newly realigned system was Anatoly Dobrynin.

Dobrynin entered the Soviet diplomatic service in 1946, seven years before Stalin's death. Like so many others during Stalin's time, he had received no specialized training in foreign affairs; in fact, he had been educated as an engineer. But he entered the Ministry of Foreign Affairs (MID) in a sufficiently junior capacity to be able to develop his career in what for the Soviet Union at that time was relative peace. Born in 1919, Dobrynin was old enough to have been thoroughly shaped by the Stalinist period—a mark he, would carry throughout his career. Perhaps it was the lingering fear of repression that eternally lingered in the back of the minds of people from his generation that would make Dobrynin into the consummate survivor. Still relatively young when he entered the MID, for the first six years of his career he served in the central MID apparat before being appointed counselor to the Soviet embassy in Washington; from that moment on he would devote his career almost exclusively to Soviet-American relations.

In 1961, Dobrynin achieved the post that he would hold through more than two decades. In January 1962, at the age of only forty-three, he arrived in the United States as the new Soviet ambassador; he would remain at that post until Gorbachev removed him in 1985. Dobrynin eludes analysis; unlike other Soviet diplomats, such as the voluble Maiskii, he chose not to publish very much. He was clearly a man on the move; he was intelligent, maneuvered well in internal politics, and had supporters and patrons within the Soviet hierarchy; too long a paper trail could prove a liability, so either from indifference or calculation he never spent much time putting his reflections on paper.

Dobrynin's political adroitness may explain why he remained so long in Washington. As in the American Foreign Service, in the Soviet MID it is customary to rotate officers from post to post to prevent them from becoming advocates of their locale's interests, rather than those of the central government. Dobrynin was a glaring exception to this rule. This may have been due to Foreign Minister Andrei Gromyko's fear that Dobrynin's political skills were somewhat too well developed; he feared his political rivalry.[36] Since the defeat of the Workers' Opposition of the early 1920s, posting abroad in the diplomatic service had been a convenient method of removing political rivals from the cockpit of the political struggle.

Dobrynin's appointment as ambassador came at a fateful time. Nineteen sixty-one had been a year of great tension in the Soviet-American relationship: the failure of the American-backed Bay of Pigs landing, tension over Berlin that led to the building of the wall, the collapse of the test-ban talks—relations between Moscow and Washington seemed to be heading into a box canyon.

In large part because of these heightened tensions, President John Kennedy had devised what he hoped would be an informal direct circuit to the Soviet leadership, using his brother Robert and Dobrynin. This was designed to be a special channel, which would allow both sides to talk informally, without the glare of a summit meeting but still confident that the views being aired would reach the highest levels of the two governments. This would be the beginning of Dobrynin's unique position in the Washington diplomatic world; throughout the remainder of his time in Washington, with a short break following the election of President Reagan, he would enjoy special protected access to the American halls of power.

This channel had drawbacks, to be sure; for instance, Dobrynin found the younger Kennedy a disquieting partner in negotiations. "Those who knew Robert Kennedy," Dobrynin said later, "knew that he was emotional; it was not so easy to conduct a discussion with him. But, all the same, within reasonable limits we conducted these conversations."[37] Despite the difficulties, this back-door channel seemed to have proven its usefulness during the Cuban missile crisis. During this fourteen-day emergency in October 1962, Dobrynin would attend seven heated meetings with Robert Kennedy, who was clearly speaking for the president and with his full approval. In finally judging the effectiveness of these talks, it would be necessary to know more than we do at present about how well-informed Dobrynin was. Certainly, Robert Kennedy was kept fully informed by his brother, who, or so Dobrynin believes, was actually in direct telephone contact during intervals during several of the meetings.[38]

As for Dobrynin, he clearly did not always know the content of messages Khrushchev was passing to the Americans. Indeed, Soviet diplomacy at this time seems to have been slipshod: Khrushchev had, notoriously, not fully consulted his military before ordering the missiles deployed in Cuba;[39] he also apparently did not tell his diplomats in Washington what his overall goals were. Dobrynin, who is not famous for criticizing his leaders or his country's foreign policies, came very close to doing both when he remarked, "Frankly speaking, I don't have the impression that everything was thought through to the last move, as in a game of chess. Undoubtedly, there was a conception [behind Moscow's policy], steps were taken, but there was also improvisation as things unfolded. At least this is what we felt in the embassy."[40]

Further complicating the situation were the poor communications of the Soviet embassy with Moscow. If Dobrynin is to be believed, he personally encoded messages to be sent to Moscow, which were then sent through the streets of Washington by Western Union bicycle messenger to be telegraphed back to the Kremlin. "See what kind of time we were living in!" Dobrynin exclaimed. "On the one hand it was the Cuban Crisis, nuclear missiles, and, on the other hand, a black man on a bicycle. Now it all seems rather colorful, but at the time it was no joke."[41]

Even at this distance, it is hard to establish Khrushchev's motives with any certainty in what the Russians call the Caribbean crisis. Did he hope to force a settlement in Germany and Berlin by ratcheting up pressure in America's backyard? Did he seek to have American nuclear missiles removed from Turkey? Did he hope to gain formal guarantees that the United States would not repeat a Bay of Pigs–style invasion? Was he simply fishing for possible gains? Owing to Khrushchev's personalization of foreign policy, any one of these theories, or some combination thereof, is plausible.

As is well known, the Cuban crisis ended in a tradeoff: the Soviets withdrew their missiles from the island, and, in return, the Americans went ahead with their already planned removal of American missiles from Turkey. In addition, the United States pledged not to attack Cuba in the future. What finally caused the Soviets to back down remains unclear. In his account of the affair, Robert Kennedy claimed that he delivered an ultimatum on 28 October: either the Soviet missiles would be withdrawn, or the United States would attack Cuba within twenty-four hours.[42] Dobrynin, by contrast, argues that Kennedy never issued such an ultimatum. Given the nature of the meetings, we may never have a definitive answer to this question either. Perhaps Kennedy delivered an implicit ultimatum, which went over Dobrynin's head; unlikely as that may seem, stranger things have occurred in fast-paced negotiations.

Whatever the actual sequence of events, the American diplomatic victory that the Kennedys and their supporters touted in the wake of the crisis looks more dubious with every passing year. Certainly, the Soviet embassy in Washington regarded the outcome as positive for Moscow: "the fundamental question" of the crisis, according to Dobrynin, was whether the United States could be induced to make a pledge not to attack Cuba in the future. "We persistantly posed this question at all discussions and meetings; in all letters and conversations, whether public or not, this was our goal."[43] One wonders whether it was Khrushchev's as well.

Two years after the Cuban crisis, Khrushchev would be ousted, but Dobrynin would go from strength to strength. He admits that the Caribbean events were "the most dramatic moment of my long experience in America";[44] but he would be centrally involved in all the major events of Soviet-American relations during the following two decades. The Cuban crisis had in a sense set the pattern; Dobrynin might be a tough negotiator and an old Stalinist, but his direct line to the Kremlin was one no future American administration felt that it could dispense with.

This was true during the Johnson administration and especially during the Nixon-Kissinger years, when Dobrynin achieved a status few ambassadors to the United States attained during the twentieth century. This is not to say, of course, that his outward affability, which soon became his trademark, represented greater personal flexibility than that of his predecessors. On the contrary, all indications are that, whether engaged in sensitive negotiations over Vietnam or complicated discussions of arms control, Dobrynin consistently adhered to the hard-line positions of his government, while persuading even so perceptive and skilled a diplomat as Secretary of State Dean Rusk that he was seeking to advance peace negotiations in good faith, although there is substantial evidence that this was not true.

Nevertheless, Rusk found Dobrynin a congenial person to deal with, and in his memoirs, published twenty years later, paid him a handsome tribute, describing him as "sociable, civilized, and well read, like Gromyko," and with "a real understanding of the complexities of American democracy." He added:

> When John Kennedy took office, the Soviets guessed that an ambassador with Dobrynin's temperament and personal style would be more effective than his predecessor, Mikhail "Smiling Mike" Menshikov, a cold warrior of the old school. Dobrynin was a great asset to the Soviets in his twenty-four years as ambassador."[45]

Henry Kissinger, in particular, both as national security adviser and as secretary of state, found Dobrynin an ambassador with whom he liked to do important business. Indeed, doubtless with the Soviet ambassador's ingratiating encouragement, Kissinger did not hesitate to conduct the most secret negotiations with him, and on one occasion, in May 1971, made important concessions on the question of offensive missiles, without telling senior State Department and arms control agency officials, who should have been kept continuously informed of these back-channel discussions.

Like Dean Rusk, Kissinger admired Dobrynin as a diplomat, and in the first volume of his memoirs he recalled their notable collaboration, which began in 1969 and continued for eight years. He wrote:

> I never forgot that Dobrynin was a member of the Central Committee of the Soviet Communist Party; I never indulged the conceit that his easy manner reflected any predisposition toward me or toward the West. I had no doubt that if the interests of his country required it he could be as ruthless and duplicitous as any other Communist leader. I took it for granted that his effectiveness depended on the skill with which he reflected his government's policies, not his personal preferences. . . .
>
> Dobrynin was free of the tendency toward petty chiseling by which the run-of-the-mill Soviet diplomat demonstrates his vigilance to his superiors; he understood that a reputation for reliability is an important asset in foreign policy. Subtle and disciplined, warm in his demeanor but wary in his conduct, Dobrynin moved through the upper echelons of Washington with consummate skill.[46]

One of those who was distinctly unimpressed by Dobrynin's successes in Washington was President Nixon's last chief of staff, General Alexander M. Haig, Jr. As he recalled in his memoirs, Haig had his share of unpleasant experiences with the Soviet ambassador, with the result that, when he became secretary of state in the Reagan administration, he ostentatiously withdrew the permission, accorded to Dobrynin by Dean Rusk and continued by his successors, to enter the State Department by a private entrance, where he would not be observed by the press. This action was soon rescinded by George P. Shultz, when he succeeded Haig in July 1982.

Despite Dobrynin's prominence in the Washington scene, from what we know about the conduct of Soviet foreign policy, it remained as rigidly centralized as it had been under Stalin. Dobrynin could not, for instance, contact Soviet ambassadors in other countries. Arkady Shevchenko, a defector from the USSR's UN delegation, writes, "It was ridiculous, but even the Soviet mission in New York was not permitted to coordinate its actions with the Soviet embassy in Washington. If it was necessary to discuss a matter with the American government, we had to cable Moscow, and Moscow would transmit it to Dobrynin, despite the fact that the Soviet mission and embassy are located less than two hundred and fifty miles apart. This does not mean that Soviet ambassadors in New York and Washington have no conversations at all, but such communications are unofficial."[47]

Unfortunately for the Russian people, this sort of massive bureaucratism was a feature of all Soviet life, and its crushing effects on the conduct of normal life would ultimately be one of the principal causes of the Soviet collapse. In its never-ending urge to centralize, the Soviet diplomatic bureaucracy had not changed much since the days of Stalin.

Where Soviet diplomacy had changed, however, was in its focus: in the early years of the Bolshevik state, the leaders in Moscow truly believed in the potency of their example. They dealt with bourgeois governments only with some distaste, preferring instead to appeal directly to the people. Even during the Second World War the Soviets had believed that their society possessed a universal appeal, and, as the heavy emphasis on propagandistic activities by Soviet ambassadors in the West showed, they acted on this belief.

By contrast, although Dobrynin could talk like a revolutionary, denounce imperialism, support "comrades" as far afield as Cuba and Vietnam, in fact his methods testified to the creeping decrepitude of Soviet foreign policy. No longer the revolutionary appealing to the people over the heads of the government, Dobrynin had become the consummate insider, or political operator. To be sure, Soviet foreign policy still hoped to persuade Western opinion to do such things as oppose the deployment of missiles in Europe or the American war in Vietnam, but gone were the days when Moscow took it for granted that the working class of the West was invariably on its side.

In retrospect, it would appear that the loss of this faith would help to seal the fate of the USSR. No state so unnatural as the Soviet system could hope long to survive once even those in charge began to believe that the whole structure had ceased to serve any higher purpose. In short, the trajectory from Maiskii and Litvinov to Dobrynin, from the first generation of true believers to the professional but mechanical bureaucrat, mirrored the transformation of the revolutionary state into a tired, top-heavy, cynical mammoth.

Notes

1. V. A. Zorin, *Osnovy diplomatecheskoi sluzhby* (Moscow, 1964), 68. Zorin had begun work in the NKID in 1941, and he went on to become, among other things, Soviet representative to the UN and ambassador to West Germany.

2. Ibid., 196.

3. Ivan Maisky, *Memoirs of a Soviet Ambassador: The War 1939–43* (New York, 1967), 210–11.

4. Leverett S. Lyon to Berle (invitation to address the Chicago Chamber of Commerce), 6 Apr. 1942, United States National Archives (hereafter NA), Record Group 59 701.6111/1129; John Marshall Club, St. Louis, to Litvinov, via the State Department, 14 Mar. 1942, NA, 701.6111/1124. There are numerous such invitations in State Department files.

5. In April 1943, for example, the military attaché at the Soviet Embassy in Washington addressed school groups and American Legion gatherings about the urgent need for a second front. The Soviet naval attaché, Captain Egorichev, and his assistant, Commander Skriabin, said that they had been sent by their embassy "to address civilian meetings in various cities in this country [the United States] regarding U.S. aide [*sic*] to the Soviet Union and the opening of a second front." Struble to Liaison Officer, State Department, 26 Apr. 1943, NA, 701.6111/1178.

6. Russkii Tsentr dlia Khraneniia i Izucheniia Nyneshnykh dokumentov (Russian Center for the Preservation and Study of Contemporary Documents, hereafter, RTsKhIND), "Stenogramma soveshchaniia u tov. Lozovskogo," 2 Oct. 1941, Fond 5, opis' 6, rolik 1352.

7. A. A. Gromyko et al., eds., *Diplomaticheskii slovar'* (Moscow, 1985), 2:172. Litvinov to Molotov, 2 June 1943, text of telegram printed in Amos Perlmutter, *FDR and Stalin: A Not So Grand Alliance, 1943–1945* (Columbia, Mo., 1993), 236.

8. He even dined with Beaverbrook on occasion, and such informal meetings could prove very useful. See, for example, "telegram of the ambassador of the USSR in Great Britain to the People's Commissariat of Foreign Affairs of the USSR," 28 June 1941, Ministerstvo inostrannykh del SSSR, *Sovetsko-angliiskie otnosheniia vo vremia velikoi otechestvennoi voiny, 1941–1945* (hereafter *SAO*) (Moscow, 1983) 1:52–53.

9. Edwards to Dowden, 25 Aug. 1944, British Public Record Office (hereafter PRO), Ministry of Information (hereafter INF), 1/678.

10. RTsKhISD, Moscow, V. Kemenov to A. Aleksandrov, 20 Aug. 1942, fond 17, opis' 125, rolik 1364.

11. Litvinov to Stalin and Molotov, 2 June 1943, text of telegram in Perlmutter, *FDR and Stalin*, 244, 246.

12. J. E. Hoover to Adolf A. Berle, Jr., 23 May 1942, NA, 701.6111/1134. Henry L. Stimson to Cordell Hull, 2 June 1941, NA, 701.6111/1013.

13. Later, after several months had passed, Maiskii explained to the NKID that, from the time of the German invasion through mid-July 1941, public opinion in Britain was characterized by "pessimism regarding the chances of the USSR." *SAO*, "From a telegram of the ambassador of the USSR in Great Britain to the People's Commissariat of Foreign Affairs of the USSR," 26 Oct. 1941, 159–63.

14. Maiskii has left an interesting and, by the admittedly low standards of officially sanctioned Soviet diplomatic memoirs, entertaining and informative account of his

years in London before and during the Bolshevik Revolution. *Journey into the Past* (London, 1962).

15. These are the words of Alexander Nekrich, the émigré Russian historian, who studied under Maiskii in Moscow following the latter's rehabilitation. Nekrich speculates that Maiskii's admissions to his captors may have been intended as a means of improving his treatment. Nonetheless, judging from Maiskii's wartime dispatches and later writing, it would seem that he developed a genuine understanding of, and even sympathy for, Britain. Alexander Nekrich, "The Arrest and Trial of I. M. Maiskii," *Survey* 22 (1976): 313–20.

16. Eden to Cooper, 28 June 1941, PRO, INF 1/913.

17. Cooper to Eden, 12 July 1941, PRO, Foreign Office (hereafter FO) 371 29602.

18. Cooper to Eden, 28 June 1941, PRO, INF 1/913.

19. Allen memorandum, 28 May 1943, PRO FO 371 37023.

20. Smollett to Grubb and Ryan, 8 Oct. 1942, PRO FO 371 32925.

21. Smollett, whose real name was H. P. Smolka, was evidently a Soviet mole. During much of the war he was responsible for all official British propaganda relating to the USSR; as a result of his unique position, Smollett was able to meet weekly with Zinchenko and regularly with Maiskii. See Christopher Andrew and Oleg Gordievsky, *KGB: The Inside Story of its Foreign Operations from Lenin to Gorbachev* (New York, 1990), 325–28.

22. Gates to Director General, 15 Oct. 1942, PRO, FO 371 32925.

23. Sargent to Radcliffe, 24 Nov. 1941, PRO, FO 371 29603.

24. The extensive correspondence on this question is contained in PRO, FO 371 29603.

25. Vladislav Krasnov, *Soviet Defectors: The KGB Wanted List* (Stanford, 1986), 18.

26. The collection of Home Office Weekly Intelligence summaries is in PRO, INF 1/292.

27. See Ralph B. Levering, *American Opinion and the Russian Alliance, 1939–1945* (Chapel Hill, 1976), 87.

28. Maisky, *Memoirs of a Soviet Ambassador,* 327, 378. Maiskii also dedicated his book *Journey into the Past* "To the memory of my old friend, M. M. Litvinov."

29. A. A. Gromyko et al., eds., *Diplomaticheskii slovar',* tom 1, (Moscow, 1985), 275, 279.

30. Andrei Gromyko, *Pamiatnoe* (Moscow, 1988), 1:77.

31. "Biographical Sketch of Mr. Andrei D. Gromyko, Counselor of the Soviet Embassy," 13 May 1941, NA, 701.6111/1012.

32. See Chapter 3.

33. Gromyko, *Pamiatnoe,* 1:76.

34. Viktor Kravchenko, *I Chose Freedom: The Personal and Political Life of a Soviet Official* (New York, 1946), 458–59. Another Soviet defector claims that this dual system was still in operation long after the war. Aleksandr Kaznacheev, *Inside a Soviet Embassy: Experiences of a Russian Diplomat in Burma* (Philadelphia, 1962).

35. State Department, *Foreign Relations of the United States, 1943,* Welles Memorandum, 7 May 1943 (Washinton, D.C., 1963), 3:522–24.

36. Such, at any rate, is the opinion of two observers who knew both men: Arkady Shevchenko, *Breaking with Moscow* (New York, 1985), 36; and Georgi Arbatov, *The System: An Insider's Life in Soviet Politics* (New York, 1992), 300 n.

37. Bruce J. Allyn, et al., eds., *Back to the Brink: Proceedings of the Moscow Conference on the Cuban Missile Crisis, January 27–28, 1989* (Cambridge, Mass., 1992), 143.

38. Ibid.

39. See the account of the crisis in Fedor Burlatskii, *Vozhdi i sovetniki: O Khrushcheve, Andropove i ne tol'ko o nikh* (Moscow, 1990), 227–46.

40. Allyn et al., *Back to the Brink,* 84.

41. Ibid., 86.

42. Robert F. Kennedy, *Thirteen Days: a memoir of the Cuban Missile Crisis* (New York, 1971), 86–87.

43. Allyn et al., *Back to the Brink,* 80–81.

44. Allyn et al., *Back to the Brink,* 83.

45. Dean Rusk, *As I Saw It* (New York, 1990), 360.

46. Henry A. Kissinger, *White House Years* (Boston, 1979), 139–40.

47. Shevchenko, *Breaking with Moscow,* 141.

22

FROM HELSINKI TO AFGHANISTAN: AMERICAN

DIPLOMATS AND DIPLOMACY, 1975–1979

Francis L. Loewenheim

I

T HE WORLD HAD SEEN nothing like it since 1945. The Conference on European Security and Cooperation, better known as the Helsinki Conference, which opened in the Finnish capital on 31 July 1975, brought together representatives of thirty-five nations, including the Holy See, and yet it was strikingly different from the San Francisco conference that gave birth to the United Nations organization thirty years earlier. The latter, attended by delegates from fifty states, lasted two months and was, in every sense, a meeting where serious negotiations, indeed hard bargaining, went on at length between its larger and smaller participants. By contrast, the Helsinki gathering lasted barely three days, and its outcome was carefully scripted in advance.

Yet there was no mistaking the historic nature of Helsinki. For nearly two decades, dating back to Soviet Foreign Minister V. M. Molotov's initial proposal in 1954, the Soviet government had repeatedly sought an agreement that would make permanent the temporary boundaries of 1945 and in effect ratify the political-territorial outcome of World War II. Led by the United States, the Western democracies had long resisted Moscow's objective, contending, at least until the late 1960s, that a final agreement on frontiers could only be reached by a formal peace conference, which, almost everyone knew or understood, was nowhere in sight.

By 1973–1974, the American negotiating position had clearly begun to change. As part of its new policy of détente, initiated by Richard Nixon and Henry Kissinger in 1969, Washington exhibited a far greater willingness to accede to Soviet desires, including diplomatic recognition of the so-called German Democratic Republic. The steadily deteriorating situation in South Vietnam further undermined Washington's longstanding determination to postpone a final peace settlement in Europe. By the summer of 1974, as the burgeoning Watergate scandals drove Richard Nixon from office, the United States finally indicated its willingness to attend an international conference that would formalize European boundaries in accordance with Moscow's longstanding wishes.

In the protracted and tortuous negotiations that paved the way for the Helsinki Conference, the United States put forth what it considered a substantial condition of its own. Twenty years had passed since Joseph Stalin's death, and some of the worst abuses of his terror state had been meliorated or abolished. But for all the changes wrought by Nikita Khrushchev and Leonid Brezhnev, human rights in the Soviet Union and the Soviet-controlled East European satellite states remained conspicuous by their absence.

The United States now insisted that this deplorable situation be formally addressed and significant reforms at least begun.[1] Months of hard bargaining ensued, but Soviet negotiators finally gave way, or appeared to do so, and a diplomatic compromise was struck. The agreement thus reached was in three parts or—a term invented by the British—baskets. The first basket concerned security, including "confidence-building measures" such as advance notification of certain military maneuvers. The second covered economic cooperation. The third concerned basic human rights, which the Soviets, in what seemed to be clear and unequivocal language, undertook to observe, while also agreeing to a series of follow-up conferences to assess progress achieved.

Not surprisingly, from the outset, East and West emphasized, or sought to emphasize, different baskets. To the Soviets, Basket I meant the territorial status quo in perpetuity, to which the West Germans, supported by President Ford, responded that there was still room for "peaceful change."[2] Indeed, the president himself sought to downplay the importance of the conference. As he told a group representing Americans of East European background at a meeting at the White House on 25 July 1975:

> I would emphasize that the document I will sign [at Helsinki] is neither a treaty nor is it legally binding on any participating state. . . . It is the policy of the United States, and it has been my policy ever since I entered public life, to support the aspirations for freedom and national independence of the peoples of Eastern Europe—with whom we have close ties of culture and blood—by every proper and peaceful means. I believe the outcome of this European Security Conference will be a step—how long a step remains to be tested—in that direction. I hope my visits to Poland, Romania, and Yugoslavia will again demonstrate our continuing friendship and interest in the welfare and progress of the fine people of Eastern Europe.[3]

The president's secretary of state, Henry Kissinger, had apparently not approved Ford's remarks in advance, and he was furious when he learned what the president planned to say. "You will pay for this!" he raged to staff members gathered outside the Oval Office. "I tell you heads will roll."[4] The most Kissinger was able to achieve, however, was to persuade Ford to drop one sentence from his departure statement at Andrews Air Force Base: "The United States has never recognized the Soviet incorporation of Lithuania, Latvia, and Estonia, and is not going to do so in Helsinki."[5] But Ron Nessen, the White House press secretary, had already distributed the planned remarks to the media, and "the President's conspicuous omission," as Robert T. Hartmann, the perceptive counselor to the president, wrote later, "made it look as if [Ford] was being muzzled by his Secretary of State and bent on appeasing Brezhnev."[6]

In a historical overview of American-Soviet relations from 1917 to 1976, published the following year, George F. Kennan referred to what he called "a bewildered Gerald Ford, by no means unresponsive to hard-line pressures."[7] The contemporary record does not bear out that harsh assessment. At Helsinki, the president held two extended meetings with Leonid Brezhnev, meetings reportedly concerned with a broad range of issues from arms control to Jewish emigration. Some Soviet commentators, including the faithful party-liner Georgi Arbatov, later effusively described Helsinki as "the high point" of the decade.[8] To Ford, on the other hand, the conference served as a welcome opportunity for him to set forth his own view of the world and the current international situation. Speaking last to assembled delegates and guests on 1 August 1975, the president expressed his deepest personal feelings. Ford declared:

> Peace is not a piece of paper. There is not a single people represented here whose blood does not flow in the veins of Americans and whose culture and traditions have not enriched the heritage which we Americans prize so highly. The people of all Europe—and I assure you the people of North America—are thoroughly tired of having their hopes raised and then shattered by empty promises. We had better say what we mean and mean what we say, or we will have the anger of our citizens to answer.

Looking straight at Brezhnev, whose appearance and performance at the conference was beginning to betray his advancing age and declining health, the president continued:

> Détente, as I have often said, must be a two way street. Tensions cannot be eased by one side alone. Both sides must want détente and work to achieve it. . . . Can there be stability and progress in the absence of justice and fundamental freedom? . . . History will judge this Conference not by what we say here today, but by what we do tomorrow—not by the promises we make, but by the promises we keep."[9]

For all the attention it received at the time, and all the ink spilled about it subsequently, the Helsinki Conference changed little or nothing either in Washington's conduct of foreign policy or in American relations with the communist world. When he first succeeded Richard Nixon as president on 9 August 1974, Gerald Ford, who had served in the House of Representatives since 1949 and as vice president since November 1973, probably knew less about foreign affairs than any new occupant of the White House since Warren G. Harding or Calvin Coolidge fifty years earlier. It was hardly surprising, therefore, that one of

Ford's first confidence-building acts was to announce that he would retain Henry Kissinger as secretary of state and national security adviser. Similarly, the new chief executive decided to make few changes at the top of the State Department or at American embassies around the world.

Not long after he became president, Ford had to make one of his most sensitive appointments, nominating someone to succeed the illustrious David K. E. Bruce as head of the United States liaison office in Beijing. Having passed over former Congressman George Bush of Houston for vice president in favor of former New York Governor Nelson A. Rockefeller, Ford gave Bush, then head of the Republican National Committee, a choice between the embassies in London and Paris and the Beijing post, and was, Bush recalled later, "obviously surprised" when he expressed his preference for the Chinese position. "An important, coveted post like London or Paris would be good for the résumé, but [Beijing] was a challenge, a journey into the unknown. A new China was emerging, and the relationship between the United States and the People's Republic would be crucial in the years to come, not just in terms of Asian but of worldwide American policy."[10]

Bush soon got a taste of Henry Kissinger's highly secretive method of operation. "Some of the most important papers I needed to know about," he wrote, "fundamental documents like Nixon's conversations with Mao that led to the Shanghai Communiqué of 1972, were closely held by Henry's staff. So closely held that I could read them only inside the private office of Richard Solomon, senior staff member of the National Security Council and one of our top China experts." And Bush went on to say:

> Henry assured me before I left for China that I'd be kept fully informed by him and his staff on everything that transpired between the United States and China. Most of the action along this front came not in Beijing but Washington, where he met frequently with Ambassador Huang Zhen, my counterpart in the Chinese Liaison Office. I'd learn, as had David Bruce, that it took a bureaucratic battle with the State Department to get any information about the Secretary's private talks with the Chinese.

As Bush's remarks confirm anew, the period from late spring 1974 to late summer 1975 probably marked the high point of Kissinger's influence and power in Washington. As a senior White House official told the columnist Richard Reeves: "There wasn't much [Ford] could do but let Henry run the show. There was never any question of moving Ford people into foreign policy. What could we do? Henry *was* foreign policy."[11] So just as Harding, for example, had followed the strong lead of his formidable secretary of state, Charles Evans Hughes, Ford readily accepted the course Kissinger mapped out for him. And while disaffection with Kissinger's policies had been growing since the early seventies—and was ventilated in the Senate Foreign Relations Committee hearings on the subject in August, September, and October

1974[12]—it was not until the following year that the president and some of his White House advisers began to appreciate the seriousness of the mounting criticism. The reasoning behind Kissinger's view and approach to détente has been and continues to be much discussed. But it is clear enough that he was anxious to preserve the existing framework of relations and the budding systems of arms control that he and Nixon had developed with Moscow, and so another of Ford's initial actions was to agree to meet with Leonid Brezhnev to continue the personal and diplomatic relationship Nixon had begun at their highly publicized summits in 1972, 1973, and 1974.

Was détente successful in limiting or reducing the nuclear arms race? As the era of nuclear weapons entered its fourth decade, its complexities and subtleties defied ready comprehension. Different analyses could reach different conclusions. Comparative weapons statistics—hard enough to calculate meaningfully before 1914 or 1939[13]—could be interpreted any number of ways and sometimes were. No one in authority in Washington in the early seventies would dwell on how the West had lost its former nuclear preeminence, and if and how that lead might be restored. Many believed, however, that, since the mid-sixties, the USSR had achieved virtual parity, if not superiority, in nuclear weapons,[14] and was continuing to widen its lead, so American arms control strategy appeared designed, in large measure, to slow that lead. A lasting new East-West nuclear balance—however tentative and unstable—seemed a chimera. All of which did not keep military spending from again becoming a volatile political issue.

Under those circumstances, the Ford-Brezhnev meeting at the Siberian port city of Vladivostok on 23–24 November 1974 marked something of a turning point in American-Soviet relations. For despite the president's evident euphoria about his initial venture into the rarefied atmosphere of superpower summitry,[15] the arms agreement the two leaders reached left the Soviets with what many, including Paul Nitze, who had recently resigned his position as deputy chief American arms control negotiator, regarded as a disturbing advantage over the United States in several important categories.[16]

Nor did Vladivostok do anything to head off the coming dénouement in Vietnam. If Nixon and Kissinger had embarked on their policy of détente with Moscow and Beijing as a way of achieving a lasting peace settlement in Vietnam—that is to say, a peace settlement that presumably assured the freedom and security of South Vietnam—that expectation was about to be put to its supreme test. For whatever hopes Nixon and Kissinger may have entertained on this point at one time or another, there is no reason to believe that either the Soviet Union or Communist China ever sought to restrain Hanoi in its avowed determination to conquer South Vietnam, the terms of the January 1973 Paris peace agreement notwithstanding.[17] With American military assistance to Saigon largely shut off by congressional action, the Republic of Vietnam found itself increasingly at the mercy of its sworn foes in Hanoi. Three months after

Vladivostok, North Vietnam at last felt ready to move in for the kill, and Ford and Kissinger knew better than to expose their diplomatic powerlessness by useless appeals to Moscow and Beijing.

To be sure, the president and the secretary appealed to Congress for one more round of American military assistance to Saigon. But the antiwar forces, led by men like Senate Majority Leader Mike Mansfield of Montana and Foreign Relations Chairman Frank Church of Idaho, were firmly in control and determined not to yield an inch. This is not the place to recount the tragic last days of South Vietnam, except to note the heroic performances of Graham A. Martin, since 1973 American ambassador in Saigon, and his embattled staff. Probably few American diplomats had ever faced a more challenging and thankless task than Martin did during those harrowing weeks in March and April 1975, when he was responsible not only for the safety of all remaining Americans in the area, but for evacuating many South Vietnamese as well.

Hanoi's triumph presented the White House with an especially intractable dilemma. For years, Ford had been a staunch supporter of American assistance to South Vietnam. Now came the problem of rationalizing—in effect historicizing—that policy. In an address at Tulane University on 23 April 1975, Ford summed up his own position succinctly. "Today," he declared, "America can regain the sense of pride that existed before Vietnam. But it cannot be achieved by refighting a war that is finished as far as America is concerned."[18] The result of Ford's remarks—which the president and Kissinger may well have welcomed under the circumstances—was that there was no further congressional or executive inquest into what had gone wrong in Vietnam, and no disposition to treat South Vietnam as occupied territory, whose continuing control by Hanoi the United States would refuse to recognize under the terms of the Stimson doctrine of 1932.[19]

The fall of South Vietnam, which Kissinger may have expected for a year or more, produced no basic change in American foreign policy. That became abundantly clear at the Helsinki conference three months later, and it was further confirmed by the White House's decision not to invite the renowned Russian writer and political dissident, Aleksandr Solzhenitsyn, to the Oval Office during his visit to the United States in July 1975, to avoid offending the Russians. "The Solzhenitsyn affair," as one of the president's speech writers recorded in his diary, became "a nightmare inside the White House,"[20] and there can be little doubt that Ford suffered serious political damage as a result. The episode may also, however, have had another, no less important consequence, leading the president to have fresh doubts about the soundness of Kissinger's policies, which were coming in for steadily increasing public and political criticism. In any case, as part of a larger administrative shakeup, in late October 1975 Ford decided to relieve Kissinger of his position as the president's national security adviser.[21] To be sure, Kissinger's position as secretary of state remained commanding, but it was clearly no longer unchallenged. Not only had the vaunted policy of détente conspicuously failed in Vietnam. It was rapidly becoming a political albatross, and as Ford looked ahead to the 1976 presidential campaign, it seemed unlikely that grandiloquent talk about the blessings of détente, real or imagined, would contribute to his election prospects as it doubtless had to Richard Nixon's 1972 race against Senator George McGovern of South Dakota in 1972.

While Ford was beginning to think about 1976, more immediately pressing storm clouds were starting to form on the international horizon, commencing in Angola. The Angolan situation was part of the larger Portuguese problem, which began in early 1974, when that country's long-ruling military junta headed by Marcelino Caetano had been overthrown and, succeeded by a distinctly left-leaning regime headed by Colonel dos Santos Vasco Gonçalves. One of the first acts of the new government, which Washington had been quick to applaud, was to announce that the Portuguese colony Angola would receive its independence effective 11 November 1975. Since Angola was ill-prepared for its new freedom, it soon became a battleground between a small pro-Western faction, the National Front for the Liberation of Angola (FLNA), and a much larger, pro-Communist Popular Movement for the Liberation of Angola (MPLA).

For nearly twenty years—that is to say since the middle years of the Eisenhower administration—American policy had sought to prevent the spread of Communist influence and power in Africa, and, on the whole, that policy had been remarkably successful. Now Angola suddenly loomed as fertile ground for Communist intervention, and Moscow and Havana were not slow to take advantage of the new opportunity. With neighboring Rhodesia and South Africa both facing increasing turmoil and political upheaval, there was no ignoring Angola's strategic and symbolic importance. The Soviet Union and Castroite Cuba, moreover, made no secret of their determination to obtain a foothold in the former Portuguese colony and, if possible, to exploit it as the beginning of a far larger involvement in Africa.[22]

Ford and Kissinger were well aware of the Angolan stakes, but when they appealed to Congress for a modest amount of assistance for the pro-Western forces, on 19 December 1975 the dovish majority in the Senate voted 54 to 22 to cut off further American help to the FLNA. The president displayed understandable exasperation:

How can the United States, the greatest power in the world, take the position that the Soviet Union can operate with impunity many thousands of miles away with Cuban troops and massive amounts of military equipment, while we refuse any assistance to the majority of local people who ask only for military equipment to defend themselves? This abdication of responsibility by a majority of the Senate will have the gravest consequences for the long-term position of the United States and for international order in general. A great nation cannot escape its responsibilities. Responsibilities abandoned today will return as more acute crises tomorrow."[23]

At a press conference on 14 January 1976, Kissinger heatedly denounced Soviet-Cuban intervention as being "counter to the crucial principles of avoidance and scrupulous concern for the interests of others which we have jointly enunciated."[24] The secretary's convoluted allusion to the portentous twelve "basic principles of mutual relations between the United States and the U.S.S.R.," signed by Nixon and Brezhnev at their first Moscow summit in May 1972, was however blithely ignored by Brezhnev and Castro, who continued to increase their support of the MPLA. By late 1975 there were an estimated five thousand Cuban troops in Angola. With the State Department bureaucracy and the Central Intelligence Agency paralyzed by internal differences or fear of adverse public reaction, the triumph of communist forces was not long in coming. As William G. Hyland, who observed much of the proceedings from the vantage point of the National Security Council, wrote later: "For the first time since the Truman Doctrine and American intervention in Greece in 1947, the United States had formally refused to contest a Communist offensive campaign."[25]

That is not to say that the developments in Angola did not affect American policy toward Africa in the larger sense. As if to head off the possibility of further Communist intrusion in the area, Kissinger soon became far more critical of the white governments of Rhodesia and South Africa. The new American policy was doubtless unappreciated by Salisbury and Pretoria,[26] but it served its purposes in limiting the further spread of Soviet and Cuban influence at a time when America's role in Southeast Asia had been dramatically reduced as a result of the Communist triumph in South Vietnam and its takeover of Cambodia and Laos, where the elaborately negotiated Geneva peace agreements of 1962 likewise proved to be little more than a scrap of paper.

If Ford-Kissinger diplomacy had proved largely ineffectual or worse vis-à-vis Moscow, Hanoi, and Havana, it was hardly more successful as far as Communist China was concerned. In December 1975, a year after his journey to Vladivostok, Ford traveled to Beijing, where he was treated to the ringing anti-Soviet pronouncements now standard fare with Communist Chinese leaders and their spokesmen. As Vice Premier Deng Xiao Ping put it in an address during a nine-course dinner in the Great Hall of the People: "Today, it is [the Soviet Union] . . . that is the most dangerous source of war. . . . Rhetoric about détente cannot cover up the stark reality of the growing danger of war."[27]

Two days later, Ford was received by the fast-failing Mao Zedong, and the eighty-one-year-old Communist party chairman proceeded to subject the president, Kissinger, national security advisor Maj. Gen. Brent Scowcroft, and George Bush to a long monologue, contending (as Ford summed it up later in his memoirs) that the Soviets wanted world domination, and if their drive was ever to be stopped, the United States would have to stand up to them. That was why [Mao continued] the U.S. would have to remain strong in the Pacific basin, why we'd have to be willing to challenge the Soviets everywhere. Mao seemed fully aware of the restrictions that Congress was placing on my ability to conduct foreign policy, and it was clear that they upset him. Would we do anything to challenge the Soviet-Cuban thrust in Africa? When was the United States going to strengthen ties with its NATO allies? Were we going to continue helping our traditional friend in Asia? Or, in the wake of our setbacks in Cambodia and South Vietnam, would the United States turn inward again?[28]

Ford and Kissinger may have regarded such summit encounters as enhancing the administration's national and international prestige. Eight months after the fall of South Vietnam, it seems more likely that the president's trip to Communist China only added fresh doubts and questions about where the administration was headed in world affairs. As for George Bush, the China mission on which he had embarked with such high hopes also ended on a doubtful note. On 3 November 1975, Ford had announced his appointment as the new director of the Central Intelligence Agency, but Mao's government seemed undisturbed by the news. "When word of my appointment reached [Beijing]," Bush remembered, "Chinese officials, far from being appalled, were openly pleased. As one of them confided, they felt they'd spent a year 'teaching' me their views on the Soviet threat and now, as America's chief intelligence officer, I'd be able to 'teach' them to the President."

Certainly the China visit did nothing to improve the president's position at home. Inflation and unemployment, both at high levels when he assumed office, had declined only modestly. Faced with an overwhelmingly Democratic Congress that sensed victory in the approaching presidential election, Ford had been unable to produce a substantial legislative program of his own. Despite some of the extraordinarily capable senior staff that he had assembled at the White House, including men like Philip W. Buchen, Richard B. Cheney, David R. Gergen, Robert T. Hartmann, Brent Scowcroft, and L. William Seidman, a number of whom were later to serve with distinction in the Reagan and Bush administrations, Ford was increasingly viewed by the media as an undistinguished president whose days were numbered. As the columnist George F. Will put it in mid-December 1975: "After 500 days in office Mr. Ford is widely regarded as a caretaker. And in presidential politics, a synonym for 'caretaker' is 'lame duck.' "[29]

Not surprisingly, the country took little notice of one of Ford's substantial achievements, his role in the development of a new kind of economic collaboration between the leading democratic industrial states, an initiative dating back to George P. Shultz's days as treasury secretary in the Nixon administration, which began with a series of economic summits at Rambouillet near Paris in mid-November 1975 and at Puerto Rico in late June 1976.[30] With the United States and most of the other large industrial states in the midst of serious recession, the idea of an economic conference had been briefly discussed at Helsinki, where West German Chancellor Helmut Schmidt had been among its leading proponents.[31] At Rambouillet, a month before his journey to Beijing, Ford had left no doubt where he stood on economic relations with the communist world (a subject on which Henry Kissinger was largely indifferent): "It is our belief that the development of strong economic ties with Eastern Europe, the Soviet Union, and the People's Republic of China represents an essential element in our overall policy. Close economic ties and increased trade enhance our ability to foster restraint and cooperation in the behavior of the Communist countries."[32] Seven months later, at Puerto Rico, in the midst of the presidential campaign, Ford found it desirable to be rather more cautious in his comments about relations with the communist world. "We agreed," he declared, without going into details, "to examine carefully the various aspects of East-West economic contacts so that they enhance overall East-West relations."[33] Clearly, political and economic circumspection was the watchword. As Leonard Silk of the *New York Times* summed it up: "Mr. Ford shows no intention of giving up any more of his cautious and conservative economic policy than he needs to for political reasons, and he can and doubtless will use the Puerto Rico joint declaration as evidence of broad international support for his brand of economics."[34]

Thus began a new international tradition on which Gerald Ford's successors would continue to build for decades, and despite their evident limitations, the first two economic summits achieved a useful economic-political dialogue and collaboration at a time when the global diplomatic-military fortunes of the Western democracies had taken a distinct turn for the worse.

II

It was against that uncertain background that Ford and Kissinger began to face the 1976 campaign. By late 1975, two determined challengers, one expected, one not, had begun to emerge. The first was former Governor Ronald Reagan of California, the great conservative Republican hope in the aftermath of the collapse of the Goldwater movement. The second was former Governor Jimmy Carter of Georgia, who soon began to make a name for himself, as his future campaign manager Hamilton Jordan had recommended to him as early as November 1972, as "a highly successful and concerned former governor of Georgia . . . speaking out on the pertinent issues of the day."[35]

If Reagan and Carter differed sharply on domestic issues, they seemed frequently to agree in their harsh criticism of Ford-Kissinger foreign policy.

Gradually abandoning his earlier decision not to criticize Ford and Kissinger, at a televised news conference in Orlando, Florida, on 4 March 1976, the Californian sharply attacked the president for what he called "the diplomatic and military decline of the United States. . . . Under Messrs. Kissinger and Ford, the nation has become No. 2 in military power in a world where it is dangerous—if not fatal—to be second best." Détente, Reagan declared, had "yielded nothing more than Soviet belligerence in the Middle East, Soviet duplicity in Southeast Asia, and Soviet imperialism in South Central Africa." Using "Castro's mercenaries," the Soviet Union "intervened decisively in the Angola civil war and routed pro-Western forces." The truth is, Reagan concluded, that "all our smiles, concessions, and boasts of détente have not brought genuine peace any closer."

Not to be outdone, Jimmy Carter took broad aim at the recent Helsinki accords. "At Helsinki," he was quoted by United Press International on 11 March 1976, "we signed an agreement approving the takeover of Eastern Europe. I would be very much tougher in the following years [in negotiations] with the Soviet Union." But Carter didn't stop there. "I don't believe," the *Chicago Tribune* quoted him on 9 May 1976, "that I would have participated in the Helsinki meeting. I don't see that we got anything tangible in return from the Soviets. I think also that in the Vladivostok agreement, on nuclear arms control, the Soviet Union simply out-traded us."

The White House lost no time tracking the Reagan-Carter attacks and their political fall-out.[36] As late as spring 1975, Kissinger had warmly defended détente. As he put it in an interview with Pierre Salinger, for *L'Express* of Paris, on 12 April 1975: "I think in America too many people have taken détente for granted and forgotten what it was like to live in the Cold War."[37] Eleven months later, the president was no longer prepared to support that view. In an interview filmed for a Miami television station in early March 1976, Ford announced: "I don't use the word détente any more. . . . Détente is only a word that was coined. I don't think it is applicable any more."[38] And in an address at Peoria, Illinois, on 5 March, the president added: "We are going to forget the use of the word détente." Henceforth, he said, American policy would be "peace through strength," language reminiscent of the Truman postwar years.[39]

In January 1976, while Kissinger was on yet another trip to Moscow, a secret meeting of the National Security Council decided not to proceed with further SALT discussions during the upcoming election year. The rationale behind the president's decision was not immediately clear. Had the administration—Ford in particular—concluded that détente had been a mistake and should therefore be abandoned? "We will never permit détente to become a license to fish in troubled waters," Ford had said on 10 April 1975.[40] Now, as if to reassure himself, he plaintively minuted General Scowcroft, his national security adviser, in February 1976: "What has U.S.S.R. done to abide by Helsinki: List if possible."[41] Had the president and secretary of state jointly agreed to drop the use of the term? And what kind of foreign policy might the Ford administration follow, assuming the president emerged victorious in November?

To these questions there were no ready answers, then or later, but at the Republican National Convention in Kansas City, Missouri, in mid-August 1976, Kissinger was carefully kept out of sight until the last day, and the final version of the platform plank on foreign policy expressed the White House's acceptance of the fact that the country had had enough of détente and henceforth wished American diplomacy to be conducted in a distinctly more assertive fashion and direction. The Republican platform declared:

> The goal of Republican foreign policy is the achievement of liberty under law and a just and lasting peace in the world. The principles by which we act to achieve peace and to protect the interests of the United States must merit the restored confidence of our people. . . .
>
> Ours will be a foreign policy which recognizes that in international negotiations we must make no undue concessions—that in pursuing détente we must not grant unilateral favors with only the hope of getting future favors in return.
>
> Agreements that are negotiated, such as the one signed in Helsinki, must not take from those who do not have freedom the hope of one day gaining it.

In the event, the Reagan challenge to Ford's nomination fell short, but once the autumn campaign got under way, Carter's attacks on administration foreign policy continued unabated. The differences between Ford and Carter on foreign policy came to a head at their nationally televised debate in San Francisco on 6 October 1976.[42] From the opening, the Georgian left the viewing audience, estimated in the tens of millions, in no doubt about what he thought of the merits of Ford-Kissinger statecraft. "We talk about détente," he declared. "The Soviets know what they want in détente, and they've been getting it. We have not known what we wanted, and we've been out-traded. . . . As far as foreign policy goes, Mr. Kissinger has been president of this country."

Such language came as no surprise to Ford and his staff. But when it came his turn to reply, the president made what is widely regarded as one of the classic gaffes in modern campaign history, a slip often considered to have cost him the election. The episode began with a carefully worded question by Max Frankel, the Sunday editor of the *New York Times*. We've recognized, said Frankel, "a permanent Communist regime in East Germany; we virtually signed, in Helsinki, an agreement that the Russians have dominance in Eastern Europe. . . . Is that what you would call a two-way street of traffic in Europe?" Doubtless recalling some of the earlier Reagan-Carter attacks on the Helsinki agreement, Ford replied that there was no Soviet dominance of Eastern Europe, and there never would be under a Ford administration, adding that Yugoslavia, Rumania, and Poland were "independent" and "autonomous."

Apparently thinking the president might have misunderstood the question or had made a slip of the tongue, Frankel decided to rephrase his question. Did the president mean to say that the Soviets "are not using Eastern Europe as their own sphere of influence in occupying most of the countries there and making sure with their troops that it's a Communist zone?"

Ford, however, was determined to stand by his earlier response: "I don't believe, Mr. Frankel, that the Yugoslavians consider themselves dominated by the Soviet Union—I don't believe that the Romanians consider themselves dominated by the Soviet Union. I don't believe that the Poles consider themselves dominated by the Soviet Union . . . and the United States does not concede that these countries are under the domination of the Soviet Union."

Carter promptly seized on the president's response. "I would like," he said, "to see Mr. Ford convince Polish-Americans and the Czech-Americans and the Hungarian-Americans in this country that those countries don't live under the domination and supervision of the Soviet Union behind the Iron Curtain."

Conventional wisdom to the contrary, the president's repeated position was no slip and no accident. As his handwritten notes, preserved at the Gerald R. Ford Library, leave little doubt, the president said exactly what was on his mind. Since the White House and the Democratic challenger had previously agreed that neither candidate would bring handwritten or printed materials to the debate, it seems virtually certain that the president made his notes either before responding to a question addressed to him, or while waiting to comment on a question first directed to Carter. Under the circumstances, his handwritten notes strongly suggest that his reply to Frankel's questions represented precisely the position he wanted to convey. Ford's notes, covering several sheets, read in part:

> Helsinki—
>
> 1) thirty-five nations—including sec. of State for Vatican.
>
> 2) No Soviet sphere of influence in Eastern Europe Agreement/borders cannot be changed by force.
>
> 3) Established standard for Human Rights.

A point-by-point comparison of the president's remarks and his handwritten notes further confirms the direct correlation between the two. For example, in response to Frankel's initial question, Ford had declared: "In the case of Helsinki, thirty-five nations signed an agreement, including the secretary of state for the Vatican. I can't under any circumstances believe that his Holiness the Pope would agree, by signing that agreement, that the thirty-five nations have turned over to the Warsaw Pact nations the domination of Eastern Europe."

It should be added that this, or something very much like it, is what the president had been telling members of the Congress, and writing to private citizens around the country, for many weeks and months. Whatever Moscow and others chose to believe, to Ford the Helsinki agreements did not legitimize Soviet overlordship over Eastern Europe. As far as he was concerned, Soviet rule was a distinctly temporary phenomenon, which he and others, including the pope, were not prepared to recognize as a permanent state of affairs.

However that may be, most of the American media, which had long been highly critical of Ford's domestic and foreign policies, promptly decided that he had committed yet another egregious blunder, all the more serious for being in a field in which the president presumably had far more experience and know-how than did his Democratic challenger. "The Blooper Heard Around the World," *Time* magazine called it.[43]

In a matter of days, the forward momentum of Ford's campaign, which had steadily reduced the Georgian's considerable lead, suddenly halted, never to resume. On 2 November 1976, Jimmy Carter was narrowly elected president with 50.1 percent of the popular vote, carrying twenty-three states and the District of Columbia, with 297 electoral votes, twenty-seven more than required. It remained to be seen, however, what Carter's own foreign policy would turn out to be, and how he would cope with the global challenges, old and new, of the late 1970s.

III

It is impossible to say what kind of foreign policy Gerald Ford might have pursued had he been elected in his own right in November 1976. But those who hoped or expected that Jimmy Carter's victory would mean a sharp break with the policies he had repeatedly denounced during the campaign were soon to be disappointed. America did not withdraw its ground forces from South Korea. The United States did not extend diplomatic recognition to Castro's Cuba. The president did not end public or covert assistance to pro-Western elements in the Angola civil war.

On the other hand, almost at once détente was back in fashion at the White House and the State Department. Indeed, in some ways Carter was determined to go beyond the concessionist course of the Ford-Kissinger years. His first objective was, as quickly as possible, to reach a final agreement, in the making since the Johnson sixties, to turn over operation of the Panama Canal to that country's government. He expected to achieve a SALT II treaty with the Soviet Union as well as the normalization of United States relations with Communist China, even if this required cancellation of the 1954 American-Taiwan mutual defense treaty and withdrawal of diplomatic recognition from Taiwan. He would seek a comprehensive settlement of long-standing Middle East problems, especially those resulting from the 1967 war. Last, but in some ways first and foremost on the Carter agenda, was the president's new emphasis on human rights and his determination to make human rights an integral part of American foreign policy as a whole.[44]

If Carter's expansive program lacked nothing in ambition, it made no concessions to his inexperience to foreign affairs.[45] Though he had briefly traveled in the Middle East before he was elected, the new president was little better versed in international affairs than his predecessor had been when he first took office, but with the difference that Ford was prepared, at least for a year or so, to accept Henry Kissinger's continued direction of American foreign policy. Carter, on the other hand, with an arrogance born of ignorance, was determined to strike out on his own almost immediately, not infrequently with unfortunate results.

The new team Carter assembled to carry out his foreign policy was a mixed bag, to say the least. Hardly had the ballots been counted than Carter chose, as his first cabinet appointee, Cyrus R. Vance as his secretary of state. Vance, it should be remembered, had served as secretary of the Army in the Kennedy administration and as deputy secretary of defense under Lyndon Johnson, and had become increasingly anti-Vietnam as time went on. His appointment was clearly a message to the country and the world that the president was determined to follow the dovish course that had characterized most of his remarks on foreign policy during the recent campaign.[46]

As if to balance Vance's views, Carter proceeded to select as his national security adviser Professor Zbigniew Brzezinski, a distinguished Columbia University political scientist and specialist on totalitarianism and Eastern Europe, a scholar whose widely known hard-line views were too readily attributed to his Polish background. Carter had begun to consult Brzezinski at length as early as 1975, when Vance was supporting Sargent Shriver, brother-in-law of the late President Kennedy and George McGovern's running mate in 1972.[47] Carter and Vance may have expected the national security adviser to take a narrow view of his office and prerogatives, as General Brent Scowcroft had done in the last years of the Ford administration; if so, they were mistaken. If Brzezinski had been "the *éminence grise* of foreign policy in the Carter camp" before the election, his influence continued to grow once the former Georgia governor was in the White House. As his voluminous papers, already available at the Carter Presidential Library, make amply clear, Brzezinski lost no time becoming the political conscience of the new administration. From his first weeks and months in office, he attracted the attention and support of numerous members of Congress, concerned interest groups, and thoughtful scholars, who soon discovered with dismay that, like Henry Kissinger before him, Cyrus Vance had a firmly established agenda, and was even less disposed than Kissinger to pay attention to dissenting views.

Despite their differences of opinion, especially during their first year or two together, as time went on Brzezinski had good reason to believe that the president was coming increasingly to appreciate and support his judgment, at the same time that Vance's influence in the White House began to wane. Indeed, it is not too much to say that, had Carter listened more attentively to his national security adviser, he might have spared himself some of the humiliating setbacks he suffered in 1979, which led to his overwhelming repudiation at the polls in November 1980.

As the third member of his foreign policy-defense troika Carter chose Dr. Harold Brown, a noted physicist, from 1965 to 1969 secretary of the Air Force in the Johnson administration, from 1969 to 1977 president of the California Institute of Technology. Brown, who brought an informed scientist's knowledge and experience to bear on the fast-changing problems of national and international security, initially leaned rather toward Cyrus Vance's views, but as time went on drew closer to Brzezinski's outlook. The remainder of Carter's new foreign policy team—there were few holdovers from the Nixon-Ford years—appeared to follow no clearly distinct ideological lines, although a number of them, including Patricia Derian, the president's Mississippi campaign manager, named assistant secretary of state for human rights and humanitarian affairs, increasingly made a name for themselves, favorable and unfavorable, on the left-liberal side of the political spectrum.[48] Centrist or conservative Democrats were conspicuous by their absence.

Doubtless the most symbolic and controversial of Carter's early diplomatic appointments was his nomination of Paul C. Warnke, an early antiwar dove in the McNamara Defense Department and former national security adviser to Senator George McGovern during the 1972 campaign, as head of the Arms Control and Disarmament Agency and chief negotiator at the SALT talks with the Soviet Union. Warnke's nomination was promptly opposed by defense-minded senators like Democrat Henry M. Jackson of Washington, who accused Warnke of being "a tireless advocate of deep . . . and irresponsible-cuts in the defense budget, of unilateral restraints in our defense programs . . . [and] of the notion that nuclear superiority is meaningless." After extended debate, the Senate eventually confirmed Warnke by a vote of 58 to 40, but the large number of senators opposing him should have alerted the president to growing public and political doubts about current American arms control policies.[49]

To assist him in choosing ambassadors, Carter appointed a special commission headed by Democratic Governor Reubin Askew of Florida, whose colleagues included W. Averell Harriman and former Secretary of State Dean Rusk. Since President Ford had made a number of senior appointments during his last year in office, Carter wisely decided against reassigning these career Foreign Service officers. Accordingly, there were few changes at the major embassies from London to Moscow. To replace Anne L. Armstrong, long closely identified with Republican party circles, at the Court of St. James's, Carter chose Kingman Brewster, the president of Yale University, whose diplomatic credentials were minimal and whom Carter repeatedly declined to see when the ambassador was back in Washington on leave.

As American ambassador to France, the president appointed Arthur A. Hartman, who had served as assistant secretary of state for European and Canadian affairs since 1973. In Moscow, Carter retained Malcolm Toon, who had previously served with distinction in Czechoslovakia, Yugoslavia, and Israel, but who soon discovered the Brezhnev-Gromyko regime to be as unhelpfully uncooperative as its predecessors had been going back to the unlamented days of Khrushchev and Molotov. In October 1979 Carter replaced Toon with Thomas J. Watson, Jr., the son of the founding head of International Business Machines, perhaps expecting to improve American-Soviet trade relations, a hope soon dashed by the invasion of Afghanistan, which led Carter to recall Watson from Moscow.

As ambassador to Bonn, Carter continued Walter J. Stoessel, Jr., who had spent the preceding two years in Moscow. But whatever Stoessel's demonstrated talents, he found himself unable to smooth relations between the president and West German Chancellor Helmut Schmidt, who regarded Carter as disturbingly lightweight, and who, though a Socialist himself, longed for the days of Gerald Ford, about whom he wrote admiringly in his memoirs, "I did not find a comparable familiarity with the history of my country in either of his successors."[50] Other, more or less prestigious or desirable posts went to deserving Carterites. Philip H. Alston, Jr., of Georgia, was appointed ambassador to Australia, Anne Cox Chambers, another Georgian, ambassador to Belgium. To Mexico, the president sent Governor Patrick J. Lucey of Wisconsin, an early Carter backer, who spoke no Spanish. To Norway, he appointed Louis A. Lerner, another early Carter supporter from Illinois.

On balance, it seems fair to say that the ambassadors played as modest a role in Carter's administration as they had done during the Nixon-Ford years. There were two conspicuous exceptions, who were to cause the president considerable difficulty. First, there was William H. Sullivan, a career officer with experience dating back to 1939, whom Carter appointed American ambassador to Iran in early 1977, and with whom he had a bitter falling out in 1979–1980 over his reports and recommendations concerning the Shah and the rising revolutionary forces there. Second, there was former Congressman Andrew J. Young of Georgia, the United States ambassador to the United Nations, with whom the president came to a parting of the ways in mid-August 1979 over the ambassador's unauthorized contacts with representatives of the Palestine Liberation Organization. About both of these episodes more will be said below.

Both at the time and in later years, Carter was frequently criticized for unwisely piling up an unmanageably large and complicated domestic agenda for Congress to debate and act upon. In the realm of foreign affairs, the president's program was hardly less ambitious, and from his first weeks and months in office, his performance raised serious questions about his judgment and steadfastness. "What's missing" in the Carter presidency, wrote David S. Broder, one of the most perceptive of Washington observers, on 8 June 1977, "is the sense of strategy, of choosing those problems that are important . . . and ignoring the rest; and of tackling the specific problems in a way that illuminates the principles, rather than contradicts them."[51]

As already noted, from the outset Carter was determined to make human rights a central feature of his foreign policy, giving it an importance far greater than it had previously enjoyed. "The passion for freedom," he declared in his inaugural address, most of which he wrote himself, "is on the rise. Tapping this new spirit, there can be no nobler nor more ambitious task for America to undertake . . . than to help shape a just and peaceful world that is truly humane."[52] He was determined, for example, that there would be no repetition of Gerald Ford's embarrassing unwillingness to receive Aleksandr Solzhenitsyn at the White House. On this score, Carter and Brzezinski clearly saw eye to eye, and it was hardly surprising, therefore, that almost immediately the national security adviser found himself inundated with numerous appeals for assistance with a wide variety of human rights problems, including some of the most moving pleas to reach 1600 Pennsylvania Avenue since the days of Franklin D. Roosevelt in the Holocaust era.

Hardly had the Carter administration taken over than the State Department commended the Russian physicist Andrei Sakharov for his courageous opposition to Soviet totalitarianism.[53] The President expanded upon this statement at a meeting with Soviet Ambassador Anatoly Dobrynin at the White House on 1 February, and in a subsequent personal letter to the Russian scientist, promptly released to the press for added international effect.[54] As Carter may or may not have expected, the Brezhnev regime declared itself affronted by his outspoken position, which the Soviet leader denounced as "direct attempts . . . to interfere in the internal affairs of the Soviet Union." Long accustomed to Henry Kissinger's seeking to downplay Jewish emigration and other human rights issues, the president's statement may have alerted the Kremlin to the unwelcome realization that the new administration was not disposed to view Basket III of the Helsinki agreement as an empty letter, and expected Moscow to live up to the accords Brezhnev had signed in August 1975.

If Carter's initial démarche on the human rights issue proved largely unproductive—indeed perhaps even counterproductive—the president's first move in the volatile field of arms control met no better fate. About Carter's determination to bring about a sharp reduction in nuclear weapons of all kinds, indeed probably armaments of every sort, there could be no serious doubt. It was a problem he had repeatedly, sometimes movingly, addressed during the presidential campaign. For example, he criticized the high weapons totals Ford and Kissinger had accepted at Vladivostok in November 1974, and it was a subject he turned to almost as soon as he took office. As early as 17 February 1977, it was announced that the United States would not make available to any foreign country the CBU 72 radiation bomb, then widely recognized as the most deadly nonnuclear weapon in existence. This was followed, on 30 June 1977, by the decision to cancel production of the Air Force's strategic new B-1 bomber, successor to the aging B-52s.[55] And in an address to the United Nations on 4 October, Carter declared the United States ready to consider reductions in nuclear weapons ranging from 10 to 20 to 50 percent. How the Kremlin might respond to his new arms control initiatives, Carter appeared at the outset to have no idea and not to be overly concerned about.[56]

To the Soviets, who regarded their enormous and steadily growing nuclear arsenal as the centerpiece of their superpower status, Carter's new approach was anathema. Again, in a sense, the Brezhnev regime had been spoiled by years of dealing with Kissinger, who, while he deplored the continuing increase in nuclear weapons, in practice did little or nothing to control or retard it. Not surprisingly, therefore, when Secretary of State Vance arrived in Moscow in late March 1977, bearing the president's new arms control proposals, he met with an icily hostile reception. As Vance reported to Carter: "My view is that they have calculated, perhaps mistakenly, that pressure will build on us to take another position. . . . we should not be discouraged. A certain testing period was probably to be expected."[57]

But Brezhnev's brusque rejection of Carter's new SALT proposals was not the end of the episode. While waiting for the final communiqué to be agreed to, back at the American Embassy Vance and Paul C. Warnke, the new chief American arms negotiator, held a news conference for American and foreign reporters, defending the president's new proposals and, as William G. Hyland, of the National Security Council staff, who was present, wrote later, "by implication [criticizing] the Soviets for turning them down." As if to teach Carter a lesson in diplomatic protocol—for having, in effect, abandoned the 1974 Ford-Brezhnev Vladivostok agreement—Soviet Foreign Minister Gromyko, after seeing Vance off at the airport, held an extraordinary press conference of his own. It was, Vance later wrote, "long and harsh and out of character with Gromyko's usual style . . . probably in an attempt to throw the blame for lack of progress on the United States . . . unfortunately, effective as a propaganda device [which] created widespread fear that the U.S.-Soviet relationship was in jeopardy."[58] Following the earlier riposte regarding human rights, here was a second crucial test for the new Carter administration. Would the president and his secretary of state stand fast behind their new proposals, and insist upon them as the basis of further negotiations? Or would they quietly abandon their initial effort and hope that the Soviets would be amenable to far more limited arm control measures?[59]

This is not to suggest that Carter had come to the presidency determined to challenge Soviet power and authority, as Eisenhower and Dulles had appeared to do twenty-five years earlier. To be sure, in an unmistakable rebuke of Kissinger-style foreign policy, he had told the Foreign Policy Association in New York on 23 June 1976 that he favored "not a condominium of the powerful but a community of the free" and "organizing free world nations to share world responsibility in collective action."[60] But his inaugural address also contained a thinly disguised antiwar message—"Let our recent mistakes bring a resurgent commitment to the basic principles of our nation"—and in his commencement address at Notre Dame University, on 22 May 1977, a speech several months in the making, Carter himself had, at the last moment, added a warning against "that inordinate fear of communism which once led us to embrace any dictator who joined us in that fear."[61]

Such remarks troubled many of Carter's middle-of-the-road and more conservative internationalist supporters, and Eugene V. Rostow, the noted Yale legal scholar and arms negotiator, doubtless spoke for not a few when he wrote Landon Butler, one of Carter's top aides, on 19 October 1977, words that must have had a haunting ring by late 1979:

> I think the biggest political issue in the country today is "Are we No. 1 or No. 2?" The party that embraces it first, and hardest, will win in 1980. I hope the President will decide soon to break out of his cage on the subject. The idea that an increase in real terms of 3% a year in the defense budget can overcome the gaps which Nixon allowed to develop is just ridiculous. Of course he would need to fire about 50 of the McGovernites who now infest the government to make such a policy effective. But that would be a good thing for many reasons. The President has followed their advice, and has been led into one swamp after another. He should not only turn a sharp corner, but be seen to do so.[62]

About Carter's determination to complete the complex and highly sensitive Panama Canal Treaty negotiations, in the works for thirteen years, there was never any doubt. It might be, indeed it proved to be, a politically thankless effort, but the new chief executive was determined to press ahead. Shortly after taking office, he added Sol M. Linowitz, an experienced Latin American hand, to the negotiating team headed by Ambassador Ellsworth Bunker, and the president's efforts reached a striking climax on 7 September 1977, when representatives of twenty-six Western Hemisphere countries witnessed the signing of the resultant treaties by Carter and Omar Torrijos, the Panamanian leader.[63]

As is not infrequently the case with highly controversial international agreements, approval by the United States Senate was far from automatic. On 14 October 1977, Carter and Torrijos agreed that the new agreements gave the United States the right to defend the canal, but that that right should not be used to justify intervention in Panama's internal affairs.[64] Opponents of the treaties, many and powerfully vocal, including former Governor Ronald Reagan of California, were unpersuaded.[65] "There is no Panama Canal! There is an American Canal at Panama. Don't let President Carter give it away!" So ran one of their many advertisements. In the end, by 18 April 1978, the Senate completed action on the two treaties by the narrowest of margins. The president had prevailed, but it added little to his political stature at home or his influence abroad. In the elections of 1978 and 1980, eighteen of the senators who voted for the treaties were defeated.

As noted above, Carter had long wanted to make a significant contribution to peacemaking in the Middle East, and by late 1977 he would benefit by President

Anwar Sadat's unexpected decision to visit Israel, the first step toward the unprecedented peace agreement signed at the White House in late March 1979. Sadat's bold action was all the more surprising because, since succeeding Colonel Gamal Abdel Nasser in 1970, he had largely followed his predecessor's policy of inflexible hostility toward the Jewish state. Now the Egyptian leader decided it was time to undertake a new initiative toward peace.

Sadat's trip to Israel on 19–21 November 1977 produced an international sensation. But both that journey and Prime Minister Menachem Begin's return visit, on 25–26 December, to Ismailia proved, initially at least, largely atmospheric. Nevertheless, Carter felt encouraged. Personally, like most Americans, he was anxious to see an early end to the decades of war and threats of war that had convulsed the region at least since the establishment of the state of Israel in 1948, and he followed subsequent developments closely, thanks to the reports of his able ambassadors in Egypt and Israel, Hermann F. Eilts and Samuel W. Lewis.

Carter's first trip to the Middle East proved largely unproductive. Looking back, probably the most illuminating, or embarrassing, moment of his journey came during his visit to Iran at the end of December 1977. Toasting the Shah and his wife at a New Year's Eve banquet in Teheran, the president remarked: "[After] the delightful visit that we received from the Shah and Empress Farah just a month ago . . . I asked my wife, 'With whom would you like to spend New Year's Eve?' And she said, 'Above all other, I think, with the Shah and Empress Farah.' So we arranged the trip accordingly and came to be with you. . . . I think it is a good harbinger of things to come—that we could close out this year and begin a new year with those in whom we have such great confidence and with whom we share such great responsibilities for the present and for the future." Iran, "because of the great leadership of the Shah," Carter went on, "is an island of stability in one of the more troubled areas of the world. This is a great tribute to you, Your Majesty, and to your leadership and to the respect and the admiration and love which your people give to you."[66] It was not a tribute Carter chose to recall in his White House memoirs.

By the summer of 1978, however, it was painfully apparent that the new peace process had reached a dead end. At this point, the president, unwilling to accept this negative result, invited Begin and Sadat to meet with him at Camp David, and on 4 September 1978 the two men, accompanied by their top diplomatic and military advisers, arrived for what was to become one of the most remarkable exercises in recent summit diplomacy. The Camp David accords, signed at the White House on 17 September 1978, have been rightly praised as the outstanding diplomatic achievement of the Carter administration. But behind the scenes, the bargaining had been long and hard, and more than once the negotiations appeared on the verge of breaking down.[67]

Whatever his personal feelings about the Israeli and Egyptian leaders, the president recognized that the Begin-Sadat agreement was only the beginning of what was bound to be a long and complex peace process that would eventually have to involve all of Israel's neighbor states. To Carter's understandable regret, the next stage of that peace process was nowhere in sight. Indeed, for both ideological and strategic reasons, neither Israel nor Egypt was prepared to take its peace efforts much further for the moment. In the meantime, although he may not have immediately recognized it, the president soon found himself confronted with a far more explosive development in the region, the nascent Islamic fundamentalist revolution in Iran, which would set the stage for the most disastrous and, as it proved, the final year of his administration.

At this point, a few words may be added about the increasingly strained relations that had been developing between the White House and William H. Sullivan, the American ambassador to Iran, difficulties that doubtless further impaired President Carter's ability to deal effectively with the deteriorating situation in that country. In his acerbic memoir, *Mission to Iran,* published in 1981, Sullivan, most recently ambassador to the Philippines, recalled his surprise at being appointed to a post in a highly sensitive part of the world with which he was not familiar. He went on to mention how, after appointing him, Carter had initially declined to meet with him, on the grounds—Sullivan said State Department officials informed him—that the president "had established a very limited quota of ambassadorial appointments with whom he would meet and that it had already been filled for that particular time." Sullivan recounted also how his mission had ended in April 1979, after he received "a most unpleasant and abrasive cable from Washington, which, in my judgement, contained an unacceptable aspersion upon my loyalty . . . [an] insulting message [that] had originated at the White House."[68]

In his memoirs, *Keeping Faith,* the former president told a very different story. He wrote:

> By early November [1978] Ambassador Sullivan [initially a strong supporter of the Shah] had become convinced that opposition leaders would have to be given a much stronger voice in Iran's affairs than the Shah was willing to consider. I could not disagree with this, but my basic choice was whether to give the Shah our complete backing in his crisis or to predicate support, as Sullivan increasingly seemed to prefer, on the Shah's acquiescence to suggestions from the American Embassy. [By early 1979, Sullivan] was recommending that we . . . insist on [the Shah's] immediate eventual departure, and try to form some kind of friendship or alliance with Khomeini.

Because, Carter continued, the ambassador "seemed unable to provide us with adequate reports from the military, which was a crucial source of information, [Defense] Secretary Brown and I concluded that we needed a strong and competent American representative in Teheran to keep me informed about the military's needs," and accordingly sent General Robert Huyser, deputy commander of United States Forces in Europe, "to carry out this assignment in Iran."[69]

Relations between the president and the ambassador soon went from bad to worse. According to Carter,

> Sullivan apparently lost control of himself, and on January 10 sent Vance a cable bordering on insolence, condemning our asking the French President to contact Khomeini instead of doing it ourselves. He used such phrases as "gross and perhaps irretrievable mistake," "plea for sanity," and "incomprehensible." He seemed unable to present an objective analysis of the complicated situation in Iran. I was well aware that he had been carrying out some of my directives halfheartedly, if at all. Now, since he had changed his mind in recent weeks about supporting the Shah, his activities and statements cost him much of the confidence he had previously enjoyed from the Shah and his associates—and from me. I told the Secretary of State to get Sullivan out of Iran, but Cy insisted that it would be a mistake to put a new man in the country in the midst of the succession of crises we probably faced. I reluctantly agreed, but from then on I relied primarily on General Huyser, who remained cool and competent.[70]

Ambassador Sullivan's eventual departure from Iran did not, however, reduce Carter's dilemma of whether to continue to support the Shah, and, if so, how far and by what means. Indeed, the president's problems with the Iranian revolution were soon to take a serious turn for the worse, and by late 1979 began to threaten the future of the Carter administration itself.

IV

As it happened, for Carter the year 1979 appeared to open on a distinctly positive note. On New Year's Day, the United States formally established diplomatic relations with Communist China, and on 29 January Deputy Premier Deng Xiaoping arrived for what was generally considered to be a highly successful six-day visit, which began with elaborate official and social formalities in Washington, and subsequently took him to Houston and Seattle. In his memoirs, Secretary Vance also waxed enthusiastic about Deng's coming, the first such visit by a senior Chinese Communist official since 1949. It was "an extravaganza and understandably so. It symbolized the attainment of one of our fundamental goals." It was also a visit not bereft of humor. As Brzezinski remembered, "[At] one stage, when Carter registered his concern for human rights, requesting Deng to be flexible on emigration, Deng leaned forward toward Carter and said, 'Fine. We'll let them go. Are you prepared to accept ten million?'"

As a further expression of satisfaction with the new relationship with mainland China, on 1 March the United States formally opened its new embassy in

Beijing, with Leonard F. Woodcock, since July 1977 chief of the United States liaison office, as the first American ambassador to Communist China. Vance was likewise delighted with Woodcock's performance. "Although he had no previous international experience," he wrote later, "Woodcock drew on his extensive experience as the [former] president of the United Automobile Workers of America and proved an instinctive and brilliant diplomat."

So as to prepare the way for the move, on 15 December 1978 Carter had announced that, as the United States was "normalizing" relations with Communist China, it was withdrawing diplomatic recognition from Taiwan and terminating the American-Taiwan mutual defence treaty, effective on 1 January 1980,[71] and he announced organization of a private "American Institute in Taiwan" to "maintain," as he explained later, "our existing commercial, cultural, and trade relations . . . through non-governmental means [and to] carry out many of the routine functions of an embassy." Unsurprisingly, the president's announcement aroused a storm of protest. "We gave all and got nothing," said George Bush, adding, "we are simply diminishing U.S. credibility around the world." Ohio Democratic Senator John H. Glenn, chairman of the Far East Subcommittee of the Senate Foreign Relations Committee said, "[The Communist Chinese] don't have the military capability of taking Taiwan right now, but it's ten years from now that I'm concerned about."[72]

In the realm of Atlantic diplomacy, the New Year had begun on a distinctly mixed note. On 5–6 January Carter met with the leaders of Britain, France, and West Germany at the Hamak, a resort on the southern coast of the French island of Guadeloupe. Carter and Vance made it clear that "we intended to pursue our interests with [Communist] China in a positive way, and not as an anti-Soviet gambit," which didn't, however, the secretary recalled in 1983, keep the Soviets from fearing "a tacit NATO-PRC encirclement." There was more inconclusive talk about how to counter Soviet deployment of their new SS-20 missiles. It was the first time the West Germans had participated in such meetings, and, as Helmut Schmidt recalled later, his "audience"—including British Prime Minister James Callaghan and French President Valéry Giscard d'Estaing—"realized . . . that the German chancellor was emphasizing matters that were clearly at odds with what was favored by the new American president."[73]

Here, in short, were the roots of serious differences to come. The Nixon-Kissinger policy of détente had reinforced existing anti-armament sentiment in Europe. Now Helmut Schmidt was calling for new weapons to match the ominous Soviet arms build-up but did not want his country alone to station the new American intermediate-range missiles.[74] Carter, who had come to office sharing his predecessors' enthusiasm for arms control, was perplexed. "The European leaders," he wrote later, "would let the United States design, develop, and produce the new weapons, but none of them was willing to agree in advance to deploy them." Renewed Soviet aggression would largely end such differences by the close of the year.

As noted above, from his first days in office one of Carter's top priorities had been in the Middle East, and there too the president's fortunes suddenly took a turn for the better, for the Camp David process, which had seemed hopelessly deadlocked for months, suddenly took on new life. Following Carter's shuttling between Cairo and Jerusalem for nearly a week, on 26 March 1979 President Sadat and Prime Minister Begin came to Washington finally to sign the agreement envisaged at Camp David or something close to it. The text, wrote Philip M. Klutznick, who witnessed its laborious evolution over many months from his vantage point as president of the World Jewish Congress, "consisted of a thick pile of documents, and three indexes dealing with the minutiae of security arrangements, maps, and the resumption of diplomatic relations. Very real blood, sweat, and tears shed over the years lay behind these formal words and graphs. Yet I have often wondered how many people in the wide world except for the negotiators—and perhaps some scattered Ph.D. candidates—read every line in the treaty and its annexes."[75]

Those were substantial achievements, the full importance of which would become clear only with time. But for the rest, 1979 would soon prove to be an *annus terribilis*, one of the darkest years in postwar American international history. The growing failure of Carter's foreign policy could no longer be disguised.

If Washington, like the rest of the Western world, had been taken aback by the dramatic Iranian upheaval that had begun in the last months of 1978, the Carter administration appeared dangerously divided on how to respond to the rapidly disintegrating situation there. On 16 January 1979, the Shah left Iran for exile in Egypt. While Brzezinski hoped to encourage the increasingly embattled government forces, and did so by establishing a back channel that Ambassador Sullivan understandably found offensive,[76] the Carter administration apparently believed that a policy of conciliation and compromise might yet lead to acceptable relations with the Shah's successors. Returning from Teheran on 5 February, General Huyser told the president that "[Ambassador] Sullivan believed that if Khomeini established an Islamic republic, the drift would be eventually toward democracy." On 12 February 1979, Washington formally recognized the new regime headed by Khomeini,[77] though the latter and his associates had long made little secret of their bitterly anti-foreign, especially anti-American, outlook. As if to demonstrate that American diplomatic recognition counted for little or nothing at this point, two days later government-inspired mobs seized the United States embassy, and retreated only after Ambassador Sullivan personally appealed to the Khomeini leadership for help.[78]

Meanwhile, the uneasily balanced political situation in Afghanistan was slowly coming apart. In late April 1978, Muhammed Daoud, since 1973 president of Afghanistan, was overthrown in a coup by army officers, who proclaimed the Democratic Republic of Afghanistan, the first country in South Asia to be ruled by communists.[79] Under Secretary of State David D. Newsom was sent to Kabul to investigate the situation. He returned, Vance recalled in his memoirs, "with a pessimistic assessment of the new regime's . . . intentions. We decided to continue several [aid] programs and to watch the situation closely." In February 1979, the recently appointed American ambassador to Afghanistan, Adolph Dubs, was kidnapped and killed. Moscow rejected American protests, and Soviet "military advisors" continued to pour into Afghanistan, but the new Communist regime was unable to suppress the Muslim resistance mounting around the country. "We refused to replace Dubs or to authorize new aid," wrote Vance. Much worse was to come later in the year.

Hoping, mistakenly as it proved, that the Iranian situation had stabilized for the time being, the Carter administration pressed ahead with final plans and preparations for another summit with Leonid Brezhnev, whom the president had never met, to be held in Vienna in mid-June. The climax of the Vienna summit was to be the signing of the SALT II treaty, seven years in the making. In addition, Carter doubtless hoped that a personal meeting with the Soviet leader would serve to improve bilateral relations, including some highly sensitive issues like trade and Jewish emigration that continued seriously to complicate relations between Washington and Moscow. "What we needed at the summit first of all," Carter wrote later, "was mutual understanding. I wanted the Soviets to know that the United States was driven by a desire for peace and an end to violence and aggression around the world."[80]

The meetings lasted for four days. The outward appearance of harmony was belied by contention behind the scenes. Carter told Brezhnev "that the Soviet Union had increased its military budget substantially each year for the last fifteen years, and until recently the United States had not matched this effort." Brezhnev said that "China threatened to encroach on the territory of its neighbors, and wanted to precipitate a world war during which it would sit on the sidelines." Carter responded that "when violence occurred in almost any place on earth, the Soviets or their proxies were most likely to be at the center of it. This kind of interventionism could precipitate a serious confrontation in the future if our own national interests should become involved." The president told Brezhnev that the "subject of human rights is very important to us in shaping our attitude toward your country. . . . you need to release [Anatoly] Shcharansky and other dissidents." Brezhnev replied coldly that "Shcharansky had been tried and convicted in a Soviet court of law and that as the leader of the nation, [he] was bound to support the laws of his country." On 18 June Carter and Brezhnev signed the SALT II treaty. "After we finished," he wrote in his memoirs, "I shook hands with President Brezhnev, and to my surprise, we found ourselves embracing each other warmly in the Soviet fashion."[81]

As it turned out, the Vienna summit did not add up to a political success for the president at home. The arms control consensus was rapidly dissolving. A number of liberal senators, including Mark Hatfield of Oregon, George McGovern of South Dakota, William Proxmire of Wisconsin, and Adlai E. Stevenson, Jr., of Illinois, opposed the new treaty on the ground that it did not go far enough and allowed the development of new weapons. Democratic Senator Henry M. Jackson of Washington lost no time denouncing SALT II treaty as "a new Munich," and no assurances from the White House and State Department about future arms control negotiations, perhaps more advantageous to the United States, succeeded in reducing Jackson's determined opposition and that of a growing number of like-minded senators. Senators John Glenn of Ohio and Sam Nunn of Georgia, both widely respected for their military expertise, doubted Soviet intentions and questioned the adequacy of verification procedures agreed to. Despite the Democrats' sizable majority in both houses, from his first days in office, Carter never had an effective working majority in Congress. Now that lack threatened to undermine an agreement he deemed vital to the security of the United States and the peace of the world.

While big storms were in the offing from the Middle East to Central America, things were not going well for Carter on the international economic front. OPEC doubled the oil price. In the United States, inflation was rising at an alarming rate as energy prices skyrocketed and long lines were forming at filling stations around the country. At the annual economic summit at Tokyo, the third of his administration, the president plainly had a bad time of it. As he recorded in his personal diary on 28 June 1979: "This is the first day of the economic summit, and one of the worst days of my diplomatic life. . . . we . . . had a luncheon that was very bitter and unpleasant. [West German Chancellor] Schmidt got personally abusive toward me. . . . for instance, he alleged that American interference in the Middle East trying to work for a peace treaty was what had caused the problems with oil all over the world." The next day Carter remarked favorably on a new member of the G-7 circle: "Margaret Thatcher is a tough lady, highly opinionated, strong-willed, cannot admit that she doesn't know something. However, I think she will be a good prime minister for Great Britain."[82]

But far more ominous foreign problems were soon to make their appearance. Serious political trouble had long been brewing in Nicaragua. For months and years, the United States had protested, both publicly and privately, what it considered flagrant human rights violations by the government of President Anastasio Somoza. In mid-January 1979, Somoza—whose family, reportedly worth $500 million, had controlled the country for forty-five years, and whose father and brother had served as president before him—rejected a proposal by the Organization of American States for an independently supervised plebescite on the presidency, with Somoza agreeing to resign if he was defeated. As further indication of its mounting displeasure, in early February 1979 the Carter administration sharply reduced the staff at the American embassy in Managua, terminated all military assistance, and withdrew all Peace Corps volunteers, meanwhile treating the Nicaraguan ambassador to the United States—the dean of the diplomatic corps on account of his longevity of service—with contemptuous disdain. Sensing that his ruling days were numbered, and with civil war raging throughout much of his country, Somoza resigned on 17 July and fled to the United States. Three days later, a Sandinista-controlled junta took power in Managua, promising to establish what it called a pluralist democracy.[83]

Of all international developments of the Carter years, the Nicaraguan turn of events was to prove the most embarrassing to the president and the secretary of state, so much so indeed that in both their memoirs, published in 1982 and 1983 respectively, the subject is virtually ignored, as it is in Brzezinski's memoirs that appeared in 1983. Carter's problem, of course, was not so much Somoza's resignation, but what followed it, which was little more than a thinly disguised Marxist takeover, inspired and supported, if not specifically directed, by Castroite forces long readied for the occasion. "The two revolutions in Iran and Nicaragua," wrote Robert A. Pastor, who served as head of Latin American and Caribbean affairs on the National Security Council from 1977 to 1981, "contained so many parallels that even the characters sometimes seemed interchangeable."

In Nicaragua, as in Iran, the Carter administration hoped that conciliation and compromise would provide the foundation for improved relations with a new revolutionary regime, and, as in Iran, the president and his administration were soon to be deeply disappointed. Lawrence A. Pezzullo, of Maryland, an imperious Foreign Service officer Carter had named ambassador in May 1979, apparently had little comprehension of the Sandinistas and their Marxist aims.[84] To judge by the available evidence, neither did the president's top Latin American experts and advisers.

As if such problems were insufficient to send the president's political stock into deep decline, in late summer he found himself unable to escape a long-simmering trouble spot at the State Department, Andrew Young, his ambassador to the United Nations. As Professor Betty Glad has summed up the president's dilemma:

> Young had come to epitomize Carter's inability to control his own people. Over the thirty-one months Young served as ambassador to the United Nations, he increasingly embarrassed the Administration by his comments on American "political prisoners," British and Swedish "racism" and Cuba's role as a stabilizing force in Africa. But Young was the symbol of black support for Carter, and to fire Young would have been to risk losing that support completely. But finally Young went too far. On August 14 [1979] Secretary of State Vance reprimanded him for having held an unauthorized meeting with the PLO and for giving the State Department inaccurate reports of the meeting. The next day Young resigned, saying that he could not stay out of controversies that would be politically embarrassing to the President. Carter accepted the resignation "reluctantly" and two weeks later chose another black career diplomat and Young's deputy at the United Nations, Donald F. McHenry, to succeed him.[85]

Meanwhile the Iranian situation had gone from bad to ominously worse. On 22 October 1979, the Shah had arrived for urgent medical treatment in New

York.[86] His condition was diagnosed as a malignant lymphoma, compounded by a possible internal blockage, which produced severe jaundice, and a first operation was performed on him two days later at Sloan-Kettering Hospital. The Iranian government announced that he was "terminally ill," a move, Vance wrote, "that we interpreted as an effort to ease the reaction in Iran." By 30 October, however, the Khomeini regime had changed its tune and was demanding the Shah's extradition for trial. Khomeini, the secretary of state believed, "evidently decided to align himself with the mob rather than the government." On 3 November, the American embassy compound was stormed by about three thousand militants demanding the return of the Shah and his wealth. Almost sixty embassy staff members were captured, and the Khomeini regime made no move to free them. "It's almost impossible to deal with a crazy man," the president wrote in his diary on 6 November. So, he recalled later, began "the most difficult period of my life."[87]

In Europe, too, the president was facing new dangers he had long hoped to ignore or avoid. The Vienna summit and the signing of SALT II notwithstanding, Soviet armaments were accelerating at an ever more disturbing rate. As early as late October 1977, in a largely unnoticed address to the International Institute for Strategic Studies in London, West German Chancellor Schmidt had voiced his growing concern about the appearance of powerful new Soviet weapons, including the SS-20, a mobile, intermediate range rocket capable of hitting every part of Europe as well as much of the Middle East.[88] While the Brezhnev regime continued to maintain its protestations of peaceful intentions—protestations that sound disturbingly hollow following the opening of long top-secret Soviet and East German military archives in 1992–1993[89]—Carter found it impossible not to respond with new weapons decisions of his own.

Accordingly, the president announced his plans in an address to the Business Council at the White House on the afternoon of 12 December. With the uniformed chiefs of staff looking on, he began with the obligatory liberal critique of Vietnam: "We've learned the mistake of military intervention in the internal affairs of another country when our own American security was not directly involved. But we must understand that not every instance of the firm application of the power of the United States is a potential Vietnam." Then Carter went on to describe his plans for a 4.5 percent annual increase in defense spending, over the yearly inflation rate, for the next five years, an increase designed, he said, to balance a twenty-year build-up by the Soviet Union. The same day, the North Atlantic Treaty Organization, meeting at Brussels, finally agreed to deploy American medium-range nuclear missiles in Western Europe, a decision opposed by the Netherlands and only partly approved by Belgium, with installations of the thousand-mile range cruise missiles to begin by late 1983.[90]

While all this was going on abroad, in mid-December the new British Prime Minister, Margaret Thatcher, arrived in Washington for her first official visit to the United States. Her domestic and international views were far closer to those of Ronald Reagan, just beginning a second campaign for the White House, and she lost no time strongly defending the president's recent military-political turnabout. She likewise left no doubt where she stood on the Iranian hostage situation. If the president asked for economic sanctions, she declared unhesitatingly after a cordial two-hour meeting with Carter, "you would expect nothing less and you would get nothing less than our full support."[91]

By this time, such words probably meant little or nothing in the Kremlin. For having taken the measure of the Carter administration, or so it thought, the Brezhnev regime was about to embark on the most audacious Soviet move since Nikita Khrushchev's placement of nuclear weapons in Cuba seventeen years earlier. For months, Soviet and East German diplomats on the scene had made no secret of Moscow's determination to achieve effective control of Afghanistan. Still, as earlier in Iran, Washington was clearly caught by surprise. Climaxing a period of growing communist-inspired terror. On the night of 25 December 1979, Soviet ground and air forces invaded Afghanistan and captured its capital Kabul.[92] President Hafizullah Amin was overthrown and executed at Moscow's instigation. Blithely dismissing strong American protests, the Soviet government brazenly maintained that its troops had been invited into the country by the Afghan authorities, leading the president to comment tartly, "The leaders who requested the Soviet presence were assassinated."

The invasion revealed an unexpected fissure at the top of the Carter administration. In September the president had told Vance and Brzezinski that greater publicity should be given to growing Soviet involvement in southwestern Asia, but as the latter noted, as late as mid-September, Under Secretary of State David Newsom opposed this "on the grounds that it might be seen by the Soviets as meddling in Afghanistani affairs."[93] Secretary Vance tended to find extenuating reasons for Moscow's aggression, holding that

> the downward spiral in U. S.-Soviet relations had released the brakes on Soviet international behavior. If, as is likely, Moscow had decided by late December that the SALT treaty was in deep trouble, that access to American trade and technology was drying up, and that the dangers of American-Chinese-Western European encirclement were growing, it probably had concluded that there was little reason to show restraint in dealing with a dangerous problem on its border. I am not suggesting that the Soviets would not have acted had relations with us been better. But it is possible that had there been more to lose in its relationship with the United States, [it] would have been more cautious.

Among America's principal allies, Vance recalled in his memoirs, he "encountered serious concern that the administration's reaction to Afghanistan was exaggerated and threatened to wreck the framework of East-West relations."[94] At first, Carter's outrage was distinctly muted too, and the *Washington Post* noted "the growing unease expressed about the government's seemingly passive, long-suffering response" to events in Afghanistan, adding that the president had "not yet found the right voice in which to speak to the American people about the perils they face in the world."[95] Carter's disillusionment, however, soon found public expression. In a televised interview on 31 December, he told Frank Reynolds of ABC News:

> My opinion of the Russians has changed most drastically in the last week. . . . It's only dawning upon the world, the magnitude of the action the Soviets undertook in invading Afghanistan. It's even more profoundly important than their going into Hungary and Czechoslovakia, because they went in, overthrew an existing government, installed a puppet, put massive forces in, and created a direct confrontation between an atheistic government on the one hand and a deeply religious people on the other who have historically fought for their own independence and freedom.[96]

The Soviet invasion, Carter said, was "the greatest threat to world peace since the second world war." "History teaches, perhaps, very few clear lessons," he declared in a televised address to the nation on 4 January 1980. "But surely one such lesson learned by the world at great cost is that aggression, unopposed, becomes a contagious disease," an unmistakable allusion to President Franklin Roosevelt's famous Quarantine Address in Chicago in October 1937.[97]

On 23 January, the president told Congress: "An attempt by any outside force to gain control of the Persian Gulf region will be regarded as an assault on the vital interests of the United States of America. And such an assault will be repelled by any means necessary, including military force."[98] In the absence of pertinent Soviet documents, it is impossible to assess the impact of this declaration. To be sure, for the time being, the United States lacked the forces necessary to contain the Soviet Union in the Middle East. But perhaps the last thing that the Kremlin wanted was another showdown with Washington like the Berlin blockade of 1948–1949 or the Cuban missile crisis of 1962. But détente seemed finally dead, and now, thanks in part to covert American assistance to the anti-Soviet resistance forces in Afghanistan, Moscow was to learn—as Stalin, Khrushchev, and Brezhnev never had—that it was one thing to invade a neighboring country and another to occupy and control it effectively.

As he surveyed the wreckage of his well-intentioned foreign policy at the close of 1979, it was difficult for President Carter to escape the painful conclusion that he had trusted the Kremlin far too much, far too long, and that his trust had been badly abused.[99] Brzezinski, long suspicious of Soviet intentions, was doubtless unsurprised by the latest turn of events. To Carter he wrote candidly that "before you [can be] a President Wilson you have to be for a few years a President Truman," and in his journal he added: "Had we been tougher sooner . . . maybe the Soviets would not have engaged in this act of miscalculation. As it is, American-Soviet relations will have been set back for a long time to come."[100] As for Cyrus Vance, he seemed ready to give Moscow yet another chance. "One of the lessons to be learned from Afghanistan," he wrote in 1983, "is the importance of giving a clear forewarning of what we viewed as unacceptable behavior. . . . we must recognize that we are but one member of the alliance . . . [and we must] adjust our position in order to achieve a unified alliance position."[101]

These fundamental disagreements at the top of the Carter administration doubtless mirrored similar differences of opinion around the country. To many in Washington and throughout America, the global balance of power and ideas was shifting steadily against the United States, and there was nothing that could be done to stop the tide. Some accepted the apparent trend with an air of resignation, fatalistically hoping that a stable new world order would somehow soon begin to emerge. Still others believed that there was nothing inevitable about the triumph of the age of anti-democratic revolution. Most people were probably agreed on one point. As the 1980s dawned, the only certainty was uncertainty itself, and where America and the world might be headed no one could say for sure.

Notes

1. See the statements of Assistant Secretary of State Arthur H. Hartman and Professor Hans J. Morgenthau in *Détente: Hearings Before the House Subcommittee on Europe*, 93d Congress, 2d sess. (Washington, D.C., 1974), 52, 139.

2. For the West German position, see Helmut Schmidt, *Men and Powers: A Political Retrospective* (New York, 1989), 173.

3. *Public Papers of the President, Gerald R. Ford, 1975*, 2: no. 430 (Washington, D.C., 1977) (henceforth cited as *Public Papers*).

4. Robert T. Hartmann, *Palace Politics: An Inside Account of the Ford Years* (New York, 1980), 342.

5. *Public Papers, Ford, 1975*, 2: no. 439.

6. Hartmann, *Palace Politics*, 342.

7. George F. Kennan, "The United States and the Soviet Union," in *Two Hundred Years of American Foreign Policy*, ed. William P. Bundy (New York, 1977), 176.

8. See Georgi A. Arbatov and Willem Oltmans, *The Soviet Viewpoint* (New York, 1983), 76. "From Moscow's perspective," John Lewis Gaddis has written, "the path from Helsinki was . . . all downhill." *The United States and the End of the Cold War* (New York, 1992), 25 f.

9. *Public Papers, Ford, 1975*, 2: no. 459.

10. George Bush with Vic Gold, *Looking Forward: An Autobiography* (New York, 1987), 129–30.

11. Richard Reeves, *A Ford, Not a Lincoln* (New York, 1975), 7.

12. *Détente: Hearings Before the Committee on Foreign Relations*, United States Senate, 93d Congress, 2d sess. (Washington, D.C., 1974), 15, 20, 21 Aug.; 10, 12, 18, 19, 24, 25 Sept; 1, 8 Oct. 1974.

13. See, for instance, Ernest R. May, ed., *Knowing One's Enemies: Intelligence Assessments Before the Two World Wars* (Princeton, 1984).

14. See the testimony of former Secretary of State Dean Rusk before the Senate Foreign Relations Committee on 18 Sept. 1974 in *Détente: Hearings, U.S. Senate*, 220.

15. See Gerald R. Ford, *A Time to Heal* (New York, 1979), 219.

16. See Paul Nitze, *From Hiroshima to Glasnost: At the Center of Decision* (New York, 1989), 343–44; and Schmidt, *Men and Powers*, 39.

17. Any restraint that the Soviets had been exercising on North Vietnam, writes Walter Isaacson, "had dissipated after the decline of détente." *Kissinger: A Biography* (New York, 1992), 636. In fact, no credible evidence of such "restraining influence" has turned up twenty years later.

18. *Public Papers, Ford, 1975*, vol. 1, no. 208.

19. For the possible application of the Stimson doctrine to Vietnam, see Francis L. Loewenheim, "Viet leaders should live up to bargain," *Houston Post*, 20 Apr. 1988. For a contemporary proposal to publish all Vietnam records immediately, which was ignored by the State Department, see Loewenheim, "Documenting the Vietnam Story," *New York Times*, 12 Aug. 1975.

20. John J. Casserly, *The Ford White House: The Diary of a Speech-Writer* (Boulder, Colo., 1977), 126.

21. According to Louis M. Thompson, Jr., a member of Ford's staff, the decision may have originated as early as April 1975. See Mark J. Rozell, *The Press and the Ford Presidency* (Ann Arbor, 1992), 204, n. 114.

22. For a defense of Soviet and Cuban policy, see Raymond Garthoff, *Détente and Confrontation: American-Soviet Relations from Nixon to Reagan* (Washington, D.C., 1985), chap. 15.

23. *Public Papers, Ford, 1975*, 2: no. 738.

24. *Department of State Bulletin* 74, no. 1910, p. 125.

25. William G. Hyland, *Mortal Rivals: Superpower Relations from Nixon to Reagan* (New York, 1987), 145.

26. Isaacson, *Kissinger*, 687 ff.

27. *New York Times*, 2 Dec. 1975.

28. Ford, *A Time to Heal*, 36.

29. Quoted in Rozell, *The Press and the Ford Presidency*, 121.

30. For a brief history of economic summitry, see Francis L. Loewenheim, "A History of Economic Summitry from Rambouillet to Rice," *Sallyport*, Rice University, October 1990, on the occasion of the Houston summit. At Puerto Rico, where Canada had been represented for the first time, Roy Jenkins wrote later that there had been "some movement away from the genuine informality of a country house gathering at Rambouillet towards the international circus trappings of more recent Western Economic Summits." *European Diary, 1977–1981* (London, 1981), 20.

31. Schmidt, *Men and Powers*, 173 f. At Helsinki, wrote former Prime Minister James Callaghan, "Gerry Ford had seemed rather unenthusiastic." *Time and Chance* (London, 1987), 478 ff. See also Denis Healey, *The Time of My Life* (London, 1989), 450 ff.

32. *Public Papers, Ford, 1975*, 2: no. 680.

33. *Public Papers, Ford, 1976–1977*, 2: no. 620 (Washington, D.C., 1979).

34. *New York Times*, 30 June 1976.

35. Burton I. Kaufman, *The Presidency of James Earl Carter* (Lawrence, Kansas, 1993), 10 ff.

36. Political opposition to Ford's foreign policy was especially widespread in Texas. "The issue," declared the influential *Dallas Morning News* on 22 Feb. 1976, "is whether we can pursue a policy that throws up no visible obstacles to Soviet designs, yet never ever insists on a Soviet quid for an American quo."

37. *Department of State Bulletin* 72, no. 1872 (12 May 1975): 609.

38. Campaign Files, Gerald R. Ford Library.

39. *Public Papers, Ford, 1976–1977,* 1: no. 185.

40. *Public Papers, Ford, 1975,* 1: no. 179.

41. Scowcroft Papers, Gerald R. Ford Presidential Library.

42. For a more detailed account of the famous Ford-Carter debate, its inner history and public and political aftermath, see Francis L. Loewenheim, "Was Ford's Gaffe Actually a Mistake?" *Houston Post,* 5 Oct. 1986.

43. Quoted in Rozell, *The Press and the Ford Presidency,* 147.

44. For Carter's own view of his foreign policy, see not only his White House memoirs, *Keeping Faith* (New York, 1983), but also the long Carter Library interview with Robert Beckels, former deputy assistant secretary for public affairs, which is illuminating on Carter's way of doing business at home and abroad.

45. Kaufman, *Presidency,* gives a useful overview. The best detailed study is Richard C. Thornton, *The Carter Years: Toward a Global New Order* (New York, 1991). On personal traits that contributed to his foreign policy problems, see Pierre Salinger, *America Held Hostage: The Secret Negotiations* (New York, 1981), 32.

46. Vance told his own story in *Hard Choices: Critical Years in America's Foreign Policy* (New York, 1983). For a sympathetic assessment, see David S. McLellan, *Cyrus Vance* (Totowa, N.J., 1985).

47. Brzezinski's account of the Carter years is to be found in his revealing memoirs, *Power and Principle: Memoirs of the National Security Adviser, 1977–1981* (New York, 1983), and his lengthy oral history interview in the Carter Library.

48. These included Leslie H. Gelb, Richard Holbrooke, Anthony Lake, and Richard Moose. On Senator McGovern's approval of most of the Carter-Vance choices, see Robert Shogan, *Promises to Keep: Carter's First Hundred Days* (New York, 1977), 217. In March 1978, George Will complained that many of them thought the United States "as much a threat to world peace as communist powers are." Quoted in Mark Rozell, *The Press and the Carter Presidency* (Ann Arbor, 1992), 94.

49. Kaufman, *Presidency,* 41. On Carter's confidence in Warnke, see his statement in *Department of State Bulletin* 76, no. 1988 (28 Feb. 1977): 157.

50. Schmidt, *Men and Powers,* 171.

51. Mark J. Rozell, *The Press and the Carter Presidency* (Boulder, 1989), 51.

52. *Public Papers, Jimmy Carter, 1977* (Washington, D.C., 1977), 1:10.

53. Ibid.

54. Carter, *Keeping Faith,* 146; Brzezinski, *Power and Principle,* 155–56.

55. Vance, *Hard Choices,* 57–58.

56. *Public Papers, Carter, 1977* (Washington, D.C., 1978), 2:1717. "It's like being in the dark," he told the cabinet, "because we don't know what the Soviet response will be." Shogan, *Promises to Keep,* 186.

57. Vance, *Hard Choices,* 51–54; Carter, *Keeping Faith,* 145.

58. Hyland, *Mortal Rivals,* 213; Vance, *Hard Choices,* 54.

59. Carter later confessed to having failed to see how important the Vladivostok agreements were to Brezhnev. Haynes Johnson, *In the Absence of Power: Governing America* (New York, 1980), 183 n.

60. Brzezinski, *Power and Principle,* 7–8.

61. *Public Papers, Carter, 1977,* 1:956.

62. Name File, Carter Library.

63. *Public Papers, Carter, 1977,* 2:1544 ff. For an inside view of the negotiations, see William J. Jorden, *Panama Odyssey* (Austin, Texas, 1981).

64. *Public Papers, Carter, 1977,* 2:1793.

65. Robert Dallek, *Ronald Reagan: The Politics of Symbolism* (Cambridge, Mass., 1989), 55. Also see David Skidmore, "Foreign Policy Interest Groups and Presidential Power: Jimmy Carter and the Battle over Ratification of the Panama Canal Treaties," *Presidential Studies Quarterly* 23, no. 3 (Summer 1993): 477–97.

66. *Public Papers, Jimmy Carter, 1977* (Washington, 1978) 2: 2220–21.

67. On Camp David, in addition to the accounts by Carter, Vance, and Brzezinski, see William B. Quandt, *Camp David: Peacemaking and Politics* (Washington, D.C., 1986), and Quandt, *Peace Process: American Diplomacy and the Arab-Israeli Conflict since 1967* (Berkeley, 1993), chaps. 10–12. An NSC staff member, Quandt was heavily involved in Middle East affairs. For a different perspective, see Perlmutter, *Begin,* chap. 34, and for the latest scholarly assessment, Shirley Telhami, "Evaluating Bargaining Performance: The Case of Camp David," *Political Science Quarterly* 107 (Winter 1992–1993): 629, 653.

68. William H. Sullivan, *Mission to Iran* (New York, 1981), 12–13, 17–18.

69. Carter, *Keeping Faith,* 440, 443. See also Robert E. Huyser, *Mission to Teheran* (New York, 1986).

70. Carter, *Keeping Faith,* 446.

71. *Public Papers, Carter, 1978* (Washington, D.C., 1979), 2:2266.

72. *Washington Post,* 16 Dec. 1978.

73. Schmidt, *Men and Powers,* 73–74, 189–91.

74. See especially Jeffrey Herf, *War by Other Means: Soviet Power, West German Resistance, and the Battle of the Euromissiles* (New York, 1991).

75. Philip M. Klutznick, *Angles of Vision: A Memoir of My Lives* (Chicago, 1991), 349–50.

76. Brzezinski, *Power and Principle,* 337 ff.; Sullivan, *Mission to Iran,* 171 f.

77. "I see continued hope for very productive and peaceful cooperation with the Government of Iran," Carter told a White House news conference on 12 Feb. 1979. *Public Papers, Carter, 1979,* 1:255.

78. Sullivan, *Mission to Iran,* 252 ff.

79. Thomas T. Hammond, *Red Flag over Afghanistan: The Communist Coup, the Soviet Invasion, and the Consequences* (Boulder, Colo., 1984), chaps. 5–8; Henry S. Bradsher, *Afghanistan and the Soviet Union* (Durham, 1983), chaps. 5–8.

80. Carter, *Keeping Faith,* 240.

81. Ibid., 246 ff., 261; Brzezinski, *Power and Principle,* 241 ff.; Vance, *Hard Choices,* 138 f.

82. Carter, *Keeping Faith,* 111 ff.

83. See Paul Coe Clarke, Jr., *The United States and Somoza, 1933–1956* (Westport, Conn., 1992); and Constantine Menges, *The Twilight Struggle: The Soviet Union and the United States Today* (Washington, D.C., 1990), 242 ff.

84. Robert A. Pastor, *Condemned to Repetition: The United States and Nicaragua* (Princeton, 1987), 117. For Pezzullo's elaborate defense, see his *At the Fall of Somoza* (Pittsburgh, 1994), and also Anthony Lake, *Somoza Falling* (Boston, 1989).

85. Betty Glad, *Jimmy Carter: In Search of the Great White House* (New York, 1980), 488 f.

86. Unknown at the time, the president was the last to agree to the Shah's admission to the United States. See Salinger, *America Held Hostage,* 15; Hamilton Jordan, *Crisis: The Last Year of the Carter Presidency* (New York, 1982), 88 ff.; Vance, *Hard Choices,* 372.

87. Vance, *Hard Choices,* 372 ff., 459 f.; Brzezinski, *Power and Principle,* 476 ff.; Carter, *Keeping Faith,* 458 f.

88. Schmidt, *Men and Powers,* 64; Thornton, *Carter Years,* 65 ff.

89. See, for instance, "Warsaw Pact Military Planning in Central Europe: Revelations from the East German Archives," *Cold War International History Project* (Woodrow Wilson International Center for Scholars, Washington, D.C.), Bulletin Issue 2 (Fall, 1992); and Marc Fisher, "A Chilling War Story: Plans Uncovered by German Military Detail East Germany's State of Readiness," *International Herald Tribune,* 17 Mar. 1993.

90. *Public Papers, Carter, 1979,* 2:2233 ff.; Carter, *Keeping Faith,* 535.

91. Quoted in Geoffrey Smith, *Reagan and Thatcher* (New York, 1991), 18.

92. Hammond, *Red Flag over Afghanistan,* chaps. 11, 13.

93. Brzezinski, *Power and Principle,* 428.

94. Vance, *Hard Choices,* 388, 393. For continued rationalizations of the Soviet invasion, see Walter LaFeber, *America, Russia and the Cold War, 1945–1992,* 7th ed. (New York, 1993), 301 ff., and Garthoff, *Détente and Confrontation,* 895 ff.

95. "Voices of the President," *Washington Post,* 30 Dec. 1979. "It was impossible not to like Jimmy Carter," former Prime Minister Margaret Thatcher wrote in her memoirs, *The Downing Street Years* (London and New York, 1993), 68–69. She added, however: "In foreign affairs, he was over-influenced by the doctrines then gaining ground in the Democratic Party that the threat from communism had been exaggerated and that US intervention in support of right wing dictators was almost as culpable. Hence he found himself surprised and embarrassed by such events as the Soviet invasion of Afghanistan and Iran's seizure of American diplomats as hostages."

96. The text of Carter's interview is inexplicably omitted from the Public Papers.

97. Quoted in Bradsher, *Afghanistan and the Soviet Union,* 189.

98. *Public Papers, Carter, 1980–1981* (Washington, D.C., 1981), 1:194 ff.

99. See the judgment of Norman A. Graebner, "The President as Commander in Chief: A Study in Power," *The Journal of Military History* 62, no. 1 (January 1993): 131.

100. Brzezinski, *Power and Principle,* 432.

101. Vance, *Hard Choices,* 393 f.

23

THE NEWS MEDIA AND DIPLOMACY

Ernest R. May

D URING THE BRIEF PERSIAN GULF WAR of 1991, the eighty-thousand-strong contingent of U.S. Marines received an enormous amount of favorable publicity. When a correspondent for the *Wall Street Journal* asked why, a Marine replied that the Marines had seen the news media "as an environmental feature of the battlefield, kind of like the rain. If it rains, you operate wet."[1]

By the end of the 1970s, diplomats all over the world "operated wet." An aide to a former American secretary of state estimated that the secretary's staff spent 80 to 90 percent of its time thinking about the news media.[2] President Anwar Sadat of Egypt hired American consultants to help him do likewise. When he and Prime Minister Menachem Begin of Israel explored possibilities for an Egyptian-Israeli détente, they signaled each other through interviews with CBS Evening News anchor Walter Cronkite. When détente proved feasible, Sadat and Begin sealed their accord by meeting with U.S. President Jimmy Carter at Camp David, Maryland, with thousands of correspondents and camera operators covering the story. The new Sandinista government of Nicaragua, Communist and anti-Western, had also retained American consultants to help in relations with the news media. Earlier, during the civil war of 1966–1970, the British Foreign Office had quietly advised the Nigerian government to hire a London media adviser.[3]

These examples not only illustrate how relations with the news media had come to preoccupy government leaders; they also illustrate the centrality of the English language news media. Sadat and Begin and the Sandinistas hired American consultants because they were most concerned with American newspapers and newsmagazines and television networks. The Nigerians needed to be concerned about London newspapers, the BBC, and ITV. The *New York Times,* the *Wall Street Journal,* the *Washington Post,* and the *Los Angeles Times* would be quoted or cited around the world. So would *The Times* of London, *The Guardian,* and the *Financial Times.* Only *Le Monde,* the *Neue Zürcher Zeitung,* and possibly, though not certainly, the *Frankfurter Allgemeine Zeitung* and Munich's *Süddeutsche Zeitung* enjoyed comparable status.

For most newspapers around the globe, news from foreign parts came via wire services, and the dominant wire services were the American Associated

Press and United Press International and Britain's Reuters Agency. Though many newsmagazines flourished within nations, only America's *Time* and *Newsweek* and Britain's *Economist* had truly international circulation and would be cited without an identifier in almost any city on the globe. Except for what issued from Radio Moscow and its affiliates, the heaviest traffic on international radio waves came from the BBC's World Service and the Voice of America. At least until the late 1970s, the BBC and the great American networks produced much of what appeared on television. There was force in the title of Jeremy Tunstall's 1977 book, *The Media Are American*, though a more accurate title might have been, "The Media Are Anglo-American."[4] Much of this essay necessarily concerns American and British news media. Equally necessarily, much of it also focuses on the American and British governments, for internal and external politics are nowhere harder to disentangle than where the news media and public opinion are central concerns.

I

The news media were, of course, factors in international relations long before the twentieth century. In his widely-read treatise *Diplomacy,* Sir Harold Nicolson comments, "The use of the printing press as an ally to diplomacy is as old as Swift and the Treaty of Utrecht." In fact, it went back at least to Louis XIV. The historian Sidney B. Fay's list of major causes of the First World War included "the poisoning of public opinion by the newspaper press."[5] Only after World War I, however, did concern with the news media become part of the routine of framing foreign policy and conducting diplomacy.

In 1908, in *The Process of Government,* Arthur Bentley exhorted analysts of international relations and politics to pay more attention to the press.[6] (He did not have to use the awful half Saxon-half Latin term, *news media.* That became necessary only with radio.)[7] The most thoughtful response to Bentley came from Walter Lippmann. His 1922 book, *Public Opinion,* had the premise that public opinion was largely "organized . . . by the press."[8] Much subsequent writing built on Lippmann's. And there was a lot of it: *International News and the Press,* a bibliography published in 1940, listed more than forty-five hundred books and articles.[9] Subsequently, analysis of public opinion, primarily to gauge markets or to forecast elections, became an industry. On the specific relationship between the news media and international affairs, a landmark work was Bernard C. Cohen's *The Press and Foreign Policy,* published in 1963.[10]

Lippmann, Cohen, and other analysts identified four major roles played by the news media. The first was map-making, primarily for the public. The second was agenda-setting, for both the public and the policy-maker. Third was the exertion of influence on government. Fourth was use by government, either for influence on public opinion or for diplomatic communication or sometimes for intragovernmental communication.

As map-makers, the news media accounted, in Lippmann's words, for the "pictures inside the heads of . . . human beings, the pictures of themselves, of others, of their needs, purposes, and relationship."[11] This included images of the globe. As Cohen observed, Latin America "takes up a lot of space on the cartographer's map, but it scarcely exists on the political map delineated by most newspapers in the United States."[12]

Map-making included stereotyping—of individuals and nationalities. Lippmann cited Marshal Joseph Joffre's press-created image as sage and hero and Western images of German "huns" shaped by press exaggerations of atrocities in Belgium. Map-making also involved establishing contexts. Thus, Lippmann wrote, the press during World War I had accustomed readers to thinking of a two-front war. As a result, American and Japanese lines in Siberia, 5,000 miles from any Germans, easily became a new "Eastern Front."

As agenda-setters, the news media guided judgments about the importance or unimportance of topics or problems. Lippmann instanced July 1914, when French newspapers featured the sensational trial of Madame Henriette Caillaux, charged with murdering a prominent Paris newspaper editor who had been tormenting her second husband, former Premier Joseph Caillaux. These papers gave little space to developments in the Balkans from the assassination of the Archduke Francis Ferdinard (on June 28, 1914) until Austria's harsh ultimatum to Serbia that touched off the final crisis on July 23, 1914. In Britain, during the same period, the press focused on continuing disorders in Ireland, ignoring the explosive situation in the Balkans, and members of the Asquith-Grey government did likewise.[13] As an influence on government, the news media functioned in three different ways. They provided facts, on the basis of which the public could judge what government was doing. Secondly, the news media acted as voices for the public, communicating to government the views and feelings of citizens or even of "world opinion." Thirdly, the news media spoke for themselves, giving advice both to the public and to governments.

As instruments of government, the news media could help government speak to the public. Shortly after taking office in late March 1913 Woodrow Wilson inaugurated presidential press conferences, saying: "I feel that a large part of the success of public affairs depends on the newspaper men . . . because the news is the atmosphere of public affairs. Unless you get the right setting to affairs—disperse the right impression—things go wrong."[14] The news media could also help governments speak to other governments. As Nicolson points out, this practice had a long, if shady, history: "Cavour in Italy and Bismarck in Germany employed the Press for the purpose of secret rather than open diplomacy, and Bismarck himself was not above fabricating articles and letters which served the uses of his policy."[15]

In the age of Roosevelt and Hitler, press and radio began to play an increasingly large role on the international scene. Before Pearl Harbor, the Nazi dictator's addresses were frequently broadcast live by shortwave to the United States, and Foreign Office and propaganda officials in Berlin kept a close tab on American press opinion and reporting and what it might portend about the future of American foreign policy. Indeed, no one on either side in World War II was a more assiduous media watcher than Dr. Goebbels, the Nazi propaganda minister. Even when the war was hopelessly lost in March and April 1945, his staff was still combing through American newspapers and magazines for signs of softening in the Allied demand for "unconditional surrender."

As for Franklin D. Roosevelt, probably no American president ever handled the media as skillfully as he did. He was admired and liked by most members of the Washington press corps, which was not always true of his successors, and this enabled him, for instance, to use his regular press conferences—though not published verbatim at the time—as a means of making sure that he got the kind of coverage that he wanted for the issues that were of greatest importance to him. He was also able on occasion to persuade individual members of the corps to launch trial balloons for him, testing potential public response to plans that he was considering but to which he was not yet fully committed.

II

After sketching the evolution of the news media after World War II, this essay appraises their performance in the roles identified by Lippmann, Cohen, and other analysts—as map-makers, agenda-setters, influences on government, and instruments of government. In 1922, Lippmann criticized the press, contending that it did badly in preparing the public to share in policy-making. Sadly, one conclusion of this essay is that, while the news media were incomparably better staffed and equipped in the decade after World War II, they did not do much better, and in some cases not as well, in the roles that Lippmann had identified. But a second conclusion is that, paradoxically, they nevertheless helped public opinion achieve more influence in foreign policy and diplomacy.

Tracing the evolution of the news media after World War II requires first some description of trends within each medium—newspapers, newsmagazines, radio news, and television news. It requires, second, some description of trends common to all.

The most noticeable trend among newspapers was toward concentration. This was most marked in the United States. At the end of World War I, New York City had twenty dailies. As late as 1963, it still had twelve. By the end of the 1970s, it was down to three (four, if Long Island's *Newsday* is added). The United Kingdom had eleven national newspapers in 1945. By 1979 it still had ten, but six were tabloids.[16] In 1947 Paris had more than a dozen large circulation dailies. By the end of the 1970s, it had only four with circulations over five hundred thousand, and one of these, *Le Parisien Libéré,* reached that figure with five out-of-Paris editions emphasizing provincial news.[17]

Another marked trend among newspapers was toward more concentrated or more sporadic coverage of international affairs. During the interwar years, many dailies maintained foreign correspondents or made regular use of stringers residing in foreign countries. After World War II, not only did many metropolitan dailies disappear, those that survived began to cut back on foreign bureaus. As of 1945, American newspapers had about twenty-five hundred reporters abroad. As of 1969, the number was under six hundred. As of the mid-1970s, it was well under five hundred. Even the *New York Times* scaled back. It had more than sixty foreign correspondents in the 1950s but as of 1978 only thirty-four.[18] Between 1965 and 1976 *The Times* of London reduced numbers of foreign correspondents from twenty-six to eighteen; the *Daily Telegraph* cut back from thirty to thirteen.[19]

The flow in international news tended to be sustained by the wire services. The New York–based Associated Press was the most widely used. The other major American service, United Press International, the result of a 1958 merger between the United Press and William Randolph Hearst's International News Service, ran second. London's Reuters Agency ran third. Each of the three services had about twelve hundred newspapers as subscribers. Reuters led the two American services in worldwide business news, but it was well behind them in subscriptions from radio and television stations. The AP and UPI each served between three thousand and four thousand stations. Except for the Soviet TASS agency, the nearest competitor to the three English-language wire services was the Agence France Presse, successor to the prewar HAVAS agency, but AFP in the 1970s had fewer than one hundred newspapers as direct subscribers. Its claim to serve twelve thousand newspapers rested on exchange arrangements with numerous small national wire services, ranging from West Germany's Deutsche Presse Agentur, Italy's Agenzia Nazionale Stampa Associata, and Japan's Kyodo to Libya's Arab News Agency and Egypt's Middle East News Agency.[20]

Because of the wire services, newspapers received bulletins from all over the world. Indicative of the breadth of coverage is the structure of the smallest of the big four, the Agence France Presse. In the 1970s, the AFP maintained twenty-one bureaus in Europe, eight in the Middle East, twenty-five in Africa, three in the United States, eighteen in Latin America, and seventeen in Asia.[21] As a rule, however, wire services provided little besides bulletins. Reuters, AP, UPI, and AFP bureaus rarely filed reportage with depth comparable to that from a daily's own foreign bureau.

Newsmagazines compensated in a small way for the decline in numbers of newspaper foreign bureaus. Before World War II, *Time* had been the dominant newsmagazine. In the postwar era, *Newsweek* and *U.S. News and World Report* gained ground on *Time*. Britain's venerable *Economist* became increasingly as much a newsmagazine as a journal of commentary. By the 1970s it would have worldwide circulation (with more subscribers in the United States than in the United Kingdom).[22] In France, *L'Express* had six hundred thousand subscribers, *Le Nouvel Observateur* about half as many.[23] In West Germany, *Der Spiegel* could sell as many as a million copies a week, and the newspaper-format weekly, *Die Zeit,* sometimes approached half that figure.[24]

The English-language newsmagazines, like the wire services, maintained strong foreign bureaus. These bureaus filed reports that often had more detail, depth, and overt analysis than reports from most newspaper bureaus. But only a tiny fraction of this reportage could reach the public. As a *Time* editor once complained, the magazine had to compress "all the important news of the week into less space than *The New York Times* has in one day."[25] Because the newsmagazines thrived partly by scooping daily newspapers, their content tended to be skewed toward the stories expected to be most arresting on the day of the weekly's publication. Comparing newsmagazine reporters to those for newspapers, the veteran AP correspondent, Mort Rosenblum, writes that they "work in a more leisurely fashion, or in a mad frenzy, depending upon the day of the week."[26]

During the interwar years, radio had become a major source of both spot news and news commentary. Interested persons in the Western world obtained their first and perhaps strongest impressions of the Munich crisis of 1938 from broadcasts rather than from newsprint. This was to be true throughout World War II, with reportage complemented by analysis (or what passed for such) from commentators as varied as Edward R. Murrow, William L. Shirer, H. V. Kaltenborn, Howard K. Smith, Jean Giraudoux, and Joseph Goebbels.[27]

Radio news expanded after World War II. In 1945 the BBC had one daily news broadcast beginning at 9 P.M. By the end of the 1980s it would have an entire frequency devoted to day-and-night broadcasting of news and discussion of current affairs.[28] In the United States, radio news was eclipsed by television news during the 1950s. It recovered some ground in the 1970s when National Public Radio began to function for Americans as did BBC News for listeners in the United Kingdom.

By the 1930s and 1940s, it might be added, a distinctively American type of foreign correspondent had developed. Well versed in the politics and diplomacy of the countries they were writing about, reporters like Edgar Ansel Mowrer, Frederick R. Kuh, Anne O'Hare McCormick, and Dorothy Thompson did much to enlighten Americans about what was happening in Europe during "the gathering storm." In succeeding decades, they were followed by men and women such as Marguerite Higgins, C. L. Sulzberger, Georgie Anne Geyer, and Jim Hoagland, whose work was no less important and widely read.

Television news became the principal rival of the newspaper. Although television existed before the war, hardly anyone had foreseen its future. As late as

1951, Churchill, newly returned to Downing Street, declined televised interviews. "Why do we need this peepshow?" he asked.[29] In the United States, the audience for television news was then just about to skyrocket. In 1950 fewer than 4 million American households had television sets. By 1955 the figure was above 30 million. In Britain, France, and West Germany a comparable surge occurred later. Between 1955 and 1964, the number of television licenses in the United Kingdom went from under 5 million to about 14 million.[30] In France, this pattern repeated itself in the 1960s. In 1954 French households had only 125,000 television sets; in 1958, just under 1 million; by 1964, almost 6 million; by 1973, more than 14 million. West German statistics were very similar to those of France.[31] In the Eastern bloc, the lag was about the same. The Soviet Union had about 5 million television sets as of 1960. By 1975 it had 55 million.[32]

For a long time television challenged the print media more in local and national than in international news. The American networks set up foreign bureaus. Eventually, each would have about fifteen. The cost of each such bureau, however, was very high, and network home offices had the same problem as newsmagazine home offices. They could use only a tiny proportion of what foreign bureaus sent in.[33] The networks therefore often covered foreign stories as national or even local stories—conducting interviews in Washington or at the UN about the foreign area in question. If the story seemed big enough, special crews would go to the actual scene, but these crews would be ordered home as soon as a story faded.

In the 1960s, the American networks and the American Telephone and Telegraph Company (not yet broken up by antitrust prosecutors) capitalized on government space research to begin beaming broadcasts by satellite. Geosynchronous satellites put up late in the decade could provide continuous broadcasting over whatever area of the earth they were positioned. In the 1970s, this transmission technology united with new reception technologies known loosely as "cable." The result was greatly to increase the number and variety of broadcasts that could reach a single television set. In American cities, channels quickly multiplied. In most of the rest of the world, including Britain and Western Europe, governments attempted to limit the numbers. They had at most modest success. Moreover, the advent of the cheap VCR, allowing video recording and replay, ended almost any technical possibility of effective government control over what the possessors of television sets would watch.[34]

Several entrepreneurs seized on satellite and cable technologies to go into competition with the major networks. Most failed. One, however, proved successful. This was Ted Turner of Atlanta, Georgia. One of Turner's most successful initiatives was the formation in 1978 of a Cable News Network (CNN), broadcasting news and commentary all day long, worldwide.[35] The full effects of satellites, cable, VCRs, and CNN would not begin to come into evidence, however, until the 1980s.

Overall, trends within the news media led by the end of the 1970s to highly concentrated reportage on international affairs. There were fewer major dailies, and they had far fewer foreign correspondents. The wire services held their own but supplied primarily spot news. While newsmagazines increased in number and devoted more resources to international reportage, at least cumulatively, they provided relatively little reportage as compared with either newspapers or the electronic media. Radio and television tended to focus on stories that seemed big enough and lasting enough to justify air fares for special teams.

At the same time, individual newspapers, magazines, and radio and television broadcasts became primary sources of information about international affairs for larger and less concentrated audiences. Before World War II, while *The Times* of London or *Le Temps* or Milan's *Corriere della Sera* might be quoted widely, the paper itself would be read mostly in its home city. By the 1970s technology had greatly increased the potential circulation of newspapers. The *New York Times* was by then delivered early in the morning to homes throughout the northeastern United States. At about the same time, it would go on sale in newsstands the world around. The *Wall Street Journal*, the *Financial Times*, *Le Monde*, the *Neue Zürcher Zeitung*, and the Paris-based *International Herald Tribune* likewise reached worldwide circles of readers.

Radio and television newscasts similarly went out to worldwide audiences. The BBC World Service, though overseen by the Foreign Office, acquired large and loyal audiences by seeming rigorously objective.[36] The United States government created a Voice of America early in 1942 and now expanded it to broadcast news to communist countries and partly to compete elsewhere with Radio Moscow and its affiliates. Channeling funds clandestinely to ostensibly private organizations, the United States government also sponsored Radio Free Europe and Radio Liberty, which beamed broadcasts across all Eastern Europe.[37]

The most essentially Anglo-American yet most international of the news media was television. The BBC and the American radio-television networks had such a head start that their programming was inevitably borrowed almost wherever television broadcasting spread. While this programming aimed primarily at entertainment, it included some news broadcasts, especially event-focused special reports or interpretive retrospectives such as Edward R. Murrow's "See It Now." By the 1960s, the original networks had become slightly less dominant. A new BBC venture, with Reuters, the Rank Organization, and some Commonwealth broadcasting authorities as partners, was the British Commonwealth International Newsfilm Agency, subsequently renamed Visnews. Becoming the equivalent of a wire service for television use, it provided footage that could be put on the air anywhere. The only sounds were those of the action on film (as Jeremy Tunstall remarks, "the thud of rifle butts on heads, perhaps"[38].) Explanation of the pictures came in writing and could be used by narrators speaking any language. By the 1970s Visnews had bureaus in sixteen capitals and fielded camera crews, including hundreds of stringers, wherever stories broke. UPITN, a partnership between the American United Press and British Independent Television News, was Visnews' major competitor. It had eight foreign bureaus of its own, supplementing those of the UP.[39]

Soviet and Communist Chinese authorities tried initially to control what could be heard or seen by people in their countries or blocs. They jammed radio broadcasts from foreign sources. Soviet and East European television sets were designed not to receive signals from Western transmitters. (East German television standards were different and made possible reception of West German broadcasts—possibly an inertial result of the early Soviet policy of pushing for reunification.)[40] But adaptations in Western transmitters and technical ingenuity among possessors of television sets made for many openings in the curtains dividing the blocs. This fact would have great impact on events in Eastern Europe and the Soviet Union in the 1970s and 1980s.[41]

III

For the news media as factors in foreign policy decisions and in diplomacy, internal changes may have been as important as external changes, and these internal changes appear to have been common to all the news media.

For one thing, the major news media ceased to be pulpits for their individual owners. For generations, dating back to the second half of the nineteenth century, particularly during and just after World War I, a number of newspaper owners believed they could mold public opinion and thereby shape public policy to their liking. Before his death in 1922, Viscount Bryce, no radical, wrote fearfully of the press's "capacity to manipulate news and report selectively according to the interests of its proprietors."[42] The British press barons, chiefly Lords Northcliffe, Harmsworth, and Beaverbrook, inspired Bryce's comment. Northcliffe had declared publicly, "God made people read so that I could fill their brains with facts, facts, facts—and later tell them whom to love, whom to hate, and what to think."[43] But Northcliffe, Harmsworth, and Beaverbrook were not unique. The United States had counterparts, particularly Roy W. Howard and William Randolph Hearst, and France had Jean Prouvost. Henry R. Luce, the cofounder of *Time*, hoped by means of his magazines to make the American government follow his guidance. He was in fact to be given much of the credit (or blame) for a thirty-year American policy of refusing to recognize the People's Republic of China. Hearst lived on until 1951, waging a final campaign in support of Douglas MacArthur against Harry Truman and thus for all-out war with the Communist Chinese. Max Aitken, Lord Beaverbrook, died in 1964. But Beaverbrook's last crusade came in the mid-1950s and was largely personal, aimed at preventing Lord Louis Mountbatten from becoming First Sea Lord. Prouvost had long since become simply an owner of journals like *Le Figaro,* favored by French readers on the political right.[44]

The change from the heyday of Hearst, Northcliffe, Rothermere, and Beaverbrook is best illustrated by the career of Axel Springer.[45] As the Western powers closed down their occupation regimes, Springer gathered into his hands a publishing empire. His *Bild-Zeitung,* consciously modeled on the *Daily Mirror,* became the most popular daily in Germany. At one point, he owned 40 percent of Germany's dailies, 80 percent of Germany's Sunday papers, and a significant proportion of all popular magazines. With the example of Hearst and the English press barons in mind, Springer acquired *Die Welt,* a Hamburg daily aspiring to be a national newspaper for Germany's elite. Springer had already given the *Bild-Zeitung*'s editorial page a raucously right-wing voice. The terms of purchase of *Die Welt* temporarily inhibited him. By the mid-1960s, however, he had assumed full control, and he turned *Die Welt* to his political purposes.

Springer's offensive against all things leftist made him in turn a target for Germany's militant student movement. Students boycotted *Die Welt.* A reporter for the newspaper tells of returning from a long assignment in Asia. "And not only could you not buy *Die Welt* anywhere on a university campus. You didn't even dare carry a copy."[46] Circulation plummeted. Before long, Springer had given *Bild-Zeitung* a new editor. While the editorial line remained unchanged, the editorial pages received less and less prominence. After a time, Springer shifted the same pragmatist editor from the *Bild-Zeitung* to *Die Welt.* For practical purposes, Springer gave up his effort to be a press lord on the old English model.[47]

The reason for Springer's failure—and for the virtual disappearance of the press baron—was largely a matter of economics. Newspapers depended on advertising. Sales of newspapers themselves rarely covered costs. In 1970 the *Washington Post* took in $13 million from subscriptions and newsstand sales. It spent $20 million just on newsprint.[48] But advertisers paid on the basis of circulation. If the publisher's political campaigns caused circulation to drop, as with *Die Welt,* there were immediate consequences. New press barons such as Rupert Murdoch and Robert Maxwell rarely let their prejudices affect their balance sheets. Though Murdoch did what he could to help conservatives, his guiding motto was "to interest the whole community"—and thus sell newspapers. Though Maxwell was actually for a time a Labour MP, he, too, interfered with editors only when circulations lagged.[49]

The same was true for other news media. Though Luce kept up his campaign against recognition of Communist China, *Time* carried on few other crusades. Television had barons temperamentally akin to Hearst and Northcliffe. At CBS, William S. Paley was known as "The Chairman," the allusion being to Mao Zedong. But the dictatorships of Paley and his counterparts seemed, like those of Murdoch and Maxwell, to be directed more toward making money than toward dictating how the news should be reported.[50]

The trend complementary to the decline of the press baron was the rise of the professional journalist. By and large, power over the content and makeup of newspapers fell to editors, most of whom had previously been reporters. Editors and reporters increasingly thought of the newspaper as *theirs*. An extreme example offered itself early in the postwar era in *Le Monde*. Founded just after World War II as a successor to the once authoritative Paris daily, *Le Temps*, discredited by its association with Vichy, *Le Monde* was supposed to be controlled by a triumvirate, one of whom was its editor, Hubert Beuve-Méry. At the turn into the 1950s, the other two fired Beuve-Méry because of his outspoken opposition to the Atlantic alliance. (Beuve-Méry argued that France would make itself a satellite of the United States.) The paper's subeditors and reporters mounted a ferocious campaign, the result of which was Beuve-Méry's reinstatement.[51] Though few other tests occurred, the principle gained ground everywhere in the West that publishers or owners should not interfere in news judgments.

The same principle acquired strength in radio and television. The apparent objectivity of the BBC World Service derived in part from rigid insistence by the BBC staff, domestic as well as foreign, on independence from the government.[51] Broadcasters for the Voice of America similarly refused to accept dictation from the State Department. They took the position that they were primarily professional journalists and only secondarily employees of the United States.[53] In television, matters were more complicated because "production values" often had greater weight than news values. The quality of pictures could determine whether a story would be featured or would run at all. The "gatekeepers"—those who determined what news the public would read or watch—included producers and directors, and in television producers and directors sometimes took precedence over news editors.[54] Nevertheless, judgments about what was to be represented as news were presumed to be determined by professional criteria. Though the news departments of American television networks often waged battles with network executives, most had to do with budgets or time allocations, not politics.

Along with the decline of the news media baron and the rise of the professional journalist went two other internal developments. One was change in technology. The newspaper of the late twentieth century differed strikingly from that of even mid-century. Computer editing and typesetting—introduced in the 1970s—greatly increased the efficiency and speed of newspaper production.[55] Satellite and cable transmission stepped up not only the reach of radio and television broadcasts but also the reception of news by editors and producers. And jet aircraft made easier the dependence on special teams as opposed to resident correspondents or bureaus.

The second development was bureaucratization. On major newspapers, editorial work subdivided. Reporters increasingly received specialized beats. Newsrooms became as compartmentalized as beehives. Gay Talese describes the *New York Times* as of 1951, when Turner Catledge became managing editor: "Each morning hundreds of people would file into the newsroom and would either seat themselves behind vast rows of desks like parishioners at church, or they would disappear in the distance behind some pillar or interior wall, some dark nook or glass-enclosed maze on the doors of which was printed 'Science' or 'Real Estate' or 'Drama' or 'Sports' or 'Society'—and even when Catledge stood outside his own office gazing around the newsroom through his binoculars he could never see at a single sweep everybody on his staff nor did he precisely know what they were all doing there."[56]

While decisions on reporters' assignments and on the space and placing of stories were based on professional criteria, they were also in some sense corporate decisions. Bargaining went on just as within large government agencies or business organizations. Leon Sigal describes battles at the *New York Times* over whether a presidential speech at the UN would belong to the metropolitan staff, the national desk's White House correspondent, or the foreign desk's UN correspondent.[57] Studying *Time, Newsweek,* and both CBS Evening News and NBC Nightly News, sociologist Herbert Gans found similar conditions. He characterizes the newsmagazines and networks as "bureaucracies staffed by professionals."[58]

Newspapers, newsmagazines, and networks developed routinized procedures for covering the news. Edwin L. James, Catledge's immediate predecessor at the *New York Times,* once wrote: "News breaks through definite channels; it cannot do otherwise. Cover those channels and you catch the news—much like casting a net across a salmon stream."[59] This principle governed reporters' assignments and decisions on closing or retaining foreign bureaus. Sensible as it was for managing resources, it meant close coverage of the expected and not much watch for the unexpected. It accounted, for example, for the news media's slowness to see unrest in Iran in the 1970s. Until late in 1978, few reporters even visited Teheran. The first major stories appeared only after the Shah brought about the Ayatollah Khomeini's departure from Iraq to Paris in 1963. Charles Peters, editor of the *Washington Monthly,* alleged that the explanation lay in a principle followed by journalists abroad: "Never Leave the City where the Good Bars and Hotels Are." Peters offered as "the Khomeini corollary" the proposition that, if a revolutionary wanted media attention, he should go to Paris or possibly London or New York.[60]

The news media developed routinized procedures for sorting stories caught in the designated channels and choosing those to be featured. Internally, since seniority and merit were major factors in promotion, there were tendencies toward institutional uniformity—the *New York Times* adhering to one set of fashions, for example, the *Washington Post* to another.

IV

As map-makers, the news media of the late twentieth century obviously had much greater capacity for showing the public worlds beyond their neighborhoods. In the interwar years, wire photos and newsreels provided increasing complements to print reportage. By the 1970s television could flood the world with pictures of events actually in progress—or almost so. Surveys indicated that, by then, television had replaced the print media as the public's preferred source for news. Though most data came from the United States, the same preferences appeared in surveys run in France and in Yugoslavia. And, at least among Americans, the preference for television over print was especially marked with regard to international news.[61]

Nevertheless, the news media of the 1970s would probably have disappointed Lippmann even more than had the newspapers of 1922. As compared with the earlier period, coverage of international news was more random and disjointed. The decline in numbers of foreign correspondents and foreign bureaus serving newspapers meant that news coming in from the field, no matter how much greater might be the volume, came from a smaller number of places. The fact that stories came increasingly to be covered by special teams increased the amount of what was sometimes termed *parachute journalism.*[62] The reporters could be stars as reporters, but they often lacked the local knowledge stored up and drawn upon by resident correspondents or stringers.

Also, as newspapers, newsmagazines, and networks sent teams out to cover stories, they were likely to send teams to the same places. This meant more coverage for those places, less for others. Given the new technologies, the teams could get on site quickly and file stories right away. They could leave equally quickly and, unlike resident correspondents, stop filing until a new assignment came along. Mort Rosenblum describes the result: "With so few reporters roaming freely, with so little backup from staff colleagues on different turf, major scoops go unscooped. With overworked editors, whose view of the world is dimmed by distance, important stories die on the desk."[63]

By the late twentieth century, news media maps were more likely than those of earlier decades to have geographical areas temporarily highlighted, then completely gone, then reappearing with little explanation of what had happened in between. This was not unknown earlier. A member of Parliament complained in 1918: "What happened in the press? We see a series of events reported with great fullness; we begin to read of them. The next day the story continues, and we read it with interest; but the day after that some domestic concern crops up, . . . and the foreign news is withdrawn, the story stops, and the country is under the impression that that particular issue is over. It may not be at all."[64] But this complaint had greater force later.

Before the Second World War, the foreign editors of newspapers, newsmagazines, and radio networks had had reason to suppose themselves selecting reportage for a special, restricted audience, for foreign policy and diplomacy were thought to interest only an elite. Survey research confirmed this supposition, calculating the potential "foreign policy public," at least in the United States, at not much more than 15 percent of the public generally interested in public affairs.[65] When foreign news was given space or air time, the selection criteria were somewhat different from those for local or national news, and foreign editors, where they existed, had some latitude for presenting the news as if to specially informed readers or listeners. By the 1970s this had long since ceased to be true. Foreign news competed for space or time on an even basis with other news. Its chances of appearing depended on what a Hearst editor once characterized as "anything that makes a reader say 'Gee whiz!' "[66]

In earlier times, when streams of copy came in from various locales, editors sometimes used the reports to show off the existence of the bureau or correspondent. And the reportage was there if space needed to be filled. These incentives persisted. A study of television news in the 1970s found that the best predictor of whether a network would give coverage to a given country or area was whether it had a permanent bureau there.[67] But newspapers and networks maintained increasingly few permanent bureaus, and wherever they had no bureaus, incentives ran in an exactly opposite direction. Since home offices paid out of pocket for sending special teams to foreign sites, they were likely to do so only for stories with strong "Gee whiz!" potential, and they were equally likely to recall the teams the moment this potential began to fade.

Reduction in coverage by regular correspondents as opposed to special teams meant more coverage by reporters short on background or sense of context. Though the British MP's comment may have been justified when he made it in 1918, newspaper stories in his era often tried to bring readers up to date on what had happened since the last period of headline attention. Thus, for example, the *New York Times* and *Times* of London reports on the early stages of the Italo-Ethiopian crisis of the 1930s included long dispatches from stringers in Addis Ababa describing developments since the Italian defeat in Ethiopia in the 1890s. Coverage by the same newspapers and by radio and television networks of the Angolan crisis of 1975 lacked anything comparable.

As a result of the 1974 revolution in Portugal, Angola had been promised independence. Fighting broke out among rival Angolan factions. Wire services and newsmagazines sent out reporters. CBS television sent a correspondent and camera crew. Boning up, the newsmen consulted American government officials and the handful of American scholars who had written on Angola. This being the Watergate era, they distrusted the officials, and they had trouble understanding the scholars. Consequently, they relied chiefly on reporters who had covered an abortive Angolan war for independence back in 1961. This was a mistake. One reason why the scholars had seemed unintelligible was that Angolan politics had turned topsy-turvy since 1961.

First reports out of Luanda used characterizations from the earlier period. Augustinho Neto's MPLA was "moderate," Holden Roberto's FNLA was "the right" (supported from Zaire), Jonas Savimbi's UNITA was "radical." (In 1961, Savimbi had had backing from China and North Korea and had been thought a protégé of Cuba's Che Guevara.) After being on the scene for a while, reporters corrected themselves, now characterizing the MPLA as "Moscow-oriented,"

Roberto's FNLA as "Peking-backed," and UNITA as "moderate." But report-age never provided clear descriptions of who stood where in Angola itself or noted that Neto, Roberto, and Savimbi all seemed ready to take help from any source. (The Vanderbilt University television archive has a clip of an on-the-scene ABC television correspondent receiving a bulletin and reading it aloud, with his voice rising in surprise: "Jonas Savimbi is receiving arms . . . *from Rumania?*")[68]

Early in 1976, Daniel Schorr, then of CBS television news, broadcast a report that the CIA had been secretly supporting one of Angola's factions. (It turned out to be Savimbi's.) Schorr reported that some senators suspected the CIA of circumventing recent laws requiring consultation with Congress. For a while thereafter, Angola was in newspaper headlines and often led evening television news broadcasts. But this was as a Washington story. Angola itself, with its bewildering politics and unphotogenic scenery, faded from view. It could as well have been in Latin America—or on the moon.

The contrast with the 1930s, when Addis Ababa datelines alternated regu-larly with ones from Rome or Geneva or Paris or London, illustrates the double effect of concentration in news media coverage of international affairs. Parts of the world other than major capitals came to be covered more sporadically and more superficially, and stories about these other parts of the world focused more often than not on what was being said, thought, or done about the areas in the handful of capitals where news personnel congregated.

As map-makers, the news media of the 1970s put in brilliant relief a few metropolitan centers but left much of the intervening space in darkness. In 1922, when Lippmann wrote *Public Opinion,* someone depending on a single major newspaper would have had a skewed and partial sense of the world. The same person in the 1970s would have had an even more skewed and partial view—and with stereotypes no less simplistic. Witness the effort to identify good guys and bad guys in Angola and the portrayal of the Angolans' war as simply part of the Cold War.

These observations about map-making apply also to agenda-setting. In com-parison to the period when Lippmann wrote *Public Opinion,* the news media by the 1970s probably focused attention more intensively on particular issues or events and in the process more often discouraged attention to other issues or events. The intensiveness of coverage of a highlighted story might be greater by orders of magnitude. In-depth reportage on fighting in Vietnam during the Tet holidays of 1968 exceeded comparable reportage on any part of World War II, except perhaps the Normandy landings.

The news media's effects as agenda-setters can be illustrated by the United States at the end of the 1970s. Day after day, press, radio, and television featured stories on Americans held hostage in Teheran. Many other stories meanwhile got short shrift. One concerned what two writers have labeled "the Mexican time bomb."[69] Less-developed countries, led by Mexico, Brazil, and

Argentina, owed debts to the nine largest American banks that, in aggregate, would soon equal more than 300 percent of the banks' total capital. Default by these governments could have shocked the world's financial system more than the Wall Street crash of 1929 or the collapse of Vienna's Creditanstalt in 1931. "Commodity, security, and foreign exchanges would be forced to shut down . . . ," writes one economist, "trade and production would halt."[70] But because the story figured in business news rather than in national or international news and, in addition, was Latin American business news, it did not catch attention either among the public or in officialdom. Worried experts within the United States government had difficulty even getting discussion of the matter on the presidential timetable.[71]

V

As for influence on government, the news media obviously gained in potential. During the Cold War, editors and reporters sometimes cooperated with officialdom in withholding facts. The *New York Times* and some other newspapers knew in detail of the Kennedy administration's plan to land anticommunist exiles in Cuba, pretending that the landing had been organized by Cubans themselves and not by the CIA. Kennedy asked journalists not to publish the story, and they obliged him. Kennedy later said he regretted his request. The actual landing at the Bay of Pigs was a bloody fiasco. If the story had come out, he implied, he might have called the landing off. The then Washington bureau chief of the *New York Times,* James Reston, drew the moral that the news media ought to publish or broadcast any stories picked up about what governments were planning to do. Early publicity, he argued, might force them to proceed more thoughtfully.[72]

Actually, the tension between what Washington was ready to disclose and what the press was anxious to print was nothing new. With Pearl Harbor, as Secretary of War Henry L. Stimson wrote later in his memoirs, "a Curtain of Fire was lowered over the problems and anxieties of the preceding months. No longer would the secret war plans of the Army's General Staff be freely published by a major newspaper—as the *Chicago Tribune* had done three days before Pearl Harbor."[73] Washington, Roosevelt declared, was "the worst rumor factory, and therefore, the source of more lies than are spoken and printed throughout the United States, than any other community."[74]

By the 1960s the news media became increasingly avid searchers for stories that governments wanted to conceal. Marvin Kalb, then of CBS television news, explains: "There was a time, pre-Vietnam, pre-Watergate, when American journalists tended to believe their government's version of events. . . . There was no discernible skepticism. By the mid-1960s, Vietnam had begun to corrode this attitude, and by the mid-1970s, Watergate turned it into sour cynicism."[75]

The best documented example is news coverage of the American war in Vietnam. The Pentagon said that American bombers were hitting only military targets in North Vietnam. Harrison E. Salisbury of the *New York Times* visited Hanoi and reported that this was not so. The *New York Times* and *Washington Post* subsequently defied the government and published the Pentagon Papers, an illicitly released, highly classified official history of the war, some of which documented deliberate efforts to deceive the public. In March 1968, after the North Vietnamese staged their surprise Tet offensive, CBS's Walter Cronkite, the dean of television anchors, declared the war a hopeless stalemate. According to George Christian, then the president's press secretary, Cronkite's broadcast sent "shock waves" through the government. Along with barrages from other television personalities and from newspapers and newsmagazines, the Cronkite broadcast is credited with producing President Johnson's decision to stop further American escalation of the war and instead renew efforts for a negotiated settlement.[76]

It seems clear in retrospect that journalists misread the Tet offensive. It was an act of desperation by the North Vietnamese, who had concluded that the Americans were on the verge of defeating them in South Vietnam, and its effect was to decimate their already weakened cadre there.[77] On the whole, nevertheless, newspaper, newsmagazine, radio, and television reportage on the Vietnam War was accurate and judicious. The interested public got a better picture of reality from the news media than from the government. The same had been true of French press reportage on the earlier Indo-China War and on the war in Algeria.[78]

The extent to which the news media gained effectiveness as voices for the public is hard to gauge. From the 1960s onward, editors and reporters rarely drew a distinction between speaking for the public and speaking for themselves. If the news media had more influence as voices for the public, the most probable reason was—in the paradox to be explored later—that the government had meanwhile acquired greater influence over the news media.

The news media did, of course, exert some influence independently—speaking for themselves rather than the public. How much influence is also hard to gauge. Some observers ascribed important roles, especially in the United States, to columnists and commentators. A London *Observer* correspondent asserted in the 1950s that there was "a small group of writers who must be included in any outline of what constitutes 'Washington'. . . . They not only check and when necessary destroy individuals, they positively affect the course of policy."[79] Lippmann, who continued writing until January 1971, certainly figured in any such group. So did Joseph and Stewart Alsop, who, like Lippmann, regularly produced columns that a syndicate placed in hundreds of newspapers. But acute onlookers such as Reston questioned the actual impact of any of these writers. Lippmann, he thought, might have helped to define major questions, but he doubted that even Lippmann had had much to do with determining the answers. Probably most columnists became so dependent on continued access to inside sources that they spoke, as a rule, for those sources more than for themselves.[80]

Regarding the influence of government on the news media, any realistic comment has to be two-edged. The wars in Indo-China, Algeria, and Vietnam showed government trying to shape news reportage and failing. In 1962, Defense Minister Franz Josef Strauss cracked down on *Der Spiegel,* accusing its editors of disclosures that crossed the line into treason. Strauss's inability to prove his accusation resulted in his own temporary disgrace and probably accounted for his never becoming chancellor.[81] British Prime Minister Harold Wilson tried to discipline first the *Daily Express* and then the *Sunday Telegraph* for publishing classified information. In both instances, the only practical result was to give the information wider currency.[82] Whether the *Spiegel* affair and these British "D-Notice" flaps or even the publication of the Pentagon Papers had any effect on the respective governments' policies is, however, impossible to judge.

Whatever the reality, officials believed the news media to be both increasingly powerful and increasingly dangerous. Those on the political right tended to see the news media as the agent of the left. American officials who agreed with Henry Luce about Communist China blamed journalists for having whitewashed the Chinese Communists during the civil war. (One whom they held particularly at fault was *Time*'s own Theodore H. White.) Similar accusations were leveled against the *New York Times* and other newspapers after Fidel Castro came to power in Cuba and again after the Sandinistas' success in Nicaragua.[83] In Britain, Tories tended to regard the BBC as a malign influence on the public. The Conservative party set up a committee to keep watch on BBC programming. (Its head was John Profumo, later the star in sex scandals that helped bring down Prime Minister Harold Macmillan.) A *Daily Mirror* cartoon once suggested that the initials should stand for "Be Bloody Careful."[84] In Belgium, Christian Democrats and Liberals constantly complained that radio and television were dominated by Socialists.[85]

Political leaders and others on the left tended to see the news media as agents of their owners and of other reactionaries. Harold Wilson worked hard on his television image because he thought the press would portray him as an ogre. He hoped to offset that by having people see him on the screen and say, "Oh look, he is an ordinary chap like the rest of us."[86] In the United States, a number of academics accused the news media of slavishly supporting government policy. Sometimes, they actually had supporting evidence.[87]

In the 1950s and 1960s, relations between democratic governments and the press appeared to deteriorate almost everywhere. Even if not making accusations of bias, officials could regard the news media as enemies just because of their ubiquity and their nosiness. The veteran Israeli diplomat, Abba Eban, says, "Any discussion of changes in the diplomatic system must begin with the most potent and far-reaching transformation of all: the collapse of reticence and privacy in negotiation. The intrusion of the media into every phase and level of the negotiation process changes the whole spirit and nature of diplomacy."[88] In his final days as secretary of state, Henry Kissinger told the National Press Club: "The days when statesmen and journalists coexisted in an atmosphere of trust and shared confidences have given way to a state of almost perpetual inquest which, at its worst, can degenerate into a relationship of hunter and hunted, deceiver and dupe."[89] Kissinger's remarks were of special interest since, as many of his listeners knew he had had few peers when it came to managing, or attempting to manage, the news.

Suspicion of and irritation with the news media caused officials to develop defenses. They invented their equivalents of the tiger tamer's chair and whip. The visible outer circle of these defenses was manned by public affairs officers specially assigned to deal with journalists. In *Public Opinion*, Lippmann quotes a fellow journalist's protests against press agents: "The great corporations have them, the banks have them, the railroads have them, all the organizations of business and social and political activity have them. . . . Even statesmen have them."[90] Note: *even* statesmen.

When Lippmann wrote, most governments had only recently begun to use press offices. The British Foreign Office created a News and Political Intelligence Department in 1919. Its head was Sir William (later Lord) Tyrell, one of the Foreign Office mandarins. He was to be long remembered by British journalists for his frankness regarding the government-press relationship, saying once to a group of reporters: "You think we lie to you. But we don't lie, really we don't. However, when you discover that, you make an even greater error. You think we tell you the truth."[91] In the United States, press offices began to take form during the 1930s, mostly to protect or propagandize for controversial New Deal agencies such as the Tennessee Valley Authority. In 1936 a congressional inquiry identified 270 federal public affairs officers, many part-time. In 1977, when Congress counted again, there were 3,366, and this for only the twenty largest agencies.[92]

These armies of public affairs officers performed many functions, the number and variety growing over time. In the early 1960s, a scholar studying press-government relations in Washington divided public affairs officers into three categories: informers ("just the facts"), educators (or explainers), and promoters.[93] In that period of high Cold War, public affairs officers in all three categories acted partly as guardians of the government's secrets, partly—even if trying only to inform or educate—as missionaries, for a not untypical attitude was that voiced by Eisenhower's first national security assistant, Robert L. Cutler: "In this world, where freedom as never before struggles rawly for survival . . . [the news media] must make clear how they will contribute to our survival; they must prove to us that the widespread, public disclosure of our secret projects will make the free world stronger, and the neutrals better disposed, will rally the subject peoples, and will put the Communist regimes at a disadvantage."[94]

Intentness on somehow controlling the news media increased during the 1960s. Robert Manning, who managed press relations for the United States State Department early in the 1960s, concluded that most officials had little understanding of the news media and little interest in trying to manage news media relations. Philip Goulding, who had a similar post in the United States Defense Department later in the decade, testifies by contrast to carefully planned campaigns playing on the prejudices, weaknesses, and strengths of particular correspondents.[95] A similar shift occurred in the American Congress. A former aide to Senator J. William Fulbright, the chairman of the Foreign Relations Committee, comments that, as of 1962–1963, Fulbright avoided both interviews with reporters and appearances on television. By 1970, said the aide, "there had been quite a change. Advance speech texts and press releases were the rule. The Senator himself was well aware that in order to make the evening news shows it was wise to do the filming around noon—never after 4 p.m.—to permit the networks to plan for it."[96]

Men and women in government used the news media for communication and competition with one another. Writing in 1959, Douglass Cater cited front page stories of 1955 about the crisis over Quemoy and the Matsus. Navy sources told reporters—off the record—that the Communist Chinese were about to attack these tiny offshore islands and that the United States planned not only to defend them but to strike targets on the Chinese mainland. When stories to this effect appeared, the president feared becoming boxed in. His press secretary called in reporters and told them—also off the record—that war was unlikely and that United States policy had not yet been determined. Other mutually contradictory stories appeared in subsequent days as "hawks" and "doves" used the press as one venue for their debates.[97]

In the early 1970s, Morton Halperin described the range of approaches to the news media that he had observed while in high positions in the Pentagon and on the National Security Council staff. In addition to conducting policy debate, as earlier regarding Quemoy and the Matsus, said Halperin, officials used the news media to transmit messages up and down the governmental chain. Knowing that the president and every other high official started the day by poring over the *New York Times* and the *Washington Post,* officials tried to plant stories there in order to get attention that they could not necessarily get through customary channels. Halperin also noted examples of officials planting stories in order to undermine rivals. To illustrate the many variations, he cited former presidential press secretary George Reedy's description of a "reverse thrust"—a story describing someone as well-thought-of and possibly in line for promotion, the object being to arouse envy, mistrust, and opposition. Halperin gave examples also of officials' use of the media for trial balloons, for trying to improve chances that the bureaucracy at large would understand and carry out a presidential policy, and for communicating with foreign governments and bureaucracies.[98]

After yet another decade, Stephen Hess surveyed government-press relations in Washington. Also experienced in government, Hess came up with findings similar to Halperin's. He described Washington reporters as "journalist bumble bees spreading pollen from White House to State Department to Pentagon to State to White House." His list of officials' uses of the news media added only three minor categories: ego-gratification (the name in the paper), good will (a credit bank with the reporter or his or her editors), and whistle-blowing (out-of-channel complaints of misdoing).

Hess also confirmed the finding of earlier scholars that officials had become increasingly discriminating in choosing leakees. They used the *Times* and *Post* or network anchors to communicate with officials or with the Eastern foreign policy establishment. They used wire service reporters or regional dailies to reach larger publics, specialized journals for population segments, and foreign journalists for communities abroad.[99]

Looking at the press-government relationship from the reporters' side, these scholars and others concluded that the relationship worked increasingly in favor of the government. Several drew analogies with markets. Officials figured as sellers, reporters as buyers. Though officials might be eager to sell their stories—for any of the reasons identified by Halperin and Hess—they had some freedom to choose among buyers. The reporters were constrained by being in some sense middlemen. Once a reporter had a piece of news, he or she still had to persuade an editor or producer to use it. The more rare the tidbit offered by the official, the more the value to the reporter in terms of his or her competition for space. The reporter was a buyer in a sellers' market but a seller in a buyers' market.[100]

Not surprisingly, officials became able in some degree to determine the terms of trade. They could stipulate that information was provided off-the-record: that is, with nothing to be published showing that any information had been provided. They could stipulate that it was "background," meaning that the informant would not be identified. The commonness of news stories citing anonymous "sources" led the reporter Ward S. Just to write: "Walter and Ann Source had four daughters, 'Highly Placed, Authoritative, Unimpeachable, and Well-Informed.' The first married a diplomat named U.S. Officials and the second a government public relations man named Reliable Informant."[101] The directly attributable statement, however, usually had less value to the reporter because it was likely to be widely distributed.

Students of the relationship saw other reasons why reporters tended to become captives of their sources. The *New York Times'* Russell Baker observed that they became assimilated to their beats: "The State Department reporter quickly learns to talk like a fuddy-duddy and to look grave, important, and inscrutable. The Pentagon man always seems to have just come in off maneuvers."[102] Case studies confirmed that there was truth in Baker's comment and suggested further that reporters sometimes became integral parts of the organizations they covered. Reporters' discourse tended to be with their sources rather than their editors or readers or even fellow reporters. A substantial body of analysis has suggested that there was more use of the news media by government than the reverse. More often than not, however, the use was cautious and respectful, not manipulative in the popular sense of the term, for few officials forgot that, if there was a last word, it would be the reporters', not theirs. In his study of newsmagazines and television networks, Herbert Gans described officials and reporters as like dancers, with both parties cooperating and keeping step but with officials giving the lead.[103]

VI

Observers of political leaders, as distinct from appointed or career officials, concluded that they, too, had become increasingly dominant in relationships with the news media. Learning from their predecessors and often studying examples in other countries, political leaders became progressively more skillful in managing these relationships.

James Margach, a newspaperman who covered every British prime minister following David Lloyd George, describes in *The Abuse of Power* how each maneuvered "the lobby," the corps of correspondents covering Westminster. Even before World War II, writes Margach, prime ministers would spend time with reporters or editors or publishers at the expense of time with their parliamentary colleagues, even their party whips. Margach characterized his book as an account of "the tempestuous and never-ending war between Downing Street and Fleet Street." He wrote, "To win this war has been the first priority of . . . Prime Ministers. . . . With almost obsessional ruthlessness the majority sought to their domination of Parliament, parties and public opinion."[104]

Many political leaders made effective use of radio. During the 1930s both Roosevelt and Hitler did so. During World War II, Churchill's broadcasts contributed powerfully not only to sustaining British morale but to building the Anglo-American alliance. De Gaulle's broadcasts were crucial to creating and maintaining the Free French movement. David Schoenbrun, Paris bureau chief for CBS television from 1947 to 1964, writes without wild exaggeration, "De Gaulle had created himself uniquely on the radio waves."[105]

When television overtook radio, political leaders gradually adapted. Eden tried to accommodate himself to what Churchill had called "the peepshow." He failed. His career had been built in part on an image as a handsome, polished diplomat. Photographs and even newsreels preserved this image. Television did not. In 1956, well before the Suez crisis, Eden appeared on television to explain the issues with Egypt. The camera showed him looking old and tired, having to grope for eyeglasses, and nevertheless stumbling over his script. Because of this, according to Michael Cockerell, Eden's support began rapidly to erode.[106]

Having witnessed Eden's fall—indeed, having contributed to it—Macmillan bent himself to make more effective use of television. He succeeded. William Deedes, his chief publicity adviser, explained why: "It was exactly to him like charades in a country house where you all put on funny clothes and funny hats and did an act; that's why he got into the spirit of it."[107] Macmillan made an art of staging travel so as to maximize television footage. He went to Moscow in February 1959 partly for this purpose, taking over a hundred newspaper and television people with him and walking down the steps of his airplane wearing a foot-high white fur hat.[108] He exploited to the full the television potential of his own subsequent trips to North America and those of Eisenhower and Kennedy to the United Kingdom. The last was staged, writes Cockerell, as "a powerful young knight comes to pay court to the wise old king."[109]

Yet Dwight D. Eisenhower's effective use of the media should not be overlooked. Beginning with the 1952 election campaign, radio and television coverage—especially certain prestige interview programs—became steadily more important. Though supposedly a novice in partisan politics, Eisenhower required little tutoring when it came to avoiding possible media pitfalls. As he wrote Senator Henry Cabot Lodge, Jr., on 20 June 1952, when it was suggested that Eisenhower appear on NBC's "Meet the Press," long the most widely followed program of its kind, headed up by the acidulous Lawrence E. Spivak: "The only [television show] I refused to have anything to do with is the Spivak program. I simply will not appear on a program where I have as little respect for an individual's integrity and probity as I have for that man's."[110]

Indeed hardly had Eisenhower been nominated by the Republicans at Chicago than he chose as his press secretary the able and tough-minded James C. Hagerty, press secretary to Governor Thomas E. Dewey of New York, whose father, James A. Hagerty, had for years been a renowned political reporter for the *New York Times*. It was Hagerty who, in effect, became the first White House spin doctor, decades before that term achieved widespread circulation.

John F. Kennedy made even more effective use of television than had Eisenhower. Political leaders elsewhere studied and imitated Kennedy. Harold Wilson did so. When remolding his persona to fit the small screen, he attempted to achieve Kennedy's blend of formality and informality. He adopted the custom of gesturing with a pipe, for example, because his advisers warned that his natural clenched-fist gestures did not fit that pattern. For a time, Wilson proved even more successful than Macmillan. The vice chairman of the Conservative party pronounced Wilson "the only really competent political TV performer this country had produced."[111]

The portion of the Downing Street–Fleet Street war conducted over television was one where both sides fought mobile actions. Prime ministers adapted, but television meanwhile changed. Competition between the BBC and a new independent network made both strive for liveliness. One innovation was the satiric program, *This Was the Week that Was* (*TW3*). Its satires on scandals in the Tory government helped bring Wilson and Labour into power. Before long, *TW3* began to mock Wilson. *TW3*'s competitors tried to outdo it. One low point came in a sequence where the questioner asked what body motions betrayed the secret that Wilson was lying. The answer: "when his lips move." By all accounts, Wilson became obsessively angry. When Labour lost in June 1970, Wilson laid all the blame on the news media.

By this time, the effort to manage television coverage had become an important and integral part of political leadership everywhere. In France, de Gaulle had proved himself as well able to use this medium as to use radio. Critics attacked his 1962 referendum as "the first electronic coup d'état." (It helped that television was a government monopoly. De Gaulle reportedly said, "The press belongs to the opposition, but the television belongs to me.")[112] Commenting not only on de Gaulle but on other world leaders, including himself, Richard Nixon wrote in 1982, "Television today has transformed the ways in which national leadership is exercised."[113] The journalist/historian Theodore H. White wrote of Jimmy Carter, "There could have been no Carter presidency without television."[114] Margaret Thatcher concentrated her considerable will on avoiding the fates of Eden and Wilson. Her highly expert television adviser, Sir Gordon Reece, analyzed for her the experiences of Carter and other Americans. The result was meticulous attention not only to her words but even more to details of scenery, setting, color, and costume. The image of the iron lady— both iron and lady—was carefully contrived.[115]

West European leaders focused similarly (though generally less effectively) on their television images. Attentiveness to television elsewhere was evident in the performances of Sadat and Begin leading to the Camp David agreements. Former Israeli Prime Minister Golda Meir sniffed that the two might not deserve Nobel Prizes but that they certainly deserved Oscars.[116]

VII

Successes in managing the news media did not necessarily mean successes in managing public opinion. In the first place, the managerial successes were not necessarily in service of a single government strategy. The various uses of the news media by officials could cancel each other out. In 1955, even attentive elite publics had been confused by the conflicting leaks regarding Quemoy and the Matsus. The dances of officials and reporters, in any event, involved different sets of partners following different rhythms in different ballrooms. Sometimes the real story turned out to involve conflict among reporters' sources.

Harold Wilson's press officer, Joe Haines, complains that a picture of the prime minister as traitor to the European Economic Community idea was deliberately drawn by press officers of the Foreign and Colonial Office "suckled by a corps of highly paid British diplomatic correspondents."[117]

In the second place, it remains unclear whether or to what extent the news media influenced public opinion. Literature on this subject is voluminous and technical. To simplify: much research has validated Paul Lazarfeld's model of how opinion takes form. The mass of interested persons take their leads from a comparatively small group of "opinion leaders," thought to be particularly knowledgeable about the topic at hand. A study by Joseph T. Klapper, published in 1960, drew on a large body of survey data to conclude that neither the mass public nor "opinion leaders" were much affected by what they read in newspapers or magazines, heard on radio, or saw on television. Most people, Klapper found, noticed news that jibed with previously formed belief or attitudes. They ignored the rest.

Reanalyzing Klapper's data, other scholars later questioned his conclusion. They suggested that, while the news media might not have much effect on what people thought, they might have much to do with determining what people thought about. These scholars, in other words, emphasized the agenda-setting role of the news media. Subsequent studies have tended, however, to weaken rather than strengthen this hypothesis. The question of whether the news media have any power over what publics think remains open.[118]

It can nevertheless be credibly hypothesized that, via the news media, public opinion influenced government policy. The reason is the very preoccupation with management of the news media just described.[119] Over the course of the twentieth century, officials and political leaders came to feel increasingly dependent on and vulnerable to public opinion. They saw the various news media as their chief sources of access to the public. What else could have given them access? Even when they addressed the public directly, they had to worry about what points the news media might choose to highlight or ignore or what fifteen-second clips would be shown on television.

Because of the intensity of concern about impacts and images, officials and political leaders became acutely sensitive when the news media brought unexpected feedback. Assuming the news media to be hostile, they might try to discount this feedback as a product of bias or malice. Lyndon Johnson complained that, if he were to cross the Potomac River on foot, proving he could walk on water, the headline would read, "President Can't Swim."[120] Officials and political leaders nevertheless paid attention. Sometimes they even changed course.

The American war in Vietnam might seem an example. Certainly, the news media brought the government evidence of antiwar demonstrations. But officials and political leaders saw these demonstrations for themselves. They may have discounted some evidence of antiwar feeling because of conviction that the reporters were deliberately playing it up. Whatever the merit of this judgment about reporters, the instinct regarding the public may have been right, for poll data showed steadily high support for the war, and some of the data suggests that reportage on antiwar demonstrations had the effect of heightening this support, not weakening it.[121]

Better examples concern nuclear weapons. In 1955 German newspapers published details about a NATO exercise entitled "Carte Blanche." The exercise involved a simulated Soviet attack across the North German Plain, which NATO sought to check with tactical nuclear bombs and artillery warheads. According to these press stories, the exercise's judges had concluded that, if the battles had been real, minimum losses for Germany and France would have been 1.7 million dead and 3.5 million wounded, taking no account of future fatalities and injuries due to radiation. This story brought on a prolonged crisis in Bonn. This crisis and lasting memories of "Carte Blanche" had much to do with subsequent efforts inside NATO aimed at guaranteeing both that the Germans would have a voice in any decision for use of nuclear weapons and that, if there were a major war, it would not be limited to Europe but would entail immediate engagement of American strategic nuclear forces based in the continental United States.[122]

In June 1977 the *Washington Post* published a front-page story charging that the United States was planning to deploy to Europe a new "neutron bomb," a nuclear weapon that would cause damage more by radiation than by blast.[123] The *Post* headline used the phrase "killer warhead." For the better part of a month, new details and charges and countercharges kept the story on or near front pages of major American dailies and in lead segments of evening television news. A movement developed in Congress to block deployment of the weapons. President Jimmy Carter brought to bear enough influence to prevent passage of such a resolution.

At this point, European newspapers put the "killer warhead" on their front pages, for West German leftists mounted their own campaign to block deployments. Despite these stories and misgivings among many members of the Bundestag, Chancellor Helmut Schmidt declared himself willing to see the weapons deployed. Hearing clamor from both sides of the Atlantic, President Carter, however, reversed himself and announced that there would be no deployments. This backdown embarrassed and angered Schmidt and poisoned American–West German relations for the remainder of Carter's term.

Both in 1955 and in 1977, the news media had powerful influence on policy and on international relations. The reason was that they acted as conveyors of public attitudes. Officials easily forgot how ordinary citizens felt about nuclear weapons. They regarded them as weapons of deterrence, possibly even of war. Though making the statement for diplomatic effect rather than as an expression of his personal opinion, Eisenhower as president had articulated a view widespread within officialdom, particularly among the military, when he declared that nuclear weapons should be regarded as weapons, like bullets.

The public at large never adopted such an attitude, either in America or in Europe.

For reasons that Spencer Weart elaborates in his book, *Nuclear Fear,* ordinary citizens thought of the radiation effects of nuclear weapons as death rays akin to the long-dreaded effects of witches' spells.[124] For a time, many seemed fatalistically to accept the likelihood of nuclear cataclysm. Their vision was not of an occurrence produced by rational processes. Rather it was the scenario of the 1959 movie, *On the Beach,* where humankind was obliterated because of something inexplicable done somewhere by God knew who. As early as the 1960s, this vision had given way to the caricatures in Stanley Kubrick's *Dr. Strangelove: How I Learned to Stop Worrying and Love the Bomb.* The premise was that nuclear war could occur but, if so, it would be the work of madmen.

In 1955 insiders could debate seriously about how, when, and where to use tactical nuclear weapons in densely populated West and East Germany. To most ordinary citizens, the basic notion was lunatic. In the late 1970s, insiders could see the advantages of neutron bombs (properly, enhanced radiation weapons). Neutron bombs could stop a Soviet tank attack without obliterating the villages through which the tanks were moving. They would leave tank crews sitting inside their vehicles like fried eggs. They would unfortunately leave villagers in the same state. But any war has its downside.

What the news media did was to force upon officials the points of view of ordinary citizens. To some officials in the United States government, the original *Washington Post* story had been just an irritant. Their first reaction was to assume that the editors and reporters did not understand and needed to be educated. They tried—and failed. What they missed was the fact that the *Post* story appeared on page one—and stayed on page one there and in other newspapers and became a lead story on television—because the concept of the "killer warhead" horrified and fascinated large numbers of readers and viewers. Gatekeepers in West Germany and elsewhere in Europe recognized that readers and viewers there, too, reacted against the notion of nuclear weapons that would kill millions but leave houses as shells to be inspected later by tourists, once the radiation had dissipated.[125]

In these instances and in a few others, particularly ones involving human rights or human misery, the news media exerted great influence. Newspaper and newsmagazine buyers, radio listeners, and television watchers showed by their responses that these stories struck chords with them. Officials and political leaders were forced by this evidence to take into account attitudes and views that they might otherwise have ignored.

VIII

The news media probably became progressively less good at providing the public the wherewithal with which to judge foreign policy issues. Reductions in numbers of major newspapers, shrinkage in numbers of permanently assigned foreign correspondents, "parachute journalism," and too narrow a focus on too small a set of capitals reduced the ability of the news media to perform a broadly educative role.

All the same, the news media played large roles in international affairs after World War II. Newspapers, newsmagazines, radio, and especially television formed more and more of the environment in which foreign policy decisions were made and diplomatic negotiations conducted. Wanting public support and fearing public criticism, decision-makers and diplomats spent more and more of their time and energy trying to control stories in the press and images broadcast over television. They were comparatively successful. The result was not, however, to give them greater control over the public. It was rather to give the public greater control over them. Simply by showing interest in particular stories, as, for example, that about the neutron bomb, the public could evidence and give force to attitudes or views that officials might have disregarded. Though the news media might in some respects have been weaker than in earlier eras, and more subject to influence from government, they were a vehicle that allowed the voice of the public to become relatively more powerful.

Despite the many and transforming changes he had witnessed during his decades as reporter, editor, and columnist, Walter Lippmann, for one, never lost faith in the importance of his craft and its relationship to the discussion and formation of public and international policy. As he told the National Press Club in Washington at a luncheon in honor of his seventieth birthday in September 1957:

> If the country is to be governed with the consent of the governed, then the governed must arrive at opinions about what their governors want them to consent to. How do they do this?
>
> They do it by hearing on the radio and reading in the newspapers what the corps of correspondents tell them is going on in Washington, and in the country at large, and in the world. Here, we correspondents perform an essential service. In some fields of interest, we make it our business to find out what is going on under the surface and beyond the horizon, to infer, to deduce, to imagine, and to guess what is going on inside, what this meant yesterday, and what it could mean tomorrow.
>
> In this we do what every sovereign citizen is supposed to do but has not the time or the interest to do for himself. This is our job. It is no mean calling. We have a right to be proud of it and to be glad that it is our work.[126]

In the years that followed, which would include Vietnam and Watergate, that special calling of which Lippmann had spoken became no less important. Indeed to the end of the 1970s—whatever the vicissitudes of the diplomats and diplomacy discussed earlier in this volume—the news media had much to do with creating the environment for all international relationships. Officials and political leaders everywhere "operated wet."

Notes

1. John J. Fialka, *Hotel Warriors: Covering the Gulf War* (Washington, D.C., 1991), 27.

2. Michael Ledeen, cited in Simon Serfaty, ed., *The Media and Foreign Policy* (London, 1990), xiv.

3. David R. Gergen, "Diplomacy in a Television Age," in Serfaty, *Media and Foreign Policy*, especially 47–48; James F. Larson, "Global Television and Foreign Policy," Foreign Policy Association *Headline Series*, no. 283 (February 1988): 48; W. A. Ajibola, *Foreign Policy and Public Opinion: A Case Study of British Foreign Policy over the Nigerian Civil War* (Ibadan, 1978).

4. Jeremy Tunstall, *The Media Are American* (New York, 1977).

5. Harold Nicolson, *Diplomacy*, 2d ed. (London, 1950), 97; Sidney B. Fay, *The Origins of the World War*, 2d ed. (New York, 1948), 1:47. Joseph Klaits, "Censorship Under Louis XIV," *Proceedings of the Annual Meeting of the Western Society for French Historians*, no. 2 (1974): 104–16, describes press management well before Utrecht, and so, despite its title, does Jeremy Black, "The Press, the Party and Foreign Policy in the Reign of George I," *Publishing History* 13 (1983): 23–40.

6. Arthur F. Bentley, *The Process of Government*, new ed. (Cambridge, Mass., 1967). See Dan Nimmo and James E. Combs, *Mediated Political Realities*, 2d ed. (New York, 1990), xi–xiii.

7. Fred Allen, a radio comedian, said that radio was called a medium "because it was seldom well done." After television had come along, newspaper columnist Jimmy Breslin suggested that "media" was "the plural of mediocre." Richard M. Clurman, *Beyond Malice: The Media's Years of Reckoning* (New Brunswick, N.J., 1988), 13.

8. Walter Lippmann, *Public Opinion* (New York, 1922), 32.

9. Ralph O. Nafziger, *International News and the Press: Communications, Organization of News-Gathering, International Affairs and the Foreign Press: An Annotated Bibliography* (New York, 1940).

10. Bernard C. Cohen, *The Press and Foreign Policy* (Princeton, 1963).

11. Lippmann, *Public Opinion*, 29.

12. Cohen, *Press and Foreign Policy*, 12–13.

13. As the authoritative *Annual Register* for 1914 put it: "Doubtless the German Government counted on civil strife [over Ireland] to paralyse British efforts at resistance to its schemes." [London, 1915], 258. For contemporary press coverage, see for instance *The History of The Times*, vol. 4 (1912–1948) (London, 1952), 193 ff.

14. Remarks to reporters at the First Press Conference, 22 Mar. 1913, Arthur S. Link et al., eds., *The Papers of Woodrow Wilson* (Princeton, 1978), 27:210–13.

15. Nicolson, *Diplomacy*, 97.

16. Anthony Smith, "The Newspaper of the Late Twentieth Century: The U.S. Model," in *Newspapers and Democracy: International Essays on a Changing Medium*, ed. Anthony Smith (Cambridge, Mass., 1980), 9–10; Colin Seymour-Ure, *The British Press and Broadcasting Since 1945* (London, 1991), chap. 3.

17. Claude Bellanger, *Histoire Générale de la Presse Française* (Paris, 1976) 5:473.

18. Mort Rosenblum, *Coups and Earthquakes: Reporting the World for America* (New York, 1979), 9, 29.

19. Oliver Boyd-Barrett, "The Collection of Foreign News in the National Press," Part A of Royal Commission on the Press, *Studies on the Press* (London, 1977), 15–19.

20. Jim Richstad, "Transnational News Agencies: Issues and Policies," 242–57, Jeremy Tunstall, "Worldwide News Agencies: Private Wholesalers of Public Information," 258–70, and Mort Rosenblum, "Reporting from the Third World," 224–26, all in *Crisis in International News: Policies and Prospects,* ed. Jan Richstad and Michael H. Anderson (New York, 1981); Bellanger, *Histoire Générale de la Presse Française,* 5:426–31.

21. Bellanger, *Histoire Générale de la Presse Française,* 5:431.

22. Gergen, "Diplomacy in a Television Age," 52.

23. Bellanger, *Histoire Générale de la Presse Française,* 5:400–401.

24. Klaus Wenger, *Kommunikation und Medien in der Bundesrepublik Deutschland* (Munich, 1988), 28–29.

25. Quoted in Barry Rubin, *International News and the American Media* (Beverly Hills, 1977), 20.

26. Rosenblum, *Coups and Earthquakes,* 28.

27. See J. Fred MacDonald, *Don't Touch that Dial: Radio Programming in American Life, 1920–1960* (Chicago, 1979), Philip M. Taylor, *The Projection of Britain: British Overseas Publicity and Propaganda, 1919–1939* (Cambridge, Eng., 1980), and Jean-Louis Crémieux-Brilhac, *Les Français de l'an 40* (Paris, 1990), 1: chap. 3.

28. Seymour-Ure, *British Press,* chap. 1.

29. Michael Cockerell, *Live from Number 10: The Inside Story of Prime Ministers and Television* (London, 1988), xiii.

30. Seymour-Ure, *British Press,* 76–77.

31. Bellanger, *Histoire Générale de la Presse Française,* 5:185, 238; Arthur Williams, *Broadcasting and Democracy in West Germany* (London, 1976), 51.

32. Ellen Propper Mickiewicz, *Media and the Russian Public* (New York, 1981), 18.

33. Larson, "Global Television and Foreign Policy," 20–21.

34. Erik Barnouw, *Tube of Plenty: The Evolution of American Television* (New York, 1990), 308–14 and 494–97; and W. E. McCavitt, ed., *Broadcasting Around the World* (Blue Ridge Summit, Pa.), summarize developments; James W. Romand, *Cablemania* (Englewood Cliffs, N.J., 1983), explains the complex reality under the label *cable;* George H. Quester, *The International Politics of Television* (Lexington, Mass., 1990), chap. 5, supplies an elegant analysis of the implications.

35. See Hank Whittemore, *CNN: The Inside Story* (Boston, 1990).

36. See Gerald Mansell, *Let Truth Be Told: 50 Years of BBC External Broadcasting* (Oxford, 1982).

37. See Sig Mickelson, *America's Other Voice: Radio Free Europe and Radio Liberty* (New York, 1983).

38. Tunstall, *The Media Are American,* 48.

39. Peter Marshall, "Visnews: TV News Flow and Satellites," 279–83, and Jonathan King, "Visnews and UPITN: News Film Supermarkets in the Sky," 283–99, both in *Crisis in International News,* ed. Richstad and Anderson.

40. Quester, *International Politics of Television,* 126 ff.

41. Ellen Propper Mickiewicz, *Split Signals: Television and Politics in the Soviet*

Union (New York, 1988); Leonard Pratt, "The Circuitry of Protest: Electronic Journalism in China, 1989," *Gannett Center Journal* (Fall 1989), unpaged.

42. Quoted in Royal Commission on the Press, Working Paper no. 2: Denis McQuail, *Review of Sociological Writing on the Press* (London, 1976), 12.

43. Hugh Cudlipp, *The Prerogative of the Harlot: Press Barons and Power* (London, 1980). The quotation is from p. 82.

44. Antoine de Tarlé, "The Press and the State in France," in Smith, *Newspapers and Democracy,* 129–33.

45. Hans Dieter Muller, *Press Power: A Study of Axel Springer* (London, 1969); Martin Walker, *Powers of the Press: Twelve of the World's Influential Newspapers* (New York, 1982), chap. 4.

46. Friedheim Kremna, quoted in Walker, *Powers of the Press,* 96.

47. On *Die Welt* after Springer's retreat, see Karl Heinz Harenberg, *"Die Welt,"* in *Porträts der deutschen Presse: Politik und Profit,* ed. Michael Wolf Thomas (Berlin, 1980), 109–26.

48. Leon V. Sigal, *Reporters and Officials: The Organization and Politics of Newsmaking* (Lexington, Mass., 1973), 9.

49. William Shawcross, *Rupert Murdoch, Ringmaster of the Information Circus* (London, 1992), 186. Joe Haines, *Maxwell* (London, 1988), 393–95. (Though Haines's book is an authorized biography, he writes with the authority of an editor who initially fought Maxwell and as a former press aide to a prime minister.)

50. Sally Bedell Smith, *In All His Glory: The Life of William S. Paley, the Legendary Tycoon and His Brilliant Circle* (New York, 1990), though an exposé, points to little political activity by the legendary "Chairman" of CBS other than cooperation with the CIA in the 1950s and flattery of Nixon in hope of an ambassadorial appointment. In fact, as Smith reports (pp. 473 ff.), Paley found CBS, along with other elements of the news media, a target of attacks by the Nixon White House inspired by hope of thus muffling criticism of the Vietnam War. For William L. Shirer's version, see his *A Native's Return, 1945–1988,* vol. 3 of *Twentieth Century Journey* (Boston, 1990).

51. Bellanger, *Histoire Générale de la Presse Française,* 5:396–99, 427–28; for more, see Hubert Beuve-Méry, *Réflexions politiques (1932–1952)* (Paris, 1951), and *Onze ans du règne (1958–1969)* (Paris, 1974).

52. Mansell, *Let Truth Be Told,* and Asa Briggs, *The BBC, the First Fifty Years* (Oxford, 1985), chap. 6.

53. Laurie Ann Alexandre, "Broadcasting Public Diplomacy: The Voice of America During Détente and Beyond" (Ph.D. thesis, 1985, University of California, Irvine); Muhammad Ibrahim Ayish, "The Voice of America Between Diplomacy and Journalism: A Case Study of the VOA Arabic Service" (Ph.D. thesis, 1986, University of Minnesota); Enoch Albert Moffett, III, "Voice of America News: An Organizational Study of its Struggle for Objectivity (Ph.D. thesis, 1987, University of Georgia). Mickelson, *America's Other Voice,* 72, notes that Radio Free Europe broadcasters were equally mulish about accepting guidance from the CIA.

54. David Manning White, "The Gate Keeper: A Case Study in Selection of News," *Journalism Quarterly* 27, no. 4 (1950): 383–90.

55. There is a good summary by Smith in his essay in Smith, *Newspapers and Democracy,* 5–48.

56. Gay Talese, *The Kingdom and the Power* (New York, 1969), 212.

57. Sigal, *Reporters and Officials* (Lexington, Mass., 1973), 21.

58. Herbert J. Gans, *Deciding What's News: A Study of CBS Evening News, NBC Nightly News, Newsweek, and Time* (New York, 1979), 84. Stephen Hess, *The Washington Reporters* (Washington, D.C., 1981), 42–43, makes the point, however, that newspaper bureaus are less bureaucratic than other organizations of comparable size and complexity, largely because of reporters' horror of bureaucracy. On the bureaucratization of journalism, see, in addition to Sigal, Gans, and Hess, Gaye Tuchman, *Making News: A Study in the Construction of Reality* (New York, 1978), which is based on extended observation of both newspaper and television newsrooms.

59. Quoted in Sigal, *Reporters and Officials,* 101.

60. "Tilting at Windmills," *Washington Monthly* 10 (February 1979): 7. J. V. Vilanilam, *Reporting a Revolution: The Iranian Revolution and the NIICO Debate* (New Delhi, 1989), makes interesting comparisons between coverage in the American press and in the Indian press, citing a number of points overlooked by the former but noticed by the latter.

61. Bellanger, *Histoire Générale de la Presse Française,* 5:211; Larson, "Global Television and Foreign Policy," 22–23.

62. Rosenblum, *Coups and Earthquakes,* 10–12. Larson, "Global Television and Foreign Policy," 40, cites criticism of this practice (also called the "firehouse model" of journalism) by television news anchors John Chancellor and Charles Collingwood.

63. Mort Rosenblum, "Special Correspondent Quixote," *Gannett Center Journal* (Fall 1989), unpaged.

64. Arthur Ponsonby, quoted in DeWitt C. Poole, *The Conduct of Foreign Relations under Modern Democratic Conditions* (New Haven, 1924), 137.

65. V. O. Key, *Public Opinion and American Democracy* (New York, 1961), 173–74; Robert W. Oldendick and Barbara Ann Bardes, "Mass and Elite Foreign Policy Opinions," *Public Opinion Quarterly* 45 (Winter 1982), 368–82.

66. Sigal, *Reporters and Officials,* 1.

67. Larson, "Global Television and Foreign Policy," 39.

68. See Vanderbilt University, *Television News Index and Abstracts* (1975–1976), under index for "Angola"; for samples of print reportage: *Time* 105 (26 May 1975): 32; *Time* 106 (28 July 1975): 25; *Time* 106 (29 Dec. 1975): 7. On the general subject, see Beverly G. Hawk, ed., *Africa's Media Image* (New York, 1992), index under "Angola," and Elaine Windrich, *The Cold War Guerrilla: Jonas Savimbi, the U.S. Media, and the Angolan War* (New York, 1992).

69. Norman A. Bailey and Richard Cohen, *The Mexican Time Bomb* (New York, 1987).

70. Penelope Hartland-Thunberg, "Vulnerabilities of the International Financial Mechanism," Georgetown University, Center for Strategic and International Studies: *Significant Issues Series* 5, no. 1 (1983): 11.

71. "What the Market Will Bear: The CIA and the International Debt Crisis," John F. Kennedy School of Government, Harvard University, Case Program Case no. C16-91-1032-0 (1991).

72. James Reston, *The Artillery of the Press: Its Influence on American Foreign Policy* (New York, 1966), 30–31.

73. Henry L. Stimson and McGeorge Bundy, *On Active Service in Peace and War* (New York, 1948), 393.

74. James MacGregor Burns, *Roosevelt: The Soldier of Freedom* (New York, 1970), 211.

75. Kalb, in the foreword to Serfaty, *The Media and Foreign Policy,* xvi.

76. Herbert Y. Schandler, *Lyndon Johnson and Vietnam: The Unmaking of a President* (Princeton, 1977); the quotation from Christian is on p. 197.

77. See *inter alia* Peter Braestrup, *Big Story: How the American Press and Television Reported and Interpreted the Crisis of Tet 1968 in Vietnam and Washington,* 2 vols. (Boulder, Colo., 1977); and Stanley Karnow, *Vietnam: A History* (New York, 1983), chap. 14.

78. Bellanger, *Histoire Générale de la Presse Française,* 3:352, 424–25, 446, 450–51; Mohamed Kirat, "Partiality and Biases: The Coverage of the Algerian Liberation War (1954–1962) by *Al-Ahram* and *Le Monde,*" *International Journal for Mass Communication Studies* 44, no. 3 (1989): 155–75.

79. Patrick O'Donovan, quoted in Douglass Cater, *The Fourth Branch of Government* (New York, 1959), 7–8.

80. Reston, *Artillery of the Press,* especially chap. 5, and *Deadline: A Memoir* (New York, 1991), 138; Cater, *Fourth Branch,* 96–101; Sigal, *Reporters and Officials,* 43, 77–78. Abundant evidence of columnists' dependence on sources is in Lloyd Tataryn, *The Pundits: Power, Politics, and the Press* (Toronto, 1985), a breezy report on interviews with columnists in the United States, the United Kingdom, and Canada.

81. Hans Kroll, *Lebenserinnerungen eines Botschafters* (Cologne, 1967), 548–54; Catherine McArdle Kelleher, *Germany and the Politics of Nuclear Weapons* (New York, 1975), 172–88.

82. Annabelle May and Kathryn Rowan, eds., *Inside Information: British Government and the Media* (London, 1982), 79–88.

83. Ross Koen, *The China Lobby in American Politics* (New York, 1974); Russ Braley, *Bad News: The Foreign Policy of The New York Times* (Chicago, 1984). The accusations were not totally fanciful. Some journalists did get China, Cuba, and Nicaragua wrong. On the other hand, in none of the three cases did all journalists report the same way. See Kenneth E. Shewmaker, *Americans and Chinese Communists 1927–1945: A Persuading Encounter* (Ithaca, 1971); Stephen R. Mackinnon and Oris Friesen, *China Reporting: An Oral History of American Journalism in the 1930s and 1940s* (Berkeley, 1987); Theodore Draper, *Castro's Revolution: Myths and Realities* (New York, 1962); and Joshua Muravchik, *News Coverage of the Sandinista Revolution* (Washington, D.C., 1988).

84. Cockerell, *Live from Number 10,* 7, 48, 134.

85. Jef Verschueren, *International News Reporting: Pragmatic Metaphors and the U-2* (Amsterdam, 1985).

86. Cockerell, *Live from Number 10,* 87.

87. See Gans, *Reporting the News,* 36–38; Mervin D. Lynch and Atiya Effendi, "Editorial Treatment of India in the *New York Times,*" *Journalism Quarterly* 41, no. 3 (1964): 430–32; Haluk Sahin, "Turkish Politics in the *New York Times,*" *Journalism Quarterly* 50, no. 4 (1973): 685–89; John A. Lent, "Foreign News in the American Media," *Journal of Communication* 27, no. 1 (1977): 46–51; Manny Paraschos, "News Coverage of Cyprus: A Case Study in Press Treatment of Foreign Policy Issues," *Journal of Political and Military Sociology* 16, no. 2 (1988): 201–13; Vilanilam, *Reporting a Revolution.* For an example of more polemical writing in this vein, see W. Lance Bennett, *News, The Politics of Illusion* (New York, 1983).

88. Quoted in Larson, "Global Television and Foreign Policy," 5.

89. Quoted in Rubin, *International News and the American Media*, 8.

90. Lippmann, *Public Opinion*, 344.

91. Quoted in Sigal, *Reporters and Officials*, 131.

92. David Morgan, *The Flacks of Washington: Government Information and the Public Agenda* (New York, 1986), 19–25.

93. Dan D. Nimmo, *Newsgathering in Washington* (New York, 1964).

94. Quoted in Cater, *Fourth Branch*, 115–16.

95. Robert Manning, *The Swamp Root Chronicle: Adventures in the Word Trade* (New York, 1992), 231; Phil G. Goulding, *Confirm or Deny* (New York, 1970), 220–21.

96. Walter Pincus, quoted in Sigal, *Reporters and Officials*, 127.

97. Cater, *Fourth Branch*, 129–30.

98. Morton H. Halperin, *Bureaucratic Politics and Foreign Policy* (Washington, D.C., 1974), chap. 10.

99. Stephen Hess, *The Government-Press Connection: Press Officers and their Offices* (Washington, D.C., 1984), and *The Ultimate Insiders: U.S. Senators in the National Media* (Washington, D.C., 1986), 106–7.

100. Both Gans, *Deciding What's News*, and Sigal, *Reporters and Officials*, develop the market analogy.

101. Quoted in Robert J. McCloskey, "The Care and Handling of Leaks," in Serfaty, *Media and Foreign Policy*, 114.

102. Quoted in Sigal, *Reporters and Officials*, 48.

103. Gans, *Deciding What's News*, 34. On the general issue: Richard V. Ericson, Patricia M. Baranek, and Janet B. L. Chan, *Negotiating Control: A Study of News Sources* (Toronto, 1989).

104. James Margach, *The Abuse of Power: The War Between Downing Street and the Media from Lloyd George to Callaghan* (London, 1978), 1.

105. David Schoenbrun, *On and Off the Air: An Informal History of CBS News* (New York, 1989), 88.

106. Cockerell, *Live from Number 10*, 45–46.

107. Ibid., 64.

108. Ibid.

109. Ibid., 93.

110. Louis Galambos et al., eds., *NATO and the Campaign of 1952*, vol. 13 of *The Papers of David Dwight Eisenhower* (Baltimore, 1989), 1257.

111. Cockerell, *Live from Number 10*, 140–41.

112. Jean-Jacques Servan-Schreiber, quoted in Bellanger, *Histoire Générale de la Presse Française*, 5:180; de Gaulle quoted in James Martin, *Telematic Society* (Englewood Cliffs, N.J., 1981), 50.

113. Richard M. Nixon, *Leaders* (New York, 1982), 342.

114. Theodore H. White, *America in Search of Itself: The Making of the President, 1956–1960* (New York, 1982), 195.

115. Cockerell, *Live from Number 10*, chaps. 12–13.

116. Rosenblum, *Coups and Earthquakes*, 134.

117. Joe Haines, *The Politics of Power* (London, 1977), 74–81. Henry James, "The Role of the Central Office of Information," in May and Rowan, *Inside Information*,

186–88, asserts that the civil service provides the press "objective statements of the truth so far as it can be determined, dispassionately, objectively and practically," unlike ministers who hand out "hundreds of politically calculated releases."

118. Paul F. Lazarsfeld and Elihu Katz, *Personal Influence: The Part Played by People in the Flow of Communications* (New York, 1955); Joseph Klapper, *The Effects of Mass Communication* (New York, 1960); Gladys E. Lang and Kurt Lang, *The Battle for Public Opinion* (New York, 1983); Maxwell E. McCombs and Donald L. Shaw, "The Agenda-setting Function of Mass Media," *Public Opinion Quarterly* 36 (Summer 1972): 176–87; Sidney Kraus and Dennis Davis, *The Effects of Mass Communication on Political Behavior* (University Park, Pa., 1976); Jack M. McLeod and Byron Reeves, "On the Nature of Mass Media Effects," in *Television and Social Behavior,* ed. Stephen B. Withey and Ronald P. Abeles (Hillsdale, N.J., 1980); Cliff Zutkin, "Mass Communication and Public Opinion," in *Handbook of Political Communication,* eds. Dan D. Nimmo and Keith R. Sanders (Beverly Hills, Calif., 1986); W. Russell Neuman, *The Paradox of Mass Politics* (Cambridge, Mass., 1986); Klaus Bruhn Jensen, *Making Sense of the News* (Aarhus, Denmark, 1986); Barrie Gunter, *Poor Reception: Misunderstanding and Forgetting Broadcast News* (Hillsdale, N.J., 1987); Leo Bogart, *Press and Public,* 2d ed. (Hillsdale, N.J., 1989); W. Russell Neuman, Marion R. Just, and Ann N. Crigler, *Common Knowledge: News and the Construction of Political Meaning* (Chicago, 1992). The last-cited puts forward a "constructionist" model, arguing that the process is interactive, with readers or viewers picking their subjects and their media but then in some degree borrowing media evaluations.

119. This point is skillfully developed in Martin Linsky, *Impact: How the Press Affects Federal Policymaking* (New York, 1986).

120. Clurman, *Beyond Malice,* 18.

121. In 1967, 64 percent said television made them feel more like "backing up the boys in Vietnam": Rubin, *International News and the American Media,* 29. J. Fred MacDonald, *Television and the Red Menace: The Video Road to Vietnam* (New York, 1985), argues that biased television reportage for a dozen years before the mid-1960s had conditioned the public to support such a war. He describes the reporters who criticized the war after the mid-1960s as showing new independence and responsibility. James D. Halloran, Philip Elliot, and Graham Murdock, *Demonstrations and Communication: A Case Study* (London, 1970), provides strong evidence that reporters did, indeed, exaggerate antiwar demonstrations.

122. Hans Speier, *German Rearmament and Atomic War* (White Plains, N.Y., 1957), is the most detailed account. Kelleher, *Germany and the Politics of Nuclear Weapons,* 34–44, and Mark Cioc, *Pax Atomica: The Nuclear Defense Debate in West Germany During the Adenauer Era* (New York, 1988), 21–37, analyze the long-term effects of the disclosures.

123. The best account is David Whitman, "The Press and the Neutron Bomb," in *How the Press Affects Federal Policymaking: Six Case Studies,* ed. Martin Linsky et al. (New York, 1986), 145–217.

124. Spencer Weart, *Nuclear Fear, A History of Images* (Cambridge, Mass., 1988), especially chap. 3.

125. As is indicated in Thomas W. Graham, *American Public Opinion on NATO, Extended Deterrence, and Use of Nuclear Weapons: Future Fission?* (Lanham, Md., 1989), attentive publics supported the general strategy of nuclear deterrence, but in

America as in Europe they recoiled from anything suggesting deliberate use of nuclear weapons. Evidence on the general skepticism of the American public regarding the "nuclear freeze" movement of the early 1980s is further testimony that reaction to the "neutron bomb" was not just unsophisticated repugnance: J. Michael Hogan and Ted J. Smith, III, "Polling on the Issues: Public Opinion and the Nuclear Freeze," *Public Opinion Quarterly* 55 (Spring 1991): 534–69.

126. Ronald Steel, *Walter Lippmann and the American Century* (Boston 1980), 515.

AFTERWORD

A S THE DECADE of the 1970s ended, a diplomatic observer with a literary bent, talking with a colleague about all the unfinished tasks of peace, might well have quoted the words of Schiller's hero Wallenstein:

> Leave them alone, Seni. Let us go.
> The new dawn breaks with Mars in the ascendant.

After the high hopes of the détente period, mankind seemed headed for a new age of conflict. The Red Army was becoming daily more deeply involved in Afghanistan, surrogate wars were raging in Angola and Nicaragua, the British were embroiled in a dispute with Argentina that was to prove irreconcilable, and in Iraq Saddam Hussein's ambitious regime had plunged into a bitter conflict with revolutionary Iran that was to rage for years. No less important was the fact that, beginning with the Carter administration in late 1979 and intensifying in the early Reagan years, the United States government was concerned that the progress made by the Soviet Union in building up its military strength during the previous twenty years was merely the prologue to a possible attack upon vital American national security interests, commencing with the invasion of Afghanistan in the oil rich Middle East.

The future, then, seemed forbidding. Yet if our imaginary diplomat had let his mind turn on history rather than literature, it is possible that he would have been consoled rather than depressed. If he had reflected upon the previous four decades, he could not have failed to remember that they had begun with mankind facing a host of problems more formidable than those that loomed before him in 1979, and that the most dangerous of them had been solved and the most persistent of them brought under some degree of control by human courage, patience, and ingenuity in devising instruments of containment, deterrence, conciliation, and compromise.

The period that has been covered in this volume began with the outbreak of a terrible war, which, in 1941–1942, in the dark months following Pearl Harbor, the Axis powers had come close to winning. That possibility, with all the grim consequences it would have brought to the free nations of the world, was avoided; but the end of the conflict in the summer of 1945 found Western diplomacy, which had not entirely distinguished itself during the war years, perilously unprepared for the trials that awaited it. Chief among these was the possibility of a confrontation with the Soviet Union, the first signs of which had begun to appear nearly a year earlier. Having failed to anticipate the renewal of ideological conflict with Moscow, it took the United States and its Western allies several years to regain their bearings in the postwar world. The war had irrevocably destroyed the international system that had laid down the rules and regulated the forms of interstate relations during most of the nineteenth century and (although much enfeebled by ideological divisions) the two decades that followed the war of 1914–1918. What was to take its place? How was the readmission of the defeated powers to the society of nations to be regulated? How was new aggression to be contained? How was peace to be assured in an ideologically torn world?

It cannot be claimed that the great powers, in the forty years that followed the war's end, succeeded in finding satisfactory answers to all of these questions, the last of them least of all. But in the most critical strategical areas in the ideological struggle, and the ones most threatened in the first postwar years, Europe and the Middle East, the democratic nations were able to establish a security system that protected local independence and provided the possibility of recovery from the ravages of the war. In a burst of creative energy unmatched in modern times, Western leaders, diplomats, and politicians responded to Soviet threats to Afghanistan, Greece and Turkey, and Berlin in the late forties with a series of striking policy initiatives that began with the Truman Doctrine in March 1947, continued with the Marshall Plan in June 1947, and culminated in the establishment of the North Atlantic Treaty Organization in April 1949, which declared in its fifth article that an attack on one of its signatories in Europe would be considered an attack on all. In the history of Western diplomacy, NATO is remarkable as representing the first permanent alliance made by the United States in peacetime, and this linkage between American policy and the fate of Europe became the central pillar of the system of containment that helped stabilize relations between Western Europe and members of the Soviet bloc of nations in the period covered by this book.

In the realm of economic policy, Western diplomacy—led by Americans like Secretary of State George C. Marshall, Under Secretary of State Dean Acheson, and Under Secretary of State for Economic Affairs William L. Clayton—was determined by a desire to avoid the experience of the interwar period, during which the United States had withdrawn behind a barrier of steadily rising protective tariffs and left Europe to its fate. In contrast, Washington now became the leading exponent of a cooperative economic order, which in turn encouraged a new generation of European leaders—men like Jean Monnet, Robert Schuman, Konrad Adenauer, Alcide de Gasperi, and Paul-Henri Spaak—to develop new economic structures that had often been talked about in the past but never attained. This was the background of the European Coal and Steel Community, established in May 1952, and the historic treaty of Rome, signed on 25 March 1957. The European Economic Community that resulted from these basic agreements—it shortened its name in 1967 to European Community—was viewed almost from the first less as a merely functional organization than as comprehensive economic-political structure, federalist and confederalist in nature. It was through membership in the EEC that the new Federal Republic of Germany became more firmly integrated into the Atlantic association and—although Charles de Gaulle, no friend of supernational ideas and institutions, might not have liked to admit it—the EEC served as an invaluable backdrop for the Franco-German Treaty of Friendship of January 1963, which brought an end to generations of conflict between the two nations.

Leaving these measures of containment and economic reinvigoration aside, Western diplomacy was less successful in addressing the more difficult task of building political structures that would bridge the gap between East and West and overcome ideological conflict. Insofar as there emerged a new international order in this period, it was the Cold War itself, a bipolar system in which two superpowers, each with its satellites and allies, competed for power and influence. As a system, it precluded neither crisis nor local war. Its precarious balance was maintained by rough parity in armaments between the superpowers, which discouraged resort to all-out war between them, and by the ability of the diplomats on both sides to defuse or control dangerous confrontations or, like the Polish foreign minister, Adam Rapacki, to emphasize the inherent dangers of the status quo by devising substitutes for it.

The achievement of the diplomats in these dangerous decades was surely not inconsiderable. In the first place, although they often failed to avert war—in Korea, for example, where it is now clear that the Soviets encouraged the North Korean aggression in June 1950, although that aggression may have been inspired by an imprecise definition of American security interests by the United States secretary of state, and in the Suez crisis in late 1956, where as Victor H. Feske has demonstrated above, the British and French governments deliberately excluded the diplomats from the decision-making process—they were successful in terminating others, like the Yom Kippur War of October 1973, and in averting those that might have led to all-out nuclear exchanges. At the same time, the fact that the United States and the Soviet Union did not go to war during these years, although there were moments during the period that extended from the Khrushchev Berlin Note to the Cuban missile crisis when resort to war seemed likely, is surely a tribute to the expedients of diplomacy and to those who wielded them. This proves perhaps the validity of Jules Cambon's remark:

Expressions such as "old diplomacy" and "new diplomacy" bear no relation to reality. It is the outward form—if you like, the "adornments"—of diplomacy that are undergoing a change. The substance must remain the same, since human nature is unalterable; since there exists no other method of regulating international differences; and since the best instrument at the disposal of a Government wishing to persuade another Government will always remain the spoken words of a decent man (la parole d'un bonnête homme).

In the case of Vietnam, the longest and bloodiest series of wars in the whole period, American diplomats were prevented from negotiating a timely and durable end to the conflict by public clamor in the Western democracies for early withdrawal, a situation North Vietnamese diplomats were able to exploit.

In the second place, the security treaties of the fifties and those that created the Common Market, as well as those that were negotiated with the states of Eastern Europe by Willy Brandt, Egon Bahr, and Georg Ferdinand Duckwitz in the seventies, had an importance that went beyond their texts. The same can be said for the summit meeting at Camp David in September 1978 (one of the rare summits in these years that had a positive issue), and the accord that was fashioned there between Egypt and Israel. Here was a precedent and a model for the "Declaration of Principles" signed by Itzhak Rabin and Yassir Arafat at the White House in September 1993 with all the hopes that it bears for peace in the Middle East.

In the third place, in some ways the best example of the varied uses to which diplomacy can be put in the modern world was the evolution of the United Nations, discussed above in the chapter of Paul Gordon Lauren. Perhaps the organization's finest hour was that in which Secretary-General Dag Hammarskjöld defied Khrushchev's attempt to subvert the organization's purpose, declaring that his duty was not to obey great power dictation but to serve the interests of its members. Hammarskjöld was reminding the Soviet leader that the UN was a global organization rather than an American-Soviet preserve, and his declaration also reflected one of the most important developments in the world of diplomacy in this and the subsequent period, namely, the increasing desire of the lesser powers to escape from great power domination.

This of course was not new. Even at the Congress of Vienna there had been complaints about the larger powers' attempts to arrogate to themselves special prerogatives. But in the years 1939–1979 the desire for independence was much stronger. It was seen in the attractions of the doctrine of nonalignment proclaimed at the Bandung conference, in the jubilation of the lesser states when the balance of power in the UN Assembly shifted in their favor in 1973, and in the way in which the small powers and neutrals at the Helsinki Conference successfully pressured the superpowers into accepting measures for the protection of human rights.

Two other developments during this period should be mentioned because of their importance after 1979 and the influence they had in overcoming the dangers and dissipating the fears mentioned at the outset of these remarks. The first, beginning in the seventies and increasing rapidly thereafter, was the atrophying of the ideological motive within each of the great power blocs. In 1980, the West German journalist Peter Bender wrote of the failure of the Afghanistan crisis to engage the passions of anybody but the Americans and the Russians: "The crisis that erupted as a result of Afghanistan was different from all comparable crises earlier. It was the first East-West conflict that did not strengthen the alliances but divided them. . . . The Europeans from the Bug to the Atlantic distanced themselves from their superpowers." In the hearts and minds of many, indeed, détente seemed to have made a more lasting impression than it had done upon their governments. This was shown by the strong opposition of liberal West Europeans to the new American rearmament policy, initially suggested and supported by the Bonn government. This opposition was reflected in an appreciable amount of anti-American feeling in West Germany in particular and was illustrated in striking fashion by the fact that in 1979, as relations between the United States and the Soviet Union reached their nadir, the relationship between the Federal Republic and the East German regime was warmer than it had been since 1949. Similarly, the Polish Communist government, facing the increasing challenge of the Solidarity movement, showed no interest in Afghanistan and, indeed, chose the year 1980 for new experiments in autonomy. This failure of communist ideology was a principal reason for the loosening, and eventually the voluntary renunciation, of Soviet control over Eastern Europe at the end of the eighties.

Allied with this was the steadily mounting cost of supporting the Cold War as the decades passed. This had always borne more heavily upon the Soviet Union than upon the United States, for, as Norman Stone has pointed out above, it was a country with a Third World economy that was incapable even of feeding its own people adequately but nevertheless insisted upon maintaining its position as a military superpower. In the end, Afghanistan and the American arms buildup proved the straws that broke the Soviet imperial back and ushered in *perestroika* and all that followed. But the other superpower was by no means exempt from these burdens, although they took somewhat longer to make themselves apparent. What Afghanistan was to the Soviet Union, Ronald Reagan's decision to spend an additional $1 trillion over four years on the armed forces was to the United States. Partly as a result of the unprecedented peacetime deficits that followed, it lost its leading position in the world economy, became heavily dependent on foreign creditors, jeopardized the health of domestic industry, and forfeited much of its ability to protect its interests abroad through the application of economic pressures. Thus did their sins of commission and omission during the years 1939–1979 avenge themselves in the end upon the two superpowers, leading to the disintegration of the Soviet Union and the serious weakening of the United States in the search for a new world order after the Cold War had come to an end in 1990–1991.

If the striking improvement in East-West relations since the middle eighties can, to a considerable extent, be attributed to the renewed operation of traditional diplomacy, so also can the peaceful reunification of Germany in October 1990, an extraordinary achievement that had eluded even Otto von Bismarck at the height of his powers in the late 1860s. It was a development that seemed unimaginable in the days of Konrad Adenauer and Willy Brandt, whose political successors lost no time rushing in to claim their share of the credit for the establishment of a free and united Germany.

But that is another story, and it, and the role played by a new generation of statesmen and diplomats—Ronald Reagan and George Bush, Margaret Thatcher and François Mitterand, Helmut Kohl and Lech Walesa, George Shultz and Eduard Shevardnadze, Mikhail Gorbachev and Boutros Boutros-Ghali—properly belongs to a sequel to *The Diplomats, 1939–1979*.

G.A.C.
F.L.L.

INDEX